PAGE 54 ON THE ROAD

YOUR COMPLETE DESTINATION GUIDE
In-depth reviews, detailed listings and insider tips

PAGE 493 SURVIVAL GUIDE

VITAL PRACTICAL INFORMATION TO HELP YOU HAVE A SMOOTH TRIP

D1041541

THIS EDITION W … HED BY

Nick Ray
Greg Bloom, Austin Bush,
Iain Stewart, Richard Waters

welcome to the Mekong Region

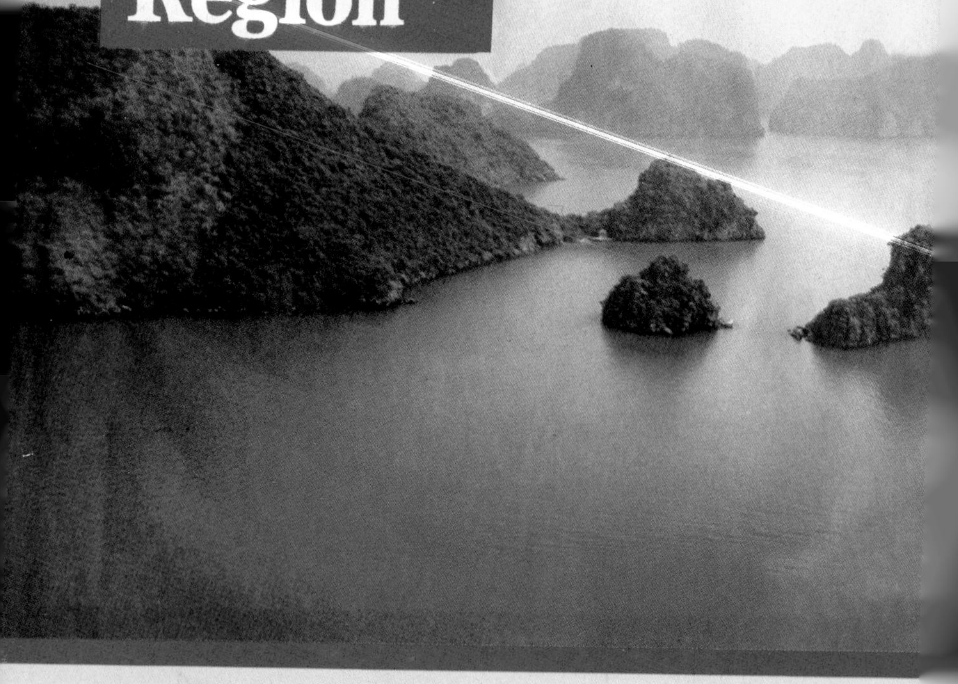

A River Runs Through It

One of the world's great rivers, the Mekong winds its way down from the foothills of Tibet to the South China Sea, encompassing some of the most diverse backdrops in Asia. Its dramatic journey southwards takes in remote national parks and immense waterfalls in Laos, traditional towns and 21st-century cities in Thailand, freshwater dolphins and forgotten temples in Cambodia and a patchwork of emerald greens in Vietnam's Mekong Delta.

Old Asia, New Asia

Experience old Asia and new Asia jostling for space. One minute it's Bangkok, riding the Skytrain to a state-of-the-art shopping mall, the next it's an elephant careering through the jungle in Cambodia. In the cities, the pace of life runs at a dizzying speed, matched only by the endless rush of motorbikes and call of commerce. In the countryside, life seems timeless, the rural rhythms the same as they have been for centuries, with pyjama-clad peasants tending the fields and monks wandering the streets in search of alms.

MARK DAFFEY / LONELY PLANET IMAGES ©

The Mekong. It's an exotic name guaranteed to fire up the imagination. Riding high on the global hotlist, it is home to such iconic sights as Angkor Wat, Halong Bay and Luang Prabang.

LA MERIDIAN

(left) Halong Bay (p79), Vietnam
(below) Prasat Preah Vihear (p229), Cambodia

TOM COCKREM / LONELY PLANET IMAGES ©

Memorable Journeys

Travelling in the Mekong region is as much about the journey as the destination, although it is not always as smooth as the brochures would have you believe. Float down the river by slow boat from Huay Xai to Luang Prabang, passing by distant minority villages in a land that time forgot. Hitch a ride on a remork (a motorbike-drawn carriage) around the ancient temples of Angkor. Or explore the bustling backstreets of old Asia from the comfort of a *cyclo* (bicycle rickshaw). Experience some rough with the smooth for the real flavour of the Mekong region.

The Spirit of the Mekong

Quench your thirst for adventure with some adrenalin-fuelled activities in the jungle before relaxing on a beautiful beach overlooking the South China Sea. Delve deeper to discern the mosaic of ethnicities and learn about their incredible cultures and lifestyles. The people are irrepressible, the experiences unforgettable and the stories impossible to re-create, but sometime during your journey, the Mekong and its people will enter your soul. Go with the flow and let the Mekong spirit course through your veins.

›Vietnam, Cambodia, Laos & Northern Thailand

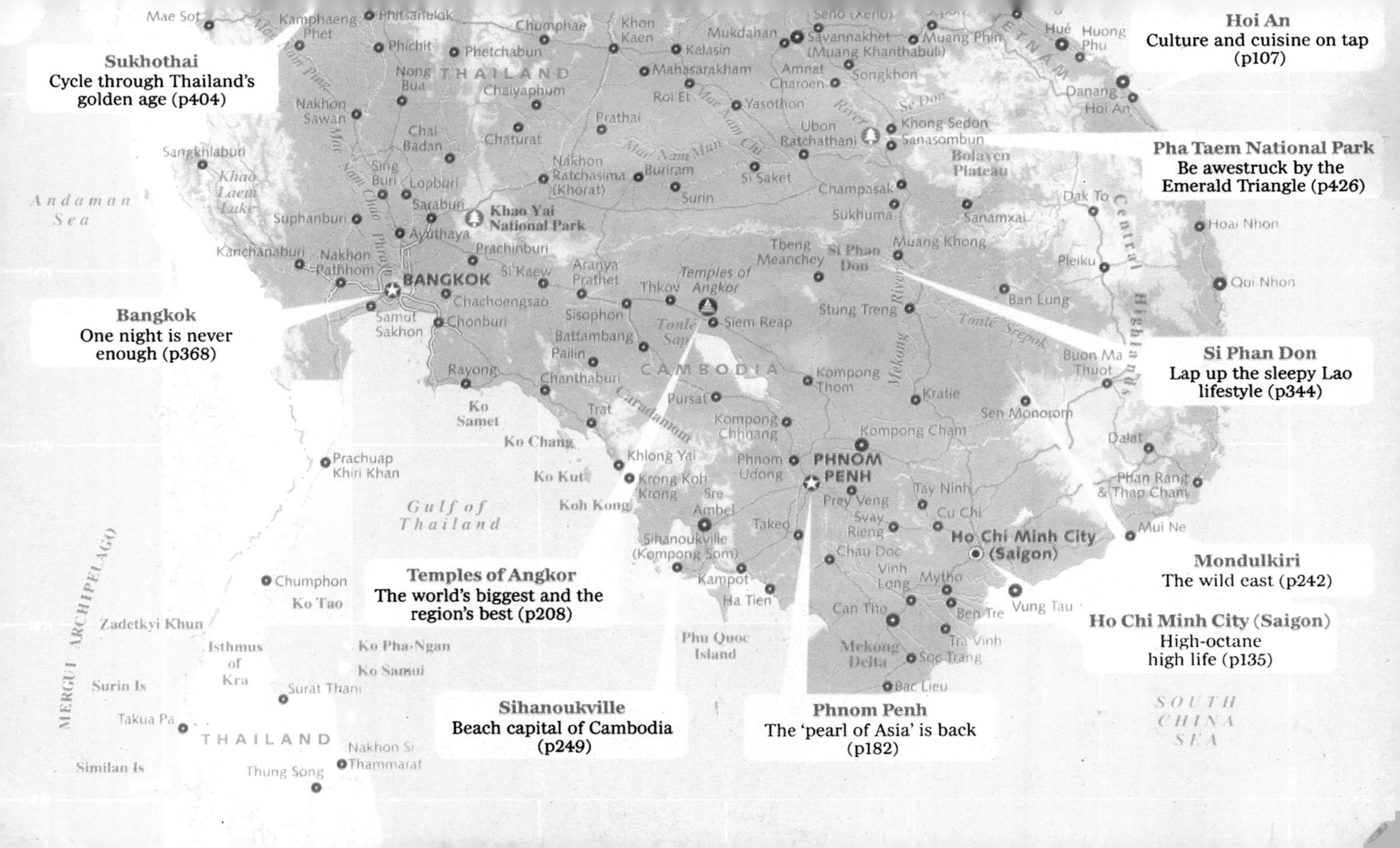
Hoi An
Culture and cuisine on tap
(p107)
Sukhothai
Cycle through Thailand's golden age (p404)
Pha Taem National Park
Be awestruck by the Emerald Triangle (p426)
Bangkok
One night is never enough (p368)
Si Phan Don
Lap up the sleepy Lao lifestyle (p344)
Mondulkiri
The wild east (p242)
Ho Chi Minh City (Saigon)
High-octane high life (p135)
Temples of Angkor
The world's biggest and the region's best (p208)
Sihanoukville
Beach capital of Cambodia (p249)
Phnom Penh
The 'pearl of Asia' is back (p182)
THAILAND
CAMBODIA
BANGKOK
PHNOM PENH
Ho Chi Minh City (Saigon)
Andaman Sea
Gulf of Thailand
SOUTH CHINA SEA
MERGUI ARCHIPELAGO
Central Highlands
Mekong Delta
Mekong River
Tonlé Sap
Tonlé Srepok
Mae Nam Mun
Mae Nam Chi
Mae Nam Ping
Mae Nam Chao Phraya
Khao Laem Lake
Bolaven Plateau
Khao Yai National Park
Temples of Angkor
Isthmus of Kra
Mae Sot
Kamphaeng Phet
Phitsanulok
Phichit
Phetchabun
Chumphae
Khon Kaen
Mukdahan
Kalasin
Mahasarakham
Savannakhet (Muang Khanthabuli)
Amnat Charoen
Songkhon
Muang Phin
Hué
Huong Phu
Danang
Hoi An
Nong Bua
Chaiyaphum
Nakhon Sawan
Chai Badan
Chaturat
Prathai
Roi Et
Yasothon
Ubon Ratchathani
Khong Sedon
Sanasombun
Sangkhlaburi
Sing Buri
Lopburi
Saraburi
Nakhon Ratchasima (Khorat)
Buriram
Si Saket
Surin
Champasak
Sukhuma
Sanamxai
Dak To
Hoai Nhon
Suphanburi
Ayutthaya
Kanchanaburi
Nakhon Pathom
Prachinburi
Si Kaew
Aranya Prathet
Tbeng Meanchey
Si Phan Don
Muang Khong
Pleiku
Qui Nhon
Samut Sakhon
Chachoengsao
Chonburi
Sisophon
Thkov
Siem Reap
Stung Treng
Ban Lung
Battambang
Pailin
Rayong
Chanthaburi
Kompong Thom
Buon Ma Thuot
Kratie
Sen Monorom
Ko Samet
Trat
Pursat
Kompong Chhnang
Kompong Cham
Ko Chang
Khlong Yai
Phnom Udong
Dalat
Prachuap Khiri Khan
Ko Kut
Krong Koh Kong
Sre Ambel
Prey Veng
Tay Ninh
Phan Rang & Thap Cham
Koh Kong
Takeo
Svay Rieng
Cu Chi
Mui Ne
Sihanoukville (Kompong Som)
Chau Doc
Kampot
Ha Tien
Vinh Long
Mytho
Ben Tre
Can Tho
Vung Tau
Tra Vinh
Soc Trang
Bac Lieu
Phu Quoc Island
Chumphon
Ko Tao
Zadetkyi Khun
Ko Pha-Ngan
Ko Samui
Surin Is
Surat Thani
Takua Pa
Nakhon Si Thammarat
Thung Song
Similan Is

20 TOP EXPERIENCES

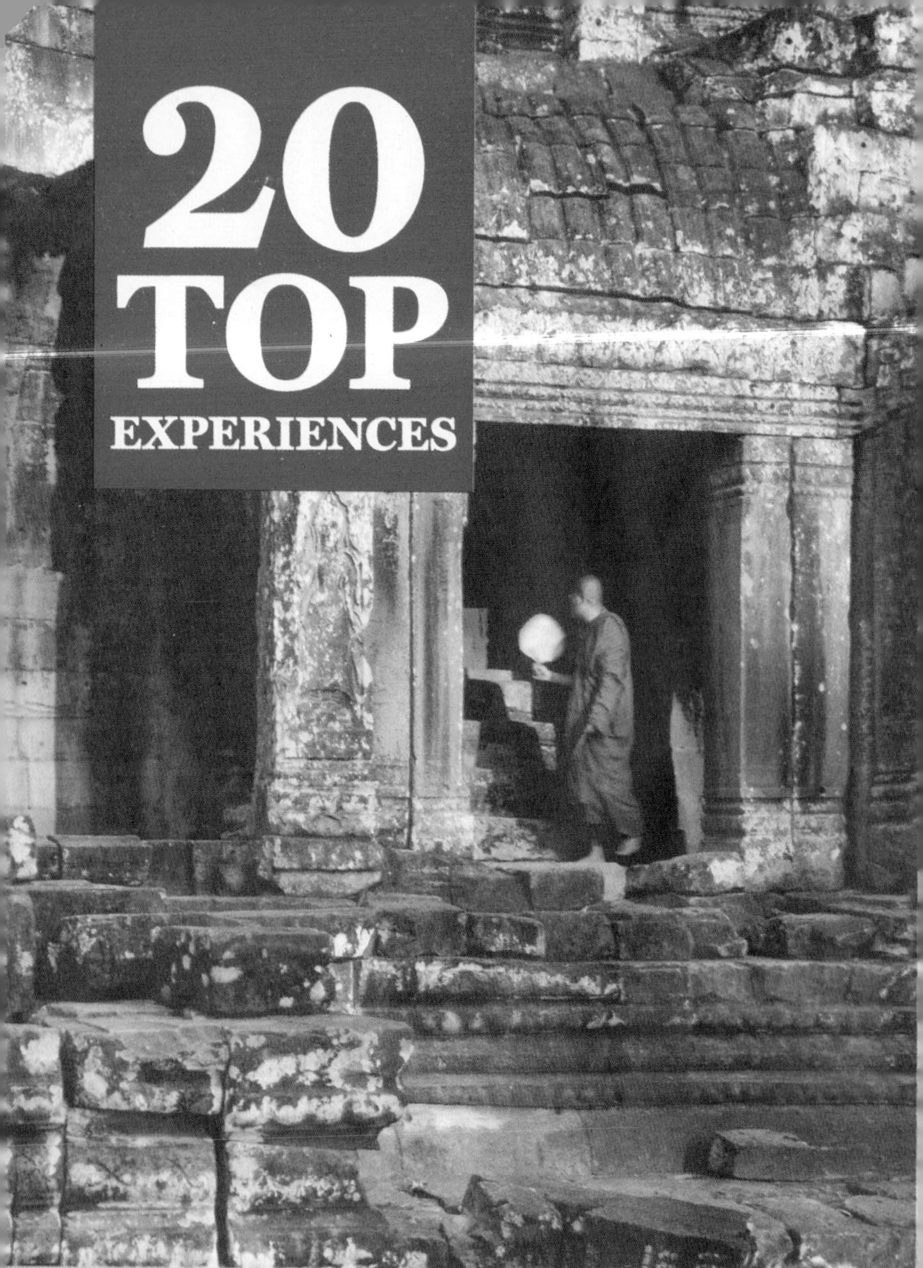

Temples of Angkor

1 One of the world's most magnificent sights, the temples of Angkor (p208) are so much better than the superlatives. Choose from Angkor Wat, the world's largest religious building; Bayon, one of the world's weirdest; or Ta Prohm, where nature runs amok. Siem Reap is the base to explore the world's grandest collection of temples and is a buzzing destination with a superb selection of restaurants and bars. Beyond the temples lie floating villages on the Tonlé Sap Lake, adrenalin activities such as quad biking and microlighting, and cultured pursuits such as cooking classes and birdwatching.

Luang Prabang

2 Hemmed in by the Mekong and Khan rivers, this ancient city of temples (p298) is a travel editor's dream; rich in royal history, Buddhist monks, stunning river views, world-class French cuisine and the best boutique accommodation in Southeast Asia. Hire a bike and explore the tropical peninsula's backstreets; take a cooking workshop, elephant trek, or just ease back with a restful massage at one of a dozen affordable spas. Prepare to adjust your timetable and stay a little longer than planned.

TONY BURNS / LONELY PLANET IMAGES ©

Hoi An

3 Medieval-looking Hoi An (p107) was once Vietnam's most cosmopolitan port. Today the good times have returned and this beautiful, ancient town is bursting with gourmet Vietnamese restaurants, hip bars and cafes, quirky boutiques and expert tailors. Immerse yourself in history in the warren-like lanes of the Old Town, shop til you drop, tour the temples and pagodas, dine like an emperor on a peasant's budget (then learn how to cook like the locals), hit glorious An Bang beach, explore the riverside and backroads. Hoi An has it all.

Halong Bay

4 Halong Bay's stunning combination of karst limestone peaks and sheltered, shimmering seas is one of Vietnam's top tourist draws, but with more than 2000 different islands, there's plenty of superb scenery to go around (p79). Definitely book an overnight cruise, and make time for your own special moments at this World Heritage wonder; rise early for an ethereal misty dawn or pilot a sleek kayak into grottoes and lagoons. If you're still hankering for more karst action, move on to less touristed, but equally spectacular, Lan Ha Bay.

PETER STUCKINGS / LONELY PLANET IMAGES ©

Bangkok

5 The original City of Angels lives up to the hype as one of Southeast Asia's most buzzing cities. Excuses to delay your trip upcountry include the city's excellent-value accommodation, cheap and spicy eats, unparalleled shopping and a rowdy but fun nightlife scene. Bangkok (p368) also functions as the unofficial gateway to the rest of the region, with cheap flights, cosy train rides, modern buses and a variety of other convenient and comfortable transport to your next destination – if you ever decide to leave, that is.

ANDERS BLOMQVIST / LONELY PLANET IMAGES ©

Gibbon Experience

6 Minus the surfboard here's your chance to become the Silver Surfer as you whiz way above the forest floor attached to a zip-line. These brilliantly engineered cables – some over 500m long – span forest valleys in the lush Bokeo Nature Reserve (p327), habitat of the black-crested gibbon and Asiatic tiger. Your money goes toward protecting the eponymous endangered primate and your guides are former poachers turned rangers. Zip into and bed down in vertiginously high treehouses by night, listening to the call of the wild. This is Laos' premier wildlife and adrenalin high.

Hanoi Old Quarter

7 Don't worry, it happens to everyone when they first get to Hanoi (p60). Get agreeably lost in the city's Old Quarter, a frantic commercial labyrinth where echoes of the past are filtered and framed by a 21st-century energy. Discover Vietnam's culinary flavours and aromas by eating iconic Hanoi dishes such as *pho bo* (beef noodle soup), *bun cha* (barbecued pork) and *banh cuon* (rice crepes). Later at night, join the socialising throngs enjoying crisp *bia hoi* (draught beer) at street-corner bars.

Phnom Penh

8 The Cambodian capital is a chaotic yet charming city which has thrown off the shadows of the past to embrace a brighter future. Boasting one of the most beautiful riverfronts in the region, Phnom Penh (p182) is in the midst of a boom, with designer restaurants, funky bars and hip hotels ready to welcome the adventurous. Experience emotional extremes at the inspiring National Museum and the depressing Tuol Sleng Prison, showcasing the best and worst of Cambodian history. Once the 'Pearl of Asia', Phnom Penh is regaining its shine.

BERNARD NAPTHINE / LONELY PLANET IMAGES ©

Si Phan Don

9 Legends don't happen by accident. Laos' hammock-flopping mecca (p344) has been catering to weary travellers for years, and with electricity just arrived (fans and air-con abound) staying on these tropical islands bounded by the turquoise waters of the Mekong has suddenly become even more appealing. Between tubing and cycling through paddy fields, grab a kayak or fish with the locals, and round off your day with a sunset boat trip to see the rare Irrawaddy dolphin.

Northeast Cambodia

10 Eventually the endless ricefields and sugar palms that characterise the Cambodian landscape give way to the rolling hills of the northeast. This is the wild east, home to a diverse group of ethnic minorities who still practise animism and ancestor worship, carving effigies of their dead in spirit cemeteries. Elephants are still in use in this part of the country, although better than riding them is visiting them in their element at the Elephant Valley Project (p244). Add freshwater dolphins and a collection of thunderous waterfalls to the mix and you have the right recipe for adventure.

Ho Chi Minh City

11 Increasingly international but still unmistakably Vietnamese, the former Saigon's visceral energy will delight big city devotees while leaving others completely flabbergasted. This city doesn't inspire neutrality. Either you'll be drawn into its thrilling vortex, hypnotised by the perpetual whir of its orbiting motorbikes, or you'll find the whole experience overwhelming. Dive in and you'll be rewarded with a wealth of history, delicious food and a vibrant nightlife that has always set the standard for the country. The heat is always on in Saigon (p135). Loosen your collar and enjoy.

GREG ELMS / LONELY PLANET IMAGES ©

Vietnamese Food

12 Perhaps Asia's greatest culinary secret, Vietnamese food (p168) is on the radar but hardly a global phenomenon. Essentially it's all about the freshness of the ingredients – chefs shop twice daily to source just-picked herbs from the market. The result? Incomparable texture and flavour combinations. For the Vietnamese, a meal should balance sour and sweet, crunchy and silky, fried and steamed, soup and salad. Wherever you are, you'll find exquisite local specialities – the 'white rose' (shrimp dumplings) of Hoi An, *canh chua* (fish sour soup) of the Mekong Delta or good ol' *pho* (noodle soup) of the north.

Sukhothai

13 Northern Thailand isn't just about hill tribes and trekking. A visit to the awesome ruins of Thailand's 'golden age' at Sukhothai (p406) and Si Satchanalai-Chaliang Historical Parks (p407) also throws a bit of history into the mix. The ruins range from towering Buddha statues to ancient kilns, many of which are amazingly well preserved. Best seen by bicycle, these two parks offer self-guided exploration at its best, and are good outdoor alternatives for those intimidated by the north's more adrenalin-based options.

Tham Kong Lo

14 Imagine your deepest nightmare, the snaggled mouth of a river cave beneath a towering limestone mountain; the boatman in his rickety longtail taking you into the heart of darkness as you putter beneath the cathedral-high ceiling of stalactites...bats whispering over your head. This extraordinary 7.5km-long subterranea (p330) in Laos' remote Khammuan Province is an awesome experience and you'll be very glad to see the light at the other end. Just remember – you have to come back!

IDEON MENDEL / CORBIS ©

Nam Ha National Protected Area (NPA)

15 'Tiger, tiger burning bright...' Step into the church-cool interior of the triple canopy Nam Ha jungle and you may just hear one, for there are still a few lurking in the depths of Laos' first established National Protected Area (p322). It's also home to a rich tapestry of ethnic groups who live off the forest. Head to Luang Nam Tha or Muang Sing for award winning eco-treks into this wonderland, or better still, try a homestay – which involves you staying with a tribe, sharing smiles over the fire.

TOM COCKREM / LONELY PLANET IMAGES ©

Battambang

16 This is the real Cambodia, far fr jetset destinations of Phnom Penh and Siem Reap. Unfurling along the banks of the Sangker River, this is one of the best-preserved colonial-era towns in the country. Streets of French shophouses play host to social enterprises ranging from fair-trade cafes to bike excursions. In a word? Charming. Beyond Battambang (p220) lies the Cambodian countryside and a cluster of ancient temples, that, while not exactly Angkor Wat, mercifully lack its crowds. Further afield lies Prek Toal Bird Reserve, a world-class bird sanctuary en route to Siem Reap.

Thai Elephant Conservation Center, Lampang

17 One of Southeast Asia's unique experiences is undoubtedly the chance to learn how to be a mahout (elephant caretaker) at Lampang's Thai Elephant Conservation Center (p400). At this program, the profits of which go to help sick elephants, you'll learn how to ride, work with, bathe and care for elephants in stints ranging from a day to a month. If you stay overnight, you have the option of crashing with the real mahouts, where there's the added bonus of picking up a bit of

Sihanoukville

18 Its reputation for backpacker hedonism notwithstanding, the real appeal of Sihanoukville (p249) is its beaches. Many of them are on nearby islands such as Koh Rong and Koh Rong Samlon, where resorts are creating a buzz for their laid-back-bungalow vibe. On the Cambodian mainland, it's only 5km from Sihanoukville's grittier central beach, Occheuteal, to Otres Beach, still mellow and sublime despite the threat of development. More central Victory Beach, Independence Beach, Sokha Beach and even Occheuteal also have their charms – and their own unique personalities.

JOHN BORTHWICK / LONELY PLANET IMAGES ©

Pha Taem National Park

19 One of northeast Thailand's most amazing natural sights is Pha Taem National Park (p427). It's here that the normally vast Mekong River narrows to a wild, rocky channel. The entrance area of the park offers fantastic views over here and neighbouring Laos from a high cliff, and it's also possible to get directly into the action via a handful of trails, some of which pass by prehistoric wall paintings. If you're lucky, you may even run into locals still fishing in the same manner as depicted on the walls – with giant bamboo baskets.

Khmer Temple Trail

20 If you want to see Angkor Wat but don't want the crowds, consider following northeast Thailand's informal Angkor temple trail from Phimai to Phanom Rung (p421). The area's Khmer-era ruins cover the spectrum from immaculate to rubble, and visiting them is a good excuse to explore Thailand on rented wheels. In addition to taking in some pretty impressive history, a visit offers a unique chance to experience the laid-back rural lifestyle and unique culture of this little-visited region.

need to know

Currency

» Cambodia: riel (r)

» Laos: kip (K)

» Thailand: baht (B)

» Vietnam: dong (d)

Language

» Cambodia: Khmer

» Laos: Laotian

» Thailand: Thai

» Vietnam: Vietnamese

When to Go

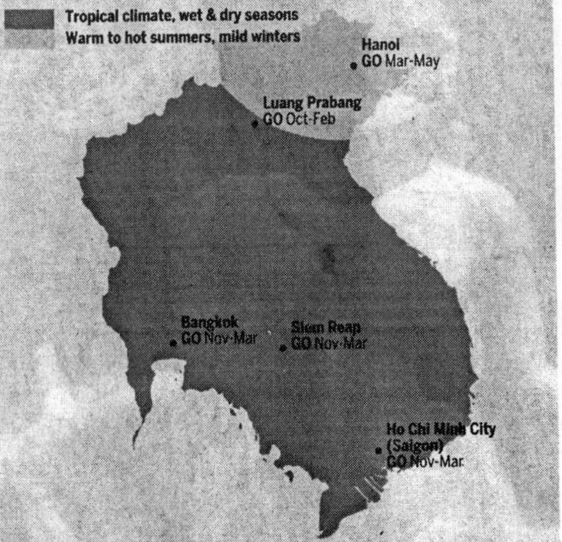

High Season
(Nov–Mar)

» Cool season in the southern part of the Mekong region.

» Cold in Hanoi and the mountains of Laos and Vietnam.

» Watch out for Chinese New Year in January/February, as everyone is on the move.

Shoulder
(Jul–Aug)

» Wet in the south, but landscapes are emerald green.

» Hot and humid in Hanoi/the north; it's local holidays, too – beaches are packed.

» Thailand is busy as many Western visitors flock here for summer holidays.

Low Season
(Apr–Jun & Sep–Oct)

» Hot season in the south when the mercury hits 40°C.

» Spring and autumn are perfect for Halong Bay with sunny days and good visibility.

» Good for trekking, with lush landscapes and a pleasant climate.

Your Daily Budget

Budget less than
US$50

» Cheap guesthouse room: US$5–10

» Local meals and street eats: US$1–2

» Local buses and trains: US$2–3 per 100km

Midrange
US$50 –150

» Air-con hotel room: US$15–50

» Decent local restaurant meal: US$5–10

» Local tour guide per day: US$20

Top End over
US$150

» Boutique hotel or resort: US$50–500

» Gastronomic meal with drinks: US$25–75

» 4WD rental per day: US$60–120

Money
» ATMs widely available in Cambodia, Thailand and Vietnam. Only found in major cities in Laos.

Visas
» Cambodia: US$20 on arrival

» Laos: US$30–42 on arrival

» Thailand: Usually no visa required

» Vietnam: US$35–60 in advance

Mobile Phones
» Roaming possible in all countries but is expensive. Local SIM cards and unlocked mobile phones available in all countries.

Driving
» Thailand drives on the left. Cambodia, Laos and Vietnam drive on the right, although in some places it isn't always apparent!

Websites
» **Lonely Planet** (www.lonelyplanet.com) The online authority in the Mekong region.

» **Travelfish** (www.travelfish.org) Opinionated articles and reviews about the region.

» **Visit Mekong** (www.visit-mekong.com) The official travel website for the Mekong.

» **Golden Triangle Rider** (www.GT-rider.com) The motorbiking website for the Mekong region.

» **Tales of Asia** (www.talesofasia.com) Inside information on overland travel in the region.

Exchange Rates

Cambodia	US$1	4000r
Laos	US$1	8000K
Thailand	US$1	30B
Vietnam	US$1	21,000d

For current exchange rates see www.xe.com.

Important Numbers
Always remember to drop the 0 from a regional (city) code when dialling into Cambodia, Laos, Thailand or Vietnam from another country.

Cambodia code	☎855
Laos code	☎856
Thailand code	☎66
Vietnam code	☎84

Arriving in the Mekong Region
» **Suvarnabhumi International Airport, Bangkok, Thailand**
Metered taxi 400B to 500B, depending on destination; three different airport bus routes cost 150B.

» **Noi Bai International Airport, Hanoi, Vietnam**
Taxi to centre 300,000d, around one hour; Vietnam Airlines minibus US$3, every 30 minutes.

» **Regional Flights**
Lots of regional carriers fly directly into Cambodia and Laos, as well as Thailand and Vietnam.

Travelling Responsibly in the Mekong Region
Much of the Mekong region experienced turbulent times in the 20th century, including war, genocide and famine, and there are many ways to put a little back into the countries you visit. Staying longer, travelling further and spreading the wealth is obvious advice, but even for those on a short stay, it is possible to engage with locals in markets and spend money in restaurants and outlets that assist disadvantaged locals.

For more on sustainable tourism and some tips on responsible travel while still having the trip of a lifetime, try the following websites:

» **Mekong Tourism** (www.mekongtourism.org) The official site of the Mekong Tourism Coordinating Office, promoting responsible and poverty-alleviating tourism in the region.

» **Stay Another Day** (www.stay-another-day.org) A great website dedicated to tempting tourists into staying another day in Cambodia, Laos, Thailand or Vietnam, packed with ideas on day trips, project visits and alternative things to see and do.

if you like...

Fabulous Food

There's no surer way to spice up your life than with a culinary odyssey through the Mekong region. Thai chilli is the stuff of legend, but throw in herbs and spices such as ginger, lemongrass, basil and cardamom and the results are a magical mix for the palate. Learn the tricks of the trade with a cooking class in the region.

Bangkok, Thailand Food capital of the Mekong region; take a hands-on cooking class at Khao or Helping Hands (p371).

Phnom Penh, Cambodia Dine to make a difference at one of Phnom Penh's many training restaurants to help the disadvantaged (p191).

Hanoi, Vietnam Dive into Hanoi's endlessly tasty street-food scene at one of the stalls famous for *bun cha* (barbecued pork), sticky rice creations, fried eels or crab noodle soup (p69).

Luang Prabang, Laos Discover the art of making *mok pa* (steamed fish in banana leaves) at Tamarind, home to traditional Lao cuisine (p301).

Markets

Get up close and personal with locals at one of the many markets of the region. These are the original super-markets; vast, sprawling cauldrons of commerce where everything has a price – if you can master the art of bargaining. From ethnic minority meets in the highlands to floating wholesalers on the local river, the region does markets like nowhere else.

Bac Ha, Vietnam See the unique costume of the Flower Hmong at Bac Ha, one of the most colourful markets in Southeast Asia (p89).

Luang Prabang, Laos The candlelit Handicraft Night Market is an endless ribbon of colourful textiles, paper lanterns and ethnic motifs (p307).

Chiang Mai, Thailand The weekend 'Walking Streets' offer the chance to shop till you drop, with a bit of culture thrown in for good measure (p395).

Mekong Delta's floating markets, Vietnam Get up early and experience the Delta's famous floating markets (p152).

Russian Market, Cambodia Phnom Penh's premier shopping destination; if it's available in Cambodia, it is somewhere in here (p194).

Temples & Tombs

The Mekong region is home to some of the world's most spectacular temples. Cambodia is the temple heavyweight thanks to incredible Angkor, but Laos and Thailand are dotted with elegant wats and ancient stupas. Vietnam is home to ancient Cham temples, emperors' tombs and pagodas that are a world apart from their Mekong neighbours.

Angkor, Cambodia The one and only, the temples that put all others in the shade. Choose from a dozen or more headline acts that carpet the pretty countryside around Siem Reap (p208).

Wat Xieng Thong, Laos The jewel in the crown of Luang Prabang's temples, with its roofs sweeping majestically low to the ground (p300).

Hué, Vietnam Vietnamese emperors constructed dazzling monuments to their rule around the city of Hué. See the extraordinarily grandiose tombs of Tu Duc and Minh Mang (p96).

Sala Kaew Ku, Thailand Bizarre and larger-than-life Buddhist- and Hindu-themed sculptures can be seen at this park outside of Nong Khai (p432).

CHRISTER FREDRIKSSON / LONELY PLANET IMAGES ©

» Mui Ne (p123), Vietnam

Spectacular Treks

Thailand was a trekking destination back when the Vietnamese were still marching up and down the Ho Chi Minh Trail and Indochina was convulsed by war. However, Cambodia, Laos and Vietnam are catching up fast and all the countries of the Mekong region offer some incredible hiking opportunities, featuring mountains, minority culture and rare wildlife.

Sapa, Vietnam Framed by cascades of verdant rice terraces, join chatty Hmong guides to explore the ethnic minority villages around Sapa (p93).

Nam Ha National Protected Area (NPA), Laos Laos' original national park offers responsibly coordinated trekking and is one of the best places to see towering original-growth forest (p322).

Chiang Rai, Thailand Home to a diversity of ethnic groups, the hills around Chiang Rai comprise one of Thailand's best areas for trekking (p408).

Mondulkiri, Cambodia Try a trek with a difference or 'walking with the herd' at the Elephant Valley Project in northeast Cambodia (p244).

Beautiful Beaches

The Mekong River is not the only well-known water in the region: both Vietnam and Cambodia boast lengthy and beautiful coastlines. Vietnam might have been late to the beach party, but it was worth the wait – there are seemingly infinite stretches of sand, hidden coves, lovely lagoons and tropical islands. Cambodia's coast is less developed and offers opportunities for aspiring Robinson Crusoes.

Phu Quoc, Vietnam Stretching for many kilometres, Long Beach offers white sand in profusion, while Sao Beach is a quieter stretch of sand (p155).

Sihanoukville, Cambodia King of the Cambodian beaches, the headland is ringed by white sands, and offshore lie countless tropical islands with only a few beach huts in sight (p249).

Mui Ne, Vietnam Squeaky sands along the shore, towering sand dunes nearby and expanses of empty beaches up the coast (p123).

Kep, Cambodia The original beach resort in Cambodia, it was devastated by war but has resurrected itself in recent years with boutique resorts, succulent seafood and palm-fringed islands (p260).

Cycling & Motorbiking

Get closer to the local population on two wheels. Choose from pancake-flat rides along the Mekong River, including the Mekong Discovery Trail in Cambodia and the Delta in Vietnam, or mountain highs in northern Vietnam and Laos. Adventure motorbiking is huge in all the countries, including along the Ho Chi Minh Trail in Vietnam and Laos.

Northwest Loop, Vietnam The spectacular road between Dien Bien Phu and Sapa offers glorious mountain scenery, river valleys and tribal villages galore (p88).

Nong Khiaw, Laos The base for adventure cycling trips through beautiful scenery, organised by responsible local operators (p310).

Sukhothai, Thailand Explore the first Thai capital, with its 200 temples and stupas, on two wheels (p404).

Preah Vihear Province, Cambodia Seek out the lost jungle temples of Preah Vihear in northern Cambodia, including Route 66 from Beng Mealea to Preah Khan. Not for novices (p229).

If you like... surreal sculpture
Buddha Park near the Lao capital Vientiane is one of the more trippy sights in the region (p283).
If you like... white-water rafting
Head to the remote province of Nan in the north of Thailand where white waters await (p416).

Boat Trips

River cruises are incredibly popular along the Mekong River's length, including northern Laos, Si Phan Don and the stretch between Phnom Penh and Ho Chi Minh City. Off the coast, Halong Bay is a natural wonder and a boat trip there is a must. Party boats patrol the waters off Nha Trang and Sihanoukville.

Halong Bay, Vietnam Cruise the myriad islands and take in the supernatural karst scenery of Halong Bay, a Unesco World Heritage Site (p81).

Tonlé Sap lake, Cambodia Discover floating villages, bamboo skyscrapers, flooded forests and rare birdlife during a boat trip on Cambodia's great lake (p207).

Tham Kong Lo, Laos Enter the underworld in the eternal night of this spooky 7.5km-long river cave beneath a mountain (p330).

Nan, Thailand Thailand's whitest waters are found in the Mae Nam Wa in remote Nan, but only at the end of the rainy season (p416).

Diving & Snorkelling

It's not all about the action on the water, as some of the most impressive sites lie under the surface for those who dive or snorkel. Thailand is the dive capital for those exploring the south, but Vietnam also offers a number of impressive dive destinations up and down its coast. Sihanoukville is Cambodia's original dive centre.

Con Dao Islands, Vietnam Unquestionably the best diving and snorkelling in Vietnam, with bountiful marine life, fine reefs and even a wreck dive (p128).

Cham Islands, Vietnam Hoi An's two dive schools head to the lovely Cham Islands, where macro life can be impressive (p166).

Nha Trang, Vietnam The country's most popular diving and snorkelling centre, where there are several reputable dive operators and fun boat trips for the non-diving fraternity (p117).

Sihanoukville, Cambodia At Cambodia's most established dive centre, the best action takes place around the more isolated islands far from the coast (p249).

Remote Villages

Arriving from the Thai islands, it's hard to believe there are still remote villages in Southeast Asia, but there are some very off-the-beaten-track destinations in the Mekong region. The hills and mountains of Cambodia, Laos and Vietnam conceal remote tribal villages that can be explored on foot or by bicycle.

Ban Bo Luang, Thailand Strategically located between the Lao border at Doi Phu Kha National Park, it doesn't get much more remote than Ban Bo Luang (p417).

Mai Chau, Vietnam Get off the beaten track by trekking, kayaking and biking around this idyllic White Thai village (p88).

Muang Sing, Laos A few kilometres from the Chinese border and surrounded by shimmering paddy fields, it's a relaxed base for trekking into Nam Ha NPA (p325).

Muang Ngoi Neua, Laos This laid-back village redefines the term 'horizontal', with great guesthouses and sunsets that should be bottled (p312).

Ratanakiri, Cambodia The red-earth roads of this remote highland province lead to isolated hill-tribe villages and traditional tribal cemeteries (p238).

month by month

Top Events

1 **Tet/Chinese New Year** January/February

2 **Khmer/Lao/Thai New Year** April

3 **Rocket Festival** May

4 **Bon Om Tuk** October/November

5 **Loi Krathong** November

January

This is peak tourist season with the region just about as busy as it gets, as Europeans and North Americans escape the cold winter. For serious revellers, it also sees the rare occurrence of two new-year celebrations in a month.

Tet

The Big One! Vietnamese Lunar New Year is Christmas, New Year and birthdays all rolled into one. Falls in late January or early February. Travel is difficult at this time, as transport is booked up and many businesses close.

Chinese New Year

Always occuring at the same time as Vietnamese New Year, these festivities are headline news in major cities in the region such as Phnom Penh and Bangkok. Expect businesses to close for a few days and dragon dances to kick off all over town.

February

Still peak season for the region, and the coastline is busy with sunseekers. Inland the first round of rice harvesting is over but in parts of Vietnam and Thailand, they are already on to round two.

Bun Wat Phu Champasak

The three-day Wat Phu Champasak Festival has an atmosphere somewhere between a kids' carnival and music festival. The central ceremonies performed are Buddhist, culminating with a dawn parade of monks receiving alms, followed that evening by a candlelit *wien thien* (circumambulation) of the lower shrines.

Makha Bucha

One of three holy days marking important moments of Buddha's life, Makha Bucha falls on the full moon of the third lunar month and commemorates Buddha preaching to 1250 enlightened monks who came to hear him 'without prior summons'. It's mainly a day for temple visits.

Flower Festival

Chiang Mai displays its floral beauty during this three-day event. Flower-bedecked floats parade through town.

April

The hottest time of year, so book an air-con room. New years are ushered in all over the region, including Cambodia, Laos and Thailand. The accompanying water fights are a guaranteed way to keep cool.

Songkran

Songkran, the Thai New Year, is a no-holds-barred countrywide water fight that has to be seen to be believed. Bangkok and Chiang Mai are some of the most raucous battlegrounds. Like Lao and Khmer new year, it always falls in mid-April.

Bun Pi Mai

Lao New Year is one of the most effusive, fun-splashed events in the Lao calendar as houses and Buddha statuary are cleaned, and the country engages in a national water fight with waterpistols and buckets of

H20 tossed with great mirth at passers-by. Protect your camera and join in the fun.

Chaul Chnam

Khmer New Year is a more subdued event than in neighbouring Laos and Thailand, but water fights still kick off in much of the countryside. It is mainly a family time when city dwellers return to the place of their ancestry to meet distant relatives.

Liberation Day

30 April is the date when Saigon fell to the north and was renamed Ho Chi Minh City. It's celebrated by the Communist Party; expect the reaction to be more subdued in the south.

May

The hottest time of year in many parts of the region; escape to northern Vietnam for spring-like weather. This is low season, when visitor numbers drop and prices follow.

Chat Preah Nengkal

The Royal Ploughing Ceremony in Cambodia determines the forthcoming harvest for the year. If the royal oxen eat, the harvest will be bountiful; should they refuse, it may spell drought. Also celebrated at the Royal Palace in Bangkok.

Rocket Festival

Villagers craft bamboo rockets (*bang fai*) and fire them into the sky to provoke rainfall in the hope that it will bring a bountiful rice harvest. Mainly celebrated in northeastern Thailand and Laos, things can get pretty wild with music, dance and folk theatre. Dates vary from village to village.

Visaka Bucha

The holy day of Visaka Bucha falls on the 15th day of the waxing moon in the sixth lunar month and commemorates Buddha's birth, enlightenment and parinibbana (passing away). Activities centre around the temple.

June

The wet season begins in much of the Mekong region. Expect a daily downpour, but much of the time it should be dry. River levels begin to rise again.

Hué Festival (Biennial)

Vietnam's biggest cultural event (www.huefestival.com) is held every two years, including 2012 and 2014. Most of the art, theatre, music, circus and dance performances, including many international acts, are held inside Hué's Citadel.

Phi Ta Khon

The Buddhist holy day of Bun Phra Wet is given a Carnival makeover in Dan Sai village in northeastern Thailand. Revellers disguise themselves in garish 'spirit' costumes and parade through the village streets wielding wooden phalluses and downing rice whisky. Dates vary.

July

A mini-high in the midst of the low season, the summer months see Europeans head to the region to coincide with long summer holidays back home. The rain keeps falling.

Khao Phansaa

Early in the monsoonal rains, Buddhist monks retreat into monasteries in Cambodia, Laos and Thailand. This is the traditional time for young men to enter the monkhood or when monks begin a retreat for study and meditation. Worshippers offer candles and donations to the temples and attend ordinations.

September

The height of the wet season: if places like Bangkok or Phnom Penh are going to flood this is when it usually happens. Occasional typhoons sweep in across Vietnam, wreaking havoc.

Pchum Ben

A sort of Cambodian All Souls' Day – respects are paid to the dead through offerings made at wats to resident monks. Many Khmers visit their home villages and try to pack in seven temples in seven days. Trung Nguyen is a similar festival celebrated in Vietnam, usually in the preceding month.

October

The rains are easing off and farmers prepare for the harvest season. A series of festivals fall around this time and the temples are packed as monks emerge from their retreat.

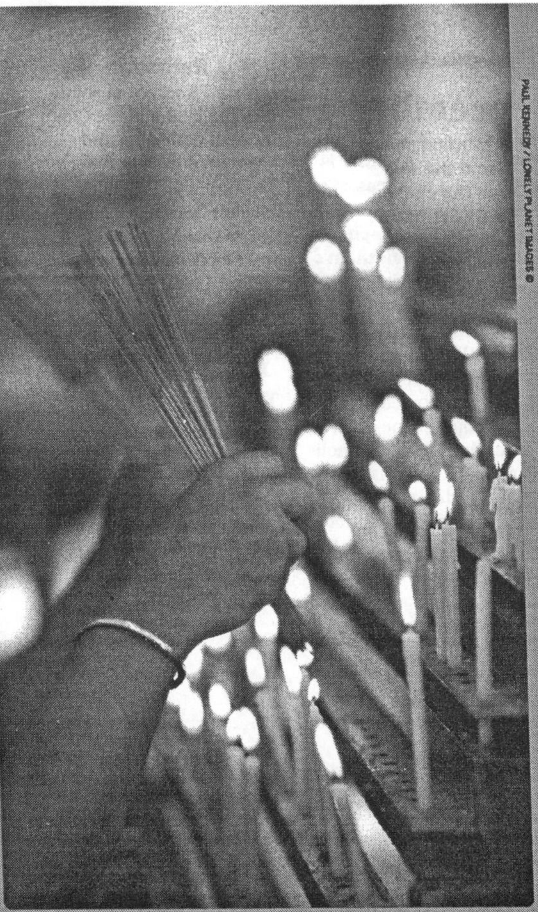

(Above) Temple ceremony, Thailand
(Below) Thailand beach

PAUL KENNEDY / LONELY PLANET IMAGES ©

DAMIEN SIMONIS / LONELY PLANET IMAGES ©

★★ Bon Om Tuk

The Water Festival celebrates Jayavarman VII's victory over the Chams in 1177 and the reversal of the Tonlé Sap river. Boat races stir local patriotism and up to two million people descend on Phnom Penh. A smaller event takes place in Siem Reap. Falls in October or November.

★★ Ork Phansaa

The end of the Buddhist Lent (three lunar months after Khao Phansaa) is marked by the *gà·tĭn* ceremony, in which new robes are given to the monks by merit-makers. The peculiar natural phenomenon known as the *'naga* fireballs' coincides with Ork Phansaa.

November

The cool, dry season begins and is an ideal time to visit for lush landscapes. In the far north of the region, temperatures begin to drop.

★★ Loi Krathong

Join Thais in launching floating candles during the festival of Loi Krathong, usually held in early November. If you happen to be in Chiang Mai, the banana-leaf boats are replaced by *yêe peng,* floating paper lanterns.

★★ Bun Pha That Luang

That Luang Festival is tied to the November full moon. Based in Vientiane and lasting a week, this celebration involves music, a lot of drinking, processions to That Luang, fireworks and a cast of many thousands who flock to the capital.

Surin Elephant Roundup

Held on the third weekend of November, Thailand's biggest elephant show celebrates this northeastern province's most famous residents. The event in Surin begins with a colourful elephant parade culminating in a fruit buffet for the pachyderms.

December

Peak tourism season is back and the weather is fine, so the chances of a white Christmas are very slim unless you happen to be climbing Vietnam's highest peak, Fansipan.

Christmas

We wish you a merry Christmas. Most of the region has adopted Christmas in some shape or form, but for the sizeable Catholic population of Vietnam, it is serious business with important services in churches and cathedrals across the country.

Ramadan

Observed in southern Thailand and the Cham areas of Cambodia and Vietnam during October, November or December, the Muslim fasting month requires that Muslims abstain from food, drink, cigarettes and sex between sunrise and sunset.

Lao National Day

This 2 December holiday celebrates the 1975 victory over the monarchy with parades and speeches. Lao national and communist hammer-and-sickle flags are flown all over the country. Celebration is mandatory.

itineraries

Whether you've got six days or 60, these itineraries provide a starting point for the trip of a lifetime. Want more inspiration? Head online to lonelyplanet.com/thorntree to chat with other travellers.

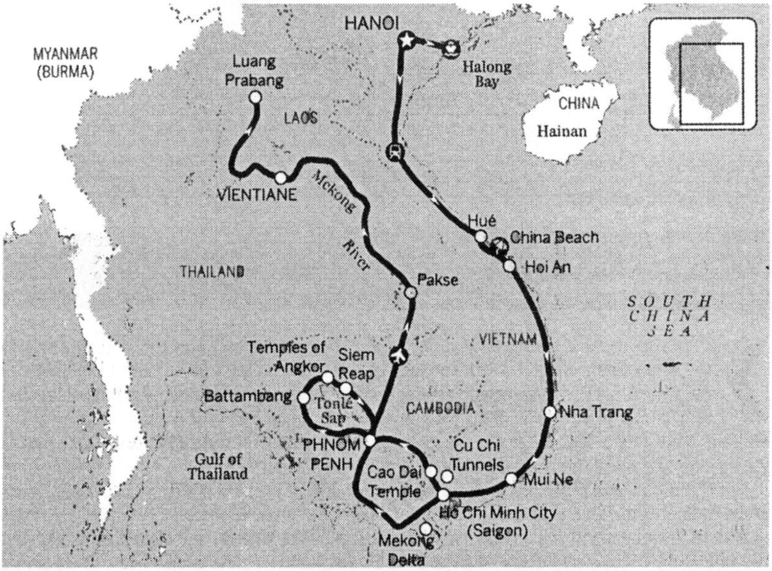

Three to Five Weeks

Indochina Explorer

Begin in the Vietnamese capital of **Hanoi**, replete with boulevards and lakes. Take a junk cruise among the spectacular karst islands of **Halong Bay**, then head south to **Hué**, the old imperial capital and cultural hub of central Vietnam. Take the coastal road to the historic trading point of **Hoi An**. Continue to party at the beach town of **Nha Trang** or the sand dunes of **Mui Ne**.

Hit **Ho Chi Minh City**, the full-throttle face of new Vietnam, head on. Go underground at the **Cu Chi Tunnels**, then join the faithful at the **Cao Dai Great Temple** before plunging into the **Mekong Delta**.

Experience the contrasts of **Phnom Penh**, then loop around the lake to the old town of **Battambang**. Continue to **Siem Reap**, home to the world's most spectacular collection of temples at **Angkor**.

Board a flight to **Pakse**, then head north to the Lao capital of **Vientiane**. Finish up in **Luang Prabang** and see monks at dawn and an old Asia that is increasingly hard to find.

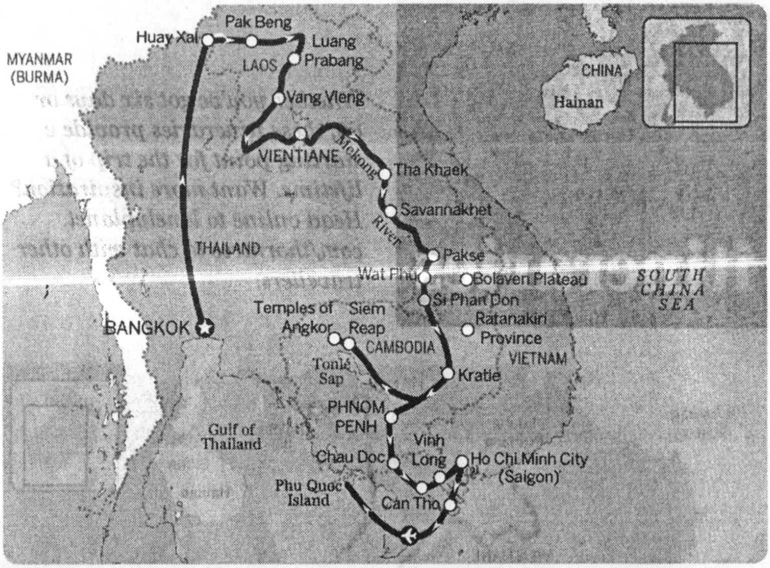

Three to Six Weeks
Mekong Meander

This trip trickles through an older Asia and includes some of the hottest spots in the region, as well as some of the less-visited backwaters. Leave behind the bustle of **Bangkok** for the **Golden Triangle**, where the borders of Laos, Myanmar (Burma) and Thailand converge. Step back in time into Laos and take a slow boat down the Mekong from **Huay Xai**, stopping the night in **Pak Beng**, to **Luang Prabang**. Soak up the magic before leaving the river for some relaxation in **Vang Vieng**.

Continue to **Vientiane** and reunite with the mother river. It's a sleepy place with some great cafes, restaurants and bars, which you won't be encountering for a while. Fly south to **Pakse** or wind your way down the river through **Tha Khaek** and **Savannakhet**. Visit the imposing Khmer sanctuary of **Wat Phu Champasak**, in the shadow of Lingaparvata Mountain; explore the waterfalls and villages of the **Bolaven Plateau**; or enjoy the laid-back islands of **Si Phan Don**.

Cross into Cambodia and visit the mountains of **Ratanakiri**, home to elephants, hill tribes and pristine nature. Back on the river, call in at **Kratie** to see the rare Irrawaddy dolphin. Continue south to the revitalised Cambodian capital of **Phnom Penh**. Make a diversion by speedboat up the Tonlé Sap river to the boom town of **Siem Reap**, your base for the majestic **Temples of Angkor**.

Back in Phnom Penh, take a fast boat down the mighty Mekong to **Chau Doc**, gateway to the Mekong Delta. Check out **Can Tho**, its commercial heart. Hotfoot it to **Ho Chi Minh City** for some fun; delve deeper into the delta with a homestay around **Vinh Long**, or make for the tropical retreat of **Phu Quoc Island**, a well-earned reward for following the mother river.

» (above) Don Det (p347) on the Mekong River, Laos
» (left) Streetside hairdresser, Ho Chi Minh City (Saigon, p135), Vietnam

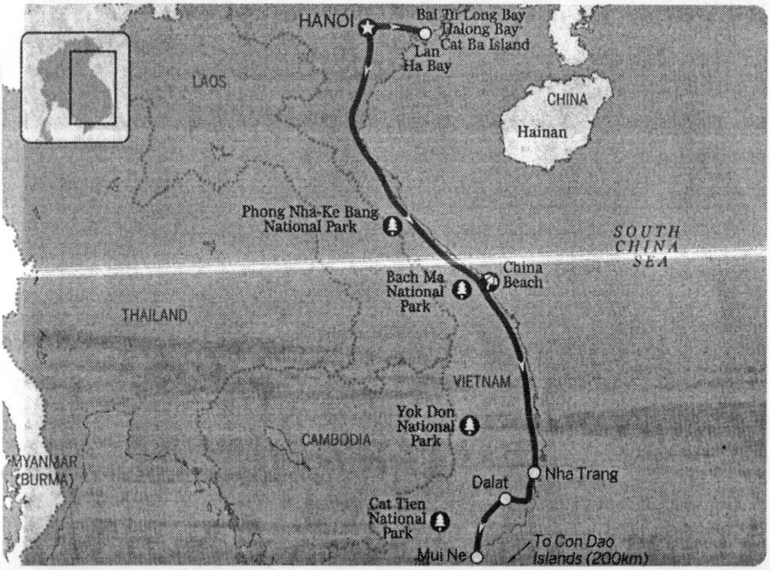

Three to Five Weeks
Natural Highs

Starting in **Hanoi**, Vietnam has plenty to offer adrenalin junkies and nature lovers. Explore **Halong Bay** for some sea kayaking among the karsts. Experienced climbers with their own gear can leave the water far below, as the limestone outcrops around **Cat Ba Island** offer some excellent ascents. Take to the waters of **Lan Ha Bay** by local boat to see the 'new' Halong Bay without the tourists. Boating, kayaking and Robinson Crusoe-style camping are possible here, and there are some beautiful hidden coves.

Heading south to central Vietnam, stop at **Phong Nha-Ke Bang National Park**, a rising star in Vietnam that is home to spectacular caves, stunning jungle scenery and the chance for a boat trip into the karst system. Continuing down the coast is **China Beach**, a great place for budding surfers to test their board skills against some of the South China Sea's biggest waves.

Go under the waves at **Nha Trang**, the dive capital of Vietnam, before heading up towards the hills of the Central Highlands. Wind up, or down, in **Dalat**, a base for abseiling, cycling and rock climbing. Don't forget two of Vietnam's best-known national parks: the birding hotspot of **Cat Tien National Park**, which is home to the new Wild Gibbon Trek, and **Yok Don National Park**, home to elephants, both domesticated and wild.

After all this inland adventure, it's back to the coast to finish up. Try kitesurfing or windsurfing in **Mui Ne** or just relax over a cocktail if you feel you have earned your rest. Then continue south to the islands of **Con Dao** to experience some underwater action. A marine national park, Con Dao is home to rare manatee (sea cow) and a nesting site for the green sea turtle.

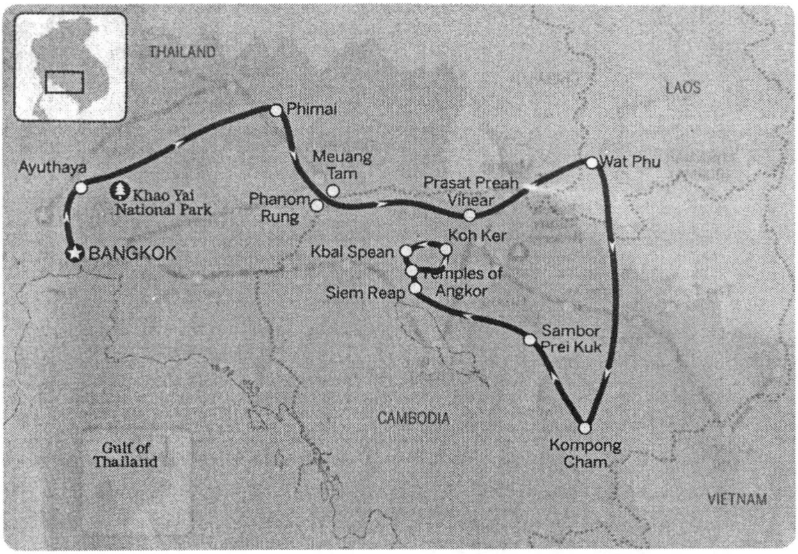

Two to Four Weeks

The Khmer Empire

Following in the footsteps of the Khmer empire is a relatively straightforward proposition: much like the Romans, the ancient Khmers built a network of roads connecting the outposts of their empire. First, escape **Bangkok** for the seldom-visited region of northeast Thailand. Forget the Khmer theme for a day or two with a visit to the lush jungle and lovely waterfalls of **Khao Yai National Park**. Continue east to the ancient city of **Phimai**, one of the most important regional capitals during the time of Angkor. Head south to see the wonderfully restored temple of **Phanom Rung**, set atop an extinct volcano, and the nearby temple of **Meuang Tam**.

Dip your toe into Cambodia by crossing the border to visit the spectacular mountaintop temple of **Prasat Preah Vihear** (Khao Praa Wihaan in Thai). Take in the dramatic views as you'll be down below on the plains of Cambodia in a couple more weeks. If politics means the border is closed, you may have to attempt this from the other side at the end of the trip.

Enter Laos and crisscross the Mekong to visit the Khmer sanctuary of **Wat Phu Champasak**, one of the oldest sacred sites in the region.

Cross into Cambodia and call in at **Kompong Cham** before swinging northwest again to the pre-Angkorian capital of **Sambor Prei Kuk**, the first great temple city in the region.

The climax of the pilgrimage is approaching: the incredible temples of **Angkor**. See the mother of all temples, **Angkor Wat**, the world's largest religious building; the **Bayon**, one of the world's weirdest temples with its enigmatic faces; and the jungle-clad **Ta Prohm**. Venture further to encounter the usurper capital of **Koh Ker**, and the River of a Thousand Lingas at **Kbal Spean** before taking a well-earned massage in **Siem Reap**.

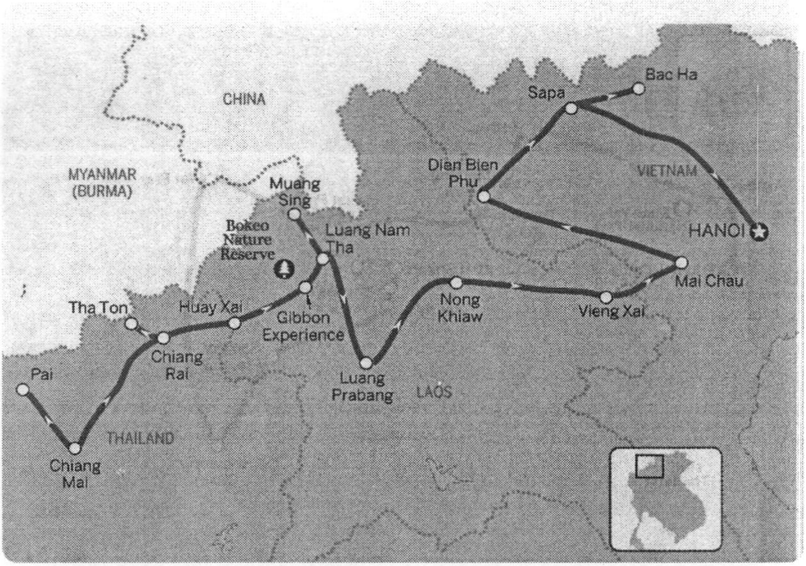

Four to Six Weeks

Minority Report

This route covers the mountainous regions of the Mekong where hill tribes have long made a home. Start in **Chiang Mai**, cultural capital of northern Thailand, and make sure you visit the **Tribal Museum**. Take the winding road to **Pai**, a mountain retreat that proves the hippy trail is alive and well. Then head on to **Tha Ton**, the entry point for rafting trips down to **Chiang Rai**, itself a good base for responsible trekking. Cross into Laos at **Huay Xai** and check out the **Gibbon Experience** at Bokeo Nature Reserve before heading for **Luang Nam Tha**. Spend a day or two trekking with the award-winning **Nam Ha Eco Trek Service**, before continuing to **Muang Sing**, the hub for one of the most diverse minority regions in all Laos.

Head south to **Luang Prabang**, a beautiful World Heritage Site on the banks of the Mekong to soak up the culture, before boomeranging north once more to **Nong Khiaw**. From here an adventurous overland trail runs east to Vietnam via **Vieng Xai** and the Pathet Lao Caves, a sort of Cu Chi Tunnels cast in stone. Once over the border in **Mai Chau**, try the northwest loop through **Dien Bien Phu** to experience incredible scenery and some of the country's most dramatic mountain passes.

Sapa, an old French hill station, is the gateway to the minority communities of this region. Consider a side trip to **Bac Ha**, home to the colourful Flower Hmong folk and great walking country. Head south to **Hanoi**, happy in the knowledge that all your ethnic souvenirs were bought direct from the minority people and not in the designer boutiques of the Old Quarter.

Visas & Borders

My Top Three Border-Crossing Experiences

Nick Ray

I've been crossing the borders in this region for 15 years. Here are some of the more memorable moments:

Cambodia–Laos (2001) The border had just opened, although even the government wasn't aware of this. Our boat got stuck on a sandbar, we reached the border after dark and the Lao immigration team were tough negotiators.

Cambodia–Thailand (1995) The land borders were officially closed, but rumour had it that travellers were making it out via Koh Kong. I ended up in Thailand via speedboat and received a tongue-lashing from Immigration in Bangkok.

Laos–Vietnam (2008) Planning to ride a Ural up the Ho Chi Minh Highway to Hanoi, I got stuck in Attapeu due to landslides. I was the first to get through as mounds of mud and rock were cleared on the road to the Phou Keua–Bo Y border.

During the bad old days of communism and the Cold War, there were pretty much no land borders open to foreigners in the Mekong region. Times have changed and there are now more than 20 border crossings connecting the neighbouring countries of the region. For a quick visual reference, see the border crossings map (p35).

In this book we give detailed instructions for every crossing open to foreigners. Before making a long-distance trip, be aware of border closing times, visa regulations and any transport scams by referring to the relevant country's Getting There & Away sections and the specific entries on border towns located in boxed texts in each chapter. Border details change regularly, so ask around or check the Lonely Planet Thorntree (www.lonelyplanet.com/thorntree).

Visas are available at some borders but not at others. As a general rule of thumb, visas are available at the land borders of Cambodia, Laos and Thailand and are not available at Vietnam border crossings. Most borders are open during the core hours of 7am to 5pm. However, some of the most popular crossings are open later in the evening and other more-remote crossings close for lunch.

There are few legal moneychanging facilities at some of the more remote border crossings, so be sure to have some small-denomination US dollars handy. The black market is also an option for local currencies, but remember that black marketeers have a well-deserved reputation for short-changing and outright theft.

Some of the immigration police at land border crossings, especially at the Cambodia, Laos and Vietnam borders, have a reputation for petty extortion. Crossing between Cambodia and Thailand can be a pain in the neck, but it's nothing compared with crossing between Laos and Vietnam, which has the most remote borders in the region with terrible transport and little room for leeway. Most travellers find it much easier to exit overland than it is to enter. Travellers at remote border crossings are occasionally asked for an 'immigration fee' of some kind, although this is less common than it used to be. Overtime surcharges are common at Cambodian and Lao immigration.

Cambodia

Cambodia shares borders with Laos, Thailand and Vietnam. Cambodian visas are available at all land borders shared with their neighbours.

From Laos

The only border crossing with Cambodia is from Dong Kalaw (L) to Trapeang Kriel (C), which connects Si Phan Don in southern Laos to Stung Treng (C). Minibuses ply the new road to Stung Treng (see p348).

From Thailand

There are up to six land crossings between Thailand and Cambodia, but only two are popular with travellers. The border at Aranya Prathet (T) to Poipet (C) is frequently used to travel between Bangkok (T) and Siem Reap (C). See p387 for more information. Down on the coast, crossings can be made from Hat Lek (T) to Cham Yeam (C) by road (see p387), which connects to Koh Kong (C) and on to Sihanoukville (C) or Phnom Penh (C).

There are also three more-remote crossings, which see little traffic. There's a crossing at Chong Chom (T) in Surin Province to O Smach (C), connecting with Samraong (C); see p423. Another crossing is at Chong Sa-Ngam (T) to Choam (C), leading to the former Khmer Rouge stronghold of Anlong Veng (C); see p423. The third is at Ban Pakard (T) to Psar Pruhm (C) leading to Pailin (C); see p387.

There is also a border at Prasat Preah Vihear (C), the stunning Cambodian temple perched atop the Dangkrek Mountains. When it's not closed due to politics or military stand-offs, this is a day crossing for tourists wanting to visit the temple from the Thai side. It may open up as a full international border during the lifetime of this book, if the two sides can agree on border demarcation.

From Vietnam

Cambodia and Vietnam share a long frontier with a glut of border crossings. The most popular option is the road border linking Moc Bai (V) and Bavet (C) for quick passage between Ho Chi Minh City and Phnom Penh (see p175). The most evocative route is the river crossing linking Chau Doc (V) to Phnom Penh (C) via the Mekong border at Vinh Xuong (V) and Kaam Samnor (C); see p154. The new crossing from Xa Xia (V) to Prek Chak (C) (see p156) is a great way to link the Cambodian coast with the Mekong Delta or Phu Quoc Island, while the Le Thanh (V) to O Yadaw (C) – see p117 – crossing is an adventurous way to link the Central Highlands of Vietnam with Cambodia's remote northeast. Then there is the rarely used option of Tinh Bien (V) to Phnom Den (C) that connects Chau Doc (V) and Takeo (C) – see p155 – plus a couple of obscure borders in the east of Cambodia.

Laos

Laos shares borders with all the Mekong region countries. Lao visas are available on arrival at all land borders with Thailand and the land border with Cambodia. The border with Vietnam is more complicated; visas are available at Dansavanh, Nam Phao, Nong Haet, Phou Keua and Sop Hun, but not at the other borders.

From Cambodia

Dong Kalaw (L) to Trapeang Kriel (C) is the only international border post with Cambodia; see p238. This border links Champasak Province and the Si Phan Don area of Laos with Stung Treng in northern Cambodia.

From China

There is only one international border crossing between Móhān (C) and Boten (L), but it's in quite a remote area of both countries. It links Yúnnán Province in China to Luang Nam Tha Province in Laos. From

Border Crossings

LEGEND
(C) Cambodia
(L) Laos
(T) Thailand
(V) Vietnam
Kūnmíng
YÚNNÁN PROVINCE (CHINA)
CHINA
Mekong River
MYANMAR (BURMA)
Hékǒu (China)
Lao Cai (V)
Youyi Guan (China)
Huu Nghi Quan (V)
Tay Trang (V)
Sop Hun (L)
HANOI
Dongxing (China)
Mong Cai (V)
Móhān (China)
Boten (L)
Nam Xoi (V)
Na Maew (L)
Chiang Khong (T)
Huay Xai (L)
LAOS
Nong Haet (L)
Nam Can (V)
Ban Huay Kon (T)
Muang Ngeun (L)
Hainan Island (China)
Paksan (L)
Beung Kan (T)
VIENTIANE
Nam Phao (L)
Cau Treo (V)
Na Phao (L)
Cha Lo (V)
SOUTH CHINA SEA
Vientiane (L)
Nong Khai (T)
Tha Khaek (L)
Nakhon Phanom (T)
Dansavanh (L)
Lao Bao (V)
Mukdahan (T)
Savannakhet (L)
THAILAND
Chong Mek (T)
Vang Tao (L)
Chong Chom (T)
O Smach (C)
Phou Keua (L)
Bo Y (V)
Aranya Prathet (T)
Poipet (C)
Chong Sa-Ngam (T)
Choam (C)
Dong Kalaw (L)
Trapeang Kriel (C)
O Yadaw (C)
Le Thanh (V)
BANGKOK
Ban Pakard (T)
Psar Pruhm (C)
CAMBODIA
VIETNAM
PHNOM PENH
Trapeang Sre (C)
Loc Ninh (V)
Hat Lek (T)
Cham Yeam (C)
Bavet (C)
Moc Bai (V)
Kaam Samnor (C)
Vinh Xuong (V)
Ho Chi Minh City
Gulf of Thailand
Prek Chak (C)
Xa Xia (V)
Phnom Den (C)
Tinh Bien (V)

MEKONG REGION BORDERS AT A GLANCE

COUNTRIES	BORDER CROSSING
Cambodia/Vietnam	Bavet (C)/Moc Bai (V)
Cambodia/Vietnam	Kaam Samnor (C)/Vinh Xuong (V)
Cambodia/Vietnam	Prek Chak (C)/Xa Xia (V)
Cambodia/Vietnam	Phnom Den (C)/Tinh Bien (V)
Cambodia/Vietnam	O Yadaw (C)/Le Thanh (V)
Cambodia/Laos	Trapeang Kriel (C)/Dong Kalaw (L)
Cambodia/Thailand	Poipet (C)/Aranya Prathet (T)
Cambodia/Thailand	Cham Yeam (C)/Hat Lek (T)
Cambodia/Thailand	O Smach (C)/Chong Chom (T)
Cambodia/Thailand	Psar Pruhm (C)/Ban Pakard (T)
Cambodia/Thailand	Choam (C)/Chong Sa-Ngam (T)
China (Yúnnán)/Laos	Móhān (China)/Boten (L)
China (Yúnnán)/Vietnam	Hékǒu (China)/Lao Cai (V)
China/Vietnam	Youyi Guan (China)/Huu Nghi Quan (V)
China/Vietnam	Dongxing (China)/Mong Cai (V)
Laos/Thailand	Vientiane (L)/Nong Khai (T)
Laos/Thailand	Paksan (L)/Beung Kan (T)
Laos/Thailand	Huay Xai (L)/Chiang Khong (T)
Laos/Thailand	Tha Khaek (L)/Nakhon Phanom (T)
Laos/Thailand	Savannakhet (L)/Mukdahan (T)
Laos/Thailand	Vang Tao (L)/Chong Mek (T)
Laos/Vietnam	Dansavanh (L)/Lao Bao (V)
Laos/Vietnam	Phou Keua (L)/Bo Y (V)
Laos/Vietnam	Na Phao (L)/Cha Lo (V)
Laos/Vietnam	Nong Haet (L)/Nam Can (V)
Laos/Vietnam	Nam Phao (L)/Cau Treo (V)
Laos/Vietnam	Na Maew (L)/Nam Xoi (V)
Laos/Vietnam	Sop Hun (L)/Tay Trang (V)

Boten, it's a two-hour journey to Luang Nam Tha, the nearest major town. See p324 for more information.

From Thailand

The most popular crossing is from Nong Khai (T) across the Thai-Lao Friendship Bridge to Vientiane (L). See p433 for more information. There is also a river crossing between Beung Kan (T) and Paksan (L), about 120km from Vientiane, but it is rarely used by travellers; see p430.

From northern Thailand, you can cross the border by boat at Chiang Khong (T) to Huay Xai (L) and continue downriver to Luang Prabang (L); see p415. A new crossing connecting Muang Ngeun (T) and Ban Huay Kon (L), which links Nan Province (T) with Sainyabuli Province (L), is also open to foreigners (see p418).

From the northeast, travellers have two options. Cross the Mekong at Nakhon Phanom (T) to Tha Khaek (L); see p429; or at Mukdahan (T) to Savannakhet (L), where there is a bridge spanning the river (see p428).

In eastern Thailand, there is a land crossing from Chong Mek (T), near Ubon Ratchathani, to Vang Tao (L), an hour west of Pakse (L); see p426.

CONNECTING TOWNS	VISA ON ARRIVAL	MORE DETAILS
Phnom Penh/Ho Chi Minh City	Cambodia (Y)/Vietnam (N)	p196/p175
Phnom Penh/Chau Doc	Cambodia (Y)/Vietnam (N)	p195/p154
Kep/Ha Tien	Cambodia (Y)/Vietnam (N)	p262/p156
Takeo/Chau Doc	Cambodia (Y)/Vietnam (N)	p260/p155
Ban Lung/Pleiku	Cambodia (Y)/Vietnam (N)	p241/p117
Stung Treng/Si Phan Don	Cambodia (Y)/Laos (Y)	p238/p348
Siem Reap/Bangkok	Cambodia (Y)/Thailand (Y)	p226/p387
Koh Kong/Trat	Cambodia (Y)/Thailand (Y)	p247/p387
Samraong/Surin	Cambodia (Y)/Thailand (Y)	p205/p423
Pailin/Chanthaburi	Cambodia (Y)/Thailand (Y)	p224/p387
Anlong Veng/Chong Sa-Ngam	Cambodia (Y)/Thailand (Y)	p228/p423
Mĕnglà/Luang Nam Tha	China (N)/Laos (Y)	p324
Kūnmíng/Hanoi	China (N)/Vietnam (N)	p90
Pingxiang/Lang Son	China (N)/Vietnam (N)	p87
Dongxing/Mong Cai	China (N)/Vietnam (N)	p87
Vientiane/Nong Khai	Laos (Y)/Thailand (Y)	p290/p433
Paksan/Beung Kan	Laos (N)/Thailand (N)	p329/p430
Huay Xai/Chiang Rai	Laos (Y)/Thailand (Y)	p328/p415
Tha Khaek/Nakhon Phanom	Laos (Y)/Thailand (Y)	p333/p429
Savannakhet/Mukdahan	Laos (Y)/Thailand (Y)	p337/p428
Pakse/Ubon Ratchathani	Laos (Y)/Thailand (Y)	p342/p426
Savannakhet/Dong Ha	Laos (Y)/Vietnam (N)	p338/p102
Attapeu/Pleiku	Laos (Y)/Vietnam (N)	p351/p115
Tha Khaek/Dong Hoi	Laos (N)/Vietnam (N)	p334/p104
Phonsovan/Vinh	Laos (Y)/Vietnam (N)	p316/p97
Tha Khaek/Vinh	Laos (Y)/Vietnam (N)	p331/p96
Sam Neua/Thanh Hoa	Laos (N)/Vietnam (N)	p320/p89
Muang Khua/Dien Bien Phu	Laos (Y)/Vietnam (N)	p312/p94

From Vietnam

The most popular crossing connects Lao Bao (V) to Dansavanh (L), linking the central city of Dong Ha (V) and the southern Lao province of Savannakhet; see p102. Further north there is another land border at Cau Treo (V) to Nam Phao (L); see p96. The nearest Vietnamese city, Vinh, is about 80km from the border and on the Lao side it's about 200km from the border to Tha Khaek, just opposite Nakhon Phanom in Thailand. There is another border in this region at Cha Lo (V) and Na Phao (L), connecting Dong Hoi (V) and Tha Khaek (see p104), but most travellers use Cau Treo (V).

It's also possible to cross at Nam Can (V) to Nong Haet (L), but this is a marathon trek starting in Vinh and aiming for Phonsavan; see p97 for more information. Another northern crossing is open at Nam Xoi (V) to Na Maew (L), connecting Thanh Hoa (V) or Hanoi to Sam Neua in Laos; see p89. However, this is pretty remote and it can take as much as four days to travel between Luang Prabang and Hanoi this way. There is a more southerly border at Bo Y (V) to Phou Keua (L) that links Pleiku (V) with Attapeu (L) and Pakse (L); see p115.

The most recent border to open, long the Holy Grail for border fanatics, connects Tay Trang (V) with Sop Hun (L) (p94), linking Dien Bien Phu (V) with Muang Khua (L).

Thailand

Thailand shares borders with Cambodia and Laos in the Mekong region, plus popular borders with Malaysia and Myanmar. Entry stamps are available at all Thailand crossings except for Beung Kan.

From Cambodia

The border at Poipet (C) to Aranya Prathet (T) is frequently used to access Siem Reap (C) or Bangkok (T); see p226. Along the coast, crossings can be made from Cham Yeam (C) to Hat Lek (T) by road for connections to Trat (T), Bangkok (T) and Koh Chang (T); see p247. There are also three more-remote crossings: from the town of Samraong through O Smach (C) to Chong Chom (T) in Surin Province (see p205); from Anlong Veng through Choam (C) to Chong Sa-Ngam (T), see p228; and from the southwest town of Pailin through Psar Pruhm (C) to Ban Pakard (T); see p224.

From Laos

The most popular crossing is from Vientiane (L) across the Thai-Lao Friendship Bridge to Nong Khai (T); see p290. There is also a river crossing between Paksan (L) and Beung Kan (T), about 120km from Vientiane, but it's rarely used by travellers; see p329.

Heading to northern Thailand, cross the border by boat at Huay Xai (L) to Chiang Khong (T) from where it is a short hop to the Golden Triangle (T) or Chiang Rai (T); see p328. There is also a crossing connecting Ban Huay Kon (L) and Muang Ngeun (T), linking Sainyabuli Province (L) with Nan Province (T), which is seldom used by foreigners (see p418).

From the south, travellers have the option of crossing the Mekong River at Tha Khaek (L) to Nakhon Phanom (T); see p333; or at Savannakhet (L) to Mukdahan (T); see p337. In the far south, there is a land crossing from Vang Tao (L), an hour west of Pakse, to Chong Mek (T), near Ubon Ratchathani; see p342.

From Malaysia

On the west coast, the crossing between Satun (T) to Pulau Langkawi (M) is made by boat. On the east coast, Sungai Kolok (T) to Rantau Panjang (M) is a dusty land crossing for travel between Kota Bharu (M) and Pulau Perhentian (M). The major transit hub in Thailand, Hat Yai, and Penang-Butterworth in Malaysia, receive bus and rail traffic through the borders at Kanger (T) to Padang Besar (M) or Sadao (T) to Bukit Kayu Hitam (M). Betong (T) to Keroh (M) is also a land crossing open to foreigners.

From Myanmar (Burma)

There are two legal crossings: Mae Sai (T) to Tachileik (My) (p413), and Ranong (T) to Kawthoung (My). Be sure to have a valid Myanmar visa when exiting and be prepared for unexpected charges from Myanmar officials at the border when crossing into Thailand.

Vietnam

Vietnam shares borders with Cambodia, China and Laos. Vietnam visas are not available at any land crossings, so be sure to arrange a visa in advance.

From Cambodia

There are plenty of border-crossing options for travel between Vietnam and Cambodia. The road border at Bavet (C) to Moc Bai (V) connects Phnom Penh and Ho Chi Minh City. More memorable is the Mekong River crossing at Kaam Samnor (C) to Vinh Xuong (V) linking Phnom Penh and Chau Doc; see p195.

The newer crossing from Prek Chak (C) to Xa Xia (V; see p262) is a great way to link the Cambodian coast with the Mekong Delta or Phu Quoc Island, while the O Yadaw (C) to Le Thanh (V) crossing – see p241 – looks set to be a popular way to link the Central Highlands of Vietnam with Cambodia's remote northeast.

Then there is the rarely used option of Phnom Den (C) to Tinh Bien (V) that connects Takeo (C) and Chau Doc (V; see p260) plus a couple of obscure borders in the east.

From China

There are three border checkpoints where foreigners are permitted to cross between Vietnam and China. The crossing from Hékǒu (Yúnnán) to Lao Cai (V) is convenient for travellers going between Yúnnán and Hanoi; see p90.

The other two crossings are located outside of Yúnnán Province. The Friendship Gate (Huu Nghi Quan on the Vietnamese side, Youyi Guan on the Chinese side) connects Pinxiang (China) to Lang Son (V), see p87. There's also a seldom-used crossing from Dongxing (China) to Mong Cai in Vietnam's far northeast; see p87.

The China–Vietnam border-crossing hours vary a little but are generally between 8am and 6pm (China time). Reset your watch when you cross the border as the time in Vietnam is one hour behind.

From Laos

The most popular crossing connects Dansavanh (L) to Lao Bao (V), linking Savannakhet (L) and Dong Ha (V); see p338. Further north there is another border connecting Nam Phao (L) to Cau Treo (V); see p331. From the Lao side it's about 200km to the border from Tha Khaek, while the nearest Vietnamese city, Vinh, is about 80km from the border. There is another border in this region at Na Phao (L) and Cha Lo (V), connecting Tha Khaek (L) and Dong Hoi (V); see p334. It's also possible to cross from Nong Haet (L) to Nam Can (V), but this is a marathon trek starting in Phonsavan and aiming for Vinh; see p316 for details. Another northern crossing is open from Na Maew (L) to Nam Xoi (V), connecting Sam Neua (L) to Thanh Hoa (V) or Hanoi (V); see p320.

There is a more southerly border at Phou Keua (L) to Bo Y (V) that links Attapeu (L) and Pakse (L) with Pleiku (V) and Quy Nhon (V); see p351.

The latest border to open, long closed to frustrated border-hoppers, connects Sop Hun (L) with Tay Trang (V) (p312), connecting Muang Khua (L) with Dien Bien Phu (V).

Outdoor Adventures

When to Go

Trekking, cycling, diving or kitesurfing: whatever your flavour, careful planning is required, as the region's climate is highly variable and subject to the annual monsoons. Cycling or trekking in the rain is not a lot of fun, but along other parts of the coast, the surf is up.

Best Trekking

Sapa Superlative views but very popular.
Nam Ha National Protected Area (NPA) Responsible treks in old-growth forest.
Chiang Rai Explore fascinating hill-tribe terrain.
Mondulkiri Walk with elephants in their habitat.

Best Cycling

Mekong Delta Backroads through Vietnam's rice bowl.
Sukhothai Pedal into Thai history.
Muang Sing Cycle through ethnic minority villages.
Angkor Freewheel past ancient wonders.

Best Diving & Snorkelling

Con Dao Remote underwater adventures.
Nha Trang Vietnam's most popular diving.
Hoi An See macro life off Cham Islands.
Sihanoukville Cambodia's top diving destination.

Dense jungles, brooding mountains, endless waterways, towering cliffs and hairpin bends: the potential for adrenalin-fuelled adventures is limitless in the Mekong region. Whether you prefer to scale the heights or plumb the depths, the Mekong region will deliver something special. Just travelling here is one long adventure, but these experiences will take it to another level.

Mountain biking and jungle hiking are taking off. On river and offshore there's kayaking from Mekong tributaries to Halong Bay. Or there is kitesurfing above the water and diving and snorkelling beneath. Even extreme sports are represented, with caving, rock climbing and ziplining all possible in the region. If this all sounds too challenging, jump on a motorbike and let the engine take the strain.

Trekking

Trekking in the Mekong region isn't quite as high and mighty as in Nepal, but the more demure peaks are home to many minority hill-tribe villages, which host overnight trekking groups. Anything is possible, from half-day hikes to assaults on Fansipan, the region's highest mountain. Less-strenuous walks include jungle hikes to pristine waterfalls and village walks in remote areas. The scenery – think plunging highland valleys, tiers of rice paddies and soaring limestone mountains in much of Laos, Thailand and Vietnam – is often remarkable. Even the coastal regions of Cambodia and Vietnam offer some DIY walking opportunities, where you can go strolling along the sands for an hour or two and experience a near-pristine coastal environment.

Trekking companies are recommended in the relevant sections. Rangers inside national parks can also help craft trekking itineraries. It may be necessary to arrange special permits, especially if you plan to spend the night in remote mountain villages in parts of Laos and Vietnam.

Prices, including all food, guides, transportation, accommodation and park fees, start at around US$25 per day for larger groups. For more specialised long treks into remote areas, prices can run into several hundred US dollars. In most cases you can trek with as few as two people, with per-person costs dropping the larger the group.

Where to Hike

Cambodia

Cambodia is the least developed trekking destination among the four neighbours. Trekking in northeast Cambodia is beginning to take off in the provinces of **Mondulkiri** (p242) and **Ratanakiri** (p238) thanks to their wild natural scenery, abundant waterfalls and ethnic minority populations. Remote **Virachey National Park** (p242) in Ratanakiri offers the possibility of multiday treks. The **Cardamom Mountains** (see Koh Kong Conservation Corridor, p247) have huge potential for the future and are starting to draw visitors.

Angkor (p208) is emerging as a good place for gentle walks between the temples – one way to experience peace and solitude as visitor numbers skyrocket.

Laos

Trekking through the mountains and forests of Laos has become so popular it's almost a mandatory part of any visit to the

TOP FIVE WILDLIFE EXPERIENCES

While wildlife-spotting may not be quite as straightforward here as in the Serengeti, it is still possible to have some world-class encounters in the Mekong region.

The Gibbon Experience, Laos

Take to the trees to live like a gibbon in the jungle canopy at this celebrated ecotourism project (p327). Hang from a zipline and glide through the forest: this is monkey business for a good cause.

Dolphinwatching, Cambodia

The freshwater Irrawaddy dolphin is one of the rarest mammals on earth, with fewer than 100 inhabiting stretches of the Mekong. View them in their natural habitat near Kratie (p234) in northeast Cambodia.

Elephant Valley Project, Cambodia

The elephant is one of the oldest forms of transport in the Mekong region. Kick the habit and see these majestic animals in their natural environment by 'walking with the herd' in the lush jungles of Mondulkiri (p244).

Khao Yai National Park, Thailand

The jungle is massive in this incredibly lush national park (p421), home to one of the world's largest monsoon forests. Track shy wildlife, including more than 200 elephants, or hike to hidden waterfalls in this remote paradise.

Wild Gibbon Trek, Vietnam

Cat Tien National Park (p135) is one of Vietnam's most accessible protected areas. Learn more about gibbon behaviour with a dawn trek to a habituated family. Listen to the forest slowly come alive with their calls before watching the family go about their everyday lives.

country. And thanks to several projects aimed at getting money into poor communities, there are now a dozen or more areas you can choose from. **Luang Nam Tha** (p322) has developed an award-winning ecotourism project for visits to local ethnic minority villages in Nam Ha NPA.

Overnight camping treks to the summit of Nong Khiaw's **Phou Nang None** (p310) are a new experience. Eat supper under the stars and take in the dizzying panoramic views of the surrounding karsts and river far below.

In southern Laos, **Xe Pian NPA**, close to Pakse, is great for elephant treks and general hikes. **Dong Natad NPA** (p338) has treks through beautiful landscapes, organised by Savannakhet's Eco Guide Unit.

Thailand

The northern Thai cities of **Chiang Mai** (p391) and **Chiang Rai** (p408) are very popular for treks, often in combination with white-water rafting and elephant rides. **Pai** (p401) has also emerged as an alternative place to trek. Many of these treks are run by ethical operators with sustainable trips to help disadvantaged minority peoples, but there are also a lot of cowboys out there. For trekking tips, see p392.

It is also possible to arrange day treks at up-and-coming **Pha Taem National Park** (see p426), whose centrepiece is a long cliff with views over to Laos and a collection of prehistoric rock paintings that are at least 3000 years old.

Vietnam

Sapa (p91) is Vietnam's trekking mecca. The scenery is remarkable, with majestic mountains, impossibly green rice paddies and some fascinating tribal villages. But the main trails are incredibly popular and some villagers see hiking groups on a hourly basis. **Bac Ha** (p89) is at a lower elevation, less rainy and the trails here are not as heavily tramped.

Phong Nha-Ke Bang National Park (p101) is just opening up to tourism. Adventure tour operators in **Hoi An** (p107) also offer some intriguing treks in the tribal areas west of town.

Hire a guide to see the best of **Cat Tien National Park** (p135) where the Wild Gibbon Trek is proving a big hit. Over in **Dalat** several adventure tour operators offer short hiking trips (p138).

Cycling

The Mekong region is steadily establishing itself as a cycling destination. Thailand has long been the most popular place for cycling tourists, but Vietnam is fast catching up. Even Cambodia and Laos see their share of cyclists these days. For hardcore cyclists, the mountains of northern Vietnam and northern Laos are the ultimate destination. For those who like a more gentle workout, meandering along Mekong villages is memorable, particularly in the Mekong Delta in Vietnam. Biking around Angkor is a great way to get around, and Thailand's northeast can be rewarding thanks to good roads and light traffic.

Throughout the region, basic bicycles can be rented for US$1 to US$3 per day and good-quality mountain bikes cost US$7 to US$12. When it comes to cycling tours,

SAFETY GUIDELINES FOR HIKERS

- Don't stray from established paths, as there are landmines and unexploded ordnance (UXO) in parts of Cambodia, Laos and Vietnam.
- Guides are worth hiring; they're inexpensive, speak the language and understand indigenous culture.
- Dogs can be aggressive; a stout stick may come in handy.
- Boots with ankle support are a great investment.
- Carry a mosquito net if trekking in malarial zones of the region.
- Consider quality socks and repellent to reduce the likelihood of leeches.
- Carry water purification tablets if you have a weak constitution.
- Invest in some snack bars or energy snacks to avoid getting 'riced out' on longer treks.

» (above) Trekking near Dalat (p129), Vietnam
» (left) Cycling around Angkor Thom (p209), Cambodia

CYCLING HIGHLIGHTS

LOCATION	DETAILS	PAGE
Angkor, Cambodia	Incredible temples, towering forest and friendly locals make exploring by bike a must	p208
Luang Nam Tha, Laos	Dramatic scenery, fecund forests and minority villages provide a dramatic backdrop	p322
Sukhothai, Thailand	Cycling through the first Thai capital, the Land of Rising Happiness, will guarantee a smile	p404
Dalat, Vietnam	Lots of dirt trails and base camp for the dramatic two-day descent to the beaches of Mui Ne	p129

Bangkok-based **Spice Roads** (www.spiceroads.com) is the acknowledged expert for the Mekong region and Asia beyond, but there are good local operators in each country.

For some laughs, as well as the low-down on cycling in the Mekong region, visit the website www.mrpumpy.net. Visit the FAQ sections for to-the-point information on what to take and packing the bike on an aeroplane.

ZIPLINING IN LAOS

Ziplining has, well, quite literally taken off in Laos. **The Gibbon Experience** (p327) in Bokeo Nature Reserve pioneered the use of ziplines to explore the jungle canopy. Visitors hang from a zipline and glide through the forest where the gibbons roam. Overnight in treehouses and test-drive the new **Gibbon Spa** for a massage in the most memorable of locations.

Ecotourism pioneer **Green Discovery** (www.greendiscoverylaos.com) now offers an alternative zipline experience for thrill-seekers in southern Laos. **Tree Top Explorer** (p340) is an exciting new network of vertiginous ziplines passing over the semi-evergreen canopy of the south's Don Hua Sao NPA. Ride so close to a giant waterfall you can taste the spray on your lips. Feel the wind on your face on its longest 450m ride, then flop into bed in your comfortable 20m-high treehouse.

Motorbiking

For those with a thirst for adventure, motorbike trips into remote areas of the region are unforgettable. The mobility of two wheels is unrivalled. Motorbikes can traverse trails that even the hardiest 4WD cannot follow. It puts you closer to the countryside – its smells, people and scenery – compared with getting around by car or bus. Just remember to watch the road, even when the passing scenery is sublime. Motorbiking is still *the* mode of transport for many Mekong residents, so you'll find repair shops everywhere. If you are not confident riding a motorbike, it's comparatively cheap to hire someone to drive it for you, particularly in Cambodia, Laos or Vietnam. For those seeking true adventure, there is no better way to go.

Motorbikes are available for rent throughout the region. Daily charges start at just US$4 to US$10 for 100cc bikes and rise to US$10 to US$25 for 250cc dirt bikes or road bikes. Thailand has serious touring and road bikes for hire, but, thankfully, a licence is usually required. No licence is required in Laos, Cambodia or Vietnam.

Specialist motorcycle touring companies can organise multiday trips into remote areas using the roads less travelled. Costs for these trips start from US$50 a day for Dalat's Easy Riders up to US$150 a day or more for the premium tours, depending on accommodation. One of the most experienced operators in the region is **Explore Indochina** (www.exploreindochina.com), which covers the Ho Chi Minh Trail in Laos and Vietnam and provided support services for the BBC 'Top Gear Vietnam' special.

Kayaking, Sailing, Rafting & Boat Trips

With the Mekong cutting a swath through the heart of the region, it is hardly surprising to find that boat trips are a major drawcard here. There are opportunities to explore small jungled tributaries leading to remote minority villages in Cambodia and Laos. It is possible to explore cave systems by boat in Vietnam, as well as experience the bustle of a floating market in the Mekong Delta. Whole villages float on the waters of the Tonlé Sap lake in Cambodia. Cruising the waters of Halong Bay on a junk is one of the most iconic boat trips in the region (see the boxed text, p81).

It is also possible to make some functional boat trips that offer beautiful scenery. The two-day boat trip from Huay Xai and the Golden Triangle down to Luang Prabang includes a stunning stretch of the Mekong. Travelling by boat from Chau Doc in the Mekong Delta to Phnom Penh offers a tantalising glimpse of rural life, or go one better with a boat cruise from Ho Chi Minh City to Siem Reap.

Kayaking has exploded in popularity in Vietnam in the past few years, particularly around Halong Bay, following in the footsteps of Krabi in Thailand. Many standard Halong Bay tours now include kayaking through the karsts, or you can choose a kayaking specialist and paddle around majestic limestone pinnacles, before overnighting on a remote bay. The rest of the nation is catching up, and other kayaking destinations now include Cat Ba, Phong Nha, Dalat and rivers of the Hoi An region.

There are also kayaking trips on many rivers in Laos and Thailand, although some of the white water is for experienced paddlers only. Given that Laos is intersected by multiple rivers, it's not surprising that a number of companies have established some easy to adrenalin-level kayaking trips. **Luang Prabang** (see p310), **Nong Khiaw** (see p309) and **Vang Vieng** (see p294) are all popular destinations for a spot of paddling.

Kayaking starts from as little as US$25 per day, but it is usually included free on Halong Bay boat trips.

Sailing trips, lessons and courses are available in Vietnam. Nha Trang is a popular watersports base. Sail to a stunning backdrop in the Halong Bay region with tours out of Cat Ba Island taking in beautiful Lan Ha Bay.

White-water rafting is in its infancy in the Mekong region and the rivers are fairly tame most of the year. Things can get a little more vigorous in the wet season.

MOTORBIKING HIGHLIGHTS

LOCATION	RIDES	VIEWS
Cambodia	Route 66 Angkor road	Ancient Angkor bridges
	Phnom Penh to Kep	Rice fields and karst
	Snuol to Mondulkiri	Mountains and jungle
	Sre Ambel to Koh Kong	Cardamom Mountains
Laos	Ho Chi Minh Trail	Jungle and war relics
	Pakse to Attapeu direct	Bolaven Plateau falls
	Luang Nam Tha	Jungle and minorities
	Luang Prabang to Vang Vieng	Karst and mountains
Thailand	Pai to Chiang Mai	Hair-raising hairpins
	Khorat to Surin	Khmer temple trail
	Chiang Rai to Nan	Jungle and parks
Vietnam	Ha Giang to Meo Vac	Incredible karst scenery
	Dien Bien Phu to Sapa	Mighty Tram Ton Pass
	Dalat to Nha Trang	High-altitude jungle pass
	Hai Van Pass	The 'Top Gear' road
	Duc Tho to Phong Nha	Ho Chi Minh Highway

CHRISTER FREDRIKSSON / LONELY PLANET IMAGES ©

» (above) Diving in Thailand
» (left) Windsurfing at Mui Ne (p123), Vietnam

Rafting in Vietnam is available out of **Dalat** and **Nha Trang** (p119). In Thailand, it is possible to include rafting in multi-activity treks out of **Chiang Mai** (p391) or **Chiang Rai** (p407) or, for something more specialised, try a two- to three-day rafting trip out of **Nan** (p415).

Diving & Snorkelling

Compared with destinations like Indonesia and the Philippines, diving and snorkelling opportunities in the Mekong region are limited. Thailand has great diving for those heading south from Bangkok.

Vietnam, and to a lesser extent Cambodia, have up-and-coming dive industries. The most popular place to dive in Vietnam is **Nha Trang** (p117), with plenty of reputable dive operators, whose equipment and training is up to international standards. Hoi An's two dive schools head to the lovely **Cham Islands** (p166) where macro life can be impressive. **Phu Quoc Island** (p166) is another popular spot. The **Con Dao Islands** (p127) offer unquestionably the best diving and snorkelling in Vietnam, with bountiful marine life, fine reefs and even a wreck dive. Two professional dive schools are based here, though it's more costly than the rest of Vietnam.

In Cambodia, **Sihanoukville** (p249) is the main place geared up for diving and snorkelling, but the best diving is further afield and requires an overnight on a boat.

Typical diving and snorkellings costs:

» Discover Scuba: US$60-80

» 2 fun dives US$60-80 (US$140 in Con Dao)

» Padi Open Water: US$350-500

» Snorkelling day trip: US$20-40

Kitesurfing & Windsurfing

Windsurfing and kitesurfing have only recently arrived on the scene, but these are quickly catching on. **Mui Ne Beach** (p123) is fast becoming an Asian windchasers' hotspot with competitions and a real buzz about the place. **Nha Trang** and **Vung Tau** are other possibilities.

If you've never kitesurfed before, go for a taster lesson (from US$75) first before you enrol in a lengthy course – a three-day course costs around US$250. It's tough to get your head (and body) around all the basics.

The best conditions in Mui Ne are in the dry season (November to April). Mornings are ideal for beginners, while in the afternoon wind speeds regularly reach 35 knots.

RESPONSIBLE DIVING

Please consider the following tips when diving and help preserve the ecology and beauty of reefs:

» Never use anchors on a reef and take care not to ground boats on coral.

» Avoid touching or standing on living marine organisms or dragging equipment across a reef. Polyps can be damaged by even the gentlest contact. If you must hold on to a reef, only touch exposed rock or dead coral.

» Be conscious of your fins. Even without contact, the surge from fin strokes near a reef can damage delicate organisms. Take care not to kick up clouds of sand, which can smother organisms.

» Practise and maintain proper buoyancy control. Major damage can be done by divers descending too fast and colliding with the reef.

» Resist the temptation to collect or buy coral or shells or to take souvenirs from marine archaeological sites (mainly shipwrecks).

» Ensure that you take home all your rubbish, and any litter you may find as well. Plastics in particular are a serious threat to marine life.

» Do not feed fish.

» Minimise your disturbance of marine animals. *Never* ride on the backs of turtles.

CHARLIE DOES SURF

First, the bad news: *that* wave scene in *Apocalypse Now* was shot in the Philippines. But the good news is that Vietnam offers decent surf at the right times of year. Surf's up between November and April when the winter monsoon blows from the north. Several typhoons form in the South China Sea each year and these produce the biggest wind swells, though the action is usually short-lived.

Dedicated surf shops are rare, though the odd guesthouse and adventure-sport tour operator have boards for hire from US$5 to US$20 per day. Surfing lessons are available from US$50 per day.

The best locations include the following:

» **Danang:** The original GI Joe break on a 30km stretch of sand. Can produce clean peaks over 2m, though watch out for pollution after heavy rains.

» **Nha Trang**: Head to Bai Dai beach, 27km south of Nha Trang, where there's a good lefthand break, up to 2m, during stormy conditions.

» **Mui Ne**: Ideal for beginners. Multiple breaks around the bay including short right- and left-handers. Occasionally barrels.

Anyone searching for fresh waves in remote locations should be extremely wary of unexploded ordnance (UXO), which litters the countryside, particularly near the DMZ. Garbage, stormwater run-off and industrial pollution are other hazards, particularly near cities. Rip tides can be powerful, so use a leash on your board.

Rock Climbing

When it comes to organised climbing, Thailand has the most on offer (see p392 for info on Chiang Mai), but the region is liberally peppered with karsts and climbing in Laos and Vietnam has really taken off. In Vietnam, the pioneers and acknowledged specialists are **Asia Outdoors** (p83), a highly professional outfit based on Cat Ba that offers instruction for beginners and dedicated trips for rock addicts. In **Dalat** (p138) there are a couple of good adventure tour operators offering climbing and canyoning too.

In Laos, **Vang Vieng** (p294) has some of the best climbing in Southeast Asia with 200 routes – many of them bolted – up the limestone cliffs, along with excellent instructors and safe equipment. Most routes are rated between 4a and 8b. **Adam's Rock Climbing School** (www.laos-climbing.com) is the only dedicated climbing outfit in town, with experienced guides and sturdy kit. Nong Khiaw has attracted the adventure specialist **Green Discovery** (www.nongkiau.com), with climbs up the limestone karsts under close and experienced instruction.

Climbing costs in the region start from about US$20 for a group of four and rise for more specialised climbs in the Halong Bay area or for instruction.

Travel with Children

Best Regions for Children

Bangkok

The City of Angels does a surprising cameo as the City of Little Angels, although you have to seek out the experiences. Boat rides on the *khlong* (canals), and shopping centres with aquariums and wax museums are fun.

Siem Reap/Angkor

If the children are Indiana Jones fans, look no further than the temples of Angkor. Ta Prohm has the jungle, Bayon has the weirdness and Angkor Wat has the proportions. Leave time for floating villages and bicycle rides.

Vietnamese Coastline

If they want beaches, they'll get them in Vietnam. Hoi An combines culture with cavorting on the sand. Nha Trang has fun boat trips, and the older kids can windsurf or sandboard in Mui Ne.

Luang Prabang

While its cultural credentials draw mature visitors in their thousands, Luang Prabang has plenty to offer younger visitors, including kayaking, cycling and elephant encounters. The waterfalls are also a hit thanks to jungle bathing opportunities.

The Mekong for Children

Children can live it up in the Mekong region, as they are always the centre of attention and almost everybody wants to play with them. This goes double for exotic-looking foreign children from faraway lands. Children become instant celebrities wherever they go in the region, locals overcoming their natural conservatism to immediately interact with the young ones.

This is great news when it comes to babes in arms and little toddlers, as everyone wants to entertain them for a time or babysit while you tuck into a plate of noodles. This works in a diverse range of environments from the market and street stall through to international restaurants, as long as they are not too pretentious or packed with customers.

As the toddler moves into childhood, a certain wariness towards strangers may develop and this can create some conflicts along the way. People in the Mekong region are not backwards in coming forwards with children and this extends to pinching cheeks and patting bums. While this might be tolerable from the great aunt they get to see once in a blue moon, it's not so fun when it is happening a dozen times a day with random people in the street. Soon enough you'll find your child wants to be carried on your shoulders whenever the opportunity arises.

For the full picture on surviving and thriving on the road, check out Lonely Planet's

Travel with Children by Cathy Lanigan, which contains useful advice on how to cope on the road, with a focus on travel in developing countries. There is also a rundown on health precautions for kids and advice on travel during pregnancy.

Children's Highlights

Among many contrasting destinations in the Mekong region, children will especially enjoy the beaches. Cambodia has the most child-friendly waters, as it faces the shallow, warm waters of the Gulf of Thailand. Sihanoukville and Kep are the most popular beaches, but the islands are also emerging as the next big thing. Vietnam has a superb selection of beaches, including the calm waters around Phu Quoc. However, many of their beaches face the South China Sea and attract some bigger rip tides, so very close supervision is required for most pre-teens.

Animal amusements abound in the region, but the conditions and treatment are often sub-par compared with standards in the West. Elephant rides are a popular experience and there are sustainable initiatives around Lampang and Chiang Mai in Thailand, Luang Prabang and Champasak in Laos and Mondulkiri in Cambodia. Rides in Vietnam are also possible but there is more of a circus feel about those in the Central Highlands.

Older children will appreciate the diverse range of activities on offer in the region, including rafting and boat trips, wildlife encounters with mammals from dolphins to primates, jungle romps to waterfalls, ruined temples in the jungle and organised watersports.

The big cities can be great fun for those in awe of construction sites, as places like Bangkok and Ho Chi Minh City are filled with cranes, jackhammers and concrete-pouring trucks. A metropolis like Bangkok also has the Skytrain for elevated city views and shopping malls complete with escalators and lifts. The city's immense shopping options will appeal to the tweens and teens and places like Hanoi, Ho Chi Minh City and Phnom Penh are slowly catching up. Many of these shopping centres also include indoor playgrounds and entertainment centres for children, which might sound hellish from afar, but can be heaven on a sweltering day when you just need air-con and the chance for the children to do some 'sightseeing' instead of the adults.

Many children are really into their transport and the Mekong region can deliver in style. For kids who have never been on a sleeper train, both Thailand and Vietnam offer a great chance to experience this in relative comfort. Unlike buses, trains allow children to walk around and children are usually assigned the lower sleeping berths with views of the stations.

Boats provide a lot of fun, provided you do a sweep for lifejackets before committing to a trip and stay vigilant along the way. River trips are generally less likely to churn the stomach and the scenery can be more dramatic: choose from the mountains of northern Laos and Thailand down to the floating markets of the Mekong Delta. From our experience, Halong Bay will stun children of any age, including youngsters, as the scenery is simply out of this world. Overnights are an adventure for many and it is also possible to cruise the Mekong from Huay Xai to Luang Prabang, and from Phnom Penh to Ho Chi Minh City.

Local transport is also a blast, providing you throw away the international health and safety manual for parenting for a while. *Cyclo* (bicycle rickshaw) rides in Cambodia, Laos and Vietnam are a timeless way to explore towns and cities. Túk-túks, or their local equivalent, are a buzz, but sometimes the drivers need to be reminded to use the brakes.

Even the temples can be engaging places for children. Climbing hilltop temples is a great way to expend energy and some forested hills have cave shrines. Merit-making at a Buddhist temple is surprisingly kid-friendly, including the burning of joss sticks, the bowing in front of the Buddha and the rubbing of gold leaf on the central image. It is a very active process that kids can enjoy. In Luang Prabang, if you can wake them up early enough (perhaps they will wake you), children can join in the dawn call to alms. As the monks snake their way through this timeless town, the kids can drop sticky rice or other donations into their bowls.

Temples schmemples. Wait until they see Angkor. Not for the youngest of children, those of four and up will be amazed by the jungle roots of Ta Prohm, the Tomb Raider temple, and immense four-faced gates of Angkor Thom. Choose wisely though, as they may only have the stamina for one or two temples a day. Still, if there is a swimming pool at the end of it, and there often is in the average midrange hotel in the Mekong region, they will be sorted.

Planning

Amenities specially geared towards young children – such as child-safety seats for cars, high chairs in restaurants or nappy-changing facilities in public restrooms – are virtually nonexistent in the Mekong region. It is sometimes possible to arrange a child seat if booking a regional tour through a high-end travel agent, but otherwise parents have to be extra resourceful in seeking out substitutes. Or just follow the example of local families, which means holding smaller children on their laps much of the time.

Cot beds (cribs) are available in international-standard midrange and top-end hotels, but not elsewhere. However, many hotels are happy to add an extra bed or a mattress for a nominal charge.

Baby formula and nappies (diapers) are available at minimarts and supermarkets in the larger towns and cities, but the sizes are usually smallish, small and smaller. For larger sizes, you will need to hit a major supermarket in one of the big cities of the region. Nappy-rash cream is sold at pharmacies. Breastfeeding in public is quite common, so there is no need to worry about crossing a cultural boundary.

Hauling around little ones can be a challenge. Pavements and footpaths are often too crowded to push a stroller, especially today's full-sized SUV versions. Instead opt for a compact umbrella pushchair that can squeeze past the fire hydrant and the mango cart and that can be folded up and thrown in a túk-túk. A baby backpack is also useful but make sure that the child's head doesn't sit higher than yours: there are lots of hanging obstacles poised at forehead level.

Health & Safety

For the most part, parents needn't worry too much about health concerns, although it pays to lay down a few ground rules (such as regular hand-washing) to head off potential medical problems.

The main worry throughout the region is keeping an eye on what strange things infants are putting in their mouths. Their natural curiosity can be a lot more costly in countries where dysentery, typhoid and hepatitis are commonplace. Keeping their hydration levels up and insisting they use sunscreen, despite their protests, are also important.

Children should be warned not to play with animals as rabies is relatively common in Thailand and many dogs are better at being barkers and garbage eaters than pets. 'Cute' monkeys are some of the biggest offenders when it comes to bites, so be extra vigilant when they are around.

Mosquito and sandfly bites often leave big welts on children. Use child-friendly repellents around dusk and arrange for them to sleep under a mosquito net in remote areas, especially in the wet season. One of the nastier bites in the region comes from innocuous looking sandflies. These are present on some beaches in Cambodia and Vietnam. The main problem is the itchiness of the bites, which if infected can cause complications. Use sticking plasters and encourage children to itch with fingers not nails. If they get bitten, there are a variety of locally produced balms that can reduce swelling and itching. All the usual health precautions apply.

Children familiar with urban environments will do well in the region's cities, where traffic is chaotic and pedestrian paths are congested. Mekong cities are very loud and can be sensory overloads for young children. Be sure that your child cooperates with your safety guidelines before heading out as it will be difficult for them to focus on your instructions amid all the street noise. Sometimes in this region, it is better to restrict your child's movements than have them wander into danger.

Parts of rural Cambodia, Laos and Vietnam are not such good travel destinations for children, as there are landmines and unexploded ordnance (UXO) littering the countryside. No matter how many warnings a child is given, you can't be certain they won't stray from the path.

countries at a glance

Many a Mekong adventure begins or ends in Bangkok. It works as the perfect decompression chamber between East and West. Thailand is a good launch pad for first-timers in Southeast Asia as it combines the exotic and familiar, sizzling street carts side by side with 7-Elevens.

Most travellers make a loop through Indochina entering Laos or Cambodia overland before continuing into Vietnam. A flight to Hanoi is also an option to cover some of the legwork.

Laos is the remote backwater of Indochina. Diverse minorities and national parks ensure this is the ecotourism darling of the region. Cambodia is the land in between – as Phnom Penh and Siem Reap race to embrace a better future, much of the country is left behind and travels to remote areas are still a challenge. Temple heavyweight of the region, it is also home to some of the friendliest people in the region, the Khmers.

Vietnam is catching up with Thailand fast. Spiralling cities, designer dining and ultra-luxury beach resorts point to the future. War relics and traditional minority lifestyles are reminders of the past.

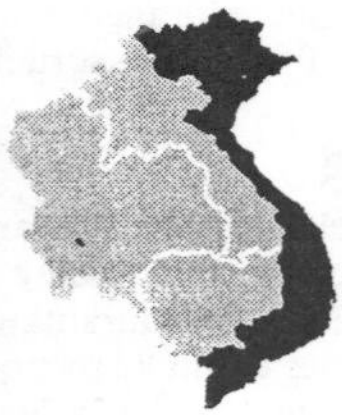

Vietnam

Blissful Beaches ✓✓✓
Delectable Dining ✓✓✓
Historic Cities ✓✓

Blissful Beaches

Vietnam has a voluptuous coastline. Hoi An, Mui Ne and Nha Trang are the big hitters, but there are hundreds of kilometres of empty beaches to discover, including islands such as Phu Quoc and Con Dao.

Delectable Dining

You don't have to be a gastronome to experience the culinary delights of Vietnam. Surf the streets for sumptuous local snacks, discover the bounty of the sea along the lengthy coastline or learn the secrets of the kitchen with a cooking class.

Historic Cities

Explore the bustling Old Quarter of 1000-year-old Hanoi, discover the tombs and royal relics of imperial Hué, and browse the backstreet galleries, cafes and bars of delightful Hoi An – in Vietnam you are literally spoilt for choice when it comes to cities with a story to tell.

p56

Cambodia

Top Temples ✓✓✓
Non-profits ✓✓✓
In the Jungle ✓✓

Top Temples
Heard enough about Angkor Wat? Well don't forget the pre-Angkorian capital of Sambor Prei Kuk, the region's first temple city, or the jungle temples of Preah Vihear Province. If Angkor Wat is the mother of all temples, Cambodia is the daddy of temple destinations.

Responsible Tourism
Cambodia is leading the way in non-profit initiatives to help the disadvantaged or downtrodden. Dine out at sumptuous training restaurants giving a helping hand to ex-street kids, buy designer silk dresses stitched by disabled seamstresses or try a community homestay deep in the countryside.

In the Jungle
Jungle is massive in Cambodia, at least for the time being. Bike into the Cardamom Mountains from a base in Chi Phat or trek through the remote and unexplored Virachey National Park in Ratanakiri. Wilderness remains a reality rather than a dream in remote Cambodia.

p178

Laos

National Parks ✓✓✓
Minority Culture ✓✓✓
Adventures ✓✓

National Parks
With around 20 National Protected Areas, Laos has more dense forest per square mile than anywhere else in Southeast Asia and is begging to be explored. Award-winning ecotreks take you deep into the jungle realm of the clouded leopard, wild elephant and Asiatic tiger.

Minority Culture
More than 65 tribes (and still counting) compose Laos' colourful ethnic quilt. In the rugged north there are homestay opportunities galore (with a minimal footprint), which allow you to immerse yourself in rural life, encounter animism and observe cultures which have changed little in the last century.

Adrenalin Adventures
Glide like gibbons on one of a number of tree-canopy ziplines, taking you up close to nature and jaw-dropping jungle views. By night sleep in a treehouse and wait for the eyes to blink on in the trees.

p278

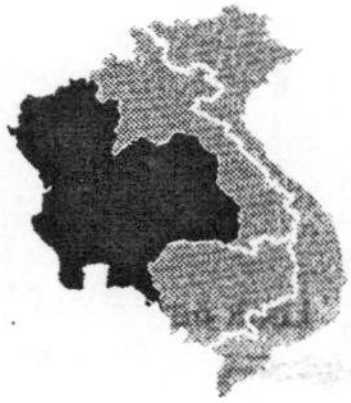

Northern Thailand

Fiery Food ✓✓✓
Shopping ✓✓✓
Upcountry ✓✓

Fiery Food
Start getting your taste buds in shape, as everything you've heard about Thai food is true. From spicy stir-fries to sadistic salads, chillies form their own food group for Thais. If it gets too much, put out the fire with some extra rice, not water.

Shopping
Believe us, you've never encountered commerce the way they do it in Thailand. From the mega-malls and hypermarkets of Bangkok to Chiang Mai's more sedate Saturday Walking Street and Sunday Walking Street, you'll work hard not to come away from Thailand with a souvenir or five.

Upcountry Adventures
If you're willing to stray from the beaten track, provincial Thailand invites you learn to how to ride an elephant, do a homestay in rice-growing country or trek to a remote hill-tribe village. Prerequisites include a Thai dictionary and a willingness to live like a local; the memories come effortlessly.

p364

Look out for these icons:

TOP CHOICE Our author's recommendation

A green or sustainable option

FREE No payment required

See the Index for a full list of destinations covered in this book.

On the Road

Vietnam

Includes »

Best Places to Eat

» Morning Glory (p112)

» Hanoi's street-food kitchens (p69)

» Cuc Gach Quan (p142)

» Veranda (p121)

Best Places to Stay

» Sofitel Metropole Hotel (p66)

» Full Moon Resort (p124)

» Pilgrimage Hotel (p97)

» Phong Nha Homestay (p101)

Why Go?

If there's one country in Southeast Asia that everyone has heard about before they discover the region, it's Vietnam. Of course, such infamy wasn't always for the right reasons, but that's history. This is the new Vietnam and it's one of the most intoxicating destinations on earth. It's a kaleidoscope of vivid colours and subtle shades, of exotic sights and curious sounds, of grand architecture and deeply moving war sites.

Nature has blessed Vietnam with soaring mountains in the north, emerald-green rice paddies in the Mekong Delta and a sensational, curvaceous coastline blessed with ravishing sandy beaches. Travelling here you'll witness children riding buffalo, see the impossibly intricate textiles of hill-tribe communities, hear the buzz of a million motorbikes and eat some the world's greatest food.

This is a dynamic nation, on the move, where life is lived at pace. Prepare yourself for the ride of your life.

When to Go

Hanoi

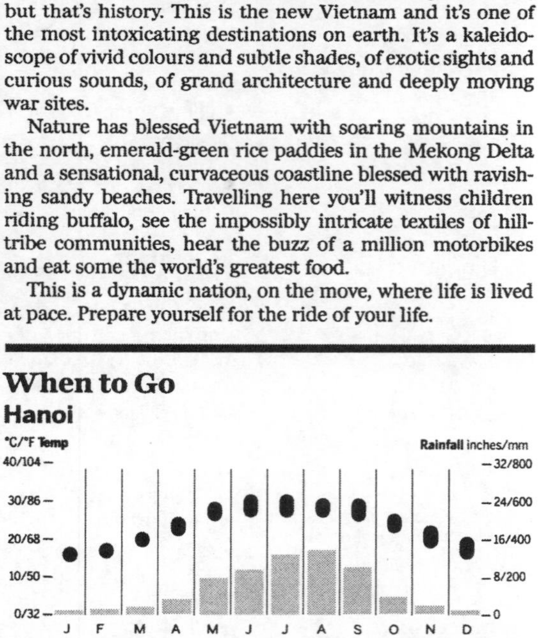

Dec–Mar Cool weather north of Hué; the winter monsoon brings cloud and drizzle.

Apr–May On balance perhaps the best time to tour the whole nation.

Jul–Aug High season on the central coast, with balmy temperatures.

Connections

Ho Chi Minh City Airport Taxi to centre 100,000d, around 30 minutes; bus (Route 152) 4000d, every 15 minutes, 6am-6pm, around 40 minutes.
Hanoi Airport Taxi to centre 300,000d, around one hour; Vietnam Airlines minibus US$3, every 30 minutes.

ITINERARIES

One Week

Begin in **Hanoi**, immerse yourself in Old Quarter life and tour the capital's sights and its famous museums for a couple of days. Then it's a day-trip to **Halong Bay** to lap up the surreal karst scenery from the deck of a boat, ideally with a cold beer in hand. Move down to **Hué** to explore the imperial citadel and any number of wonderful pagodas on the banks of the Perfume River. Then shift to **Hoi An** for two days of foodie treats, old-world ambience and beach time. Finish off with a night in **Ho Chi Minh City (HCMC)**.

Two Weeks

Acclimatise in the capital, **Hanoi**, see the sights, then wine and dine. Tour incomparable **Halong Bay** by boat, then take in the extraordinary caves and karsts of **Phong Nha**. **Hué**, city of pagodas and tombs, beckons next before pushing on to charming **Hoi An**. Rest up here. Party in **Nha Trang**, Vietnam's beach king, then continue south to idyllic **Mui Ne Beach** and hit lovely An Bang beach nearby if the climate is benign. Round things off Saigon-style in Vietnam's liveliest metropolis, **HCMC**.

What to Take

» Calculator – for all those tricky sums; the Vietnamese currency is notoriously hard to fathom.

» Mobile phone – get yourself a local SIM card and domestic calls and international texts (SMS) cost next to nothing.

» Earplugs – sleep deeper in the cities with every traveller's best friend.

» Hiking boots – ideal for tackling both tough highland trails and rough city streets. It's best to bring your own as large sizes are hard to find.

NEED TO KNOW

» **Currency** Dong (d)

» **Language** Vietnamese

» **Money** ATMs are widespread

» **Visas** Required in advance for most nationalities

» **Mobile phones** Prepay SIM cards for a few dollars

Fast Facts

» **Area** 329,566 sq km

» **Capital** Hanoi

» **Country Code** ☎84

» **Population** 90 million

Exchange Rates

Australia	A$1	21,700d
Canada	C$1	20,600d
Europe	€1	28,900d
Japan	¥100	27,500d
New Zealand	NZ$1	16,700d
UK	£1	33,600d
USA	US$1	21,000d

Set Your Budget

» **Budget hotel room** US$8–15

» **Memorable restaurant meal** US$5–10

» **Beer in bar** from US$0.75

» **Short taxi ride** US$2

Vietnam Highlights

❶ Hoi An (p107) Charming despite the tourists, this maze of cobbled lanes offers a magical trip back in time

❷ Hanoi (p60) The capital is a seductive blend of Parisian grace and Asian pace, bubbling with commerce and buzzing with motorbikes

❸ Halong Bay (p79) Island peaks tower above the shimmering sea at this natural wonder

❹ Ho Chi Minh City (p135) Saigon's visceral energy will delight big-city devotees with its history and vibrant nightlife

❺ Northwest Highlands (p91) Banks of clouds and mist ebb and flow across this dramatic mountainous area, dotted with tribal villages

❻ Mui Ne (p123) Lie back on the pristine beach, clamber immense sand dunes or kitesurf sick waves

❼ Phong Nha-Ke Bang National Park (p101) Limestone highlands riddled with extraordinary cave systems

❽ Con Dao Islands (p127) Idyllic islands fabled for their remote beaches, pristine dive sites and diverse nature

❾ Hué (p95) Follow in the footsteps of emperors in this majestic imperial city

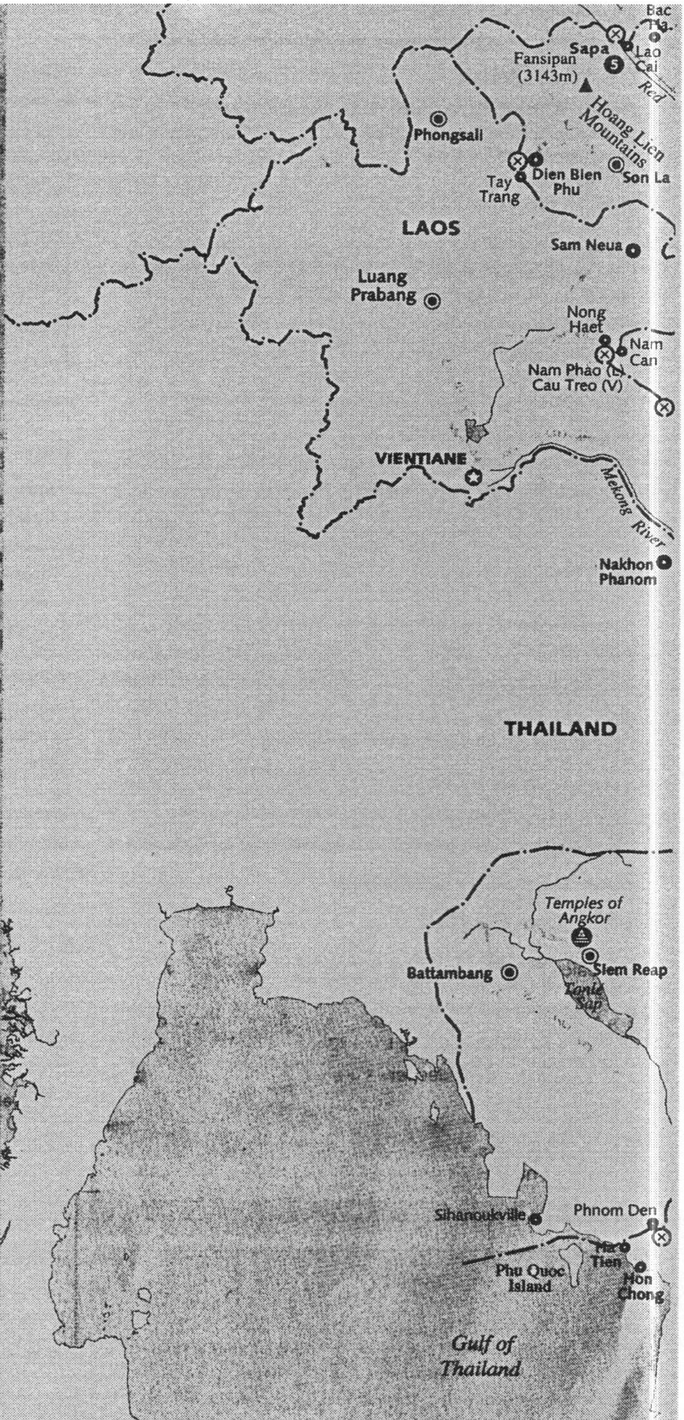

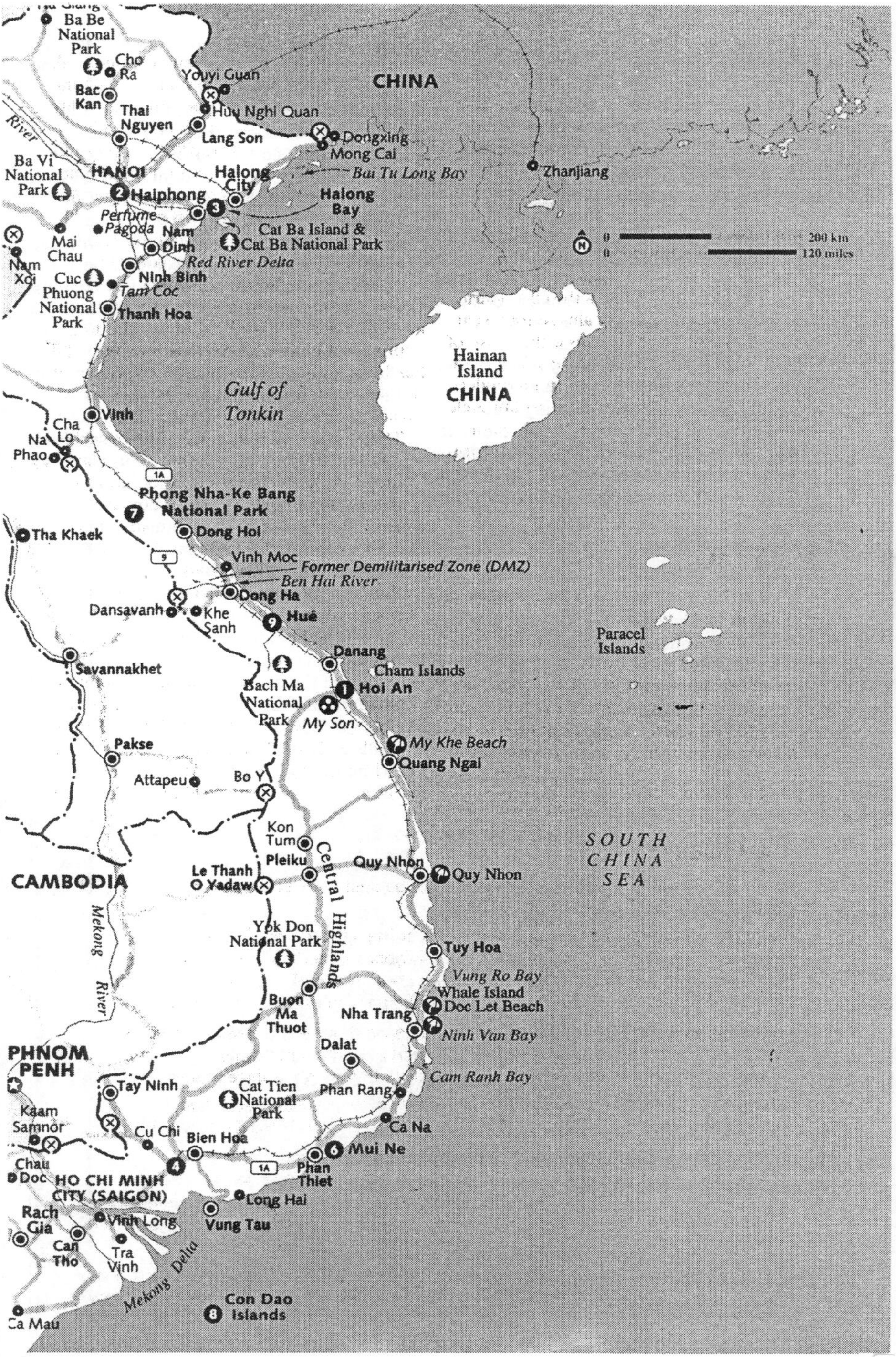

Ba Be National Park
Cho Ra
Bac Kan
Thai Nguyen
River
Youyi Guan
Huu Nghi Quan
Lang Son
CHINA
Dongxing
Mong Cai
Zhanjiang
Ba Vi National Park
HANOI
Haiphong
Halong City
Bai Tu Long Bay
Halong Bay
Perfume Pagoda
Mai Chau
Nam Xoi
Nam Dinh
Cat Ba Island & Cat Ba National Park
Red River Delta
Ninh Binh
Cuc Phuong National Park
Tam Coc
Thanh Hoa
0 200 km
0 120 miles
Hainan Island
CHINA
Gulf of Tonkin
Vinh
Cha Lo
Na Phao
1A
Phong Nha-Ke Bang National Park
Dong Hoi
Tha Khaek
9
Vinh Moc
Former Demilitarised Zone (DMZ)
Ben Hai River
Dong Ha
Dansavanh
Khe Sanh
Hué
Paracel Islands
Danang
Savannakhet
Cham Islands
Bach Ma National Park
Hoi An
My Son
My Khe Beach
Quang Ngai
Pakse
Attapeu
Bo Y
Kon Tum
SOUTH CHINA SEA
Pleiku
Central Highlands
Quy Nhon
Quy Nhon
Le Thanh
Yadaw
CAMBODIA
Mekong River
Yok Don National Park
Tuy Hoa
Vung Ro Bay
Whale Island
Doc Let Beach
Buon Ma Thuot
Nha Trang
Ninh Van Bay
Dalat
PHNOM PENH
Cam Ranh Bay
Tay Ninh
Cat Tien National Park
Phan Rang
Kaam Samnor
Ca Na
Cu Chi
Bien Hoa
Mui Ne
Chau Doc
HO CHI MINH CITY (SAIGON)
1A
Phan Thiet
Long Hai
Rach Gia
Vinh Long
Vung Tau
Can Tho
Tra Vinh
Mekong Delta
Con Dao Islands
Ca Mau

HANOI

☎04 / POP 6.4 MILLION

The grand old dame of the Orient, Hanoi is the most graceful, atmospheric and captivating capital city in the region. Here exotic old Asia blends seamlessly with the dynamic face of the continent, an architectural museum piece evolving in harmony with its history, rather than bulldozing through it.

A mass of motorbikes swarms through the tangled web of streets that is the Old Quarter, a cauldron of commerce for almost 1000 years and still the best place to check the pulse of this resurgent city. Hanoi has it all: the ancient history, a colonial legacy and a modern outlook. There is no better place to untangle the paradox that is contemporary Vietnam.

Known by many names down the centuries, Thanh Long (City of the Soaring Dragon) is the most evocative, and let there be no doubt that this dragon is on the up once more.

Sights

TOP CHOICE Old Quarter NEIGHBOURHOOD

This is the Asia we dreamed of from afar. Steeped in history, pulsating with life, bubbling with commerce, buzzing with motorbikes and rich in exotic scents, the Old Quarter is Hanoi's historic heart. Hawkers pound the streets bearing sizzling, smoking baskets that hide a cheap meal. *Pho* (noodle soup) stalls and *bia hoi* (draught beer) dens hug every corner, resonant with the sound of gossip and laughter. It's modern yet medieval, and there's no better way to spend some time in Hanoi than walking these streets, simply soaking up the sights, sounds and smells.

Hoan Kiem Lake (Map p70) is the liquid heart of the Old Quarter and a good landmark. Legend has it that in the mid-15th century, heaven gave Emperor Ly Thai To (Le Loi) a magical sword that he used to drive the Chinese out of Vietnam. One day after the war, while out boating, he came upon a giant golden tortoise; the creature grabbed the sword and disappeared into the depths of the lake. Since that time, the lake has been known as Ho Hoan Kiem (Lake of the Restored Sword) because the tortoise returned the sword to its divine owners.

The **Ngoc Son Temple** (Jade Mountain Temple; Map p70; admission 3000d; ⊙8am-5pm), founded in the 18th century, is on an island in the northern part of Hoan Kiem Lake. It's a meditative spot to relax, but also worth checking out for the embalmed remains of a gigantic tortoise. Keep your eyes peeled for Cu Rua ('Great Grandfather'), a 200kg turtle that still inhabits the lake. This revered reptile was fished out of the lake in April 2011 for medical treatment (caused by pollution) before being returned to his watery domain.

One of the oldest temples in Hanoi, **Bach Ma Temple** (Map p64; cnr P Hang Buom & P Hang Giay; ⊙8-11.30am & 2.30-5.30pm) was originally built by King Ly Thai To in the 11th century (to honour a white horse that guided him

SCAM ALERT!

Hanoi is a very safe city on the whole and crimes against tourists are extremely rare. That said, the city certainly has its share of scams.

» **Fake Hotels** Beware of taxis and minibuses at the airport that take unwitting tourists to the wrong hotel. Invariably, the hotel has appropriated the name of another popular property and will then attempt to swindle as much of your money as possible. Check out a room before you check in, and walk on if you have any suspicions.

» **Hotel Tours** Some budget-hotel staff have been verbally aggressive and threatened physical violence towards guests who've declined to book tours through their in-house tour agency. Don't feel pressured, and if it persists find another place to stay.

» **Women** Walking alone at night is generally safe in the Old Quarter but you should always be aware of your surroundings. Hailing a taxi is a good idea if it's late and you have a long walk home.

» **The Kindness of Strangers** There's a scam going on around Hoan Kiem Lake in which a friendly local approaches you, offering to take you out. You end up at a karaoke bar or a restaurant, where the bill is upwards of US$100. Gay men have been targeted in this way. Exercise caution and follow your instincts.

Make sure you report scams to the **Vietnam National Administration of Tourism** (☎3356 0789; www.hanoitourism.gov.vn; 3 Tran Phu), which might well pressure the cowboys into cleaning up their act.

Hanoi

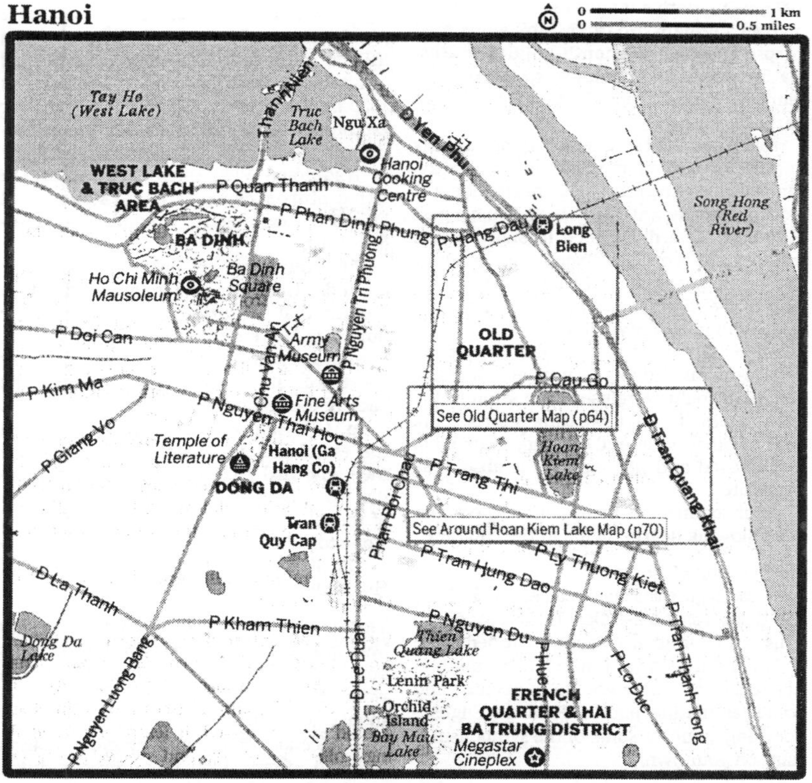

to this site, where he chose to construct his city walls). Pass through the wonderful old wooden doors of the pagoda to see a statue of the legendary white horse, as well as a beautiful red-lacquered funeral palanquin.

Stepping inside **St Joseph Cathedral** (Map p70; P Nha Tho; ⏲5-7am & 5-7pm) is like being transported to medieval Europe. This neo-Gothic cathedral (inaugurated in 1886) is noteworthy for its square belltowers, elaborate altar and stained-glass windows. The main gate is open when Mass is held. At other times you have to enter the compound via a side street, at 40 P Nha Chung. During Sunday Mass (usually at 6pm), the congregation spills out onto the streets, hymns are beamed out, and the devout sit on motorbikes listening intently to the sermon.

Memorial House (Map p64; 87 P Ma May; admission 5000d; ⏲8.30am-5pm) is well worth a visit. Thoughtfully restored, this traditional Chinese-style dwelling gives you an insight into how local merchants used to live in the Old Quarter.

FREE Ho Chi Minh Mausoleum Complex MONUMENT

(Map p61; Ba Dinh Square; ⏲8-11am Tue-Thu, Sat & Sun Dec-Sep, last entry at 10.15am) This is the holiest of holies for many Vietnamese. In the tradition of Lenin, Stalin and Mao, the final resting place of Ho Chi Minh is a glass sarcophagus set deep within a monumental edifice. As interesting as the man himself are the crowds coming to pay their deep respects. Ho (see p162) is honoured for his role as the liberator of the Vietnamese people from colonialism, as much as for his communist ideology. This view is reinforced by Vietnam's educational system, which emphasises Ho's deeds and accomplishments.

Built contrary to his last will to be cremated, the Ho Chi Minh Mausoleum Complex was constructed between 1973 and

1975, using native materials gathered from all over Vietnam. Ho Chi Minh's embalmed corpse gets a three-month holiday to Russia for yearly maintenance, so the mausoleum is closed from September through early December.

You join a long queue, which usually snakes for several hundred metres to the mausoleum entrance itself. Inside, adopt a slow but steady walking pace as you file past Ho's body. Guards, regaled in snowy white military uniforms, are posted at intervals of five paces, giving an eerily authoritarian aspect to the slightly macabre spectacle of the body with its wispy white hair.

All visitors must register and leave their bags, cameras and mobile phones at a reception hall. You'll be refused admission to the mausoleum if you're wearing shorts, tank tops or other 'indecent' clothing. Hats must be removed and photography is absolutely prohibited.

After exiting the mausoleum, check out the following nearby sights in the complex.

Ho Chi Minh Museum

(www.baotanghochiminh.vn; admission 15,000d; ⏲8-11.30am daily & 2-4.30pm Tue-Thu, Sat & Sun) This is a triumphalist monument dedicated to Ho and the onward march of revolutionary socialism. There are Ho mementos and some fascinating photos. Find an English-speaking guide, as some of the symbolism is hard on your own.

Ho Chi Minh's Stilt House

(admission 15,000d; ⏲summer 7.30-11am & 2-4pm, winter 8-11am & 1.30-4pm, closed all day Mon, & Fri afternoon) Behind the mausoleum, this was supposedly Ho's official residence, on and off, between 1958 and 1969. Its simplicity reinforces his reputation as a man of the people.

One Pillar Pagoda

(Chua Mot Cot) Built by Emperor Ly Thai Tong (r 1028–54) and designed to represent a lotus blossom, a symbol of purity, rising out of a sea of sorrow.

Presidential Palace

In stark contrast to Ho's stilt house, this imposing restored colonial building was constructed in 1906 as the palace of the Governor General of Indochina. It's not open to the public.

TOP CHOICE Temple of Literature TEMPLE

(Van Mieu; Map p64; P Quoc Tu Giam; admission 10,000d; ⏲8am-5pm) Hanoi's peaceful Temple of Literature was dedicated to Confucius in 1070 by Emperor Ly Thanh Tong, and later established as a university for the education of mandarins. A well-preserved jewel of traditional Vietnamese architecture in 11th-century style with roofed gateways and low-eaved buildings, this temple is an absolute must.

Five courtyards are enclosed within the grounds. The front gate is inscribed with a request that visitors dismount from their horses before entering. Make sure you do. There's a peaceful reflecting pool in the front courtyard, and the Khue Van Pavilion at the back of the second courtyard.

In 1484, Emperor Le Thang Tong ordered the establishment of stelae honouring the men who had received doctorates in triennial examinations dating back to 1442. Each of the 82 stelae that stands here is set on a stone tortoise.

The Temple of Literature is 2km west of Hoan Kiem Lake.

Vietnam Museum of Ethnology MUSEUM

(www.vme.org.vn; Đ Nguyen Van Huyen; admission 25,000d; ⏲8.30am-5.30pm Tue-Sun) The wonderful Vietnam Museum of Ethnology should not be missed. It features a fascinating collection of art and everyday objects gathered from Vietnam's diverse tribal people. From the making of conical hats to the ritual of a Tay shamanic ceremony, the museum explores Vietnam's cultural diversity.

In the grounds are examples of traditional village houses – a Tay stilt house, impressive Bahnar communal structure and a Yao home. Don't miss the soaring, thatched-roofed Giarai tomb, complete with risqué wooden statues. Displays are labelled in Vietnamese, French and English. A fair-trade craft shop sells books, beautiful postcards, and arts and crafts from ethnic communities.

The museum is in Cau Giay District, about 7km from the city centre. A metered taxi here is around 120,000d (one way); *xe om* (motorbike taxi) about 50,000d. The cheapest way to arrive is to take bus 14 (3000d) from Hoan Kiem Lake and get off at the junction between Đ Hoang Quoc Viet and Đ Nguyen Van Huyen.

Women's Museum MUSEUM
(Bao Tang Phu Nu; off Map p70; www.baotangphunu.org.vn; 36 P Ly Thuong Kiet; admission 30,000d; ⏲8am-4.30pm Tue-Sun) Recently reopened after a long renovation, this excellent museum concentrates on women's role in Vietnamese society and culture. Superbly laid out and labelled in English and French, it's the memories of the wartime contribution of individual heroic women that are most poignant. There are wartime propaganda posters and tribal artefacts, and regular special exhibitions are held on topics as diverse as human trafficking, street vendors and traditional medicine.

Fine Arts Museum MUSEUM
(Map p61; www.vnfineartsmuseum.org.vn; 66 P Nguyen Thai Hoc; admission 20,000d; ⏲9.15am-5pm Tue-Sun) There are superb textiles, furniture and ceramics in the first building, which also showcases some terrific temporary exhibitions. Over in the magnificent main building, artistic treasures include ancient Chapa stone carvings, astonishing effigies of Guan Yin (the thousand-eyed, thousand-armed Goddess of Compassion) and lacquered-wood statues of robed Buddhist monks from the Tay Son dynasty. There's also a large collection of contemporary art.

National Museum of Vietnamese History MUSEUM
(Map p70; 1 P Trang Tien; admission 20,000d; ⏲8am-4.30pm) A must for both the architecture and the collection, this museum occupies an elegant, ochre-coloured structure built between 1925 and 1932 that has French and Chinese design influences.

Highlights include some excellent bronzes from the Dong Son culture (3rd century BC to 3rd century AD), striking Hindu statuary from the Khmer and Champa kingdoms, and beautiful jewellery and accoutrements from imperial Vietnam.

Everything is comprehensively labelled in English and French.

Tay Ho (West Lake) LAKE
(Map p61) The city's largest lake, Tay Ho is around 13km in circumference and ringed by upmarket suburbs. On the south side of the lake, along Đ Thuy Khue, is a string of popular seafood restaurants, and to the east, the Xuan Dieu strip is lined with restaurants, cafes, boutiques and luxury hotels. You'll also find two temples on its shores; the Tay Ho and Tran Quoc pagodas.

A newly installed pathway now circles the lake, making for a great bicycle ride.

Hoa Lo Prison Museum MUSEUM
(Map p70; 1 P Hoa Lo; admission 10,000d; ⏲8am-5pm) The museum is all that remains of the notorious Hoa Lo Prison, ironically nicknamed the 'Hanoi Hilton' by US POWs. Exhibits concentrate on the Vietnamese struggle for independence from France, including a guillotine used to behead Vietnamese revolutionaries. Other displays focus on American pilots incarcerated here, including Pete Peterson (the first US Ambassador to a unified Vietnam in 1995) and Senator John McCain.

Lenin Park PARK
(Map p61; admission 5000d; ⏲4am-9pm) The nearest green lung to the Old Quarter, Lenin Park is about 2km south of Hoan Kiem Lake. It's a great place to escape urban Hanoi (and incorporates Bau Mau Lake, where there are pedal boats) and has a couple of cafes. Its shady paths are popular with joggers.

Army Museum MUSEUM
(Bao Tang Quan Doi; Map p61; www.btlsqsvn.org.vn; P Dien Bien Phu; admission 20,000d; ⏲8-11.30am & 1-4.30pm, closed Mon & Fri) Displays Soviet and Chinese equipment alongside French- and US-made weapons captured during years of warfare – check out the Soviet-built MiG-21 jet fighter and US F-111.

Activities

Massage & Spa

Hanoi has a good choice of spas and massage centres.

La Siesta Spa SPA
(Map p64; ☎3935 1632; www.hanoielegancehotel.com/spa; 32 P Lo Su) Escape from the incessant energy of the Old Quarter and indulge in a spa, massage or beauty treatment. Located at the Hanoi Elegance Diamond Hotel.

QT Anam Spa SPA
(☎3928 6116; www.qtanamspa.com; 26-28 Ly Thai Tho) Excellent spa, massage and beauty treatments hidden away inside the Hanoi Horison Hotel. It's 2km west of Hoan Kiem Lake.

Sports & Swimming

Hanoi Water Park SWIMMING
(Ho Tay; admission 30,000-50,000d; ⏲9am-9pm Wed-Mon Apr-Nov) A family-geared water park around 5km north of the city centre with

Old Quarter

0 200 m
0 0.1 miles

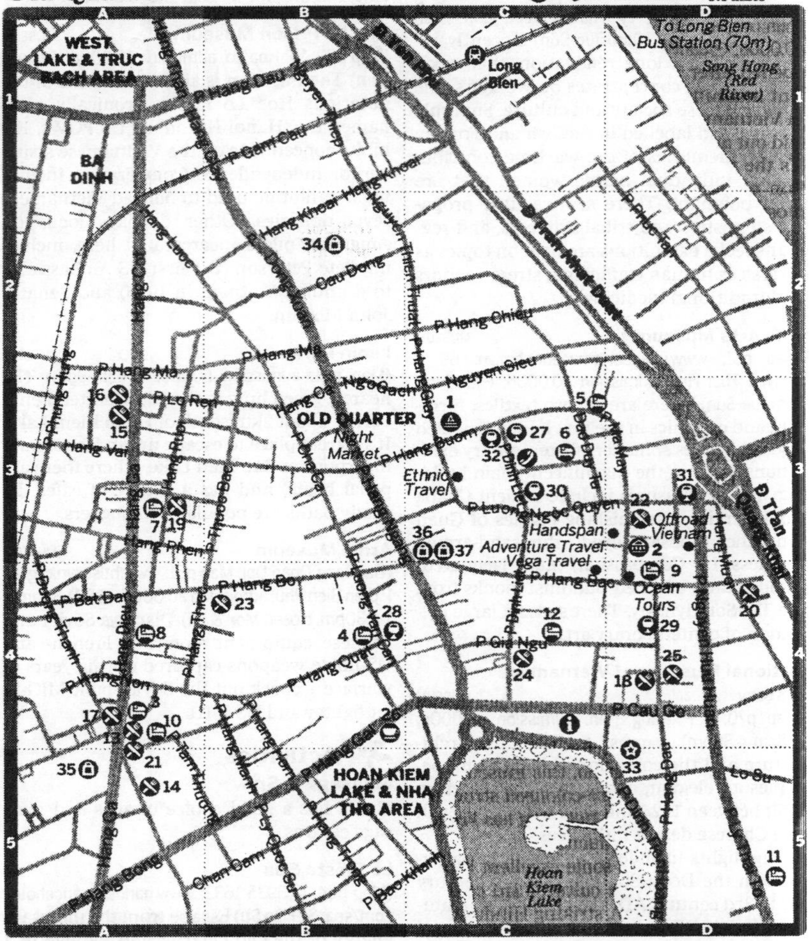

pools, slides and a lazy river. It gets extremely busy here on hot summer afternoons.

Daewoo Hotel Fitness Centre HEALTH & FITNESS
(☎3835 1000; www.hanoi-daewoohotel.com; 360 Đ Kim Ma; 🅿) The day-use fee is US$25 for all facilities including the pool. There's also a good spa. It's 5km west of Hoan Kiem Lake.

Army Hotel SWIMMING
(33C P Pham Ngu Lao) In central Hanoi, the pool is big enough for laps and open all year.

Courses

Hanoi Cooking Centre COOKING
(Map p61; ☎3715 0088; www.hanoicookingcentre.com; 44 Chau Long; per class US$50) Excellent interactive classes including market visits and a special kids club. Also offers a highly recommended walking tour exploring Hanoi's street-food scene.

Highway 4 COOKING
(Map p64; ☎3715 0577; www.highway4.com; 3 Hang Tre; per class US$50) Incorporates a *cyclo* ride and market tour, before continuing to Highway 4's Tay Ho restaurant. Also

Old Quarter

Sights
1 Bach Ma Temple C3
Dong Xuan Market .... (see 34)
2 Memorial House D3

Activities, Courses & Tours
Free Wheelin' Tours .... (see 32)

Sleeping
3 Art Hotel A4
4 Green Mango B4
5 Hanoi Backpackers 2 .... C3
6 Hanoi Elite C3
7 Hanoi Guesthouse A3
8 Hanoi Rendezvous Hotel A4
9 La Siesta Spa D4
10 New Gallery Hotel A4
11 QT Anam Spa D5
12 Tirant Hotel C4

Eating
13 Bun Bo Nam Bo A4
14 Bun Cha A5
Bun Oc Saigon .... (see 12)
Bun Rieu Cua .... (see 10)
15 Buon Cuon A3
16 Cha Ca Thang Long A3
17 Che A4
18 Green Tangerine D4
19 Highway 4 .... A3
20 Highway 4 .... D4
21 Mien Xao Luon A5
22 Nola D3
23 Pho Bo B4
24 Quan Bia Minh C4
25 Spot D4
Xoi Yen .... (see 3)

Drinking
26 Café Pho Co B4
27 Cheeky Quarter C3
28 Jazz Club By Quyen Van Minh B4
29 Le Pub D4
30 Mao's Red Lounge C3
31 Roots D3
32 Tet C3

Entertainment
33 Municipal Water Puppet Theatre D5

Shopping
34 Dong Xuan Market B2
35 Hang Da Market A5
36 Hanoi Gallery C3
37 Old Propaganda Posters C3

cocktail-making classes (per person US$29) using Son Tinh liquors.

Sleeping

Most budget and midrange visitors make for the Old Quarter or the neighbouring Hoan Kiem Lake area for accommodation. Luxury places tend to be further afield.

OLD QUARTER

TOP CHOICE Hanoi Elite BOUTIQUE HOTEL $$
(Map p64; ☎3828 1711; www.hanoielitehotel.com; 10/5032 Dao Duy Tu; r US$45-55; ❄@📶) Hanoi Elite features cool and classy decor, top-notch staff, and the kind of touches – rainforest shower-heads, breakfasts cooked to order, in-room computers – you'd expect only in more expensive accommodation.

Art Hotel HOTEL $$
(Map p64; ☎3923 3868; www.hanoiarthotel.com; 75 P Hang Dieu; 5;.s/d from US$38/44; ❄@📶) The young, friendly and very welcoming crew at the Art Hotel make this new opening really stand out. Rooms are spacious with spotless bathrooms and wooden floors, and there's tons of street food close by.

Tirant Hotel HOTEL $$
(Map p64; ☎6269 8899; www.tiranthotel.com; 38 Gia Ngu; s/d from US$55/65; ❄@📶) Trendy decor, switched-on English-speaking staff and spacious bedrooms all conspire to make this one of Hanoi's best new hotels. The buffet breakfast is superb and the huge Grand Suite (US$145) is undoubtedly the Old Quarter's best room.

New Gallery Hotel HOTEL $$
(Map p64; ☎3923 3366; www.hanoinewgalleryhotel.com; 75 P Hang Dieu; US$50-55; ❄@📶) One of a cluster of great-value midrange hotels, the New Gallery offers spacious bedrooms, balcony views, and spotless modern bathrooms.

Hanoi Rendezvous Hotel HOTEL $
(Map p64; ☎3828 5777; www.hanoirendezvous.com; 31 P Hang Dieu; dm/s/d/tr US$7.50/25/30/35; ❄@📶) Aussie-run Hanoi Rendezvous features spacious rooms, good dorms, friendly staff and well-run tours.

SPECIALITY FOOD STREETS

To combine eating with exploration, head to these locations crammed with interesting restaurants and food stalls.

Pho Cam Chi This narrow lane is crammed with local eateries turning out cheap, tasty food for a few dollars a hit. Adjoining Tong Duy Tan is an up-and-coming area for hip cafes and restaurants. Cam Chi is about 500m northeast of Hanoi train station.

Duong Thuy Khue On the southern bank of Tay Ho, Đ Thuy Khue features dozens of outdoor seafood restaurants with a lakeside setting. You can eat well here for about 150,000d per person.

Truc Bach Around the northeast edge of Truc Bach Lake you'll find *lau* (hotpot) restaurants huddled together in a near-continuous strip. Perfect on a cool Hanoi night.

Pho Nghi Tam About 10km north of central Hanoi, P Nghi Tam has about 60 dog-meat *(thit cho)* restaurants; meals start at 120,000d. Eating dog in the first half of the lunar month brings bad luck, so the restaurants are deserted. Business picks up in the second half of the month and the last day is a particularly auspicious with the restaurants packed. Now we know why dogs howl at the moon!

Don't miss the reproductions of classic Vietnam-themed movies in the downstairs breakfast bar.

Hanoi Backpackers 2 HOSTEL $
(Map p64; ☎3935 1890; www.hanoibackpackershostel.com; 9 Ma May; dm US$6-9, tw & d US$40; ❄@📶) Spanking-new hostel offering an excellent location, spotless dorms and designer doubles. There's a very social restaurant and bar, good travel info and tours.

Hanoi Guesthouse GUESTHOUSE $
(Map p64; ☎3824 5732; www.hanoiguesthouse.com; 14 Bat Su; r US$20-22; @📶) A quiet location, eager young English-speaking staff, and Hanoi's weekend night market is just a couple of blocks away. Heritage Asian decor flows from reception through to the simple but immaculate rooms.

AROUND HOAN KIEM LAKE

TOP CHOICE **Sofitel Metropole Hotel** HOTEL $$$
(Map p70; ☎3826 6919; www.sofitel.com; 15 P Ngo Quyen; r from US$210; ❄@📶🏊) A historic hotel and a supremely refined place to stay. Boasts a beautifully restored colonial facade, mahogany-panelled reception rooms, two well-regarded restaurants and the delightful Bamboo Bar. Rooms in the old wing offer unmatched colonial style.

6 on Sixteen BOUTIQUE HOTEL $$
(Map p70; ☎6673 6729; www.sixonsixteen.com; 16 Bao Kanh; r US$50-88; ❄@📶) Decked out with designer textiles, ethnic art and interesting locally made furniture, 6 on Sixteen has a warm and welcoming ambience. There are only six rooms, but lots of shared areas to encourage guests to mix. Breakfast includes freshly baked pastries and robust Italian coffee.

Hotel L'Opera HOTEL $$$
(Map p70; ☎6282 5555; www.mgallery.com; 29 P Trang Tien; r from US$150; ❄@📶) Effortlessly combines French colonial style with a sophisticated design aesthetic. Rooms are trimmed in silk and Asian textiles, and glamorous features include a spa and the hip late-night vibe of the La Fée Verte (Green Fairy) bar.

Cinnamon Hotel BOUTIQUE HOTEL $$
(Map p70; ☎3938 0430; www.cinnamonhotel.net; 26 P Au Trieu; r US$70-80; ⊖❄@📶) Hip hotel overlooking St Joseph Cathedral. The design is outstanding, combining the historic features of the building – wrought-ironwork and window shutters – with Japanese-influenced interiors and modern gadgetry. Only six rooms: book 'Lime' for cathedral views.

Golden Lotus Hotel HOTEL $$
(Map p70; ☎3938 0901; www.goldenlotushotel.com.vn; 32 P Hang Trong; s/d incl breakfast from US$52/62; ❄@📶) Atmospheric little hotel, which blends Eastern flavours and Western chic. All rooms have wooden floors, silk trim and art aplenty, though most at the rear do not enjoy any natural light.

Madame Moon Guesthouse GUESTHOUSE $
(Map p70; ☎3938 1255; www.madammoonguesthouse.com; 17 Hang Hanh; r US$22-25; ❄@📶)

Keeping it simple and tasteful, Madame Moon has surprisingly chic rooms and a (relatively) traffic-free location in a street filled with cafes.

Church Hotel BOUTIQUE HOTEL **$$**
(Map p70; ☎3928 8118; www.churchhotel.com.vn; 9 P Nha Tho; r US$50-88; ❄@🛜) Classy minihotel with real boutique appeal. Some rooms are smallish, but all have stylish furnishings and the location is superb.

Hanoi Backpackers Hostel HOSTEL **$**
(Map p70; ☎3828 5372; www.hanoibackpackershostel.com; 48 P Ngo Huyen; dm US$6, r US$25-36; ❄@🛜) Impressively organised, perennially popular hostel with custom-built bunk beds and lockers, and the dorms all have en-suite bathrooms. There's a rooftop terrace for barbecues and a bar downstairs.

Central Backpackers Hanoi HOSTEL **$**
(Map p70; ☎3938 1849; www.centralbackpackershostel.com; 16 P Ly Quoc Su; dm US$5; @🛜) Well-run hostel close to good cafes and street eats. It's a pretty social spot, possibly due to the 'Free Beer' (very) happy hour every night from 8pm to 9pm.

Joseph's Hotel HOTEL **$$**
(Map p70; ☎3939 1048; www.josephshotel.com; 5 P Au Trieu; r US$50-55; ❄@🛜) Compact hotel featuring pastel tones, mod-Asian decor and breakfasts cooked to order; some rooms have church views.

Especen Hotel HOTEL **$**
(Map p70; ☎3824 4401; www.especen.vn; 28 P Tho Xuong & 41 P Ngo Huyen; s/d US$17/20; ❄@🛜) Spacious, light, well-kept rooms and a relatively tranquil Old Quarter location.

OTHER AREAS

InterContinental Westlake Hanoi HOTEL **$$$**
(☎6270 8888; www.intercontinental.com/hanoi; 1A Nghi Tam, Tay Ho; d from US$120; ❄@🛜🏊) The most luxurious address in the north of the city, this hotel in the Ho Tay area features a contemporary Asian-design theme, and the whole complex juts out into the lake. Many of the stunning rooms (all with balconies) are set on stilts above the water.

The Drift HOSTEL **$**
(☎3944 8415; www.thedriftbackpackershostel.com; 42 Truong Han Sieu; dm US$6, r US$20-25; ❄@🛜) Aussie-run hostel with a social ambience, free breakfast, movie room and cafe specialising in comfort food. It's a 20-minute walk south of the Old Quarter.

✖ Eating

Whatever your budget (or your tastes) it's available here. Get stuck into the local cuisine, which is wonderfully tasty, fragrantly spiced and inexpensive. And don't miss the essential experience of dining on street food or a memorable meal in one of Hanoi's gourmet Vietnamese restaurants.

OLD QUARTER

TOP CHOICE **Highway 4** VIETNAMESE **$$**
(Map p64; ☎3926 0639; www.highway4.com; 3 P Hang Tre; meals 100,000-200,000d) The original location (inside a tottering old house) of an expanding family of restaurants that specialise in Vietnamese cuisine from the northern mountains. Feast on bite-sized snacks like superb *nem ca xa lo* (catfish spring rolls) and wash it all down with a bottle or two of delicious Son Tinh liquor made from sticky rice.

Green Mango MEDITERRANEAN **$$**
(Map p64; ☎3928 9917; www.greenmango.vn; 18 P Hang Quat; meals 180,000-250,000d) This hip restaurant-cum-lounge has a real vibe as well as great cooking. The stunning dining rooms, complete with rich silk drapes, evoke the feel of an opium den and there's a huge rear courtyard. Menu-wise there's everything from pizza and pasta to mod-Asian fusion creations.

Cha Ca Thang Long VIETNAMESE **$$**
(Map p64; 21 P Duong Thanh; cha ca fish 150,000d; ⊙10am-3pm & 5-10pm) Grill your own succulent fish with a little shrimp paste and plenty of herbs. *Cha ca* is an iconic Hanoi dish.

The Spot INTERNATIONAL **$$**
(Map p64; P Hang Be; mains 100,000-200,000d) Decorated with propaganda posters, The Spot is good for Western-style grub: salads, grilled tuna, and Greek-style salmon sandwiches. There's a good range of wines by the glass. Occasionally DJs spin tunes later on.

Green Tangerine FUSION **$$$**
(Map p64; ☎3825 1286; www.greentangerinehanoi.com; 48 P Hang Be; mains US$10-20; 🚭) Experience the mood and flavour of 1950s Indochine at this elegant restaurant located in a beautifully restored colonial house with a cobbled courtyard. French-Vietnamese cuisine.

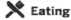

Quan Bia Minh VIETNAMESE $

(Map p64; 7A Dien Liet; mains 80,000-120,000d) A *bia hoi* joint with well-priced Vietnamese food and excellent service. Bag an outdoor table, grab a cold beer and tuck in.

Nola CAFE $

(Map p64; 89 P Ma May; snacks 30,000-60,000d) There's retro furniture and a boho ambience at this fine bar-cafe, so it's coffee and cake in the day and beer after dark. A good place to meet Hanoi's hip young things.

AROUND HOAN KIEM LAKE

TOP CHOICE **Ly Club** VIETNAMESE $$

(Map p70; ☎3936 3069; www.lyclub.vn; 4 Le Phung Hieu; meals US$10-15) Set in an elegant French colonial mansion, this restaurant's impressive dining room is a great location for a gourmet meal. The menu excels at both Asian and Vietnamese flavours as well as international dishes. When someone asks, 'So where did you go for your last night in Hanoi?', this is the correct answer.

Madame Hien VIETNAMESE $$

(Map p70; ☎3938 1588; www.verticale-hanoi.com; 15 P Chan Cam; mains US$10-15) Housed in a restored 19th-century villa, this is a place to go for Hanoi street food (without the street). Try the '36 Streets' fixed menu (435,000d) or a good-value set lunch (200,000d).

La INTERNATIONAL $$

(Map p70; ☎3928 8933; 49 P Ly Quoc Su; mains US$13-18) Intimate, modest-looking and yet atmospheric bistro with a creative menu that includes roast pork loin with mango, coriander and garlic. Offers wines by the glass.

Cart CAFE $

(Map p70; 18 P Au Trieu; www.thecartfood.com; baguettes 40,000d; ⊙7.30am-5pm; ☑) Superlative pies, interesting baguettes and excellent juices (try the apple, carrot and ginger juice) at this little haven of creative, healthy Western food.

Khazaana INDIAN $$

(Map p66; www.khazaana.vn; 1C P Tong Dan, meals 100,000-270,000d; ☑) Very pukka, upmarket Indian restaurant with delicious cooking from the north and south of the subcontinent. There's plenty of vegetarian choices and filling thalis.

Mediterraneo ITALIAN $$

(Map p70; www.mediterraneo-hanoi.com; 23 P Nha Tho; mains US$10-15) Popular, authentic little Italian restaurant that serves up homemade pasta and pizza from a wood-fired oven.

San Ho Restaurant SEAFOOD $$$

(☎3934 9184; 58 P Ly Thuong Kiet; meals around 300,000d) Set in a French-era villa, this classy seafood restaurant has crustaceans and molluscs bathed in delicious sauces. Most prices are by the kilogram.

WEST OF THE OLD QUARTER

TOP CHOICE **Quan An Ngon** VIETNAMESE $

(15 P Phan Boi Chau; dishes 35,000-80,000d; ⊙11am-11pm) Fancy that street-food experience, but afraid to take the plunge? Try this incredibly busy and popular place where mini-kitchens turn out terrific food, including specialities from all over the nation, like squid with lemongrass and chilli. Be prepared to wait for a table.

La Badiane INTERNATIONAL $$$

(☎3942 4509; www.labadiane.hanoi.sitew.com; 10 Nam Ngu; mains US$15) A restored French villa is the setting for some inspired French cuisine, plus a few Asian and Mediterranean flavours. Menu highlights include sea bass tagliatelle with smoked paprika.

KOTO CAFE $$

(www.koto.com.au; 59 P Van Mieu; meals 95,000-140,000d; ⊙closed dinner Mon; ⊛🍸) Stunning four-storey modernist cafe-bar-restaurant by the Temple of Literature with daily specials, excellent Vietnamese food and modern Western flavours. KOTO is an extraordinarily successful not-for-profit project that provides career training and guidance to disadvantaged kids.

Southgate FUSION $$

(www.southgatehanoi.com; 28 Tong Duy Tan; tapas 90,000-120,000d, mains 130,000-250,000d) Tempting tapas – try the double-cooked pork belly – and superb desserts feature at this stylish restaurant and bar.

Puku CAFE $

(18 28 Tong Duy Tan; mains 60,000-110,000d; ⊙24hr; 🍸⊛) Kiwi cafe culture: great burgers, Mexican wraps and all-day eggy breakfasts.

Net Hue VIETNAMESE $

(cnr P Hang Bong & P Cam Chi; mains 30,000-60,000d) Exceptional and well-priced Huế cuisine including *banh nam* (steamed rice pancake with minced shrimp). Run by a friendly family.

DON'T MISS

THE OLD QUARTER'S TOP STREET FOOD

Instead of just walking on by (and wondering what might have been), squat down on one of those teeny-tiny plastic stools next to a smoking charcoal burner and chow down with the masses. Many stalls have been operating for decades, and most specialise in just one dish. Note that opening hours can be somewhat flexible.

Bun Cha (Map p64; 67 Duong Thanh; ⊙11am-3pm) Visiting Hanoi and not eating *bun cha* (barbecued pork) should be classed as a capital offence. Try the combination of grilled pork patties, crab spring rolls, vermicelli noodles and mountains of fresh herbs at **Bun Cha Nem Cua Be Dac Kim**.

Buon Cuon (Map p64; 14 P Hang Ga; ⊙8am-4pm) Gossamer-light *banh cuon* – steamed rice crêpes filled with minced pork, mushrooms and ground shrimp.

Pho Bo (Map p64; 49 P Bat Dan; ⊙7-10am) Head to **Pho Gia Truyen** for classic *pho* (hearty broth with noodles and tender beef), a breakfast of champions. Be prepared to queue.

Banh Ghoi (Map p70; 52 P Ly Quoc Su; ⊙10am-7pm) Under a banyan tree near St Joseph Cathedral, this stall turns out *banh ghoi*, moreish deep-fried pastries crammed with pork, vermicelli and mushrooms.

Bun Oc Saigon (Map p64; cnr P Nguyen Huu Huan & P Hang Thung; ⊙11am-11pm) Shellfish specials here include *bun oc* (snail noodle soup) with a hearty dash of tart tamarind.

Bun Bo Nam Bo (Map p64; 67 P Hang Dieu; ⊙11am-10pm) *Bu bo nam bo* (dry noodles with beef) is a zingy southern Vietnam dish mixed with bean sprouts, garlic, lemongrass and green mango.

Xoi Yen (Map p64; cnr P Nguyen Huu Huan & P Hang Mam; ⊙7am-11pm) Specialises in sticky rice topped with goodies including sweet Asian sausage, gooey fried egg and slow-cooked pork.

Mien Xao Luon (Map p64; 87 P Hang Dieu; ⊙7am-2pm) Crunchy fried eels prepared three different ways. Try them stir-fried with vermicelli, egg, bean sprouts and shallots.

Bun Rieu Cua (Map p64; 40 P Hang Tre; ⊙7-9am) A Hanoi breakfast classic, *bun rieu cua* (crab noodle soup) is a rice-paddy noodle broth laced with fried shallots and garlic, and topped with shrimp paste and chilli.

Che (Map p64; 76 P Hang Dieu; ⊙7am-3pm) For a sweet treat. In winter try *che banh troi tau*, mung beans laced with sesame and ginger. In summer, refreshing *che thap nam* has up to 10 colourful ingredients including coconut milk, crushed peanuts, lotus seeds and dried apples.

GREATER HANOI

Quan Hai San Ngon SEAFOOD $$
(☎3719 3169; 198 Nghi Tam, Tay Ho; mains 150,000-200,000d) Just maybe Hanoi's most atmospheric dining space, arrayed elegantly around giant al fresco reflecting pools, and showcasing excellent Vietnamese seafood – try the briny Halong Bay oysters topped with wasabi. It's a 10-minute taxi ride from central Hanoi.

Drinking

Hanoi has sophisticated bars, congenial pubs, grungy clubs and *bia hoi* joints by the barrel-load.

Cafes come in every persuasion too, from old-school to hip young thing.

Cafes

Coffee meccas include P Trieu Viet Vuong, around 1km south of Hoan Kiem Lake, which has scores of cafes – some modern spots with iPad-toting teens, others more traditional.

Cafe Duy Tri CAFE
(43A P Yen Phu) In the same location since 1936, this caffeine-infused labyrinth is a Hanoi classic. Negotiate the tiny ladders and stairways to the 3rd floor balcony and order the delicious *caphe sua chua* (iced coffee with yoghurt). It's a couple of blocks east of Truc Bach Lake.

Café Pho Co CAFE
(Map p64; 11 P Hang Gai) One of Hanoi's best-kept secrets, this place has plum views over Hoan Kiem Lake. Enter through the silk

Around Hoan Kiem Lake

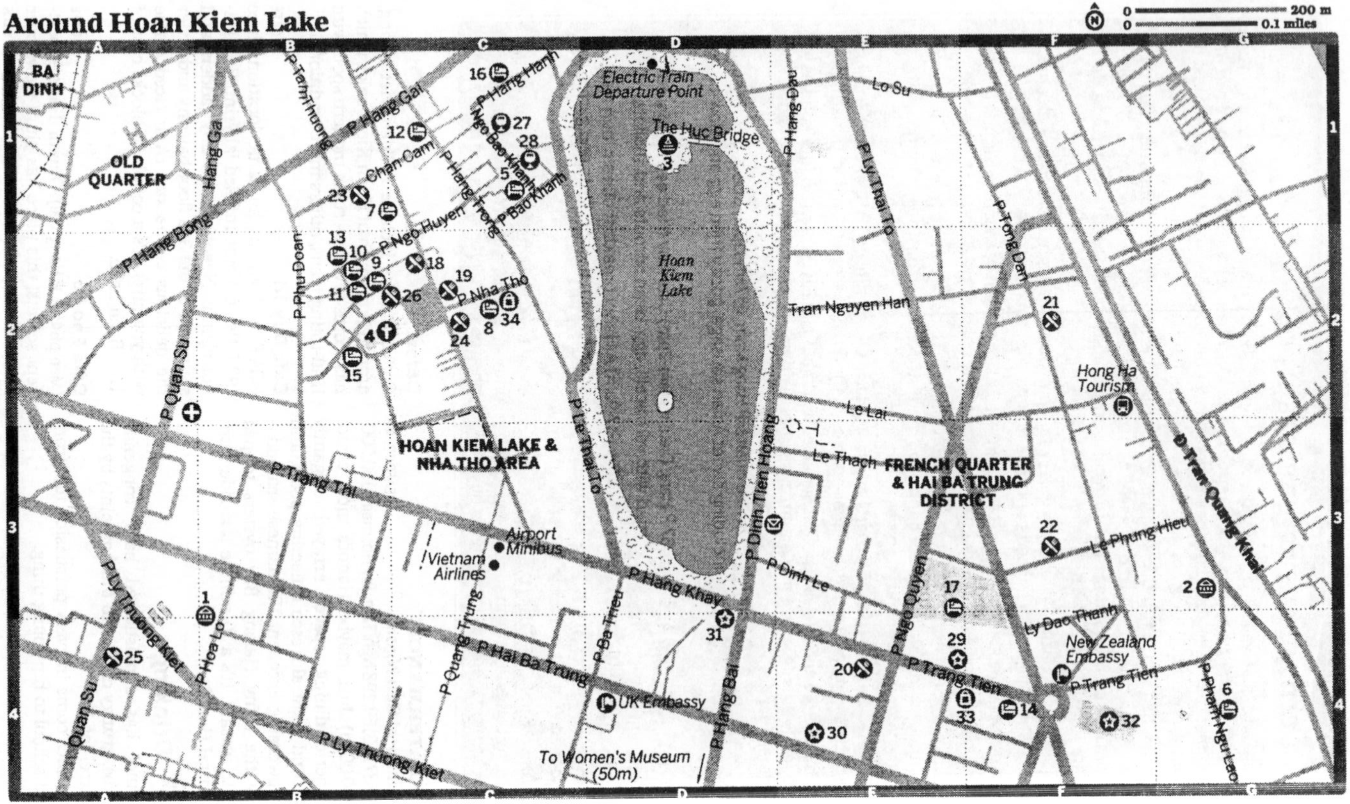

Around Hoan Kiem Lake

Sights
1 Hoa Lo Prison Museum B3
2 National Museum of Vietnamese History G3
3 Ngoc Son Temple D1
4 St Joseph Cathedral B2

Sleeping
5 6 on Sixteen C1
6 Army Hotel G4
7 Central Backpackers Hanoi B1
8 Church Hotel C2
9 Cinnamon Hotel B2
10 Especen Hotel B2
11 Especen Hotel B2
12 Golden Lotus Hotel C1
13 Hanoi Backpackers Hostel B2
14 Hotel L'Opera F4
15 Joseph's Hotel B2
16 Madame Moon Guesthouse C1
17 Sofitel Metropole Hotel E3

Eating
18 Banh Ghoi C2
19 Hanoi House C2
20 Kem Trang Tien E4
21 Khazaana F2
La ..... (see 24)
22 Ly Club F3
23 Madame Hien B1
24 Mediterraneo C2
25 San Ho A4
26 The Cart C2

Drinking
27 Factory C1
28 GC Pub C1

Entertainment
29 Centre Culturel Francaise de Hanoi E4
30 Cinematheque E4
31 Face Club D4
32 Hanoi Opera House F4
Tunnel ..... (see 27)

Shopping
33 Chi Vang F4
34 Things of Substance C2

shop and continue up to the top floor for the mother of all vistas. For something deliciously different try the *caphe trung da*, coffee with a silky-smooth beaten egg white.

Kinh Do Café CAFE
(252 P Hang Bong) Featured in Catherine Deneuve's *Indochine* and serves tasty French pastries and feisty coffee. It's a kilometre west of Hoan Kiem Lake.

Cong Caphe CAFE
(152 P Trieu Viet Vuong) The caffeine scene here features eclectic beats and kitsch communist memorabilia.

Bars

Ha Tien in the Old Quarter has a choice of bars and is a good starting or finishing point for a crawl.

TOP CHOICE **Quan Ly** BAR
(82 Le Van Hu) Traditional *ruou* (Vietnamese liquor) bar complete with ginseng, snake and gecko creations. An English-language menu makes it easy to choose, and there's also cheap *bia hoi* and good Vietnamese food. Yes, that is the genial owner meeting Ho Chi Minh in the photograph on the wall. It's in the French Quarter, south of Hoan Kiem Lake.

Factory BAR
(Map p70; www.factory.org.vn; 11A P Bao Khanh) Combines a spacious roof terrace with a dramatic interior featuring interesting socialist paintings. There's even a shisha lounge. Regularly hosts music and arts events – check the website for listings.

Cheeky Quarter BAR
(Map p64; 1 P Ta Hien; open late) A tiny, quirky, sociable little bar that has table footy (foosball) and drum and bass or house music.

Mao's Red Lounge BAR
(Map p64; 5 P Ta Hien; open late) The most popular place on P Ta Hien, this is rammed with a sociable crowd on weekend nights. It's a classic dive bar with dim lighting and swirling smoke.

Green Mango LOUNGE
(Map p64; 18 P Hang Quat) Lounge bar with stylish seating, a tempting cocktail list and plenty of beautiful people enjoying the relaxed vibe.

GAY & LESBIAN HANOI

There are very few gay venues in Hanoi, but plenty of places that are gay-friendly. However, official attitudes are still fairly conservative and Hanoi is home to these official attitudes. Police raids in the name of 'social reform' aren't unknown and that tends to ensure gays and lesbians keep a low profile.

The website www.utopia-asia.com has up-to-date information about gay Hanoi. See also the Vietnam information section on www.cambodiaout.com.

Note the warning on p60 for possible scams in the area around Hoan Kiem Lake.

Le Pub PUB
(Map p64; 25 P Hang Be) British-style pub with a street-facing terrace popular with travellers and foreign residents. Good comfort grub.

Roots BAR
(Map p64; 2 Luong Ngoc Quyen; ⊙8pm-late) Primarily a reggae bar, this is *the* place for some serious bassline pressure and can be a riot on the right night. Lock-ins have been known.

21N Club BAR
(49 Lang Yen Phu, Tay Ho) A lakeside location spills out onto waterfront seating, there's regular live music and 'Sailor' microbrewed beer.

GC Pub PUB
(Map p70; 7 P Bao Khanh) Looks pretty rundown from the street but it gets very lively on weekend nights. Popular with gay Hanoians and has pool tables.

Tet BAR
(Map p64; 2A P Ta Hien) Compact bar that's best *very* late at night when the music is turned up and it morphs into one of Hanoi's smallest clubs.

☆ Entertainment

Cinemas

Megastar Cineplex CINEMA
(Map p61; www.megastarmedia.net/en; 6th fl, Vincom Tower, 191 Ba Trieu) Multiplex cinema with international standards and tickets from just US$2.50.

Cinematheque CINEMA
(Map p70; 22A Hai Ba Trung) A mecca for arthouse film lovers, this is a Hanoi institution.

Classical Music

Hanoi Opera House OPERA
(Map p70; www.hanoioperahouse.org.vn; P Trang Tien) This magnificent 900-seat venue, built in 1911, hosts occasional classical music performances and the atmosphere is incredible.

Clubbing

Hanoi is definitely not the Ibiza of the north, and the often-enforced midnight curfew means dance action is very limited. Also check out the bar-clubs in the Old Quarter.

Face Club CLUB
(Map p70; 6 P Hang Bai) Face Club dishes up lots of lasers, music from hip hop to techno, and a booming sound system. Popular with well-off Hanoians.

Tunnel CLUB
(Map p70; 11B P Bao Khanh) Happy-hour promotions and DJ nights make this a happening multifloor late-night spot.

Live Music

Live music is performed daily at the Temple of Literature.

Hanoi Rock City LIVE MUSIC
(www.hanoirockcity.com; 27/52 To Ngoc Van, Tay Ho) A great new venue for live music, hip hop, reggae, Hanoi punk, and regular electronica nights. Located about 7km north of the city near Tay Ho.

Jazz Club By Quyen Van Minh JAZZ
(Map p64; ☎3825 7655; www.minhjazzvietnam.com; 31-33 P Luong Van Can; ⊙performances 9-11.30pm) *The* place in Hanoi to catch some live jazz. Jams feature father-son team Minh and Dac, plus other local and international jazz acts.

Centre Culturel Française de Hanoi LIVE MUSIC
(Map p64; ☎3936 2164; www.ifhanoi-lespace.com; 24 P Trang Tien) Music and art in the modernist L'Espace building.

Water Puppetry

Municipal Water Puppet Theatre THEATRE
(Roi Nuoc Thang Long; Map p64; www.thanglongwaterpuppet.org; 57B P Dinh Tien Hoang; admission 60,000-100,000d; ⊙performances 2.15pm, 3.30pm, 5pm, 6.30pm, 8pm & 9.15pm) This fascinating art form originated in northern Vietnam, and

Hanoi is the best place to catch a show. An absolute must for children.

Shopping

The Old Quarter is brimming with temptations; price labels signal set prices. As you wander around you'll find cosmetics, fake sunglasses, luxury food, T-shirts, musical instruments, herbal medicines, jewellery, spices, propaganda art, fake English Premier football kits and much, much more.

Art & Handicrafts

You can find a selection of ethnic minority garb and handicrafts in Hanoi; P Hang Bac or P To Tich are good hunting grounds.

North and northwest of Hoan Kiem Lake around P Hang Gai, P To Tich, P Hang Khai and P Cau Go you'll be tripping over shops offering Vietnamese handicrafts (lacquerware, mother-of-pearl inlay, ceramics), as well as watercolours, oil paintings, prints and assorted antiques – real and fake.

Private art galleries are concentrated on P Trang Tien, between Hoan Kiem Lake and the Opera House. **Viet Art Centre** (www.vietartcentre.vn; 42 P Yet Kieu) is a fine place to browse contemporary Vietnamese art, photography and sculpture. It's a kilometre southwest of Hoan Kiem Lake.

Craft Link (www.craftlink-vietnam.com; 43 P Van Mieu) is a not-for-profit organisation near the Temple of Literature that sells quality tribal handicrafts and weavings at fair-trade prices.

For communist propaganda art posters, there are several good places on Hang Bac in the Old Quarter including **Hanoi Gallery** (Map p64; 110 P Hang Bac) and **Old Propaganda Posters** (Map p64; 122 P Hang Bac).

Books

Bookworm BOOKS
(www.bookwormhanoi.com; 44 Chau Long)
Hanoi's best selection of new and used English-language books, including plenty of fiction. It's 1.2km west of Hoan Kiem Lake.

Markets

Dong Xuan Market MARKET
(Map p64) Hundreds of stalls and not touristy at all – catch a flavour of Hanoian street life here.

Hang Da Market MARKET
(Map p64; Yen Thai) Small, but good for imported foods, wine, beer and flowers.

Silk Products & Clothing

P Hang Gai, about 100m northwest of Hoan Kiem Lake, and its continuation, P Hang Bong, are good places to look for embroidery and silk (including tailored clothes). Also check out the chic boutiques in the streets around St Joseph Cathedral.

Chi Vang (Map p64; 17 P Trang Tien) Exquisite lace creations, including clothing and homeware.

Things of Substance (Map p64; 5 P Nha Tho) Tailored fashions at moderate prices.

Information

Emergency

Ambulance (☎115)
Fire (☎114)
Police (☎113)

Internet Access

Most budget and midrange hotels offer free internet access as standard, with computers in the lobby and wi-fi. Chances are you won't have to venture into a cybercafe, but you'll find several on P Hang Bac in the Old Quarter. Rates start at 5000d per hour.

Internet Resources

To get the most out of Hanoi, try the following websites:

Hanoi Grapevine (www.hanoigrapevine.com) A culture-vulture's paradise, this site has a useful events calendar.

New Hanoian (www.newhanoian.com) The city's premier online resource, well worth checking out for its up-to-date restaurant, bar and accommodation reviews.

Sticky Rice (http://stickyrice.typepad.com) Foodie website *par excellence*.

The Word (www.wordhanoi.com) Online version of the excellent, free monthly magazine, *The Word*.

> **THE 36 STREETS**
>
> In the 13th century Hanoi's 36 guilds established themselves in the city, each taking a different road – hence the original name '36 Streets'. *Hang* means 'merchandise' and is usually followed by the name of the product that was traditionally sold in that street. Thus, P Hang Gai translates as 'Silk Street'.

Medical Services

Hanoi Family Medical Practice (☎3843 0748; www.vietnammedicalpractice.com; Van Phuc Diplomatic Compound, 298 P Kim Ma) Includes a team of well-respected international physicians and dentists and has 24-hour emergency cover. Prices are high, so check your medical insurance is in order.

L'Hopital Français de Hanoi (☎3577 1100, emergency ☎3574 1111; www.hfh.com.vn; 1 Phuong Mai; ⊙24hr) Long-established, international-standard hospital with A&E, intensive care, dental clinic and consulting services.

SOS International Clinic (☎3826 4545; www.internationalsos.com; 51 Xuan Dieu; ⊙24hr) English, French, German and Japanese are spoken and there's a dental clinic. It's 5km north of central Hanoi.

Money

Hanoi has many ATMs, and on the main roads around Hoan Kiem Lake are international banks where you can change money and get cash advances on credit cards.

Post

Main post office (75 P Dinh Tien Hoang)

International post office (cnr P Dinh Tien Hoang & P Dinh Le)

Telephone

Guesthouses and internet cafes are convenient for local calls. For international services, internet cafes using Skype offer the cheapest rates.

International Call Service (3 P Ta Hien; ⊙7am-10pm) 1500d to 2000d per minute to most countries.

Tourist Information

Even though this is the capital, forget anything really useful like a helpful tourist office that dishes out free information. In the cafes and bars of the Old Quarter look for the excellent local magazine, *The Word*.

Tourist Information Center (P Dinh Tien Hoang; ⊙8.30am-9pm) City maps and brochures, but privately run with an emphasis on selling tours. Pick up a free copy of the handy pocket-sized *Hanoi City Pass*.

Travel Agencies

Hanoi has hundreds of budget travel agencies. It's not advisable to book trips or tickets through guesthouses and hotels. Dealing directly with tour operators will give you a much better idea of what you'll get for your money, and how many other people you'll be travelling with. Try to seek out tour operators that stick to small groups and use their own vehicles and guides.

Successful tour operators often have their names cloned by others looking to trade on their reputation, so check addresses and websites carefully. Consider the following places in the Old Quarter:

Ethnic Travel (Map p64; ☎3926 1951; www.ethnictravel.com.vn; 35 P Hang Giay) Off-the-beaten-track trips across the north in small groups. Some trips are low-impact using public transport and homestays, others are activity based (including hiking, cycling and cooking). Offers Bai Tu Long Bay tours and also has an office in Sapa.

Handspan Adventure Travel (Map p64; ☎3926 2828; www.handspan.com; 78 P Ma May) Handspan is highly recommended for its wide range of tours, including sea-kayaking trips using an ecocamp in Lan Ha Bay, jeep tours, mountain biking, trekking and community-based tourism.

Ocean Tours (Map p64; ☎3926 0463; www.oceantours.com.vn; 22 P Hang Bac) A professional, well-organised tour operator with options to Halong Bay and Ba Be National Park, and 4WD road trips around the north-east region.

Travel (Map p64; ☎3926 3678; www.itravel-online.com; 25 P Hang Be) Offering culturally and environmentally sensitive trips across Vietnam.

Vega Travel (Map p64; ☎392 62092; www.vegatravel.vn; cnr P Ma May & 24A P Hang Bac) Well-run tours around the north and throughout Vietnam. Financially supports minority kindergartens and schools around Sapa and Bac Ha.

For nationwide operators offering tours of Hanoi and northern Vietnam, see p176. For motorbike tours see p176.

Getting There & Away

Air

Hanoi has fewer international flights than Ho Chi Minh City (HCMC), but with a change of aircraft in Hong Kong or Bangkok you can get almost anywhere. For more on international flights into and out of Hanoi, see p174.

Vietnam Airlines (Map p70; ☎1900 545 486; www.vietnamair.com.vn; 25 P Trang Thi) Links Hanoi to destinations throughout Vietnam. Popular routes include Hanoi to Dalat, Danang, Dien Bien Phu, HCMC, Hué and Nha Trang, all served daily.

Jetstar Airways (☎1900 1550; www.jetstar.com) Operates low-cost flights to Danang, HCMC and Nha Trang.

Bus

Hanoi has three main long-distance bus stations, each serving a particular area. It's a good idea to arrange your travel the day before you want to leave. The stations are pretty well organised with ticket offices, displayed schedules and fixed prices.

Gia Lam bus station (Đ Ngoc Lam), 3km northeast of the centre on the far bank of the Song Hong (Red River), is the place for buses to points east and northeast of Hanoi.

DESTINATION	TRAVEL TIME (HR)	COST (D)	FREQUENCY
Cao Bang	8	180,000	5 daily
Ha Giang	7	170,000	hourly
Haiphong	2	70,000	every 20 minutes
Halong City (Bai Chay)	3½	100,000	every 30 minutes
Lao Cai	9	250,000	1pm & 7pm

Loung Yen bus station (Tran Quang Khai & Nguyen Khoai) is 3km southeast of the Old Quarter and serves destinations to the south and the east, including sleeper buses to Hué, Dalat and Nha Trang and transport to Cat Ba Island.

Note that taxis at Luong Yen are notorious for their dodgy meters. Walk a couple of blocks and hail one off the street.

DESTINATION	TRAVEL TIME (HR)	COST (D)	FREQUENCY
Dalat	24	440,000	11am & 6pm
Danang	13	240,000	hourly from 2pm to 6pm
Hué	12	220,000	hourly from 2pm to 6pm
Nha Trang	7	170,000	10am & 6pm
Ninh Binh	2½	55,000	every 20 minutes from 6am to 6pm

My Dinh bus station (Đ Pham Hung), 7km west of the city, provides services to the west and the north, including sleeper buses to Dien Bien Phu.

DESTINATION	TRAVEL TIME (HR)	COST (D)	FREQUENCY
Cao Bang	10	135,000	every 45 minutes
Dien Bien Phu	11½	260,000	11am & 6pm
Ha Giang	7	140,000	from 4am to 6am
Mai Chau	2½	65,000	6.30am & 2.30pm
Son La	7½	150,000	from 7am to 8am

Some buses from Ninh Binh and the south use **Giap Bat bus station** (Đ Giai Phong), 7km south of the Hanoi train station.

Tourist-style minibuses can be booked through most hotels and cafes. Popular destinations include Halong Bay and Sapa. Prices are usually about 30% to 40% higher than the regular public bus, but include a hotel pick-up.

Open-tour bus tickets are available in Hanoi for destinations including Ninh Binh and Hué.

Buses also connect Hanoi with Nanning in China, see p174.

Car & Motorcycle

Car hire is best arranged via a travel agency, hotel or tour operator. The roads in the north are in pretty good shape but expect an average speed of 35km to 40km per hour. You'll definitely need a 4WD. Daily rates start at about US$110 a day (including driver and petrol). For more see p175.

Hanoi is a nightmare to negotiate on a motorbike – we suggest you leave it to the locals. If you're really up for the challenge, try the Hanoi tour operators on p176 for reliable machines.

Train

The main **Hanoi train station** (Ga Hang Co; Map p61; 120 Đ Le Duan; ⏲ticket office 7.30am-12.30pm & 1.30-7.30pm) is at the western end of P Tran Hung Dao. Trains from here go to destinations south.

To the right of the main entrance of the train station is a separate ticket office for northbound trains to Lao Cai (for Sapa) and China (see p174). Note that all northbound trains leave from a separate station (just behind the main station) called **Tran Quy Cap station** (B Station; P Tran Qui Cap).

To make things even more complicated, some northbound (Lao Cai and Lang Son included) and eastbound (Haiphong) trains depart from **Gia Lam** (Nguyen Van Cu, Gia Lam District) on the eastern side of the Song Hong (Red River), and **Long Bien** on the western (city) side of the river. Be sure to ask just where you need to go to catch your train.

TRAINS FROM HANOI

DESTINATION	STATION	COST (AIR-CON SOFT SEAT–SOFT BERTH) (D)	DURATION (HR)
Danang	Hanoi	570,000-915,000	15½-21
Haiphong	Long Bien & Gia Lam	47,000-60,000	2-3
HCMC	Hanoi	1,175,000-1,690,000	30-41
Hué	Hanoi	508,000-833,000	12-16
Lao Cai	Tran Quy Cap	210,000-450,000	8½-9½
Nha Trang	Hanoi	1,030,000-1,510,000	19-28

In theory, **Vietnam Rail** (www.vr.com.vn) has timetables and prices in English, though it's rarely updated; try the rail website www.seat61.com.

It's best to buy tickets at least one day before departure to ensure a seat or sleeper. Travel agents will book train tickets for a commission.

Getting Around

Bicycle

Many Old Quarter guesthouses and cafes rent bikes for about US$2 per day. Good luck with that traffic.

Bus

Plenty of local buses (fares from 3000d) serve routes around Hanoi but very few tourists bother with them. Pick up a copy of the *Xe Buyt Hanoi* (Hanoi Bus Map; 5000d) from bookshops if you want to tackle the system.

Cyclo

A few *cyclo* drivers still frequent the Old Quarter. Settle on a price first and watch out for overcharging.

Aim to pay around 25,000d for a shortish journey; night rides cost more. Not many *cyclo* drivers speak English so take a map with you.

Electric Train

Hanoi's eco-friendly **electric train** (per person 15,000d; ⊙8.30am-10.30pm) is actually a pretty good way to get your bearings. It traverses a network of 14 stops in the Old Quarter and around Hoan Kiem Lake. Catch one at the northern end of Hoan Kiem Lake; a circuit takes around 40 minutes.

Motorcycle

Offers for *xe om* rides are ubiquitous. A short ride should be about 30,000d, about 5km around 70,000d.

Forget getting around Hanoi by motorbike unless you're very familiar with the city – traffic is relentless, road signs are missing, road manners are nonexistent and it's dangerous.

Taxi

Taxis are everywhere. Flag fall is around 15,000d, which takes you 1km or 2km; every kilometre thereafter costs around 10,000d. Some dodgy operators have high-speed meters, so use the following reliable companies:

Thanh Nga Taxi (☎3821 5215)

Mai Linh Taxi (☎3822 2666)

Van Xuan (☎3822 2888)

AROUND HANOI

Perfume Pagoda

The **Perfume Pagoda** (Chua Huong; admission incl return boat trip 55,000d) is a striking complex of pagodas and Buddhist shrines built into the karst cliffs of Huong Tich Mountain (Mountain of the Fragrant Traces). This is a domestic drawcard and it is an interesting experience just to see the Vietnamese tourists at play.

If you want to do the scenic river trip, travel from Hanoi by car to My Duc (two hours), then take a small boat rowed by two women to the foot of the mountain (1½ hours).

The main pagoda area is about a 4km walk up from where the boat lets you off. The good news is that there is now a **cable car** (one way/return 60,000/100,000d) to the summit. A smart combination is to use the cable car to go up and then walk down.

Hanoi travel agents (see p74) offer day tours to the pagoda from US$10, inclusive of transport, guide and lunch (drinks excluded). A small-group tour is around US$25.

Handicraft Villages

There are numerous villages surrounding Hanoi that specialise in particular cottage industries. Visiting these villages can make a rewarding day trip, though you'll need a good guide to make the journey worthwhile.

Bat Trang, 13km southeast of Hanoi, is known as the ceramic village. You can watch artisans create superb ceramic vases and other masterpieces in their kilns.

So, known for its delicate noodles, mills the yam and cassava flour for noodles. It's about 25km southwest of Hanoi.

You can see silk cloth being produced on a loom in **Van Phuc**, a village 8km southwest of Hanoi. There's also a small produce market every morning.

Dong Ky, 15km northeast of Hanoi, produces beautiful, traditional furniture inlaid with mother-of-pearl.

Ninh Binh

☎030 / POP 130,000

The city of Ninh Binh, 93km south of Hanoi, isn't a destination in itself, but a good base for exploring some quintessentially Vietnamese karst scenery and bucolic countryside. The town, though industrial, has its pleasant aspects, but the proximity of sights, including the limestone mountains of Tam Coc and Cuc Phuong National Park, is the real draw. Tours of these sights from Hanoi are popular.

Sleeping & Eating

Accommodation is excellent value here. All the places listed can arrange tours, and hire out motorbikes and bicycles. Restaurant choices are very limited but try the local speciality, *de* (goat meat), usually served with fresh herbs and rice paper.

TOP CHOICE **Thanhthuy's Guest House & New Hotel** HOTEL $
(☎387 1811; www.hotelthanhthuy.com; 128 Đ Le Hong Phong; guesthouse r US$7-10, hotel r US$15-25;) Probably the best place to mingle with other travellers, this popular hotel is run by a friendly crew, including some very switched-on tour guides. Rooms, all very clean and some with balcony, vary quite a bit in price and comfort level.

Thuy Anh Hotel HOTEL $$
(☎387 1602; www.thuyanhhotel.com; 55A Đ Truong Han Sieu; s/d old wing US$20/25, new wing US$30/45;) A well-run hotel with good-value rooms, particularly the spotless, modern options at the rear. The restaurant serves Western food (including a hearty complimentary breakfast) and Vietnamese dishes.

Ninh Binh Legend Hotel HOTEL $$$
(☎389 9880; www.ninhbinhlegendhotel.com; Tien Dong Zone; r/ste from US$77/126;) Landmark new four-star hotel with well-appointed rooms. There's a decent gym, spa, tennis courts and huge, though pricey, restaurant.

Thanh Binh Hotel HOTEL $
(☎387 2439; www.thanhbinhhotelnb.com.vn; 31 Đ Luong Van Tuy; s/d US$10-25/15-30;) Popular with budget travellers – the rooms are good, the owner is friendly and there's a restaurant.

Information

You'll find a cluster of internet cafes on Đ Luong Van Tuy and several ATMs on Đ Tran Hung Dao.

Getting There & Away

Public buses leave regularly from Giap Bat and Loung Yen bus terminals in Hanoi (55,000d, 2½ hours). The bus station is on the east side of the Van River. Ninh Binh is also a hub on the open-tour bus route (see p175).

Ninh Binh is a scheduled stop for some trains travelling between Hanoi and HCMC, but travelling by road is faster.

Around Ninh Binh

TAM COC

Known as 'Halong Bay on the Rice Paddies' for its huge rock formations jutting out of paddies, **Tam Coc** (admission 30,000d, boat 60,000d) boasts breathtaking scenery.

The only way to see Tam Coc is by rowboat on the Ngo Dong River. The boats row through karst caves on this beautiful two-hour trip. Boats seat two passengers (and have no shade). Arrive before 9am to beat the crowds, as it can be a bit of a circus thanks to the pushy vendors.

Tam Coc is 9km southwest of Ninh Binh. By car or motorbike, follow Hwy 1 south and turn west at the Tam Coc turn-off, marked by a pair of tall stone pillars.

HOA LU

The scenery here resembles nearby Tam Coc, though Hoa Lu has an interesting historical twist. It was the capital of Vietnam under the Dinh (968–80) and Le dynasties (980–1009). The site was a suitable choice for a capital city due to its proximity to China and the natural protection afforded by the region's bizarre landscape.

The **ancient citadel** (admission 12,000d) of Hoa Lu, most of which, sadly, has been destroyed, once covered an area of about 3 sq km.

There is no public transport to Hoa Lu, which is 12km north of Ninh Binh. Most travellers get here by bicycle, motorbike or car.

CHUA BAI DINH

FREE **Chua Bai Dinh** (⊙7am-5.45pm), a vast new Buddhist complex, attracts thousands of Vietnamese visitors. The sheer scale of the compound is astonishing, but think twice if you're seeking spiritual enlightenment – the crowds here don't facilitate feelings of peace and harmony.

Cloister-like walkways pass 500 stone arhats that line the route up to the triple-roofed Phap Chu pagoda, which contains a 10m, 100-tonne bronze Buddha. Some of the wood detailing, lacquerwork and stone-carving is impressive.

An additional 13-storey pagoda and a temple with Vietnam's largest bell are other key attractions at this bombastic sight.

Chua Bai Dinh is 11km northwest of Ninh Binh. You'll pass dozens of goat-meat restaurants on the way.

Cuc Phuong National Park

☎030 / ELEV 150-648M

This **national park** (☎384 8006; www.cucphuongtourism.com; adult/child 20,000/10,000d) is one of Vietnam's most important nature preserves. Ho Chi Minh personally took time off from the war in 1963 to dedicate the area as a national park, Vietnam's first. The hills are laced with many grottoes, and the climate is subtropical at the park's lower elevations.

Excellent trekking opportunities abound in the park, including a hike (8km return) to an enormous 1000-year-old tree (*Tetrameles nudiflora*, for botany geeks), and to a Muong village where you can also go rafting. A guide is mandatory for longer treks.

During the rainy season (July to September) leeches are common; the best time to visit is between December and April. Try to avoid visiting on weekends and during school holidays, when it gets hectic.

Endangered Primate Rescue Center (www.primatecenter.org; ⊙9.30-11.30am & 1.30-4.30pm) here is home to around 150 rare monkeys bred in captivity or confiscated from illegal traders. These gibbons, langurs and lorises are rehabilitated, studied and, whenever possible, released back into their native environments or into semi-wild protected areas. Seeing them in full swing (quite literally) is a sight.

Turtle Conservation Center (⊙9-11.15am & 2-4.45pm) houses over 1000 turtles, many of them confiscated from smugglers. You'll find excellent information displays, and there are incubation and hatchling viewing areas. The centre successfully breeds and releases turtles from 11 different species including six native turtles.

Sleeping & Eating

There are three accommodation areas in the park.

At the visitor centre are dark, basic **rooms** (per person US$7), en-suite **guesthouse rooms** (r US$23-27), and 2km away are attractive **bungalows** (r US$25) overlooking Mac Lake.

The main park centre, 18km from the gate, has simple **rooms** (per person US$7), large **four-bed rooms** (r US$20) and a few **bungalows** (r US$28).

There are **restaurants** (meals 25,000-50,000d) at both the park centre and visitor centre. Call ahead and place your order for each meal (except breakfast).

Cuc Phuong can get very busy at weekends and holidays, when you should make a reservation.

Getting There & Away

Cuc Phuong National Park is 45km west of Ninh Binh, and there are irregular bus connections (18,000d).

NORTHERN VIETNAM

Welcome to the roof of Vietnam, where the mountains of the Tonkinese Alps soar skyward, delivering some of the most spectacular scenery in the country. The attractive old French hill station of Sapa remains the main base in the far north, but nearby Bac Ha is emerging as a less-visited alternative for trekking and exploring hill-tribe villages. South of here, the sublime scenery and idyllic lakes of Ba Be National Park are well worth a diversion.

Bizarre but beautiful, Halong Bay is geology gone wild, with hundreds of limestone pinnacles emerging from the waters. North of Halong Bay is less-visited Bai Tu Long Bay, where nature's spectacular show continues all the way to the Chinese border. Or head to rugged Cat Ba, a verdant island renowned for its hiking, biking, sailing, and world-class rock climbing.

Halong Bay

Majestic and mysterious, inspiring and imperious – words alone cannot do justice to the natural wonder that is Halong Bay, where 3000 or more incredible islands rise from the emerald waters of the Gulf of Tonkin. Designated a World Heritage Site in 1994, this mystical seascape of limestone islets is a vision of breathtaking beauty.

Ha long means 'where the dragon descends into the sea'. Legend says that the islands of Halong Bay were created by a great dragon that lived in the mountains. As it ran towards the coast, its flailing tail gouged out valleys and crevasses; as it plunged into the sea, the areas dug up by its tail became filled with water, leaving only pockets of high land visible.

The islands are dotted with wind- and wave-eroded grottoes, many now illuminated with technicolour lighting effects. Sadly, litter and trinket-touting vendors are now also part of the experience.

From February through until April, the weather can often be cold and drizzly, and the ensuing fog can cause low visibility, although the temperature rarely falls below 10°C. Tropical storms are frequent during the summer months (running from July to September).

Most visitors sensibly opt for tours that include sleeping overnight on a boat in the bay. Some dodge the humdrum gateway Halong City completely and head independently for Cat Ba Town, from where trips to less-visited, equally alluring Lan Ha Bay can be easily set up. See the boxed text on p81 for more details on organised trips.

Halong Bay Management Department (033-384 6592; http://halong.org.vn/; 166 Đ Le Thanh Tong), 2km west of Halong City, regulates independent cruises on the bay. It's easy to hook up with other people to share a boat with here; rates start at around 50,000d per hour.

Halong City

033 / POP 193,700

Halong City is the main gateway to Halong Bay. Overdeveloped but underloved, the seafront is blighted by high-rise hotels. That said, it has good-value accommodation and its waterside setting is breathtaking on a fine day.

An elegant suspension bridge connects the western, touristy side of town (known as Bai Chay) with the much more Vietnamese entity (Hon Gai) to the east.

Sleeping & Eating

The 'hotel alley' of Đ Vuon Dao has more than 50 minihotels, most of them almost identical with comfortable doubles for around US$12. Midrange and top-end hotels are scattered along Đ Halong.

For cheap, filling food there are modest places at the bottom of Đ Vuon Dao with English menus. Seafood lovers should gravitate to the harbourfront Đ Halong, where there's a cluster of good places.

TOP CHOICE **Novotel** HOTEL $$$
(384 8108; www.novotelhalongbay.com; Đ Halong; r from US$115;) This hip hotel fuses Asian and Japanese influences with contemporary details. The rooms are simply stunning, with teak floors, marble bathrooms and sliding screens to divide living areas. Check online for rates of around US$80.

BMC Thang Long Hotel HOTEL $$
(384 6458; Đ Halong; www.bmcthanglonghotel.com; r US$25-75;) Large hotel with spacious and recently renovated rooms, some with ocean views. Staff are warm and personal, and Bai Chay tourist docks are just across the road.

Tung Lam Hotel HOTEL $
(364 0743; 29 Đ Vuon Dao; r US$10-12;) This minihotel is making a little more effort than most. Rooms all have two beds, TV, minibar and en-suite bathrooms, and those at the front are spacious and include a balcony.

Information

Post office (Đ Halong) Internet access available.
Vietcombank (Đ Halong) Exchange services and ATM.

Getting There & Away

The bus station is 6km south of central Bai Chay, just off Hwy 18.

DESTINATION	TRAVEL TIME (HR)	COST	FREQUENCY
Haiphong	1½	50,000d	every 20 minutes
Hanoi	3	90,000d	every 15 minutes
Lang Son	5½	120,000d	12.30pm
Mong Cai	4	90,000d	every 30 minutes

Getting to Cat Ba Island from Halong City can be a pain, see boxed text p82.

Hydrofoil connections from Bai Chay to Mong Cai are no more.

Cat Ba Island

031 / POP 13,500

Rugged, craggy and jungle-clad Cat Ba, the largest island around Halong Bay, is emerging as northern Vietnam's adventure-sport and ecotourism mecca. There's a terrific roll-call of activities here – sailing trips, birdwatching, biking, hiking and rock climbing – and some fine tour operators organising them.

Lan Ha Bay, off the eastern side of the island, is especially scenic and offers numerous beaches to explore. You could spend a year here discovering a different islet every day, while swimming and snorkelling the bay's turquoise waters. While the vast majority of Halong Bay's islands are uninhabited vertical rocks, Cat Ba has a few fishing villages, as well as a fast-growing town.

Much of Cat Ba Island was declared a national park in 1986 in order to protect the island's diverse ecosystems and wildlife, including the endangered golden-headed langur, the world's rarest primate. There are beautiful beaches, numerous lakes, waterfalls and grottoes in the spectacular limestone hills.

In recent years Cat Ba Town has experienced a hotel boom, and a chain of ugly concrete hotels now frames a once-lovely bay. But its ugliness is skin deep, as the rest of the island and Lan Ha Bay are so alluring.

Sights

TOP CHOICE Lan Ha Bay ISLANDS

The 300 or so karst islands of Lan Ha Bay are directly south and east of Cat Ba Town. Geologically they are very much an extension of Halong Bay. They share the same emerald sea, and the limestone pinnacles and scenery are every bit as beautiful as Halong Bay, but with the additional attraction of numerous white-sand beaches. Few tourist boats venture here, giving Lan Ha Bay a more isolated, off-the-beaten-track appeal. There's a 20,000d admission fee to the bay, but this is often incorporated into the cost of tours.

Around 200 species of fish, 500 species of mollusc, 400 species of arthropod and numerous hard and soft coral live in Lan Ha Bay. Larger marine animals in the area include seals and three species of dolphin.

Sailing and kayak trips here are best organised in Cat Ba Town. With hundreds of **beaches** to choose from it's easy to find your own private patch of sand for the day. Camping is permitted on gorgeous **Hai Pie beach** (also known as Tiger Beach), which is used as a base camp by the Cat Ba adventure tour operators and even hosts occasional full-moon parties.

Blue Swimmer offers wonderful sailing excursions at reasonable rates in Lan Ha Bay. The islands also offer superb rock climbing, and are the main destination for trips run by Asia Outdoors (p83).

Cat Ba National Park NATIONAL PARK

(admission 30,000d; guide 60,000-170,000d; dawn-dusk) The main habitat of the golden-headed langur (officially the world's most endangered primate with around 65 remaining), Cat Ba National Park is a vitally important ecosystem. Macaques, wild boar, deer, civets, several species of squirrel including the giant black squirrel, and more than 70 species of birds including hawks, hornbills and cuckoos are all present.

There's excellent trekking too, such as a very challenging 18km trek (five to six hours) through the park. You'll need a guide, transport to the trailhead and a boat to return, all of which can be arranged in Cat Ba Town through hotels, Asia Outdoors or Cat Ba Ventures. Proper trekking shoes, rainwear, a generous supply of water, plus food are recommended. Shorter, less hardcore hiking options are possible.

To reach the national park headquarters at Trung Trang, get a QH public bus from the hydrofoil docks at Cat Ba Town (15,000d, 20 minutes). Buses leave at 5am, 8.10am, 11.10am and 4pm. Another option is to hire a *xe om* for around 60,000d one way, or rent your own motorbike for the day.

DON'T MISS

CRUISING THE KARSTS: TOURS TO HALONG BAY

There are many ways to experience the ethereal beauty of Halong Bay. Unless you have a private yacht (or you're an Olympian kayaker), you'll have to take a tour of some kind.

For a serious splurge, cruising the karsts aboard a luxury junk or a French colonial-style paddle ship is hard to beat. But be aware that nearly all of these luxury trips operate on a fixed itinerary, taking in the well-known caves and islands, and simply do not have the time to stray far from Halong City. Many 'two-day' tours actually involve less than 24 hours on a boat (and cost hundreds of dollars per person).

At the other end of the scale, budget tours sold out of Hanoi start from a rock-bottom US$35 per person for a dodgy day trip, rising to around US$150 for two nights on the bay with kayaking. For around US$80 to US$90, you should get a worthwhile overnight cruise.

Lonely Planet gets many complaints about poor service, bad food and rats running around boats, but these tend to be on the ultra-budget tours. Spend a little more and enjoy the experience a lot more. In February 2011, a budget tour boat sank with the loss of 12 lives. Consequently, new regulations have been introduced to tighten up safety issues.

Most tours include transport, meals and, sometimes, island hikes. Drinks are extra. Boat tours are sometimes cancelled in bad weather and you'll probably be offered a full or partial refund. Ascertain in advance what that will be.

If you've got more time and want to experience Halong Bay without the crowds, consider Cat Ba Island. Here you'll find operators who concentrate on Lan Ha Bay, which is less frequented and relatively untouched, with sublime sandy beaches. See p83.

Boat Operators

There are hundreds of boats plying the waters these days. The following is just a selection of the most interesting.

Cruise Halong (☎04-3984 2807; www.cruisehalong.com; d from US$467) Three beautiful junks that are well finished throughout.

Emeraude Classic Cruise (☎04-3934 0888; www.emeraude-cruises.com; d US$255-490) A replica paddle steamer that cruises the waters of Halong Bay daily.

Handspan (☎04-3926 2828; www.handspan.com; US$144-379) Offers excellent cruises and also the only true sailing ship (the *Treasure Junk*), so there's no diesel engine to disturb the peace. Crack open a cold Bia Hanoi and you'll be in heaven.

Indochina Sails (☎04-3984 2362; www.indochinasails.com; cabins from US$375) A traditional junk kitted out to a three-star standard.

Indochina Junk (☎04-3926 4085; www.indochinajunk.com; from US$178) Sail in style on board these elegant craft.

For a list of reliable Hanoi-based tour operators with trips to Halong Bay see p74.

Fort Cannon WAR MONUMENT

(admission 20,000d; ⊙sunrise-sunset) For one of the best views in all of Vietnam head to Fort Cannon. Underground tunnels and gun emplacements were first installed by the Japanese in WWII and later utilised by the French and Vietnamese during subsequent conflicts.

Well-labelled paths guide visitors around, and the astounding vistas include the colourful tangle of fishing boats in Cat Ba harbour and nearby coves and beaches. The views out to a karst-punctuated sea are quite sublime, and there's even a terrific cafe and juice bar.

The entrance gate is a steep 10-minute walk or a 10,000d *xe om* ride from Cat Ba Town. From the gate, a **tourist train** (40,000d) trundles the last uphill journey, or it's another stiff 20-minute walk.

Hospital Cave WAR MONUMENT

(admission 15,000d; ⊙7am-4.30pm) This cave is a very intriguing site. It was used as a (bomb-proof) secret hospital during the war in Vietnam and as a safe house for VC leaders. This incredibly well-constructed three-storey feat of engineering was in constant use until 1975. A guide will show you around

HALONG BAY TO CAT BA ISLAND (WITHOUT THE HASSLE)

Warning! Travelling from Halong City to Cat Ba Island can be fraught with hassles.

Tourist boats (US$8, four hours) depart from Halong Bay around 1pm for Cat Ba Island. The trouble is they dock at Gia Luan, which is 40km from Cat Ba Town – and local taxi and *xe om* mafia frequently demand up to US$50 for the ride. There *is* actually a local bus (15,000d) – the QH Green Bus – at 5pm, but this usually departs just before the boats arrive. Funny that...

Many boat owners in Halong Bay are part of the scam, so check if onward transport to Cat Ba Town is included. Some operators, including Cat Ba Ventures (www.catbaventures.com), do include it.

An alternative route is taking the **passenger and vehicle ferry** (per person 40,000d, one hr; ⊙on the hr 5am-5pm May-Sep & 8am, 11.10am & 3pm Oct-Apr) that travels from the resort island of Tuan Chau to Gia Luan. (A taxi from Halong City to Tuan Chau is around 130,000d, *xe om* 35,000d.) You can then catch a QH Green bus (departures at 6am, 9.30am, 1.10pm, 4pm and 5pm for 15,000d) to Cat Ba Town.

To travel in the other direction contact Cat Ba Ventures in Cat Ba Town for the latest information.

the 17 rooms, point out the old operating theatre, cinema and small swimming pool. It's about 10km north of Cat Ba Town.

Cat Co Beaches BEACHES

The white-sand Cat Co beaches (called simply Cat Co 1, Cat Co 2 and Cat Co 3) are perfect places to lounge around for the day; however, Cat Co 1 and 3 have been taken over by big resorts. Luckily, Cat Co 2 is the most attractive beach, also offering simple accommodation and camping. The beaches are about 1km from Cat Ba Town.

Activities

Cat Ba is a superb base for adventure sports.

Mountain Biking

Hotels can arrange Chinese mountain bikes (around US$4 per day), and Blue Swimmer Adventures rents Trek bikes for US$12 per day.

One possible route traverses the heart of the island, past Hospital Cave down to the west coast's mangroves and crab farms, and then in a loop back to Cat Ba Town past tidal mudflats and deserted beaches.

Rock Climbing

Cat Ba Island and Lan Ha Bay's spectacular limestone cliffs make for world-class rock climbing. Based in Cat Ba, Asia Outdoors (formerly known as Slo Pony Adventures) pioneered climbing in Vietnam, and uses fully licensed and certified instructors. Other, less-qualified Cat Ba operators also offer climbing trips, but Asia Outdoors is the absolute authority on the island.

Full-day climbing trips including instruction, transport, lunch and gear start at US$52 per person for Cat Ba Island, or US$75 if you head for Lan Ha Bay. These longer trips by boat incorporate kayaking, beach stops and exploring the amazing karst landscape.

See the boxed text Climbing the Karsts (p84).

Sailing & Kayaking

Don't miss exploring the spectacular islands and beaches of Lan Ha Bay on a **sailing excursion**. Overnight trips through Lan Ha Bay to Nam Cat beach, including a night sleeping in a bamboo hut, cost US$39 per person. Also available are private boat charters with a skipper, and full-day trips on a Chinese junk to Long Chau lighthouse, built by the French in the 1920s and still bearing bomb scars from the war in Vietnam.

Plenty of hotels in Cat Ba rent kayaks (per half-day around $8). Blue Swimmer has good-quality kayaks (single/double per day US$12/20), ideal for exploring the Cat Ba coast independently.

Guided overnight kayak tours from Blue Swimmer (per person $108) include Lan Ha Bay, sea caves, and camping on a deserted beach.

Trekking

Most of Cat Ba Island consists of protected tropical forest. For details of trekking routes see Cat Ba National Park. Asia Outdoors and Blue Swimmer both offer a great hike around Cat Ba Island, including taking in Butterfly Valley.

Tours

Tours of the island and boat trips around Halong Bay are offered by nearly every hotel in Cat Ba. Typical prices are around US$20 for day trips including kayaking and US$70 for two-day, one-night tours.

We receive unfavourable feedback – cramped conditions and dodgy food – about some of these trips. The following adventure tour operators understand travellers' needs and will steer you away from the tourist trail to really special areas of Cat Ba, Lan Ha Bay, and beyond.

Asia Outdoors ROCK CLIMBING
(☎368 8450; www.slopony.com; Noble House, Đ 1-4) Formerly known as Slo Pony, this highly professional company is run by two uber-passionate climbers and explorers, Onslow Carrington and Erik Ferjentsik. Climbing instruction is their real expertise, but they also offer excellent, well-structured sailing, biking and hiking trips. Rock up to their office in Noble House at 6pm every night to see what's planned.

Blue Swimmer SAILING, KAYAKING
(☎369 6079; www.blueswimmersailing.com; 265 Đ Nui Ngoc) A very well-organised, environmentally conscious outfit offering superb sailing and kayaking trips; trekking and biking excursions are also offered. At the time of writing, it had also just finalised the lease on its new Blue Swimmer Adventure Hotel.

Cat Ba Ventures BOAT TRIPS, KAYAKING
(☎368 8237; www.catbaventures.com; 223 Đ 14) Locally owned and operated company offering boat trips to Halong Bay, kayaking, and hiking. Excellent service from Mr Tung is reinforced by multiple reader recommendations.

Sleeping

Most of the island's 40 or so hotels are concentrated along the bayfront in Cat Ba Town. Room rates fluctuate greatly between high-season summertime and the slower winter months. The following are low-season prices.

CAT BA TOWN

Duc Tuan Hotel HOTEL $
(☎388 8783; 210 Đ 1-4 178; www.catbatravelservice.com; r US$8-15;) Family-owned place with simple but colourfully furnished rooms; those at the back are quieter, but lack windows. Downstairs is a good restaurant offering seafood *lau* (hotpot) meals, and Cat Ba excursions are offered.

Cat Ba Dream HOTEL $
(☎388 8274; 226 Đ 1-4; www.catbadream.com.vn; r US$10-15;) A recent addition to the town's coastal cavalcade of accommodation. Service is a tad perfunctory, but if you can angle for a seafront room, you'll have a cinematic scroll of Cat Ba action right in front of you.

Vien Dong HOTEL $
(☎388 8555; 225 Đ Nui Ngoc; www.viendong-hotel.com.vn; r US$12-15;) A good choice, with sterling views of the bay, well-kept and spacious rooms, and a good grasp of English at reception.

Phong Lan Hotel HOTEL $
(☎388 8605; Đ 1-4; r US$8-12;) Request a room at the front of this hotel, right in

BAI TU LONG BAY

There's more to northeastern Vietnam than Halong Bay. The sinking limestone plateau, which gave birth to the bay's spectacular islands, continues for some 100km to the Chinese border. The area immediately northeast of Halong Bay is part of **Bai Tu Long National Park**.

Bai Tu Long Bay is every bit as beautiful as its famous neighbour. Indeed, in some ways it's more beautiful, since it's relatively undeveloped. It's definitely a laid-back alternative to the touristy hustle and bustle of Halong Bay.

Charter boats can be arranged to Bai Tu Long Bay from Halong Bay; rates start at around 300,000d per hour and the trip there takes about five hours. A cheaper and more flexible alternative is to travel overland to Cai Rong and visit the outlying islands by boat from there. An increased frequency of ferry sailings definitely makes this a more viable alternative than in earlier years.

Hanoi travel agencies, including Ethnic Travel, run trips into the Bai Tu Long area. Another Hanoi contact for Bai Tu Long is **Le Pont Travel** (☎04-3935-1889; 102 P Ma May, Old Quarter; www.letponttravel.com).

CLIMBING THE KARSTS

If you've ever been tempted to climb, Halong Bay is a superb place to go for it – the karst cliffs here offer exceptional climbing amid stunning scenery. Most climbers in Cat Ba are complete novices, but as the instruction is excellent, many leave Cat Ba completely bitten by the bug.

You don't need great upper-body strength to climb, as you actually use your legs far more. The karst limestone of Halong Bay is not too sharp and quite friendly on the hands. As many of the routes are sheltered by natural overhangs that prevent the climbable portion of the rock from getting wet, climbing is almost always possible, rain or shine.

Climbing opportunities for beginners are located on walls inland on Cat Ba Island or out on beautiful Lan Ha Bay. You'll be kitted up with a harness and climbing shoes, given instruction and taught the fundamentals of the climbing and belaying technique, then given a demonstration. Then it's over to you (with your climbing instructor talking you through each move, and anchoring you, of course!). Most people are able to complete a couple of climbs at Hai Pai and Moody's Beach, both ideal for beginners.

The vertical cliffs of Halong and Lan Ha Bays are also perfect for deep-water soloing, which is basically climbing alone, without ropes or a harness, and using the ocean as a waterbed in case you fall. This is obviously only for the experienced, and it's essential to know the depth of water and tidal patterns. It's customary to finish with a controlled freefall (or 'tombstone') into the sea and a swim.

A few inexperienced locals offer climbing excursions, but beginners should sign up with the experienced crew at Asia Outdoors (p83).

the middle of the seafront strip, which has balconies overlooking the harbour. The English-speaking owner is helpful and there's a travel agency here too.

Thu Ha HOTEL $

(☎388 8343; Đ 1-4; r US$8-12; ❄☜) Offering a super-central seafront location, the recently refurbished Thu Ha offers great value. Negotiate hard for a front room with a balcony, and wake up to sea views.

Cat Co 2 BUNGALOW $

(☎093 447 8156; d 400,000d) On the sandy beach at Cat Co 2, there are basic, thatched wooden bungalows with a fan in an attractive, leafy beachside plot. There's a shower block and cafe for meals (around 70,000d). At the time of writing, a five-star resort was planned for Cat Co 2, so this may change.

AROUND CAT BA ISLAND

TOP CHOICE **Sui Goi Cat Ba Resort** LODGE $$

(☎368 8966; Cat Ba Island; www.suoigoicatbaresort.vn; d from US$45; ❄☜) This new ecoresort celebrates a wonderfully quiet village location 12km from Cat Ba Town. Spacious wooden stilt houses sit around a breezy bar and restaurant, and activities include trekking, and riding bicycles to a beach 2km away. Most nights there's a seafood barbecue (US$10), and free pickups can be arranged from the ferry or Cat Ba Town.

Whisper of Nature GUESTHOUSE $

(☎265 7678; Viet Hai Village; www.vietbungalow.com; dm US$12, d US$22-28) Located in the hamlet of Viet Hai, these simple concrete-and-thatch bungalows are arrayed around a stream on the edge of the forest. Arrival is an adventure, with the final stage a bike ride through lush scenery. Ask about transport when you book, or hire a bamboo boat from Cat Ba Town to the Viet Hai village jetty (200,000d), and then a *xe om* (30,000d) for the final 5km to the village.

NEARBY ISLANDS

Nam Cat Island Resort RESORT $$

(☎098 955 5773; Nam Cat Island; namcatisland@gmail.com; d US$25-60; ❄) Enjoys a secluded cove location with simple bungalows plus flashier villas with private facilities. Spend your days swimming and kayaking, and kick back with seafood barbecues and beach bonfires after dark. Nam Cat is included on some itineraries arranged by Cat Ba Ventures (p83).

Monkey Island Resort RESORT $$

(☎04-3926 0572; www.monkeyislandresort.com; d US$40-60; ❄) There's a nice social vibe going down at Monkey Island, with a nightly seafood buffet, cool R&B beats and volleyball. Accommodation is in comfortable private bungalows, and there are kayaks for hire. Free transfers from Cat Ba Town are offered. The eponymous primates lurk close by on a karst peak.

Eating & Drinking

For a memorable dining experience, try the floating seafood restaurants in Cat Ba or Ben Beo harbours, where you choose your own seafood from pens underneath the restaurant. A rowing boat there and back should cost 100,000d with waiting time; a feast for two should cost 200,000d or so. Overcharging is a possibility, so work out meal prices beforehand.

All of the following are in Cat Ba Town.

TOP CHOICE Bamboo Café VIETNAMESE $
(Đ 1-4; dishes 80,000-120,000d) The best option for a casual bite on the seafront, this enjoyable little place has a small harbour-facing terrace and an intimate bamboo-walled interior. The genial owner is a fluent English-speaker and serves up generous portions of Vietnamese and international food. The beer is super-cold and there's wine available by the glass.

Vien Duong VIETNAMESE $$
(12 Đ Nui Ngoc; meals from 100,000d) One of the most popular of the seafood spots lining Đ Nui Ngoc, and often heaving with Vietnamese tourists diving into local crab, squid and steaming seafood hotpots.

Family Bakery BAKERY $
(196 Đ 1-4; dishes 80,000-120,000d; ⊙7am-4pm) Friendly place that opens early for goodies like Turkish bread and almond pastries. Pop in for a coffee and croissant.

Thao May VIETNAMESE $
(18 Đ Nui Ngoc; mains 80,000-120,000d) Family-run spot that's recommended by in-the-know expats for authentic local grub and cheap beer.

Good Bar BAR
(Đ 1-4; 📶) A social HQ for travellers with pool tables and a lively vibe.

Flightless Bird BAR
(Đ 1-4; 📶) This tiny, Kiwi-owned bar is another good seafront place for a drink.

Information

Agribank has a branch 1km north of town for changing dollars, and an ATM on the harbourfront. **Vu Binh Jewellers** by the market cashes travellers cheques at 3% commission and does credit-card cash advances at 5%.

There are several internet cafes on Cat Ba's seafront. The **main post office** (Đ 1-4) is here too.

Getting There & Away

Cat Ba Island is 45km east of Haiphong and 30km south of Halong City. Various boat and bus combinations make the journey, starting in either Hanoi or Haiphong. It's possible to travel by boat from Halong City to Cat Ba Island, but it is a journey often blighted by scams (p82).

To/From Hanoi

The easiest way to/from Hanoi is via the city's Luong Yen bus station. Here **Hoang Long** (☎031-268 8008) offers a combined bus-boat-bus ticket (210,000d, 4½ hours) straight through to Cat Ba Town. Buses depart Hanoi at 10am, 2pm and 4pm, and return from Cat Ba Town at 7.15am, 9.15am, 1.15pm and 3.15pm.

To/From Haiphong

Fast boats depart Haiphong's Ben Binh harbour to Cat Ba's Cai Vieng harbour at 7am and 10am. From there a bus takes passengers into Cat Ba Town; this boat-bus combo takes around 90 minutes (130,000d). The other way, Haiphong-bound buses depart from the waterfront in Cat Ba Town at 2pm and 4pm.

A second option to/from Haiphong is a bus from Ben Binh harbour in Haiphong to Dinh Vu port. A fast boat then skips across to Cai Vieng on Cat Ba, and another bus then continues into Cat Ba Town. The journey takes around two hours (150,000d). Buses depart Ben Binh at 6.40am, 8.15am, 9.45am, 1.40pm, 3.10pm and 4.35pm. Return buses from Cat Ba depart at 6.10am, 7.50am, 9.10am, 1.10pm, 2.50pm and 4.10pm.

Getting Around

Rented bicycles are a good way to explore the island (see Activities).

Motorbike rentals (with or without driver) are available from most of the hotels from US$5 per day. If you're heading to the beaches or national park, pay the parking fee to ensure your bike isn't stolen.

Haiphong

☎031 / POP 1.67 MILLION

Vietnam's third-largest city, Haiphong has a graceful air and the verdant tree-lined boulevards conceal some classic colonial-era structures. It's an important seaport, industrial centre and transport hub, but very few visitors linger long.

Cafe culture is very strong here and many places have street tables perfect for people-watching.

Sights & Activities

Though there isn't a whole lot to see in Haiphong, its slow-paced appeal is enhanced by the French colonial architecture lining the streets.

FREE **Haiphong Museum** MUSEUM
(66 P Dien Bien Phu; ⊙8am-12.30pm & 2-4pm Mon-Fri, 7.30-9.30pm Wed & Sun) In a splendid colonial building, the Haiphong Museum concentrates on the city's history. Some displays have English translations, and the museum's garden harbours a ragtag collection of war detritus.

Du Hang Pagoda PAGODA
(Chua Du Hang; 121 P Chua Hang; ⊙7-11am & 1.30-5.50pm) Founded three centuries ago and rebuilt several times since, this pagoda has architectural elements that look Khmer. Equally enjoyable is wandering along the narrow alley, P Chua Hang, to get here; it buzzes with Haiphong street life.

Queen of the Rosary Cathedral CATHEDRAL
(P Hoang Van Thu) Haiphong's elegant cathedral was built in the 19th century and comprehensively restored in 2010. The building's grey towers are a local landmark, and the inner courtyard is spacious and relaxing.

Sleeping

Monaco Hotel HOTEL $$
(☎374 6468; monacohotel@vnn.vn; 103 P Dien Bien Phu; r US$25, ste US$35-50; ❄📶) This modern and central hotel has a real polish about it, including the smart lobby. Spacious, spotless rooms come with two double beds and breakfast is included.

Harbour View Hotel HOTEL $$$
(☎382 7827; www.harbourviewvietnam.com; 4 P Tran Phu; s/d incl breakfast US$118/132; ⊘❄@📶🏊) Built in neo-colonial style, this stately hotel has comfortable rooms and excellent facilities, including a gym, spa and restaurant.

Hoa Viet Hotel HOTEL $
(☎384 2409; www.hoaviethotel.vn; 50 P Dien Bien Phu; r incl breakfast 250,000-400,000d; ❄📶) Excellent value in central Haiphong, with simply furnished rooms arranged around a courtyard in a restored colonial building.

Eating & Drinking

Haiphong is noted for fresh seafood. Visit P Quang Trung for places with point-and-cook tanks as well as *bia hoi* joints. For more stylish cafes and restaurants take a wander along P Minh Khai.

Big Man Restaurant VIETNAMESE $$
(7 P Tran Hung Dao; mains from 80,000d; ⊙11am-11pm) Upmarket, sociable restaurant-cum-beer garden with a great outdoor terrace and an extensive menu – try the seafood or Vietnamese salads. Doubles as a microbrewery.

BKK THAI $$
(☎382 1018; 22 P Minh Khai; mains 70,000-150,000d) The card proclaims 'trendy Thai restaurant' and it's absolutely true. All the Thai tastes are here, plus a serious amount of seafood.

Com Vietnam VIETNAMESE $
(4A P Hoang Van Thu; mains 30,000-80,000d) Diminutive, unpretentious restaurant that hits the spot for its affordable local seafood and Vietnamese specialities.

Phone Box BAR
(79 P Dien Bien Phu; ⊙noon-11.30pm) This tiny bar is run by a musician and is a great place for a relaxed drink, with live music (usually acoustic) on Monday and Friday. Expect good tunes at other times from the owner's extensive vinyl collection.

Information

There are internet cafes on P Dien Bien Phu; many cafes have free wi-fi. ATMs dot the city centre.

Haiphong International Hospital (☎395 5888;124 Nguyen Duc Canh) Newly built and modern with some English-speaking doctors.

Getting There & Away

Vietnam Airlines (☎381 0890; www.vietnamair.com.vn; 30 P Hoang Van Thu) has flights to HCMC and Danang. **Jetstar Pacific** (www.jetstar.com) has flights to HCMC.

For boat connections to Cat Ba, see p85.

Buses for Hanoi (70,000d, two hours) leave from the **Tam Bac bus station** (P Tam Bac), 4km from the waterfront. Buses heading to points south including Ninh Binh (90,000d, 3½ hours, every 30 minutes) leave from **Niem Nghia bus station** (Đ Tran Nguyen Han). **Lac Long bus station** (P Cu Chinh Lan) has buses to Halong City (50,000d, 1½ hours).

GETTING TO CHINA: THE NORTHEAST BORDERS

There are two borders in northeast Vietnam where foreigners can cross into China.

Huu Nghi Quan to Youyi Guan

This is the most popular border crossing. The border post itself is at Huu Nghi Quan (Friendship Gate), 3km north of Dong Dang. Catch a bus from Hanoi to Dong Dang (130,000d, 3¼ hours) and a *xe om* (20,000d) to the border. On the Chinese side, it's a 20-minute drive from the border to Pingxiang by bus or a shared taxi. Pingxiang is connected by train and bus to Nanning.

Three trains also link Hanoi and Lang Son daily, but these are very slow, taking over five hours – the bus is a better option. Trains from Hanoi to Nanning and Běijīng pass through this border, but it's not possible to jump aboard these services in Lang Son or Dong Dang. For the full picture about these cross-border trains see p176.

Mong Cai to Dongxing

Mong Cai is on the Chinese border in the extreme northeastern corner of Vietnam, but is rarely used by foreigners.

There are four trains a day to Hanoi (48,000-60,000d, 2-3 hours) from **Haiphong train station** (Đ Luong Khanh Thien & Đ Pham Ngu Lao).

Ba Be National Park

☎0281 / ELEV 145M

Boasting mountains high, rivers deep, and waterfalls, lakes and caves, **Ba Be National Park** (☎389 4014; www.babenationalpark.org; admission per person 20,000d) is an incredibly scenic spot. The region is surrounded by steep peaks (up to 1554m) while the park contains tropical rainforest with more than 400 plant species. Wildlife in the forest includes bears, monkeys, bats and lots of butterflies. Surrounding the park are Tay minority villages, whose people live in stilt homes.

Ba Be (Three Bays) is actually three linked lakes, with a total length of 8km and a width of about 400m. The Nang River is navigable for 23km between a point 4km above Cho Ra and the **Dau Dang Waterfall** (Thac Dau Dang), which is a series of spectacular cascades between sheer walls of rock. **Puong Cave** (Hang Puong) is about 30m high and 300m long, and passes completely through a mountain. A navigable river flows through the cave.

Park staff can organise tours. Costs depend on the number of people, starting at about US$30 per day for solo travellers, less for a group. The most popular excursion is a **boat trip** (boat hire around 550,000d). The boats can carry about 12 people and you should allow at least seven hours to take in most sights. The boat dock is about 2km from park headquarters.

Other options include dugout-canoe tours or combination cycling, boating and walking possibilities. Longer treks can also be arranged.

An optional guide, worth considering, costs US$12 per day.

Sleeping & Eating

There are two accommodation options not far from the park headquarters.

Accommodation in the newer **Park Guesthouse** (☎389 4026) is fine, if a little overpriced, and includes semi-detached bungalows (350,000d), each with two double beds, and chalets (220,000d) that are small and fairly basic. The complex has two **restaurants** (meals from 50,000d), though you should place your order a few hours before you want to eat.

There are about a dozen **stilt houses** (per person 70,000d) at Pac Ngoi village on the lakeshore which take guests. The park office can help organise this. Meals (40,000d to 60,000d), which can include fish from the lake, are available.

Only cash is accepted and the nearest ATM and internet access are in Cho Ra.

Getting There & Around

Ba Be National Park is 240km from Hanoi and 18km from Cho Ra.

Most visitors get here by chartered vehicle from Hanoi (six hours) or on a tour.

By public transport, the most direct route is on a daily bus at noon from the Gia Lam bus station in

Hanoi to Cho Ra (150,000d, six hours). You overnight in Cho Ra before continuing on to Ba Be by boat (or motorbike taxi) the following morning.

Mai Chau

0218 / POP 47,500

In an idyllic valley, the Mai Chau area is a world away from the hustle and bustle of Hanoi. The White Thai villages are surrounded by lush paddy fields, there's minimal traffic, and the rural soundtrack is defined by gurgling irrigation streams and birdsong.

Most villagers no longer wear traditional dress, but the women are masterful weavers producing plenty of traditional-style clothing and souvenirs. Locals do not employ strong-arm sales tactics here: polite bargaining is the norm.

Dozens of local families have signed up to a highly successful homestay initiative, and for visitors the chance to sleep in a traditional stilt house is a real appeal. That said, some find the experience too sanitised, as the villages are firmly on the tour-group agenda. If you're looking for hardcore exploration this is not the place, but for biking, hiking and relaxation, Mai Chau fits the bill nicely.

Sights & Activities

There's fine **walking** past rice fields and **trekking** to minority villages. A typical trek further afield covers 7km to 8km; a local guide costs about US$10. Most homestays also rent bikes to explore the village at your own pace.

A popular 18km trek is from **Lac village** (Ban Lac) in Mai Chau to Hmong **Xa Linh village**, near a mountain pass (elevation 1000m) on Hwy 6. This trek takes in a 600m climb in altitude and usually involves an overnight stay.

Many travel agencies in Hanoi run inexpensive trips to Mai Chau.

Sleeping & Eating

Most visitors stay in **Thai stilt houses** (per person incl breakfast around 150,000d) in the villages of Lac or Pom Coong, just a five-minute stroll apart. It's perfectly feasible to just pitch up and find a bed – there's always space. All the stilt-house homestays have electricity, running water, hot showers, mosquito nets and roll-up mattresses.

Most people eat where they stay. Establish the price of meals first as some places charge up to 150,000d for dinner. Warning: cheesy song-and-dance routines follow dinner at some places.

DON'T MISS

EXPLORING THE FAR NORTH

Motorcycling in Vietnam's wild northern territory is unforgettable. If you're not confident riding a motorbike yourself, it's possible to hire someone to drive you. 4WD trips are also recommended, though the mobility of travelling on two wheels is unrivalled.

One of the most popular routes is the 'Northwest Loop', which follows Hwy 6 through the heart of the Tonkinese Alps. There are many variations, but the standard route involves starting in **Lao Cai**, heading to **Sapa** (p91), the queen of the mountains, then west via a spectacular road to the historic battlefield of **Dien Bien Phu**. Next is a stop in **Son La**, before dropping into the **White Thai villages** around Mai Chau and hitting the highway (to hell) back to Hanoi.

Some companies also specialise in taking bikers right off the trail into the far north of **Ha Giang** or the beautiful northeast province of **Cao Bang** and the nearby lakes of **Ba Be National Park**.

It's certainly possible to organise a motorcycling trip on your own. Northwest Loop roads are almost completely paved, though things can deteriorate in rainy season. Signposts are rare so bring a good map. The busy, long route north to Lao Cai is not a great ride so let the train take the strain and load your bike into a goods carriage while you sleep in a berth. Then in Lao Cai, pick it up, fill up, and take off.

Minsks used to be the bike of choice, but many now favour more reliable Japanese bikes. Daily hire rates for a quality bike range from US$20 to US$40 and are best organised in Hanoi. Check out p176 for recommended motorbike tour operators, most of which offer quality rental bikes too.

GETTING TO LAOS: NAM XOI TO NA MAEW

This is the most remote border in a mountainous area 175km northwest of Thanh Hoa city and 70km east of Sam Neua (Laos). If at all possible take a direct bus. There's a daily 8am bus from Thanh Hoa's western bus station (Ben Xe Mien Tay) to Sam Neua (275,000d) inside Laos, but expect overcharging. It's best not to get stuck on the Laos side of the border as transport is extremely irregular and there's no accommodation. Na Maew has several basic, serviceable guesthouses.

For information on crossing this border in the other direction, see p320.

Mai Chau Nature Place HOMESTAY $
(www.maichaunatureplace.com; dm/d US$5/20) A step up from other Mai Chau homestays, this friendly operation in Lac village offers comfortable private rooms decked out with bamboo furniture and local textiles. Visitors are also welcome to join the cooks in the kitchen.

Mai Chau Lodge HOTEL $$$
(386 8959; www.maichaulodge.com; r US$90-160, meals US$10-16;) 'Live the culture but stay in comfort' it says in the brochure. This means contemporary rooms with wooden floors and designer lighting, most with rice-paddy views. Various activities, including cookery classes, guided walks and kayaking, are offered.

Getting There & Around

Direct buses to Mai Chau leave Hanoi's My Dinh bus station regularly from 6am to 2pm (80,000d, 3¾ hours). Alternatively, catch a regular Son La or Dien Bien Phu bus to Tong Dau junction (80,000d, 3½ hours). From the junction it's another 5km to Mai Chau; *xe om* charge 20,000d.

Lao Cai

020 / POP 46,700

One of the gateways to the north, Lao Cai lies at the end of the train line, 3km from the Chinese border. The border crossing slammed shut during the 1979 war between China and Vietnam and remained closed until 1993. Lao Cai is now a major hub for travellers journeying between Hanoi, Sapa and Kūnmíng.

There are ATMs next to the train station, plus internet cafes close by.

With Sapa just up the mountain, there's no need to stay the night, but you'll find plenty of good hotels around the station. **Terminus Hotel & Restaurant** (383 5470; 342 P Nguyen Hue; r 200,000-300,000d, meals 20,000-45,000d;) is one option, with clean, tidy rooms and filling meals available.

Getting There & Around

Nine daily buses (240,000d, nine hours) ply the Hanoi–Lao Cai route, but virtually everyone prefers the train. Minibuses for Sapa (40,000d, one hour) wait by the train station while services to Bac Ha (50,000d, 2½ hours) at 6am, 7am, 10am, noon and 3pm leave from a terminal next to the Red River Bridge.

Rail tickets to Hanoi (8½ to 11 hours) start at 110,000d for a hard seat (bad choice) to 450,000d for an air-con soft sleeper, and rise by about 10% at weekends. There are three night trains and two day trains in either direction.

Several companies operate special private carriages with comfortable sleepers, including the affordable **ET Pumpkin** (www.et-pumpkin.com) and the more expensive **Victoria Express** (www.victoriahotels-asia.com).

Bac Ha

020 / POP 7400

An unhurried and friendly town, Bac Ha makes a relaxed base for exploring the northern highlands and hill-tribe villages. The atmosphere is very different from Sapa, and you can walk the streets freely without being accosted by hawkers. The climate here is also noticeably warmer than in Sapa.

Bac Ha has a certain charm, though its stock of traditional old adobe houses is dwindling and being replaced by concrete structures. Wood-smoke fills the morning air and chickens and pigs poke around the back lanes. For six days a week Bac Ha slumbers, but its lanes fill up to choking point each Sunday when tourists and Flower Hmong flood in for the weekly market.

Sights

Bac Ha's **Sunday market** is a riot of colour and commerce, and while the influx of day-trippers from Sapa is changing things, it's

GETTING TO CHINA: LAO CAI TO HÉKǑU

The Lao Cai–Hékǒu crossing (⏰7am-10pm) connects northern Vietnam with Yúnnán in China.

The border is about 3km from Lao Cai train station; *xe om* charge 20,000d. Travellers have reported Chinese officials confiscating Lonely Planet *China* guides at this border, so you may want to try masking the cover.

Trains no longer run from Hékǒu to Kūnmíng, but there are several 'sleeper' buses (Y150). One bus leaves at 7pm and arrives in Kūnmíng around 7am, but there are earlier departures. You'll need to have a pre-arranged visa for China.

still a worthwhile and relatively accessible place to visit.

The *ruou* corn hooch produced by the Flower Hmong is so potent it can ignite; there's an entire area devoted to it at the Sunday market.

While you're here check out the outlandish **Vua Meo** ('Cat King' House; admission free; ⏰8am-5.30pm), a palace constructed in a kind of bizarre 'oriental baroque' architectural style.

Beyond town lie several interesting markets:

Can Cau market One of Vietnam's most exotic, this Saturday market is 20km north of Bac Hã, just 9km south of the Chinese border.

Coc Ly market Takes place on Tuesday, about 35km from Bac Ha. There's a pretty good road, or you can go by road and river; ask at hotels in Bac Ha.

Lung Phin market Between Can Cau market and Bac Ha, about 12km from the town. It's less busy than Bac Ha's market, and operates on Sunday.

Activities

There's great hiking to hill-tribe villages around Bac Ha. The Flower Hmong village of **Ban Pho** is one of the nearest to town, from where you can walk to the Nung settlement of **Na Kheo** then head back to Bac Ha. Other nearby villages include **Trieu Cai**, an 8km return walk, and **Na Ang**, a 6km return walk; it's best to set up a trip with a local guide.

Tour guides in Bac Ha can arrange visits to rural schools as part of a motorbike or trekking day trip. There's also a **waterfall** near Thai Giang Pho village, about 12km east of Bac Ha, which has a pool big enough for swimming.

Take a peek at the website www.bachatourist.com for more inspiration. It's operated by English-speaking **Mr Nghe** (☎091 200 5952; hoangvutours@hotmail.com), Bac Ha's one-man tourism dynamo. All hotels recommended below offer excursions too.

Sleeping & Eating

Room rates tend to increase on weekends, when tourists arrive for a piece of the Sunday market action. Weekday rates are quoted here.

Hoang Vu Hotel HOTEL $
(☎388 0264; r from US$8) Number one for budget travellers in town. It's nothing fancy, but the large spacious rooms are good value, with TV and fan. Mr Nghe is based here.

Ngan Nga Gia Huy HOTEL $$
(☎388 0231; www.nganngabacha.com; 133 Ngoc Uyen; r US$25-35; ❄📶) A friendly place above a popular restaurant that does a roaring trade in tasty steamboats. Its new rooms are spotless and quiet and some are almost ridiculously roomy.

Congfu Hotel HOTEL $$
(☎388 0254; www.congfuhotel.com; 152 Ngoc Uyen; r US$30, meals from 40,000d; ❄@📶) Boasts attractive rooms demonstrating a notable absence of chintz. All have good-quality bed linen, and some enjoy floor-to-ceiling windows overlooking Bac Ha market. There's a good restaurant here too.

Hoang Yen VIETNAMESE $
(mains 40,000-80,000d) Bar-restaurant with a well-priced menu of good breakfast options, tasty rice and noodle dishes, and robust pumpkin soup. Cheap beer and Dalat wine are both available.

Information

There's no ATM in Bac Ha but the **Agribank** will cash dollars and the **Sao Mai Hotel** will change other currencies.

You'll find a **tourist information office** (⏲7.30-11.30am & 1.30-5pm) at the Vua Meo and internet access next to the Hoang Vu Hotel, also home base for the irrepressible Mr Nghe.

Getting There & Away

DESTINATION	TRAVEL TIME (HR)	COST (D)	FREQUENCY
Hanoi	11	400,000	8pm
Lao Cai	2½	60,000	6am, 8am, noon, 1pm, 2pm

Car & Motorbike

Tours to Bac Ha from Sapa cost from US$15 per person; on the way back you can bail out in Lao Cai and catch the train back to Hanoi.

A motorbike/taxi to Lao Cai costs US$20/60, or to Sapa US$25/75.

Sapa

☎020 / POP 36,200 / ELEV 1650M

Perched on a steep slope, Sapa overlooks a plunging valley of cascading rice terraces, with mountains towering above the town on all sides. Founded as a French hill station in 1922, Sapa is the premier tourist destination in northern Vietnam. Views of this epic scenery are often subdued in thick mist rolling across the peaks, but even if it's cloudy Sapa is a fascinating destination, especially when local hill-tribe people fill the town with colour.

Don't forget your winter woollies – Sapa is known for its cold, foggy winters (down to 0°C). The dry season for Sapa is approximately January to the end of June – afternoon rain showers in the mountains are frequent.

The town's colonial villas fell into disrepair during successive wars with the French, Americans and Chinese, but following the advent of tourism, Sapa has experienced a renaissance. The downside is a hotel building boom, including numerous soaring concrete constructions.

Inherent in this prosperity is cultural change for the hill-tribe people. The Hmong are canny (though very persistent) traders and will urge you to buy handicrafts and trinkets. Many have had little formal education, yet all the youngsters have a good command of English, French and a handful of other languages.

Sights & Activities

Surrounding Sapa are the Hoang Lien Mountains, including **Fansipan**, which at 3143m is Vietnam's highest peak. The trek from Sapa to the summit and back can take several days. Some of the better-known sights around Sapa include the epic **Tram Ton Pass**; the pretty **Thac Bac** (Silver Falls); and **Cau May** (Cloud Bridge), which spans the Muong Hoa River.

Be sure to check out the fascinating **market**, which is a riot of colour and commerce.

Treks can be arranged at many guesthouses and travel agencies (see Information); the following are Hmong owned:

Sapa O'Chau TOURS
(☎091 535 1479; www.sapaochau.com) Helmed by the livewire Shu Tan, who used to peddle handicrafts to tourists. Profits from this tour agency provide training to Hmong children in a learning centre. Excellent day walks, longer homestay treks, and Fansipan hikes are offered. Volunteers are welcome.

Sapa Sisters TOURS
(☎097 621 6140; www.sapasisters.webs.com) Operated by four enterprising teenage Hmong girls. Email them to arrange day treks, two- to three-day village homestays, or ascents of Fansipan. Excellent English is spoken, and some French, Spanish and Japanese.

Sleeping

Hmong Mountain Retreat LODGE $$
(☎650 5228; www.hmongmountainretreat.com; 6km west of Sapa on Lao Cai Rd; full board per person US$55; ⏲Mar-Dec) Accommodation in bungalows is simple, but the real attraction here is sleeping above a verdant cascade of rice paddies. Meals are served in an 80-year-old tribal house. Up to 95% of ingredients are sourced within a 2km radius, and the stunning grounds are dotted with the owner's artworks.

Boutique Sapa Hotel BOUTIQUE HOTEL $$
(☎387 2727; www.boutiquesapahotel.com.vn; 41 Đ Phan Si; s/d from US$40/55;) Features classy furniture, flat-screen TVs, and superb vistas from the terrace cafe. Pay a little more for valley views. The downstairs dining room does great pizza (US$5 to US$8).

Luong Thuy Family Guesthouse GUESTHOUSE $
(☎387 2310; www.familysapa.com; 028 Đ Muong Hoa; s/d US$10-15;) Simple and spotless

Sapa

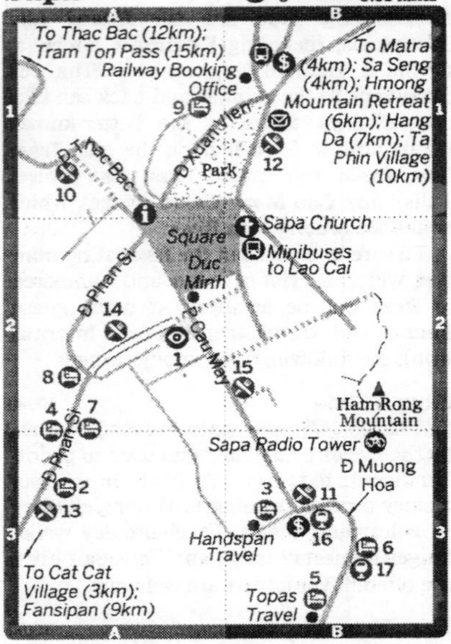

Sapa

Sights

1 Sapa Market A2

Sleeping

2 Boutique Sapa Hotel A3
3 Casablanca Sapa Hotel B3
4 Cat Cat View Hotel A2
5 Luong Thuy Family Guesthouse B3
6 Pinocchio Hotel B3
7 Sapa Hostel A2
8 Sapa Rooms A2
9 Victoria Sapa Resort & Spa A1

Eating

10 Baguette & Chocolat A1
11 Delta Restaurant B3
12 Gecko B1
13 Nature View A3
14 Restaurants A2
15 Viet Emotion B2

Drinking

16 Mountain Pub & Bar B3
17 Red Dragon Pub B3

rooms in a friendly, family-owned guesthouse a short stroll from the hubbub of downtown Sapa. The misty valley view from the front balconies is quite superb.

Cat Cat View Hotel HOTEL $$
(387 1946; www.catcathotel.com; 1 Đ Phan Si; s/d US$10-90;) This excellent spot has 40 rooms over nine floors, many with great views. There's something for every budget, with homely, comfortable pine-trimmed accommodation. Cheaper rooms are the best value.

Sapa Rooms BOUTIQUE HOTEL $$
(650 5228; www.saparooms.com; Đ Phan Si; r incl breakfast US$57-72;) Billing itself as a boutique hotel, this place has hip rooms and a quirky-looking lobby cafe.

Pinocchio Hotel HOTEL $
(387 1876; www.pinocchiohotel.com; 15 Đ Muong Hoa; r US$15-20;) The friendly staff that run this excellent guesthouse really make the place. The rooms have simple but attractive decor, some with impressive views.

Victoria Sapa Resort & Spa RESORT HOTEL $$$
(387 1522; www.victoriahotels-asia.com; r from US$175;) Immaculate hilltop hotel, right down to the manicured lawns. Rooms aren't large, but they are classy. There's a heated swimming pool, fitness centre and the best spa in town.

Topas Eco Lodge ECOLODGE $$$
(387 2404; www.topas-eco-lodge.com; s/d US$131/143) Perched on a slope overlooking a plunging valley about 18km from Sapa, this ecolodge has gorgeous bungalows, most with magnificent views. Solar power, wastewater management and minority staff are part of the set-up here.

Baguette & Chocolat GUESTHOUSE $
(387 1766; www.hoasuaschool.com; Đ Thac Bac; r US$22;) Operated by Hoa Sua (a group helping disadvantaged youth), this four-room place has style and an excellent French cafe. Rates include a great breakfast.

Sapa Hostel GUESTHOUSE $
(387 3073; www. sapahostel.com; 9 & 33 Đ Phan Si; dm/s/d/tr US$5/12/15/18;) Spacious rooms in two locations with a laidback travellers' vibe.

Casablanca Sapa Hotel HOTEL $
(387 2667; www.sapacasablanca.com; Đ Dong Loi; s/d/tr US$17/20/25;) Good value rooms in a central location. Mr Kien, the attentive owner, speaks fluent English.

Eating

For eating options on a tight budget, cheap Vietnamese restaurants are huddled below the market, and night market stalls south of the church serve *bun cha* (barbecued pork).

Vietnamese-style hotpot is a very popular local dish; try the area just south of the bus station.

Sapa Rooms CAFÉ $
(www.saparooms.com; Đ Phan Si; snacks 50,000d, meals around 90,000d) Sapa Rooms is a flamboyantly decorated cafe that's great for a snack (think corn fritters or a BLT baguette), meal (try the 'caramelised' pork fillet or fish and chips), or just a pot of tea and a piece of cake. Cookery classes are offered, too.

Baguette & Chocolat CAFE $$
(Đ Thac Bac; cakes from 20,000d, snacks & meals 70,000-160,000d; ☑) Fine breakfasts, *tartines*, baguettes, cakes, salads, pasta and Asian and Vietnamese dishes are served in elegant premises. On a misty and chilly Sapa day, a warming mug of ginger tea is impossible to beat.

Nature View VIETNAMESE $
(Đ Phan Si; meals from 60,000d) Newish place offering a good mix of Vietnamese and Western flavours and a great set lunch. Some of Sapa's best pizzas and terrific fruit smoothies effortlessly tick the box marked 'comfort food'.

Viet Emotion MEDITERRANEAN $$
(www.vietemotion.com; 27 P Cau May; meals 70,000-150,000d) Stylish bistro that features a cosy fireplace, and, if the weather really sets in, there are books, magazines and board games. Try the trekking omelette, homemade soup, or something from the tapas menu.

Delta Restaurant ITALIAN $$
(P Cau May; mains US$7-12) Renowned for its pizzas, the most authentic in town, plus pretty decent pasta too.

Gecko FRENCH $$
(Đ Ham Rong; mains US$7-10) French-owned place that resembles an *auberge* (inn), with a rustic feel and a Gallic menu.

Drinking

Mountain Bar & Pub BAR
(2 Đ Muong Hoa) Dangerously strong cocktails, cold beer, and ultra-competitive games of table football feature at this bar. If it's freezing outside, a shisha beside the open fire will soon perk up the chilliest of travellers.

Red Dragon Pub PUB
(23 Đ Muong Hoa) Genteel place that resembles a Welsh tea room. Good for a quiet drink, and serves filling pub grub.

Information

Internet access, including complimentary wi-fi, is available at hotels, restaurants and cafes around town.

BIDV (Đ Ngu Chi Son) Has an ATM, exchanges travellers cheques and cash.

Duc Minh (☑387 1881; www.ducminhtravel.vn; 10 P Cau May) Friendly English-speaking operator organising transport and treks.

Handspan Travel (☑387 2110; www.handspan. com; Chau Long Hotel, 24 Dong Loi) Offers trekking and mountain-biking tours to villages and markets.

Main post office (Đ Ham Rong)

Sapa Tourism (☑387 3239; www.sapa -tourism.com; 103 Đ Xuan Vien; ☉7.30-11.30am & 1.30-5pm) Helpful English-speaking staff offering transport, trekking and weather information. The website is a mine of useful information.

Topas Travel (☑387 1331; www.topastravel.vn; 24 Đ Muong Hoa) High-quality trekking, biking and village encounters. Many options include a stay in the Topas Eco Lodge.

Getting There & Away

The gateway to Sapa is Lao Cai, 38km away to the west. Minibuses (40,000d, 1½ hours) make the trip regularly until midafternoon.

FLOWER POWER

Flower Hmong women wear several layers of dazzling clothing. These include an elaborate collar-cum-shawl that's pinned at the neck and an apron-style garment, both made of tightly woven strips of multicoloured fabric, often with a frilly edge. Highly ornate cuffs and ankle fabrics are also part of their costume as is a checked headscarf (often electric pink or lime green).

GETTING TO LAOS: TAY TRANG TO SOP HUN

This crossing is 34km from Dien Bien Phu (DBP). Buses (135,000d, seven to eight hours) leave DBP daily at 5.30am for Muang Khua in Laos. Book your ticket the day prior to travelling if you can. The journey can take longer depending on the roads and border formalities (expect to have to pay a small fee to cross here).

It's possible to hire a *xe om* from DBP to the border for around 200,000d, but you'll probably then have to walk 5km to the nearest Lao village for transport to Muang May. Muang May has basic guesthouses and onward travel options to Muang Khua but make sure you have cash dollars or Lao kip.

For information on crossing this border in the other direction, see p312.

A minibus to Bac Ha for the Sunday market is around US$15 per person; departure from Sapa is at 6am and from Bac Ha at 1pm. It's cheaper to go by public minibus, changing in Lao Cai. A daily bus leaves at 7.30am for Dien Bien Phu (170,000d, eight hours) and there are regular buses for Lai Chau (70,000d; 6am to 4pm).

Travel agencies and cafes in Hanoi offer weekend trips to Sapa, but DIY is straightforward and offers maximum flexibility.

There is an official **Railway Booking Office** (P Cau May; ⌚7.30-11am & 1.30-4pm), which charges a small commission. For more information on trains to Hanoi, see Lao Cai (p89).

Getting Around

Downtown Sapa can be walked in 20 minutes. For excursions further out, you can hire a motorbike for US$5 to $US10 per day, or take one with a driver from US$12.

Dien Bien Phu

☎0230 / POP 72,700

On 7 May 1954 French colonial forces were defeated by the Viet Minh in a decisive battle at Dien Bien Phu (DBP), and the days of their Indochine empire were numbered.

Previously just a minor settlement, DBP only became a provincial capital in 2004. Boulevards and civic buildings have been constructed and the airport now has daily flights from Hanoi. With the nearby border with Laos now open to foreigners, many travellers are passing through the city.

The scenery to or from DBP is stunning, with approach roads scything through thick forests and steep terrain. The city itself lies more prosaically on a broad, dry plain.

Sights

Dien Bien Phu Museum MUSEUM
(Đ 7-5; admission 5000d; ⌚7-11am & 1.30-5pm) Commemorating the 1954 battle, this well-laid-out museum features an eclectic collection. Alongside weaponry and guns, there's a bicycle capable of carrying 330kg of ordnance, and plenty of photographs and documents, some with English translations.

Bunker Headquarters WAR MEMORIAL
(admission 3000d; ⌚7-11am & 1.30-5pm) Across the river, the command bunker of Colonel Christian de Castries has been recreated. You'll probably see Vietnamese tourists mounting the bunker and waving the national flag.

A1 Hill WAR MEMORIAL
(admission 5000d; ⌚7-11am & 1.30-5pm) There are more tanks and a monument to Viet Minh casualties on this former French position. Elaborate trenches at the heart of the French defences have been recreated here.

Sleeping

Muong Thanh Hotel HOTEL $$
(☎381 0043; www.muongthanhthanhnien.com; Đ Muong Thanh; r US$45-75; ❄📶🏊) An excellent recent renovation has resulted in modern rooms with satellite TV, elegant furniture, and marble bathrooms. Added attractions include a wood-lined pub and pool.

Viet Hoang Hotel GUESTHOUSE $
(☎373 5046; 67 Đ Tran Dang Ninh; s/d 100,000/120,000d; ❄@📶) Right opposite the bus station, this friendly guesthouse has small, neat rooms. Owner Mr Duc and his family are very hospitable.

Binh Long Hotel GUESTHOUSE $
(☎382 4345; 429 Đ Muong Thanh; d/tw US$10; ❄📶) Another small, friendly, family-run place, but on a busy junction. Offers neat, tidy twin rooms and transport info.

Eating & Drinking

Dining options are limited. Muong Thanh Hotel has a good restaurant and **Lien Tuoi Restaurant** (Đ Hoang Van Thai; mains 60,000-90,000d) is famous for its filling Vietnamese and Chinese food.

For a cheap bite, check out the *pho* stalls and simple restaurants opposite the bus station. *Bia hoi* gardens on Đ Hoang Van are ideal for a local brew or two.

Information

Internet cafes are on Đ Hoang Van Thai.

Agribank (Đ 7-5) ATM and changes US dollars.

Main post office (Đ 7-5)

Getting There & Away

Air

Vietnam Airlines (☎382 4948; www.vietnamairlines.com; Nguyen Huu Tho) operates two flights daily between DBP and Hanoi. The office is near the airport, about 1.5km from the town centre, along the road to Muong Lay.

Bus

DBP's bus station is on Hwy 12, at the corner of Đ Tran Dang Ninh.

DESTINATION	TRAVEL TIME (HR)	COST (D)	FREQUENCY
Hanoi	11½	from 300,000	frequent until noon
Lai Chau	6	130,000	from 5am to 2pm
Muong Lay	6	57,000	from 5am to 2pm
Son La	6	97,000	frequent until noon

Car & Motorbike

The 480km drive from Hanoi to DBP on Hwys 6 and 279 takes around 11 hours.

CENTRAL VIETNAM

With ancient history, compelling culture, incredible food and terrific beaches, central Vietnam is one of the must-see regions of the country. This is a region that packs in Huế (the country's former imperial capital), the DMZ battle sites, and Hoi An, an exquisite architectural gem that time forgot. Throw in the ancient religious capital of My Son, extraordinary cave systems of Phong Nha and nature reserves so dense that scientists discover new creatures in them every few years, and the region's appeal is overwhelming.

Danang and Huế airports are the perfect gateways for visitors who want to avoid long overland journeys.

Huế

☎054 / POP 286,400

Huế is the intellectual, cultural and spiritual heart of Vietnam. Palaces and pagodas, tombs and temples, culture and cuisine, history and heartbreak – there's no shortage of poetic pairings to describe Huế. A World Heritage Site, the capital of the Nguyen emperors is where tourists come to see the decaying, opulent royal tombs and the grand, crumbling Citadel. Most of these architectural attractions lie along the northern side of the Song Huong (Perfume River). For rest and recreation, plus a little refreshment, the south bank is where it's at.

The city hosts a biennial arts festival, the **Festival of Huế** (www.huefestival.com), on even-numbered years, featuring local and international artists and performers.

Sights & Activities

Citadel HISTORIC SITE

One of Vietnam's treasures, the former imperial city on the northern bank of the Perfume River is immensely impressive. Though it was heavily bombed by the Americans its scope and beauty still endure, as more and more buildings are being reconstructed.

Emperor Gia Long began building the moated Citadel in 1804. The emperor's official functions were carried out in the **Imperial Enclosure** (Dai Noi, or Hoang Thanh; admission 55,000d; ⊙6.30am-5.30pm Apr-Sep, 7am-5pm Oct-Mar), a 'citadel within the Citadel'. Inside the 6m-high, 2.5km-long wall is a surreal world of deserted gardens, palaces and ceremonial halls.

Be sure to check out the **Thai Hoa Palace**, a spacious hall with an ornate timber roof supported by 80 carved and lacquered columns, which was used for the emperor's official receptions.

Within the Imperial Enclosure is the holy-of-the-holy **Forbidden Purple City** (Tu Cam Thanh), which was reserved for the private life of the emperor. The only servants allowed inside were eunuchs, who posed no threat to the royal concubines. Nowadays, all are welcome. Drop by the beautiful (though crumbling) little **Emperor's Reading Room** (Thai Binh Lau) to admire its Gaudi-esque roof mosaics.

West of here is the beautifully restored **To Mieu Temple Complex** that encompasses the three-tiered Hien Lam Pavilion and its nine dynastic urns *(dinh)*, each dedicated to one Nguyen sovereign. On the other side of the courtyard, To Mieu Temple houses shrines to each of the emperors, each topped with a photo.

You could spend hours exploring the rest of the Citadel, stumbling across other ruined palaces, exploring overgrown gardens, fortifications and lakes.

Royal Tombs MONUMENTS

(⊙6.30am-5.30pm Apr-Sep, 7am-5pm Oct-Mar) Set like royal crowns on the banks of the Perfume River, the Royal Tombs are spread 2km to 16km south of Hué.

The **Tomb of Tu Duc** (admission 55,000d) is a majestic site, laced with frangipani and pine trees and set alongside the Luu Khiem Lake. The temples and buildings here are beautifully designed. Near the entrance, the Xung Khiem pavilion is where the concubines used to lounge overlooking the lake. Just around the lakeshore is the Honour Courtyard; you pass between a guard of elephants, horses and diminutive mandarins to reach it.

Perhaps the most majestic is the **Tomb of Minh Mang** (admission 55,000d), who ruled from 1820 to 1840. This tomb is renowned for its architecture, which blends harmoniously into the natural setting, surrounded by a forest and lakes. Sung An Temple, which is dedicated to Minh Mang and his empress, is reached via three terraces and the rebuilt Hien Duc Gate.

The elaborate, hilltop **Tomb of Khai Dinh** (admission 55,000d), who ruled from 1916 to 1925, stands out from the other tombs for its unique structure. The buildings and statues reflect a distinct mix of Vietnamese and European features.

FREE **Pagodas** PAGODAS

Thien Mu Pagoda (Đ Le Duan) is one of the most iconic structures in Vietnam. Its 21m-high octagonal tower, Thap Phuoc Duyen, was constructed under the reign of Emperor Thieu Tri in 1844. Each of the seven storeys is dedicated to a manushi-buddha (a Buddha that appeared in human form). Thien Mu is on the banks of the Perfume River, 4km southwest of the Citadel.

Dieu De National Pagoda (Quoc Tu Dieu De; 102 Đ Bach Dang) was built under Emperor Thieu Tri (1841–47). It is one of Hué's three 'national pagodas', once under the direct patronage of the emperor. It's famous for its four low towers and was a stronghold of Buddhist and student opposition to the South Vietnamese government and the war in Vietnam.

Bao Quoc Pagoda (Ham Long Hill) was founded in 1670 by Giac Phong, a Chinese Buddhist monk. It has a striking triple-gated entrance reached via a wide staircase. On the right is a centre for training monks. It's 250m south of the train station.

Tours

Song Huong Cruises BOAT TOURS

Many sights around Hué, including Thien Mu Pagoda and several Royal Tombs, can be reached by boat via the Perfume River. Rates for chartering a boat are around US$10 for an hour's sightseeing on the river; a half-day charter to one or more sites will cost from US$20.

GETTING TO LAOS: CAU TREO TO NAM PHAO

This crossing (open 7am to 6pm) is 96km west of Vinh and about 30km east of Lak Sao in Laos.

This border has a dodgy reputation with travellers, who report chronic overcharging and hassle on local buses (such as bus drivers ejecting foreigners in the middle of nowhere unless they cough up extra bucks).

If you do decide to travel step-by-step, local buses leave Vinh to Tay Son (formerly Trung Tam) regularly from 6am (70,000d, three hours). From Tay Son, it's another 25km to the border. Morning buses to Lak Sao may be available, but if not motorbikes ask for up to 150,000d for the ride. On the Laos side, a jumbo or *sŏrngtăaou* (pick-up truck) between the border and Lak Sao costs about 45,000 kip (bargain hard).

For information on crossing this border in the other direction, see p331.

GETTING TO LAOS: NAM CAN TO NONG HAET

This often mist-shrouded border is 119km east of Phonsavan and 250km northwest of Vinh. Buses between Vinh and Phonsavan cross here, leaving on Wednesday, Friday, Saturday and Sunday (235,000d).

For a DIY journey, head to Muong Xen where you'll need a motorbike to take you uphill 25km to the border (around US$7). Transport on the Laos side to Nong Haet is erratic, but once you get there, you can pick up a bus to Phonsavan.

For information on crossing this border in the other direction, see p316.

Ask directly at the moorings on the south side of the river; it's cheaper than going through an agency. Work out an itinerary then fix a price.

Most hotels and travellers' cafes offer shared day tours from as little as US$3 per person. Note that many tombs are some distance from the river, and given the time constraints you'll probably want to hire motorbikes to get from the moorings to some tombs.

Once the various fees have been factored in, many travellers wish they had cycled or arranged a motorbike tour instead. Motorbike guides from local travellers' cafes can do customised day tours of the Royal Tombs, the Citadel, the Demilitarised Zone (DMZ) and the surrounding countryside.

Cafe on Thu Wheels TOURS
(☎383 2241; minhthuhue@yahoo.com; 3/34 Đ Nguyen Tri Phuong) Inexpensive cycling, motorbiking (from US$10pp) and car tours (DMZ is US$40pp) around Huế and beyond.

Mandarin Café TOURS
(☎382 1281; www.mrcumandarin.com; 24 Đ Tran Cao Van) Boss Mr Cu organises transport and tours.

Stop & Go Café TOURS
(☎382 7051; www.stopandgo-hue.com; 3 Đ Hung Vuong) Personalised motorbike and car tours, including the DMZ.

Sleeping

TOP CHOICE **Pilgrimage Village** LODGE $$$
(☎388 5461; www.pilgrimagevillage.com; 130 Minh Mang; r/bungalow from US$121/172;) A wonderful hideaway, this chic, imposing lodge feels more like a Zen retreat than a hotel. It's been designed around a verdant valley and lotus ponds. Rooms are all supremely comfortable, the bungalows boast private plunge pools and there's a fine restaurant, spa and yoga space. It's about 3km south of the centre.

Mercure HOTEL $$
(☎393 6688; www.mercure.com; 38 Đ Le Loi; r from US$58;) Soaring above the Perfume River, this elegant new hotel offers exceptional value for money, a prime location and great service standards. Stunning rooms, complete with polished wood furnishings, hip bathrooms, balconies and all mod cons, are beautifully finished.

Google Hotel HOTEL $
(☎383 7468; www.googlehotel-hue.com; 26 Đ Tran Cao Van; d/tr US$15/18;) Offering flashpacker chic at backpacker cheap, the light, spacious rooms here have luxurious beds, huge flat-screen TVs and modish en-suite bathrooms. The large bar-restaurant is a good place to socialise.

Orchid Hotel HOTEL $$
(☎383 1177; www.orchidhotel.com.vn; 30A Đ Chu Van An; r US$35-60;) This hotel receives rave reviews for its impeccable service and sterling accommodation. Every room has a DVD player, and some even have a jacuzzi bath with city views.

La Residence Hotel & Spa HOTEL $$$
(☎383 7475; www.la-residence-hue.com; 5 Đ Le Loi; r from US$151;) This chic escape is housed in the former French governor's residence, offering river views, lush gardens and beautiful rooms.

Huenino GUESTHOUSE $
(☎625 2171; www.hueninohotel.com; 14 Đ Nguyen Cong Tru; r incl breakfast US$14-22;) The family owners here are super-attentive and rooms are very attractively presented with artwork, minibar, cable TV and good-quality beds.

Huế

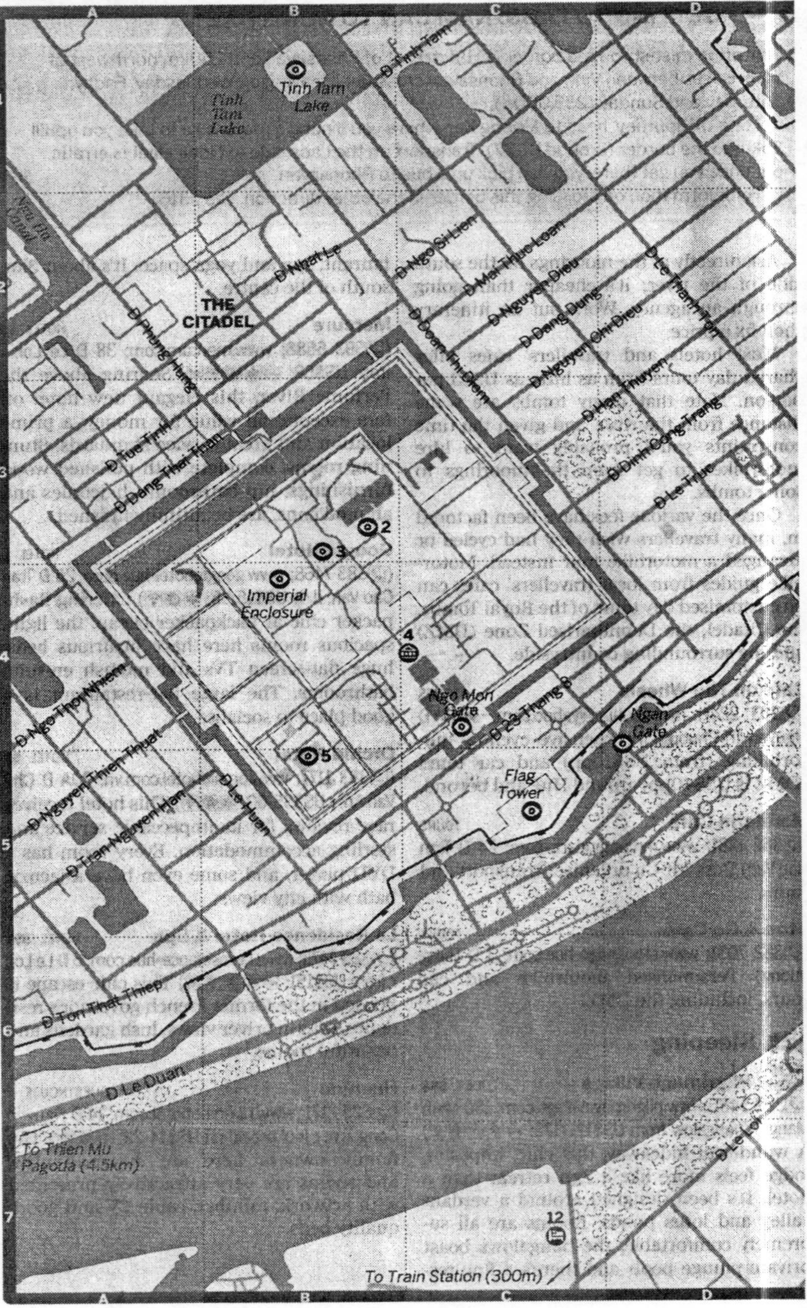
A
B
C
D
1
2
3
4
5
6
7
Tinh Tam Lake
Tinh Tam Lake
Đ Tinh Tam
THE CITADEL
Đ Ngat Le
Đ Phung Hung
Đ Tue Tinh
Đ Dang Thai Than
Đ Ngo Si Lien
Đ Mai Thuc Loan
Đ Nguyen Dieu
Đ Doan Thi Diem
Đ Dang Dung
Đ Nguyen Chi Dieu
Đ Le Thanh Ton
Đ Han Thuyen
Đ Dinh Cong Trang
Đ Le Truc
2
3
Imperial Enclosure
4
Ngo Mon Gate
Đ 23 Thang 8
Ngan Gate
Flag Tower
5
Đ Ngo Thoi Nhiem
Đ Nguyen Thien Thuat
Đ Nguyen Nhan
Đ Le Huan
Đ Tran Nguyen Han
Đ Ton That Thiep
Đ Le Duan
To Thien Mu Pagoda (4.5km)
12
Đ Le Loi
To Train Station (300m)

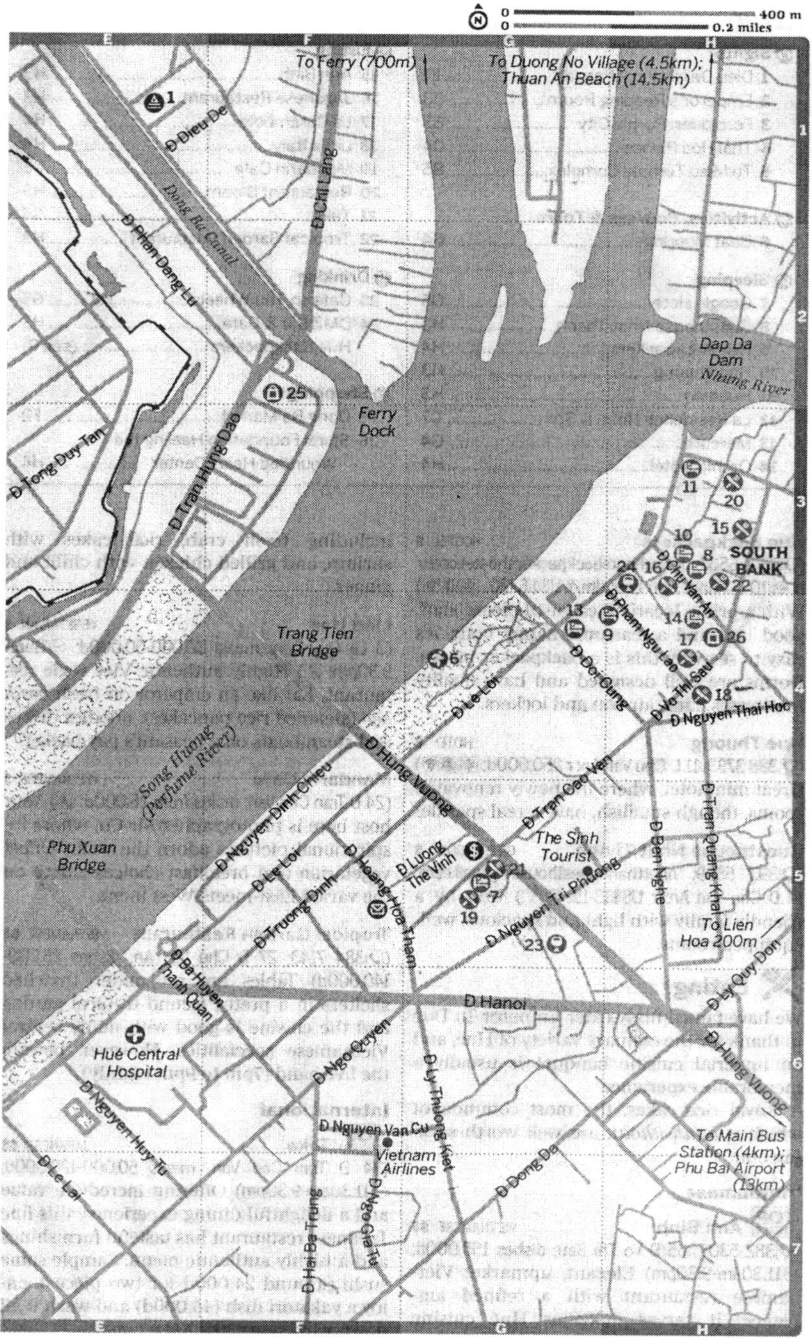
0 400 m
0 0.2 miles
To Ferry (700m)
To Duong No Village (4.5km); Thuan An Beach (14.5km)
Đ Dieu De
Dong Ba Canal
Đ Chi Lang
Đ Phan Dang Lu
Dap Da Dam
Nhung River
Ferry Dock
Đ Tong Duy Tan
Đ Tran Hung Dao
SOUTH BANK
Đ Chu Van An
Đ Pham Ngu Lao
Trang Tien Bridge
Đ Doi Cung
Đ Vo Thi Sau
Đ Le Loi
Đ Nguyen Thai Hoc
Song Huong (Perfume River)
Đ Hung Vuong
Đ Nguyen Dinh Chieu
Đ Tran Cao Van
The Sinh Tourist
Phu Xuan Bridge
Đ Le Loi
Đ Luong The Vinh
Đ Hoang Hoa Tham
Đ Truong Dinh
Đ Nguyen Tri Phuong
Đ Ben Nghe
Đ Tran Quang Khai
To Lien Hoa 200m
Đ Ba Huyen Thanh Quan
Đ Hanoi
Đ Ly Quy Don
Hue Central Hospital
Đ Ngo Quyen
Đ Ly Thuong Kiet
Đ Hung Vuong
Đ Nguyen Huy Tu
Đ Nguyen Van Cu
Vietnam Airlines
To Main Bus Station (4km); Phu Bai Airport (13km)
Đ Le Lai
Đ Dong Da
Đ Ngo Gia Tu
Đ Hai Ba Trung
1
25
6
11
20
15
10
8
24
16
22
13
9
14
17
26
18
21
7
19
23

Hué

Sights
1 Dieu De National Pagoda ... E1
2 Emperor's Reading Room ... B3
3 Forbidden Purple City ... B3
4 Thai Hoa Palace ... C4
5 To Mieu Temple Complex ... B5

Activities, Courses & Tours
6 Boat Moorings ... G4

Sleeping
7 Google Hotel ... G5
8 Guesthouse Nhat Thanh ... H3
9 Hue Backpackers ... H4
10 Hue Thuong ... H3
11 Huenino ... H3
12 La Residence Hotel & Spa ... C7
13 Mercure ... G4
14 Orchid Hotel ... H4

Eating
15 Anh Binh ... H3
16 Japanese Restaurant ... H3
17 La Carambole ... H4
18 Little Italy ... H4
19 Mandarin Cafe ... G5
20 Restaurant Bloom ... H3
21 Take ... G5
22 Tropical Garden Restaurant ... H3

Drinking
23 Café on Thu Wheels ... G5
24 DMZ Bar & Cafe ... H3
Hue Backpackers ... (see 9)

Shopping
25 Dong Ba Market ... F2
26 Spiral Foundation Healing the Wounded Heart Center ... H4

Hue Backpackers HOSTEL $
(382 6567; www.hanoibackpackershostel.com/hue; 10 Đ Pham Ngu Lao; dm/r US$6/20;) With a prime location, eager-to-please staff, good info and a fearsome happy hour, it's easy to see why this is a backpacker mecca. Dorms are well designed and have quality mattresses, fans, air-con and lockers.

Hue Thuong HOTEL $
(388 3793; 11 Đ Chu Van An; r 250,000d;) Great minihotel, where the newly renovated rooms, though smallish, have a real sparkle.

Guesthouse Nhat Thanh GUESTHOUSE $
(393 5589; nhatthanhguesthouse@gmail.com; 17 Đ Chu Van An; r US$13-15;) Run by a friendly family with light and spacious, well-equipped rooms.

Eating

We have famed fussy-eater Emperor Tu Duc to thank for the culinary variety of Hué, and an imperial cuisine banquet is usually a memorable experience.

Royal rice cakes, the most common of which is *banh khoai*, are well worth seeking out.

Vietnamese

TOP CHOICE **Anh Binh** VIETNAMESE $$
(382 5305; 65 Đ Vo Thi Sau; dishes 155,000d; 11.30am-9.30pm) Elegant, upmarket Vietnamese restaurant with a refined ambience. It serves delicious Hué cuisine including fresh crab, rice cakes with shrimp, and grilled chicken with chilli and ginger.

Lien Hoa VEGETARIAN $
(3 Le Quy Don; meals 30,000-50,000d; 11am-9.30pm;) Highly authentic Viet vegie restaurant. Eat like an emperor on fresh *banh beo* (steamed rice pancakes), noodles dishes and steamboats on a peasant's pay packet.

Mandarin Café VIETNAMESE $
(24 Đ Tran Cao Van; mains from 26,000d;) Your host here is photographer Mr Cu, whose inspirational pictures adorn the walls. Offers vegetarian and breakfast choices galore on the varied East-meets-West menu.

Tropical Garden Restaurant VIETNAMESE $$
(384 7143; 27 Đ Chu Van An; dishes 25,000-140,000d) Tables are set under thatched shelters in a pretty, fecund tropical garden and the cuisine is good with many central Vietnamese specialities. However, beware the live band (7pm to 9pm nightly).

International

TOP CHOICE **Take** JAPANESE $$
(34 Đ Tran Cao Van; meals 50,000-120,000d; 11.30am-9.30pm) Offering incredible value and a delightful dining experience, this fine Japanese restaurant has tasteful furnishings and a highly authentic menu. Sample some sushi (around 24,000d for two pieces), enjoy a yakatori dish (45,000d) and wash it all down with sake (30,000d a cup).

PHONG NHA-KE BANG NATIONAL PARK

A Unesco World Heritage Site, the remarkable **Phong Nha-Ke Bang National Park** contains the oldest karst mountains in Asia and is riddled with hundreds of cave systems – many of extraordinary scale and length – including the largest cave in the world. This is nature on a very grand scale indeed.

Above the ground, most of this mountainous national park is near-pristine tropical evergreen jungle, over 90% of which is primary forest.

Sight and Activities

The most popular excursion is the boat trip into 55km-long **Phong Nha Cave** (adult/child 40,000/20,000d, boat 220,000d; ⊙7am-4pm) – though only the first kilometre or so is open to visitors. Boats leave Son Trach and cruise along the Son River past bathing buffalo until you reach the jaws of the cave. Then the engine is cut and you're transported to another world as you're paddled through cavern after cavern – quite a surreal experience. There's also the opportunity to hike up to nearby Tien Son Cave where there are Cham altars and inscriptions.

Only open to the public since 2011, remote **Paradise Cave** (adult/child 120,000/60,000d; ⊙7.30am-4.30pm) extends for 31km and is said to be the longest dry cave in the world. Once you've climbed the 500-step approach staircase its sheer scale becomes truly apparent as you enter a cathedral-like space replete with glimmering stalactites of white crystal that resemble glass pillars. The whole experience is a lot less commercial than the Phong Nha trip. Paradise Cave is located deep in the national park, 18km from Son Trach. Phong Nha Farmstay's national park tour (from 900,000d) includes Paradise Cave.

A beautiful riverside retreat, **Nuoc Mooc Eco-Trail** (adult/child 50,000/30,000d; ⊙7am-5pm) has riverside paths and is a gorgeous place for a swim. Bring a picnic; it's 12km southwest of Son Trach.

Established around a small hill, a semi-wild **primate reserve** has been set up as a breeding centre for critically endangered Ha Tien langurs. You can walk around the perimeter fence via a 1.8km trail. It's 3km from Son Trach.

At the time of research there was no public access to the world's largest cave, **Hang Son Doong**. The sheer scale of the principal cavern (5km long, 150m wide and over 200m high) was only confirmed in 2009. Oxalis (see Practicalities) offers a great two-day trek (three to four people, US$170 per person) to the mouth of Hang Son Doong.

Sleeping and Eating

There are a dozen or so **guesthouses** (r 200,000d) and cheap eateries in Son Trach village.

Phong Nha Farmstay (☎052-367 5135; www.phong-nha-cave.com; dm/r US$8/25-35; meals 30,000-90,000d; ❄@🛜🏊), an impressive place run by a welcoming Australian-Vietnamese couple, is where most travellers stay. Overlooking rice paddies, it has a great vibe, bar, local and Western food, and offers outstanding tours including kayaking, tubing, biking and hiking. It's in Cu Nam, 13km southeast of Son Trach; pick-ups can be arranged in Dong Hoi.

Practicalities

The coastal city of Dong Hoi, 166km north of Hué on Hwy 1 and on the north–south train line, is the gateway to Phong Nha.

Phong Nha-Ke Bang National Park abuts Son Trach village, which is 50km northwest of Dong Hoi. Local buses (45,000d) offer irregular connections between Dong Hoi and Son Trach. There's also a daily minibus between Phong Nha Farmstay and Danang (200,000d), stopping in Dong Ha and Hué (150,000d) en route.

Independent travellers wanting to explore the national park might find some officials less than helpful; try entering via the Tro Mung entrance.

Organised tours are an excellent way to explore Phong Nha – those run by Phong Nha Farmstay are highly recommended and cost 1,100,000d by motorbike or 900,000d by minibus. **Oxalis** (☎090 337 6776, www.oxalis.co.vn, Son Trach) is a professional locally owned adventure tourism outfit offering treks inside the National Park.

GETTING TO LAOS: LAO BAO TO DANSAVANH

The Lao Bao border (⊙7am to 6pm) is the most popular and least problematic border crossing. Buses to Savannakhet run from Hué via Dong Ha and Lao Bao. From Hué, there's a 7am air-con bus (280,000d, nine hours), on odd days only, that leaves from Sinh Cafe. This travels via Dong Ha, where it makes a stop at the Sepon Travel office around 8.30am and picks up more passengers (Dong Ha to Savannakhet costs 210,000d) before getting to Savannakhet at 4pm.

It's also easy to cross the border on your own; Dong Ha is the gateway. Buses, roughly every 15 minutes, leave the town to Lao Bao bus station (50,000d , two hours, 85km). From here *xe om* (motorbike taxi) charge about 12,000d to the border, or it's a 20-minute walk. Between the Vietnam and Laos border posts is a short walk of a few hundred metres.

For information on crossing this border in the other direction, see p338.

Restaurant Bloom CAFE $
(14 Đ Nguyen Cong Tru; snacks from 15,000d;) Ideal for a sandwich, baguette, croissant or homemade cake (baked on the premises), this likeable little cafe employs disadvantaged youths.

Stop & Go Café INTERNATIONAL $
(3 Đ Hung Vuong; meals 20,000-60,000d;) Casual little place with tasty Vietnamese and backpacker fare, including good rice cakes, pizza and pasta and filling Western breakfasts.

La Carambole FRENCH, VIETNAMESE $$
(☎381 0491; www.lacarambole.com; 19 Đ Pham Ngu Lao; mains 32,000-155,000d) Long-running bistro with Gallic and local cuisine, including imperial-style Hué specialities. Popular with French tour groups, so book ahead.

Little Italy ITALIAN $$
(www.littleitalyhue.com; 2A Đ Vo Thi Sau; mains 45,000-115,000d) Large trattoria with a decent line-up of Italian favourites: pasta, calzone, pizzas and seafood.

Japanese Restaurant JAPANESE $
(12 Đ Chu Van An; dishes US$1.50-9; ⊙6-9pm) Simple place for all your usual Japanese faves. Employs street children and supports a home for them.

Drinking

In the evening, travellers gather over Huda beers in the cafes along Đ Hung Vuong.

Hue Backpackers BAR
(10 Đ Pham Ngu Lao;) Party central for backpackers, this hostel bar packs 'em in with its 8pm to 9pm happy hour, infused vodkas and (unashamedly tacky) cocktail list.

Café on Thu Wheels BAR
(10/2 Đ Nguyen Tri Phuong;) Hole-in-the-wall with cheap grog, graffiti-splattered walls, a sociable vibe and good info from the feisty owner, Thu.

DMZ Bar & Cafe BAR
(44 Đ Le Loi) As popular as ever, this joint's always abuzz with rocking music, free pool and lively conversation. It serves food till midnight.

Shopping

Hué produces the finest conical hats in Vietnam and is renowned for rice paper and silk paintings. As ever, bargain hard.

Spiral Foundation Healing the Wounded Heart Center HANDICRAFTS
(www.hwhshop.com; 69 Đ Ba Trieu) Gorgeous eco-friendly handicrafts and souvenirs (including picture frames from recycled beer cans) made by disabled artisans. Profits aid heart surgery for children in need.

Dong Ba Market MARKET
(Đ Tran Hung Dao; ⊙6.30am-8pm) Anything and everything – clothing, food and coffee – can be bought here.

Information

There are lots of internet cafes on the tourist strips of Đ Hung Vuong and Đ Le Loi. See Tours for a list of good local tour operators.

Hué Central Hospital (Benh Vien Trung Uong Hue; ☎382 2325; 16 Đ Le Loi)

Main post office (Đ Hoang Hoa Tham)

The Sinh Tourist (☎382 3309; www.thesinhtourist.vn; 7 Đ Nguyen Tri Phuong) Open-tour buses, and buses to Laos.

Vietinbank (12 Đ Hung Vuong) An ATM plus exchange services.

Getting There & Away

Air

Vietnam Airlines (☎382 4709; 23 Đ Nguyen Van Cu; ⊙Mon-Sat) offers three daily flights to both Hanoi and HCMC. **Jetstar Pacific** (☎395 5955; Đ 176 Hung Vuong; ⊙Mon-Sat) also connects Hué with HCMC daily

Phu Bai airport is 14km south of town. Metered taxis meet all flights and cost about 175,000d to the centre, or use the minibus service for 40,000d. Vietnam Airlines also runs an airport shuttle, which can collect you from your hotel (tickets 55,000d).

Bus

The **main bus station** is 4km to the southeast of the centre on the continuation of Đ Hung Vuong. **An Hoa bus station** (Hwy 1A), northwest of the Citadel, serves northern destinations, including Dong Ha.

From smaller **Mien Bac bus station** there's also a privately operated minibus to Phong Nha Farmstay (p101) at 1pm (150,000d, 7½ hours).

Hué is also a regular stop on the open-tour bus routes. Mandarin and Stop & Go cafes can arrange bookings for the bus to Savannakhet, Laos.

Train

Hué train station (2 Đ Bui Thi Xuan) is at the southwestern end of Đ Le Loi.

Getting Around

Bicycles (US$1 to US$2), motorbikes (US$4 to US$10) and cars (from US$35 per day) can be hired through hotels all over town. **Mai Linh** (☎389 8989) has air-con taxis with meters. *Cyclos* and *xe om* will find you when you need them - and when you don't.

Around Hué

THUAN AN BEACH

Thuan An Beach (Bai Tam Thuan An), 15km northeast of Hué, is on a lovely lagoon near the mouth of the Perfume River.

DEMILITARISED ZONE (DMZ)

From 1954 until 1975, the Ben Hai River served as the dividing line between South Vietnam and North Vietnam. The DMZ, 90km north of Hué, consisted of the area 5km on either side of the line.

Many of the 'sights' around the DMZ are places where historical events happened, and may not be worthwhile unless you're into war history. To make sense of it all, and to avoid areas where there's still unexploded ordnance (UXO), take a guide. Group day tours from Hué cost from US$11 for a budget bus trip to up to US$100 for a specialised car tour with a Viet vet.

Significant sites include:

Vinh Moc Tunnels (admission 20,000d; ⊙7am-4.30pm) Highly impressive complex of tunnels from the remains of a coastal village that literally went underground in response to unremitting American bombing. Explore the 2km warren of tunnels, subterranean bedrooms, meeting rooms and even a maternity unit; 110km from Hué.

Truong Son National Cemetery (Nghia Trang Liet Si Truong Son) A memorial to the tens of thousands of North Vietnamese soldiers killed along the Ho Chi Minh Trail. Row after row of white tombstones stretch across the hillsides; about 105km from Hué.

TRAVELLING FROM HUÉ

DESTINATION	CAR/MOTORBIKE TRAVEL TIME	BUS TRAVEL TIME/COST/FREQUENCY	TRAIN TRAVEL TIME/COST/FREQUENCY	AIR TRAVEL TIME/COST/FREQUENCY
Danang	2½-4 hours	3 hours/US$3/every 20 minutes	2½-4 hours/US$3-6/8 daily	N/A
Dong Hoi	3½ hours	3½ hours/US$4-7/12 daily	3-5½ hours/US$5-10/8 daily	N/A
Hanoi	16 hours	13-16 hours/US$18-27/8 daily	12-16½ hours/US$20-41/5 daily	1 hour/3 daily/from US$30
HCMC	22 hours	19-24 hours/US$23-37/8 daily	19½-22 hours/US$27-54/4 daily	1¼ hours/4 daily/from US$32

GETTING TO LAOS: CHA LO TO NA PHAO

Bus services link Dong Hoi and Tha Khaek (260,000d, 11 hours) on Monday, Wednesday and Friday, returning from Tha Khaek the next morning. For information on crossing this border in the other direction, see p334.

Khe Sanh Combat Base (admission 20,000d; ⊙7am-5pm) The site of the most famous battle of the war in Vietnam, this former USA base was never overrun, but about 500 Americans and 10,000 North Vietnamese troops died here in 1968. There's a small museum. About 130km from Hué.

BACH MA NATIONAL PARK

A French-era hill station known for its cool weather, **Bach Ma National Park** (☎054-387 1330; www.bachma.vnn.vn; adult/child 20,000/10,000d) is 45km southeast of Hué. There's currently a lot of construction going on inside Bach Ma to upgrade the road to the summit; at the time of research only the lower reaches were open. Work is scheduled to finish sometime in 2013.

There's some decent trekking in the lower reaches through subtropical forest to villages on the fringes of the park. You can book village and birdwatching tours and English- or French-speaking guides (200,000d per day) at the visitor centre. Unexploded ordnance is still in the area, so stick to the trails.

There's a **guesthouse** (☎054-387-1330; bachmaeco@gmail.com; r with fan/air-con 180,000/270,000d) at the park entrance. When the upper sections reopen, you'll find more accommodation close to the summit.

Danang

☎0511 / POP 788,500

Danang, Vietnam's fifth-biggest city, is on the move. For decades it had a reputation as a slightly mundane provincial backwater, but big changes are brewing. The Han riverfront is resplendent with gleaming new modernist hotels and restaurants. Beachside, five-star hotel developments are emerging on the My Khe strip. And a revamped international airport should open in 2012.

The city itself still has few conventional sightseeing spots, except for an outstanding museum. So for most travellers, a day or two off the tourist trail enjoying the city's restaurants and nightlife is probably enough.

Sleeping

An excellent selection of new minihotels has opened along the riverside in central Danang, though good budget hotels aren't as easy to find.

CITY CENTRE

TOP CHOICE **New Moon Hotel** HOTEL $$
(☎382 8488; info@newmoonhotel.vn; 126 Đ Bach Dang; r 300,000-800,000d; ❄@☎) This new hotel offers unrivalled value for money, with a selection of beautifully finished rooms in different price categories, all with flat-screen TV and inviting en-suite marble bathrooms. Book a river-view room for breathtaking vistas.

Rainbow Hotel HOTEL $$
(☎382 2216; rainbowkhachsan@yahoo.com; 220 Đ Bach Dang; r 450,000-600,000d; ❄@☎) A spanking-new place with a prime riverfront location, the Rainbow is a hip hotel with a budget price tag. Rooms have contemporary decor and all mod cons.

Winn Hotel HOTEL $
(☎388 8571; ngockhanh_nk@yahoo.com; 36 Hung Vuong; r US$17-20; ❄@☎) Excellent little hotel with 15 modern rooms, painted white and pale pink, all with a good TV and in-room wi-fi. The cheaper options don't have windows.

CHINA BEACH

TOP CHOICE **Eena Hotel** HOTEL $
(☎222 5123; www.geocities.jp/eenahotel; Khu An Cu 3; s/d/tw incl breakfast US$14/19/24; ❄@☎) Offering astonishing value, this Japanese-owned minihotel has immaculately clean, light and spacious white rooms, some with sea or mountain views. There's fast wi-fi and friendly English-speaking staff. It's about 3km west of the centre, just off the beach.

Hoa's Place GUESTHOUSE $
(☎396 9216; 215/14 Đ Huyen Tran Cong Chua; My An Beach; hoasplace@hotmail.com; r US$9) Shabby but not chic, Hoa's is nevertheless a popular backpacker haunt thanks to the fantastic hospitality, food and beachside location. Check it's still open as big resorts

are planned nearby. It's on My An beach, 6km southwest of Danang.

Eating & Drinking

TOP CHOICE Waterfront INTERNATIONAL $$
(www.waterfrontdanang.com; Đ 150-152 Bach Dang; meals 90,000-300,000d; ⊙10am-11pm;) Hip new riverfront lounge-cum-restaurant that has really helped put Danang on the map. Upstairs is a superb restaurant with stunning river vistas. Gourmet sandwiches (90,000d), light snacks (like salt-and-pepper calamari) and select mains are the order of the day. Also operates as a bar, and serves some of the best cocktails in town.

Red Sky INTERNATIONAL $$
(Đ 248 Tran Phu; meals 80,000-200,000d; ⊙11.30am-10.30pm;) Casual bar-restaurant that scores highly for Western grub including good-value steaks, generous salads and Italian food; Vietnamese dishes are also reliable. Beer is very cheap (La Rue is just 15,000d); happy hour is 5pm to 8pm.

Com Nieu VIETNAMESE $
(☎386 7026; 25 Đ Yen Bai; dishes 18,000-140,000d) Very popular with locals, this contemporary restaurant has hearty meals and affable staff. Try the succulent seafood or the claypot rice signature dish.

Bread of Life INTERNATIONAL $$
(www.breadoflifedanang.com; Đ 4 Dong Da; meals 40,000-100,000d; ⊙Mon-Sat) American-style diner-cum-bakery where the pancakes, burgers, sandwiches, pizza and other comfort foods hit the spot. Run by deaf staff and benefits deaf people.

Vietnamese Home VIETNAMESE $$
(34 Đ Bach Dang; meals 50,000-250,000d) Huge, rustic-style restaurant with an open courtyard. The menu takes in lots of seafood (including steamboats), meat, noodles, soups and filling Western breakfasts.

Le Funk BAR
(166 Đ Bach Dang) Lively riverfront hole-in-the-wall run by a genial French DJ, so expect pumping house tunes.

Chillout Cafe BAR, RESTAURANT
(36 Đ Thai Phien) Hospitable Vietnamese-Western-owned place with relaxed atmosphere, filling food, quiz nights and great local information.

Tulip Brewery BREWERY
(174 Đ 2/9) Huge Czech-style microbrewery pub that draws locals in their hundreds. Offers lager-style and dark beer on tap plus a menu of Western and Vietnamese dishes. It's 2km south of the centre.

Information

There are internet cafes scattered all over Danang. Consult the website www.indanang.com for reviews and information.

Agribank (202 Đ Nguyen Chi Thanh) ATM and exchange service.

Dana Tours (☎382 5653; 76 Đ Hung Vuong; ⊙Mon-Sat) Offers car hire, boat trips, visa extensions and day trips.

Danang Family Medical Practice (☎358 2700; www.vietnammedicalpractice.com; 50-52 Đ Nguyen Van Linh) One of Vietnam's most trusted foreign-owned clinics.

Hospital C (Benh Vien C; ☎382 2480; 35 Đ Hai Phong) The most advanced hospital in Danang.

Main post office (☎383 7407; 64 Đ Bach Dang)

The Sinh Tourist (☎384 3258; www.thesinhtourist.vn; 154 Đ Bach Dang) Books open-tour buses.

Trong's Real Easy Riders (☎090 359 7971; trongn59@yahoo.com) A branch of the Easy Riders group, which operates out of Danang.

Vietcombank (140 Đ Le Loi) Exchange services and ATM.

DON'T MISS

MUSEUM OF CHAM SCULPTURE

Danang's jewel is its famed **Museum of Cham Sculpture** (1 Đ Trung Nu Vuong; admission 30,000d; ⊙7am-5pm). This classic, colonial-era building houses the finest collection of Cham sculpture to be found anywhere on earth. More than 300 pieces on display include altars, lingas, garudas, apsaras, Ganeshas and images of Shiva, Brahma and Vishnu – all dating from the 5th to 15th centuries. These intricately carved sandstone pieces come from Cham sites all over Vietnam.

Guides hang out at the museum's entrance.

Danang

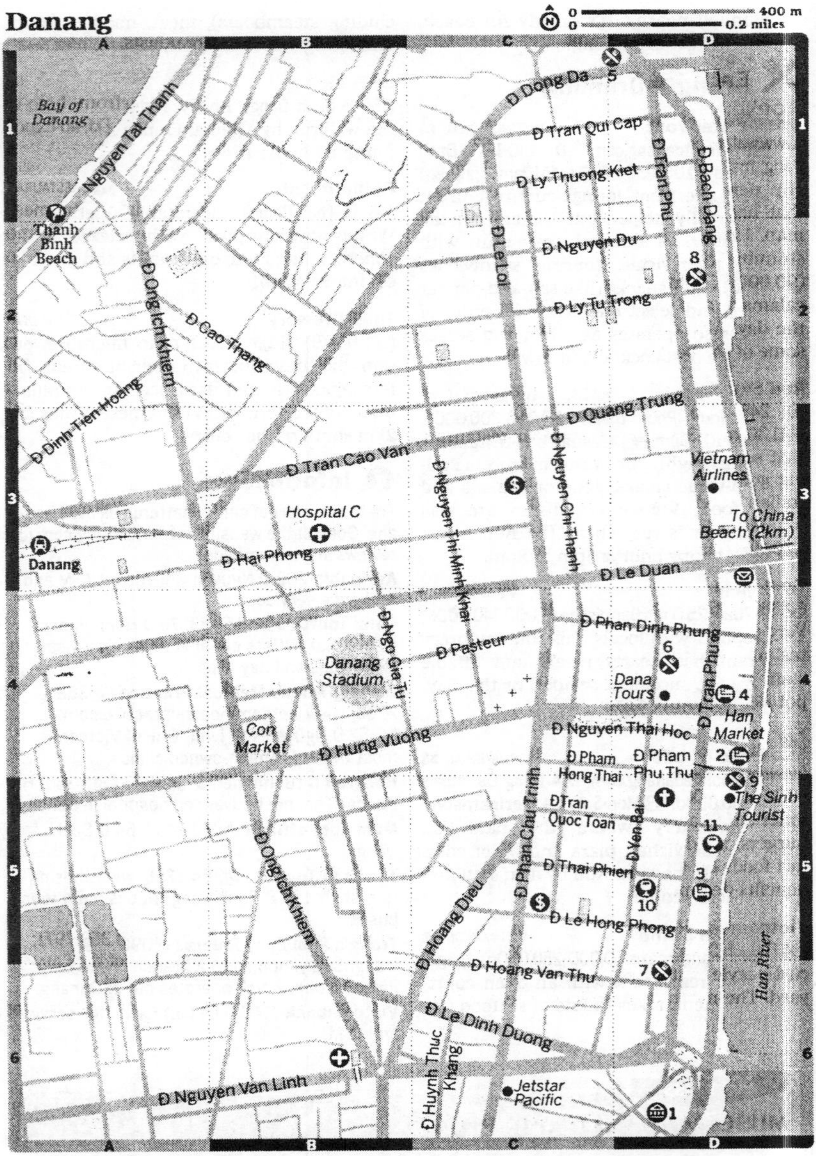

Getting There & Away

Air

Danang's only scheduled international connection at the time of research was **Silk Air** (☎356 2708; www.silkair.com; HAGL Plaza Hotel, Đ 1 Nguyen Van Linh) flights (four per week) to Singapore, but expect more routes when the new airport terminal opens in 2012 or 2013. For domestic connections, **Jetstar Pacific** (☎358 3538; www.jetstar.com; 307 Đ Phan Chu Trinh) has daily flights from Danang to HCMC and Hanoi while **Vietnam Airlines** (☎382 1130; www.vietnamairlines.com; 35 Đ Tran Phu) operates

Danang

Sights

1	Museum of Cham Sculpture	D6

Sleeping

2	New Moon Hotel	D4
3	Rainbow Hotel	D5
4	Winn Hotel	D4

Eating

5	Bread of Life	D1
6	Com Nieu	D4
7	Red Sky	D6
8	Vietnamese Home	D2
9	Waterfront	D5

Drinking

10	Chillout Cafe	D5
11	Le Funk	D5

direct flights to Hanoi, HCMC, Haiphong, Buon Ma Thuot and Nha Trang.

Bus

The **bus station** (Đ Dien Bien Phu) is 3km west of the city centre. Buses run to Hué (64,000d, three hours) and to points up and down the coast to HCMC and Hanoi. For Laos, there are three weekly services to Savannakhet at 8pm (130,000d, 14 hours), crossing the border at Lao Bao. There's also a daily service to Pakse at 6.30am (190,000d, 14 hours). Buses to the Lao Bao border alone are 95,000d (six hours); you may have to change buses at Dong Ha.

Yellow public buses to Hoi An (18,000d, one hour, hourly) travel along Đ Tran Phu in the heart of town.

Travel agencies can also arrange passage on open-tour minibuses running between Danang and both Hoi An and Hué.

Train

Danang **train station** is 1.5km from the city centre on Đ Hai Phong at Đ Hoang Hoa Tham. The city is served by all the main north–south trains. Try to take the railway journey up to Hué (from 60,000d, 2½ to four hours, eight daily), it's one of the most beautiful stretches in the country.

Taxis & Motorbikes

A taxi to Hoi An officially costs around 400,000d but most will drop to 300,000d, while *xe om* charge around 90,000d. Bargain hard if you want to stop at the Marble Mountains or China Beach en route. A ride to the airport is around 55,000d. Call **Mai Linh** (☎356 5656) for a cab.

Around Danang

About 10km south of Danang are the striking **Marble Mountains** (admission 15,000d; 7am-5pm), consisting of five craggy marble outcrops topped with jungle and pagodas. With natural caves sheltering small Hindu and Buddhist sanctuaries and stunning views of the ocean and surrounding countryside, they're worth exploring.

Thuy Son is the largest and most famous of the five mountains. Of the two paths heading up the mountain, the one closer to the beach (at the end of the village) makes for a better circuit and includes a mini-gorge.

China Beach (Bai Non Nuoc), once an R'n'R hang-out for US soldiers during the war, is actually a series of beaches stretching 30km between Hoi An and Danang. Nearest to central Danang, My Khe Beach is well touristed and accordingly has beachside restaurants and roving vendors. Opposite the Marble Mountains is Non Nuoc Beach, and in between the two are countless spots to spread your beach towel.

For surfers, China Beach's break gets a decent swell from mid-September to December. The best time for swimming is from May to July, when the sea is at its calmest. There's a mean undertow, so take care.

Buses and minibuses running between Danang and Hoi An can drop you off at the entrance to the Marble Mountains and China Beach, and it's easy to find onward transport.

Hoi An

☎0510 / POP 122,000

Graceful, historic Hoi An is Vietnam's most atmospheric and delightful town. Once a major port, it boasts the grand architecture and beguiling riverside setting that befits its heritage, but 21st-century curses of traffic and pollution are almost entirely absent.

Hoi An owes its easy-going ambience and remarkably harmonious character more to luck than planning. Had the Thu Bon River not silted up in the late 19th century, Hoi An would doubtless be very different today.

The city's allure and importance dwindled until an abrupt revival in fortunes in the 1990s, when a tourism boom transformed the local economy. Today Hoi An is once again a cosmopolitan melting pot, one of the nation's most wealthy towns and a culinary mecca.

In the Old Town, an incredible legacy of tottering Japanese merchant houses, Chinese temples and ancient tea warehouses has been preserved and converted into stylish restaurants, wine bars and a glut of tailor shops. And yet, down by the market and over in neighbouring An Hoi peninsula you'll find life has changed little.

Travel a few kilometres further – you'll find some superb bicycle, motorbike and boat trips – and some of central Vietnam's most enticing bucolic scenery and beaches are within easy reach.

Sights

HOI AN OLD TOWN

A Unesco World Heritage Site, Hoi An Old Town levies an admission fee to most of its historic buildings, which goes towards funding the preservation of the town's architecture. Buying the **ticket** (admission 90,000d) gives you a choice of five heritage sites to visit, including a traditional musical concert or stage play. Booths dotted around the Old Town sell tickets.

The following list of sites is by no means comprehensive.

FREE Japanese Covered Bridge BRIDGE
(Đ Tran Phu & Đ Nguyen Thi Minh Khai) Hoi An's iconic bridge was constructed in 1593 and has a roof and a temple built into its northern side. According to one story, the bridge's construction began in the year of the monkey and finished in the year of the dog; thus one entrance is guarded by monkeys, the other by dogs (neither pair will confirm or deny this story).

Assembly Halls

The Chinese who settled in Hoi An identified themselves according to their province of origin. Each community built its own assembly hall, known as *hoi quan* in Vietnamese, for social gatherings, meetings and celebrations.

Assembly Hall of the Fujian Chinese Congregation TEMPLE
(opposite 35 Đ Tran Phu; admission by Old Town ticket; ⌚7am-5.30pm) Founded for community meetings, this hall later became a temple to worship Thien Hau, a deity born in Fujian Province in China. Check out the elaborate mural, the unhealthy skin of the statuary, and the replica of a Chinese boat.

FREE Chinese All-Community Assembly Hall HISTORIC BUILDING
(64 Tran Phu; ⌚8am-5pm) The hall has been used by Chinese congregations since 1773. The well-restored main temple is a total assault on the senses with great smoking incense spirals, demonic-looking deities and dragons, and lashings of red lacquer – it's dedicated to Thien Hau.

Assembly Hall of the Cantonese Chinese Congregation HISTORIC BUILDING
(176 Đ Tran Phu; admission by Old Town ticket; ⌚8am-5pm) Founded in 1786, this assembly hall has a tall, airy entrance hall that opens onto a splendidly over-the-top mosaic statue of a dragon and a carp. The main altar is dedicated to Quan Cong. The garden behind has an even more incredible dragon statue.

Temples & Pagodas

Quan Cong Temple TEMPLE
(Chua Ong; 24 Đ Tran Phu; admission by Old Town ticket) Dedicated to Quan Cong, this temple has some wonderful papier mâché and gilt statues, as well as carp-shaped rain spouts on the roof surrounding the courtyard. When someone makes an offering to the portly-looking Quan Cong, the caretaker solemnly strikes a bronze bowl. Shoes should be removed before mounting the platform in front of the deity.

FREE Chuc Thanh Pagoda PAGODA
(Khu Vuc 7, Tan An; ⌚8am-6pm) Founded in 1454, this pagoda is the oldest in Hoi An. Among the antique ritual objects still in use are several bells, a stone gong that is two centuries old, and a carp-shaped wooden gong said to be even older.

To get to Chuc Thanh Pagoda, head north all the way to the end of Đ Nguyen Truong To and turn left. Follow the small road for 500m.

Historic Houses & Museums

Tan Ky House HISTORIC HOME
(101 Đ Nguyen Thai Hoc; admission by Old Town ticket; ⌚8am-noon & 2-4.30pm) This is a lovingly preserved house from the 19th century, which once belonged to a Vietnamese merchant. Japanese and Chinese influences are evident throughout the architecture. The house is a private home, and the owner – whose family has lived here for seven generations – speaks French and English.

Museum of Trading Ceramics MUSEUM
(80 Đ Tran Phu; admission by Old Town ticket; ⏲7am-5.30pm) Occupies a simply restored wooden house and contains artefacts from all over Asia, with oddities from as far afield as Egypt. The displays are mediocre but the small exhibition on the restoration of Hoi An's old houses provides a useful crash-course in Old Town architecture.

Tran Family Chapel HISTORIC HOME
(21 Đ Le Loi; admission by Old Town ticket; ⏲7.30am-noon & 2-5.30pm) This chapel was built for worshipping family ancestors in 1802 by Tran Tu, who ascended to the rank of mandarin and served as an ambassador to China. His picture is to the right of the chapel. Its architecture reflects the influence of Chinese (the 'turtle' style roof), Japanese (triple beam) and vernacular (look out for the bow and arrow detailing) styles.

Phung Hung Old House MUSEUM
(4 Đ Nguyen Thi Minh Khai; ⏲8am-7pm) Has a wide, welcoming entrance hall decorated with exquisite lanterns, wall hangings and embroidery.

Arts & Crafts Villages

All those neat fake antiques sold in Hoi An's shops are manufactured in nearby villages. Cross the An Hoi footbridge to reach the **An Hoi peninsula,** noted for its boat factory and mat-weaving factories. South of the peninsula is **Cam Kim island,** where people are engaged in woodcarving and boat-building. Cross the Cam Nam bridge to **Cam Nam** village, a lovely spot also noted for arts and crafts.

Activities

Vietnamese Cooking Courses

TOP CHOICE **Morning Glory Cooking School**
(☎224 1555; www.hoianhospitality.com/morning_c.htm; 106 Đ Nguyen Thai Hoc) Classes are directed by the acclaimed Vy, owner of several restaurants in town, or Lu, her protégé. You'll learn how to tackle local recipes including *banh khoai* and white rose, plus regional Vietnamese dishes in a professionally organised environment.

Red Bridge Cooking School (☎393 3222; www.visithoian.com; half-/full-day per person US$23/39) Runs a course that starts with a trip to the market, and is followed by a cruise down the river to its relaxing retreat about 4km from Hoi An.

Informal classes are offered by **Gioan** (☎386 3899; 98B Đ Bach Dang; US$16), **Phone Café** (US$12), and the **Lighthouse Café & Restaurant** (US$21).

Diving & Snorkelling

Two reputable dive schools offer trips to the Cham Islands. Both charge the same rates: two fun dives are US$75. The diving is not world-class, but can be intriguing, with good macro life – and the daytrip to the Cham islands is superb. Snorkellers pay US$30 to US$40. Trips only leave between February and September; conditions are best in June, July and August.

Blue Coral Diving (☎627 9297; www.divehoian.com; 77 Đ Nguyen Thai Hoc)

Cham Island Diving Center (☎391 0782; www.chamislanddiving.com; 88 Đ Nguyen Thai Hoc)

Spa & Massage

TOP CHOICE **Palmarosa** SPA
(☎393 3999; www.palmarosaspa.vn; 90 Đ Ba Trieu; 1hr massage from US$19) Palmarosa is a highly professional spa that offers a full range of massages, treatments, facials, and hand and foot care.

Duyen Que SPA
(☎350 1584; Đ 512 Cua Dai; 1hr massage from US$15) Staff here are well-trained and know their stuff. Try the foot beauty ritual (US$15). It's 2km west of town on the beach road.

Life Spa SPA
(☎391 4555 ext 525; www.liferesorts.com; Life Heritage Resort, 1 Đ Pham Hong Thai; 1hr massage from US$58) This luxury hotel's spa has the full gamut of treatments and massages.

Festivals & Events

Hoi An Legendary Night FESTIVAL
Takes place on the 14th day (full moon) of every lunar month from 5.30pm to 10pm. These festive evenings feature traditional food, song and dance, and games along the lantern-lit streets in the town centre.

Sleeping

Hoi An is awash with excellent accommodation options.

TOP CHOICE **Ha An Hotel** HISTORIC HOTEL $$
(☎386 3126; www.haanhotel.com; 6-8 Đ Phan Boi Chau; r US$58-115; ❄@🛜) This colonial-style hotel has rooms set around a gorgeous central garden. Rooms have nice individual

Hoi An

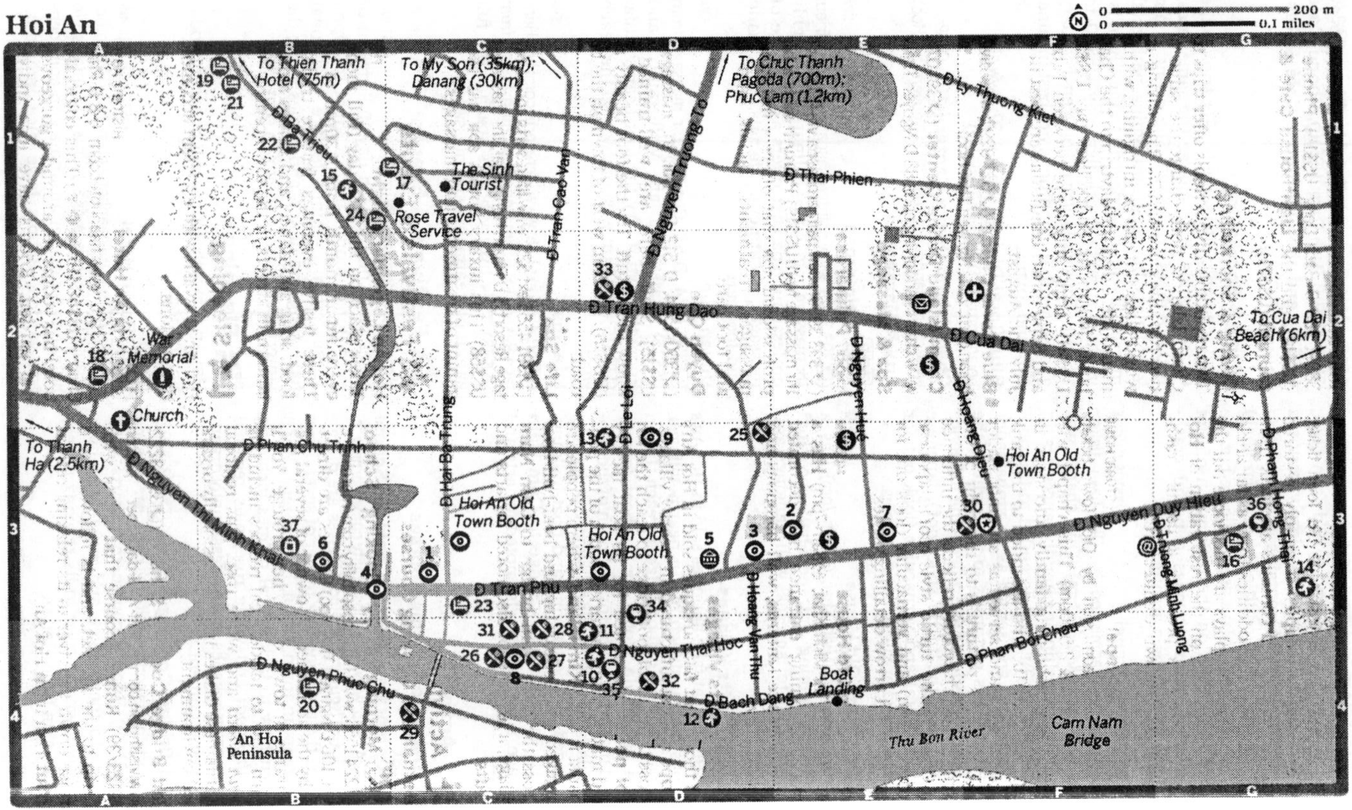
0 200 m
0 0.1 miles
To Thien Thanh Hotel (75m)
To My Son (35km); Danang (30km)
To Chuc Thanh Pagoda (700m); Phuc Lam (1.2km)
Đ Ly Thuong Kiet
Đ Ba Trieu
The Sinh Tourist
Rose Travel Service
Đ Tran Cao Van
Đ Nguyen Truong To
Đ Thai Phien
Đ Tran Hung Dao
Đ Cua Dai
To Cua Dai Beach (6km)
War Memorial
Church
To Thanh Ha (2.5km)
Đ Phan Chu Trinh
Đ Le Loi
Đ Nguyen Hue
Đ Hoang Dieu
Hoi An Old Town Booth
Đ Phan Hong Thai
Đ Hai Ba Trung
Hoi An Old Town Booth
Hoi An Old Town Booth
Đ Nguyen Duy Hieu
Đ Nguyen Thi Minh Khai
Đ Tran Phu
Đ Truong Minh Luong
Đ Hoang Van Thu
Đ Nguyen Thai Hoc
Đ Phan Boi Chau
Đ Nguyen Phuc Chu
Boat Landing
Đ Bach Dang
An Hoi Peninsula
Thu Bon River
Cam Nam Bridge

Hoi An

Sights

1	Assembly Hall of the Cantonese Chinese Congregation	C3
2	Assembly Hall of the Fujian Chinese Congregation	E3
3	Chinese All-Community Assembly Hall	D3
	Conkhi Cocktail Classes	(see 11)
4	Japanese Covered Bridge	B3
5	Museum of Trading Ceramics	D3
6	Phung Hung Old House	B3
7	Quan Cong Temple	E3
8	Tan Ky House	C4
9	Tran Family Chapel	D3

Activities, Courses & Tours

10	Blue Coral Diving	D4
11	Cham Island Diving Center	D4
12	Gioan	D4
13	Hoi An Motorbike Adventures	D3
14	Life Heritage Resort	G3
	Life Spa	(see 14)
	Morning Glory Street Food Restaurant	(see 31)
15	Palmarosa	B1

Sleeping

16	Ha An Hotel	G3
17	Hoa Binh Hotel	C1
18	Hoang Trinh Hotel	A2
19	Long Life Hotel	B1
20	Long Life Riverside	B4
21	Phuong Dong Hotel	B1
22	Thien Nga Hotel	B1
23	Vinh Hung 1 Hotel	C3
24	Vinh Hung 3	B1

Eating

25	Bale Well	D3
26	Cargo Club	C4
27	Casa Verde	C4
28	Hai Cafe	C4
29	Mango Mango	C4
30	Mermaid Restaurant	F3
31	Morning Glory Street Food Restaurant	C4
32	Phone Café	D4
33	Shree Ganesh Indian Restaurant	D2

Drinking

34	Before & Now	D3
	Dive Bar	(see 11)
	Q Bar	(see 11)
35	White Marble	D4
36	Why Not?	G3

Shopping

37	Art Galleries	B3
	Lotus Jewellery	(see 28)
	Reaching Out	(see 26)

touches – perhaps a tribal textile or original painting. The helpful, well-trained staff make staying here a very special experience.

Long Life Riverside HOTEL $$
(☎391 1696; www.longlifehotels.com; 61 Nguyen Phuc Chu; r US$45-90;) Enjoys a terrific location just over the bridge from the heart of the Old Town and has incredibly spacious rooms with tasteful modern furnishings and state-of-the-art bathrooms. The only drawback is the cramped pool area.

Thien Nga Hotel HOTEL $$
(☎391 6330; thienngahotel@gmail.com; 52 Đ Ba Trieu; r US$30-35;) Excellent value all round with lovely, spacious, airy rooms all with balcony and a contemporary feel – book one at the rear for garden views. Staff are smiley and accommodating.

Hoang Trinh Hotel HOTEL $
(☎391 6579; www.hoianhoangtrinhhotel.com; 45 Đ Le Quy Don; r incl breakfast US$20-28;) Well-run place with helpful, friendly service. Rooms here are a little cluttered but spacious and clean, with high ceilings and cable TV.

Hoa Binh Hotel HOTEL $
(☎391 6838; www.hoianbinhhotel.com; 696 Đ Hai Ba Trung; r US$12-18;) With a good selection of simple but modern and comfortable rooms, all with wi-fi, minibar, cable TV and air-con, this is getting close to budget chic. However the pool layout (in the lobby!) is bizarre and room rates change according to demand.

Life Heritage Resort RESORT HOTEL $$$
(☎391 4555; www.life-resorts.com; 1 Đ Pham Hong Thai; r US$141, ste from US$216;) This large colonial-style resort has beautifully furnished rooms with a real hip-hotel feel.

Immaculately maintained grounds, a classy bar, restaurant, cafe, spa and pool area.

Vinh Hung 3 Hotel HOTEL $$

(☏391 6277; www.hoianvinhhung3hotel.com; 96 Đ Ba Trieu; r US$35-40; ✲◉⊜⊜) Recently upgraded, this smart four-storey minihotel has elegant modish rooms with good attention to detail and facilities: huge beds, dark wood furniture, writing desks and satellite TV; some have balconies.

Windbell Homestay HOMESTAY $$

(☏393 0888; www.windbellhomestay.com.vn; Chau Trung, Cam Nam Island; r US$55, villa US$80-110; ✲◉⊜⊜⊜) Popular Vietnamese luxury homestay where all the lovely, spacious rooms and villas have either pool or garden view.

Vinh Huy HOTEL $

(☏391 6559; www.vinhhuyhotel.com; 203 Đ Ly Thoung Kiet; r US$10-12; ⊜✲◉⊜) All the clean, well-appointed rooms here represent a great deal and have minibars, fan and cable TV; some have large bathrooms with tubs. It's a 15-minute walk north from the Old Town.

Vinh Hung 1 Hotel HISTORIC HOTEL $$$

(☏386 1621; www.vinhhunghotels.com.vn; 143 Đ Tran Phu; r US$80-100; ✲◉⊜⊜) This 200-year-old timber-townhouse simply oozes history and mystique, and featured in Michael Caine's version of *The Quiet American*. Rooms at the rear are a little dark, but all are classy and spacious.

Thien Thanh Hotel HOTEL $$

(☏391 6545; www.hoianthienthanhhotel.com; 16 Đ Ba Trieu; r US$40-60; ✲◉⊜⊜) Spacious, inviting and well-equipped rooms with Vietnamese-style decor, DVD player and bathtubs and a lovely breakfast terrace.

Long Life Hotel HOTEL $$

(☏391 6696; www.longlifehotels.com; 30 Đ Ba Trieu; r US$45-55; ✲◉⊜⊜) Rooms are in fine shape here and the secret garden and pool area is a delight.

Phuong Dong Hotel HOTEL $

(☏391 6477; www.hoianphuongdonghotel.com; 42 Đ Ba Trieu; s/d/tr US$10/12/15; ✲◉⊜) Plain, good-value rooms with comfortable mattresses, reading lights, fan and air-con and in-room wi-fi.

✖ Eating

Hoi An offers a culinary tour de force, including several amazing local specialities.

Be sure to try *banh bao* ('white rose'), an incredibly delicate dish of steamed dumpling stuffed with minced shrimp. *Cao lau*, doughy flat noodles mixed with croutons, bean sprouts and greens, topped with pork slices and served in a savoury broth, is also delicious. The other two culinary treats are fried *hoanh thanh* (wonton) and *banh xeo* (crispy savoury pancakes rolled with herbs in fresh rice paper).

⟨TOP CHOICE⟩ Morning Glory Street

Food Restaurant VIETNAMESE $$

(☏224 1555; www.restaurant-hoian.com; 106 Đ Nguyen Thai Hoc; dishes 42,000-120,000d; ⊜⊘) Simply outstanding restaurant in historic premises that concentrates on street food and traditionally prepared Vietnamese cooking. The exceptional dishes include shrimp mousse on sugarcane skewers, caramelised pork with young bamboo, and wonderful salads.

⟨TOP CHOICE⟩ Cargo Club INTERNATIONAL $

(☏391 0489; www.restaurant-hoian.com; 107 Đ Nguyen Thai Hoc; dishes 35,000-105,000d; ⊜) For all things Western, from a snack to fine dining, Cargo Club excels: the best breakfasts, delectable patisserie selections and mains like grilled sea bass and lamb shank rate very highly indeed. Head for the upper terrace for stunning river views.

Casa Verde EUROPEAN $$

(☏391 1594; www.casaverde-hoian.com; 99 Đ Bach Dang; mains 85,000-190,000d; ⊘noon-10pm) Casa Verde's riverside premises are relatively modest but the cooking is not: Mediterranean classics, thin-crust pizzas and authentic Asian dishes. Be sure to leave room for ice cream, which is unquestionably the best in town and made on the premises.

Shree Ganesh Indian Restaurant INDIAN $$

(www.ganeshindianrestaurant.com; 24 Đ Tran Hung Dao; meals 60,000-120,000d; ⊘noon-10.30pm) Highly authentic Indian with tantalising thalis, fiery curries and nans freshly baked in a tandoor oven. Prices are reasonable and portions are generous.

Mermaid Restaurant VIETNAMESE $

(www.restaurant-hoian.com; 2 Đ Tran Phu; dishes 35,000-90,000d) One of the original Hoi An eateries (established 1992), this renowned yet simple-looking place serves up wonderful Hoi An specialities and unique family recipes.

Bale Well VIETNAMESE $
(45-51 Đ Tran Cao Van; meals 40,000-75,000d; ⌚11.30am-10pm) Local place that's famous for one dish – delicious barbecued pork, served up satay-style, which you then combine with fresh greens and herbs to create your own fresh spring roll.

Mango Mango FUSION $$$
(☎391 0839; www.mangorooms.com; 111 Đ Nguyen Thai Hoc; meals US$30; wi-fi) Celeb chef Duc Tran's third and most beautiful Hoi An restaurant is situated just over the bridge in An Hoi with fine Old Town views. Puts a global spin on Vietnamese cuisine, with fresh, unexpected combinations.

Hai Cafe INTERNATIONAL $
(www.visithoian.com; 98 Đ Nguyen Thai Hoc; mains 60,000-105,000d; wi-fi) Occupying a wonderful Old Town trading house and courtyard, the menu here features good sandwiches, Western breakfasts, Vietnamese dishes, European mains and vegie specials.

Lighthouse Cafe & Restaurant VIETNAMESE $
(☎393 6235; www.lighthousecafehoian.com; To 5 Khoi Xuyen Trung, Cam Nam Island; mains 20,000-100,000d; ⌚Wed-Mon) A cosy restaurant on Cam Nam Island, it has good Vietnamese food and great views. Reservations are advisable.

Phone Café VIETNAMESE $
(80B Đ Bach Dang; dishes 22,000-62,000d) Humble-looking place that serves up the usual faves as well as some good claypot specialities.

Drinking

TOP CHOICE Dive Bar BAR
(88 Đ Nguyen Thai Hoc; wi-fi) Expect a great vibe here thanks to the welcoming service, electronic tunes and party atmosphere. Check out the gorgeous cocktail garden and bar at the rear.

Why Not? BAR
(10B Đ Pham Hong Thai; internet) Great late-night hang-out with pool table and YouTube jukebox run by a friendly local character who's been in the bar game for decades.

Q Bar LOUNGE
(94 Đ Nguyen Thai Hoc; wi-fi) The hippest bar in town, Q Bar offers stunning lighting, lounge music and electronica and the best cocktails in town. It's also gay-friendly.

White Marble WINE BAR
(www.visithoian.com; Đ 99 Le Loi; wi-fi) Gorgeous new wine-bar-cum-restaurant in historic premises. Offers a fine selection of wines (12 are available by the glass, from US$4).

Before & Now BAR
(www.beforennow.com; 51 Đ Le Loi; wi-fi) Your standard-issue backpackers' bar, complete with (slightly clichéd) pictures of the likes of Che, Marilyn, er... Charles Manson. Expect mainstream pop and rock. Happy hour from 6pm to 9pm.

Shopping

Tailor-made clothing is one of Hoi An's best trades, and there are more than 200 tailor shops in town that can whip up an *ao dai* (traditional Vietnamese tunic and trousers), Western suits, shirts and much more. Other hot items include handmade shoes and silk lanterns.

Hoi An also boasts a growing array of interesting art galleries, especially on the west side of the Japanese Covered Bridge.

Reaching Out SOUVENIRS
(www.reachingoutvietnam.com; 103 Đ Nguyen Thai Hoc) A great place to spend your dong, this is a fair-trade gift shop with profits going towards assisting disabled artisans.

Lotus Jewellery JEWELLERY
(www.lotusjewellery-hoian.com; 100 Đ Nguyen Thai Hoc) Very affordable and attractive handcrafted pieces.

Information

For the most part, Hoi An is very safe at any hour. However, late-night bag snatchings in the unlit market have been known and women should avoid walking home alone late at night.

Most hotels have lobby computers and free wi-fi.

Agribank (Đ Cua Dai) With ATM.

Hoi An Hospital (☎386 1364; 4 Đ Tran Hung Dao) Serious problems should be addressed in Danang.

Hoi An police station (☎386 1204; 84 Đ Hoang Dieu)

Main post office (48 Đ Tran Hung Dao)

Min's Computer (2 Truong Minh Luong; per hr 5000d) You can also print, scan, burn and Skype here.

Randy's Book Xchange (www.randysbookxchange.com; To 5 Khoi Xuyen Trung)

Rose Travel Service (☎391 7567; www.rosetravelservice.com; Đ 111 Ba Trieu) Tours, car rental, bus bookings and boat, jeep and motorbike trips.

The Sinh Tourist (☎386 3948; www.thesinhtourist.vn; 587 Đ Hai Ba Trung) For open-tour buses.

Vietinbank (4 Đ Hoang Dieu) Full exchange services, plus ATMs.

Getting There & Away

Most north–south bus services do not stop at Hoi An, but you can head for the town of Vinh Dien (10km to the west) and catch one there. If you're heading for Hué or Nha Trang, open-tour buses are easier.

Hoi An bus station (96 Đ Hung Vuong), 1km west of the centre, mainly serves local destinations including Danang (16,000d, one hour).

The nearest airport and train station are both in Danang.

Getting Around

Metered taxis and motorbike drivers wait for business over the bridge in An Hoi. Call **Hoi An Taxi** (☎391 9919) or **Mai Linh** (☎392 5925) for a pick-up.

Many hotels offer bicycles/motorbikes for rent from 20,000/100,000d per day.

Around Hoi An

BEACHES

The nearest beach to Hoi An, **Cua Dai** is subject to intense development and the domain of hard-selling beach vendors. There are seafood restaurants here. The 5km of coastline south to Cua Dai port is being totally transformed, as a strip of five-star resorts emerges from the sand dunes.

Just 3km north of Cua Dai, **An Bang** is fast emerging as one of Vietnam's most happening and enjoyable beaches. There's a wonderful stretch of fine sand here and lots of cool little beachfront bar-restaurants. **Soul Kitchen** (www.soulkitchen.sitew.com; meals around 90,000d; 📶) and **La Plage** (www.laplagehoian.com; meals from 100,000d; 📶) both offer terrific European food.

The coastline immediately to the north of An Bang remains pristine, a glorious broad beach lined with casuarina and pandan trees and dotted with the curious coracles of local fishermen.

CHAM ISLANDS

☎0510 / POP 2700

A breathtaking cluster of granite islands around 15km directly offshore from Hoi An, the serene **Cham Islands** are blissfully undeveloped – for now. Trips to dive or snorkel the reefs and visit the main island of **Hon Lao** make an excellent day out. The Chams are only accessible for about seven months of the year (March to September), as the ocean is usually too rough at other times.

The islands are protected as a marine park and the underwater environment includes 135 species of soft and hard coral and varied macro life. Fishing and the collection of birds' nests (for soup) are the two key industries here.

Bai Lang, Hon Lao's pretty little port, is the only real settlement. Drop by the tiny but very curious temple **Ong Ngu**, dedicated to whales. Locals worshipped whales as oceanic deities that would provide protection at sea. There are two good, simple guesthouses in town, **Luu Ly** (☎393 0240; r 200,000d) and **Thu Trang** (☎393 0007; r 200,000d), both of which serve meals.

A dirt track heads southwest from Bai Lang for 2km past a couple of glorious little coves to a fine, sheltered beach. There's great swimming in azure waters, powdery sand and hammocks, and the excellent **Cham Restaurant** (☎224 1108; meals 50,000-90,000d); call ahead to book your meal.

Getting There & Away

Most visitors arrive on tours (US$25 to US$40) organised by dive schools in Hoi An (p166). There's also a scheduled daily boat connection from Đ Bach Dang in Hoi An (20,000d, two hours, 7.30am). Note foreigners are routinely overcharged – as much as 100,000d. Boats do not sail during heavy seas. Bring a copy of your passport and visa.

MY SON

The ancient Cham city of **My Son** (admission 60,000d; ⏲6.30am-4pm) is one of the most stunning sights in the area, and another Unesco World Heritage Site. The ruins are nestled in a lush valley surrounded by hills and the massive Hon Quap (Cat's Tooth Mountain). My Son became a religious centre under King Bhadravarman in the late 4th century and was occupied until the 13th century – the longest period of development of any city in the Mekong region.

My Son's temples are in poor shape today – only about 20 structures survive where at least 68 once stood – after American bombing devastated the temples. Note that only a handful of the monuments are properly labelled and there are virtually no information panels on site.

Look out for temples **C1**, an 8th-century structure used to worship Shiva; **B1**, dedicated to Bhadresvara; **B5**, built in the 10th century, which has some original Cham masonry; and **B3**, which has an Indian-influenced pyramidal roof typical of Cham towers.

Buildings **D1** and **D2** were once meditation halls and now house small displays of Cham sculpture.

Group A was almost completely destroyed by US bombs. **A1** was previously My Son's largest temple, reaching 24m, but only its foundations remain.

The ruins are 55km southwest of Hoi An. Day tours to My Son can be arranged in Hoi An for US$4 to US$7, not including admission, and some trips return to Hoi An by boat. Independent travellers can hire a motorbike, *xe om* or car. Get here early (preferably pre-dawn) or late in the afternoon to beat the tour groups.

SOUTH-CENTRAL COAST

Vietnam has an incredibly curvaceous coastline and it's in this region that it is at its most alluring with sweeping sands, towering cliffs and concealed bays. Many of the voluptuous beaches along this stretch are yet to be discovered and developed. Not for long.

Nha Trang, Mui Ne and Con Dao are the key destinations, but the beach breaks come thick and fast in this part of Vietnam. If your idea of paradise is reclining in front of turquoise waters, weighing up the merits of a massage or a mojito, then you have come to the right place.

On hand to complement the sedentary delights are activities to set the pulse racing, including scuba diving, snorkelling, surfing, windsurfing and kitesurfing. Action or inaction, this region bubbles with opportunities.

Quy Nhon

☎056 / POP 275,000

This sprawling city is not a destination in itself, but it's still worth a stop. Close by are some blissful beaches, the countryside is dotted with ancient Cham temples and you'll find some excellent seafood.

Sights & Activities

The long sweep of Quy Nhon's **beachfront** extends from the port in the northeast to the hills in the south: a beautiful stretch of sand.

Queen's Beach (5000d) is popular with locals and has great views back over Quy Nhon. It's just over the hill to the south of town.

Quy Hoa Beach is a popular weekend hang-out for the city's small expat community.

The partly ruined **Thap Doi Cham Towers** (admission 5000d; 8-11am & 1-6pm) sit in a pretty little park. They're about 1.5km south of Quy Nhon, beyond Queen's Beach.

Sleeping & Eating

Hotel Au Co-Ben Bo Bien HOTEL **$**
(☎374 7699; hotel_auco@yahoo.com; 8 & 24 Đ An Duong Vuong; r 180,000-300,000d; ❄) These two hotels share the same name and ownership. Number 8 is slightly better, offering genuine sea views and balconies.

GETTING TO LAOS: BO Y TO PHOU KEUA

This border connects Kon Tum and Attapeu (Laos). Lao visas are available here on arrival. Buses leave Pleiku at 8am daily for Attapeu (240,000d, eight hours, 250km), continuing to Pakse (320,000d, 12 hours, 440km). Kon Tum Tourist can arrange for you to join the bus when it passes through Kon Tum at 9.30am. Mai Linh Express also runs daily buses on this route.

Buses also depart Quy Nhon several times a week, passing through Pleiku and Kon Tum en route to Attapeu and Pakse, but as the schedule fluctuates it's best to check locally for the latest details.

Crossing the border is a challenge. On the Vietnam side, the nearest major town is Ngoc Hoi, which can be reached by bus (30,000d, 1½ hours, 60km) from Kon Tum. You'll have to catch a minibus or *xe om* from Ngoc Hoi to cover the 14km to the border. On the Laos side, things are even quieter and you'll be at the mercy of passing traffic to hitch a ride onwards. Take a through bus.

For information on crossing this border in the other direction, see p351.

Hoang Yen Hotel HOTEL $$
(☎374 6900; www.hoangyenhotel.com.vn; 5 Đ An Duong Vuong; r 400,000-950,000d; ❄@📶) A 10-storey pad overlooking the beach with smart rooms that represent a good deal.

Life Resort BOUTIQUE HOTEL $$$
(☎384 0132; www.life-resorts.com; Bai Dai Beach; r US$106-120, ste US$147; ❄@📶) This gorgeous resort is set on a private beach about 18km south of town.

Barbara's: The Kiwi Connection CAFE $
(102 Đ Xuan Dieu; mains 25,000-75,000d) Popular for comfort food like Western breakfasts; draws backpackers and expats.

2000 SEAFOOD $$
(1 Đ Tran Doc; dishes 40,000-250,000d) Renowned for its crabs, shrimp and fish, and particularly its hotpots.

Information

Barbara's: The Kiwi Connection (☎389 2921; nzbarb@yahoo.com; 102 Đ Xuan Dieu) Free tourist information, bike and motorbike hire, local maps and connections with English-speaking drivers.

Main post office (197 Đ Phan Boi Chau) Plus cheap internet.

Vietcombank (148 Đ Le Loi) With ATM.

Getting There & Away

Air

Vietnam Airlines (☎382 5313; 1 Đ Nguyen Tat Thanh) has daily flights to HCMC (983,000d) plus flights to Hanoi via Danang four times a week. Also runs a minibus transfer (40,000d) between the office and Phu Cat airport, 36km north of the city.

Bus

Quy Nhon bus station (Đ Tay Son) is on the south side of town. Buses run regularly to Quang Ngai (60,000d, 3½ hours), Danang (75,000d, six hours), Nha Trang (80,000d, five hours), Kon Tum (80,000d, five hours) and irregularly to Buon Ma Thuot (120,000d, seven hours).

There's also a connection to Pakse in Laos (from 250,000d, 20 hours, four per week); see the boxed text, p115.

Train

The nearest mainline station is Dieu Tri, 10km west of the city. Destinations include: Quang Ngai (82,000d, five hours), Danang (178,000d, seven hours) and Nha Trang (132,000d, four hours).

Nha Trang

☎058 / POP 375,000

Welcome to the beach capital of Vietnam. Visually, it's immediately attractive, with towering mountains looming up behind the city and a sweeping beach that stretches into the distance. Offshore islands add to the appeal, offering decadent boat trips and diving in turquoise waters.

Nha Trang is a study in contrasts, as the main city is still a bustling Vietnamese entity, buzzing along oblivious to the tourist crowds lining the shore. Hugging the coast for a few blocks is a fully-fledged international resort, complete with high-rise hotels, souvenir shops and stylish restaurants.

It's a party town at heart, like any self-respecting resort should be; people play late here. Yes, the nightlife rocks!

This part of the country has its own microclimate and the rains tend to come from October until December – not the best time for beach bums or scuba divers.

Sights

Nha Trang Coast BEACHES
Coconut palms provide shade for sunbathers and strollers along most of Nha Trang's 6km beachfront. The best beach weather is generally before 1pm, as the afternoon sea breezes can whip up the sand.

Beach chairs are available for rent and vendors peddle food and massages. Popular lounging spots include the Sailing Club and Louisiane Brewhouse. Head further south and it's still possible to find a stretch of sand to yourself.

Hon Chong Promontory, 3km north of central Nha Trang, is a scenic collection of granite rocks jutting into the South China Sea. The promontory borders a rustic beach cove with island views.

Po Nagar Cham Towers TEMPLE
(Đ 2 Thang 4; admission 16,000d; ⊙6am-6pm) Built between the 7th and 12th centuries on a site used by Hindus for linga (phallic symbols) worship, the Po Nagar Cham Towers are 2km north of central Nha Trang on the left bank of the Cai River. The hill offers blue views of the harbour below.

In centuries past, a person coming to pray passed through the pillared meditation hall, 10 pillars of which can still be seen, before proceeding up the steep staircase to the towers. Originally there were seven or eight towers; four remain. All of the temples face east.

The 28m-high **North Tower** (Thap Chinh), with its terraced pyramidal roof, vaulted interior masonry and vestibule, is a superb example of Cham architecture. It was built in 817 after the original temples here were sacked and burned.

Cham, ethnic Chinese and Vietnamese Buddhists come to Po Nagar to pray and make offerings, according to their respective traditions.

FREE Long Son Pagoda PAGODA

(Chua Tinh Hoi Khanh Hoa; Đ 23 Thang 10; ⏲7.30-11.30am & 1.30-8pm) This impressively adorned pagoda is decorated with mosaic dragons covered with glass and ceramic tiles. Founded in the late 19th century, the pagoda still has resident monks. At the top of the hill, behind the pagoda, is the **Giant Seated Buddha** visible from town. Around the statue's base are fire-ringed relief busts of Thich Quang Duc and six other Buddhist monks who died in self-immolations in 1963. Seated near the Buddha, you can contemplate their struggle and the view of Nha Trang.

Watch out for scammers claiming to work 'for the monks' here, who will attempt to guide you round the site then demand a hefty fee.

The pagoda is about 500m west of the train station.

Alexandre Yersin Museum MUSEUM

(10 Đ Tran Phu; admission 26,000d; ⏲7.30-11am & 2-4.30pm Mon-Fri, 8-11am Sat) Dr Alexandre Yersin (1863–1943) founded Nha Trang's **Pasteur Institute** in 1895. He learned to speak Vietnamese fluently, introduced rubber- and quinine-producing trees to Vietnam, and discovered the rat-borne microbe that causes bubonic plague. At his request, Dr Yersin was buried near Nha Trang.

Yersin's library and office are now an interesting museum, particularly for those who have an interest in medicine. Tours are in French, English and Vietnamese.

Photographic Galleries ART GALLERIES

The **Long Thanh Gallery** (www.longthanhart.com; 126 Đ Hoang Van Thu; ⏲9am-7pm Mon-Fri) showcases the work of Vietnam's most prominent photographer and his extraordinary black-and-white images of everyday Vietnamese moments.

Do Dien Khanh Gallery (www.ddk-gallery.com; 126B Đ Hong Bat; ⏲8am-6pm Mon-Fri) has hauntingly beautiful portraits of Cham communities.

Nha Trang Cathedral CHURCH

(cnr Đ Nguyen Trai & Đ Thai Nguyen) Built between 1928 and 1933 in French Gothic style, complete with stained-glass windows, Nha Trang Cathedral is a surprisingly elegant building with colourful Vietnamese touches.

Oceanographic Institute MUSEUM

(Vien Nghiem Cuu Bien; 1 Cau Da; adult/child 15,000/7000d; ⏲6am-6pm) Floating in tanks in the Oceanographic Institute (a French colonial building) are colourful representatives of squirming sea life and 60,000 jars of pickled specimens. It's 5km south of central Nha Trang.

Activities

Diving

Nha Trang is Vietnam's premier diving destination, with around 25 dive sites in the area. Visibility averages 15m, but can be as much as 30m depending on the season (late October to early January is the worst time of year). There are some good drop-offs and small underwater caves to explore, and an amazing variety of corals. Among the colourful reef fish, stingrays are occasionally spotted.

A full-day outing, including two dives and lunch, costs between US$40 and US$70.

GETTING TO CAMBODIA: LE THANH TO O YADAW

Remote and rarely used by foreigners, this border crossing links Pleiku and Ban Lung, Cambodia. Visas are available on arrival in Cambodia.

From Pleiku, local buses leave several times a day for Moc Den (30,000d, two hours, 80km), where another bus (20,000d, 15km) heads to the border. After entering Cambodia at O Yadaw, minibuses (30,000r or US$7.50) or motorbikes (US$15) head to Ban Lung. Departing early should make it easier to arrange affordable transport on the Cambodian side.

For information on crossing this border in the other direction, see p241.

Nha Trang

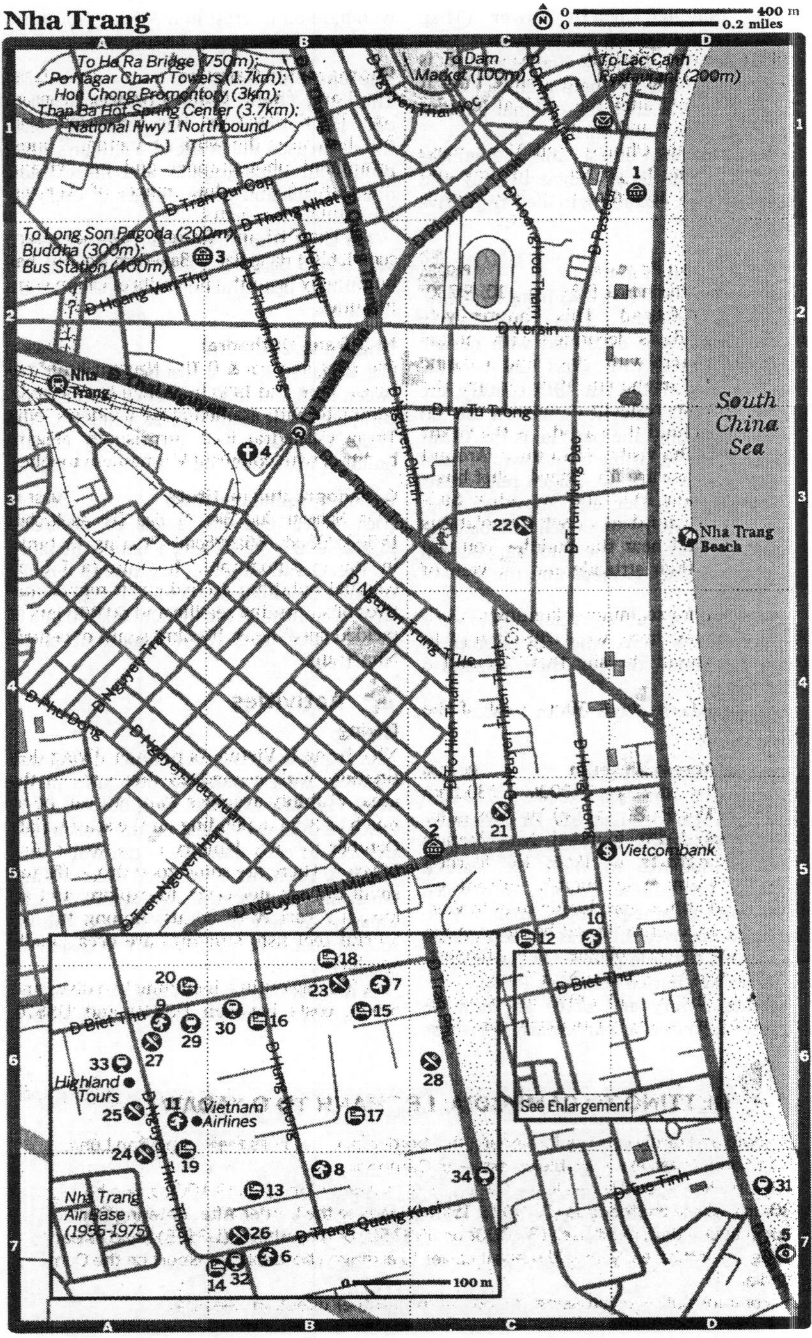

0 400 m
0 0.2 miles
A
B
C
D
1
2
3
4
5
6
7
To Ha Ra Bridge (750m); Po Nagar Cham Towers (1.7km); Hon Chong Promontory (3km); Thap Ba Hot Spring Center (3.7km); National Hwy 1 Northbound
To Dam Market (100m)
To Lac Canh Restaurant (200m)
To Long Son Pagoda (200m); Buddha (300m); Bus Station (400m)
D Tran Quy Cap
D Thong Nhat
D Hoang Van Thu
D Phan Chu Trinh
D Pasteur
D Yersin
D Thai Nguyen
D Ly Tu Trong
D Nguyen Chanh
D Tran Hung Dao
D Nguyen Trung Truc
D Nguyen Trai
D Phu Dong
D Nguyen Thien Thuat
D Hung Vuong
D Nguyen Thi Minh Khai
D Biet Thu
D Tue Tinh
D Tran Quang Khai
Nha Trang
South China Sea
Nha Trang Beach
Vietcombank
Highland Tours
Vietnam Airlines
Nha Trang Air Base (1955-1975)
See Enlargement
0 100 m
1
2
3
4
5
6
7
8
9
10
11
12
13
14
15
16
17
18
19
20
21
22
23
24
25
26
27
28
29
30
31
32
33
34

Nha Trang

Sights

1	Alexandre Yersin Museum	D1
2	Do Dien Khanh Gallery	C5
3	Long Thanh Gallery	A2
4	Nha Trang Cathedral	B3
5	Phu Dong Water Park	D7

Activities, Courses & Tours

6	Angel Dive	B7
7	Crazy Kim Spa & Gym	B6
8	Funky Monkey	B7
9	Mama Linh's	A6
10	Rainbow Divers	C5
	Sailing Club Divers	(see 34)
11	Su Spa	A6
	Waves Watersports	(see 31)

Sleeping

12	AP Hotel	C5
13	Axar Hotel	B7
	Golden Rain Hotel	(see 16)
14	Ha Van Hotel	B7
15	Hotel An Hoa	B6
16	King Town Hotel	B6
	La Suisse Hotel	(see 14)
17	Mai Huy	B6
18	Perfume Grass Inn	B5
19	Sao Mai Hotel	A6
20	Violet Hotel	A6

Eating

21	Artful Ca Phe	C5
22	Au Lac	C3
23	Kirin Restaurant	B6
24	La Mancha	A7
25	Lanterns	A6
26	Le Petit Bistro	B7
	Louisiane Brewhouse	(see 31)
27	Omar's Tandoori	A6
	Sandals Restaurant at the Sailing Club	(see 34)
	Truc Ling 2	(see 9)
28	Veranda	C6

Drinking

29	Crazy Kim Bar	A6
30	Guava	B6
31	Louisiane Brewhouse	D7
	Nghia Bia Hoi	(see 17)
32	Oasis	B7
33	Red Apple Club	A6
34	Sailing Club	C7

Dive operators also offer a range of courses. Recommended centres include:

Angel Dive (☎352 2461; www.angeldivevietnam.info; 1/33 Đ Tran Quang Khai)

Rainbow Divers (☎352 4351; www.divevietnam.com; 90A Đ Hung Vuong)

Sailing Club Divers (☎352 2788; www.sailingclubdivers.com; 72-74 Đ Tran Phu)

Other Watersports

Waves Watersports WATERSPORTS
(☎090 544 7393; www.waveswatersports.com; Louisiane Brewhouse, 29 Đ Tran Phu) Windsurfing, sea kayaking, wakeboarding, waterskiing, surfing and sailing lessons.

Whitewater Rafting RAFTING
(☎090 515 0978; www.shamrockadventures.vn; Đ Tran Quang Khai; per person inc lunch from US$35) Can be combined with mountain biking.

More Watery Fun

Thap Ba Hot Spring Center THERMAL BATHS
(☎383 4939; www.thapbahotspring.com.vn; 25 Ngoc Son; from 100,000d; ⏲7am-7.30pm) The only way to get really clean in Nha Trang is to get deep down and dirty at these hot thermal mud baths. Also home to hot and cold mineral swimming pools (50,000d).

Phu Dong Water Park SWIMMING
(Đ Tran Phu; adult/child 40,000/20,000d; ⏲9am-5pm) Hydroslides, shallow pools and fountains, right on the beachfront.

Vinpearl Land WATER PARK
(☎359 0111; www.vinpearlland.com; Hon Tre Island; adult/child 250,000/175,000d; ⏲9am-10pm) This island resort has funfair rides, a fantastic water park, aquarium, the world's longest over-the-sea cable car and a huge wave pool.

Spas

Crazy Kim Spa & Gym (☎352 7837; 1D Đ Biet Thu) Indulgence for a good cause, massages start at 160,000d.

Su Spa (☎352 3242; www.suspa.vn; 93 Đ Nguyen Thien Thuat) A designer spa; facials are priced from US$27 and body massages from US$21.

DON'T MISS

TRIPPING THE BAY BY BOAT

The 71 offshore islands around Nha Trang are renowned for remarkably clear water and boat trips (from just 100,000d) to these islands are a huge draw. Booze cruises are wildly popular with young backpackers but there are less-raucous snorkelling excursions and luxury trips too.

There's a working fish farm on **Hon Mieu** (Mieu Island) that's also an impressive outdoor **aquarium** (admission 50,000d). From here, you can rent canoes, or hire someone to paddle you out to the nearby islands of **Hon Mun** (Ebony Island) or **Hon Yen** (Swallow Island).

Idyllic **Hon Tre** (Bamboo Island) is the largest island in the area. You can get a boat to **Bai Tru** (Tru Beach) at the northern end of the island. There's great snorkelling and diving off Hon Mun, Hon Tam and Hon Mot.

Virtually every hotel and travel company in town books island-hopping boat tours. Note that the once-notorious hedonistic trips involving free marijuana joints are no more, though others continue the party tradition – minus the ganja – with cheesy DJs and floating bars.

Boat tours include the following:

Con Se Tre (☎381 1163; www.consetre.com.vn; 100/16 Đ Tran Phu) Snorkelling trips from US$13. The office is 3km south of the centre.

Funky Monkey (☎352 2426; www.funkymonkeytour.com.vn; 75A Đ Hung Vuong) Booze cruise (100,000d) with 'live entertainment' from the er...Funky Monkey boy band.

Mama Linh (☎352 2844; mamalinhvn@yahoo.com; 23C Đ Biet Thu) Still a popular party option.

Van Phong Bay (☎352 2844; 23C Đ Biet Thu; incl lunch 349,000d) This trip takes in remote and secluded beaches and bays far from the tourist crowd.

Sleeping

TOP CHOICE **Ha Van Hotel** HOTEL $$
(☎352 5454; www.in2vietnam.com; 3/2 Đ Tran Quang Khai; r US$22-32;) Under French management, this hotel strives to offer a higher standard of service than the local competition. The rooms are well appointed and show a welcome decorative flair. There's an inviting rooftop restaurant-bar and an ice-cream counter in reception.

TOP CHOICE **Violet Hotel** HOTEL $$
(☎352 2314; www.violethotelnhatrang.com; 12 Đ Biet Thu; r incl breakfast 450,000-800,000d;) It's hard to beat this new hotel for location and value for money. Rooms are tastefully finished and facilities include a small courtyard swimming pool.

Evason Ana Mandara Resort & Spa RESORT HOTEL $$$
(☎352 2222; www.evasonresorts.com; Đ Tran Phu; villa US$279-537;) A charming cluster of beach villas on an exclusive strip of sand, 3km south of the central strip. There's more than a hint of Bali evident in the design, classic furnishings and four-poster beds here. Boasts two swimming pools and an indulgent spa.

Mai Huy HOTEL $
(☎352 7553; maihuyhotel.vn@gmail.com; 7H Quan Tran, Đ Hung Vuong; r US$7-15;) The family here really makes their guests feel at home. Rooms are great value, meticulously clean and include cheaper fan options for those counting the dong.

AP Hotel HOTEL $
(☎352 7545; 34 Đ Nguyen Thien Thuat; r 290,000-450,000d;) Offers excellent facilities including flat-screen TV, minibar and bathtub. Cheaper rooms have no window but the VIPs have balconies with distant sea view.

Axar Hotel HOTEL $
(☎352 1655; axarhotel@vnn.vn; 148/10 Đ Hung Vuong; r US$12;) A new hotel tucked away down a side alley. Rooms are spacious and light and the trim is a cut above the competition, making it excellent value.

Perfume Grass Inn HOTEL $$
(☎352 4286; www.perfume-grass.com; 4A Đ Biet Thu; r US$12-30;) Consistently popular, this welcoming inn has rooms with a

touch of character, particularly the pricier options with wood panelling. Cheaper fan rooms include satellite TV and hot shower.

La Suisse Hotel HOTEL $$
(☎352 4353; www.lasuissehotel.com; 3/4 Đ Tran Quang Khai; r US$22-45; ❄@📶) La Suisse is renowned for its efficient service. All rooms have smart furnishings and the family suites include a jacuzzi-style tub and a huge balcony with sunloungers.

King Town Hotel HOTEL $$
(☎352 5818; www.kingtownhotel.com.vn; 92 Đ Hung Vuong; r US$20-40; ❄@📶🏊) A smart new hotel where the rooms have silk trim and stylish bathrooms. Rooftop swimming pool.

Golden Rain Hotel HOTEL $$
(☎352 7799; www.goldenrainhotel.com; 142 Đ Hung Vuong; r US$26-55; ❄@📶🏊) New in 2010 with elegant rooms, some of them with large windows; also has a rooftop pool and gym.

Hotel An Hoa HOTEL $
(☎352 4029; www.anhoahotel.com.vn; 64B/6 Đ Tran Phu; r US$8-14; ❄@📶) A reliable, friendly option in budget alley with a variety of rooms – some fan-cooled, others larger with air-con.

Sao Mai Hotel HOTEL $
(☎352 6412; saomai2hotel@yahoo.com; 99 Đ Nguyen Thien Thuat; dm US$4, r US$6-12; ❄@📶) Budget crash pad with no-nonsense rooms and rooftop terrace. Receptionist Mr Mao Loc runs customised photographic tours.

Eating

Nha Trang is a diner's delight, with a diverse mix of international flavours.

For authentic Vietnamese food, head away from the main strip. **Dam Market** (Đ Trang Nu Vuong) has good stalls, including vegie options.

Vietnamese

TOP CHOICE **Lac Canh Restaurant** VIETNAMESE $
(44 Đ Nguyen Binh Khiem; dishes 30,000-150,000d) Locals flock here in numbers to fire up the tabletop barbecues and grill their own tasty meats, squid, prawns, lobsters and more. There are plenty of accompaniments on the menu.

Lanterns VIETNAMESE $$
(72 Đ Nguyen Thien Thuat; dishes 35,000-178,000d) Predominantly Vietnamese flavours, such as braised pork in claypot, and international offerings for anyone who is riced out. Lanterns supports a local orphanage and offers cooking classes (US$18).

Truc Linh 2 VIETNAMESE $$
(www.truclinhrest.vn; 21 Đ Biet Thu; dishes 40,000-190,000d) The Truc Linh empire includes several eateries in the heart of backpackerville. Number 2 has a pretty garden setting and serves authentic dishes at affordable prices.

Nha Trang Xua VIETNAMESE $$
(Thai Thong, Vinh Thai; dishes 50,000-180,000d) A classic Vietnamese restaurant set in a beautiful old house in the countryside around Nha Trang. Expect a refined menu, beautiful presentation and atmospheric surrounds.

Lang Nuong Phu Dong Hai San SEAFOOD $
(Đ Tran Phu; dishes 30,000-150,000d; ⏲2pm-3am) It may be plastic-chair fantastic but the seafood is fresh and delicious: choose from scallops, crab, prawns and lobster, all at market prices.

Au Lac VEGETARIAN $
(28C Đ Hoang Hoa Tham; meals from 12,000d; ✎) A long-running I-can't-believe-it's-not-meat restaurant. Tasty and cheap.

Kirin Restaurant VIETNAMESE $
(1E Đ Biet Thu; dishes 20,000-120,000d) Colonial surrounds and authentic, affordable Vietnamese cuisine.

International

TOP CHOICE **Veranda** INTERNATIONAL $
(66 Đ Tran Phu; mains 40,000-120,000d) This stylish little restaurant offers a small menu of food with flair, blending Vietnamese ingredients with an international outlook to create some highly original flavours. There's a huge variety of three-course set menus on offer from just US$5, including a drink.

Sandals Restaurant at the Sailing Club INTERNATIONAL $$
(72-74 Đ Tran Phu; mains 50,000-250,000d; @) A local institution offering Vietnamese, Italian and Indian menus. The beachfront terrace is the nicest of the dining areas with people-watching by day and brisk breezes by night.

BUCKET OF WHAT?

There have been a number of reports of dodgy cocktail buckets (laced with moonshine or drugs) doing the rounds in bars and clubs. Keep an eye on what goes into the bucket or avoid them completely – you don't want your night to end in paranoia, illness or robbery.

Le Petit Bistro FRENCH $$
(☎352 7201; 26D Đ Tran Quang Khai; mains 50,000-250,000d) Nha Trang's most popular French restaurant, this is the place for the *fromage* you have been pining for, some select cold cuts or duck specialities.

La Mancha SPANISH $$
(78 Đ Nguyen Thien Thuat; mains 45,000-210,000d; ⏲10am-midnight) Offers an extensive tapas menu plus delicious mains. Try *gambas con ajillo* (garlic prawns) or serrano ham.

Louisiane Brewhouse INTERNATIONAL $$
(29 Đ Tran Phu; www.louisianebrewhouse.com.vn; mains 50,000-350,000d; ⏲7am-1am; @✉) Microbrewery with a pool that also has an eclectic menu of Thai, Vietnamese and Japanese food plus great cakes and pastries.

Omar's Tandoori INDIAN $
(89B Đ Nguyen Thien Thuat; dishes 40,000-120,000d) Authentic curries plus tandoori specialities.

Artful Ca Phe CAFE $
(20A Đ Nguyen Thien Thuat; mains 20,000-100,000d) Part photography gallery, part cafe, it's ideal for a coffee, juice or light bite.

Drinking

Oasis BAR
(3 Đ Tran Quang Khai) Popular for cocktail-drinking and shisha-smoking with happy hours rolling on from 4pm to midnight. The garden terrace is great for sporting events. Stays open until dawn.

Sailing Club BAR
(72-74 Đ Tran Phu; @) Despite its evident gentrification, this remains the definitive Nha Trang nightspot. Drinks are more expensive than in other venues, so it tends to fill up as the night wears on. Popular nights attract a cover charge.

Crazy Kim Bar BAR
(www.crazykimbar.com; 19 Đ Biet Thu; @wi-fi) Busy bar that's home to the 'Hands off the Kids!' campaign, which works to prevent paedophilia. Regular themed party nights, great music and profits go towards the cause. There's a classroom for vulnerable street kids on the premises, and volunteer English teachers are needed.

Louisiane Brewhouse BREWERY
(☎352 1948; 29 Đ Tran Phu; @✉) Homebrew, Nha Trang–style. Elegant microbrewery with an inviting swimming pool and a private strip of sand.

Guava LOUNGE
(www.clubnhatrang.com; 17 Đ Biet Thu; @) A hip lounge bar, with sunken sofas inside and a leafy garden patio outside. There are regular drink promotions and great food is served here.

Red Apple Club BAR
(54H Đ Nguyen Thien Thuat; @) Backpacker party HQ with cheap beer, flowing shots and indie anthems.

Nghia Bia Hoi BAR
(7G/3 Đ Hung Vuong) Probably the cheapest beer in Nha Trang, including a light lager and a darker brown beer.

Information

Nha Trang has dozens of internet cafes and most hotels and bars have free wi-fi. ATMs are widespread too.

Highland Tours (☎352 4477; www.highlandtourstravel.com; 17B Đ Hung Vuong) Affordable tours in the Central Highlands.

Main post office (4 Đ Le Loi)

Mama Linh's Boat Tours (☎352 2844; 23C Đ Biet Thu) Famed for its raucous boat tours, Mama Linh can also arrange trips around the province and the highlands.

Pasteur Institute (☎382 2355; 10 Đ Tran Phu) Medical consultations and vaccinations.

The Sinh Tourist (☎352 2982; www.thesinhtourist.vn; 2A Đ Biet Thu) Cheap local tours and open-tour buses.

Vietcombank (17 Đ Quang Trung; ⏲Mon-Fri) Changes travellers cheques and offers cash advances.

Dangers & Annoyances

Though Nha Trang is generally a safe place, be very careful on the beach during the day (theft) and at night (robbery). Pickpocketing is a perennial problem. Bags with valuables left behind in bars for 'safekeeping' are regularly relieved of

TRANSPORT CONNECTIONS WITH NHA TRANG

DESTINATION	CAR/MOTORBIKE TRAVEL TIME	BUS TRAVEL TIME/ COST/FREQUENCY	TRAIN TRAVEL TIME/ COST/FREQUENCY	AIR TRAVEL TIME/COST/ FREQUENCY
Dalat	4 hours	5 hours/US$3.50-6/regular	N/A	N/A
Danang	11 hours	12 hours/US$9-12/ regular	12-15 hours/US$9-24/frequent	1 hour/1 daily/ from US$49
HCMC	10 hours	11 hours/US$9-12/ frequent	9-12 hours/US$8-23/ frequent	1 hour/3 daily/ from US$34
Mui Ne	5 hours	6 hours/US$5-7/ regular	N/A	N/A
Quy Nhon	4 hours	5 hours/US$5-7/ frequent	4-6 hours/US$3-7/ frequent	N/A

cash and phones. Drive-by bag snatching is on the rise – take great care on the back of *xe om*. And note the warning about cocktail buckets.

Getting There & Away

Air

Vietnam Airlines (☎352 6768; 91 Đ Nguyen Thien Thuat) connects Nha Trang with HCMC (from 680,000d), Hanoi (from 1,700,000d) and Danang (from 980,000d) daily. **Jetstar Pacific** (www.jetstar.com) offers cheaper connections with Hanoi starting at 775,000d.

Bus

Phia Nam Nha Trang bus station (Đ 23 Thang 10) has regular buses to Quy Nhon (100,000d, five hours), with a few continuing to Danang. Regular buses head south to Phan Rang (40,000d, two hours), and HCMC (180,000d, 11 hours), including sleeper buses from 7pm. Buses also run west to Dalat (100,000d, five hours) and Buon Ma Thuot (85,000d, four hours).

Open-bus tours are the best option for Mui Ne (four to five hours), continuing on to HCMC. Open buses also head to Dalat (five hours) and Hoi An (11 hours).

Train

Nha Trang train station (Đ Thai Nguyen; ⊙ticket office 7am-10pm) is in the middle of town. Destinations include Quy Nhon (132,000d, four hours) and Danang (soft seat/sleeper 285,000/475,000d, 10 hours).

Getting Around

Nha Trang is now served by Cam Ranh Airport, about 28km south of the city. Shuttle buses (40,000d) ply this route leaving from the site of the old airport (near 86 Đ Tran Phu) two hours before scheduled departure times, taking about 40 minutes. **Nha Trang Taxi** (☎382 6000) charges 320,000d from the airport to a downtown destination, or only 190,000d in reverse.

Cyclos and *xe oms* cost 20,000d for a shortish ride. Hotels and cafes rent out bicycles from 30,000d per day. **Mai Linh** (☎382 2266) taxis are safe and reliable.

Mui Ne

☎062 / POP 15,000

Once upon a time, Mui Ne was an isolated stretch of sand, but it was too beautiful to be ignored and it's now a string of resorts. Mercifully, most of these are low-rise and set amid pretty gardens by the sea. The original fishing village is still here, but tourists outnumber locals these days. Mui Ne is definitely moving upmarket, as more exclusive resorts open their doors, but there is still a surfer vibe to the town.

Mui Ne is the adrenalin capital of southern Vietnam. Surf's up from August to December. Windsurfing and kitesurfing are huge here. It's also the 'Sahara' of Vietnam, with the most dramatic sand dunes in the region looming large.

Sights

Sand Dunes BEACH

Mui Ne is known for its enormous sand dunes. Be sure to try the sand-sledding. The Fairy Spring (Suoi Tien) is a stream that flows through a patch of the dunes and rock formations near town. Also nearby are a red stream, a market and a fishing village. 4WD tours of the dunes are popular.

Po Shanu Cham Tower TEMPLE
(Km 5; admission 5000d; ⏲7.30-11.30am & 1.30-4.30pm) On Route 706 heading towards Phan Thiet, the small Po Shanu Cham Tower occupies a hill with sweeping views of Phan Thiet, including the boat-filled estuary, and a cemetery filled with candy-like tombstones.

Activities

Taste of Vietnam COOKING
(☎091 665 5241; atasteofvietnam@gmail.com; Sunshine Beach Resort, 82 Đ Nguyen Dinh Chieu; US$20-25) Learn the secrets of Vietnamese cuisine with a cooking class by the beach.

Nina Spa SPA
(☎384 7577; 165 Đ Nguyen Dinh Chieu; massages from US$21; ❄) Set in a beautiful traditional house, this is the most alluring spa in Mui Ne.

Jibes KITESURFING, WINDSURFING
(☎384 7405; www.windsurf-vietnam.com; 90 Đ Nguyen Dinh Chieu) The original kitesurfing school, Jibes is watersports heaven, offering lessons and renting state-of-the-art gear like windsurfers, surfboards, kitesurfers and kayaks. Insurance costs extra.

Sankara Kitesurfing Academy KITESURFING
(☎091 491 0607; www.kiteschoolmuine.com; 78 Đ Nguyen Dinh Chieu) Based at ultra-hip Sankara, this place offers kitesurfing and equipment rentals.

Vietnam Kitesurfing Tours KITESURFING, SURFING
(☎090 946 9803; www.vietnamkitesurfingtours.com) Located in Mellow Guesthouse, this company takes you to parts others cannot reach. Day trips cost US$80 and two-day trips start at US$180.

Sleeping

TOP CHOICE **Mui Ne Backpackers** GUESTHOUSE $
(☎384 7047; www.muinebackpackers.com; 88 Đ Nguyen Dinh Chieu; dm US$6-10, r US$20-60; ❄@☎❄) Highly popular, sociable place with hospitable Aussie management, where you'll find smart four-bed dorms, full-renovated private rooms and beachfront bungalows with unrestricted sea views.

TOP CHOICE **Full Moon Resort** BOUTIQUE HOTEL $$
(☎384 7008; www.windsurf-vietnam.com; 84 Đ Nguyen Dinh Chieu; r US$48-165; ❄@☎❄) One of the pioneering resorts in Mui Ne, this well-maintained place has beachfront bungalows with wall-hangings and jacuzzi-like bathtubs. Family rooms are available that include a sofa bed for the kiddies.

Cham Villas BOUTIQUE HOTEL $$$
(☎374 1234; www.chamvillas.com; 32 Đ Nguyen Dinh Chieu; r US$150-185; ❄@☎❄) Arguably the most boutique of many 'boutique' resorts in Mui Ne, with just 20 stylish villas. Verdant gardens surround the large pool and there's a 60m strip of private beach. Book ahead.

Indochina Dreams BOUTIQUE HOTEL $$
(☎384 7271; www.indochinadream.com; 74 Đ Nguyen Dinh Chieu; r US$40-55; ❄@☎❄) Expanding place in extensive gardens where the newer bungalows are finished in local stone. The swimming pool is a great place to unwind.

Mia Resort BOUTIQUE HOTEL $$$
(☎384 7440; www.sailingclubvietnam.com; 24 Đ Nguyen Dinh Chieu; r US$66, bungalows US$85-170; ❄@☎❄) Also known as the Sailing Club, this is a sophisticated resort offering sensibly priced rooms with designer furnishings and private balconies. The pool is beachside, as is the excellent in-house Sandals Restaurant.

Shades BOUTIQUE HOTEL $$$
(☎374 3236; www.shadesmuine.com; 98A Đ Nguyen Dinh Chieu; r US$74-380; ❄@☎❄) Small in size but big on personality, Shades offers luxurious studio apartments with sleek contemporary lines.

Sunsea Resort BOUTIQUE HOTEL $$$
(☎384 7700; www.sunsearesort-muine.com; 50 Đ Nguyen Dinh Chieu; r US$75-150; ❄@☎❄) Luxurious rooms in beautiful banda-style buildings with views over the pool and sea, plus cheaper rooms with garden view. Home to a great Thai restaurant.

Bien Dua Resort GUESTHOUSE $
(Coconut Beach; ☎384 7241; www.bienduaresort.com; 136 Đ Nguyen Dinh Chieu; r US$10-20; ❄@☎) Intimate, friendly French-run place with bungalow-style rooms that are enticing value for the prime beachfront location. Budget fan-cooled rooms are available too.

Rang Garden Bungalow HOTEL $
(☎374 3638; 233A Đ Nguyen Dinh Chieu; r US$10-30; ❄@☎❄) New in 2011, this place offers seriously smart rooms around a generously proportioned pool.

Mui Ne Beach

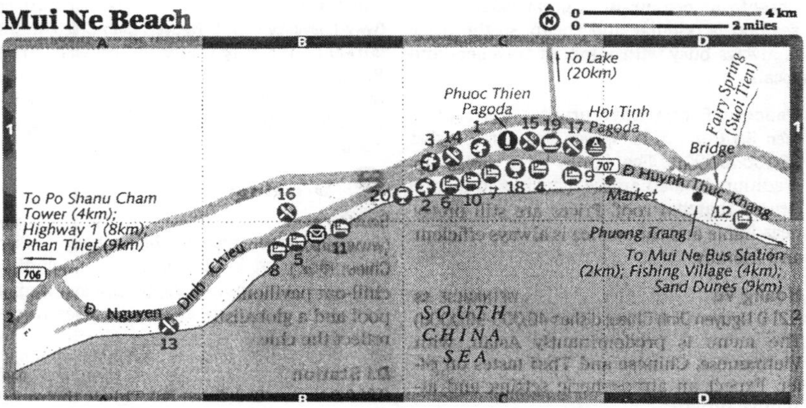

Mui Ne Beach

Activities, Courses & Tours

- Jibes .... (see 6)
- 1 Nina Spa C1
- 2 Sankara Kitesurfing Academy C1
- Taste of Vietnam .... (see 2)
- 3 Vietnam Kitesurfing Tours C1

Sleeping

- 4 Bien Dua Resort C1
- 5 Cham Villas B2
- 6 Full Moon Resort C1
- Indochina Dreams .... (see 2)
- 7 Lu Hoang Guesthouse C1
- 8 Mia Resort B2
- Mui Ne Backpackers .... (see 6)
- Paradise Huts .... (see 6)
- Rang Garden Bungalows .... (see 15)
- 9 Salina Resort C1
- 10 Shades C1
- 11 Sunsea Resort B2
- 12 Thai Hoa Mui Ne Resort D1

Eating

- 13 Hoa Vien Brauhaus A2
- 14 Hoang Vu C1
- 15 La Taverna C1
- Lam Tong .... (see 6)
- 16 Peaceful Family Restaurant B1
- 17 Phat Hamburgers C1

Drinking

- 18 DJ Station C1
- Fun Key .... (see 18)
- 19 Info Café C1
- Sankara .... (see 2)
- 20 Wax B1

Paradise Huts HOTEL $$
(☎384 7177; www.chezninaresort.com; 86 Đ Nguyen Dinh Chieu; r US$35-50; ❄@🏊) Pretty bungalows in a leafy garden with the beachfront on your doorstep.

Thai Hoa Mui Ne Resort HOTEL $$
(☎384 7320; www.thaihoaresort.com; 56 Đ Huynh Thuc Khang; r US$20-50; ❄@🏊) Popular, attractive bungalows fronting a spacious garden.

Lu Hoang Guesthouse HOTEL $
(☎350 0060; 106 Đ Nguyen Dinh Chieu; r US$15-20; ❄@🏊) Welcoming hosts and lovingly decorated rooms, some with sea view and breezy balconies.

Salina Resort HOTEL $$
(☎374 3666; www.salinaresort.net; 130D Đ Nguyen Dinh Chieu; r 600,000-700,000d; ❄@🏊) New family-run place around the Km16 mark offering the atmosphere of a boutique homestay.

Eating

Vietnamese

Venture beyond the Km14 mark and there is a host of seafront shacks that serve affordable seafood (mains 30,000d to 80,000d) from sundown.

TOP CHOICE **Lam Tong** VIETNAMESE $
(92 Đ Nguyen Dinh Chieu; dishes 25,000-75,000d) It doesn't look like much but this family-run

beachfront restaurant is great value. Fresh seafood is popular and cheap, so the place is always busy with a mix of travellers and locals.

Peaceful Family Restaurant VIETNAMESE $
(Yen Gia Quan; 53 Đ Nguyen Dinh Chieu; dishes 30,000-70,000d) The family here serves up traditional Vietnamese cuisine under a breezy thatched roof. Prices are still pretty reasonable and the service is always efficient and friendly.

Hoang Vu VIETNAMESE $$
(121 Đ Nguyen Dinh Chieu; dishes 40,000-90,000d) The menu is predominantly Asian, with Vietnamese, Chinese and Thai tastes on offer. Expect an atmospheric setting and attentive service.

International

TOP CHOICE **La Taverna** ITALIAN $$
(374 3272; 229C Đ Nguyen Dinh Chieu; mains 50,000-150,000d;) A new Italian restaurant in Mui Ne around the Km16 mark, La Taverna is already popular thanks to its thin-crust pizzas and homemade pastas. The extensive menu also includes Vietnamese faves, fresh seafood and Italian vino.

TOP CHOICE **Phat Hamburgers** INTERNATIONAL $$
(374 3502; 253 Đ Nguyen Dinh Chieu; burgers 50,000-75,000d;) Vietnam's finest burgers are available here in a variety of shapes and sizes. Try Baby Phat if you are only snacking, or experiment with the Phatarella, including cashew-nut pesto and mozzarella cheese.

Hoa Vien Brauhaus INTERNATIONAL $$
(www.hoavien.vn; 2A Đ Nguyen Dinh Chieu; mains 50,000-150,000d;) Freshly brewed draft Pilsner Urquell is the big draw, though the huge restaurant offers some Czech and international dishes, as well as a dizzying array of live seafood.

Drinking

Sankara BAR
(www.sankaravietnam.com; 78 Đ Nguyen Dinh Chieu;). A sleek beach bar, including chill-out pavilions and daybeds, a swimming pool and a globalista menu. However, prices reflect the chic.

DJ Station BAR
(120C Đ Nguyen Dinh Chieu;) This is the most popular late-night spot in Mui Ne, with a resident DJ and dastardly drink promotions. Gets going after 10pm.

Info Cafe CAFE
(241 Đ Nguyen Dinh Chieu; drinks 20,000-50,000d; 7am-10pm;) Travellers are wild about the coffee here, which comes in all styles and flavours. Also a reliable spot for travel info.

Fun Key BAR
(124 Đ Nguyen Dinh Chieu;) New in 2011, this is another 'in' spot with the backpacker crowd looking for the Ko Pha Ngan experience in Mui Ne.

Wax BAR
(68 Đ Nguyen Dinh Chieu;) Wax has happy hours until midnight when they light up the beach bonfire.

BEAUTIFUL BEACHES

Beach meccas Mui Ne, Nha Trang and Quy Nhon are fully covered in this guide, but there are many pristine stretches of sand along this coast, some of which see very few tourists. Here's our top five from north to south:

» **My Khe** Located near the site of the infamous My Lai Massacre, My Khe (not to be confused with the other My Khe Beach near Danang) is a great beach, with fine white sand and clear water.

» **Vung Ro Bay** The most easterly point on the mainland and famed for its beautiful and isolated bays, which hide some unspoilt beaches.

» **Whale Island** Off the coast to the north of Nha Trang, Whale Island is a tiny speck on the map, home to the lovely and secluded **Whale Island Resort** (www.whaleislandresort.com) and a great spot for diving.

» **Doc Let** Within commuting distance of busy Nha Trang, the beachfront is long and wide, with chalk-white sand and shallow water, and there are several blissful resorts.

» **Ninh Van Bay** This place doesn't really exist – except in an alternate reality populated by European royalty, film stars and the otherwise rich and secretive. It's home to the **Six Senses Ninh Van Bay** (www.sixsenses.com).

Information

A great resource for information on Mui Ne is www.muinebeach.net.

Internet and wi-fi is widely available and there are several ATMs.

Main post office (348 Đ Huynh Thuc Khang)

The Sinh Tourist (www.thesinhtourist.vn; 144 Đ Nguyen Dinh Chieu) Operates out of Mui Ne Resort, booking open-tour buses.

Getting There & Around

Mui Ne is connected to Hwy 1 via branch roads to the north and south but few regular buses serve the town.

Open-tour buses are the best option for Mui Ne; try The Sinh Tourist for destinations including HCMC (90,000d, six hours), Nha Trang (90,000d, five hours) and Dalat (100,000d, five hours). There are also night buses to HCMC (160,000d), Nha Trang (160,000d) and Hoi An (200,000d).

Local buses run from nearby Phan Thiet to Mui Ne, or take a *xe om* (60,000d). **Mai Linh** (☎389 8989) operates metered taxis. *Xe om* charge 20,000d to 40,000d for rides up and down the coast.

Vung Tau

☎064 / POP 270,000

A popular escape from HCMC for expats and locals alike, Vung Tau has been a beach resort since about 1890. It's big and brash, with a somewhat seedy underbelly.

Sights & Activities

Welcome to Rio di Vietnam, where a 32m **giant Jesus** (parking 2000d; ⊙7.30-11.30am & 1.30-5pm) stands atop Small Mountain with arms outstretched to embrace the South China Sea.

The grand colonial-era **White Villa** (Bach Dinh or Villa Blanche; Đ Tran Phu; admission 15,000d) was the weekend retreat of the French governor; wander the extensive gardens.

Surf Station (☎352 6101; www.vungtausurf.com; 8 Đ Thuy Ban), based at the Vung Tau Beach Club, offers kitesurfing and surfing classes if the wind is up.

Sleeping & Eating

Binh An Village BOUTIQUE HOTEL **$$$**
(☎351 0016; www.binhanvillage.com; 1 Đ Tran Phu; r & ste US$85-250; ❄@≋) *The* desirable address in Vung Tau, this oasis feels like it has been transported straight from Bali. The bungalows are beautifully decorated with Asian antiques, set amid serene oceanfront scenery.

Lua Hong Motel HOTEL **$**
(☎381 8992; 137 Đ Thuy Van; r 250,000-350,000d; ❄@📶) This 'motel' has a touch (but only a touch, mind you) more decorative flair than some of the neighbouring places, plus sea views.

Lan Rung Resort & Spa HOTEL **$$**
(☎352 6010; www.lanrungresort.com; 3-6 Đ Ha Long; s/d from US$60/80; ❄@📶≋) Smart beachside place with pristine rooms, plus all the usual extras.

Ganh Hao VIETNAMESE **$$**
(3 Đ Tran Phu; mains 40,000-180,000d) Set above the bay on the road to Mulberry Beach, this popular local restaurant offers seafood including lobster and king crab at very reasonable prices.

Someplace Else INTERNATIONAL **$$**
(3 Đ Ba Cu; mains 50,000-300,000d; 📶) Also known as Tommy's 3. The menu is predominantly international, including imported Aussie meats and regular barbecues, but also some authentic Vietnamese dishes.

Information

Check out www.vungtau-city.com for up-to-date information.

Main post office (8 Đ Hoang Dieu)

Vietcombank (27-29 Đ Tran Hung Dao) Full exchange services and an ATM.

Getting There & Around

From Mien Dong bus station in HCMC, air-con minibuses (40,000d, three hours) leave for Vung Tau throughout the day until around 4.30pm.

It's much more enjoyable to catch a hydrofoil; there are services every half-hour until about 4.30pm to HCMC (adult/child 200,000/100,000d, 75 minutes) from Cau Da pier.

Bikes and motorbikes are widely available for rent. Call **Mai Linh** (☎356 5656) for a taxi.

Con Dao Islands

☎064 / POP 5500

Isolated from the mainland, the Con Dao Islands are one of the star attractions in Vietnam. Long the Devil's Island of Indochina - the preserve of political prisoners and undesirables - this place is now turning heads thanks to its striking natural beauty. Con

PENNILESS IN PARADISE

Make sure you have sufficient funds before travelling to the Con Dao Islands. There's one bank, but its two ATMs are temperamental. Most midrange hotels accept credit cards, but local exchange rates are notoriously poor.

Son, the largest of this chain of 15 islands and islets, is ringed with lovely beaches, coral reefs and scenic bays, and remains partially covered in thick forests. Hiking, diving and deserted beaches are all a big draw. .

More than three-quarters of the land area in the island chain is part of Con Dao National Park, which protects Vietnam's most important **sea turtle nesting grounds**.

◉ Sights

The entrance fees for Phu Hai is valid for the other sights.

Phu Hai Prison HISTORIC BUILDING
(admission 20,000d; ⊘7-11.30am & 1-5pm Mon-Sat) The largest of the 11 jails on the island, this prison dates from 1862. It houses several enormous detention buildings, one with about 100 shackled and emaciated mannequins that are all too lifelike.

The notorious **tiger cages** were used by the French to incarcerate nearly 2000 political prisoners. These tiny cells had ceiling bars, where guards could peer down on the prisoners like tigers in a zoo.

Revolutionary Museum HISTORIC BUILDING
(⊘7-11am & 1.30-5pm Mon-Sat) This museum has exhibits on Vietnamese resistance to the French, communist opposition to the Republic of Vietnam, and the treatment of political prisoners. An impressive-looking new **Con Dao Museum** is located at the eastern end of Ð Nguyen Hue; exhibits from the Revolutionary Museum will be moved here once it opens its doors.

BEACHES

Bai Dam Trau is arguably the best all-round beach, a secluded cove on the southern end of the island. Other options include tiny **Bai Nhat**, though it's exposed only during low tide. **Bai Loi Voi** is another possibility.

🏃 Activities

Con Dao offers the most pristine marine environment in the country. Diving is possible

year-round, but March to September is considered the best time.

Two good dive operators are based here:

Dive! Dive! Dive! (☑383 0701; www.dive-condao.com; 36 Ð Ton Duc Thang)

Rainbow Divers (☑090 557 7671; www.divevietnam.com; Six Senses Con Dao)

There are lots of treks around Con Son Island, as much of the interior remains heavily forested. It's necessary to take a national park guide (150,000d to 250,000d) when venturing into the forest. Trekking destinations include **Bamboo Lagoon** (Dam Tre), **Ong Dung Bay** and **So Ray**.

🛏 Sleeping & Eating

Con Dao Camping HOTEL $$
(☑383 1555; www.condaocamping.com; Ð Nguyen Duc Thuan; r 600,000d; ✳◉🛜) Curious triangular bungalows with satellite TV, minibar and al fresco showers are great value for the beachfront location.

Six Senses Con Dao BOUTIQUE HOTEL $$$
(☑383 1222; www.sixsenses.com; Dat Doc Beach; villas from US$685; ✳◉🛜🌊) This is the designer castaway experience complete with stunning rustic-chic seafront villas, each with its own pool. The food is in a league of its own.

Hai Nga Mini Hotel HOTEL $
(☑363 0308; 7 Ð Tran Phu; r 200,000-550,000d; ✳◉🛜) Small hotel run by a friendly family that speaks English, French and German. Rooms are basic but good value, including air-con, TV and hot showers.

Thu Tam VIETNAMESE $
(Ð Nguyen Hue; mains 20,000-100,000d) Fresh from bubbling tanks, you'll find seafood galore plus fish huge enough to feed a family here.

Tri Ky VIETNAMESE $$
(7 Ð Nguyen Duc Thuan; mains 40,000-200,000d) Ocean-fresh treats including squid grilled in five spices and seafood hotpots.

ℹ Information

The **National Park HQ** (☑383 0669; www.condaopark.com.vn; 29 Ð Vo Thi Sau; ⊘7-11.30am & 1.30-5pm) is a good place to get information about excursions and hikes.

There is a branch of **Vietinbank** (Ð Le Duan) with two ATMs. However, these are notorious for running out of dong and the bank does not change foreign currency.

Internet access and wi-fi are available at hotels in town.

Getting There & Around

Vasco (☎383 1831; www.vasco.com.vn; 44 Đ Nguyen Hue) offers three flights daily from HCMC at 863,000d one way, although it often has specials on the website. **Air Mekong** (www.airmekong.info) has daily flights too. The tiny airport is about 15km from the town centre. Big hotels provide free airport transfers; you can hitch a ride on one of these for about 60,000d.

Boat trips (2,000,000d to 5,000,000d per day) can be arranged through the national park office. Bicycles (US$2) and motorbikes (from US$7) are available for rent from hotels.

CENTRAL HIGHLANDS

The undulating landscape that once sheltered VC soldiers down the Ho Chi Minh Trail offers an off-the-beaten-track destination for travellers. There's a rugged charm to its hill-tribe villages and valleys, waterfalls and winding roads.

Looking for big nature? Check out the national parks of Cat Tien and Yok Don – both give visitors the opportunity to explore Vietnam's all-too-rare wild side.

Despite a fraught history, the Central Highlands are safe and easy to travel. Dalat is perfect for a weekend's respite from the heat, and the rest of the highlands are ideal for a week-long immersion in a life far from the madding crowd.

Dalat

☎063 / POP 205,000 / ELEV 1475M

Dalat is the alter-ego of lowland Vietnam. The weather is spring-like cool instead of tropical hot. Days are fine, but nights can be chilly. The town is dotted with elegant French colonial villas instead of squat socialist architecture, and farms are thick with strawberries and flowers, not rice. As a highland resort it's been welcoming tourists for a century, and it has all the attractions to prove it.

Dalat is small enough to remain charming, and the surrounding countryside is blessed with lakes, waterfalls, evergreen forests and gardens. The town is a big draw for domestic tourists for whom it is 'Le Petit Paris', a honeymoon capital and the City of Eternal Spring all rolled into one.

Sights & Activities

Perhaps there's something in the cool mountain air that fosters the distinctly artistic vibe that veers towards cute kitsch in Dalat. Whatever the reason, Dalat has attractions you won't find elsewhere in Vietnam.

Hang Nga Crazy House NOTABLE BUILDING
(3 Đ Huynh Thuc Khang; admission 30,000d; ⊙7am-5pm; s US$25-57, d US$35-70) Southeast of central Dalat, this is a funky place that's earned the moniker Crazy House from local residents. It's notable for its *Alice in Wonderland* architecture, where you can perch inside a giraffe or get lost in a giant spiderweb. Architecture buffs will marvel at the echoes of Antoni Gaudí, children will simply enjoy getting lost in the maze of tunnels, walkways and ladders. You can even stay here.

Crémaillère TRAIN TRIP
(Ga Da Lat; 1 Đ Quang Trung; ⊙6.30am-5pm) The Crémaillère is a cog railway that linked Dalat and Thap Cham-Phan Rang from 1928 to 1964. It's about 500m east of Xuan Huong Lake. The line has now been partially repaired and is a tourist attraction. You can ride 8km down the tracks to Trai Mat village, where you can visit the ornate Linh Phuoc Pagoda.

There are five scheduled trains to Trai Mat (return ticket 100,000d, 30 minutes, 8km) every day between 7.45am and 4.05pm.

Bao Dai's Summer Palace PALACE
(off Đ Trieu Viet Vuong; admission 10,000d; ⊙7am-5pm) This art deco–influenced villa was constructed in 1933 and was one of three palaces Bao Dai kept in Dalat. The decor has not changed in decades, making a visit here akin to wandering on to a film set.

In Bao Dai's office, the life-sized white bust above the bookcase is of the man himself (he died in 1997). Upstairs are the living quarters. The huge semicircular couch was used by the emperor and empress for family meetings.

Bao Dai's Summer Palace is set in a pine grove, 2km southwest of the city centre.

Xuan Huong Lake LAKE
Created by a dam in 1919, this banana-shaped lake was named after a 17th-century Vietnamese poet known for her daring attacks on the hypocrisy of social conventions and the foibles of scholars, monks, mandarins and

Dalat

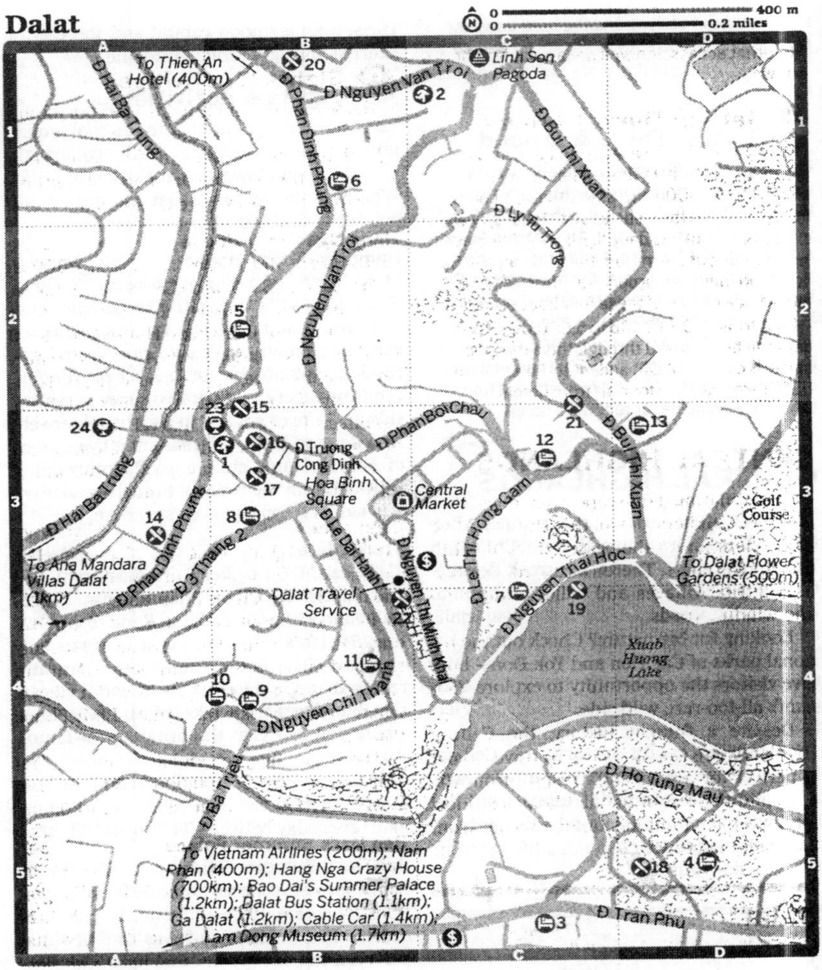

kings. The lake can be circumnavigated along a 7km sealed path that leads past several of Dalat's main sights, including the flower gardens.

Dalat Flower Gardens GARDENS

(Vuon Hoa Thanh Pho; Đ Tran Nhan Tong; admission 10,000d; ⊙7.30am-4pm) Established in 1966, flowers here include hydrangeas, fuchsias and orchids.

Like any good Dalat park, the gardens have also been embellished with kitschy topiary. To amuse the kids (or the couples), there are horse-drawn carriage rides.

Lam Dong Museum MUSEUM

(4 Đ Hung Vuong; admission 10,000d; ⊙7.30-11.30am & 1.30-4.30pm Mon-Sat) Housed in a modern pink building, this hillside museum displays ancient artefacts and pottery, as well as costumes and musical instruments of local ethnic minorities. There are informative exhibits about Alexandre Yersin and the history of Dalat.

Groovy Gecko Adventure Tours TOURS

(☎383 6521; www.groovygeckotours.net; 65 Đ Truong Cong Dinh) Experienced agency offering canyoning, hiking and mountain-biking trips.

Dalat

Phat Tire Ventures TOURS
(☎382 9422; www.ptv-vietnam.com; 109 Đ Nguyen Van Troi) Reputable operator offering adventure sports including trekking (from US$26), kayaking (from US$37). Bike trips include two-day rides to Mui Ne (US$169).

Sleeping

TOP CHOICE **Dreams Hotel** HOTEL $
(☎383 3748; dreams@hcm.vnn.vn; 151 Đ Phan Dinh Phung; r US$20-25; @) Quite simply the friendliest and most comfortable place to stay in Dalat. The buffet breakfast spread is legendary and there's no hassling over tours. Dreams includes a sauna, steam room and hot tub, free for guests from 4pm to 7pm. There's a second branch at 164B offering more of the same.

TOP CHOICE **Dalat du Parc** COLONIAL HOTEL $$
(☎382 5777; www.hotelduparc.vn; 7 Đ Tran Phu; r US$55-85, ste US$105; @) A class apart for those seeking the Dalat of old, this respectfully refurbished 1932 building offers colonial-era class at enticing prices. The old lobby lift sets the tone and rooms here include wooden furnishings, historic photos and modern touches such as flat-screen TVs.

Thi Thao Hotel HOTEL $$
(Gardenia Hotel; ☎383 3333; www.thithaohotel.com; 29 Đ Phan Boi Chau; r from US$25; @) Offers the best-value places in town; rooms are new and spacious with superb bathrooms and a flat-screen TV. All very tasteful.

Ana Mandara Villas Dalat BOUTIQUE HOTEL $$$
(☎355 5888; www.anamandararesort.com; Đ Le Lai; r US$142-259, ste US$372-435; @) A truly memorable experience, Ana Mandara consists of 70 rooms with period furnishings spread across 17 lovingly restored French colonial-era villas.

Hotel Chau Au – Europa HOTEL $
(☎382 2870; europa@hcm.vnn.vn; 76 Đ Nguyen Chi Thanh; r US$10-20; @) A likeable, homely hotel run by a delightful owner. Rooms at the front with balconies have views over Dalat.

Trung Cang Hotel HOTEL $
(☎382 2663; www.thesinhtourist.vn; 4A Đ Bui Thi Xuan; r US$15-25; @) Smart Sinh establishment with tastefully decorated rooms, including local silks, and good tour and transport information.

Le Phuong Hotel HOTEL $
(☎382 3743; lephuonghotel@gmail.com; 80 Đ Nguyen Chi Thanh; r 250,000-330,000d; @) A new family-run hotel on a busy accommodation strip with large rooms, oversized beds and tasteful bathrooms.

Empress Hotel HOTEL $$
(☎383 3888; www.empresshotelvn.com; 5 Đ Nguyen Thai Hoc; r from US$60; @) This is an intimate, atmospheric place with a prime lakeside location and 20 spacious, tasteful rooms.

Dalat Palace COLONIAL HOTEL $$$
(☎382 5444; www.dalatpalace.vn; 12 Đ Tran Phu; s US$246-306, d US$260-320, ste US$446-510; @) The grande dame of Dalat hotels (1922) has unimpeded views of Xuan Huong

Lake and offers the *magnifique* opulence of French colonial life.

Hoan Hy Hotel HOTEL $
(☎351 1288; hoanhyhotel@yahoo.com; 16 Đ 3 Thang; r US$15;) New hotel above a bakery where the rooms are serious value for money and well equipped.

Thien An Hotel HOTEL $
(☎352 0607; thienanhotel@vnn.vn; 272A Đ Phan Dinh Phung; r US$18-25;) Spacious rooms, glorious breakfasts and warm hospitality. It's a little far from the centre, but free bicycles are provided.

Ngoc Lan Hotel BOUTIQUE HOTEL $$
(☎382 2136; www.ngoclanhotel.vn; 42 Đ Nguyen Chi Thanh; r from US$65;) Boutique-ish hotel with clean white lines, stylish purple accents and a dash of colonial character for good measure.

Eating

There are vegetarian food stalls and cheap eats in the market area.

Vietnamese

Art Cafe VIETNAMESE $$
(70 Đ Truong Cong Dinh; dishes 25,000-75,000d;) Owned by an artist whose work adorns the walls, this elegant eatery has intimate tables and soft lighting. The menu features Vietnamese dishes with a twist, including plenty of vegetarian options. Linger over a glass of wine.

Da Quy VIETNAMESE $
(Wild Sunflower; 49 Đ Truong Cong Dinh; dishes 25,000-65,000d) With a sophisticated ambience but unsophisticated prices, this place earns consistently good reviews from travellers of all taste buds. Try the traditional claypot dishes with fish or shrimp.

Nam Phan GOURMET VIETNAMESE $$$
(☎381 3816; 7 Đ Tran Hung Dao; dishes 55,000-1,500,000d) This stunning Vietnamese restaurant is set in a beautifully restored colonial-era mansion with manicured gardens and sweeping views. Set dinners run from US$20 to US$90 and include superb seafood and artfully presented classics.

An Lac VEGETARIAN $
(71 Đ Phan Dinh Phung; meals from 10,000d;) There's an English menu here, and options range from noodle soups to *banh bao* or steamed rice-flour dumplings stuffed with a savoury filling.

Trong Dong VIETNAMESE $
(220 Đ Phan Dinh Phung; mains 25,000-80,000d) A friendly and unpretentious eatery designed in French bistro style, this place is popular for its rabbit and eel dishes.

International

V Cafe INTERNATIONAL $
(1/1 Đ Bui Thi Xuan; dishes 25,000-79,000d) A travellers' favourite, this friendly restaurant serves a mix of Asian and Western mains, most with sides of mash and fresh vegetables. Owned by an American muso, there's a live duo performing here most nights.

Chocolate Cafe INTERNATIONAL $
(40A Đ Truong Cong Dinh; dishes 20,000-70,000d) In the busy backpacker strip, this place has affordable pizzas and pastas and well-presented Vietnamese dishes. The decor is stylish and the coffee includes espresso-based options.

Cafe de la Poste FRENCH $$$
(☎382 5777; 7 Đ Tran Phu; dishes US$6-58) Set in a gorgeous old French-era building, this stylish restaurant's menu is ambitious indeed. Salads, sandwiches, pastas and fresh bakery products represent the best value.

Thanh Thuy Blue Water Restaurant INTERNATIONAL $
(2 Đ Nguyen Thai Hoc; dishes 30,000-105,000d) Boasts an unbeatable location right on the lake. Feast from an eclectic menu of Cantonese, Vietnamese and Western dishes.

Le Rabelais FRENCH $$$
(☎382 5444; 12 Đ Tran Phu; mains US$10-47) For gourmet French cuisine, the Dalat Palace's signature restaurant and its refined dining room really impresses. Feeling flush? Try the seven-course degustation menu at...US$85.

Drinking

Hangout DIVE BAR
(71 Đ Truong Cong Dinh) Acts as a HQ for some of Dalat's Easy Riders, as well as visiting backpackers, with cheap beers and a pool table.

Saigon Nite DIVE BAR
(11A Đ Hai Ba Trung) Run-down yet friendly bar where people come for the beer and pool, not for the decor.

Shopping

Hoa Binh Square and the **market** building adjacent to it are the places to purchase ethnic handicrafts including Lat rush baskets that roll up when empty. Coffee is another smart purchase.

Information

Dalat has numerous ATMs and internet cafes. Wi-fi is available in most hotels and cafes.

Dalat Travel Service (☎382 2125; dalattravelservice@vnn.vn; 7 Đ 3 Thang 2) Tours and vehicle rentals.

Lam Dong Hospital (☎382 1369; 4 Đ Pham Ngoc Thach)

Main post office (14 Đ Tran Phu)

The Sinh Tourist (☎382 2663; www.thesinhtourist.vn; 4A Đ Bui Thi Xuan) Tours and open-tour bus bookings.

Vietcombank (☎351 0586; 6 Đ Nguyen Thi Minh Khai) Exchanges cash and travellers cheques, and has an ATM.

Getting There & Around

Vietnam Airlines (☎383 3499; www.vietnamairlines.com; 2 Đ Ho Tung Mau) has daily services to HCMC (680,000d), Danang (980,000d) and Hanoi (1,700,000d). Lien Khuong Airport is 30km south of the city. Vietnam Airlines operates a shuttle bus (35,000d, 30 minutes) timed around flights. Taxis cost about US$12.

Long-distance buses leave from the **station** (Đ 3 Thang 2) about 1km south of the city centre. Services are available to most of the country, including HCMC (110,000d to 160,000d, six to seven hours), Nha Trang (70,000d to 100,000d, new road four hours, old road seven hours) and Buon Ma Thuot (from 85,000d, four hours). Open-tour minibuses to Saigon, Mui Ne and Nha Trang can be booked at travellers' cafes.

Car rental with a driver starts from about US$40 a day. Full-day tours with local motorbike guides (from US$10) are a great way to see the area, as many of the sights lie outside Dalat's centre. Many hotels offer bicycle and motorbike hire. For a taxi call **Mai Linh** (☎352 1111).

Around Dalat

Dalat's **waterfalls** are obviously at their gushing best in the wet season but still flow during the dry. We advise skipping Prenn Falls, which are overdeveloped and include an appalling collection of caged animals, as well as the commercial kitsch-fest of Cam Ly Falls.

Datanla Falls (admission 5000d) are 7km southeast of Dalat off Hwy 20. It's a nice walk through the rainforest and a steep hike downhill to the falls. You can also take a **bobsled ride** (40,000d return) down a winding elevated track. On weekends expect crowds and loud music.

An uneven and sometimes hazardous path heads down to **Elephant Falls** (admission free), which are best seen from below. The falls are situated near Nam Ban village, 30km west of Dalat.

The largest waterfall in the Dalat area, **Pongour Falls** (admission 6000d) are about 55km in the direction of HCMC. The stepped falls are beautiful at any time but most spectacular during the rainy season when they form a full semicircle.

Dambri Falls (admission 10,000d), 75km from Dalat, are the tallest falls (90m) in the area – walking down to feel the spray from the bottom is divine on a hot day. You can trek your way down and take the cable car back up.

You'll need your own wheels to access these waterfalls.

EASY DOES IT

For many travellers, the highlight of their trip to the Central Highlands is an off-the-beaten-track motorcycle tour with an Easy Rider. The flip side to the popularity of the Easy Riders is that now everyone claims to be one – some have started wearing official jackets, others are now disdainful of the term. In central Dalat, you can't walk down the street without being invited (sometimes harassed) for a tour.

Hiring a rider (official or not) can be a great way to explore the countryside. It's highly recommended that you test-drive a rider first before committing to a longer trip. Most guides speak great English and/or French. The going rate starts at US$20 for a day tour, or US$50 per day for an extended trip.

Rider-guides can be found in hotels and cafes in Dalat. Read testimonials from past clients. Check the bike over. Then discuss the route in detail – for scenery, the new coastal highways that link Dalat with Mui Ne and Nha Trang, plus the old road to the coast via Phan Rang, are wonderful.

CAT TIEN NATIONAL PARK

One of the outstanding natural spaces in Vietnam, Unesco-listed **Cat Tien National Park** (☎063-366 9228; www.cattiennationalpark.vn; adult/child 50,000/20,000d; ⌚7am-10pm) comprises an amazingly biodiverse area of lowland tropical rainforest. The hiking, mountain biking and birdwatching are outstanding.

Fauna in the park includes 326 bird species, 100 mammals (including elephants), 79 reptiles plus an incredible array of insects, including 400 or so species of butterfly. Tiny numbers (as few as eight) of Javan rhinoceros still exist here, and leopards are also believed to be present. Rare birds in the park include the orange-necked partridge and Siamese fireback. There's also a healthy population of monkeys. Leeches are less-desirable natives. Visitors rarely see any of the larger mammals resident in the park, so don't come expecting to encounter tigers and elephants.

Always call ahead for reservations as the park can accommodate only a limited number of visitors.

Sight & Activities

Cat Tien National Park can be explored on foot, by mountain bike, by 4WD and also by boat along the Dong Nai River. There are many well-established hiking trails in the park, though you'll need a **guide** (from 250,000d).

Trips to the **Crocodile Swamp** (Bau Sau; entry 100,000d, guide fee 300,000d, boat trip 300,000d), taking in a three-hour jungle trek, are popular. **Night safaris** (300,000d) are another option, although deer are the only animals usually seen. Wherever you decide to go, be sure to book a guide in advance and take plenty of insect repellent.

Dao Tien Endangered Primate Species Centre (www.go-east.org; entry adult/child incl boat ride 150,000/50,000d; ⌚8am & 2pm) is located on an island in the Dong Nai River. Its a rehabilitation centre hosting gibbons, langurs and loris that have been confiscated as pets or from traffickers; the eventual goal is to release the primates back into the wild.

Wild Gibbon Trek (ecotourism@cattiennationalpark.vn; US$60, maximum four people) runs daily and involves a 4am start to get out to the gibbons in time for their dawn chorus. Relax in a hammock as the forest slowly comes alive with their calls before watching the family go about their everyday lives. The trip finishes off with a fully-guided tour of the primate species centre. Book ahead.

Sleeping & Eating

Avoid weekends and holidays if possible, as this is when the Vietnamese descend in numbers.

Forest Floor Lodge (☎063-166 9890; www.forestfloorlodge.com; from US$100; ❄@) is a fine new privately-run ecolodge that has several lovely safari tents overlooking the Dong Nai River and a range of rooms set in reclaimed traditional wooden houses. There's a great **restaurant** (meals from 75,000d). It's located across from the primate centre, so it is often possible to see and hear gibbons.

Cat Tien National Park (☎063-366 9228; small tent/big tent 200,000/300,000d, bungalow from 500,000d; ❄) offers basic bungalow rooms and tented accommodation close to the park headquarters. There are two small **restaurants** (meals 35,000-200,000d) here.

Getting There & Away

Cat Tien is 125km north of HCMC and 175km south of Dalat. Turn off Hwy 20 at Tan Phu and it's another 25km up a paved access road to the entrance.

Buses between Dalat and HCMC pass the access road; ask for Vuon Quoc Gia Cat Tien. Waiting motorbikes (around 150,000d) will then take you to the park entrance.

We've received mixed reviews about budget tours to Cat Tien. For a reputable customised birding, bike or hiking tour, contact Sinhbalo Adventures (p148).

Bicycles are available for hire in the park, from 20,000d per day.

OFF THE BEATEN TRACK IN THE CENTRAL HIGHLANDS

It's easy to get off the beaten track in this scenic part of the country. Only Dalat makes it onto most tourists' radars, meaning that the rest of the region still offers adventure in abundance. This is a great part of the country to see from the back of a motorbike.

The upgrading of the historic **Ho Chi Minh Trail** has made it easier than ever to visit out-of-the-way places such as **Kon Tum**, one of the friendliest cities in Vietnam. So far Kon Tum remains largely unspoiled and the authorities are blessedly invisible. It remains to be seen whether increased tourism will leave these delightful backwaters unchanged.

Buon Ma Thuot is the major city in the region, but the biggest buzz you'll get is from the coffee beans. Nearby **Yok Don National Park** (☎050-378 3049; www.yokdonnationalpark.vn) is home to 38 endangered mammal species, including plenty of elephants and a handful of tigers. Impressive waterfalls in this area include **Gia Long** and **Dray Nur Falls** along the Krong Ana River.

Be sure to also explore **Cat Tien National Park** (p135) southwest of Dalat.

Lang Bian Mountain NATURE RESERVE
(Nui Lam Vien; admission 10,000d) With five volcanic peaks ranging in altitude from 2100m to 2400m, Lang Bian Mountain, 13km north of Dalat, makes a scenic trek (three to four hours from Lat Village). You might spot some semi-wild horses grazing on the side of the mountain, where rhinoceros and tigers dwelt only half a century ago. Views from the top are tremendous.

The nine hill-tribe hamlets of **Lat Village** are about 12km northwest of Dalat at the base of Lang Bian Mountain.

HO CHI MINH CITY (SAIGON)

☎08 / POP 7.2 MILLION

Ho Chi Minh City (HCMC) is a metropolis on the move and we are not just talking about the city's motorbikes. Yes, Saigon is Vietnam at its most dizzying, a high-octane city of commerce and culture that has driven the whole country forward with its limitless energy and booming economy.

Wander through alleys to ancient pagodas or teeming markets, past ramshackle wooden shops selling silk and spices, before fast-forwarding into the future beneath skyscrapers and mammoth malls. The ghosts of the past live on in the churches, temples, former GI hotels and government buildings that one generation ago witnessed a city in turmoil.

Whether you want to relive the colonial experience in sumptuous French-era hotels or seek out the cheapest guesthouse, classiest restaurants or street food, designer boutiques or the scrum of the markets, Saigon has it all. Put simply, there's nowhere else quite like it.

Sights

Museums & Historic Buildings

War Remnants Museum MUSEUM
(Map p137; Bao Tang Chung Tich Chien Tranh; 28 Đ Vo Van Tan; admission 15,000d; ⊙7.30am-noon & 1.30-5pm) Documenting the atrocities of war, the War Remnants Museum is unique, brutal and an essential stop. On display are retired artillery pieces, a model of the tiger cages used to house VC prisoners, and a heartbreaking array of photographs of the victims of war – those who suffered torture as well as those who were born with birth defects caused by the use of defoliants. The exhibits are labelled in Vietnamese, English and Chinese, and propagandist, but still very powerful in tone. Many of the atrocities documented here are well publicised but rarely do Westerners have the opportunity to hear the victims of US military action tell their own stories.

Upstairs, look out for the **Requiem Exhibition**. Compiled by legendary war photographer Tim Page, this striking collection documents the work of photographers killed during the course of the conflict, on both sides, and includes works by Larry Burrows and Robert Capa.

Reunification Palace HISTORIC BUILDING
(Map p137; Dinh Thong Nhat; Đ Nam Ky Khoi Nghia; adult/child 30,000/3000d; ⊙7.30-11am & 1-4pm) Built in 1966 to serve as South Vietnam's Presidential Palace, today this landmark is known as the Reunification Palace. It was designed by Paris-trained Vietnamese architect Ngo Viet Thu, and is an outstanding

example of 1960s architecture, with an airy and open atmosphere.

The first communist tanks in Saigon crashed through the gates of this building on the morning of 30 April 1975 when Saigon surrendered to the North. The building is a time warp, having been left just as it looked on that momentous day.

Highlights include the president's living quarters and its shagadelic card-playing room, complete with groovy three-legged chairs set around a flared-legged table. There's also a cinema and a rooftop nightclub, complete with helipad: James Bond/Austin Powers – eat your heart out.

In the basement are a telecom centre, war room and network of tunnels. An information film documents the palace's history, after which the national anthem is played. At the end you are expected to stand up – it would be rude not to.

English- and French-speaking guides are available.

HCMC Museum MUSEUM

(Map p144; www.hcmc-museum.edu.vn; 65 Đ Ly Tu Trong; admission 15,000d; ⏲8am-4pm) A grand, neoclassical structure built in 1885, HCMC's city museum is a singularly beautiful and impressive building.

It tells the story of the city through archaeological artefacts, ceramics, old city maps and curios. The struggle for independence is extensively covered.

Deep beneath the building is a network of reinforced concrete bunkers and fortified corridors once used by President Diem but not open to the public because most of the tunnels are flooded.

In the gardens around the museum are various items of military hardware, including the American-built F-5E jet used by a renegade South Vietnamese pilot to bomb the Presidential Palace (now Reunification Palace) on 8 April 1975.

History Museum MUSEUM

(Map p138; Bao Tang Lich Su; Đ Nguyen Binh Khiem; admission 15,000d; ⏲8-11am & 1.30-4.30pm Tue-Sun) The impressive collection of HCMC's History Museum is housed in a stunning Sino-French building constructed in 1929 by the Société des Études Indochinoises. It displays artefacts from almost 4000 years of human activity in what is now Vietnam, including Dong Son, Funan, Cham and Khmer relics.

The museum is located by the main gate to the city's botanic gardens and zoo, which animal lovers will find thoroughly depressing.

Fine Arts Museum ART GALLERY

(Bao Tang My Thuat; www.baotangmythuattphcm.vn; 97A Đ P Duc Chinh; admission 10,000d; ⏲9am-5pm Tue-Sun) The city's Fine Arts Museum covers art from the earliest civilisations in Vietnam – Funan and Cham – to contemporary work. There's also lacquer- and enamelware and oil paintings by Vietnamese and foreign artists.

Pagodas, Temples & Churches

CENTRAL HO CHI MINH CITY

Jade Emperor Pagoda PAGODA

(Map p138; Phuoc Hai Tu or Chua Ngoc Hoang; 73 Đ Mai Thi Luu) Built in 1909 by the Cantonese (Quang Dong) Congregation, this is a real gem among Chinese temples. It's filled with statues of phantasmal divinities and grotesque heroes, and the pungent smoke of burning joss sticks fills the air. The roof is covered with elaborate tilework, while the statues, which represent characters from both the Buddhist and Taoist traditions, are made of reinforced papier mâché. To get to the pagoda, go to 20 Đ Dien Bien Phu and walk half a block in a northwest direction.

Notre Dame Cathedral CHURCH

(Map p144; Đ Han Thuyen; ⏲Mass 9.30am Sun) Built between 1877 and 1883, Notre Dame stands regally in the heart of the government quarter looking like it's been beamed

DON'T MISS

SKYHIGH SAIGON

Opened in late 2010, the magnificent Carlos Zapata–designed **Bitexco Financial Tower** (Map p144; 36 Đ Ho Tung Mao; admission 200,000d; ⏲1-9pm Mon-Fri, 10am-10pm Sat & Sun) peaks at 262m and dwarfs all around it. It's meant to be shaped like a lotus bulb, but we can't help thinking it looks a little like a CD rack with tambourine shoved into it. That tambourine is actually the **Saigon Skydeck**, on the 48th floor. The views are, of course, extraordinary (on a clear day).

Ho Chi Minh City

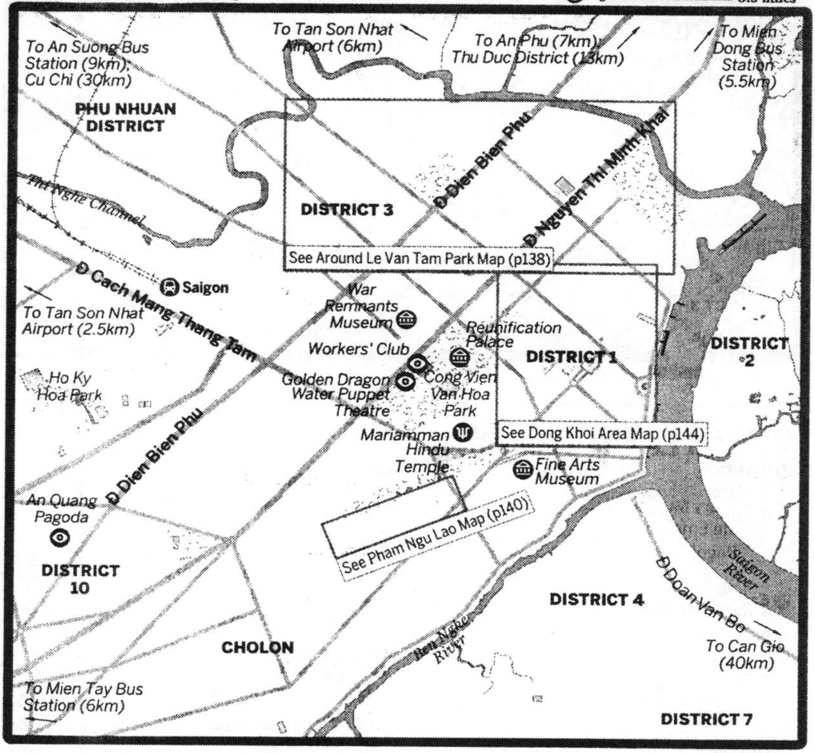

in directly from Normandy. Romanesque arches and twin 40m-high towers create an imposing facade but the church itself is relatively unadorned.

Mariamman Hindu Temple TEMPLE
(Map p137; Chua Ba Mariamman; 45 Đ Truong Dinh; ⏲7.30am-7.30pm) A splash of southern India's colour in Saigon, this temple was built at the end of the 19th century and is dedicated to the Hindu goddess Mariamman. It is also considered sacred by many ethnic Vietnamese and Chinese. After reunification, the government turned part of it into a factory for joss sticks.

Saigon Central Mosque MOSQUE
(Map p144; 66 Đ Dong Du) Constructed by South Indian Muslims in 1935, this is an immaculately clean and well-kept island of calm in the middle of bustling central Saigon. Remove your shoes before entering. Clustered around this mosque are several Malaysian and Indian restaurants serving halal food.

CHOLON

The following pagodas are in the Cholon district, about a kilometre southwest of the Pham Ngu Lao area.

Thien Hau Pagoda PAGODA
(Ba Mieu or Pho Mieu; 710 Đ Nguyen Trai) Cholon has a wealth of wonderful Chinese temples, including this one dedicated to Thien Hau, the Chinese goddess of the sea. As she protects maritime travellers, you might stop by to ask for a blessing for your Mekong Delta trip. Though there are guardians to each side of the entrance, it is said that the real protectors of the pagoda are the two land turtles that live here.

Phuoc An Hoi Quan Pagoda PAGODA
(184 Đ Hung Vuong) Stands as one of the most beautifully ornamented constructions in the

Around Le Van Tam Park

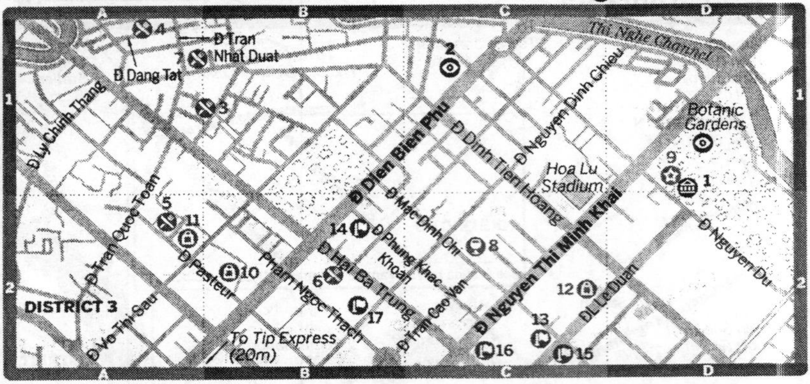

Around Le Van Tam Park

Sights
- 1 History Museum D1
- 2 Jade Emperor Pagoda C1

Eating
- 3 Banh Xeo 46A B1
- 4 Cuc Gach Quan A1
- 5 Pho Hoa A2
- 6 Tib B2
- 7 Tib Vegetarian A1

Drinking
- 8 Hoa Vien C2

Entertainment
- 9 Saigon Water Puppet Theatre D1

Shopping
- 10 Adidas Puma Factory Shop B2
- 11 Cham Khanh A2
- 12 Thu Quan Sinh Vien C2

Information
- 13 American Consulate C2
- 14 Cambodian Consulate B2
- 15 Dutch Consulate C2
- 16 French Consulate C2
- 17 German Consulate B2

city. Of special interest are the many small porcelain figures, the elaborate brass ritual objects and the fine woodcarvings on the altars, walls and hanging lanterns. This pagoda was built in 1902 by the Fujian Chinese congregation.

Quan Am Pagoda PAGODA
(12 Đ Lao Tu) . The roof of this 1816 pagoda is decorated with fantastic scenes, rendered in ceramic, from traditional Chinese plays and stories. The front doors of the pagoda are decorated with very old gold-and-lacquer panels.

GREATER HO CHI MINH CITY

Beautiful **Giac Lam Pagoda** (118 Đ Lac Long Quan; Tan Binh District; ⏲6am-noon & 2-8.30pm) dates from 1744 and is believed to be the city's oldest. Like many Vietnamese Buddhist pagodas it also incorporates aspects of Taoism and Confucianism. The architecture hasn't changed since 1900, and the compound is a meditative place to explore. It's in the west of the city, 3km north of Cholon.

Activities

Massage

HCMC offers some truly fantastic settings for pampering – the perfect antidote to a frenetic day dodging motorbikes. While many midrange and upmarket hotels offer massage service, some are more legitimate than others.

L'Apothiquaire (Map p144; ☎3932 5181; www.lapothiquaire.com; 64A Đ Truong Dinh; 1hr massage from 740,000d; ▣) Long considered the city's most elegant spa, it is housed in a pretty white mansion and offers body wraps, massages, facials, foot treatments and herbal baths.

Vietnamese Traditional Massage Institute (Map p140; ☎3839 6697; 185 Đ Cong Quynh; per hr 50,000-60,000d) It's not the classiest act in town, but it does offer inexpensive, no-nonsense massages performed by well-trained blind masseurs.

River Cruises

Bach Dang jetty (Map p144) is the place to arrange a boat to tour the Saigon River. Small boats cost around US$10 per hour, larger boats US$15 to US$30.

Bonsai River Cruise CRUISE
(☎3910 5095; www.bonsaicruise.com.vn; tickets US$36) Dinner cruises featuring live music and a buffet dinner.

Tau Sai Gon CRUISE
(☎3823 0393; www.tausaigon.com) Floating restaurant that offers an Asian or European dinner menu and a Sunday buffet lunch (150,000d).

Swimming Pools & Water Parks

Most of HCMC's luxury hotels have swimming pools with gyms attached. Non-guests can indulge for a fee of US$12 to US$30 per day.

Dam Sen Water Park WATER PARK
(☎3858 8418; www.damsenwaterpark.com.vn; 3 Đ Hoa Binh, District 11; adult/child 50,000/80,000d; ⏲9am-6pm) Water slides, rivers with rapids (or slow currents) and rope swings. It's 3km northwest of Cholon.

Workers' Club SWIMMING POOL
(55B Đ Nguyen Thi Minh Khai, District 3; admission 14,000d) The swimming pool of the old Cercle Sportif still has its colonnades and some art deco charm.

Cooking Courses

Saigon Cooking Class COOKING
(Map p144; ☎3825 8485; www.saigoncookingclass.com; 74/7 Hai Ba Trung, District 1; class US$39; ⏲10am & 2pm Tue-Sun) Prepare three mains and one dessert with the chefs from Hoa Tuc. A market visit is optional.

Vietnam Cookery Centre COOKING
(☎3512 7246; www.vietnamcookery.com; 362/8 Đ Ung Van Khiem, Binh Thanh District) Introductory classes, market visits and 'VIP premium' classes.

Festivals & Events

Saigon Cyclo Race CHARITY RACE
(mid-March) Professional and amateur *cyclo* drivers find out who's fastest; money raised is donated to local charities.

Sleeping

Budget travellers often head straight to the Pham Ngu Lao area. Those seeking upscale digs go to Dong Khoi, home to the city's best hotels, restaurants and bars.

PHAM NGU LAO

Saigon's backpacker ghetto has more than 100 places to stay, most between US$10 and US$35. There are also some excellent midrange deals here, with most minihotels priced at US$25 to US$55.

TOP CHOICE **Giang & Son** GUESTHOUSE $
(Map p140; ☎3837 7548; www.giangson.netfirms.com; 283/14 Đ Pham Ngu Lao; r US$16-25; ❄@🛜) A clean, comfortable and friendly place on a surprisingly quiet alley. Tall and thin, with three rooms on each floor, the only downer here is that there's no lift. It's worth upgrading to a US$20 room for a window.

Hong Han Hotel GUESTHOUSE $
(Map p140; ☎3836 1927; www.honghan.netfirms.com; 238 Đ Bui Vien; r incl breakfast US$20-25; ❄@🛜) Another guesthouse in the tall and skinny mode (seven floors and no lift), Hong Han offers style and comfort. The front rooms have thrilling views to the Bitexco Tower but the smaller rear rooms are quieter and cheaper.

Bich Duyen Hotel GUESTHOUSE $
(Map p140; ☎3837 4588; bichduyenhotel@yahoo.com; 283/4 Đ Pham Ngu Lao; r US$17-25; ❄@🛜) This welcoming place on a quiet lane has excellent rooms – pay more for the luxury of a window. The showers are excellent.

Diep Anh GUESTHOUSE $
(Map p140; ☎3836 7920; dieptheanh@hcm.vnn.vn; 241/31 Đ Pham Ngu Lao; r US$20; ❄@🛜) A step above most guesthouses, figuratively and literally (there are endless stairs), Diep Anh's tall and narrow shape makes for light and airy upper rooms. The gracious staff ensure they're kept in good nick.

An An Hotel HOTEL $$
(Map p140; ☎3837 8087; www.anan.vn; 40 Đ Bui Vien; r US$40-50; ❄@🛜) Unassuming, unpretentious and affable, An An is a smart minihotel with well-proportioned, businesslike rooms that come with deposit boxes, in-room computers and bathtubs.

Pham Ngu Lao

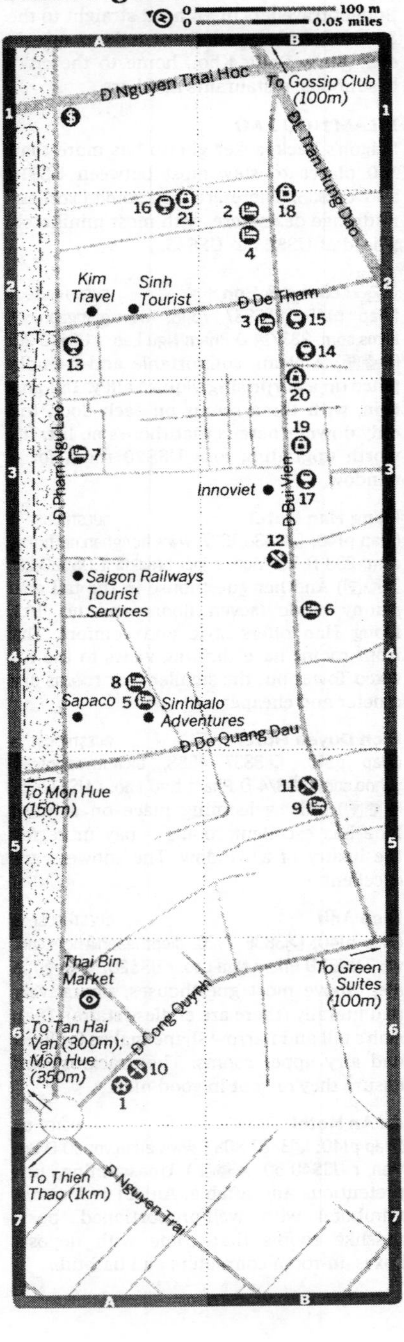

Pham Ngu Lao

Activities, Courses & Tours

1	Vietnamese Traditional Massage Institute	A6

Sleeping

2	An An Hotel	B2
3	Beautiful Saigon	B2
4	Beautiful Saigon 2	B2
5	Bich Duyen Hotel	A4
6	Diep Anh	B4
7	Elios Hotel	A3
8	Giang & Son	A4
9	Hong Han Hotel	B5

Eating

10	Dinh Y	A6
11	Mumtaz	B5
12	Sozo	B3

Drinking

13	Allez Boo Bar	A2
14	Bobby Brewers	B2
15	Go2	B2
16	Le Pub	A2
17	Spotted Cow	B3

Shopping

18	Blue Dragon	B2
19	Hanoi Gallery	B3
20	Mekong Creations	B2
21	SahaBook	A2

Elios Hotel HOTEL $$
(Map p140; ☎3838 5584; www.elioshotel.vn; 233 Đ Pham Ngu Lao; s US$48-102, d US$53-107; ❄@📶) Boasts a very swish lobby and clean and modern rooms, with safes and writing desks. Enjoy your free breakfast on the rooftop restaurant.

Beautiful Saigon 2 HOTEL $$
(Map p140; ☎3920 8929; www.beautifulsaigon2hotel.com; 40/19 Đ Bui Vien; s US$26-37, d US$29-42; ❄@📶) This new minihotel lurks down a back lane and its deluxe rooms have balconies.

Beautiful Saigon HOTEL $$
(Map p140; ☎3836 4852; www.beautifulsaigonhotel.com; 62 Đ Bui Vien; s US$26-45, d US$29-55; ❄@📶) The original Beautiful Saigon has tidy rooms; the cheaper ones are small and windowless.

DONG KHOI AREA

The Dong Khoi area is home to most of HCMC's top-notch hotels but also some excellent midrange options.

TOP CHOICE Park Hyatt Saigon HOTEL $$$
(Map p144; ☎3824 1234; www.saigon.park.hyatt.com; 2 Lam Son Sq; r around US$350;) Setting the standard as the smartest hotel in Saigon, the Park Hyatt has a prime location opposite the Opera House. This neoclassical structure is as easy on the eye as its lavishly appointed rooms. There's an inviting pool, the acclaimed Xuan Spa, and a highly regarded (yet affordable) Italian restaurant, Opera.

Intercontinental Asiana Saigon HOTEL $$$
(Map p144; ☎3520 9999; www.intercontinental.com; cnr ĐL Hai Ba Trung & ĐL Le Duan; r from US$189;) Modern and tasteful without falling into generic blandness, the Intercontintental's rooms have separate shower cubicles and free-standing baths, and many have wonderful views. A neighbouring tower of apartment-style residences caters to longer stayers.

Caravelle Hotel HOTEL $$$
(Map p144; ☎3823 4999; www.caravellehotel.com; 19 Lam Son Sq; r from US$218;) One of the first luxury hotels to reopen its doors in post-war Saigon, the Caravelle has quietly elegant, well-equipped rooms spread over 16 new floors and the historic 'signature' wing. The rooftop bar is a spectacular spot for a cocktail.

Spring Hotel HOTEL $$
(Map p144; ☎3829 7362; www.springhotelvietnam.com; 44-46 Đ Le Thanh Ton; s US$35-55, d US$40-60, ste US$72-97;) An old favourite, this welcoming hotel is handy to dozens of restaurants and bars on the popular Le Thanh Ton and Hai Ba Trung strips. The rooms are a little dated but bas-reliefs and moulded cornices give it a touch of class.

Northern Hotel HOTEL $$$
(Map p144; ☎3825 1751; www.northernhotel.com.vn; 11A Đ Thi Sach; s US$70-110, US$80-120;) Asian glam at an affordable price, the Northern's rooms are seriously smart for this kind of money. The bathrooms are a cut above the average, plus there's a rooftop bar and gym.

King Star Hotel HOTEL $$
(Map p144; ☎3822 6424; www.kingstarhotel.com; 8A ĐL Thai Van Lung; r US$40-70;) Verging on boutique business, all the contemporary rooms have flat-screen TVs and snazzy showers.

Riverside Hotel HOTEL $$
(Map p144; ☎3822 4038; www.riversidehotelsg.com; 18 Đ Ton Duc Thang; s US$59-150, d US$69-169;) Dating all the way back to the 1920s, the Riverside Hotel still delivers excellent value for money given its prime location.

OTHER NEIGHBOURHOODS

TOP CHOICE Ma Maison Boutique Hotel HOTEL $$
(☎3846 0263; www.mamaison.vn; 656/52 Cach Mang Thang Tam, District 3; s US$65-90, d US$75-95;) Down a peaceful lane halfway between the airport and the city centre and, decor-wise, partly in the French countryside. Wooden shutters soften the exterior of the modern, medium-rise block, while in the rooms, painted French provincial-style furniture and first-rate bathrooms add a touch of panache.

Thien Thao HOTEL $$
(☎3929 1440; www.thienthaohotel.com; 89 Đ Cao Thang, District 3; r US$32-60;) All you'd want from a midrange hotel, Thien Thao has affable staff and clean, comfortable, smallish rooms. Deluxe rooms are quieter but otherwise very similar to standard. From the Pham Ngu Lao area, take Đ Bui Thi Xuan, which becomes Đ Cao Thang.

Eating

Ho Chi Minh City is the reigning culinary king of Vietnam. Restaurants here range from dirt-cheap sidewalk stalls to atmospheric villas, each serving its own unique interpretation of Vietnam sustenance. Besides brilliant native fare, Saigon offers world cuisine, with Indian, Japanese, Thai, French, Spanish, Korean and Argentinian all on offer.

Good foodie neighbourhoods include the Dong Khoi area, with a high density of top-quality restaurants, as well as nearby District 3. Pham Ngu Lao's eateries are generally less memorable.

Banh mi – sandwiches with a French look and a very Vietnamese taste – are sold by street vendors. They're fresh baguettes which are stuffed with something resembling pâté (don't ask), pickled gherkins and various other fillings.

DONG KHOI AREA

TOP CHOICE Nha Hang Ngon VIETNAMESE $
(Map p144; ☎3827 7131; 160 Đ Pasteur; mains 35,000-205,000d; ⏰7am-10pm; ❄📶) This is one of the most popular places in town, offering street food in stylish surroundings. Set in a leafy garden ringed by food stalls, each cook serves up a specialised traditional dish, ensuring an authentic taste. Follow your nose and browse the stalls.

TOP CHOICE Temple Club VIETNAMESE $
(Map p144; ☎3829 9244; 29 Đ Ton That Thiep; mains 59,000-98,000d; 🍷📶❄) A classy establishment in a beautiful colonial-era villa and there's a massive selection of delectable Vietnamese dishes on offer, including a range of vegetarian specialities. The spirited cocktails are a good way to prepare for the experience.

Huong Lai VIETNAMESE $
(Map p144; 38 Đ Ly Tu Trong; mains 40,000-120,000d) Set in the airy loft of an old French-era shophouse, this is dining with a difference. All of the staff are from disadvantaged families or are former street children. A must for beautifully presented, traditional Vietnamese food.

Xu GOURMET VIETNAMESE $$
(Map p144; ☎3824 8468; www.xusaigon.com; 1st fl, 75 Đ Hai Ba Trung; lunch 50,000-165,000d, dinner 175,000-340,000d; ⏰11am-midnight; 📶) Super-stylish restaurant-lounge renowned for Vietnamese-inspired fusion dishes. The name means 'coin' and it is expensive, but well worth it. Top service, a classy wine list and the happening lounge-bar round things off nicely. Try the tasting menu (850,000d).

Flow MODERN EUROPEAN $$
(Map p144; ☎3915 3691; www.flowsaigon.com; 88 Đ Ho Tung Mau; mains 130,000-365,000d; ⏰7.10am-midnight Mon-Fri, 10am-midnight Sat, 10am-3.30pm Sun; ❄📶) Going with the Flow has a lot to recommend it: rock-star-chic decor, wonderfully creative cuisine, an appealing terrace and occasional after-hours performances. One of Saigon's hippest new establishments.

Warda MIDDLE EASTERN $$
(Map p144; ☎3823 3822; 71/7 Đ Mac Thi Buoi; 140,000-258,000d; ⏰8am-midnight; ❄📶) Suitably located in a medina-like alley, head here for sensuous flavours covering the distance from Morocco to Persia, including tagines, kebabs and mezze. Round things off with a shisha.

El Gaucho ARGENTINEAN $$
(Map p144; ☎3825 1879; www.elgaucho.com.vn; 5 Đ Nguyen Sieu; 250,000-690,000d; ⏰4-11pm) Nirvana for the serious meat-lover, El Gaucho offers fall-apart lamb shanks, tender skewers and juicy steaks in a fine-dining environment. It even makes its own chorizo and *salchicha* (spicy sausage).

Hoa Tuc VIETNAMESE $$
(Map p144; ☎3825 1676; 74/7 ĐL Hai Ba Trung; mains 50,000-190,000d; ⏰10.30am-10.30pm; ❄📶) Excellent Vietnamese cuisine in the trendy courtyard of a former opium refinery. Signature dishes include mustard leaves rolled with crispy vegetables and shrimp. Pick up tricks at an in-house cooking class (p139).

Golden Elephant THAI $$
(Map p144; ☎3822 8544; 34 Đ Hai Ba Trung; mains 75,000-250,000d; ⏰11am-10pm; ❄) Steaming and sizzling plates of Thai favourites (along with a few Cambodian add-ons) and linen-dressed tables.

Augustin FRENCH $$
(Map p144; ☎3829 2941; 10 Đ Nguyen Thiep; mains 140,000-380,000d; ⏰Mon-Sat) Unassuming little bistro that serves delectable French food accompanied by wines from the old country.

DA KAO & AROUND

TOP CHOICE Cuc Gach Quan VIETNAMESE $
(Map p138; ☎3848 0144; http://en.cucgachquan.com; 10 Đ Dang Tat; mains 50,000-200,000d; ⏰9am-midnight) Cleverly renovated old villa with rustic-chic decor and delectable food that balances authentic flavours of the countryside with metropolitan presentation. Despite its tucked-away location in the northernmost reaches of District 1, this is no secret hideaway; book ahead.

TOP CHOICE Pho Hoa VIETNAMESE $
(Map p138; 260C Đ Pasteur; mains 45,000-50,000d; ⏰6am-midnight) A contender for the title of Saigon's best *pho* restaurant, this long-running establishment is more upmarket than most but is definitely the real deal – as evidenced by its popularity with regular Saigonese patrons.

Banh Xeo 46A VIETNAMESE $
(Map p138; 46A Đ Dinh Cong Trang; mains 25,000-50,000d) This renowned spot serves some of

the best *banh xeo* in town. These Vietnamese rice-flour pancakes stuffed with bean sprouts, prawns and pork (vegetarian versions available) are the stuff of legend.

Tib VIETNAMESE $$
(Map p138; www.tibrestaurant.com.vn); Hai Ba Trung (3829 7242; 187 Đ Hai Ba Trung; mains 60,000-240,000d;); Express (Map p138; 162 Đ Nguyen Dinh Chieu; mains 28,000-50,000;); Vegetarian (11 Đ Tran Nhat Duat; mains 30,000-40,000;) Justifiably famous atmospheric old house that showcases imperial Huế cuisine in a wonderful setting. Tib Express and Tib Vegetarian offer a cheaper, more relaxed take on the same.

REUNIFICATION PALACE & AROUND

TOP CHOICE **Lion City** SINGAPOREAN $$
(www.lioncityrestaurant.com; 45 Đ Le Anh Xuan; mains 65,000-200,000d; 7am-3pm;) Representing its country's culinary heritage with aplomb, Lion City is acclaimed for its frog porridge and chilli crab but we also adore the Malaysian-style curry and sambal dishes.

Shri JAPANESE, FUSION $$
(3827 9631; 23rd fl, Centec Tower, 72-74 Đ Nguyen Thi Minh Khai; mains 200,000-400,000d; 11am-midnight;) Perched up a tower block, classy Shri has the best views in town bar none. Offers Japanese-influenced Western mains and a more traditional Japanese section. Book ahead.

PHAM NGU LAO AREA

Mumtaz INDIAN $
(Map p140; www.mumtazrest.com; 226 Đ Bui Vien; mains 45,000-90,000d; 11am-11pm;) Excellent service, pleasant surrounds and succulent vegetarian options, tandoori dishes and the greatest hits of both North and South Indian cuisine. The lunch buffet is a steal.

Dinh Y VEGETARIAN $
(Map p140; 171B Đ Cong Quynh; mains 12,000-40,000d) Run by a friendly Cao Dai family, this humble eatery is in a very 'local' part of PNL near Thai Binh Market. The food is delicious and cheap, plus there's an English menu.

Mon Hue VIETNAMESE $
(Map p140; 98 Đ Nguyen Trai; mains 29,000-150,000d; 6am-11pm) Huế's famous cuisine is now accessible to HCMC's discerning proletariat. This branch offers a good introduction for travellers who don't make it to the old capital.

Sozo CAFE $
(Map p140; www.sozocentre.com; 176 Đ Bui Vien; bagels 40,000d; 7am-10.30pm Mon-Sat;) A classy little cafe ideal for excellent smoothies, doughy cinnamon rolls and other sweet treats. The cafe trains and employs poor, disadvantaged Vietnamese.

Drinking

Wartime Saigon was known for its riotous nightlife. Liberation in 1975 put a real dampener on evening activities, but the bars and clubs have staged a comeback. However, periodic 'crack-down, clean-up' campaigns continue to calm the fun.

Action is concentrated around the Dong Khoi area, with everything from dives to designer bars. However, places in this area generally close around 1am while Pham Ngu Lao rumbles on into the wee hours.

DONG KHOI AREA

Many of Dong Khoi's coolest bars double as restaurants (see Flow and Pacharan) or hover at the top of hotels.

TOP CHOICE **Vasco's** BAR, NIGHTCLUB
(Map p144; www.vascosgroup.com; 74/7D ĐL Hai Ba Trung; 4pm-late;) Vasco's is one of the hippest hang-outs in town. Downstairs is a breezy spot for cocktails and pizza, while upstairs a nightclub-like space regularly plays host to DJs and live bands.

Ala Mezon BAR
(Map p144; 10 Đ Chu Minh Trinh; 11.30am-1am;) Chic Japanese-themed bar with inventive cocktails and Japanese tapas. Play board games, Wii or Xbox in a frilly pink room or head up to the roof terrace for an altogether more elegant tipple.

Rooftop Garden Bar BAR
(Map p144; www.rexhotelvietnam.com; 141 ĐL Nguyen Hue; 24hr) The Rex Hotel's decor is several shades of camp: life-size elephants, birdcage lanterns, topiary draped in fairy lights and, to cap it all off, a giant, rotating, golden crown. There's also live music most nights.

2 Lam Son COCKTAIL BAR
(Map p144; www.saigon.park.hyatt.com; 2 Lam Son Sq, enter ĐL Hai Ba Trung;) The Park Hyatt's cocktail bar is the city's most stylish watering hole – and also one of its most expensive.

Dong Khoi Area

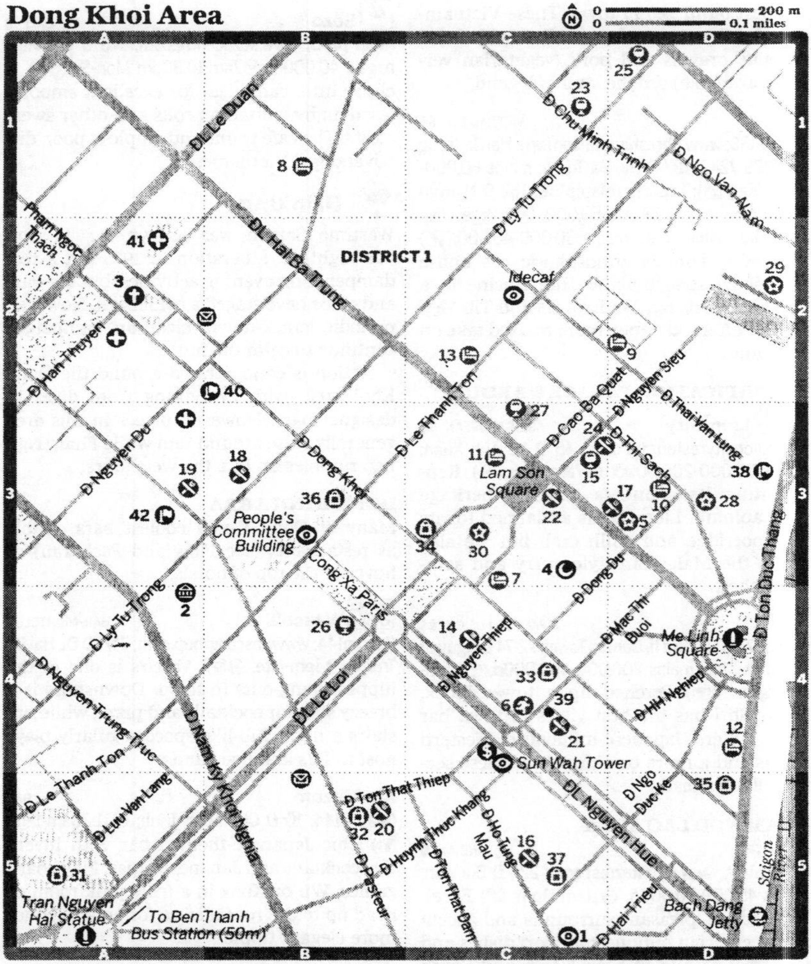

Alibi COCKTAIL BAR

(Map p144; www.alibi.vn; 5A Đ Nguyen Sieu; ⏲10am-late; ⊜📶) A happening New York-looking bar, with black-and-white photographs, creative cocktails and, upstairs, excellent fusion food.

Q Bar BAR

(Map p144; www.qbarsaigon.com; 7 Lam Son Sq) The mother of all trendy nightspots in HCMC. An enduring and endearing spot, it pulls the beautiful people thanks to hip music and sophisticated decor.

Lush BAR, NIGHTCLUB

(Map p144; www.lush.vn; 2 Đ Ly Tu Trong) Once you're done chatting in the garden zone, move to the central bar for serious people-watching and ass-shaking. DJs spin most nights, with Fridays devoted to hip hop.

DA KAO & AROUND

Hoa Vien BREWERY

(Map p138; www.hoavien.vn; 28 Đ Mac Dinh Chi; ⏲8am-midnight; ⊜📶) An unexpected find in the backstreets of HCMC, this Czech-style restaurant brews up fresh pilsner daily.

Dong Khoi Area

Sights
- 1 Bitexco Financial Tower C5
- 2 Ho Chi Minh City Museum A4
- 3 Notre Dame Cathedral A2
- 4 Saigon Central Mosque C3

Activities, Courses & Tours
- 5 Exotissimo D3
- 6 L'Apothiquaire C4
- Saigon Cooking Class .... (see 27)

Sleeping
- 7 Caravelle Hotel C3
- 8 Intercontinental Asiana Saigon B1
- 9 King Star Hotel D2
- 10 Northern Hotel D3
- 11 Park Hyatt Saigon C3
- 12 Riverside Hotel D4
- 13 Spring Hotel C2

Eating
- 14 Augustin C4
- 15 El Gaucho C3
- 16 Flow C5
- 17 Golden Elephant D3
- Hoa Tuc .... (see 27)
- 18 Huong Lai B3
- 19 Nha Hang Ngon A3
- 20 Temple Club B5
- 21 Warda C4
- 22 Xu C3

Drinking
- 2 Lam Son .... (see 11)
- 23 Ala Mezon C1
- 24 Alibi C3
- 25 Lush D1
- Q Bar .... (see 30)
- 26 Rooftop Garden Bar B4
- 27 Vasco's C3

Entertainment
- 28 Apocalypse Now D3
- 29 Fuse D2
- 30 Municipal Theatre C3

Shopping
- 31 Ben Thanh Market A5
- 32 Dogma B5
- 33 Khai Silk C4
- 34 Mai's C3
- 35 Nguyen Freres D5
- 36 Song B3
- 37 Vietnam Quilts C5

Information
- 38 Australian Consulate D3
- 39 Buffalo Tours C4
- 40 Canadian Consulate B2
- 41 HCMC Family Medical Practice A2
- 42 Lao Consulate A3
- New Zealand Consulate .... (see 40)

REUNIFICATION PALACE & AROUND

Serenata CAFE

(6D Đ Ngo Thoi Nhiem; ⏲7.30am-10.30pm; 📶) This grand house is the perfect setting for a coffee – the garden is scattered with tables around a pond-filled courtyard. Hosts live music every evening from 8.30pm and a tinkling piano on weekend mornings. It's 700m northwest of the Reunification Palace.

Cloud 9 BAR

(6th fl, 2 bis Cong Truong Quoc Te) Fashionable young things flock to the rooftop bar, while dance music pounds in the room below.

PHAM NGU LAO AREA

Le Pub PUB

(Map p140; www.lepub.org; 175/22 Đ Pham Ngu Lao; ⏲7am-late; 📶) Popular with expats and travellers alike, Le Pub has an extensive beer list, nightly promotions, cocktail jugs and tasty pub grub.

Go2 BAR

(Map p140; 187 Đ De Tham; 📶) There's no better street theatre than watching the crazy goings-on from the outside seats of this all-night venue. The music is usually excellent and there's a club upstairs if you feel the need to boogie, plus a rooftop bar if you want to cool off.

Allez Boo BAR

(Map p140; 195 Đ Pham Ngu Lao; ⏲7am-late) Proudly displays its tropical kookiness on a prominent street corner: think bamboo-lined walls and a rattan-shaded bar. A merry-go-round of backpackers and the late-night action upstairs ensures its popularity.

Spotted Cow SPORTS BAR

(Map p140; 111 Đ Bui Vien; ⏲11am-midnight) Aussie-run sports bar with lots of drink specials and a cow-print fetish.

Bobby Brewers CAFE

(Map p140; www.bobbybrewers.com; 45 Đ Bui Vien; 📶🚭) Contemporary cafe set over three floors, offering juices, sandwiches, pastas and salads, plus movies upstairs.

Entertainment

Pick up *The Word HCMC, Asialife HCMC* or *The Guide* to find out what's on during your stay in Saigon, or log onto www.anyarena.com or www.thewordhcmc.com.

Clubs

HCMC's hippest club nights include the semi-regular **Everyone's a DJ** (www.everyonesadjvietnam.wordpress.com) loft party, **dose** and **The Beats Saigon** (www.thebeats-saigon.com).

Apocalypse Now CLUB
(Map p144; 2C Đ Thi Sach; ⊙7pm-2am) 'Apo' has been around since the early days and remains one of the must-visit clubs. It's quite a circus with a cast comprising travellers, expats, Vietnamese movers and shakers, plus the odd hooker (some odder than others). The 150,000d charged on weekends includes a free drink.

Gossip CLUB
(Map p140; 79 79 Đ Tran Hung Dao; admission 120,000d; ⊙9.30pm-2.30am) Housed in the Dai Nam Hotel, this long-running club heats up at the weekend with a hard techno soundtrack.

Fuse CLUB
(Map p144; 3A Đ Ton Duc Thang; ⊙7pm-late) Small club, big beats.

Live Music

Acoustic BAR
(6E1 Đ Ngo Thoi Nhiem; ⊙7pm-midnight; 🍸) Don't be misled by the name: most of the musicians are fully plugged and dangerous when they take to the intimate stage of the city's leading live-music venue. It's 1km northwest of the Reunification Palace.

Municipal Theatre CONCERT HALL
(Nha Hat Thanh P Ho Chi Minh; Map p144; ☎3829 9976; Lam Son Sq) The French-era opera house is home to the HCMC Ballet, Symphony Orchestra & Opera (www.hbso.org.vn) and hosts performances by visiting artists.

Conservatory of Music CONCERT HALL
(Map p137; Nhac Vien Thanh P Ho Chi Minh; ☎3824 3774; 112 Đ Nguyen Du) Performances of both traditional Vietnamese and Western classical music are held here.

Water Puppetry

Golden Dragon Water Puppet Theatre THEATRE
(Map p137; 55B Nguyen Thi Minh Khai) The main water puppet venue, with shows starting at 5pm and 6.30pm and lasting about 50 minutes.

Saigon Water Puppet Theatre THEATRE
(Map p138; History Museum, Đ Nguyen Binh Khiem; entry 40,000d) Within the History Museum, this small theatre has performances at 9am, 10am, 11am, 2pm, 3pm and 4pm, lasting about 20 minutes.

Shopping

Among the tempting wares to be found in Saigon are embroidered silk shoes, miniature *cyclos*, fake Zippos engraved with GI philosophy and toy helicopters made from beer cans. Boutiques along Đ Le Thanh Ton and Đ Pasteur sell handmade ready-to-wear fashion. In Pham Ngu Lao, shops sell ethnic-minority fabrics, handicrafts, T-shirts and various appealing accessories.

Ben Thanh Market (Cho Ben Thanh; Map p144) is the best place to start. Part of the market is devoted to normal everyday items, but the lucrative tourist trade also has healthy representation. Đ Dong Khoi (Map p144) is one big arts-and-crafts tourist bazaar, but prices can be outrageous – negotiate if no prices are posted.

Check out the following shops around town:

DONG KHOI AREA

Vietnam Quilts HANDICRAFTS
(Map p144; (www.mekong-quilts.org; 64 Đ Ngo Duc Ke) The place to buy handmade quilts sewn by the rural poor in support of a sustainable income.

Dogma SOUVENIRS
(Map p144; (www.dogmavietnam.com; 1st fl, 43 Đ Ton That Thiep) Reproduction propaganda posters, as well as politically kitsch coffee mugs, coasters, and T-shirts.

Mai's CLOTHING
(Map p144; www.mailam.com.vn; 132-134 Đ Dong Khoi) Insanely hip boutique that sells beautiful but pricey hand-stitched men's and women's clothing and accessories.

Nguyen Freres ANTIQUES, HANDICRAFTS
(Map p144; 2 Đ Dong Khoi) Stocks a lovely assortment of new and antique furnishings

and textiles, pillowcases, silks, pottery and lamps.

Khai Silk CLOTHING
(Map p144; www.khaisilkcorp.com; 107 Đ Dong Khoi) This is one of several branches in HCMC of the nationwide silk empire. Expensive but high quality.

Song CLOTHING
(Map p144; 76D Đ Le Thanh Ton) A central boutique that specialises in sophisticated linens and cottons for men and women.

DA KAO & AROUND

Thu Quan Sinh Vien BOOKS
(Map p138; 2A ĐL Le Duan; ⊙8am-10pm; 🛜) Upmarket bookstore that stocks imported books and magazines in English, French and Chinese.

Adidas Puma Factory Shop SHOES, CLOTHING
(Map p138; 232 Đ Pasteur) Authentic trainers/sneakers at a fifth of the price you'll pay back home.

Cham Khanh TAILOR
(Map p138; 256 Đ Pasteur) One of several *ao dai* shops on this stretch of Đ Pasteur.

PHAM NGU LAO AREA

Mekong Creations HANDICRAFTS
(Map p140; www.mekong-creations.org; 141 Đ Bui Vien) Profits from the sale of bamboo bowls and platters benefit remote Mekong villages.

Hanoi Gallery SOUVENIRS
(Map p140; 79 Đ Bui Vien) Original (or so we're told) and repro propaganda posters.

SahaBook BOOKS
(Map p140; www.sahabook.com; 175/24 Đ Pham Ngu Lao) Specialises in guidebooks and travel literature including genuine Lonely Planet guides.

Blue Dragon HANDICRAFTS
(Map p140; 1B Đ Bui Vien) Popular souvenir store that stocks objets d'art made from recycled motorbike parts, among other things.

OTHER NEIGHBOURHOODS

Mai Handicrafts HANDICRAFTS
(www.maihandicrafts.com; 298 Đ Nguyen Trong Tuyen, Tan Binh District; ⊙Mon-Sat) A fair-trade shop dealing in ceramics, ethnic fabrics and other gift items. It's located about 5km northwest of the centre, off the road to the airport.

Information

For up-to-date information on what's going on in town, check out **The Word HCMC** (www.wordhcmc.com) or **Asialife HCMC** (www.asialifehcmc.com), both quality listings magazines.

Cultural Centres

British Council (☎3823 2862; www.britishcouncil.org/vietnam; 25 ĐL Le Duan) Attached to the British Consulate.

Institute of Cultural Exchange with France (Idecaf; Map p144; ☎3829 5451; 31 Đ Thai Van Lung)

Dangers & Annoyances

Be careful in the Dong Khoi area and along the Saigon riverfront, where motorbike 'cowboys' operate and specialise in bag and camera snatching. See the transport section for common taxi and *xe om* scams.

Emergency

Ambulance (☎115)

Fire (☎114)

Police (☎113)

Internet Access

Internet cafes are everywhere in HCMC. Many hotels, cafes, restaurants and bars offer free wi-fi.

Medical Services

HCMC Family Medical Practice (Map p144; 24hr emergency ☎3822 7848; www.vietnammedicalpractice.com; Diamond Plaza, 34 ĐL Le Duan; ⊙24hr) One of the best places, with prices to match.

International Medical Centre (Map p144; ☎3827 2366, 24hr emergency ☎3865 4025; fac@hcm.vnn.vn; 1 Đ Han Thuyen; ⊙24hr) A nonprofit organisation with English-speaking French doctors.

International SOS (Map p144; ☎3929 8424, 24hr emergency ☎3829 8520; www.internationalsos.com; 65 Đ Nguyen Du; ⊙24hr) Has an international team of doctors speaking English, French and Japanese.

Money

There are ATMs and exchange counters (most offering decent rates) in the airport hallway of arrivals, just after clearing customs.

ANZ Bank (Map p144; 11 Me Linh Sq) With ATM.

Citibank (Map p144; 115 Đ Nguyen Hue) Its ATM allows up to 8,000,000d in one hit.

Sacombank (Map p140; 211 Đ Nguyen Thai Hoc) Conveniently located in the backpacker zone, with ATM.

Post

Main post office (Map p144; 2 Cong Xa Paris) Saigon's striking French-era post office is next to Notre Dame Cathedral.

Tourist Information

Tourist Information Center (Map p144; ☎3822 6033; www.vietnamtourism.com; 4G Le Loi; ⏰8am-8pm) Distributes city maps and brochures and offers limited advice.

Travel Agencies

There are lots of travel agents offering tours of the Mekong Delta and other jaunts beyond HCMC. Some of the better ones include the following:

Buffalo Tours (Map p144; ☎3827 9170; www.buffalotours.com; 81 Đ Mac Thi Buoi)

Cafe Kim Tourist (Map p140; ☎3836 5489; www.thekimtourist.com; 270 Đ De Tham)

Exotissimo (Map p144; ☎3827 2911; www.exotissimo.com; 64 Đ Dong Du; ⏰Mon-Sat)

Handspan Adventure Travel (☎3925 7605; www.handspan.com; 7th fl, Titan Bldg, 18A Đ Nam Quoc Cang, District 1) Known for its innovative, non-generic tours and professional approach.

Innoviet (Map p140; ☎6291 5406; www.innoviet.com; 158 Đ Bui Vien)

Sinhbalo Adventures (Map p140; ☎3837 6766; www.sinhbalo.com; 283/20 Đ Pham Ngu Lao; ⏰closed Sat afternoon & Sun) For customised tours, this is one of the best agencies in Vietnam. Specialises in cycling trips, but also arranges special-interest journeys to the Mekong Delta, Central Highlands and further afield.

The Sinh Tourist (Map p140; ☎3838 9593; www.thesinhtourist.vn; 246 Đ De Tham; ⏰6.30am-10.30pm)

Getting There & Away

Air

For more information on international air travel, see p173.

Vietnam Airlines (☎3832 0320; www.vietnamairlines.com) Flies to/from Hanoi, Hai Phong, Vinh, Dong Hoi, Huế, Danang, Quy Nhon, Nha Trang, Dalat, Buon Ma Thuot, Pleiku, Rach Gia and Phu Quoc Island.

Air Mekong (☎3846 3666; www.airmekong.com.vn) Flies to/from Hanoi, Quy Nhon, Dalat, Buon Ma Thuot, Pleiku, Con Dao Islands and Phu Quoc Island.

Jetstar Pacific (☎1900 1550; www.jetstar.com) Flies to/from Hanoi, Hai Phong, Vinh, Huế and Danang.

Vietnam Air Service Company (VASCO; www.vasco.com.vn) Flies to/from Tuy Hoa, Chu Lai, Con Dao Islands and Ca Mau.

Boat

Hydrofoils (adult/child 200,000/100,000d, 1¼ hours) depart for Vung Tau almost hourly from **Bach Dang Jetty** (Map p144; Đ Ton Duc Thang). The main companies based here:

Greenlines (☎3821 5609; www.greenlines.com.vn)

Petro Express (☎3821 0650)

Vina Express (☎3825 3333; www.vinaexpress.com.vn)

Bus

Intercity buses operate from three main bus stations around HCMC. Local buses (3000d) travelling to the intercity bus stations leave from the local bus station opposite Ben Thanh Market (Map p144).

An Suong bus station Buses to Tay Ninh and points northeast of HCMC; in District 12, west of the centre. Buses to/from Cu Chi leave from here but tours are far more convenient.

Mien Dong bus station Buses heading north of HCMC; about 5km from downtown on Hwy 13. Express buses depart from the east side of the station, and local buses connect with the west side of the complex.

Mien Tay bus station Serves all the main Mekong Delta towns; located about 10km southwest of Saigon in An Lac.

Open-tour buses Depart and arrive in the Pham Ngu Lao area. Destinations include Mui Ne (US$5 to US$10), Nha Trang (US$7 to US$20), Dalat (US$8 to US$15), Hoi An (US$15 to US$37) and Hanoi (US$31 to US$49).

There are plenty of **international bus services** connecting HCMC and Cambodia, most with departures from the Pham Ngu Lao area. **Sapaco** (Map p140; ☎3920 3623; 309 Pham Ngu Lao) has nine direct daily services to Phnom Penh (US$10; departing between 6am and 3pm), as well as one to Siem Reap (US$20).

Car & Motorcycle

Hotels and travellers' cafes can arrange car rentals (from US$35 per day). Pham Ngu Lao is the neighbourhood to look for motorbike rentals (US$5 to US$10 per day).

Train

Trains from **Saigon train station** (Ga Sai Gon; Map p137; 1 Đ Nguyen Thong, District 3; ticket office ⏰7.15-11am & 1-3pm) head north to destinations including:

Danang (616,000d to 1,019,000d, 15½ to 20¾ hours, six daily)

Dong Hoi (759,000d to 1,199,000d, 21 to 26 hours, five daily)

Huế (655,000d to 1,100,000, 18 to 24½ hours, six daily)

Nha Trang (272,000d to 550,000d, 6½ to nine hours, eight daily)

In Pham Ngu Lao, purchase tickets from **Saigon Railway Tours** (Map p140; ☎3836 7640; www.railtour.com.vn; 275C Đ Pham Ngu Lao; ⌚7.30am-8pm) or from most travel agents for a small fee.

Getting Around

To/From the Airport

Tan Son Nhat Airport is 7km northwest of central HCMC. **Metered taxis** are your best bet and cost around 100,000d to/from the centre. English-speaking controllers will shuffle you into a waiting cab and tell the driver your destination. The driver may try to claim your hotel of choice is closed, burned down, is dirty and dangerous, or anything to steer you somewhere else for a commission. Stick to your guns.

Air-conditioned buses (route 152; 4000d, every 15 minutes, 6am to 6pm) also run to and from the airport. These make regular stops along Đ De Tham (Pham Ngu Lao area) and international hotels along Đ Dong Khoi.

Bicycle

Bicycles are available for hire (US$2) from many budget hotels and cafes. Use parking lots to safeguard against theft.

Car & Motorcycle

HCMC is *not* the place to learn to ride a motorbike. They are nevertheless available for hire around Pham Ngu Lao for US$5 to US$10 per day. Give it a test-drive first; you'll be asked to leave your passport as collateral.

Cyclo

Cyclos are an interesting way to get around town, but avoid them at night. They're banned from many streets so pedal merchants are often forced to take circuitous routes. Overcharging tourists is the norm, so negotiate a price beforehand and have exact change. Short hops around the city centre are 15,000d to 25,000d; District 1 to central Cholon costs about 40,000d.

Taxi

Metered taxis cruise the streets. Flagfall is around 15,000d for the first kilometre and most rides in the city centre cost just two or three bucks. Be wary of dodgy taxi meters that are rigged. Reliable companies:

Mai Linh (☎3822 6666)

Saigon Taxi (☎3823 2323)

Xe Om

Xe om drivers hang out on parked bikes touting for passengers. The accepted rate is 20,000d for short rides, an hour/day cost about US$3/15.

AROUND HO CHI MINH CITY

Cu Chi

If the tenacious spirit of the Vietnamese can be symbolised by a place, then Cu Chi could be the one. Its fame is such that it's become a place of pilgrimage for many Vietnamese, and a must-see for travellers.

Chu Chi Tunnels HISTORIC SITE

(www.cuchitunnel.org.vn; adult/child 80,000/20,000d) The tunnel network at Cu Chi was the stuff of legend during the 1960s for its role in facilitating Viet Cong control of a large rural area only 30km from Saigon. At its height, the tunnel system stretched from Saigon to the Cambodian border. In the district of Cu Chi alone, there were more than 200km of tunnels. After ineffective ground operations targeting the tunnels claimed large numbers of casualties, the Americans turned their artillery and bombers on the area, transforming it into a moonscape.

TRAVELLING FROM HO CHI MINH CITY

DESTINATION	AIR TRAVEL TIME/ COST	BUS TRAVEL TIME/ COST	TRAIN TRAVEL TIME/ COST
Dalat	50 minutes/from US$39	7 hours/$8-15	N/A
Hanoi	2 hours/from US$70	41 hours/$31-49	30 hours/$50-79
Hué	80 minutes/from US$37	29 hours/$26-37	18 hours/$32-54
Nha Trang	55 minutes/from US$44	13 hours/$7-20	6½ hours/$13-27

Parts of this remarkable tunnel network have been reconstructed and two sites are open to visitors; one near the village of Ben Dinh and the other at Ben Duoc. It's possible to descend into the tunnels themselves. Although some sections have been widened, others remain in their original condition. If you can fit into the narrow passageways, you'll gain an empathetic, if claustrophobic, appreciation for the people who spent weeks underground.

Day tours operated by travellers' cafes charge around US$8 per person (transport only); most include a stop at the Cao Dai Great Temple in Tay Ninh.

Cu Chi Wildlife Rescue Station WILDLIFE CENTRE
(www.wildlifeatrisk.org; adult/child US$5/free; ⏲7.30-11.30am & 1-4.30pm) Just a few kilometres down the road from the tunnels of Ben Dinh, this small rescue centre provides protection to wildlife confiscated from illegal traders. Animals here include bears, otters and gibbons. The centre is expanding its enclosures to create more comfortable habitats and there is an informative display on the rather depressing state of wildlife in Vietnam.

It's tough to find the centre, so talk to a travel agent about incorporating it into a Cu Chi Tunnels trip.

Tay Ninh

☎066 / POP 127,000

Tay Ninh town, capital of Tay Ninh Province, serves as the headquarters of Cao Dai, one of Vietnam's most interesting indigenous religions (see boxed text, p481). The **Cao Dai Great Temple** was built between 1933 and 1955. Victor Hugo is among the Westerners especially revered by the Cao Dai; look for his likeness at the Great Temple.

Tay Ninh is 96km northwest of HCMC. The Cao Dai Holy See complex is 4km east of Tay Ninh. One-day tours from Saigon, including Tay Ninh and the Cu Chi Tunnels, cost around US$8.

Beaches

There are several beach resorts within striking distance of downtown Saigon, although most travellers make for Mui Ne. If time is short and you want a quick fix, consider Vung Tau, which you can reach by hydrofoil.

MEKONG DELTA

The 'rice bowl' of Vietnam, the Mekong Delta is a landscape carpeted in a dizzying variety of greens. It's also a water world where boats, houses, restaurants and even markets float upon the innumerable rivers, canals and streams that flow through like arteries.

Although the area is primarily rural, it is one of the most densely populated regions in Vietnam and nearly every hectare is intensively farmed. Visitors can experience southern charm in riverside cities where few tourists venture, sample fruits traded in the colourful floating markets, or dine on home-cooked delicacies before overnighting as a homestay guest. There are also bird sanctuaries, impressive Khmer pagodas and, inevitably, war memorials.

Those seeking a tropical hideaway will find it on Phu Quoc, an island lined with white-sand beaches and crisscrossed by empty dirt roads.

By far the easiest and cheapest way to see the delta is by taking a tour with a travel agency in Ho Chi Minh City (p148). It's also possible to travel independently, although it can be time-consuming.

My Tho

☎074 / POP 169,300

Gateway to the Mekong Delta for day trippers to the region, the slow-paced capital of Tien Giang Province is an important market town, but to visit floating markets you'll need to continue on to Can Tho (p152).

On the riverfront, the **My Tho Tourist Boat Station** (8 Đ 30 Thang 4) is home to several tour companies offering cruises to the neighbouring islands and through the maze of small canals. Destinations usually include a coconut-candy workshop, a honey farm (try the banana wine) and an orchid garden. A 2½-hour boat tour costs around 350,000d for one person or 450,000d for two. Prices are significantly better if you can join a group.

Sleeping

Song Tien Annex HOTEL $$
(☎387 7883; www.tiengiangtourist.com; 33 Đ Thien Ho Duong; r US$30-40; ❄📶) The phrases 'boutique hotel' and 'state tourist company' rarely go together, but in this case, they've pulled it off. Rooms have polished wooden floors and hip bathrooms complete with

claw-footed bathtubs. There's a rooftop restaurant too.

Song Tien HOTEL $
(☎387 2009; www.tiengiangtourist.com; 101 Đ Trung Trac; r from 400,000d; ❄📶) Reliable seven-storey hotel where the rooms include satellite TV, minibars and hot water; 'suites' have fancier furniture.

Eating

My Tho is well known for a special vermicelli soup called *hu tieu My Tho*, which is richly garnished with fresh and dried seafood, pork, chicken, offal and fresh herbs. Carnivores will enjoy **Hu Tieu 44** (44 Đ Nam Ky Khoi Nghia; soups 20,000d), while vegetarians should try **Hu Tieu Chay 24** (24 Đ Nam Ky Khoi Nghia; soups 15,000d; ✓).

Ngoc Gia Trang VIETNAMESE $$
(196 Đ Ap Bac; mains 45,000-150,000d) Tables are set alongside ponds amid lots of greenery and the lengthy menu is translated into English and French. The seafood is excellent and beautifully presented.

Quan Oc 283 VIETNAMESE, SEAFOOD $
(283 Đ Tet Mau Than; mains 15,000-100,000d) Seafood is the speciality here, including clams, scallops, mussels and snails, or venture behind to the tanks of live fish, crab and shrimp.

Getting There & Around

New bridges and roads have considerably shortened travel distances to My Tho. The **bus station** (Ben Xe Tien Giang; 42 Đ Ap Bac) is 3km west of the town centre on Đ Ap Bac, the main road to HCMC. Buses head to HCMC's Mien Tay bus station (30,000d, around 75 minutes), Can Tho (50,000d), Cao Lanh (25,000d), Chau Doc (51,000d) and Ca Mau (100,000d).

Ben Tre

☎075 / POP 120,000

Famous for its *keo dua* (coconut candy), Ben Tre is now plugged into the 'mainland' of My Tho thanks to a new bridge. The town's sleepy waterfront, lined with ageing villas, is easy to explore on foot, as is the rustic settlement across the bridge to the south of the centre. Located off the main trail, it receives far fewer visitors than My Tho and makes a lovely stop on a Mekong tour.

Try the modern **Ham Luong** (☎356 0560; www.hamluongtourist.com.vn; 200 Đ Hung Vuong; r US$18-29; ❄@📶) on the riverfront for nicely furnished rooms. A multistorey barge moored in the river, **Noi Ben Tre** (Đ Hung Vuong; mains 20,000-60,000d) has piquant prawn salads, delicious frog in lemongrass and other local delicacies.

Ben Tre Tourist (☎382 9618; www.bentretourist.vn; 65 Đ Dong Khoi; ⊙7-11am & 1-5pm) rents out bikes and motor boats (per hour US$10) and arranges excursions including a motorcart/canal-boat trip to the honey farm and coconut-candy workshop (per one/two/three/four people $25/30/42/52) and an 'ecological tour' by bike to coconut, guava and grapefruit groves.

Buses leave regularly from the new bus terminal 5km northeast of town for HCMC (67,000d, last bus between 4pm and 5pm), Can Tho (55,000d), Ca Mau (103,000d) and Ha Tien (134,000d).

Slow boats can be rented at the public pier near the market for about 70,000d to 90,000d per hour.

Vinh Long

☎070 / POP 130,000

It may not be the largest town in the Mekong Delta, but as a major transit hub Vinh Long can be noisy and chaotic nonetheless. Escape to the riverfront away from the mayhem, where there are plenty of cafes and restaurants. Vinh Long is the gateway to island life and some worthwhile sites, including Cai Be floating market, abundant orchards and atmospheric homestays, which can be a highlight of a Mekong journey.

What makes a trip to Vinh Long worthwhile are the beautiful islands in the river. Charter a boat through Cuu Long Tourist for around US$12 per person or pay substantially less for a private operator (US$7 per hour).

The bustling **Cai Be floating market** (⊙5am-5pm) is worth including on a boat tour from Vinh Long. It's best to arrive early in the morning. Wholesalers on big boats moor here, each specialising in one or a few types of fruit or vegetable.

We suggest you don't stay in town; instead opt for a homestay, see the boxed text on p153.

Dong Khanh (49 Đ 2 Thang 9; mains 30,000-50,000d) offers lots of hotpots and rice dishes and has an English-language menu.

Cuu Long Tourist (☎382 3616; www.cuulongtourist.net; 2 Phan Boi Chau) is one of the more capable state-run tour outfits with boat tours ranging from three hours to three days. **Vietcombank** (143 Đ Le Thai To) can exchange cash and travellers cheques.

Frequent buses go between Vinh Long and HCMC (70,000d, three hours), from the terminal in the middle of town. Buses to other locations including Can Tho (34,000d), leave from a provincial bus station 3km south of town.

Can Tho

☎071 / POP 1.1 MILLION

The epicentre of the Mekong Delta, Can Tho feels like a veritable metropolis after exploring the backwaters. As the political, economic, cultural and transportation centre of the Mekong Delta, Can Tho hums with activity. It's a buzzing town with a waterfront lined with sculpted gardens and an appealing blend of narrow backstreets and wide boulevards that make for some rewarding exploration.

Can Tho also makes the perfect base for visiting nearby floating markets. **Cai Rang** is the biggest floating market in the Mekong Delta, 6km from Can Tho towards Soc Trang. Although the lively market goes on until around noon daily, show up before 9am for the best photo opportunities. You can hire boats (about US$6 per hour) on the river near the Can Tho market. Cai Rang is one hour away by boat, or you can drive to Cau Dau Sau boat landing, where you can get a **rowing boat** (per hr around 80,000d) to the market, 10 minutes away.

Less crowded and less motorised is the **Phong Dien market**, with more stand-up rowboats. It's best between 6am and 8am. Twenty kilometres southwest of Can Tho, it's easy to reach by road and you can hire a boat on arrival.

Sleeping

TOP CHOICE **Kim Tho Hotel** HOTEL $$
(☎381 7517; www.kimtho.com; 1A Đ Ngo Gia Tu; r US$40-120; ❄📶) A smart hotel verging on the boutique, Kim Tho sets the standard for midrange properties in the Mekong Delta. The rooms are stylish throughout and include designer bathrooms, and there's a rooftop coffee bar.

Victoria Can Tho Resort RESORT $$$
(☎381 0111; www.victoriahotels.asia; Cai Khe Ward; r US$91-230, ste US$277-310; ❄@📶🏊) Classy French colonial-style hotel with rooms set around an inviting pool that looks out over the river. Facilities include an excellent restaurant, an open-air bar and a riverside spa. There are plenty of activities on offer too.

Kim Lan Hotel HOTEL $
(☎381 7049; www.kimlancantho.com.vn; 138A Đ Nguyen An Ninh; r US$18-50; ❄@📶) Chic rooms at this solar-powered hotel include contemporary furnishings in bamboo and wood, and artwork. Even the small, windowless standard rooms are perfectly adequate.

Xuan Mai Minihotel HOTEL $
(☎382 3578; tcdac@yahoo.com; 17 Đ Dien Bien Phu; r US$12; ❄📶) This place has a real local feel as it's on a lane which doubles as An Lac Market by day. Offers spacious, clean and surprisingly quiet rooms with TV, fridge and hot shower.

Eating & Drinking

Hop Pho VIETNAMESE, CAFE $
(6 Đ Ngo Gia Tu; mains 30,000-130,000d; 📶) For discount designer dining, look no further. Serves Vietnamese favourites at fair prices and it's a great spot for a coffee or a cocktail, either in air-conditioned comfort inside or outside in the lush garden.

Sao Hom FUSION $
(☎381 5616; 50 Đ Hai Ba Trung; mains 35,000-150,000d; ⊙8am-midnight) Set in the (now upmarket) former market, Sao Hom has an atmospheric riverside setting for Vietnamese, international and some fusion dishes.

Mekong VIETNAMESE, PIZZA $
(38 Đ Hai Ba Trung; mains 25,000-105,000d; ⊙8am-2pm & 4-10pm) A travellers' favourite thanks to the good local and international food at very reasonable prices. Doubles as a bar at night.

Xe Loi BAR
(Hau Riverside Park; ⊙5pm-late) The most happening nightspot with tables in the large garden, a fake beach on the riverside (yes!) and a full-on club with DJs and regular live music.

Information

Can Tho Tourist (☎382 1852; www.cantho tourist.com.vn; 50 Đ Hai Ba Trung) Has helpful English- and French-speaking staff. Tours are available, and there's a booking desk for both Vietnam Airlines and Jetstar Pacific.

There are plenty of ATMs and internet cafes dotted around town.

ℹ Getting There & Around

Air

Can Tho opened a new international airport in early 2011, but at the time of writing the only services were **Vietnam Airlines** (www.vietnamairlines.com) flights to Phu Quoc Island (from 500,000d, daily), the Con Dao Islands (from 400,000d, four per week) and Hanoi (from 1,700,000d, daily). The airport is 10km northwest of the city centre.

Bus

Can Tho's **bus station** (cnr Đ Nguyen Trai & Đ Hung Vuong) is centrally located. Regular buses (75,000d, five hours) and express minibuses (90,000d, four hours) run to HCMC's Mien Tay bus station. Other services include Cao Lanh (30,000d), My Tho (50,000d), Tra Vinh (55,000d), Vinh Long (34,000d), Soc Trang (50,000d), Ca Mau (65,000d) and Ha Tien (83,000d).

Boat

Boat services include hydrofoils to Ca Mau (150,000d, three to four hours), passing through Phung Hiep.

Chau Doc

☎076 / POP 112,000

Perched on the banks of the Bassac River, Chau Doc is a charming town near the Cambodian border with sizeable Chinese, Cham and Khmer communities.

Chau Doc is a place rich in cultural diversity – something apparent in the mosques, temples, churches and nearby pilgrimage sites – making it fascinating to explore.

The popular river crossing between Vietnam and Cambodia means many travellers pass through. Nearby Sam Mountain is a local beauty spot with terrific views over Cambodia.

War remnants near Chau Doc include Ba Chuc, the site of a Khmer Rouge massacre, with a bone pagoda similar to that of Cambodia's Choeung Ek memorial; and Tuc Dup Hill, where an expensive American bombing campaign during 1963 earned it the nickname Two Million Dollar Hill. It's also possible to visit some fish farms established underneath floating houses on the river.

A NIGHT ON THE MEKONG

Spending the night on board a boat on the Mekong River is an excellent way to help bring you closer to life on the river and explore the waterways. The more interesting options include the following:

Bassac (☎0710-382 9540; www.transmekong.com) Offers a range of beautiful wooden boats for small groups. The standard itinerary is an overnight between Cai Be and Can Tho, but custom routes are possible.

Exotissimo (☎08-3827 2911; www.exotissimo.com) Upmarket single- or multiday tours of the delta by boat.

Le Cochinchine (☎08-3993 4552; www.lecochinchine.com) Cruises on a luxurious converted rice barge and a traditional sampan that are akin to floating hotels. The main routes are Cai Be to Can Tho (overnight) or Cai Be to Sa Dec, Ving Long and Can Tho (two nights). Private trips are available.

Mekong Eyes (☎0710-246 0786; www.mekongeyes.com) A stunningly converted traditional rice barge that travels between Can Tho and Cai Be; it's also available for charter.

As well as these options, there are boats plying the waters between HCMC and Phnom Penh or Siem Reap, including **Pandaw Cruises** (www.pandaw.com) and **Compagnie Fluviale du Mekong** (www.cfmekong.com). Newcomers **Indochina Sails** (www.indochina-sails.com), operating RV *La Marguerite*, and the **Jayavarman VII** (www.heritage-line.com) boat look to be taking the competition to a new level on this route. **Ama Waterways** (www.amawaterways.com) offers tours from Siem Reap to My Tho on commodious boats with balconies and jacuzzis.

Sleeping & Eating

TOP CHOICE **Victoria Chau Doc Hotel** HOTEL $$$
(☎386 5010; www.victoriahotels-asia.com; 32 Đ Le Loi; r/ste from US$162/220, meals from US$12;) Seriously stylish colonial-style riverfront hotel with grand rooms that have timber floors, classy drapes and inviting bathrooms. There's a small spa, and tours can be arranged. The restaurant here is the best in town, with beautifully presented Vietnamese food and inventive French dishes.

TOP CHOICE **Trung Nguyen Hotel** HOTEL $
(☎386 6158; trunghotel@yahoo.com; 86 Đ Bach Dang; r US$13-15;) Best of the budget places, with a trim and panache that is decidedly more midrange. Rooms feature balconies overlooking the market. It's on a busy corner site, so pack earplugs.

Hai Chau HOTEL $
(☎626 0026; www.haichauhotel.com; 61 Đ Suong Nguyet Anh; r 360,000-560,000d;) Sixteen rooms spread over four floors; all smartly fitted out with dark wooden furniture and good showers.

Good local eateries in Chau Doc include **Bay Bong** (22 Đ Thuong Dang Le; mains from 40,000d), with excellent hotpots and soups, and **Mekong** (41 Đ Le Loi; mains from 35,000d), where you can try the *ca kho to* (fish in claypot).

Information

Mekong Tours (☎386 8222; www.mekongvietnam.com; 14 Đ Nguyen Huu Canh) is a reliable travel agent offering boat/bus transport to Phnom Penh, Mekong boat trips, and cars with drivers.

Getting There & Away

Buses to Chau Doc depart HCMC's Mien Tay station (120,000d, six hours).

Ha Tien

☎077 / POP 93,000

Ha Tien may be part of the Mekong Delta, but lying on the Gulf of Thailand it feels a world away from the rice fields and rivers that typify the region. Dramatic limestone formations define the area, pepper-tree plantations dot the hillsides and the town itself has a sleepy tropical charm. Visitor numbers have recently soared thanks to the opening of the border with Cambodia at Xa Xia–Prek Chak and the new fast-boat service to Phu Quoc.

Sleeping & Eating

Hai Phuong HOTEL $
(☎385 2240; So 52, Đ Dong Thuy Tram; r 200,000-700,000d;) Friendly and family-run, this smart, six-level hotel offers good-value, well-presented rooms, some with excellent river views from their balconies.

Anh Van Hotel HOTEL $
(☎395 9222; So 2, Đ Tran Hau; d/tw/f 200,000/400,000/500,000d;) In the new part of town near the bridge, this large hotel has cheap, small windowless rooms brimming with amenities and pricier options with river views.

It's happy days when shrimp is the cheapest dish on the menu. Local eatery **Xuan Thanh** (20 Đ Tran Hau; mains 30,000-60,000d) has an English menu boasting a range of Vietnamese favourites.

Be sure to try the local coconut; its flesh is mixed with ice and sugar and served in restaurants all over town. For a beer try **Oasis** (www.oasisbarhatien.com; 42 Tuan Phu Dat; ⌚9am-9pm;), run by an expat and his Vietnamese wife; it's also a great source of impartial travel information.

GETTING TO CAMBODIA: VINH XUONG TO KAAM SAMNOR

One of the most enjoyable ways to enter Cambodia is via this crossing just northwest of Chau Doc along the Mekong River. Cambodian visas are available at the crossing, but minor overcharging is common.

Several companies in Chau Doc sell boat journeys from Chau Doc to Phnom Penh via the Vinh Xuong border. **Hang Chau** (Chau Doc ☎076-356 2771; www.hangchautourist.com.vn) has boats departing Chau Doc at 7.30am (US$24, five hours).

The more upmarket **Blue Cruiser** (www.bluecruiser.com; HCMC ☎08-3926 0253) pulls out at 7am (US$55, 4½ hours) from the Victoria Hotel, as do speedboats exclusive to Victoria Hotel guests.

For information on crossing this border in the other direction, see p195.

GETTING TO CAMBODIA: TINH BIEN TO PHNOM DEN

This is a little-used border crossing that connects Chau Doc to Takeo Province in Cambodia. Buses from Chau Doc to Phnom Penh depart at 7.30am and can be booked through Mekong Tours in Chau Doc (US$15 to US$21, five hours).

For information on crossing this border in the other direction, see p260.

Information

The **post office** (3 Đ To Chau) has internet access and **Agribank** (37 Đ Lam Son), one block from the waterfront, has an ATM.

Getting There & Away

Passenger ferries dock at the **ferry terminal**, opposite the Ha Tien Hotel. See the Phu Quoc Island transport section for details of services.

Buses connect HCMC (from 132,000d, 10 hours) and Ha Tien, and also run to destinations including Chau Doc (52,000d), Rach Gia (38,000d) and Can Tho (83,000d). **Ha Tien bus station** is on the road to Mui Nai Beach and the Cambodian border.

Rach Gia

☎077 / POP 206,000

Rach Gia is something of a boom town, flush with funds from its thriving port and an injection of Viet Kieu money. The population here includes significant numbers of ethnic Chinese and ethnic Khmers. Most travellers give the busy centre short shrift, heading straight to Phu Quoc Island. Those who do linger can explore the lively waterfront and bustling backstreets, where there are some inexpensive seafood restaurants to be found.

Sleeping & Eating

Linda HOTEL $

(☎391 8818; cnr Đ 3 Thang 2 & Nguyen An Ninh; r 180,000-400,000d; ❄📶) New hotel on the emerging seafront strip with some of the smartest rooms in Rach Gia. The priciest are corner suites with two balconies and a massage bath, but the cheapest are a tight squeeze.

Kim Co Hotel HOTEL $

(☎387 9610; www.kimcohotel.com; 141 Đ Nguyen Hung Son; r 300,000d; ❄📶) Centrally located and the rooms are in good shape, some including decadent bathtubs, making it tempting value. Most rooms face the corridor, so you'll need to pull the shades to get some privacy.

Hong Yen HOTEL $

(☎387 9095; 259 Đ Mac Cuu; r 150,000-250,000d; ❄@📶) Stretching over four pink floors, Hong Yen is a likeable minihotel with sizeable, clean rooms (some with balcony) and friendly owners.

Than Binh VIETNAMESE $

(2 Đ Nguyen Thai Hoc; mains 18,000-35,000d) Humble streetside restaurant rammed with fish-noodle-soup-slurping locals. No menu, so try the point-and-gesture 'I'll have what she's having' approach.

Hai Au VIETNAMESE $$

(2 Đ Nguyen Trung Truc; mains 25,000-200,000d; 📶) This place is fancy by local standards, with a great location along the Cai Lon River. Seafood is popular, including crayfish and crab, and Western-style dishes are available, too.

Information

Banks, ATMs and internet cafes are scattered around town. **Kien Giang Tourist** (Du Lich Lu Hanh Kien Giang; ☎386 2081; ctycpdulichkg@vnn.vn; 5 Đ Le Loi) is the provincial tourism authority.

Getting There & Away

Vietnam Airlines flies daily between HCMC (from 500,000d) and Rach Gia, continuing on to Phu Quoc Island (from 500,000d). The airport is about 10km outside town; taxis cost about 160,000d.

For details on getting to Phu Quoc by hydrofoil, see p159. Stop by the **Rach Gia hydrofoil terminal** (☎387 9765) the day before, or phone ahead to book a seat.

There are regular services to Ca Mau (50,000d, three hours), Ha Tien (38,000d, two hours), HCMC (120,000, six to seven hours) and other cities from the **bus station** (Đ Nguyen Binh Khiem), 7km south of Rach Gia.

Phu Quoc Island

☎077 / POP 85,000

Fringed with white-sand beaches and with large tracts still covered in dense, tropical

GETTING TO CAMBODIA: XA XIA TO PREK CHAK

This crossing connects Ha Tien with Kep and Kampot on Cambodia's south coast. Direct buses cross the border twice a day, terminating in Sihanoukville or Phnom Penh. Casinos have sprung up in the no-man's-land between the two border posts.

Direct buses leave Ha Tien for Cambodia at noon and 4pm daily, heading to Kep (US$12, one hour, 47km), Kampot (US$15, 1½ hours, 75km), Sihanoukville (US$20, four hours, 150km) and Phnom Penh (US$18, four hours, 180km). Bookings can be made through Ha Tien Tourism. *Xe om* drivers in Ha Tien will also take you to Kep for around US$15.

For information on crossing this border in the other direction, see p262.

jungle, Phu Quoc has been quickly morphing from a sleepy backwater to a favoured beach escape. Beyond the chain of resorts lining Long Beach, it's still largely undeveloped – and unlike Phuket, to which it aspires, you won't find a lot to do here after dark. Opt instead for daytime adventures by diving the reefs, kayaking in the bays or exploring the backroads on a motorbike – or live the life of a lotus eater by lounging on the beach, indulging in a massage and dining on fresh seafood.

The tear-shaped island lies in the Gulf of Thailand, 15km south of the coast of Cambodia. Phu Quoc is Vietnam's largest island but is also claimed by Cambodia; its Khmer name is Koh Tral. Despite the impending development (of a new international airport, a golf course and a casino), close to 70% of the island is protected as Phu Quoc National Park.

Phu Quoc's rainy season is from July to November. The peak season for tourism is between December and March when the sky is blue and the sea is calm.

At the time of research, several road projects seemed to have stalled – leaving a confusing hotchpotch of incomplete roads and diversions. Expect a bit of confusion as you scoot about, but rest assured you're unlikely to get lost for long – it's a relatively small island, after all.

Hydrofoils to the mainland dock at Bai Vong on the east of the island. Most beachside accommodation options can be found at Long Beach, located on the western side of the island just south of Duong Dong town.

Sights & Activities

Deserted white-sand beaches ring around Phu Quoc.

Duong Dong NEIGHBOURHOOD

The island's bustling main town is not that exciting, though the excellent night market is filled with delicious food stalls. Take a peek at **Cau Castle** (Dinh Cau; Đ Bach Dang), actually more of a temple-cum-lighthouse, built in 1937 to honour Thien Hau, the Chinese goddess of the sea.

Phu Quoc is famous for the quality of its fish sauce, and the factory **Nuoc Mam Hung Thanh** (admission free; ⊗8-11am & 1-5pm), located a short walk from the market, exports all over the world. At first glance, the giant wooden vats may make you think you've arrived for a wine tasting, but one sniff of the festering *nuoc mam* essence brings you right back to reality.

Long Beach BEACH

(Bai Truong) Aptly-named Long Beach stretches from Duong Dong southwards to An Thoi port. The main resort section is concentrated in the northern part, a motorbike or bicycle is necessary to reach some of the remote bays towards the south. You'll find bamboo huts for drinks, and beachside massages are popular.

Phu Quoc National Park FOREST

About 90% of the island is forested and the trees and adjoining marine environment now enjoy official protection. In July 2010 the park was declared a Unesco Biosphere Reserve.

The forest is most dense in the northern half of the island, which forms the Khu Rung Nguyen Sinh reserve. You'll need a motorbike or mountain bike to explore its rough dirt roads; there are no real hiking trails.

Vung Bau, Dai & Thom Beaches BEACHES

(Bai Vung Bau, Bai Dai & Bai Thom) Retaining their isolated, tropical charm, these northern beaches are rarely peopled, let alone crowded. The road from Dai to Thom via Ganh Dau is very beautiful, passing through dense forest with tantalising glimpses of the coast below.

Sao, Dam & Vong Beaches BEACHES
(Bai Sao, Bai Dam & Bai Vong) On the east side of the island, Sao and Dam are two beautiful white-sand beaches, just a few kilometres from An Thoi, the main shipping port. North of here is Vong Beach, where the fast boats from the mainland dock. It's also home to Mui Duong Watersports and you'll find kayaks (60,000d per hour) for rent here.

Cua Can & Ong Lan Beaches BEACHES
(Bai Cua Can & Bai Ong Lan) Cua Can beach, about 11km north of Duong Dong, is mercifully quiet during the week, but busy at weekends. Just south of here Ong Lan, forming a series of sandy bays sheltered by rocky headlands, is home to several midrange resorts.

Suoi Da Ban WATERFALL
(admission 3000d, motorbike 1000d) Suoi Da Ban (Stony Surface Spring) is a white-water creek tumbling across some attractive large granite boulders. There are deep pools and it's nice enough for a dip. By the end of the dry season there's little more than a trickle though.

Activities

Diving & Snorkelling

There's plenty of underwater action around Phu Quoc, but only during the dry months (from November to May). Two fun dives cost from US$40 to US$80; four-day PADI Open Water US$320 to US$360; snorkelling trips US$20 to US$30. The following schools are based in the Doung Dong area:

Rainbow Divers DIVING, SNORKELLING
(☎091 340 0964; www.divevietnam.com; 17A Đ Tran Hung Dao) This reputable PADI outfit offers a wide range of diving and snorkelling trips.

Coco Dive Center DIVING, SNORKELLING
(☎398 2100; www.cocodivecenter.com; 58 Đ Tran Hung Dao)

Searama DIVING, SNORKELLING
(☎629 1679; www.searama.com; 50 Đ Tran Hung Dao) French- and English-speaking operators, with new equipment.

Vietnam Explorer DIVING
(☎384 6372; 36 Đ Tran Hung Dao)

Fishing & Boat Trips

Anh Tu's Tours BOAT TRIPS
(☎399 6009; anhtupq@yahoo.com) Snorkelling, squid fishing and island tours, plus motorbike rental.

John's Tours BOAT TRIPS
(☎091 910 7086; www.johnsislandtours.com; 4 Đ Tran Hung Dao) Snorkelling, island-hopping and fishing trips.

Sleeping

Accommodation prices yo-yo depending on the season. Price fluctuations are more extreme than anywhere else in Vietnam, but tend to affect budget and midrange places more than the top-end resorts.

DUONG DONG

Sea Breeze HOTEL $
(Gio Bien; ☎399 4920; www.seabreezephuquoc.com; 62A Đ Tran Hung Dao; r with fan US$15, air-con US$25-40; ❄📶) New place with smart, contemporary rooms and a breezy rooftop

OFF THE BEATEN TRACK IN THE MEKONG DELTA

It's not hard to get off the beaten track in the Mekong Delta, as most tourists are on hit-and-run day trips from HCMC or passing through on their way to or from Cambodia. Here are some lesser-known regional gems:

» Check out some Khmer culture in **Tra Vinh**, home to a significant population of Cambodians and their beautiful temples.

» The Khmer kingdom of Funan once held sway over much of the lower Mekong; its principal port was at **Oc-Eo**, located near Long Xuyen. Archaeologists have found ancient Persian and Roman artefacts here.

» Birding enthusiasts will want to make a diversion to **Tram Chin Reserve** near Cao Lang, a habitat for the rare eastern sarus crane. These huge birds are depicted on the bas-reliefs at Angkor and only found here and in northwest Cambodia.

» The small and secluded beach resort of **Hon Chong** has the most scenic stretch of coastline on the Mekong Delta mainland. The big attractions here are Chua Hang Grotto, Duong Beach and Nghe Island.

terrace. It's handy for the night markets and beach road.

Hiep Phong Hotel GUESTHOUSE $
(384 6057; nguyet_1305@yahoo.com; 17 Đ Nguyen Trai; r 280,000d;) Very friendly, family-run minihotel in the town centre. The rooms include satellite TV, fridge and hot water.

LONG BEACH

TOP CHOICE La Veranda RESORT HOTEL $$$
(398 2988; www.laverandaresort.com; 118/9 Đ Tran Hung Dao; r US$275-375;) Elegant and classy, colonialesque La Veranda is small enough to remain intimate, with just 44 rooms. All rooms feature large beds and designer bathrooms. There's a spa, pretty beach, and cafe and restaurant.

Sea Star Resort RESORT HOTEL $$
(398 2161; www.seastarresort.com; r US$40, bungalow US$50-75;) A fun and friendly place to stay, the extensive compound includes 37 rooms and bungalows, many fronting a manicured stretch of sand with sea-view balconies.

Beach Club RESORT HOTEL $$
(398 0998; www.beachclubvietnam.com; r US$25-35;) This chilled retreat, run by an English-Vietnamese couple, has tightly grouped, well-kept and spacious bungalows. Good local info, plus a breezy beachside restaurant for stunning sunsets.

AROUND THE ISLAND

TOP CHOICE Chen Sea Resort & Spa RESORT HOTEL $$$
(399 5895; www.chenla-resort.com; Ong Lang Beach; bungalows US$234-473;) Upmarket On Lang resort has attractive villas that are designed to resemble ancient terracotta-roofed houses. Offers a beautiful sandy beach, large pool, spa and plenty of activities.

Bamboo Cottages & Restaurant RESORT HOTEL $$
(281 0345; www.bamboophuquoc.com; Vung Bau Beach; r US$50-85;) Run by a friendly family, Bamboo Cottages has Vung Bau beach largely to itself. Boasts an open-sided shorefront restaurant and bar, and the 14 attractive villas have private, open-roofed bathrooms with solar-powered hot water.

Mango Garden B&B $$
(629 1339; mangogarden.inn@gmail.com; US$35; Sep-Apr;) Isolated B&B reached by a bumpy dirt road (turn left just before Sao Beach), run by a Vietnamese-Canadian. Surrounded by gorgeous gardens and mango trees, it has just a handful of rooms. Book ahead.

Mango Bay RESORT HOTEL $$$
(398 1693; www.mangobayphuquoc.com; Ong Lang Beach; r US$75-80, bungalows US$90-145;) Set around a small cove, this eco-friendly resort's bungalows all include a private terrace. A romantic, if simple, getaway for those who want some privacy.

Freedomland HOMESTAY $$
(399 4891; www.freedomlandphuquoc.com; Ong Lang Beach; r US$30-40;) More like a little hippy commune than a resort, the 11 basic bungalows (with mosquito nets and fans, although no hot water) at Freedomland are scattered around a shady plot. The communal vibe and shared meal experience makes it a popular place with solo travellers.

Eating & Drinking

Most hotels have their own lively cafes or restaurants in-house.

Duong Dong's **night market** (Đ Vo Thi Sau;) is one of the most atmospheric (and affordable) places to dine with a delicious range of Vietnamese seafood, grills and vegetarian options.

The seafood restaurants in the fishing village of Ham Ninh also offer an authentic local experience and taste; try **Kim Cuong I** (mains 30,000-300,000d).

DUONG DONG

Buddy Ice Cream ICE CREAM $
(www.visitphuquoc.info; 26 Đ Nguyen Trai; mains 25,000-130,000d;) New Zealand ice cream (per scoop 25,000d), plus toasted sandwiches, fish and chips and snacks. Doubles as a tourist information centre and there's free internet.

Le Giang VIETNAMESE $
(289 Đ Tran Hung Dao; mains 40,000-80,000d) A wide range of Vietnamese favourites in a local-style place with a breeze-catching terrace. Try the caramelised fish claypots.

LONG BEACH

Mondo TAPAS $
(82 Đ Tran Hung Dao; tapas 50,000-90,000d) Head here for Spanish tapas (chorizo, spicy meatballs, garlic prawns), Western breakfasts and Asian flavours in a chic setting.

Ganesh INDIAN $$
(www.ganeshindianrestaurant.com; 97 Đ Tran Hung Dao; mains 52,000-99,000d; ⊙11am-10pm; ⊘) Authentic North and South Indian cuisine is served in this attractive, airy restaurant, including tandoori dishes and ample vegetarian selections.

Hop Inn VIETNAMESE $
(Đ Tran Hung Dao; mains 50,000-130,000d) The best Vietnamese food on the Tran Hung Dao strip, including plenty of seafood, as well as sandwiches if you fancy more familiar fare.

Pepper's Pizza & Grill ITALIAN $
(☎384 8773; 89 Đ Tran Hung Dao; mains 65,000-190,000d) Terrific pizzas, and they'll even deliver to your hotel.

AROUND THE ISLAND

My Lan VIETNAMESE $$
(mains 55,000-110,000d, Sao Beach) Located on the white sands of Sao Beach, this place has succulent barbecued seafood and fish in claypots.

Bo Resort FRENCH $$$
(☎398 6142; www.boresort.com; mains around US$13) The restaurant at this French-run resort is renowned for its wonderful Gallic grub.

Information

There are ATMs in Duong Dong and in many resorts on Long Beach. **Buddy Ice Cream** (see Eating) offers free internet and wi-fi.

Getting There & Away

Air

Demand can be high in peak season, so book ahead. A new international airport should open towards the end of 2011.

Vietnam Airlines (☎399 6677; www.vietnamairlines.com; 122 Đ Nguyen Trung Truc) Flies to/from Rach Gia (from 500,000d, daily), Can Tho (from 500,000d, daily) and HCMC (from 450,000d, 10 daily).

Air Mekong (☎04-3718 8199; www.airmekong.com.vn) Flies to/from HCMC (from 450,000d, four daily) and Hanoi (from 2,230,000d, two daily).

Boat

Fast boats connect Phu Quoc to both Ha Tien (1½ hours) and Rach Gia (2½ hours). Phu Quoc travel agents, such as **Green Cruise** (☎397 8111; www.greencruise.com.vn; 14 Đ Tran Hung Dao), have the most up-to-date schedules and can book tickets.

From Ha Tien there are two small boats, departing 8am (180,000d) and 1.30pm (230,000d) and a car ferry (departing 9.30am from Ha Tien and 2.30pm from Phu Quoc; per passenger/motorbike/car 145,000d/100,000d/US$50) departing daily.

Rach Gia has two reputable operators servicing the route:

Savanna Express (☎369 2888; www.savannaexpress.com; adult/child 295,000/200,000d) Departs Rach Gia at 8.05am and Phu Quoc at 1.05pm; 2½ hours.

Superdong (Rach Gia ☎077-387 7742, Phu Quoc ☎077-398 0111; www.superdong.com.vn; adult/child 295,000/225,000d) Departs Rach Gia at 8am, 1pm and 1.30pm and Phu Quoc at 8am, 8.30am and 1pm; 2½ hours.

Ferries depart from the pier at Vong Beach (Bai Vong). Buses, timed to meet the ferries, pick up on Đ Tran Hung Dao and Đ 30 Thang 4 (20,000d).

DON'T MISS

AN THOI ISLANDS

Just off the southern tip of Phu Quoc Island, these 15 islands and islets can be visited by chartered boat. It's a fine area for sightseeing, fishing, swimming and snorkelling. Hon Thom (Pineapple Island) is about 3km in length and is the largest in the group. Other islands include Hon Dua (Coconut Island), Hon Roi (Lamp Island), Hon Vang (Echo Island), Hon May Rut (Cold Cloud Island), the Hon Dams (Shadow Islands), Chan Qui (Yellow Tortoise) and Hon Mong Tay (Short Gun Island). As yet, there is no real development on the islands, but expect some movement in the next few years.

Most boats depart from An Thoi on Phu Quoc, but you can make arrangements through hotels and resorts on Long Beach. You can also inquire at the dive operators, as they have boats heading down there regularly for diving. Boat trips are seasonal and generally do not run during the rainy season.

Getting Around

Phu Quoc's airport is in central Duong Dong. Motorbike drivers charge US$1 to US$2 to most places on Long Beach. A metered taxi costs around 90,000d to Long Beach and 250,000d to Ong Lang Beach.

Bicycle rentals are available through most hotels from US$3 per day.

There is a skeletal bus service (every hour or two) between An Thoi and Duong Dong. A bus (20,000d) waits for the ferry at Bai Vong to take passengers to Duong Dong.

Rental motorbikes cost US$7 to US$10 (automatic) per day. Motorbike taxis are everywhere. Short hops cost 20,000d; figure on around 50,000d for about 5km.

Call **Mai Linh** (☎397 9797) for a reliable taxi; Duong Dong to Vong Beach costs about 250,000d.

UNDERSTAND VIETNAM

Vietnam Today

Few places on earth have changed as much as Vietnam in the last few decades. One of the poorest, war-wounded corners of the globe has transformed itself into a stable, prospering nation through industriousness, ingenuity and ambition. The overall standard of living has risen incredibly, education and healthcare have greatly improved. Blue-chip finance has flooded into a red-flag communist society. Rice paddies have become business parks. Comrades have become entrepreneurs. It's been a breathtaking, and largely successful, transformation.

And yet. Take a peek beneath those headline-grabbing growth figures and there are concerns. Double-digit growth has faltered as the economy has cooled. Corruption remains systemic: the nation is rated 116 out of 182 on Transparency International's global index. Vietnamese people have to pay backhanders for everything from getting an internet connection to securing a hospital appointment. At the highest level, corrupt politicians have been caught demanding millions of dollars to facilitate infrastructure projects.

Observers argue this is why Vietnam needs to embrace democracy, to hold those in power accountable for their actions. Such a prospect seems a distant dream; there's no sign that the Communist Party is contemplating relaxing control. Not only is political dissent a complete no-no but the entire nation's internet operates behind a firewall that blocks anything – including Facebook – that might potentially lead to trouble.

Most Vietnamese have accepted this status quo for now. They're living in an age of rising prosperity. Times are pretty good, for most, though inflation (running at 25% in 2011) is a huge concern. The population is young, the country is stable, foreign investment is considerable. Much will depend on how the Party manages to continue creating jobs and growth. And with only two million paid-up members of the Communist Party and 90 million Vietnamese, it is a road they must tread carefully.

History

Vietnam has a history as rich and evocative as anywhere on earth. Sure, the war with the USA captured the attention of the West, but centuries before that the Vietnamese were scrapping with the Chinese, the Khmers, the Chams and the Mongols. Vietnamese civilisation is as sophisticated as that of its mighty northern neighbour China, from where it drew many of its influences under a 1000-year occupation. Later came the French and the humbling period of colonialism from which Vietnam was not to emerge until the second half of the 20th century. The Americans were simply the last in a long line of invaders who had come and gone through the centuries and, no matter what was required or how long it took, they too would be vanquished. If only the military planners in Washington had paid a little more attention to the history of this proud nation, the trauma and tragedy of a long war might have been avoided.

Early Vietnam

The sophisticated Indianised kingdom of Funan flourished from the 1st to 6th centuries AD in the Mekong Delta area. Archaeological evidence reveals that Funan's busy trading port of Oc-Eo had contact with China, India, Persia and even the Mediterranean. Between the mid-6th century and the 9th century, the Funan empire was absorbed by the pre-Angkorian kingdom of Chenla.

Meanwhile, around present-day Danang, the Hindu kingdom of Champa emerged in the late 2nd century AD. Like Funan, it adopted Sanskrit as a sacred language and borrowed heavily from Indian art and culture.

By the 8th century Champa had expanded to include what is now Nha Trang and Phan Rang. The Cham warred constantly with the Vietnamese to the north and the Khmers to the south and ultimately found themselves squeezed between these two great powers.

Chinese Occupation

The Chinese conquered the Red River Delta in the 2nd century BC and over the following centuries attempted to impress a centralised state system on the Vietnamese. There were numerous small-scale rebellions against Chinese rule – which was characterised by tyranny, forced labour and insatiable demands for tribute – between the 3rd to 6th centuries, but all were defeated.

However, the early Viets learned much from the Chinese, including advanced irrigation for rice cultivation and medical knowledge, as well as Confucianism, Taoism and Mahayana Buddhism. Much of the 1000-year period of Chinese occupation was typified by Vietnamese resistence while at the same time adopting many Chinese cultural traits.

In AD 938 Ngo Quyen destroyed Chinese forces on the Bach Dang River, winning independence and signaling the start of a dynastic tradition. During subsequent centuries the Vietnamese successfully repulsed foreign invaders, including the Mongols, and absorbed the kingdom of Champa in 1471 as they expanded south.

Contact with the West

In 1858 a joint military force from France and the Spanish colony of the Philippines stormed Danang after several missionaries were killed. Early the next year, Saigon was seized. By 1883 the French had imposed a Treaty of Protectorate on Vietnam. French rule often proved cruel and arbitrary. Ultimately, the most successful resistance came from the communists, first organised by Ho Chi Minh in 1925.

During WWII, the only group that significantly resisted the Japanese occupation was the communist-dominated Viet Minh. When WWII ended, Ho Chi Minh – whose Viet Minh forces already controlled large parts of the country – declared Vietnam independent. French efforts to reassert control soon led to violent confrontations and full-scale war. In May 1954, Viet Minh forces overran the French garrison at Dien Bien Phu.

The Geneva Accords of mid-1954 provided for a temporary division of Vietnam at the Ben Hai River. When Ngo Dinh Diem, the anti-communist Catholic leader of the southern zone, refused to hold the 1956 elections, the Ben Hai line became the border between North and South Vietnam.

The War in Vietnam

Around 1960, the Hanoi government changed its policy of opposition to the Diem regime from one of 'political struggle' to one of 'armed struggle'. The National Liberation Front (NLF), a communist guerrilla group better known as the Viet Cong (VC), was founded to fight against Diem.

An unpopular ruler, Diem was assassinated in 1963 by his own troops. When the Hanoi government ordered North Vietnamese Army (NVA) units to infiltrate the South in 1964, the situation for the Saigon regime became desperate. In 1965 the USA committed its first combat troops, soon joined by soldiers from South Korea, Australia, Thailand and New Zealand in an effort to bring global legitimacy to the conflict.

As Vietnam celebrated the Lunar New Year in 1968, the VC launched a surprise attack, known as the Tet Offensive, marking a crucial turning point in the war. Many Americans, who had for years believed their government's insistence that the USA was winning, started demanding a negotiated end to the war. The Paris Agreements, signed in 1973, provided for a ceasefire, the total withdrawal of US combat forces and the release of American prisoners of war.

Reunification

Saigon surrendered to the NVA on 30 April 1975. Vietnam's reunification by the communists meant liberation from more than a century of colonial oppression, but was soon followed by large-scale internal repression. Hundreds of thousands of southerners fled Vietnam, creating a flood of refugees for the next 15 years.

Vietnam's campaign of repression against the ethnic Chinese, plus its invasion of Cambodia at the end of 1978, prompted China to attack Vietnam in 1979. The war lasted only 17 days, but Chinese-Vietnamese mistrust lasted for well over a decade.

Post–Cold War

After the collapse of the Soviet Union in 1991, Vietnam and Western nations sought

UNCLE OF THE PEOPLE

Father of the nation, Ho Chi Minh ('Bringer of Light') was the son of a fiercely nationalistic scholar-official. Born Nguyen Tat Thanh near Vinh in 1890, he was educated in Hué and adopted many pseudonyms during his momentous life. Many Vietnamese affectionately refer to him as Bac Ho ('Uncle Ho') today.

In 1911 he signed up as a cook's apprentice on a French ship, sailing the seas to North America, Africa and Europe. While odd-jobbing in England and France as a gardener, snow sweeper, waiter, photo-retoucher and stoker, his political consciousness developed.

Ho Chi Minh moved to Paris, where he mastered languages including English, French, German and Mandarin, and began to promote the issue of Indochinese independence. He was a founding member of the French Communist Party in 1920.

In 1941 Ho Chi Minh returned to Vietnam for the first time in 30 years, and established the Viet Minh (whose goal was independence from France). As Japan prepared to surrender in August 1945, Ho Chi Minh led the August Revolution, and his forces then established control throughout much of Vietnam.

The return of the French compelled the Viet Minh to conduct a guerrilla war, which ultimately led to victory against the colonists at Dien Bien Phu in 1954. Ho then lead North Vietnam until his death in September 1969 – he never lived to see the North's victory over the South.

Since then the party has worked hard to preserve the image and reputation of Bac Ho. His image dominates contemporary Vietnam. This cult of personality is in stark contrast to the simplicity with which Ho lived his life. For more Ho, check out *Ho Chi Minh*, the excellent biography by William J Duiker.

rapprochement. The 1990s brought foreign investment and Association of Southeast Asian Nations (Asean) membership. The US established diplomatic relations with Vietnam in 1995, and in 2000 Bill Clinton became the first US president to visit north Vietnam. George W Bush followed suit in 2006, as Vietnam was welcomed into the World Trade Organisation (WTO) in 2007.

Relations have also greatly improved with the historic enemy, China. China may still secretly think of Vietnam as 'the one that got away', but Vietnam's economic boom has caught Běijīng's attention and trade and tourism are booming across mutual borders.

Culture

People

The Vietnamese are battle-hardened, proud and nationalist, as they have earned their stripes in successive skirmishes with the world's mightiest powers. But that's the older generation, which remembers every inch of the territory for which it fought. For the new generation, Vietnam is a place to succeed, a place to ignore the staid structures set in stone by the communists, and a place to go out and have some fun.

As in other parts of Asia, life revolves around the family; there are often several generations living under one roof. Poverty, and the transition from a largely agricultural society to that of a more industrialised nation, sends many people seeking their fortune to the bigger cities, and is changing the structure of the modern family unit. Women make up 52% of the nation's workforce but are not well represented in positions of power.

Vietnam's population is 84% ethnic Vietnamese (Kinh) and 2% ethnic Chinese; the rest is made up of Khmers, Chams and members of more than 50 minority people, who mainly live in highland areas.

Politics

Vietnam's political system could not be simpler: the Communist Party is the sole source of power. Officially, according to the Vietnamese constitution, the National Assembly (or parliament) is the country's supreme authority, as it selects the president and prime minister and manages the legal system. The reality is that National Assembly is a tool of the Party and its carefully controlled elections typify the kind of voting process you'd expect in a one-party state. Currently, 90% of delegates are Communist Party members.

Officially, communism is still king, but there can be few party hacks who really believe Vietnam is a Marxist utopia. Market-oriented socialism is the new mantra, although socially responsible capitalism might be nearer the mark. Foreign investment is booming. Capitalism thrives like never before, with the dynamic private sector driving the economy. On the street, everyone seems to be out to make a fast buck. Fast.

Yet the reality is that the state still controls a vast swath of the economy. More than 100 of the 200 biggest companies in Vietnam are state-owned and the key sectors of oil production, shipbuilding, cement, coal and rubber are government controlled.

Economic liberalisation is ongoing, though any meaningful democratic change still seems a long, long way off. Everything is geared to safeguard the Party's grip on power. The media is tightly controlled and critics of the Party are silenced. In 2007, democracy movement members Nguyen Van Dai and Le Thi Cong Nhan were sent to prison for spreading 'anti-state propaganda'.

Religion

Over the centuries, Confucianism, Taoism and Buddhism have fused with popular Chinese beliefs and ancient Vietnamese animism to form what's collectively known as the Triple Religion (Tam Giao). Most Vietnamese people identify with this belief system but, if asked, they'll usually say they're Buddhist.

Vietnam has a significant percentage of Catholics (8% to 10% of the total population).

The unique and colourful Vietnamese sect Cao Daism (see p481) was founded in the 1920s. It combines secular and religious philosophies of the East and West, and is based on seance messages revealed to the group's founder, Ngo Minh Chieu.

There are also small numbers of Muslims (around 60,000) and Hindus (50,000).

Arts

CONTEMPORARY ART

It is possible to catch modern dance, classical ballet and stage plays in Hanoi and Ho Chi Minh City (HCMC).

The work of contemporary painters and photographers covers a wide swath of styles and gives a glimpse into the modern Vietnamese psyche.

Youth culture is most vibrant in HCMC where there is more freedom for musicians and artists.

ARCHITECTURE

The Vietnamese were not great builders like their neighbours the Khmer. Most early Vietnamese buildings were made of wood and other materials that proved highly vulnerable in the tropical climate. The grand exceptions are the stunning towers built by Vietnam's ancient Cham culture. These are most numerous in central Vietnam. The Cham ruins at My Son (p114) are a major draw.

SCULPTURE

Vietnamese sculpture has traditionally centred on religious themes and has functioned as an adjunct to architecture, especially that of pagodas, temples and tombs.

The Cham civilisation produced exquisite carved sandstone figures for its Hindu and Buddhist sanctuaries. The largest single collection of Cham sculpture is at the Museum of Cham Sculpture (p105) in Danang.

WATER PUPPETRY

Vietnam's ancient art of *roi nuoc* (water puppetry) originated in northern Vietnam at least a thousand years ago. Developed by rice farmers, the wooden puppets were manipulated by puppeteers using water-flooded rice paddies as their stage. Hanoi is the best place to see water-puppetry performances, which are accompanied by music played on traditional instruments.

THE NORTH–SOUTH DIVIDE

The north–south divide lingers on. The war may be history, but prejudice is alive and well. Ask a southerner what they think of northerners and they'll say they have a 'hard face', that they are too serious and don't know how to have fun. Ask a northerner what they think of southerners and they will say they are too superficial and business-obsessed.

When it comes to the older generation, the south has never forgiven the north for bulldozing its war cemeteries, imposing communism and blackballing whole families. The north has never forgiven the south for siding with the Americans against its own. For Vietnam, however, today's generation seems to have less interest in this harrowing history.

Environment

Environmental consciousness is low in Vietnam. Rapid industrialisation, deforestation and pollution are major problems facing the country.

Unsustainable logging and farming practices, as well as the US's extensive spraying of defoliants during the war in Vietnam, have contributed to deforestation. This has resulted not only in significant loss of biological diversity, but also in a harder existence for many minority people.

The country's rapid economic and population growth over the last decade – demonstrated by the dramatic increase in industrial production, motorbike numbers and helter-skelter construction – has put additional pressure on the already-stressed environment.

The Land

Vietnam stretches more than 1600km along the east coast of the Indochinese peninsula. The country's land area is 329,566 sq km, making it slightly larger than Italy and a bit smaller than Japan.

As the Vietnamese are quick to point out, it resembles a *don ganh*, or the ubiquitous bamboo pole with a basket of rice slung from each end. The baskets represent the main rice-growing regions of the Red River Delta in the north, and the Mekong Delta in the south.

Of several interesting geological features found in Vietnam, the most striking are its spectacular karst formations (limestone peaks with caves and underground streams). The northern half of Vietnam has a spectacular array of karst areas, particularly around Halong Bay (p79), Tam Coc (p77) and Phong Nha (p101).

Wildlife

Because Vietnam has such a wide range of habitats, fauna here is enormously diverse; its forests are estimated to contain 12,000 plant species, only 7000 of which have been identified. Vietnam is home to more than 275 species of mammal, 800 species of bird, 180 species of reptile and 80 species of amphibian. In the 1990s, one species of muntjac (deer) and an ox similar to an oryx were discovered in Vietnam – the only newly identified large mammals in the world in the last 60 years.

Tragically, Vietnam's wildlife is in precipitous decline as forest habitats are destroyed and waterways become polluted. Illegal hunting has also exterminated the local populations of certain animals, in some cases eliminating entire species. Officially, the Vietnamese government recognises 57 mammal species (including

LOCAL KNOWLEDGE

VINH VU: FOUNDER, HANDSPAN TRAVEL

In a nation of cloned tour operators, few stand out. Handspan is one company that does, with its highly innovative trips. We grilled Handspan founder Vinh Vu for his insider tips.

Where's Vietnam's most spectacular scenery? The Ha Giang rock plateau of Dong Van and Meo Vac area, and Phong Nha-Ke Bang National Park.

Where do you like to escape the crowds? In the northern mountains, especially where road conditions are not great. Also I love island beaches such as Co To, Quan Lan, Con Dao and Con Co.

Which regions are emerging? Improved roads have opened up Ngoc Son Ngo Luong in Hoa Binh Province, which is a Muong tribal area with great countryside, rice paddies and innocent people. The Moc Chau plateau, which has a cool climate, tea plantations and Hmong and Thai culture, is another.

Your tips for travellers to get more out of Vietnam? Try to balance between must-see and off-the-beaten-track places for better impact on the country and to diversify your experience. Must-see places are already popular so you won't feel that special. Off-the-beaten-track destinations require more study, organising and costs but your experiences are unique and these places are changing too, so be quick.

several primates) and 64 bird species as endangered.

Many officials still turn a blind eye to the trade in wildlife for export and domestic consumption, though laws are in place to protect the animals. Poachers continue to profit from meeting the demand for exotic animals for pets and traditional medicines. Tragically, one of mainland Asia's few remaining Javan rhino (there are thought to be less than 10) was killed for its horn inside Cat Tien National Park in 2010.

Animal welfare is not yet a priority in Vietnamese culture, evidenced by the appallingly inadequate conditions for caged wildlife found throughout Vietnam.

National Parks

The number of national parks in the country has been rapidly expanding and there are now 30, covering about 3% of Vietnam's total territory. In the north the most interesting and accessible include Cat Ba (p80), Bai Tu Long (see boxed text, p83), Ba Be (p87) and Cuc Phuong (p78). Heading south, Phong Nha (p101), Bach Ma National Park (p104), Yok Don National Park (p135) and Cat Tien National Park (p135) are well worth investigating.

With the help of NGOs, the Vietnamese government is taking steps to expand national park boundaries, crack down on illegal poaching and educate and employ people living in national park buffer zones. It's a long process.

Flora and Fauna International produces the excellent *Nature Tourism Map of Vietnam,* which includes detailed coverage of all the national parks in Vietnam. All proceeds from sales of the map go towards supporting primate conservation.

SURVIVAL GUIDE

Directory A–Z

Accommodation

In general, accommodation in Vietnam offers superb value for money and excellent facilities. In big cities and the main tourism centres you'll find everything from hostel dorm beds to uber-luxe hotels. Cleanliness standards are generally good and there are very few real dumps.

Most hotels in Vietnam quote prices in Vietnamese dong and/or US dollars. Prices are quoted in dong or dollars throughout this chapter based on the preferred currency of the particular property.

In this chapter, the budget breakdown is: budget (**$**), rooms less than US$25 a night (dorm-bed prices are given individually); midrange (**$$**), US$25 to US$75; and top end (**$$$**), US$75 and above. These reflect high-season rates, though discounts are often available at quiet times of year.

Family-run guesthouses are usually the cheapest option; they often have private bathrooms and room rates range from around US$7 to US$20. A step up from the guesthouses, minihotels typically come with more amenities: satellite TV and free wi-fi. Rates often go down the more steps you have to climb; upper floors are cheaper.

When it comes to midrange places, flash a bit more cash and three-star touches are available, such as chic decor or access to a swimming pool.

At the top end you'll find everything from faceless but comfortable business hotels to colonial places resonating with history and lovely boutique hotels.

Be aware that some hotels apply a 10% sales tax. Check carefully before taking a room to avoid any unpleasant shocks on departure.

Accommodation is at a premium during Tet (late January or early February), when the whole country is on the move and overseas Vietnamese flood back into the country. Prices can rise by 25% or more. Christmas and New Year represent another high season.

HOMESTAYS

Homestays are popular in parts of Vietnam, but it's highly advisable not to just drop into a random tribal village and hope things work out, as there are strict rules about registering foreigners who stay overnight.

Areas that are well set up include the Mekong Delta (p153), the White Thai villages of Mai Chau (p88) and Ba Be (p87).

Activities

Vietnam's roads, rivers, sea and mountains have ample opportunity for active adventures.

Travel agencies and travellers' cafes all over the country can arrange local trips,

TOP READS ON VIETNAM

There's a great deal been written about the war in Vietnam and the US role in the conflict. Up-to-date books about contemporary Vietnam are harder to find. Some of the best books about Vietnam include the following:

» *The Quiet American* (1955) by Graham Greene is a classic account of Vietnam in the 1950s as French Indochina is crumbling.

» *The Sorrow of War* by Bao Ninh (1994) is a deeply poignant war tale told from the North Vietnamese perspective.

» *Shadows and Wind* (1999) by Robert Templer is a snappily-written exploration of Vietnam.

» *Catfish & Mandala* by Andrew X Pham (1999) is a biographical tale of a Vietnamese-American.

» *Vietnam: Rising Dragon* by Bill Hayton (2010) is a candid assessment of the nation today.

from kayaking on Halong Bay to trekking up Fansipan or kitesurfing in Mui Ne.

CYCLING

If you love exploring on a saddle, Vietnam is ideal. You'll find cheap bicycles for hire (US$1 to US$2 per day) in virtually every town in the country.

For extended trips the flatlands and back roads of the Mekong Delta are wonderful to cycle through and observe the vibrant workaday agricultural life. Another spot well away from the insane traffic of National Hwy 1 is Hwy 14, winding through the Central Highlands.

Tour companies with good cycling trips include:

Handspan Adventure Travel (☎04-3926 0581; www.handspan.com; 80 P Ma May, Hanoi) Hanoi-based, with many trips across the north.

Sinhbalo Adventures (☎08-3837 6766; www.sinhbalo.com; 283/20 Đ Pham Ngu Lao, HCMC) Meander in the Mekong Delta or further afield.

DIVING & SNORKELLING

Vietnam's diving is not world class, but there are several established dive destinations. The Con Dao Islands (p128) are considered the best, while the beach resort of Nha Trang (p117) has numerous sites and scuba schools. Others possibilities include the lovely Cham Islands (p166) near Hoi An, and Phu Quoc Island (p155) in the deep south.

KAYAKING

For an even closer look at those limestone crags, it's possible to paddle yourself around Halong Bay or Lan Ha Bay. Talk to travel agencies in Hanoi and Cat Ba about kayaking trips.

The rest of the nation is catching up, and other kayaking destinations now include Phong Nha, lakes near Dalat and rivers of the Hoi An region.

TREKKING

The most popular region for trekking is the north, notably around Sapa (p91), which includes Vietnam's tallest mountain, Fansipan, and offers walks through majestic mountain scenery and past fascinating tribal villages. Bac Ha, Mai Chau and Ba Be are other bases.

There's also good trekking in the forests of Cat Ba (p80), Cuc Phuong (p78) and Phong Nha (p101) and Cat Tien (p135) national parks.

WATERSPORTS

Mui Ne (p123) is a world-class kitesurfing and windsurfing destination, with several excellent schools that run courses and classes. Nha Trang (p116) is another good locale for windsurfing, sailing or wakeboarding. Vung Tau (p127) is a third option.

Vietnam is not a surf mecca and boards and gear are hard to find. Conditions are best between November and April when the winter monsoon blows from the north. The China Beach (p107) area south of Danang is renowned; there are also waves to ride around Nha Trang, Mui Ne and Vung Tau.

Business Hours

Offices and other public buildings are usually open from 7am or 8am to 11am or 11.30am and again from 1pm or 2pm to 4pm or 5pm. Banks tend to be open during these hours, and until 11.30am on Saturday.

Post offices are generally open from 6.30am to 9pm. Government offices are usually open until noon on Saturday and closed Sunday. Most museums are closed on Monday. Temples are usually open all day, every day.

Many small, privately owned shops, restaurants and street stalls stay open seven days a week, often until late at night.

By law, most bars in Vietnam officially close at midnight and the fun police often enforce this. However, in major centres such as HCMC there are always a few late-night places.

Children

Children get to have a good time in Vietnam. There are some great beaches, but pay close attention to any playtime in the sea, as there are some big rip tides.

Kids generally enjoy local cuisine, which is rarely too spicy; the range of fruit is staggering. Comfort food from home (pizzas, pasta, burgers and ice cream) is available in most places.

Baby supplies are available in the major cities. Cot beds are rare, and car safety seats virtually non-existent. Breastfeeding in public is fine.

The main worry throughout Vietnam is keeping an eye on what strange things infants are putting in their mouths: remember dysentery, typhoid and hepatitis are common. Keep their hydration levels up, and slap on the sunscreen.

Customs Regulations

Bear in mind that customs may seize suspected antiques or other 'cultural treasures'. If you do purchase authentic or reproduction antiques get a receipt and customs clearance form from the seller.

Electricity

220V, 50 cycles. Socket are two pin, round head.

Embassies & Consulates

Australia (www.vietnam.embassy.gov.au) Hanoi (☎3774 0100; 8 Đ Dao Tan, Ba Dinh District); HCMC (Map p144; ☎3521 8100; 5th fl, 5B Đ Ton Duc Thang)

Cambodia Hanoi (☎3942 4788; cambocg@hcm.vnn.vn; 71A P Tran Hung Dao); HCMC (Map p138; ☎3829 2751; 41 Đ Phung Khac Khoan)

Canada (www.canadainternational.gc.ca/vietnam) Hanoi (☎3734 5000; 31 Đ Hung Vuong); HCMC (Map p144; ☎3827 9899; 10th fl, 235 Đ Dong Khoi)

China (http://vn.china-embassy.org/chn) Hanoi (☎8845 3736; 46 P Hoang Dieu); HCMC (☎3829 2457; 39 Đ Nguyen Thi Minh Khai)

France (www.ambafrance-vn.org) Hanoi (☎3944 5700; P Tran Hung Dao); HCMC (Map p138; ☎3520 6800; 27 Đ Nguyen Thi Minh Khai)

Germany (www.hanoi.diplo.de) Hanoi (☎3845 3836; 29 Đ Tran Phu); HCMC (Map p138; ☎3829 1967; 126 Đ Nguyen Dinh Chieu)

Japan (www.vn.emb-japan.go.jp) Hanoi (☎3846 3000; 27 P Lieu Giai, Ba Dinh District); HCMC (☎3822 5341; 13-17 ĐL Nguyen Hue)

Laos (www.embalaohanoi.gov.la) Danang (12 Đ Tran Qui Cap); Hanoi (☎3942 4576; 22 P Tran Binh Trong); HCMC (Map p144; ☎3829 7667; 93 Đ Pasteur)

Netherlands (www.netherlands-embassy.org.vn) Hanoi (☎3831 5650; 6th fl, Daeha Office Tower, 360 Kim Ma St, Ba Dinh) HCMC (Map p138; ☎3823 5932; Saigon Tower, 29 ĐL Le Duan)

New Zealand (www.nzembassy.com/viet-nam) Hanoi (Map p70; ☎3824 1481; Level 5, 63 P Ly Thai To); HCMC (Map p144; ☎3827 2745; 8th fl, The Metropolitan, 235 Đ Dong Khoi)

Philippines Hanoi (☎3943 7948; hanoi.pe@dfa.gov.ph; 27B P Tran Hung Dao)

Singapore (www.mfa.gov.sg/hanoi) Hanoi (☎3848 9168; 41-43 Đ Tran Phu)

Sweden (www.swedenabroad.com) Hanoi (☎3726 0400; 2 Đ Nui Truc)

Thailand (www.thaiembassy.org) Hanoi (☎3823 5092; 63-65 P Hoang Dieu); HCMC (☎3932 7637; 77 Đ Tran Quoc Thao)

UK (http://ukinvietnam.fco.gov.uk) Hanoi (Map p70; ☎3936 0500; Central Bldg, 31 P Hai Ba Trung); HCMC (☎3829 8433; 25 ĐL Le Duan)

HIGHLIGHTS FOR CHILDREN

ATTRACTION	DETAILS	PAGE
HCMC's water parks	Cool off with a big grin on your face	p139
Hanoi's water-puppet performances	Always goes down well	p63
Cuc Phuong Primate Rescue Centre	Monkey business (and conservation education)	p78
Halong Bay	Bobbing about on a boat	p79

THERE'S SOMETHING FISHY AROUND HERE...

Nuoc mam (fish sauce) is the one ingredient that is quintessentially Vietnamese and it lends a distinctive character to Vietnamese cooking. The sauce is made by fermenting highly salted fish in large ceramic vats for four to 12 months. Connoisseurs insist high-grade sauce has a much milder aroma than the cheaper variety. Dissenters insist it is a chemical weapon. It's very often used as a dipping sauce, and takes the place of salt on a Western table.

USA (http://vietnam.usembassy.gov) Hanoi (☎3850 5000; 7 P Lang Ha, Ba Dinh District); HCMC (Map p138; ☎3822 9433; 4 ĐL Le Duan)

Food & Drink

FOOD

Vietnamese food is one of the world's greatest cuisines; there are said to be nearly 500 traditional dishes. It varies a lot between north, central and south. Soy sauce, Chinese influence and hearty soups like *pho* typify northern cuisine. Central Vietnamese food is known for its prodigious use of fresh herbs and intricate flavours; Hué imperial cuisine and Hoi An specialities are key to this area. Southern food is sweet, spicy and tropical; its curries will be familiar to lovers of Thai and Cambodian food. Everywhere you'll find Vietnamese meals are superbly prepared and excellent value.

As an approximate guide, prices for a meal when eating out are under US$5 for budget, US$5 to US$15 for midrange and more than US$15 for top-end places. For any prices in dong, use the conversion rate given in the box at the start of the chapter.

Fruit

Aside from the usual delightful Southeast Asian fruits, Vietnam has its own unique *trai thanh long* (green dragon fruit), a bright fuchsia-coloured fruit with green scales. Grown mainly along the coastal region near Nha Trang, it has white flesh flecked with edible black seeds, and tastes something like a mild kiwifruit.

Meals

Pho is the noodle soup that built a nation and is eaten at all hours of the day, but especially for breakfast. *Com* are rice dishes. You'll see signs saying *pho* and *com* everywhere. Other noodle soups to try are *bun bo Hue* and *hu tieu*.

Spring rolls (*nem* in the north, *cha gio* in the south) are a speciality. These are normally dipped in *nuoc mam* (fish sauce), though many foreigners prefer soy sauce (*xi dau* in the north, *nuoc tuong* in the south).

Because Buddhist monks of the Mahayana tradition are strict vegetarians, *an chay* (vegetarian cooking) is an integral part of Vietnamese cuisine.

Snacks

Street stalls or roaming vendors are everywhere, selling steamed sweet potatoes, rice porridge and ice-cream bars even in the wee hours.

There are also many other Vietnamese nibbles to try:

Bap xao Made from fresh, stir-fried corn, chillies and tiny shrimp.

Bo bia Nearly microscopic shrimp, fresh lettuce and thin slices of Vietnamese sausage rolled up in rice paper and dipped in a spicy-sweet peanut sauce.

Sinh to Shakes made with milk and sugar or yoghurt, and fresh tropical fruit.

Sweets

Many sticky confections are made from sticky rice, like *banh it nhan dau,* made with sugar and bean paste and sold wrapped in banana leaf.

Most foreigners prefer *kem* (ice cream) or *yaourt* (yoghurt), which is generally of good quality.

Try *che,* a cold, refreshing sweet soup made with sweetened black bean, green bean or corn. It's served in a glass with ice and sweet coconut cream on top.

DRINK

Alcoholic Drinks

Memorise the words *bia hoi,* which mean 'draught beer', probably the cheapest beer in the world. Starting at around 4000d a glass, anyone can afford a round and you can get 'off yer heed' for just a few bucks. Places that serve *bia hoi* usually also serve cheap food.

Several foreign labels brewed in Vietnam under licence include Tiger, Carlsberg and Heineken.

National and regional brands include Halida and Hanoi in the north, Huda and Larue in the centre, and BGI and 333 *(ba ba ba)* in the south of the country.

Wine and spirits are available but at higher prices. Local brews are cheaper but not always drinkable.

Nonalcoholic Drinks

Whatever you drink, make sure that it's been boiled or bottled. Ice is generally safe on the tourist trail, but not guaranteed elsewhere.

Vietnamese *cà phê* (coffee) is fine stuff and there is no shortage of cafes in which to sample it.

Foreign soft drinks are widely available in Vietnam. An excellent local treat is *soda chanh* (carbonated mineral water with lemon and sugar) or *nuoc chanh nong* (hot, sweetened lemon juice).

Gay & Lesbian Travellers

Vietnam is pretty hassle-free for gay travellers. There's not much in the way of harassment, nor are there official laws on same-sex relationships. Vietnamese same-sex friends often walk with arms around each other or holding hands, and guesthouse proprietors are very unlikely to question the relationship of same-sex travel companions. But be discreet – public displays of affection are not socially acceptable whatever your sexual orientation.

Check out **Utopia** (www.utopia-asia.com) to obtain contacts and some useful travel information.

Insurance

Insurance is a *must* for Vietnam, as the cost of major medical treatment is prohibitive. A travel insurance policy to cover theft, loss and medical problems is the best bet.

Some insurance policies specifically exclude such 'dangerous activities' as riding motorbikes, diving and even trekking. Check that the policy covers an emergency evacuation in the event of serious injury.

Worldwide travel insurance is available at www.lonelyplanet.com/travel_services. You can buy, extend or claim anytime – even if you're already on the road.

Language Courses

Vietnamese language courses are offered in HCMC, Hanoi and elsewhere. Lessons usually cost from US$5 to US$10 per hour. Decide whether you want to study in northern or southern Vietnam, because the regional dialects are very different.

Legal Matters

If you lose something really valuable such as your passport or visa, you'll need to contact the police. Few foreigners experience much hassle from police and demands for bribes are rare – it's a different story for the Vietnamese though...

The Vietnamese government is seriously cracking down on the burgeoning drug trade. You may face imprisonment and/or large fines for drug offences, and drug trafficking can be punishable by death.

Maps

A *must* for its detailed road maps of every province is the *Viet Nam Administrative Atlas,* published by Ban Do. Basic road maps of major cities such as Hanoi, HCMC, Huế and Nha Trang are readily available.

Money

Vietnam's official currency is the dong (d). Banknotes come in denominations of 500d, 1000d, 2000d, 5000d, 10,000d, 20,000d, 50,000d, 100,000d, 200,000d and 500,000d. Coins include 500d, 1000d and 5000d. US dollars are also widely used.

ATMS

ATMs are widespread. They're present in virtually every town in the country and accept foreign cards. Watch out for stiff withdrawal fees (typically 20,000d to 30,000d) and low withdrawal limits – most are around 3,000,000d, but Agribank allows up to 6,000,000d.

A RIGHT ROYAL FOOD CRITIC

Emperor Tu Duc (1848–83) expected 50 dishes to be prepared by 50 cooks to be served by 50 servants at every meal. And his tea had to be made from the dew that accumulated on leaves overnight.

BEWARE YOUR BLEND

Some consider *chon* to be the highest grade of Vietnamese coffee. It is made of beans fed to a certain species of weasel and later collected from its excrement.

BARGAINING

For *xe om* and *cyclo* trips, as well as anywhere that prices aren't posted, bargaining is possible. In tourist hotspots, you may be quoted as much as five times the going price, but not everyone is trying to rip you off. In less-travelled areas, foreigners are often quoted the Vietnamese price but you can still bargain a little bit.

CASH

The US dollar acts as a second local currency. Many hotels and travel agencies quote their prices in dollars. Paying by dong is usually a bit cheaper.

Other major currencies can be exchanged at leading banks including Vietcombank and HSBC.

CREDIT CARDS

Visa and MasterCard are accepted in most top hotels, upmarket restaurants and shops but not in many budget places. Getting cash advances on credit cards is also possible, but a 3% commission is common.

MONEYCHANGERS

If you need to exchange money after hours, jewellery shops will exchange US dollars at fair rates.

TIPPING

Tipping isn't expected in Vietnam, but it's enormously appreciated. For someone making US$100 per month, the cost of your drink can equal half a day's wages. Many guests take up a collection for tour guides and drivers after tours or for outstanding service.

TRAVELLERS CHEQUES

Travellers cheques in US dollars can be exchanged for local dong at Vietcombank, although it will charge a commission of 0.5% – or no commission on Amex cheques. Most hotels and airline offices will not accept travellers cheques.

Photography

Memory cards are pretty cheap in Vietnam. Most internet cafes can also burn photos onto a CD or DVD to free up storage space. Photo-processing shops and internet cafes in bigger cities can burn digital photos onto DVDs. Colour print film is widely available; slide film is available in HCMC and Hanoi.

Vietnam's gorgeous scenery and unique character makes for memorable photographs. Inspiration will surely strike when you see a row of colourfully dressed hill-tribe women walking to market, but remember to maintain an appropriate level of respect for the people and places you visit. Ask permission before snapping a photo of someone.

Post

International mail from Vietnam is not unreasonably priced when compared with most countries, though parcels mailed from smaller cities and towns may take longer to arrive at their destinations. Be aware that customs inspect the contents before you ship anything other than documents, so don't show up at the post office with a carefully wrapped parcel ready to go. It will be dissected on the table.

Poste restante works in the larger cities but don't count on it elsewhere. All post offices are marked with the words *buu dien*.

Public Holidays

Politics affects everything, including many public holidays, in Vietnam. If a Vietnamese public holiday falls on a weekend, it is observed on the following Monday.

New Year's Day (Tet Duong Lich) 1 January

Vietnamese New Year (Tet) A three-day national holiday; late January or February

Anniversary of the Founding of the Vietnamese Communist Party (Thanh Lap Dang CSVN) 3 February – the date the Party was founded in 1930

Hung Kings Commemorations (Hung Vuong) 10th day of the 3rd lunar month, late March or April

Liberation Day (Saigon Giai Phong) 30 April – the date on which Saigon's surrender is commemorated nationwide as Liberation Day

International Workers' Day (Quoc Te Lao Dong) 1 May

Ho Chi Minh's Birthday (Sinh Nhat Bac Ho) 19 May

Buddha's Birthday (Phat Dan) Eighth day of the fourth moon (usually June)

National Day (Quoc Khanh) 2 September – commemorates the Declaration of Independence by Ho Chi Minh in 1945

Safe Travel

All in all, Vietnam is an extremely safe country to travel in. The police keep a pretty tight grip on social order and we very rarely receive reports about muggings, armed robberies and sexual assaults. Sure there are scams and hassles in some cities, particularly in Hanoi and Nha Trang; see those sections.

Watch out for petty theft. Drive-by bag snatchers on motorbikes are not uncommon, and thieves patrol buses, trains and boats. Don't be flash with cameras and jewellery.

Since 1975 many thousands of Vietnamese have been maimed or killed by rockets, artillery shells, mortars, mines and other ordnance left over from the war. Stick to defined paths and *never* touch any suspicious war relic you might come across.

Telephone

INTERNATIONAL CALLS

It's usually cheapest to use a mobile phone to make international phone calls – rates can be as little as US$0.10 a minute.

Otherwise you can webcall from any phone in the country; just dial ☎17100, the country code and your number – most countries cost a flat rate of just US$0.50 per minute. Many budget hotels operate even cheaper webcall services, as do post offices.

Of course, using services such as Skype costs next to nothing, and many budget and midrange hotels now have Skype and webcams set up for their guests.

Directory assistance (☎116)

General information (☎1080)

International operator (☎110)

International prefix (☎00)

Time (☎117)

LOCAL CALLS

Phone numbers in Hanoi, HCMC and Haiphong have eight digits. Elsewhere around the country phone numbers have seven digits. Telephone area codes are assigned according to the province.

Local calls from hotels are often free – though confirm this first!

MOBILE PHONES

Vietnam has an excellent, comprehensive cellular network. The nation uses GSM 900/1800, which is compatible with most of Asia, Europe and Australia but not with North America.

VIET SIM CARDS

It's well worth getting a local SIM card if you're planning to spend any time in Vietnam: you'll be able to send texts (SMS) anywhere in the world for around 2500d per message. Local handsets are available for as little as US$20, often with US$10 of credit included.

There are three main mobile phone companies (Viettel, Vinaphone and Mobifone), all with offices nationwide.

ROAMING

If your phone has roaming, it's easy enough (although it can be outrageously expensive) to use your handset in Vietnam – particularly if you use the internet.

Time

Vietnam is seven hours ahead of Greenwich Mean Time/Universal Time Coordinated (GMT/UTC) and there's no daylight-saving or summer time.

Toilets

Western-style sit-down toilets are the norm but the odd squat bog still survives in some cheap hotels and bus stations. Hotels usually supply a roll of toilet paper, but it's wise to BYO (bring your own) while on the road.

Tourist Information

Tourist offices in Vietnam have a different philosophy from the majority of tourist offices worldwide. These government-owned enterprises are really travel agencies whose primary interests are booking tours and turning a profit.

Travellers' cafes, travel agencies and your fellow travellers are a much better source of information than most of the so-called 'tourist offices'.

Visas

Most nationalities need a visa (or approval letter) in order to enter Vietnam. Entry and exit points include Hanoi, HCMC and Danang airports, or any of the plentiful land borders shared with Cambodia, China and Laos.

Certain favoured nationalities (see table) including Asean nations, Russia, Sweden and Norway, qualify for an automatic visa on arrival. Everyone else has to sort out a visa in advance. Arranging the paperwork has become fairly straightforward, but it remains expensive and unnecessarily time-consuming. Processing a tourist-visa application typically takes four or five working days in countries in the West.

Tourist visas are valid for a 30-day or 90-day stay (and can be single or multiple entry).

In Asia the best place to pick up a Vietnamese visa is Cambodia, where it costs around US$35 and can be arranged the same day. Bangkok is also a popular place.

If you plan to spend more than a month in Vietnam, or if you plan to exit Vietnam and enter again from Cambodia or Laos, arrange a 90-day multiple-entry visa. These cost around US$95 in Cambodia, but are not available from all Vietnamese embassies.

In our experience, personal appearance influences the reception you receive from immigration – if you wear shorts or scruffy clothing, or look dirty or unshaven, you can expect problems. Try your best to look 'respectable'.

BUSINESS VISAS

Business visas are usually valid for 90 days (sometimes 180 days in Cambodia) and allow both single and multiple entries as you wish. They're easy to obtain, although more expensive than a tourist visa.

MULITIPLE-ENTRY VISAS

It's possible to enter Cambodia or Laos from Vietnam and then re-enter without having to apply for another visa. However, you must apply for a multiple-entry visa *before* you leave Vietnam.

Multiple-entry visas are easiest to arrange in Hanoi or HCMC, but you will almost certainly have to ask a travel agent to do the paperwork for you. Travel agents charge about US$45, and the procedure takes up to seven days.

VISA EXTENSIONS

If you've got the dollars, they've got the rubber stamp. Tourist-visa extensions officially cost as little as US$10, but it's advisable to pay more and go via a travel agency as the bureaucracy is deep. The process can take seven days, and extensions are 30 to 90 days.

Extensions are best organised in major cities such as HCMC, Hanoi, Danang and Hué.

Volunteering

For information on volunteer work opportunities, chase up the full list of non-government organisations (NGOs) at the **NGO Resource Centre** (☎04-3832 8570; www.ngocentre.org.vn; Hotel La Thanh, 218 P Doi Can, Hanoi), which keeps a database of all of the NGOs assisting Vietnam. Projects in need of volunteers include the following:

KOTO (www.koto.com.au) Donate your skills, time or money to help give street children career opportunities. Street Voices' primary project is KOTO Restaurant in Hanoi.

Volunteers for Peace (www.vpv.vn) Always looking for volunteers to help in an orphanage on the outskirts of Hanoi.

Women Travellers

While it always pays to be prudent (avoid dark lonely alleys at night), foreign women

VIETNAM VISA AGENTS

If you're arriving by air, it's now usually easiest and cheapest to get your visa approved in advance through a visa service company or travel agent. This system does *not* operate at land border crossings.

They will need passport details, and then email you an approval document two to three days later which you need to print and bring with you to the airport. On arrival you need to present the approval document and passport picture then pay a stamping fee (US$25 for single-entry, US$50 for multiple-entry visas).

Recommended companies include **Vietnam Visa Center** (www.vietnamvisacenter.org) and **Visa Vietnam** (www.visatovietnam.org).

rarely report problems in Vietnam. That said, you may receive unwanted (although usually pretty harmless) advances if travelling alone. Be aware that exposing your upper arms (by wearing a vest top) will attract plenty of attention – local women rarely expose much flesh.

East Asian women travelling in Vietnam may want to dress quite conservatively. Very occasionally some ill-educated locals may think an Asian woman accompanying a Western male could be a Vietnamese prostitute.

Most Vietnamese women enjoy relatively free, fulfilled lives and a career. The sexes mix freely and society does not expect women to behave in a subordinate manner.

Work

At least 90% of foreign travellers seeking work in Vietnam end up teaching English, though there is some demand for French teachers too. Pay can be as low as US$5 per hour at a university and up to US$20 per hour at a private academy.

Jobs in the booming private sector or with NGOs are usually procured outside of Vietnam before arriving.

It's best to arrange a business visa if you plan on job hunting (see p172).

Getting There & Away

Most travellers enter Vietnam by plane or bus, but there are also train links from China and boat connections from Cambodia via the Mekong River.

Flights, tours, rail tickets and other travel services can be booked online at www.lonelyplanet.com/travel_services.

Entering Vietnam

Formalities at Vietnam's international airports are generally smoother than at land borders. Crossing overland from Cambodia and China is now also relatively stress-free. Crossing the border between Vietnam and Laos can be slow.

PASSPORT

Your passport must be valid for six months upon arrival in Vietnam. Most nationalities need to arrange a visa in advance (see p172).

Air

AIRPORTS

There are three established international airports in Vietnam. A fourth major international airport, in Phu Quoc, should become fully operational in late 2011.

Ho Chi Minh City (SGN; ☎08-3845 6654; www.tsnairport.com) Tan Son Nhat airport is Vietnam's busiest international air hub.

Hanoi (HAN; ☎04-3827 1513) Noi Bai airport serves the capital.

Danang airport (DAD; ☎051-1383 0339) Only has a few international flights, but a new terminal should result in additional connections.

AIRLINES

Vietnam Airlines (www.vietnamairlines.com.vn) Hanoi (☎04-3832 0320); HCMC (☎08-3832 0320) is the state-owned flag carrier and has flights to 28 international destinations, mainly in east Asia.

The airline has a modern fleet of Airbuses and Boeings, and has a good recent safety record.

TICKETS

From Europe or North America it's usually more expensive to fly to Vietnam than other Southeast Asian countries. Consider buying a discounted ticket to Bangkok, Singapore or Hong Kong and picking up a flight from there: Air Asia and other low-cost airlines fly to Vietnam.

It's hard to get reservations for flights to/from Vietnam during holidays, especially Tet, which falls between late January and mid-February.

VISA ON ARRIVAL

Citizens of the following countries do not have to apply in advance for a Vietnamese visa. Always double-check visa requirements before you travel as policies regularly change.

COUNTRY	VISA VALIDITY
Thailand, Malaysia, Singapore, Indonesia, Laos, Cambodia	30 days
Philippines	21 days
Japan, Korea, Russia, Norway, Denmark, Sweden, Finland, Brunei	15 days
Kyrgyzstan	90 days

Land & River

BORDER CROSSINGS

Vietnam shares land border crossings with Cambodia, China and Laos. See the map on p35 for more about travelling around the region. Vietnam visas were not available at any land borders at the time of research.

Cambodia

Cambodia and Vietnam share a long frontier with seven (and counting) border crossings. One-month Cambodian visas are issued on arrival at all border crossings for US$20, but overcharging is common except at Bavet (the most popular crossing).

There's also a river border crossing between Cambodia and Vietnam at Kaam Samnor–Vinh Xuong on the banks of the Mekong. Regular fast boats ply the route between Phnom Penh in Cambodia and Chau Doc in Vietnam via this border.

Cambodian border crossings are generally open daily between 7am and 5pm.

China

There are currently three border checkpoints where foreigners are permitted to cross between Vietnam and China: Lao Cai (p90), Huu Nghi Quan (the Friendship Pass) and Mong Cai (p87).

International trains link China and Vietnam, connecting Hanoi with Nanning (and even on to Běijīng!).

Trains are currently not operating on the Chinese side Lao Cai–Hékǒu border.

It is necessary to arrange a Chinese visa in advance.

Laos

There are seven (and counting) overland crossings between Vietnam and Laos. Thirty-day Lao visas are now available at all borders. All of the border crossings between north and central Vietnam and Laos have a degree of difficulty. Lao Bao (p102) is the simplest route.

Try to use direct city-to-city bus connections between the countries as the potential hassle is greatly reduced – immigration and transport scams are very common on the Vietnamese side of these borders. Bus drivers lie about journey times and some stop in the middle of nowhere and renegotiate the price.

Transport links on both sides of the border can be very hit and miss, so don't use the more-remote borders unless you have plenty of time to spare.

Getting Around

Air

Vietnam has good domestic flight connections, and very affordable prices (if you book early). Airlines accept bookings on international credit or debit cards. However, note that cancellations are not unknown.

There are two main airlines:

Vietnam Airlines (www.vietnamairlines.com.vn) The leading local carrier with the most comprehensive network and best reliability.

Jetstar Pacific (www.jetstar.com/vn/en/home) This budget airline has very affordable fares though only serves the main cities.

And these offer additional services:

Air Mekong (www.airmekong.com.vn) Links HCMC with Phu Quoc, Dalat, Con Dao and Hanoi.

Vasco (www.vasco.com.vn) Flies to the Con Dao Islands from HCMC.

Bicycle

Bikes are a great way to get around Vietnam, particularly when you get off the main highways. With the loosening of borders in the Mekong region, more and more people are planning overland trips by bicycle.

The main hazard is the traffic, and it's wise to avoid certain areas (notably Hwy 1). The best cycling is in the northern mountains and the Central Highlands, although you'll have to cope with some big hills. The Mekong Delta is a rewarding option for those who prefer the flat.

Purchasing a good bicycle in Vietnam is hit and miss. It's recommended that you bring one from abroad, along with a good helmet and spare parts.

Bicycles can also be hired locally from guesthouses for about US$2 per day, and are a great way to get to know a new city.

Boat

The extensive network of canals in the Mekong Delta makes getting around by boat feasible in the far south. Travellers to Phu Quoc Island can catch ferries from Ha Tien (p154) or Rach Gia (p155).

In the country's northeast, hydrofoils connect Haiphong with Cat Ba Island (near Halong Bay), and cruises on Halong Bay are extremely popular. Day trips to islands off the coast of Nha Trang, to the Chams off Hoi An, and in Lan Ha Bay are also good excursions.

Bus

Vietnam has an extensive network of buses that reach the far-flung corners of the country. Most are painfully slow and seriously uncomfortable local services but modern buses are now increasingly available on all the main routes.

Whichever class of bus you're on, bus travel in Vietnam is never speedy – reckon on just 50kph on major routes including Hwy 1.

BUS STATIONS

Many cities have several bus stations so make sure you get the right one! Bus stations all look chaotic but many now have ticket offices with official prices and departure times displayed.

RESERVATIONS & COSTS

Always buy a ticket from the office, as bus drivers are notorious for overcharging. Reservations aren't usually required for most of the frequent, popular services between towns and cities.

On rural runs, foreigners are typically charged anywhere from twice to 10 times the going rate. As a benchmark, a typical 100km ride is between US$2 and US$3.

BUS TYPES

Deluxe Buses

On most popular routes, modern air-conditioned Korean and Chinese buses offer comfortable reclining seats or padded flat beds for really long trips. These sleeper buses can be a good alternative to long-distance trains, and costs are comparable.

Deluxe buses are non-smoking. On the flip side most of them are equipped with TVs and some with dreaded karaoke machines.

Open Tours

Connecting backpacker haunts across the nation, open-tour buses are wildly popular in Vietnam. These air-con buses depart from convenient, centrally located departure points and allow you to hop-on, hop-off at any major city along the main north-to-south route.

Prices are reasonable. A through ticket from Ho Chi Minh City to Hanoi costs around US$45, Nha Trang to Hoi An around US$12.

Travellers' cafes, tour agencies and budget hotels sell tickets. Sinh Café (www.sinhcafe.com) started the concept and has a good reputation.

Local Buses

Short-distance buses, most of them pretty decrepit, drop off and pick up as many passengers as possible along the route, so the frequent stops make for a slow journey. Conductors tend to routinely overcharge foreigners on these local services so they're not popular with travellers.

Car & Motorcycle

Having your own wheels gives you maximum flexibility to visit remote regions and to stop when and where you please. Car hire always includes a driver. Motorbike hire is good value and this can be self-drive or with a driver.

DRIVING LICENCE

In order to drive a car in Vietnam, you need a Vietnamese licence and an International Driving Permit. However, all rental companies only rent out cars with drivers. When it comes to renting motorbikes, it's a case of no licence required.

FUEL

Unleaded gasoline costs 21,000d per litre. Even isolated communities usually have someone selling petrol by the roadside.

HIRE

The major considerations are safety, the mechanical condition of the vehicle, the reliability of the rental agency, and your budget.

Car & Minibus

Renting a vehicle with a driver and guide is a realistic option even for budget travellers, providing there are enough people to share the cost.

Costs per day:

Standard model US$40 to US$60

4WD/Minibus US$80 to US$115

Motorbike

Motorbikes can be rented from virtually anywhere, including cafes, hotels and travel agencies. Some places will ask to keep your passport as security. Ask for a signed agreement stating what you are renting, how much it costs, the extent of compensation and so on.

It is compulsory to wear a helmet when riding a motorbike in Vietnam, even when travelling as a passenger.

Costs per day:

Moped (semi-auto) US$4 to US$6

Moped (fully auto) US$8 to US$10

Trail and road bikes from US$15 to US$30

Plenty of local drivers will be willing to act as a chauffeur and guide for around US$10 to US$20 per day.

INSURANCE

If you are travelling in a tourist vehicle with a driver, then it is almost guaranteed to be insured. When it comes to motorbikes, many rental bikes are not insured and you will have to sign a contract agreeing to a valuation for the bike if it is stolen.

ROAD CONDITIONS & HAZARDS

Road safety is definitely not one of Vietnam's strong points. Vehicles drive on the right-hand side (in theory). Size matters and small vehicles get out of the way of big vehicles. Even Hwy 1 is only a two-lane highway for most of its length and high-speed head-on collisions are all too common.

In general, the major highways are hard surfaced and reasonably well maintained, but seasonal flooding can be a problem. Non-paved roads are best tackled with a 4WD vehicle or motorbike. Mountain roads are particularly dangerous: landslides, falling rocks and runaway vehicles can add an unwelcome edge to your journey.

Local Transport

Cyclos are bicycle rickshaws. Drivers hang out in touristy areas and some speak broken English. Bargaining is imperative; settle on a fare before going anywhere. A short ride costs about 10,000d, over 2km about 20,000d.

Taxis with meters are found in all cities and are very, very cheap by international standards and a safe way to travel around at night. Average tariffs are about 10,000d to 15,000d per kilometre. Only travel with reputable or recommended companies. **Mai Linh** (www.mailinh.vn) is an excellent nationwide firm.

Xe om, or motorbike taxis, are everywhere. Fares are comparable with those for a *cyclo*. Drivers hang out around street corners, markets, hotels and bus stations. They will find you before you find them...

Tours

The following are Vietnam-based travel agencies that offer premium tours throughout Vietnam:

Buffalo Tours (Map p144; ☎04-3828 0702; www.buffalotours.com; 94 P Ma May, Hanoi)

Exotissimo (Map p144; ☎08-3995 9898; www.exotissimo.com; 80-82 Đ Phan Xich Long, Phu Nhuan District, HCMC)

Handspan (☎04-3926 2828; www.handspan.com; 78 P Ma May, Hanoi)

Ocean Tours (☎04-3926 0463; www.oceantours.com.vn; 22 P Hang Bac, Hanoi)

Sisters Tours (☎04-3562 2733; www.sisterstoursvietnam.com; 37 Đ Thai Thinh, Hanoi)

Train

The Vietnamese railway system, operated by **Vietnam Railways** (Duong Sat Viet Nam; ☎04-3747 0308; www.vr.com.vn) is an ageing, slow but fairly dependable service, and offers a relaxing way to get around the nation. Travelling in an air-con sleeping berth sure beats

MOTORBIKE TOURS

Specialised motorbike tours offer an unrivalled way to explore Vietnam's scenic excesses on traffic-light back roads. A little experience helps, but many of the leading companies also offer tuition for first-timers.

Explore Indochina (☎09-1309 3159; www.exploreindochina.com) Excellent tours in the far north on vintage 650 Urals or modified Minsks; US$150 to US$200 per day. Good rental bikes also available.

Free Wheelin' Tours (☎04-3926 2743; www.freewheelin-tours.com) Trips and custom-made tours utilising the company's own homestays. From US$100 per day (per group of four).

Hoi An Motorbike Adventure (☎0510-391 1930; www.motorbiketours-hoian.com) Specialises in short trips (from US$35) in the Hoi An region on well-maintained Minsk bikes.

Offroad Vietnam (☎04-3926 3433; www.offroadvietnam.com) Well-organised tours on Honda road and dirt bikes to remote areas of northern Vietnam for around US$100 per day. Also rents quality Honda road bikes (from US$20)

Voyage Vietnam (☎04-3926 2373; www.voyagevietnam.net) Trips in the north, Mekong Delta and along HCMC highway; from around US$85 per day.

TRAIN FARES FROM HANOI

STATION	SOFT SEAT AIR-CON	TOP HARD AIR-CON (6 BERTH)	BOTTOM SOFT AIR-CON (4 BERTH)
Danang	570,000d	853,000d	915,000d
HCMC	1,175,000d	1,590,000d	1,690,000d
Hué	508,000d	785,000d	833,000d
Lao Cai	210,000d	310,000d	450,000d
Nha Trang	1,030,000d	1,340,000d	1,510,000d

a hairy overnight bus journey along Hwy 1. And of course there's some spectacular scenery to lap up too.

ROUTES

The main line connects HCMC with Hanoi. Three rail-spur lines link Hanoi with other parts of northern Vietnam: to Haiphong; Lang Son; and Lao Cai.

The train journey between Hanoi and HCMC takes from 30 to 41 hours, depending on the train.

CLASSES & COSTS

Trains classified as SE are the smartest and fastest. There are four main ticket classes: hard seat, soft seat, hard sleeper and soft sleeper. These are also split into air-con and non air-con options. Presently, air-con is only available on the faster express trains. Hard-seat class is usually packed, and is tolerable for day travel, but expect plenty of cigarette smoke.

Ticket prices vary depending on the train; the fastest trains are the most expensive.

RESERVATIONS

Reservations should be made at least one day in advance, especially for sleeping berths. You'll need to bring your passport when buying train tickets.

Many travel agencies, hotels and cafes sell train tickets for a small commission.

Cambodia

Includes »

Best Places to Eat

» Friends (p191)
» Sugar Palm (p203)
» Blue Pumpkin (p203)
» Chez Claude (p253)
» Kimly (p261)

Best Places to Stay

» La Résidence d'Angkor (p202)
» Blue Lime (p185)
» Mushroom Point (p253)
» Terres Rouges Lodge (p239)
» Elephant Valley Project (p244)

Why Go?

Ascend to the realm of the gods at Angkor Wat, a spectacular fusion of spirituality, symbolism and symmetry. Descend into the darkness of Tuol Sleng to witness the crimes of the Khmer Rouge. This is Cambodia, a country with a history both inspiring and depressing, a captivating destination that casts a spell on all those who visit.

Fringed by beautiful beaches and tropical islands, sustained by the mother waters of the Mekong River and cloaked in some of the region's few remaining emerald wildernesses, Cambodia is an adventure as much as a holiday. This is the warm heart of Southeast Asia, with everything the region has to offer packed into one bite-sized chunk.

Despite the headline attractions, Cambodia's greatest treasure is its people. The Khmers have been to hell and back, but thanks to an unbreakable spirit and infectious optimism, they have prevailed with their smiles and spirits largely intact.

When to Go

Phnom Penh

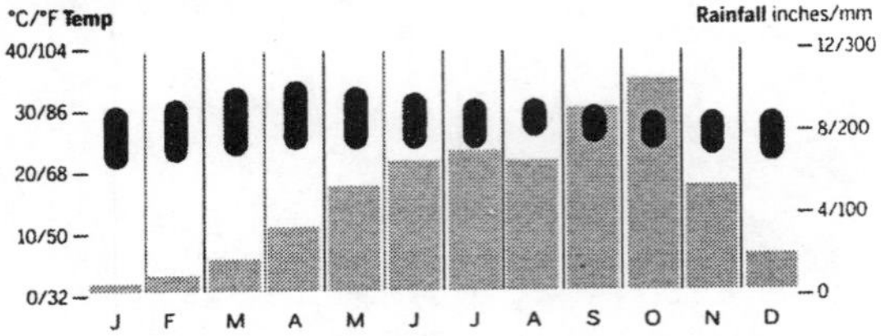

Nov–Feb The windy season, with Mediterranean-like temperatures; the best all-round time to explore.

Apr–May Khmer New Year is in mid-April, the hottest time of the year, when the mercury hits 40°C.

Jul–Sep Green season; rice paddies glisten; thunderous downpours bring relief from the humidity.

Connections

Phnom Penh Airport (p182) Taxi to centre US$9, around 30 minutes.
Siem Reap Airport (p276) Taxi to centre US$7, 15 minutes.

ITINERARIES

One Week

Soak up the sights, sounds and smells of **Phnom Penh**, Cambodia's dynamic and fast-changing capital. Travel by road to **Siem Reap**, gateway to the majestic temples of **Angkor**, passing by the pre-Angkorian temples of **Sambor Prei Kuk** or a longer detour via the charming colonial-era city of **Battambang**. Explore Angkor in depth, as no one does temples quite like Cambodia.

Two Weeks

Explore the ancient abode of the god-kings, the incredible temples of **Angkor**, including a side trip to the water world of the **Tonlé Sap lake**. Travel down to **Phnom Penh** to savour the dining and drinking scene. Head south to Cambodia's up-and-coming coastline, including the silvery sands of **Sihanoukville**. Finish up with the languid charms of **Kampot** and **Kep** if heading overland to Vietnam, or the adrenalin adventures on offer around **Koh Kong** if continuing to Thailand.

Internet Resources

» **Andy's Cambodia** (blog.andybrouwer.co.uk) A great gateway to all things Cambodian; includes comprehensive links and daily Cambodia musings.

» **Cambodia Tribunal Monitor** (www.cambodiatribunal.org) Detailed coverage of the Khmer Rouge trials, including up-to-date information on the trials of Ieng Sary and Khieu Samphan.

» **Heritage Watch** (www.heritagewatch.org) Works to safeguard Cambodia's architectural heritage and promotes 'heritage-friendly' tourism.

» **Phnom Penh Post** (www.phnompenhpost.com) The online version of Cambodia's newspaper of record.

» **Tales of Asia** (www.talesofasia.com) Comprehensive overland travel information.

NEED TO KNOW

» **Currency** Riel (r)

» **Language** Khmer

» **Money** ATMs are common in major cities

» **Visas** Available on arrival for most countries

» **Mobile phones** Prepay SIM cards are cheap but need passport to register

Fast Facts

» **Area** 181,035 sq km

» **Capital** Phnom Penh

» **Country Code** ☎855

» **Population** 15 million

Exchange Rates

Australia	A$1	4100r
Canada	C$1	4000r
Europe	€1	5600r
Japan	¥100	5200r
New Zealand	NZ$1	3200r
UK	£1	6400r
USA	US$1	4100r

Set Your Budget

» **Budget hotel room** US$5–20

» **Decent restaurant meal** US$5–10

» **Beer in bar** US$1–3

» **Short moto ride** US$0.50

Cambodia Highlights

1 The eighth wonder of the world, the **temples of Angkor** (p208) include the mother of all temples, Angkor Wat; the weirdest of all temples, the Bayon; and the jungle ruins of Ta Prohm

2 The laid-back capital of **Phnom Penh** (p182) boasts fine cuisine, a thriving nightlife and a promenade along the mighty Mekong

3 Explore the wild east of Cambodia in **Mondulkiri** (p242), a land of rolling hills, thundering waterfalls, indigenous minorities and the unique Elephant Valley Project

4 Discover the soporific pace of **Kampot** (p256), with its colonial-era architecture and atmospheric guesthouses

5 Get away from it all and go **island hopping** (p255) on idyllic Koh Rong and Koh Rong Saloem

6 Base yourself in **Battambang** (p220), a charming old-world town, and explore the pretty countryside

7 Ecotourism has taken off in the rainforests of **Koh Kong** (p244), a tiny pocket of the country near the Thai border

8 In **Kratie** (p234) soak up some of the community tourism experiences on offer on the Mekong Discovery Trail and see some of the world's rarest freshwater dolphins

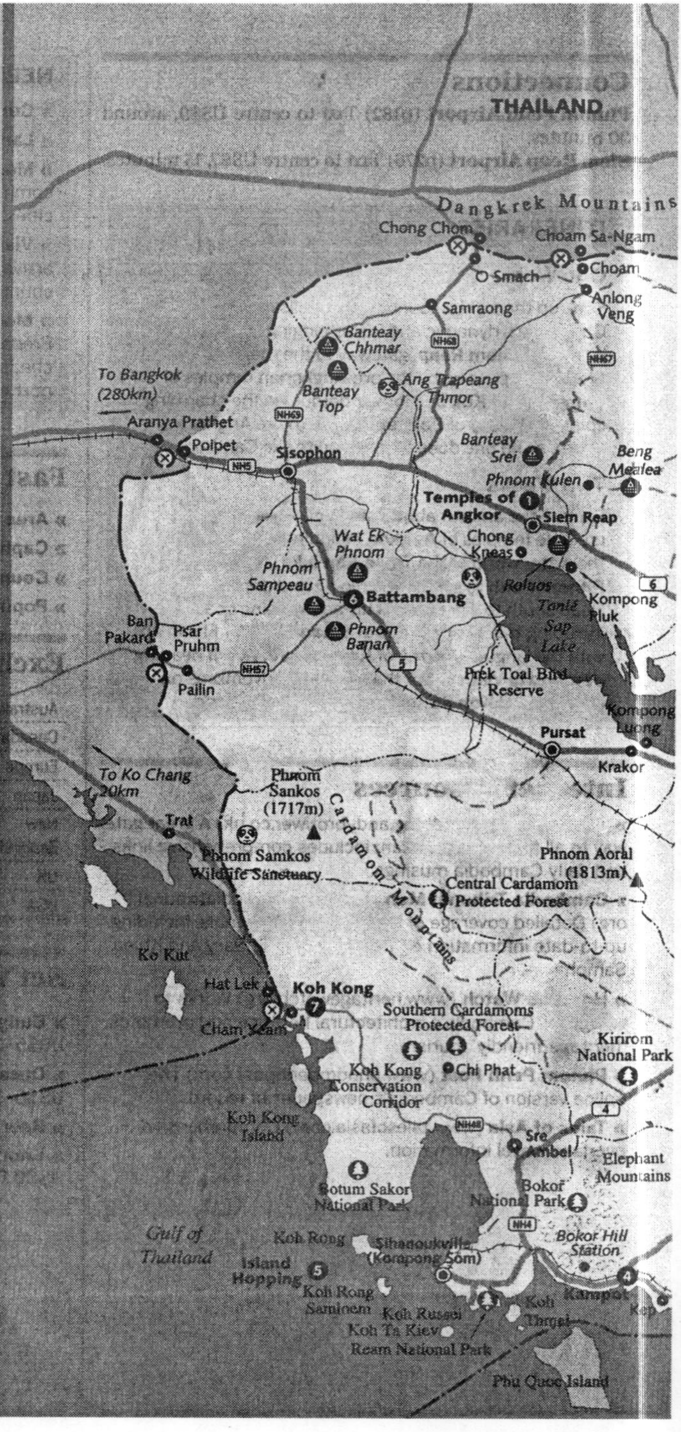

0 100 km
0 60 miles
LAOS
VIETNAM
SOUTH CHINA SEA
Eastern Highlands
Virachey National Park
RATANAKIRI
Le Thanh
Ban Lung
Yadaw
Lumphat
Tonlé San
Tonle Srepok
NH78
Koh Nhek
3 Mondulkiri
Bou Sraa Falls
Sen Monorom
Snuol
Trapaeng Sre
Loc Ninh
Prasat Preah Vihear
Sra Em
Dong Kalaw
Trapeang Knel
Koh Ker
Tbeng Meanchey
Srayong
PREAH VIHEAR
NH64
Stung Treng
Mekong
Preah Khan
Mekong Discovery Trail
River
7
Sambor Prei Kuk
Kompong Thom
Kakoah
Phnom Sontuk
Kampi
Kratie 8
5
Tonlé Sap River
6
Chhlong
Kompong Chhnang
Skuon
NH6
Kompong Cham
Wat Maha Leap
Udong
Trapaeng Plong
Xa Mat
NH11
PHNOM PENH 2
Kompong Speu
Prey Veng
NH1
Tonlé Bati
Phnom Tamao Wildlife Sanctuary
Phnom Chisor
Neak Luong Ferry
Tay Ninh
Bavet
Moc Bai
1
Takeo
Angk Tasaom
Angkor Borei
Kaam Samnor
Vinh Xuong
Tonlé Bassac
3
2
Phnom Da
Chau Doc
Phnom Den
Tinh Bien
Kompong Trach
Prek Chak
Xa Xia
Ha Tien
Long Xuyen
Mekong River
Mytho
Ho Chi Minh City (Saigon)

PHNOM PENH

☎023 / POP 1.5 MILLION

Phnom Penh: the name can't help but conjure up an image of the exotic. This is the Asia that many dreamt of when first planning their adventures overseas. Phnom Penh is a crossroads of Asia's past and present, a city of extremes of poverty and excess, of charm and chaos, but one that never fails to captivate.

Once the 'Pearl of Asia', Phnom Penh's shine was tarnished by the impact of war and revolution. But that's history and Phnom Penh has risen from the ashes to take its place among the 'in' capitals of Asia. Delve into the ancient past at the National Museum or struggle to make sense of the recent trauma at Tuol Sleng Museum. Browse the city's markets for a bargain or linger in the beautiful boutiques that are putting Phnom Penh on the style map. Street-surf through the local stalls for a snack or enjoy the refined surrounds of a designer restaurant. Whatever your flavour, no matter your taste, it's all here in Phnom Penh.

The riverfront Sisowath Quay, lined with myriad restaurants and a brand-new promenade, is where most visitors gravitate. The city sprawls west from there. The main thoroughfares, Sihanouk Blvd and Norodom Blvd, intersect a few blocks east of the river at lotus-flower-like Independence Monument, a useful landmark and the point from which distances to the provinces are measured.

Sights

Royal Palace & Silver Pagoda PALACE

(Map p184 & Map p188; Sothearos Blvd; admission incl camera/video 25,000r; ⏲8-11am & 2-5pm) The Royal Palace dominates the diminutive skyline of the riverfront where the Tonlé Sap and Mekong meet, with its classic Khmer roofs and ornate gilding. It is a striking structure, bearing a remarkable likeness to its counterpart in Bangkok. Hidden away behind protective walls and beneath shadows of striking ceremonial buildings, it's an oasis of calm with lush gardens and leafy havens.

The Silver Pagoda is so named because it is constructed with 5000 silver tiles weighing 1kg each. It is also known as Wat Preah Keo (Pagoda of the Emerald Buddha) thanks to a 17th-century Buddha statue made of Baccarat crystal. Check out the life-sized gold Buddha, weighing in at 90kg, and decorated with 9584 diamonds.

Upper arms must be covered and shorts must reach the knee while visiting the palace.

National Museum MUSEUM

(Map p184; Ph 13; admission US$3, camera/video US$1/3; ⏲8am-5pm) The National Museum of Cambodia is home to the world's finest collection of Khmer sculpture, a millennia's worth and more of masterful Khmer design. Housed in a graceful terracotta structure of traditional design (built 1917–20), it provides the perfect backdrop to an outstanding array of delicate objects.

The Angkor collection includes a giant pair of wrestling monkeys, an exquisite frieze from Banteay Srei, and the sublime statue of Jayavarman VII (r 1181–1219) meditating.

No photography is allowed except in the beautiful central courtyard.

Tuol Sleng Museum MUSEUM

(Map p188; Ph 113; admission US$2, video US$5; ⏲7am-6pm) Once a centre of learning, Tuol Svay Prey High School was taken over by Pol Pot's security forces and transformed into Security Prison 21 (S-21). The classrooms were turned into torture chambers and equipped with various instruments to inflict pain, suffering and death. Now Tuol Sleng Museum, it was the largest incarceration centre in the country. The long corridors are hallways of ghosts containing

GETTING INTO TOWN

An official booth outside the airport arrivals area arranges taxis/remorks (túk-túk) to anywhere in the city for a flat US$9/7. You can get a remork for $US4 and a moto (motorcycle taxi) for half that if you walk one minute out to the street. A taxi/remork/moto will cost about US$9/4/2 heading to the airport from central Phnom Penh.

If you arrive by bus, chances are you'll be dropped off near Psar Thmei (aka Central Market), a short ride to most hotels and guesthouses. Figure on 2000r to 6000r for a moto, and US$2 to US$3 for a remork. Prices are about the same from the tourist boat dock on Sisowath Quay, where arriving boats from Vietnam and Siem Reap incite moto-madness.

Phnom Penh

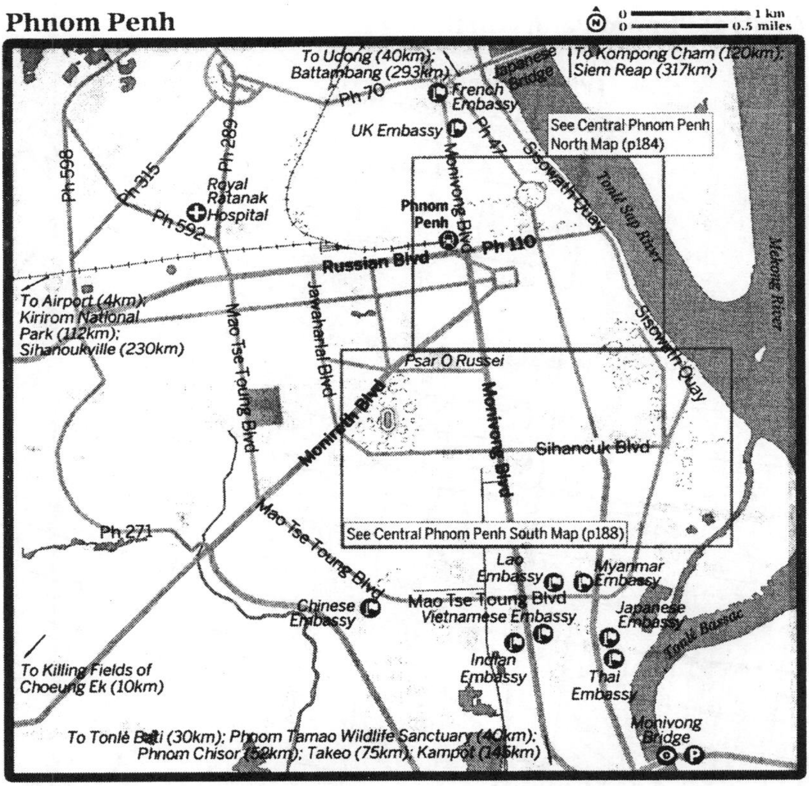

haunting photographs of the victims, their faces staring back eerily from the past.

Like the Nazis, the Khmer Rouge leaders were meticulous in keeping records of their barbarism and each prisoner who passed through S-21 was photographed. When the Vietnamese army liberated Phnom Penh in early 1979, there were only seven prisoners alive at S-21, all of whom had used their skills such as painting or photography to stay alive.

For more on stories from Tuol Sleng and the Cambodian genocide, visit the **Documentation Center of Cambodia** (DC-Cam; www.dccam.org) website or the website of Yale University's **Cambodian Genocide Program** (www.yale.edu/cgp).

Killing Fields of Choeung Ek MEMORIAL

(off Map p183; admission incl audio tour US$5; ⏲7am-5.30pm) Most of the 17,000 detainees held at the S-21 prison were executed at the Killing Fields of Choeung Ek. Prisoners were often bludgeoned to death to avoid wasting precious bullets. It is hard to imagine the brutality that unfolded here when wandering through this peaceful, shady former orchard, but the memorial stupa soon brings it home, displaying more than 8000 skulls of victims and their ragged clothes. See p465 for more on the Khmer Rouge.

Choeung Ek is 14km southwest of Phnom Penh. A trip out here will cost US$5 round trip on a moto or about US$20 by taxi.

Wat Phnom TEMPLE

(Map p184; admission US$1) Wat Phnom, meaning Hill Temple, is appropriately set on the only hill (more like a mound at 27m) in Phnom Penh. The wat is highly revered among locals, who flock here to pray for good luck. Legend has it that in the year 1373, the first temple was built by a lady named Penh to house four Buddha statues that she found floating in the Mekong.

Central Phnom Penh North

Penh's statue is in a shrine dedicated to her behind the *vihara* (temple sanctuary).

Wat Ounalom TEMPLE

(Map p184) Wat Ounalom is the headquarters of Cambodian Buddhism. It is unexceptional, but might be worth visiting just for the one eyebrow hair of Buddha himself, preciously held in a stupa located behind the main building.

Independence Monument MONUMENT

(Map p188; cnr Norodom & Sihanouk Blvds) This monument is modelled on the central tower of Angkor Wat and was built in 1958 to commemorate independence from France in 1953.

Activities

Boat Tours

There are many private operators that offer boat cruises up and down the Mekong, stationed along Sisowath Quay, and most offer a sunset cruise from US$10 per hour.

Cooking Classes

Cambodian Cooking Class (Map p188; ☎012 524801; www.cambodian-cooking-class.com; booking office at 67 Ph 240, classes on Ph

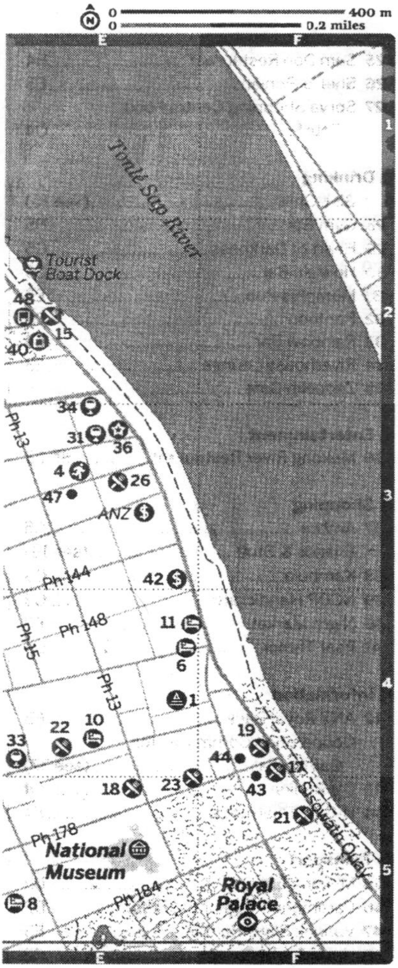

19; half/full day US$12.50/20; ⊙closed Sun) Learn the art of Khmer cuisine at Frizz Restaurant. Reserve ahead.

Cycling

Vicious Cycle (Map p184; ☎012 462165; www.grasshopperadventures.com; 29 Ph 130; bicycles per day US$4-8) Runs great cycling tours to Mekong islands and Udong. Plenty of mountain and other bikes available, including a couple of family bikes with kiddie seats for US$10. Request a map of local bicycle routes.

Massage & Spas

Bliss Boutique (Map p188; ☎215754; 29 Ph 240) One of the most established spas in town, set in a lovely old French house.

Seeing Hands Massage Ph 108 (Map p184; 34 Ph 108) Riverside (Map p184; 12 Ph 13) Eases those aches and pains, and helps blind masseurs stay self-sufficient. Massages average US$7 per hour.

Bodia Spa (Map p184; ☎226199; cnr Sothearos Blvd & Ph 178; massages from US$26) About the best rub-downs in town, in a Zen-like setting (albeit with some street noise).

Swimming

Most pool-equipped boutique hotels, such as Villa Langka and The 252, will let you swim if you buy a few bucks worth of grub or cocktails. The following hotels have larger pools fit for swimming laps.

Himawari Hotel (Map p188; ☎214555; 313 Sisowath Quay; admission Mon-Fri/Sat & Sun US$7/8)

Hotel Cambodiana (Map p188; ☎424888; 313 Sisowath Quay; admission Mon-Fri/Sat & Sun US$8/15)

Sleeping

Against all odds, the few establishments that remained in Phnom Penh's traditional backpacker area around Boeng Kak Lake were thriving at the time of research. Given that the lake was 90% filled in and slated for massive development, this surely can't last. Or can it? A trio of miniature backpacker colonies are lying in wait as potential heirs apparent to Boeng Kak: Ph 258, near the riverside; a strip of Ph 172; and the area south of Psar O Russei. Ph 278 – aka 'Golden St' – is a flashpacker district of sorts.

Midrange hotels are terrific value and there are plenty of stylish ones to choose from. All midrange and top-end hotels include breakfast and have non-smoking rooms.

CENTRAL PHNOM PENH NORTH

TOP CHOICE **Blue Lime** BOUTIQUE HOTEL **$$**
(Map p184; ☎222260; www.bluelime.asia; 42 Ph 19z; r US$40-75; ✱@🛜≋) The follow-up act of the team behind the Pavilion outdoes its predecessor with smart, minimalist rooms and a leafy pool area done just right. The pricier rooms are true gems, with private

Central Phnom Penh North

Top Sights
- National Museum ... E5
- Royal Palace ... F5

Sights
- 1 Wat Ounalom ... E4
- 2 Wat Phnom ... C2

Activities, Courses & Tours
- Bodia Spa ... (see 44)
- 3 Seeing Hands Massage ... D2
- Seeing Hands Massage ... (see 13)
- 4 Vicious Cycle ... E3

Sleeping
- 5 11 Happy Guesthouse ... A1
- 6 Amanjaya Pancam Hotel ... E4
- 7 Billabong ... C5
- 8 Blue Lime ... E5
- 9 Grand View Guesthouse ... A1
- 10 Last Home ... E4
- 11 Quay ... E4
- 12 Raffles Hotel Le Royal ... B1

Eating
- 13 Armand's ... D2
- 14 Bayon Supermarket ... A3
- 15 Bopha Phnom Penh Restaurant ... E2
- Cantina ... (see 19)
- 16 Ebony Apsara Café ... D5
- 17 Foreign Correspondents' Club ... F4
- 18 Friends ... E5
- 19 Happy Herb Pizza ... F4
- 20 Kebab ... C5
- 21 Khmer Borane Restaurant ... F5
- 22 Laughing Fat Man ... E4
- 23 Le Wok ... E5
- Psar Thmei ... (see 41)
- 24 Romdeng ... C5
- 25 Sam Doo Restaurant ... B4
- 26 Sher-e-Punjab ... E3
- 27 Sorya Shopping Centre Food Court ... C4

Drinking
- Blue Chilli ... (see 16)
- 28 Gym Bar ... D5
- 29 Heart of Darkness ... C5
- 30 Howie's Bar ... C5
- 31 Memphis Pub ... E3
- 32 Pontoon ... C5
- 33 Rainbow Bar ... E4
- 34 Riverhouse Lounge ... E3
- 35 Zeppelin Cafe ... C5

Entertainment
- 36 Mekong River Restaurant ... E3

Shopping
- 37 Ambre ... C5
- Friends & Stuff ... (see 18)
- 38 Kambuja ... C3
- 39 NCDP Handicrafts ... C3
- 40 Night Market ... E2
- 41 Psar Thmei ... C4

Information
- 42 ANZ Royal Bank ... E3
- Cooperation Committee for Cambodia ... (see 37)
- 43 D's Books ... F4
- 44 U-Care Pharmacy ... F4

Transport
- 45 Mekong Express ... D2
- 46 Paramount Angkor Express ... D2
- 47 Vannak Bikes Rental ... E3
- 48 Virak Buntham ... E2

plunge pools, four-poster beds and contemporary concrete love seats. No kids.

TOP CHOICE Raffles Hotel Le Royal HISTORIC HOTEL $$$
(Map p184; ☎981888; www.raffles.com; cnr Monivong Blvd & Ph 92; r from US$200;) A grandee from the golden age of travel, this is one of Asia's opulent addresses. Indulgent diversions include two swimming pools, a gym, a spa, and bars and restaurants with lavish dining and drinking.

The Quay BOUTIQUE HOTEL $$$
(Map p184; ☎224894; www.thequayhotel.com; 277 Sisowath Quay; r/ste US$90/170;) The Quay is a temple of contemporary style right on the riverfront. The long, narrow suites have fabulous desks if you want to work, and flat-screen TVs if you don't. Standard quarters are much smaller but equally slick. Ascend to the rooftop Chow bar to catch breezes off the Tonlé Sap.

Amanjaya Pancam Hotel LUXURY HOTEL $$$
(Map p184; ☎219579; www.amanjaya.com; 1 Ph 154; r US$155-250;) One of Phnom

Penh's original Asian Zen-style boutiques, Amanjaya boasts a superb riverfront location and spacious, stylish rooms with dark-wood floors, elegant Khmer drapes and tropical furnishings.

Billabong GUESTHOUSE $$
(Map p184; ☎223703; www.thebillabonghotel.com; 5 Ph 158; d US$36-70; ❄@☜≋) Near Psar Thmei but an oasis of calm by comparison, Billabong has a big open courtyard and 20 rooms set around a large swimming pool. Standard rooms are smallish. Wi-fi costs extra.

Last Home HOSTEL $
(Map p184; ☎6921009; 21 Ph 172; www.lasthomecambodia.com; d with fan/air-con from US$7/15; ❄@☜) This was the first budget guesthouse to plant its flag on up-and-coming Ph 172. It has a loyal following among regular visitors, who undoubtedly appreciate extras like cable TV and newish bathrooms.

CENTRAL PHNOM PENH SOUTH

TOP CHOICE **Top Banana Guesthouse** HOSTEL $
(Map p188; ☎012 885572; www.topbanana.biz; 9 Ph 278; r US$6-15; ❄@☜) A great location high above Golden St, a comfy open-air chill-out area and popular bar make it the Penh's top backpacker crash pad. Cheap rooms don't come with hot water, but the more expensive ones include brisk air-con. Book way ahead.

Villa Langka BOUTIQUE HOTEL $$
(Map p188; ☎726771; www.villalangka.com; 14 Ph 282; r US$44-121; ❄@☜≋) One of the first players in the poolside-boutique game, it's now firmly cemented as a Phnom Penh favourite. Rooms ooze post-modern panache. The pool gets crowded with walk-in guests on weekends.

The 252 BOUTIQUE HOTEL $$
(Map p188; www.the-252.com; 19 Ph 252; r US$45-55; ❄@☜≋) Just a tick down from Blue Lime and Pavilion in style and comfort, it's nonetheless terrific value. The attractive lime-striped rooms are a tad small for hangin', but around the pool prime lounging spots lurk.

Anise HOTEL $$
(Map p188; ☎222522; 2C Ph 278; www.anisehotel.com.kh; s/d from US$37/40-55; ❄☜) If the 'leafy boutique around pool' thing isn't for you, Anise is the best midrange high-rise in town. Indigenous textiles and lovely wood trim add character to rooms that already boast extras like DVD players.

Pavilion BOUTIQUE HOTEL $$
(Map p188; ☎222280; www.thepavilion.asia; 227 Ph 19; r US$50-90; ❄@☜≋) Housed in an elegant French villa, this immensely popular and atmospheric place helped popularise the Phnom Penh poolside boutique hotel. Furnishings show a Chinese-Khmer touch and some rooms have pool views. No children allowed.

Manor House GUESTHOUSE $$
(Map p188; ☎992566; www.manorhousecambodia.com; 21 Ph 262; s/d from US$42/49; ❄@☜≋) Set in a small villa, this gay-friendly guesthouse offers artfully decorated rooms and a small swimming pool. Kids aren't allowed.

Sofitel LUXURY HOTEL $$$
(Map p188; ☎999200; www.sofitel.com; 26 Sothearos Blvd; r from US$190; ❄@☜≋) Phnom Penh's latest five-star property boasts spacious rooms and a gazillion facilities, including numerous tennis courts, several restaurants and the city's best gym.

Lazy Gecko Guest House HOSTEL $
(Map p188; ☎078 786025; Ph 258; d US$5-15; ❄@☜) Well-known as a cafe in its lakeside days, it tacked on an equally appealing guesthouse upon moving to its new location amid the backpacker haunts of Ph 258. Probably the best rooms in town at this price range.

Okay Guesthouse HOSTEL $
(Map p188; ☎986534; 3B Ph 258; okay.2001@hotmail.com; s US$4-10, d US$6-15; ❄@☜) Okay is more than just OK thanks to a popular restaurant, cheap rooms and a friendly vibe. Budget rooms start with shared bathroom, and top whack brings air-con, TV and hot water.

The Willow BOUTIQUE HOSTEL $$
(Map p188; ☎996256; www.thewillowpp.com; 1 Ph 21; r US$40-55; ❄☜) The latest of many fashionable boutique hotels to open in the capital, The Willow has seven spacious rooms in a splendid 1960s villa. Also known for its build-your-own-sandwich bar.

Hotel Nine GUESTHOUSE $
(Map p188; ☎215964; www.hotel-nine.com; 48 Ph 9; r US$17-38; ❄@☜≋) This new white-washed hotel was just getting its sea legs when we checked in. Pluses: nice little pool,

Central Phnom Penh South

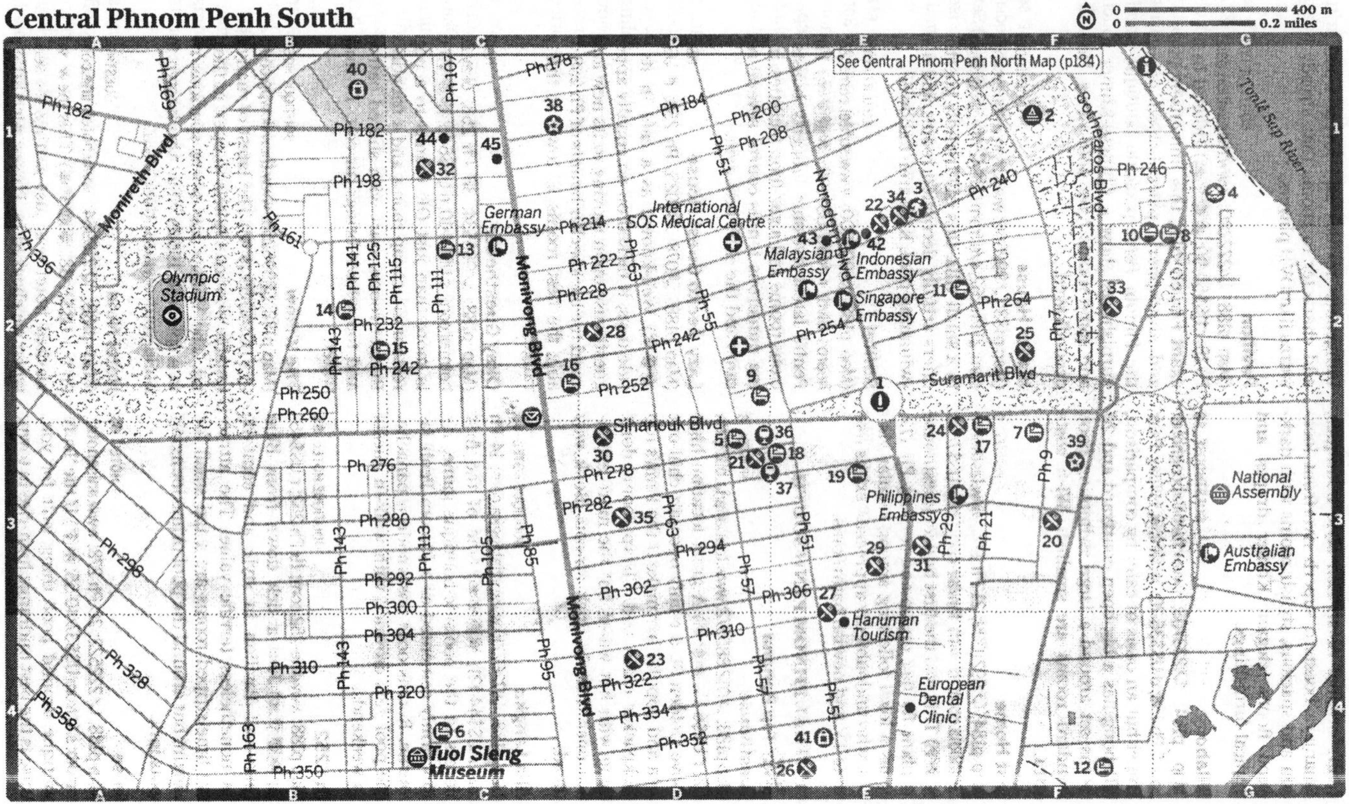

Central Phnom Penh South

Top Sights
Tuol Sleng Museum ... C4

Sights
1 Independence Monument ... E2
2 Silver Pagoda ... F1

Activities, Courses & Tours
3 Bliss Boutique ... E1
Cambodian Cooking Class ... (see 22)
4 Himawari Hotel Swimming Pool ... G1
Hotel Cambodia Swimming Pool ... (see 4)

Sleeping
5 Anise ... D3
6 Boddhi Tree Umma ... C4
7 Hotel Nine ... F3
8 Lazy Gecko Guest House ... G2
9 Manor House ... D2
10 Okay Guesthouse ... F2
11 Pavilion ... F2
12 Sofitel ... F4
13 Spring Guesthouse ... C2
14 Sunday Guesthouse ... B2
15 Tat Guesthouse ... B2
16 The 252 ... C2
17 The Willow ... F3
18 Top Banana Guesthouse ... E3
19 Villa Langka ... E3

Eating
20 Boat Noodle Restaurant ... F3
21 Chayyam ... D3
Freebird ... (see 22)
22 Frizz Restaurant ... E1
23 Hagar ... D4
24 Java Café ... E3
25 K'nyay ... F2
26 Le Jardin ... E4
27 Le Lotus Blanc ... E3
28 Le Rit's ... D2
29 Living Room ... E3
30 Lucky Supermarket ... D3
31 Malis ... E3
32 Mama Restaurant ... C1
33 Origami ... F2
34 Shop ... E1
35 Yumi ... D3

Drinking
Elsewhere ... (see 18)
36 Equinox ... D3
37 Score ... D3

Entertainment
38 French Cultural Centre ... C1
39 Meta House ... F3

Shopping
Nyemo ... (see 28)
40 Psar O Russei ... B1
41 Tabitha ... E4
Water Lily ... (see 34)

Information
42 D's Books ... E2
43 Monument Books ... E2

Transport
44 Capitol Tour ... C1
45 Lucky! Lucky! ... C1
New! New! ... (see 45)

cosy beds, creative menu and booming water pressure. Fusses: mozzies and street noise.

Boddhi Tree Umma GUESTHOUSE $
(Map p188; www.boddhitree.com; 50 Ph 113; s/d with fan & shared bathroom from US$12/24, r with air-con from US$30;) Some might be spooked by the location opposite Tuol Sleng, but it's a wonderfully atmospheric place. There is a divine restaurant in the verdant garden.

WEST OF MONIVONG

11 Happy Guesthouse HOSTEL $
(Map p184; 012 999921; http://www.happy11ghcambodia.com/Guest_House.html; 4 Ph 93; r US$2-15;) The friendly, informative staff put smiles on backpackers' faces with cheap laundry and good rooms at these prices.

Grand View Guesthouse HOSTEL $
(Map p184; 430766; www.grandview.netfirms.com; 4 Ph 93; r US$4-10;) This tall, skinny structure has unrivalled views of the sandlot formerly known as Boeng Kak.

Tat Guesthouse HOSTEL $
(Map p188; 099 801000; tatguesthouse@yahoo.com; 52 Ph 125; s/d from US$3/6;) A friendly, family-run place with cheap and cheerful rooms, plus a breezy rooftop hang-out area.

Spring Guesthouse HOSTEL $
(Map p188; ☎222155; 34 Ph 111; r US$6-10;) This five-storey walk-up was the first of a new generation of smart guesthouses in this area. It offers bright, spotless rooms with cable TV.

Sunday Guesthouse HOSTEL $
(Map p188; ☎211623; gech_sundayguesthouse@hotmail.com; 97 Ph 141; r US$8-12;) The rooms aren't quite as spiffy as at Spring but the service is friendlier and staff can help with travel arrangements.

Eating

For foodies, Phnom Penh is real delight, boasting a superb selection of restaurants that showcase the best in Khmer cooking, as well as the greatest hits from world cuisines such as Chinese, Thai, Indian, Japanese, French, Mexican and more.

CENTRAL PHNOM PENH NORTH

TOP CHOICE **Foreign Correspondents' Club** FUSION $$
(FCC; Map p184; www.fcccambodia.com; 363 Sisowath Quay; mains US$6-15; 6.30am-midnight;) A PP institution, the FCC is housed in a colonial gem with great views and cool breezes. The Asian and international dishes are delicious. One of those must-see places in Cambodia, almost everyone swings by for a drink – happy hour is from 5pm to 7pm.

Le Wok FUSION $$
(Map p184; 33 Ph 178; mains US$7-15) One of the better fusion restaurants in town, the name says it all – French flair with an Asian flavour.

Khmer Borane Restaurant CAMBODIAN $
(Map p184; 389 Sisowath Quay; mains US$4-5.50; 7am-midnight) A great little restaurant for traditional Khmer recipes; choose from *trey kor* (steamed fish with sugar palm) or *lok lak* (fried diced beef with a salt, pepper and lemon dip).

Tepui INTERNATIONAL $$$
(off Map p184; ☎991514; 45 Sisowath Quay; mains US$12-17; 6-10pm Tue-Sun) One of the city's true colonial-era masterpieces, formerly a bar, is now a restaurant with a diminutive menu that includes red snapper, duck and a succulent rib-eye steak.

Armand's FRENCH $$$
(Map p184; ☎015 548966; 33 Ph 108; meals US$12-25; from 5pm, closed Mon;) The best steaks in town are served flambé style by the eponymous owner of this French bistro. The steaks are nonpareil, and every item on the chalkboard menu shines. Space is tight so book ahead.

Bopha Phnom Penh Restaurant CAMBODIAN $$
(Map p184; Sisowath Quay; mains US$6.50-15; 6am-11pm) It's right on the river and designed to impress, with Angkorian-style carvings, and heavy furniture. The menu is heavy on the exotic, especially water buffalo, and there's a Western menu for the less adventurous.

Sher-e-Punjab INDIAN $
(Map p184; ☎216360; 16 Ph 130; mains US$3-6; 11am-11pm;) The top spot for a curry fix according to many members of Phnom Penh's Indian community; the tandoori dishes are particularly good.

Sam Doo Restaurant CHINESE $
(Map p184; 56-58 Kampuchea Krom Blvd; mains US$2.60-10; 7am-3am;) Chinese-Khmers swear this has the best food in town. Try the delicious dim sum.

Happy Herb Pizza PIZZA $
(Map p184; ☎362349; 345 Sisowath Quay; pizzas US$4-8; 8am-11pm;) No, happy doesn't mean it comes with free toppings, it means pizza *à la* ganja. The non-marijuana pizzas are also pretty good, but don't involve the free trip. Good place to sip a cheap beer as well. Delivery available.

Laughing Fat Man BACKPACKER CAFE $
(Map p184; Ph 172; mains US$2-4; 7.30am-11pm) This is a welcoming place with cheap food and big breakfasts, formerly Oh My Buddha. 'New name, same body,' the jovial corpulent owner joked.

Kebab QUICK EATS $
(Map p184; Ph 57; wraps US$2.50-3; 9pm-6am) One of several shacks that exist solely to provide late-night edibles to Ph 57 bar-crawlers, this is the pick of the bunch, best known for its vegie falafel wraps. Opposite the Heart of Darkness club.

Bayon Supermarket SUPERMARKET $
(Map p184; 33-34 Russian Blvd; 8am-9pm) Phnom Penh's best all-round supermarket.

Ebony Apsara Café CAMBODIAN $
(Map p184; 42 Ph 178; mains US$3.50-6; 11am-midnight Sun-Thu, to 2am Fri & Sat;) A stylish little cafe serving health shakes,

vegetarian treats and Khmer food. Forty per cent of profits go to the Apsara Arts Association (p193).

Cantina MEXICAN $
(Map p184; 347 Sisowath Quay; mains US$3-6; ⌚2.30pm-11pm Sun-Fri) This is the spot for tostadas, fajitas and other Mexican favourites, all freshly prepared. It's also a journo hangout and a lively bar with well-made margaritas and tequilas.

CENTRAL PHNOM PENH SOUTH

TOP CHOICE **Malis** CAMBODIAN $
(Map p188; ☎221022; 136 Norodom Blvd; mains US$4-15) The leading Khmer restaurant in the Cambodian capital, Malis is a chic place to dine al fresco. The original menu includes beef in bamboo strips, sand goby (fish) with ginger, and traditional soups and salads.

TOP CHOICE **Shop** DELI $
(Map p188; 39 Ph 240; mains US$2-5; ⌚7am-8pm; ❄📶🅥) If you are craving the local deli back home, then make for this haven, which has a changing selection of sandwich and salad specials. The pastries and cakes are delectable and worth the indulgence.

K'nyay CAMBODIAN $
(Map p188; 25K Suramarit Blvd; mains US$2-5; ⌚noon-9pm Mon-Fri, 7am-9pm Sat; 📶🅥) A stylish little Cambodian restaurant with a generous selection of vegetarian and vegan options, original health shakes and homemade ice cream with ginger and honey.

Living Room CAFE $
(Map p188; 9 Ph 306; mains US$3.50-7; ⌚7am-8.30pm; ❄📶🅥) Family-friendly place in a colonial house with a wonderfully healthy menu and fresh fruit drinks to die for (try the mango passion smoothie or the blueberry lassi). Garden seating available.

Origami JAPANESE $$
(Map p188; ☎012 968095; 88 Sothearos Blvd; set menus US$8-30; ⌚11.30am-2pm & 6-10pm; ❄) This outstanding Japanese eatery takes the art of Japanese food to another level. Set menus include beautifully presented sushi, sashimi (US$15) and tempura boxes.

Le Jardin CAFE $
(Map p188; 16 Ph 360; mains US$3.50-6; ⌚Tue-Sun) Taking full advantage of a garden laden with jackfruit trees, this family-oriented cafe has a sandpit and a playhouse. Snacks and salads for adults, pastas and titbits for kids.

Yumi FUSION $$
(Map p188; ☎092 163903; 29a Ph 288; meals US$7-10; ⌚noon-2.30pm & 6-11pm Mon-Sat) With a compact menu of refreshingly original tapas and light Asian fare, it's the perfect spot for

TOP FIVE: GOOD-CAUSE DINING

These fantastic eateries act as training centres for young staff and help fund worthy causes in the capital.

» **Romdeng** (Map p184; 74 Ph 174; mains US$4-7; ⌚11am-9pm; 📶) Set in a gorgeous colonial villa with a small pool, the elegant Romdeng specialises in Cambodian country fare, including deep-fried spiders.

» **Friends** (Map p184; www.friends-international.org; 215 Ph 13; tapas US$2-5, mains from US$6; ⌚11am-9pm) One of Phnom Penh's best-loved restaurants, this place is a must, with tasty tapas bites, heavenly smoothies and creative cocktails. It offers former street children a head start in the hospitality industry.

» **Le Rit's** (Map p188; 71 Ph 240; mains US$2.50-7, set lunch US$6; 📶) The three-course lunches and dinners here are a relaxing experience in the well-groomed garden. Proceeds assist disadvantaged women with re-entering the workplace.

» **Hagar** (www.hagarcambodia.com) Ph 310 (Map p188; 44 Ph 310) Ph 163 (9 Ph 163, cnr Ph 292) The all-you-can-eat Asian fusion lunch buffet at the Ph 310 main restaurant costs US$6.50 and all proceeds go towards assisting destitute or abused women. If you can't afford that, the branch on Ph 163 charges only US$2.50 for its Cambodian lunch buffet.

» **Le Lotus Blanc** (Map p188; 152 Ph 51; mains US$6; ⌚Mon-Sat) This suburban restaurant acts as a training centre for youths who previously scoured the city dump. Run by French NGO Pour un Sourire d'Enfant (For the Smile of a Child), it serves classy Western and Khmer cuisine.

LOCAL FLAVOURS

Experience the real flavour of Phnom Penh with a meal at one of the city's many markets, where the food is fresh, tasty and cheap. **Psar Thmei** (p193) and **Psar Tuol Tom Pong** (p194) are two of the most popular places to combine some browsing with some bites. Both have plenty of produce available for self-caterers, plus dozens of food stalls with dishes for 3000r to 6000r. If the market stalls look a little raw and street-surfing doesn't appeal, then consider the air-conditioned alternative, **Sorya Shopping Centre Food Court** (Map p184; cnr Ph 63 & Ph 154; meals 5000r), located on the 4th floor.

Also worthwhile for cheap barbecue fare washed down with cheap beer are any of the numerous open-air 'beer gardens' scattered around town – look for the illuminated Anchor or Angkor beer signs. For something a bit more upmarket, cross the Japanese Friendship Bridge, over the Tonlé Bassac River just north of the centre, where there are plenty of big Cambodian restaurants built on stilts over the floodwaters.

a late dinner before a night out on nearby Ph 278.

Freebird AMERICAN $$
(Map p188; 69 Ph 240; mains US$5-15; ⊙7am-11pm; ❄📶) An American-style bar-diner with a great selection of burgers, wraps, salads and Tex-Mex.

Java Café CAFE $
(Map p188; www.javaarts.org; 56 Sihanouk Blvd; mains US$3.50-7; ❄📶) Consistently popular thanks to a breezy balcony and air-conditioned interior. The creative menu includes crisp salads, homemade sandwiches, towering burgers and daily specials, plus excellent coffee from several continents. Doubles as an art gallery.

Chayyam FUSION $
(Map p188; 8A Ph 278; mains US$4-6) Chayyam has some of the best Thai food in the city, along with Khmer specialities, conveniently located in the heart of Golden St. Traditional Khmer dances take place some nights.

Café Yejj CAFE $
(www.yejj.com; 92A Ph 432; mains US$3.50-6; ❄📶🖉) An air-con escape from Psar Tuol Tom Pong (Russian Market), this bistro-style cafe specialises in pastas and salads. Promoting fair trade and responsible employment.

Boat Noodle Restaurant THAI $
(Map p188; ☎012 200426; Ph 294; mains 8000-20,000r) This wooden house in a leafy garden brimming with water exudes old-school ambience and serves decent-value Thai and Cambodian food.

Mama Restaurant BACKPACKER CAFE $
(Map p188; 10C Ph 111; mains 6000-14,000r) The menu at this long-running hole-in-the-wall includes a bit of Khmer, Thai, French and even African.

Lucky Supermarket SUPERMARKET $
(Map p188; 160 Sihanouk Blvd; ⊙7am-9pm) The leading supermarket chain in town with a professional deli counter.

Drinking

Several of the aforementioned restaurants moonlight as popular bars, including Cantina and the Foreign Correspondents' Club. Keep an eye out for happy hours around town as these include two-for-the-price-of-one offers.

TOP CHOICE **Equinox** BAR
(Map p188; 3A Ph 278; ⊙7am-late) At the heart of the action on Ph 278, this is a popular place with a lively outdoor bar downstairs and excellent live music upstairs on any given night.

Zeppelin Cafe BAR
(Map p184; 109 Ph 51; ⊙6.30pm-late) Who says vinyl is dead? It lives on here thanks to this old-skool rock bar with a serious '60s and '70s music collection.

Elsewhere BAR
(Map p188; 2 Ph 278; ⊙8am-late) With ambient vibes, a great drinks menu, and two plunge pools for punters, it's sedate by day but sexy by night. It's in the heart of the action on Ph 278.

Heart of Darkness BAR, NIGHTCLUB
(Map p184; 26 Ph 51; ⊙8pm-late) This Phnom Penh institution with the alluring Angkor theme has evolved into more of a nightclub than a bar. It goes off every night of the week, attracting all sorts.

Pontoon NIGHTCLUB
(Map p184; www.pontoonclub.com; 80 Ph 172; admission Fri & Sat US$3-5, Sun-Thu free; ⊙9.30pm-late) The city's premier nightclub often sees big foreign acts at the stacks. Thursday is gay-friendly night, with a 1am lady-boy show.

Riverhouse Lounge LOUNGE
(Map p184; cnr Ph 110 & Sisowath Quay; ⊙4pm-2am) Almost a club as much as a lounge, it has DJs and live music through the week. It's chic and cool with a minimalist bar-restaurant downstairs.

Blue Chili BAR
(Map p184; 36 Ph 178; ⊙6pm-late) The owner of this gay-friendly bar stages his own drag show every Friday and Saturday at 10.30pm.

Memphis Pub LIVE MUSIC
(Map p184; 3 Ph 118; ⊙5pm-1am Mon-Sat) A good bet for live rock 'n' roll.

Score SPORTS BAR
(Map p188; ☎221357; 5 Ph 282; ⊙8am-late) The best place to watch a big game, with its ginormous screen.

Rainbow Bar BAR
(Map p184; 36 Ph 172) Laid-back, gay-friendly bar.

Gym Bar SPORTS BAR
(Map p184; 42 Ph 178; ⊙11am-late) The only workout going on here is raising glasses; the most comprehensive sports coverage in town.

Howie's Bar BAR
(Map p184; 32 Ph 51; ⊙7pm-6am) Friendly and fun place that's the perfect spillover when the Heart of Darkness is packed.

☆ Entertainment

Entertainment listings can be found in the *Phnom Penh Post* and *Cambodian Daily.*

TOP CHOICE **Meta House** CINEMA
(Map p188; www.meta-house.com; 37 Sothearos Blvd; ⊙6pm-midnight Tue-Sun) This night gallery has a diverse program of arthouse films, documentaries and shorts from Cambodia and around the world. Films are sometimes followed by Q&As with those involved.

French Cultural Centre CINEMA
(Map p188; Ph 184) Movie screenings in French during the week, starting at 6.30pm.

Mekong River Restaurant CINEMA
(Map p184; ☎991150; cnr Ph 118 & Sisowath Quay; ⊙24hr) Screens two original films, one covering the Khmer Rouge and the other about landmines (admission US$3).

Apsara Arts Association DANCE
(☎012 979335, 011 857424; 71 Ph 598) Hosts performances of classical dance and folk dance most Saturdays at 7pm (call to confirm; tickets US$5). It's in Tuol Kork district, in the far north of the city.

Sovanna Phum Arts Association DANCE
(☎987564; 16 Ph 99, cnr Ph 484) Impressive traditional shadow-puppet performances and classical dance shows are held at 7.30pm on Friday and Saturday nights (tickets US$5).

Shopping

An affirmation of identity, the *krama* (chequered scarf) is worn around the neck, shoulders and waist of nearly every Khmer. The scarves make superb souvenirs, as do Cambodia's sculptures and handicrafts.

Good shops to check out:

Ambre TEXTILES
(Map p184; ☎217935; 37 Ph 178; ⊙10am-6pm) Leading designer Romady Keth has turned this French-era mansion into a showcase for her stunning silk collection.

Kambuja CLOTHING
(Map p184; 165 Ph 110; ⊙9am-8pm) Blending the best of East and West, the Cambodian and American designers focus on female fashion but also produce some quality embroidered men's shirts.

Water Lily ACCESSORIES
(Map p188; 37 Ph 240; ⊙9am-7pm) Popular jewellery and accessory shop with strikingly original designs.

Markets

Bargains galore can be found at Phnom Penh's vibrant markets. Navigating the labyrinths of shoes, clothing, bric-a-brac and food is one of the most enjoyable ways to earn a foot massage. Markets are open from 6.30am to 5.30pm.

Psar Thmei MARKET
(New Market; Map p184) Often also referred to as Central Market, this art deco landmark resembles a Babylonian ziggurat. It houses an array of stalls selling jewellery, clothing and curios. The food section is enormous with produce spilling onto the streets. It's looking in fine fettle these days after

undergoing a much-needed facelift with French funding.

Psar Tuol Tom Pong MARKET

Best known as the Russian Market, this was the Russians' retail outlet of choice back in the 1980s. It's a good location to practise your haggling skills in purchasing designer clothing labels hot out of the factory, bootleg music and films, and carvings in wood, stone or bronze. This is the one market all visitors should come to at least once during a trip to Phnom Penh.

Psar O Russei MARKET

(Map p188) Housed in a sprawling mall-like space, this less-touristy market is the place to come if you want to lose the legion of attentive remork (túk-túk) drivers. It is a complete rabbit warren, selling everything you can think of and some you can't.

Night Market MARKET

(Psar Reatrey; Map p184; Ph 106 & Sisowath Quay; ⌚Fri-Sun) A cooler al fresco version of Psar Tuol Tom Pong, it's mainly souvenirs, silks and knick-knacks. Bargain vigorously, as prices can be on the high side.

Information

Check out *Phnom Penh Drinking and Dining* (www.cambodiapocketguide.com) for the low-down on bars and restaurants. The *Phnom Penh Visitors' Guide* (www.canbypublications.com) is brimming with useful information on the capital, while *AsiaLife Phnom Penh* (www.asialifecambodia.com) is a reliable read.

Bookshops

D's Books Ph 240 (Map p188; 79 Ph 240; ⌚9am-9pm) Ph 178 (Map p184; 7 Ph 178; ⌚9am-9pm) The largest chain of secondhand bookshops in the capital, with a good range of titles.

Monument Books (Map p188; ☎223 622; 111 Norodom Blvd; ⌚7am-8pm) The best-stocked bookshop in town, with almost every Cambodia-related book available, good maps and lots of LP titles.

Dangers & Annoyances

Phnom Penh is a big bustling city, but in general it is no more dangerous than most capitals. Bag snatching is a possibility in busy tourist areas; keep your valuables close or concealed and be prepared to let go rather than be dragged into the road. Keep shoulder bags in front of you when riding on motos. Be aware of traffic rules that seem to only apply to foreigners or you may have to pay some on-the-spot fines.

Emergency

Ambulance (☎119)

Fire (☎118)

Police & Medical (☎117)

Internet Access

It is not difficult to find somewhere to log on in Phnom Penh. Internet cafes are everywhere and usually charge US$0.50 to US$1 per hour. Most hotels and many cafes and restaurants also offer wi-fi connections, usually free.

TOP FIVE: GOOD-CAUSE SHOPPING

These stores sell high-quality silk items and handicrafts to provide the disabled and disenfranchised with valuable training for future employment, plus a regular flow of income to improve lives.

» **Friends & Stuff** (Map p184; 215 Ph 13; ⌚11am-9pm Mon-Sat) The closest thing to a charity shop or thrift store in Phnom Penh, with a good range of new and secondhand products sold to generate money to help street children.

» **NCDP Handicrafts** (Map p184; www.ncdpcam.org; 3 Norodom Blvd; ⌚8am-7pm) Run by the National Centre for Disabled Persons (NCDP), the collection includes exquisite silk scarves, throws, bags and cushions.

» **Nyemo** (Map p188; 71 Ph 240; ⌚7am-5pm Mon-Sat) In Le Rit's restaurant and with a branch at the Russian Market, Nyemo's focus is on quality silk and soft toys for children. It helps disadvantaged women return to work.

» **Rajana** (170 Ph 450; ⌚10am-6pm) Promoting fair wages and training, Rajana offers a beautiful selection of cards, some quirky metalware products, quality jewellery and bamboo crafts. Near the Russian Market.

» **Tabitha** (Map p188; 239 Ph 360; ⌚8am-6pm Mon-Sat) A leading NGO shop with a good collection of silk bags, tableware, bedroom decorations and children's toys. Proceeds go towards rural community development, such as well drilling.

GETTING TO VIETNAM: KAAM SAMNOR TO VINH XUONG (CHAU DOC)

The most scenic way to end your travels in Cambodia is to sail the Mekong to Kaam Samnor, about 100km south-southeast of Phnom Penh, cross the border to Vinh Xuong in Vietnam, and proceed to Chau Doc on the Tonlé Bassac River via a small channel or overland. Chau Doc has onward land and river connections to points in the Mekong Delta and elsewhere in Vietnam.

Various companies do trips all the way through to Chau Doc using a single boat or some combination of bus and boat; prices vary according to speed and level of service. **Capitol Tour** (023 217627; US$21) departs Phnom Penh at 8.30am and **Hang Chau** (017 336307; US$24) departs at noon. The more upmarket and slightly faster **Blue Cruiser** (016 868887; US$35) pulls out at 1pm. These companies take about four hours, including a slow border check, and use a single boat to Chau Doc. Backpacker guesthouses and tour companies in Phnom Penh offer the cheaper bus/boat combo trips. All boats depart from Phnom Penh's tourist dock.

Another option is to make your own way overland to Neak Luong, on the Mekong east of Phnom Penh, and sail down the Mekong to Kaam Samnor. Plenty of buses, minibuses and share taxis ply NH1 to Neak Luong, where speedboats are available for hire to Kaam Samnor (US$50, one hour) at a pier 300m south of the ferry landing on the west bank of the Mekong. A scheduled slow passenger boat to Kaam Samnor leaves daily at 9am from the same pier. In Vinh Xuong, local Vietnamese transport waits to transfer you to Chau Doc, an hour away.

The 45km road from Neak Luong to Kaam Samnor, paralleling the west bank of the Mekong, is passable for motorbikes but don't count on finding a moto.

For information on crossing this border in the other direction, see p154.

Medical Services

Calmette Hospital (off Map p184; 426948; 3 Monivong Blvd) A reputable hospital in Phnom Penh.

International SOS Medical Centre (Map p188; 216911; www.internationalsos.com; 161 Ph 51; 8am-5.30pm Mon-Fri, 8am-noon Sat, emergency 24hr) International standards for health and teeth.

U-Care Pharmacy (Map p184; 222499; 26 Sothearos Blvd; 8am-10pm) International-style pharmacy with a convenient location near the river.

Tropical & Travellers Medical Clinic (Map p184; 306802; www.travellersmedicalclinic.com; 88 Ph 108) Well-regarded British-run clinic.

Money

There are exchange services and banks with viable ATM machines all over Phnom Penh. Supermarkets, malls, high-end hotels and Caltex petrol stations usually have an ATM or two.

ANZ Royal Bank (Map p184; 265 Sisowath Quay) With multiple locations, it offers cash advances and ATM withdrawals.

Canadia Bank (Map p184; 265 Ph 110) Cash advances on MasterCard and Visa, plus an ATM.

Post

Main Post Office (Ph 13; 7am-6pm)

Telephone

The cheapest local and domestic calls in Phnom Penh are found at private stalls with the mobile telephone prefixes displayed.

Many internet cafes offer low-cost international calls via the internet (or free via Skype).

Tourist Information

There is not much in the way of official tourist information in the Cambodian capital. Pick up the free listings mags or ask around guesthouses and other travellers for up-to-date information.

Travel Agencies

Travel agencies abound on the riverfront. Most offer a city tour plus the standard day tours, and can sort you out with bus and boat tickets to just about anywhere.

Reliable operators:

Exotissimo (Map p184; 218948; www.exotissimo.com; Norodom Blvd)

Hanuman Tourism (Map p188; 218396; www.hanumantourism.com; 12 Ph 310)

GETTING TO VIETNAM: DIRECT TO HO CHI MINH CITY (SAIGON)

The easiest way to get to Ho Chi Minh City (Saigon) is to catch an international bus (US$12, six hours). Several companies offer direct services, including Capitol Tour, Mekong Express, Phnom Penh Sorya and Vietnamese company Sapaco.

For information on making the trip in the other direction see p148.

Getting There & Away

Air

See p276 for a list of airlines including those flying in to/out of Phnom Penh. See the boxed text, p182, for details on getting to/from the airport.

Boat

Speedboats depart daily to Siem Reap (US$35, five to six hours) at 7.30am from the **tourist boat dock** (Map p184; Sisowath Quay) at the eastern end of Ph 104, but the tickets are well overpriced compared with the bus.

Following the river to Chau Doc in Vietnam is a gorgeous way to go – see the boxed text p195.

Bus

Phnom Penh is connected to all of the provincial capitals by bus. Healthy competition keeps transport prices reasonable and all the companies are similar in terms of comfort and price.

See the relevant sections for individual destinations and details on prices and journey times. Some of the leading companies:

Capitol Tour (Map p188; ☎011 601341; 14 Ph 182) Services to Battambang, Kep/Kampot, Poipet, Siem Reap and Sihanoukville, plus Ho Chi Minh City (Saigon).

GST (Map p184; ☎097 5979791; Psar Thmei) Services to Battambang, Poipet, Siem Reap, Kratie/Stung Treng and Sihanoukville.

Mekong Express (Map p184; ☎427518; 87 Sisowath Quay) Upmarket services to Battambang, Siem Reap and Sihanoukville, plus Ho Chi Minh City.

Paramount Angkor Express (Map p184; ☎427567; 24 Ph 102) Double-decker buses to Battambang, Kampot, Koh Kong, Kompong Cham, Kratie, Pailin, Pakse (Laos), Poipet, Siem Reap and Sihanoukville.

Phnom Penh Sorya (Map p184; ☎210359; Psar Thmei) Long-running company serving most provincial destinations, plus Bangkok, Ho Chi Minh City and Pakse (Laos).

Virak Buntham Express (Map p184; ☎016 786270; Ph 106) Night buses to Siem Reap, plus buses to Battambang, Koh Kong, Sihanoukville, and Ho Chi Minh City and Ha Tien (Vietnam).

Car & Motorcycle

Guesthouses and travel agencies can arrange a car and driver from US$25 to US$60 a day, depending on the destination. See below for motorcycle rental details.

Share Taxi, Pick-Up & Minibus

Share taxis are an option for those in a rush. For Kampot, Koh Kong and Sihanoukville they leave from **Psar Dang Kor** (Mao Tse Toung Blvd) while minibuses, pick-ups and taxis for most other places leave from the northwest corner of Psar Thmei (p193). Vehicles for the Vietnam border leave from **Chbah Ampeau taxi park** (Hwy 1).

Getting Around

Bicycle

Simple bicycles can be hired from some guesthouses and hotels from US$1 a day, or contact Vicious Cycle (p185) for something more reliable and/or rugged.

Cyclo, Moto & Remork

Motos are everywhere; near the tourist areas they can generally speak a good level of street English. Short rides around the city cost 2000r; it's US$1 to venture out a little further. At night these prices double. To charter one for a day, expect to pay US$6 to US$8. Remorks usually charge double the price of a moto, possibly more if you pile on the passengers.

Cyclos aren't so common now that remorks have invaded the city. *Cyclos* cost about the same as motos. Arrange a *cyclo* tour through the **Cyclo Centre** (☎991178; www.cyclo.org.uk), dedicated to supporting *cyclo* drivers in Phnom Penh.

Motorcycle

Exploring Phnom Penh and the surrounding areas on a motorbike is a very liberating experience if you are used to chaotic traffic conditions. You usually get what you pay for when choosing a steel steed.

Lucky! Lucky! (Map p188; 413 Monivong Blvd) Has well-maintained trail bikes for US$13 per day.

New! New! (Map p188; 417 Monivong Blvd) Cheapest bikes.

Vannak Bikes Rental (Map p184; 46 Ph 130) Has good quality trail bikes up to 600cc for US$15 to US$30 per day.

Taxi

Taxis are cheap at 3000r per kilometre but don't expect to flag one down on the street. Call **Global Meter Taxi** (☎011 311888) or **Choice Taxi** (☎888023) for a pickup.

AROUND PHNOM PENH

There are several sites close to Phnom Penh that make for interesting excursions. Tonlé Bati, Phnom Tamao and Phnom Chisor are all near each other on NH2 and make a great full-day remork excursion (US$40) or self-drive motorbike ride. Udong is a separate half-day trip.

Tonlé Bati

Locals love to come to this **lake** (admission incl drink US$3) for picnics, as along the way they can stop off at the two 12th-century temples: Ta Prohm and Yeay Peau. Ta Prohm is the more interesting of the two; it has some fine carvings in good condition, depicting scenes of birth, dishonour and damnation.

The well-marked turnoff to Tonlé Bati is on the right about 31km south of Independence Monument in Phnom Penh. Buses going to Takeo can drop you here; find a moto to the temples (about 2.5km from the highway).

Phnom Tamao Wildlife Sanctuary

This **wildlife sanctuary** (admission US$5) for rescued animals is home to gibbons, sun bears, elephants, tigers, lions, deer and a massive bird enclosure. They were all taken from poachers or abusive owners and receive care and shelter here, as part of a sustainable breeding program.

The access road to Phnom Tamao is signposted on the right, 6.5km south of the turnoff to Tonlé Bati on NH2. The sanctuary is 5km from the highway on an incredibly dusty road often lined with elderly beggars.

Phnom Chisor

This 11th-century structure is a well-preserved laterite **temple** (admission US$3) that is aligned with the temples of Angkor. It has a peaceful setting on the summit of the hill, with stunning views of the countryside and the sacred pond below, Tonlé Om.

The access road for Phnom Chisor is signposted (in Khmer) on the left, 12km south of the turn-off to Phnom Tamao on NH2. The temple is 4.5km from the highway – motos wait at the turn-off.

Udong

Before the capital moved to Phnom Penh in 1866, it was based 40km north in Udong, ruling over the country for more than two centuries from its hilltop. Now it seems rather abandoned, with only a few scattered temples and stupas left standing, some of which contain the royal remnants of old kings. The 10-minute climb up the main hill is hot but offers great views of the surrounding countryside.

To get to Udong take a Phnom Penh Sorya bus bound for Kompong Chhnang (10,000r, one hour to Udong). They drop you off at the access road and from there it's 3km (4000r by moto).

WORTH A TRIP

WORTH THE TRIP: KIRIROM NATIONAL PARK

You can really get away from it all at this lush elevated **park** (admission US$5) just a couple of hours' drive southwest from Phnom Penh. Winding walking trails lead to cascading wet-season waterfalls and cliffs with amazing views of the Cardamom Mountains, and there's some great mountain-biking to be done if you're adventurous. Or you could just relax and forget about the outside world for a few days at **Kirirom Hillside Resort** (☎012 938 920; www.kiriromresort.com; r from US$50; ❄@≋) near the park entrance. With plastic dinosaurs, it's tacky at first glance, but scattered around the grounds are some great Scandinavian-style bungalows in various shapes and sizes. The pool has a lovely setting with the hills of Kirirom as a backdrop and is open to non-guests for US$5 per day. Nearby are camping and basic budget sleeping options, and a **Community-Based Ecotourism Program** (admission adult/child US$3/1) 10km from the park entrance in Chambok commune, where attractions include a 40m-high waterfall, traditional ox-cart rides and nature walks. A taxi from Phnom Penh is about US$60.

SIEM REAP

☎063 / POP 135,000

The life-support system for the one and only temples of Angkor, Siem Reap was always destined for great things. Back in the 1960s, Siem Reap (*see*-em ree-*ep*) was the place to be in Southeast Asia and saw a steady stream of the rich and famous. After three decades of slumber, it's well and truly back and one of the most popular destinations on the planet right now. It has reinvented itself as the epicentre of the new Cambodia, with more guesthouses and hotels than temples, and sumptuous spas and world-class wining and dining.

At heart, though, Siem Reap – whose name rather undiplomatically means 'Siamese Defeated' – is still a little charmer, with old French shophouses, shady tree-lined boulevards and a slow-flowing river.

Sights

Angkor National Museum MUSEUM
(Map p200; ☎966601; www.angkornationalmuseum.com; 968 Charles de Gaulle Blvd; adult/child under 1.2m US$12/6, audio guide US$3; 8.30am-6pm) A worthwhile introduction to the glories of the Khmer empire, the state-of-the-art Angkor National Museum will help clarify Angkor's history, religious significance, and cultural and political context. Displays include 1400 exquisite stone carvings and artefacts. Wheelchair accessible.

Les Chantiers Écoles HANDICRAFT WORKSHOP
(Map p200; 7am-5pm Mon-Fri & Sat morning) Tucked down a side road, Les Chantiers Écoles teaches traditional Khmer artisanship, including lacquer-making and wood- and stone-carving, to impoverished youngsters. Tours of the workshops are possible when school is in session. On the premises is an exquisite shop, Artisans d'Angkor (p205).

To see the entire silk-making process, from mulberry trees to silkworms and spinning to weaving, visit Les Chantiers Écoles' **silk farm** (7.30am-5.30pm), 16km west of town. Shuttle buses leave the school at 9.30am and 1.30pm for a three-hour free tour.

Cambodia Landmine Museum MUSEUM
(off Map p210; ☎012 598951; www.cambodialandminemuseum.org; admission US$2; 7.30am-5pm) Popular with travellers thanks to its informative displays on one of the country's postwar curses, the non-profit Cambodia Landmine Museum has a mock minefield where visitors can search for deactivated mines. It's situated about 25km from Siem Reap and 6km south of Banteay Srei temple.

Banteay Srei Butterfly Centre BUTTERFLY CENTRE
(off Map p210; ☎011 348460; www.angkorbutterfly.com; adult/child US$4/2; 9am-5pm) This is a worthwhile place to include on a trip to Banteay Srei and the Landmine Museum. The largest fully enclosed butterfly centre in Southeast Asia, there are more than 30 species of Cambodian butterflies fluttering about. It is a good experience for children, as they can see the whole process from egg to caterpillar, cocoon to butterfly. It is located about 7km before Banteay Srei on the right-hand side of the road.

Bayon Information Centre MUSEUM
(Map p210; ☎092 165083; www.angkor-jsa.org/bic; entry US$2; 8am-4pm Tue, Wed & Fri-Sun) This exhibition introduces the visitor to the history of the Khmer empire and the restoration projects around Angkor through a series of short films and displays. Set in the beautiful Japanese team for Safeguarding Angkor (JSA) compound, it's considerably cheaper than the Angkor National Museum, although there is no statuary on display.

Centre for Friends Without a Border EXHIBITION
(Map p200; ☎963409; www.fwab.org; 8am-noon & 1-6pm Mon-Fri, 8am-noon Sat) This small centre houses an elegant photography gallery whose proceeds go to the adjacent Angkor Hospital for Children.

Khmer Ceramics Centre POTTERY CENTRE
(Map p210; ☎017 843014; www.khmerceramics.com; Charles de Gaulle Blvd; 8am-7.30pm) At this centre you can see ceramics being turned, decorated and fired using the traditional techniques that were almost lost because of the Khmer Rouge. Half-day courses are also available if you fancy taking the wheel. It's situated on the road to Angkor Wat.

Cambodian Cultural Village CULTURAL VILLAGE
(Map p210; ☎963836; www.cambodianculturalvillage.com; NH6; US$9, child under 1.1m free; 8am-7pm) The Cambodian Cultural Village tries to represent all of Cambodia in a whirlwind tour of recreated houses and villages. It may be kitschy and overpriced, but it's very

Kiri 063966747

popular with Cambodians and the dance and music performances will keep the kiddies entertained.

War Museum MUSEUM

(Map p210; admission US$3; 7.30am-5.30pm) The War Museum, 1km north of NH6 from the Royal Angkor International Hospital, displays old mines, rusty Soviet tanks, a Russian-built Mi-8 helicopter and a Chinese-built MiG-19 in a peaceful garden. All bear silent witness to decades of bloodshed.

Tonlé Sap Exhibition EXHIBITION

(Map p210; 8am-noon & 1.30-5.30pm) On the main road to Angkor Wat, on the grounds of the Siem Reap School for Deaf or Blind, is the Tonlé Sap Exhibition, which has a low-tech but interesting exhibition about the Tonlé Sap ecosystem. Like the adjacent **Massage by Blind** it is run by the NGO Krousar Thmey.

Wat Thmei TEMPLE

(Map p210; 6am-6.30pm) Modern-day pagodas offer an interesting contrast to the ancient sandstone structures of Angkor. On the left fork of the road to Angkor Wat, Wat Thmei, built in 1992, has a memorial stupa containing the skulls and bones of people killed here when the site served as a Khmer Rouge prison. Some of the young monks are keen to practise their English.

Activities

Cooking Courses

Cooks in Tuk Tuks COOKING CLASS

(Map p210; 963400; www.therivergarden.info; classes US$25; 10am-1pm) The course starts at 10am daily with a visit to Psar Leu market, then returns to the peaceful River Garden boutique hotel for a professional class.

Le Tigre de Papier COOKING CLASS

(Map p200; 760930; www.letigredepapier.com; Pub St; classes US$12; 10am-1pm) Starts at 10am daily and includes a visit to the market. Proceeds go to supporting Sala Bai (p203).

Golf

Siem Reap has several international-standard golf courses. Greens fees are around US$100, plus more for clubs, a caddy and buggy. Two of the best:

Phokheetra Country Club (off Map p210; 964600; www.sofitel.com) Includes an ancient Angkor bridge amid its manicured fairways and greens.

Angkor Golf Resort (Map p210; 761139; www.angkor-golf.com) World-class course designed by legendary British golfer Nick Faldo.

Horse Riding

Happy Ranch HORSE RIDING

(Map p210; 012 920002; www.thehappyranch.com; 30min-4hr rides US$17-80) Ride 'em cowboy. Take the chance to explore Siem Reap on horseback, taking in surrounding villages and secluded temples. Riding lessons are also available for children or beginners. Book direct for the best prices.

Massage & Spa

You may well need a massage if you have been exploring the rollercoaster roads of Preah Vihear Province.

Foot massage is a big hit in Siem Reap, hardly surprising given all those steep stairways at the temples. Some are more authentic than others, so dip your toe in first before selling your sole.

For an alternative foot massage, brave the waters of **Dr Fish**. It's basically a paddling pool full of cleaner fish, which nibble away at your dead skin. Heaven for some, tickly as hell for others; places have sprung up all over town, including along Pub St.

The following are worthwhile massage places:

Seeing Hands Massage 4 (Map p200; 012 836487; 324 Ph Sivatha; per hr fan/air-con $5/7) Trains blind people in the art of massage.

Krousar Thmey (Map p210; massage US$7) Also has massage by the blind in the same location as its free Tonlé Sap Exhibition. Watch out for copycats, as some of these are just exploiting the blind for profit.

There are also some indulgent spas to pamper that inner princess:

Bodia Spa (Map p200; 761593; www.bodia-spa.com; Ph Pithnou; 10am-midnight) Sophisticated spa offering a full range of scrubs, rubs and natural remedies, including its own line of herbal products.

Bodytune (Map p200; 764141; www.bodytune.co.th; 293 Pokambor Ave; massages US$12-37; 10am-10pm) Lavish outpost of a popular Thai spa, this is a fine place to relax and unwind on the riverfront.

Siem Reap

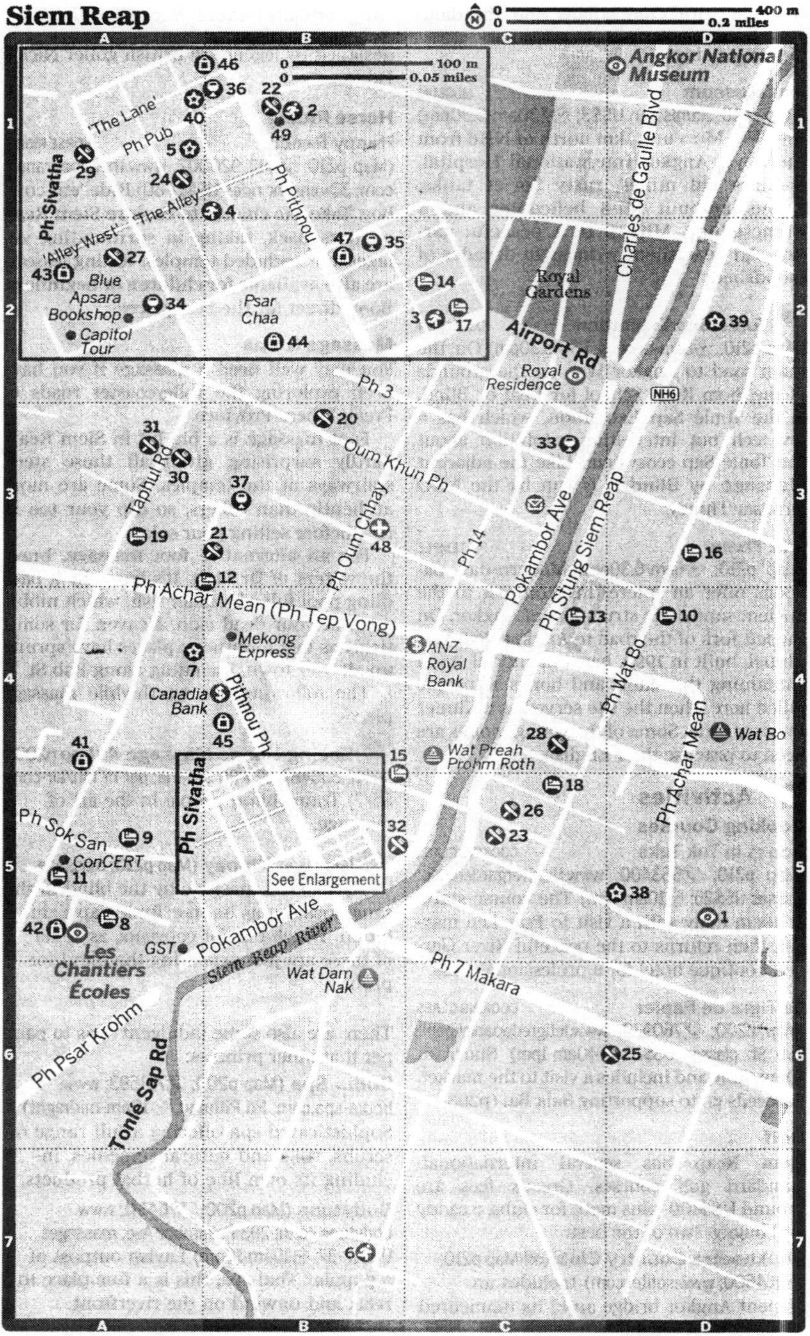

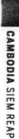

0 400 m
0 0.2 miles
A
B
C
D
1
2
3
4
5
6
7
0 100 m
0 0.05 miles
46
36
22
2
40
49
'The Lane'
Ph Pub
5
29
Ph Sivatha
24
Ph Pithnou
'The Alley'
4
'Alley West'
47
35
27
43
Blue Apsara Bookshop
34
Psar Chaa
14
3
17
Capitol Tour
44
Angkor National Museum
Charles de Gaulle Blvd
Royal Gardens
Airport Rd
Royal Residence
NH6
39
Ph 3
20
31
Taphul Rd
30
Oum Khun Ph
33
37
Ph Oum Chhay
Ph 14
Pokambor Ave
Ph Stung Siem Reap
19
21
48
16
12
Ph Achar Mean (Ph Tep Vong)
13
10
Mekong Express
ANZ Royal Bank
7
Ph Wat Bo
Canadia Bank
Pithnou Ph
45
41
28
Wat Bo
15
Wat Preah Prohm Roth
Ph Achar Mean
18
Ph Sivatha
32
26
Ph Sok San
9
23
ConCERT
11
See Enlargement
38
1
42
8
Les Chantiers Écoles
GST
Pokambor Ave
Siem Reap River
Wat Dam Nak
Ph 7 Makara
Ph Psar Krohm
Tonlé Sap Rd
25
6

Siem Reap

Top Sights
- Angkor National Museum D1
- Les Chantiers Écoles A5

Sights
- Centre for Friends Without a Border ..... (see 48)
- 1 Sam Veasna Center for Wildlife Conservation D5

Activities, Courses & Tours
- 2 Bodia Spa B1
- 3 Bodytune C2
- 4 Frangipani B1
- 5 Le Tigre de Papier A1
- 6 Quad Adventure Cambodia B7
- 7 Seeing Hands Massage 4 ..... A4

Sleeping
- 8 EI8HT Rooms A5
- 9 Encore Angkor Guesthouse A5
- 10 Frangipani Villa Hotel D4
- 11 Golden Temple Villa A5
- 12 Hotel de la Paix B3
- 13 La Résidence d'Angkor C4
- 14 Neth Socheata Guesthouse C2
- 15 Prohm Roth Guesthouse B5
- 16 Seven Candles Guesthouse D3
- 17 Shadow of Angkor Guesthouse C2
- 18 Soria Moria Hotel C5
- 19 Villa Siem Reap A3

Eating
- 20 Angkor Market B3
- 21 Barrio B3
- 22 Blue Pumpkin B1
- 23 Butterflies Garden Restaurant C5
- Café de la Paix ..... (see 12)
- 24 Cambodian BBQ A1
- Chamkar ..... (see 24)
- 25 Kanell D6
- 26 Karavansara C5
- 27 La Trattoria A2
- 28 Le Café C4
- Le Tigre de Papier ..... (see 5)
- 29 Local Food Stalls A1
- Psar Chaa ..... (see 44)
- 30 Sala Bai A3
- 31 Sugar Palm A3
- 32 Swensen's Ice Cream B5

Drinking
- 33 FCC Angkor C3
- 34 Joe-to-Go A2
- 35 Laundry Bar B2
- 36 Miss Wong B1
- 37 Nest B3
- Warehouse ..... (see 47)

Entertainment
- 38 Apsara Theatre D5
- 39 La Noria D2
- 40 Temple Club A1

Shopping
- 41 Angkor Night Market A4
- 42 Artisans d'Angkor A5
- 43 Keo Kjay A2
- 44 Psar Chaa B2
- 45 Rajana B4
- 46 Samatoa A1
- 47 Senteurs d'Angkor B2

Information
- 48 Angkor Hospital for Children B3
- 49 U Care Pharmacy B1

Frangipani (Map p200; ☎964391; www.frangipanisiemreap.com; The Alley; ⊙10am-10pm) This delightful place offers massage and a whole range of spa treatments.

Quad Biking

Quad Adventure Cambodia QUAD BIKING
(Map p200; ☎092 787216; www.q-adventure-cambodia.com; 15min to full-day rides US$25-195) Offers sunset rides through the rice fields or longer rides to pretty temples following back roads through traditional villages. Quad Adventure Cambodia is well signposted in the Wat Dam Nak area.

Swimming

It's hot work clambering about the temples and there is no better way to wind down than with a dip in a swimming pool. Pay by the day at most hotels for use of the swimming pool and/or gym, ranging from just US$5 at some of the midrange hotels to US$20 at the five-star palaces.

Sleeping

Siem Reap now has more hotels and guesthouses than temples and that means there are hundreds to choose from, from simple shacks with shared toilets to sumptuous six-star suites.

PSAR CHAA & AROUND

TOP CHOICE Shadow of Angkor Guesthouse GUESTHOUSE $
(Map p200; 964774; www.shadowofangkor.com; 353 Pokambor Ave; r US$15-25;) In a grand old French-era building overlooking the river, this friendly 15-room place offers affordable air-con in a superb setting.

Golden Temple Villa HOTEL $
(Map p200; 012 943459; www.goldentemplevilla.com; r US$13-23;) Independent travellers love this place thanks to its funky, colourful decor and fun outlook. Their new Golden Temple Hotel offers the four-star high life.

Hotel de la Paix LUXURY HOTEL $$$
(Map p200; 966000; www.hoteldelapaixangkor.com; Ph Sivatha; r from US$240;) This place is all about funky, contemporary design, trendy interiors and minimalist style. Rooms include open-plan bathrooms and iPods, plus house restaurant Meric serves up cutting-edge cuisine.

Prohm Roth Guesthouse GUESTHOUSE $
(Map p200; 012 466495; www.prohmroth-guesthouse.com; r US$9-25;) Central, yet tucked away down a side street which runs parallel to Wat Preah Prohm Roth, this is a friendly place. Free pick-up from airport, port or bus station.

EI8HT Rooms GUESTHOUSE $
(Map p200; 969788; www.ei8htrooms.com; r US$12-24;) A smart, gay-friendly guesthouse with boutique touches, bright silks, DVD players and free internet. So popular there are now 16 rooms set in two buildings.

Encore Angkor Guesthouse HOTEL $$
(Map p200; 969400; www.encoreangkor.com; 456 Ph Sok San; r US$20-50;) The stylish lobby sets the tone for a budget boutique experience. Rooms include oversized beds and an in-room safe.

Villa Siem Reap HOTEL $$
(Map p200; 761036; www.thevillasiemreap.com; Taphul Rd; r US$20-55;) Homely service in intimate surrounds make this a popular place. Popular tours are available to some of the far-flung sights.

Neth Socheata Guesthouse GUESTHOUSE $$
(Map p200; 963294; www.angkorguesthouseneth socheata.com; near Psar Chaa; r US$22-33;) This place has a likeable location in the warren of alleys to the north of the market. Tasteful furnishings, sparkling bathrooms and free wi-fi add up to an affordable deal.

EAST BANK

This area is quieter than around Psar Chaa, with plenty of charm near the river.

TOP CHOICE Frangipani Villa Hotel BOUTIQUE HOTEL $$
(Map p200; 999930; www.frangipanihotel.com; Ph Wat Bo; r US$40-60;) The Siem Reap outpost of the growing Frangipani empire, this is chic boutique on the cheap. Rooms include stylish touches like flat-screen TVs and there is an inviting pool.

TOP CHOICE La Résidence d'Angkor BOUTIQUE RESORT $$$
(Map p200; 963390; www.residencedangkor.com; Ph Stung Siem Reap; r from US$275;) The 54 wood-appointed rooms, among the most tasteful and inviting in town, come with verandahs and huge jacuzzi-sized tubs. The gorgeous swimming pool is perfect for laps. The new wing is ultra-contemporary.

Soria Moria Hotel BOUTIQUE HOTEL $$
(Map p200; 964768; www.thesoriamoria.com; Ph Wat Bo; r US$40-65;) A Norwegian-owned hotel with bright, attractive rooms and a rooftop sun deck with a spa room, jacuzzi and bar. Promotes local causes to help the community.

Seven Candles Guesthouse GUESTHOUSE $
(Map p200; 963380; www.sevencandlesguesthouse.com; 307 Ph Wat Bo; r US$7-15;) A warm and welcoming good-cause guesthouse; profits help a local foundation seeking to promote education to rural communities. Rooms include hot water, TV and fridge.

Karavansara BOUTIQUE HOTEL $$$
(Map p200; 760678; www.karavansara.com; Ph 25 Acha Sva; r from US$87;) Set in an iconic building from Cambodia's new architecture heyday, this boutique hotel offers tasteful rooms and, across the road, larger apartments for families. The restaurant is set in a delightful relocated traditional house.

Mens Resort & Spa BOUTIQUE HOTEL $$
(Map p210; 963503; www.mens-resort.com; r US$49-90;) The latest gay resort among a growing scene in Siem Reap, this is designed along slick minimalist lines.

CRAVING ICE CREAM

After a hot day exploring the temples, there is nothing quite like an ice-cream fix and Siem Reap delivers some superb surprises:

Blue Pumpkin (Map p200; Ph Pithnou; cones US$1.50; ☺6am-10pm) Homemade ice cream in original tropical flavours from ginger to passion fruit.

Cafe de la Paix (Map p200; Hotel de la Paix, Ph Sivatha; cones US$1.50; ☺6am-10pm) Velvety ice creams including Mars flavour and tangy sorbets.

Swenson's Ice Cream (Map p200; Pokambor Ave; cones US$1.25; ☺9am-9pm) One of America's favourites has become one of Siem Reap's favourites, located in the Angkor Trade Centre.

Rooms include funky artworks and the discreet premises includes a pool and spa.

Borann L'Auberge des Temples HOTEL $$
(Map p210; ☑964740; www.borann.com; r US$49-69; ✵@☎⛱) Set in a lush tropical garden with a pretty swimming pool, the rustic rooms (without TV) are decorated with shadow puppets.

FURTHER AFIELD
Siddharta Boutique Hotel BOUTIQUE HOTEL $$$
(Map p210; ☑768769; www.siddharta-hotel.com; r from US$75; ✵@☎⛱) Offering enlightened prices for this level of comfort, this new hotel is finished in colonial-era style. Rooms include sophisticated amenities and their own adjoined seating area with a rattan egg chair to unwind.

My Home Tropical Garden Villa HOTEL $
(Map p210; ☑760035; www.myhomecambodia.com; Ph Psar Krom; r US$14-26; ✵@☎⛱) Offering hotel standards at guesthouse prices, this is a fine place to rest your head. The decor includes some subtle silks and the furnishings are tasteful.

The Samar BOUTIQUE RESORT $$$
(Map p210; ☑762449; www.samarvillas.com; r US$160-300; ✵@☎⛱) The most boutique of many boutique places in Siem Reap, the Samar offers sumptuous all-wooden suites, each with individual taste and character. Rates include a daily shave for gents and a hand massage for women.

Paul Dubrule Hotel & Tourism School HOTEL $$
(Map p210; ☑963673; www.ecolepauldubrule.org; NH6; r US$20-35; ✵@☎) Paul Dubrule cofounded the Accor hotel group, so it's no surprise that his four-room training hotel offers smart rooms and slick service. A great deal.

Golden Mango Inn HOTEL $
(Map p210; ☑761857; www.goldenmangoinn.com; r US$15-20; ✵@☎) We are not normally so keen on this busy side of town, but Golden Mango is a lively guesthouse tucked away down a quiet side street.

✗ Eating

Worthy restaurants are sprinkled all around town but Siem Reap's culinary heart is the Psar Chaa area, whose focal point, The Alley, is literally lined with mellow eateries offering great atmosphere. It is wall-to-wall with good Cambodian restaurants, many family-owned. Cheap eats can be found at the nearby **local food stalls** (Map p200; Ph Sivatha; mains 4000-8000r; ☺4pm-3am), around Pub St's western end.

For self-caterers, markets have fruit and vegies. **Angkor Market** (Map p200; Ph Sivatha; ☺7.30am-10pm) can supply international treats.

Blue Pumpkin INTERNATIONAL $
(Map p200; Ph Pithnou; mains US$2-6; ☺6am-10pm; ✵☎) Upstairs is a world of white minimalism with beds to lounge on and free wi-fi. Light bites, great sandwiches, filling specials, divine shakes and superb cakes keep them coming.

Sugar Palm KHMER $
(Map p200; Taphul Rd; mains US$4-8; ☺11.30am-3pm & 5.30-10pm) Set in a beautiful wooden house, this is an excellent place to sample traditional flavours infused with herbs and spices. Owner-chef Katana taught Gordon Ramsay some tricks during his 'Great Escape' shoot.

Sala Bai INTERNATIONAL $$
(Map p200; www.salabai.com; Taphul Rd; set lunch US$8; ☺7-9am, noon-2pm Mon-Fri) This school

trains young Khmers in the art of hospitality and serves an affordable three-course lunch menu of Western and Cambodian cuisine.

Cambodian BBQ BARBECUE $$
(Map p200; ☎966052; The Alley; mains US$5-9; ⏰11am-11pm) Crocodile, snake, ostrich and kangaroo meat add an exotic twist to the traditional *phnom pleung* (hill of fire) grills. It has spawned a dozen or more copycats in the surrounding streets.

Le Tigre de Papier INTERNATIONAL $
(Map p200; Pub St; Khmer mains US$3-6.50; ⏰24hr) Established spot with a wood-fired oven and a great menu of Italian, French and Khmer food. The 24-hour opening means it's a good place if the midnight munchies strike.

Butterflies Garden Restaurant INTERNATIONAL $
(Map p200; www.butterfliesofangkor.com; mains US$3-7; ⏰8am-10pm) In a blooming garden aflutter with butterflies, this place serves Khmer flavours (including vegie and vegan) with an international touch. Supports good causes.

Le Café FRENCH $
(Map p200; Wat Bo area; mains US$4-5; ⏰7.30am-8pm) Brings five-star, Paul Dubrule-inspired sandwiches, salads and shakes to the French Cultural Centre, where it serves as the in-house eatery.

Chamkar VEGETARIAN $
(Map p200; The Alley; mains US$3-5; ⏰11am-11pm) A creative menu of Asian vegetarian flavours includes stuffed pumpkin or vegetable kebabs in black pepper sauce. A good spot for watching the world go by on The Alley.

La Trattoria ITALIAN $
(Map p200; Alley West; mains US$4-10 ⏰11am-11pm) Formerly Samot, and famous for seafood, the house speciality is now authentic pizzas and pasta. Lunch specials are a good way to take a break from the boutiques on Alley West.

Kanell INTERNATIONAL $$
(Map p200; Ph 28; mains US$5-15; ⏰11am-midnight; 📶🏊) Set in a handsome Khmer villa on the edge of town, Kanell offers extensive gardens and a swimming pool for those seeking to dine and unwind. The menu includes French-accented dishes, plus some Cambodian favourites.

Wat Damnak Cuisine KHMER $$
(Map p210; set menus from US$15; ⏰lunch & dinner) The new restaurant from Siem Reap celeb chef Johannes Rivieres, its menu promises the ultimate contemporary Khmer dining experience. A little out of the way, set in a traditional wooden house.

Barrio FRENCH $
(Map p200; Ph Sivatha; mains US$4-10; ⏰11am-11pm) One of the longest-running French bistros in town, it's popular with European expats thanks to its Gallic menu and continental vibe.

Drinking

Siem Reap is now firmly on the nightlife map of Southeast Asia, with many of the most interesting places situated in the vicinity of Psar Chaa, on or near Pub St or The Alley.

Many of the high-end hotels offer two-for-one happy hours. **FCC Angkor** (Pokambor Ave; 5-7pm) is well worth stopping by for a jar or two to take in the sophisticated surrounds.

Laundry Bar LOUNGE.BAR
(Map p200; Psar Chaa area; ⏰5pm-3am) One of the most alluring bars in town thanks to discerning decor, low lighting and a laid-back soundtrack. Happy hour is 5pm to 9pm.

Miss Wong COCKTAIL BAR
(Map p200; ☎092-428332; The Lane; ⏰6pm-1am or later) Miss Wong carries you back to the chic of 1920s Shanghai. A gay-friendly bar, the cocktails are the draw here.

Warehouse BAR
(Map p200; Ph Pithnou; ⏰10.30am-3am) A popular bar opposite Psar Chaa; indie anthems, table football, a pool table and devilish drinks.

Nest BAR-RESTAURANT
(Map p200; Ph Sivatha; ⏰4pm-late) A memorable watering hole thanks to its sweeping sail-like shelters and stylish seating, this place has one of the most creative cocktail lists in town.

Joe-To-Go CAFE
(Map p200; Psar Chaa; ⏰7am-9.30pm) If you need gourmet coffee to course through your veins before you muster the lustre to tackle the temples, then head here.

Entertainment

Classical dance shows take place all over town, but only a few are worth considering. Children perform **apsara dances** at 7pm on Friday at the Soria Moria Hotel (p202).

The performance is free with a set menu (US$6/8 for Khmer/Western food).

Apsara Theatre CLASSICAL DANCE
(Map p200; www.angkorvillage.com; show incl dinner US$25) Nightly performances in a wat-style wooden pavilion opposite Angkor Village.

La Noria SHADOW PUPPETS
(Map p200; River Rd; US$12; ⏲8pm Wed & Sun) See the traditional art of shadow puppetry performed over a set dinner. Part of the fee goes to the NGO Krousar Thmey.

Temple Club CLASSICAL DANCE
(Map p200; Pub St; buffet incl dance show US$5) A very popular bar-restaurant that offers the best-value classical dance show in town. Cultural performances upstairs, late-night mayhem downstairs.

Shopping

Siem Reap has an excellent selection of Cambodian-made handicrafts. **Psar Chaa** (Map p200) is well stocked. There are bargains to be had if you haggle patiently and humorously.

Angkor Night Market (Map p200; www.angkornightmarket.com; near Ph Sivatha; ⏲4pm-midnight) is packed with silks, handicrafts and souvenirs. Up-and-coming **Alley West** is also a great strip to browse socially responsible fashion boutiques.

Several shops support Cambodia's disabled and disenfranchised:

Artisans d'Angkor HANDICRAFTS
(Map p200; www.artisansdangkor.com; ⏲7.30am-7.30pm) One of the best places in Cambodia for quality souvenirs and gifts, with everything from silk clothing and accessories to elegant reproductions of Angkorian-era statuary. Branches in town, opposite Angkor Wat, and at the airport.

Keo Kjay FASHION
(Map p200; www.keokjay.org; Alley West; ⏲11am-10pm) Translating as 'fresh' in Khmer, this hip little boutique is a fair-trade fashion enterprise that aims to provide HIV+ women with a sustainable income.

Rajana HANDICRAFTS
(Map p200; www.rajanacrafts.org; Ph Sivatha; ⏲8am-10pm Mon-Sat, 2-10pm Sun) Sells quirky wooden and metalware objects, silver jewellery and handmade cards. Rajana promotes fair trade and employment opportunities for Cambodians.

Samatoa FASHION
(Map p200; Ph Pithnou; ⏲8am-11pm) Fair-trade fashion in Siem Reap, select designer clothes finished in silk, with the option of a tailored fit in 48 hours.

Senteurs d'Angkor HEALTH & BEAUTY
(Map p200; www.senteursdangkor.com; Ph Pithnou; ⏲7am-10pm) Has a wide-ranging collection of silk, stone carvings, beauty products, massage oils, spices, coffees and teas. Visit their **Botanic Garden** (Airport Rd; ⏲7.30am-5.30pm), a sort of Willy Wonka's for the senses.

Information

Hotels, pubs and restaurants have the free *Siem Reap Angkor Visitors Guide* (www.canbypublications.com) and two handy booklets produced by *Pocket Guide Cambodia* (www.cambodiapocketguide.com).

There are ATMs at the airport and in banks and minimarts all over central Siem Reap, especially along Ph Sivatha. The greatest concentration of internet shops is along Ph Sivatha and around Psar Chaa. Free wi-fi is available at many of the leading cafes, restaurants and bars, not forgetting most guesthouses and hotels.

GETTING TO THAILAND: O SMACH TO CHONG CHOM

This is not the easiest border crossing to reach. Share taxis (30,000r, four hours) link Siem Reap with Samraong, the backwater provincial capital, where you can hire a moto (US$10) or a private taxi (US$25) for the punishing drive to O Smach (nearly two hours, 40km) and its frontier casino zone. On the Thai side it's easy – *sŏrngtăaou* (pick-up trucks) and motos take arrivals to the stop for buses to Surin (1½ to two hours, 70km). Cambodian visas are available for US$20 plus a US$2 'processing fee'. Sometimes 1000B is requested.

For information on crossing this border in the other direction, see the boxed text, p423.

TRANSPORT CONNECTIONS FROM SIEM REAP

DESTINATION	CAR/MOTORBIKE TRAVEL TIME	BUS TRAVEL TIME/ COST/FREQUENCY	BOAT TRAVEL TIME/ COST/FREQUENCY	AIR TRAVEL TIME/ COST/FREQUENCY
Bangkok	8 hours	10 hours/US$12-15/frequent	N/A	1 hour/from US$144/5 daily
Battambang	3 hours	4 hours/US$4-5/ regular	6-8 hours/ US$20/7am	N/A
Kompong Thom	2 hours	2½ hours/US$5/ frequent	N/A	N/A
Phnom Penh	5 hours	6 hours/US$5-11/ frequent	5 hours/ US$35/7am daily	30 minutes/from US$90/3 daily
Poipet	3 hours	4 hours/US$4-5/ regular	N/A	N/A

Angkor Hospital for Children (Map p200; ☎963409; http://angkorhospital.org; Ph Achar Mean; ⏲24hr) A paediatric hospital that's free for anyone under 16, tourists included. Non-emergency hours are 7am to 5pm Monday to Friday and 7am to noon Saturday.

ANZ Royal Bank (Map p200; Ph Achar Mean) Plus ATMs conveniently dotted about town.

Blue Apsara Bookshop (Map p200; ⏲8am-11pm) Used books in several languages.

D's Books (Map p200; Pub St; ⏲9am-10pm) The largest chain of secondhand bookshops in Cambodia, this is conveniently located for night browsing.

Main post office (Map p200; Pokambor Ave; ⏲7am-5.30pm) Services are more reliable these days, but it doesn't hurt to see your stamps franked. Also offers EMS express international postal service.

Royal Angkor International Hospital (Map p210; ☎761888; www.royalangkorhospital.com; NH6; ⏲24hr) A modern, international-standard facility affiliated with the Bangkok Hospital Medical Center. Call to arrange an ambulance or a house call by a doctor.

Tourist police (Map p210; ☎012 969991) At the main Angkor ticket checkpoint.

U-Care Pharmacy (Map p200; Ph Pithnou; ⏲8am-9pm) Smart pharmacy and shop like Boots in Thailand (and the UK). English spoken.

Getting There & Away

Air

Siem Reap International Airport (Map p210; www.cambodia-airports.com) is a work of art set 7km west of the centre and offers regular connections to most neighbouring Asian cities. Domestic flights are limited to Phnom Penh, but it is hoped that direct flights will resume to Sihanoukville at some stage. For airline details see p276.

Boat

Boats for the trip to Battambang (US$20; p224) and the faster ride to Phnom Penh (US$35) depart at 7am from the tourist boat dock at Chong Kneas, 11km south of town. Tickets are sold at guesthouses, hotels and travel agencies, and include pick-up from your hotel or guesthouse around 6am.

Bus

All buses depart from the **bus station** (Map p210), which is 3km east of town and about 200m south of NH6. Tickets are available at guesthouses, hotels, bus offices, travel agencies and ticket kiosks. Some bus companies send a minibus around to pick up passengers at their place of lodging. Most departures to Phnom Penh are between 7am and 1pm; buses to other destinations generally leave early in the morning. Upon arrival in Siem Reap, be prepared for a rugby scrum of eager moto drivers meeting the bus.

There are lots of bus companies that serve Siem Reap. All have ticket offices at the bus station. Most travellers buy tickets through their guesthouse or hotel, including a transfer to the bus station:

Capitol Tour (☎963883)

GST (☎092 905016)

Mekong Express (☎963662)

Neak Kror Horm (☎964924)

Paramount Angkor Express (☎966469)

Phnom Penh Sorya (☎012 235618)

Rith Mony (☎012 344377)

Virak Bunthan (☎015 958989)

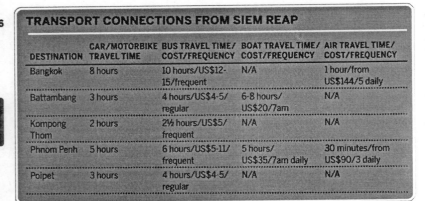

Tickets to Phnom Penh (six hours), via NH6, cost US$5 to US$11, depending on the level of service (air-con, comfy seats, a toilet, a hostess), whether foreigners pay more than locals, and whether there's hotel pick-up. Many companies charge the same price to Kompong Thom as they do to Phnom Penh. Virak Bunthan offers the only night bus services to Phnom Penh and through to Sihanoukville, departing between 8pm and midnight.

Several companies offer direct services to Kompong Cham (US$6, five or six hours), Battambang (US$5, four hours) and Poipet (US$5, four hours). GST has a bus to Anlong Veng (15,000r, three hours).

Share Taxi & Pick-Up

Share taxis – quicker than buses – to most destinations stop along NH6 just north of the bus station (Map p210). Destinations include Phnom Penh (US$10, 4½ hours), Kompong Thom (US$5, two hours), Sisophon (US$5, 1½ hours) and Poipet (US$7, 2½ hours).

To get to Banteay Chhmar, head to Sisophon and catch transport from there. For details on getting to Anlong Veng, see p229.

Getting Around

From the airport, an official moto/taxi/van costs US$2/7/8; remorks (US$5 or so) are available outside the terminal. From the bus station, a moto/remork to the city centre should cost about US$1/2.

Short moto trips around the centre of town cost 2000r or 3000r (more at night). A remork should be about double that, more with lots of people.

Most guesthouses and small hotels can usually help with bicycle rental for about US$2 per day. Look out for guesthouses and hotels supporting the **White Bicycles** (www.thewhitebicycles.org; per day US$2) project whose proceeds go to local development projects.

Hiring a moto with a driver costs US$8 to US$10 for the whole day, while a remork is about US$12 and up. Prices rise for far-flung destinations like Kbal Spean or Beng Mealea.

Hiring a car should cost about US$30 for a whole day of cruising around Angkor, US$45 to Kbal Spean and Banteay Srei, US$70 to Roluos and Beng Mealea, and US$90 out to Koh Ker.

AROUND SIEM REAP

Floating Villages

The famous floating village of **Chong Kneas** is now so popular with visitors that it's become something of a floating cash cow, at least insofar as hiring a boat (US$11 per person plus US$2 entry fee) is concerned. Unfortunately, large tour groups tend to take over, and boats end up chugging up and down the channels in convoy. The small, floating **Gecko Environment Centre** (www.tsbr-ed.org; admission free; ⏰7am-4pm) has displays on the Tonlé Sap's remarkable annual cycle. **Tara Boat** (☎092-957765; www.taraboat.com) offers all-inclusive trips with a meal aboard their converted cargo boat. Prices include transfers, entry fees, local boats, a tour guide and a two-course meal, starting from US$27 for a trip with lunch.

To get to the floating village from Siem Reap costs US$2 by moto each way (more if the driver waits), or US$15 or so by taxi. The trip takes 20 minutes. Or rent a bicycle in town and just pedal out here – it's a leisurely 11km through pretty villages and rice fields.

More memorable than Chong Kneas, but also harder to reach, is the friendly village

WORTH A TRIP

BIRDWATCHING AROUND SIEM REAP

Sam Veasna Center for Wildlife Conservation (Map p200; ☎963710; www.samveasna.org) runs birding and ecotourism trips to several globally important sites managed by the **Wildlife Conservation Society** (www.wcs.org), proceeds from which benefit local communities. Book at least three days ahead for overnight trips and 24 to 48 hours ahead for day trips.

Prek Toal Bird Reserve (210 sq km), the closest birdwatching site to Siem Reap on the northwestern tip of Tonlé Sap lake, is a seasonally inundated forest unmatched anywhere in Southeast Asia for its dry-season populations of endangered waterbirds. These include lesser and greater adjutant storks, milky storks and spot-billed pelicans. An all-day excursion to this ornithologist's fantasy land costs from US$98 per person, including land and lake transport, meals, fees and guides.

Also accessible on an SVC day trip from Siem Reap is the **Ang Trapeng Thmor Reserve**, a wetland bird sanctuary 100km northwest of Siem Reap that's home to the extremely rare Sarus crane, depicted on bas-reliefs at the Bayon, and 200 other bird species. Overnight stays are possible.

of **Kompong Pluk**, an other-worldly place built on soaring stilts. Most of the houses are almost bamboo skyscrapers and it looks like it's straight out of a film set. In the wet season you can explore the nearby flooded forest by canoe. To get here, either catch a boat (US$55 return) at Chong Kneas or come via the small town of Roluos by a two-hour combination of road (about US$7 return by moto) and boat (US$8 per person). An all-weather elevated access road is under construction, which no doubt means a private company will start levying charges to visit Kompong Pluk.

TEMPLES OF ANGKOR

Where to begin with Angkor? There is no greater concentration of architectural riches anywhere on earth. Choose from the world's largest religious building, Angkor Wat; one of the world's weirdest, the Bayon; or the riotous jungle of Ta Prohm. All are global icons and have helped put Cambodia on the map as the temple capital of Asia. Today, the temples are a point of pilgrimage for all Khmers, and no traveller to the region will want to miss their extravagant beauty.

Beyond the big three are dozens more temples, each of which would be the star were it located anywhere else in the region. Banteay Srei, the art gallery of Angkor; Preah Khan, the ultimate fusion temple uniting Buddhism and Hinduism; or Beng Mealea, the Titanic of temples suffocating under the jungle. The most vexing part of a visit to Angkor is working out what to see, as there are simply so many spectacular sites.

The hundreds of temples surviving today are but the sacred skeleton of the vast political, religious and social centre of the ancient Khmer empire. Angkor was a city that, at its zenith, boasted a population of one million when London was a small town of 50,000. The houses, public buildings and palaces of Angkor were constructed of wood – now long decayed – because the right to dwell in structures of brick or stone was reserved for the gods.

Angkor is one of the most impressive ancient sites on earth, with the epic proportions of the Great Wall of China, the detail and intricacy of the Taj Mahal and the symbolism and symmetry of the Egyptian pyramids all rolled into one.

Angkor Wat

The traveller's first glimpse of Angkor Wat, the ultimate expression of Khmer genius, is simply staggering and is matched by only a few select spots on earth such as Machu Picchu or Petra.

Angkor is, quite literally, heaven on earth. Angkor is the earthly representation of Mt Meru, the Mt Olympus of the Hindu faith and the abode of ancient gods. Angkor is the perfect fusion of creative ambition and spiritual devotion. The Cambodian 'god-kings' of old each strove to better their ancestors in size, scale and symmetry, culminating in the world's largest religious building, Angkor Wat.

Angkor Wat is the heart and soul of Cambodia. It is the Khmers' national symbol, the epicentre of their civilisation and a source of fierce national pride. Unlike the other Angkor monuments, it was never abandoned to the elements and has been in virtually continuous use since it was built.

DON'T MISS

TOP ANGKOR EXPERIENCES

» See the sun rise over the holiest of holies, **Angkor Wat** (p208), the world's largest religious building.

» Contemplate the serenity and splendour of the **Bayon** (p209), its 216 enigmatic faces staring out into the jungle.

» Witness nature reclaiming the stones at the mysterious ruin of **Ta Prohm** (p216), the *Tomb Raider* temple.

» Stare in wonder at the delicate carvings adorning **Banteay Srei** (p216), the finest seen at Angkor.

» Trek deep into the jungle to discover the River of a Thousand Lingas at **Kbal Spean** (p217).

ON LOCATION WITH *TOMB RAIDER* NICK RAY

Several sequences for the 2001 film *Tomb Raider*, starring Angelina Jolie as Lara Croft, were shot around the temples of Angkor. The Cambodia shoot opened at Phnom Bakheng with Lara looking through binos for the mysterious temple. The baddies were already trying to break in through the East Gate of Angkor Thom by pulling down a giant polystyrene *apsara* (celestial nymph). Reunited with her custom Land Rover, Lara made a few laps around the Bayon before discovering a back way into the temple from Ta Prohm, where she plucked a sprig of jasmine and fell through into... Pinewood Studies. After battling a living statue and dodging Daniel Craig (aka 007) by diving off the waterfall at Phnom Kulen, she emerged in a floating market in front of Angkor Wat, as you do. She came ashore here before borrowing a mobile phone from a local monk and venturing into the Gallery of a Thousand Buddhas, where she was healed by the abbot.

Nick Ray worked as location manager for Tomb Raider *in Cambodia*

Angkor Wat is surrounded by a moat, 190m wide, which forms a giant rectangle measuring 1.5km by 1.3km. Stretching around the outside of the central temple complex is an 800m-long series of bas-reliefs, designed to be viewed in an anticlockwise direction. Rising 31m above the third level is the central tower, which gives the whole ensemble its sublime unity.

Angkor Wat was built by Suryavarman II (r 1113–52), who unified Cambodia and extended Khmer influence across much of mainland Southeast Asia. He also set himself apart religiously from earlier kings by his devotion to the Hindu deity Vishnu, to whom he consecrated the temple, built around the same time as European Gothic heavyweights such as Westminster Abbey and Chartres.

The sandstone blocks from which Angkor Wat was built were quarried more than 50km away and floated down the Stung Siem Reap on rafts. The logistics of such an operation are mind-blowing.

The upper level of Angkor Wat is once again open to modern pilgrims, but visits are strictly timed to 20 minutes.

Angkor Thom

It is hard to imagine any building bigger or more beautiful than Angkor Wat, but in Angkor Thom the sum of the parts add up to a greater whole. It is the gates that grab you first, flanked by a monumental representation of the Churning of the Ocean of Milk, 54 demons and 54 gods engaged in an epic tug of war on the causeway. Each gate towers above the visitor, the magnanimous faces of the Bodhisattva Avalokiteshvara staring out over the kingdom. Imagine being a peasant in the 13th century approaching the forbidding capital for the first time. It would have been an awe-inspiring yet unsettling experience to enter such a gateway and come face to face with the divine power of the god-kings.

The last great capital of the Khmer empire, Angkor Thom took monumental to a whole new level, set over 10 sq km. Built in part as a reaction to the surprise sacking of Angkor by the Chams, Jayavarman VII (r 1181–1219) decided that his empire would never again be vulnerable at home. Beyond the formidable walls is a massive moat that would have stopped all but the hardiest invaders in their tracks.

THE BAYON

Right at the heart of Angkor Thom is the Bayon, the mesmerising if slightly mind-bending state temple of Jayavarman VII. It epitomises the creative genius and inflated ego of Cambodia's legendary king. Its 54 gothic towers are famously decorated with 216 enormous, coldly smiling **faces of Avalokiteshvara** that bear more than a passing resemblance to the great king himself. These huge visages glare down from every angle, exuding power and control with a hint of humanity – precisely the blend required to hold sway over such a vast empire, ensuring that disparate and far-flung populations yielded to the monarch's magnanimous will.

The Bayon is decorated with 1.2km of extraordinary **bas-reliefs** incorporating more than 11,000 figures. The famous carvings on the outer wall of the first level vividly depict everyday life in 12th-century Cambodia.

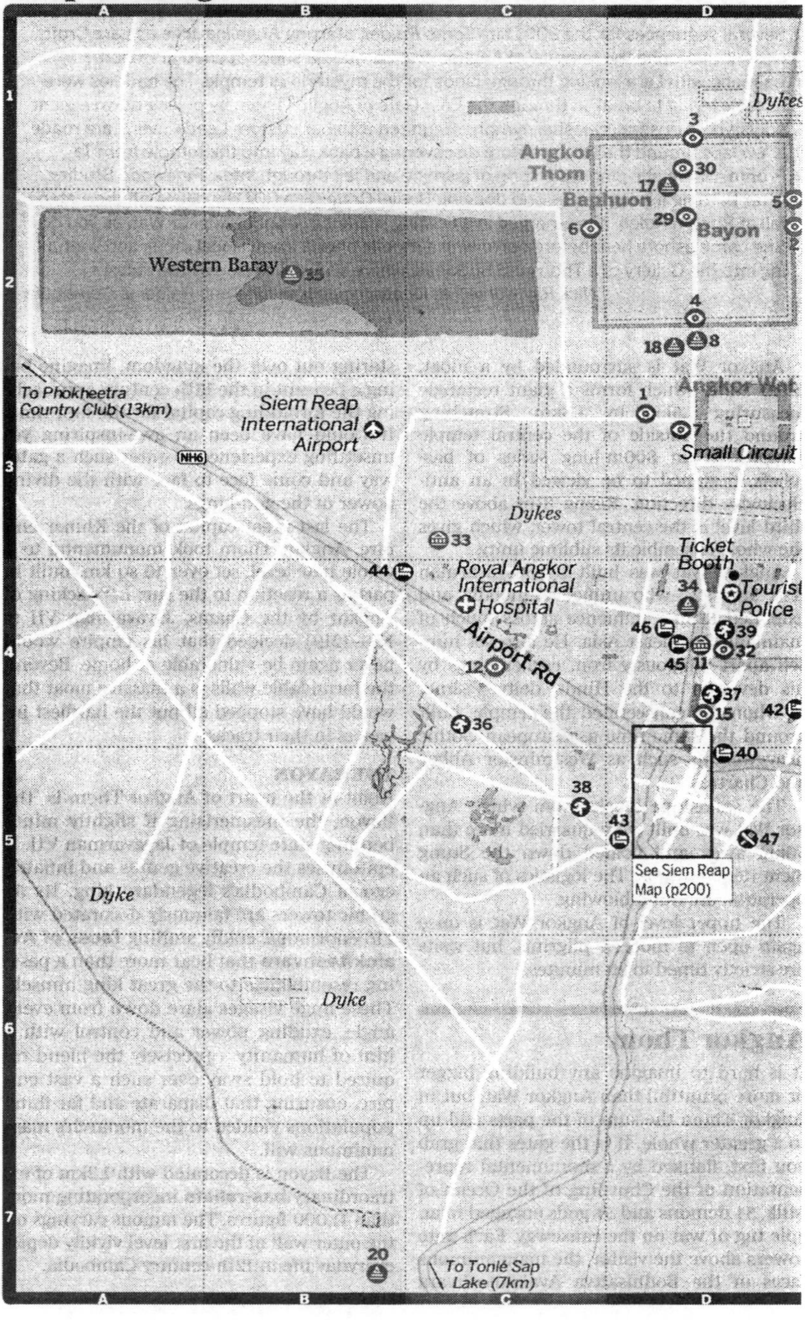

Dykes
3
Angkor Thom
30
17
Baphuon
5
29
6
Bayon
2
Western Baray
35
4
18
8
Angkor Wat
To Phokheetra Country Club (13km)
Siem Reap International Airport
1
7
Small Circuit
NH6
Dykes
33
Ticket Booth
44
Royal Angkor International Hospital
34
Tourist Police
46
39
Airport Rd
45
11
32
12
37
42
15
36
40
38
43
47
See Siem Reap Map (p200)
Dyke
Dyke
20
To Tonlé Sap Lake (7km)

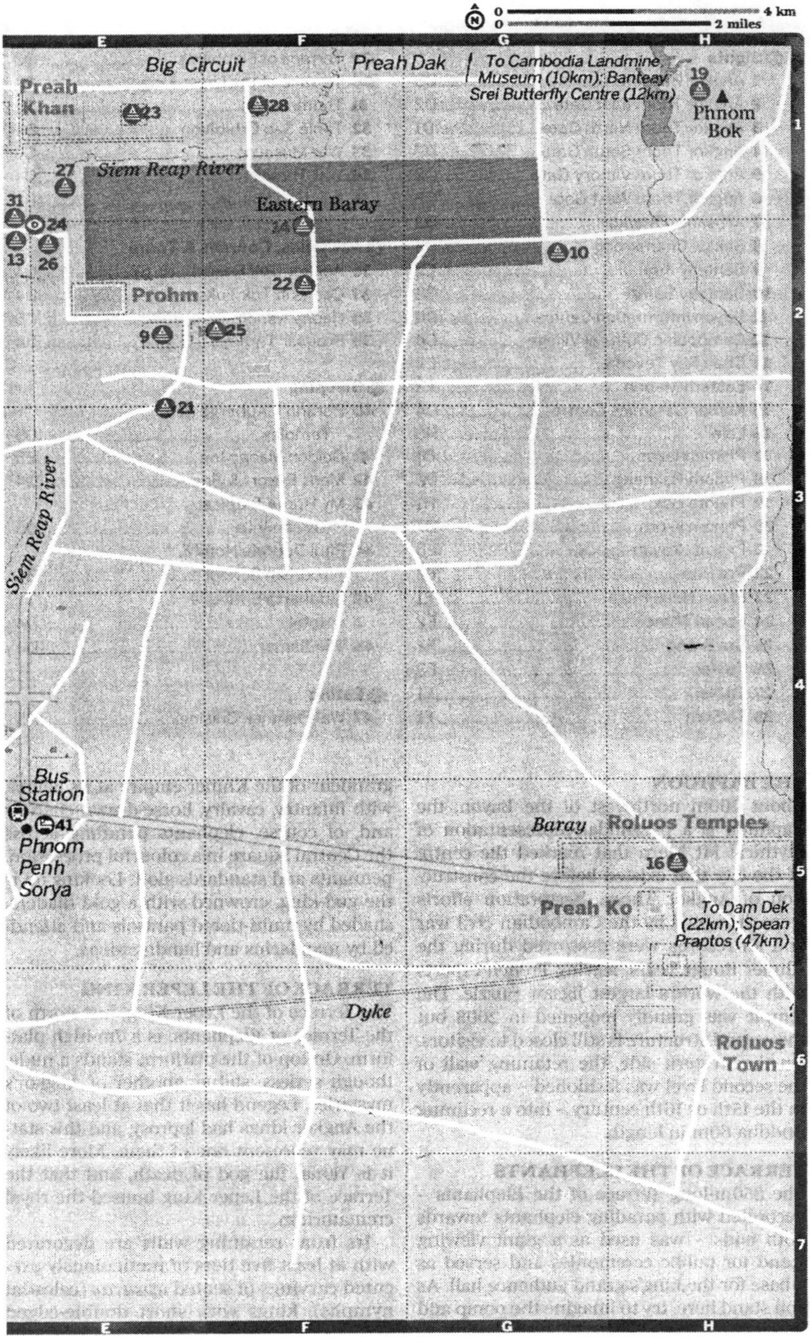
0 4 km
0 2 miles
E
F
G
H
Big Circuit
Preah Dak
To Cambodia Landmine Museum (10km); Banteay Srei Butterfly Centre (12km)
19
Phnom Bok
Preah Khan
23
28
1
27
Siem Reap River
Eastern Baray
31
24
14
13
26
10
22
Prohm
2
9
25
21
Siem Reap River
3
4
Bus Station
41
Phnom Penh Sorya
Baray
Roluos Temples
16
5
Preah Ko
To Dam Dek (22km); Spean Praptos (47km)
Dyke
Roluos Town
6
7

Temples of Angkor

Sights

1	Angkor Balloon	D3
2	Angkor Thom East Gate	D2
3	Angkor Thom North Gate	D1
4	Angkor Thom South Gate	D2
5	Angkor Thom Victory Gate	D2
6	Angkor Thom West Gate	C2
7	Artisans d'Angkor	D3
8	Baksei Chamkrong	D2
9	Banteay Kdei	E2
10	Banteay Samré	G2
11	Bayon Information Centre	D4
12	Cambodian Cultural Village	C4
13	Chau Say Tevoda	E2
14	Eastern Mebon	F2
15	Khmer Ceramics Centre	D4
16	Lolei	H5
17	Phimeanakas	D1
18	Phnom Bakheng	D2
19	Phnom Bok	H1
20	Phnom Krom	B7
21	Prasat Kravan	E3
22	Pre Rup	F2
23	Preah Neak Poan	E1
24	Spean Thmor	E2
25	Sra Srang	F2
26	Ta Keo	E2
27	Ta Nei	E1
28	Ta Som	F1
29	Terrace of Elephants	D2
30	Terrace of the Leper King	D1
31	Thommanon	E1
32	Tonlé Sap Exhibition	D4
33	War Museum	C3
34	Wat Thmei	D4
35	Western Mebon	B2

Activities, Courses & Tours

36	Angkor Golf Resort	C4
37	Cooks in Tuk Tuks	D4
38	Happy Ranch	C5
39	Krousar Thmey	D4

Sleeping

40	Borann L'Auberge des Temples	D5
41	Golden Mango Inn	E5
42	Mens Resort & Spa	D4
43	My Home Tropical Garden Villa	D5
44	Paul Dubrule Hotel & Tourism School	B4
45	Siddharta Boutique Hotel	D4
46	The Samar	D4

Eating

47	Wat Damnak Cuisine	D5

THE BAPHUON

About 200m northwest of the Bayon, the Baphuon is a pyramidal representation of mythical Mt Meru that marked the centre of the city that existed before the construction of Angkor Thom. Restoration efforts were disrupted by the Cambodian civil war and all records were destroyed during the Khmer Rouge years, leaving French experts with the world's largest jigsaw puzzle. The temple was grandly reopened in 2008 but the central structure is still closed to visitors. On the western side, the retaining wall of the second level was fashioned – apparently in the 15th or 16th century – into a reclining Buddha 60m in length.

TERRACE OF THE ELEPHANTS

The 350m-long Terrace of the Elephants – decorated with parading elephants towards both ends – was used as a giant viewing stand for public ceremonies and served as a base for the king's grand audience hall. As you stand here, try to imagine the pomp and grandeur of the Khmer empire at its height, with infantry, cavalry, horse-drawn chariots and, of course, elephants parading across the Central Square in a colourful procession, pennants and standards aloft. Looking on is the god-king, crowned with a gold diadem, shaded by multi-tiered parasols and attended by mandarins and handmaidens.

TERRACE OF THE LEPER KING

The Terrace of the Leper King, just north of the Terrace of Elephants, is a 7m-high platform. On top of the platform stands a nude, though sexless, statue, another of Angkor's mysteries. Legend has it that at least two of the Angkor kings had leprosy, and this statue may represent one of them. More likely it is Yama, the god of death, and that the Terrace of the Leper King housed the royal crematorium.

Its front retaining walls are decorated with at least five tiers of meticulously executed carvings of seated *apsaras* (celestial nymphs), kings with short double-edged

EXPLORING THE TEMPLES

One Day

Hit Angkor Wat for sunrise, then explore the mighty temple while it's still quiet. From there continue to Ta Prohm before breaking for lunch. In the afternoon, explore the temples within the walled city of Angkor Thom and the beauty of the Bayon in the late-afternoon light.

Three Days

With three days it's possible to see most of the important sites. One approach is to see as much as you can on the first day or two (as above), then spend the final days visiting other sites such as Roluos and Banteay Kdei. Better still is a gradual build-up to the most spectacular places. After all, if you see Angkor Wat first, then a temple like Ta Keo just won't cut it.

One Week

In addition to what you can see in three days, take in Beng Mealea and even Koh Ker. For a change of pace, take a boat to the watery villages of the Tonlé Sap (p207).

Tickets

The **ticket booth** (Map p210; 1-day/3-day/1-week tourist pass US$20/40/60; ⊙5am-5.30pm) is on the road from Siem Reap to Angkor. Tickets issued after 5pm (for sunset viewing) are valid the next day. Tickets are not valid for Phnom Kulen or Beng Mealea.

Eating

All the major temples have some kind of food near the entrance The most extensive eating area is opposite the Angkor Wat entrance. There are many noodle stalls north of the Bayon.

Guides

The **Khmer Angkor Tour Guide Association** (www.khmerangkortourguide.com) can arrange certified tour guides in 10 languages (US$25 to US$50 a day).

Tours

One of the best ways to see Angkor's temples, especially some of the distant ones, is to take a tour. Ask other travellers for recommendations, or keep an eye out for these companies:

» **Beyond** (www.beyonduniqueescapes.com) Beng Mealea, Kompong Pluk, cycling trips and cooking classes.

» **Buffalo Trails** (www.buffalotrails-cambodia.com) Ecotours and lifestyle adventures around Siem Reap.

» **Grasshopper Adventures** (www.grasshopperadventures.com) Cycling tours around Angkor or to Beng Mealea.

» **Khmer Ways** (www.khmerways.com) Upscale moto tours to remote temple sites around Angkor and beyond.

» **Sam Veasna Center** (www.samveasna.org) Has day trips that combine birdwatching with visits to outlying temples.

Transport

Bicycles are a great way to get around the temples, which are linked by good, flat roads.

Motos, zippy and inexpensive, are a popular way to explore the temples (US$8 to US$10 per day, more for distant sites). Drivers accost visitors from the moment they set foot in Siem Reap but they often end up being knowledgeable and friendly.

Remorks (US$12 to US$15 a day, more for distant sites) take a little longer than motos but offer protection from the rain and sun. Even more protection is offered by cars (US$30 a day, more for distant sites), though these tend to isolate you from the sights, sounds and smells.

Temples of Angkor

THREE-DAY EXPLORATION

The temple complex at Angkor is simply enormous and the superlatives don't do it justice. This is the site of the world's largest religious building, a multitude of temples and a vast, long-abandoned walled city that was arguably Southeast Asia's first metropolis, long before Bangkok and Singapore got in on the action.

Starting at the Roluos group of temples, one of the earliest capitals of Angkor, move on to the big circuit, which includes the Buddhist-Hindu fusion temple of **1 Preah Khan** and the ornate water temple of **2 Neak Poan**.

On the second day downsize to the small circuit, starting with an atmospheric dawn visit to **3 Ta Prohm**, before continuing to the temple pyramid of Ta Keo, the Buddhist monastery of Banteay Kdei and the immense royal bathing pond of **4 Sra Srang**.

Next venture further afield to Banteay Srei temple, the jewel in the crown of Angkorian art, and Beng Mealea, a remote jungle temple.

Saving the biggest and best until last, experience sunrise at **5 Angkor Wat** and stick around for breakfast in the temple to discover its amazing architecture without the crowds. In the afternoon, explore **6 Angkor Thom**, an immense complex that is home to the enigmatic **7 Bayon**.

Three days around Angkor? That's just for starters.

TOP TIPS

» **Dodging the Crowds** Early morning at Ta Prohm, post sunrise at Angkor Wat and lunchtime at Banteay Srei does the trick.

» **Extended Explorations** Three-day passes can now be used on non-consecutive days over the period of a week but be sure to request this.

MICK ELMORE / LONELY PLANET IMAGES ©

Bayon
The surreal state temple of legendary king Jayavarman VII, where 216 faces bear down on pilgrims, asserting religious and regal authority.

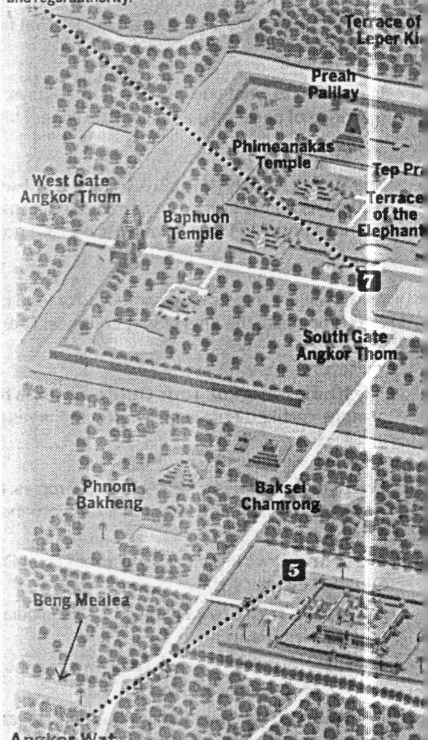

Angkor Wat
The world's largest religious building. Experience sunrise at the holiest of holies, then explore the beautiful bas-reliefs – devotion etched in stone.

JOHN BANAGAN / LONELY PLANET IMAGES ©

ANDERS BLOMQVIST / LONELY PLANET IMAGES ©

Angkor Thom

The last great capital of the Khmer empire conceals a wealth of temples and its epic proportions would have inspired and terrified in equal measure.

ANDERS BLOMQVIST / LONELY PLANET IMAGES ©

Preah Khan

A fusion temple dedicated to Buddha, Brahma, Shiva and Vishnu; the immense corridors are like an unending hall of mirrors.

Neak Poan

If Vegas ever adopts the Angkor theme, this will be the swimming pool, a petite tower set in a lake, surrounded by four smaller ponds.

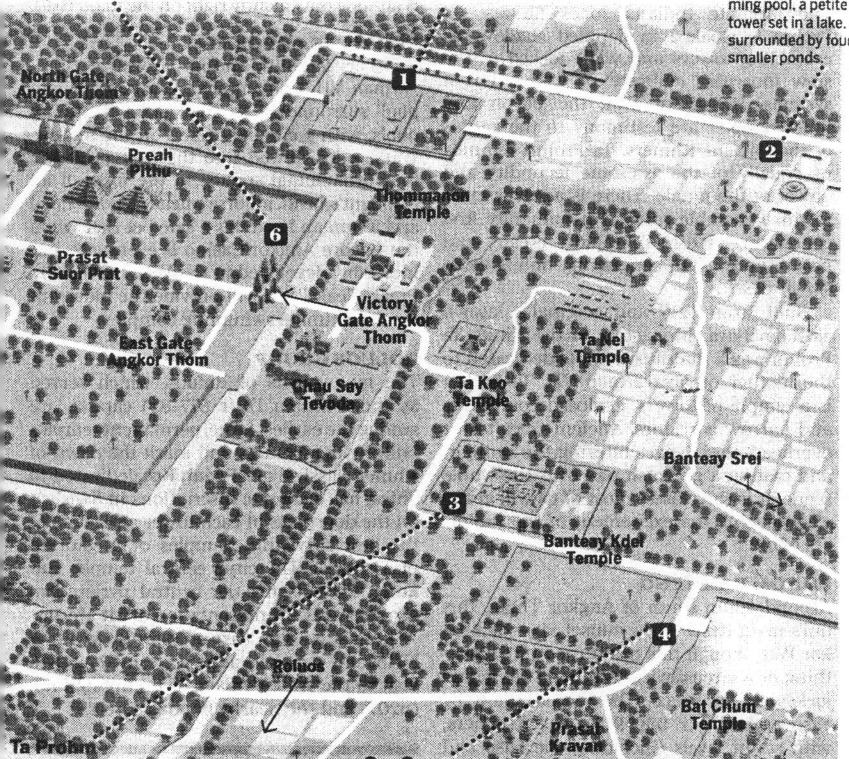

Ta Prohm

Nicknamed the *Tomb Raider* temple, *Indiana Jones* would be equally apt. Nature has run riot, leaving iconic tree roots strangling the surviving stones.

Sra Srang

Once the royal bathing pond, this is the ablutions pool to beat all ablutions pools and makes a good stop for sunset.

ARIADNE VAN ZANDBERGEN / LONELY PLANET IMAGES ©

swords and princesses, the latter adorned with beautiful rows of pearls. At the base on the southern side, there is narrow access to a hidden terrace that was covered up when the outer structure was built. The figures, including *nagas* (mythical serpent-beings), look as fresh as if they had been carved yesterday.

Around Angkor Thom

TA PROHM

The ultimate Indiana Jones fantasy, Ta Prohm is cloaked in dappled shadow, its crumbling towers and walls locked in the slow muscular embrace of vast tree-root systems. If Angkor Wat, the Bayon and other temples are testimony to the genius of the ancient Khmers, Ta Prohm reminds us equally of the awesome fecundity and power of the jungle. There is a poetic cycle to this venerable ruin, with humanity first conquering nature to rapidly create, and nature once again conquering humanity to slowly destroy.

Built from 1186 and originally known as Rajavihara (Monastery of the King), Ta Prohm was a Buddhist temple dedicated to the mother of Jayavarman VII. Ta Prohm is a temple of towers, enclosed courtyards and narrow corridors. Ancient trees tower overhead, their leaves filtering the sunlight and casting a greenish pall over the whole scene. It is the closest most of us will get to experiencing the excitement of the explorers of old.

PHNOM BAKHENG

Around 400m south of Angkor Thom, this hill's main draw is the sunset view of Angkor Wat, though this has turned into something of a circus, with hundreds of visitors jockeying for space. The temple, built by Yasovarman I (r 889–910), has five tiers, with seven levels (including the base and the summit).

> **FUSION TEMPLE**
>
> Preah Khan is a genuine fusion temple, the eastern entrance dedicated to Mahayana Buddhism with equal-sized doors, and the other cardinal directions dedicated to Shiva, Vishnu and Brahma with successively smaller doors, emphasising the unequal nature of Hinduism.

PREAH KHAN

The temple of Preah Khan (Sacred Sword) is one of the largest complexes at Angkor – a maze of vaulted corridors, fine carvings and lichen-clad stonework. Constructed by Jayavarman VII, it covers a very large area, but the temple itself is within a rectangular wall of around 700m by 800m.

Unless wet-season conditions preclude it, try to enter via the historic east gate so the complex unfolds before you as its architects intended, rather than via the west gate, which is all-too-conveniently right on the main road.

PREAH NEAK POAN

Another late-12th-century work of Jayavarman VII, this temple has a large square pool surrounded by four smaller square pools, with a circular 'island' in the middle. Water once flowed into the four pools via four ornamental spouts, in the form of an elephant's head, a horse's head, a lion's head and a human head. It's a safe bet that when the Encore Angkor Casino is eventually but inevitably developed in Las Vegas or Macau, Preah Neak Poan will provide the blueprint for the ultimate swimming complex.

ROLUOS GROUP

The monuments of Roluos, which served as Indravarman I's (r 877–89) capital, are among the earliest large, permanent temples built by the Khmers and mark the dawn of Khmer classical art. **Preah Ko**, dedicated to Shiva, has elaborate inscriptions in Sanskrit on the doorposts of each tower and some of the best surviving examples of Angkorian plasterwork. The city's central temple, **Bakong**, with its five-tier central pyramid of sandstone, is a representation of Mt Meru.

Roluos is 13km east of Siem Reap along NH6 and can be easily combined with a visit to the stilted village of Kompong Pluk (p207) and the nearby flooded forest.

Further Afield

BANTEAY SREI

Considered by many to be the jewel in the crown of Angkorian art, Banteay Srei is cut from stone of a pinkish hue and includes some of the finest stone carving anywhere on earth. Begun in AD 967, it is one of the few temples around Angkor not to be commissioned by a king, but by a Brahman, perhaps a tutor to Jayavarman V.

Banteay Srei means 'Citadel of the Women' and it is said that it must have been built

LOCAL KNOWLEDGE

PROFESSOR ANG CHOULEAN – KHMER ANTHROPOLOGIST & ARCHAEOLOGIST

What is the most important Khmer temple? Angkor Thom is the most striking and challenging for archaeologists, since it was a living city, with humans and gods co-habiting there.

What is the most important archaeological site in Cambodia? Sambor Prei Kuk is among the most important for its homogeneity, given the period and its artistic style.

Who is the most important king in Cambodian history? Suryavarman I, who had a real political vision which can be measured by the monuments he built, such as Preah Vihear and Wat Phu.

What is your position on the debate between romance and restoration at Ta Prohm? It is a matter of balance. The trees are most impressive, but maintaining the monument is our duty.

Which other civilisation interests you greatly? Japanese civilisation, as it is so different from Khmer civilisation, allowing me to better understand mine.

Professor Ang Choulean is one of Cambodia's leading experts on anthropology and archaeology and a renowned scholar on Cambodian history. He was awarded the 2011 Grand Fukuoka Prize for his outstanding contribution to Asian culture.

by women, as the elaborate carvings are too fine for the hand of a man.

Banteay Srei, 21km northeast of the Bayon and about 32km from Siem Reap, can be visited along with Kbal Spean and the Cambodia Landmine Museum (p198). Transport out to here will cost a little more than the prices quoted for the central temples of Angkor.

KBAL SPEAN

Kbal Spean is a spectacularly carved riverbed, set deep in the jungle about 50km northeast of Angkor. More commonly referred to in English as the 'River of a Thousand Lingas', it's a 2km uphill walk to the carvings, which include phallic lingas and Hindu deities. From the carvings you can work your way back down to the waterfall to cool off. Carry plenty of water.

Kbal Spean was only 'discovered' in 1969, when ethnologist Jean Boulbet was shown the area by a local hermit; the area was soon off-limits due to the civil war, only becoming safe again in 1998.

At the nearby **Angkor Centre for Conservation of Biodiversity** (ACCB; www.accb-cambodia.org), trafficked animals are nursed back to health. Free tours generally begin at 1pm daily except Sunday.

PHNOM KULEN

The most sacred mountain in Cambodia, Phnom Kulen (487m) is where Jayavarman II proclaimed himself a *devaraja* (god-king) in AD 802, giving birth to Cambodia. It's a popular place of pilgrimage during weekends and festivals; the views it affords are absolutely tremendous.

At no point during a visit to Phnom Kulen should you leave well-trodden paths, as there may be landmines in the area.

Phnom Kulen is 50km from Siem Reap and 15km from Banteay Srei. The road toll is US$20 per foreign visitor; none of this goes towards preserving the site. It is possible to buy a cheaper entrance ticket to Phnom Kulen for US$12 from the City Angkor Hotel in Siem Reap.

BENG MEALEA

Built by Suryavarman II to the same floor plan as Angkor Wat, **Beng Mealea** (admission US$5) is the Titanic of temples, utterly subsumed by jungle. Nature has well and truly run riot here. Jumbled stones lie like forgotten jewels swathed in lichen, and the galleries are strangled by ivy and vines.

Beng Mealea is about 65km northeast of Siem Reap on a sealed toll road.

REMOTE TEMPLES OF THE NORTHWEST

See the relevant sections under Northwestern Cambodia for more information on remote temples such as **Koh Ker** (p230), **Banteay Chhmar** (p227), **Preah Khan** (p230) and **Prasat Preah Vihear** (p229).

NORTHWESTERN CAMBODIA

Offering highway accessibility and outback adventure in equal measure, northwestern Cambodia stretches from the Cardamom Mountains to the Dangkrek Mountains, with Tonlé Sap lake at its heart.

Battambang attracts the most visitors thanks to an alluring blend of mellowness, colonial-era architecture and excellent day tripping. Kompong Thom is also popular as gateway to the pre-Angkorian temples of Sambor Prei Kuk.

Northwestern Cambodia's remote plains and jungles conceal some of the country's most inspired temples, including spectacular Prasat Preah Vihear, declared a World Heritage Site in 2008, and Koh Ker, a rival capital to Angkor dating from the 10th century.

Kompong Chhnang Province

Kompong Chhnang is a relatively wealthy province thanks to its proximity to the capital and its fishing and agricultural industries, supported by abundant water resources.

KOMPONG CHHNANG

☎026 / POP 43,000

Kompong Chhnang (Clay Pot Port) is a tale of two cities: the leafy centre, its focal point a grassy park, and the bustling dockside. Nearby sights include two floating villages and a hamlet famous for its pottery.

Sights & Activities

A short ride from Kompong Chhnang's **waterfront** takes you to two colourful, ethnic-Vietnamese floating villages, **Phoum Kandal** to the east and **Chong Kos** to the northwest. To get a waterborne look at the floating villages, you can take a one-hour **excursion** (per person US$2.50, minimum 10 people) from the Tourism Port. Chartering an entire vessel is US$20 per hour. A cheaper, quieter and more ecological option, available about 300m to the west, is to get around like the floating villagers do: on a **wooden boat** (per hr US$5).

The quiet village of **Ondong Rossey**, where the area's famous red pottery is made under every house, is a delightful 7km ride west of town through serene rice fields dotted with sugar palms. **Phnom Santuk**, 2km southwest of Kompong Chhnang, affords stunning views of the countryside. By bicycle or moto (US$6), combining Ondong Rossey and Phnom Santuk makes for a truly magical circuit, especially early in the morning or late in the afternoon.

Sleeping & Eating

Sokha Hotel HOTEL $
(☎988622; r US$8-15; ❄) Set in a shady garden, this 31-room family pad offers the most charming accommodation in town. Situated a very long block west of Independence Monument.

Asia Hotel HOTEL $
(☎989666; thydaasia@gmail.com; NH5; r US$6-25; ❄@📶) One of cluster of smart new places on the main road to Phnom Penh; fan rooms are a bargain for their size and comfort. Upgrade yourself to VIP status for just US$18.

Mittapheap Restaurant KHMER $
(NH5; mains 6000-20,000r; ⊙6am-9pm) Facing Independence Monument, this airy eatery serves mainly Khmer dishes.

Information

The city centre is anchored by Psar Leu (Central Market), which is two blocks west of the Acleda Bank and the bus and taxi station. Independence Monument is 500m south of the bank; the waterfront is 3km northeast.

Acleda Bank (NH5) Has an ATM.

Internet Terminals (⊙7am-8pm) Inside two mobile-phone shops around the corner from the Acleda Bank.

Getting There & Around

Kompong Chhnang is 91km northwest of Phnom Penh and 202km southeast of Battambang.

Buses on the Phnom Penh–Battambang–Poipet run will stop if they're not full. A share taxi is probably the best bet to Phnom Penh (15,000r).

Sokha Hotel rents out bicycles (US$1 per day) and motorbikes (US$5 per day).

Pursat Province

Pursat Province stretches from the remote forests of Phnom Samkos, on the Thai border, eastwards to the floating villages and marshes of the Tonlé Sap lake, encompassing the northern reaches of the Cardamom Mountains.

PURSAT

☎052 / POP 59,000

This town, known for its marble carvers and oranges, makes an ideal base for a day trip to the floating village of Kompong Luong. Roads head from here into the Cardamoms.

Sights & Activities

For a pleasant **stroll**, walk north along Ph 1, cross the river on the vertiginous, Khmer Rouge–era cement **dam**, and then head south along the east bank of the river, where you'll come upon a number of small **marble-carving shops**.

The **Bun Rany Hun Sen Development Centre** (☑951606; Ph 9; ☻7-11am & 2-5pm Mon-Fri & Sat morning) teaches weaving, sewing and marble carving to young people. Travellers are welcome to visit classes and purchase craft items.

Sleeping & Eating

Pursat Century Hotel HOTEL $

(☑951446; pursatcenturyhotel@yahoo.com; r with fan/air-con from US$7/15; ✱◉🛈) This multi-storey establishment has set new standards for Pursat. The 110 rooms offer two-star comfort, including (cue contented sleep) imported linens.

New Toun Sour Hotel HOTEL $

(☑951506; thansourthmey@yahoo.com; Ph 2; r US$6-15; ✱🛈) This hotel, popular with the NGO crowd, has 41 large, pleasant rooms. The restaurant has great fries but at prices slightly higher than local joints.

Community Villa KHMER $

(NH5; mains 8000-22,000r; ☻7am-10pm) Run by a Cambodian NGO that gives job skills to at-risk young people, this place serves Khmer dishes, including ginger fish, salads, and the best pancakes and *tukalok* (fruit shakes) in town. Situated on the Phnom Penh side of town.

Information

Pursat's main commercial street, Ph 3, is two blocks west of Ph 1, which runs along the river-front. Both roads lead south from NH5.

Acleda Bank (NH5) Has an ATM.

Department of Tourism (☻7-11am & 2-5pm Mon-Fri) Has maps and photos on the walls and a few handouts. Two blocks north of the market.

Getting There & Around

Dozens of buses pass through Pursat daily, shuttling between Poipet (30,000r), Sisophon and Battambang (10,000r, 1½ hours, 105km) to the northwest, and Kompong Chhnang and Phnom Penh (15,000r, three hours, 188km) to the southeast.

Buses stop along NH5, including many stops about 200m west of the bridge (near the Phnom Penh Sorya office). Rith Mony has an early-morning bus to Siem Reap (35,000r).

Share taxis to Phnom Penh (30,000r) can be found on NH5 just east of the bridge; those to Battambang (15,000r) stop in front of the old train station.

Ask your hotel about bicycle and motorbike rentals.

KOMPONG LUONG
POP 10,000

Kompong Luong has all the amenities you would expect to find in a large fishing village, including cafes, mobile-phone shops, chicken coops, ice-making factories, a pagoda, a church – except that here everything floats.

The result is an ethnic-Vietnamese Venice without the dry land. In the dry season, when water levels drop and the Tonlé Sap shrinks, the entire aquapolis is towed, boat by boat, a few kilometres north. **Homestays** (per night US$6) are available with local families and meals are available for US$1 to US$2 per person.

Kompong Luong is between 39km and 44km east of Pursat, depending on the time of year. From Pursat, transport options include moto (US$7 return) and private taxi (about US$30 return). At the dock, the official tourist rate to charter a four-passenger wooden motorboat around Kompong Luong is US$7 per hour for one to three passengers (US$10 for four or five).

NORTHERN CARDAMOM MOUNTAINS

The **Central Cardamoms Protected Forest** (CCPF) and adjacent wildlife sanctuaries are slowly opening up to ecotourism, with Pursat as the gateway. This area is still pretty wild: roads are heavily rutted, bridges have holes big enough for a car tyre to fall through, and some areas are still being demined. For details on accessing the Cardamoms from the south, see p247.

Conservation International (CI; www.conservation.org) provides technical and financial support to the CCPF's armed enforcement ranger teams, some of whose rough-and-ready ranger stations (including Kravanh and Rovieng, one and two hours southwest of Pursat) now welcome overnight visitors. Surrounded by confiscated Toyota Camrys crammed to the gills with raw luxury timber, these have the feel of a remote military outpost and offer only basic amenities.

To stay overnight at a ranger station, you will need to contact CI's **Ouk Kimsan** (☑012-256777; oukkimsan@yahoo.com) or **Seng Bunra** (☑012-835352; sbunra@conservation.org).

Promoui, the main town in **Phnom Samkos Wildlife Sanctuary** (3338 sq km; highest point 1717m), is 125km and four hours from Pursat over a ruinous road. The town has three **guesthouses** (r US$5-10) and motos you can hire for forays into the forest.

From Promoui, an even worse track heads south to **O Som** (where there's a ranger station) and **Veal Veng** (where there are several guesthouses). In the dry season, it may be possible to hire a moto from Promoui all the way to the south coast and the Koh Kong Conservation Corridor (p247).

In Pursat, pick-ups to Promoui leave from the **old market** (Ph 6), a parking lot two blocks north of NH5.

Battambang Province

Said by proud locals to produce Cambodia's finest rice, tastiest oranges and sweetest coconuts, Battambang (Bat Dambang) has a long border with Thailand and a short stretch of the Tonlé Sap shoreline. Thailand controlled the area from 1795 to 1907 and 1941 to 1946.

BATTAMBANG

☎053 / POP 145,000

Thanks to its colonial architecture and urbane conviviality, Battambang is emerging as one of Cambodia's leading visitor destinations. Highlights include taking a bicycle or moto through the lush countryside to several hilltop temples.

Sights

Colonial-era Architecture NEIGHBOURHOOD

Much of Battambang's special charm lies in its early-20th-century French architecture. Some of the finest **colonial buildings** are along the waterfront (Ph 1), especially just south of **Psar Nat**, itself quite an impressive structure. There are also some old **French shophouses** along Ph 3, including some just east of the train station. The two-storey **Governor's Residence**, with its balconies and wooden shutters, is another handsome legacy of the very early 1900s.

Battambang Museum MUSEUM

(Ph 1; admission US$1; ⌚8-11am & 2-5pm Mon-Fri) This small museum displays Angkorian lintels and statuary from all over the province, including Phnom Banan.

Wats TEMPLES

A number of the monks at **Wat Phiphétaram, Wat Damrey Sar** and **Wat Kandal** speak English and are glad for a chance to practise; they're often around in the late afternoon.

Train Station TRAIN STATION

Here the time is always 8.02. Just along the tracks just south of here, you can explore a treasure trove of crumbling, French-era repair sheds, warehouses and rolling stock.

Activities

FREE **Heritage Walking Tour** SIGHTSEEING

(http://battambang-heritage.org/downloads.htm) Phnom Penh–based **KA Architecture Tours** (www.ka-tours.org) is highly regarded for its specialist tours in and around the capital; it has collaborated with Battambang Municipality to create two heritage walks in the historic centre of Battambang. There are two downloadable PDFs including a colour map and numbered highlights. A great way to spend half a day exploring the city.

Soksabike CYCLING

(☎012-542019; www.soksabike; ⌚7.30am departures) Based at 1½ Street Cafe, Soksabike is a social enterprise aiming to connect visitors with the Cambodian countryside and its people. The half-day trip costs US$18 per person, covering about 30km, and the price includes a fresh coconut, seasonal fruits and a shot of rice wine.

DON'T MISS

PHARE PONLEU SELPAK CIRCUS SCHOOL

Roll up, roll up, the circus is now in town – every Monday and Thursday, at least. **Phare Ponleu Selpak** (☎952424; www.phareps.org) is a multi-arts centre for disadvantaged children that hosts internationally acclaimed circus *(cirque nouveau)* performances (admission adult/child US$8/4), often preceded by dinner (US$6; book a day ahead). Time your visit to Battambang to catch the spectacle. To get here from the Vishnu Roundabout on NH5, head west for 900m and then turn right (north) and continue another 600m.

Green Orange Kayaks KAYAKING

(☑077-204121; feda@online.com.kh; ⊙7am-5pm Mon-Fri) One- to three-person kayaks can be rented from Green Orange Kayaks, run by an NGO, Friends Economic Development Association (FEDA; www.fedacambodia.org), that offers free English classes. The half-day trip costs US$12 per person (including lifejackets); an optional guide is US$3. To rent at weekends, make contact during the week.

Seeing Hands Massage MASSAGE

(☑092-379903; per hr US$6; ⊙7am-10pm) Trained blind masseurs and masseuses offer soothing work-overs.

Australian Centres
for Development LANGUAGE CLASSES

(☑952370; acd@online.com.kh) Near the old train station, offers well-regarded Khmer language classes.

🛏 Sleeping

CITY CENTRE

Most of the city's veteran hotels are within a few bustling blocks of Psar Nat. The rival Chhaya and Royal Hotels dominate the backpacker market and can help arrange guides and transport.

TOP CHOICE Chhaya Hotel & Apartments HOTEL $

(☑952170; www.chhayahotel.com; 118 Ph 3; dm US$1, r US$3-12, apt US$15-25; ❋❀🛜) One of the longest-running budget hotels in Battambang, it has the cheapest beds in town if you don't mind a dorm. The new serviced apartments are incredible value, offering tasteful decoration, acres of space and a kitchen for self-catering.

Golden Land Hotel HOTEL $

(Sovanphoom Hotel; ☑6903790; sovanphoom@yahoo.com; NH5; d US$10-15; ❋❀🛜) Still looking brand-spanking new during our visit, this riverfront pad offers excellent value for money. Be a VIP for the night and enjoy space and a swish bathroom.

Royal Hotel HOTEL $

(☑016 912034; www.asrhotel.com.kh; r with fan/aircon from US$8/10; ❋❀🛜) Deservedly popular with independent travellers, the 45-room Royal is clean, friendly and very central.

Banan Hotel HOTEL $$

(☑012 739572; www.bananhotel.doodlekit.com; NH5; r US$20-30; ❋❀🛜) A modern hotel that combines two-star comfort with Khmer-style wooden decor. The 30 rooms come with all the mod cons, plus there is a new annex with a rooftop pool.

Tomato Guesthouse GUESTHOUSE $

(☑6907374; r from US$3) A new budget crash pad with very few frills but the odd thrill. The friendly owners have opened a rooftop restaurant that is a good place to relax in after dark.

EAST BANK

TOP CHOICE Bambu Hotel BOUTIQUE HOTEL $$$

(☑953900; www.bambuhotel.com; Ph KO; r US$70-110; ❋❀🛜☀) One of the newest boutique hotels in Battambang, Bambu is designed in Franco-Khmer style with spacious and stylish rooms. As well as the pool, there is a well-regarded restaurant here and a bar that simply invites lingering.

Spring Park Hotel HOTEL $

(☑730999; spparkhotel@yahoo.com; Old NH5; r US$6-35; ❋❀🛜) This place keeps on improving and now offers 78 rooms running from basic fan jobs through to deluxe mini-suites. Excellent value all-round.

Phka Villa Hotel BOUTIQUE HOTEL $$

(☑953255; Ph KO; r fromUS$50;-❋❀🛜☀) This homely boutique resort offers a series of tastefully decorated bungalows set around an inviting swimming pool. Breakfast is included and there is a small bar.

La Villa HOTEL $$

(☑730151; www.lavilla-battambang.com; East River Rd; d US$55-85; ❋❀🛜☀) One of the most romantic boutique hotels in Cambodia, this attractive hostelry occupies a French-era villa renovated in vintage 1930s style. The only drawback is that it has now been hemmed in by looming apartment blocks on both sides.

🍴 Eating

CITY CENTRE

Cheap dining is available in and around Psar Nat. There's a riverside **night market** (Ph 1; ⊙approx 3pm-midnight) opposite the Battambang Museum.

Fresh Eats Café INTERNATIONAL $

(Ph 2½; mains US$1.50-3; ⊙6am-9pm; 🛜) Run by an NGO that helps children whose families have been affected by HIV/AIDS, this little place serves cheap, tasty food, including Western breakfasts, bagels, fried spring rolls and Khmer curry.

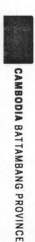

Battambang

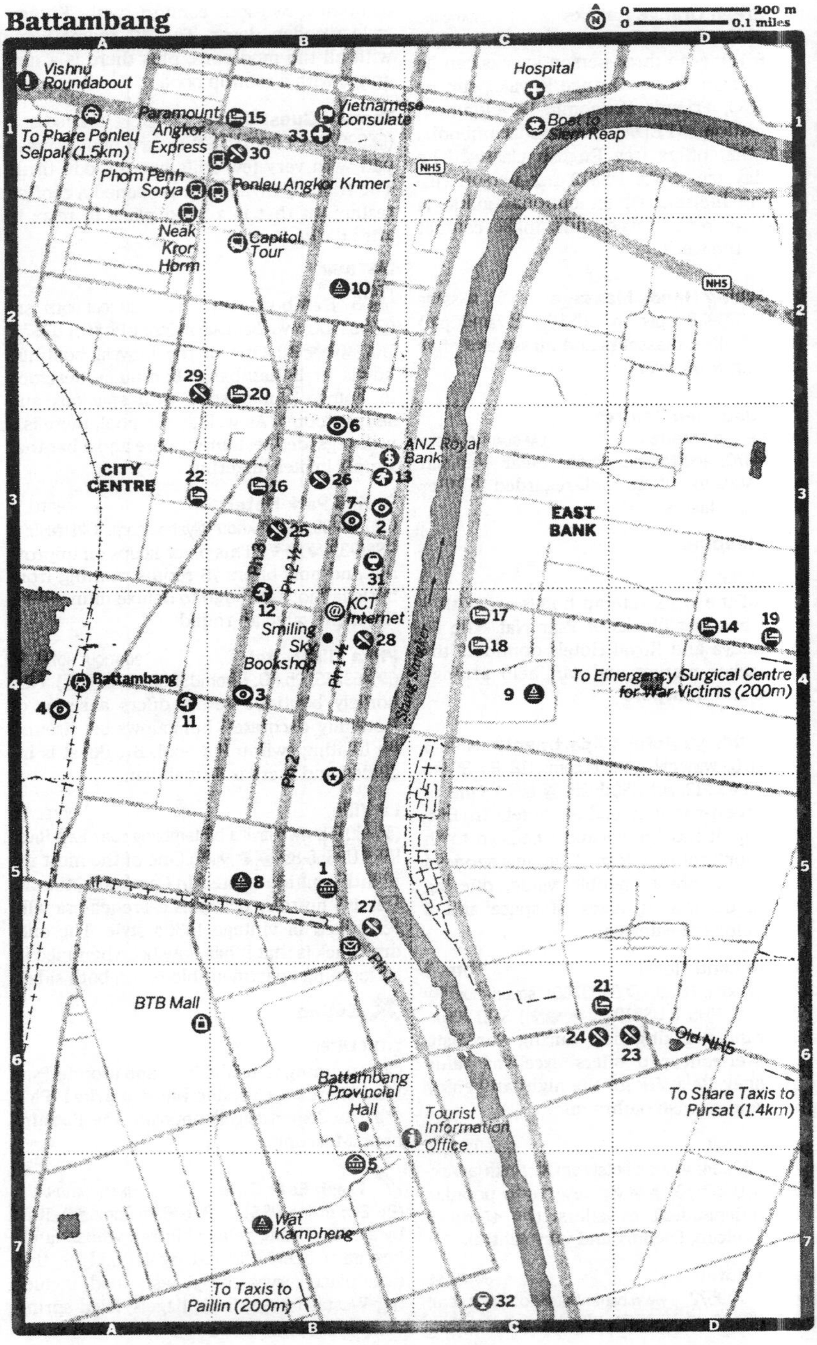

0 200 m
0 0.1 miles
Vishnu Roundabout
To Phare Ponleu Selpak (1.5km)
Paramount Angkor Express
15
30
33
Vietnamese Consulate
Hospital
Boat to Siem Reap
NH5
Phom Penh Sorya
Ponleu Angkor Khmer
Neak Kror Horm
Capitol Tour
10
29
20
6
ANZ Royal Bank
CITY CENTRE
22
16
26
13
7
2
25
EAST BANK
Ph 3
Ph 2½
31
12
KCT Internet
Smiling Sky Bookshop
28
Ph 1½
17
18
14
19
Stung Sangker
Battambang
4
11
3
9
To Emergency Surgical Centre for War Victims (200m)
Ph 2
8
1
27
Ph 1
BTB Mall
21
24
23
Old NH5
To Share Taxis to Pursat (1.4km)
Battambang Provincial Hall
Tourist Information Office
5
Wat Kampheng
To Taxis to Paillin (200m)
32

Battambang

Sights

1 Battambang Museum ... B5
2 Colonial Buildings ... B3
3 French Shophouses ... B4
4 French-Era Train Repair Sheds ... A4
5 Governor's Residence ... B7
6 Psar Nat ... B3
Smokin' Pot Cooking Classes ... (see 28)
7 The Colonial ... B3
8 Wat Damrey Sar ... B5
9 Wat Kandal ... C4
10 Wat Phiphétaram ... B2

Activities, Courses & Tours

11 Australian Centres for Development ... A4
12 Seeing Hands Massage ... B4
13 Soksabike ... B3

Sleeping

14 Bambu Hotel ... D4
15 Banan Hotel ... B1
16 Chhaya Hotel & Apartments ... B3
17 Golden Land Hotel ... C4
18 La Villa ... C4
19 Phka Villa Hotel ... D4
20 Royal Hotel ... B2
21 Spring Park Hotel ... C6
22 Tomato Guesthouse ... A3

Eating

23 Bamboo Train Cafe ... D6
24 Battambang BBQ & Buffet ... C6
Fresh Eats Café ... (see 26)
25 Gecko Café ... B3
26 Pomme d'Amour ... B3
Psar Nat ... (see 6)
27 Riverside Night Market ... B5
28 Smokin' Pot ... B4
29 Sunrise Coffee House ... A2
30 Vegetarian Foods Restaurant ... B1

Drinking

1½ Street Cafe ... (see 13)
31 Cafe Eden ... B3
32 Riverside Balcony Bar ... C7

Information

33 Polyclinique Visal Sokh ... B1

Sunrise Coffee House INTERNATIONAL $
(mains 8000-14,000r; 6.30am-8pm Mon-Sat;) Better than Starbucks, this is a great place for coffee, fresh-baked banana bread, California-style wraps, homemade tortillas, vegie or chicken quesadillas, and all-day breakfasts.

Gecko Café INTERNATIONAL $
(www.geckocafecambodia.com; Ph 3; mains US$2.75-5; 8am-1pm;) This is Battambang's answer to the Foreign Correspondents' Club (FCC) thanks to the glorious setting in an old French shophouse. Mellow and atmospheric, it's a good place for some international bites or an evening drink.

Vegetarian Foods Restaurant VEGETARIAN $
(mains 1500-3000r; 6am-11am;) Serves some of the most delicious vegetarian dishes in Cambodia, including rice soup and homemade soy milk. Open only for breakfast and brunch.

Smokin' Pot KHMER $
(012 821400; vannacksmokinpot@yahoo.com; mains US$2-3.50; 7am-11pm) This cheery, laid-back restaurant serves good Khmer, Thai and Western food – burgers and fried beef with ginger are popular choices. Offers cooking classes (US$8) every morning.

Pomme d'Amour FRENCH $$
(63 Ph 2½; mains US$5-8.50; 11am-10pm) The French-run 'Apple of Love' serves fine French cuisine at elegantly set tables. Specialities include local beef with black Kampot pepper sauce and authentic crêpes.

The Colonial INTERNATIONAL $
(near Ph 1; mains US$3-6; 11am-10pm) A new steakhouse in Battambang, this place has the atmosphere of a French bistro. There are four sauces to choose from, including green pepper and blue cheese. Pies and pasta also available.

EAST BANK

A lively restaurant scene is developing on the East Bank, especially along Old NH5.

Bamboo Train Cafe INTERNATIONAL $
(Old NH5; mains 4000-24,000r; 7am-10pm) The affable owner ensures this place is always popular. As well as an eclectic menu with pizzas, pastas, curries and a delicious tofu *amok* (steamed fish curry with coconut and lemongrass), there is a pool table and regular movie screenings.

GETTING TO THAILAND: PSAR PRUHM TO PONG NAM RON

This out-of-the-way crossing is 102km southwest of Battambang and 22km northwest of the town of Pailin.

In Battambang, taxis leave from the west side of **Psar Leu** (southern end of Ph 3). A share taxi to Pailin town (two hours) costs 25,000r. An onward share taxi from Pailin to the frontier costs about 10,000r. A private taxi from Battambang direct to the border (US$50) offers the option of stopping off at Phnom Sampeau and Sneng.

On the Thai side, you can avoid being overcharged for transport to Chanthaburi (150B by minibus, one hour) by hopping on a moto (50B) to the nearby *sŏrngtăaou* (pick-up truck) station. From Chanthaburi's bus station there are buses to Bangkok.

For information on crossing this border in the other direction, see the boxed text, p387.

Battambang BBQ & Buffet ASIAN $
(Old NH5; US$4; ⊙11am-10pm) Offering an all-inclusive tabletop barbecue and serve-yourself buffet, this place is unbelievably popular with local Khmers and domestic tourists. Exceptional value.

Drinking

Riverside Balcony Bar BAR
(cnr Ph 1 & NH57; mains US$3.50-7.50; ⊙4pm-midnight Tue-Sun) Set in a gorgeous wooden house high above the riverfront, this is Battambang's original bar and still the best spot in town. Renowned for its burgers.

Cafe Eden BAR
(www.cafeedencambodia.com; 85 Ph 1; ⊙8am-9pm Wed-Mon) Located in an old colonial block on the riverfront, this is a social enterprise offering a relaxed space for an afternoon drink, great food and an original boutique out the back.

1½ Street Cafe CAFE
(1 Ph 1½; ⊙7am-7pm) The home base of Soksabike, this tiny cafe offers a welcome refuge from the backstreets of Battambang. Choose from global coffees, infused teas and some homemade cakes.

Information

The focal point of Battambang's city centre, on the west bank of Stung Sangker, is Psar Nat (Meeting Market). There are lots of restaurants and bars dotting the old French-era streets running between the riverfront and Ph 3. The liveliest street on the up-and-coming East Bank is Old NH5.

We've heard reports of persistent locals asking foreigners to come teach English to needy kids – or, in lieu of actually teaching, to make a donation. They then pocket the cash.

ANZ Royal (Ph 1) One of several banks facing Psar Nat. Has an ATM.

Emergency Surgical Centre for War Victims (☎370065; ⊙24hr for emergencies) This 106-bed surgical hospital *cannot* help with tropical diseases or routine illness but may be able to save your life if you need emergency surgery (such as for traffic accidents or appendicitis).

KCT Internet Café (⊙7am-9pm) Internet access.

Polyclinique Visal Sokh (☎952401; NH5; ⊙24hr) For minor medical problems, including snake bites, malaria and rabies shots.

Smiling Sky Bookshop (113 Ph 2; ⊙8am-7.30pm) Sells used books in English, French and German.

Tourist Information Office (☎730217; www.battambang-town.gov.kh; Ph 1; ⊙7.30am-5.30pm) Has brochures and maps of Battambang, Siem Reap and Phnom Penh.

Vietnamese Consulate (☎952894; ⊙8-11am & 2-4pm Mon-Fri) Issues 15-day visas (US$35) in 15 minutes; one-month visas (US$40) take two or three days.

Getting There & Away

BOAT

The riverboat to Siem Reap (US$20, five to nine or more hours, departure at 7am) squeezes through narrow waterways and passes by protected wetlands. It's a bird-watcher's paradise. It's operated on alternate days by **Angkor Express** (☎012-601287) and **Chann Na** (☎012-354344). In the dry season, passengers have to be driven to a navigable section of the river. Try to sit as far from the noisy motor as possible. It may be possible to alight at the Prek Toal Bird Reserve (boxed text, p207) and then be picked up there the next day for US$5 extra. Be aware that these fast boats are not always so popular with local communities along the way, as the wake has caused small boats to capsize and fishing nets are regularly snagged.

BUS

Battambang does not have a central bus station. Rather, bus companies have offices and stops on or near NH5. All companies serve Phnom Penh (US$5 to US$8, five hours, 293km), Pursat (US$2.50, two hours), Sisophon (US$2 to US$3, one hour) and Poipet (US$3 to US$4, three hours). Capitol Tour and Neak Kror Horm have buses to Bangkok (US$13 to US$15) and Siem Reap (US$5); Paramount Angkor Express also goes to Siem Reap (US$5). Phnom Penh Sorya has a service to Kompong Cham (US$9).

Bus companies include:

Capitol Tour (☎953040)
KSO Transport (☎012 320737)
Neak Kror Horm (☎953838)
Phnom Penh Sorya (☎092 181804)
Paramount Angkor Express (☎092 575572)
Ponleu Angkor Khmer (☎092 517792)
Rith Mony (☎012 823885)

TAXI

At the **taxi station** (NH5), share taxis to Poipet (20,000r), Sisophon (15,000r) and Siem Reap (30,000r) leave from the north side while taxis to Pursat (15,000r) and Phnom Penh (40,000r) leave from the southeast corner. Budget hotels can assist with arranging a private chartered taxi if you crave more space.

Getting Around

A moto ride in town costs 1000r to 3000r, plus a bit more at night.

Hiring a moto driver who speaks English or French costs US$6 to US$8 for a half-day in and around town and US$12 for an all-day trip out of the city.

Gecko Moto (☎089 924260; www.geckocafecambodia.com; Ph 3; ⊙8am-7pm) rents out 100cc/250cc motorbikes for US$6/12 a day. It's located in the Gecko Cafe (p223). The Chhaya Hotel charges US$5/7 a day for an old/new motorbike, while the Royal Hotel charges US$8.

Bicycles (US$2 a day at Gecko Moto or the Royal Hotel) are a great way to get around and can be ridden along either bank of the river in either direction.

AROUND BATTAMBANG

Before setting out, try to link up with an English-speaking moto driver, as it really adds to the experience. Possible itineraries include a loop along the river to Phnom Banan and back to town via Phnom Sampeau.

Admission to Phnom Sampeau, Phnom Banan and Wat Ek Phnom is US$2. If you purchase a ticket – sold by the tourist police, which have a booth at each site – at one of the three *phnoms* (hills), it's valid all day at the other two.

Return travel by moto/remork costs US$7/10 to Phnom Sampeau, US$8/12 to Phnom Banan and US$6/10 to Wat Ek Phnom; a full-day trip to several sights is about US$12/20.

PHNOM SAMPEAU

At the summit of this fabled limestone outcrop, 12km southwest of Battambang (towards Pailin), a complex of **temples** (admission US$2) affords gorgeous views. Some of the macaques that live here, dining on bananas left as offerings, are pretty ornery.

Between the summit and the mobile-phone antenna, a **deep canyon** descends steeply through a natural arch to a 'lost world' of stalactites, creeping vines and bats. Nearby, two government **artillery pieces** still point west towards **Phnom Krapeu** (Crocodile Mountain), a one-time Khmer Rouge stronghold.

About halfway up the hill, a turn-off leads 250m up to the **Killing Caves of Phnom Sampeau**. An enchanted staircase, flanked by greenery, leads into a cavern where a golden reclining Buddha lies peacefully next to a glass-walled memorial filled with the bones and skulls of some of the people bludgeoned to death by Khmer Rouge cadres before being thrown through the overhead skylight.

PHNOM BANAN

Exactly 358 stone steps lead up a shaded slope to 11th-century **Prasat Banan** (admission US$2), 28km south of Battambang, whose five towers are reminiscent of the layout of Angkor Wat. Indeed, locals claim it was the inspiration for Angkor Wat. The views are well worth the climb.

From the temple, a narrow stone staircase leads south down the hill to **three caves**, two of which are not mined and can thus be visited with a torch-/flashlight-equipped local guide.

On the main road from Battambang to Phnom Banan (about midway between the two), in an area famous for its hot red chillies, you can visit Cambodia's only winery, **Prasat Phnom Banon Winery** (☎012 665238; Bot Sala Village; ⊙6am-6pm), growing shiraz and cabernet sauvignon grapes to make reds.

WAT EK PHNOM

This atmospheric, partly collapsed, 11th-century **temple** (admission US$2) is 11km north of Battambang. A lintel showing

GETTING TO THAILAND: POIPET TO ARANYA PRATHET

This is by far Cambodia's most popular land crossing with Thailand. From the roundabout at the western terminus of NH5, go through **passport control** (⏲7am-8pm), walk through the casino zone and cross the Friendship Bridge (don't look down). On the Thai side you can catch a túk-túk (60B) for the 6km ride to Aranya Prathet, where buses can get you into Bangkok in about four hours. You can also catch the train to Hualamphong station in Bangkok (six hours). We've heard repeated reports of fake bus tickets being sold at the border for onward bus trips to other places in Thailand.

For information on crossing this border in the other direction, see the boxed text, p387.

the Churning of the Ocean of Milk can be seen above the east entrance to the central temple, whose upper flanks hold some fine bas-reliefs. This is a great place for a shady picnic.

On the way from Battambang by bicycle or moto, it's possible to visit a 1960s **Pepsi bottling plant** (1.2km north of Battambang's ferry landing), frozen in time since 1975, and, 1km further out, the **Slaket crocodile farm**.

Banteay Meanchey Province

Sandwiched between the casinos and sleaze of Poipet and the glories of Angkor, agricultural Banteay Meanchey (Fortress of Victory) – which claims to grow Cambodia's best rice – is home to the Angkorian temples of Banteay Chhmar.

POIPET

☎054 / POP 45,000

Long the armpit of Cambodia, notorious for its squalor, sleaze and scams, Poipet (poi-*peh*) has recently applied some thick make-up and deodorant, at least in the border-adjacent casino zone. The Khmers' gentle side is little in evidence here but don't worry, the rest of the country does not carry on like this.

Sleeping

Hotels in the baht-only casino zone advertise rooms for 500B to 1500B, good value given the facilities. Cheap guesthouses, some of them brothels, are strung out along NH5 and around the bus station, but we don't advise staying here unless you get stuck.

Orkiday Angkor Hotel HOTEL $
(Orchidée Angkor Hotel; ☎967502; oa_tour@online.com.kh; NH5; r US$13-20; ❄) Right outside the casino zone, rooms have terracotta floors, huge beds and hot water. There's no lift, so rates drop as you ascend the stairs.

Information

There's a **Canadia Bank** (NH5) 1km east of the roundabout and an **ANZ Bank** (NH5) 500m further east. ANZ Bank has ATMs at the border. Internet shops can be found along NH5.

Getting There & Away

Poipet is 48km west of Sisophon and 153km west of Siem Reap. NH5 between Poipet and Sisophon has at long last been paved.

BUS

Apart from the scam of the official tourist bus stations, there are some independent bus companies based here, including **Capitol Tour** (☎967350), **Phnom Penh Sorya** (☎092 181802) and **GST** (☎012 727771). Destinations include Sisophon (US$2 to US$3, 40 minutes), Siem Reap (US$5, 2½ hours to four hours), Battambang (US$3.75, two hours) and Phnom Penh (US$7.50, seven hours). Phnom Penh Sorya has a direct service to Kompong Cham. Almost all departures are between 6.15am and 10.30am. Several companies, including Capitol, offer mid-afternoon services to Bangkok (300B).

TAXI

Six-person share taxis are available all day along NH5 about 1.3km east of the roundabout (near the bus station turn-off), if you can avoid the bus station mafia. Destinations include Sisophon (100B, 40 minutes), Siem Reap (250B, three hours), Battambang (US$5 to 200B, two hours) and Phnom Penh (500B).

SISOPHON

☎054 / POP 41,000

Strategically situated at northwest Cambodia's great crossroads, the intersection of NH5 and NH6, Sisophon (often called Svay or Banteay Meanchey by locals) makes a convenient first stop if you're coming from Poipet and is a good base for exploring the Angkorian temples of Banteay Chhmar.

Sleeping

Botoum Hotel HOTEL $
(☎012 687858; r US$8-15;) A new hotel near the Provincial Hall, the rooms are a real find compared with what is on offer elsewhere in town. The small coffee shop out front brews a good cuppa.

Golden Crown Guesthouse HOTEL $
(☎958444; r US$6-13;) One of the most central hotels in town, rooms are fair value, including hot-water showers and satellite TV. Downstairs is a cheap and mildly cheerful restaurant.

Information

A block or two south of NH6 in the triangular town centre, Acleda Bank has an ATM as does Canadia Bank. There are several internet places along NH6 between NH5 and NH69.

Getting There & Away

Long-haul buses and most share taxis stop at the bus station, about 400m south of NH6. Companies including **Capitol Tour**, **Rith Mony** and **Phnom Penh Sorya** serve Poipet (5000r to 10,000r), Siem Reap (15,000r to 20,000r), Battambang (7000r to 10,000r), Phnom Penh (US$5 to US$6) and Bangkok (US$10). Buses heading west depart between 6.30am and 10.30am; buses to Poipet and Bangkok leave in the early afternoon.

Share taxis link the bus station with Phnom Penh (US$10, five hours), Siem Reap (US$5) and Battambang (15,000r, one hour); a private taxi to Siem Reap costs about US$30. Share taxis to Poipet (10,000r) stop on NH5.

BANTEAY CHHMAR

The temple complex of **Banteay Chhmar** (www.globalheritagefund.org; admission US$5) was constructed by Cambodia's most prolific builder, Jayavarman VII (r 1181–1219), on the site of a 9th-century temple. One of a handful of Angkorian sites to feature the towering heads of Avalokiteshvaras, with their enigmatic smiles, the 12th-century temple is also renowned for its intricate carvings. These include two multi-armed Avalokiteshvaras and a bas-relief that dramatically depicts naval warfare between the Khmers (on the left) and the Chams (on the right).

A pioneering community-based **homestay project** (☎012 435660, cbtbanteaychhmar@yahoo.com; r US$7) makes it possible to stay in and around Banteay Chhmar. Rooms come with mosquito nets, fans that run when there's electricity (6pm to 10pm) and downstairs bathrooms. Bikes can be rented for US$1.50 a day.

Near the temple's eastern entrance, rustic **Banteay Chhmar Restaurant** (mains US$2-3) serves tasty Khmer food.

POIPET TRANSPORT SCAMS

The moment you enter Cambodia at Poipet, whether you know it or not, you are the duly purchased client of a monopoly that has paid for the exclusive right to provide you with onward land transport.

Poipet now has two international terminals. The **Poipet Tourist Passenger International Terminal**, situated 9km east of town in the middle of nowhere, and the **International Tourist Terminal**, 1.5km east of the tourist zone. Posted fares at both these places are higher than the prices locals pay by up to 250%.

As you exit the immigration police office (where passports are stamped), fencing herds you into the 'Free Shuttle Bus Station', departure point for **OSP buses** (⊙7am-6pm) to the international terminals. OSP's job is straightforward: to operate the **bus station** (⊙7am-6pm) and make sure tourists get there.

Transport out of Poipet is orchestrated by three 'associations' that work out of the bus station on a rotational basis: each handles all buses and taxis for tourists on every third day. All charge the same fares, offering buses/four-passenger share taxis to Sisophon (US$5/5), Siem Reap (US$9/12), Battambang (US$10/10) and Phnom Penh (US$15/25).

For the cash-strapped traveller, the obvious solution is to find a taxi the way Cambodians do. Readers have reported that 'association' enforcers, with police backing, often intervene to prevent independent taxi drivers from accepting foreign tourists. When they declined OSP's shuttle offer, an 'association' agent followed them for blocks and intimidated any taxi driver they came upon. The trick, therefore, is to give the agent the slip, perhaps by saying you'll be overnighting in Poipet.

GETTING TO THAILAND: CHOAM TO CHONG SA-NGAM

This crossing is 16km north of Anlong Veng (10,000r by moto) and 134km north of Siem Reap. From Anlong Veng, a sealed road heads up the Dangkrek escarpment to a new Thai border complex, in mothballs because the Cambodians say it's on their territory. Head instead to the old crossing, a few hundred metres east, next to the smugglers market. On the Thai side, it should be possible to find a *sŏrngtăaou* to Phusing and from there a bus to Kantharalak. You might also suss out transport to Si Saket.

The border is open from 7am to 5pm. There are no fixed fees, but visa overcharging is commonplace at most borders with Thailand or Laos. There are also overtime fees between noon and 2pm.

For information on crossing this border in the other direction, see the boxed text, p423.

In Sisophon, share taxis to Banteay Chhmar (61km via a terrible road) leave from near Psar Thmei, on NH69 1km north of NH6. A moto from Sisophon to Banteay Chhmar should cost about US$12 return. There's no public transport from Banteay Chhmar northeast to Samraong, although the road is now in good shape.

Oddar Meanchey Province

The remote, dirt-poor province of Oddar Meanchey produces very little apart from opportunities for aid organisations. Khmer Rouge sites around Anlong Veng are starting to attract visitors appalled and fascinated by evil and its banality.

ANLONG VENG

For almost a decade this was home to the most notorious leaders of Democratic Kampuchea. For those with a keen interest in contemporary Cambodian history, the Khmer Rouge sites around Anlong Veng are an important, if somewhat disturbing, part of the picture.

Sights

Pol Pot's military enforcer, Ta Mok, was responsible for thousands of deaths in successive purges during the terrible years of Democratic Kampuchea. Widely known as 'The Butcher', he was arrested in 1999 and died in July 2006 in a Phnom Penh hospital, awaiting trial for genocide and crimes against humanity. **Ta Mok's house** (admission incl English tour US$2), a spartan structure decorated with childish murals, is on a peaceful lakeside site 2km north of the roundabout and then a few hundred metres east.

Ta Mok's grave, next to a modest pagoda, is 7km further north in Tumnup Leu. Further north still, about 2km before the frontier, look out for a group of **statues** – hewn entirely from the surrounding rock by the Khmer Rouge – depicting a woman and two uniformed Khmer Rouge soldiers.

A few hundred metres before the frontier, under a rusted corrugated-iron roof, is the **cremation site of Pol Pot**, who was hastily burned in 1998 on a pile of old tyres and rubbish, a fittingly inglorious end, perhaps.

From the frontier smugglers market, a dirt road heads east between minefields, parallel to the escarpment. After about 4km you come to another **Ta Mok residence**, the cement shell of the Khmer Rouge's **radio station** and **Peuy Ta Mok** (Ta Mok's Cliff), where domestic tourists come to enjoy spectacular views of Cambodia's northern plains.

From here a half-hour moto ride takes you to **Khieu Samphan's house**, buried in the jungle on the bank of a stream, from where it's a few hundred metres along an overgrown road to **Pol Pot's house**, a modest complex that includes a low brick building whose courtyard hides an underground bunker.

Sleeping & Eating

Monorom Guesthouse HOTEL $
(☎012 603339; r with air-con from US$15; ❄) Anlong Veng's finest hostelry, with big, modern rooms with air-con and hot water. The new wing includes VIP rooms but is often full of visiting, well, VIPs.

Phkay Preuk Restaurant KHMER $
(NH67; mains 5000-20,000r; ⊙6am-10pm) Situated about 2km north of town, this popular eatery serves tasty and good-value Khmer dishes in private pavilions.

Information

Acleda Bank (⌚7.30am-2pm Mon-Fri, to noon Sat) The only bank in town; has an ATM.

VTC Computer (per hr US$1; ⌚6am-9pm) Anlong Veng's first internet shop.

Getting There & Around

Anlong Veng is 118km north of Siem Reap along the excellent Thai-built NH67; 16km south of the Choam border crossing; 80km northeast of Samraong; and 90km west of Sra Em, gateway to Prasat Preah Vihear.

Share taxis to Siem Reap (20,000r, two hours) are available a few hundred metres south of the main roundabout; a private taxi is about US$40. **GST** (☎092-905026) has a 7am bus to Siem Reap (15,000r, three hours). Share taxis to Sra Em (20,000r, two hours) leave in the morning.

A moto circuit to the border costs US$6 (or US$10 or so including a tour of Pol Pot's house).

Preah Vihear Province

Bordering Thailand and Laos to the north, vast Preah Vihear Province is home to three of Cambodia's most impressive legacies of the Angkorian era, including stunning Prasat Preah Vihear, high atop the Dangkrek escarpment. Much of this province was heavily forested and extremely remote, but it is now on the frontline of development thanks to the border conflict with Thailand. The government plans to motivate its regular soldiers to protect Cambodian territory by offering them parcels of land in the province.

TBENG MEANCHEY

☎064 / POP 22,000

Tbeng Meanchey, often referred to by locals as Preah Vihear (not to be confused with Prasat Preah Vihear), is sprawling and dusty-red (or muddy-red, depending on the season). The town makes a good staging post for the long trip to Prasat Preah Vihear, 110km north.

The centre of town, insofar as there is one, is around the taxi park and the market, Psar Kompong Pranak. Acleda Bank, a block south of the market, has an ATM.

Prom Tep Guesthouse (☎012 964645; Ph Koh Ker; r with fan/air-con from US$6/16; ❄@) is large enough to be a hotel and offers 25 spacious rooms, all with cable TV and Western toilets.

The 10-room **Heng Heng Guesthouse** (☎012 900992; NH64; r with fan/air-con US$8/16; ❄) has the nicest rooms in town. It's situated one block west and one block south of the taxi park.

Dara Raksmey Restaurant (Ph Mlou Prey; mains 8000-20,000r; ⌚6.30am-9pm) is Tbeng Meanchey's finest and fanciest eatery, with mirror-clad columns, massive wood tables and the usual selection of Khmer favourites.

Getting There & Away

For details on public transport to/from Kompong Thom, 157km to the south via the execrable NH64, see p231. For details on transport to Prasat Preah Vihear, 110km to the north, see p230.

PRASAT PREAH VIHEAR

The most dramatically situated of all the Angkorian monuments, 800m-long **Prasat Preah Vihear** (elevation 625m; www.preahvihearauthority.org) consists of a series of four cruciform *gopura* (sanctuaries) decorated with exquisite carvings, including some striking lintels. Starting at the Monumental Stairway, a walk south takes you to the **Gopura of the Third Level**, with its early rendition of the Churning of the Ocean of Milk, and finally, perched at the edge of the cliff, the **Central Sanctuary**. The stupendous views of Cambodia's northern plains make this a fantastic spot for a picnic.

Before the armed stand-off, visitors could visit Prasat Preah Vihear from Thailand, crossing into Cambodia with a special no-visa day pass (US$10). However, the border has been closed since 2008 and the only way to visit is from the Cambodian side. The temple has remained open during much of the stand-off for visitors who are willing to take the risk. Check on the latest situation while in Phnom Penh, Siem Reap, Tbeng Meanchey or Sra Em before attempting to visit the temple.

The village of Koh Muy, at the base of the hill, was evacuated during the on-and-off fighting, so the nearest accommodation is in **Sra Em**, 27km away. Guesthouses are rudimentary to say the least. The best of the lot is the **Tuol Monysophon Guesthouse** (☎099 620757; r without/with private bathroom US$7.50/10). It has 25 rooms with mosquito nets and wood-plank floors. **Pkay Prek Restaurant** (mains 4000-15,000r; ⌚6am-10pm)

MINE YOUR STEP

Stick to well-marked paths, as the Khmer Rouge laid huge numbers of landmines around Prasat Preah Vihear as late as 1998.

serves delicious *phnom pleung* ('hill of fire'; US$3.75), which you BBQ yourself.

Getting There & Away

Visiting Prasat Preah Vihear from the Cambodian side is much easier as the road has been fully sealed in order to ensure rapid access for Cambodian soldiers travelling to the border area.

Share taxis now link Sra Em with Siem Reap (30,000r, three hours), Anlong Veng (20,000r, two hours) and Tbeng Meanchey (25,000r, two hours).

For travel from Sra Em to Koh Muy (22km), a share taxi costs 10,000r per person while a moto is about 15,000r. From there, the return trip up to the temple (5km each way), past sandbagged machine-gun positions, costs US$5 by moto or US$25 by pick-up truck. Some *motodups* (moto drivers) – many are off-duty army officers – are happy to act as guides.

KOH KER

Abandoned to the forests of the north, **Koh Ker** (admission US$10), capital of the Angkorian empire from AD 928 to 944, was long one of Cambodia's most inaccessible temple complexes. However, this has now changed thanks to recent de-mining and the opening of a new toll road from Dam Dek (via Beng Mealea) that puts Koh Ker within day-trip distance of Siem Reap.

Most visitors start at **Prasat Krahom** (Red Temple), whose stone archways and galleries lean hither and thither; impressive stone carvings grace lintels, doorposts and slender window columns.

The principal monument is **Prasat Thom** (Prasat Kompeng), a 55m-wide, 40m-high, sandstone-faced pyramid whose seven tiers offer spectacular views across the forest. The upper level has been closed for some years due to ongoing safety concerns.

Some of the largest Shiva *linga* (phallic symbols) in Cambodia can be seen inside four temples about 1km northeast of Prasat Thom.

About 8km south of Prasat Krahom, the quiet **Mom Morokod Koh Ker Guesthouse** (☎011 935114; r from US$10) has 11 clean, spacious rooms with fancy carved-wood doors, painted wood-plank walls and en-suite bathrooms.

In the quiet village of Srayong, 2km from the toll plaza, the family-run **Ponloeu Preah Chan Guesthouse** (☎012 489058; r US$5) has 12 small rooms. Only one room has its own plumbing.

Getting There & Away

Koh Ker is 127km northeast of Siem Reap (2½ hours by car) and 72km west of Tbeng Meanchey (two hours). From Siem Reap, hiring a private car for a day trip to Koh Ker costs about US$80. From Tbeng Meanchey, a private taxi costs US$70 return, a moto US$15.

PREAH KHAN

Covering almost 5 sq km, **Preah Khan** (admission US$5) is the largest temple enclosure constructed during the Angkorian period – quite a feat when you consider the competition. Originally dedicated to Hindu deities, it was reconsecrated to Mahayana Buddhist worship by Jayavarman VII in the late 12th and early 13th centuries. Thanks to its back-of-beyond location, the site is astonishingly quiet and peaceful.

At the eastern end of the 3km-long *baray* (reservoir) is a small pyramid temple called **Prasat Damrei** (Elephant Temple), with several impressive carvings of *devadas* (goddesses). At the *baray's* western end stands **Prasat Preah Stung**, known to locals as Prasat Muk Buon (Temple of the Four Faces) because of its four Bayon-style faces. Tragically, the central temple complex was devastated by looters in the 1990s.

Getting There & Away

There's no public transport to Preah Khan, so your best bet is to hire a moto or pick-up truck in Kompong Thom (four hours, 120km), Phnom Den (on NH64, 35km east of the temple) or Tbeng Meanchey (three hours). If you've got more cash, you might consider chartering a 4WD. Only *very* experienced bikers should attempt to get to Preah Khan on rental motorcycles, as conditions are extremely tough from every side.

Preah Khan is not accessible in the wet season.

Kompong Thom Province

An easy stopover if you're travelling overland between Phnom Penh and Siem Reap, Kompong Thom is starting to draw more visitors thanks to several unique sites, including the pre-Angkorian temples of Sambor Prei Kuk and the extraordinary hilltop shrines of Phnom Santuk.

KOMPONG THOM

☎062 / POP 66,000

A bustling commercial centre, Kompong Thom is situated on NH6 midway between Phnom Penh and Siem Reap.

Sleeping & Eating

TOP CHOICE Sambor Village Hotel BOUTIQUE HOTEL $$
(☎961391; Ph Prachea Thepatay; r US$50, ste US$80;) This atmospheric place brings boutique to Kompong Thom. Rooms are set in spacious bungalows and the verdant gardens include an inviting pool. International dishes at the restaurant.

Arunras Hotel HOTEL $
(☎961294; 46 Sereipheap Blvd; r with fan/air-con US$6/15;) Dominating the accommodation scene in Kompong Thom, this seven-storey corner establishment has 58 smart, good-value rooms.

Bayon Restaurant KHMER $
(Ph Prachea Thepatay; mains incl rice 6000r; 5am-9pm) Lacking English signs or even a printed menu, this is a popular feeding station with locals. Situated one long block west of the Arunras Hotel.

American Restaurant INTERNATIONAL $
(Ph Prachea Thepatay; mains US$3-7.50; 7am-9pm;) This outpost of culinary Americana specialises in thin-crust Neapolitan pizzas, spaghetti, sandwiches, burgers and homemade ice cream, as well as Khmer dishes and freshly brewed coffee.

Psar Kompong Thom Night Market KHMER $
(NH6; mains 2000-4000r; 4pm-2am) Sit on a plastic chair at a neon-lit table and dig into chicken rice soup, chicken curry noodles, Khmer-style baguettes or a *tukalok* (fruit shake).

Information

Acleda Bank (NH6) Just north of the bridge. Has an ATM.

Internet pharmacy (NH6; per hr 4000r; 6.30am-7pm) Internet access one block north of the market.

Getting There & Around

Kompong Thom is on NH6 165km north of Phnom Penh and 150km southeast of Siem Reap.

Dozens of buses on the Phnom Penh–Siem Reap (both US$5) route pass through Kompong Thom and can easily be flagged down near the Arunras Hotel. Share taxis, which leave from the taxi park (one block east of the Arunras Hotel).

THE FIGHT FOR PRASAT PREAH VIHEAR

For generations, Prasat Preah Vihear (Prasat Phra Viharn to the Thais) has been a source of tension between Cambodia and Thailand. This area was ruled by Thailand for several centuries, but was returned to Cambodia during the French protectorate, under the treaty of 1907. In 1959 the Thai military seized the temple from Cambodia and then Prime Minister Sihanouk took the dispute to the International Court of Justice in the Hague, gaining worldwide recognition of Cambodian sovereignty in a 1962 ruling.

Prasat Preah Vihear hit the headlines again in May 1998 because the Khmer Rouge regrouped here after the fall of Anlong Veng and staged a last stand that soon turned into a final surrender. The temple was heavily mined during these final battles and de-mining was ongoing up until the outbreak of the conflict with Thailand. Re-mining seems to be the greater threat right now, with both sides accusing the other of using landmines.

In July 2008 Prasat Preah Vihear was declared Cambodia's second Unesco World Heritage Site. The Thai government, which claims 4.6 sq km of territory right around the temple (some Thai nationalists even claim the temple itself), initially supported the bid, but the temple soon became a pawn in Thailand's chaotic domestic politics. Within a week, Thai troops crossed into Cambodian territory, sparking an armed confrontation that has taken the lives of several dozen soldiers and some civilians on both sides. The Cambodian market at the bottom of the Monumental Stairway, which used to have a guesthouse, burned down during an exchange of fire in April 2009. In 2011, exchanges heated up once more and long-range shells were fired into civilian territory by both sides – including the controversial use of cluster munitions by the Thai army, according to reports from the Cluster Munition Coalition (www.stopclustermunitions.org).

In July 2011, the International Court of Justice ruled that both sides should withdraw troops from the area to establish a demilitarised zone. It is hoped that with a new pro-Thaksin (therefore possibly Hun Sen–friendly) government in Bangkok, the border dispute may finally come to an end. At the time of going to press, relations were rapidly normalising and Preah Vihear was once again at peace.

are faster and cost US$5 to either Phnom Penh (three hours), Siem Reap (two hours) or Kompong Cham (two hours); minibuses cost just 15,000r.

Heading north to Tbeng Meanchey (often referred to as Preah Vihear), pick-ups (20,000/15,000r inside/on the back, three to four hours) are the most common form of transport, although when NH64 is in decent condition share taxis also do the run.

Moto drivers can be found across NH6 from the Arunras Hotel. Count on paying US$6 to US$8 per day, plus petrol.

Bicycles can be rented at **Piseth Bike Rental** (Ph 103; per day US$3; ⏲6am-5pm), a block north of the bridge.

AROUND KOMPONG THOM

SAMBOR PREI KUK

Cambodia's most impressive group of pre-Angkorian monuments, **Sambor Prei Kuk** (admission US$3) encompasses more than 100 brick temples scattered through the forest. Originally called Isanapura, it served as the capital of Chenla during the reign of the early-7th-century King Isanavarman and continued to be an important learning centre during the Angkorian era.

Forested and shady, Sambor Prei Kuk has a serene and soothing atmosphere. The main temple area consists of three complexes, each enclosed by the remains of two concentric walls. The principal group, **Prasat Sambor**, is dedicated to Gambhireshvara, one of Shiva's many incarnations (the other groups are dedicated to Shiva himself). **Prasat Yeay Peau** (Prasat Yeai Poeun) feels lost in the forest, its eastern gateway both held up and torn asunder by an ancient tree.

Prasat Tao (Lion Temple), the largest of the Sambor Prei Kuk complexes, boasts excellent examples of Chenla carving in the form of two large, elaborately coiffed stone lions. It also has a fine, rectangular pond, **Srah Neang Pov**.

If you're interested in the chronological evolution of Cambodian temple architecture, you might want to see Sambor Prei Kuk before heading to Angkor.

Just past the ticket booth, the **Isanborei Crafts Shop** sells a worthwhile English brochure (2000r) and high-quality craft items. Nearby are several **small eateries** offering a very basic selection of Khmer dishes.

From Kompong Thom, a moto ride out here (45 minutes) should cost about US$10.

PHNOM SANTUK

Phnom Santuk (Phnom Sontuk; elevation 207m; admission US$2), its flanks decorated with Buddha images and a series of pagodas, is the most important holy mountain in this region. Exactly 809 stairs wend their way up an especially colourful wat.

The turn-off to Phnom Santuk intersects NH6 18km towards Phnom Penh from Kompong Thom, just past the village of **Kakoah**, famed for its stonemasons. Also nearby is **Santuk Silk Farm** (☎012-906604; budgibb@yahoo.com; admission free), where you can see the entire silk production cycle. The peaceful garden site has clean, top-quality Western toilets; complimentary coffee, tea and cold water are on offer. Try to call ahead a couple of hours before your visit.

From Kompong Thom, a round trip by moto costs about US$5 or so, depending on wait time.

EASTERN CAMBODIA

Eastern Cambodia is home to a diversity of landscapes and peoples, shattering the illusion that the country is all paddy fields and sugar palms. There are plenty of those in the lowland provinces, but in the northeast they yield to the forested mountains of Mondulkiri and Ratanakiri, both up-and-coming ecotourism areas.

If it is a walk on the wild side that fires your imagination, then the northeast – home to thundering waterfalls, crater lakes, meandering rivers, rare forest elephants and freshwater dolphins – is calling you. Trekking, biking, kayaking and elephant adventures are all activities beginning to take off. The rolling hills and lush forests provide a home to many ethnic minority groups. Do the maths: it all adds up to an amazing experience.

Kompong Cham Province

Gateway to the northeast, Kompong Cham is a land of picturesque villages and quiet Mekong meanders. Some of Cambodia's finest silk is woven here.

KOMPONG CHAM

☎042 / POP 60,000

This quiet Mekong city, an important trading post during the French period, serves as the gateway to Cambodia's northeast thanks to a vast bridge spanning the Mekong here.

INCY WINCY SPIDER

Locals in the small Cambodian town of Skuon (otherwise known affectionately as Spiderville) eat eight-legged furry friends for breakfast, lunch and dinner. Most tourists travelling between Siem Reap and Phnom Penh pass through Skuon without ever realising they have been there. This is hardly surprising, as it has nothing much to attract visitors, but it is the centre of one of Cambodia's more exotic culinary delights – the deep-fried spider.

Buses usually make a bathroom stop in Spiderville, so take a careful look at the eight-legged goodies the food sellers are offering. The creatures, decidedly dead, are piled high on platters, but don't get too complacent as there are usually live samples lurking nearby.

The spiders are hunted in holes in the hills to the north of Skuon and are quite an interesting dining experience. They are best treated like a crab and eaten by cracking the body open and pulling the legs off one by one, bringing the juiciest flesh out with them – a cathartic experience indeed for arachnophobes. They taste a bit like...mmm, chicken. Alternatively, for a memorable photo, just bite the thing in half and hope for the best. Watch out for the abdomen, which seems to be filled with some pretty nasty-tasting brown sludge, which could be anything from eggs to excrement; spider truffles, perhaps?

Ph Preah Bat Sihanouk, home to several hotels and eateries, runs along the riverfront. Psar Thmei (New Market) is a few blocks inland (west); Preah Monivong Blvd is one block further west.

Sights & Activities

Koh Paen ISLAND

For a supremely relaxing bike ride, it's hard to beat Koh Paen, a rural, traffic-free island that's connected to the mainland about 600m south of the Mekong bridge by a motorised ferry in the wet season and an elaborate bamboo toll bridge – totally rebuilt from scratch each December – in the dry season.

Wat Nokor TEMPLE

(admission US$2) The ultimate fusion temple, Wat Nokor is a modern Buddhist pagoda squeezed into the walls of an 11th-century Mahayana Buddhist shrine of sandstone and laterite. Located about 1km west of town.

Sleeping

The best hotels are strung out along the riverfront.

Monorom 2 VIP Hotel HOTEL $

(092 777102; Ph Preah Bat Sihanouk; r US$15-25; air-con, wi-fi) Currently the smartest hotel in town, rooms include heavy wood furnishings and inviting bathtubs. Most include a balcony with a Mekong view.

Mekong Hotel HOTEL $

(941536; Ph Preah Bat Sihanouk; r with fan/air-con US$7/15; air-con) This old-timer has been around for years and is still popular thanks to renovated rooms on the riverfront. The corridors are wide enough for an ultimate Frisbee tournament.

Eating & Drinking

Psar Thmei has fruit stalls in its northwest and southeast corners. After the sun goes down there's a cluster of night stalls along the river opposite the Mekong Hotel.

TOP CHOICE **Destiny Coffee House** CAFE $

(12 Ph Pasteur; mains US$2-5; 7am-4.30pm Mon-Sat; wi-fi) An unexpected oasis in little old Kompong Cham, this stylish cafe has relaxing sofas and a contemporary look. The international menu includes some delicious hummus with dips, lip-smacking homemade cakes and freshly prepared shakes.

Smile Restaurant KHMER $

(Ph Riverside; www.bdsa-cambodia.org; mains US$2.50-4.50; wi-fi) This non-profit restaurant run by the Buddhism and Society Development Association is a big hit with the NGO crowd for its big breakfasts, healthy menu and free wi-fi.

Lazy Mekong Daze INTERNATIONAL $

(Ph Riverside; mains US$2.50-4.50) With a pool table and a big screen for sports and movies, this is the place to be after dark. The menu parades a range of Khmer, Thai and Western food, and it has delicious Karem ice-cream available.

Information

ANZ Royal Bank (Preah Monivong Blvd) One of several banks with an ATM.

Sophary Internet (cnr Ph Preah Bat Sihanouk & Vithei Pasteur; 7am-9pm) Internet access.

GETTING TO VIETNAM: TRAPEANG SRE TO LOC NINH

To get to this crossing (⊙7am-5pm), seldom used by foreigners, catch a moto (US$5) in the much-maligned junction town of Snuol for an 18km trip southeastward along NH74, which is little more than a rutted dirt track. Snuol, on nicely paved NH7, is linked by bus, share taxi and minibus with Sen Monorom, Kratie and Kompong Cham. On the Vietnamese side, the nearest town is Binh Long, 40km to the south.

Getting There & Around

Phnom Penh is 120km southwest. NH7 is in excellent shape all the way to the Lao border.

Phnom Penh Sorya and **GST**, with offices on Preah Monivong Blvd, run direct buses to Phnom Penh (13,000r, three hours). **Rith Mony** has two direct trips to Siem Reap per day (US$5, five hours). GST also has a daily trip to Battambang (30,000r, six hours).

Rith Mony buses from Phnom Penh to Sen Monorom (US$7.50), Ban Lung (US$10) and Stung Treng (US$7, six hours) pass through here, as do Sorya's buses to Stung Treng and Pakse in Laos. Most buses come through around 10am. Most Stung Treng and Ban Lung buses take the long road via Snuol and stop in Kratie (US$4, three hours).

You can catch a faster share taxi to Phnom Penh (15,000r, two hours) on the northeast side of the market.

Several hotels and restaurants rent bicycles for US$1 to US$2 a day.

AROUND KOMPONG CHAM

PHNOM PROS & PHNOM SREI

'Man Hill' and 'Woman Hill', the subject of a rich variety of local legends, offer fine views of the countryside, especially during the wet season, and a very strokeable statue of the sacred bull Nandin (Shiva's mount). Phnom Pros is a good place for a cold drink among the inquisitive monkeys that populate the trees.

The hills are about 7km northwest of town (towards Phnom Penh) and can be visited by moto/remork for about US$5/10 return (depending on wait time), including a stop at Wat Nokor.

WAT MAHA LEAP

More than a century old, Wat Maha Leap is one of the most sacred Buddhist temples in Cambodia because it's one of the few wooden wats to have survived the destruction wrought by the Khmer Rouge, as they converted it into a hospital. Look for the 20m-long **racing boat**, which competes in Phnom Penh's annual Water Festival.

The wat is about 20km south of Kompong Cham (across the Mekong) but is hard to find without a guide or some knowledge of Khmer. A moto should cost about US$10 return. It may also be possible to take a minibus (5000r) from near the western end of Kompong Cham's Mekong bridge.

WEAVING VILLAGES

Kompong Cham Province is famous for its high-quality silk. In tiny villages such as **Dom Na Prin**, 4.5km west of Wat Maha Leap, and **Prey Chung Kran**, a few kilometres further south, the women and men of nearly every household turn raw silk into exquisite bolts of hand-woven silk (US$70 for 4m). Under the cool shade provided by their stilted homes, they work deftly to produce *sampots* (sarong-like garments worn on important occasions) and traditional *kramas* (chequered scarves). It's fascinating to watch the painstaking dyeing process – the traditional diamond and dot tessellations are formed by tying off precise lengths of silk and dyeing them various colours.

Getting to these villages by moto from Kompong Cham should cost about US$12 return, including a stop at Wat Maha Leap.

RUBBER PLANTATIONS

The rubber industry has bounced back in recent years, and Kompong Cham is the heartland of Cambodian rubber country. About 20km east of Kompong Cham (eg around Chup, aka Chob), you can turn off NH7 or NH11 and find yourself in deep, refreshing shade, surrounded by neat rows of rubber trees, a backbone of the regional economy since the 1920s.

Kratie Province

In this pretty province spanning the Mekong, much of Kratie's population makes its living from the mother river's waters. Away from the river, though, it's a remote and wild land that sees few outsiders.

KRATIE

☎072 / POP 31,000

Kratie (pronounced kra-*cheh*) is a lively riverside town with a rich legacy of French-era architecture and some of the best Mekong

Kratie

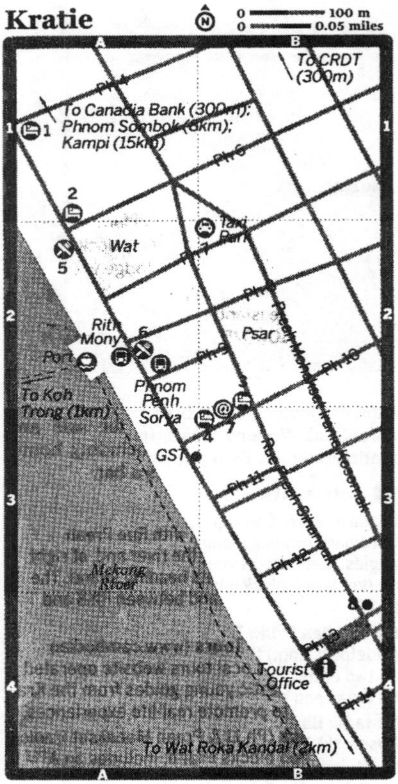

Kratie

Sleeping

1 Balcony Guesthouse A1
2 Oudom Sambath Hotel A1
3 Star Guesthouse B2
4 You Hong II Guesthouse B3

Eating

5 Food Stalls A2
6 Red Sun Falling A2

Information

7 Ly Kheang Web B3

Transport

8 Rent Bike B4

sunsets in Cambodia. A thriving travel hub, it's the natural place to break the overland journey between Kompong Cham and Laos, or to pick up the Mekong Discovery Trail (p237).

Sights & Activities

Dolphin Viewing WILDLIFE

Approximately 75 critically endangered **freshwater Irrawaddy dolphins** (Mekong River dolphin; Latin *Orcaella brevirostris;* Khmer *trey pisaut*), recognisable by their bulbous foreheads and puny dorsal fins, live in the Mekong between Kratie and the Lao border. In the last few years, an alarming number of calves have been dying for reasons that are not clear to scientists. Groups working to ensure the survival of this rare creature and to promote sustainable dolphinwatching include the **WWF** (www.panda.org).

These gentle mammals can be seen at **Kampi**, about 15km north of Kratie (on the road to Sambor). A return moto/remork ride costs about US$5/10, depending on how long the driver has to wait and whether you stop off at **Phnom Sombok**, a 70m-high hill with an active wat and fine Mekong views. Cycling is also an option.

Motorboats shuttle visitors out to the middle of the river to view the dolphins at close quarters. It costs US$9 per person for one to two persons and US$7 per person for groups of three or more. Encourage the boat driver to use the engine as little as possible once near the dolphins, as the noise is sure to disturb them. The best viewing times are in the morning and late afternoon.

Wat Roka Kandal TEMPLE

(www.cambodian-craft.com; admission 2000r) Serene little Wat Roka Kandal, 2km south of Kratie on the road to Chhlong, was built about two centuries ago and is the only extant Khmer pagoda of its type. To see the beautifully restored interior, which serves as a showroom for local wicker handicrafts, ask around for someone with the key.

The riverside road heading south from here towards Chhlong makes for a nice **bicycle ride**.

Sleeping

As well as the guesthouses and hotels covered here, there are also homestays and an upmarket lodge on the island of Koh Trong opposite Kratie town.

You Hong II Guesthouse GUESTHOUSE $

(☎085 885168; youhong_kratie@yahoo.com; 119 Ph 10; r US$5-13;) A great little shoes-off

WORTH A TRIP

KOH TRONG – AN ISLAND IN THE MEKONG

Lying just across the water from Kratie is the island of Koh Trong, an almighty sandbar in the middle of the river. Cross here by boat and enjoy a slice of rural island life. This could be the Don Det of Cambodia in years to come and attractions include an **old stupa** and a small **floating village**, as well as the chance to encounter one of the rare **Mekong mud turtles** that inhabit the western shore.

There are two homestays on the island. Best is **Koh Trong Community Homestay I** (per person US$4), set in an old wooden house, offering two proper bedrooms and fancy-pants bathrooms, meaning thrones not squats. It is located about 2km north of the ferry dock.

Sala Koh Trong (☎012 938984; www.kohtrong.com; r US$30-60) is a new lodge with attractive bungalows providing the best accommodation in the Kratie region. A swimming pool is planned for 2012. It's located at the northern tip of the island.

Catch the little ferry from the port (with/without bicycle 1000/500r). Bicycle rental is available on the island for US$1.

guesthouse between the market and riverfront. As well as a good mix of rooms, there's a lively little bar-restaurant plastered wall-to-wall with travel info, and internet access.

Balcony Guesthouse GUESTHOUSE $
(☎016 604036; balcony@y7mail.com; Rue Preah Suramarit; r US$7-15;) The sign proclaims it a Gust House, but don't be put off by the windbags, as this place attracts some bright young things thanks to good-value rooms, a gay-friendly vibe and impressive food.

Oudom Sambath Hotel HOTEL $
(☎971502; 439 Rue Preah Suramarit; r US$8-20;) Long one of the smartest hotels in town, with a popular breakfast restaurant downstairs. Fan rooms are a good deal, but it's a long hike to the upper floors.

Star Guesthouse GUESTHOUSE $
(☎017 491906; khmermao@yahoo.com; Ph 10; r US$3-5;) Back under the stewardship of the original family, this budget crash pad looks set to take off again thanks to cheap rooms and wholesome meals.

Eating & Drinking

Along the riverfront, **food stalls** (Rue Preah Suramarit) sell two famous Kratie specialities: *krolan* (sticky rice, beans and coconut milk steamed inside a bamboo tube), displayed on tables that look like miniature church organs; and *nehm* (tangy, raw, spiced river fish wrapped in edible fresh leaves that are in turn wrapped in a cube of banana leaves).

Red Sun Falling INTERNATIONAL $
(Rue Preah Suramarit; mains 6000-14,000r) One of the liveliest spots in town, with a relaxed cafe ambience, used books for sale and Asian and Western meals, including home-made brownies. By night it's a bar.

Information

Kratie is laid out on a grid, with Rue Preah Suramarit running along the river and, at right angles, numbered streets heading inland. The market is one block inland between Ph 8 and Ph 10.

Cambodian Pride Tours (www.cambodianpridetours.com) Local tours website operated by two enthusiastic young guides from the Kratie area keen to promote real-life experiences.

Canadia Bank (Ph 11 & Preah Mohaksat Iranie Kosomak) Two blocks inland; includes an ATM.

Ly Kheang Web (Ph 10; 7am-9.30pm) One block inland; reliable internet.

Mekong Discovery Trail Office (cnr Rue Preah Suramarit & Ph 13) Supposedly located inside the Department of Tourism building, but rarely open.

Getting There & Around

Kratie is 348km northeast of Phnom Penh (250km via Chhlong) and 141km south of Stung Treng.

Express minivans, which pick you up from your guesthouse at 6am, are the fastest and most comfortable way to Phnom Penh (US$8, four hours). Buses depart from along the riverfront around Ph 8 and Ph 10. **GST**, **Phnom Penh Sorya** and **Rith Mony** operate buses to Phnom Penh (25,000r, six hours) via Snuol (US$2) and Kompong Cham (US$4, three hours); Stung Treng (20,000r, two hours); Ban Lung (US$10, six hours) in Ratanakiri; and Sen Monorom (25,000r) in Mondulkiri. There are also direct buses to Pakse (US$17, 12.30pm) in southern Laos.

Share taxis gather just north of the market, at Ph 7. Travelling via Chhlong (NH73) rather than along NH7, they can make it to Phnom Penh (US$10) in as little as four hours. Other destinations include Snuol (10,000r), Kompong Cham (30,000r) and Stung Treng (25,000r).

Hiring a moto driver costs US$10 a day plus petrol. Most guesthouses can arrange a motorbike (US$6 a day). Bicycles (6000r per day) are available from **Rent Bike** (124 Rue Preah Sihanouk; ⏲6am-6pm), facing the post office.

Stung Treng Province

A particularly beautiful and environmentally rich stretch of the Mekong flows through Stung Treng.

STUNG TRENG

☎074 / POP 28,000

Stung Treng is a relaxed provincial capital on the banks of the Sekong (Tonlé San), which flows into the Mekong just west of the city. While there is almost nothing to do here, it makes a good base for exploring the many Mekong islands upriver towards Laos.

Sights & Activities

See the entire silk-making process, from rearing silkworms to dyeing and hand-loom weaving, at NGO-run **Mekong Blue** (☎012 622096; www.mekongblue.com; ⏲7.30-11.30am & 1.30-5pm Mon-Sat), 4km east of town (4000r by moto).

A handful of **Irrawaddy dolphins** live in the Mekong up towards the Lao border. Talk to the Riverside Guesthouse's restaurant about speedboat excursions (US$80 for up to four people) to observe them and visit **waterfalls, islands** and Ramsar-recognised **wetlands**. The northern village of **O'Svay** provides a gateway to several ecotourism initiatives including kayaking out to a pod of rare Irrawaddy dolphins near the Laos border, passing islands, waterfalls, and bird-infested wetlands on the way.

Sleeping & Eating

TOP CHOICE **Tonlé Tourism Training Centre** GUESTHOUSE $
(☎973638; fieldco@tourismforhelp.org; s/d from US$6/8) Located on the riverfront about 500m west of the ferry dock, this small guesthouse doubles as a training centre to help underprivileged locals get a start in the tourism industry. Rooms are simple but tastefully furnished. The restaurant serves tasty Khmer dishes.

Golden River Hotel HOTEL $
(☎973790; r US$15-35; ❄@📶) The smartest hotel in town by a country mile. Set on the riverfront, it has the province's only lift and 50 well-appointed rooms, many with panoramic views.

Riverside Guesthouse GUESTHOUSE $
(☎012 439454; riverside.tour@yahoo.com; r US$5-7; @) Overlooking the riverfront area, the Riverside is a popular travellers' crossroads. Rooms are basic, but so are the prices. Good for travel information and there is a popular bar-restaurant downstairs.

THE MEKONG DISCOVERY TRAIL

The **Mekong Discovery Trail** (www.mekongdiscoverytrail.com) is a new initiative to open up stretches of the Mekong River around Stung Treng and Kratie to community-based tourism. The project deserves support, as it intends to provide fishing communities with an alternative income in order to protect the Irrawaddy dolphin and other rare species on this stretch of river.

An excellent booklet outlining half-day to several-day excursions around Kratie is available in some guesthouses, hotels and restaurants in Kratie and Stung Treng. Ideal for cycling, it is being signposted so that travellers interested in pedalling their way through a slice of rural life can follow the trail for a few hours or several days, overnighting in village **homestays**. This stretch of the Mekong includes two 'biodiversity hotspots': the trail's northernmost section traverses Ramsar-recognised wetlands. Routes criss-cross the Mekong frequently by ferry and traverse several Mekong islands, including Koh Trong (boxed text, p236).

As well as homestays on Koh Trong, the **Cambodian Rural Development Team** (CRDT; ☎072 633 3644; www.crdt.org.kh; 695 Ph 2, Kratie) can arrange homestays on **Koh Pdao**, an island 35km north of Kratie, and less popular **Koh Preah**, in southern Stung Treng province. Participants do some serious interacting with locals and even get their hands dirty on volunteer building or farming projects. Diversions include cycling and dolphinspotting from the shore. It costs US$35/50 for one/two nights including all meals and transport.

GETTING TO LAOS: TRAPEANG KRIEL TO DONG KALAW

Minibuses link Kratie and Stung Treng (64km south of the frontier along smoothly paved NH7) with **Trapeang Kriel** (8am-5pm) and Laotian destinations further north. From Stung Treng there are minibuses (US$5) heading north to the border at around 7am and again after lunch (some continuing to Pakse). Onward transport is not easily available at the border so book a minibus at far as Don Det (US$9 from Stung Treng).

Cambodian (US$20) and Lao visas (US$30 to US$42 depending on nationality) are available at the border, but petty overcharging is common on both sides. The Laotians charge an 'overtime' fee if you pass through after 'working hours', ie on weekends, holidays or after 4pm.

For information on crossing in the other direction, see the boxed text, p348.

Ponika's Place INTERNATIONAL $
(mains US$2-5) Need a break from *làap* after Laos? Burgers, pizza and English breakfast grace the menu, along with Indian food and wonderful Khmer curries. Owner Ponika speaks English.

Information

Acleda Bank Has an ATM; half a block east of the market.

Internet Service (7am-7pm) Internet access next to the GST bus office.

Mlup Baitong (012 425172; www.mlup.org) NGO that organises dolphinwatching trips and homestays along the Mekong Discovery Trail.

Riverside Guesthouse Specialises in transport around the northeast, plus boat trips to Kratie (four hours) and to the Lao border via the resident dolphin pod.

Xplore-Asia (012 675413) Offers cycling-and-kayak combo tours. Kayaks (US$30), motorbikes (US$7) and Trek mountain bikes (US$5) for rent.

Tourist Information Centre (638 8867; 8-11am & 2.30-4pm) Inconveniently located near the new bridge, it's run by the helpful Theany, who also works at Xplore-Asia.

Getting There & Away

Rith Mony, **Phnom Penh Sorya** and **GST** all have 7am buses to Phnom Penh (US$8 to US$10, nine hours) via Kratie (20,000r, two hours) and Kompong Cham (30,000r, six hours). Rith Mony has a 3pm bus to Ban Lung (US$5).

From the riverfront taxi park, share taxis and minibuses go to Phnom Penh (50,000r, eight hours) and Ban Lung (30,000r, four hours).

Ratanakiri Province

Up-and-coming Ratanakiri is making a name for itself as a diverse region of outstanding natural beauty that's also a remote home for a mosaic of minority peoples – Jarai, Tampuen, Brau and Kreung – with their own languages, traditions and customs.

Adrenalin activities abound. Swim in clear volcanic lakes, shower under waterfalls, or trek in the vast Virachey National Park, it's all here. Tourism looks all set to take off, but that's if the lowland politicians and generals don't plunder the place first. Ratanakiri is the frontline in the battle for land, and the slash-and-burn minorities are losing out thanks to their tradition of collective ownership. Hopefully someone wakes up and smells the coffee – there's plenty of that as well – before it's too late.

BAN LUNG

075 / POP 25,000

Affectionately known as '*dey krahorm*' (red earth) after its rust-coloured affliction, Ban Lung provides a popular base for a range of Ratanakiri romps. It is one of the easiest places in Cambodia to arrange a jungle trek and has several beautiful lakes and waterfalls nearby (see p241). Members of highland minorities, woven baskets on their backs, come from nearby villages to buy and sell at the market.

Sights

Boeng Yeak Laom LAKE
(admission US$1) Boeng Yeak Laom is one of the most serene and sublimely beautiful sites in all of Cambodia. This clear blue crater lake, surrounded by dark green jungle, is sacred to the indigenous minority peoples. It's a great place to take a dip, although Cambodians jump in fully clothed. The NGO-run **Cultural & Environmental Centre** (8am-5.30pm), 500m around the lake, displays traditional Tampuen crafts. The adjacent **kiosk** sells au-

Ban Lung

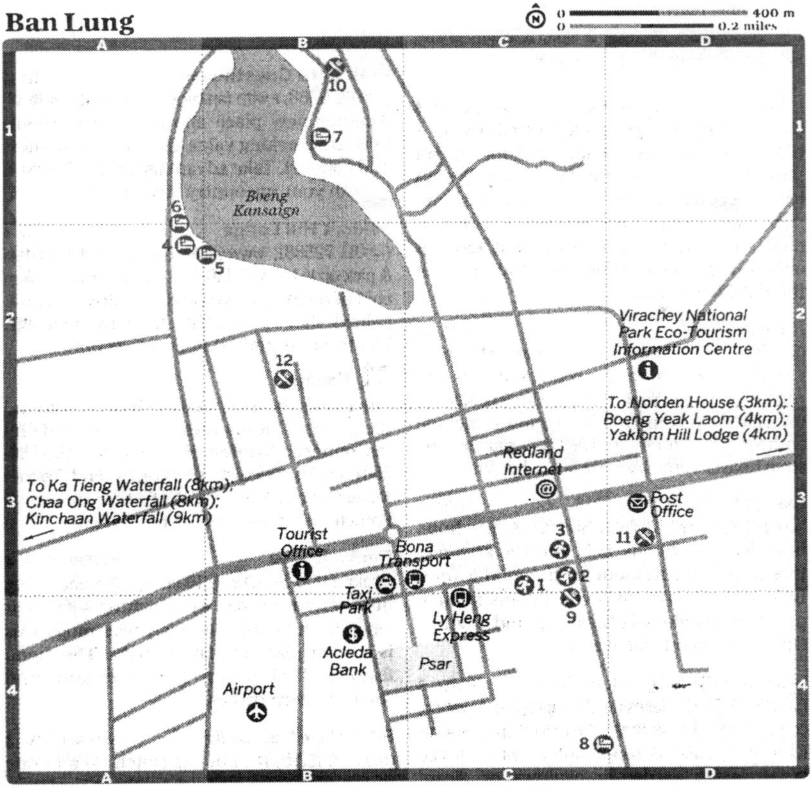

Ban Lung

Activities, Courses & Tours

1 Dutch Couple C3
2 Parrot Tours C3
3 Smiling Tours C3

Sleeping

4 Lakeside Chheng Lok Hotel A2
5 Lakeside Hotel B2
6 Prak Dara Guesthouse A1
7 Terres Rouges Lodge B1
8 Tree Top Ecolodge C4

Eating

9 A'Dam Restaurant C4
10 Coconut Shake Restaurant B1
11 Gecko House D3
12 Lay Lay Restaurant B2
Rik's Cafe Cambodge .... (see 1)
Terres Rouges Lodge .... (see 7)

thentic Tampuen crafts and rents inner tubes (3000r).

Boeng Yeak Laom is 4km east of Ban Lung; turn right at the statue of the minority family. Motos cost about US$4 return, a bit more if the driver has to wait around.

Sleeping

TOP CHOICE **Terres Rouges Lodge** BOUTIQUE HOTEL $$

(974051; www.ratanakiri-lodge.com; r US$40-
) In a gorgeous lakeshore g
this atmospheric complex has 2
including superb Balinese-style

with open-plan bathrooms and antique decor. Amenities include a spa, Khmer sauna and an inviting swimming pool.

TOP CHOICE Tree Top Ecolodge GUESTHOUSE $
(☑012 490333; www.treetop-ecolodge.com; r US$7-15; ☎) Setting the standard for budget digs in the northeast, rough-hewn walkways lead to all-wood bungalows with mosquito nets, thatch roofs and verandahs with verdant valley views. The restaurant dangles over a lush ravine, affording great views of the hillside beyond.

Norden House LODGE $$
(☑690 0640; www.nordenhouseyaklom.com; r US$25; ✹☺) In a peaceful spot on the road to Boeng Yeak Laom, the six stylish international-standard bungalows include embroidered linens and a DVD player. The smart bathrooms include solar hot water.

Lakeside Hotel HOTEL $
(☑012 233312; r US$10-25; ✹☺☎) A new hotel next door to Chheng Lok, and the architecture is an improvement on the mod-Khmer that predominates in town. Rooms include nice touches like silk hangings and a kettle. Opt for a balcony lakeview.

Lakeside Chheng Lok Hotel HOTEL $
(☑012 957422; lakeside-chhenglokhotel@yahoo.com; r US$5-20; ✹☺☎) Overlooking Boeng Kansaign, this 65-room hotel has a choice of attractive garden bungalows or clean,

spacious rooms, all with cable TV. Good all-rounder.

Prak Dara Guesthouse HOTEL $
(☑666 6068; r with fan/air-con US$6/10; ✹☺☎) Another new place above the lake, rooms here are cracking value given the cleanliness and comfort. Take advantage of the free wi-fi to plan your upcountry adventures.

Yaklom Hill Lodge ECOLODGE $
(☑011 725881; www.yaklom.com; r incl breakfast & pick-up in town US$10-20) In lush forest 5km east of town, this ecolodge has all-wood bungalows that are starting to show their age. Electricity is limited to evenings only.

🍴 Eating

Ban Lung's cheapest food can be found around the market. Guesthouses offer some good dining options: **Norden House** (mains US$5.50-7.50) serves Swedish specialities and **Terres Rouges Lodge** (mains US$4.50-13) serves some French dishes, as well as Khmer ones.

Gecko House INTERNATIONAL $
(mains 6000-18,000r; ☺10am-11pm) A charming little restaurant-bar with inviting sofas, soft lighting and famously frosty beer mugs, this is a great place by day or night. The menu features Thai tastes, Khmer classics and some Western dishes.

Rik's Cafe Cambodge INTERNATIONAL $
(mains US$2-5) Run by the Dutch Couple, one of the more experienced trekking outfits in

RESPONSIBLE TREKKING AROUND RATANAKIRI

Overnight trekking has really started to take off around Ratanakiri but make sure you link up with a guide who is culturally and ecologically sensitive and is clear about your expectations. Popular routes take in minority villages, including Kreung villages near the road to Ta Veng and Jarai villages up in Andong Meas district. Only official national-park rangers can take you into Virachey National Park. With deforestation continuing apace, last year's lush forest may be this year's barren expanse of tree stumps.

A newly formed association of **Tampuen guides** (yeak.loam@yahoo.com) is a good source when looking for an indigenous guide. The association also runs an exclusive tour of several Tampuen villages around Boeng Yeak Laom.

Ban Lung places that run their own treks include Tree Top, Terres Rouges and Yaklom Hill Lodge; Norden House is the place to go for motorcycle tours. Day hikes, elephant rides, kayaking and overnight treks are offered by a number of tour companies:

» **Dutch Couple** (☑097 679 2714; www.trekkingcambodia.com; ☺Oct-Aug) One of the most experienced trekking operators in the province, run by — wait for it — a friendly Dutch couple.

» **Parrot Tours** (☑012 764714; www.jungletrek.blogspot.com) Sitha Nan is a national-park-trained guide with expert local knowledge.

» **Smiling Tours** (☑012 247713; smeyadventure@gmail.com) Smey often hangs out at Tree Top Ecolodge and offers a range of trips and treks.

Ratanakiri (see boxed text, p240), this relaxed cafe offers great valley views. Good for coffee and light bites by day and a spot of pre- or post-trek beer drinking by night.

A'Dam Restaurant INTERNATIONAL $
(mains US$2-4; ⏲11am-3pm & 5.30pm-midnight) This mellow restaurant warmly welcomes locals, expats and travellers, and is an animated bar by night thanks to a pool table and dartboard to tempt barflies.

Lay Lay Restaurant ASIAN $
(meals 4000-20,000r; ⏲7am-10pm) A new restaurant set in a cavernous yellow-green complex off the main drag, the extensive menu includes tasty Khmer, Chinese and Asian dishes.

Coconut Shake Restaurant CAFE $
(northeast cnr of Boeng Kansaign; meals 4000-10,000r; ⏲7am-8pm) The best coconut shakes in the northeast. Dare to try the 'fish and ship' or the 'friend toes' (French toast?).

Information

For recommended tour companies, see the boxed text on p240. Check out www.yaklom.com for ideas on what to do around Ratanakiri.

Acleda Bank Has an ATM.

Redland Internet Café (⏲7am-8pm)

Tourist Information Centre (☎974125; ⏲7.30-11.30am & 2-5pm Mon-Fri) Has brochures on Ratanakiri.

Getting There & Around

Ban Lung is 588km northeast of Phnom Penh and 150km east of Stung Treng. The road between Ban Lung and O Pong Moan on NH7 was still under construction at the time of writing.

Buses to Phnom Penh (US$10, 11 hours) operate only in the dry season. Hong Ly, Rith Mony and Ly Heng Express make the trip, with early morning departures in either direction via Kratie, Snuol and Kompong Cham.

Speedy express minibus services offer guesthouse pick ups at 6am and take the shortcut to Phnom Penh via Chhlong (US$12, nine hours). Try Ly Heng Express or **Bona Transport** (☎012-567161).

Share taxis go from the taxi park to Kratie (US$10 to US$12.50) and Phnom Penh (US$15 to US$17.50, seven hours). Pick-ups are slightly cheaper if you ride out back.

Tree Top Ecolodge can arrange transport to Laos.

For details on the punishing overland trip to Sen Monorom, see the boxed text, p243.

Most guesthouses and hotels offer motorbike rentals from US$5 to US$7. Norden House rents out 250cc dirt bikes (US$25 per day). 4WDs start from US$50 and rise depending on the distance travelled.

> **GETTING TO VIETNAM: O YADAW TO LE THANH**
>
> Remote and rarely used by foreigners this **border crossing** (⏲7am-5pm) lies 64km from Ban Lung and 90km from Pleiku, Vietnam for onward connections to Hoi An or Quy Nhon. Visas are available on arrival in Cambodia, but not in Vietnam. From Ban Lung, take a through minibus to the O Yadaw border (30,000r, 7.30am). On the Vietnamese side of the frontier, *xe oms* (motos) await to take you to Duc Co (20km), where there are buses (20,000d) to Pleiku.
>
> For information on crossing this border in the other direction, see p117.

AROUND BAN LUNG

WATERFALLS

Within 10km of Ban Lung, you can visit spectacular **Chaa Ong**, set in a jungle gorge; **Ka Tieng** (Kateng), with a rock shelf that offers the opportunity to clamber behind and vines to swing over the splashpool; and **Kinchaan** (Kachanh). Directions are signposted 3km west of town on the road to Stung Treng and admission to each is 2000r.

VOEN SAI

Situated 37km (1½ hours) northwest of Ban Lung, Voen Sai is on the banks of the Tonlé San about 15km south of Virachey National Park. A ferry (500r) links a cluster of eateries with the river's northern bank.

The Khmer Leu (Upper Khmer or ethnic minorities) of Ratanakiri bury their dead amid the ancient jungle, carving wooden effigies of the deceased – some holding sunglasses and mobile phones – to stand guard over the graves. In the village of **Kachon**, a 40-minute long-tailed motorboat ride upriver from Voen Sai, you can visit a **Tampuen cemetery** (admission US$1). The boat trip from Voen Sai costs US$15 for up to three people, including stops at an orderly **Chinese village** five minutes downriver from Voen Sai, and a nearby **Lao village**.

Voen Sai is 37km northwest of Ban Lung on an average-to-poor road, passable only by 4WD in the wet season.

TREKKING IN VIRACHEY NATIONAL PARK

Cambodia's most developed ecotourism program takes visitors deep into 3325-sq-km **Virachey National Park** (admission US$5), an ecological gem in the country's far northeastern tip that's so remote it has yet to be fully explored. The park's forests and grasslands are home to elephants, gibbons and an amazing variety of birds, including hornbills and vultures. The area was once traversed by the Ho Chi Minh Trail and war relics are still lying around.

There are two treks available in Virachey. Prices listed are per-person for a group of two and include transport by moto to the trailhead, park admission, food, guides, porters, hammocks and boat transport where necessary. Prices rise for smaller groups or individuals.

» **Kalang Chhouy Sacred Mountain Trek** (2 days/1 night from US$59) This short trek starts from near Koklak village and includes a night by the Chai Chanang Waterfall. On the second day, continue to Phnom Gong, a sacred mountain for the Brau people, and swim at the Tju Preah rapids.

» **Phnom Veal Thom Wilderness Trek** (7/8 days from US$258/286) The longest trek starts from Ta Veng with an overnight homestay in a Brau village. The trek goes deep into the heart of the Phnom Veal Thom grasslands, an area rich in wildlife such as Sambar deer, gibbon, langur, wild pig, bear and hornbill.

Bookings must be made at least a day or two ahead, via the park's official **Eco-Tourism Information Centre** (☎075 974176, virachey@camintel.com; ⊙8-11.30am & 2-3pm Mon-Fri) in Ban Lung.

Mondulkiri Province

Mondulkiri (Meeting of the Hills), the original Wild East of the country, is a world apart from the lowlands with not a rice paddy or palm tree in sight. Home to the hardy Bunong people and their noble elephants, this upland area is a seductive mix of grassy hills, pine groves and rainforests of jade green. Conservationists have grand plans for the sparsely populated province but are facing off against loggers, poachers, prospectors and well-connected speculators.

SEN MONOROM

☎073 / POP 10,000

A charming community where the famous hills meet, the area around Sen Monorom is peppered with minority villages and picturesque waterfalls, making it the ideal place to spend some time. Many Bunong people from nearby villages come to Sen Monorom to trade and the distinctive baskets they carry on their backs make them easy to spot. Set at more than 800m, the town can get quite chilly so bring warm clothing.

Sights & Activities

Not much happens in Sen Monorom itself but there's plenty to see and do nearby, including trips out to **Bunong villages** and **waterfalls**.

Head to the observation deck of **Phnom Bai Chuw** (Raw Rice Mountain), 6km northwest of Sen Monorom (accessible on foot or by moto), for a jaw-dropping view of the emerald forest, known to locals as **Samot Cheur** (Ocean of Trees).

Sleeping

TOP CHOICE **Nature Lodge** GUESTHOUSE $
(☎012 230272; www.naturelodgecambodia.com; r US$10-30) Located on a windswept hilltop near town, this quirky ecoresort has basic bungalow accommodation with hot showers and some incredible Swiss Family Robinson–style chalets. The inviting restaurant is decorated with abandoned tree trunks and has a good range of traveller fare, plus a pool table.

Emario Mondulkiri Resort HOTEL $$
(☎652 3344; r from US$35; ❄@📶) Looking rather like a bungalow retirement community beamed down to Cambodia, this resort offers the smartest rooms in Mondulkiri, with parquet flooring, comfortable beds and bathroom amenities.

Phanyro Guesthouse GUESTHOUSE $
(☎017 770867; r US$8-12) This is a favourite with visiting volunteers and NGOs, offering a clutch of cottages perched on a ridge

overlooking the river valley. Clean with a capital C.

Sum Dy Guesthouse HOTEL $
(☎099 250543; r US$12-30; ✱@☰) Once occupied by mining conglomerate BHP Billiton, the rooms include sturdy wooden beds and slick if slightly uncoordinated bathroom decor. Fan rooms are a steal for US$12.

Long Vibol Guesthouse GUESTHOUSE $
(☎012 944647; r US$5-20) An attractive wooden resort with 20 rooms set amid a lush garden; staff here are knowledgeable about the area. Includes a restaurant popular with visiting Khmers.

Eating & Drinking

All the guesthouses have restaurants. Nature Lodge is probably the best all-rounder for atmosphere and food.

Khmer Kitchen KHMER $
(mains US$2-4; ⏲6am-9pm) This unassuming streetside eatery whips up some of the most flavoursome Khmer food in the hills. The *kari saik trey* (fish coconut curry) and other curries are particularly scrumptious.

Greenhouse Restaurant INTERNATIONAL $
(mains US$1.50-3.50; ⏲6.30am-late) As well as internet access and tour information, Greenhouse is a popular place for inexpensive Khmer and Western dishes. By night, this place draws the drinkers to sup beers and cocktails against a backdrop of ambient reggae beats.

Bananas INTERNATIONAL $$
(mains US$6.50-8; ⏲9am-10pm) Set in a small banana grove, this homey restaurant-bar has, hands down, Mondulkiri's best Western cuisine, served *table d'hôte*-style, including *coq au vin* and Flemish stew.

Information

Acleda Bank An ATM is located on the road to Phnom Penh.

Bunong Place (☎012 474879; www.bunong center.org; ⏲6am-6pm) This NGO-run 'drop-in centre' for Bunong people is a good source of information on sustainable tourism, village homestays and elephant rides. Sells authentic Bunong textiles, and local coffee, sodas and beers are available. Also provides trained Bunong guides for local tours, costing US$15/25 per half-/full day, including motorbike.

Greenhouse (☎017 905659; www.green house-tour.blogspot.com) Offers internet access and the most comprehensive tour progam around the province.

Getting There & Away

NH76 to Sen Monorom is now in fantastic shape, and includes some impressive bridges across deep river valleys.

Rith Mony and Phnom Penh Sorya run morning buses to/from Phnom Penh (US$7.50, eight hours) via Snuol (US$3.75, three hours) and Kompong Cham (US$6.25, five hours). Faster morning share taxis (US$12.50) and minivans (US$10) to Phnom Penh are best reserved a day in advance.

Minivans are a good option for Kratie (30,000r, 4½ hours). Count on at least one

THE OVERLAND TRAIL RUNS DRY

Glance at a map and it seems obvious: the best way to visit both Mondulkiri and Ratanakiri without backtracking is to make a grand loop via the remote villages of Koh Nhek and Lumphat. Alas, while the road from Sen Monorom to Koh Nhek (93km) is in good shape and takes just a couple of hours, north of there – until the Tonlé Srepok River – the road vanishes into a spider's web of ox-cart trails. Over the past few years, a handful of hardcore bikers have been using this route during the dry season (wet-season travel is close to impossible), but only attempt it if you have years of biking experience and an iron backside. A local guide who knows the route, as well as spare parts for your bike, copious amounts of water and a compass, should make for a smoother journey.

A few intrepid moto drivers in both Ban Lung and Sen Monorom ply this route. The journey takes about nine hours, with a few long breaks along the way, and costs a hefty US$50 to US$70. A cheaper option is to use a minibus between Sen Monorom and Koh Nhek (15,000r) and charter a moto driver from there to Lumphat for about US$25. In the reverse direction, make your way to Lumphat and negotiate a moto south to Koh Nhek. Cheaper again but a little less adventurous is a combination of two buses via Kratie.

Work has started on upgrading the road and a new overland trail is expected to be up and running in 2013.

DON'T MISS

THE ELEPHANT VALLEY PROJECT

For an original elephant experience, visit the **Elephant Valley Project** (☎099 696041; www.elephantvalleyproject.org). The project entices local mahouts to bring their often overworked and wounded elephants to this sanctuary, where, in the words of project coordinator Jack Highwood, 'they can learn how to act like elephants again.'

Most tour companies in Mondulkiri make a point of stressing that their tours employ only humanely treated elephants. Highwood wonders whether it's possible to know the truth. 'Most elephants in Mondulkiri are in a highly abused state,' he says. 'They are beaten on the head and made to do things they aren't meant to be doing. In Mondulkiri, the elephant is basically seen as a cheap tractor.'

Highwood no longer allows visitors to ride the elephants. Instead, you simply walk with the herd through the forest and observe them in their element. In the process you learn a lot about not only elephant behaviour but also Bunong culture and forest ecology.

A two-day stay, including all meals, transport to the site and a night's accommodation in exquisite bungalows tucked into the jungle on a ridge overlooking the valley, costs US$100 per person. A day trip costs US$50, but don't show up unannounced. **Bunong Place** (☎012 474879; www.bunongcenter.org; ⊙6am-6pm) in Sen Monorom can handle bookings. Short- and long-term volunteers who want to help the project while learning mahout skills are welcome, although volunteers must pay extra to cover training costs.

early-morning departure and two or three departures around lunchtime.

Share taxis and minivans usually depart from the market, but will pick up from guesthouses and hotels on request.

Getting Around

Motorbike rental (US$5 to US$10 a day) can be arranged through guesthouses and hotels in town. Greenhouse Restaurant has 250cc dirt bikes (US$15) for rent. 4WD or pick-up rental starts from US$50 per day, depending on the destination.

AROUND SEN MONOROM

The Ho Chi Minh Trail passed through the hills of Mondulkiri and was bombed by the Americans: never touch anything that looks vaguely like unexploded ordnance.

Monorom Falls, set in the forest a walkable 3km northwest of town, is the closest thing to a public swimming pool for Sen Monorom. Motos take people out here for about US$3 return.

Two-tiered **Bou Sraa Waterfall** (admission 5000r), 35km east of Sen Monorom along an unfinished toll road, is famous throughout the country. Continuing to levy the toll, given the state of the second half of the road, seems a little impertinent. Hire a moto for the day (US$15) or charter a car (US$60) for a group.

SOUTH COAST

Cambodia's coast offers an alluring mix of tropical seaside fun and undiscovered nature: unspoilt islands, pristine mangrove forests and national parks of global ecological importance.

Koh Kong Province

Cambodia's far southwestern province, vast and sparsely populated, boasts deserted beaches, offshore islands and lush rainforests with ecotourism potential as vast as their mountains, streams and hamlets are remote.

KOH KONG CITY

☎035 / POP 35,000

Once Cambodia's Wild West, its frontier economy dominated by smuggling, prostitution and gambling, Koh Kong is striding towards respectability as ecotourists scare the sleaze away. The town serves as the gateway to the Koh Kong Conservation Corridor (p247).

Sights & Activities

Koh Kong's main draw is seeking adventure in and around the Cardamom Mountains and the Koh Kong Conservation Corridor.

Wat Neang Kok TEMPLE

A rocky promontory on the right (western) bank of the estuary is decorated with **life-size statues** demonstrating the violent punishments that await sinners in the Buddhist hell. This graphic tableau belongs to **Wat Neang Kok**, a Buddhist temple. To get there, cross the bridge and turn right 600m past the toll booth (motos cost 1200r). The statues are 150m beyond the temple.

Peam Krasaop Wildlife Sanctuary
MANGROVES

Anchored to alluvial islands – some no larger than a house – the millions of magnificent mangroves of this 260-sq-km sanctuary's protect the coast from erosion, serve as a vital breeding and feeding ground for fish, shrimp and shellfish, and provide a home to myriad birds (see www.ramsar.org). The area, which is part of the Koh Kong Conservation Corridor, is all the more valuable from an ecological standpoint because similar forests in Thailand have been trashed by short-sighted development.

To get a feel for the delicate mangrove ecosystem – and to understand how mangrove roots can stop a tsunami dead in its tracks – head to the 600m-long concrete **mangrove walk** (admission 5000r; ⏲6.30am-6pm), which wends its way above the briny waters to a 15m observation tower. The walk begins at the sanctuary entrance, about 5.5km southeast of the city centre. A moto/remork costs US$5/10 return.

Unfortunately, a new resort has built 30 stilted bungalows amid the mangroves near the sanctuary entrance. The resort is a shrine to wood-crete that falls well short of blending with the beauty of the surroundings.

You can avoid confronting this eyesore by hiring a motorboat to take you through the park. Wooden boats are available for hire near the observation tower (per hour US$10), but a better plan is to take a boat tour out of Koh Kong proper.

Tours

Boat tours are excellent way to view Koh Kong's many coastal attractions. If you speak some Khmer you can try hiring open-top fibreglass outboards at the boat dock (at the corner of Ph 1 and Ph 9), but it's easier and not much more expensive to take an organised tour. Most guesthouses can arrange these. Popular destinations include Koh Kong Island via Peam Krasaop Wildlife Sanctuary (full day per person including lunch US$25), and Koh Por Waterfall (four-/eight-person speedboat US$45/60). There's a good chance of spotting endangered Irrawaddy dolphins early in the morning en route to Koh Kong Island. Bring sunscreen, a hat and plenty of bottled water.

Recommended operators for boat and other tours:

Koh Kong Eco Tours (☎012 707719; oasis resort@netkhmer.com; Ph 3) Rithy's excursions include boat tours, birdwatching, guided mountain-biking odysseys (full day per person including food US$30), and a two-day/one-night hike in the Cardamoms (per person including food costs US$60).

Blue Moon Guesthouse (p246) Mr Neat, a former park ranger, offers a range of boat trips (dry season only) and other tours.

Sleeping

TOP CHOICE Oasis Bungalow Resort
RESORT $$

(☎092 228342; http://oasisresort.netkhmer.com; d/tr US$25/30;) In a quiet rural area 2km north of the centre, this oasis of calm has a gorgeous infinity pool with views of the Cardamoms and five cheerful, spacious bungalows with all the amenities. Blue signs point the way from Acleda Bank.

Koh Kong City Hotel
HOTEL $

(☎936777; http://kkcthotel.netkhmer.com; Ph 1; d US$15-20;) Ludicrous value for what you get: a huge bathroom, two double beds, 50 TV channels, full complement of toiletries, free H2O and – in the US$20 rooms – glorious river views.

Paddy's Bamboo Guesthouse
GUESTHOUSE $

(☎015 533223; ppkohkong@gmail.com; dm US$2, r US$4-6;) Paddy's targets backpackers with a (planned) dormitory, basic rooms, a balcony for chillin', a pool table and tours. Shoot for the wood-floored rooms with shared bathrooms upstairs.

Koh Kong Guesthouse
GUESTHOUSE $

(☎015 522005; Ph 1; d without/with bathroom US$5/6;) This great budget choice has woody rooms sharing a bathroom upstairs off an appealing common area with river views and floor pillows. Concrete rooms downstairs are less appealing.

Asian Hotel
HOTEL $

(☎936667; www.asiankohkong.com; Ph 1; r US$15-20;) A virtual clone of the newer City Hotel across the street, only with views of City Hotel instead of the river.

Koh Kong City

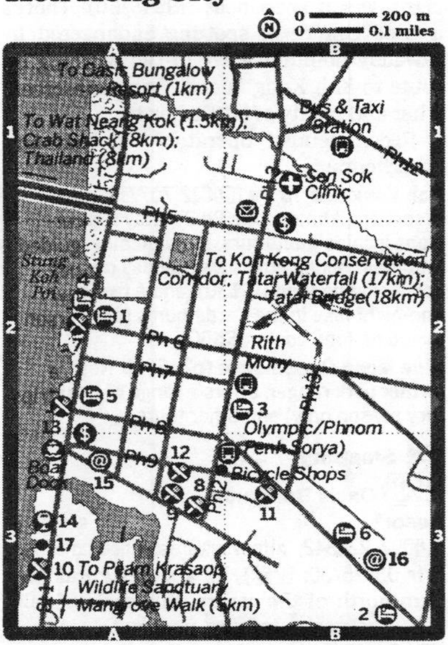

Dugout Hotel GUESTHOUSE $
(☎936220; thedugouthotel@yahoo.com; Ph 3; r with fan/air-con US$10/14; ❄✉) Smack in the centre of town, it's another nice value place, just a small step down in cleanliness and amenities from the Asian Hotel. Five of the rooms are arrayed around a small pool.

Blue Moon Guesthouse GUESTHOUSE $
(☎012 575741; bluemoonkohkong@yahoo.com; r with fan/air-con US$6/10; ❄📶) Nine neat, clean rooms with spiffy furnishings and hot water line a long, narrow courtyard. It's off the street so peace and quiet is a real possibility.

✕ Eating & Drinking

The best cheap food stalls are in the southeast corner of Psar Leu (the market); fruit stalls can be found near the southwest corner. Riverfront food carts sell noodles and cans of beer for 2000r to 3000r.

TOP CHOICE **Café Laurent** INTERNATIONAL $
(Ph 1; mains US$4-7; ⊙7am-midnight; ❄📶) This chic, French-style cafe and restaurant has an old Citroën Deux Chevaux out front and refined Western and Khmer cuisine inside. Add seating in over-water pavilions and it's a slam dunk as Koh Kong's top restaurant.

Koh Kong City

Activities, Courses & Tours

Koh Kong Eco Tours ....(see 3)

Sleeping

1 Asian Hotel A2
2 Blue Moon Guesthouse B3
3 Dugout Hotel B2
4 Koh Kong City Hotel A2
5 Koh Kong Guesthouse A2
6 Paddy's Bamboo Guesthouse B3

Eating

Asian Hotel Minimart ....(see 1)
Blue Moon Shop ....(see 2)
7 Café Laurent A2
8 Food Stalls A3
9 Fruit Stalls A3
Ice Cream Shop ....(see 5)
10 Le Phnom A3
11 Paddy's Bamboo Pub B3
12 Psar Leu A3
13 Riverfront Food Stalls A2

Drinking

14 Aqua Sunset Bar A3
Paddy's Bamboo Pub ....(see 11)

Information

15 Mary Internet A3
16 Resmey Angkor Internet Corporation B3

Transport

17 Dive Inn A3
Virak Buntham Bus Office ....(see 3)

Le Phnom CAMBODIAN $
(Ph 1; meals US$2-4; ⊙9am-10pm) The speciality at this authentic Khmer eatery is *banh chhev* – meat, herbs and other goodies wrapped inside a pancake wrapped inside a lettuce leaf and hand-dipped in sweet sauce.

Crab Shack CRAB SHACK $
(Koh Yor Beach; mains US$3-5) A family-run place on a lonely, windswept stretch of beach 7km southwest of town. It's known for perfect sunsets and heaping portions of fried crab with pepper (by request).

Ice Cream Shop CAFE $
(Ph 1; mains US$2-4) Popular Bob's Bar has moved to the riverfront under a new name. Don't be fooled: while the ice cream,

imported from Thailand, is great, it's mainly a bar and restaurant.

Paddy's Bamboo Pub PUB $
(mains US$2-3) Paddy's angles for the backpacker market with US$1 beers and affordable Khmer food.

Aqua Sunset Bar PUB $
(Ph 1; snacks & sandwiches US$2-4) It's mystifyingly quiet given its attractive wood decor, pool table and breezy riverside locale. Nonetheless, a worthy spot for a sundowner.

Self caterers can purchase snacks and drinks at the **Asian Hotel Minimart** (Ph 1; ⊙7am-11pm) and fancier Western meats and other goodies at the **Blue Moon Shop** (⊙7am-9pm).

Information

Guesthouses, hotels and pubs are the best places to get the local low-down. Thai baht are widely used so there's no urgent need to change baht into dollars or riels. To do so, use one of the many Hello mobile phone shops around Psar Leu – look for blue-and-yellow signs and glass counters with little piles of banknotes inside. Moto drivers who offer to help you change money are probably setting you up for a rip-off.

Acleda Bank (cnr Ph 3 & Ph 5) ATM accepts Visa cards.

Canadia Bank (Ph 1) New bank with ATM accepting most Western plastic.

Mary Internet (Ph 2; per hr 40B; ⊙7am or 8am-9pm) Has five computers.

Resmey Angkor Computer Corporation (per hr 3000r; ⊙8am-9pm) Lofty name for a modest internet cafe.

Sen Sok Clinic (☎012 555060; kkpao@camintel.com; cnr Ph 3 & Ph 5; ⊙24hr) Has doctors who speak English and French.

Getting There & Around

Rith Mony (☎015 558185; Ph 3), **Olympic/Phnom Penh Sorya** (☎012 308014; Ph 3) and **Virak-Buntham** (☎6363900; Ph 3) each run two or three buses to Phnom Penh (US$7, five hours, last trips at 11.30am) and one or two trips to Sihanoukville (US$7, four hours). Trips to Kampot (US$12, four hours) and Kep (US$14, 4½ hours) involve a change or two.

Most buses pick up passengers in town but may drop you off at Koh Kong's unpaved **bus station** (Ph 12), where motos and remorks await, eager to overcharge tourists. Don't pay more than US$1 to US$2 (preferably less) for a moto/remork into the centre.

From the **taxi station** next to the bus station, shared taxis head to Phnom Penh (US$11, 3½ hours) and occasionally to Sihanoukville (US$10, three hours). Travel agents can easily set you up with shared or private taxis (to Phnom Penh/Sihanoukville US$55/50).

Paddy's Bamboo Guesthouse (per day US$1) and **Dive Inn** (Ph 1; US$2) rent out cheap bicycles, while **Koh Kong Eco Tour** (US$10) has fancier mountain bikes. Motorbike hire is available from most guesthouses and from Koh Kong Eco Tour for US$5.

KOH KONG CONSERVATION CORRIDOR

Stretching along both sides of NH48 from Koh Kong to the Gulf of Kompong Som (the bay north of Sihanoukville), the Koh Kong Conservation Corridor encompasses many of Cambodia's most outstanding natural sites, including the most extensive mangrove forests on mainland Southeast Asia and the southern reaches of the fabled **Cardamom Mountains,** an area of breathtaking beauty and astonishing biodiversity.

While forests and coastlines elsewhere in Southeast Asia were dramatically altered by developers and well-connected logging companies, the Cardamom Mountains and the adjacent mangrove forests were protected from much of this due to their sheer remoteness and, at least in part, by Cambodia's long civil war. As a result, much of the area is still in pretty good shape, ecologically speaking.

The next few years will be critical in determining the future of the Cardamom Mountains. NGOs such as **Conservation International** (www.conservation.org), **Flora &**

GETTING TO THAILAND: CHAM YEAM TO HAT LEK

To travel the 8km from Koh Kong to the Thai border, a private taxi costs about US$8, while a moto/remork can be had for US$3/6. On the Thai side minibuses can take you to Trat, where you can connect to Ko Chang.

Cambodian officials at this border often try to charge tourists coming over from Thailand an unwarranted US$2 to US$5 service charge on top of the standard US$20 visa fee. If you are faced with this charge, you should refuse to pay it and eventually they will let you go through.

For information on crossing this border in the other direction, see the boxed text, p387.

WORTH A TRIP

CHI PHAT

Once notorious for its loggers and poachers, Chi Phat is now home to a pioneering **community-based ecotourism project** (CBET; www.ecoadventurecambodia.com) offering hardy travellers a unique opportunity to explore the Cardamoms ecosystem while contributing to its protection. Visitors can take day treks through the jungle, go sunrise birdwatching by boat, mountain bike to several sets of rapids, and look for monkeys and hornbills with a former poacher as a guide (US$6 to US$10 per day). Also possible are one- to five-night mountain-bike trips and jungle treks deep into the Cardamoms (US$30 per day, including guide and food). In the village, visitors can relax by playing volleyball, badminton or pool with the locals.

Basic accommodation options in Chi Phat include nine CBET-member guesthouses (US$5 per person) and eight homestays (US$3 per person). Reserve through the **CBET office** (☎092 720925; ecotourism@wildlifealliance.org) in Chi Phat.

Chi Phat is on the Preak Piphot River 21km upriver from Andoung Tuek, which is 98km east of Koh Kong on NH48 (any Koh Kong–bound bus can drop you in Andoung Tuek). From Andoung Tuek to Chi Phat it's a two-hour boat ride or a one-hour motorbike ride on an unpaved but smooth road. Call the CBET office to arrange a boat (US$25 for a four-passenger boat) or moto (US$5 to US$7).

Fauna International (www.fauna-flora.org) and the **Wildlife Alliance** (www.wildlifealliance.org) are working to help protect the region's 16 distinct ecosystems from loggers and poachers. Ecotourism, too, can play a role in spurring sustainable development by generating income for local people, which is why the Wildlife Alliance is launching a project to transform the **Southern Cardamoms Protected Forest** (1443 sq km) into a world-class ecotourism destination.

KOH KONG ISLAND

Cambodia's largest island towers over seas so crystal clear you can make out individual grains of sand in a couple of metres of water. Its west coast shelters **seven pristine beaches** fringed with coconut palms and lush vegetation, just as you'd expect in a tropical paradise. At the **sixth beach** from the north, a narrow channel leads to a *Gilligan's Island*-style lagoon.

The island, about 25km south of Koh Kong City, is not part of any national park and thus has few protections against rampant development, which may soon arrive. The best way to get here is on a tour from Koh Kong (p245).

KOH POR WATERFALL

Upriver from Koh Kong, this waterfall pours over a stone shelf in a lovely jungle gorge, though the site's tranquillity has recently been threatened by a new road. For now, the only way to get here is by boat (see p245).

TATAI RIVER & WATERFALL

About 18km east of Koh Kong on NH48, the Phun Daung (Tatai) Bridge spans the Tatai River. Nestled in a lushly forested gorge upstream from the bridge is the **Tatai Waterfall**, a thundering set of rapids in the wet season, plunging over a 4m rock shelf. Water levels drop in the dry season but you can swim year-round in refreshing pools around the waterfall.

A short kayak away from the waterfall is the supremely tranquil **Rainbow Lodge** (☎099 744321, 012 1602585; www.rainbowlodgecambodia.com; s/d incl all meals US$40/65). About 6km downriver from the bridge is a more upscale rainforest retreat, the **Four Rivers Floating Ecolodge** (☎035 6900650, 097 6434032; www.ecolodges.asia; s/d incl breakfast May-Sep US$97/118, Oct-Apr US$119/139; 📶). Access to both resorts is by boat; call ahead for a free pick-up from the bridge.

You can access Tatai Waterfall by car or motorbike. The clearly marked turn-off is about 15km southeast of Koh Kong, or 2.8km northwest of the Tatai Bridge. From Koh Kong, a half-day moto/remork excursion to Tatai Waterfall costs US$10/15 return, or less to go one-way to the bridge. If travelling from Phnom Penh to one of the resorts, tell the driver to let you off at the bridge.

CENTRAL CARDAMOMS PROTECTED FOREST

Encompassing 4013 sq km of dense rainforest, most of the Central Cardamoms

Protected Forest (CCPF) is completely inaccessible except on foot. Dry-season trekking options include a three-day hike from **Chumnoab**, east of Thma Bang, eastwards to **Roleak Kang Cheung**, linked to Kompong Speu by road. Between the two is **Knong Krapeur** (1000m), set amid high-elevation grassland and pines, an area known for its giant ceramic funeral jars. Trekking from **Chamnar** (linked to Thma Bang by road) over the mountains to **Kravanh** takes about five days. Ask tour operators in Koh Kong about organised treks out of Thma Bang. Overnights are in hammocks, homestays, or in forest ranger stations. Bring warm clothes as temperatures can drop to as low as 10°C.

Except in the wet season, when travel may be difficult or impossible, Thma Bang is about 1½ hours from Koh Kong; turn off NH48 about 10km east of the Tatai bridge.

BOTUM SAKOR NATIONAL PARK

Occupying almost the entirety of a 35km-wide peninsula, this 1834-sq-km national park, encircled by mangroves and beaches, is home to a profusion of wildlife, including elephants, deer, leopards and sun bears. It's not yet geared up for tourism, but at the sleepy **park headquarters**, on NH48 about 3.5km west of Andoung Tuek, it should be possible to arrange a hike with a ranger (US$5 a day). Long-tail boat excursions from Andoung Tuek or Sihanoukville are also possible.

Grandiose tourist development is on the cards for the park's beach-lined west coast and a 12-island archipelago offshore: in 2009 a Chinese company broke ground on a $US5 billion project, but it may take decades to complete. A few islands – namely Koh Sdach – have resorts, accessible by boat from Sihanoukville.

Sihanoukville

☎034 / POP 155,000

Surrounded by beaches and idyllic tropical islands, Sihanoukville (Kompong Som) is Cambodia's premier seaside resort. Visitor numbers have risen in recent years, but despite the boomtown rents, the city's bars and sands remain laid-back. Most of the action takes place not far from the scruffy city centre on busy Occheuteal Beach; for peace and quiet, venture south of town to Otres Beach or hit one of the islands.

Sights & Activities

Beaches

Sihanoukville's sandy beaches are in a state of flux as developers move in and murky leases are signed to cash in on the tourism boom. Most central is **Occheuteal Beach**, lined with ramshackle restaurants, whose northwestern end – a tiny, rocky strip – has emerged as a happy, easy-going travellers' hang-out known as **Serendipity Beach**.

South of Occheuteal, gloriously quiet **Otres Beach** is a seemingly infinite strip of almost-empty white sand, populated by casuarinas and a small colony of mellow resorts at the south end. Developers have long been eyeing Otres Beach, and in 2010 a stretch of resorts was forcibly removed. But at press time developers had yet to build on the land they claimed, which is sealed off by a fence.

Northwest of Serendipity, all but a tiny stretch of pretty 1.5km-long **Sokha Beach** now belongs to the Sokha Beach Resort. **Independence Beach** is a good stretch of clean sand but is being developed. A bit north of tiny, secluded **Koh Pos Beach**, a bridge links the mainland with **Koh Pos** (Snake Island), where a Russian firm has plans to build a resort city. The original backpacker beach, **Victory Beach**, under Russian management, is clean, orderly and devoid of buzz.

Diving

The diving near Sihanoukville isn't terrific. It gets better the further you go out, although you still shouldn't expect anything on par with the western Gulf of Thailand or the Andaman Sea. Most serious trips will hit Koh Rong Saloem while overnight trips target the distant islands of **Koh Tang** and **Koh Prins**. Overnight trips cost about US$85 per day including two daily dives, food, accommodation on an island and equipment. Two-tank dives out of Sihanoukville average US$70 including equipment.

Marine Conservation Cambodia (www.marineconservationcambodia.org) is working to protect the area's reefs and coastal breeding grounds and occasionally has volunteer positions available.

Dive operators:

Chez Claude (Map p250; ☎934100; www.bestcambodia.com; above 2 Ph Thnou) Claude specialises in longer trips to distant reefs.

Dive Shop (Map p252; ☎933664; www.diveshopcambodia.com; Road to Serendipity) PADI five-star dive centre offering National Geographic Diver certification.

Sihanoukville

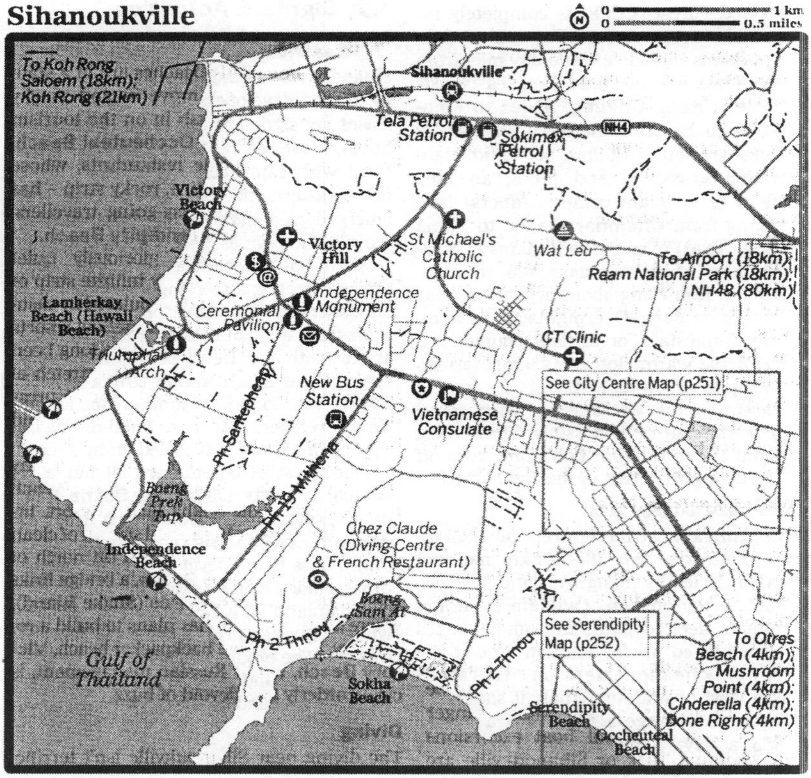

EcoSea Dive (Map p252; ☎012 606646; 736949; www.ecoseadive.com; Road to Serendipity) Offers PADI and SSI courses.

Scuba Nation Diving Center (Map p252; ☎012 604680; www.divecambodia.com; Ph Serendipity) Cambodia's first PADI five-star dive centre. Four-day PADI open-water courses here include two days on Koh Rong Saloem.

Massage

NGO-trained blind and disabled masseurs deftly ease away the tension at **Seeing Hands Massage 3** (Map p251; 95 Ph Ekareach; per hr US$6; ⊙8am-9pm) and **Starfish Bakery & Café** (Map p251; ☎012 952011; 62 7 Ph Makara; per hr US$6-10; ⊙7am-6pm).

Tours

Popular day tours go to some of the closer islands and to Ream National Park (p256).

Coasters (Map p252; ☎933776; www.cambodia-beach.com; Ph Serendipity) A good bet for boat and snorkel trips. A daily trip to Koh Ta Kiev/Koh Russei (per person US$15/20) departs at 9am and includes breakfast and lunch, or hire a private boat (US$50).

Eco-Trek Tours (Map p252; ☎012 987073; ecotrektourscambodia@yahoo.com; Road to Serendipity; ⊙8am-10pm) Associated with the knowledgeable folks at Mick & Craig's, this travel agency has information on just about anything. They also hire out mountain bikes (per day US$2) and can direct you to good rides.

Courses

Traditional Khmer Cookery Classes (☎092 738615; www.cambodiacookeryclasses.com; 335 Ph Ekareach; half-/full-day course per person US$15/25; ⊙Mon-Sat) Teaches traditional culinary techniques in classes with

Sihanoukville City Centre

0 200 m
0 0.1 miles

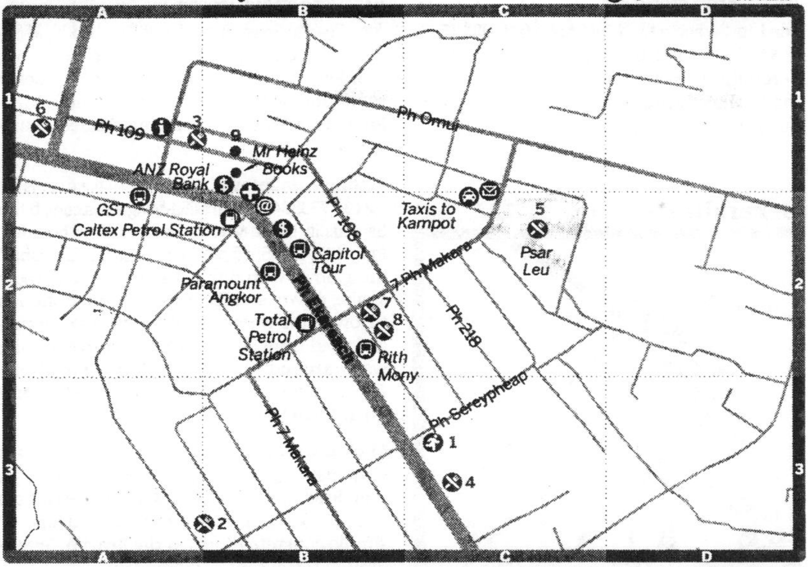

Sihanoukville City Centre

Activities, Courses & Tours

1 Seeing Hands Massage 3 .... C3
Starfish Bakery & Café .... (see 8)

Eating

2 Cabbage Farm Restaurant B3
3 Gelato Italiano A1
4 Holy Cow C3
5 Psar Leu C2
6 Psar Pinechikam A1
7 Samudera Supermarket B2
8 Starfish Bakery & Café B2

Transport

9 Virak Buntham B1

no more than eight participants. Reserve a day ahead.

Sleeping

SERENDIPITY AREA

The area between Serendipity Beach and the Golden Lions Roundabout, including the Road to Serendipity, is the main travellers' hang-out. It's worth paying a premium to stay right on the beach. The names of the resorts along this rocky outcrop – Cloud 9, Tranquility, Above Us Only Sky, Aquarium – suggest some supremely mellow vibes. Grab that hookah and pen some verse. Expect major low-season discounts here.

Backpacker central is back up the hill on the busy Road to Serendipity.

TOP CHOICE **Above Us Only Sky** BUNGALOWS $$
(☎089 822318; www.aboveusonlysky-cambodia.com; Serendipity Beach; r incl breakfast $40-60; ❄📶) The bungalows are attractively minimalist inside, but chances are you'll be hangin' on the cosy balcony, where satellite chairs stare at the sea. The bar perched over the rocks by the seashore is a gem.

The Cove BUNGALOWS $$
(☎012 380296; www.thecovebeach.com; Serendipity Beach; r with fan incl breakfast US$24-29, with air-con US$33-35; ❄📶) Another hillside place with bungalows, balconies and a bar lapped by waves. Most bungalows face the sea and all have hammocks. Request a room high up for the best views.

Reef Resort HOTEL $$
(Map p252; ☎934281; www.reefresort.com.kh; Road to Serendipity; d incl breakfast US$35-50;) The apex of comfort and style in the Serendipity area. A good choice if you're doing business around here or can't live without your modcons.

Serendipity

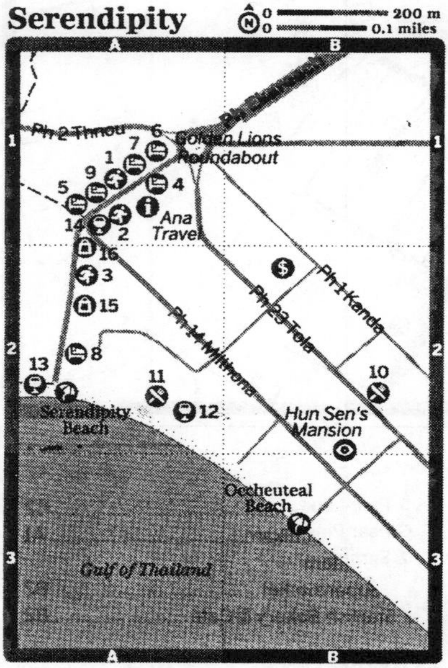

Monkey Republic HOSTEL $
(Map p252; ☎012 490290; http://monkeyrepublic.info; Road to Serendipity; dm US$3, r US$10;) A favourite of the young backpacker crowd, Monkey Republic has an eight-bed dorm room and several dozen bright-blue bungalows set around two banana-shaded courtyards.

Malibu Bungalows BUNGALOWS $$
(☎012 733334; www.malibu-bungalows.com; b'twn Serendipity Beach & Sokha Beach; s/d incl breakfast from US$40/45;) The rattan-furnished bungalows with pitched Balinese-style roofs snake down a hillside to within a stone's throw of the waterline. It's accessible by rugged road from Sokha Beach or a five-minute walk around the point from Serendipity Beach. Offers a measure of seclusion and great breakfasts.

Mick & Craig's GUESTHOUSE $
(Map p252; ☎012 727740; www.mickandcraigs.com; Road to Serendipity; r with fan/air-con from US$8/15;) A popular restaurant and 17 simple concrete rooms in the heart of Serendipity's restaurant and bar strip.

Beach Road Hotel HOTEL $
(Map p252; ☎017 827677; www.beachroad-hotel.com; Road to Serendipity; r with fan/air-con from US$15/20;) Well-located and efficiently run, Beach Road has 76 modern rooms, some set around the pool. They are clean and well kept, but have a few quirks (sneeze-inducing air freshener, hard pillows).

Serendipity

Activities, Courses & Tours
- Coasters .... (see 13)
- 1 Dive Shop A1
- 2 EcoSea Dive A1
- Eco-Trek Tours .... (see 6)
- 3 Scuba Nation Diving Center A2

Sleeping
- 4 Beach Road Hotel A1
- 5 Cool Banana A1
- 6 Mick & Craig's A1
- 7 Monkey Republic A1
- 8 New Sea View Villa A2
- 9 Reef Resort A1

Eating
- Happa .... (see 5)
- 10 Happy Herb Pizza B2
- 11 Kuren A2

Drinking
- 12 Dolphin Shack A2
- 13 JJ's Playground A2
- Monkey Republic .... (see 7)
- 14 Utopia A1

Shopping
- 15 Cambodia Children's Painting Project A2
- 16 M'lop Tapang Gift Shop A2

Information
- Utopia Information Centre .... (see 14)

Transport
- Mick & Craig's .... (see 6)

Cloud 9 BUNGALOWS $$
(☎012 479365; www.cloud9bungalows.com; Serendipity Beach; r incl breakfast US$20-35; 📶) Another fine choice at Serendipity Beach's terminus.

Cool Banana HOSTEL $
(Map p252; ☎934649; www.coolbananabungalows.com; Road to Serendipity; d with cold/hot water US$8/10, q $14; 📶) Backpacker fave has basic bungalows with balconies.

New Sea View Villa HOTEL $$
(Map p252; ☎092 759753; www.sihanoukville-hotel.com; Ph Serendipity; d with fan/air-con from US$15/20; ❄📶) Decent rooms and good food near beach.

OTRES BEACH

Otres is a place for serious chilling. Shortly after most bars and guesthouses were cleared out in 2010, a new colony of funky guesthouses sprung up at the far (southern) end of the beach. It's a US$2/5 moto/remork ride to get here from Serendipity Beach (more at night).

TOP CHOICE **Mushroom Point** GUESTHOUSE $
(off Map p250; ☎078 509079, 097 7124365; mushroompoint.otres@gmail.com; dm US$5-7, bungalows US$25; 📶) The open-air dorm over the restaurant in the shape of – what else – a mushroom wins the award for most awesome dorm room in Cambodia. Even those averse to communal living will be content in the mozzie-net-draped pods, good for two. The 'shroom-shaped private bungalows and food get high marks too. It's across the road from the beach.

Cinderella GUESTHOUSE $
(off Map p250; ☎088 9907588; s/d without bathroom $5/9, bungalows US$15) Way down at the far south end of the beach, this is your spot if you just want some alone time. The beach is a bit dishevelled here and the A-frame cottages basic, but you can't argue with the beachfront setting. Castaways Beach Bar next door has wi-fi.

Done Right GUESTHOUSE $
(off Map p250; ☎088 6678668, 097 9361441; s/d without bathroom $5/9, bungalows US$15) Space-age, ecofriendly bungalows known as 'geodomes' are done right here – a bit like concrete yurts, with skylights in lieu of windows. Above the restaurant are nine simple rooms with clapboard walls and lino floors. It's next to Mushroom Point.

Eating

Sihanoukville's centre of culinary gravity has shifted to the Serendipity area, but the main drag of Victory Hill still has some good-value restaurants. The gritty commercial centre also holds a few pleasant surprises.

SERENDIPITY AREA

For romance, nothing beats dining on the water, either at one of the resorts at Serendipity Beach or – more cheaply – in one of the shacks along adjacent Occheuteal Beach. Of the resorts, the best food is found at New Sea View Villa (good for candlelight dinners) and Reef Resort.

Happa JAPANESE $
(Map p252; Road to Serendipity; mains US$4-7; ⊙5pm-midnight) Authentic teppanyaki with a variety of sauce options is served amid tropical decor with Japanese touches.

Grand Kampuchea CAMBODIAN $
(23 Ph Tola; mains US$2.50-5) This popular outdoor eatery serves some of the best *amok* (fish in coconut leaves) in town, succulent grilled marlin and other sea beasts, and bargain *loc lak* (peppery stir-fried beef cubes).

Kuren BARBECUE $
(Map p252; Occheuteal Beach; mains US$2.50-3.50) Kuren's generous mixed seafood grill, fantastic value at US$3, separates it from the pack of barbecue shacks lining Occheuteal Beach.

Happy Herb Pizza WEED PIZZA $
(Map p252; ☎012 632198; 23 Ph Tola; small/medium/large pizza from US$4/7/9.50) Serves Khmer dishes (US$1.50 to US$3) and 23 kinds of pizza, all available 'happy' (ie ganja-fortified). Free delivery.

AROUND THE CITY

For Sihanoukville's cheapest dining, head to the **food stalls** in and around **Psar Leu** (Map p251; 7 Ph Makara; ⊙7am-9pm) – the vendors across the street, next to the Kampot taxis, are open 24 hours – as well as at the smaller and slightly more expensive **Psar Pinechikam** (Map p251; Ph Boray Kamakor).

TOP CHOICE **Chez Claude** FRENCH $$
(Map p250; ☎934100; www.claudecambodge.com; above 2 Ph Thnou; mains US$5.50-14) Dou Dou and Claude are your hosts at this all-wood eyrie – perched high above Sokha Beach – with outstanding French, Vietnamese and Cambodian cuisine, especially seafood. Order paella

48 hours in advance. Access is via an innovative tractor-pulled cable car that would make MacGyver proud.

Holy Cow ORGANIC $
(Map p251; 83 Ph Ekareach; mains US$2.50-4.50; ⊙8.30am-11pm;) Options at this chic-funky cafe-restaurant include pasta, sandwiches on homemade bread and two vegan desserts, both involving chocolate.

Starfish Bakery & Café ORGANIC $
(Map p251; www.starfishcambodia.org; behind 62 7 Ph Makara; sandwiches US$3.50-4.50; ⊙7am-6pm;) This relaxing, NGO-run garden cafe specialises in filling Western breakfasts and healthy, innovative sandwiches heavy on Mexican and Middle Eastern flavours. Add a cookie and drink to your sandwich for $1. Income goes to sustainable development projects.

Cabbage Farm Restaurant CAMBODIAN $
(Map p251; small/large mains 8000/15,000r; ⊙11am-10pm) Known to locals as Chom Ka Spey, it gets rave reviews for its seafood and spicy seasonings. An authentic Khmer dining experience. A sign in English on Ph Serepheap points the way.

Gelato Italiano ICE CREAM $
(Map p251; 49 7 Ph Makara; per gelato scoop $0.75; ⊙8am-9pm;) Run by students from Sihanoukville's Don Bosco Hotel School, this Italian-style cafe specialises in gelatos (Italian ices) and also serves various coffee drinks and light meals in a bright, airy space.

Samudera Supermarket SUPERMARKET $
(Map p251; 64 7 Ph Makara; ⊙6am-10pm) Has a good selection of fruits, vegies and Western favourites, including cheese and wine.

Drinking

Occheuteal Beach is lined with beach bars that are perfect for sundowners; hit the north end of Serendipity Beach for a more laid-back scene. A few longstanding and genuinely cool regular bars remain standing amid the girlie bars of Victory Hill. Rambunctious late-night action takes place either side of the pier dividing Occheuteal and Serendipity Beaches.

JJ's Playground BEACH BAR
(Map p252; Serendipity Beach) The scene changes frequently on Serendipity Beach, but for a while now JJ's has been the go-to spot for those seeking pure late-night debauchery.

Dolphin Shack BEACH BAR
(Map p252; Occheuteal Beach) Like JJ's, it has a host of specials designed to get you drunk fast and bevies of beautiful backpackers pouring drinks and passing out flyers. Peaks earlier than JJ's.

Monkey Republic BAR
(Map p252; Road to Serendipity) The bar and upstairs chill-out area are ideal for meeting other travellers.

Utopia BAR
(Map p252; cnr Road to Serendipity & 14 Ph Milthona; ⊙24hr) The prime backpacker warm-up bar was starting to get a bit sleazy when we went. Then it wasn't, then it was again. One look in will tell.

Retox Bar BAR
(Victory Hill; ⊙noon-1am or later) This pub, plastered in posters and album covers, often has live music (from 8.30pm) and jam sessions (instruments available).

Happy Dayz CAFE
(Victory Hill; ⊙6pm-whenever) There's weed being smoked every way weed can be smoked at this virtual shrine to Bob Marley.

Shopping

M'lop Tapang Gift Shop TEXTILES
(Map p252; www.mloptapang.org; Ph Serendipity) Run by a local NGO that works with at-risk children, it sells bags, scarves and good-quality T-shirts. Several other handicrafts shops are nearby.

Cambodia Children's Painting Project ART
(Map p252; www.letuscreate.org; Ph Serendipity) Another NGO that works with underprivileged kids; you can buy small paintings here. The volunteer backpackers are happy to tell you more about the project.

Information

Details on local activities and businesses appear in two free brochures, *The Sihanoukville Visitors Guide* and *The Sihanoukville Advertiser*. Also see www.sihanoukville-cambodia.com.

Internet cafes (per hour 4000r) are sprinkled along the Road to Serendipity and, in the city centre, along Ph Ekareach near Ph Sophamongkol.

Theft is a problem on Occheuteal Beach so leave your valuables in your room. At night, both men and women should avoid walking alone along dark, isolated beaches and roads.

Ana Travel (Map p252; ☎016 499915; www.anatravelandtours.com; Road to Serendipity; ⏰8am-10pm) Handles Cambodia visa extensions (US$50/85/160/295 for one/three/six/12 months) and arranges Vietnam visas in one hour (US$45 plus US$3 service charge).

ANZ Royal Bank (Map p251; 215 Ph Ekareach) One of several ATM-equipped banks along Ph Ekareach. Another ANZ ATM is in front of the Golden Sand Resort on 23 Ph Tola in the Serendipity area.

CT Clinic (Map p250; ☎081 886666; 47 Ph Boray Kamakor; ⏰24hr for emergencies) The best medical clinic in town. Can administer rabies shots and snake serum.

Vietnamese Consulate (Map p250; ☎934039; 310 Ph Ekareach; ⏰8am-noon & 2-4pm Mon-Sat) Issues some of the world's speediest Vietnamese visas (US$45/90/120 for one/three/six months), often on the spot. Bring a passport photo.

Getting There & Away

Temple-beach combo holidays will be an easy option when and if newly reconstructed Sihanoukville International Airport, 18km east of town, resumes flights to/from Siem Reap. At press time the de facto national carrier, Cambodia Angkor Air, continued to resist opening this route, and the airport remained essentially mothballed.

All of the major bus companies have frequent connections with Phnom Penh (US$3.75 to US$6, four hours) from early morning until at least 2pm, after which trips are sporadic. The cheapest is **Capitol Tour** (Map p251; ☎934042; Ph Ekareach). **Virak Buntham** (Map p251; ☎011 558988; Ph Ekareach) runs the last trip at 8.30pm, while Capitol Tour, **GST** (Map p251; ☎6339666; Ph Ekareach) and **Paramount Angkor** (Map p251; ☎017 525366; Ph Ekareach) have late-afternoon trips. Most travel agents only work with two or three bus companies, so ask around if you need to leave at a different time than what's being offered.

Cramped share taxis (US$6 per person, US$45 per car) and minibuses (15,000r) to Phnom Penh depart from the **new bus station** (Map p250; 19 Ph Mithona) until about 8pm. Avoid the minibuses if you value things like comfort and your life. Hotels can arrange taxis to Phnom Penh for US$45 to US$55.

Virak Buntham and **Kampot Tours & Travel** (in Kampot ☎092 125556) run minibuses to Kampot (US$6, 1½ hours) that continue to Kep (US$10, 2½ hours) and Ha Tien in Vietnam (US$16, five hours). Travel agents can arrange hotel pick-ups. See the boxed text, p262, for details on crossing the border with Vietnam at Prek Chak.

Share taxis to Kampot (US$5, 1½ hours) leave mornings only from an open lot across 7 Ph Makara from Psar Leu. This lot and the new bus station are good places to look for rides to Koh Kong or the Thai border. If nobody's sharing, expect to pay US$45 to US$60 to the Thai border.

Virak Buntham and **Rith Mony** (Map p251; ☎012 644585; Ph Ekareach) have morning buses to Bangkok (US$25, change buses on the Thai side) via Koh Kong (US$7, four hours). Paramount Angkor has daily services to Koh Kong, Siem Reap, Battambang and Ho Chi Minh City. GST has a night bus to Siem Reap and day buses to Battambang and Ho Chi Minh City.

Bus companies all have terminals downtown on Ph Ekareach. Most departures originate at these terminals and stop at the new bus station on the way out of town.

Getting Around

Arriving in Sihanoukville, buses stop at the bus terminal then most (but not all) continue to their central terminals. Prices to the Serendipity Beach area from the new bus station are fixed at a pricey US$2/6 for a moto/remork, so continue to the centre if possible and get a cheaper, shorter remork ride from there.

A moto/remork should cost about US$1/2 from the centre to Serendipity, Occheuteal and Victory Beaches and Victory Hill. Serendipity to Victory Hill costs US$1.50/3.

Motorbikes can be rented from many guesthouses for US$5 to US$7 a day. For fundraising purposes, the police sometimes 'crack down' on foreign drivers. Common violations: no driving licence, no helmet, no wing mirrors and – everybody's favourite – driving with the lights on during the day.

Bicycles can be hired from many guesthouses for about US$1.50 a day.

Around Sihanoukville

ISLANDS

More than a dozen tropical islands dot the waters off Sihanoukville. Developers have been drooling over the islands for years, but so far wide-scale development has been kept at bay.

The most appealing of the islands are neighbouring **Koh Rong** and **Koh Rong Saloem**, both about two hours offshore and ringed by white-sand beaches that count among Cambodia's best. Plans to turn Koh Rong into a Cambodian version of Thailand's Koh Samui, complete with ring road and airport, have stalled. Instead, the opening of several simple, extremely appealing beach resorts has turned Koh Rong into an ideal spot to escape civilisation. Koh Rong Saloem has a few lonely resorts of its own and some amazing wildlife, including macaques, black squirrels and sea eagles.

Closer to Sihanoukville, little **Koh Ta Kiev** has two resorts and a long white beach, while you can snorkel off **Koh Russei** (Bamboo Island), where development plans are forcing most resorts to shut down.

Sleeping

Most island resorts run their generators from about 6pm to midnight.

Lazy Beach BUNGALOWS $$
(☎016 214211; www.lazybeachcambodia.com; Koh Rong Saloem; q US$30) Alone on the southwest coast of Koh Rong Saloem, its idyllic bungalows come with sea-facing balconies and hammocks.

Paradise Bungalows BUNGALOWS $$
(☎034 933664; www.diveshopcambodia.com; Koh Rong; d/q US$20/35) This is the most upscale of several options on the southeast side of Koh Rong. The German manager, Rudy, opens the more backpacker-friendly Mango Lounge nearby in the high season only.

Monkey Island BUNGALOWS $
(☎016 594177; Koh Rong; cottage US$15-25) Another gem on the southeast coast of Koh Rong, this one is run by Sihanoukville backpacker haven Monkey Republic. Most of the 19 bungalows share a bathroom.

Treehouse Bungalows BUNGALOWS $$
(☎081 830992; Koh Rong; beach/tree cottage US$20/30) Treehouse Bungalows has six beach bungalows and five tree houses on the southeast side of Koh Rong.

M'pay Bay Bungalows BUNGALOWS $$
(☎085 242257; Koh Rong Saloem; cottage US$20) A cluster of simple bungalows in a fishing village on the north side of the island; the friendly owners bill it as a more ecofriendly option.

Getting There & Away

Island-hopping tours usually take in the closer islands such as Koh Ta Kiev and Koh Russei; book through a tour company or your guesthouse. For Koh Rong and Koh Rong Saloem, make arrangements through your resort.

REAM NATIONAL PARK

Also known as Preah Sihanouk National Park, this park – now seriously endangered by commercial development – comprises 150 sq km of primary forests and is an excellent place to see wildlife. Fascinating two- to three-hour **jungle walks** (per person US$8) are led by rangers (most, but not all, speak English), and are easy to arrange (hiking unaccompanied is not allowed) at the **park headquarters** (☎016 767686, 012 875096; ⊙7am-6pm), across the road from the airport.

Ranger-led **boat trips** (1-5 people US$50) on the Prek Toeuk Sap Estuary and its mangrove channels are another option. Travel agencies in Sihanoukville offer day trips out to the park.

The park is 18km east of Sihanoukville. A return trip by moto should cost US$8 to US$14 depending on how long you stay.

Kampot Province & Kep

Kampot Province is endowed with an alluring combination of old colonial towns, abundant natural attractions and easy intraregional transport. Kampot produces some of the world's finest pepper (www.kampotpepper.biz).

KAMPOT

☎033 / POP 33,000

More and more independent travellers are discovering this charming riverside town, with its relaxed atmosphere and a run-down French architectural legacy. It makes an excellent base for exploring the area between Bokor National Park and Kep, or for just lazing by the river for a few days.

Sights & Activities

The most enjoyable activity is strolling along the riverside promenade and along streets lined with decrepit French-era shophouses. Some of the best colonial architecture can be found in the triangle delineated by 7 Ph Makara, the central Durian Roundabout and the post office. The **old cinema** (7 Ph Makara), **Kampot Prison** and the **old governor's mansion** – the latter two are very French – are worth a look (from the outside).

Kampot Traditional Music School MUSIC
(⊙6-9pm Mon-Fri) Visitors are welcome to observe training sessions and/or performances every evening at this school that trains orphaned and disabled children in traditional music and dance.

Seeing Hands Massage 5 MASSAGE
(per hr US$4; ⊙7am-11pm) Blind masseurs and masseuses offer soothing bliss.

Tours

One of the best ways to explore Kampot Province is on an organised day trip. Popular destinations include Kep and Bokor National Park (see p259), while various companies run sunset river cruises and countryside tours that include visits to pepper plantations. The following run interesting tours:

Kampot Dreamtime Tours (☎089 908417; www.kampotluxurytours.com) Runs upmarket countryside trips in air-con vans (per person US$35) and wine-and-cheese river cruises in a boat formerly owned by King Norodom Sihanouk.

Sok Lim Tours (☎012 719872, 012 796919; www.soklimtours.com) Kampot's oldest and largest outfit, well regarded all around. Has trained pepper-plantation guides.

Kampot Tours & Travel (☎633 5556, 092 125556) Its van fleet can get you a shared ride to just about anywhere; also does the standard area excursions.

Captain Chim's (☎012 321043) Sunset cruises on a traditional boat cost US$5 per head and include a cold beer.

Sleeping

TOP CHOICE **Les Manguiers** RIVER RESORT $
(☎092 330050; www.mangomango.byethost18.com; r US$10-17, bungalows US$25-44;) This rambling garden complex, on the river 2km north of the new bridge, is rich with activities for kids and adults, including kayaking

Kampot

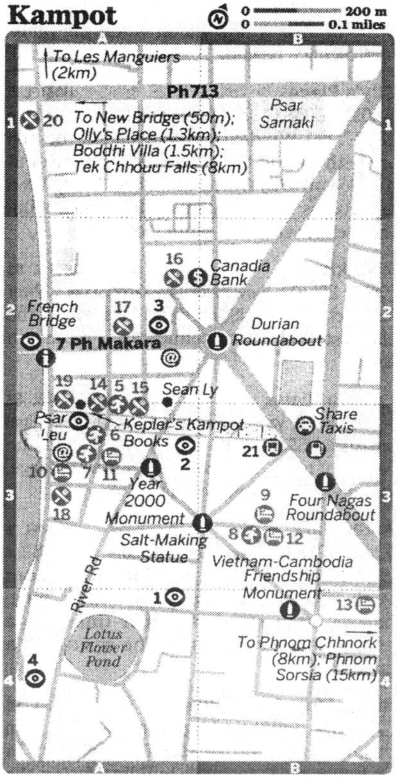

Kampot

Sights
1 Kampot Prison ... A4
2 Kampot Traditional Music School ... A3
3 Old Cinema ... A2
4 Old Governor's Mansion ... A4

Activities, Courses & Tours
Captain Chim's ... (see 14)
5 Kampot Dreamtime Tours ... A3
6 Kampot Tours & Travel ... A3
7 Seeing Hands Massage 5 ... A3
8 Sok Lim Tours ... B3

Sleeping
9 Blissful Guesthouse ... B3
10 Bokor Mountain Lodge ... A3
11 La Java Bleue ... A3
12 Orchid Guesthouse ... B3
Rikitikitavi ... (see 18)
13 Ta Eng Guesthouse ... B4

Eating
14 Captain Chim's ... A2
15 Epic Arts Café ... A3
16 Fruit Stalls & Little Eateries ... A2
Jasmine ... (see 19)
17 Night Market ... A2
18 Rikitikitavi ... A3
19 Rusty Keyhole ... A2
20 Ta Ouv Restaurant ... A1

Transport
Capitol Tour ... (see 21)
Hua Lian ... (see 21)
Paramount Angkor ... (see 21)
21 Phnom Penh Sorya ... B3

(free), swimming and firefly-watching boat trips (best on a new moon when the phosphorescence peaks).

Olly's Place
HOSTEL $
(☐092 605837; www.ollysplacekampot.com; r US$3-7; 🛖) Windsurfers and paddle boards are both free on the other side of the river at Aussie-run Olly's. The thatched bungalows and rooms are ridiculous value considering the mellow vibe and plum location.

Rikitikitavi
BOUTIQUE HOTEL $$
(☐012 235102; www.rikitikitavi-kampot.com; River Rd; r incl breakfast US$40; 🖭🛖) Has five of the classiest and most comfortable rooms in town.

La Java Bleue
BOUTIQUE HOTEL $$
(☐667 6679; www.lajavableue-kampot.com; r incl breakfast US$35; 🖭🛖) Newly opened in the centre of town, it's a colonial gem with large, tastefully decorated rooms.

Bodhi Villa
HOSTEL $
(☐012 728884; www.bodhivilla.com; dm US$2, r US$5-12; 🛖) Boddhi is popular with Phnom Penh expats on weekends, when huge parties often erupt. At other times it's a peaceful hideaway across the river with a good bar.

Bokor Mountain Lodge
HISTORIC HOTEL $$
(☐932314; www.bokorlodge.com; River Rd; r in back/front incl breakfast US$30/40; 🖭🛖) In an imposing French-era building facing the river, it's a bit torn and frayed these days, but undeniably charismatic.

Orchid Guesthouse
GUESTHOUSE $
(☐092 226996; orchidguesthousekampot@yahoo.com; r with fan/air-con US$5/15, bungalow US$10; 🖭🛖) Set in a manicured garden, this hostelry has comfortable air-con rooms, less-comfortable fan rooms and three bungalows by a fish pond toward the back.

Blissful Guesthouse
GUESTHOUSE $
(☐092 494331; www.blissfulguesthouse.com; 3-bed dm US$2, r without/with bathroom US$4/8) An old-time backpacker vibe lives on at this atmospheric wooden house. Has a popular bar-restaurant with a Sunday roast and slightly shabby rooms.

Ta Eng Guesthouse
GUESTHOUSE $
(☐012 330058; r US$5-10; 🖭🛖) Ta Eng is the best of the Khmer-style high-rises thanks to squeaky-clean rooms and friendly family ownership.

✖ Eating & Drinking

Quite a few restaurants line River Rd south of the old French bridge. There are fruit stalls and little eateries (⊙7am-10pm) next to the Canadia Bank and, nearby, a night market (7 Ph Makara) with both mains and desserts.

TOP Rikitikitavi
FUSION $$
(☐012 235102; www.rikitikitavi-kampot.com; River Rd; mains US$5-8; 🛖🖉) Rikitikitavi's riverview restaurant, known for its Kampot pepper chicken, slow-cooked curry and salads, matches its guesthouse in style and ambience.

Jasmine Restaurant
FUSION $
(☐077 933352; 25 River Rd; mains US$4-9; ⊙9am-10pm; 🖉) California meets Cambodia at this semiformal place. Wonderful sweet-and-sour fish, and wine by the glass for US$3.50.

🖉 Epic Arts Café
CAFE $
(www.epicarts.org.uk; mains US$2-4; ⊙7am-6pm; 🛖) A great place for breakfast, homemade cakes or tea, this mellow eatery is staffed by deaf and disabled young people. Profits fund arts workshops for disabled Cambodians.

Rusty Keyhole
FUSION $$
(☐092 758536; River Rd; small/large/extra-large ribs US$5/7.50/10; 🛖) Popular riverfront bar-restaurant serves widely praised food. Order the famous ribs in advance or they may sell out.

Captain Chim's
CAFE $
(mains US$1-3; ⊙7am-10pm) Kampot's best budget eats are here. It's best known for breakfast, but Khmer faves like *loc lak* will fill you up any time of day. Ask about Cambodian cooking classes.

Ta Ouv Restaurant
CAMBODIAN $$
(River Rd; mains US$5; ⊙10am-2pm & 6-10pm) Built on stilts over the river by the new bridge, it specialises in seafood (crab with peppercorns is a favourite), with plenty of other meat and vegie options.

ⓘ Information

There's a strip of copy shops with internet access southwest of the Durian Roundabout on 7 Ph Makara.

Canadia Bank Has an ATM.

Kepler's Kampot Books (⊙8am-8pm) Second-hand books plus pepper, *kramas* (chequered scarves) and fine T-shirts.

Tourist Information Centre (☐6555541, 012 462286; lonelyguide@gmail.com; River Rd; ⊙7am-7pm) Led by the knowledgeable Mr Pov,

WORTH A TRIP

ANGKOR BOREI & PHNOM DA

The city of Takeo, roughly halfway between Kampot and Phnom Penh on NH2, is the jumping-off point for one of Cambodia's great thrill rides: the 20km open-air motorboat ride along Canal No 15, dug in the 1880s, to the impoverished riverine hamlet of **Angkor Borei** (45 minutes). Angkor Borei is home to a small **archaeological museum** (admission US$1; ⊙8am-4.30pm) featuring locally discovered Funan- and Chenla-era artefacts. The boat then continues for 15 minutes to **Phnom Da** (admission US$2), spectacularly isolated Mont-St-Michel-style by annual floods, which is topped by a temple whose foundations date from the 6th century (the temple itself was rebuilt in the 11th century). Hiring a boat for the trip at Takeo's boat dock costs US$40 return for up to four people.

Kampot's new tourist office is the main point of contact for assembling groups for Bokor National Park trips. Also doles out free advice and can arrange transport to area attractions like caves, falls and Kompong Trach.

Getting There & Away

Kampot is 105km from Sihanoukville and 148km from Phnom Penh.

Paramount Angkor, Capitol Tour, Phnom Penh Sorya and Hua Lian sell tickets from offices opposite the Total petrol station near the Four Nagas Roundabout. All have two or three daily trips to Phnom Penh (US$3.50 to US$4.50, four hours), the last of which depart at 1pm; some go via Kep (US$2, 45 minutes). Across the street you can catch share taxis (US$6), packed-to-the-gills minibuses (16,000r) and private taxis (US$40) to Phnom Penh. Sorya also has daily trips to Siem Reap and Battambang.

Share taxis to Sihanoukville cost US$5 and a private taxi is US$30. Daily Kampot Tours & Travel and Virak Buntham minibuses go west to Sihanoukville (US$6, 1½ hours) and Koh Kong (US$13, four hours with a bus transfer); and east to Ha Tien, Vietnam (US$10, 2½ hours). Guesthouses can arrange tickets and pick-ups.

A moto/remork/taxi to Kep should run about US$6/10/20.

Getting Around

Bicycles can be hired or borrowed for free from many guesthouses, which can also arrange motorbike hire, or try the following:

Captain Chim's Motorbike hire for US$4 per day.

Sean Ly (☎012 944687; ⊙7am-9pm) Rents 125cc bikes for US$3 a day (US$5 for a new one) and 250cc trail bikes for US$10.

BOKOR NATIONAL PARK

This 1581-sq-km **national park** (Preah Monivong National Park; admission US$5) is famed for its abandoned French hill station, refreshingly cool climate and lush primary rainforest. A massive resort project including a golf course and casino is planned for the summit, but it appears to be a few years off. A new road up to the hill station has been completed, but is only open to the public on selected holidays. Plans are to open it full-time in 2013.

At the park entrance, an informative (if low-budget) **ranger station** has displays about Bokor's fauna and the challenges of protecting the area's ecosystems in the face of encroachment, poaching, illegal logging and the Kamchay hydropower project. Threatened animals that live in the park include the leopard, Indian elephant, Asiatic black bear, Malayan sun bear, pileated gibbon, pig-tailed macaque, slow loris and pangolin. Don't expect to see much wildlife, though – most of the animals survive by staying in more remote areas and, in addition, are nocturnal.

Sights & Activities

In the early 1920s the French – ever eager to escape the lowland heat – established the **Bokor Hill Station** atop Phnom Bokor (1080m), known for its dramatic vistas of the coastal plain – and for frequent pea-soup fogs. A grand, four-storey hotel-casino, the **Bokor Palace**, opened in 1925, but the entire holiday village, including the **Catholic church** and the **post office**, was abandoned to the howling winds in 1972 when Khmer Rouge forces infiltrated the area. The hill station became a ghost town, its once-grand buildings turned into eerie, windowless shells. Over time they became carpeted with a bright-orange lichen that gives them an other-worldly cast. Appropriate, then, that the foggy showdown that ends the Matt Dillon crime thriller *City of Ghosts* (2002) was filmed here. Other Phnom Bokor sights include lichen-caked **Wat Sampeau Moi Roi** (Five Boats Wat), from which an 11km trail (four or five hours) leads to two-tiered **Popokvil Falls**.

GETTING TO VIETNAM: PHNOM DEN TO TINH BIEN

NH2 runs 58km from Takeo to the rarely used **Phnom Den border crossing** (⊙7am-5pm). Transport options from Takeo include early-morning minibuses (5000r), share taxis and motos (US$8). It may be necessary (or quicker) to change to a moto or remork at Kirivong, 8km from the frontier. On the other side, motos and taxis go to Chau Doc.

For information on crossing this border in the other direction, see the boxed text, p155.

Getting There & Around

To visit the park you must take an organised tour. The standard full-day tour takes you up to the hill station and involves a bit of on-road driving, a bit of off-road driving and a bit of trekking. First you'll be driven 7km to the ranger station west of Kampot. There you'll jump into the ranger's truck and drive about 30 minutes before getting out to start the trekking leg of your journey. After walking for 1¼ hours, the ranger truck again picks you up and takes you the remaining 1½ hours to the top.

The standard tour costs US$25 per person (minimum four people) and includes all transport, food and water, an English-speaking guide and the park entry fee. Bring your own protection against mosquitoes, leeches, snakes and rain. It's usually easy to hook up with a group through the Tourist Information Centre in Kampot or any travel agent or guesthouse.

Variations on the standard tour, including overnight trips, are possible. Walking the whole way up takes six to seven hours and costs US$40 to US$50 per person including overnight accommodation in a ranger station at the top.

AROUND KAMPOT

About 8km from Kampot, picnic platforms, eateries and refreshing rapids make the **Tek Chhouu Falls** hugely popular with locals. A moto/remork costs US$5/8 return.

The limestone hills east towards Kep are honeycombed with caves, some of which can be explored with the help of local kids and a reliable torch. The temple cave of **Phnom Chhnork** (admission US$1), surrounded by blazingly beautiful countryside, is a real gem, known for its 7th-century (Funan-era) **brick temple**. The turn-off is 6km east of Kampot, from where it's 6km to the cave on a bumpy road. A return moto/remork ride costs about US$8/10. Less interesting is **Phnom Sorsia** (admission free), 15km southeast of Kampot, which has a gaudily painted modern temple and several natural caves.

KEP

☎036 / POP 10,300

The seaside resort of Kep-sur-Mer, famed for its spectacular sunsets and splendid seafood, was founded as a colonial retreat for the French elite in 1908. In the 1960s, Cambodian high rollers continued the tradition but Khmer Rouge rule brought evacuation followed by systematic looting. Today, scores of Kep's luxurious prewar villas are still blackened shells, relics of a once-great (or at least rich and flashy) civilisation that met a sudden and violent end.

Sleepy Kep lacks a centre and its accommodation options are spread out all over the place. As a result, some find it somewhat soulless. Others revel in its sleepy vibe, content to relax at their resort, nibble on crab at the famed Crab Market and poke around the mildewed shells of modernist villas that speak of happier, carefree times.

Sights & Activities

Beaches & Swimming BEACH

Most of Kep's beaches are too shallow and rocky to make for good swimming. The best is centrally located **Kep Beach**, but it's still somewhat pebbly and tends to fill up with locals on weekends. The best place for sunset viewing is the long wooden pier in front of Knai Bang Chatt's **Sailing Club**, where there's also a small but shallow beach. For **swimming**, you might be better off at one of the resort pools; Kep Lodge and Veranda Natural Resort have good ones that are free if you order some food.

Kep National Park NATIONAL PARK

The interior of Kep peninsula is occupied by Kep National Park, degraded in recent years by illegal logging, but finally guarded by a complement of rangers. An 8km circuit around the park, signposted in yellow, starts at the park entrance behind Veranda Natural Resort. Directly behind the Beach House guesthouse overlooking Kep Beach, the signposted Stairway to Heaven leads 800m up the hill to a pagoda, a nunnery and – 400m further on – Sunset Rock, with superb views.

Koh Tonsay ISLAND

Offshore, rustic Koh Tonsay (Rabbit Island) has a lovely beach with several family-run clusters of rudimentary bungalows where you can overnight for US$5 per day. Boats to the island (25 minutes) leave from a pier 2.7km east of the Kep Beach roundabout. Your guesthouse can arrange to get you on a boat for US$10 per person return – make it clear which day you want to be picked up. A scheduled trip departs daily at 9am for the same price. A private boat arranged at the pier costs US$30 one way for up to seven passengers.

Sleeping

Rooms at all midrange and top-end places listed include breakfast.

TOP CHOICE Kep Lodge GUESTHOUSE $
(092 435330; www.keplodge.com; r US$15-38;) A friendly place whose bungalows have thatch roofs, tile floors and verandahs with breathtaking sunset views. The grounds are lush, the common area relaxing and the food great. The one US$15 bungalow is often booked out. The turn-off is 600m north of the northern roundabout towards Kampot.

Le Bout Du Monde BOUTIQUE HOTEL $$
(011 964181; http://leboutdumonde.new.fr; r US$20-85;) The French-owned 'end of the earth,' the highest up of all the hillside resorts, has a dozen gorgeous bungalows with wraparound verandahs, Angkorian sculptures, beautiful wood furniture and stone-walled bathrooms. The view from the restaurant is Kep's best.

Jasmine Valley Eco-Resort BOUTIQUE HOTEL $$
(097 7917635; www.jasminevalley.com; r US$24-64;) This ecolodge has funky bungalows raised dramatically amid dense jungle foliage just below Kep National Park. There are good hikes around, and green credits include solar power and a natural swimming pool complete with pond critters. It's about 2.5km in from the Rabbit Island pier (follow the signs). A moto/remork from the Crab Market should cost US$2/3.

Tree Top Bungalows HOSTEL $
(012 515191; khmertreetop@hotmail.com; r US$4-25;) The highlights here are the towering stilted bamboo bungalows with sea views; each pair shares a bathroom. Otherwise unspectacular. Cool off at nearby Kep Lodge's pool.

Veranda Natural Resort BOUTIQUE HOTEL $$
(012 888619; www.veranda-resort.com; r with fan/air-con from US$40/60;) This rambling colony of hillside bungalows built of wood, bamboo and stone and connected by a maze of stilted walkways is a memorable spot for a romantic getaway. The food is excellent and sunset views from the restaurant pavilion are stunning.

Knai Bang Chatt BOUTIQUE HOTEL $$$
(078 888556; www.knaibangchatt.com; r US$165-325;) This chic 11-room boutique hotel, occupying three waterfront villas from the 1960s, has a beachside infinity pool and its own sailing club.

Kukuluku Beach Club HOSTEL $
(6300150; www.kukuluku-beachclub.com; dm US$3.50-5, d with fan/air-con US$10/20;) The rooms are nothing special and the pool tiny, but it's a great place to meet other travellers and party on weekends, when live music – and expat crowds – are sometimes imported from Phnom Penh.

Kep Seaside Guesthouse HOTEL $
(012 684241; r with fan/air-con from US$7/15;) This three-storey place is a bit decrepit but you can't argue with the location, right on the water (although beachless) next to exclusive Knai Bang Chatt.

Eating & Drinking

Eating crab at the 'Crab Market,' a row of wooden waterfront shacks next to a wet fish market, is a quintessential Kep experience. Most guesthouses also grill up eight-legged crustaceans.

Kimly Restaurant CRAB SHACK $
(mains US$2.50-7; 9am-10pm) The longest-running and still the best of the Crab Market eateries, it does crab every which way – 27 ways, to be exact, all US$6 to US$7, or super-size it for an extra two bucks. The Kampot pepper crab is truly mouthwatering.

Breezes FUSION $$
(mains US$5-8; 9am-9pm) Just 10m from the waterline, this Dutch-owned restaurant boasts sleek furnishings, excellent food and fine views of Koh Tonsay.

Information

There are no banks or ATMs in Kep.

Kampot Information Centre (097 7998777; pheng_say@yahoo.com; Kep Beach) Host Pheng is a font of information on buses and borders.

GETTING TO VIETNAM: PREK CHAK TO XA XIA

The easiest way to get to the border crossing at **Prek Chak** (⊙6am-5.30pm) and on to Ha Tien, Vietnam, is on a direct bus from Phnom Penh (US$16, five hours), Sihanoukville (US$16, five hours), Kampot (US$10, two hours), or Kep (US$8, 1½ hours). Virak Buntham has a bus from Phnom Penh; Virak Buntham and two other companies ply the Sihanoukville–Kampot–Kep–Ha Tien route.

A more flexible alternative from Phnom Penh or Kampot is to take any bus to Kompong Trach, then a moto (about US$3) for 15km, on a good gravel road, to the frontier.

In Kep, tour agencies and guesthouses can arrange a direct moto (US$8, 40 minutes), remork (US$13, one hour) or taxi (US$20, 30 minutes). Rates and times are almost double from Kampot. Private vehicles take a new road that cuts south to the border 10km west of Kompong Trach.

At Prek Chak, motos ask US$5 to take you to the Vietnamese border post 300m past the Cambodian one, and then all the way to Ha Tien (7km). You'll save money walking across no-man's land and picking up a moto on the other side for US$2 to US$3.

Because Ha Tien is a free economic zone, foreigners do not need a visa to visit, but they must limit their stay to 14 days and cross back over the same border. While technically you are required to have a visa to travel beyond the free economic zone, at the time of writing travellers were reportedly being allowed to travel on to Phu Quoc Island visa-free. But the same caveats applied: you get 14 days and must return from whence you came.

Vietnam visa holders bound for Phu Quoc should arrive in Ha Tien no later than 12.30pm to secure a ticket on the 1pm ferry (230,000d, 1½ hours). Extremely early risers may be able to make it to Ha Tien in time to catch the (slower) 8.20am car ferry to Phu Quoc. Scheduled buses from Cambodia to Ha Tien arrive before the 1pm boat departs.

For information on crossing this border in the other direction, see the boxed text, p156.

Rith Travel Center (☎016 789994; Crab Market) Specialises in island tours and handles bus tickets.

Getting There & Away

Kep is 25km from Kampot and 41km from the Prek Chak–Xa Xia border crossing to Vietnam. Phnom Penh Sorya, Capitol Tour and Hua Lian buses link the town with Kampot (US$2, 45 minutes) and Phnom Penh (US$4, four hours, last trips at 2pm). Stops are on request but usually include the northern roundabout and Kep Beach; guesthouses have details. A private taxi to Phnom Penh (2½ hours) costs US$40 to US$45, to Kampot US$20.

See p262 for details on getting across the Vietnamese border to Ha Tien (Vietnam). Virak Buntham's Ha Tien–Sihanoukville bus rumbles through Kep, and Kampot Tours & Travel can also get you to Sihanoukville (US$10, 2½ hours). You can also board Virak Buntham's Kampot–Siem Reap night bus in Kep.

A moto/remork to Kampot runs about US$7/10; private taxis are US$15 to US$20. Drivers hang out at the northern and Kep Beach roundabouts.

Motorbike rental averages US$7 per day, mountain-bike rental is US$3 per day. Hiring a remork for a full day, including a trip to Kompong Trach and a pepper plantation, costs US$20.

AROUND KEP

Near the town of Kompong Trach, 28km north of Kep, you'll find **Wat Kiri Sela** (admission US$1), a Buddhist temple built at the foot of **Phnom Kompong Trach**, a dramatic karst formation riddled with over 100 caverns and passageways. From the wat, an underground passage leads to the centre of a fishbowl-like karst formation, surrounded by vine-draped cliffs and open to the sky. Various stalactite-laden caves shelter reclining Buddhas and miniature Buddhist shrines. There's major **rock-climbing** (www.rockclimbingincambodia.com) opportunities around here.

Friendly local kids with torches, eager to put their evening-school English to use, are eager (overeager?) to serve as guides; make sure you tip them if you use them.

Getting There & Away

Kompong Trach makes an easy day trip from Kep or Kampot, or you can hop off the bus on the way to/from Phnom Penh. To get to Wat Kiri Sela, take the dirt road opposite the Acleda Bank for 2km.

UNDERSTAND CAMBODIA

Cambodia Today

Cambodia is at a crossroads on its path to recovery from the brutal years of Khmer Rouge rule. Compare Cambodia today with the dark abyss into which it plunged under the Khmer Rouge and the picture looks pretty optimistic, but look to its more successful neighbours and it's easy to be pessimistic. Cambodia must choose its path: pluralism, progress and prosperity or intimidation, impunity and injustice. The jury is still very much out on which way things will go.

Another jury still out is that of the Khmer Rouge trial, sidelined by the politics of the Cold War for two decades, and then delayed by bureaucratic bickering at home and abroad. The Extraordinary Chambers in the Courts of Cambodia (ECCC) trial is finally under way, but it is by no means certain that the wheels of justice will turn fast enough to keep up with the rapid ageing of the surviving Khmer Rouge leaders. Military commander Ta Mok died in custody in 2006 and both Ieng Sary and Nuon Chea are suffering from health complications. However, the trial of Kaing Guek Eav, aka Comrade Duch, dominated headlines for much of 2010 and an appeal verdict is anticipated in 2011. Many Cambodians were dismayed by the lenient sentence of 35 years (only 19 of which remain to be served) initially passed, given the magnitude of his crimes.

Cambodia remains one of the poorest countries in Asia and it's a tough existence for much of the population. According to the UN Development Programme (UNDP; www.undp.org), Cambodia remains in worse shape than Congo and the Solomon Islands, just scraping in ahead of Myanmar, while Transparency International (www.transparency.org), the anticorruption watchdog, rates the country a lowly 158 out of the 180 countries ranked.

Cambodia is like the teen starlet who has just been discovered by an adoring public: everyone wants something from her but not everyone wants what is in her best interests. The government, long shunned by international big business, is keen to benefit from all these newfound opportunities. Contracts are being signed off like autographs and there are concerns for the long-term development of the country. The Chinese have come to the table to play for big stakes and have pledged US$1.1 billion in assistance in the last couple of years, considerably more than all the other donors put together – ostensibly with no burdensome strings attached.

There are two faces to Cambodia: one shiny and happy, the other dark and complex. For every illegal eviction of city dwellers or land grab by a general, there will be a new NGO school offering better education, or a new clean-water initiative to improve the lives of the average villager. Such is the yin and yang of Cambodia, a country that both inspires and confounds. Like an onion, the more layers you unravel, the more it makes you want to cry, sometimes in sorrow, sometimes in joy.

The royal family has been a constant in contemporary Cambodian history and no one more so than the mercurial monarch King Sihanouk, who once again surprised the world with his abdication in 2004. His relatively unknown son, King Sihamoni, assumed the throne and has brought renewed credibility to the monarchy, untainted as he is by the partisan politics of the past. Meanwhile, the political arm of the royal family, Funcinpec, has continued to haemorrhage.

But there's a new royal family in town, the Cambodian People's Party (CPP), and it is making plans for the future with dynastic alliances between offspring. At the head of this elite is Prime Minister Hun Sen, who has proved himself a survivor, personally as well as politically, for he lost an eye during the battle for Phnom Penh in 1975. It would appear that for the time being at least, with a poorly educated electorate and a divided opposition, 'in the country of the blind, the one-eyed man is king.'

History

The good, the bad and the ugly is a simple way to sum up Cambodian history. Things were good in the early years, culminating in the vast Angkor empire, unrivalled in the region during four centuries of dominance. Then the bad set in, from the 13th century, as ascendant neighbours steadily chipped away at Cambodian territory. In the 20th century it turned downright ugly, as a brutal civil war culminated in the genocidal rule of the Khmer Rouge (1975–79), from which Cambodia is still recovering.

Funan & Chenla

The Indianisation of Cambodia began in the 1st century as traders plying the sea route from the Bay of Bengal to southern China brought Indian ideas and technologies to what is now southern Vietnam. The largest of the era's nascent kingdoms, known to the Chinese as Funan, embraced the worship of the Hindu deities Shiva and Vishnu and, at the same time, Buddhism, and was crucial in the transmission of Indian culture to the interior of Cambodia.

From the 6th to 8th centuries Cambodia seems to have been ruled by a collection of competing kingdoms. Chinese annals refer to 'Water Chenla', apparently the area around the modern-day town of Takeo, and 'Land Chenla', along the upper reaches of the Mekong River and east of Tonlé Sap lake, around Sambor Prei Kuk.

Rise & Fall of Angkor

The Angkorian era lasted from 802 to 1432, encompassing periods of conquest, turmoil and retreat, revival and decline, and fits of remarkable productivity.

In 802 Jayavarman II (reigned c 802–50) proclaimed himself a 'universal monarch', or *devaraja* (god-king). He instigated an uprising against Javanese domination of southern Cambodia and, through alliances and conquests, brought the country under his control, becoming the first monarch to rule most of what we now call Cambodia.

The Angkorian empire was made possible by *baray* (reservoirs) and irrigation works sophisticated and massive enough to support Angkor's huge population. The first records of such works date to the reign of Indravarman I (r 877–89), whose rule was marked by the flourishing of Angkorian art, including the building of temples in the Roluos area.

In the late 9th century Yasovarman I (r 889–910) moved the capital to Angkor, creating a new centre for worship, scholarship and the arts.

After a period of turmoil and conflict, Suryavarman II (r 1113–52) unified the kingdom and embarked on another phase of territorial expansion, waging successful but costly wars against both Vietnam and Champa. His devotion to the Hindu deity Vishnu bequeathed the world the incredible temple of Angkor Wat.

The tables soon turned. Champa struck back in 1177 with a naval expedition up the Mekong, taking Angkor by surprise and putting the king to death. But the following year a cousin of Suryavarman II – soon crowned Jayavarman VII (r 1181–1219) – rallied the Khmers and defeated the Chams in another epic naval battle. A devout follower of Mahayana Buddhism, it was he who built the city of Angkor Thom.

Scholars believe that Angkor's decline was already on the horizon when Angkor Wat was built – and that the reasons were partly environmental. The 1000-sq-km irrigation network had begun silting up due to deforestation and erosion, and the latest climate data from tree rings indicates that two prolonged droughts also played a role. After the era of Jayavarman VII's reign, temple construction effectively ground to a halt.

During the twilight years of the empire, the state religion changed back and forth several times and religious conflict and internecine rivalries were rife, and the empire began to implode. The Thais, who were in the ascendency, made repeated incursions into Angkor, sacking the city in 1351 and again in 1431 and making off with thousands of intellectuals, artisans and dancers from the royal court whose profound impact on Thai culture can be seen to this day.

From 1600 until the arrival of the French, Cambodia was ruled by a series of weak kings whose intrigues often involved seeking the protection of either Thailand or Vietnam – granted, of course, at a price. The commercial metropolis that is now Ho Chi Minh City (Saigon) in Vietnam was, in the 17th century, a small Cambodian trading port called Prey Nokor.

French Colonialism

The era of yo-yoing between Thai and Vietnamese masters came to a close in 1864, when French gunboats intimidated King Norodom I (r 1860–1904) into signing a Treaty of Protectorate. An exception in the annals of colonialism, the French presence really did protect the country at a time when it was in danger of going the way of Champa and vanishing from the map.

The French maintained Norodom's court in a splendour unseen since the heyday of Angkor, helping to enhance the symbolic position of the monarchy. In 1907 the French pressured Thailand into returning the northwest provinces of Battambang, Siem Reap and Sisophon, bringing Angkor under Cambodian control for the first time in more than a century.

THE LAST OF THE GOD-KINGS

Norodom Sihanouk has been a constant presence in the topsy-turvy world of Cambodian politics. A colourful character with many interests and shifting political positions, he became the prince who stage-managed the close of French colonialism, autocratically led an independent Cambodia, was imprisoned by the Khmer Rouge and, from privileged exile, finally returned triumphant as king, only to abdicate dramatically in 2004. A political chameleon, he is many things to many people, but whatever else he may be, he has proved himself a survivor.

Sihanouk, born in 1922, was not an obvious contender for the throne. He was crowned in 1941, at just 19 years old, with his education incomplete. By the mid-1960s Sihanouk had been calling the shots in Cambodia for more than a decade. The conventional wisdom was that 'Sihanouk is Cambodia' – his leadership was unassailable. But as government troops battled with a leftist insurgency in the countryside and the economy unravelled, Sihanouk came to be regarded as a liability. His involvement in the film industry and his announcements that Cambodia was 'an oasis of peace' suggested a leader who was losing touch with everyday realities.

Following the Khmer Rouge victory on 17 April 1975, Sihanouk realised he had been used as a Trojan Horse to propel the Khmer Rouge into power and found himself confined to the Royal Palace as a prisoner. He remained there until early 1979 when, on the eve of the Vietnamese invasion, he was flown to Běijīng. It was to be more than a decade before Sihanouk finally returned to Cambodia.

Sihanouk never quite gave up wanting to be everything for Cambodia: international statesman, general, president, film director, man of the people. He will be a hard act to follow – the last in a long line of Angkor's god-kings.

Led by King Sihanouk (r 1941–55 and 1993–2004), Cambodia declared independence on 9 November 1953.

Independence

The period after 1953 was one of peace and great prosperity, Cambodia's golden years, a time of creativity and optimism. Phnom Penh grew in size and stature and the temples of Angkor were the leading tourist destination in Southeast Asia. Dark clouds were circling, however, as the war in Vietnam became a black hole, sucking in neighbouring countries.

In 1955 Sihanouk renounced the throne and established his own political party, becoming prime minister after that year's elections. He would dominate Cambodian politics, veering this way and that, for the next 15 years, alienating the USA by his support for China and North Vietnam; the army and urban elite with his anti-American 'neutrality' and nationalisations; young leftists by his repression; and just about everyone else thanks to pervasive corruption.

As the 1960s drew to a close, the North Vietnamese and the Viet Cong were using Cambodian territory in their battle against South Vietnam, prompting devastating American bombing and a land invasion into eastern Cambodia.

In 1967 a countryside-based leftist rebellion began and clashes with the army soon spread.

Sihanouk was overthrown by General Lon Nol in March 1970 and took up residence in Běijīng, where he set up a government-in-exile in alliance with an indigenous Cambodian revolutionary movement that Sihanouk had dubbed the Khmer Rouge. This was a defining moment in contemporary Cambodian history: talk to many former Khmer Rouge fighters and they all say that they 'went to the hills' to fight for their monarch and knew nothing of Marxism or Mao.

Khmer Rouge Rule

Upon taking Phnom Penh on 17 April 1975 – two weeks before the fall of Saigon – the Khmer Rouge implemented one of the most radical and brutal restructurings of a society ever attempted. Its goal was to transform Cambodia – renamed Democratic Kampuchea – into a giant peasant-dominated agrarian cooperative untainted by anything that had come before. Within days, the entire populations of Phnom Penh and provincial towns, including the sick, elderly and infirm, were forced to march into the countryside and work as slaves for 12 to 15 hours a day. Disobedience of any sort often brought immediate execution. The advent of Khmer Rouge rule was proclaimed Year Zero.

The revolution soon set about wiping out all intellectuals – wearing glasses was reason enough to be killed. It soon began 'devouring its own children', liquidating cadres seen as insufficiently doctrinaire, or too closely associated with North Vietnam or Sihanouk.

Leading the Khmer Rouge was Saloth Sar, better known as Pol Pot. As a young man, he won a scholarship to study in Paris, where he began developing the radical Marxist ideas that later metamorphosed into extreme Maoism. Under his rule, Cambodia became a vast slave-labour camp. Meals consisted of little more than watery rice porridge twice a day, meant to sustain men, women and children through a backbreaking day in the fields. Disease stalked the work camps, malaria and dysentery striking down whole families.

Khmer Rouge rule was brought to an end by the Vietnamese, who liberated the almost-empty city of Phnom Penh on 7 January 1979. It is still not known exactly how many Cambodians died during the three years, eight months and 20 days of Khmer Rouge rule. The most accepted estimate is that at least 1.7 million people perished at the hands of Pol Pot and his followers. The Documentation Center of Cambodia (www.dccam.org) records the horrific events of the period.

A Sort of Peace

As Vietnamese tanks neared Phnom Penh, the Khmer Rouge fled westward with as many civilians as it could seize, taking refuge in the mountains along the Thai border. The Vietnamese installed a new government led by several former Khmer Rouge officers, including current Prime Minister Hun Sen, who had defected to Vietnam in 1977 and 1978 when fleeing internal purges of the Eastern Zone. In the dislocation that followed liberation, little rice was planted or harvested, leading to a massive famine.

In 1984 the Vietnamese overran all the major Khmer Rouge camps inside Cambodia and the Khmer Rouge and its allies, including Pol Pot, retreated into Thailand. From there, they waged guerrilla warfare aimed at demoralising their opponents, shelling towns, attacking road transport, targeting civilians and planting countless mines.

In September 1989 Vietnam, its economy in tatters and eager to end its international isolation, announced the withdrawal of all of its forces from Cambodia.

In February 1991 all parties – including the Khmer Rouge – signed the Paris Peace Accords, according to which the UN Transitional Authority in Cambodia (Untac) would rule the country for two years. Although Untac is still heralded as one of the UN's success stories (elections with a 90% turnout were held in 1993), to many Cambodians who had survived the 1970s it was unthinkable that the Khmer Rouge was allowed to play a part in the process. The Khmer Rouge ultimately pulled out before polling began, but the smokescreen of the elections allowed them to re-establish a guerrilla network throughout Cambodia. Untac is also remembered for causing a significant increase in prostitution and HIV/AIDS.

The last Khmer Rouge hold-outs, including Ta Mok, were not defeated until the capture of Anlong Veng and Prasat Preah Vihear by government forces in the spring of 1998. Pol Pot cheated justice by dying a sorry death near Anlong Veng, cremated on a pile of old tyres.

Culture

People & Population

Nearly 15 million people live in Cambodia. With a rapid growth rate of about 2% a year, the population is predicted to reach 20 million by 2025. According to official statistics, around 96% of the people are ethnic Khmers, making the country the most homogeneous in Southeast Asia, but in reality anywhere between 10% and 20% of the population is of Cham, Chinese or Vietnamese origin. Cambodia's diverse Khmer Leu (Upper Khmer) or Chunchiet (minorities), who live in the country's mountainous regions, probably number between 75,000 and 100,000.

The official language is Khmer, spoken by 95% of the population. English has taken over from French as the second language of choice, although Chinese is also growing in popularity. Life expectancy is currently 62 years.

Lifestyle

For untold centuries, life in Cambodia has centred on family, food and faith.

Extended families stick together, solving problems collectively, pooling resources and coming together to celebrate festivals and mourn deaths. Ties remain strong despite the fact that increasing numbers of young people are migrating to the cities in search of opportunity.

Food is extremely important to Cambodians as they have tasted what it is like to be without. Famine stalked the country in the late 1970s and even today there are serious food shortages in times of drought or inflation. For country folk – still the vast majority of the population – survival depends on what they can grow, and the harvest cycle dictates the rhythm of rural life.

Faith is a rock in the lives of many older Cambodians, and Buddhism has helped them to survive the terrible years and then rebuild their lives after the Khmer Rouge.

Economy

Badly traumatised by decades of conflict, Cambodia's economy was long a gecko amid the neighbouring dragons. This has slowly started to change, as the economy has been liberalised and investors are circling to take advantage of the new opportunities.

Before the civil war, rubber was the leading industry and it has been bouncing back with new plantations. Other plantation industries taking off include palm oil and paper pulp. Virgin forest is being cut down on the pretext of replanting, but the ecosystem never recovers.

The garment sector is important to the economy, with factories ringing the Cambodian capital. Cambodia is trying to carve a niche for itself as an ethical producer, with good labour relations and air-conditioned factories. It's no picnic for workers in the factories, but the alternative is often the rice fields or the shadowy fringes of the entertainment industry, which is often a one-way ticket into prostitution.

Tourism is a big deal in Cambodia with more than two million visitors arriving in 2008, a doubling of numbers in just a few years. Thousands of jobs are being created every year and this is proving a great way to integrate the huge number of young people into the economy.

Foreign aid was long the mainstay of the Cambodian economy, supporting half the government's budget, and NGOs have done a lot to force important sociopolitical issues onto the agenda. However, with multibillion-dollar investments stacking up and the Chinese government loaning vast sums, it looks like their days in the sun could be numbered, and the government may no longer be influenced by their lobbying.

Corruption remains a way of life in Cambodia. It is a major element of the Cambodian economy and exists to some extent at all levels of government. Sometimes it is overt, but increasingly it is covert, with private companies often securing very favourable business deals on the basis of their connections. It seems everything has a price, including ancient temples, national parks and even genocide sites.

Religion

The majority of Khmers (95%) follow the Theravada branch of Buddhism. Buddhism in Cambodia draws heavily on its predecessors, incorporating many cultural traditions from Hinduism for ceremonies such as birth, marriage and death; as well as genies and spirits, such as Neak Ta, which link back to a pre-Indian animist past.

Under the Khmer Rouge, the majority of Cambodia's Buddhist monks were murdered and nearly all of the country's wats (more than 3000) were damaged or destroyed. In the late 1980s, Buddhism once again became the state religion.

Other religions found in Cambodia are Islam, practised by the Cham community; animism, among the hill tribes; and Christianity, which is making inroads via missionaries and Christian NGOs.

Arts

The Khmer Rouge regime not only killed the living bearers of Khmer culture, it also destroyed cultural artefacts, statues, musical instruments, books and anything else that served as a reminder of a past it was trying to efface. The temples of Angkor were spared as a symbol of Khmer glory and empire, but little else survived. Despite this, Cambodia is witnessing a resurgence of traditional arts and a growing interest in cross-cultural fusion.

Cambodia's royal ballet is a tangible link with the glory of Angkor and includes a unique *apsara* dance. Cambodian music, too, goes back at least as far as Angkor. To get some sense of the music that Jayavarman VII used to like, check out the bas-reliefs at Angkor Wat.

TONLÉ SAP: HEARTBEAT OF CAMBODIA

The Tonlé Sap, the largest freshwater lake in Southeast Asia, is an incredible natural phenomenon that provides fish and irrigation water for half the population of Cambodia – and a home for 90,000 people, many of them ethnic Vietnamese, who live in 170 floating villages.

Linking the lake with the Mekong, at Phnom Penh, is a 100km-long channel known as the Tonlé Sap River. From June to early October, wet-season rains rapidly raise the level of the Mekong, backing up the Tonlé Sap River and causing it to flow northwestward into the Tonlé Sap lake. During this period, the lake increases in size by a factor of four or five, from 2500 to 3000 sq km up to 10,000 to 16,000 sq km, and its depth increases from an average of about 2m to more than 10m. An unbelievable 20% of the Mekong's wet-season flow is absorbed by the Tonlé Sap. In October, as the water level of the Mekong begins to fall, the Tonlé Sap River reverses direction, draining the waters of the lake back into the Mekong.

This extraordinary process makes the Tonlé Sap an ideal habitat for birds, snakes and turtles, and one of the world's richest sources of freshwater fish: the flooded forests – deciduous during the high-water months – make for fertile spawning grounds, while the dry season creates ideal conditions for fishing. Experts believe that fish migrations from the lake help to restock fisheries as far north as China.

This unique ecosystem was declared a Unesco **Tonlé Sap Biosphere Reserve** (www.tsbr-ed.org) in 2001 but this may not be enough to protect it from the twin threats of upstream dams and rampant deforestation.

In the mid-20th century a vibrant Cambodian pop music scene developed, but it was killed off (literally) by the Khmer Rouge. After the war, overseas Khmers established a pop industry in the USA and some Cambodian-Americans, raised on a diet of rap, are now returning to their homeland. The Los Angeles-based sextet Dengue Fever, inspired by 1960s Cambodian pop and psychedelic rock, is the ultimate fusion band.

The people of Cambodia were producing masterfully sensuous sculptures - much more than mere copies of Indian forms - in the age of Funan and Chenla. The Banteay Srei style of the late 10th century is regarded as a high point in the evolution of Southeast Asian art.

Environment

The Land

Modern-day Cambodia covers 181,035 sq km, making it a little more than half the size of Vietnam. It has 435km of coastline along the island-specked Gulf of Thailand.

Cambodia's two dominant geographical features are the mighty Mekong and the Tonlé Sap. The rich sediment deposited during the annual wet-season flooding has made central Cambodia incredibly fertile.

In Cambodia's southwest quadrant, much of the land mass is covered by the Cardamom Mountains (Chuor Phnom Kravanh) and, near Kampot, the Elephant Mountains (Chuor Phnom Damrei). Along Cambodia's northern border with Thailand, the plains collide with the Dangkrek Mountains (Chuor Phnom Dangkrek), a striking sandstone escarpment more than 300km long and up to 550m high.

In the northeastern corner of the country, in the provinces of Ratanakiri and Mondulkiri, the plains give way to the Eastern Highlands, a remote region of densely forested mountains and high plateaus.

Wildlife

It's estimated that 212 species of mammal live in Cambodia. Creatures under serious threat include the Asian elephant, tiger, banteng (a wild ox), gaur, black gibbon, clouded leopard, fishing cat, marbled cat, sun bear and pangolin.

A whopping 720 bird species find Cambodia a congenial home, thanks in large part to its year-round water resources, especially the marshes around the Tonlé Sap. The Sam Veasna Center (boxed text, p207) runs birding trips.

Cambodia has some of the last remaining freshwater Irrawaddy dolphins (p235). The Mekong giant catfish, which can weigh up to

300kg, is critically endangered due to habitat loss and overfishing.

About 240 species of reptile can be found here. Four types of snake are especially dangerous: the cobra, king cobra, banded krait and Russell's viper.

The surest way to see Cambodian animals up close is to drop by the Phnom Tamao Wildlife Sanctuary (p197) near Phnom Penh, or the Angkor Centre for Conservation of Biodiversity (ACCB; p217) near Siem Reap.

National Parks

The good news is that national parks, wildlife sanctuaries, protected landscapes and multiple-use areas now cover 43,000 sq km, or around 25% of Cambodia's surface area. The bad news is that the government does not have the resources – or, in some cases, the will – to protect these areas beyond drawing lines on a map.

Cambodia's most important national parks, all of them threatened by development and/or deforestation, are Bokor (p259), Botum Sakor (p249), Kirirom (p197), Ream (p256), Virachey (p242) and the Mondulkiri Protected Forest.

Environmental Issues

The greatest threat to Cambodia's globally important ecosystems is logging, which is done to provide charcoal and timber and to clear land for cash-crop plantations. The environmental watchdog **Global Witness** (www.globalwitness.org) keeps an eye on the network of well-connected businesspeople who work hand-in-glove with corrupt members of the government and army.

In the short term, deforestation is contributing to worsening floods along the Mekong, but the long-term implications of deforestation are mind-boggling. Siltation, combined with overfishing and pollution, may lead to the eventual death of the Tonlé Sap lake, a catastrophe for future generations of Cambodians.

Environmentalists fear that damming the mainstream Mekong may be nothing short of disastrous for the flow patterns of the Mekong, the migratory patterns of fish, the survival of the freshwater Irrawaddy dolphin and the very life of the Tonlé Sap (see the boxed text, p268). Plans now under consideration include the Sambor Dam, a massive project 35km north of Kratie.

A new challenge is oil, which has been discovered off Sihanoukville. Sloppy extraction could devastate Cambodia's lovely coast, including pristine mangrove forests, and may inevitably add fuel to the fires of corruption than burn the Cambodian economy.

Detritus of all sorts, especially plastic bags and bottles, can be seen in distressing quantities all over the country.

SURVIVAL GUIDE

Directory A–Z

Accommodation

Accommodation is great value in Cambodia, just like the rest of the Mekong region. Rooms with private bathroom and satellite TV are generally available for US$5 to US$10. Hotels improve significantly once you start spending more than US$10 a night, and for US$15 it's usually possible to get air-con and hot water. For US$20 to US$50 you can arrange something very comfortable with the possible lure of a swimming pool.

Most hotels quote in US dollars, but some places in the provinces quote in riel, while those near the Thai border quote in baht. We provide prices based on the currency quoted to us at the time of research.

NGOS ON THE ENVIRONMENTAL FRONT LINE

The following environmental groups – staffed in Cambodia mainly by Khmers – are playing leading roles in protecting Cambodia's wildlife:

- **Conservation International** (www.conservation.org)
- **Fauna & Flora International** (www.fauna-flora.org)
- **Maddox Jolie-Pitt Foundation** (www.mjpasia.org)
- **Wildlife Alliance** (formerly WildAid; www.wildlifealliance.org)
- **Wildlife Conservation Society** (www.wcs.org)
- **World Wildlife Fund** (WWF; www.worldwildlife.org)

In this chapter, the budget breakdown is: budget ($), US$3 to US$20; midrange ($$), US$20 to US$60; and top end ($$$), US$60 and above.

International-standard luxury hotels can be found in Siem Reap, Phnom Penh, Sihanoukville and Kep. Most quote hefty walk-in rates and whack 12% tax and 10% service on as well; book through the internet for lower rates.

Hotels are fullest – and prices highest – from mid-November to March. Discounts are most in evidence during the green season (June to October).

Homestays, often part of a **community-based ecotourism project** (www.ccben.org), are a good way to meet the local people and learn about Cambodian life.

Activities

Cambodia is steadily emerging as an eco-tourism destination and now offers rainforest trekking in the Cardamom Mountains (p248) and Ratanakiri (p240), walking with elephants in Mondulkiri (p244), scuba diving and snorkelling near Sihanoukville (p249), birdwatching in Siem Reap province and beyond (p207), and cycling along the Mekong Discovery Trail (p237) and around the temples of Angkor (p213). It's also a popular destination for adventurous dirt biking for those with some experience.

Business Hours

Most Cambodians get up very early and it is not unusual to see people out and about at 5.30am.

Government offices, open from Monday to Friday and Saturday morning, theoretically begin the working day at 7.30am, break for a siesta from 11.30am to 2pm, and finish the day at 5pm. However, it's a safe bet that few people will be around early in the morning or after 3.30pm or 4pm, as their real income is earned elsewhere.

Banking hours vary slightly according to the bank, but most keep core hours of 8am to 3.30pm Monday to Friday, plus Saturday morning.

Tourist attractions such as museums are normally open seven days a week.

Local restaurants are generally open from about 6.30am until 9pm, tourist-oriented places until a little later.

Local markets *(psar)* operate seven days a week and usually open and close with the sun, running from 6.30am to 5.30pm. Shops in cities and larger towns tend to be open from about 8am until 7pm, sometimes later.

Customs Regulations

If Cambodia has official customs allowances it's close-lipped about them, though a 'reasonable amount' of duty-free items is allowed in. Like any other country, Cambodia does not allow travellers to import weapons, explosives or narcotics – some would say there are enough in the country already. It is illegal to take antiquities out of the country.

Electricity

The usual voltage is 220V, 50 cycles, but power surges and power cuts are common, particularly in the provinces. Electrical sockets are usually two-prong, flat or round pin.

TOP FIVE READS ON CAMBODIA

A whole bookcase-worth of volumes examines Cambodia's recent history, including the French colonial period, the spillover of the war in Vietnam into Cambodia, the Khmer Rouge years and the wild 1990s. The best include:

» *A Dragon Apparent* by Norman Lewis (1951) is a classic account of the author's 1950 travels in Indochina.

» *First They Killed My Father* by Luong Ung (2001) is a personal memoir of Democratic Kampuchea. One of the best of many survivor accounts.

» *A History of Cambodia* by David Chandler (1994) describes the full sweep of Cambodian history, from the prehistoric period through the glories of Angkor to the present day.

» *River of Time* by John Swain (1995) takes readers back to old Indochina, lost to the madness of war.

» *The Gate* by Francois Bizot (2003) is a heartfelt account of the author's survival of interrogation by Comrade Duch and his incarceration in the French Embassy after the fall of Phnom Penh on 17 April 1975.

Embassies & Consulates

Some of the embassies located in Phnom Penh:

Australia (Map p188; ☎213413; 16 Ph National Assembly)

France (Map p183; ☎430020; 1 Monivong Blvd)

Germany (Map p188; ☎216381; 76-78 Ph 214)

Laos (Map p183; ☎982632; 15-17 Mao Tse Toung Blvd)

Thailand (Map p183; ☎726306; 196 Norodom Blvd)

UK (Map p183; ☎427124; 27-29 Ph 75)

USA (Map p184; ☎728000; 1 Ph 96)

Vietnam Phnom Penh (Map p183; ☎362531; 436 Monivong Blvd); Sihanoukville (Map p250; ☎012 340495; Ph Ekareach)

Food & Drink

Some traditional Cambodian dishes are similar to those of neighbouring Laos and Thailand (though not as spicy), others closer to Chinese and Vietnamese cooking. The French left their mark, too.

Thanks to the Tonlé Sap, freshwater fish – often *ahng* (grilled) – are a huge part of the Cambodian diet. The great national dish, *amok,* is fish baked with coconut and lemongrass in banana leaves. *Prahoc* (fermented fish paste) is used to flavour foods, with coconut and lemongrass making regular cameos.

A proper Cambodian meal almost always includes *samlor* (soup), served at the same time as other courses. *Kyteow* is a rice-noodle soup that will keep you going all day. *Bobor* (rice porridge), eaten for breakfast, lunch or dinner, is best sampled with some fresh fish and a dash of ginger.

As an approximate guide, prices for main dishes when eating out are under US$5 for budget, US$5 to US$10 for midrange and more than US$10 for top-end places.

Tap water *must* be avoided, especially in rural areas. Bottled water is widely available but coconut milk, sold by machete-wielding street vendors, is more ecological and may be more sterile. The beers of choice are Angkor, Anchor (pronounced 'An-Chore' to differentiate it from Angkor), locally brewed Tiger, newcomer Kingdom Beer and many popular imports from Beerlao to Tsingtao. Rural folk drink palm wine, tapped from the sugar palms that dot the landscape. *Tukaloks* (fruit shakes) are mixed with milk, sugar and sometimes a raw egg.

> **BOTTOMS UP**
>
> When Cambodians propose a toast, they usually stipulate what percentage must be downed. If they are feeling generous, it might be just *ha-sip pea-roi* (50%), but more often than not it is *moi roi pea-roi* (100%). This is why they love ice in their beer, as they can pace themselves over the course of the night. Many a *barang* (foreigner) has ended up face down on the table at a Cambodian wedding when trying to outdrink the Khmers without the aid of ice.

Gay & Lesbian Travellers

Cambodia is a very tolerant country when it comes to sexual orientation and the scene is slowly coming alive in the major cities. But as with heterosexual couples, amorous displays of public affection are a basic no-no. Handy websites include:

Cambodia Out (www.cambodiaout.com) Promoting the GLBT community in Cambodia and the gay-friendly Adore Cambodia campaign.

Sticky Rice (www.stickyrice.ws) Gay travel guide covering Cambodia and Asia.

Insurance

Make sure your medical insurance policy covers emergency evacuation: limited medical facilities mean that you may have to be airlifted to Bangkok for problems such as a traffic accident or dengue fever.

See p511 for information on health insurance and p508 for motorcycle and car insurance. Worldwide travel insurance is available at www.lonelyplanet.com/travel_services. You can buy, extend and claim online anytime, even if you're already on the road.

Internet Access

Internet access is widespread and there are internet shops in all but the most remote provincial capitals. Charges range from 2000r to US$2 per hour. In this chapter, guesthouses and hotels that offer access to an online computer are indicated by an internet icon (@).

RESPONSIBLE TRAVEL IN CAMBODIA

Cambodia has been to hell and back and there are many ways in which you can put a little back into the country. Eating locally grown food is just one of many.

The looting of stone carvings from Cambodia's ancient temples has devastated many temples. Don't contribute to this cultural rape by buying antiquities of any sort – classy reproductions are available in Phnom Penh and Siem Reap, complete with export certificates.

Cambodians dress very modestly and are offended by skimpily dressed foreigners. Just look at the Cambodians frolicking in the sea – most are fully dressed. Wearing bikinis on the beach is fine but cover up elsewhere. Topless or nude bathing is a definite no-no.

The sexual exploitation of children is now taken very seriously in Cambodia. Report anything that looks like child sex tourism to the **ChildSafe Hotline** (☎012-311112; www.childsafe-international.org) or to the national **police hotline** (☎023-997919). Tourism establishments that sport the ChildSafe logo have staff trained to protect vulnerable children and, where necessary, intervene.

Websites with lots of practical ideas for responsible travel:

» **Cambodia Community-Based Ecotourism Network** (www.ccben.org) Promotes community-based ecotourism in Cambodia, with projects and initiatives across the country.

» **ConCERT** (Map p200; ☎963511; www.concertcambodia.org; 560 Phum Stoueng Thmey; ⊙9am-5pm Mon-Fri) Siem Reap–based organisation 'connecting communities, environment and responsible tourism'. It offers information on anything from ecotourism initiatives to volunteering opportunities.

» **Heritage Watch** (www.heritagewatch.org) The home of the heritage-friendly tourism campaign to raise interest in remote heritage sites and their protection.

» **Mekong Discovery Trail** (www.mekongdiscoverytrail.org) The official website for the Mekong Discovery Trail, promoting community-based tourism initiatives on the upper Mekong.

» **Sam Veasna Center for Wildlife Conservation** (www.samveasna.org) The best source of information on sustainable visits to Cambodia's world-class bird sanctuaries.

Many hotels, guesthouses and cafes now offer wi-fi, although connections are easiest to find in Phnom Penh and Siem Reap. Places offering wi-fi are shown with the wi-fi icon (📶).

Legal Matters

All narcotics, including marijuana, are illegal in Cambodia. However, marijuana is traditionally used in food preparation so you may find it sprinkled across some pizzas.

Many Western countries have laws that make sex offences committed overseas punishable at home.

Maps

The best all-round map is Gecko's *Cambodia Road Map* at a 1:750,000 scale.

Money

Cambodia's currency is the riel, abbreviated here by a lower-case r written after the sum. Riel notes (there are no coins) come in denominations of 50r, 100r, 200r, 500r, 1000r, 2000r, 5000r, 10,000r, 20,000r, 50,000r and 100,000r, though you'll rarely see the highest-denomination bills. Cambodia's second currency (some would say its first) is the US dollar, which is accepted everywhere. In far western Cambodia, the Thai baht is also commonly used.

Throughout this chapter, prices are in the currency quoted to the average punter – so get ready to think in three currencies.

ATMS

Debit- and credit-card-friendly ATMs are found in all major cities and a growing number of provincial towns and border crossings. Banks with ATMs include Acleda Bank in most provinces, ANZ Royal with good coverage in cities, and Canadia for most major provincial towns.

BARGAINING

Bargaining is expected in local markets, when travelling by share taxi or moto and, sometimes, when taking a cheap room. The Khmers are not ruthless hagglers so a persuasive smile and a little friendly quibbling is usually enough to get a good price.

CASH

The US dollar is accepted everywhere in Cambodia and US cash is the currency of most ATMs, so there's no need to buy riel at the border (don't believe the touts). US$1 banknotes are particularly useful; banks can supply them if you run out. Avoid ripped banknotes, which Cambodians often refuse. Near the Thai border, many transactions are in Thai baht.

When paying in dollars or baht, change is often given in riel, which is handy since small-denomination riel notes can be useful when paying for things such as moto rides and drinks. When calculating change, the US dollar is usually rounded off to 4000r.

CREDIT CARDS

Top-end hotels, airline offices and upmarket boutiques and restaurants generally accept most major credit cards (Visa, MasterCard, JCB, sometimes American Express) but they usually pass the charges on to the customer, meaning an extra 3% or more on the bill.

Photography

Many internet cafes in Phnom Penh, Siem Reap, Battambang and Sihanoukville will burn CDs (about US$1.50) or DVDs (about US$2.50) from digital images using card readers or USB connections. The price is about US$2.50 if you need a CD or US$1.50 if you don't. Digital memory sticks are widely available in Cambodia and are pretty cheap. Digital cameras are a real bargain in Cambodia thanks to low tax and duty, so consider picking up a new model in Phnom Penh rather than Bangkok or Ho Chi Minh City.

Make sure you have the necessary charger, plugs and transformer for Cambodia. Take care with some of the electrical wiring in guesthouses around the country, as it can be pretty amateurish.

Post

The postal service is hit and miss. When sending postcards and letters, make sure the stamps are franked before they disappear from your sight. Phnom Penh's main post office has a poste restante service.

Courier services include EMS, which has offices at all major post offices.

Public Holidays

Holidays may be rolled over if they fall on a weekend. Some people take off a day or two extra during major festivals (see p23). It is widely believed that Cambodia has more public holidays than any other country on earth.

International New Year's Day 1 January

Victory over Genocide Day 7 January

International Women's Day 8 March

International Labour Day 1 May

King's Birthday 13 to 15 May

International Children's Day 1 June

King Mother's Birthday 18 June

Constitution Day 24 September

Coronation Day 29 October

King Father's Birthday 31 October

Independence Day 9 November

International Human Rights Day 10 December

Safe Travel

MINES & MORTARS

Cambodia is one of the most heavily mined countries in the world, especially in the northwest of the country near the Thai border. Many mined areas are unmarked so *do not* stray from well-worn paths and *never, ever* touch any unexploded ordnance (UXO) you come across, including mortars and artillery shells. If you find yourself in a mined area, retrace your steps only if you can clearly see your footprints. If not, stay where you are and call for help. If someone is injured in a minefield, do not rush in to help even if they are crying out in pain – find someone who knows how to enter a mined area safely.

TRAFFIC ACCIDENTS

Traffic in Cambodia is chaotic, with vehicles moving in both directions on both sides of the road. Get in a serious accident in a remote area and somehow you'll have to make it to Phnom Penh, Siem Reap or Battambang for treatment. The horn is used to alert other drivers to a vehicle's presence – when walking, cycling or on a motorbike, get out of the way if you hear one honking behind you.

CRIME

Cambodia is now a generally safe place to travel as long as you exercise common sense. Hold-ups are rare but petty theft is still a problem in the major cities and at beaches.

Late at night, walking alone in unlit areas is not advisable, particularly for unaccompanied women.

In the major cities, drive-by bag snatchings happen and are especially dangerous when you're riding a moto as you can fall and hit your head. Never put a bag or purse in the front basket of a motorbike. Shoulder bags are an attractive target, so on a moto hold them tightly in front of you so that thieves – approaching from behind – don't have a strap to slash.

DRUGS

The local version of crystal meth, concocted in backstreet labs and known ominously as *yama* (the Hindu god of death), is often laced with toxic substances like mercury and lithium. Much of what is sold as 'cocaine' is actually pure heroin. Every year several travellers die from accidental overdose.

SCAMS

Cambodia is legendary for its inventive (and often well-connected) scammers. No need to be alarmed, but it helps to arrive with an idea of their repertoire.

The scam action often starts right at the Cambodian frontier – or, in many cases (such as Poipet), before you even get there – with shameless overcharging for visas. In fact, you may encounter your first Cambodia-related scam in Bangkok – remember, if that bus fare to Siem Reap sounds too good to be true, it probably is and may involve arriving very late at night and being taken to a substandard, overpriced guesthouse.

Upon setting foot on Cambodian territory, you are likely to meet your first moto drivers' cartel. These seemingly aggressive fellows (usually quite friendly once you get to know them) are intent on convincing you (or forcing you, by making sure there's a dearth of other options) to pay over the odds to get to the nearest town.

Moto fares have been rising in recent years, in part because of the skyrocketing price of petrol – a fact oft-cited by moto drivers – but prices that are two or three times those quoted in this book are probably a gouge, not a cost-of-living adjustment.

If possible, frontier moto drivers would also like to help you to 'change money', at rip-off rates. Remember, if you have US dollars (or, near Thailand, baht), there's absolutely no need to buy riel at the border. If you do want to exchange currency, never go to the exchange place 'recommended' by a moto driver, even if it bills itself as 'official'.

Both at borders and at inland bus stations, members of moto cartels with semi-official monopoly status (local officials get kick-backs for letting them operate) will make a determined effort to overcharge for rides. In Sihanoukville, particularly notorious for this sort of thing, all you need to do to pay the usual price is walk out of the bus station to the main road.

In parallel, they'll try to steer you to guesthouses and hotels that pay them fat commissions. Don't believe age-old lines such as 'that place is closed' – if you want to go to a specific establishment, insist on being taken there. Smiling also usually helps, as it does with everything in Cambodia.

We have also heard very occasional reports of local taxi drivers who stop midroute and ask for a higher fare.

Telephone

Landline area codes appear under the name of each city but in many areas service is spotty. Mobile phones, whose numbers start

SHOPPING TIPS

High-quality handmade crafts, including silk clothing and accessories, stone and wood carvings, and silver, are widely available, especially in Siem Reap, Phnom Penh and towns with particular handicraft specialities. Hill tribes in Mondulkiri and Ratanakiri produce hand-woven cotton in small quantities. In the Cambodia chapter of this book, we focus on shops and organisations that contribute to reviving traditional crafts and support people who are disadvantaged or disabled.

The ubiquitous cotton *krama* (chequered scarf) is a symbol of Cambodia and, for many Khmers, wearing one is an affirmation of their identity. Its main function is to provide protection from the sun, wind and dust, but it can also be worn as a mini-sarong, serve as a towel, be tied across the shoulders as a baby carrier and be stuffed inside a motorbike tyre in the event of a puncture. The most famous silk *kramas* come from Kompong Cham (p234) and Takeo Provinces.

with 01, 07, 08 or 09, are hugely popular with both individuals and commercial enterprises. Foreigners need to present a valid passport to get a local SIM card. For listings of businesses and government offices, check out www.yellowpages-cambodia.com.

Many internet shops offer cheap international calls for 100r to 1000r per minute, though in places with broadband speeds you can Skype for the price of an internet connection (usually 2000r to 4000r *per hour*). International calls from mobile phone shops cost about 1000r per minute.

Time

Cambodia, like Laos, Vietnam and Thailand, is seven hours ahead of Greenwich Mean Time or Universal Time Coordinated (GMT/UTC).

Visas

For most nationalities, one-month tourist visas (US$20) are available on arrival at Phnom Penh and Siem Reap airports and all land border crossings. Unfortunately, except at the airports and the land crossings with Vietnam, overcharging is rampant, and uniformed Cambodian border officials – and touts who work with them – are often very creative in compelling travellers to pay more than official rates.

At the notorious Poipet–Aranya Prathet crossing and at Cham Yeam–Hat Lek, visitors are told they must pay in baht, with fees set at 1000B (US$34) to 1200B (US$40), plus 100B for a photo. A few valiant travellers insist on paying in US dollars, but you'll be unlikely to get away with less than US$25. Avoid the Thai-side touts who will swear that visas are not issued at the frontier.

One-month tourist e-visas (US$20 plus a US$5 processing fee), which take three business days to issue and are valid for entry to Cambodia at the airports, Bavet, Poipet and Cham Yeam, are available from www.mfaic.gov.kh.

Tourist visas can only be extended once for one month, so if you're planning a longer stay, ask for a one-month business visa (US$25) when you arrive. Extensions for one/three/six/12 months cost about US$40/75/150/250 and take three or four business days; bring a passport photo. It may be cheaper to do a 'visa run' to Thailand, getting a fresh visa when you cross back into Cambodia. Overstayers are charged US$5 per day at the point of exit.

Thailand issues free 30-day visas to qualifying passport holders at all border crossings, but at least at Psar Pruhm–Ban Pakard (near Pailin) you'll have to show an onward ticket out of Thailand. Vietnamese visas are available in Phnom Penh, Sihanoukville and Battambang. Lao visas are issued in Phnom Penh.

Volunteering

Some of the many non-governmental organisations (NGOs) working in Cambodia welcome volunteers, though they may require a commitment of at least several months.

Cambodia hosts a huge number of NGOs, some of whom do require volunteers from time to time. The best way to find out who is represented in the country is to drop in on the **Cooperation Committee for Cambodia** (CCC; Map p184; ☎023-214152; 35 Ph 178) in Phnom Penh.

Professional Siem Reap–based organisations helping to place volunteers include **ConCERT** (Map p200; ☎063-963511; www.concertcambodia.org; 560 Phum Stoueng Thmey; ⏲9am-5pm Mon-Fri) and **Globalteer** (www.globalteer.org), but their programs do involve a weekly charge.

Women Travellers

Women will generally find Cambodia a safe country to travel in. As is the case anywhere in the world, walking or cycling alone late at night can be risky, and if you're planning to go off the beaten track it's a good idea to find a travelling companion.

Khmer women dress fairly conservatively, and it's best to follow suit, particularly when visiting wats. In general, long-sleeved shirts and long trousers or skirts are preferred. Miniskirts aren't too practical on motos, even if – like local women – you ride side-saddle.

Tampons and sanitary napkins are widely available in major cities and provincial capitals, as is the contraceptive pill.

Work

Jobs are available throughout Cambodia, but apart from English teaching or helping out in guesthouses or bars, most are for professionals and arranged in advance. Places to look for work include the classifieds sections of the *Phnom Penh Post* and the *Cambodia Daily*, and the noticeboards at guesthouses and restaurants in Phnom Penh.

Getting There & Away

Entering Cambodia

Most travellers enter Cambodia by plane or bus, but there are also boat connections from Vietnam via the Mekong River.

Formalities at Cambodia's international airports are generally smoother than at land borders. That said, crossing overland from Vietnam is relatively stress-free. Crossing the borders between Cambodia and Laos or Thailand often involves being overcharged for visa fees or unpublicised overtime fees.

Air

Cambodia's two major international airports, Phnom Penh and Siem Reap, have frequent flights to destinations all over eastern Asia. International departure tax of US$25 is now included in the ticket price.

Air Asia (www.airasia.com) Flights from Phnom Penh and Siem Reap to Kuala Lumpur, plus Phnom Penh to Bangkok.

Air France (www.airfrance.com) Flights from Phnom Penh to Paris via Bangkok.

Asiana Airlines (http://flyasiana.com/english) Flights to Seoul.

Bangkok Airways (www.bangkokair.com) Flights from Phnom Penh and Siem Reap to Bangkok.

Cambodia Angkor Airways (www.cambodiaangkorair.com) Daily connections from Phnom Penh and Siem Reap to Ho Chi Minh City (Saigon).

China Airlines (www.china-airlines.com) Phnom Penh to Taipei.

China Eastern Airlines (www.flychinaeastern.com) Links Siem Reap with Kūnmíng.

China Southern Airlines (www.cs-air.com/en) Links Phnom Penh with Guangzhou.

Dragon Air (www.dragonair.com) Phnom Penh and Siem Reap to Hong Kong.

Eva Air (www.evaair.com) Phnom Penh to Taipei.

Jetstar Asia (www.jetstarasia.com) Cheapest flights from Phnom Penh and Siem Reap to Singapore.

Korean Air (www.koreanair.com) Phnom Penh and Siem Reap to Seoul.

Lao Airlines (www.laos-airlines.com) Flights to Vientiane, Luang Prabang and Pakse.

Malaysia Airlines (www.malaysia-airlines.com) Phnom Penh and Siem Reap to Kuala Lumpur.

Shanghai Airlines (www.shanghai-air.com) Links Phnom Penh with Shanghai.

Silk Air (www.silkair.com) Phnom Penh and Siem Reap to Singapore, plus Siem Reap to Danang in Vietnam.

Thai Airways International (www.thaiair.com) Links Phnom Penh with Bangkok.

Vietnam Airlines (www.vietnamairlines.com) Has flights to Ho Chi Minh City, Hanoi, Vientiane and Luang Prabang, so offers useful Indochina loop options.

Land & River

BORDER CROSSINGS

For details on border crossings in the region, see p33. Cambodia shares land borders with Laos, Thailand and Vietnam. There is also a popular river crossing offering boat connections between Phnom Penh and the Mekong Delta in Vietnam. As well as daily fast boats between Phnom Penh and Chau Doc, there are also some boutique cruise options taking between three and seven days (the latter including Kompong Cham and Siem Reap). Popular companies include:

Indochina Sails (www.indochina-sails.com) Operates luxurious *La Marguerite*.

Jayavarman VII (www.heritage-line.com) Arguably the smartest boat on the Mekong.

Pandaw Cruises (www.pandaw.com) Several boats operating.

Toum Teav Cruises (www.cf-mekong.com) Smaller boats than the competition.

Getting Around

Air

The only scheduled domestic flights link Phnom Penh with Siem Reap (from US$90) and all are currently operated by **Cambodia Angkor Airways** (www.cambodiaangkorair.com), a monopolistic joint-venture with Vietnam Airlines.

Bicycle

Cambodia is a great country for adventurous cyclists as travelling at gentle speeds allows for lots of interaction with locals. Cycling around Angkor is an awesome experience as it really gives you a sense of the size and scale of the temple complex.

Adventure mountain biking is likely to take off in the Cardamom Mountains and in Mondulkiri and Ratanakiri Provinces over the coming years.

Much of Cambodia is pancake flat or only moderately hilly. Safety, however, is a considerable concern on paved roads as trucks, buses and cars barrel along at high speed.

Some guesthouses and hotels rent out bicycles for US$2 or so day. If you'll be doing lots of cycling, bring along a bike helmet, which can also provide some protection on a moto.

For the full story on cycle touring in Cambodia, see Lonely Planet's *Cycling Vietnam, Laos & Cambodia,* which has the low-down on planning a major ride.

Boat

For details on the fast boats from Phnom Penh to Siem Reap (via Kompong Chhnang) and the leisurely boats linking Siem Reap with Battambang, see p277 and p224.

Bus

About a dozen bus companies serve all populated parts of the country. The largest and, often, least expensive is **Phnom Penh Sorya** (www.ppsoryatransport.com). Comfort levels and prices vary, and a few companies charge foreigners more than they do locals, so if you're on a tight budget it pays to shop around. Booking bus tickets through guesthouses and hotels is convenient but incurs a commission.

Car & Motorcycle

Cambodia's main national highways (NH) are generally in excellent condition but can be quite dangerous due to the prevalence of high-speed overtaking/passing.

Travel is riskier around dusk and at night as there may be drunk drivers (or pedestrians) about. Aim to avoid road travel after dark.

Guesthouses and hotels can arrange hire cars with a driver for about US$30 or so a day, plus petrol, and lodging and food for the driver.

In many towns (Siem Reap and Sihanoukville are exceptions), 100cc and 125cc motorbikes can be hired for US$4 to US$10 a day. 250cc bikes are available in some places for US$10 to US$20 per day. No licence is required except by the occasional policeman when fishing for some cash. Use a strong lock and always leave the bike in guarded parking where available.

Local Transport

A few *cyclos* (pedicabs) can still be seen on the streets of Phnom Penh and Battambang, but they have been almost completely replaced by motos (or *motodups*), unmarked motorbike taxis. It used to be that moto prices were rarely agreed in advance, but with the increase in visitor numbers a lot of drivers have gotten into the habit of overcharging foreigners.

Chartering a moto for the day costs US$7 to US$10, more if a greater distance is involved or the driver speaks good English.

The vehicle known in Cambodia as a túk-túk is, technically speaking, a remork (or *remorque-moto*), ie a roofed, two-wheeled trailer hitched to the back of a motorbike. Fares are roughly double those of motos, though in some places you pay per passenger. Still, for two or more people a remork can be cheaper than a moto and much more comfortable if it's raining.

Local taxis can be ordered via guesthouses and hotels in Phnom Penh, Siem Reap and Sihanoukville. There are now some metered taxi companies in Phnom Penh.

Share Taxi, Minibus & Pick-Up

Share taxis (usually jacked-up old Toyota Camrys), which depart when full, are a bit faster and slightly more expensive than buses. The custom in Cambodia is that each share taxi carries six or seven passengers, in addition to the driver. That's two in the front seat and four in the back, with a seventh passenger sometimes squished between the driver and his door. Pay double the regular fare and you get the front seat all to yourself; pay six fares and you've got yourself a private taxi.

Minibuses are even more jam-packed, which is why they're a bit cheaper than share taxis – that, and the fact that some are driven by maniacs. On some routes you can join the locals on a pick-up. Riding out back with the masses is cheaper than a place in the cab, but bring a *krama*, sunscreen and, in the wet season, rain gear.

Laos

Includes »

Best Places to Eat

» Tamarind (p306)
» L'Elephant Restaurant (p306)
» La Terrasse (p288)
» Jasmine Restaurant (p341)
» Le Camargue (p288)

Best Places to Stay

» Auberge Les 3 Nagas (p304)
» Apsara (p305)
» Boat Landing Guest House & Restaurant (p323)
» Auberge Sala Don Khone (p348)

Why Go?

Imagine a country where your pulse relaxes, smiles are genuine and locals are still curious about you. A place where it's easy to make a quick detour and find yourself well and truly off the traveller circuit, in a landscape straight out of a daydream: jagged limestone cliffs, brooding jungle and the snaking Mekong River. Welcome to Laos, home to as many as 132 ethnic groups and a history steeped in war, imperialism and mysticism. Paddy fields glimmering in the post-monsoon light, Buddhist temples winking through morning mist as monks file past French colonial villas... Laos deserves all the hyperbole thrown at it, and more. Adrenalin junkies can lose themselves in underground river-caves, white-water rapids or jungle ziplines; wildlife nuts can trek through Southeast Asia's most pristine forests, still home to tigers and leopards. From hedonist to gourmand, every type of traveller seems to find what they're looking for here.

When to Go

Vientiane

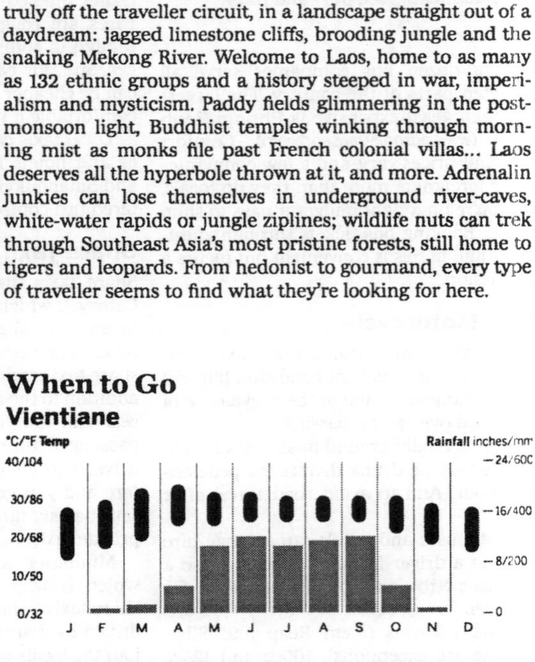

Jan Cool-season breezes; even the infernal south is pleasant.

Oct Mercifully cool weather. Bun Awk Phansa sees the floating of candle-bearing boats down rivers.

Nov–Dec Bun That Luang sees celebrations in Luang Prabang and Vientiane. Cool weather.

Connections

Well-placed Laos is sandwiched between Vietnam, Cambodia, Thailand, Myanmar (Burma) and China. Roads have improved over recent years thanks to the creation of Chinese trade routes, and many ailing public buses have also been updated. Air travel has recently progressed, with the national carrier, Lao Airlines, enjoying a new fleet of planes, better safety records and daily flights to Bangkok, Hanoi, Kuala Lumpur and Siem Reap; its routes cover the entire country, making it easier than ever to see more in less time.

ITINERARIES

One Week

After spending a few days in riverside **Vientiane** sampling its Soviet-Franco architecture, sophisticated bars and Asian-fusion cuisine, travel north to the unforgettable ancient city of **Luang Prabang** to experience its temples, crumbling villas, pampering spas, myriad monks and Gallic cuisine.

Two Weeks

Fly to **Vientiane**, imbibe its fine accommodation and cuisine for a few days then head north to **Vang Vieng** for climbing, kayaking and tubing in serene karst scenery. Leisurely move on up to **Luang Prabang**, the jewel of Southeast Asia and a place so bedecked with charming bakeries, temples, boutiques and restaurants you may not want to leave. After a few days here take a two-day slow boat up the Mekong River to **Huay Xai**, having already booked yourself in for the memorable **Gibbon Experience** and an overnight stay in a jungle tree house. If you've got time, head up to **Luang Nam Tha** for an ecoconscious trek in the wild **Nam Ha National Protected Area (NPA)**. From here you can fly back to Vientiane to catch your flight out.

Internet Resources

» **Ecotourism Laos** (www.ecotourismlaos.com) Focusing on trekking, the environment and eco-activities.

» **Lonely Planet** (www.lonelyplanet.com) Head to the Thorntree forum for the latest news from the road.

» **Lao Bumpkin** (www.laobumpkin.blogspot.com) Travel, food and all things Lao.

» **Lao National Tourism Authority** (www.tourismlaos.gov.la) Mostly up-to-date travel information from the government.

» **Vientiane Times** (www.vientianetimes.org.la) Website of the country's only English-language newspaper. Operated by the government.

NEED TO KNOW

» **Currency** Kip (K)

» **Language** Lao

» **Money** Plenty of ATMs in every major town and city

» **Visas** 30-day visa available upon arrival

» **Mobile phones** Prepay SIM cards available across Laos for as little as 10,000K

Fast Facts

» **Area** 236,000 sq km

» **Capital** Vientiane

» **Country Code** ☎856

» **Population** 6.1 million

Exchange Rates

Australia	A$1	8600K
Canada	C$1	8300K
Europe	€1	11,000k
Japan	¥100	10,000K
New Zealand	NZ$1	6500K
UK	£1	13,100K
USA	US$1	8000K

Set Your Budget

» **Budget hotel room** US$20

» **Evening meal** US$3–10

» **Museum admission** US$1

» **Beer** US$1–3 for a big bottle

Laos Highlights

❶ Explore the fabled city of **Luang Prabang** (p298) to find French cuisine, Buddhist temples, colonial villas, stunning river views and some of the best boutique accommodation in Southeast Asia

❷ Take a boat ride through the exhilarating yet spooky 7.5km **Kong Lo Cave** (p330), home to fist-sized spiders and stalactite woods

❸ Zip through the treetops, sleeping among the wild things in a cosy jungle tree house, on the **Gibbon Experience** (p327), Laos' premier eco adventure

❹ Take an eco-responsible trek through some of the wildest, densest jungle in the country, in **Nam Ha National Protected Area (NPA)** (p322), home to tigers and a rich variety of ethnic tribes

❺ Lower your pulse in the travellers' Mecca of Four Thousand Islands, **Si Phan Don** (p344), where the Mekong River turns turquoise and the night air is flecked with fireflies

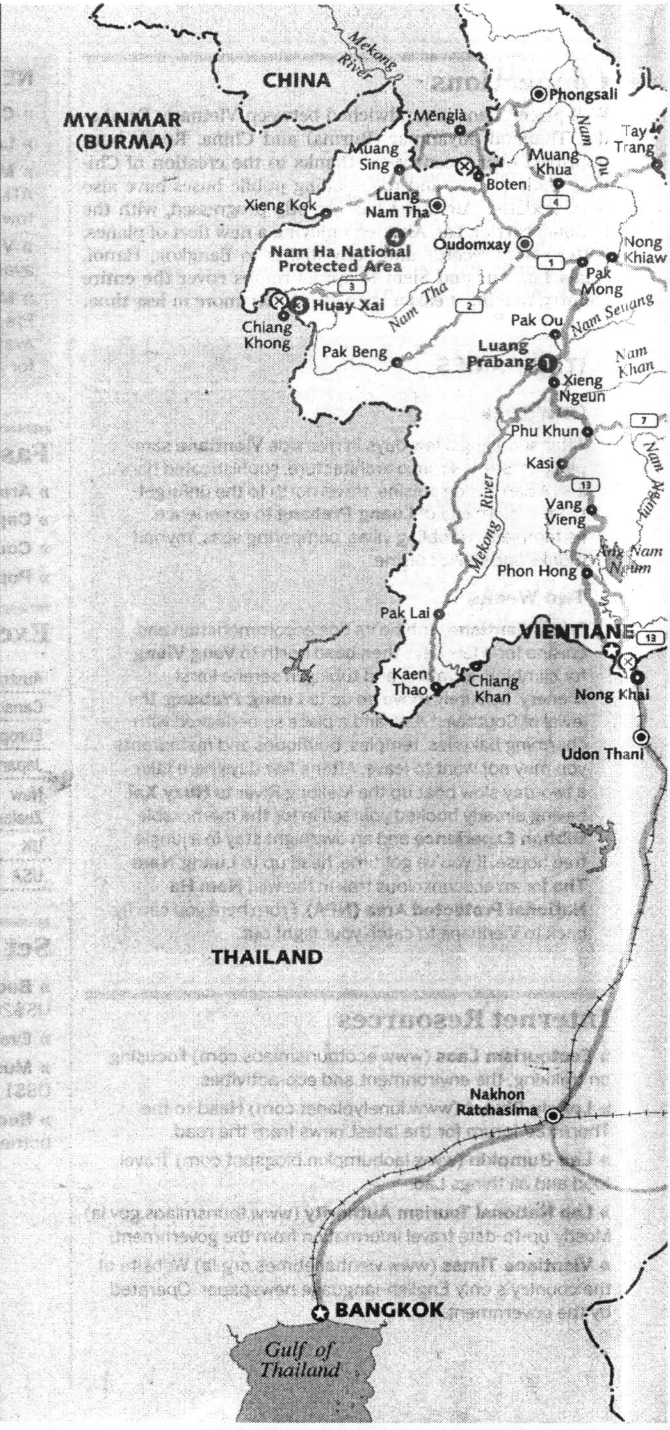

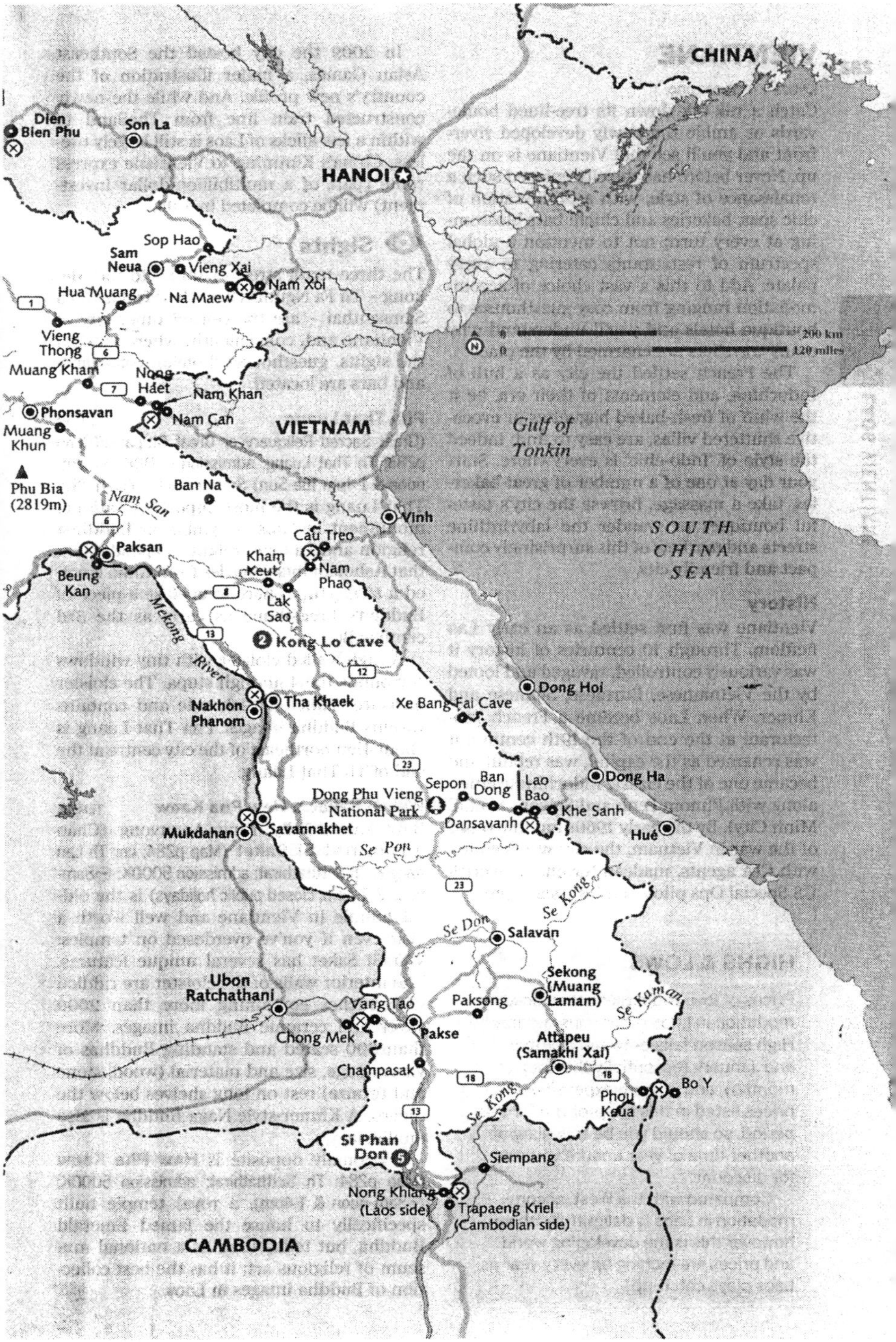

CHINA
Dien Bien Phu
Son La
HANOI
Sop Hao
Sam Neua
Vieng Xai
Na Maew
Nam Xoi
Hua Muang
1
Vieng Thong
6
Muang Kham
Nong Haet
7
Nam Khan
Phonsavan
Nam Can
Muang Khun
VIETNAM
0 200 km
0 120 miles
Gulf of Tonkin
Phu Bia (2819m)
Nam San
Ban Na
6
Vinh
Cau Treo
Paksan
Kham Keut
Nam Phao
Beung Kan
8
Lak Sao
Mekong River
13
2 Kong Lo Cave
SOUTH CHINA SEA
12
Dong Hoi
Nakhon Phanom
Tha Khaek
Xe Bang Fai Cave
23
Dong Ha
Sepon
Ban Dong
Lao Bao
Dong Phu Vieng National Park
Khe Sanh
Dansavanh
Mukdahan
Savannakhet
Se Pon
Hué
23
Se Kong
Se Don
Salavan
Sekong (Muang Lamam)
Se Kaman
Ubon Ratchathani
Paksong
Vang Tao
Pakse
Chong Mek
Attapeu (Samakhi Xai)
Champasak
18
18
Bo Y
Phou Keua
Se Kong
13
Si Phan Don 5
Siempang
Nong Khiang (Laos side)
Trapaeng Kriel (Cambodian side)
CAMBODIA

VIENTIANE

☎021 / POP 237,000

Catch a túk-túk down its tree-lined boulevards or amble the newly developed riverfront and you'll see that Vientiane is on the up. Never before has the city enjoyed such a renaissance of style, with a proliferation of chic spas, bakeries and chichi bars blossoming at every turn; not to mention a global spectrum of restaurants catering to every palate. Add to this a vast choice of accommodation ranging from cosy guesthouses to boutique hotels and you'll understand why many travellers are charmed by the place.

The French settled the city as a hub of Indochina, and elements of their era, be it the whiff of fresh-baked baguettes or evocative shuttered villas, are easy to find; indeed the style of 'Indo-chic' is everywhere. Start your day at one of a number of great bakeries, take a massage, browse the city's tasteful boutiques or wander the labyrinthine streets and markets of this surprisingly compact and friendly city.

History

Vientiane was first settled as an early Lao fiefdom. Through 10 centuries of history it was variously controlled, ravaged and looted by the Vietnamese, Burmese, Siamese and Khmer. When Laos became a French protectorate at the end of the 19th century, it was renamed as the capital, was rebuilt and became one of the classic Indochinese cities, along with Phnom Penh and Saigon (Ho Chi Minh City). By the early 1960s and the onset of the war in Vietnam, the city was teeming with CIA agents, madcap Ravens (maverick US Special Ops pilots) and Russian spies.

HIGHS & LOWS

Prices of low-and high-season accommodation in Laos differ considerably. High season falls between October and January (essentially the cooler months), and is more expensive. All prices listed in this chapter are for this period, so should you be travelling at another time of year ensure you ask for discount.

Compared with the West, accommodation in Laos is delightfully cheap, however this is the developing world and prices are inching up every year as Laos plays catch-up.

In 2009 the city hosted the Southeast Asian Games, a major illustration of the country's new profile. And while the newly constructed train line from Thailand to within a few klicks of Laos is still largely useless, China's Kūnmíng to Vientiane express route (part of a multibillion-dollar investment) will be completed in 2014.

Sights

The three main streets parallel to the Mekong – Th Fa Ngum, Th Setthathirat and Th Samsenthai – are the central inner city of Vientiane and, conveniently, where most of the sights, guesthouses, hotels, restaurants and bars are located.

Pha That Luang STUPA

(Great Sacred Reliquary or Great Stupa; off Map p283; Th That Luang; admission 5000K; ⌚8am-noon & 1-4pm Tue-Sun) Svelte and golden Pha That Luang is the most important national monument in Laos; a symbol of Buddhist religion and Lao sovereignty. Legend has it that Ashokan missionaries from India erected a *tâht* (stupa) here to enclose a piece of Buddha's breastbone as early as the 3rd century BC.

A high-walled cloister with tiny windows surrounds the 45m-high stupa. The cloister measures 85m on each side and contains various Buddha images. Pha That Luang is about 4km northeast of the city centre at the end of Th That Luang.

Wat Si Saket & Haw Pha Kaew TEMPLE

Built in 1818 by King Anouvong (Chao Anou), **Wat Si Saket** (Map p284; cnr Th Lan Xang & Th Setthathirat; admission 5000K; ⌚8am-noon & 1-4pm, closed public holidays) is the oldest temple in Vientiane and well worth a visit even if you've overdosed on temples. Wat Si Saket has several unique features. The interior walls of the cloister are riddled with niches containing more than 2000 silver and ceramic Buddha images. More than 300 seated and standing Buddhas of varying age, size and material (wood, stone and bronze) rest on long shelves below the niches. A Khmer-style Naga Buddha is also on display.

Diagonally opposite is **Haw Pha Kaew** (Map p284; Th Setthathirat; admission 5000K; ⌚8am-noon & 1-4pm), a royal temple built specifically to house the famed Emerald Buddha, but today used as a national museum of religious art; it has the best collection of Buddha images in Laos.

Vientiane

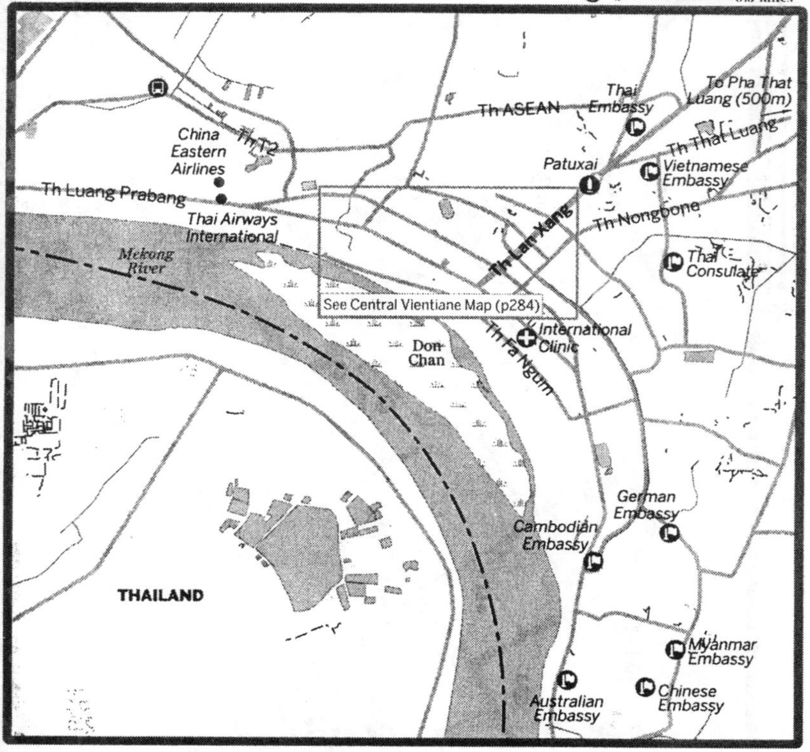

Patuxai MONUMENT
(Victory Monument; Map p283; Th Lan Xang; admission 3000K; ⏲8am-5pm) Vientiane's Arc de Triomphe replica is a slightly incongruous sight, dominating the commercial district around Th Lan Xang. Officially called 'Victory Monument' *and* commemorating the Lao who died in prerevolutionary wars, it was built in 1969 with cement donated by the USA intended for the construction of a new airport; hence expats refer to it as 'the vertical runway'. Climb to the summit for panoramic views over Vientiane.

Lao National Museum MUSEUM
(Map p284; ☎212461; Th Samsenthai; admission 10,000K; ⏲8am-noon & 1-4pm) This French-era building flanked by cherry blossom and magnolia trees was formerly known as the Lao Revolutionary Museum, and much of its collection retains an unshakeable revolutionary zeal. Downstairs – a potted account of Khmer culture in the south, accompanied by tools and Buddha statuary; upstairs – ponderous displays tell the story of the Pathet Lao, peppered with busts of Lenin and Ho Chi Minh.

Xieng Khuan (Buddha Park) MUSEUM
(Suan Phut; admission 5000K, camera 3000K; ⏲8am-4.30pm) Twenty-five kilometre southeast of Vientiane, eccentric Xieng Khuan thrills with other-worldly Buddhist and Hindu sculptures, and was designed and built in 1958 by Luang Pu, a yogi-priest-shaman who merged Hindu and Buddhist philosophy, mythology and iconography into a cryptic whole.

Bus 14 (8000K, one hour, 24km) leaves the Talat Sao Bus Station every 15 or 20 minutes throughout the day and goes all the way to Xieng Khuan. Alternatively, charter a túk-túk (145,000K return).

Central Vientiane

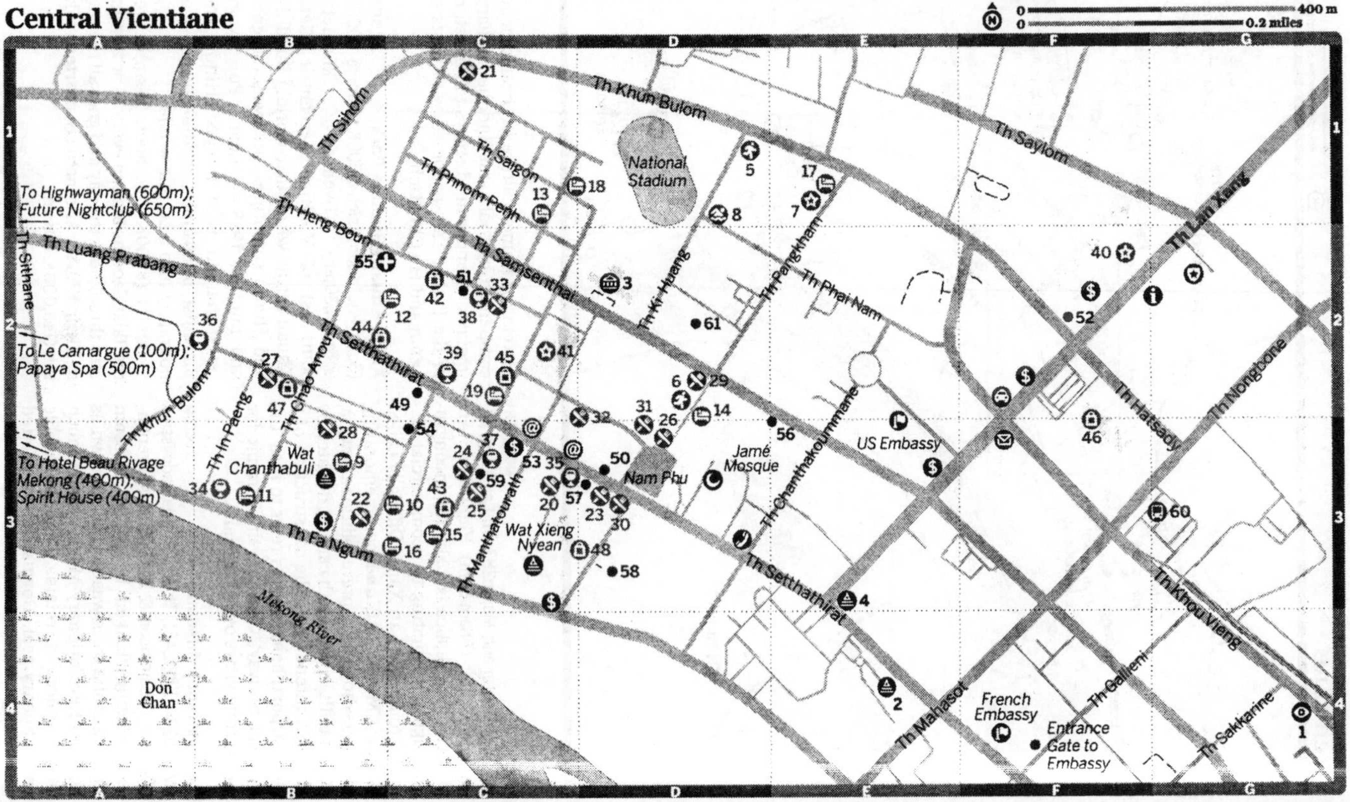

Central Vientiane

Sights
1 COPE Centre G4
2 Haw Pha Kaew E4
3 Lao National Museum D2
4 Wat Si Saket E3

Activities, Courses & Tours
5 Lao Bowling Centre D1
6 Mandarina Massage D2
7 Settha Palace Hotel Swimming Pool E1
8 Vientiane Swimming Pool D1

Sleeping
9 Ansara Hôtel B3
10 Best Western Hotel C3
11 Intercity Hotel B3
12 Lani Guest House C2
13 Lao Heritage Hotel C1
14 Mali Namphu Guest House D2
15 Mixay Guest House C3
16 Orchid Guesthouse C3
17 Settha Palace Hotel E1
18 Syri 1 Guest House C1
19 Vayakorn House C2

Eating
20 Amphone C3
21 Ban Anou Night Market C1
22 Douang Deuane Restaurant B3
23 JoMa Bakery Café D3
24 La Terrasse C3
25 Le Banneton C3
26 Le Provencal D3
27 Le Vendôme B2
28 Makphet B3
29 Nam Phu Restaurant D2
30 PhimPhone Market D3
31 Scandinavian Bakery D3
32 Taj Mahal Restaurant D2
33 YuLaLa Cafe C2

Drinking
34 Bor Pennyang B3
35 Jazzy Brick C3
36 Loft B2
37 Martini Bar C3
38 Noy's Fruit Heaven C2
39 Samlo Pub C2

Entertainment
40 Centre Culturel et de Coopération Linguistique F2
41 Lao Traditional Show C2

Shopping
42 Book Cafe C2
43 Camacrafts C3
44 Indochina's Handicrafts B2
45 Monument Books C2
46 Talat Sao F3
47 T'Shop Lai Gallery B2
48 Vientiane Book Center D3

Information
49 A-Rasa Tours C2
50 Green Discovery D3
51 Green Discovery C2
52 Immigration Office F2
53 Lao Development Bank C3
54 Lasi Ticketing C3
55 Poppy's Pharmacy C2

Transport
56 Europcar E3
57 Jule's Classic Rental D3
58 Lao Airlines D3
59 PVO C3
60 Talat Sao Bus Station G3
Thai-Lao International Bus .... (see 60)
61 Vietnam Airlines D2

Activities

Bowling

Lao Bowling Centre BOWLING
(Map p284; ☎218661; Th Khun Bulom; per frame with shoe hire 16,000K; ⊙9am-midnight) Bright lights, Beerlao and boisterous bowlers are what you'll find here. It's good fun.

Cooking Classes

Thongbay Guesthouse COOKING COURSE
(☎242292; www.thongbay-guesthouses.com; Ban Nong Douange; half-day class 125,000K) Courses at beautiful Thongbay Guesthouse are organised on demand (maximum 10 people) and start at 9am, finishing at 4pm. The price includes a trip to the market, cooking and feasting on your culinary creations.

Gym & Aerobics

Sengdara Fitness HEALTH & FITNESS
(☎414061; 5/77 Th Dong Palan; ⊙6am-10pm) Sengdara has top-notch facilities and contemporary equipment, offering sauna, pool, massage, aerobics and yoga classes. Visitors can buy a 32,000K day pass, which includes

COPE: LIGHT IN THE DARKNESS

An estimated 260 million sub-munition 'bombies' were dropped on Laos between 1964 and 1973 – sadly, 78 million of them failed to explode. Since the end of the war more than 12,000 people have fallen prey to UXO (unexploded ordnance) – many of them children – rendering the work that takes place at the excellent **COPE centre** (Map p284; ☎021 218 427; www.copelaos.org; Th Khou Vieng; admission free; ⊙9am-6pm) among the most vital in the country.

A 1km bike ride from the city centre, the excellent COPE is an inspiring not-for-profit organisation dedicated to supporting the victims of UXO. Since 1992 it has provided clinical mentoring and training programs for local staff in the manufacture of artificial limbs and related rehabilitation activities. There are five COPE centres across Laos where high-tech but low-cost artificial limbs are made, transforming the lives of people who've had to make do with their own improvised limbs.

The recently updated UXO exhibition is fascinating, with photographs portraying the salvaged lives of victims, as well as 'The Cave cinema', a bunker-style screening room showing a number of documentaries. There's also the new Karma Café, where you can grab a homemade ice cream and cool off between exploring the centre. Take a free tour around the centre accompanied by an English-speaking guide.

COPE often has openings for for those with the following skills: orthopaedic surgery, physiotherapy, occupational therapy and IT and graphic design. Get in touch with Kerryn Clarke on cope@laopdr.com.

use of everything. Also has evening tae kwon do classes.

Massage & Herbal Saunas

Wat Sok Pa Luang MASSAGE, SPA

(Th Sok Pa Luang; ⊙1-7pm) For a traditional massage and meditation class, head to this wat located in a semirural setting (*wat pàa* means 'forest temple'). It's famous for herbal saunas (10,000K) and massages (25,000K). It's 3km from the city centre. Avoid rush hour between 3pm and 6pm.

Mandarina Massage MASSAGE

(Map p284; ☎218703; Th Pangkham; ⊙10am-10pm) Offers a range of foot, herbal and oil massages in tasteful, eucalyptus-scented surroundings (50,000K to 300,000K per hour; aromatic deep-tissue massages from 150,000K).

Papaya Spa SPA

(off Map p284; ☎020 5561 0565; www.papayaspa.com; Th Phagna Sy; ⊙9am-7pm) Perhaps the best place to lose yourself in pampered heaven, this faded villa crowded with plants is an oasis of cool and the perfect spot to unwind. Massages start at 110,000K. Try the Papaya Honey Moon package (810,000K) comprising a massage, facial, scrub and sauna. It's less than a kilometre out of town.

Meditation

Foreigners are welcome at a regular Saturday-afternoon sitting at Wat Sok Pa Luang (p286). The session runs from 4pm until 5.30pm with an opportunity to ask questions afterwards.

Swimming

Vientiane Swimming Pool (Map p284; ☎020 5552 1002; Th Ki Huang; admission 10,000K; ⊙8am-7pm) is a 25m al fresco delight favoured by the local cops' swim team, but buy some goggles (25,000K) – there's enough chlorine in there to strip the barnacles off Davy Jones. The **Australian Embassy Recreation Club** (AERC; ☎314921; Km 3, Th Tha Deua; ⊙9am-8pm) is another option, but for Hollywood glamour sample the kidney-shaped pool at the **Settha Palace Hotel** (Map p284; ☎217581; 6 Th Pangkham; admission 50,000K, ⊙7am-8pm).

Sleeping

There's been a positive shift in accommodation of late, with few crappy box-rooms surviving, replaced instead by boutique accommodation in revived French villas, and decent midrange options. December to February are peak tourist months, so book ahead.

TOP CHOICE **Settha Palace Hotel** HOTEL $$$

(Map p284; ☎217581; www.setthapalace.com; 6 Th Pangkham; r standard/deluxe US$187/280; ❄@📶🏊) The Palace is a study in taste, evoking Indo-chic with a modern twist. Jazz music pipes down marble corridors while the kidney-shaped pool and Belle Epoque restaurant exude old-world charm.

Trad-luxe rooms are spacious and fragrant. Impeccable.

Lao Heritage Hotel GUESTHOUSE $$
(Map p284; ☎265093; Th Phnom Penh; s/d US$20/25; ❄🅟📶) This stunning midrange place is a cut above the rest thanks to its lovely outside terraced gardens and tasteful rooms with boutique flourishes: white walls, stained-wood floors, cable TV and an ever-vigilant sense of taste. Rooms 1 and 2 are our favourites.

Best Western Hotel HOTEL $$
(Map p284; ☎216906; Th Francois Ngin; r incl breakfast US$66; ❄🅟📶🏊) Sugar-white, modern rooms close to the river with great street views (earplugs essential!), cable TV, fresh linen and luxuries such as a gym, exquisite garden and plunge pool. Check out the lobby's freaky fish in the domed aquarium.

Lani Guest House GUESTHOUSE $$
(Map p284; ☎214919; www.laniguesthouse.com; Th Setthathirat; r US$33-38; ❄) Located down a quiet street, Lani's art deco building has traditional rooms boasting wall hangings, mosquito nets and bamboo-framed beds. Its atmospheric lobby is festooned with handicrafts and stuffed animals.

Syri 1 Guest House GUESTHOUSE $
(Map p284; ☎212682; Th Saigon; r 70,000-150,000K; ❄) This budget favourite with its flame-muralled lobby is a great place to meet other travellers. It has generously sized rooms, bikes for rent, and the owner, Air, can take you on his own tailored bike tour of the city.

Orchid Guesthouse GUESTHOUSE $
(Map p284; ☎252825; Th Fa Ngum; r 90,000-160,000K; ❄🅟) Teetering into the sky like some lantern-festooned Jenga tower, Chinese-owned Orchid is short on charm, but its maze of rooms, many windowless, boast en suites and a great sundown terrace overlooking the Mekong.

Hotel Beau Rivage Mekong GUESTHOUSE $$
(off Map p284; ☎243375; www.hbrm.com; Th Fa Ngum; r incl breakfast US$42-50; ❄🅟📶) This beautiful boutique hotel on a quiet stretch of the river has 16 pastel-shaded rooms with terrazzo floors and wooden screens, enjoying a lush garden out back.

Ansara Hôtel HOTEL $$$
(Map p 284; ☎213514; www.ansarahotel.com; off Th Fa Ngum; r/ste incl breakfast US$105-170; ❄🅟) Achingly beautiful Ansara is housed in a recently revived French villa with heavy whiffs of Indochina. Its al fresco dining terrace is as refined as its Gallic cuisine.

Vayakorn House HOTEL $$
(Map p284; ☎241911; 91 Th Nokeo Khumman; s/d/tr 140,000/220,000/280,000K; ❄📶) Long a stalwart for no-nonsense comfort, popular Vayakorn has 21 rooms with fresh linen, en suites, TV and air-con. Accepts credit cards.

Intercity Hotel HOTEL $$
(Map p284; ☎242843/4; www.laointercity.com; 24-25 Th Fa Ngum; s/d/ste incl breakfast US$35/55/75; ❄🅟📶) This quirky river-facing hotel with its deceptively shabby exterior is an oasis of oxblood-coloured walls, silk drapes and Buddhist statuary. The superior rooms boast the most romance.

Mixay Guest House GUESTHOUSE $
(Map p284; ☎262210; 39 Th Nokeo Khumman; dm 50,000K, s/d without bathroom 70,000/85,000K, r with air-con & bathroom 110,000K; ❄) Great-value, fan-cooled rooms. Some have hot-water bathrooms, while others are bereft of windows. Also a left-luggage facility.

Mali Namphu Guest House GUESTHOUSE $$
(Map p284; ☎215093; 114 Th Pangkham; r incl breakfast 170,000-250,000K; ❄📶) A lush courtyard forms the centrepiece of this lovely midrange place with fragrant rooms decked in Lao handicrafts, and enjoying impeccably clean bathrooms. There's also cable TV.

Eating

If you were looking to lose a few pounds in Vientiane, forget it. This is a gourmand's heaven, and it's possible to eat your way round a global route from Japan to France – with just about everything in between – in a vast selection of top-flight restaurants as well as informal cafes, juice bars and roadside vendors alchemising delicious grilled fare.

Makphet LAOTIAN $
(Map p284; Th Setthathirat; mains 40,000K; ⏰11am-9pm Mon, Wed, Thu, Fri & Sat, 6-9pm Tue) Managed by Friends International (www.friends-international.org), Makphet helps disadvantaged kids build a future as chefs and waiters, while reviving the country's traditional cuisine. Guacamole-green walls and hardwood furnishings add style to delicious dishes such as spicy green papaya salad. It's located opposite Wat Inpeng.

Le Provencal FRENCH $
(Map p284; Nam Phu; mains 40,000K; ⊙lunch Mon-Sat, dinner daily; ❄) This seasoned trusty has an old-world ambience with its shadowy, wooden interior. The menu excels, with wood-fired pizzas and succulent steaks at surprisingly affordable prices. It may be as old as Nam Phu circle but Le Provencal seems to get better with age.

Amphone LAOTIAN $$
(Map p284; 10/3 Th Wat Xieng Nyean; mains 20,000-65,000K; ⊙11am-2pm & 5.30-10pm; ❄) Featured on celebrity chef Anthony Bourdain's 'Discovery' TV series, Amphone replicates traditional Laotian dishes based on owner Mook's grandmother's creations. 'Luang Prabang sausage' and 'fish citronella' are but a few.

La Terrasse FRENCH $$
(Map p284; Th Nokeo Khumman; mains 40,000-100,000K; ⊙11am-6pm Mon-Sat) With its old-fashioned French ambience, this place is a real gem for perfectly executed Gallic cuisine. As proof, its menu – heavy on *steak au frites* and boeuf bourguignon – is patronised by French expats.

Le Vendôme FRENCH $$
(Map p284; 39 Th Inpeng; mains 75,000K; ⊙5-10pm Tue-Sun) Hidden behind a cascade of ivy, it's almost as if this vintage French restaurant is in hiding. Candlelit ambience accompanies very reasonably priced soufflés, pâtés, salads and wood-fired pizzas, plus a good wine selection.

Le Camargue FRENCH $$$
(off Map p284; 164 Th Sibouaban; mains 80,000-120,000K; ⊙11.30am-2pm & 5-10pm Mon-Sat) A colonial-era villa with old bullfighting posters hung on exposed-brick walls is the setting for this stylish new restaurant producing specialities from the Camargue region: tapas, fish, meat, fondue, salads and paella, plus an extensive wine cellar.

JoMa Bakery Café BAKERY $
(Map p284; Th Setthathirat; mains 28,000K; ⊙7am-9pm Mon-Sat; ❄📶) Vientiane's busiest bakery is thick with the tang of arabica, and its comfy couches, free wi-fi, American breakfasts, cinnamon buns, bagels and bespoke subs will keep you coming back for more.

Le Banneton BAKERY $
(Map p284; Th Nokeo Khumman; breakfasts 45,000K; ⊙7am-9pm; ❄) Creating the city's best croissants, Banneton's Doisneau-spattered interior makes for a nice place to read a paper over a tart, salad, panini or tasty omelette. Get there first thing in the morning to really make the most of the pastry.

Scandinavian Bakery BAKERY $
(Map p284; Nam Phu; mains 10,000-30,000K; ⊙7am-7pm; ❄) Having had more facelifts than a Hollywood starlet, Vientiane's oldest bakery has an expanded upstairs lounge with BBC News and an al fresco balcony. Its pastries, donuts, eclairs, gateaux, sandwiches and brownies are life-affirming.

PhimPhone Market SELF-CATERING $
(Map p284; 94/6 Th Setthathirat; ⊙7am-9pm Mon-Sat; 📶) This self-catering oasis stocks everything from Western magazines to ice cream, salami, bread, biscuits and chocolate, as well as Western toiletries. Don't miss its cafe serving great coffees, juices and tasty baguette sandwiches.

Nam Phu Restaurant LAOTIAN $
(Map p284; Th Pangkham; mains 20,000K; ⊙11am-10pm) Hidden next to a tailor's on the corner of Th Pangkham and Th Samsenthai, this authentic locals' favourite has been creating tasty Laotian grub for years. Try the alluring 'drunken fish'.

Douang Deuane Restaurant LAOTIAN $
(Map p284; Th François Nginn; mains 40,000K; ⊙8.30am-11.30pm Mon-Sat) Exudes a sense of old Laos with its wood-beamed walls festooned with hill-tribe baskets and rural tapestries. The fried fish in tamarind sauce leaves a zing on your taste buds.

Ban Anou Night Market LAOTIAN $
(Map p284; meals 10,000-15,000K; ⊙5-10pm) Setting up on a small street off the north end of Th Chao Anou every evening, this atmospheric open-air market dishes up Lao cuisine from grilled meats to chilli-based dips with vegetables and sticky rice.

YuLaLa Cafe JAPANESE $
(Map p284; Th Heng Boun; meals 40,000K; 11.30am-2pm & 6-9pm Tue-Sun; ❄) YuLaLa has a cosy interior with hardwood floors and scatter cushions. The menu features vegie delights such as 'fried tofu dumpling with radish sauce' and meat dishes such as sautéed salt pork, accompanied by jazz music.

Taj Mahal Restaurant INDIAN $
(Map p284; Th Setthathirat; meals 11,000-25,000K; ⊙10am-10.30pm Mon-Sat, 4-10.30pm Sun; ❄🍃) Located in little street just

behind Th Setthathirat, this place offers flavoursome Indian fare. Portions are generous and you can sit semi-al fresco. Good vegie selection too (20 dishes).

Drinking

The river plays host to a parade of American-style bars. For more chic refinement comb the backstreets radiating from Th Setthathirat.

Noy's Fruit Heaven JUICE BAR
(Map p284; Th Heng Boun; fruit shakes 7000K; ⌚7am-9pm) This juice-bar-cum-snack-cafe turns out mouth-watering salads. Noy's vitamin-bursting fruit shakes are also a great antidote to Beerlao headaches.

Spirit House COCKTAIL BAR
(off Map p283; ☎262530; Th Fa Ngum; ⌚7am-11pm) An upmarket alternative to Sala Sunset Khounta, this sensual bar pipes chillsome tunes to complement the dark woods and comfy couches of its stylish interior. Even Richard Burton would have been excited by its expansive drinks menu.

Sala Sunset Khounta BAR
(Map p283; ☎251079; Th Fa Ngum; ⌚11am-11pm) Shipwrecked against the banks of the Mekong, this serene sunset institution is in danger of closure due to riverfront redevelopment. Beerlao in hand, sit back and watch the sky turn a burnt peach.

Bor Pennyang BAR
(Map p284; ☎020 787 3965; Th Fa Ngum; ⌚10am-midnight) A friendly cast of locals, expats, bar girls and travellers assembles here. The setting is a rooftop bar overlooking the river with pool tables, pumping cheesy rock and cheap beer, and sports on TV.

Martini Bar BAR
(Map p284; ☎020 771 1138; Th Nokeo Khumman; ⌚7pm-late) This ubersleek watering hole has myriad cocktails, ochre walls and a vibe as chilled as the resident fish tank. Indie films are shown at 8pm Monday to Wednesday in the lounge upstairs.

Samlo Pub BAR
(Map p284; ☎222308; Th Setthathirat; ⌚7pm-late) A seasoned haunt with a roguish cast of hookers, lady-boys and shady expats patronising the darkness. Duck in for a beer but don't hang around.

Jazzy Brick BAR
(Map p284; ☎020 244 9307; Th Setthathirat; ⌚7pm-late) Stylish, low-lit, exposed-brick interior adorned in old jazz posters. Great mojitos and bloody Marys, and occasional live Latin and bossa nova.

Loft BAR
(Map p284; ☎242991; Th Khounboulom; ⌚7pm-midnight) Vientiane's answer to 'urban-slick', Loft has rectangular lily-peppered pools, gyrating girls on plasma screens, blood-red couches, orange low lighting and cheesy lounge music.

Entertainment

By law, entertainment venues close at 11.30pm, though a number of places push the envelope. Vientiane has movies, cultural shows, circus, Lao boxing and a clutch of nightclubs to keep you busy, as well as music concerts.

Conveniently, two of Vientiane's better nightclubs – **Future Nightclub** (Th Luang Prabang; ⌚8pm-1am) and **Highwayman** (Th Luang Prabang; ⌚8pm-midnight) are near each other on the airport road. Expect a lot of noise and a very up-for-it Lao crowd. Elsewhere, **Lunar 36** (Don Chan Palace Hotel; ⌚6pm-3am Wed, Fri & Sat), off Th Fa Ngum, is Vientiane's official late-night altar to hedonism, with a decent disco, outside verandah and cosmopolitan cast of working ladies and expats.

Centre Culturel et de Coopération Linguistique CINEMA
(French Cultural Centre; Map p284; ☎215764; www.ambafrance-laos.org/centre; Th Lan Xang; ⌚9.30am-6.30pm Mon-Fri, to noon Sat) Dance, art exhibitions, literary discussions and live music all take place in this Gallic hive of cultural activity. As well as cult French films (shown Tuesday, Thursday and Saturday at 7.30pm; 10,000K), the centre also offers French and Lao language lessons.

Lao Traditional Show LIVE MUSIC
(Map p284; ☎5017773; Lao National Culture Hall, Th Manthatulat; adult/child US$7/4) Traditional music and dancing performed by the Laos National Theatre is aimed directly at tourists, and plays from Monday to Saturday at 5.30pm.

Shopping

Numerous handicraft and souvenir boutiques are dotted around streets radiating from Nam Phu, particularly Th Pangkham and Th Setthathirat.

GETTING TO THAILAND: VIENTIANE TO NONG KHAI

The Thai-Lao Friendship Bridge is 22km southeast of Vientiane. The border is open between 6am and 10pm, and the easiest way to cross is on the comfortable **Thai-Lao International Bus** (100,000K, 90 minutes), which leaves Vientiane's Talat Sao Bus Station at 7.30am, 9.30am, 12.40pm, 2.30pm, 3.30pm and 6pm. From Nong Khai in Thailand, it leaves at the same times for 55B. Similar buses run to Udon Thani (20,000K, two hours) six times a day. Visas are issued on arrival in both countries. International VIP buses to Thailand's Udon Thani (100,000K) leave Talat Sao Bus Station at 10.30am and 11.30am. Alternative means of transport between Vientiane and the bridge include taxi or jumbo (500/20B), or regular public bus 14 (Tha Duea) from Talat Sao (15,000K) between 7.30am and 6pm. At the bridge, regular shuttle buses ferry passengers between immigration posts. The sleeper train for Bangkok costs 420,000K.

For information on crossing this border in the other direction, see p433.

T'Shop Lai Gallery BEAUTY, HOMEWARES
(Map p284; www.laococo.com/tshoplai.htm; off Th In Paeng; ⊙8am-8pm Mon-Sat, 10-6pm Sun) Exquisite furniture recycled from eggshell, coconut, bamboo and rattan, made by Les Artisans Lao, an organisation providing opportunities for disadvantaged Lao. French owner, Michel, is an inspiration – a self-taught furniture designer and *parfumier*, his soaps and aromatic oils are all made from locally sourced materials. Check out his sensual range while enjoying a coffee in the gallery's beautiful surroundings.

Camacrafts HANDICRAFTS
(Map p284; www.camacrafts.org; Th Nokeo Khumman; ⊙10am-6pm Mon-Sat) Non-profit Camacrafts markets handicrafts created by Hmong (highland dwellers) women using traditional skills, with a range of silk pashminas, quilts and wall hangings. Your purchase goes directly to help the artisans' families.

Indochina's Handicrafts HANDICRAFTS
(Map p284; Th Setthathirat; ⊙9am-8pm) This cave of a place would have kept Aladdin quiet with its antique Russian watches, waxed gold and wooden Buddhas, opium pipes, Hmong earrings and bracelets. Upstairs there's a bijou cafe.

Talat Sao MARKET
(Morning Market; Map p284; Th Lan Xang; ⊙7am-5pm) This once-memorable Vientiane shopping experience has undergone a facelift; two-thirds of its weave-world of stalls selling opium pipes, jewellery and traditional antiques have been ripped down and replaced with a eunuch of a modern mall. The remaining building's fabric merchants are hanging by a thread.

Book Café BOOKS
(Map p284; Th Heng Boun; ⊙8am-8pm Mon-Fri) Good range of thrillers and general fiction, plus works by Laos-based authors. Owner Robert Cooper is an expert on the Hmong.

Monument Books BOOKS
(Map p284; 124 Th Nokeo Khumman; ⊙9am-8pm Mon-Fri, to 6pm Sat & Sun) Glossy travel pictorials, thrillers and magazines, as well as a few toys for kids.

Vientiane Book Center BOOKS
(Map p284; laobook@hotmail.com; Th Pangkham; ⊙8.30am-5.30pm Mon-Fri, 9am-4.30pm Sat) Decent selection of secondhand thrillers and insightful books on Laos.

Information

Dangers & Annoyances

As Vientiane is one of the most laid-back capitals in the world, you're reasonably safe here. However, during big festivals – when half the country comes to visit – crime goes through the roof, with dangerous drunk driving (Laos has one of the highest rates of motorcycle-related deaths in the world) and bag snatching top of the misdemeanours list.

Emergency

Ambulance (☎195)
Fire (☎190)
Police (☎191)
Tourist police (Map p284; ☎251128; Th Lan Xang)

Internet Access

There are several internet cafes on Th Samsenthai and Th Setthathirat. Rates are around 7000K per hour with a decent broadband speed. Most have international telephone facilities.

Apollo Net (Map p284; Th Setthathirat; ⊙8.30am-11pm) Broadband (6000K per hour) and telephone kiosk (3000K per minute for calls to US, Australia and UK).

True Coffee Internet (Map p284; Th Setthathirat; ⊙9am-9pm) This swish, cool cafe makes writing home a pleasure. Enjoy a posh latte or delicious homemade yoghurt as you Skype, email (8000K per hour) or use its wi-fi (10,000K per hour) outside on your own laptop.

Media

Your only option for local news and upcoming events is the state-censored *Vientiane Times*. French speakers should look for the weekly *Le Rénovateur*. *Bangkok Post*, the *Economist*, *Newsweek* and *Time* can also be found in minimarts and bookshops.

Medical Services

Vientiane's medical facilities will do for broken bones and the diagnosis of dengue fever and malaria, but for anything more serious we strongly recommend you cross to Thailand for the **Aek Udon International Hospital** (☎0066-4234 2555; www.aekudon.com; Posri Rd, Amphur Muang, Udon Thani Province), which can dispatch an ambulance, or in critical situations an airlift, to take you to Udon Thani. The Thai-Lao Friendship Bridge is closed between 10pm and 6am, but Thai/Lao immigration will open for ambulances.

In Vientiane try the following:

Australian Embassy Clinic (☎353840; ⊙8.30am-5pm Mon-Fri) For nationals of Australia, Britain, Canada, Papua New Guinea and New Zealand only. This clinic's Australian doctor treats minor problems by appointment; it doesn't have emergency facilities. Accepts cash or credit cards.

International Clinic (Map p283; ☎214021/2; Th Fa Ngum; ⊙24hr) Part of the Mahasot Hospital; probably the best place for not-too-complex emergencies. Some English-speaking doctors. Take ID and cash.

Poppy's Pharmacy (Map p284; ☎030 981 0108;Th Heng Boun ⊙8am-9pm) Fully-stocked new apothecary with English-speaking staff, selling malaria pills, Imodium and headache pills, as well as Western-brand toiletries.

Setthathirat Hospital (☎351156) Thanks to a recent overhaul by the Japanese, this hospital northeast of the city is another option for minor ailments.

Money

There are plenty of ATMs in Vientiane, especially along Th Setthathirat. Several banks change cash and travellers cheques and will do cash advances against credit cards for a commission. The unofficial moneychangers near Talat Sao have good rates and keep longish hours.

Banque pour le Commerce Extérieur Lao (BCEL; Map p284; cnr Th Pangkham & Th Fa Ngum; ⊙8.30am-7pm Mon-Fri, to 3pm Sat & Sun) Best rates; longest hours. Exchange booth on Th Fa Ngum and three ATMs attached to the main building.

Joint Development Bank (Map p284; 75/1-5 Th Lan Xang) Usually charges the lowest commission on cash advances. Also has an ATM.

Lao Development Bank (Map p284; Th Setthathirat; ⊙8.30-11.30am & 2-4pm Mon-Fri)

Siam Commercial Bank (Map p284; 117 Th Lan Xang) ATM and cash advances on Visa.

Post

Post, Telephone & Telegraph (PTT; Map p284; cnr Th Lan Xang & Th Khou Vieng; ⊙8am-5pm Mon-Fri, to noon Sat & Sun) Come here for post restante and stamps.

Telephone

Lao Telecom Numphu Centre (Map p284; Th Setthathirat; ⊙9am-7pm) International fax, and domestic and international calls. For cheaper local calls have your mobile unlocked and buy a pay-as-you-go SIM card. Tigo and M-Phone top-up cards are widely available.

Tourist Information

Tourist information centre (NTAL; Map p284; www.ecotourismlaos.com; Th Lan Xang; ⊙8.30am-noon & 1.30-4pm) With bags of informative visual displays detailing provincial attractions, there are helpful English-speaking staff, brochures and regional maps. Staff can arrange trips to Phu Khao Khuay National Protected Area (NPA) for no charge.

Travel Agencies

A couple of the most dependable tour agents:

A-Rasa Tours (Map p284; ☎213633; Th Francois Ngin; ⊙8.30am-5pm Mon-Fri, 8.30am-noon Sat) Run by Mrs Inthavong, dependable A-Rasa organises tours to Phongsali, and books international/domestic plane tickets and sleeper trains to Bangkok.

Green Discovery (Map p284; ☎218373; www.greendiscoverylaos.com; Th Setthathirat) Offers three-day motorbike trips on the Ho Chi Minh Trail (two-person group US$330 per person) on 250cc Baja bikes (experience essential), as well as exciting new kayaking, trekking and ziplining two-day packages staying in a jungle camping ground by the Nam Lik river (three persons US$167 per person). One day's ziplining costs US$100 per person for a group of two people, but as with all Green Discovery prices, it gets cheaper the more of you there are. Dependable and safe nationwide outfit. An additional office has now opened on Th Heng Boun.

Lasi Ticketing (Map p284; ☎222851; www.lasiglobal.com; Th Francois Ngin; ⊙8.30am-5pm Mon-Fri, 8.30am-noon) With helpful English-speaking staff, Lasi sells air, VIP bus and train tickets.

LEAVING VIENTIANE BY BUS

Journeys often take longer than advertised. For buses to China, contact **Tong Li Bus Company** (☎242657) at the Northern Bus Station. For Vietnam, **S.D.T.** (☎720175) has buses leaving daily from the Southern Bus Station to Hanoi (US$25, 24 hours, 6pm), via Vinh (US$30, 16 hours); Hué (US$23, 19 hours, midnight), Danang (US$25, 19 hours, 6pm) and Ho Chi Minh City (US$60, up to 48 hours, 8am).

DESTINATION	FARE (K)	DISTANCE (KM)	DURATION (HR)	DEPARTURES
Talat Sao Bus Station				
Vang Vieng	40,000	153	4	7am, 8am, 9.30am, 10.30am, 11.30am, 1.30pm, 2pm, 3pm
Nong Khai	15,000	22	1½	7.30am, 9.30am, 12.40pm, 3.30pm, 6pm
Udon Thani	22,000	77	2½	8am, 10.30am, 11.30am, 2pm, 4pm, 6pm
Northern Bus Station				
Huay Xai	210,000	869	30-35	5.30pm
Kūnmíng	610,000	781	30	2pm
Luang Nam Tha	180,000	676	18	8.30am
Luang Prabang	110,000	384	11	6.30am, 7.30am, 8.30am, 11am, 1.30pm
	130,000 (VIP)		9	8am & 9am (VIP)
Oudomxay	150,000	578	13-15	7am, 1.35pm, 4pm, 5pm
Phongsali	190,000	811	26	7am
Phonsavan	110,000	374	9-11	6.30am, 7.30am, 9.30am, 4pm, 6.30pm, 8pm
	130,000 (VIP)			8pm (VIP)
Sainyabuli	110,000 (local)	485	14-16	9am (local)
	130,000 (air-con)			6pm (air-con)
Sam Neua	170,000-190,000	612	15-17	7am, 9.30am, 12.30pm (VIP), 12.30pm (via Phonsavan)
Southern Bus Station				
Attapeu	140,000 (local)	812	22-24	9.30am, 5pm (local)
	200,000 (VIP)			8.30pm (VIP)
Lak Sao	35,000	334	7-9	5am, 6am, 7am, 6.30pm
Paksan	30,000	143	3-4	take any bus going south, roughly every 30min from 7am to 5pm
Pakse	110,000	677	14-16	7am, 10.30am, noon, 1pm; then buses every 30min to 8pm
	180,000 (VIP)		9½	8.30am, 9pm (VIP)
Salavan	100,000 (local)	774	15-20	4.30pm, 7pm (local)
	200,000 (VIP)			8.30pm (VIP)
Savannakhet	75,000 (local)	457	8-11	every 30min from 5.30am to 9.30am; or catch any bus to Pakse (local)
	120,000 (VIP)		8-10	8.30am (VIP)
Tha Khaek	40,000 (local)	332	7	4am, 5am, 6am, noon (local)
	80,000 (VIP)			1pm (VIP)

Getting There & Away

Air

Wattay International Airport is the main transport hub for the rest of the country (for more detailed information about flights to Laos, see p362). Beside it is the rickety Domestic Terminal.

Airline Offices

China Eastern Airlines (www.ce-air.com; Th Luang Prabang; ⏲8am-noon & 1-4pm Mon-Sat, to 11.30am Sat) Flies daily to Kūnmíng and Na Ning (US$209).

Lao Airlines (Map p284; www.laoairlines.com; Th Pangkham; ⏲8am-noon & 1-4pm Mon-Sat, to noon Sun), based at Wattay airport, has daily flights to Luang Prabang (US$87) and Pakse (US$131), with five flights per week to Xieng Khuang (US$87) and three flights per week to Oudomxay, Huay Xai, Savannakhet and Luang Nam Tha (all US$112). Internationally it flies daily to Bangkok (US$125), Hanoi (US$130), Siem Reap (US$170), Phnom Penh (US$165), Kūnmíng (US$180), Ho Chi Minh City (US$172) and Chiang Mai (US$160).

Lao Capricorn Air (www.lao.capricornair.net; Wattay International Airport, Domestic Terminal; ⏲8am-5pm) Operates flights twice weekly to Sam Neua (US$105) and once a week to Phongsali and Sainyabuli (US$80).

Thai Airways International (www.thaiairways.com.com; Th Luang Prabang; ⏲8am-noon & 1-4pm Mon-Sat, to noon Sun) Has twice-daily flights to Bangkok (US$149).

Vietnam Airlines (Map p284; www.vietnamairlines.com; 1st fl, Lao Plaza Hotel, Th Samsenthai; ⏲8am-noon & 1-4.30pm Mon-Sat, to noon Sun) Conducts flights to Ho Chi Minh City, Hanoi and Phnom Penh.

Boat

Rare, no-frills cargo boats head upstream to Luang Prabang (taking four days to one week) from Kiaw Liaw Pier, 3.5km west of the fork in the road where Rte 13 heads north in Ban Kao Liaw. Go there and speak with the boatmen in advance to see if, when and how far they're running. During the dry season (November to April) it's out of the question.

Bus & Sŏrngtăaou

Buses use three different stations in Vientiane, all with some English-speaking staff. The **Northern Bus Station** (Th Asiane), about 2km northwest of the centre, serves all points north of Vang Vieng, including China, and has some buses to Vietnam.

The **Southern Bus Station** (Rte 13 South), commonly known as Dong Dok Bus Station or just *khíw lot lák kão* (Km 9 bus station), is 9km out of town and serves everywhere south. Buses to Vietnam stop here.

The **Talat Sao Bus Station** (Map p284) is where desperately slow local buses depart for destinations within Vientiane Province, including Vang Vieng, and some more distant destinations, though for these you're better off going to the Northern or Southern stations. International VIP buses to Thailand's Udon Thani (100,000K) leave here at 10.30am and 11.30am. There's also a VIP bus for Bangkok; see p290.

Getting Around

Central Vientiane is entirely accessible on foot.

Bicycle, Motorcycle & Car

Bicycles can be rented for 8000K per day from tour agencies and guesthouses. Scooters are also a great way to get about town, but remember to keep your helmet on (the police fine is a movable feast).

Europcar (Map p284; ☎223867; www.europcarlaos.com; Th Samsenthai; ⏲8am-6pm Mon-Sat) Rents vehicles from US$59 per day, US$20 extra for a driver; 4WD vehicles cost $69 per day and become more expensive the further you're deviating from the capital.

Jules' Classic Rental (Map p284; ☎020 7760 0813; www.bike-rental-laos.com; Th Setthathirat; per day US$30) Next to PhimPhone Market; has well-maintained scooters and heavy-duty 450cc motocross giants with fully comprehensive insurance.

P.V.O. (Map p284; ☎254354; Th Nokeo Khumman; ⏲8am-6pm Mon-Sat) Rents scooters (70,000K) or Honda Baja motocross bikes (250,000K per day) on a flexible 24-hour basis. It's also possible to drop the bike off in Pakse for an extra 400,000K – perfect if you're headed to Cambodia – freeing you up from sweaty, cramped buses.

Túk-Túk

Many túk-túks have a laminated list of vastly inflated tourist prices. These guys are usually found in queues outside tourist sights, and won't budge for less than the price already agreed upon with the other drivers (starting at 15,000K). You can also flag down shared, fixed-route túk-túks (with passengers already inside), which cost from 2000K to 5000K, depending on your destination.

GETTING INTO TOWN

Wattay International Airport is about 4km northwest of the city centre. Taxis into town cost 50,000K (less than US$6). Or, walk 500m to the airport gate, where you can get a túk-túk for about 30,000K.

Phu Khao Khuay National Protected Area

Covering more than 2000 sq km of mountains to the east of Vientiane, **Phu Khao Khuay National Protected Area (NPA)** (www.trekkingcentrallaos.com) is home to a herd of wild elephants and three major rivers flowing off into the Ang Nam Leuk Reservoir.

The **wild elephants** make regular appearances at their favourite salt lick, an easy walk from the village of **Ban Na**. Tragically, in 2009, six of the estimated herd of 40 were butchered – undoubtedly the work of poachers. Several tour operators in Vientiane work with the local community in running treks that involve staying overnight in the elephant observation tower, which overlooks the salt lick. Remember: they're wild and the chances of them turning up are only about 50/50.

The best way to see the elephants is through the tourist information centre in Vientiane (see p291). In the case of Ban Na, you could also get a Lao-speaker to call **Mr Bounthanom** (☎020 220 8286) directly and arrange it with him, as well as a homestay in the village (30,000K excluding food and transportation from Vientiane). Other treks, including visits to several impressive **waterfalls**, depart from **Ban Hat Khai**. Prices vary depending on the number of trekkers; eg a three-day trek from Ban Hat Khai is 680,000K per person, but much cheaper if there are more people in your group (with at least five people). A one-day trip is 150,000K. From Ban Na trekking prices are higher if you stay in the elephant tower, which has a 110,000K per-person fee that goes to the Elephant Conservation & Research Fund. All proceeds go to the villages and NPA.

Getting There & Away

Buses from the Southern Bus Station in Vientiane leave regularly for Ban Tha Bok and Paksan. For Ban Na get off at Tha Pha Bat near the Km 81 stone; Ban Na is about 2km north.

For Ban Hat Khai, stay on the bus until a turn-off left (north) at Km 92, just before Ban Tha Bok. Then take any passing *sǒrngtǎaou* the 5km to Ban Huay Leuk. Ban Hat Khai is 2km further. For the various waterfalls, find detailed information at www.trekkingcentrallaos.com, or through the tourist information centre in Vientiane (see p291). If you need a bed en route, there are two decent guesthouses in Tha Bok.

Vang Vieng

☎023 / POP 30,000

Nowhere else divides opinion among travellers like Vang Vieng; 'paradise lost' to some, heaven to others. Whatever your impression, the scene of cattle grazing the banks of the Nam Ou river backdropped by jagged, coal-black karsts is a sight for tired eyes. Over the last few years the tubing scene has mutated into raving platforms upstream complete with zipwires and nonstop amphetamine-fuelled noise. There are two camps in town: the outdoor, tranquillity-seeking crowd that heads to the boutique hotels and upmarket guesthouses downstream; or the younger partyheads flouting Lao modesty and looking as if they're off to a bikini contest.

Locals here are less happy than they used to be, knowing that with continual development and greater numbers of travellers, they're losing more of their once bucolic way of life. Trekking, caving, cycling, kayaking and climbing – there's plenty of scope to make the most of Vang Vieng's abundant natural beauty without leaving a toxic *falang* (foreigner) footprint.

Sights & Activities

Kayaking & Rafting

Given the lush landscape, kayaking is ideal, with day trips (150,000K per person) taking you down a few rapids and stopping at caves and villages. Before using a cheap operator, check guides' credentials and the quality of their kit. Reliable stalwart **Green Discovery** (☎511230; www.greendiscoverylaos.com; Th Luang Prabang) runs half-day excursions for as little as US$24 per person if there are at least four of you. **V.L.T.** (☎511369; www.vangviengtour.com) charges US$18 for similar trips, and has good kit.

Rock Climbing

Adam's Rock Climbing School (☎020 5501 0832; www.laos-climbing.com; Th Luang Prabang) has experienced guides and sturdy kit. The main centre is the branch at the northern end of town. **Green Discovery** (☎511230; www.greendiscoverylaos.com; Th Luang Prabang) runs half-day courses on moderate to easy climbs as well as offering caving and trekking. All climbs are based on the dramatic limestone cliffs and for a half/full day typically cost US$16/22.

Vang Vieng

0 200 m
0 0.1 miles

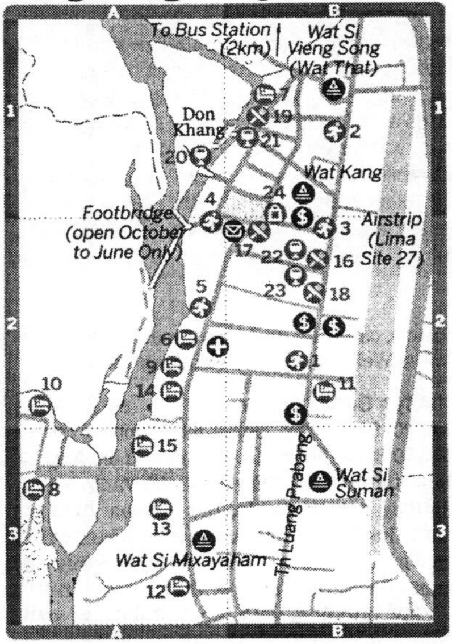

Vang Vieng

Activities, Courses & Tours

1 Adam's Rock Climbing School............B2
2 Adam's Rock Climbing School............B1
3 Green Discovery............B2
4 Tubing Operators............A2
5 V.L.T. Natural Tours............A2

Sleeping

6 Ban Sabai Bungalows............A2
7 Champa Lao............B1
8 Chez Mango............A3
9 Elephant Crossing............A2
10 Maylyn Guest House............A2
11 Pan's Place............B2
12 Seng Duen Guesthouse............A3
13 Thavisouk Hotel............A3
14 Villa Ao Kham............A2
15 Villa Nam Song............A3

Eating

16 Babylon Restaurant............B2
17 Nokeo............B2
18 Organic Mulberry Farm Cafe............B2
19 Phad Thai Restaurant............B1

Drinking

20 Bucket Bar............A1
21 Jaidee's Bar............B1
22 Rising Sun............B2
23 Sakura............B2
Smile Bar............(see 20)

Shopping

24 BKC Bookshop............B1

Hot Air Ballooning
Best enjoyed first thing in the morning, and the perfect way to take in the jaw-dropping scenery, flights take place at 6.30am, 7.30am and 4pm (adult/child US$70/40), lasting approximately 40 minutes. Call **Travel With Your Eyes** (☎020 9691 82222) to book a flight.

Caves
The stunning limestone karst around Vang Vieng is honeycombed with tunnels and caverns. After tubing, caving has to be the town's main attraction. You can buy a map from BKC Bookshop (p307) and do the caves yourself, or it's possible to go in an organised group. Wear proper shoes, as the caves are dark and slippery, and absolutely make sure you have your own torch (flashlight), not the dim ones they rent; it's very easy to get lost.

The most famous cave, **Tham Jang** (admission 15,000K), south of town, was used as a hideout from marauding Yúnnánese Chinese in the early 19th century. A set of stairs leads up to the main cavern entrance. There's also a cool spring at the foot of the cave.

Another popular cave is **Tham Phu Kham** (Blue Lagoon; admission 10,000K). To reach it, cross the **bamboo footbridge** (walking/cycling toll 4000/6000K) then walk or pedal 6km along a scenic, unsealed road to Ban Na Thong, from where you have to walk 1km to a hill on the northern side of the village. It's a tough final 200m climb, but worth it for a dip in the turquoise pool afterwards.

The **Tham Sang Triangle** is a popular half-day trip that's easy to do on your own; it takes in Tham Sang plus three other caves within a short walk of each other. Begin this odyssey by riding a bike or taking a *sŏrngtăaou* 13km north along Rte 13, turning left a few hundred metres beyond the barely readable Km 169 marker. A rough road leads to the river, where a boatman will ferry you across to Ban Tham Sang for a small fee. **Tham Sang** (admission 5000K), meaning 'Elephant Cave', is a small cavern containing a few Buddha images and a Buddha 'footprint', plus the elephant-shaped stalactite that gives the cave its name.

MINDFUL TRAVELLER

Reefer on tap, rave music, bikinis, fluorescent body paint and beautiful people – sounds like every young man's fantasy. Except this is Laos, where for centuries people have covered their bodies out of religious observation. And the drugs and pounding beat are a new phenomenon. Get caught with a joint and it's a US$600 fine and your passport is confiscated until the payment is made. Get sprung with crystal meth – and there's plenty of it in Vang Vieng – and you're talking US$1500, while the dealer who sold it to you (unless he's in cahoots with the cops) will be quietly taken away and dealt with. This is the dark flip side of Vang Vieng's nonstop bacchanalia. Plain-clothes cops are everywhere and guesthouse theft is on the rise, so be careful.

It's best visited in the morning, when light enters the cave.

From here a signed path takes you 1km northwest through rice fields to the entrances of **Tham Loup** and **Tham Hoi** (combined admission 10,000K). Tham Hoi reportedly continues about 3km into the limestone and an underground lake. About 400m south of Tham Hoi, along a well-used path, **Tham Nam** (admission 5000K) is the highlight of this trip. This cave is about 500m long and a tributary of the Nam Song flows out of its low entrance. From Tham Nam an easy 1km walk brings you back to Ban Tham Sang.

Tubing

Hire an inner tube from the tubing operators by the old market (50,000K rental, 20,000K deposit, US$7 fine if not returned on time), who will take you about 3km upriver and leave you to drift back in your own time. This usually takes three hours, as you can stop for a dance and refreshment at the many riverside bars. Be warned: at least one person a year loses their life tubing, usually because they've had an overload of beer and reefer and the river is running too quick. The 10m-high ziplines over the river are dangerous in the dry season too; one *falang* recently broke his neck landing in perilously shallow water.

Sleeping

At last count there were 120 guesthouses in Vang Vieng! Avoid the ugly town and head downriver.

TOP CHOICE Elephant Crossing HOTEL $$
(☎511232; www.theelephantcrossinghotel.com; r 350,000-650,000K; ❄@☎) Upmarket riverfacing guesthouse with a breakfast terrace beside the Nam Ou. Rooms are comfortable with hardwood floors, art deco glass wall panels, cable TV and Hmong art gracing the walls. Welcoming staff and lush gardens.

Maylyn Guest House GUESTHOUSE $
(☎020 560 4095; jophus_foley@hotmail.com; r 50,000-80,000K; ❄) Over the bridge, Maylyn is a stalwart of peace and old Vang Vieng. Run by gregarious Jo, the cabana huts are set in lush gardens bursting with butterflies and lantana flowers, affording possibly the most dramatic views of the karsts. There's a new building with immaculate en-suite rooms plus a natty little cafe to chill in.

Champa Lao GUESTHOUSE $$
(☎020 501 8501; www.thelongwander.com; r 40,000-100,000K; ☎) Champa has evolved from fluffy duckling to elegant swan, with an ambient-lit garden restaurant casting off heavenly aromas and comfortable rooms in the main building or in bungalows down the bank by the river. Fan-only rooms with or without bathroom.

Chez Mango GUESTHOUSE $
(☎020 7758 9733; r 40,000-60,000K; ❄) Located over the bridge, Mango is new, scrupulously clean and has seven colourful cabanas (some with bathrooms) in its flowery gardens. Head to the market with owner Mango to choose the ingredients for the Laotian dinner she can teach you to make, or play boules with her French husband, Noah.

Seng Duen Guesthouse GUESTHOUSE $
(☎511138; r 60,000-70,000K; ❄) Friendly digs south of town with cool, functional rooms. It also has million-dollar river views and a pleasant chilling balcony, plus a plunge pool, lush gardens and wi-fi. Great value.

Villa Nam Song GUESTHOUSE $$$
(☎511637; www.villanamsong.com; r US$90-120; ❄☎) Popular with European tour groups happy to pay the steep prices, Villa has luxurious pink adobe-and-wood cabanas set

in spotless manicured gardens overlooking the cliffs. The views are stunning from the breezy, wind-chimed restaurant, which has a decent Asian fusion menu.

Pan's Place GUESTHOUSE $
(☎511484; neilenolix@hotmail.com; Th Luang Prabang; r 60,000-90,000K) Friendly Pan's has basic en-suite rooms, plus cosy bungalows out back with shared bathroom. There's an internet cafe and tasty restaurant with a Western-leaning menu, plus a TV room with a choice of 400 films, all of which make up for the lack of a view.

Villa Ao Kham GUESTHOUSE $
(☎511357; r 150,000K; ❄) Newly built riverside digs with uninterrupted views of the karsts. Rooms are large with TV, fridge, air-con, fresh linen and firm beds. The owners are genuine and they also rent bikes and have a laundry service.

Thavisouk Hotel GUESTHOUSE $$
(☎511124; r US$20-25; ❄📶) Thavisouk has 30 riverside bungalows with rattan walls and wood floors overlooking the river; as well as air-con rooms in a new block. The view is to die for, there's a restaurant and the place feels safe.

Ban Sabai Bungalows GUESTHOUSE $$
(Xayoh Riverside Bungalows; ☎511088; r US$34-58; ❄) Next to Elephant Crossing, Sabai has 13 rustically finished bungalow rooms with exposed-brick walls and elevated verandahs, from where you can take in the panorama of the river. Great-looking elevated bar and restaurant terrace for sundowners.

Eating

It's easy to forget you're in Laos given Vang Vieng's plethora of try-hard Western-style joints, but look around and you'll see there's a number of authentic Laotian eateries.

TOP CHOICE **Organic Mulberry Farm Cafe** LAOTIAN $
(meals 20,000-30,000K) Down the quieter, southern end of Th Luang Prabang, this is a real find for vegetarians and carnivores alike, with fresh produce directly from its farm a few miles away. It has stir-fries, curries and seafood.

Nokeo LAOTIAN $
(meals 8000-20,000K; ⏲8am-8pm) This authentic Laotian eatery has almost been subsumed by the development around it, but if you're tiring of burgers and fries, try its delicious variations of *làap* (spicy salad of minced meat, poultry or vegetables).

Babylon Restaurant LAOTIAN $
(Th Luang Prabang; meals 25,000K) With its cushioned lounging areas and rattan furnishing, Babylon feels like a slice of Ko Pha-Ngan. Salads, tofu, sandwiches and soups complement a laid-back atmosphere. And guess what, it doesn't play 'Friends'. Yippee!

Phad Thai Restaurant THAI $
(Th Luang Prabang; meals 25,000K) Next to Villa Nam Song Garden, and strung with green lanterns and bags of atmosphere, this juicy little joint features the usual suspects of Thai cuisine, and when we passed, a very satisfied crowd.

Drinking

Choose between relaxed chilling bars and open-air, anything-goes haunts on Don Khang (aka 'party island'), such as the **Bucket Bar** and **Smile Bar**, which don't close until 4am.

Jaidee's Bar BAR
(⏲9am-1am) Hendrix would have dug this low-lit, riverside cave piping out '60s and '70s classics. Owner Jaidee is friendly and there's a nightly firepit.

Sakura BAR
(⏲5-11.30pm) Still packed to the gills thanks to a plasma widescreen tuned to sports channels, attractive bamboo interior and upbeat sounds.

Rising Sun PUB
(⏲5pm-midnight) Especially for homesick Brits, the only Irish pub in town has a blokey atmosphere with Guinness and Magners cider served for all thirsty leprechauns. Britpop and pool table.

Shopping

BKC Bookshop BOOKS
(⏲7am-7pm) Vang Vieng's oldest bookshop is useful for a range of guidebooks, thrillers and maps.

Information

Internet cafes in Vang Vieng charge around 400K per minute.

BCEL (☎511434; Th Luang Prabang; ⏲8.30am-3.30pm) Exchanges cash and travellers cheques, and handles cash advances on Visa, MasterCard and JCB. Has two ATMs in

TIMBER!

Increasingly China is turning to imports to slake its thirst for timber, and Laos, hungry for the income, is often too willing to oblige. Added to this, the Environmental Investigation Agency (EIA) claims that the furniture industry in Vietnam has grown tenfold since 2000, with Laos facilitating the flow of its timber to enable this. An estimated 500,000 cu metres of logs find their way over the border every year. While an outwardly hard-line approach has been taken against mass logging by the government, it's the self-funded military and local officials in remote areas who can fall prey to bribes.

Western countries, too, play a major role in the depletion of Laos' forests, with 90% of furniture produced in Vietnam being exported. Then there's the obvious impact on endangered mammals and thousands of amphibians, insects and plants endemic to the same forests, and deforestation accounts for an estimated 15% to 20% of the world's annual carbon emissions.

town including at its other branch by the old market.

Post office (☎511009) Beside the old market.

Provincial Hospital (☎511604) This new hospital has X-ray facilities and is fine for broken bones, cuts and malaria. When we visited, the doctor spoke reasonable English.

Getting There & Away

Most buses arrive at the **bus station** (Rte 13) 2km north of the main town. From the bus station, buses leave for Luang Prabang (100,000K, seven to 11 hours, 168km, 9am and 2pm), Vientiane (60,000K, 3½ to 4½ hours, 156km, 10am and 1pm) and Phonsavan (100,000K, six to seven hours, 219km, daily at about 9am). For Vientiane, pick-ups (30,000K, 3½ to 4½ hours) leave every 20 minutes from 5am until 4pm.

Tickets for minibuses and VIP buses with air-con travelling directly to Vientiane (80,000K, three hours, 2.30pm and 3.30pm) or Luang Prabang (120,000K, six to eight hours, noon) are sold at guesthouses, tour agencies and internet cafes in town. Sadly, there is no VIP bus to Phonsavan (and the route is serpentine, so don't sit at the back!).

Note that on arrival from Vientiane you'll be dropped in town, not at the bus station.

Getting Around

The township is small enough to walk around. Bicycles can be rented for around 10,000K per day, scooters for around 70,000K per day. A túk-túk up to the Organic Mulberry Farm or Tham Sang Triangle costs around 15,000K per person.

NORTHERN LAOS

Whether you're here to trek, elephant ride, zipline, kayak, cycle or try a homestay, a visit to northern Laos is for many the highlight of their Southeast Asian trip. Hemmed in by China to the far north, Vietnam to the east and Myanmar to the west, there's a fascinating cast of ethnic peoples; their rustic, tribal beliefs are a world away from the Thai-influenced urbanites of Vientiane. Hidden amid this rugged simplicity is Southeast Asia's premier Shangri La, Luang Prabang; with its chic restaurants, photogenic temples and revitalised French villas, it's something of an architectural phenomenon. Beyond it are unfettered, dense forests still home to tigers, gibbons and a cornucopia of animals, with a well-established ecotourism framework to take you to the very heart of them.

Luang Prabang

☎071 / POP 62,000

Luang Prabang is arguably one of the most sophisticated places in Southeast Asia. Nowhere else can lay claim to the city's old-world romance of 33 gilded wats, colourful monks, faded Indochinese villas and exquisite Gallic cuisine. Not to mention its many affordable spas, trekking operators, elephant walks, river cruises and outstanding natural beauty. This Unesco-protected gem, which sits at the sacred confluence of the Mekong and Nam Khan rivers, has rightfully gained mythical status as a travellers' Shangri La, and since its airport opened a decade ago the town has seen a flood of investment, with once-leprous French villas being revived as fabulous – though affordable – boutique hotels. Pootle around languid peninsula backstreets by bike, hire a scooter to visit the menthol-blue Kuang Si cascades, temple-hop, ecotrek, take a cooking course... It's guaranteed you'll stay

Luang Prabang

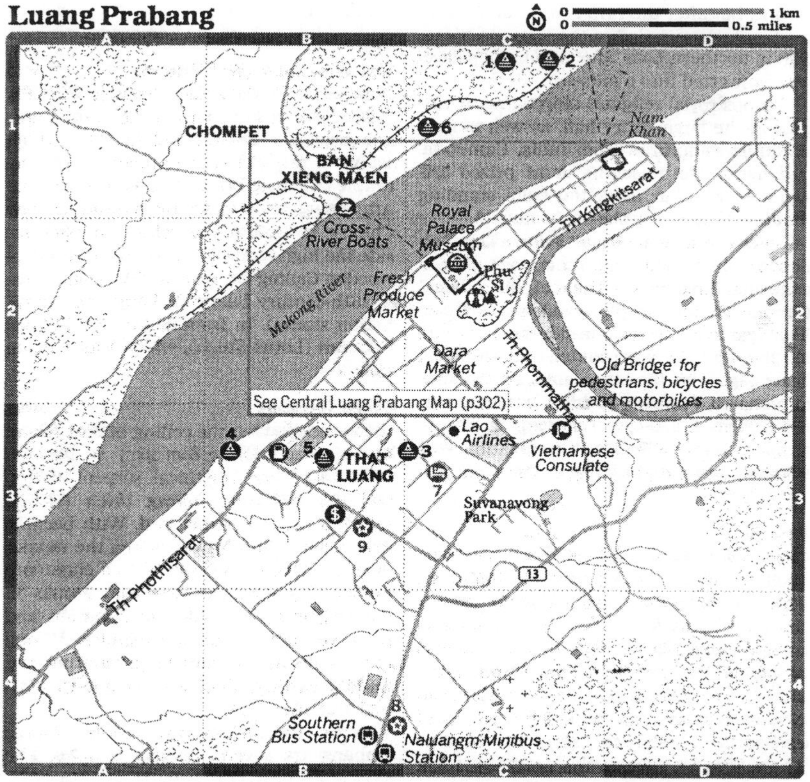

longer than planned. Let's just hope the Kūnmíng–Vientiane express train, due to pass through here in 2014, doesn't alter the city's serene charm.

Sights

Most of the tourist sights are in the old quarter on the peninsula bounded by the Mekong and Nam Khan rivers. Dominating the centre of town, Phu Si is an unmissable landmark. The majority of restaurants, accommodation, tour companies and internet cafes line and radiate from Th Sisavangvong, while additional bars are to be found on Th Kingkitsarat. For the best detailed, regularly updated map of the city keep an eye out for *Hobo Maps Luang Prabang* (www.hobomaps.com; 25,000K).

Royal Palace Museum (Ho Kham) MUSEUM
(Map p302; ☎212470; Th Sisavangvong; admission US$2; ⊙8.30-10.30am & 2-4pm Wed-Mon, last entry 3.30pm) Known to locals as Haw Kham (Golden Hall), the Royal Palace Museum was constructed in 1904 for King Sisavangvong and his family. When the king died in 1959 his son, Savang Vattana, inherited the

Luang Prabang

Sights

1 Wat Chomphet C1
2 Wat Long Khun C1
3 Wat Manorom C3
4 Wat Phabaht B3
5 Wat That Luang B3
6 Wat Xieng Maen C1

Sleeping

7 Alila Luang Prabang Hotel C3

Entertainment

8 Dao Fah B4
9 Muangsua By Night B3

throne, but after the 1975 revolution he and his family were exiled to the caves of Vieng Xai in northern Laos, after which the palace was converted into a museum.

Various royal religious objects are on display in the large entry hall, as well as rare Buddhist sculptures from India, Cambodia and Laos. The museum's most prized artwork is the Pha Bang, the gold standing Buddha after which the city is named.

Take a look at the **Royal Palace Car Collection** in a new exhibition, including a concours Lincoln Continental, dilapidated Citroën DS and an old wooden speedboat. Footwear can't be worn inside the museum, no photography is permitted and you must leave bags with the attendants. At the time of research, **Floating Buddha** (admission free; ⏲8-11.30am & 1.30-4pm Wed-Mon), a photographic study of Buddhist meditation, was showing in an outbuilding in the royal palace grounds.

Phu Si HILL

(Map p302; admission 20,000K; ⏲8am-6pm) The tiring climb to the summit of 100m-high Phu Si is more than justified by the view. A favourite haunt for sunset junkies, it's also an opportune place to chat to novice monks at the modest temple of **That Chomsi**, the starting point for a colourful Pii Mai (Lao New Year) procession. Behind this is a small cave-shrine sometimes referred to as **Wat Tham Phu Si**. Around the northeast flank are the ruins of **Wat Siphoutthabat Thippharam**, which was originally constructed in 1395 during the reign of Phaya Samsenthai on the site of a Buddha footprint.

Wat Xieng Thong TEMPLE

(Map p302; off Th Sakkarin; admission 20,000K; ⏲8am-5pm) Near the northern tip of the peninsula formed by the Mekong and Nam Khan rivers, Wat Xieng Thong is the jewel in the crown of Luang Prabang's temples. Built by King Setthathirat in 1560, it remained under royal patronage until 1975. The *sĭm* (chapel) represents classic Luang Prabang temple architecture, with roofs sweeping low to the ground. The rear wall features an impressive tree-of-life mosaic and, inside, richly decorated wooden columns support a ceiling that's vested with *dhammacakka* (dharma wheels). Near the compound's eastern gate stands the royal funeral chapel; inside are an impressive 12m-high funeral chariot and various funeral urns for each member of the royal family. The exterior of the chapel features gilt panels depicting erotic episodes from the Ramayana.

Wat Wisunalat (Wat Visoun) TEMPLE

(Map p302; Th Wisunalat; admission 20,000K; ⏲8am-5pm) To the south of the town centre and originally constructed in 1513 (which makes it the oldest continually operating temple in Luang Prabang) is Wat Wisunalat. After being burnt down by marauding Haw Chinese in 1887, it was rebuilt in 1898. Inside the high-ceilinged *sĭm* is a collection of wooden Calling for Rain Buddhas and 15th- to 16th-century Luang Prabang *sima* (ordination stones). In front of the *sĭm* is **That Pathum** (Lotus Stupa), which was built in 1514.

Other Temples TEMPLE

In the old quarter, the ceiling of **Wat Xieng Muan** (Map p302; ⏲8am-5pm) is painted with gold *naga* (mythical serpent-beings) and the elaborate *háang thíen* (candle rail) has *naga* at either end. With backing from Unesco and New Zealand, the monks' quarters have been restored as a classroom for training young novices and monks in the artistic skills needed to maintain and preserve Luang Prabang's temples. Among these skills are woodcarving, painting and Buddha-casting, all of which came to a virtual halt after 1975.

Across the Mekong from central Luang Prabang are several notable temples. The ferry stops near **Wat Long Khun** (Map p299; admission 5000K; ⏲8am-5pm), which features a few fading jatakas (stories of the Buddha's past lives) murals. When the coronation of a Luang Prabang king was pending, it was customary for him to spend three days in retreat here before ascending the throne.

Wat Tham Xieng Maen (admission 5000K; ⏲8am-5pm) is in a 100m-deep limestone cave, Tham Sakkarin Savannakuha, a little to the northwest of Wat Long Khun. At the top of a hill, peaceful **Wat Chomphet** (Map p299; ⏲8am-5pm) offers undisturbed views of the Mekong.

TAEC ARTS CENTRE

(Map p302; ☎253364; www.teaclaos.org; admission 20,000K; ⏲9am-6pm Tue-Sun) Learn to distinguish between the Hmong, Akha and Khamu tribes through the differences in their ethnic garb and jewellery. This clear and visually descriptive exhibition is based in a 1920s building up the hill by Dara market. There's also a shop and pleasant cafe (mains 25,000K).

Fibre2Fabric EXHIBITION
(Map p302; ☎254761; www.ockpoptok.com; 73/5 Ban Wat Nong; ⊙8am-9pm) In collaboration with OckPopTok, this is an illuminating exposition into the history of Lao textiles and how they transform experience into design (check out the motifs of Huey helicopters and soldiers depicting the Secret War). Talks are given every Thursday at 6pm.

Activities

The best way to really explore the city is by **bike**, meandering through the peninsula past scenes of monastic life and children playing. Once you've got your bearings, head out beyond Talat Phosy toward the Kuang Si waterfalls through some particularly spectacular scenery. Basic/mountain bikes cost 20,000/50,000K per day and can be hired along Th Sisavangvong. For easier journeys, automatic one-gear scooters cost around US$20 to US$25 per day. And should you want a more old-fashioned mode of transport there are numerous **elephant treks** on offer (see Tours).

Luang Prabang isn't just about style, it's about pampering, and what better way to ease those trekked-out muscles than sampling the city's affordable **spa parlours**; try a basic herbal sauna, traditional Lao massage, Swedish massage or hot-stone massage (to name a few).

Lao Red Cross Massage MASSAGE, SPA
(Map p302; ☎253448; Th Sisavangvong; ⊙7am-10.30pm) In traditional surroundings of wood rafters, cool fans and stone floors, sample a range of head and body massages, steams, reflexology and aromatherapy. Your donations go directly to improving the lives of the poorest villages in Laos. Prices range from 10,000K to 50,000K.

Hibiscus Massage MASSAGE
(Map p302; ☎030 923 5079; Th Sakkarin; 10am-10pm) Set in a former gallery in an old French building, Hibiscus wafts chillsome tunes through its silk-draped walls while you get pummelled to perfection. Traditional massage from 60,000K.

Lotus du Lao Massage SPA
(Map p302; ☎253448; Th Sisavangvong; ⊙9am-10.30pm) This central spa has years of experience and air choking on essential oils. Choose from a range of massage, facials and reflexology. Prices start at 60,000K.

Courses

Cooking

Tamarind COOKING COURSE
(Map p302; ☎020 777 0484; www.tamarindlaos.com; Ban Wat Nong; 1-day course 250,000K, ⊙9am-3pm Mon-Sat) Join Tamarind at its lakeside pavilion for a day's tuition in the art of Lao cuisine, meeting first at its restaurant (p306) before heading to the market for ingredients for classic dishes such as *mok pa* (steamed fish in banana leaves).

Tum Tum Cheng Cooking School COOKING COURSE
(Map p302; ☎253388; 29/2 Th Sakkarin; 1-day course incl cookbook 250,000K) Celebrated chef Chandra teaches you the secrets of his alchemy. Includes a visit to the market to select your vegetables. The day usually starts at the school on the peninsula at 8.30am and finishes at 2pm.

Weaving

OckPopTock COURSE
(☎212597; www.ockpoptock.com; 1-day course US$59, ⊙8.45am-4pm Mon-Sat) Learn to weave your own scarf and textiles with OckPopTok's dyeing classes, as well as its half-day basket weaving (US$40). Teachers are master craftspeople, you get to keep your handiwork and lunch is included. Situated 2km past Phousy market; a free túk-túk will pick you up and bring you back.

RESPECT THE BAT

The Tak Bat, where apprentice orange-robed monks form a line down Luang Prabang's pretty Th Sisavangvong to receive alms at dawn, has become a cause for concern. In their hunger for a photogenic keepsake, some Western visitors consider it OK to get uncomfortably close to the monks during this ancient and solemn ceremony. Consider these basic courtesies: observe the ritual in silence and at a respectful distance; only make an offering if it means something personal to you and the food is fresh; and do not make physical contact with the monks or talk to them. Finally, do not follow the monks on your bus.

Central Luang Prabang

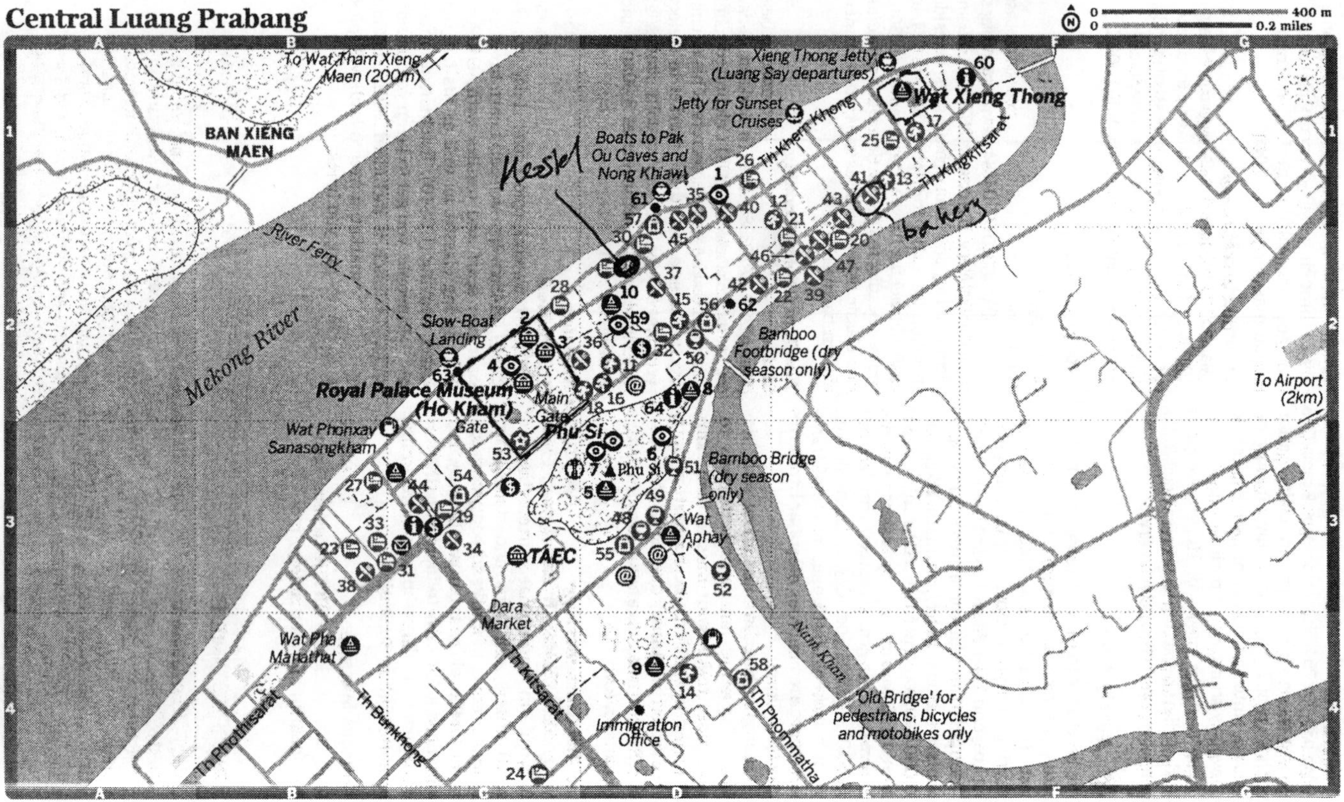

Central Luang Prabang

Top Sights

	Phu Si	D3
	Royal Palace Museum (Ho Kham)	C2
	TAEC	C3
	Wat Xieng Thong	E1

Sights

1	Fibre2Fabric	D1
2	'Floating Buddha' Photographs	C2
3	Royal Palace Car Collection	C2
4	Royal Palace Exhibition Halls	C2
5	That Chomsi	D3
6	That Chomsi Ticket Booth	D3
7	That Chomsi Ticket Booth	D3
8	Wat Siphoutthabat Thippnaran	D2
9	Wat Wisunalat (Wat Visoun)	D4
10	Wat Xieng Muan	D2

Activities, Courses & Tours

11	All Lao Service (Elephant Camp)	D2
12	Big Brother Mouse	E1
13	Hibiscus Massage	E1
14	Lao Red Cross Massage	D4
15	Lotus Du Lao Massage	D2
	Tamarind	(see 47)
16	Tiger Trail	D2
17	Tum Tum Cheng Cooking School	E1
18	White Elephant	D2

Sleeping

19	Ancient Luang Prabang Hotel	C3
20	Apsara	E2
21	Auberge les 3 Nagas	E2
22	Chittana Guesthouse	E2
23	Hoxieng 2 Guesthouse	B3
24	Jaliya Guesthouse	C4
25	Khoum Xiengthong Guesthouse	E1
26	Kongsavath Guesthouse	D1
27	Oudomphone Guesthouse	B3
28	Phousi 2 Guesthouse	C2
29	Sala Prabang	D2
30	Sayo River Guesthouse	D2
31	Souksavath Guesthouse	B3
32	Thanaboun Guesthouse	D2
33	Xayana Guesthouse	B3

Eating

34	Baguette Stalls	C3
35	Big Tree Café	D1
36	Blue Lagoon	D2
37	Café Toui	D2
38	JoMa Bakery Cafe	B3
39	Kon Kai	E2
40	L'Elephant Restaurant	D1
41	Le Banneton	E1
42	Le Café Ban Vat Sene	D2
43	Morning Glory Cafe	E1
44	Night Food Stalls	C3
45	Saffron	D1
46	Sala Cafe	E2
47	Tamarind	E2

Drinking

48	Hive Bar	D3
49	House Bar	D3
50	Ikon Club	D2
51	Lao Lao Garden	D3
52	Utopia	D3

Entertainment

	L'Etranger Books & Tea	(see 55)
53	Royal Theatre	C3

Shopping

	Big Tree Gallery	(see 35)
54	Handicraft Night Market	C3
55	L'Etranger Books & Tea	D3
	Monument Books	(see 1)
56	OckPopTok	D2
	OckPopTok	(see 1)
57	Orange Tree	D1
58	Pathana Boupha Antique House	D4

Information

59	Heritage House Information Centre	D2
60	Unesco World Heritage Information	F1

Transport

	All Lao Travel	(see 11)
	Bangkok Airways	(see 32)
61	Longboat Ticket Office	D1
62	Luang Say Office	D2
63	Navigation Office	C2
64	Treasure Travel	D2

Tours

If you have a few days in town, whimsical Kuang Si waterfalls and Pak Ou Caves are well worth a visit. There's a plethora of tour companies down Th Sisavangvong. We recommend **All Lao Travel** (☎253522; Th Sisavangvong; ⊙8am-10pm) as a one-stop shop for flights, boat and VIP bus tickets, and visa extensions. **Treasure Travel** (☎254682; www.treasuretravellaos.com; Th Sisavangvong; ⊙8am-9pm) also offers these services, and can organise trips to Pak Ou (80,000K per person) and Kuang Si (300,000K).

The following operators are good for trekking, rafting, elephant-riding and cycling excursions.

All Lao Service (Elephant Camp) TOUR
(Map p302; ☎253522; www.mahoutecolodge.com; Th Sisavangvong) Based in the same office as All Lao Travel, this outfit offers elephant treks; through stunning rural locations. One-day treks (minimum two people) cost US$45; two-day treks including a night's accommodation at a mahout lodge cost US$64.

White Elephant TOUR
(Map p302; ☎254481; www.white-elephant-adventures-laos.com; Th Sisavangvong) White Elephant is hailed for its relationships with remote Hmong and Khamu villages, allowing you a deeper insight into ethnic life without bumping into another *falang*. You can do this on a trek or by cycle in solid two- and three-day tours. Look for the old BMW and communist flag.

Tiger Trail TOUR
(Map p302; ☎252655; www.laos-adventures.com; Th Sisavangvong; ⊙8.30am-9pm) Focusing on socially responsible tours benefitting local people, Tiger Trail offers intimate treks through Hmong and Khamu villages. All tours can be tailored to include kayaking, elephant riding, rafting and mountain biking. Prices range from 350,000K, with elephant rides costing from US$40 to US$75.

Festivals & Events

The two most important annual events in Luang Prabang are **Pii Mai** (Lao or Lunar New Year) in April, when the town is packed to the gills with locals armed with water pistols (book accommodation well in advance), and **Bun Awk Phansa** (End of the Rains Retreat), which sees boat races in October.

Sleeping

Accommodation varies from basic guesthouse digs to five-star hotels and achingly perfect boutique hotels. The most atmospheric place to stay is on the peninsula; guesthouses radiate off Th Sakkarin toward both rivers. Cheaper accommodation can be found in the silversmithing district near the Mekong; a neighbourhood known as Ban Wat That (named for nearby Wat Pha Mahathat) and the adjacent Ban Ho Xiang have become a centre for a cluster of modest guesthouses.

TOP CHOICE **Auberge les 3 Nagas** BOUTIQUE HOTEL $$$
(Map p302; ☎253888; www.alilahotelsss.com/3nagas; Th Sakkarin; r US$165-260; ❄@🅿) Luang Prabang style was minted at this boutique hotel, bookended by mango trees and a burgundy 1950s Mercedes. The 100-year-old Lao-style building (there's another section of the hotel over the road) brims with old-world atmosphere and was once owned by a family that supplied the king with ice cream. Palatial suites sport swallow-you-up four-poster beds, tanned-wood bathrooms and a modern Asian design fusing colonial French roots. Service is top-flight.

Alila Luang Prabang Hotel BOUTIQUE HOTEL $$$
(Map p299; ☎260777; www.alilahotels.com; Old Prison Rd, Ban Mano; r incl breakfast US$340; ❄@≋) Housed within the stark walls of the city's old prison lies a minimalist's dream; take a dip in the plum and copper-tiled swimming pool, or retire to your suite with its private garden, elephant-grey walls and creature comforts. There's also a firepit, library, spa (treatments from US$60) and

BIG BROTHER MOUSE

If you want to get involved in improving local literacy, seek out **Big Brother Mouse** (BBM; ☎071-254937; www.bigbrothermouse.com; Th Sothikuman, Luang Prabang), a home-grown initiative that brings the delights of the written word to infants who, for lack of materials, rarely get the chance to read. BBM employees set out on sometimes difficult trips by boat, pedi power and truck to bring books to distant villages. If you sponsor a book party (2,135,000K), you can go with them. Alternatively, hang out at your local BBM for a couple of hours and read to the kids who attend; the more *falang* drop in, the more children will come to listen. Look out for the Big Brother books in Luang Nam Tha, and the organisation's offices in Luang Prabang and Vientiane.

refined longhouse restaurant. Discounts available in low season.

Apsara BOUTIQUE HOTEL $$$
(Map p302; ☎212420; www.theapsara.com; Th Kingkitsarat; r incl breakfast US$75-150; ❄📶) Apsara commands fine views of the sleepy Nam Khan. Its Indochinese lobby is peppered with silk lanterns, the bar springs from an old classic film, while each of the open-plan rooms is individually designed. From its turquoise walls to its coloured glass Buddhas, everything about this place screams style.

Sala Prabang HOTEL $$
(Map p302; ☎252460; www.salalao.com; 102/6 Th Khem Khong; r incl breakfast US$75-85; ❄📶) Housed in an old French villa, Sala's rooms have limewashed walls, guacamole-coloured linen, hardwood floors and are separated from the bathrooms by Japanese-style screens. Opt for a quieter room at the back.

Thanaboun Guesthouse GUESTHOUSE $$
(Map p302; ☎260606; Th Sisavangvong; r US$25; ❄@) In the heart of town, Thanaboun excels with clean, tastefully finished rooms. Rooms out back backing on to the temple grounds are quieter. There's also an internet cafe (8000K per hour).

Oudomphone Guesthouse GUESTHOUSE $
(Map p302; ☎252419; r with/without bathroom 100,000/60,000K; 📶) This budget favourite with fan-cooled, tile-floored rooms is run by a pleasant family. The owners also run cooking classes and rent scooters. Add yourself to the rogues' gallery with a passport photo.

Ancient Luang Prabang Hotel HOTEL $$
(Map p302; ☎212264; www.ancientluangprabang.com; Th Sisavangvong; s/d incl breakfast US$73-80; ❄@📶) Close to the start of the Handicraft Night Market, this hotel has a boutique feel, with river-facing rooms enjoying teak floors, baths, flat-screen TVs and DVD players. Its breezy cafe sells juices and pastries, and there's also a spa centre. Free transfer to the airport.

Khoum XiengthongZ Guesthouse GUESTHOUSE $$
(Map p302; ☎212906; www.luangprabang-ktg.com; Th Sisalernsak; r US$50-70; 📶) Bedecked in tea lights by night, by day this delightful guesthouse with a strong whiff of Indo-chic nestles around a pretty garden. Stone-floored, white-walled rooms enjoy golden tapestries and chrome fans.

Jaliya Guesthouse GUESTHOUSE $
(Map p302; ☎252154; Th Pha Mahapatsaman; r 70,000-120,000K; ❄) Jaliya has pleasant motel-style bungalows in its garden out back – perfect for a bit of sun-worshipping – as well as decent rooms in the old house itself. Air-con or fan rooms with en suite.

Chittana Guesthouse GUESTHOUSE $
(Map p302; ☎212552; off Th Sakkarin; r without bathroom 150,000K) Its prices may have skyrocketed but, given its enviable position, it's worth it. Atmospheric, wood-varnished, fan-only rooms with basic loos, colourful linen and house-proud touches. The room by the street on the 1st floor is the best.

Souksavath Guesthouse GUESTHOUSE $
(Map p302; ☎212043; Th Hoxieng; r 150,000-180,000K; ❄📶) Souksavath has house-proud rooms with fresh paint, bureaus and wall-mounted flat-screen TVs. Good value and just around the corner from JoMa Bakery.

Sayo River Guesthouse GUESTHOUSE $$
(Map p302; ☎252614; www.sayoguesthouse.com; Th Khem Khong; r incl breakfast US$30-50; ❄) Service is brisk but this colonial-era building compensates with its wood floors, TVs, mosquito nets and trad-Lao decor, with a few rooms enjoying balconies and baths.

Xayana Guest House GUESTHOUSE $
(Map p302; ☎260680; www.mylaohome.com; Th Hoxieng; r 80,000-160,000K) Next to Souksavath Guesthouse, this place has immaculately clean dorms, plus fresh en-suite rooms. There's a nice space out front to read, drink coffee and meet other travellers.

Phousi 2 Guesthouse GUESTHOUSE $
(Map p302; ☎253717; www.phousiguesthouse.com; Th Khem Khong; r 70,000-100,000K) Small, clean rooms with white walls and ornamental conch-shell lights. Rooms out back are dark; opt for a Mekong-facing one. There's also an internet cafe and riverside restaurant.

Kongsavath Guesthouse GUESTHOUSE $$
(Map p302; ☎212994; khongsavath@hotmail.com; Th Khem Khong; r US$40-60; ❄) This lovely, vine-choked villa has wood-panelled rooms reminiscent of a captain's bunk in an old schooner. The family suite overlooking the river is the best.

Hoxieng 2 Guesthouse GUESTHOUSE $$
(Map p302; ☎212703; off Th Hoxieng; r 250,000K; ❄📶) In a peaceful *ban* (village), this tidy guesthouse has clean, nicely finished, wood-floored rooms and an attractive lobby with free internet.

Eating

Munching your way through a spectrum of Gallic, international and Lao cuisine is part of the Luang Prabang experience. If you're hankering for a snack of local noodles or fire-grilled meat, head for the night food stalls down Th Chao Phanya Kang. Many of the better restaurants – especially French – are further down the peninsula.

For fresh Mekong fish and delicious local fare, head for one of the many riverside restaurants on Th Khem Khong.

Quick, cheap eats are to be found with baguette vendors opposite the tourist office from early morning till sunset. After this, the adjacent night market is packed with interesting barbecued food (it's dark, so be sure of what you're eating!), and local dishes such as Mekong fish steamed in banana leaves.

TOP CHOICE **Tamarind** LAOTIAN $
(Map p302; ☎020 777 0484; www.tamarindlaos.com; Th Kingkitsarat; mains 40,000K; ⊙11am-10pm) On the banks of the Nam Khan next to Apsara hotel, chic Tamarind has invented its very own strain of 'Mod Lao' cuisine. The à la carte menu boasts delicious sampling platters with bamboo dip, stuffed lemongrass and *meuyang* (DIY parcels of noodles, herbs, fish and chilli pastes, and vegetables). Its cooking courses (p301) are recommended.

TOP CHOICE **Le Banneton** BAKERY $
(Map p302; Th Sakkarin; meals 35,000K; ⊙6.30am-6pm; 📶) Easily offering the best croissants in Laos, and our personal favourite, this peaceful peninsula cafe is celebrated by pastry buffs for the quality of its flour. It has a sweet-toothed menu of *pain au chocolat*, fruit shakes, sandwiches, quiches and homemade sorbets.

L'Elephant Restaurant FRENCH $$$
(Map p302; www.elephant-restau.com; Ban Wat Nong; mains 140,000K; ⊙11.30am-10pm) Arguably the best cuisine in the city, in a renovated villa with wooden floors, stucco pillars, stencilled ochre walls and bags of atmosphere. The menu (à la carte menu 240,000K) is all terrines, soups, seafood and other Gallic specialities. The buffalo steak tartare is amazing.

Le Café Ban Vat Sene FRENCH $
(Map p302; Th Sakkarin; mains 30,000K; ⊙6.30am-10pm; 📶) Retro fans whir over an Indochinese scene of flower-shaded lights and stylish refinement. This is the place to work, sip an afternoon pastis and read a paper. French wine, salads, quiche, pasta and pizza... *parfait!*

Morning Glory Café WESTERN $
(Map p302; Th Sakkarin; mains 30,000K; ⊙7am-9pm; 📶) Housed in an old French-era building under the shade of jackfruit and mango trees, Morning Glory's al fresco seating is a choice spot to have breakfast. Juices, coffees, sandwiches and Laotian food. The red curry with chicken is tasty.

Saffron WESTERN $
(Map p302; Th Khem Khong; mains 30,000K; ⊙7am-9pm; 📶) The perfect riverside stop for breakfasts, this stylish cafe hung with lush black-and-white photography turns out great pasta dishes, has excellent coffee and warm service, as well as a choice of interior and al fresco dining. Great place to work with free wi-fi.

Café Toui FUSION $
(Map p302; Th Sisavang Vatthana; mains 40,000K; ⊙7am-10pm) Candlelit tunes harmonise with gold-stencilled oxblood walls at this chichi little eatery. The vegetarian-friendly menu is Asian fusion with standout dishes such as tofu *làap*, plus an inviting sampler menu (80,000K).

JoMa Bakery Cafe BAKERY $
(Map p302; Th Chao Fa Ngum; mains 10,000-30,000K; ⊙7am-9pm; ❄📶) This haven of cool with comfy chairs and a contemporary vibe is one of the city's busiest bakeries. While the Danish pastries aren't a match for Le Banneton's, the muffins, sandwiches and salads certainly are.

Sala Cafe FRENCH $$
(Map p302; Th Kingkitsarat; mains 60,000K; ⊙7.30-9.30am) With its Parisian-inspired interior, Sala is perfect for watching the afternoon light turn golden the banks of the Nam Khan opposite. Heavily French menu with dishes such as duck breast in honey sauce.

Kon Kai LAOTIAN $
(Map p302; Th Kingkitsarat; mains 35,000K; ⊙8am-10pm) With unbroken views of the Nam Khan, this heavily Lao-Chinese eatery has brick floors and al fresco tables shaded by tamarind trees. Tasty spring rolls and delicious *oh pa daek* (Luang Prabang pork casserole). Come for late lunch onwards, for the best light.

Big Tree Café KOREAN $
(Map p302; www.bigtreecafe.com; Th Khem Khong; mains 30,000K; ⊙9am-9pm) Korean food made by a genuine Korean! Eat in the cafe – which is full of Adri Berger's alluring Lao photography (also for sale) – or outside on the sun terrace overlooking the Mekong. There's also a choice of Western and Japanese dishes.

Blue Lagoon WESTERN $
(Map p302; www.blue-lagoon-restaurant.com; next to Royal Palace; mains 70,000K; ⊙10am-10pm) A favourite with expats, for its lantern-festooned walls, leafy patio and jazz-infused atmosphere. The menu features Luang Prabang sausage, pasta, salads and very tasty *làap*.

Drinking

Mercifully, the ancient city is insulated by an 11.30pm curfew. That said, the following do their valiant best to squeeze as much hedonistic juice from the restrictions as possible.

Hive Bar BAR
(Map p302; Th Kingkitsarat) A stylish den of hidden coves. Out back in the garden there's a dance floor, projector wall and more tables. Check out the excellent ethnic fashion show every night at 7pm. Tapas, happy hour and cocktails.

Ikon Klub BAR
(Map p302; Th Sisavang Vatthana) Less a club and more of a boudoir, there's something deliciously subversive about this boho bar; the lights are low, the decor tinged with elements of the 1930s, plus a room upstairs with hidden potential. Tom Waits croaking through the speakers finishes it off perfectly.

Lao Lao Garden BAR
(Map p302; Th Kingkitsarat) Lit up like a jungle Vegas, this garden bar on the skirts of Mount Phousi calls you to chill by candlelight, listen to easy sounds and warm your cockles by the firepit. Happy hour all day for bloody Mary and mojito enthusiasts.

Utopia BAR
(Map p302; take turn off top of Th Phommatha) This vernal oasis with a Khmer twist has celestial views of the Nam Khan. Utopia is all recliner cushions, low-slung tables and hookah pipes. Sounds wrong but it works perfectly. Chill over a fruit shake, play a board game or volleyball, or lose yourself in a sea of candles come sunset. Bar snacks too (mains 25,000K).

House Bar BAR
(Map p302; Th Kingkitsarat) Fairy-lit House is a pleasant stop for a Belgian beer. The gardens are pretty, the snacks and breakfasts delicious. Try the beef stew (58,000K).

Entertainment

L'Etranger Books & Tea (Map p302; booksinlaos@yahoo.com; Th Kingkitsarat) screens blockbusters nightly at 7pm. When we passed, **Utopia** was also looking into running documentaries and indie films.

Royal Theatre THEATRE
(Map p302; Th Sisavangvong; admission US$8-20; ⊙shows 6pm Mon, Wed, Fri & Sat) Inside the Royal Palace Museum compound, local performers put on a show that includes a *bąsǐ* ceremony, traditional dance and folk music. There are also traditional dances of Lao ethnic minorities, such as the Phoo Noi and Hmong people.

Dao Fah CLUB
(Map p299; ⊙9-11.30pm) A young Lao crowd packs this cavernous club, located off the road to the southern bus terminal. Live bands playing Lao and Thai pop alternate with DJs who spin rap and hip hop.

Muangsua By Night CLUB
(Map p299; ☎212263; Th Phu Vao; ⊙9-11.30pm) In a low-ceilinged room behind the hotel, a Lao band plays the usual mix of Lao and Thai pop to very happy line-dancers. Only Beerlao is sold.

Shopping

The first visit to Luang Prabang's **Handicraft Night Market** (Map p302; Th Sisavangvong; ⊙5.30-10pm) is magical. A seemingly endless ribbon of colourful textiles, paper lanterns, T-shirts and weavings adorn the candlelit street. Vendors are low-pressure, and, satisfyingly, your money goes straight into their pockets.

Be it locally designed jewellery, the finest Sam Neua pashminas or paintings by local artists, you're sure to find something to commemorate your trip in Luang Prabang's stylish boutiques. And remember – you can still haggle in shops.

TOP CHOICE **Big Tree Gallery** GALLERY
(Map p302; ☎212262; Th Khem Khong; ⊙9am-10pm) Photographer Adri Berger's compositions of rural Lao are exquisite and appear all over the globe. Nobody else captures that honeyed afternoon light like he does. His gallery-cum-restaurant has a range of his work on the walls, with prints starting at an affordable US$100.

Orange Tree ANTIQUES
(Map p302; ☎2121580; Th Khem Khong; ⊙10am-6pm Mon-Sat) This riverfront antiques shop is a testament to its owners' magpie wanderings, with Hong Kong tea tins, Chinese retro alarm clocks, Mao revolutionary crockery, Bakelite inkwells, Vietnamese clocks and Burmese Buddhist statuary. Curio heaven!

Pathana Boupha Antique House ANTIQUES
(Map p302; ☎212262; 29/4 Ban Visoun; ⊙8.30am-5.30pm) Follow the sweeping stairs in the garden to this Aladdin's cave of antique Buddhas, golden *naga*, silver betel-nut pots, Akha-style bracelets and Hmong necklaces. Also sells belle époque busts and fine silk scarves from Sam Neua.

OckPopTok CLOTHING, HANDICRAFTS
(Map p302; www.ockpoptok.com) Ban Wat Nong (☎254761; 73/5 Ban Wat Nong; ⊙8am-9pm); Ban Xieng Mouane (☎254406; Th Sisavangvong; ⊙8am-9pm) OckPopTok works with 16 different tribes to preserve their handicraft traditions. Fine silk and cotton scarves, chemises, dresses, wall hangings and cushion covers make perfect presents.

L'Etranger Books & Tea BOOKS
(Map p302; booksinlaos@yahoo.com; Th Kingkitsarat; ⊙8am-10pm Mon-Sat, 10am-10pm Sun) The cheapest spot for secondhand travel books and thrillers – upstairs there's a comfy lizard-lounge cafe in which to read them. Films shown nightly.

Monument Books BOOKS
(Map p302; www.monument-books.com; Ban Wat Nong; ⊙9am-9pm Mon-Fri, to 6pm Sat & Sun) Next to OckPopTok; new novels and magazines, French and English.

ℹ Information

Internet Access

For free wi-fi access try Le Café Ban Vat Sene (p306) or JoMa Bakery Café (p288). Internet cafes are peppered along Th Sisavangvong and charge 4000K per hour.

All Lao Travel (Map p302; Th Sisavangvong; ⊙8am-6pm)

Thanaboun Guest House (Map p302; Th Sisavangvong; ⊙8am-11pm)

Medical Services

Provincial Hospital (☎254025; Ban Naxang; doctor's consultation 100,000K) OK for minor problems but for any serious illnesses consider flying to Bangkok or returning to Vientiane for **Aek Udon International** (☎0066-4234 2555; www.aekudon.com; Posri Rd, Amphur Muang, Udon Thani Province) just over the Thai border. Note that the hospital in Luang Prabang charges double for consultations at weekends or anytime after 4pm.

There are plenty of pharmacies in the centre of town.

Pharmacie (Th Sakkarin; ⊙8.30am-8pm) Stocks basic medicines. On weekends, hours are variable.

Money

BCEL (Map p302; Th Sisavangvong; ⊙8.30am-3.30pm Mon-Sat) Changes major currencies in cash or travellers cheques, has a 24-hour ATM and allows you to make cash advances against Visa and MasterCard.

Lao Development Bank (Map p302; 65 Th Sisavangvong; ⊙8.30am-3.30pm Mon-Sat) Has a 24hr ATM.

Post

Post office (Map p302; Th Chao Fa Ngum; ⊙8.30am-3.30pm Mon-Fri, to noon Sat) Phone calls and Western Union facilities too.

Telephone

Most internet cafes in Luang Prabang town have Skype, and also offer international calls for 3000K and mobile calls for 4000K per minute.

Tourist Information

Provincial Tourism Department (Map p302; www.tourismlaos.com; Th Sisavangvong; ⊙8am-4pm Mon-Fri) General info stop on festivals and ethnic groups as well as selling Hobo maps. Pointlessly, staff speak little or no English.

Unesco World Heritage Information (www.unesco.org; Villa Xiengmouane, Th Sakkarin; ⊙9am-6pm Mon-Fri) Without Unesco, Luang Prabang's architectural uniqueness would have been ruined years ago. Its office is situated in an old French customs house; visit to learn more about Unesco's work.

Getting There & Away

Air

By the time you read this there could well be international flights to Hong Kong, Kuala Lumpur, Singapore and Tokyo from **Luang Prabang International Airport**, which is currently undergoing expansion. **Lao Airlines** (☎212172; www.laoairlines.com; Th Pha Mahapatsaman) flies from Luang Prabang to Vientiane (one way US$88, three times daily) and Pakse (one way US$168, three times per week). By the time you read this, a route may be operating from Luang Prabang to Phonsavan and also to Huay Xai. Internationally, flights go daily to Chiang Mai in Thailand (one way US$120, daily), Bangkok (one way US$160, daily), Hanoi (one way US$144, daily), Siem Reap (one way US$190, daily) and occasionally to Udon Thani.

Bangkok Airways (☎253334; www.bangkokair.com; Th Sisavangvong) flies from Luang Prabang to Bangkok (one way US$215, daily). **Vietnam Airlines** (☎213049; www.vietnamairlines.com; Luang Prabang International Airport) flies to both Hanoi (US$170, daily) and Siem Reap (US$260, daily).

The terminal is 4km from the city centre; it costs 50,000K in a túk-túk to get there.

Boat

PAK BENG & HUAY XAI

Slow boats motor northwest daily to Huay Xai (200,000K), departing at 8am by the **Navigation Office** (⏲8-11am & 2-4pm), located behind the Royal Palace. You can buy tickets direct from them or from a travel agent. The trip takes two days with an overnight stop in Pak Beng (100,000K, nine hours). From Pak Beng it's also possible to take the bus northeast to Oudomxay. Another, more memorable option is the luxurious accommodation on the 34m luxury **Luang Say** (☎254768; www.luangsay.com; 50/4 Th Sakkarin, Luang Prabang; ⏲9.30am-9.30pm) river barge, which takes two days and costs US$467, including an overnight stop in a luxury lodge in Pak Beng. Buy your ticket at the office in Luang Prabang.

White-knuckle **speedboats** up the Mekong leave at 8.30am daily from Ban Don pier, a 7km, 10,000K shared túk-túk ride from the centre. Compared to the slow boat, they rocket to Pak Beng (190,000K, three hours) and Huay Xai (300,000K, six hours) in a fraction of the time, but with 10 times the danger, endangering both your life and the equilibrium of the animals that live along the river. Are you really in such a hurry that you'd place your life in their riverine hands?

NONG KHIAW

Although it's quicker by road, many travellers charter a boat for the beautiful limestone scenery up the Nam Ou to Nong Khiaw (110,000K, seven hours). Inquire at the Navigation Office in Luang Prabang or with travel agents in town, where you can add your name to the passenger list of impending departures.

Bus & Sŏrngtăaou

Most inter-provincial buses and *sŏrngtăaou* heading north depart from the northern bus terminal (on Rte 13 about 4km north of town), while south-bound vehicles use the southern bus terminal, 3km south of town. On all these routes the durations can vary wildly during monsoonal weather.

A better option is the **Naluang Minibus Station** – opposite the southern bus terminal – that runs new minibuses to Nong Khiaw (55,000K, 9.30am), Vang Vieng (95,000K, 8.30am), Phonsavan (95,000K, 9am), Luang Nam Tha (105,000K, 8.30am), Hanoi (320,000K, 6pm) and Kūnming (420,000K, sleeper bus, 7am). If you've got sufficient numbers it's possible to charter a bus; short journeys such as to Phonsavan and Vang Vieng will cost around US$120.

VIENTIANE & VANG VIENG

Several local buses leave the southern bus terminal for Vientiane (110,000K, 10 to 14 hours) at 6.30am, 11am, 4pm and 6.30pm. VIP buses en route to Vientiane (130,000K, about 10 hours, 8am, 9am and 7.30pm) stop in Vang Vieng (100,000K, six to nine hours).

OUDOMXAY, LUANG NAM THA, NONG KHIAW & SAM NEUA

From the northern bus terminal, daily *sŏrngtăaou* and local buses go to Oudomxay (60,000K, four hours, four daily), Luang Nam Tha (100,000K, nine hours, 9am), Nong Khiaw (40,000K, four hours, two to five daily), Sam Neua (130,000K, 16 hours, 9am and 5pm), Huay

MEKONG COWBOYS

Beware some of Luang Prabang's boatmen scam claiming they can't leave until the boat is full. You and the other *falang* (foreigners) end up clubbing together for the 'ghost' fare and then magically the last person appears stage left – and you don't get your cash back. Also, if you're running behind on your halfway pit stop at Pak Beng to Huay Xai, the driver might complain it's too late and start heading back to Luang Prabang. This is one instance when you need to make yourself heard as a group. These boatmen illustrate anything but the gentle side of Lao people.

Xai (120,000K, local bus, 5.30pm; 140,000K, VIP bus, 7pm) and Phongsali (120,000K, 13 hours, 5.30pm).

PHONSAVAN & SAINYABULI

From the southern terminal local buses leave daily to Phonsavan (95,000K, eight hours, 8.30am) and Sainyabuli (60,000K, five hours, 9am and 2pm).

Getting Around

From the airport into town, jumbos or minitrucks charge a uniform 50,000K per vehicle, and up to six passengers can share the ride. In the reverse direction you can usually charter an entire jumbo for 30,000K to 40,000K.

Most of the town is accessible on foot. Jumbos usually ask foreigners for 15,000K a ride. Motorcycles can no longer be hired due to frequent accidents; however, mountain/ordinary bikes are available for 50,000/20,000K per day.

Around Luang Prabang

PAK OU CAVES

About 25km upstream on the Mekong and at the mouth of the Nam Ou, the dramatic **Pak Ou Caves** (admission 20,000K) are set into limestone cliffs and are crammed with hundreds of Buddha images; a kind of statue's graveyard where unwanted images are placed. This pantheon of statuary is split into two levels, with the lower being more impressive. A steep climb (10 minutes) up dark slippery steps yields a view of the mysterious **Naga vessel**. Bring a torch.

Most boat trips stop at small villages along the way, especially **Ban Xang Hai**. Boatmen call this tourist-dominated place 'Whisky Village', as it's known for its free-flowing *lào-lâo* (rice whisky).

You can hire long-tail boats to Pak Ou from Luang Prabang's charter boat landing at 130,000K for one to three people or 170,000K for four to five people, including petrol. The trip takes two hours upriver and one hour down, plus stops. Túk-túks make the trip for about half the price.

TAT KUANG SI

Kuang Si falls, 32km from the city, are a tonic for sore eyes, with a multitiered cascade tumbling over limestone formations into menthol-green pools below. The waterfall is set in a beautifully lush, well-manicured **public park** (admission 16,000K), and there's nothing more Eden-like than plunging into the turquoise water to cool off after making the vertiginous ascent. Near the entrance are enclosures housing sun bears rescued from poachers.

On the way to Kuang Si, you'll pass **Ban Tat Paen**, a scenic Khamu village with a cool stream, rustic dam and several miniature waterfalls. **Vanvisa 2 Guest House** (per person incl breakfast & dinner 85,000K) is a simple Lao-style wooden building in this village; with notice staff can arrange cooking classes for 130,000K per person.

Some visitors come by hired bicycle (only for the fit), stopping in villages along the way. Freelance guides proliferate down Th Sisavangvong and offer trips by jumbo, or boat and jumbo (both for about 100,000K per person).

Luang Prabang Province

NONG KHIAW (MUANG NGOI)

☎071

Nestled along the riverbank of the Nam Ou and towered over by forest-clad karsts, Nong Khiaw is a travellers' haven of cafes, soporific guesthouses and – thanks to the arrival of Green Discovery and Tiger Trail – plenty of things to keep you busy; finally it's exploiting its handsome outdoor potential with a range of activities. Relax with a herbal massage, watch a cult film at the video lounge or eat at a couple of tasty restaurants. After years in the shadow of neighbour Muang Ngoi Neua, Nong Khiaw is on the rise. Note – the opposite side of the river where most guesthouses are based is called Ban Sop Houn.

Sights & Activities

TREKKING & CYCLING

You can walk by yourself to **Tham Pha Tok**, an enormous, many-levelled cave where villagers hid out during the Second Indochina War, but be careful heading down the rickety ladder. To get there, walk 2.5km east of the bridge then look for a clearly visible cave mouth in the limestone cliff on the right (it's about 100m from the road).

Tiger Trail rents mountain bikes for 30,000K per day, as does Green Discovery, which charges 50,000K for superior bikes.

Tiger Trail TREKKING, CYCLING
(☎252655; info@laos-adventures.com; based at Delilah's Place, Nong Khiaw) This ecoconscious outfit has treks around the local area, including one-day trips to the '100 waterfalls' (270,000K per person, group of four). A two-day trek through Hmong villages incorporating a

homestay costs 410,000K per person, again based on at least four of you.

Green Discovery TREKKING, CYCLING
(☎020 336 6110; www.nongkiau.com; Nong Kiau Riverside Resort, Ban Sop Houn) Offers panoramic, overnight camping treks (50,000K per person for a group of four) near the summit of Phou Nang None. Cycling through Khamu, Thai Lü and Hmong villages (390,000K per person for a group of four) is recommended.

KAYAKING, TUBING, FISHING & CLIMBING

As well as tubing and kayaking (210,000K per person for a group of four) on the Nam Ou, Tiger Trail organises fishing classes with local fishermen. Green Discovery runs one-day (330,000K per person) and three-day kayaking excursions to Luang Prabang. Run by the able Mr Somneuk, Green Discovery is the outfit to scale the karsts with; climbs for a group of four cost 150,000K per person.

MASSAGE

Sabai Sabai MASSAGE
(Ban Sop Houn) Has a peaceful Zen-style garden in which to repair your spirit and aching limbs. Body massages cost 40,000K; herbal steam baths, 15,000K. It's just past the turn-off for Sunset Guest House.

Sleeping & Eating

Guesthouses in Nong Khiaw are near the bridge on the west side of the river, and in the more popular village of Ban Sop Houn, on the east side.

TOP CHOICE Nong Kiau Riverside Guest House GUESTHOUSE $$
(☎020 5570 5000; www.nongkiau.com; Ban Sop Houn; s/d incl breakfast 310,000/350,000K; @☎) As well as its excellent menu spanning spaghetti, Lao beef jerky, chocolate pancakes and chicken *làap*, Riverside's elegant A-frame cabanas are romantically finished in mosquito nets, ambient lighting, wood floors and woven bedspreads. Enjoy its sumptuous views of the river and opposite karsts.

Delilah's Place WESTERN, LAOTIAN $
(Nong Khiaw; mains 30,000K; ⊙7am-10pm) Strung with creeper vines, this tasteful eatery offers an eclectic selection ranging from delicious pancakes, bagels, salads, spring rolls and Lao green curries to hamburgers and Western breakfasts. You can even get a proper latte here.

Deen INDIAN $
(Ban Sop Houn; mains 25,000K; ⊙8.30am-10pm) Recently migrated from Huay Xai, with its wood-fired naan bread, moreish tandoori dishes, zesty curries and homely atmosphere, Deen is always packed. There's also a bank of computers (internet costs 15,000K per hour, wi-fi is free).

TONY POE: THE HORROR, THE HORROR

Exceptional secret agent or flipped-out crazoid? CIA Special Ops agent Anthony Poe was every communist guerilla's worst nightmare, famous for going native à la Colonel Kurtz, collecting Pathet Lao ears and dropping heads on his enemy's porch from a Cessna plane. In many ways he became as savage as the forests in which he made his home.

In 1961 Poe was sent to the mountainous north to ignite 'Operation Momentum', an American attempt to repel North Vietnamese forces from Laos (see p352) as well as providing home-grown resistance to national communist sympathies. His assignment: to train up a crack force of 10,000 hill-tribe warriors. He chose the Hmong, plucky, naturally suspicious of communism and eager to make a trade of guns and money in return for their opium and courage. Poe won the loyalty of his warriors – contravening his paymasters' orders – by fighting beside them and intrepidly attacking enemy-infested strongholds such as Luang Nam Tha on the Chinese border – risking China's intervention in the Secret War. Furious, the CIA considered its man a liability, their prodigy now a Frankenstein's monster. Pathet Lao ears were stapled by Poe to progress reports and sent to the CIA 'Bubble' in Bangkok. As far as he was concerned: 'War is hell, if you're gonna do it you've gotta do it with gusto.

After the Pathet Lao victory of '75 Poe retired to Thailand; a renegade scorned, he would drunkenly shoot off his pistol in Bangkok bars, never forgiving the CIA for yanking him out of Laos before 'the job was done'. The precursor and partial inspiration to Coppola's Colonel Kurtz, cinema's most enduring icon of the war in Vietnam, Poe died in 2003.

CT Restaurant and Bakery WESTERN, LAOTIAN $
(Ban Sop Houn; mains 20,000K; ⏲7am-10pm) At the end of the bridge, lit up like a beacon of doughy smells and good cheer, CT has a Western-friendly menu of pancakes, breakfasts, sandwiches and staple Lao dishes. It also does decent cakes and takeaway sandwiches for trekking.

Sunset Guest House GUESTHOUSE $
(☎020 559 7103; sunsetgh@hotmail.com; Ban Sop Houn; r 100,000-150,000K) Ever-evolving Sunset has an excellent new roof cafe and, along with its cheaper offerings, two lovely new cabanas isolated in a little meadow. The owner speaks English and French.

Sengdao Chittavong Guest House GUESTHOUSE $
(☎030 923 7089; Nong Khiaw; r 80,000-100,000K) Sizeable cabanas located in gardens of cherry blossom by the river. En-suite rooms are rattan-walled, with simple decoration, fresh flowers, clean linen, and balconies.

ℹ Getting There & Away

BOAT

In high season, boats heading up the Nam Ou to Muang Ngoi Neua (one way 20,000K, one hour) leave at 11am and 2pm. Tickets are bought at an office at the bus station. Boats sometimes continue to Muang Khua (88,000K, seven hours) from Muang Ngoi Neua.

Public boats make the six- to nine-hour trip through striking karst scenery to Luang Prabang; with a minimum of 10 people tickets cost 100,000K per person – or you can charter the boat for 1,500,000K. See p309 for information on boat travel from Luang Prabang.

BUS & SŎRNGTĂAOU

Sŏrngtăaou going to Oudomxay (45,000K) leave daily at 11am from the new bus station roughly a kilometre from town. If you miss this don't worry – you can take one of the more frequent *sŏrngtăaou* southwest to Pak Mong (20,000K, 1½ hours), then change to another *sŏrngtăaou* to Oudomxay (17,000K, two to three hours from Pak Mong) and anywhere further west. *Sŏrngtăaou* and small local buses to Luang Prabang (50,000K, three hours) depart every two hours between 8.30am and 1.30pm. If the bus is full, gather 10 of you and charter one for 50,000K.

If you're heading east towards Huah Phan or Xieng Khuang, you can get a bus to Sam Neua (120,000K, 13 hours, daily at 11.30am), or catch the local bus stopping briefly at the Ban Sop Houn side of the bridge every night between 6pm and 7pm.

MUANG NGOI NEUA

Nets drying in the breeze, roosters strutting, wood houses wilting, while indolent villagers sleep in the shadows; this roadless village fortressed by karst cliffs and caressed by the gentle Nam Ou might just be the most languid place in Laos. Stalls fry up pancakes in the morning street, mist hangs on the pyramid-shaped karst as river life crackles to life. Unlike Vang Vieng, a recent crackdown on drugs here ensured Muang Ngoi Neua didn't become a stoner casualty, and thankfully locals are still welcoming. Between trekking the serene surroundings and kayaking, worth a visit are the caves locals used to hide in during the aerial bombardment suffered during the war in Vietnam (the village lies directly in the path of the Ho Chi Minh Trail).

Generators provide electricity from 6pm to around 10pm. There are no banks here and barely a local phone signal, so bring sufficient cash to get back.

ℹ GETTING TO VIETNAM: SOP HUN TO TAY TRANG

The border (open 8am to 5pm) at Sop Hun in Phongsali Province, just across from Tay Trang (34km west of Dien Bien Phu), has now opened as an international border. If you're headed into Vietnam, there are three buses a week bound for Dien Bien Phu, leaving from the Lao village of Muang Khua (50,000K, 6.30am). Unless you get here early to buy your ticket, you'll lose all chance of a decent seat. During the wet season the road, which crosses a number of creeks, may become impassable. A 40,000K 'processing' fee is demanded by Lao immigration. The same applies from the other side – catch a return bus to Laos from Dien Bien Phu. However, while you can get a visa on arrival in Laos, you'll need to organise a visa for Vietnam in advance while in Vientiane. If leaving from Nong Khiaw, ask around to see whether a boatman can take you upriver to Muang Khua.

For information on crossing this border in the other direction, see p94.

Sights & Activities

In town you'll find a sea of signs advertising guides for **fishing trips, tubing, kayaking** and **trekking**. Treks cost 80,000K per day and tubing costs around 13,000K per day.

Recommended English-speaking tour operators include **Lao Youth Travel** (☎030 514 0046; www.laoyouthtravel.com; ⊙7.30-10.30am & 1.30-6pm), which ploughs part of its profits into supporting primary education in northern Laos. It offers kayaking (group of four costs US$28 per person), trekking (group of two costs US$28), cookery classes, homestays and boat trips. **Muang Ngoi Tours** (☎020 213 6219; top of the boat-landing stairs; ⊙8am-9pm), run by friendly Chang, has similar and slightly cheaper offerings. Finally, **Kongkeo Tours** (☎020 2386 3648; kongkeoteacher@yahoo.com), run by an affable English-speaking teacher, offers one- to five-day treks to the caves and Khamu and Hmong villages.

Sleeping

Many guesthouses feature river views, shared cold-water bathrooms, hammocks and attached family-run restaurants.

TOP CHOICE **Bungalows Ecolodge** GUESTHOUSE $
(main street; r 80,000K) Decent-sized new bungalows hidden down a side street, with sliding shutters that allow you to lie in bed and watch the sky turn amber over the karsts. Tasteful linen, solar-heated showers, mosquito nets and locally sourced food elevate it above the crowd.

Aloune Mai Guest House GUESTHOUSE $
(r 70,000K) Not to be confused with rickety Aloune Mai by the river, this hidden gem, found down a dirt track and over a bridge, sits beside a meadow and has 10 fresh rooms in a handsome rattan building with heated showers. Better still, there's a little restaurant and stunning views of the cliffs on the other side.

Lattanavongsa Guest House GUESTHOUSE $
(☎030 514 0770; r 100,000K) In a palm-filled garden, Lattanavongsa's sun-terraced cabanas enjoy views of the karsts. Inside rooms are tasteful with house-proud flourishes, including gas-fired showers. Manager Mr Touy can also take you trekking (one-day trek US$28 per person).

Ning Ning Guest House GUESTHOUSE $
(☎020 386 3306; r incl breakfast US$17-20) Nestled around a peaceful garden, Ning Ning has immaculate wood cabanas with mosquito nets, verandahs, fresh en suites and bedlinen, and walls ornamented with ethnic tapestries. There's a nice restaurant out front too.

Saylom Guest House GUESTHOUSE $
(r 40,000-50,000K) A spit from the boat ramp, this powder-blue guesthouse has clean, tiled-floor en-suite rooms, an adjoining restaurant, and verandahs with hammocks.

Rainbow Guest House GUESTHOUSE $
(☎020 2295 7880; r 50,000K) Close to the boat ramp, this newly constructed house has clean if charmless rooms. Fragrant linen, large en suites and communal verandah, and a sunset-facing cafe.

Eating

Well-priced Laotian and Western fare are available in abundance, though there are no gastronomic prodigies here.

TOP CHOICE **Riverside Restaurant** LAOTIAN $
(meals 35,000K; ⊙7.30am-10pm) Shaded by a mature mango tree festooned with lanterns, this lively haunt has lovely views of the Nam Ou. The menu encompasses noodles, fried dishes and *làap*. A real traveller magnet, it deserves all the attention it receives.

Phetdavanh street buffet LAOTIAN $
(⊙7pm) Phetdavanh runs an excellent nightly buffet that draws in locals and travellers alike. It sets up on the street around 7pm, serving barbecued pork, chicken, fish, sticky rice and vegetables. Lip-smacking.

Lao Friend Coffeeshop LAOTIAN $
(☎020 389 1827; meals 25,000K; ⊙noon-10pm) New chilling bar with a garden strewn with plants and bomb casings repurposed as flowerpots. Cocktails, lounging chairs, glowing lanterns by night and a menu including steaks and fresh fish.

Lattanavongsa Restaurant LAOTIAN $
(mains 20,000K; ⊙6.30am-9pm) Overlooking the river with an umbrella-shaded sun terrace. Come here for tasty papaya salads, spring rolls, *làap* and sweet-and-sour fish.

Getting There & Away

Boats to Nong Khiaw leave at 9am (or when full) and cost 20,000K. Heading north, a boat goes most days to Muang Khua (minimum 10 people, 100,000K, seven hours) for those headed for the Sop Hun to Tay Trang border crossing. Buy tickets at the **Boat Office**, halfway up the

AN ENDURING LEGACY

Between 1964 and 1973, the USA conducted one of the largest sustained aerial bombardments in history, flying 580,344 missions over Laos and dropping two million tons of bombs, costing US$2.2 million a day. Around 30% of the bombs dropped on Laos failed to detonate, leaving the country littered with unexploded ordnance (UXO).

For people all over eastern Laos (the most contaminated provinces being Xieng Khuang, Salavan and Savannakhet), living with this appalling legacy has become an intrinsic part of daily life. Since the British **Mines Advisory Group** (MAG; www.mag.org.uk; Rte 7; ⊙4-8pm) began clearance work in 1994, only a tiny percentage of the quarter of a million pieces in Xieng Khuang and Salavan has been removed. At the current rate of clearance it will take more than 100 years to make the country safe.

boat-landing stairs next to Lattanavongsa Restaurant. A list for each day gives an indication of how many have signed up for Muang Khua. There's a boat to Nong Khiaw from Muang Khua that stops in Muang Ngoi Neua at 1.30pm.

Xieng Khuang Province

Rainswept and cratered by American bombs that fell by the planeload every eight minutes for an unbelievable nine years, Xieng Khuang Province will make you either want to stay a while or hotfoot it to the nearest Lao Airlines office. Virtually all of the province was bombed between 1964 and 1973, and a sense of that tragedy endures today with the pernicious legacy of UXO (unexploded ordnance; see boxed text p314). Despite its alpine landscape, the shadow of the past looms large, with entire areas still denuded. Most come here to see the mystical Plain of Jars, but there are also several fascinating sites relating to the war that are open to tourists.

PHONSAVAN

☎061 / POP 60,000

Often mist-shrouded and chilly, with locals gathering collars around weather-beaten faces, this dusty old town (latterly known as Xieng Khouang) has heaps of charm if you look past its nondescript, Soviet facade – blame that on its hasty rebuild after it was decimated. Stoic locals make the most of decommissioned UXO, using it to decorate houses and foyers, and craters have morphed into duck ponds. Touchingly, while other areas of Laos erupt in boutique villas and pockets of sophistication, Phonsavan, like some retro-leaning Muscovite, barely changes.

Its two main streets are peopled by an intriguing cosmopolitan cast of Chinese, Vietnamese, Lao and Hmong, thanks to its location as a trade hub. The town is well serviced by an airport, a handful of OK guesthouses and restaurants, plus a wet and dry goods market.

Sights

Most come here to witness the mysterious Plain of Jars, considered to be funeral urns dating back to the Stone Age. It's possible you're also here to learn more about the Secret War, so pop into the **Mines Advisory Group** (MAG; www.mag.org.uk; Rte 7; ⊙4-8pm), whose tireless detection, detonation and diffusion of UXO is helping to make Laos a safer place. To deepen your understanding watch the harrowing documentaries *Bombies* and *On War*, screened daily at 4.30pm, 5.45pm and 6.30pm. Two doors down, **Xieng Khouang UXO-survivors; Information Centre** (www.laos.worlded.org; ⊙8am-8pm) displays prosthetic limbs and UXO, adding further insight.

Sleeping

Forget Indo-chic: the accommodation in Phonsavan, but for a few inviting exceptions, is as unimaginative as the Soviet buildings.

TOP CHOICE **Auberge de La Plaine des Jarres** CABIN $$
(☎020 5599 9192; r US$60) Hillside elevation, Scotch pines and Swiss-style wooden interiors give these inviting hobbit-hole cabins an incongruously alpine feel. There's a great French and Lao restaurant with a nightly fire, library of books and walls decked in animal horns like some hunter's eyrie. It's 10 minutes' drive from town.

Kong Keo Guesthouse GUESTHOUSE $
(☎211354; www.kongkeojar.com; r 60,000-80,000K) The most welcoming central digs, with an open-pit barbecue, cabins with en suites and overly hard beds, as well as a newish block of more comfortable rooms.

Phonsavan

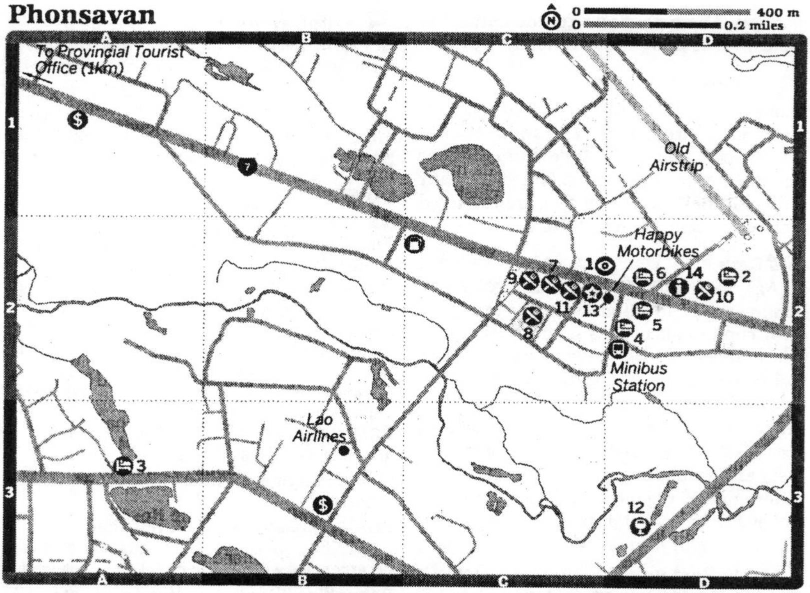

Phonsavan

Sights

1 Mines Advisory Group (MAG) C2
Xieng Khouang UXO-survivors' Information Centre .... (see 1)

Sleeping

2 Kong Keo Guesthouse D2
3 Maly Hotel A3
4 Nam Chai Guesthouse D2
5 Nice Guesthouse D2
6 White Orchid Guesthouse D2

Eating

7 Craters Bar & Restaurant C2
8 Fresh Food Market C2
9 Jars Café C2
Maly Hotel .... (see 3)
10 Nisha Restaurant D2
11 Simmaly Restaurant C2

Drinking

12 Barview D3

Entertainment

13 Sousath Travel C2

Information

14 Amazing Lao Travel D2
Post Office .... (see 9)

Eccentric owner Mr Keo runs excellent tours to the jars, as well as specialised trips.

Maly Hotel GUESTHOUSE $$
(☎312031; www.malyht.laotel.com; r incl breakfast 230,000-260,000K; ❄@) In a frigid accommodation landscape, Maly excels with wood beams and candlelit ambience. Rooms beckon with en suite, TV and hot water.

Nice Guesthouse GUESTHOUSE $
(☎312454; r 70,000-110,000K) With fresh and fragrant rooms, clean bathrooms, spotless rooms and firm beds, Nice shows no signs of ageing. Chinese lanterns cast a ruby glow into the chill.

Nam Chai Guesthouse GUESTHOUSE $
(☎312095; r 80,000K) Still smelling pine-fresh, this new guesthouse is functional with clean rooms with fan, TV and en suite. That said, it's nondescript.

White Orchid Guesthouse GUESTHOUSE $$
(☎312403; r incl breakfast 250,000K; ❄☎) Average-looking rooms with menthol-green walls, clean en suites and appealing

blankets. The higher you go, the better the rooms, views and – unfortunately – price.

Eating & Drinking

Phonsavan is still waiting to light up the gastronomic horizon. The **fresh food market** (⌚6am-5pm) sells everything from fruit to Korean, Indian and Laotian fare at its many stalls. All the following places are clustered around the central area of Rte 7.

Jars Café WESTERN $
(Sa-Nga; mains 30,000K; ⌚7am-10pm;) Finally, somewhere in Phonsavan you can get a great cup of coffee! This homely cafe offers cakes, spring rolls, sandwiches, pancakes and omelettes. Comfy retro leather couches and wi-fi make it a cool place to work in.

Nisha Restaurant INDIAN $
(meals 12,000K; ⌚breakfast, lunch & dinner) Tasty and value for money, Nisha has a wide range of vegetarian options, and makes lovely dosa (flat bread), tikka masala and rogan josh, as well as great lassi.

Simmaly Restaurant LAOTIAN $
(meals 15,000-20,000K; ⌚breakfast, lunch & dinner) Dishes up a tasty line of rice dishes, noodles and spicy meats. The pork with ginger is lovely.

Maly Hotel LAOTIAN $
(meals 25,000K; ⌚breakfast, lunch & dinner) Maly serves Laotian dishes, Thai food and wholesome soups, and is a great place to warm those chilly pinkies after the jars sites.

Craters Bar & Restaurant WESTERN $
(meals 30,000K; ⌚breakfast, lunch & dinner) A mainstay of NGOs, Craters has CNN on the tube as you munch through its toasties, soups, burgers, fried chicken, steaks and pizzas.

Barview BAR
(⌚8am-11pm) Try this simple place for sunset beers over the rice-paddy fields.

Entertainment

At 7pm every evening **Sousath Travel** pulls down the drapes and surreptitiously screens an insightful documentary (currently banned in Laos) called *The Most Secret Place on Earth*; essential viewing for a revelatory perspective on US involvement during the war.

Information

Amazing Lao Travel (☎020 234 0005; www.amazinglao.com; Rte 7) Runs treks to the jar sites and two-day treks in the mountains including a homestay in a Hmong village. As ever, the more the merrier, with prices falling for larger groups. Three jar sites including food and driver will cost around 120,000K per person. It also books minibuses and bus tickets and has a bank of internet terminals.

BCEL (☎213291; Rte 7) Located past the dry goods market. Has a 24-hour ATM.

Lao Development Bank (☎312188) Currency exchange.

Lao-Mongolian Friendship Hospital (☎312166) Good for minor needs, but medical emergencies will need to be taken to Thailand.

Post office (⌚8am-4pm Mon-Fri, to noon Sat) Domestic phone service.

Provincial tourist office (☎312217) Next to the *sǒrngtǎaou* station about a kilometre southwest of town is Phonsavan's useful provincial tourist office. Now organising treks, it also produces a great two-page document called 'Do-it yourself activities around Phonsavan', detailing how to invite yourself to a local wedding, info on war memorials, local lakes and more.

Sousath Travel (☎312031; Rte 7) Rasa runs reliable tours to the Plain of Jars and Ho Chi Minh Trail as well as homestays in Hmong villages. He also rents scooters (100,000K per day). By the time you read this he'll be able to take you to the formerly forbidden Long Tien Airbase (a former CIA site during the Secret War) in the infamous Special Zone.

GETTING TO VIETNAM: NONG HAET TO NAM CAN

The Nong Haet–Nam Can crossing is little-used by travellers because it's difficult, potentially expensive if you get ripped off, and not really convenient if you're heading north in Vietnam (you have to go 200km south to grim Vinh first). Nam Can (in Vietnam) is 13km from Nong Haet. You can get between Nong Haet and Phonsavan by bus (20,000K, three to four hours, four daily). There is also a direct bus between Phonsavan and Vinh (150,000K, 11 hours, Tuesday, Thursday and Sunday). The border crossing is open from 8am to 3pm. You can get a Lao visa on arrival; however, this is not possible when entering Vietnam.

For information on crossing this border in the other direction, see p97.

Getting There & Away

Lao Airlines (☎212027) flies to/from Vientiane (one way US$87, daily except Tuesday, Thursday and Saturday). Jumbos to the airport cost around 8500K per person.

Buses leave from the bus station 4km west of town, while minibuses leave from the centre of town behind Sousath Travel. Most long-distance buses depart between 7am and 8am – check times the day before. Buses run to Sam Neua (80,000K, eight hours, two daily), Vientiane (local bus/VIP 110,000/130,000K, 11 hours, several daily commencing 7am, one VIP ride at 8pm), Vang Vieng (local bus 80,000K, six hours, daily at 7.30am; minibus 100,000K, daily at 8am) and Luang Prabang (local bus 85,000K, 10 hours, daily at 8.30am; minibus 100,000K, daily at 8.30am). For Paksan (local bus 100,000K, daily at 7.30am) the road is improved but still unsealed in parts and takes 10 hours.

There are public buses and *sŏrngtăaou* to Muang Kham (30,000K, two hours, four daily), Muang Sui (30,000K, one hour, three daily) and Nong Haet (40,000K, four hours, four daily). These *sŏrngtăaou* leave from the little station next to the provinvcial tourist office a kilometre southwest, on the outskirts of town.

Other destinations include Lat Khai (Plain of Jars Site 3; 20,000K, 30 minutes, one daily) and Muang Khoun (20,000K, 30 minutes, six daily). Buses also go all the way through to Vinh in Vietnam (138,000K, 11 hours, 6.30am Tuesday, Thursday and Sunday).

PLAIN OF JARS

The Plain of Jars represents a huge area of Xieng Khuang scattered with thousands of limestone jars of undetermined age. Thought to be funerary urns after bones were discovered within them, the jars have been divided into 160 sites, three of which represent the greatest concentration. These are the designated UXO-cleared tourist areas you should visit.

Site 1 (Thong Hai Hin; admission 10,000K), the biggest and most accessible site, is 15km southwest of Phonsavan and features 250 jars, most of which weigh from 600kg to 1 tonne each. The largest jar weighs as much as 6 tonnes and is said to have been the victory cup of mythical King Jeuam, and so is called Hai Jeuam.

Two other jar sites are readily accessible by road from Phonsavan. **Site 2** (Hai Hin Phu Salato; admission 10,000K), about 25km south of town, features 90 jars spread across two adjacent hillsides. Vehicles can reach the base of the hills, then it's a short, steep walk to the jars.

Plain of Jars

More impressive is 150-jar **Site 3** (Hai Hin Lat Khai; admission 10,000K). It's about 10km south of Site 2 (or 35km from Phonsavan) on a scenic hilltop near the charming village of **Ban Xieng Di**, where there's a small monastery containing the remains of Buddha images damaged in the war. The site is a 2km hike through rice paddies and up a hill.

Getting There & Away

It's possible to charter a *sŏrngtăaou* to Site 1 for about 85,000K return, including waiting time, for up to six people. All three sites are reachable by bike or motorcycle (per day 160,000K through guesthouses). **Happy Motorbikes** (☎213233; Rte 7, Phonsavan; ⏲8am-6pm) rents bicycles (40,000K per day) and scooters (90,000K per day).

Otherwise, you're on a tour. Guesthouses and a number of travel agents (p316) offer tours for 120,000K to 200,000K per person in a minivan with around eight passengers. **Sousath Travel** (☎061-312031; Rte 7) and **Kong Keo Tours** (☎061-211354; www.kongkeojar.com; off Rte 7) receive consistently good reports.

Tours are often extended to include other interesting sites, including a crashed US F-105 Thunderchief, a Russian tank, Viet Cong bunkers, the US Lima Site 108 airstrip supposedly used for drug-running, and hot springs.

Huah Phan Province

Rugged and beautiful, Huah Phan is unlike any other province in Laos. Although home to 22 different ethnic groups, including Yao, Hmong, Khamu, Thai Khao and Thai Neua, the strong Vietnamese influence is evident. The province's high altitude means the climate can be cool – even in the hot season – and forested mountains are shrouded in mist. Road journeys to Huah Phan are memorably scenic, described by one local as 'a journey of a million turns'.

Despite the remote border to Vietnam and Hanoi opening to foreigners, this remains one of the least-visited provinces in Laos, which is a great reason to get off the beaten track and come – your exploration will be well rewarded.

SAM NEUA

064 / POP 40,170

Easier to reach thanks to the planes running again from Vientiane, a trip to remote Sam Neua rewards with its pine-ridged valleys, emerald rice paddies, charcoal-black karsts and fascinating nearby caves of Vieng Xai. During the Secret War this was a major stronghold of the communist Pathet Lao and there's still a sense of this with a Soviet-nodding memorial and Russian hats worn by the old boys in the market. Laos' finest silk scarves are woven here, so keep an eye out for them as you wander the dry goods market, and don't miss the eye-opening wet market over the river. This is one of the few places in Laos where the temperature can really plummet, so bring a sweater!

Sleeping & Eating

Sam Neua's digs are unspectacular, but clean and reasonable value; those listed here are found beside the Nam Sam river and dry goods market.

Kheamxam Guest House GUESTHOUSE $
(312111; r 40,000-70,000K) Rooms vary from basic to larger ones with immaculate en suites and TV. The friendly owner speaks English and has a minibus available for hire (300,000K per day), ideal for a group trip to the caves. Free airport pick-up/drop-off too.

Sam Neua Hotel HOTEL $$
(314777; snhotel_08@yahoo.com; s/d/tw incl breakfast 120,000/150,000/200,000K;) Located over the bridge on the same side as the food market, this well-maintained accommodation place has 17 luxurious rooms, with fresh linen, TVs and en suites with hot water.

Shuliyo Guest House GUESTHOUSE $
(312462; r 70,000K) The beds could be comfier, the furniture less dated, but the bathrooms are clean, the water hot, the sheets clean and travellers seem to like it. The nearest you'll get to a smile might be Ho Chi Minh's picture in the lobby, but Shuliyo is good value for money.

Dan Nao Restaurant LAOTIAN $
(mains 15,000K; breakfast, lunch & dinner) Fronting the main road by the bridge, this diminutive hole-in-the-wall has a few tables for eating basic fare such as noodles, grilled chicken, fried eggs, tender beef salad and egg fried rice.

Sokdee Restaurant LAOTIAN $
(mains 15,000K breakfast, lunch & dinner) Given the Lao proclivity for eating anything with fur and four legs, it's no surprise Sokdee is a favourite with locals but repellent among vegetarians. Come here for fried intestines and other exotic carnivorous fare.

For cheap *fŏe* (rice noodles), samosas, spring rolls and fried sweet potato, the **market** (6am-6pm) is the place to go.

Information

Agricultural Promotion Bank (8am-noon & 1.30-4pm Mon-Fri) On the main road north out of town, this bank exchanges Thai baht and Vietnamese dong, though you'll get better exchange rates at the fabric stalls in the dry goods market.

Lao Development Bank (312171; 8am-4pm Mon-Fri) On the main road 400m north of the bus station on the left; exchanges cash and travellers cheques.

Post office (8am-4pm Mon-Fri) In a large building directly opposite the bus station. A telephone office at its rear offers international calls.

Provincial tourist office (312567; 8am-noon & 1.30-4pm Mon-Fri) An excellent tourist office with English-speaking staff eager to help.

Getting There & Away

The **airport** is 3km from town and a motorcycle taxi to/from there costs about 85,000K. **Lao Capricorn Air** (www.laocapricornair.net; Wattay International Airport, Vientiane) flies to Vientiane on Wednesdays and Saturdays (850,000K, 1½ hours) at 11.20am.

Sam Neua's **bus station** is roughly 1.2km away (túk-túk 8500K). There are two buses

NAM ET-PHOU LOUEY NATIONAL PROTECTED AREA

PAUL ESHOO, LAO ECOTOURISM CONSULTANT

Covering 595,000 hectares over three provinces (Huah Phan, Luang Prabang and Xieng Khuang), **Nam Et-Phou Louey NPA** (☎064-810008; www.namet.org) is one of the largest protected areas in Laos and is home to many rare and endangered species including tigers, leopards, gaur, Sambar deer, white-cheeked gibbons, Asian red wolf, black bears and sun bears. Its tigers are the last breeding population in Indochina and are estimated at 15 to 25 individuals. With support from the Wildlife Conservation Society and a staff of more than 50 park rangers, the government is implementing a host of activities to protect tigers, including forest patrols, anti-wildlife-trade campaigns, and alternative livelihood development projects. Experts say that the area has the potential to support up to 80 tigers.

An ecotour, the **Nam Nern Night Safari**, is being piloted by the project with the hopes of providing local people with direct incentives to protect tigers and other endangered species. The tour is a unique experience involving wildlife spotlighting at night by boat with local guides. Although the possibility of seeing a tiger is extremely rare, visitors regularly see other rare species such as Sambar and barking deer, civets, otters, porcupine and loris. Benefits from the tour are split among nine villages and depend on the number of wildlife seen by visitors. Both one-night and two-night programs are available, with prices ranging from US$100 to US$225 per person based on a maximum group size of six people. The tour should be booked in advance directly with the NPA's English-speaking guide, Mr Sivilay, by contacting info@namet.org.

The park is located near Vieng Thong on the road between Luang Prabang and Sam Neua. Public buses between Luang Prabang (10 hours) and Sam Neua (five hours) can drop you here. The long drive from Luang Prabang is best broken up with a rest in Nong Khiaw.

a day to Phonsavan (80,000K, eight to 10 hours, 9am and noon). It's a sinuous but beautiful hike through the mountains. The bus then continues on to Vientiane (from Sam Neua 130,000K, 20 to 24 hours) on a winding sealed road. A VIP bus also runs to Vientiane (150,000K, 18 hours, noon).

A daily bus heads west to Nong Khiaw (80,000K, 12 hours, 8am) and continues on to Luang Prabang (from Sam Neua 110,000K, 16 hours, 7.30am). If you're heading for Oudomxay, take this bus and change at Pak Mong (120,000K).

Nathong Bus Station is 1km to the east heading for Vieng Xai. *Sŏrngtăaou* run from here to Vieng Xai (8000K, 50 minutes, 29km, 6.20am to 5.20pm) at 8am, 10am, 11am, 2.30pm and 4pm – the scenery is among the most stunning in Laos. The 8am bus to Than Hoa in Vietnam (180,000K, 11 hours) leaves the main bus station at around 7am then swings around the town collecting passengers before leaving Nathong Bus Station at around 8am. Ensure you buy a ticket from the kiosk to avoid being overcharged once on the bus.

VIENG XAI

☎064 / POP 32,800

Set amid valleys glistening with rice paddies and majestic karst fangs, beautiful Vieng Xai seems an unlikely place to have suffered a decade's worth of American air assaults. Its 450 limestone caves provided sanctuary for more than 23,000 people during the US Secret War, playing host to bakeries, a hospital, school, a metalwork factory and, more importantly, the political headquarters of the communist Pathet Lao party. As the bombs fell near the virtually unassailable caves, President Kaysone Phomvihane plotted the transformation of his country in a dank grotto, undecorated but for a framed photo of Che Guevara and a few other keepsakes.

Today, the most historically significant caves are open to tourists. Vieng Xai is a fascinating and peaceful place in which to spend a day or two. A wooden board in front of the market features a map of town.

Vieng Xai Cave Tourist Office (☎314321; admission 50,000K; ⊙8-11.30am & 1-4.30pm) is a 2km walk from the bus station. Admission to the four major caves includes the mandatory guide. Bicycles are available for 10,000/20,000K per tour/day and allow you to see more of the area. It's another 40,000K for a camera. Two-hour tours leave the office between 9am and 11am, and 1pm and 4pm and take in three or four caves. At other times you will need to pay an additional fee of 40,000K per tour to cover staff costs.

GETTING TO VIETNAM: NA MAEW TO NAM XOI

The easiest option is to take the direct bus between Sam Neua and Thanh Hoa in Vietnam, where there's a night train you can catch bound for Hanoi (11.30pm, arriving 4am). This remote, seldom-used and often difficult border (open 7.30am to 11.30am and 1.30pm to 4.30pm) at Na Maew in Laos and Nam Xoi in Vietnam is an adventurer's delight and the nearest crossing to Hanoi. There's a daily *sǒrngtǎaou* from Sam Neua (20,000K, four hours, 6.30am), or several from Vieng Xai (13,000K, two hours, 8am to 11am). Visas are not available on arrival. In Vietnam you can negotiate a motorbike to Thanh Hoa or to Ba Thuoc. Both options can be pricey and drivers will probably rip you off. There are a couple of guesthouses on the Vietnamese side. For information on crossing this border in the other direction, see p89.

Fringed in frangipani trees, the beautiful gardens that now adorn the caves can easily make you forget what their inhabitants had to endure. Perhaps the most atmospheric, as it housed the long-reigning president himself and hosted his politburo meetings, is Phomvihane's eponymously named **Tham Than Kaysone**. The electricity is often out, so you'll most likely be exploring by candlelight, your flame falling on Phomvihane's meagre library, a Russian oxygen machine poised for a chemical attack, a bust of Lenin...

Tham Than Souphanouvong, named after the communist-leaning 'Red Prince', has a crater from a 230kg bomb near the entrance, while **Tham Than Khamtay**, where up to 3000 Pathet Lao hid, is the most spectacular of the caves.

Sleeping & Eating

Thavisay Hotel GUESTHOUSE $
(020 571 2392; r 90,000K) Hands down the best accommodation in town, this place is nicer than anything Sam Neua has to offer. With its quiet lakeside setting, hot-water bathrooms, comfy beds and TVs, you'll be glad you stayed here. There's also a restaurant selling basic Laotian grub (meals 20,000K).

Naxay Guest House GUESTHOUSE $
(314336; r 50,000K) Naxay has six basic rattan huts with hobbit-hole interiors of wood and tidy linen. The fan-only en suites have no warm water. You may need to wear an extra jumper in bed.

Getting There & Away

Sǒrngtǎaou run regularly between Sam Neua's Nathong Bus Station and Vieng Xai (10,000K, 50 minutes, 29km, 6.20am to 5.20pm). From Vieng Xai market to Sam Neua, *sǒrngtǎaou* run at 7am, 10am, 1pm, 2.30pm and 4pm.

Oudomxay Province

Home to some of northern Laos' thickest forests, this rugged province is a great place to visit Hmong and Khamu villages. Close to China's Yúnnán Province, you'll find 15 ethnic minorities in the area but the dominant group is increasingly the Yúnnánese, working in construction and plantation operations. While Oudomxay town is undesirable, the surrounding hills are beautiful and shouldn't be overlooked if you have time to trek here.

OUDOMXAY

081 / POP 25,000

Dusty Oudomxay is something of an anomaly – a Lao-Chinese hybrid (25% of its population is Chinese). Dust devils skirt past mechanic's shops and gruff expressions, while construction sees unimaginative flat-topped buildings add to the unappealing aesthetic. There are no two ways about it, Oudomxay may be the ugliest town in Laos. On a more positive note, there's an excellent tourist office that can point you to a number of natural treasures in the hills a short distance away. Arrive and head out on a trek the next day.

Sleeping & Eating

There are some decent new options to make your stay a little more enjoyable. Most places are along – or just off – Rte 1.

Villa Keoseumsack GUESTHOUSE
(312170; r 120,000-140,000K) The town's best rooms, with varnished floors, en suites, TVs, Hmong-woven bed runners and freshly plumped pillows. Free wi-fi and a cool reading balcony finish it off.

Lithavixay Guest House GUESTHOUSE
(212175; Rte 1; r 60,000-120,000K;) A longtime traveller fave with a welcoming lobby and cosy breakfast and internet

cafe. Though some rooms look tired, they enjoy TVs, couches, tables and homely touches.

Xayxana Guest House GUESTHOUSE
(☎020 578 0429; off Rte 1; r 60,000-80,000K; ✱) Fresh-looking Xayxana is lovely and cool, with immaculate white rooms, tiled floors and very comfy beds. All rooms with en suite.

Meuang Neua Restaurant LAOTIAN
(meals 30,000K; ⏰7am-11pm) A pint-sized cafe on a dusty side road. Its walls are decorated with arabesques and there's an equally imaginative menu, from salads through pumpkin soup, curry, fish and stir-fry.

Sinphet Restaurant LAOTIAN
(mains 20,000K; ⏰breakfast, lunch & dinner) A bit dusty (it's almost on the road), and almost falling down with age, this place near the bridge and festooned in Beerlao bunting has noodles, steak and salads.

Siso Bakery BAKERY
(sandwiches 10,000K; ⏰7am-9pm) Head here for cookies, burgers, banana fritters and cake (as well as internet, 6000K per hour).

ℹ Information

Air Computer (Rte 1; per min 200K; ⏰8am-7pm) Speedy connection.

BCEL (☎211260; Rte 1) Changes foreign currency into kip; 24-hour ATM.

Oudomxay provincial tourism office (☎212483; Rte 1; ⏰8am-noon & 1.30-6.30pm) Just west of the bridge, the well-run office conducts its own ecotreks to Khamu villages, caves, pristine forests and waterfalls, as well as the recently discovered Chom Ong Cave. There are six different packages to choose from. Speak to Mr Sikounavong.

ℹ Getting There & Away

Lao Airlines (☎312047; airport) flies to Vientiane (one way 695,000K) every Tuesday, Thursday and Saturday.

The Chinese-built bitumen roads that radiate from Oudomxay are in fair condition (except for the road to Pak Beng). The **bus terminal** at the southwestern edge of town has buses to Luang Prabang (all VIP buses, 60,000K, five hours, 8.30am, 11.30am and 3pm daily), Nong Khiaw (30,000K, four hours, four daily), Pak Beng (45,000K, five hours, 8am and 10am daily), Pakmong (30,000K, 9am and 2pm daily), Luang Nam Tha (40,000K, four hours, 8am, noon and 3pm daily), Muang Khua (35,000K, four hours, 8.30am, noon and 3pm daily), Boten (35,000K, four hours, 8am daily), Phongsali (75,000K, eight to 12 hours, 8.30am, daily) and Vientiane (ordinary 100,000K, 16 hours, two daily; VIP 140,000K, 11 hours, 11am and 2pm).

PAK BENG

Essentially a one-street town, Pak Beng is the halfway point on the Mekong River between Huay Xai and Luang Prabang. You'll probably stop here for lunch (speedboats) or an obligatory night (two-day slow boats). The town itself is perched on the vertiginous slopes of the riverbank and to call it listless is going overboard – barely a chicken stirs. If you're here for the night there's a couple of plush hotels in which to stay.

There's little in the way of attractions, but the **Elephant Camp** (☎071 254130; from US$47) across the Mekong offers elephant rides and a chance to see the Dumbos taking their ablutions in the river.

Monsavan Guest House (☎212619; r US$30) has house-proud rooms on the main street close to the boat landing. White walls, a few sticks of furniture and clean bathrooms; upstairs the rooms are better. Nicer still is the homely **Santisouk Guest House** (☎020 5578 1797; r 135,000K) with its warm orange walls, partial wood interiors, tasteful furniture, river views and friendly management. **Villa Salika** (☎212306; r 125,000K) has private bathrooms and river views. **Phetsokxay Guest House** (☎212299; r US$30-35), opposite Santisouk Guest House, offers inviting wood-panelled rooms, fresh bathrooms, springy beds, bureaus and fine views from its elevated verandah.

For greater comforts, the **Pak Beng Lodge** (☎212304; r 255,000K; ✱) and the ecofriendly, traditional **Luang Say Lodge** (☎212296; www.mekongcruises.com; r from 500,000K) should satisfy.

For budget accommodation, **Dokhoun Guest House** (☎212540; r 100,000K) has decent river-facing rooms with tiled floors and double locks on the door. The restaurant has lovely views and does an OK steak and chips (20,000K).

Pak Beng has long been associated with bags disappearing from guesthouse rooms. Pick a room with a sturdy lock on the door and stow valuables away from open grilled windows.

For eats, check out tasty Indian at **Hashan** (mains 15,000K; ⏰8am-9pm; ✓), near the boat landing, where there's a good range of vegie options. Directly opposite Monsavan Guest House is newish **Phakdee Bakery** (mains

10,000K; ⏲7am-4pm), a handy pit stop for bagel sandwiches.

A **tourist office** (www.oudomxay.info; ⏲7am-noon & 2-9pm) up the hill is surprisingly well endowed with illustrative info and leaflets on things to do including exploring the Chom Ong cave system.

See p328 for details on river travel between Pak Beng, Luang Prabang and Huay Xai, as well as the boxed text, p309. *Sŏrngtăaou* head along potholed Rte 2 towards Oudomxay (40,000K, five hours, 8.30am and 9.30am) from a bus station 1.5km from the boat landing.

Luang Nam Tha Province

Bordered by Myanmar (Burma) and China, this heavily forested province suffered a hammering during the Second Indochina War, particularly its capital, Luang Nam Tha town. Nowadays it's a mecca for ecotourism, with award-winning tours into the Nam Ha National Protected Area. If it's trekking, mountain biking, rafting or birdwatching you're seeking, you couldn't have come to a better place. The area is also rich in cultural diversity, with more than 20 ethnic tribes. To learn more about ethnology visit the excellent Muang Sing Tourism Information & Nam Ha Eco Trek Service Center (p325).

LUANG NAM THA

☎086 / POP 18,000

Thanks to its location next to the Nam Ha National Protected Area (one of the largest and the first of Laos' 20 NPAs), Luang Nam Tha enjoys an influx of intrepid travellers. It also invites exotic appearances from Hmong tribeswomen in full rainbow-hemmed garb at the candlelit night market. Heavily bombed during the Secret War, the town itself is relatively new, nestled in a valley ringed by distant mountains, while the original town is some 10km away near the airport. It's a friendly place with plenty of guesthouses, tasty restaurants and a lively market, serviced by banks, internet cafes and cycle-hire shops. Many spend a day pedalling around local waterfalls and temples before setting out into the wilds of Nam Ha NPA.

Sights & Activities

You can pop in to the **Luang Nam Tha Museum** (admission 5000K; ⏲8.30-11.30am & 1.30-3.30pm Mon-Thu, 8.30-11.30am Fri) to see its varied collection of hunting weapons, ceramics, bronze drums, Buddha images and tribal wear, but most likely you're here to spend your time **trekking** the natural wonders of nearby **Nam Ha National Protected Area (NPA)**; a vast citadel of dense jungle, home to clouded leopards, gaur, tigers and elephants. The guides here are the country's pioneers of ecotourism and also offer **rafting**, **canoeing** and **mountain biking** along the Nam Ha river, as well as **homestays**.

There are a number of excellent trekking companies in town, including **Jungle Eco-Guide Services** (☎212025; www.thejungle-ecotour.com; ⏲8am-9pm), which offers 11 different trips ranging from one-day treks in Nam Ha NPA (group of two people, 280,000K per person), to Khamu homestay and trekking (group of two people, 590,000K per person). It also runs three-day treks (staying at jungle camps), which take you deeper into the interior.

The daddy of Laos trekking, **Green Discovery** (☎211484; www.greendiscoverylaos.com; ⏲8am-9pm) offers a panoply of activites ranging from one- to three-day treks, involving a combo of kayaking and trekking in the Nam Ha NPA, as well as cycling trips to ethnic villages. Larger groups keep the prices down.

Namtha River Experience (☎212047; www.namtha-river-experiece-laos.com; ⏲8am-9pm), specialising in one-day to four-day kayaking and rafting trips through Khamu and Lenten villages, also facilitates Khamu homestays. Typically a group of two costs US$30 per person for a one-day trip.

Places of interest within easy cycling or motorbiking distance include **Wat Ban Vieng Tai** and **Wat Ban Luang Khon**, near the airfield; a hilltop stupa, **That Phum Phuk**, about 4km west of the airfield; a small **waterfall** about 6km northeast of town past **Ban Nam Dee**; plus a host of Khamu, Lenten, Thai Dam and Thai Lü villages dotted along dirt roads through rice fields. Pick up a map and brochures at the provincial tourism office before setting off.

Sleeping & Eating

In high season (December to March) the town gets busy, so it's worth calling ahead to book a room. If you're here for a few nights make sure one of them is spent at the **night market**; bursting with steam, smoke and meat crackling on glowing braziers.

TOP CHOICE Boat Landing Guest House & Restaurant GUESTHOUSE $$
(☎312398; www.theboatlanding.laopdr.com; r incl breakfast US$40-55) Laos' premier ecolodge has riverside acacia groves hugging tastefully finished wooden bungalows with solar-heated showers. The vaulted longhouse restaurant serves award-winning (meals 42,000K) pot roasts, *làap* and Western food. It's located 7km south of the new town and about 150m off the main road; catch a túk-túk here for 20,000K.

Zuela Guesthouse GUESTHOUSE $
(☎312183; r 70,000-120,000K) Located in a leafy courtyard, Zuela evolves every time we visit. Now there's a second villa, constructed of wood and exposed brick, and a great restaurant serving 'power breakfasts', pancakes, shakes, salads and chilli-based Akha dishes. Rooms have wood floors, fans and fresh linen. It also rents scooters and operates an air-con minivan service to Huay Xai (120,000K).

Khamking Guesthouse GUESTHOUSE $
(☎312238; r 70,000K) Fresh and colourful with interior flourishes such as bedside lights and attractive curtains and bedcovers, Khamking is good value. Be warned though – you're in the chicken zone with a coop just behind you, so earplugs are essential!

Manychan Guest House & Restaurant GUESTHOUSE $
(☎312209; r 60,000-120,000K) Justifiably one of the town's best-loved traveller joints, Manychan's cafe, with walls spattered in ethnic photography, covers the bases with salads, steaks and breakfasts. Rooms are adequate with hot-water showers and TVs.

Thoulasith Guesthouse GUESTHOUSE $
(☎212166; r 70,000-90,000K; wi-fi) An injection of taste and value to rival Zuela Guesthouse, rooms are spotless with bedside lamps, art on the walls, and a comfortable wi-fi-enabled balcony to read or work on.

Aysha Restaurant INDIAN $
(mains 30,000K; ⏲7am-10pm; vegetarian) This little eatery has delicious Madras cuisine, dished up with flair and spice. Homemade nan bread, vegie options galore and chicken korma that could make you weep for joy after a day in the boonies.

Minority Restaurant LAOTIAN $
(mains 10,000-15,000K; ⏲7am-10.30pm) This inviting, wood-beamed restaurant hidden down a little street gives you a chance to sample typically ethnic dishes from the Khamu, Thai Dam and Akha tribes. If the sound of rattan shoots and banana-flower soup doesn't appeal, there's also a range of stir-fries.

Panda Restaurant WESTERN, LAOTIAN $
(mains 15,000K; ⏲6.30am-noon) Overlooking a pond, paddy fields and distant mountains,

Luang Nam Tha

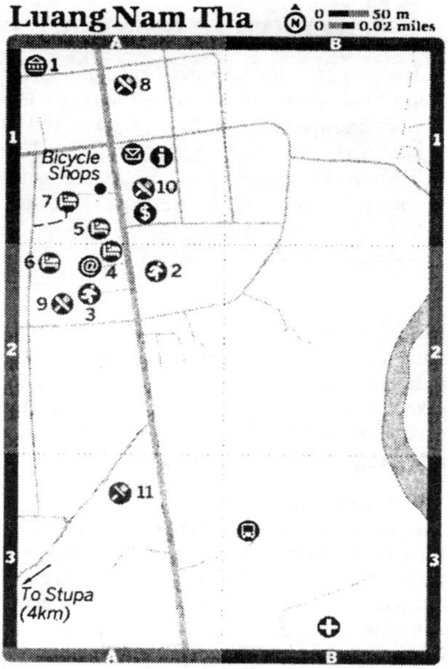

Luang Nam Tha

Sights
1 Luang Namtha Museum ... A1

Activities, Courses & Tours
2 Jungle Eco Guide Service ... A2
3 Namtha River Experience ... A2

Sleeping
4 Khamking Guesthouse ... A2
5 Manychan Guest House & Restaurant ... A1
6 Thoulasith Guesthouse ... A2
7 Zuela Guesthouse ... A1

Eating
8 Aysha Restaurant ... A1
9 Minority Restaurant ... A2
10 Night Market ... A1
11 Panda Restaurant ... A3

GETTING TO CHINA: BOTEN TO MÓHĀN

The only crossing between China and Laos that is open to foreigners is between Móhān, in Yúnnán Province, and Boten, in Luang Nam Tha Province. Laos issues 30-day visas on arrival; China does not (though some travellers claim to have bought 14-day visas on the spot here). The crossing is open from 7.30am to 4.30pm on the Laos side and 8.30am to 5.30pm in China. In both directions, onward transport is most frequent in the mornings, soon after 8am. In Laos, transport runs to Luang Nam Tha and Oudomxay. Buses from Muang Sing run to Boten from 8am every morning. If you get stuck in Boten, there are a couple of cheap guesthouses.

Panda's wood beams are interestingly strung with bees' nests (minus the bees) and buffalo horns. The menu is equally random, with dishes such as fish and chips and spaghetti carbonara as well as Lao and Thai soups and a few vegie options.

Information

The provincial tourism office has information on trips, as well as maps and excellent photocopied brochures on responsible tourism, local flora and fauna, local ethnic minorities, customs and etiquette.

BCEL (8.30am-3.30pm Mon-Fri) Changes US-dollar travellers cheques and cash; gives cash advances on credit cards; has ATM.

Lao Development Bank (8.30am-noon & 2-3.30pm Mon-Fri) Exchanges US-dollar travellers cheques and cash.

Lao Telecom Long-distance phone calls.

Post office (8am-noon & 1-4pm Mon-Fri)

Provincial Hospital (24hr) Adequately equipped for X-rays, dealing with broken limbs and dishing out antibiotics. Ask for English-speaking Dr Veokham.

Provincial tourism office (211534; 8am-noon & 2-5pm) Excellent tourist office with English-speaking staff, who can help you with treks in the nearby NPA.

Smile Internet Cafe (per hr 12,000K; 8.30am-9pm)

Getting There & Away

For now, **Lao Airlines** (312180; www.laoairlines.com) has regular flights to/from Vientiane (one way US$112, one hour, Tuesday, Thursday and Saturday) but there are plans to expand the flights servicing Luang Nam Tha. See the website for updates on new routes.

Charter boats make the wonderful trip along the Nam Tha through remote country to Pak Tha on the Mekong, or all the way to Huay Xai. They leave from the boat landing, 7km south of town on the Nam Tha, at 9.30am (between June and October) and cost 1,800,000K to Pak Tha, or 1,900,000K to Huay Xai. Sign up before your departure to share the charter costs for this two-day trip in an open long-tail boat. In high season a boat leaves almost every day, depending on passenger numbers. An additional 50,000K covers food and lodgings with the boatman's family. Bring sun protection, plus plenty of water and snacks. Go to the boat-landing office opposite the Boat Landing Guest House & Restaurant to sign up for the trip.

The **bus terminal** (312164) has relocated 11km south, beyond the airport. A *sŏrngtăaou* should cost 20,000K to/from Luang Nam Tha's new town. Buses run to Oudomxay (40,000K, five hours, 8.30am, 12.30pm and 2.30pm). A VIP bus leaves for Vientiane (190,000K, eight hours, 8.30am) followed by a local bus at (170,000K, 19 hours, 2.30pm). There's only one bus to Luang Prabang (90,000K, eight hours, 9am), and Měnglà (55,000K, 8am), while two buses run daily to Huay Xai – marked as Bokeo – (55,000K, 9am and 12.30pm). Finally, there's one daily service to both Phonsavan – marked as Xieng Khuang – (100,000K, 8am) and Phongsaly (80,000K, 8.30am). Arrive in good time to buy your ticket and get a decent seat.

The local bus station is about 500m south on the outskirts of town. *Sŏrngtăaou* travel daily to Vieng Phoukha (20,000K, four hours, 9am and noon). About six *sŏrngtăaou* run to Muang Sing daily (22,000K, two hours); one bus goes to Muang Long (40,000K, five hours, 8.30am) and Boten (45,000K, two hours, one daily, 8am) on the Laos–China border.

Getting Around

Jumbos from the main street to the airport, 7km away, cost 10,000K per person for a minimum of three people. To the Nam Tha boat landing, or the nearby Boat Landing Guest House & Restaurant, figure on 15,000K per person on a shared jumbo.

Mountain/one-speed bicycles cost 15,000/10,000K per day from the **bicycle shop** (9am-6pm) on the main street, which also rents motorcycles for 70,000K for a decent Honda – avoid cheap Chinese models for long journeys. Luang Nam Tha to Muang Sing by scooter is an exhilarating experience and gives you a chance to pass through Nam Ha NPA and visit waterfalls en route. It should take about two to three hours. Bring a jumper as it gets mighty cold up there.

MUANG SING

☎081 / POP 8000

Bordering Myanmar and almost within grasp of the green hills of China; at the heart of the Golden Triangle, rural Muang Sing has a backwater feel that transports you to a less complicated time. Formerly on the once infamous opium trail, it's a sleepy town of wilting, Thai Lü–style houses and, happily, trekking has overtaken smuggling contraband (though tribeswomen still approach you to sell rocks of opium). Hmong, Thai Lü, Akha, Thai Dam and Yao are all seen here in traditional dress at the morning market (get there for dawn), giving the town an exciting frontier feel.

Visitors who venture the extra 60km from Luang Nam Tha to Muang Sing are rewarded with some of the most scenic, ecoconscious trekking opportunities in the Nam Ha NPA, and if you want to visit ethnic minorities, this is your best bet in Southeast Asia (45% of Muang Sing's population is Akha).

Sights & Activities

The main draw for Muang Sing is its proximity to tribal villages and trekking in Nam Ha NPA. You can go with a handful of well-organised trek outfits or, if you're just here to cycle, grab a map (Wolfgang Kom's excellent 'Muang Sing Valley map') from the tourist office, hire a bike and make your own explorations. In order to leave a more positive footprint and avoid the 'human zoo' syndrome we recommend you engage a guide (100,000K per day).

Tribal Museum MUSEUM

(admission 5000K; ⏲8.30am-4.30pm Mon-Fri, 8-11am Sat) Set in a delightful old wooden building, the museum has an interesting display of traditional textiles, woven baskets, handicrafts, amulets and cymbals, as well as photographic exhibitions and a documentary on the Akha (40,000K extra).

Muang Sing Tourism Information & Nam Ha Eco Trek Service Center ADVENTURE

(☎020 239 3534; msnamhaecotrek@hotmail.com; ⏲8-11am & 1.30-5pm Mon-Fri, 8-10am & 3-5pm Sat & Sun) This is an excellent government-run resource for travellers keen to explore the natural wonders and ethnological diversity of the area. It has plenty of visual information and maps.

Muang Sing

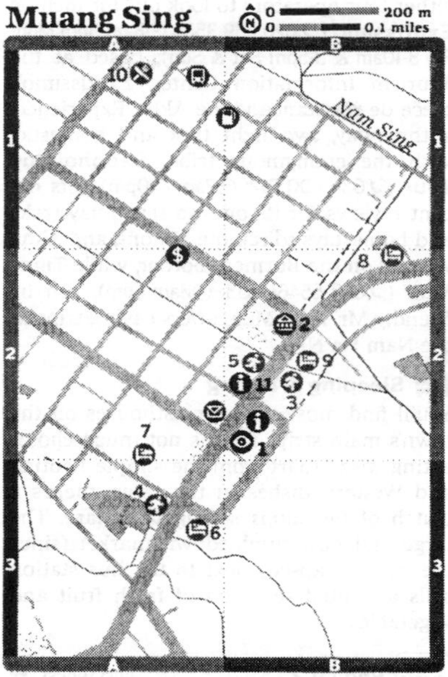

Muang Sing

Sights

1	Old Market	B2
2	Tribal Museum	B2

Activities, Courses & Tours

	Exotissimo	(see 11)
3	Nam Ha Eco Trek Service	B2
4	Saophoudoy Tour	A3
5	Tiger Man	B2

Sleeping

6	Chanthimeng Guest House	A3
7	Pho lu 2 Guest House	A2
8	Sengduan Bungalows	B2
9	Thai Lü Guest House	B2

Eating

10	New Market	A1

Information

11	Tourist Office	B2

Nam Ha Eco Trek Service (☎030 511 404; ⏲8am-5pm Mon-Fri) operates one- to four-day treks in the Nam Ha NPA, visiting Akha villages, forest camping and homestays. A one-day trek for a group of two costs 300,000K per person. Talk to English-speaking Mr Sendy.

Other tour operators to look out for include **Exotissimo** (☎020 239 3534 ⊙8am-5pm Mon-Fri, 8-10am & 3-5pm Sat & Sun); based at the Tourism Information Center, Exotissimo's pièce de résistance is the Akha Experience, a three-day, two-night trek and homestay with the eponymous tribe. **Saophoudoy Tour** (☎086-400 012; ⊙7am-7.30pm) gets decent reviews for its one- to seven-day treks and homestays to remote Hmong and Akha villages on the Burmese border, while **Tiger Man** (☎020 5546 7833; ⊙8am-6pm), run by friendly Mr Tong Mua, offers caving trips in the Nam Ha NPA.

Sleeping & Eating

You'll find most of the guesthouses on the town's main strip. There's not much choice eating-wise; apart from the simple Laotian and Western dishes in the cafes, there's a clutch of *fŏe* shops selling tasty fare. The large and now tumbledown market (since the roof collapsed) next to the bus station sells a limited selection of fresh fruit and vegetables.

TOP CHOICE **Pho Lu 2** GUESTHOUSE $$
(☎030 511 0326; r US$15-45) In a lush oasis chequered with mangos and palms, its 22 bamboo and rattan cabanas are tastefully finished with Hmong handicraft, fresh linen and an air of sophistication. There's a choice of small, double or family rooms. The nicest digs in Muang Sing.

Stupa Mountain Lodge & Restaurant GUESTHOUSE $
(☎020 286 0819; stupamtn@laotel.com; r 50,000K) Vertiginously perched on stilts on a hill overlooking paddy fields and distant China, cabanas here are cosy, with rattan walls and wood terraces to chill on. There's an edible menu, but the place is spooky if you're travelling solo.

Chanthimeng Guest House GUESTHOUSE $
(☎212351; r 70,000K) House-proud, well-sized rooms in a huge villa overlooking the rice paddies to the south. Tiled floors, fresh bedspreads, firm mattresses and clean showers make this an OK stay for the night.

Thai Lü Guest House GUESTHOUSE $
(☎212375; r 30,000-40,000K) Looking like a backdrop in an old Bruce Lee flick, this creaky wooden building has charm aplenty – even if the rattan-walled, squat-loo rooms are uninspiring. The restaurant downstairs (meals 8000K to 12,000K; open for breakfast, lunch and dinner) serves Thai, Laotian and Western dishes.

Sengduan Bungalows GUESTHOUSE $
(r 45,000K) Colourful en-suite cabanas in a back garden; rooms here have brick and rattan walls and their terraces catch the afternoon light.

Information

There's a **Lao Development Bank** (⊙8am-noon & 2-3.30pm Mon-Fri), which changes cash but has no ATM, and a **post office** (⊙8am-4pm Mon-Fri).

Getting There & Around

Sŏrngtăaou ply back and forth between Muang Sing and Luang Nam Tha (20,000K, two hours, 8am, 9.30am, 11am, 12.30pm, 2pm and 3.30pm), and the Chinese border (15,000K, 8am), and Měnglà in China (40,000K, 8am and 1pm). There are also about four *sŏrngtăaou* a day to Xieng Kok (30,000K, three to four hours) on the Myanmar border, from where speedboats race down to Huay Xai. Most passenger vehicles depart from the bus station opposite the market on the northwest edge of town. Buy your tickets at the kiosk and get here a little early to ensure your seat. You can rent bikes from shops and guesthouses.

Bokeo Province

The smallest province in the country and once a major artery on the infamous opium trail of contraband smuggled in and out of the Golden Triangle, these days Bokeo Province is home to a flourishing ecotreasure known as the Gibbon Experience, based in the rugged Bokeo Nature Reserve. Home to a rich biodiversity of large mammals, this area offers great trekking, and you may come across a colourful cast of 34 different ethnic groups.

HUAY XAI

☎084 / POP 17,800

Allegedly a US heroin processing plant was based here during the Secret War – these days the only things trafficked through Huay Xai are travellers en route to Luang Prabang. Separated from Thailand by the cocoa-brown Mekong River, it is for many their first impression of Laos (don't worry, it gets better!). By night its central drag dons its fairy lights and fires up roadside food vendors, and there are some welcoming traveller guesthouses and tasty cafes. Huay Xai is also the HQ of the now-fabled Gibbon Experience, the most talked-about

THE GIBBON EXPERIENCE

Adrenalin meets conservation in this ecofriendly adventure in the 106,000 hectares of the Bokeo Nature Reserve wilderness. The **Gibbon Experience** (212021; www.gibbon experience.org; Th Saykhong, Huay Xai; Classic & Waterfall 3-day trek/Gibbon Spa US$290/340) is essentially a series of navigable 'ziplines' criss-crossing the canopy of some of Laos' most pristine forest, home to tigers, clouded leopards, black bears and the eponymous black-crested gibbon.

Seven years ago poaching was threatening the extinction of the black-crested gibbon, but thanks to Animo, a conservation-based tour group, the hunters of Bokeo were convinced to become the forest's guardians. As guides they now make more for their families than in their old predatory days.

You'll stay in fantastical tree houses perched 60m up in the triple canopy. Admitting a maximum of eight, they're complete with cooking facilities and running rainwater showers! In between scouting for wildlife, the ziplining is life-affirming. Your safety harness with a wheel on the end of a cable is attached to a zipline; all you need then is a little faith and an adventurous spirit. It's a heart-stopping, superhero experience.

Your day also involves a serious amount of trekking. Bring a pair of hiking boots and long socks to deter the ever-persistent leeches, plus a torch (flashlight) and earplugs – the magnified sound of a million crickets may just keep you awake. The guides are helpful, though make sure you're personally vigilant with the knots in your harness. Should it rain, remember you need more time to slow down with your humble brake.

There are three options to choose from. The 'Classic' experience gives you a little more time to ponder the jungle and less time trekking. The 'Waterfall' has an increased amount of slog balanced by a wonderful dip in a refreshing cascade. Fees include transport to and from the park, plus all food and refreshments. Both of these options are for two nights. Recently added for sybarites who need a little more comfort, the 'Gibbon Spa' incorporates the best of the Classic with gourmet food, improved lodgings and massages. Whichever you choose – book weeks in advance – this is one funky gibbon you'll *never* forget.

environmentally conscious jungle adventure in the country.

Sleeping & Eating

Most guesthouses are on the main street parallel with the river. There are numerous barbecue food stalls (try the one next to BCEL) and cafes to choose from.

Oudomphone 2 Guest House GUESTHOUSE $
(211308; Th Saykhong; r 80,000-120,000K;) Decent-sized rooms and a bijou cafe make this a worthwhile place to stay – but for the resident rooster out back with the faulty body clock. Come morning, even vegetarians may be tempted to turn carnivore!

Gateway Villa Guest House GUESTHOUSE $$
(212180; Th Saykhong; r 80,000-190,000K;) Close to the boat landing, these are tastefully furnished rooms with hardwood floors, wicker chairs, TVs and contemporary-looking linen. Some rooms are more prettified than others. It has singles, doubles and triples.

Kaupjai Guest House GUESTHOUSE $
(020 5568 3164; Th Saykhong; r 130,000K;) Kaupjai has super-fresh, en-suite and air-con rooms with Persil-white walls and cool tiled floors. Although they could use a little more decoration, this is a decent new option.

Sabaydee Guest House GUESTHOUSE $
(212252; Th Saykhong; r incl breakfast 90,000-130,000K;) Sabaydee has unfailingly clean rooms with comfy beds, TVs, fans and en suites. Decked in bright colours and pleasant furnishings, some overlook the river. There's also a nice communal area with internet (10,000K per hour).

Arimid Guest House GUESTHOUSE $$
(211040; Ban Huay Xai Neua; s/d 80,000-190,000K;) Two hundred metres from the slow-boat pier but isolated from the town, Armid has rustic cabanas with pleasant balconies set in manicured gardens peppered with statues. Denim-blue walls, decent beds, fresh en suites and a nice restaurant to hang in.

GETTING TO THAILAND: HUAY XAI TO CHIANG KHONG

Long-tail boats (one way 10,000K, five minutes, 8am to 6pm) run across the Mekong River between Huay Xai in Laos and Chiang Khong in Thailand. A huge vehicle ferry (per car 1000B) also does the trip. On the Huay Xai side, the Lao immigration post is alongside the pedestrian ferry landing and issues 30-day visas on arrival, costing US$30 to US$42 depending on nationality. Free Thai visas are also available on arrival in Chiang Khong. There's an exchange booth on the Chiang Khong side and you'll have to pay a port tax fee of 30B and another 30B for the túk-túk to the bus station. The nearest ATM on the Thai side is 2km south. Boats from Pak Beng and buses from Luang Nam Tha always seem to arrive just after the border shuts. For information on crossing this border in the other direction, see p415.

BAP Guest House GUESTHOUSE $
(☎211083; bapbiz@live.com; Th Saykhong; r 60,000-160,000K; ❄) Run by English-speaking Mrs Changpeng, this wayfarer's fave has a pleasant restaurant dishing up snacks, vegie dishes and Lao staples (mains 14,000K). Rooms vary wildly in specs, with the best ones facing the river (air-con and TV come as extras).

TOP CHOICE **Gecko Bar** LAOTIAN, WESTERN $
(aka Muang Ner Café; Th Saykhong; meals 30,000K; ⌚6.30am-11pm) With its worn turquoise walls adorned in animal horns, Gecko is still the best traveller magnet in town. Mouthwatering *làap*, Western breakfasts and wood-fired pizzas all complement the welcoming vibe.

Nut Pop Restaurant LAOTIAN $
(Th Saykhong; meals 30,000K; ⌚4.30-10pm) Reached via a bridge and by night alluringly lit with ropes of golden light, this tree-house-style restaurant makes for a romantic dinner. It serves up tasty Laotian and Vietnamese food.

Drinking

Bar How BAR
(Th Saykhong; ⌚6am-11.30pm; 📶) Funky How has walls suspended with muskets and coolie hats. Perfect for chilling, it also does a mean Western breakfast, tasty Lao fare and takeaway sandwiches (mains 25,000K). Free wi-fi.

Information

BCEL (⌚8.30am-4.30pm Mon-Fri) Opposite BAP Guest House; 24-hour ATM, exchange facility and Western Union. Bring plenty of cash if you're going on the Gibbon Experience in case the ATM is out of order.

Lao Airlines (☎211471; Th Saykhong; ⌚8am-4.30pm) New office south of the boat ramp.

Luang Prabang Travel (☎211095; Th Saykhong; ⌚8am- 4.30pm) Government-sanctioned tour company offering homestays, rafting, kayaking and treks. Speak to Mr Loon.

Post office (Th Saykhong) Contains a telephone office (open from 8am to 10pm).

Yon Computer Internet Cafe (Th Saykhong; per hr 15,000K; ⌚9am-9pm) Decent connection with Skype; also fixes laptops. Next door to Bar How.

Getting There & Away

AIR

Huay Xai's airport lies a few kilometres south of town. **Lao Airlines** (☎211026; www.laoairlines.com) flies to/from Vientiane (one way 895,000K, Tuesday, Thursday and Saturday).

BOAT

The **slow boat** down this scenic stretch of the Mekong River to Luang Prabang (200,000K per person, two days) is hugely popular among travellers. However, your experience will depend on the condition of the boat and how many are on it. Boats should hold about 70 people, but captains try to cram in more than 100. If this happens, passengers can refuse en masse and a second boat might be drafted in. Even better, you can try to charter your own boat and captain for around 4,250,000K and enjoy the trip with plenty of space.

Boats leave from the boat landing at the north end of town at 10.30am and stop for one night in Pak Beng (100,000K, six to eight hours). Tickets are available from the boat landing the afternoon before you travel, or from guesthouses. Don't bother buying an overpriced ticket from a tour company. If possible opt for a boat with adapted airline seats; less authentic but more gentle on your behind.

Another more memorable option is the luxurious accommodation on the teak-interior, 34m luxury **Luang Say** (☎254768; www.luangsay.com; 50/4 Th Sakkarin, Luang Prabang; ⌚9.30am-9.30pm) river barge, which takes two days and costs US$467, including all meals and an overnight stop in Luang Say's luxury lodge in Pak Beng. It runs three times a week in each direction.

Six-passenger **speedboats** to Pak Beng (190,000K, three hours) and Luang Prabang (300,000K, six hours) leave from a landing about 2km south of town at 9.30am daily, though only when full. If there are few takers and you're in a hurry, you'll have to pay extra. Buy your ticket at any one of the guesthouses or on arrival at the kiosk above the boat landing. Deaths are not uncommon, and given the recklessness of the drivers this is no great surprise. Bring earplugs and sit at the stern; alternatively close your eyes, sit at the front and stretch your legs over the bags. Either way it's unpleasant.

Slow boats also run to Luang Nam Tha (1,530,000K to 1,700,000K per boat split between passengers, plus 40,000K each for food and accommodation) via Ban Na Lae. However from March to June the river can be so shallow you'll need to wade some of the way. Ask at BAP Guest House (p328) for more information.

For any journey take plenty of water, food supplies and padding for your back.

BUS & SŎRNGTĂAOU

Buses and large *sŏrngtăaou* ply the road northeast to Vieng Phoukha (50,000K, five hours, three to four daily), Luang Nam Tha (60,000K, four hours, daily at 9am and noon) and Oudomxay (85,000K, six hours, daily at 8.30am). There are also local buses (120,000K, eight hours, 9am and 2pm) and a VIP bus (145,000K, 5pm daily) to Luang Prabang, and a VIP bus to Vientiane (230,000K, 18 hours, 11.30am). There's also a bus to Mĕnglà in China (120,000K, 8.30am).

Travel companies operate on the main drag and boat ramp. They can arrange minibuses to Chiang Mai, Thailand (average price 95,000K, five hours, 10.30am and 6.30pm daily).

SOUTHERN LAOS

Compared with the mountainous north, the south is flatter, but – given the gothic karst formations of Khammuan Province, and chilly Bolaven Plateau – no less dramatic. Riverine life prevails, with cities based along the Mekong flourishing through trade with neighbouring Thailand. Little happens here and that's half its charm; old men play boules by the riverside while faded French villas continue to wilt with the passage of time.

Not long ago an average visit to Laos would have eschewed the steamy charms of former Indochinese cities Pakse and Savannakhet; but now, thanks to them finessing their facilities and trekking options, both are on the map. Rush straight to the lotus-eater charms of Four Thousand Islands at your peril, for in between are also the likes of charming Tha Khaek and the mysterious 7.5km subterranean Kong Lo Cave, not forgetting sleepy Champasak with its beautiful Khmer ruins.

Bolikhamsai & Khammuan Provinces

Bolikhamsai and Khammuan form the narrow girdle of Laos, straddling the Annamite Chain, which heads east from Laos to Vietnam, with the Mekong River and Thailand to the west. Thanks to the presence of Vietnam's Ho Chi Minh Trail passing through Laos here, the area was heavily bombed during the Secret War, and the UXO problem is still a major challenge for NGOs.

If you're passing this way to see Kong Lo Cave, languid Tha Khaek is a pleasant base, or nearer still – if you're in a hurry – head to the rural village of Ban Khoun Kham (Ban Na Hin), a mere 20 minutes from the cave.

PAKSAN

☎054 / POP 27,000

Sitting at the confluence of Nam San and the Mekong River, Paksan is something of a nonentity and needn't feature on your itinerary unless you're using its international border to cross to Thailand. **BK Guest House** (☎212638; r 50,000-80,000K; ❄) makes for a budget stop, with clean but small rooms. If you run into English-speaking owner Mr Koth, he is pretty helpful. Midrange, Vietnamese-run **Paksan Hotel** (☎791333;

GETTING TO THAILAND: PAKSAN TO BEUNG KAN

The Mekong River crossing (open 8am to noon and 1.30pm to 4.30pm) between Paksan and Beung Kan is rarely used and Thailand does not issue visas on arrival (nor does Laos). The boat (60B, 20 minutes) leaves when eight people show up or you charter it (480B). To get there, go west along Rte 13 from Paksan for about 1.5km and turn south, heading past Manolom Guest House and looking for the 'Port' sign.

For information on crossing this border in the other direction, see p430.

fax 791222; Rte 13; s/d 100,000/180,000K; ⊛), located a little east of the bridge, is probably the best digs on offer, with clean rooms enjoying air-con, en suites, hot water and TV.

All buses going to/from Vientiane stop on Rte 13 outside the Talat Sao (Morning Market) and leave regularly between 6.30am and 4.30pm, with most departures in the morning.

ROUTE 8 TO LAK SAO

Wind your way through a lost world of jungle bursting with bamboo, eucalyptus and palm. The upsurging rock formations are both dramatic and enchanting, the streams you pass over flickering with fluorescent clouds of butterflies – this is some of the country's most trippy landscape. The first major stop is **Ban Khoun Kham** (also known as Ban Na Hin), 41km east of Rte 13. While the village is less than desirable, its setting in the lush Hin Bun valley is beautiful and a great base from which to explore the wilds of Phu Hin Bun NPA. It's a good base to catch your forward bus to the extraordinary **Kong Lo Cave** or visit the twin-cataract of **Tat Namsanam**, 3km north of town. Community-based treks are gearing up at the **tourist information centre** (Rte 8) just south of the Tat Namsanam entrance.

Walk 400m north from the market to **Xok Xai Guesthouse** (☎051-233629; Rte 8; r 50,000-100,000K; ⊛) and you'll find a couple of timbered buildings with OK, fan-only rooms. Opt for the more recently built rooms in preference to the faded older ones. Motorbikes for rent at US$10 make for an easy DIY trip to Kong Lo Cave.

Mi Thuna Restaurant Guesthouse (☎020 224 0182; Rte 8; r 50,000-100,000K; ⊛) is another decent place to stay, with, TV, air-con, modern bedrooms and quirky management. The restaurant serves Lao food. It's 800m south of the market, past the Shell fuel stop; it also rents scooters (100,000K per day). Judging by its forgettable facade, **Seng Chan Guesthouse** (☎2425838; r 50,000K) might not look like much, but inside all is cosy with tastefully finished en-suite rooms, comfortable beds and pleasant bedspreads. Bring some earplugs to avoid the dawn public-address speaker a few feet away!

All transport along Rte 8 stops at Ban Khoun Kham. Buses for Vientiane (70,000K) usually stop between 7am and 10.30am. For Tha Khaek (50,000K, three hours, 143km), there are a couple of buses in the morning; for Lak Sao take any passing bus or *sǒrngtǎaou* (25,000K).

KONG LO CAVE

If you were to realise the ancient Greek underworld, you might end up with **Kong Lo Cave**. Situated in the 1580-sq-km wilderness of **Phu Hin Bun NPA**, this 7.5km tunnel running beneath an immense limestone mountain is unlike anything you can imagine. In the words of Aussie traveller Megan: 'I've done loads of caves, but this is the creepiest and the best I've ever seen.'

Puttering upriver (long-tail boat is the only means to enter the subterranean cave) past frolicking kids, you witness the gaping mouth of the cave, your breath stolen before you've even entered the eerie, black cavern. Passing into the church-high darkness (100m in some places) and watching the light of the cave mouth recede is an unnervingly spooky experience. As you moor up to the riverbank, strolling through a stalactite wood, you feel like you've wandered onto an old *Star Trek* set.

Remember to bring a decent torch, plus rubber sandals. You can make a long day trip to Kong Lo Cave from Ban Khoun Kham, but it's more fun to stay overnight near the cave. At the edge of Phon Nyaeng, about 12km from Kong Lo Cave, **Auberges Sala Hinboun** (☎020 561 4016; www.salalao.com; r incl breakfast 160,000-260,000K), run by style-meister Sala Lao, is an ecolodge perched by the banks of syrupy Nam Hin Bun. Rooms here are a cut above the usual ecolodge, with thoughtful decor, en suites and natty little private balconies. There's also a restaurant serving Laotian and Western dishes (mains 40,000K). Bring plenty of mosquito repellent. In Ban Tiou, about 6km closer to Ban Kong Lo, the same outfit runs the simpler **Sala Kong Lor** (☎020 7776 1846; www.salalao.com; r 80,000-265,000K), where half a dozen new rooms have been built.

In response to the growing number of visitors, Kong Lo village (about 1km downstream from the cave mouth) has recently started to develop. Should you arrive too late to do the cave and want to stay the night, head for the Swiss-style chalet of **Chantha Guest House** (☎020 210 0002; r 80,000K), which has 16 comfortable rooms. More memorable – though less comfortable – are the **homestay options** (per person incl breakfast & dinner 50,000K). Simply ask around and a family will take you in. For dinner head to **Mithuna Restaurant** (Kong Lo village; mains

30,000K; ⌚7am-8pm) for Western breakfasts and snacks and well-cooked Laotian cuisine.

Getting There & Away

From Ban Khoun Kham to Ban Kong Lo, it's an easy and picturesque 20-minute journey by scooter or *sǒrngtǎaou* (25,000K).

In Ban Kong Lo boatmen charge 120,000K per boat, as well as a 5000K entrance fee, for the return trip through the cave (about 2½ hours, maximum three people). If you're travelling solo you'll have to pay the entire 120,000K fee. If you're doing 'the loop' (p334) and returning to Tha Khaek, ask the ever-helpful Mr Somkiad at Tha Khaek's tourist information centre (p333) for more details.

LAK SAO

☎054 / POP 31,400

Deep in logging territory, with trucks rumbling over the Vietnamese border to Vinh, Lak Sao sits in the shadow of handsome karst formations. It's not much to look at, but thanks to Kong Lo Cave it's now enjoying a few more visitors.

The **Phoutthavong Guest House** (☎341074; Rte 8B; r 30,000-70,000K; ✱) has expanded recently and improved its offerings with cable TV and 10 new rooms with shared bathrooms or en suites to choose from.

There's a **Lao Development Bank** (Rte 8B) but no internet cafe.

Scheduled buses leave from near the market for Vientiane (65,000K, six to eight hours, 334km) at 5am, 6am, 8am and 5.30pm, stopping at Vieng Kham (Thang Beng; 30,000K, 1½ to 2½ hours, 100km), while other transport to Vieng Kham leaves throughout the day. One bus goes to Tha Khaek (50,000K, six hours, 202km) at 7.30am.

THA KHAEK

☎051 / POP 30,000

Romantic, authentically Lao, riverside Tha Khaek barely looks up from its game of boules to acknowledge your arrival. Its busiest days are over, the French colonial taskmasters who built the place in 1910 long gone. What remains of them are the elegant ghosts of shuttered villas yearning for restoration, and boulevards of tree-lined streets. Grab a seat in a riverfront bar and let the afternoon's honey light work its magic, animating the place with Indochinese nostalgia. With its centrepiece fountain and tree-shaded streets glowing with braziers, Tha Khaek is reminiscent of Vientiane 10 years ago.

Sleeping

TOP CHOICE **Tha Khek Travel Lodge** GUESTHOUSE $
(☎212931; travell@laotel.com; dm 25,000K, r 50,000-110,000K; ✱@☎) This travellers' oasis, five minutes east out of town in a túk-túk, excels with 17 immaculate rooms (as well as a dorm) with boutique flourishes. The best of the bunch enjoy fridges, firm mattresses, mosquito nets and en suites. And with the courtyard's nightly firepit drawing you to the company of others, this is the perfect place to swap stories about doing 'the loop' (see p334) by scooter (85,000K per day; ask for details at reception). It also runs one-day trips to Kong Lo Cave by minibus (group of four, 550,000K per person, departs 8am).

Inthira Hotel Sikotabong HOTEL $$
(☎251237; www.inthirahotels.com; Th Chao Annou; r US$29-49; ✱☎) Set in an old colonial-era trading house, fusing traditional elements with contemporary chic – oxblood walls, New York–style open-plan kitchen and chi-chi bar – Inthira is the best place in town. The rooms are heavenly, with rain showerheads, hardwood floors and teak furnishings. Try for one with a balcony overlooking the square. The restaurant has an Asian fusion menu (mains 80,000K).

GETTING TO VIETNAM: NAM PHAO TO CAU TREO

The border at Nam Phao (Laos) and Cau Treo (Vietnam) through the Kaew Neua Pass is 30km from Lak Sao and is open from 7am to 4.30pm. *Sǒrngtǎaou* (20,000K, 45 minutes) leave every hour or so from Lak Sao market. Alternatively, direct buses from Lak Sao to Vinh (120,000K, five hours) leave several times between about noon and 2pm; you might need to change conveyance at the border. You'll need your Vietnamese visa in advance. Laos issues 30-day visas on arrival.

From the border to Lak Sao, jumbos and *sǒrngtǎaou* leave when full or cost about 170,000K to charter. There's a good chance you'll get ripped off crossing here, particularly on the Vietnamese side. For information on this, and on crossing this border the other way, see p96.

Tha Khaek

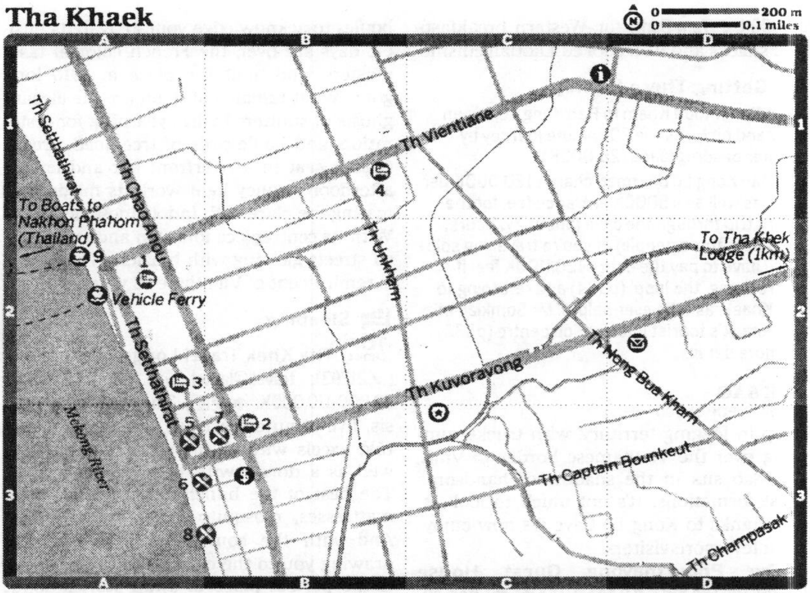

Tha Khaek

Sleeping

1 Hotel Riveria A2
2 Inthira Hotel Sikotabong B3
3 Mekong Hotel A2
4 Thakhek Mai B1

Eating

5 Duc Restaurant A3
Inthira Restaurant .... (see 2)
6 Phavilai Restaurant A3
7 Sabaidee Thakhaek B3
8 Smile Barge Restaurant B3
Thakhek Restaurant .... (see 4)

Information

9 Boats to Nakhon Phanom (Thailand) A2
Green Discovery .... (see 2)
Immigration Office .... (see 9)

Hotel Riveria HOTEL $$$
(☎251222; Th Setthathirat; r US$58-120; ❄📶) Given its marbled lobby, sports bar and plush restaurant, this is the Asian businessman's choice. Rooms are finished to international tastes, but to be honest you could be anywhere. Opt for a room with a balcony overlooking the Mekong.

Mekong Hotel HOTEL $$
(☎250777; Th Setthathirat; r 100,000-170,000K; 📶) Pleasant rooms in this elephant-grey, Soviet-style monolith have parquet floors, cupboards, fresh walls and fridges, TVs, spotless bathrooms and fine river views of the Mekong through a column of acacia trees. Good value.

Thakhek Mai GUESTHOUSE $
(☎212551; Th Vientiane; r 120,000K) Beside its cavernous restaurant, this large house has 16 rooms. The ones on the 1st floor away from the road are preferable; with mint-coloured walls, TV, wood floors, fresh linen and en suites.

Eating & Drinking

Several *khào jī* (baguette) vendors can be found on or near Fountain Sq in the morning, and the adjacent riverfront is good for a cheap meal any time. **Duc Restaurant** (meals 10,000K; ⊙6am-10pm), unnamed but for an ETL sign, looks like someone's front room (hung with family photos and portraits of Ho Chi Minh) and serves delicious *fõe hàeng* (noodle broth), while **Phavilai Restaurant** (Fountain Sq; meals 10,000-15,000K; ⌚6am-9pm), though short on charm, is wallet-friendly, with a wide choice of rice and noodles.

Smile Barge Restaurant LAOTIAN $
(meals 25,000K; ⌚noon-11.30pm) Smile pleases with its old wooden building and decked verandah overlooking the river. Fried food galore: fish, chicken, squid and, sorry Jiminy, crickets! Avoid the dingy Smile barge bar on the river.

Inthira Restaurant FUSION $
(Th Chao Annou; mains 30,000K; ❄) Complementing the Lao/international theme of the hotel, the Asian fusion menu here features spicy salads, *steak au frites*, Thai stir-fries and steamed fish. With its open-plan kitchen and adjacent bar, it's perfect for breakfast or evening dinner.

Sabaidee Thakhaek LAOTIAN $
(Th Chao Annou; mains 30,000K; ⌚7.30am-10pm) A welcoming travellers' haunt in the centre of town, with chequered tablecloths, Western-style grub, tasty Lao curries, memorable *tom yum* soup (shrimp and vegetables), and curiously, amid the secondhand thrillers, gay hard porn.

Thakhek Mai Restaurant LAOTIAN $
(Th Vientiane; meals 40,000K; ⌚7am-10.30pm) A favourite with locals, this large unpretentious eatery offers plenty of seafood, such as steamed lemon fish, crab and spiced minced fish.

ℹ Information

BCEL (Th Vientiane) Changes major currencies and travellers cheques, and makes cash advances on Visa. Including the ATM in Fountain Sq there are three ATMs in town plus one at the bus station.

Green Discovery (☎251390; Inthira Hotel, Th Chao Annou; ⌚8am-9pm) Has a desk at the Inthira Hotel and runs a range of treks and kayaking excursions in the lush Phou Hin Boun NPA including Kong Lo Cave. Cycling, kayaking and a homestay can also be combined.

Lao Development Bank (Th Kuvoravong) Cash only.

Post office (Th Kuvoravong) Also offers expensive international phone calls.

Tha Khaek Hospital (cnr Th Chao Anou & Th Champasak) Tha Khaek Hospital is fine for minor ailments or commonly seen problems including malaria and dengue. Seek out English-speaking Dr Bounthavi.

Tourist information centre (☎212512; Th Vientiane; ⌚8.30-9pm) This excellent tourist office is one of the best in the country, with exciting one- and two-day treks in Phou Hin Boun NPA (where you have a 50% chance of spotting the red-footed Douc lemurs), including a homestay with a local village (group of four, 590,000K per person). There are also treks to the waterfall by Ban Khoun Kham and Kong Lo Cave, as well as to the awe-inspiring and remote Xe Bang Fai Cave.

Tourist police (☎250610; Fountain Sq)

Wangwang Internet (Fountain Sq, opposite Inthira Hotel; per hr 7000K; ⌚7.30am-9.30pm)

ℹ Getting There & Away

Tha Khaek's **bus station** (Rte 13) is about 3.5km from the centre of town. For Vientiane (60,000K, six hours, 332km), buses leave every hour or so between 5.30am and noon. There's also a VIP bus (80,000K, six hours, 9.15am). Any buses going north stop at Vieng Kham (Thang Beng; 30,000K, 90 minutes, 102km) and Paksan (40,000K, three to four hours, 193km). There are daily services to Attapeu (85,000K, 10 hours, 3.30pm), Salavan (85,000K, 11pm) and Sekong (75,000K, 10am and 3.30pm).

Southward buses to Savannakhet depart at 10.30am, noon, 12.30pm, 1pm and 1.30pm then every half-hour till 3pm, and there's a VIP bus

GETTING TO THAILAND: THA KHAEK TO NAKHON PHANOM

Boats cross the Mekong from Tha Khaek to Nakhon Phanom in Thailand about every hour from the boat landing and **Immigration office** (⌚8am-6pm), about 400m north of Fountain Sq in Tha Khaek. The ferry costs about 15,000K. On weekends boats might be less frequent and you'll be asked for an extra 10,000K on the Lao side, and an extra 10B in Thailand.

In Tha Khaek, Laos immigration issues 30-day tourist visas on arrival and there is a **money exchange service** (⌚8.30am-3pm) at the immigration office. A free 15-day Thai visa is granted on arrival in Nakhon Phanom. On arrival in Thailand it's a 30B shared túk-túk ride to the bus station, from where buses leave Nakon Phanom for Udon Thani and Bangkok. For information on crossing this border in the other direction, see p429.

(60,000K, six hours) to Pakse that leaves at 8.15am. For Vietnam, buses leave at 8am for Hué (100,000K), 8pm for Danang (100,000K) and 8.30pm for Hanoi (160,000K, 17 hours), as well as Dong Hoi (85,000K, 10 hours, 7am Wednesday and Sunday).

If you're headed direct to Don Khong (80,000K, 15 hours, 452km) in the Four Thousand Islands, a bus from Vientiane stops around 5.30pm.

Sŏrngtăaou heading east along Rte 12 depart every hour or so from the main bus terminal, Talat Lak Sam Bus Terminal (aka Sooksomboon Bus Terminal), between 7am and 3pm for Mahaxai (15,000K, 1½ hours, 50km), Nyommalat (30,000K, two to three hours, 63km), Nakai (35,000K, 2½ to 3½ hours, 80km) and Na Phao (for the Vietnam border; 45,000K, five to seven hours, 142km).

There's also a daily bus from here to Ban Khoun Kham (50,000K, 7.30am), for those of you headed to Kong Lo Cave. If you miss this, catch an hourly bus from the main bus station to Vieng Kham (30,000K, 90 minutes) from where you can catch a túk-túk to Kong Lo village.

Getting Around

Chartered jumbos cost about 15,000K to the bus terminal out of town. **Mr Ku's Motorbike rental** (020 220 6070; Tha Khaek Travel Lodge; 7.30am-4.30pm) at Tha Khek Travel Lodge rents Chinese 110cc bikes for 90,000K a day. The tourist information centre can arrange bicycle hire. Alternatively, try **Wangwang Internet** (Fountain Sq, opposite Inthira Hotel; 7.30am-9.30pm), which rents scooters at 80,000K per day and cycles for 20,000K per day.

AROUND THA KHAEK

The main reason for staying in Tha Khaek are the caves along Rte 12 east of the city and the stunning limestone terrain in the nearby **Phu Hin Bun NPA**. Treks into the NPA come in one-, two- and three-day varieties operated by the guides at the **tourist information centre** (051-212512; Th Vientiane, Tha Khaek) in Tha Khaek; speak to **Mr Somkiad** (020 571 1797; somkiad@yahoo.com). Overnight trips involve village homestays – the centre has loads of brochures and photos to give you an idea of what you'll get. A party of two going to Kong Lo with a guide will cost 770,000K.

Travellers also hire motorbikes and take on **the loop**, a three- or four-day motorbike trip through the province via Nakai, Lak Sao, Khoun Kham (Na Hin) and Kong Lo Cave; for scooters and details look at the travellers' log at Tha Khek Travel Lodge (p331).

EAST ON ROUTE 12

The first 22km of Rte 12 east of Tha Khaek is an area with several **caves**, an abandoned railway line and a couple of swimming spots that make a great day trip. All these places can be reached by túk-túk, bicycle or hired motorcycle.

The first cave is **Tham Xang** (Elephant Cave; admission free), also known as Tham Pha Ban Tham after the nearby village – Ban Tham. The cave is famous for its stalagmite 'elephant head'. Take the right fork about 2.5km east of the Rte 13 junction and follow the road or, if it's too wet, continue along Rte 12 and turn right (south) onto a dirt road shortly after a bridge.

Back on Rte 12, turn north to **Tham Pha Pa** (Buddha Cave; admission 2000K; 8am-noon & 1-4pm), discovered by a villager hunting for bats. It's home to 229 bronze Buddha images, believed to have sat untouched for the last 600 years, and reached by a sturdy staircase that takes you 200m up a cliff face. In the rainy season the entrance floods, so you have to take a little boat to get here. It's also possible to go 50m into the mountain by boat (3000K) along a turquoise river. To get here, take a laterite road north from Rte 12 about 4km after you cross Rte 13. Turn right after about 500m and follow the old railway bed before taking the left fork. The tourist information centre in Tha Khaek also runs day treks to the cave.

GETTING TO VIETNAM: NA PHAO TO CHA LO

This border (open from 7am to 4pm) is so out of the way it might be easier to opt for a more popular crossing. No visas are issued here and transport on either side is infrequent. The best way to get close is by catching a *sŏrngtăaou* from Tha Khaek (45,000K, four hours, 142km) at 8.15am and noon, which will take you to Lang Khang, 18km short of the border. Over in Vietnam the nearest town is Dong Hoi; a direct bus goes here from Tha Khaek (85,000K, 10 to 14 hours) at 7am only on Wednesday and Sunday, and returns from Dong Hoi at 6am Monday and Friday. For information on crossing this border in the opposite direction, see p104.

Back on Rte 12 are several other caves. A track heading south for about 400m at Km 14, near the bridge over the Huay Xieng Liap and the village of Ban Songkhone (about 10.5km from Rte 13), leads to the stunning limestone cave **Tham Xieng Liap**, the entrance of which is at the base of a dramatic 300m-high cliff. Rte 12 continues through a narrow pass (about 11.5km from Rte 13), with high cliffs on either side, and immediately beyond, a track leads north to the holy cave of **Tham Sa Pha In** (Tham Phanya Inh).

The new buzz is about **Xe Bang Fai Cave**; located at the edge of Hin Namno NPA, and even longer than Kong Lo, this 9.5km subterranean cave boasts some of the tallest caverns and stalagmites (not to mention 25cm spiders) of any river cave on earth. Two-day trips here are in their infancy but involve a homestay in nearby Ban Nong Ping village (group of four, 1,800,000K per person). This is such a remote location that presently there's no tourist infrastructure to support an independent visit – difficult to reach and difficult to evacuate if you run into trouble on the rapids at the entrance or carrying your canoes over the jagged rocks. Instead, talk to English-speaking Mr Somkiad at Tha Khaek tourist information centre to arrange a visit.

Savannakhet Province

Savannakhet is the country's most populous province and has become an increasingly important trade corridor between Thailand and Vietnam. Most people stop here to experience a bit of Mekong city life and/or to go trekking in the Dong Natad and Dong Phu Vieng protected areas.

SAVANNAKHET (MUANG KHANTHABULI)

☎041 / POP 77,000

With its honey-coloured French villas, their facades crumbling in the unrelenting southern sun, the faded architecture of Savannakhet evokes a grand sense of nostalgia. There's little to do but wander by old boys busy with their pétanque, and past vendors cooking up grilled prawns by the slow, rolling Mekong. This is a sleepy city, at least in its desirable 'old town area'. A recent tourist drive has seen local activites being re-marketed, with improved signage for cultural highlights. Savannakhet is a busy, unpretentious city retaining some of its industry experienced in former days as a crucial Indochinese trading centre. Don't expect Luang Prabang, but do expect to be charmed by its languid authenticity.

Sights & Activities

Your best bet is to hire a bicycle and pedal through the cracked streets and along the riverfront, or take a trek in the neighbouring protected areas through Savannakhet's Eco Guide Unit (p337).

Savannakhet Provincial Museum MUSEUM
(Th Khanthabuli; admission 5000K; ⏲8-11.30am & 1-4pm Mon-Sat) The Savannakhet Provincial Museum is a good place to see war relics, artillery pieces and inactive examples of the deadly UXO that has claimed the lives of more than 12,000 Lao since the end of the Secret War.

Musee Des Dinosaures MUSEUM
(☎212597; Th Khanthabuli; admission 5000K; ⏲8am-noon & 1-4pm) In 1930 a major dig in a nearby village unearthed 200-million-year-old dinosaur fossils. The enthusiastically run Dinosaur Museum is an interesting place to divert yourself for an hour or so. Savannakhet Province is home to five dinosaur sites.

Wat Sainyaphum TEMPLE
(Th Tha He) The oldest and largest monastery in southern Laos; the large grounds include some centuries-old trees and a workshop near the river entrance that's a veritable golden-Buddha production line.

Sleeping

There are some decent options in town; the following are our favourites.

Saisouk Guesthouse GUESTHOUSE $
(☎212207; Th Phetsalat; r 30,000-70,000K; ❄) For sheer value, this atmospheric old villa with its shadowy corridors hung with coolie hats, buffalo horns and curios is unbeatable. Rooms are basic and cosy with a pleasant chilling balcony plus a lobby to hang in.

Leena Guesthouse GUESTHOUSE $
(☎212404; Th Chaokeen; r 40,000-80,000K; ❄📶) Fairy-lit Leena is something of a motel with kitsch decor in comfortable clean rooms with tiled floors, hot-water showers, TVs and a pleasant breakfast area. An oldie but a goodie; the air-con rooms are bigger.

Sayamungkhun Guest House GUESTHOUSE $
(☎212426; Th Ratsavongseuk; r 50,000-70,000K; ❄) Rambling guesthouse accommodation in

Savannakhet

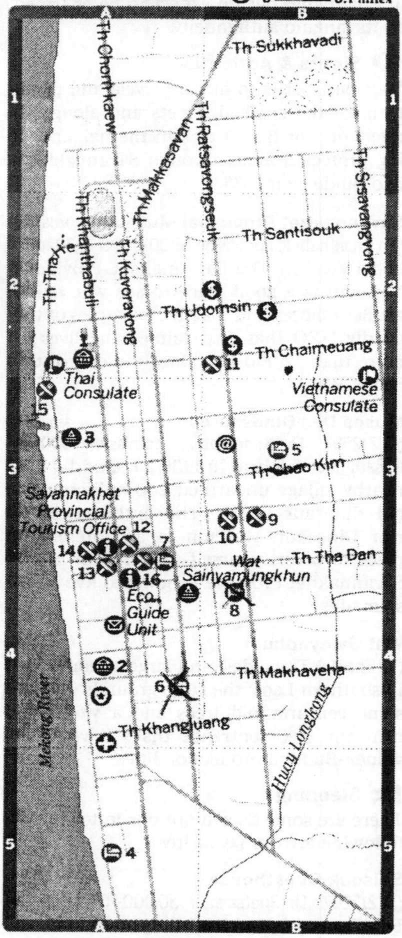

an atmospheric colonial-era building, rooms in the main house are preferable to the faded bungalows out back. Ask for one away from the busy arterial road.

Salsavan Guesthouse GUESTHOUSE $$
(☎212371; Th Kuvoravong; r incl breakfast US$20-25; ✱☎) Salsavan Guesthouse has banana-hued rooms with high ceilings and wood floors evoking a scent of old Indochine. Located in the former Thai consulate, the villa has a nice garden to read in, but feels overpriced.

Savannakhet

Sights

1 Musee des Dinosaures A2
2 Savannakhet Provincial Museum A4
3 Wat Sainyaphum A3

Sleeping

4 Daosavanh Resort & Spa Hotel A5
5 Leena Guesthouse B3
6 Saisouk Guesthouse A4
7 Salsavan Guesthouse A3
8 Sayamungkhun Guest House B4

Eating

9 Baguette Vendors B3
10 Cafe Anakot B3
11 Café Chez Boune B2
12 Dao Savanh A3
13 Friendship Bakery A4
14 Friendship Bakery A3
15 Riverside Snack and Drink Vendors A3
16 Xokxay Restaurant A3

Daosavanh Resort & Spa Hotel HOTEL $$$
(☎212188; Th Tha He; r US$66-100; ✱☎) Well-appointed though uninspiring rooms in the city's flashiest hotel. The lobby is elegant and there's a nice bar by the kidney-shaped pool, but you can find more atmosphere elsewhere.

✕ Eating & Drinking

Akin to its French-era buildings, there's some great Gallic cuisine here as well as Lao, Japanese and Thai restaurants. For quick eats, a couple of bakeries and road-side vendors operate on the corners of Th Ratsavongseuk and Th Phagnapui.

Opposite Wat Sainyaphum, the riverside **snack and drink vendors** (⊙afternoon & evening) are great for sundowners.

TOP CHOICE **Cafe Anakot** JAPANESE $
(Th Ratsavongseuk; mains 20,000K; ⊙8.30am-9pm) Run by a charming former NGO, we love this place for its Japanese cuisine and ubercool tempo. The menu features homemade youghurt, fruit, vegie spring rolls and terrific shakes. It also sells a good range of secondhand books, cool T-shirts and handicraft.

Friendship Bakery BAKERY $
(Th Tha Dan; mains 15,000K; ⊙9am-10pm) This welcoming house of pastry and all things bad for the waistline creates a range of brownies, fudge cake, apple or blueberry pie and decent coffees, as well as sealed ice lollies (you'll need them!).

Xokxay Restaurant LAOTIAN $
(Th Si Muang; mains 15,000K; ⊙9am-9pm) A mainstay for authentic Laotian food, this clean and friendly hole-in-the-wall is renowned for its noodle dishes, fried rice and salads. The crispy fried shrimp is lovely.

Café Chez Boune FRENCH $$
(Th Ratsavongseuk; mains 60,000K; ⊙7am-10pm) With its wood-panelled interior hung with Parisian oils, you get a clue that the food is going to be cooked to well and truly French tastes. We found the filet mignon with pepper sauce to be perfect. Other dishes include pasta and pizza.

Dao Savanh FRENCH $$$
(Th Si Muang; mains 100,000-150,000K; ⊙7am-10pm; 🅘🅦) This elegant villa facing the plaza is perfect for lunch in the downstairs cafe, with a menu of salads, sandwiches and *croque monsieur*. Upstairs the decor is classier still, with a French-heavy evening menu boasting dishes like grilled duck breast, tenderloin steak and lamb chops Provençal. There are also a couple of internet terminals here (5000K per hour).

Information

BCEL (Th Ratsavongseuk; ⊙8.30am-4pm) Cash exchange and credit-card advances; ATM.

Dao Savanh (☎260888; Th Si Muang; ⊙7am-10pm; 🅘🅦) With internet access for 5000K per hour, this is the perfect place to catch up on your emails over a glass of vino.

Eco Guide Unit (☎214203; www.savannakhet-trekking.com; Th Ratsaphanith; ⊙8-11.30am & 1.30-5pm Mon-Sat) Your best bet for making the most of this city and its surrounding treasures, this excellent office (run by lovely Nikki) provides free city maps, wi-fi, one-day tours to Turtle Lake, as well as day trips on the fascinating Ho Chi Minh Trail. It also arranges homestays with Katang minorities, camping, or cycling tours in Dong Natad NPA. If that doesn't whet your appetite, try a cooking class (50,000K per person). It rents bikes (15,000K) and book flights and VIP bus tickets too.

Lao Development Bank (Th Udomsin; ⊙8.30-11.30am & 1.30-3.30pm) Same services as BCEL.

Police (☎212069; Th Ratsaphanith)

Post office (☎212205; Th Khanthabuli)

Provincial hospital (☎212051; Th Khanthabuli)

Savannakhet provincial tourism office (☎212755; Th Muang Sing; ⊙8-11.30am & 1.30-4.30pm) With helpful city maps and English-speaking staff with suggestions of things to do from food to local sights.

GETTING TO THAILAND: SAVANNAKHET TO MUKDAHAN

Regular buses (13,000K, 45 minutes) leave from Savannakhet's main bus terminal for Thailand's Mukdahan, between 8.15am and 7pm. Thirty-day visas (around US$35, depending on which passport you hold) are available on arrival in Laos. A 15-day free visa is available on arrival in Thailand. For information on crossing this border in the other direction, see p428.

Getting There & Away

Savannakhet's airport fields flights to and from Vientiane (US$62, Wednesday, Friday and Sunday) and Pakse (US$62, Wednesday, Friday and Sunday). There are also flights to Bangkok (US$135) on the same days.

Savannakhet's **bus terminal** (☎212143), 2km out of town on Th Makkasavan, is at the northern edge of town. Buses leave for Vientiane (70,000K, nine hours, 470km) hourly from 6am to 11.30am. Thereafter you'll have to catch buses headed to Pakse that pass through Tha Khaek (30,000K, 2½ to four hours, 125km) until 10pm. A sleeper VIP bus to Vientiane (120,000K, six to seven hours) leaves at 9.30pm. For Salavan (45,000 K, seven hours, 190km), catch the 12.30pm bus.

Heading south, at least nine buses either start here or pass through from Vientiane for Pakse (40,000K, five to six hours, 230km) and Don Khong (70,000K, six to eight hours) between 7am and 10pm. Buses for Dansavanh (40,000K, five to seven hours) on the Laos–Vietnam border leave at 7am and noon, stopping at Sepon (40,000K, four to six hours). A local bus to Hué (80,000K) and Danang (110,000K) leaves daily at 10pm, continuing on to Hanoi (200,000K, 24 hours, 650km). *Sŏrngtăaou* leave more frequently for local destinations such as Tha Khaek (25,000K).

Getting Around

A túk-túk to the bus terminal will cost about 20,000K; prices double after dark. The town is fairly sprawled out, so it might be a good idea to

GETTING TO VIETNAM: DANSAVANH TO LAO BAO

The busy border (open 7am to 7.30pm) at Dansavanh (Laos) and Lao Bao (Vietnam) is regularly used by travellers. Buses leave from Savannakhet (40,000K, five to seven hours) at 7am and noon, and regularly from Sepon (12,000K, one hour, 45km). It's a 1km walk between the border posts (hop on a motorbike taxi on the Vietnamese side for 10,000d), but formalities don't take long if you have your Vietnam visa; Laos issues 30-day visas (around US$35) on arrival. Vietnam visas must be arranged in advance. Entering Laos, *sŏrngtăaou* to Sepon leave fairly regularly. There is simple accommodation on both sides of the border. Alternatively, a daily 8am bus runs from Savannakhet to Dong Ha (US$12, about eight hours, 329km), while a 10am and 10pm bus services Hué (local/VIP 80,000/110,000K, about 12 hours, 409km). The same VIP bus continues to Danang (110,000K, about 14 hours, 508km). No matter what you are told, you *will* have to change buses at the border. For information on crossing this border in the other direction, see p102.

rent a bicycle/scooter for 15,000/70,000K per day from Eco Guide Unit.

EAST ON ROUTE 9

If you're heading east towards Vietnam, there are several places worth stopping at including **Dong Natad Provincial Protected Area**, just 15km from Savannakhet. The provincial tourism office (p337) runs informative day and overnight treks here, with local guides explaining the myriad uses of the forest, and overnighters staying in a village home. Three-day treks into the remote **Dong Phu Vieng NPA** offer a similar but more extreme experience, staying in Katang villages.

Further east is **Sepon**, with a couple of decent guesthouses. About 20km east is **Ban Dong**, a sleepy village on what was once an important branch of the Ho Chi Minh Trail. Today there are a couple of rusting American-built tanks (kids will direct you) that are among the most accessible war relics in southern Laos.

Buses and *sŏrngtăaou* head in both directions along Rte 9 between Savannakhet and Dansavanh; your best bet is to travel in the morning.

Champasak Province

PAKSE

☎031 / POP 119,000

Sitting at the confluence of the Se Don and Mekong rivers, it's hard to imagine sultry Pakse was once the French capital of southern Laos. Thanks to its location near the Khmer ruins of Wat Phu and the Bolaven Plateau (the country's fertile coffee-growing region), as well as its proximity to Vietnam, Thailand and Cambodia, it enjoys a fair flow of travellers. Many are bound for the backpacker mecca of Si Phan Don (Four Thousand Islands), and end up spending a night here. Bar a few wats there's little to see, but by night the Mekong River and its waterfront bars are invitingly aglow, and there are some excellent restaurants, guesthouses and cafes in town to hang in. Pakse's Green Discovery branch has recently come on in leaps and bounds with the new Tree Top Explorer ziplining adventure.

Sights & Activities

Central Pakse is bound by the Mekong to the south and the Se Don to the north and west. Rte 13 cuts through the northern edge of town. On and below Rte 13 towards the Mekong are most of Pakse's guesthouses, shops and restaurants. Heading west across Se Don takes you to the northern bus terminal. The southern bus terminal and market are 8km in the opposite direction.

There are 20 wats in town, the largest being **Wat Luang**, featuring ornate concrete pillars and carved wooden doors and murals, and **Wat Tham Fai**, which has a small Buddha footprint shrine in its grounds.

The **Champasak Historical Heritage Museum** (Rte 13; admission 5000K; ⊙8-11.30am & 1-4pm) documents the history of the province, with historical photos and ethnological displays.

A massage and sauna at the **Clinic Keo Ou Done** (Traditional Medicine Hospice; ☎251895, 020 543 1115; 1hr massage 20,000K; ⊙4-9pm Mon-Fri, 10am-9pm Sat & Sun) is a real Lao experience. Go east on Rte 13, turn right about 100m before the Km 3 marker, and follow the 'Massage Sauna' signs another 800m. Alternatively, try **Dok Champa Massage** (☎020 269 6999; Th 5; 1hr massage 35,000-60,000K;

Pakse

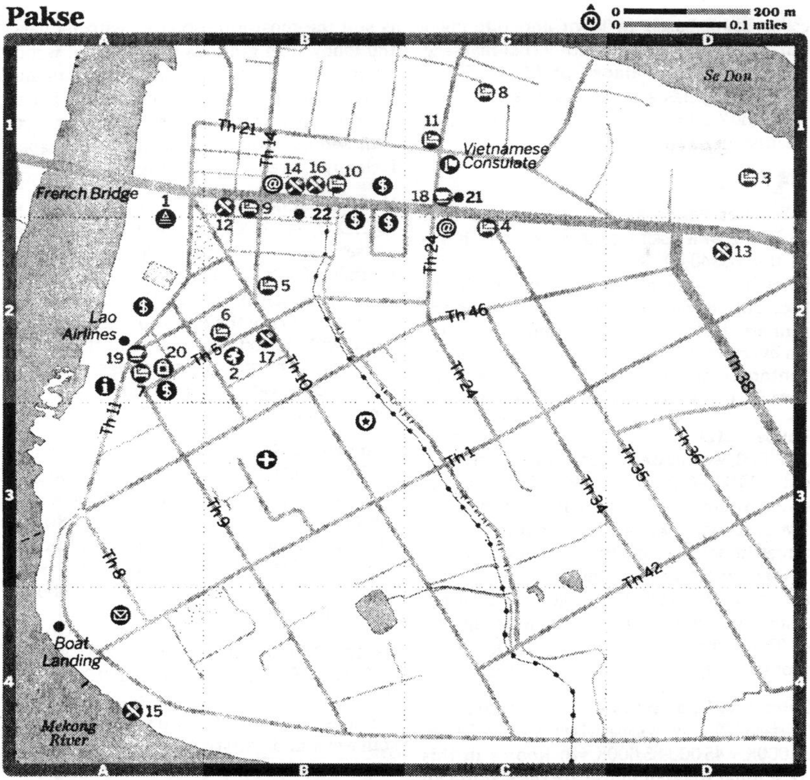

Pakse

Sights

1 Wat Luang A2

Activities, Courses & Tours

Champasak Palace Hotel Gym .... (see 3)
2 Dok Champa Massage B2

Sleeping

3 Champasak Palace Hotel D1
4 Daovieng 2 Hotel C2
5 Hotel Salachampa B2
6 Pakse Hotel B2
7 Residence Sisouk A2
8 Sabaidy 2 Guesthouse C1
9 Saigon Champasak Hotel B1
10 Sang Aroun Hotel B1
11 Thalaung Hotel C1

Eating

12 Champady B1
13 Delta Coffee D2
14 Jasmine Restaurant B1
15 Khem Khong Restaurant A4
Lankham Noodle Shop .... (see 22)
16 Mengky Noodle Shop B1
17 Xuan Mai Restaurant B2

Drinking

18 Katuad Cafe C1
19 Sinouk Coffee Shop A2

Shopping

20 Monument Books A2

Information

21 Green Discovery C1
Xplore Asia .... (see 9)

Transport

22 Lankham Hotel B1
Mai Linh Express .... (see 9)

(⊙9am-9pm), based in town and offering a range of traditional, oil and herbal massage. The **Champasak Palace Hotel** (☎212777; Rte 13; ⊙2-10pm) has a decent gym, and it costs just 7000K for visitors. It also offers massage, a sauna and a spa.

Sleeping

TOP CHOICE Residence Sisouk HOTEL $$
(☎214716; www.residence-sisouk.com; cnr Th 9 & Th 11; r US$40-80; ❄📶) This new boutique hotel has lovely rooms enjoying hardwood floors, flat-screen TVs, verandahs, Hmong bed runners, lush photography and fresh flowers everywhere. Its ace card is the excellent penthouse cafe with 360-degree views. Head here for breakfast and use the free wi-fi.

Pakse Hotel HOTEL $$
(☎212131; www.paksehotel.com; Th 5; r incl breakfast 200,000-450,000K; ❄📶) This central trad-luxe hotel is immaculate, stylish and a favourite with well-heeled visitors. Rooms range in scope from boxy singles to lovely doubles and family rooms, some with striking views (for which you pay extra) of the distant mountains and nearby Mekong River. The al fresco restaurant up top is a great spot to work and enjoy a sundowner.

Sabaidy 2 Guesthouse GUESTHOUSE $
(☎/fax 212992; www.sabaidy2laos.com; Th 24; dm 30,000K, r 45,000-85,000K; ❄) Rooms in this traditional wooden house are decked in Lao textiles; some have en suites. The beds may occasionally be itchy, but the real benefits of staying here are its leafy courtyard bar and the chance to meet other travellers. Another draw is the gregarious owner, Mr Vong, who runs treks to the Bolaven Plateau.

Champasak Palace Hotel HOTEL $$$
(☎212263; www.champasak-palace-hotel.com; Rte 13; r incl breakfast US$23-200; ❄@📶) Despite swish usurpers, this ageing grande dame is still the most atmospheric, with its palatial lobby, lush grounds and graceful wood-columned restaurant. The double rooms and suites in the hotel, while comfortably faded, are far superior to the ones in the more recent Sedone wing – which though cheaper, lack any character whatsoever.

Hotel Salachampa HOTEL $$
(☎212273; fax 212646; Th 14; r US$20-48; ❄) Pakse's oldest French villa, Salachampa has a range of solid bungalow accommodation, some of which is fresher than others. But the real stars are the rooms in the old house itself, with period furniture, and their walls hung with antique Lao paintings. Attached is a pleasant cafe serving a mix of Lao and Western fare (mains 20,000K).

Daovieng 2 Hotel HOTEL $
(☎214331; Rte 13; r incl breakfast 100,000-130,000K; ❄📶) New kid on the block, a couple of blocks down the main drag. Rooms here vary from cramped singles to attractive fresh doubles with en suites, comfy beds, sparkling linen and TV. Ensure you choose one away from the busy road.

Saigon Champasak Hotel GUESTHOUSE $
(☎254181; Th 14; s/d 120,000/160,000K; ❄) Barely seven years old, these Vietnamese-run digs need a freshen-up with threadbare stairwells and thirsty walls. But the rooms are spacious and clean, with fridges, TVs, en suites and air-con.

Thaluang Hotel GUESTHOUSE $
(☎251399; Th 21; r 60,000-70,000K; ❄) Well-run Thaluang has a range of ordinary bungalow rooms and nicer ones in the house itself, with ochre walls, fantasy art, TV and en suite. A mynah bird hails your arrival.

Sang Aroun Hotel HOTEL $$
(☎252111; Rte 13; r 140,000-250,000K; ❄📶) Don't be put off by the nondescript exterior,

SUPER FLY GUY

Pakse's Green Discovery branch runs exhilarating excursions to the recently (January 2011) opened **Tree Top Explorer** (☎252908; www.greendiscoverylaos.com; Rte 13), a series of 11 ziplines in the Bolaven Plateau that looks set to rival the Gibbon Experience for its sheer adrenalin rush. The longest ride is 450m but the most dramatic cable is that which crosses directly in the spray of a huge waterfall. Trek through jungle and stay in ecoconscious 20m-high tree houses in the semi-evergreen forests of Don Hua Sao NPA on two-day, one-night excursions (a group of two people costs US$187 per person). Reviews are effervescent: 'It was fantastic – really safety-conscious staff and magical jungle. And even though they can fit a max of 16 people in the different tree houses, we had the place to ourselves. There were only four of us!'

this place is immaculate with spacious, sugar-white rooms, plush furniture and even an in-house masseuse. A nice family option; extra beds cost 50,000K.

Eating

Tucking into a plate of noodles with locals is an authentic way to experience Pakse cuisine; try the Mengky Noodle Shop on Rte 13. For a light snack there are baguette vendors near Jasmine Restaurant, and by night the braziers light up with barbecued skewers of meat along Rte 13.

TOP CHOICE Delta Coffee ITALIAN $
(Rte 13; mains 20,000K; ⊙7am-10pm) Delta deservedly packs them in with a carb-heavy menu of tasty Italian dishes such as gnocchi with tomato and basil, numerous steaks and uninspiring pizzas. It also sells its own coffee and has set up schools for its plantation-workers' children.

TOP CHOICE Jasmine Restaurant INDIAN $
(Rte 13; mains 20,000-30,000K; ⊙8am-10pm) Could this simple hole-in-the-wall be the best Indian restaurant in Laos? Delicious curries and Malaysian fare such as nasi goreng with mutton, plus sizzling chicken tikka masala so tasty you'll be wiping the bowl with their pillow-soft naan.

Xuan Mai Restaurant LAOTIAN, VIETNAMESE $
(Th 4; mains 20,000K; ⊙6am-11.30pm) On the corner opposite the Pakse Hotel, Vietnamese-run Xuan Mai serves top-notch *fõe* (8000K), *khào pûn* (white flour noodles with sweet-spicy sauce), fruit shakes and even garlic bread. The house *làap* is full of zing.

Katuad Café WESTERN $
(Rte 13; mains 30,000K; ⊙7am-9pm; wi-fi) This breezy modern cafe does a good trade with Western breakfasts, sandwiches, hamburgers and ice cream, as well as stir-fries and spicy salads. Great coffee, fruit shakes and there's quick wi-fi connection too.

Khem Khong Restaurant SEAFOOD $
(Th 11; mains 24,000K; ⊙9am-11pm) You need decent sea legs here as you tuck into a seafood-focused menu of smoked fish and beer-grilled prawns, crab meat, spicy shrimp *làap* and *pîing pąa* (grilled fish) – this place is set upon pontoons on the Mekong River. Pleasantly rowdy and fairy-lit, this is a memorable Pakse experience.

Lankham Noodle Shop LAOTIAN $
(Rte 13; meals 8000-15,000K; ⊙7am-10pm) The best time to come here is during the morning rush-hour, when locals stock up on noodle broths before the daily commute. The food is cooked in front of you in a great steaming pot.

Champady CAFE $
(Rte 13; mains 20,000K; ⊙7am-11pm Mon-Fri) Red walls and chrome chairs give this new haunt a sleek feel, but the best bit is the fair-trade, locally grown coffee. The menu features Pakse sweet sausage as well as Western breakfasts, ice cream and fruit shakes.

Drinking

The best evenings in Pakse are nonprescriptive wanders down the Mekong riverfront stopping at a terrace bar of your liking. Alternatively, for a bit more style head to Pakse Hotel's al fresco Le Panorama Restaurant, decked out in 1930s Parisian-style lamps and glass tables, it's the perfect place to nurse a cocktail and savour the sunset.

Sinouk Coffee Shop CAFE
(cnr Th 9 & Th 11; mains 20,000K; ⊙7am-8pm; wi-fi) Thanks to a facelift, Sinouk is a good stop to come to read, work using its wi-fi, or imbibe the rich taste of its arabica coffee grown on the Bolaven Plateau. All the usual suspects such as latte, cappuccino and espresso, as well as a formidable range of temptations – apple pie, chocolate or sponge cake, *pain au chocolat*, juices and breakfast.

Shopping

Monument Books BOOKS
(Th 5; ⊙9am-8pm) Upmarket bookshop selling lavish pictorials on Laos as well as historical and cultural titles to enrich your understanding of the country. It also sells postcards and a range of maps.

Information

EMERGENCY

Hospital (☎212018; cnr Th 10 & Th 46)

Police (☎212145; Th 10)

INTERNET ACCESS

There are several places on Rte 13 with decent broadband connections, which can also burn CDs.

Lankham Internet (Rte 13; per hr 5000K; ⊙7.30am-10pm) Plus free wi-fi.

SK Internet (Rte 13; per hr 5000K; ⊙8am-10pm)

GETTING TO THAILAND: VANG TAO TO CHONG MEK

The busy crossing between Vang Tao (Laos) and Chong Mek (Thailand) is open from 5am to 6pm. From Pakse, *sŏrngtăaou* (10,000K, 75 minutes, 37km) and taxis (20,000K per person or 120,000K for the whole vehicle, 45 minutes) run between Talat Dao Heung (New Market) and Vang Tao. Easier is the Thai-Lao International Bus (55,000K, 2½ to three hours, 126km) direct from the VIP Bus Station to Ubon Ratchathani at 7am, 8.30am, 2.30pm and 3.30pm, returning at 7.30am, 9.30am, 2.30pm and 3.30pm. Alternatively, continue on to Bangkok (210,000K) on the same bus. At the border you have to walk a bit, but formalities are straightforward. Laos issues visas on arrival (around US$35, depending on what passport you hold), as do the Thais. For details on crossing the border in the other direction, see p426.

MONEY

There are now plenty of 24-hour ATMs clustered in the centre of town on Rte 13.

BCEL (Th 11; ⏲8.30am-3.30pm Mon-Fri, to 10am Sat) South of Wat Luang, this has the best rates for cash and travellers cheques. Cash advances against Visa and MasterCard. Plus ATM.

Lao Development Bank (Rte 13; ⏲8am-4pm Mon-Fri, to 3pm Sat & Sun) Changes cash and travellers cheques in the smaller exchange office; cash advances (Monday to Friday only) in the main building. Also houses a Western Union (money transfers only available weekdays). There's an ATM on the opposite side of the road.

POST

Post office (cnr Th 1 & Th 8; ⏲8am-noon & 1-5pm Mon-Fri)

TOURIST INFORMATION

Provincial tourism office (☎212021; Th 11; ⏲8am-noon & 1.30-4pm Mon-Fri) Beside the Lao Airlines office, English-speaking staff can book you onto community-based two- or three-day treks in Xe Pian NPA and Phou Xieng Thong NPA, involving kayaking and camping combos; and homestays on Don Kho and Don Daeng taking in Wat Phu (group of four, US$65 per person). It also now runs two-day elephant treks up Phou Asa (group of four, US$65 per person).

TRAVEL AGENCIES

Most hotels and guesthouses can arrange day trips to the Bolaven Plateau, Wat Phu Champasak and Si Phan Don.

Green Discovery (☎252908; www.greendiscoverylaos.com; Rte 13) As well as the excellent new Tree Top Explorer zipline adventure, Green Discovery operates one- and two-day treks in Phou Xieng Thong NPA as well as three-day elephant treks in Xe Pian NPA (group of four, US$172 per person); also, cycling and kayaking combo trips (group of four, US$195 per person including food, guide, accommodation and transport) to Si Phan Don.

Xplore-Asia (☎251983; www.xplore-laos.com; Rte 14) One- and two-day treks to Xe Pian NPA as well as one-day treks to Tad Lo (170,000K per person), Tad Fane and Katang ethnic villages. There's also a two-day kayaking trip to Don Dhet (Four Thousand Islands; US$75 per person), overnighting on Don Khon.

Getting There & Away

AIR

Lao Airlines (☎212252; www.laoairlines.com; Th 11; ⏲8-11.30am & 1.30-4.30pm Mon-Fri) flies between Pakse and Vientiane daily (one way US$131, 70 minutes), and usually three times a week to Luang Prabang (US$168, one hour 40 minutes). International flights go to Siem Reap (US$140, 45 minutes) daily, and Bangkok (US$150, one hour 10 minutes) and Ho Chi Minh City (US$95, 35 minutes) three times a week.

The airport is 3km northwest of town and has a BCEL exchange office. Note: you can't buy tickets at the airport, so purchase them at the Lao Airlines office.

BOAT

Speak to Joe at Pakse's provincial tourism office to book a seat on a boat to Champasak (100,000K, 8.30am daily). If there are 10 of you it's possible to charter a boat to the Four Thousand Islands for as little as US$20 per person, and takes six hours.

BUS & SŎRNGTĂAOU

Pakse has several bus and *sŏrngtăaou* terminals. 'Sleeper' VIP buses leave the **VIP Bus Station** (Km 2 Bus Station), off Rte 13, for Vientiane (170,000K, eight to 10 hours, 677km) every evening, though they usually also stop in town. The handy Thai-Lao International Bus headed to Bangkok (210,000K, 8.30am and 3.30pm) and Ubon (55,000K, same bus) also departs from here; see the boxed text, p342 for details. Finally, there's a bus to Phnom Penh (230,000K, 7.30am).

From the **northern bus terminal** (Rte 13), usually called *khíw lot lák jét* (Km 7 bus terminal), agonisingly slow, local buses (without air-con) rattle north every 40 minutes or so between 6.30am and 4pm for Savannakhet (40,000K, four to five hours, 277km), Tha Khaek (60,000K, eight to nine hours) and, for those with a masochistic streak, Vientiane (110,000K, 16 to 18 hours).

For buses or *sǒrngtǎaou* anywhere south or east, head to the **southern bus terminal** (Rte 13), which is usually called *khíw lot lák pąet* (Km 8 bus terminal). The terminal is 8km south of town and costs 15,000K on a túk-túk. For Si Phan Don, transport departs for Muang Khong (including ferry 40,000K, three hours, 120km) between 8.30am and 3pm, and for Ban Nakasang (for Don Det and Don Khon; 35,000K, three to four hours) hourly between 7.30am and 4pm. A *sǒrngtǎaou* runs to Kiet Ngong (Xe Pian NPA) and Ban Phapho (20,000K, two to three hours) at 1pm.

To the Bolaven Plateau, transport leaves for Paksong (25,000K, 90 minutes) hourly between 7am and 4pm, stopping at Tat Fan if you ask. Transport leaves for Salavan (30,000K, three to four hours, 115km) five times daily between 7.45am and 2pm, most going via Tat Lo (35,000K). Transport also leaves for Sekong (35,000K, 3½ to 4½ hours, 135km) hourly between 7.30am and 4pm, and for Attapeu (40,000 K, 4½ to six hours, 212km) at 6.30am, 8am and 10.30am.

Regular buses and *sǒrngtǎaou* leave Talat Dao Heung (New Market) for Champasak (20,000K, one to two hours) and Ban Saphai (for Don Kho; 8000K, about 40 minutes).

Mai Linh Express (☎254149) operates a daily minibus service from outside the Saigon Champasak Hotel to Lao Bao (140,000K, leaves 6.30am) on the Vietnam border, Hué (180,000K, leaves 7am) and Danang (220,000K, leaves 7am).

Getting Around

A jumbo to the airport should cost about 10,000K. Pakse's main attractions are accessible by foot. Bicycles/scooters (around 15,000/70,000K per day) can be hired from **Lankham Hotel** (☎213314; latchan@laotel.com; Rte 13), which also has some decent Honda Bajas for 230,000K a day, excellent for expedient trips to the Bolaven Plateau.

CHAMPASAK

☎031 / POP 14,500

If you're looking for activity beyond the somnolent to and fro of the ferryman and children playing in flower-choked backyards, you may have come to the wrong place. This serene riverside town drips with charm thanks to its backdrop of a hazy mountain fringed by emerald rice paddies. Among faded colonial villas there's a sprinkling of high-end style with a boutique hotel and a couple of upmarket restaurants, but the real high point is the picturesque ruins of Wat Phu Champasak.

The town stirs once a year when pilgrims gravitate here for **Bun Wat Phu Champasak**, a three-day Buddhist festival (usually held in February) of praying, offerings, traditional music, Thai boxing, comedy shows and cockfights.

Guesthouses are mainly found near the fountain south of Champasak's only roundabout.

Sights & Activities

Wat Phu Champasak TEMPLE

(admission 30,000K; ⊙8am-4.30pm) Beautifully positioned on a hill bursting with frangipani and overlooking the Mekong River valley, Wat Phu Champasak is one of the most important archaeological sites in Laos. It was built in the 6th century as a tribute to the Hindu god Shiva; it's possible, too, that it may have been the blueprint for Angkor Wat and other Khmer temples in Cambodia.

The complex is divided into lower and upper parts and joined by a steep stone stairway – this will stretch your calves a bit so take a break halfway and take in the fertile vista below. The lower part consists of two ruined palace buildings at the edge of a large square pond (itself split in two by a causeway) used for ritual ablutions. The upper section is the temple sanctuary itself, which once enclosed a large Shiva phallus. Some time later the sanctuary was converted into a Buddhist temple, but original Hindu sculpture remains in the lintels.

CHAMPASAK EXPRESS

A new 28km road from Pakse allows you to avoid taking the ferry from Ban Muang to Champasak, and makes for an easy hour's ride by scooter. Head from Pakse over the Lao-Japanese Bridge, and after almost exactly 2km there's a turn-off on your left at the 'Welcome to Champasak' billboard. From here it's a straight ride, though be careful of the last stretch, which was still unpaved when we tried it. If travelling at night, keep to the centre of the road to avoid random chickens, buffalo and villagers without lights.

Just north of the Shiva linga sanctuary you'll find the elephant stone and the mysterious crocodile stone (if you can locate it!). The *naga* stairway leading to the sanctuary is lined with *dawk jampaa* (jacaranda) trees. The upper platform affords spectacular views of the Mekong River valley below.

As well as Bun Wat Phu Champasak, a ritual water-buffalo sacrifice to the ruling earth spirit for Champasak, called Chao Tengkham, is performed in February each year. The blood of the buffalo is offered to a local shaman who serves as a medium for the appearance of this spirit.

Much more history is available in the pamphlet you should receive with your ticket, and in the small but accessible **museum** (admission with Wat Phu ticket; ⊙8am-4.30pm) near the ticket office. Try to see the ruins at sunrise or sunset.

If you've got time, visit the fishing island of **Don Daeng**, diminutive (8km long) and utterly unblemished by the tourist trail. You can stay in a basic community guesthouse (per person 30,000K) – ask at the **Champasak District Visitor Information Centre** (☎020 220 6215; ⊙8am-4.30pm Mon-Fri) for details. It's a short ferry trip (50,000K return), but make sure you agree upon a time for your boatman to pick you up.

Just when you thought you couldn't get any more relaxed, **Champasak Spa** (☎020 5649 9739; www.champasak-spa.com; ⊙10am-noon & 1-7pm) offers a perfect sensual antidote to tired muscles in its fragrant oasis overlooking the Mekong River. Traditional Lao body massage (55,000K), herbal massage (75,000K) and body scrubs (120,000K) are among the offerings, all of which use organic bio products.

Sleeping & Eating

TOP CHOICE Inthira Hotel Champanakone BOUTIQUE HOTEL $$
(☎511011; r US$44-69, ste US$71-79; ❄📶) The belle of the river, Inthira's sumptuous rooms and low-lit Asian fusion restaurant (mains 35,000K) give us yet another reason to stay another day in Champasak. Based in an old Chinese shophouse and in a new complex over the road (facing the river), rooms boast brick floors, ambient lighting, flat-screen TVs, rain showerheads and marble baths. A swimming pool was due to be built when we passed.

Anouxa Guest House GUESTHOUSE $
(☎511006; r 100,000-150,000K; ❄) Friendly Anouxa has homely bungalows (some facing the river), with air-con and peach and lime interiors, and immaculately clean bathrooms and linen. Add to this its pleasant gardens and tempting restaurant to sit with a sundowner Beerlao and it's a winner.

Frice and Lujane Restaurant ITALIAN $
(mains 40,000K) Offering cuisine from the Friulian alpine region of Italy, this atmospheric restaurant based in a renovated villa has a menu encompassing gnocchi, marinated pork ribs and goulash. Owner Marco is especially proud of his homemade sausage!

Getting There & Around

Regular buses and *sǒrngtǎaou* run between Champasak and Pakse (20,000K, one hour) from about 6.30am until 3pm; early morning is busiest.

If you're heading south to Ban Nakasang (for Don Det) or Muang Khong (on Don Khong), get to Ban Lak 30 (on Rte 13), where you can flag down anything going south.

Bicycles (10,000K to 15,000K per day) and scooters (50,000/80,000K per half-/full day) can be hired from guesthouses. A return túk-túk to Wat Phu costs from 80,000K, including waiting time.

SI PHAN DON

☎031

Also known as the Four Thousand Islands, Si Phan Don is one of Southeast Asia's most talked-about traveller meccas. The islands are celebrated for their horizontal vibe and location in the widest stretch of the Mekong; it's as if the great river herself is taking a breath here after her long journey from Tibet. In the cool and dry season (well after and before monsoon) the river is at her most perfect, passing around thousands of sandbars sprouting with betel trees and sugar palms, her colour a rich peacock green. At night the waters are dotted with the lights of fishing boats and fireflies, the soundtrack provided by braying buffalo and cicadas. Si Phan Don is also home to rare Irrawaddy dolphins, which can sometimes be seen at the southern tip of Don Khon, plus two impressive waterfalls. Islands Det and Khon are the best places for hammock-flopping and tubing, while neighbour Don Khong is much larger but has less of a traveller scene.

DON KHONG
POP 13,000

Less claustrophobic than islands Det and Khon thanks to its space and under-development, Khong is avoided by younger travellers. A shame for them but better for you if you're seeking a lower density of *falang*; for apart from its little town of Muang Khong, the island is largely unpeopled. Essentially a one-street town, Muang Khong has some lovely hotels and guesthouses to stay a few days in, plus a couple of decent al fresco restaurants. Wander past fishing nets drying in the sun or take a sunset boat ride to Cambodian waters, read by the river or hire a bike to explore the island.

🛏 Sleeping & Eating

You'll find all these guesthouses located in Muang Khong.

⌜TOP⌝ Pon Arena Hotel HOTEL $$
(☑253065; www.ponarenahotel.com; r with mountain/river view US$40/50; ☺7am-11.30pm; ▣▣) This river-facing hotel has fresh rooms with blonde tiled floors, white walls ornamented in silk tapestries, cable TV and granite bathrooms with giant tubs. There's also a pleasant, stilted restaurant over the river for breakfast. Friendly owner.

Villa Kang Khong GUESTHOUSE $
(☑213539; r 50,000-60,000K) The most romantic budget digs in town, this stalwart teak house creaks with uneven floors and nostalgic furnishings. Rooms are basic, fan-cooled, and with their colourful wood interiors, remind vaguely of Romany gypsy caravans.

Senesothxeune Hotel HOTEL $
(☑030 526 0577; www.ssxhotel.com; r US$45-60; ▣▣▣) This Thai-style modern hotel has upmarket rooms boasting hardwood floors, TV, deep baths, milk-white minimalism and a pleasant restaurant with a view of the river through its magnolia-blossoming garden.

Pon's River Guest House & Restaurant GUESTHOUSE $
(☑214037, 020 227 0037; r 80,000-150,000K; ▣) Welcoming guesthouse with 18 cosy rooms decked in carved wooden lights, fresh linen and immaculate bathrooms. The rooms upstairs facing the river are lovely. You can now pay with Visa and MasterCard.

Done Khong Guesthouse GUESTHOUSE $
(☑214010; r 80,000-100,00K; ▣) Welcoming, fresh rooms with tiled floors, sugar-white linen and homely furnishings in an old

house run by a French-speaking lady. Try to bag a river-facing room. Also serves meals (mains 30,000K).

Villa Muong Khong HOTEL $
(☑213011; r incl breakfast US$40-50; ▣) There are 52 comfortable rooms in this sparkling hotel, which wards off tropical mildew with an annual repaint. Rooms are well appointed with en suites and cable TV. Free sunset boat trip at 5.30pm for residents.

Lattana Guest House GUESTHOUSE $
(☑213673; r 50,000-100,000K; ▣▣) Recently renovated with comfortable river-facing rooms (avoid the drab originals out back) enjoying origami lotus folded towels, marble floors, Siberian air-con and handsome furnishings. Ground-floor rooms have enormous windows close to the road – ever felt like a goldfish? – so get one upstairs.

There's not much choice eating-wise on Don Khong, but **Pon's River Guest House & Restaurant** (mains 40,000K) is shaded by mature trees, has a lovely sun terrace and serves *làap*, grilled fish, steamed fish and fish, fish, fish! For the *poisson*-averse there are also fried rice dishes and pancake variants. Further down the road near the village green, **Done Khong Restaurant** (☑214010; mains 20,000-50,000K; ☺6.30am-10pm), run by Madame Khampiew, has a wide range of Western dishes as well as Lao fare such as grilled pork with honey.

❶ Information

One road back from the river, 400m south of the distinctive *naga*-protected Buddha at Wat Phuang Kaew, the **Agricultural Promotion Bank** (☺8.30am-3.30pm Mon-Fri) exchanges travellers cheques and cash (no sterling) at poor rates. There's no ATM on the island but you can get cash advances on your card at Pon's River Guest House & Restaurant, which charges a 5% commission.

For any medical complaints, the hospital is a little further south of the bank; ask for English-and French-speaking Dr Souban.

The **telephone office** (☺8am-noon & 2-4pm Mon-Fri) is west of the boat landing, while the **post office** (☺8am-noon & 2-4pm Mon-Fri) is just south of the bridge. **Lattana Guesthouse** (☑213673; per min 500K; ☺8am-7.30pm) has mediocre-speed internet connection.

Khong Island Travel (☑213011; www.khongislandtravel.com), based at Villa Muong Khong, can organise boat trips to Don Det and Don Khon, and forward travel/visas to Cambodia.

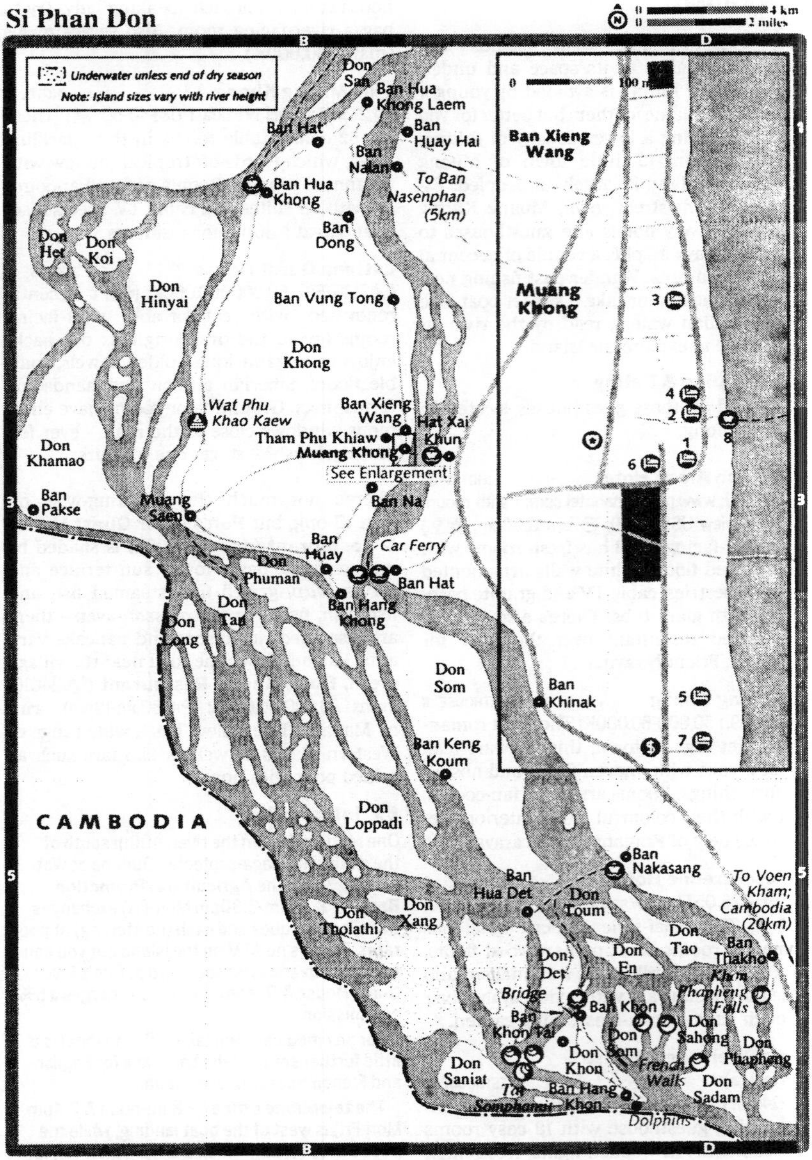

Getting There & Away

From Don Khong to Pakse, buses (50,000K, 2½ to three hours, 128km) and *sŏrngtăaou* leave from outside Wat Phuang Kaew between 6am and 10am. After that, head over to Rte 13 and wait for anything going north.

For the Cambodian border there's usually a 9am connection that costs US$10 to Stung Treng, US$13 to Kratie, US$20 to Ban Lung and US$20 to Siem Reap and Phnom Penh.

There are regular boats between Hat Xai Khun and Don Khong's Muang Khong town – 27,000K

Si Phan Don

Sleeping

1	Done Khong Guesthouse	D3
2	Lattana Guest House	D3
3	Pon Arena Hotel	D2
4	Pon's River Guest House & Restaurant	D2
5	Senesothxeune Hotel	D4
6	Villa Kang Khong	D3
7	Villa Muong Khong	D4

Eating

Done Khong Restaurant	(see 1)

Information

Khong Island Travel	(see 7)

Transport

8	Boats to Hat Xai Khun	D3

per boat for one to three people, or 10,000K per person for more.

Boats for Don Det and Don Khon (130,000K, 1½ hours) leave whenever you stump up the cash – boatmen hang out under the tree near the bridge (40,000K per person). For the same price, dependable Mr Pon's (p345) boat leaves daily at 8.30am.

Getting Around

Bicycles (10,000K per day) and motorbikes (80,000K per day) can be hired from guesthouses and elsewhere along the main street.

DON DET & DON KHON

Paradisial Don Det and Don Khon are a sight for sore eyes and, despite the volume of travellers en route to and from Cambodia, they retain their rural identities whilst proving very accommodating to weary *falang*. Chill in a hammock, cycle around or languidly drift downstream in an inner tube in the turquoise arms of the Mekong. Expect to see fishermen in pirogues, doe-eyed buffalo in the shallows and villagers taking morning ablutions. Directly after the wet season the river is churned an unappealing chocolate brown, though the paddy fields shimmer a rich leprechaun-green; while in the dry and cool season the land is parched and the river its most beautiful blue-green.

Most of the activity centres around **Ban Hua Det**, on the northern tip of Don Det. A younger crowd is drawn to its gauntlet of bars and 'cheap as chips' cabanas, loosely called 'Sunrise Boulevard', though better restaurants and digs are found elsewhere as you head south on the same side. Meanwhile, Don Khon has a calmer pace, feels more authentic and has a few upmarket hotels and restaurants targeting the more discerning traveller. It's also home to the waterfalls and the rare Irrawaddy dolphin.

Sights & Activities

With gill-net fishermen now playing a hand in the conservation of the rare **Irrawaddy dolphin**, the cetaceans' numbers have increased to beyond 20 in this area. Sadly they're on the brink of extinction, with as many as 88 dying (most of which were babies) since 2003 due to high levels of mercury and toxic pesticides in the 190km stretch of water they inhabit between Laos and Cambodia. You can sometimes see them – early evening and first thing in the morning are the best times – off the southern tip of Don Khon, right beside Cambodia, where they congregate in a 50m-deep pool. Boats are chartered (90,000K, maximum six people) from the old French pier. Sightings are regular, but the journey through the unearthly, rocky waterway is worth the money alone.

There's plenty to do here should you wish to stir from your lotus-eater's hammock: there's **tubing** (5000K) down the Mekong (avoid during monsoon when the river runs dangerously quick), which usually starts at Ban Hua Det and finishes after the French bridge; or hiring a **bicycle** (13,000K) from any of a number of places on the 'sunrise' side and meandering down the dirt paths that cross the islands. The defunct **railway line** links the two French loading piers, but it's a pretty hot trail and using alternative shaded paths is more pleasant. Heading east from the bridge on Don Khon, turn south through a wat (past Sala Phae) to see a local village and the French-built **concrete channels** once used to direct logs through the falls. In the other direction, go through Wat Ban Khon and follow the shaded path about 1km to the dramatic **Tat Somphamit** waterfalls, also known as Li Phi Falls, which means 'spirit trap', because locals believe bad spirits are trapped here as they wash downstream. Two travellers have drowned here, so be careful. There's a charge of 20,000K per day to cross the bridge, including entry to Tat Somphamit.

At the muscular **Khon Phapheng Falls** (admission 20,000K), millions of litres of water

GETTING TO CAMBODIA: DONG KALAW TO TRAPEANG KRIEL

This border crossing (open 7am to 5pm) was once the subject of much confusion – it had two different entry points, road and river – but now we're glad to report it's much more straightforward, with only one road crossing. Thirty-day visas are issued for around US$35 (depending on what passport you hold) without a hitch on both sides. The route south goes to Stung Treng in Cambodia. Many travellers en route from the Four Thousand Islands take a minibus to Stung Treng (US$8, three hours), Kratie (US$13, five hours), Ban Lung in Ratanakiri Province (US$11, six hours), or Phnom Penh (US$18, 11 hours). If you're heading north to the islands from Stung Treng, catching a minibus is a very straightforward affair.

For information on crossing in the other direction, see the boxed text, p238.

crash over the rocks and into Cambodia every second at the largest (by volume, not height) waterfall in Southeast Asia. The falls are often included on the itinerary of dolphin-viewing trips.

One-day **kayaking** and **rafting** trips (a group of two costs 180,000K per person) are also possible with Xplore-Asia (p350), based in Ban Hua Det. See p515 for information on water-borne parasites.

Sleeping

Electricity has just arrived on the islands, heralding fan-cooled nights – imagine how infernal it was before! Accommodation on Det's Sunrise Boulevard varies from decent to uberbasic. It's claustrophobic, crowded and noisy, but if you want to keep the party going (at least till the 11pm curfew) this is the place for you.

Increasingly, digs are becoming more upmarket further south and on sedate Don Khon. Boatmen will drop you near your chosen guesthouse – saving you a walk – if you insist.

TOP CHOICE Little Eden Guest House GUESTHOUSE $$
(☎020 7773 9045; www.littleedenguesthouse-dondet.com; Ban Hua Det, Don Det; bungalows 220,000-260,000K; ❄📶) Little Eden is set in lush gardens of sugar palms and betel trees, on the northern tip of the island. Fragrant rooms have cool, tiled floors, optional air-con and modern furnishings. The restaurant is the perfect place to watch the sun setting over Cambodia over a frappé. You can also get cash advances on your credit card for a 5% commission charge.

TOP CHOICE Auberge Sala Don Khone GUESTHOUSE $$
(☎260940; www.salalao.com; Don Khon; r incl breakfast US$55-65) This handsomely renovated villa delights with trompe l'œil floor tiles, four-poster beds and art deco signatured rooms. In a word, they're beautiful. Outside are new A-frame bungalows built in the classic Lao style with ambient-lit, minimalist interiors. Don't miss the floating Lao restaurant either, with its range of vegie dishes, delicious soups and various fish incarnations. Nothing beats a sunset drink here watching the light cast its amber net over the Mekong.

Seng Ahloune Guest House & Restaurant GUESTHOUSE $$
(☎260934; Don Khon; r US$35-50) Beautifully appointed bungalows right next to the bridge, with cream-white rattan walls, pink mosquito nets, wood floors and ornate lamps adding interior flair. Its restaurant, Mekong De Fleur (meals 30,000K), is a fine place for a sundowner. Salads, fried fish, and chicken and ginger are but a few of the dishes on offer.

Don Dhet Bungalows GUESTHOUSE $
(☎020 7772 1572; Sunrise Blvd, Don Det; bungalows 130,000K) Vastly superior new bungalows set back from the river with unimpaired sunrise views. The floors are varnished wood, the colourful bedspreads fragrant, and there's a lively restaurant over the way with *de rigeur* reclining cushions and an elevated decked area.

Souksan Guest House GUESTHOUSE $
(☎020 5469 0168; Sunrise Blvd, Ban Hua Det, Don Det; bungalows 60,000-70,000K) Nestled around a leafy courtyard bursting with mango trees and butterflies, Souksan's basic en-suite bungalows are immaculate and fan-cooled. The restaurant may have diminished but the helpful manager can assist you with forward travel.

Pan's Guesthouse & Restaurant GUESTHOUSE $$
(☎020 4463 1437; Don Khon; r 100,000-250,000K; @✱) A range of soporific bungalows finished in stained wood with rattan interiors, pebble-floor showers, immaculate en suites and balconies slung with hammocks. All rooms have fans or optional air-con. Try for a new one fronting the river, then sample Pan's excellent cafe (mains 20,000K) over the road.

Santiphab Guesthouse GUESTHOUSE $
(☎020 5461 4231; Don Det; r 40,000-80,000K) This old trusty by the bridge has much-improved bungalows with basic interiors and en suites, but the real draw is the unbroken view of the bridge and river. The homely cafe offers everything from fried Western breakfasts to *làap*.

Sengthavan Guesthouse & Restaurant GUESTHOUSE $
(☎020 5613 2696; Sunset Blvd, Ban Hua Det, Don Det; r 80,000K) Probably the best 'Sunset' side has to offer in the budget range, its en-suite rooms are fastidiously clean and enjoy uncluttered balcony views of Cambodia. Its low-key cafe has recliner cushions, checked-cloth tables and a Lao menu.

River Garden GUESTHOUSE $
(☎020 7770 1860; near old bridge, Don Det; r 50,000-80,000K) Gay-friendly River is house-proud, its pristine cabanas enjoying fine river views. There's also a Western and Laotian restaurant (mains 35,000K) hung with Buddha paintings, plus a shaded sun terrace on which to read.

Mekong Dream Guesthouse GUESTHOUSE $
(near old bridge, Don Det; r 40,000-60,000K) Four basic rooms with fan and en suites; the hammock lounge facing the French Bridge is the perfect statement of relaxation. The Lao-accented menu is pretty attractive too, with fried or barbecued fish (mains 25,000K).

Mr Phao's Riverview Guesthouse GUESTHOUSE $
(☎020 5656 9651; near old bridge, Don Det; r 30,000-60,000K) Sturdy stilted cabanas with en suites, wood floors, hammock-strung verandahs (boasting serene views) and a colourful cafe out front.

✖ Eating & Drinking

Establishments open for breakfast early, and close anytime around 11pm – some a little later.

TOP CHOICE **Little Eden Restaurant** WESTERN $$
(www.littleedenguesthouse-dondet.com; Ban Hua Det, Don Det; mains 60,000K; ✱📶) Catching the breeze from the tip of the island, Little Eden lives up to its name and is one of the best places to eat upmarket Laotian and Western cuisine. Owner Matt Verborg is a professional chef and his eclectic menu features tender *steak au poivre*, fillet of catfish, spaghetti carbonara and stir-fried fish with chilli, to name a few. Perfection.

Jasmine Restaurant INDIAN $
(Sunrise Blvd, Ban Hua Det, Don Det; meals 25,000K) Sister of the excellent Jasmine in Pakse, this fan-cooled eatery is hugely popular thanks to its central location and excellent Malaysian and Indian grub. All the usual suspects on offer, but irritatingly slow service.

Chanthounma's Restaurant LAOTIAN $
(Don Khon; mains 20,000K) This tumbledown long-timer has dished up its tasty spring rolls, papaya salads and vegie options to happy travellers for years. Fastidiously clean and friendly service thanks to Mama Chanthounma.

PARADISE RETAINED!

Don Det has distanced itself from its stoner image by cultivating a range of activities such as cycling and kayaking; despite bleak forecasts it hasn't become a Vang Vieng-type casualty and you're more likely to see travellers fishing with locals than buying joints from them. Villagers are grateful for your trade and there's a few things you can do to keep the smiles genuine and your footprint positive. If you do partake of a little spliff, be subtle. Also, the beach on Ban Hua Det has become a cool spot for sunbathing and nightly bonfires, but make sure you pick up your cigarette butts and litter here, even if the locals don't seem to bother. And finally: girls, the village chief has asked you to keep more than just a bikini on around the island – it's a pain because it's hot, but the Lao find it culturally offensive. Here endeth the tropical sermon.

Anny Restaurant LAOTIAN $

(Don Khon; mains 30,000K) Just after Chanthounma's, this is essentially a high-ceilinged wooden shack: nice and breezy. Its menu comprises fried rice dishes, stir-fries, seafood and steak. Especially tempting by night.

Streetview Café Bar BAR $

(Sunrise Blvd, Ban Hua Det, Don Det; meals 25,000K) Piping out decent rock and roll, this shadowy hole-in-the-wall has a few tables and chairs and an inviting bar turning out shooters, beer and cocktails. Thanks to its baker owner there are some scrumptious munchies antidotes such as cinnamon buns, doughnuts and chocolate and carrot cakes.

Pool Bar BAR

(Ban Hua Det, Don Det) Near the boat landing and Souksan Guest House, this traveller magnet is a cool place to meet others, play pool (surprise, surprise) and find a second-hand book to read. About as busy as it gets.

Information

You'll find a few internet services by the boat landing in Ban Hua Det (400K per minute). There's no bank here, so stock up on funds before you leave Pakse or else head to Little Eden Guesthouse on Don Det and ask for a cash advance on your card (5% commission charge). There's no post office either.

Xplore-Asia (☎212893; www.xplore-asia.com; Ban Hua Det) offers kayaking, rafting and forward travel to Pakse as well as Cambodian destinations (Kratie, Stung Treng, Phnom Penh and Siem Reap), while **Happy Island Tours** (☎020 267 7698; Ban Hua Det), run by Boun, takes its kayaking seriously, with solid kit and one-day trips down grade-2 to grade-3 rapids. Finally, Souksan Guest House can organise one-day fishing trips (a two-person group costs 100,000K per person) with locals using traditional nets. You get to barbecue your catch on a beach and swim.

Getting There & Away

Boats regularly leave Don Det for Ban Nakasang (30,000K per boat, 15,000K per person). Boats for Don Khong leave according to demand, though you're looking at an extortionate price of 200,000K per boat. For the same price, Little Eden (p348) will also bring you back. Boats can be hired to go anywhere in the immediate islands for about 100,000K an hour.

For Pakse (60,000K, 2½ to three hours, 148km), buses or *sǒrngtǎaou* leave Ban Nakasang at 6am, 8am, 9am and 10am. See p342 for buses from Pakse. **Wonderfull Tours** (☎020 5570 5173; Ban Hua Det, Don Det) organises daily VIP buses to Stung Treng (US$6), Ban Lung (US$6), Kratie (US$13), Phnom Penh (US$13) and Siem Reap (US$20) in Cambodia, all of which leave at 9am from the other side of the river. Buses to Vietnam leave at 11.30am and include Dong Ha ((260,000K), Hué (220,000K) and Danang (260,000K).

BOLAVEN PLATEAU

This beautiful landscape of lush forests, rivers, waterfalls and lavender-hued mountains is Laos' principal coffee-growing region. Back in the 19th century the French, looking to maximise the yield of their colony, decided the fertile soil on the 1000m Bolaven Plateau (Phu Phieng Bolaven in Lao) merited being turned into coffee plantations, and enjoying a frothy cappuccino in nearby Pakse, you'll be very glad they did.

The plateau is a centre for several Mon-Khmer ethnic groups, including the Alak, Laven (Bolaven means 'land of the Laven'), Ta-oy, Suay and Katu. The Alak and Katu are known for a water-buffalo sacrifice they perform yearly, usually on a full moon in March. But the main draw are the plateau's several spectacular waterfalls, including the dramatic twin cascades of **Tat Fan**, a few kilometres west of **Paksong**. The **Tad Fane Resort** (☎020 555 31400; www.tadfane.com; r incl breakfast US$27-30) has tastefully finished, vegetation-crowded log cabanas overlooking the falls. It offers short treks to the top of the waterfall (US$5), but don't attempt this after rain as the near-vertical muddy slopes are lethal.

TAT LO

☎034

Something of a traveller's secret, about 90km from Pakse on the Salavan road (Rte 20), secluded Tat Lo is a wide waterfall with mint-green pools to swim in. On a baking-hot day it's paradise as you cool off in the icy shallows accompanied by the chirrup of local kids. Accommodation varies from basic and forgettable cabanas to really atmospheric digs at affordable prices. This is a place to chill and best enjoyed on an overnight visit by scooter from Pakse, giving you the scope to explore the surrounding area. Speak to Bah, the friendly owner of Palamy Guest House, about half-day treks (45,000K per person) to see three nearby waterfalls on the plateau.

The nearest cascade to town is **Tat Hang**, which can be seen from the bridge, while **Tat Lo** itself is about 700m upriver via a path leading through Saise Guest House.

The spectacular third cascade is **Tat Suong**, about 10km from town and best reached by motorbike or bicycle – get directions from Bah.

Sleeping & Eating

The village is a one-street affair, with most accommodation either side of the bridge (budget places are concentrated on the east side). The best cuisine, not surprisingly, is found at the more upmarket resorts.

TOP CHOICE Tad Lo Lodge HOTEL $$
(☎211885; r US$40-57; ✿) Situated above the falls with an Edenic view of the teal-green river, this is a slice of style just where you need it. The main building is finished in traditional Lao style, with parquet floors and Buddha statuary. The menu comprises dishes such as fried pork chop to grilled Mekong fish and steaks (mains 45,000K). Rooms are stylish, with some new bungalows over the river. Elephant treks from here run at 8am, 10pm, 1pm and 3pm (100,000K per person).

Palamy Guest House & Restaurant GUESTHOUSE $
(r 30,000-60,000K) Overlooking a pretty meadow out back, the better rooms have mosquito nets, terraces with tables, and in some cases, fridges. The cheaper cabanas have shared bathrooms. Management is friendly and also rents scooters (70,000K per day) and bikes (15,000K per day). Internet is 2000K per 10 minutes – though you need your own laptop – and there's a communal dinner.

Saise Guest House & Restaurant HOTEL $
(☎/fax 211886; r 60,000-150,000K) Right beside the bottom of the falls, this is a soothing place to stop. There's a range of bungalows, the cheapest being at the back, away from the cascades. All are comfortable and good value. Meanwhile, its restaurant is almost in the water and has a simple menu of stir-fries, salads and various fish incarnations (mains 40,000K).

Tim Guesthouse & Restaurant GUESTHOUSE $
(☎211885; soulideth@gmail.com; r 40,000-60,000K; ✿) Tim's has seven rooms – all of which are basic. The gardens have become cramped with new cabanas being built. That said, there's a nice cafe plus an adjoining internet room (30,000K per hour), and if – and only if – you're staying here, the owner is full of ideas for making the most of your trip.

Getting There & Away

Just say 'Tat Lo' at Pakse's southern bus station and you'll be pointed to one of the several morning buses to Salavan that stop at Ban Khoua Set. Regular buses in the morning run from Pakse to Ban Khoua Set (25,000K, two hours) and from Pakse to Paksong (25,000K, 1½ hours). It's 1.8km to Tat Lo from Ban Khoua Set. To Paksong, get yourself up to Ban Beng, at the junction, and jump on a bus coming through from Salavan.

UNDERSTAND LAOS

Laos Today

Up until 2008 it was all going extremely well. Correction – throughout the early part of '08 it was still going well, with record figures of visitors catching the buzz about this little nation switched on to responsible eco-tourism. Not to mention the hydroelectric power dams, newly built and ready to roll; the copper and gold mining concessions, the largely foreign investors keen to climb into bed with Laos' natural resources. Then the economic axe fell on the US and those sub-prime mortgages started impacting on every

GETTING TO VIETNAM: PHOU KEUA TO BO Y

In far southeastern Attapeu Province, a border with Vietnam links Phou Keua to Bo Y. Lao visas are issued on entry but Vietnamese visas must be obtained in advance (Pakse, Vientiane and Phnom Penh are your best bet; US$40 same day). It's 113km southeast of attractive Attapeu town, where there are several guesthouses. Transport is sketchy, but at least three Vietnamese-run buses are operating each week from Attapeu to Pleiku via Kon Tum (118,000K, 12 hours). Buses depart Attapeu 8am Monday, Wednesday and Friday, and come the other way on Tuesday, Thursday and Saturday. Tickets are sold in Attapeu at the Thi Thi Restaurant west of the bridge. For information on crossing this border in the other direction, see p115.

aspect of Laos' attempt to escape its hated status as one of the 20 poorest nations by 2020. Suddenly the foreign investors pulled out, because of their own lack of liquidity; mining concessions collapsed as the price of copper was slashed…even the garment factories newly opened had to lay off most of their workers. Through no fault of its own Laos looked to be heading back to the dark days of stagnation.

Times haven't been easy, but they could have been worse – despite global gloom, by 2010 Laos was back on track with a GDP of 7.7%. And now as China flourishes, Laos is reaping the rewards of its close association as a crossroads state. And China, ever the opportunist, has moved in with celerity to grab what it can in return for improving transport infrastructure. Běijīng's multibillion-dollar rail investment in a Southeast Asian rail network, due to be finished in 2014, will connect the red giant with countries as far afield as Pakistan, India and Singapore, and to achieve this it will be passing directly through Laos. Rte 3, from Kūnmíng to Vientiane, via Luang Prabang, should be ready by 2014. It's predicted that in the next 10 years you'll be able to travel at speeds of up to 400km/h through this beautiful green nation. How this will impact on this sleepy country is anyone's guess, but all the more reason for your well-timed visit right now.

History

From the early Khmer influence around Wat Phu in southern Laos, right up to the present day, the people living in what we now know as Laos have mainly been reacting to the politics and aspirations of more-powerful neighbours in Cambodia, Vietnam, Thailand and China. Even its first taste of nationhood, with the rise of the Lan Xang kingdom, was achieved thanks to Khmer military muscle.

Kingdom of Lan Xang

Before the French, British, Chinese and Siamese drew a line around it, Laos was a collection of disparate principalities subject to an ever-revolving cycle of war, invasion, prosperity and decay.

In the 14th century a Khmer-backed Lao warlord named Chao Fa Ngum conquered Viang Chan (Vientiane), Xieng Khuang and Muang Sawa (Luang Prabang). Declaring himself sovereign over the kingdom of Lan Xang (Land of a Million Elephants), he also made Theravada Buddhism the state religion and adopted the symbol of Lao sovereignty that remains in use today – the Pha Bang Buddha image, after which Luang Prabang is named. Within 20 years, Lan Xang had expanded to the Annamite Chain in Vietnam and east to Champa, relentlessly driven by Fa Ngum's warlike preoccupation. His son, King Samsenthai, was a little more tranquil; under his rule the country developed into an important trade centre, reaching its peak in the 17th century, when it was briefly the dominant force in Southeast Asia.

By the 18th century though, Lan Xang had crumbled, falling under the control of the Siamese, who coveted much of modern-day Laos as a buffer zone against the expansionist French. Any hope of a restoration of Lao power was savagely crushed in 1828, when the Siamese put down a rebellion led by Lao king Chao Anou by razing Vientiane to the ground and carting off most of the population.

The French

After taking over Annam and Tonkin (modern-day Vietnam) in 1883, the French negotiated with Siam to relinquish its territory east of the Mekong; Laos was thus born and absorbed into French Indochina.

The country's diverse ethnic make-up and short history as a nation state meant nationalism was slow to form. The first nationalist movement, the Lao Issara (Free Lao), was created to prevent the country's return to French rule after the invading Japanese left at the end of WWII. In 1953, without any regard for the Lao Issara, sovereignty was granted to Laos by the French. Internecine struggles followed with the Pathet Lao (Country of the Lao) army forming an alliance with the Vietnamese Viet Minh (which had also been opposing French rule in its own country). Laos was set to become a stage on which the clash of communist ambition and US anxiety over the perceived Southeast Asian 'domino effect' played itself out.

The Secret War

In 1954 at the Geneva Conference, Laos had been declared a neutral nation; as such neither Vietnamese nor US forces could cross its borders. Thus began a game of cat and mouse as a multitude of Central Intelligence Agency (CIA) operatives secretly entered the country to train anticommunist Hmong fighters in the jungle (see boxed text, p311). From 1964 to 1973, the US, in response to the Viet Minh funnelling massive amounts of war munitions down the Ho Chi Minh Trail, devastated eastern and northeastern Laos with nonstop carpet-bombing (reportedly, a planeload of ordnance was dropped every eight minutes). The intensive campaign exacerbated the war between the Pathet Lao and US-backed Royal Lao Army and, if anything, intensified domestic support for the communists.

The US withdrawal in 1973 saw Laos divided up between Pathet Lao and non-Pathet Lao, but within two years the communists had taken over completely and the Lao People's Democratic Republic (PDR) was created under the leadership of Kaysone Phomvihane.

Around 10% of Laos' population fled, mostly into Thailand. The remaining opponents of the government – notably tribes of Hmong who fought with and were funded by the CIA – were suppressed or sent to re-education camps for indeterminate periods. It's alleged that two of these camps still endure in the far north, though this is hotly denied.

A New Start

Since the 1980s, socialism, following its rather unsuccessful attempt to flourish, has been softened to allow for private enterprise and foreign investment. Laos has successfully reinvented itself as the crossroads state between China, Thailand and Vietnam. Following the 2008 global recession, which badly affected Laos, the country's annual GDP is back to a healthy 7% to 8%, keeping Laos on track to escape its hated status as one of the world's 20 poorest nations by 2020. Laos' hydroelectric power endeavours are now beginning to bear fruit and the country is being considered for entry into the World Trade Organization, so things are definitely improving. In 2011 Laos implemented its first ever stock exchange in Vientiane.

China has become Laos' new best friend as it muscles in on the country's rich timber resources (see p298). In return for its building stadiums and improved sealed highways, Laos allows the red giant carte blanche. A huge area of land in Vientiane has been leased to the Chinese to allow 50,000 migrant workers to come and settle in a satellite town in coming years.

Politically, the Party (Laos has been a one-party state since 1975) remains firmly in control, and with patrons such as one-party China and Vietnam, there seems little incentive for Laos to move towards any meaningful form of democracy. The 35-year-long Hmong 'insurgency' has seen thousands of guerrillas reduced to a few hundred and forced into the upper reaches of Xaisomboun District. Most have now surrendered, emerging from the jungle as ragged protagonists in a war almost forgotten. This formerly forbidden and beautiful area is tipped to become a popular adventure playground.

Culture

People & Population

As many as 132 ethnic groups comprise the people of Laos (see p479 for more). Sixty per cent of these people are Lao Loum (lowland Lao); they have the most in common with their Thai neighbours, and it's their cultural beliefs and way of life that are known as 'Lao culture'. The remainder are labelled according to the altitude their groups live at: Lao Thai (living in valleys up to an altitude of 400m, composed of Black Thai and White Thai); Lao Thoeng (midlevel mountain slopes, including Khamu, Lamet and Alak); and Lao Soung (living 1000m or more above sea level, including the Hmong, Mien and Akha).

Trying to homogenise the people and psyche of Laos is precarious, as the country is really a patchwork of different beliefs, ranging from animism to the prevailing presence of Theravada Buddhism, and often both combined. But certainly there's a commonality in the laid-back attitude you'll encounter. Some of this can be ascribed to Buddhism, with its emphasis on controlling extreme emotions by keeping *jai yen* (cool heart) and making merit, ie doing good in order to receive good. But the rest is a Lao phenomenon. Thus you'll rarely hear a heated argument, and can expect a level of kindness unpractised to such a national degree in neighbouring countries.

The Lao are very good at enjoying the 'now', and they do this with a mixture of the *baw pen nyăng* (no problem) mentality and a devotion to *múan* (fun). If a job is *baw múan* (no fun), it is swiftly abandoned in pursuit of another, even if it means less income. *Kamma* (karma), more than devotion, prayer or hard work, is believed to determine

SPIRITS ARE YOU THERE?

The life of a Lao person involves a complex appeasement of spirits through a carousel of sacrifices and rituals designed to protect the supplicant and engender health and fortune. The *phī hēuan* (good spirits) represent both the guardian spirits of the house and ancestral spirits. In order to promote domestic happiness they're fed with Pepsi, and come crisis time it's their job to recalibrate the troubled household.

In the backyard or garden, you'll often see what look like miniature ornamental temples, the *pha phum* (spirits of the land). Their task is to protect the grounds from any malignant spirits – for in Laos the air is thick with them. Before anything is built within their grounds, offerings must be made and permission granted. The same goes for a tree that must be knocked down to make way for a bridge, a field before a harvest and so on – it's an endless animistic communion between the seen and unseen, the prosaic and the spiritual.

If ghosted by bad luck, you may have to consult a *mŏw phī* (shaman), who will place himself in a trance to mediate between you and the bad spirit. Payment might be made in eggs or chickens and is refundable if your *kwăn* (guardian spirit of the body) doesn't enjoy a rapid recovery. The Lao soul is composed of 32 components, each protecting various body organs and mental faculties. In order to prevent a weak link straying, propelling the person's body into chaos, the *sukwăn* ('calling of the soul') ritual is practised. It involves binding the *kwăn* by tying little threads to a person's wrist, which are then worn for three days. The *sukwăn* ritual also strengthens the collective wellbeing of a community.

one's lot in life, so the Lao tend not to get too worked up over the future.

Government spending on education amounts to 11.7% of public spending. Education has improved in recent years, with school enrolment rates at 85%, though many drop out by the time they reach secondary education – the planting and harvesting of crops, especially among the highlands, is seen as more important than education, as the whole family is involved.

Opium & Yaa Baa (Methamphetamine)

Up until the introduction of the anti-opium program in 2001, Laos was estimated to be producing most of the world's opium. This mantle was passed on to Afghanistan, yet in many mountainous regions of northern Laos – far from the reach of doctors – opium is grown as a medicinal drug or painkiller and used by many tribes. Given its prime location in the heart of the Golden Triangle it's understandable that Laos has often been a pawn and facilitator in the trafficking of drugs intended for the West, with even US involvement during the Secret War making a profit from opium cultivation.

In 2008 CIA reports based on satellite images suggested opium production had increased by an alarming 78%, however the trafficking of *yaa baa* (methamphetamine) gives much more pause for concern. Ethnic Wa (a minority group from Myanmar) warlords have been establishing themselves on the banks of the Mekong in northwestern Laos. For corrupt officials willing to be turned by huge payoffs, there's big money to be made for turning a blind eye and allowing the production and transit of the drug as it is moved through the country to Cambodia, Vietnam and Thailand for international shipment.

Finally, an alleged five amphetamine factories have gone into production in Laos since the Thai police drove them out from the Thailand and Myanmar borders back in 2001. That said, unless you go poking around it won't affect you; the closest encounter with narcotics you can expect is the offer of pot from a cabbie in Vientiane, or a rock of opium from an old Hmong lady in Muang Sing.

Religion

Most lowland Lao are Theravada Buddhists and many Lao males choose to be ordained temporarily as monks, typically spending anywhere from a month to three years at a wat. Indeed, a young man is not considered 'ripe' until he has completed his spiritual term. After the 1975 communist victory, Buddhism was suppressed, but it soon became clear its religious omnipresence was too strong and by 1992 the government relented. However, monks are still forbidden to promote *phī* (spirit) worship, which has been officially banned in Laos along with *sǎiyasàht* (folk magic).

Despite the ban, *phī* worship remains the dominant non-Buddhist belief system. Even in Vientiane, Lao citizens openly perform the ceremony called *sukwǎn* ('calling of the soul') or *bąsī*, in which the 32 *kwǎn* (guardian spirits of the body) are bound to the guest of honour by white strings tied around the wrists.

Outside the Mekong River valley, the *phī* cult is particularly strong among tribal Thai. *Mŏr* (priests) who are trained to appease and exorcise troublesome spirits preside at important festivals and other ceremonies. The Khamu, Hmong and Mien tribes also practise animism.

Arts & Architecture

The true expression of Lao art is found in its religious sculpture, temples and handicrafts. Distinctively Lao is the Calling for Rain Buddha, a standing image with hands held rigidly at his sides. Similarly widespread is the Contemplating the Bodhi Tree Buddha, with crossed hands at the front.

Wats in Luang Prabang feature *sǐm* (chapels), with steep, low roofs. The typical Lao *thât* (stupa) is a four-sided, curvilinear, spirelike structure. There are also hints of classical architectural motifs entering modern architecture, as with Vientiane's Wattay International Airport.

Many of the beautiful villas from the days of Indochina were torn down by the new regime in favour of harsh Soviet designs, though fortunately there are plenty of villas left, with their distinctive shuttered windows and classic French provincial style.

Traditional Lao art has a more limited range than that of its Southeast Asian neighbours, partly because Laos has a more modest history as a nation state and partly because its neighbours have stolen or burnt what art did exist.

Upland crafts include gold- and silversmithing among the Hmong and Mien tribes, and tribal Thai weaving (especially among the Thai Dam and Thai Lü). Classical music and dance have all but evaporated, partly due to the vapid tentacles of Thai pop and itinerant nature of Laos' young workforce.

Environment

Deforestation & Hydroelectric Power

With a land mass of 236,000 sq km, Laos is a little larger than the UK, and thanks to its relatively small population and mountainous terrain, it's one of the least altered environments in Southeast Asia. Unmanaged vegetation covers an estimated 85% of the country, and 10% of Laos is original-growth forest with some of the most varied and best-preserved ecosystems in Southeast Asia. A hundred years ago this last statistic was nearer 75%, which provides a clear idea of the detrimental effects of relentless logging and slash-and-burn farming. The government has clear targets to raise the level of forestation to 70% by 2020 – massively optimistic perhaps, but thanks to the encouraged (some say forced) relocation to lowland ground of tribes practising slash-and-burn farming, there's a possibility the land may have a chance to regenerate – at least a little.

Sadly, the same can't be said of areas like Attapeu Province, which has fallen victim to rampant commercial logging since 2005. Once home to dense forests, this Vietnam-bordering province is now denuded in huge areas like a lunar landscape. Just a decade ago Attapeu's remote village of Tahoy was home to a healthy population of tigers; by night you could allegedly hear them roaring at the edge of the forest. The only thing you're likely to see these days are trucks laden with rare timber openly heading over the border into Thailand. And while the flooding of lowland forests can be partly justified for the national goal of creating dams for hydroelectric power and the subsequent wealth it will bring the country (the World Bank estimated that sales of Lao hydropower to Thailand alone could be around US$2 billion per year once new dams like Nam Theun 2 are operating to full capacity), the same can't be said for logging Attapeu so fiercly. Ironically, furniture makers in Vientiane often complain that they have to buy Lao wood from Thais.

The problem Laos faces always comes down to 'needs must feed the devil' dilemmas. For example, the Laos army is self-funded, which can often lead to it making questionable decisions when it comes to granting logging licences and clearing roads as firebreaks rather over-enthusiastically, with ancient hardwood trees mysteriously disappearing into Vietnam-bound trucks (and their proceeds into army coffers).

The government's long-term economic goals tend to take precedence over the environment, and despite its pledge to retain the country's natural riches by creating 20 National Protected Areas (NPAs), it continues to sacrifice swaths of its land to the industrial logging requirements of China. The ecosystem of the Mekong River is also being disrupted by China, which is predicted to build some 20 dams on its own stretch of the Mekong over the next 20 years.

On the bright side, an estimated half of the country's revenue is generated by tourists (1.3 million visitors in 2008 was its best year yet until the global recession), which gives the landscape a limited insurance policy. The protection of its forests is also written into the responsibilities of Laos' constitution. With an internationally created blueprint to monitor and increase ecotourism, there may be some hope for these wild places. And if the country can keep its industrial ambitions in line with its delicate ecosystem, there is a chance Laos will achieve the economic independence it yearns for without squandering its natural heritage. But profit will always take precedence over well-meaning eco-pressure groups and green-minded trends, and should the tourists stop coming Laos' forests will be the first thing to be sacrificed to industry.

Wildlife

Laos is home to wild elephants, jackals, Asiatic black bears, black-crested gibbons, langurs, Asian elephants, leopards, tigers, pythons, king cobras, 437 kinds of bird and the rare Irrawaddy dolphin – to name a few! Driven by neighbours – particularly China – that seek body parts of endangered animals for traditional medicine and aphrodisiac purposes, the wildlife trade is flourishing. It's difficult for a father of five living in a forest to turn down a year's wages for killing a tiger, just as it is difficult to police poachers. In certain circumstances an altogether more revolutionary approach needs to be taken, as in the case of the Gibbon Experience (see p327), where former poachers are encouraged to make more money as guides and forest rangers. However, compared with Vietnam and Thailand – much of which is now deforested, urbanised and farmed – the wildlife in Laos is a veritable hothouse of biodiversity.

Thanks to some excellent environmentally responsible treks run in a number of Laos' 20 NPAs, there's a chance you'll come into contact with some of Laos' abundant wildlife; be it from the safety of a tree house or possibly closer contact still (though hopefully not with one of its big cats, as was the case with one of our authors!). Here's a guide to some of the more charismatic, endangered animals you might meet or hear.

ASIAN TIGER

Historically, hundreds of thousands of tigers populated Asia, yet today there may be as few as 3000 left in the entire world, and occupying a mere 7% of their original range. The survivors in Laos face a constant threat of poaching, habitat loss and conflict with humans. The NPAs in the northeast of Laos with deep, intractable forest are thought to harbour the densest populations. During your trek, look out for tiger scat and deep scratch marks on the trunks of trees. And should you hear one, it's louder and more resonant than a church organ.

MEKONG CATFISH

Growing up to 3m in length and weighing in at 300kg, the world's largest freshwater fish is unique to the Mekong River. Over the past 10 years or so their numbers have dropped an astonishing 90% due to over-fishing, but more pointedly, due to the building of hydroelectric dams that block their migratory paths. There may only be a few hundred left.

IRRAWADDY DOLPHIN

Beak-nosed and less extrovert than its bottlenose counterparts, this shy and critically endangered mammal inhabits a 190km stretch of the Mekong River between Cambodia and Laos. Recent estimates suggest between 64 and 76 members still survive. The best place to see them in Laos is off the southern tip of Don Khon, where a small pod congregates in a deepwater pool. Gill-net fishing and pollution have wiped out their numbers. During their short reign in the late 1970s, the Khmer Rouge used to dynamite them indiscriminately.

BLACK-CRESTED GIBBON

The jungle's answer to Usain Bolt racing through the canopy is an awesome, majestic sight. These heavily poached, soulful apes sing with beautiful voices – usually at dawn – which echo hauntingly around the forest.

Males are black and females golden, and in Laos, only exist in Bokeo Province, home of the Gibbon Experience. The black-crested gibbon is one of the world's rarest, most endangered species of gibbon.

SURVIVAL GUIDE

Directory A–Z

Accommodation

Since the borders opened to foreigners in the early 1990s, guesthouses have been steadily multiplying, and most villages that merit a visit will have some form of accommodation. In cities such as Vientiane and Luang Prabang, prices vary wildly, with some truly exceptional boutique hotels that could excite even the most jaded *New York Times* or *Hip Hotels* editor. At the other end of the scale, budget digs – usually a room with a fan and sometimes an en suite – are getting better every year. Even though guesthouse prices are rising, they're still unbeatable value when compared with the West; at less than 80,000K (about US$10) a night, who can argue? The cheapest accommodation is in the far north and deepest south.

Accommodation prices listed in this chapter are for the high season, for rooms with attached bathroom, unless stated otherwise. An icon (❄) is included to indicate if air-con is available; otherwise assume a fan will be provided. In this chapter, the budget breakdown is: budget ($), less than 160,000K (about US$20); midrange ($$), 160,000K (about US$20) to 660,000K (about US$80); and top end ($$$), 660,000K (about US$80) and above.

HOMESTAYS

For more than 75% of Laotians, the 'real Laos' is life in a village. Minority people in villages across the country now welcome travellers into their homes to experience life Lao-style. This means sleeping, eating and washing as they do. It's not luxury – the mattress will be on the floor and you'll 'shower' by pouring water over yourself from a 44-gallon (170L) drum while standing in the middle of the yard (men and women should take a sarong). But it's exactly this level of immersion that makes a homestay so worthwhile. It's also good to know that the 50,000K you'll pay for bed, dinner and breakfast is going directly to those who need it most.

If you're up for it, remember to pack a sarong, torch, thongs (flip-flops) or sandals, a phrasebook and some photos from home. If you can, gift a children's book from one of the many Big Brother Mouse outlets (see p304).

Activities

CYCLING

With cyclists bringing their own specialised bikes over the border without a hitch, cycling in Laos is becoming an increasingly appropriate way to see the country – leisurely transport for a languid country. Given the low population, Laos' roads are uncongested and many are now sealed, though post-monsoon there are myriad potholes in the best of them. If drivers see you in trouble, they are more than likely to stop and help or give you a lift. Alternatively, should some of those mountains become too back-breaking, just flag down a passing bus or *sǒrngtǎaou* (literally 'two rows'; a common name for small pick-up trucks with two benches in the back, used as buses/taxis). And – it goes without saying – always bring plenty of water with you.

Off-the-beaten-path places have pretty dire road surfaces, so bring plenty of inner tubes or stock up in Vientiane or Luang Prabang. During the monsoon, mud roads in places such as the Bolaven Plateau churn into a mire of mud.

In cities be careful about leaving bags in the front basket, as passing motorcyclists have been known to lift them and this seems to be happening more regularly, especially during festivals.

Several companies offer mountain-bike tours, particularly from Luang Nam Tha (see Boat Landing Guest House & Restaurant, p323) and Luang Prabang (see White Elephant, p304).

KAYAKING & RAFTING

Kayaking and white-water rafting have taken off and Laos has several world-class rapids, as well as lots of beautiful, although less challenging, waterways. Unfortunately, the industry remains dangerously unregulated and you should not go out on rapids during the wet season unless you are completely confident about your guides and equipment. Vang Vieng has the most options. **Green Discovery** (☎023-511230; www.greendiscoverylaos.com; Th Luang Prabang, Vang Vieng) has a good reputation, as does **Happy Island Tours** (☎020 267 7698; Ban Hua Det, Don Det).

LAOS IN WORDS

Lonely Planet's *Laos* has all the information you'll need for extended travel in Laos, with more detailed descriptions of sights and wider coverage to help get you off the beaten track.

» *A Dragon Apparent* (1951) Sees Norman Lewis travelling through the twilight of French Indochina, animating his subjects with atmosphere and pathos, as the colonies are about to be lost.

» *The Lao* (2008) Robert Cooper's locally published book (available in Vientiane) is a pithy yet frequently penetrating insight into Lao culture, its psyche and the practicalities of setting up here as an expat.

» *The Ravens: Pilots of the Secret War of Laos* (1987) Christopher Robbins' page-turning account of the Secret War and the role of American pilots and the Hmong is an excellent read.

» *Shooting at the Moon: The Story of America's Clandestine War in Laos* (1998) Roger Warner's well-respected book exposes the Secret War against the Ho Chi Minh Trail, and the CIA and Hmong role in it.

» *Stalking the Elephant Kings: In Search of Laos* (1998) by Christopher Kremmer Unravelling the mystery of the fate of Laos' last king, Savang Vatthana, and his subsequent exile and death in the Caves of Viengsai.

ROCK CLIMBING

Organised rock-climbing operations are run by **Green Discovery** (☎023-511230; www.greendiscoverylaos.com; Th Luang Prabang, Vang Vieng) and **Adam's Rock Climbing School** (☎020 5501 0832; www.laos-climbing.com; Th Luang Prabang, Vang Vieng) in the karst cliffs around Vang Vieng, while Green Discovery is the only real operator in Nong Khiaw. Vang Vieng has the most established scene, with dozens of climbs ranging from beginner to expert. Nong Khiaw is also gaining repute for its limestone ascents.

TREKKING

Where else can you wander through Kling-esque forests, past ethnic hill-tribe villages and rare wildlife, the triple canopy towering above you? Best of all, this is possible largely in a sustainable fashion, thanks to a blueprint drawn up by various international advisors that were determined to help Laos retain its natural wealth while harnessing its economic possibilities. Several environmentally and culturally sustainable tours have been developed, allowing you to enter these pristine areas and experience the lives of the indigenous people without exploiting them.

These treks are available in several provinces and are detailed on www.ecotourismlaos.com. You can plan to trek from Luang Nam Tha, Muang Sing, Oudomxay, Luang Prabang, Vientiane, Tha Khaek, Savannakhet and Pakse. Treks organised through the provincial tourism offices are the cheapest, while companies such as **Green Discovery** (www.greendiscoverylaos.com) offer more expensive and professional operations.

TUBING

Something of a Lao phenomenon, 'tubing' involves a huge tractor inner tube that carries you downriver. Climb in, sit back and tune out. But be mindful of how much you drink and what time it is. Vang Vieng is the tubing capital, with Muang Ngoi Neua and Si Phan Don popular runners-up; and when the Nam Ou river runs high and swift it's at its most dangerous, with at least one traveller a year losing their life to the river.

Business Hours

Government offices are typically open from 8am to 11.30am or noon, and 1pm to 4pm or 5pm, Monday to Friday. Banking hours are generally 8.30am to 4pm Monday to Friday. Shops have longer hours and are often open on weekends. Most businesses close Sunday, but not restaurants, which typically open early and close by 10pm or 11pm. Bars stay open until the officially mandated closing time of 11.30pm, sometimes a little later.

Customs Regulations

You can expect borders to be fairly sleepy affairs, and customs officers – so long as you're not carrying more than 500 cigarettes and 1L of spirits – are not too interested. If you're caught with drugs, knives or guns on your person, this may change very quickly.

Embassies & Consulates

Australia (Map p283; ☎021-353800; fax 021-353801; www.laos.embassy.gov.au; Th Tha Deua, Ban Wat Nak, Vientiane) Also represents nationals of Britain, Canada and New Zealand.

Cambodia (Map p283; ☎021-314952; fax 021-314951; Km 3, Th Tha Deua, Ban That Khao, Vientiane) Issues visas for US$20.

China (Map p283; ☎021-315105; fax 021-315104; Th Wat Nak Nyai, Ban Wat Nak, Vientiane) Issues visas in four working days.

France (Map p284; ☎021-215258/9; www.ambafrance-laos.org; Th Setthathirat, Ban Si Saket, Vientiane)

Germany (Map p283; ☎021-312111, 312110; Th Sok Pa Luang, Vientiane)

Myanmar (Map p283; ☎021-314910; Th Sok Pa Luang, Vientiane) Issues tourist visas in three days for US$20.

Thailand Vientiane embassy (Map p283; ☎021-214581; www.thaiembassy.org/vientiane; Th Kaysone Pomvihane, Vientiane; ⊙8.30am-noon & 1-3.30pm Mon-Fri) Savannakhet consulate (Map p336; ☎041-212373; cnr Th Tha He & Th Chaimeuang, Savannakhet) Vientiane consulate (Map p283; ☎021-214581; 15 Th Bourichane, Vientiane; ⊙8am-noon & 1-4.30pm) Head to the Vientiane consulate for visa renewals.

USA (Map p284; ☎021-267000; www.laos.usembassy.gov; Th Bartholomie, Vientiane)

Vietnam Vientiane embassy (Map p283; ☎021-413400; Th That Luang, Vientiane); Savannakhet consulate (Map p336; ☎041-212418; Th Sisavangvong, Savannakhet) Luang Prabang consulate (Map p299; Th Naviengkham, Luang Prabang) The embassy in Vientiane issues tourist visas in three working days (US$45) or while you wait (US$60). The consulate in Savannakhet issues a one-/three-month tourist visa for US$50/60 (one photo, three working days).

Food & Drink

FOOD

Lao cuisine lacks the variety of Thai food, but there are some distinctive dishes to try. The standard Lao breakfast is *fŏe* (rice noodles), usually served floating in a broth with vegetables and a meat of your choice. The trick is in the seasoning, and Lao people will stir in some fish sauce, lime juice, dried chillies, mint leaves, basil, or one of the wonderful speciality hot chilli sauces that many noodle shops make, testing it along the way.

Làap is the most distinctively Lao dish, a delicious spicy salad made from minced beef, pork, duck, fish or chicken, mixed with fish sauce, small shallots, mint leaves, lime juice, roasted ground rice and lots and lots of chillies. Another famous Lao speciality is *tąm màak hung* (known as *som tam* in Thailand), a salad of shredded green papaya mixed with garlic, lime juice, fish sauce, sometimes tomatoes, palm sugar, land crab or dried shrimp and, of course, chillies by the handful.

In lowland Lao areas almost every dish is eaten with *khào nĭaw* (sticky rice), which is served in a small basket. Take a small amount of rice and, using one hand, work it into a walnut-sized ball before dipping it into the food.

In main centres, delicious French baguettes are a popular breakfast food. Sometimes they're eaten with condensed milk, or with *khai* (eggs) in a sandwich that also contains Lao-style pâté and vegetables.

As an approximate guide, prices for main dishes when eating out are less than 40,000K (US$5) for budget places, 40,000K to 80,000K (US$5 to US$10) for midrange and more than 80,000K (US$10) for top-end places.

DRINK

Alcoholic Drinks

Beerlao remains a firm favourite with 90% of the nation, while officially illegal *lào-lâo* (Lao liquor, or rice whisky) is a popular drink among lowland Lao. It's usually taken neat and offered in villages as a wecoming gesture.

Nonalcoholic Drinks

Water purified for drinking purposes is simply called *nâam deum* (drinking water), whether it's boiled or filtered. All water offered to customers in restaurants or hotels will be purified, and purified water is sold everywhere. Having said that, do be careful of the water you drink – there was an outbreak of E.coli in 2008, so check the ice in your drink originated from a bottle.

Juice bars proliferate around Vientiane and Luang Prabang, and smoothies are usually on the menu in most Western-leaning cafes. Lao coffee is usually served strong and sweet. Thankfully, lattes and cappuccinos are springing up across the country with pasteurised milk coming from Thailand.

Chinese-style green tea is the usual ingredient in *nâam sáa* or *sáa láo* – the weak, refreshing tea traditionally served free in restaurants. If you want Lipton-style tea, ask for *sáa hâwn* (hot tea).

Gay & Lesbian Travellers

Laos has a liberal attitude towards homosexuality, but a very conservative attitude towards public displays of affection. Gay couples are unlikely to be given frosty treatment anywhere. Laos doesn't have an obvious gay scene, though Luang Prabang has Laos' first openly gay bar, Khob Chai (opposite Hive Bar), and has the rainbow-coloured gay pride flag flying in a few places around town.

Lesbians won't be bothered, but do expect some strange looks from Lao men.

Internet Access

You can now get internet access in all major towns for around 7000K per hour. Most internet cafes have air-con, fans and also Skype (some with cameras). Wi-fi is widely available in most upmarket bars, hotels and Western-style bakeries.

Legal Matters

There are virtually no legal services in Laos. If you get yourself in legal strife, contact your embassy in Vientiane, though the assistance it can provide may be limited. For Brits, contact your embassy in Bangkok.

It's against the law for foreigners and Lao to have sexual relations unless they're married. Travellers should be aware that a holiday romance could result in being arrested and deported.

Maps

The best all-purpose country map available is *Laos* by GT-Rider (http://gt-rider.com), a sturdy laminated affair with several city maps. Look for the 2005 edition or more recent ones.

Hobo Maps has produced a series of decent maps for Vientiane, Luang Prabang and Vang Vieng. These maps are widely available in the relevant destinations.

Money

Despite recent nationalistic attempts by the government to impose the Lao kip (K) more rigorously, US dollars and Thai baht are still widely accepted. At the time of research the US dollar was yielding a mere 8000K, but by the time you read this, it may have recovered and you'll possibly get cheaper rates than those quoted in this book.

ATMS

ATMs are now proliferating in the main cities, with many spread around Vientiane, Luang Prabang, Pakse, Vang Vieng, Luang Nam Tha, Phonsavan, Oudomxay, Huay Xai and Savannakhet. For a list of all the BCEL ATMs, try www.bcellaos.com/atm locator.php.

BARGAINING

With the exception of túk-túk drivers in Vientiane (who are a law unto themselves), most Lao are not looking to rip you off – it's not worth losing all that merit they've accrued. Take your time when haggling: start lower and gradually meet in the middle.

CASH

Kip notes come in denominations of 500, 1000, 2000, 5000, 10,000, 20,000 and 50,000K; the 50,000K note looks deceptively like the 20,000K note.

CREDIT CARDS

A number of hotels, upmarket restaurants and gift shops in Vientiane and Luang Prabang accept Visa and MasterCard, and to a much lesser extent Amex and JCB. Visa is most widely accepted. Banque pour le Commerce Extérieur Lao (BCEL) branches in Vientiane, Luang Prabang, Vang Vieng, Savannakhet and Pakse offer cash advances/withdrawals on Visa credit/debit cards for a 3% transaction fee.

MONEYCHANGERS

US dollars and Thai baht can be exchanged all over Laos. Banks in Vientiane and Luang Prabang – and in some provinces – change euro, Thai baht, UK pounds, Japanese yen, and Canadian, US and Australian dollars. US-dollar travellers cheques can be exchanged in most provincial capitals and usually attract a much better rate than cash.

Generally, the best overall exchange rate is usually offered by BCEL. In rural areas exchange rates can be significantly lower. For the latest rates check www.bcellaos.com

TRAVELLERS CHEQUES

Banks in most provincial capitals will exchange US-dollar travellers cheques. If you are changing cheques into kips, there is usually no commission, but changing into dollars attracts a minimum 2% charge.

Post

Postal services from Vientiane are generally reliable, from the provinces less so. If you have valuable items or presents to post home, there is a **Federal Express** (☎021-223278; ⊙8am-noon & 1-5pm Mon-Fri, 9am-noon Sat) office inside the main post office (Map p284) compound in Vientiane.

Public Holidays

Schools and government offices are closed on these official holidays, and the organs of state move pretty slowly, if at all, during festivals. Most Chinese- and Vietnamese-run businesses close for three days during Vietnamese Tet and Chinese New Year in February. International Women's Day is a holiday for women only.

International New Year 1 January

Army Day 20 January

International Women's Day 8 March

Lao New Year (Bun Pii Mai) 14-16 April

International Labour Day 1 May

International Children's Day 1 June

Bun Nam (Boat Racing Festival) Usually October

Bun Pha That Luang (Full Moon) Early November

Lao National Day 2 December

Safe Travel

Urban Laos is generally safe. You should still exercise vigilance at night, but thanks to the country's comparatively gentle psyche the likelihood of your being robbed, mugged, harassed or assaulted is much lower than in most Western countries. Since the 1975 revolution, there have been occasional shootings by Hmong guerrillas on Rte 13 between Vang Vieng and Luang Prabang, though it seems pacific at the moment and has been since 2003.

In the eastern provinces, particularly Xieng Khuang, Salavan and Savannakhet, UXO (unexploded ordnance) is a hazard. Never walk off well-used paths.

Finally, the transport infrastructure in Laos is barely recognisable compared with what existed just a few years ago. Huge, foreign-funded road construction projects have transformed a network of rough dirt tracks into comparatively luxurious sealed affairs.

Telephone

Laos' country code is ☎856. To dial out of the country press ☎00 first, or ask for the local mobile operator's cheaper code. For long-distance calls use a post office, Lao Telecom centre (rates vary in these, but in Vientiane are very reasonable) or internet cafes.

As a guide, all mobile-phone numbers have the prefix ☎020 followed by seven digits, while the newer WIN Phones (fixed phones without a landline) begin with ☎030.

MOBILE PHONES

With recently improved signals, you can use your own GSM mobile phone in Laos, either on roaming (prohibitively expensive) or by buying a local SIM card for about US$5, then purchasing prepaid minutes for a further US$5. Domestic calls are reasonably cheap. In our experience, Lao Telecom, M-Phone and ETL have the widest network coverage.

Tourist Information

The Lao National Tourism Administration (NTAL) and provincial tourism authorities have offices throughout Laos. The offices in Tha Khaek, Savannakhet, Pakse, Luang Nam Tha, Sainyabuli, Phongsali and Sam Neua are excellent, with well-trained staff and plenty of brochures.

NTAL also has three good websites:

Central Laos Trekking www.trekkingcentrallaos.com

Ecotourism Laos www.ecotourismlaos.com

Lao National Tourism Administration www.tourismlaos.gov.la

Visas

Laos issues 30-day tourist visas on arrival at several popular airports and borders. They are available at Vientiane, Luang Prabang and Pakse airports. For land borders, see the table, p36. Visas on arrival cost between US$30 and US$42, payable in US dollars, Lao kip or Thai baht, in cash, depending on what passport you hold. You'll also need two passport photos.

However, regulations and prices change regularly, so it's worth checking online or through the traveller grapevine, before turning up to some remote border. If you want to be doubly sure, or plan to use a border where visas are not issued, consulates and travel agents in Vietnam, China, Cambodia and Thailand can all issue/arrange visas.

VISA EXTENSIONS

Visa extensions cost US$2 per day from the **Immigration Office** (Map p284; ☎021-212250; Th Hatsady; ⏰8am-4.30pm Mon-Fri), which is in the Ministry of Public Security building in Vientiane. Extensions are available up to a maximum of 30 days. If you overstay your visa, you'll have to pay a fine on departure (US$10 for each day over).

Volunteering

It's not easy to find short-term volunteer work in Laos. The Organic Mulberry Farm in Vang Vieng needs volunteers occasionally, as does Big Brother Mouse (p304). If you're professionally skilled as an orthoptist, physio or surgeon, you may be able to work at the COPE Centre in Vientiane (see p286).

Women Travellers

Stories of women being hassled are few. Lao men are more likely to be a little intimidated by you than anything else. Much of the time any attention will be no more than curiosity, as Western women are so physically different to Lao women.

Remember, you're in a strictly Buddhist country so the revealing of flesh, despite the heat, is seen as cheap, disrespectful and possibly asking for trouble. Sarongs and long-sleeved T-shirts are a good idea. Lao people will almost never confront you about what you're wearing, but to them wearing a bikini is no different to wandering around in your underwear.

Work

English teaching is the most common first job for foreigners working in Laos, and schools in Vientiane are often hiring. There is also an inordinate number of development organisations – see www.directoryofngos.org for a full list – where foreigners with technical skills and volunteer experience can look for employment. Ask around.

Getting There & Away

With over a dozen border crossings into Laos, visiting the country has never been easier. Also, the once wobbly Lao Airlines has replaced its ailing fleet with Chinese planes, and is servicing most corners of the country and neighbouring countries with frequent flights.

Entering Laos

It's possible to enter Laos by land and air from Thailand, China, Vietnam and Cambodia. Land borders are often remote and can be quite tough-going with scant transport and accommodation on either side. But the actual frontier crossing itself is usually pretty quick and simple. A 30-day visa is now available at most Laos border crossings.

Air

There are no intercontinental flights operating to Laos. You can fly into or out of Laos at Vientiane (from or to Cambodia, China, Thailand, Malaysia and Vietnam), Luang Prabang (Cambodia, Thailand and Vietnam) or Pakse (from or to Vietnam, Cambodia and Thailand).

The following airlines fly to and from Laos. All fares are one way. See also the Mekong Region Air Routes map, p506.

Bangkok Airways (☎071-253334; www.bangkokair.com; 57/6 Th Sisavangvong, Ban Xiengmuan, Luang Prabang)

China Eastern Airlines (☎021-212300; www.ce-air.com; Th Luang Prabang, Vientiane)

Lao Airlines (Map p284; ☎021-212051; www.laoairlines.com; Th Pangkham, Vientiane)

Thai Airways International (☎021-222527; www.thaiair.com; Th Luang Prabang, Vientiane)

Vietnam Airlines (Map p284; ☎021-217562; www.vietnamairlines.com; 1st fl, Lao Plaza Hotel, Th Samsenthai, Vientiane)

Land

BORDER CROSSINGS

Laos has open land borders with Cambodia, China, Thailand and Vietnam, but not Myanmar. Under current rules, 30-day tourist visas are available on arrival at several (but not all) international checkpoints. These crossings are outlined in the table, p36, and in detail in boxes in the relevant chapters. However, we still recommend checking the **Thorn Tree** (lonelyplanet.com/thorntree) and with other travellers before setting off because things change frequently. Note that most crossings involve changing transport at the border.

CAR & MOTORCYCLE

If you have your own car or motorcycle, you can import it for the length of your visa after filling in forms and paying fees at the border; it's much easier if you have a carnet. Motorcyclists planning to ride through Laos should check out the wealth of info at www.gt-rider.com.

Getting Around

Air

Lao Airlines (www.laoairlines.com) handles all domestic flights in Laos. Fortunately, its revamped new fleet has slick MA60s, with the airline rapidly improving its safety record. Check the Lao calendar for public festivals before you fly, as it can be difficult getting a seat. In provincial Lao Airlines offices you'll be expected to pay in cash.

Always reconfirm your flights a day before departing, as undersubscribed flights may be cancelled or you could get bumped off the passenger list.

Bicycle

The light and relatively slow traffic in most Lao towns makes for favourable cycling conditions. Bicycles are available for rent in major tourist destinations, costing around 10,000K per day for a cheap Thai or Chinese model. See also p357.

Boat

Given the much-improved trade roads, the days of mass river transport are almost over. The most popular river trip in Laos – the slow boat between Huay Xai and Luang Prabang – remains a daily event. Other popular journeys – between Pakse and Si Phan Don, or between Nong Khiaw and Luang Prabang – are all recommended if you have time. For information on luxury boat charters, try **Asian Oasis** (www.asian-oasis.com), which provides two trips down the Mekong both in the north and south of the country.

River ferries are basic affairs and passengers usually sit, eat and sleep on the wooden decks; it's worth bringing some padding. The toilet (if there is one) is an enclosed hole in the deck at the back of the boat. For shorter river trips, such as Luang Prabang to the Pak Ou Caves, you can easily hire a river taxi.

Between Luang Prabang and Huay Xai and between Xieng Kok and Huay Xai, deafeningly loud and painfully uncomfortable speedboats operate, covering the same distance in six hours as that of a river ferry in two days. They kill and injure people every year when they disintegrate on contact with floating debris, or flip when they hit a standing wave.

Bus & Sǒrngtǎaou

Long-distance public transport in Laos is either by bus or *sǒrngtǎaou* (literally 'two rows'), which are converted trucks or pickups with benches down either side. Buses are more frequent and go further than ever. Privately run VIP buses operate on some busier routes, but slow, simple standard buses (occasionally with air-con) remain the norm.

Sǒrngtǎaou usually service shorter routes within a given province. Most decent-sized villages have at least one *sǒrngtǎaou*, which will run to the provincial capital daily except Sunday, stopping wherever you want.

Car & Motorcycle

Second-rate Chinese and sturdier Japanese-made 100cc scooters can be rented for 50,000K to 90,000K a day in Vientiane, Tha Khaek, Savannakhet, Pakse and Luang Nam Tha. Try to get a Japanese bike if you're travelling any distance out of town (or across mountains). In Vientiane and Pakse it's also possible to rent dirt bikes for around 250,000K per day. Three-day motorcycle tours of the Ho Chi Minh Trail are newly offered by **Green Discovery** (Map p284; ☎218373; www.greendiscoverylaos.com; Th Setthathirat, Vientiane). Meanwhile, **Jules' Classic Rental** (Map p284; ☎020 760 0813; www.bike-rental-laos.com; Th Setthathirat, Vientiane; per day US$30) and **P.V.O.** (Map p284; ☎254354; Th Nokeo Khumman; ⊙8am-6pm Mon-Sat) have a range of performance bikes and the option to rent in Vientiane and drop off in Luang Prabang or Pakse for an additional charge.

Car rental in Laos is a great if relatively costly way of reaching remote places. **Europcar** (Map p284; ☎223867; www.europcarlaos.com; Th Samsenthai; ⊙8am-6pm Mon-Sat) offers vehicles from US$59 per day, charging US$20 extra for a driver.

Hitching

Hitching is possible in Laos, if not common. It's never entirely safe and not recommended, especially for women, as the act of standing beside a road and waving at cars might be misinterpreted.

Northern Thailand

Includes »

Best Places to Eat

» nahm (p379)
» Lung Eed Locol Food (p409)
» Bao Phradit (p428)
» Palaad Tawanron (p394)
» MBK Food Court (p378)

Best Places to Stay

» Siam Heritage (p375)
» Riverside Guest House (p401)
» Villa Duang Champa (p393)
» Poonsawasdi Hotel (p433)
» Kham Pia Homestay (p429)

Why Go?

Thailand is arguably the 'safest' introduction to Southeast Asia, but this doesn't mean that it represents any sort of compromise. In fact, we suspect that the secret of Thailand's popularity is rooted in the fact that it packs a bit of everything.

Bangkok is one of the most vibrant cities in Southeast Asia, yet if contemporary Thai living is not your thing, you can delve into the country's past at historical parks such as Sukhothai or Phanom Rung. Similarly, fresh air fiends will be satiated by upcountry expeditions ranging from a rafting trip in Nan to the cliff-top views from Ubon Ratchathani's Pha Taem National Park. And culture junkies can get their fix at a homestay in the country's northeast or via a trek in northern Thailand.

And lest we forget that Thailand also functions as a convenient gateway to Cambodia, Laos and Myanmar (Burma). What's not to love?

When to Go

Chiang Mai

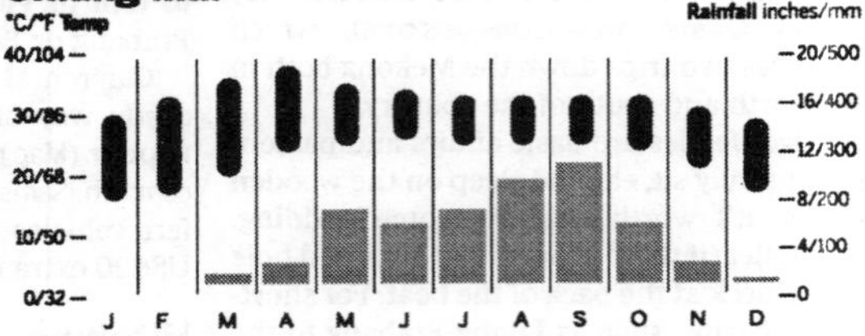

Nov–Feb Thailand's 'winter' is the best time to visit.

Mar–Jun The least desirable time to visit is during Thailand's hot season.

Late Jun–Oct Monsoon rains, although storms are usually confined to an hour's downpour.

Connections

Bangkok is one of Southeast Asia's most important air hubs, and has frequent air links to multiple destinations in Cambodia, southern China, Laos, Myanmar and Vietnam.

Bus, minivan and train links to eastern, northern and northeastern Thailand lead to numerous land (or sometimes river) border crossings with Cambodia, Laos and Myanmar.

Infrequent river and overland links connect northern Thailand and southern China.

ITINERARIES

One Week

Bangkok is the most likely place to land after a long-haul international flight and the easiest place to book onward travel. Give yourself a couple of days to adjust by exploring the old royal district of **Ko Ratanakosin** and taking a **Thai cookery course**. Experience the urban side of northern Thailand in **Chiang Mai** or **Chiang Rai** before escaping cities altogether with a side trip to the 'Golden Triangle' town of **Mae Salong**. At this point, you'll be in prime position to cross to Laos at **Chiang Khong**.

Two Weeks

With more time, you can really dive into Thailand's north via a trek in the mountains surrounding **Chiang Rai** or **Nan**. Alternatively, head to **northeast Thailand**, the country's most traditional rice-growing region. Visit the Khmer ruins at **Phanom Rung** and **Phimai**. Savour the riverine landscape around the parks that make up the **Emerald Triangle** and follow the river in reverse to laid-back **Nong Khai** before crossing to Cambodia or Laos.

Internet Resources

- **Bangkok Post** (www.bangkokpost.com) English-language daily covers breaking news and opinion pieces
- **Lonely Planet** (www.lonelyplanet.com/thailand) Country profile and what to do and see
- **Tourism Authority of Thailand** (TAT; www.tourismthailand.org) National tourism department covers introductory information and special events

AT A GLANCE

- **Currency** baht (B)
- **Language** Thai
- **Money** ATMs all over; banks open Monday to Friday
- **Visas** Not required for citizens of the EU, Australia or USA
- **Mobile phones** Prepay SIM card from 69B

Fast Facts

- **Area** 514,000 sq km
- **Population** 66,720,153
- **Capital** Bangkok
- **Emergency** 191

Exchange Rates

Australia	A$1	30.64B
Canada	C$1	30.13B
Europe	€1	42.22B
Japan	¥100	40.48B
New Zealand	NZ$1	24.34B
UK	UK£1	48.12B
USA	US$1	31B

Set Your Budget

- **Budget hotel room** from 200B
- **Two-course evening meal** from 150B
- **Museum entrance** from 100B
- **Beer** from 60B

Northern Thailand Highlights

❶ Learning to be a mahout (elephant caretaker) at Lampang's **Thai Elephant Conservation Center** (p400)

❷ Cycling around the awesome ruins of Thailand's 'golden age' at **Sukhothai** (p406) and **Si Satchanalai-Chaliang Historical Parks** (p407)

❸ Getting awestruck by the scenery in **Pha Taem National Park** (p426)

❹ Picking up some bargains at Chiang Mai's **Saturday Walking Street** (p395) and **Sunday Walking Street** (p395)

❺ Go from Phimai to Phanom Rung along Thailand's **Angkor temple trail** (p420 & p421)

❻ Getting into the groove of rural northern Thailand in laid-back **Pai** (p401)

❼ Recover from the hardships of the upcountry in **Bangkok** (p368), Thailand's modern and decadent capital

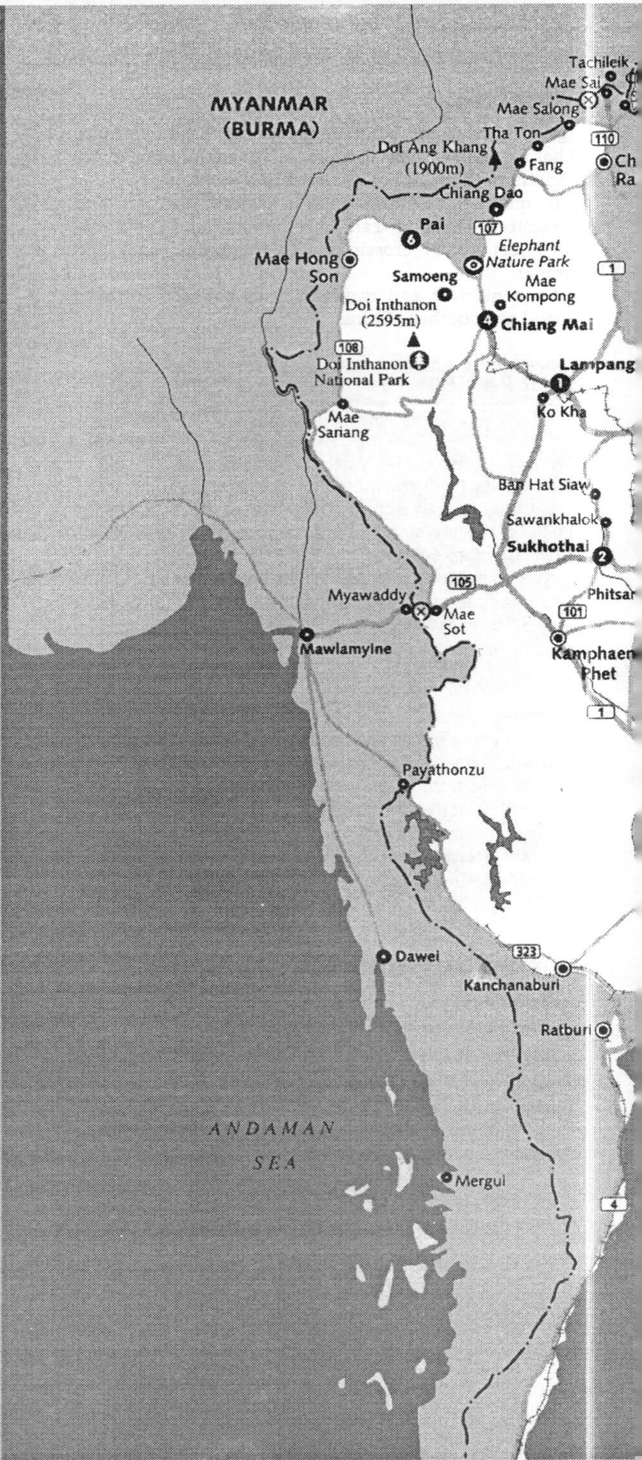

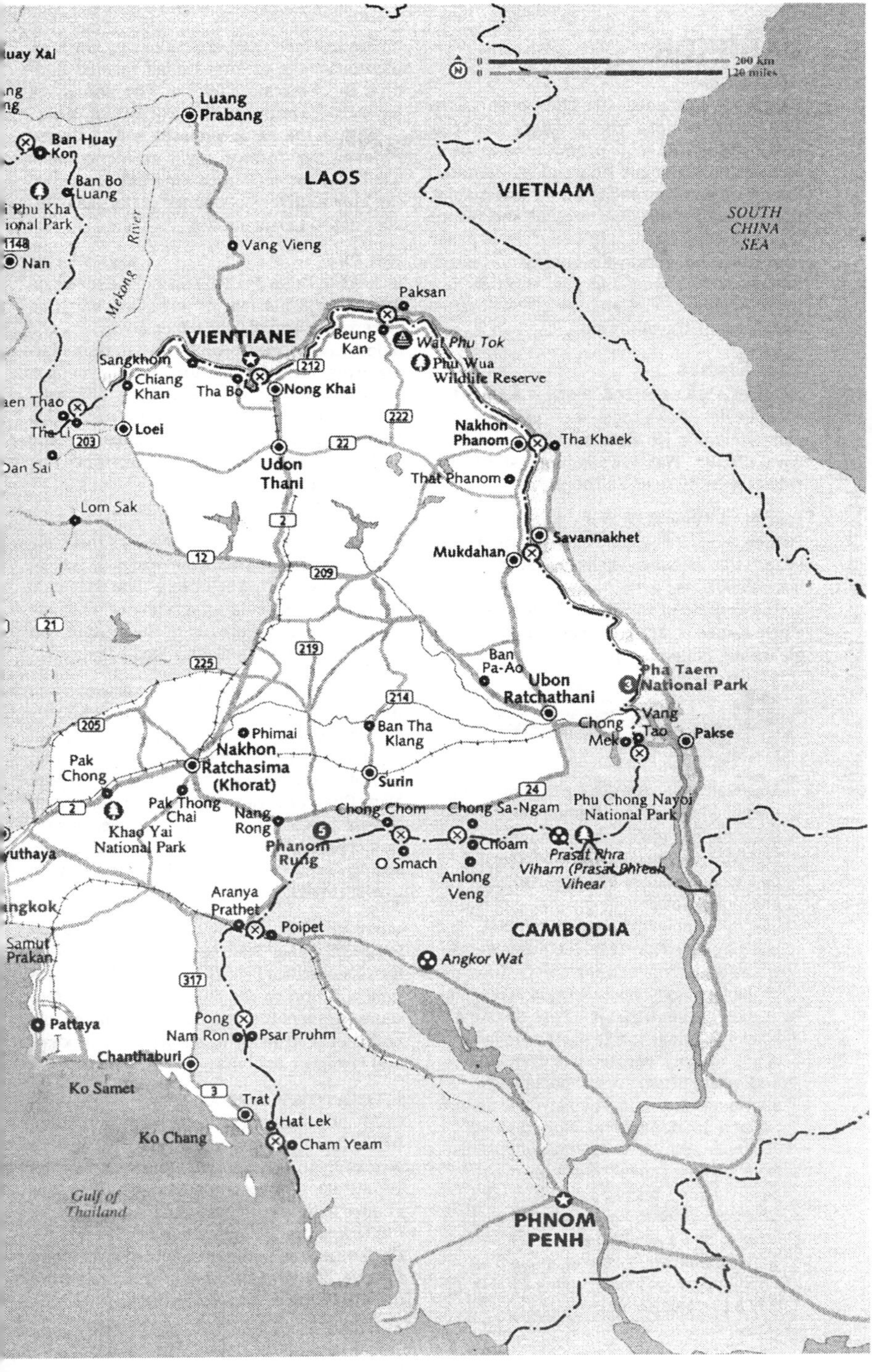

Huay Xai
Luang Prabang
Ban Huay Kon
Ban Bo Luang
Phu Kha National Park
Nan
LAOS
VIETNAM
SOUTH CHINA SEA
0 200 km
0 120 miles
Vang Vieng
Mekong River
Paksan
VIENTIANE
Beung Kan
Wat Phu Tok
Phu Wua Wildlife Reserve
Sangkhom
Chiang Khan
Tha Bo
Nong Khai
Loei
Tha Li
Dan Sai
Udon Thani
Nakhon Phanom
Tha Khaek
That Phanom
Lom Sak
Savannakhet
Mukdahan
Ban Pa-Ao
Ubon Ratchathani
Pha Taem National Park
Vang Tao
Chong Mek
Pakse
Phimai
Ban Tha Klang
Pak Chong
Nakhon Ratchasima (Khorat)
Surin
Pak Thong Chai
Khao Yai National Park
Nang Rong
Phanom Rung
Chong Chom
O Smach
Chong Sa-Ngam
Choam
Anlong Veng
Phu Chong Nayoi National Park
Prasat Phra Viharn (Prasat Phreah Vihear)
Aranya Prathet
Poipet
CAMBODIA
Angkor Wat
Samut Prakan
Pattaya
Pong Nam Ron
Psar Pruhm
Chanthaburi
Ko Samet
Trat
Hat Lek
Cham Yeam
Ko Chang
Gulf of Thailand
PHNOM PENH
212
222
22
2
12
209
21
219
225
214
205
24
203
317
3
1148

BANGKOK

POP 9.1 MILLION

Bangkok's influence stretches beyond the Thai borders into the greater Southeast Asian region due to its prominence as an international transport hub and its manufacturing of entertainment and consumables. Encompassing the past, present and future, this sprawling city is a full-on dose of urban sophistication, megawatt energy and ceaseless chaos. You'll need to pass through here to get anywhere else and the city will tattoo itself to your travelling skin.

Sights

KO RATANAKOSIN & BANGLAMPHU

Most of Bangkok's must-sees reside in compact, walkable Ko Ratanakosin, the former royal district. Wat Arun is just a short ferry ride across the river in Thonburi.

Wat Phra Kaew & Grand Palace BUDDHIST TEMPLE

(Map p370; admission 350B; ⏲8.30am-3.30pm; bus 503, 508, river ferry Tha Chang) Also known as the Temple of the Emerald Buddha, **Wat Phra Kaew** is an architectural wonder of gleaming gilded stupas, mosaic-encrusted pillars and rich marble pediments. The temple houses the country's most revered Buddha, the Emerald Buddha. The admission fee includes entrance to Dusit Palace Park.

Within the same grounds is the **Grand Palace**, the former royal residence now used only for certain ceremonial occasions; the king's current residence is Chitlada Palace (closed to the public).

Wat Pho BUDDHIST TEMPLE

(Map p370; Th Sanamchai; admission 50B; ⏲8am-9pm; bus 508, 512, river ferry Tha Tien) Wat Pho sweeps the awards for superlatives: it's the oldest and largest temple in Bangkok, dating from the 16th century. But the *biggest* attraction is the reclining Buddha, 46m long and 15m high. The temple is the traditional training ground for Thai massage and the affiliated school operates massage pavilions on the temple grounds.

National Museum MUSEUM

(Map p370; ☎0 2224 1402; Th Na Phra That 1; admission 200B; ⏲9am-3.30pm Wed-Sun; bus 32, 123, 503, river ferry Tha Chang) The National Museum provides an overview of Thai art and culture; get more out of the museum on a docent-led **tour** (⏲9.30am Wed & Thu).

Wat Arun BUDDHIST TEMPLE

(Map p370; Thonburi; admission 50B; ⏲8.30am-4.30pm; cross-river ferry from Tha Tien) Wat Arun is a striking temple named after the Indian god of dawn, Aruna. It looms large on Mae Nam Chao Phraya's west bank, looking as if it were carved from granite; a closer inspection reveals a mosaic made of broken porcelain covering the imposing 82m Khmer-style *prang* (tower).

Museum of Siam MUSEUM

(Map p370; Th Maha Rat; admission 300B; ⏲10am-6pm Tue-Sun; bus 32, 524, river ferry Tha Tien) A new addition to the royal district, this museum explores the origins of the Thai people and their culture with surprisingly modern and engaging exhibits.

CHINATOWN & PHAHURAT

Gold shops, towering neon signs and shopfronts spilling out onto the sidewalk – welcome to Chinatown (also known as Yaowarat). The neighbourhood's energy is at once exhilarating and exhausting, and it's fun to explore at night when it's lit up like a Christmas tree and there's lots of street food for sale. Much of the area is accessible from the MRT stop at Hua Lamphong.

MAKING SENSE OF BANGKOK

Mae Nam Chao Phraya (the Chao Phraya River) divides Bangkok from the older city of Thonburi. Bangkok can be further divided into east and west by the main railway line feeding Hualamphong station. The older part of the city, crowded with historical temples, bustling Chinatown and the popular travellers' centre of Banglamphu (home of the famous Khao San Rd) is sandwiched between the western side of the tracks and the river. East of the railway is the new city, devoted to commerce and its attendant skyscrapers and shopping centres, particularly the Siam Sq, and Sukhumvit and Silom districts.

A note about streets: throughout this book, *thànŏn* (street) is abbreviated as 'Th'. A *soi* is a small street that runs off a larger street. The address of a site located on a *soi* will be written as 33 Soi 3, Th Sukhumvit, meaning on Soi 3 off Th Sukhumvit. Smaller than a *soi* is a *tràwk* (meaning alley).

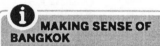

Greater Bangkok

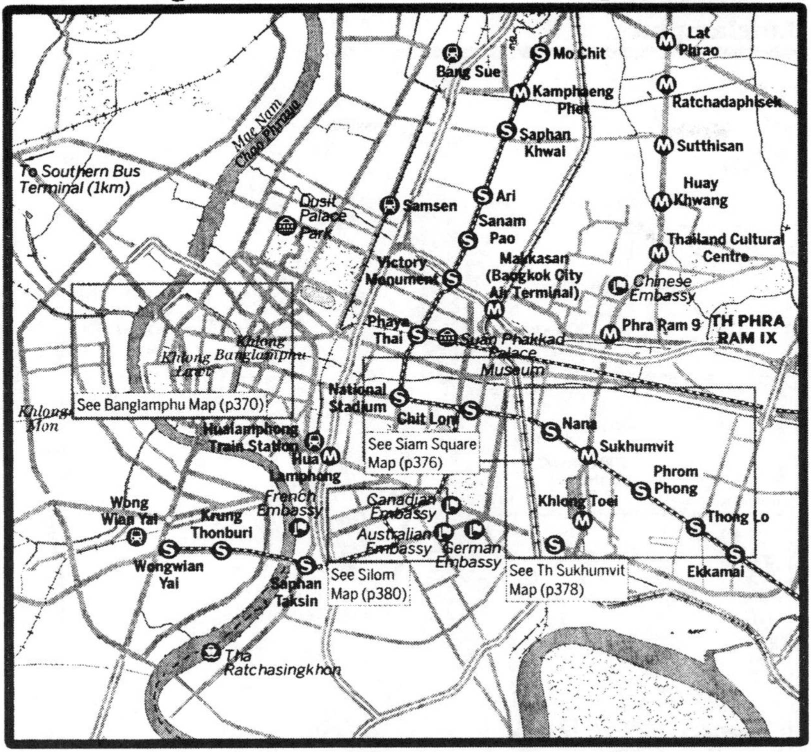

Slicing through the centre of the district, the famous **Sampeng Lane** (Soi Wanit 1; bus 73, 159, 507, MRT Hua Lamphong, river ferry Tha Ratchawong) is jam-packed with the useful and the useless, all at bargain prices.

The labyrinthine **Wat Mangkon Kamalawat** (Th Charoen Krung; ⏲9am-6pm; bus 73, 159, 507, MRT Hua Lamphong, river ferry Tha Ratchawong) is the focus of Vegetarian Festival activities and holds Buddhist, Taoist and Confucian shrines. Nearby is **Talat Mai** (Trok Itsaranuphap; bus 73, 159, 507, MRT Hua Lamphong, river ferry Tha Ratchawong), an alley market that caters to cooking ingredients and Chinese devotional items.

Wat Traimit (Temple of the Golden Buddha; cnr Th Yaowarat & Th Charoen Krung; admission 40B; ⏲8am-5pm Tue-Sun; MRT Hua Lamphong, river ferry Tha Ratchawong) shelters a 3m, 5.5-tonne, gold Buddha image that was 'discovered' when it was being moved in the 1960s and the stucco exterior hiding it cracked.

At the western edge of Chinatown is a small but thriving Indian district, generally called Phahurat. Here, dozens of Indian-owned shops sell all kinds of fabric and clothes.

OTHER AREAS

Jim Thompson's House MUSEUM
(Map p376; www.jimthompsonhouse.com; 6 Soi Kasem San 2; adult/child 100/50B; ⏲9am-5pm, compulsory tours in English & French every 20min; BTS National Stadium, klorng taxi Tha Hua Chang) This is the beautiful house of the American entrepreneur Jim Thompson, who successfully promoted Thai silk to Western markets. Atmospherically sited on a small *klorng* (canal), the house was built from salvaged components of traditional Thai houses. His collection of Thai art and furnishings is equally superb.

Banglamphu

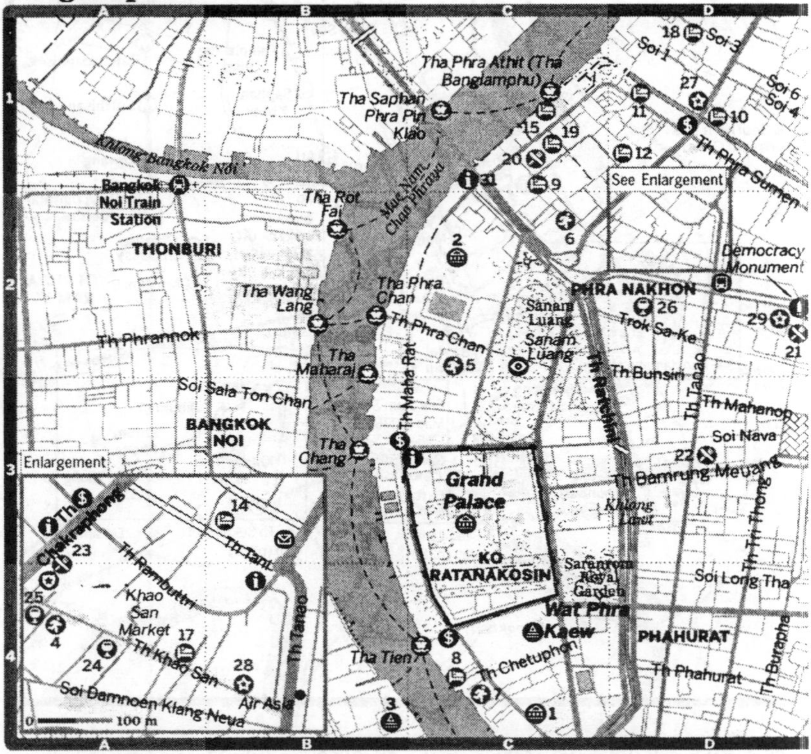

Suan Phakkad Palace Museum MUSEUM
(Map p369; Th Sri Ayuthaya; admission 100B; ⊙9am-4pm; BTS Phaya Thai) An overlooked treasure, Suan Phakkad is a collection of eight traditional wooden Thai houses that was once the residence of Princess Chumbon of Nakhon Sawan and before that a lettuce farm – hence the name. Within the stilt buildings are displays of art, antiques and furnishings, and the landscaped grounds are a peaceful oasis complete with ducks, swans and a semi-enclosed garden.

Dusit Palace Park ROYAL PALACE
(Map p369; bounded by Th Ratchawithi, Th U-Thong Nai & Th Ratchasima; adult/child 100/50B, free with Grand Palace ticket; ⊙9.30am-4pm; bus 18, 28, 515) Elegant Dusit Palace Park is a former royal palace with serene green space and multiple handicraft museums. The must-see is the 1868 Vimanmek Teak Mansion, reputedly the world's largest golden teakwood building.

Activities

Depending on the neighbourhood, prices for massages tend to stay fixed: around 250B for a foot massage and around 500B for a body massage.

Wat Pho Traditional Thai Medical and Massage School MASSAGE
(Map p370; ☎0 2622 3550; 392/25-28 Soi Pen Phat; Thai massage per hr 220B; ⊙8am-6pm; bus 508, 512, river ferry Tha Tien) This is the nation's premier massage school and offers air-con service in this location, but the pavilions inside the temple are more atmospheric. Lessons in Thai massage are also available.

Health Land SPA, MASSAGE
(Map p380; ☎0 2637 8883; www.heathlandspa.com; 120 Th Sathon Neua; Thai massage 2hr 450B; ⊙9am-11pm; BTS Chong Nonsi) Spas are becoming increasingly popular in Thailand, and while this is more down-to-earth than most, the pamper factor is still first-class.

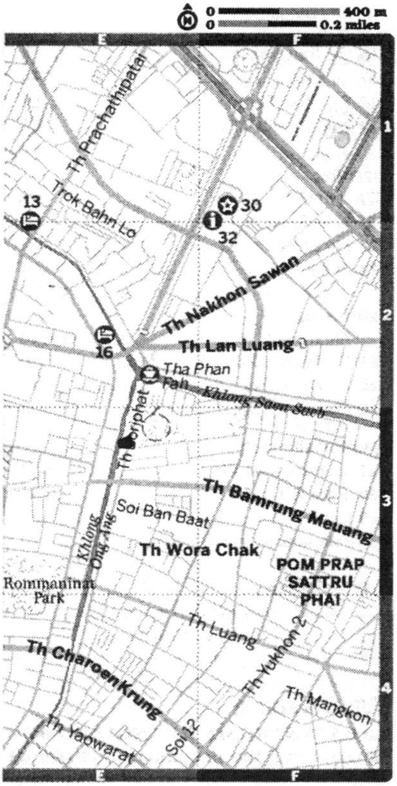

Courses

Khao COOKERY COURSE
(Map p370; ☎08 9111 0947; www.khaocookingschool.com; D&D Plaza, 68-70 Th Khao San; lessons 1500B; ⌚9.30am-12.30pm & 1.30-4.30pm) Khao was established by an authority on Thai food and features instruction on a wide variety of authentic dishes. Located in the courtyard behind D&D Inn.

Helping Hands COOKERY COURSE
(☎08 4901 8717; www.cookingwithpoo.com) This popular cookery course was started by a native of Khlong Toey's slums and is held in her neighbourhood. Courses, which must be booked in advance, span four dishes and include a visit to Khlong Toey Market and transportation to and from the Emporium Shopping Centre.

Wat Pho Thai Traditional Medical and Massage School THAI MASSAGE
(Map p370; ☎0 2622 3550; www.watpomassage.com; 392/25-28 Soi Phen Phat; tuition from 5000B; ⌚8am-6pm; bus 508, 512, river ferry Tha Tien) Offers basic and advanced courses in traditional massage. The school is outside the temple compound in a restored Bangkok shophouse on unmarked Soi Phen Phat – look for Coconut Palm restaurant.

Sor Vorapin Gym THAI BOXING GYM
(Map p370; ☎0 2282 3551; www.thaiboxings.com; 13 Th Kasab, Th Chakraphong; tuition per day/month 500/9000B; bus 2, 15, 44, 511, river ferry Tha Phra Athit) Specialising in training foreign students of both genders, this gym is sweating distance from Th Khao San.

Wat Mahahat MEDITATION
(Map p370; 3 Th Maha Rat; bus 32, 201, 503, river ferry Tha Maharaj or Tha Chang) This temple is home to two independently operating meditation centres. The **International Buddhist Meditation Center** (☎0 2222 6011; www.centermeditation.org; Section 5, Wat Mahathat; donations accepted) offers daily meditation classes at 7am, 1pm and 6pm. Taught by English-speaking Phra Suputh, classes last three hours. The **Meditation Study and Retreat Center** (☎0 223 6878; www.meditation-watmahadhat.com; Wat Mahathat; donations accepted) offers a regimented daily program of meditation.

Festivals & Events

In addition to the national holidays, there's always something going on in Bangkok.

DRESS FOR THE OCCASION

Thai temples, especially those with a royal connection, are sacred places, and visitors should dress and behave appropriately. Wear shirts with sleeves, long pants or skirts past the knees, and closed-toed shoes. Sarongs and baggy pants are available on loan at the entry area for Wat Phra Kaew. Shoes should be removed before entering buildings. When sitting in front of a Buddha image, tuck your feet behind you in the 'mermaid' position to avoid the offence of pointing your feet towards a revered figure.

Banglamphu

Top Sights

Grand Palace C3
Wat Phra Kaew & Grand Palace C4

Sights

1 Museum of Siam C4
2 National Museum C2
3 Wat Arun B4

Activities, Courses & Tours

4 Khao A4
5 Meditation Study and Retreat Center C2
6 Sor Vorapin Gym C2
7 Wat Pho Thai Traditional Medical and Massage School C4

Sleeping

8 Arun Residence C4
9 Baan Sabai C1
10 Diamond House D1
11 Fortville Guesthouse D1
12 Lamphu House D1
13 Lamphu Tree House E1
14 NapPark Hostel B3
15 Navalai River Resort C1
16 Old Bangkok Inn E2
17 Rikka Inn A4
18 Sam Sen Sam D1
19 Wild Orchid Villa C1

Eating

20 Hemlock C1
21 Krua Apsorn D2
22 Poj Spa Kar D3
23 Shoshana A4

Drinking

Amarosa's .... (see 8)
24 Center Khao San A4
25 Hippie de Bar A4
26 Pranakorn Bar D2

Entertainment

27 Ad Here the 13th D1
28 Brick Bar B4
29 Café Democ D2
30 Ratchadamnoen Stadium F1

Information

31 Bangkok Information Center C1
32 Tourism Authority of Thailand F1

Check the website of **TAT** (www.tourismthailand.org) or the **Bangkok Information Center** (www.bangkoktourist.com) for exact dates.

Chinese New Year
Thai-Chinese celebrate the lunar New Year with a week of housecleaning, lion dances and fireworks; February/March.

Songkran
Thai New Year has morphed into a water war; mid-April.

Royal Ploughing Ceremony
The crown prince commences rice-planting season at Sanam Luang; early May.

Vegetarian Festival
Chinese-Thais visit temples and eschew meat for 10 days in September/October.

Loi Krathong
Small lotus-shaped boats made of banana leaves and containing a lit candle are set adrift on Mae Nam Chao Phraya; early November.

Bangkok World Film Festival
(www.worldfilmbkk.com) Mid-November.

Sleeping

KO RATANAKOSIN & BANGLAMPHU

Banglamphu, the neighbourhood that includes the backpacker street of Th Khao San, is a well-padded landing zone for jet-lagged travellers. This doesn't necessarily mean it's the only or even the best place to stay in town, but prices are generally low and standards relatively high. Neighbouring Ko Ratanakosin is seeing an increasing number of boutique-type riverside places.

TOP CHOICE **Lamphu Tree House** BOUTIQUE HOTEL $$
(Map p370; ☎0 2282 0991; www.lamphutreehotel.com; 155 Wanchat Bridge, Th Prachatipatai; r incl breakfast 1500-2100B; bus 56, 58, 516, klorng taxi Tha Phah Fah, river ferry Tha Phra Athit) Despite the name, this attractive mid-ranger has its feet firmly on land and as such, represents brilliant value. Rooms are attractive and inviting, and the rooftop bar, pool, internet, restaurant and quiet canal-side location ensure that you may never feel the need to leave.

Diamond House BOUTIQUE HOTEL $$
(Map p370; ☎0 2629 4008; www.thaidiamondhouse.com; 4 Th Samsen; ❄@📶; r 2000-2800B, ste 3600B; bus 32, 516, river ferry Tha Phra Athit) Despite sharing real estate with a rather brash Chinese temple, there's no conflict of design at this eccentric, funky hotel. Most rooms are loft style, with beds on raised platforms, and are outfitted with stained glass, dark, lush colours and chic furnishings.

Arun Residence BOUTIQUE HOTEL $$$
(Map p370; ☎0 2221 9158; www.arunresidence.com; 36-38 Soi Pratu Nok Yung, Th Maha Rat; r incl breakfast 3500-3800B, ste 5500B; ❄@📶; bus 123, 508, river ferry Tha Tien) The six rooms here manage to feel both homey and stylish, some being tall and loftlike, while others cojoin two rooms (the best is the top-floor suite with its own balcony). There are inviting communal areas, including a library, a rooftop bar and a restaurant.

NapPark Hostel HOSTEL $
(Map p370; ☎0 2282 2324; www.nappark.com; 8 Th Tani; dm 550-750B; river ferry Tha Tien; ❄@📶) This exceedingly well-done hostel features dorm rooms of various sizes, the smallest and most expensive of which boasts six pod-like beds outfitted with power points, mini-TV, reading lamp and wi-fi.

Fortville Guesthouse BUDGET HOTEL $
(Map p370; ☎0 2282 3932; www.fortvilleguesthouse.com; 9 Th Phra Sumen; r 650-970B; ❄@📶; bus 32, 33, 64, 82, river ferry Tha Phra Athit) The design concept of this unique new hotel can be a bit hard to pin down, but rooms are stylishly minimal, and the more expensive include perks such as fridge, balcony and free wi-fi.

Navalai River Resort HOTEL $$$
(Map p370; ☎0 2280 9955; www.navalai.com; 45/1 Th Phra Athit; r incl breakfast 2900-4800B; ❄@📶🏊; bus 32, 33, 64, 82, river ferry Tha Phra Athit) The latest thing to go up on Th Phra Athit, this chic hotel has 74 modern rooms, many looking out over Chao Phraya Mae Nam.

Old Bangkok Inn BOUTIQUE HOTEL $$$
(Map p370; ☎0 2629 1787; www.oldbangkokinn.com; 609 Th Phra Sumen; r incl breakfast 3190-6590B; ❄@📶; klorng taxi to Tha Phan Fah) The 10 rooms in this refurbished antique shophouse are decadent and sumptuous, making it the perfect honeymoon hotel.

Baan Sabai BUDGET HOTEL $
(Map p370; ☎0 2629 1599; baan sabai@hotmail.com; 12 Soi Rongmai; r 190-600B; ❄@; bus 53, 516, river ferry Tha Phra Athit) Truly living up to its name (Comfortable House), this rambling

VENICE OF THE EAST

In Bangkok's early days, *klorng* (also spelled *khlong*, canals), not roads, transported goods and people, and the mighty Mae Nam Chao Phraya was the superhighway leading to the interior of the country. All life centred on the waterways, and central Thais regarded themselves as *jôw nám* (water lords). Most of the canals are gone now, but aqua transport still flows through Bangkok and offers a glimpse into the past, and is sometimes the swiftest way to get around.

Chao Phraya River Express (☎0 2623 6001; www.chaophrayaboat.co.th; tickets 13-32B) runs up and down the Mae Nam Chao Phraya with boats stopping at different piers depending on their designation: express (indicated by yellow, orange or yellow-and-green flags), local (without a flag) and the larger tourist boat (19B per trip) that stops at piers convenient for sightseers. There are also small flat-bottomed boats that do cross-river trips to Thonburi (3.5B per trip). The main pier (called Tha Sathon or Central Pier) is near Saphan Taksin BTS station, and services run roughly from 6am to 6.30pm.

The **klorng taxis** (9-21B; ⏰6am-7pm) on Khlong Saen Saep are the quickest option for getting from Banglamphu to points east, such as Siam Sq (Tha Hua Chang).

The loveliest and leafiest trips are through the remaining canals in Thonburi such as Khlong Bangkok Noi and Khlong Mon. **Long-tail boats** can be hired from the busier piers (Tha Chang and Tha Tieng) for about 1000B per hour.

Another option is to combine river transport with dining for a unique Bangkok experience. **Wan Fah Cruises** (☎0 2222 8679; www.wanfah.in.th; cruises 1200B; ⏰7-9pm; river ferry to Tha Si Phraya) operates a wooden boat complete with Thai music and dance. Or for a more regal touch, **Manohra Cruises** (☎0 2477 0770; www.manohracruises.com; Bangkok Marriott Resort & Spa, Thonburi; cocktail cruise, dinner cruise child/adult 1712/2343B; ⏰7.30-10pm; hotel shuttle boat from Tha Sathon/Central Pier) runs a fleet of converted teak rice barges.

WORTH A TRIP

MONUMENTS IN MINIATURE

East of Bangkok in the suburb of Samut Prakan is an unusual attraction. The **Ancient City** (Muang Boran; www.ancientcity.com; adult/child 400/300B; ☺8am-5pm) is an 80-hectare outdoor museum with 109 scaled-down replicas of Thailand's most famous historic monuments, including some that no longer survive. Visions of Legoland may spring to mind, but the Ancient City is architecturally sophisticated and definitely worth the trip.

Air-con bus 511 travels from the east end of Th Sukhumvit to Samut Prakan's bus terminal; then you board minibus 36, which passes the entrance to Ancient City.

old building holds dozens of plain but comfy rooms, at a variety of prices.

Wild Orchid Villa BUDGET HOTEL $
(Map p370; ☎0 2629 4378; www.wildorchidvilla.com; 8 Soi Chana Songkhram; r 280-1800B; ☀@☎; bus 32, 33, 64, 82, river ferry Tha Phra Athit) The cheapies here are some of the tiniest we've seen anywhere, but all rooms are clean and neat, and come in a bright, friendly package.

Lamphu House BUDGET HOTEL $
(Map p370; ☎0 2629 5861; www.lamphuhouse.com; 75-77 Soi Ram Buttri; r 200-950B; ☀@☎; river ferry Tha Phra Athit) Tucked off Soi Ram Buttri, you'll forget how close to Th Khao San you are in this quiet, homey budget hotel.

Rikka Inn BUDGET HOTEL $$
(Map p370; ☎0 2282 7511; www.rikkainn.com; 259 Th Khao San; r 1150-1450B; ☀@☎☒; bus 53, 516, river ferry Tha Phra Athit) Boasting tight but attractive rooms, a rooftop pool and a central location, the new Rikka is one of several great-value hotels changing the face of Th Khao San.

Sam Sen Sam GUESTHOUSE $
(Map p370; ☎0 2628 7067; www.samsensam.com; 48 Soi 3, Th Samsen; r 590-2400B; ☀@☎; river ferry to Tha Phra Athit) This bright, refurbished villa gets good reports about its friendly service and quiet location.

CHINATOWN & PHAHURAT

Bangkok's Chinatown isn't the most hospitable part of town, but for those who wish to stay off the beaten track it's an area where travellers can remain largely anonymous.

Shanghai Mansion BOUTIQUE HOTEL $$$
(☎0 2221 2121; www.shanghai-inn.com; 479-481 Th Yaowarat; r 2500-3500B, ste 4000B; ☀@☎; river ferry Tha Ratchawong) This award-winning boutique hotel screams Shanghai c 1935 via stained glass, an abundance of lamps, bold colours and tongue-in-cheek Chinatown kitsch.

Baan Hualampong GUESTHOUSE $
(☎0 2639 8054; www.baanhualampong.com; 336/20-21 Trok Chalong Krung; dm incl breakfast 250B, r 290-800B; ☀@☎; MRT Hua Lamphong) Simple but homey, this guesthouse is a short walk from Hualamphong, Bangkok's main train station.

@ Hua Lamphong BUDGET HOTEL $$
(☎0 2639 1925; www.at-hualamphong.com; 326/1 Th Phra Ram IV; dm 200B, r 690-1000B; ☀@☎; MRT Hua Lamphong, river ferry Tha Ratchawong) Tidy hostel across the street from the train station.

SIAM SQUARE

Siam Sq lies conveniently along both BTS lines. A low-key, DIY traveller community bunks down on Soi Kasem San 1.

TOP CHOICE **Siam@Siam** HOTEL $$$
(Map p376; ☎0 2217 3000; www.siamatsiam.com; 865 Th Phra Ram I; r incl breakfast 4050-6750B; ☀@☎☒; BTS National Stadium) A seemingly random mishmash of colours and materials result in a style one could only describe as 'junkyard' – but in a good way, of course. The rooms, which continue the theme, are between the 14th and 24th floors, offer terrific city views, free wi-fi and breakfast.

Lub*d HOSTEL $
(Map p376; ☎0 2634 7999; www.lubd.com; Th Pha Ram I; dm 550B, r 1350-1800B; ☀@☎; BTS National Stadium) There are 24 dorms (including ladies-only dorms) here, each with four beds, and a few private rooms, both with and without bathrooms. There's an inviting communal area stocked with free internet, games and a bar, and thoughtful facilities ranging from washing machines to a theatre room.

Reno Hotel BUDGET HOTEL $$
(Map p376; ☎0 2215 0026; www.renohotel.co.th; 40 Soi Kasem San 1; r incl breakfast 1280-1890B; ; BTS National Stadium, klorng taxi to Tha Ratchathewi) Most of the rooms reflect the renovations evident in the lobby and exterior, but the cafe and classic pool of this Vietnam War–era hotel still cling to the past.

A-One Inn BUDGET HOTEL $
(Map p376; ☎0 2215 3029; www.aoneinn.com; 25/13-15 Soi Kasem San 1; s/d/tr 600/750/950B; ; BTS National Stadium, klorng taxi to Tha Ratchathewi) A repeat visitors' fave on this 'secret soi', A-One has simple but good-value rooms.

SILOM, SATHON & RIVERSIDE

The city's financial district along Th Silom is not the most charming area of town, but it is conveniently located for nightspots and the BTS and MRT. The adjacent riverside area is home to some of Bangkok's most famous luxury hotels.

TOP CHOICE **Siam Heritage** BOUTIQUE HOTEL $$$
(Map p380; ☎0 2353 6101; www.thesiamheritage.com; 115/1 Th Surawong; r incl breakfast 3000-3500B, ste 4500-9000B; BTS Sala Daeng, MRT Si Lom;) Tucked off busy Th Surawong, this classy boutique hotel oozes with homey Thai charm – probably because the owners also live in the same building. The rooms are decked out in silk and dark woods with genuinely thoughtful design touches, not to mention thoughtful amenities.

Oriental Hotel LUXURY HOTEL $$$
(☎0 2659 9000; www.mandarinoriental.com; 48 Soi 40/Oriental, Th Charoen Krung; r incl breakfast 12,799-14,799B, ste 23,999-140,999B; ; hotel shuttle boat from Tha Sathon/Central Pier) While the rest of the city jumps overboard for the new Zen trend, the classic Oriental stays rooted in its Victorian past. It is consistently rated one of the best hotels in the world.

Swan Hotel HOTEL $$
(☎0 2235 9271; www.swanhotelbkk.com; 31 Soi 36, Th Charoen Krung; s/d incl breakfast 1200/1500B; ; river ferry Tha Oriental) A recent facelift has this classic Bangkok hotel looking better than ever, although the room furnishings are still stuck in the 1970s.

HQ Hostel HOSTEL $
(Map p380; ☎0 2233 1598; www.hqhostel.com; 5/3-4 Soi 3, Th Silom; dm 380-599B, r 1300-1700B; ; BTS Sala Daeng, MRT Si Lom) This new hostel combines basic but stylish rooms and dorms with inviting communal areas, smack dab in the middle of Bangkok's financial district.

SUKHUMVIT

This seemingly endless urban thoroughfare is Bangkok's unofficial International Zone and also boasts much of the city's accommodation, ranging from the odd backpacker hostel to sex tourist hovels and five-star luxury.

TOP CHOICE **AriyasomVilla** BED & BREAKFAST $$$
(Map p378; ☎0 2254 880; www.ariyasom.com; 65 Soi 1, Th Sukhumvit; r incl breakfast 4248-9138B; ; BTS Phloen Chit) If you can score a reservation, you'll be privy to one of the 24 spacious rooms here, meticulously outfitted with thoughtful Thai design touches and beautiful antique furniture. There's a spa and an inviting tropical pool, and breakfast is vegetarian and is served in the original villa's stunning glass-encased dining room.

72 Ekamai BOUTIQUE HOTEL $$
(Map p378; ☎02 714 7327; www.72ekamai.com; 72 Soi 63/Ekamai, Th Sukhumvit; r incl breakfast 2100B, ste 2500-2850B; ; BTS Ekkamai) This fun, young-feeling, design-conscious hotel is a great choice. The junior suites are huge, and like all rooms, are well equipped and conveniently located.

Suk 11 BUDGET HOTEL $
(Map p378; ☎0 2253 5927; www.suk11.com; 1/33 Soi 11, Th Sukhumvit; s incl breakfast 535-695B, d 749-963B, tr 963-1284B; ; BTS Nana) This guesthouse is an oasis of woods and greenery in the urban jungle that is Th Sukhumvit. The cheaper rooms have shared bathrooms, and although there's nearly 100 rooms, you'll still need to book at least two weeks ahead.

Eugenia BOUTIQUE HOTEL $$$
(Map p378; ☎0 2259 9017-19; www.theeugenia.com; 267 Soi 31/Sawatdi, Th Sukhumvit; ste incl breakfast 8107-9911B; ; BTS Phrom Phong & access by taxi) Colonial manor houses aren't an indigenous legacy in Thailand but this anachronistic 12-guestroom hotel indulges in the anomaly.

Sacha's Hotel Uno HOTEL $$
(Map p378; ☎0 2651 2180; www.sachas.hotel-uno.com; 28/19 Soi 19, Th Sukhumvit; r incl breakfast 1800-2500B; ; BTS Asok, MRT Sukhumvit)

Siam Square

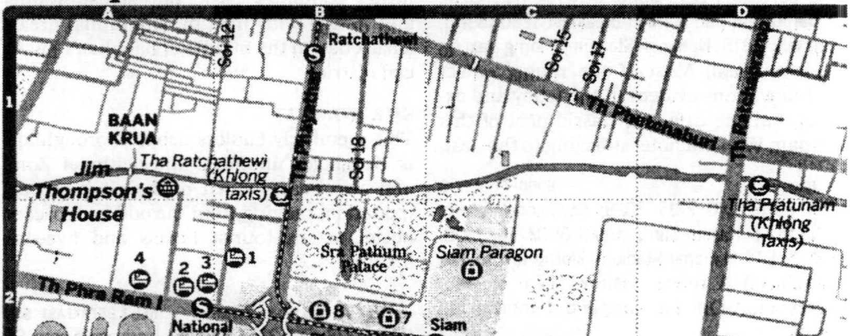

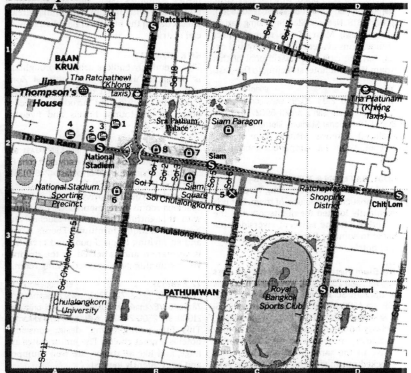

Surprisingly sophisticated rooms at budget price. Convenient location, too.

Stable Lodge BUDGET HOTEL $$
(Map p378; ☎0 2653 0017; www.stablelodge.com; 39 Soi 8, Th Sukhumvit; r 1495-1695B; BTS Nana) A recent renovation has given a bit of life to the simple rooms here, and the spacious balconies still offer great city views.

HI-Sukhumvit HOSTEL $
(Map p378; ☎0 2391 9338; www.hisukhumvit.com; 23 Soi 38, Th Sukhumvit; dm/s incl breakfast 320B/650B, d 900-1300B, tr 1200-1500B; BTS Thong Lo) At the quieter end of Sukhumvit, this friendly hostel excels in its neat dorms and immense bathrooms. There is a rooftop deck, laundry and kitchen.

Seven BOUTIQUE HOTEL $$$
(Map p378; ☎0 2662 0951; www.sleepatseven.com; 3/15 Soi 31/Sawatdi, Th Sukhumvit; r incl breakfast 3290-5290B; BTS Phrom Phong) Tiny hotel with hip rooms and easy-to-befriend staff.

Eating

No matter where you go in Bangkok, food is always there. There is so much variety just on the street that you can go days without stepping inside a restaurant. When the need comes for a restaurant, Bangkok's best are the decorless mom-and-pop shops. Higher prices always bring more ambience, and dining in Bangkok's fashionable or touristy restaurants is sometimes more for show than for flavour. All the great international cuisines, from French to Japanese, are available too.

KO RATANAKOSIN & BANGLAMPHU

The old areas of town near the river are full of simple Thai eats and, because of the traveller presence, Western and vegetarian food as well.

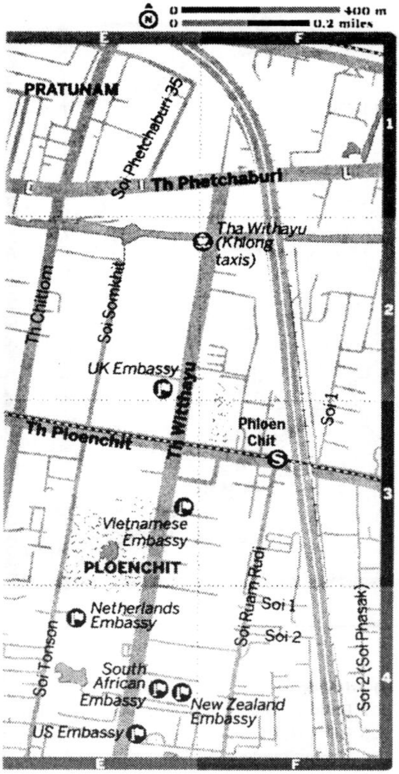

Siam Square

Top Sights

Jim Thompson's House A1

Sleeping

1 A-One Inn B2
2 Lub*d A2
3 Reno Hotel A2
4 Siam@Siam A2

Eating

5 Coca Suki C3
MBK Food Court .... (see 6)

Shopping

6 MBK Center B3
7 Siam Center B2
8 Siam Discovery Center B2

TOP CHOICE Krua Apsorn THAI $$
(Map p370; Th Din So; mains 70-320B; ⌚lunch & dinner Mon-Sat; ✱; bus 2, 25, 44, 511, klorng taxi to Tha Phan Fah) This homey dining room has served the Thai royal family and, back in 2006, was recognised as Bangkok's Best Restaurant by the *Bangkok Post*. Must-eat dishes include mussels fried with fresh herbs, the decadent crab fried in yellow chilli oil and the tortilla Española-like crab omelette.

Poj Spa Kar THAI $$
(Map p370; 443 Th Tanao; mains 100-200B; ⌚lunch & dinner; ✱; bus 2, 25, 44, 511, klorng taxi to Tha Phan Fah) Pronounced *pôht sà pah kahn*, this is allegedly the oldest restaurant in Bangkok, and continues to maintain recipes handed down from a former palace cook.

Hemlock THAI $$
(Map p370; 56 Th Phra Athit; mains 60-220B; ⌚4pm-midnight; ✱; bus 32, 33, 64, 82, river ferry Tha Phra Athit) This cosy gem has an eclectic range with many items that don't usually pop up on menus.

Shoshana ISRAELI $$
(Map p370; 88 Th Chakraphong; mains 90-220B; ⌚lunch & dinner; ✱; bus 32, 516, river ferry Tha Phra Athit) This is one of Khao San's best and longest-running Israeli restaurants, tucked away in an unnamed, almost secret alley beside the former petrol station.

CHINATOWN & PHAHURAT

When you mention Chinatown, Bangkokians begin dreaming of noodles, usually prepared by street vendors lining Th Yaowarat, near Trok Itsaranuphap (Soi 16, Th Yaowarat), after dark. Of course, the dining is good in the Indian district of Phahurat too.

Old Siam Plaza THAI $
(ground fl, Old Siam Plaza, cnr Th Phahurat & Th Triphet; mains 15-50B; ⌚9am-6.30pm; river ferry Tha Saphan Phut) The Thai version of Willy Wonka's factory turns seemingly savoury ingredients like beans and rice into syrupy sweet desserts, right before your eyes.

Th Phadungdao Seafood Stalls THAI $$
(cnr Th Phadungdao & Th Yaowarat; mains 180-300B; ⌚dinner Tue-Sun) After sunset, this frenetic street sprouts outdoor barbecues, iced seafood trays and sidewalk seating.

Royal India INDIAN $$
(392/1 Th Chakraphet; mains 65-250B; ⌚lunch & dinner; river ferry Tha Saphan Phut) A Lonely Planet staple that still delivers reliable North Indian cuisine.

Th Sukhumvit

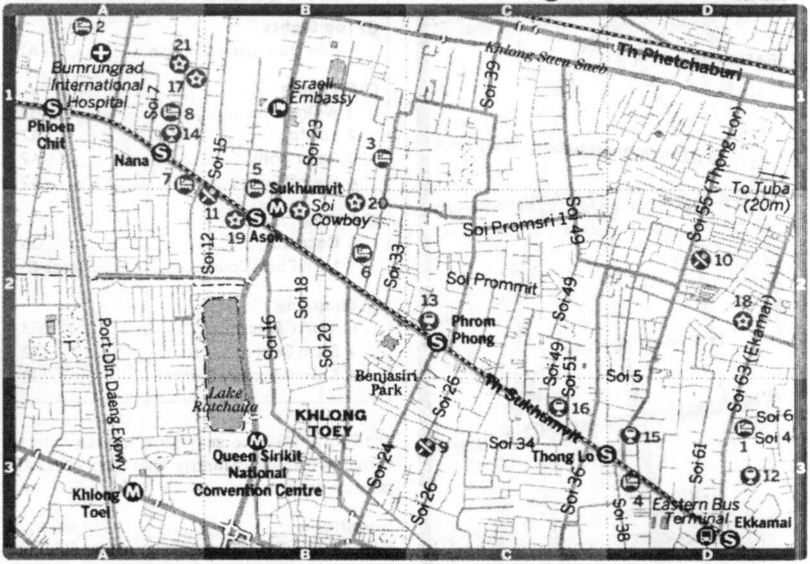

Th Sukhumvit

Sleeping
- 1 72 Ekamai D3
- 2 AriyasomVilla A1
- 3 Eugenia B1
- 4 HI-Sukhumvit D3
- 5 Sacha's Hotel Uno B1
- 6 Seven B2
- 7 Stable Lodge A1
- 8 Suk 11 .... A1

Eating
- 9 Bo.lan C3
- 10 Boon Tong Kiat Singapore Hainanese Chicken Rice D2
- 11 Myeong Ga B2

Drinking
- 12 Bangkok Bar D3
- 13 Bull's Head C2
- 14 Cheap Charlie's A1
- 15 Soul Food Mahanakorn D3
- 16 WTF C3

Entertainment
- 17 Bed Supperclub A1
- 18 Ekamai Soi 5 .... D2
- 19 Living Room B2
- 20 Narz B2
- 21 Q Bar A1

SIAM SQUARE

If you find yourself hungry in this part of central Bangkok, you're largely at the mercy of shopping-mall food courts and chain restaurants.

TOP CHOICE **MBK Food Court** THAI $

(Map p376; 6th fl, MBK Center, cnr Th Phra Ram I & Th Phayathai; ⏲10am-9pm; ❄; BTS National Stadium) A great introduction to Thai food for recent arrivals, this mall food court has fresh and flavourful street-stall eats that are deciphered into English and in air-con comfort. Buy coupons from the ticket desk and then cash in whatever you don't spend.

Coca Suki THAI-CHINESE $$

(Map p376; 416/3-8 Th Henri Dunant; mains 60-200B; ⏲11am-11pm; ❄; BTS Siam) Immensely popular with Thai families, *sù gêe* takes the form of a bubbling hotpot of broth and the raw ingredients to dip therein.

SILOM, SATHON & RIVERSIDE

Office workers swarm the shanty villages of street vendors for lunch, and simple Indian restaurants proliferate towards the western end of Th Silom and Th Surawong, but this area is known for its elegant restaurants preparing international fusion and royal Thai cuisine.

TOP CHOICE nahm THAI $$$

(off Map p380; 0 2625 3333; Metropolitan Hotel, 27 Th Sathon Tai; set meal 1500B; dinner; ; MRT Lumphini) Australian chef/author David Thompson is behind what is quite possibly the best Thai restaurant in Bangkok. Dishes range from the exotic (spicy stir-fried frog with chillies, turmeric holy basil and cumin leaves) to the adventurous (fermented fish simmered with minced prawns and pork with chillies, galangal and green peppercorn), with bold flavours and artful presentation as a unifying thread. Reservations recommended.

Chennai Kitchen INDIAN $

(Map p380; 10 Th Pan; mains 50-150B; 10am-3pm & 6-9.30pm; ; BTS Surasak) This thimble-sized restaurant puts out some of the most solid southern Indian vegetarian around.

Somtam Convent THAI $

('Hai'; Map p380; 2/4-5 Th Convent; mains 20-120B; 10.30am-9pm; BTS Sala Daeng, MRT Si Lom) A less intimidating introduction to the wonders of *lâhp* (a minced meat 'salad'), *sôm-đam* (papaya salad) and other Isan delights can be had at this popular restaurant.

Soi 10 Food Centres THAI $

(Map p380; Soi 10, Th Silom; mains 20-60B; lunch Mon-Fri; BTS Sala Daeng, MRT Si Lom) These two adjacent hangar-like buildings tucked behind Soi 10 are the main lunchtime fuelling stations for this area's office staff.

SUKHUMVIT

This avenue is the communal dining room of Bangkok's expat communities.

Bo.lan THAI $$$

(Map p378; 0 2260 2962; www.bolan.co.th; 42 Soi Rongnarong Phichai Songkhram, Soi 26, Th Sukhumvit; set meal 1500B; dinner Tue-Sun; BTS Phrom Phong) This Australian/Thai couple's scholarly approach to Thai cooking takes the form of seasonal set meals featuring dishes you're not likely to find elsewhere. Reservations recommended.

Nasir Al-Masri MIDDLE EASTERN $$$

(Map p378; 4/6 Soi 3/1, Th Sukhumvit; mains 80-350B; 24hr; ; BTS Nana) The glimmering stainless-steel exterior beckons to passers-by at this Soi Arabia fave. Middle Eastern meals can be consumed streetside or upstairs for the ambience of a genuine *sheeshah* (waterpipe) cafe.

Myeong Ga KOREAN $$$

(Map p378; 0 2229 4658; cnr Soi 12 & Th Sukhumvit; mains 200-550B; dinner; ; BTS Asok, MRT Sukhumvit) Located on the ground floor of Sukhumvit Plaza, the multistorey complex known around Bangkok as Korean Town, this restaurant is the city's best destination for authentic Seoul food.

Bed Supperclub INTERNATIONAL $$$

(Map p378; 0 2651 3537; www.bedsupperclub.com; 26 Soi 11, Th Sukhumvit; mains 450-990B, set meals 790-1850B; 7.30-10pm Tue-Thu, dinner 9pm Fri & Sat; ; BTS Nana) Crawl into Bed, a long-standing cutting-edge leader that dabbles in 'modern eclectic cuisine'.

Boon Tong Kiat Singapore Hainanese Chicken Rice SINGAPOREAN $

(Map p378; 440/5 Soi 55/Thong Lor, Th Sukhumvit; dishes 60-150B; lunch & dinner; ; BTS Thong Lo) Order a plate of the restaurant's namesake and bear witness to how a dish can be simultaneously simple and profound.

Drinking

Once infamous as an anything-goes nightlife destination, in recent years Bangkok has been edging towards teetotalism with strict regulations limiting the sale of alcohol and increasingly conservative closing times, with most bars closing around 1am. Also, keep in mind that smoking has been outlawed at all indoor (and some quasi-outdoor) entertainment places since 2008.

KO RATANAKOSIN & BANGLAMPHU

The area around Th Khao San is one of the city's best destinations for a fun night out.

Amorosa BAR

(Map p370; www.arunresidence.com; rooftop, Arun Residence, 36-38 Soi Pratu Nok Yung; 6-11pm; bus 123, 508, river ferry Tha Tien) It may be the only bar in the area, but that doesn't mean it's any sort of compromise; Amorosa's rooftop location packs killer views of Wat Arun, making it one of the best spots in Bangkok for a riverside sundowner.

Silom

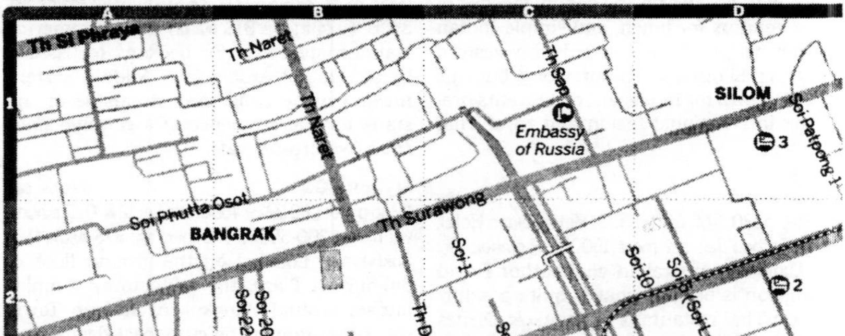

NORTHERN THAILAND BANGKOK

Silom

Activities, Courses & Tours
1 Health Land C4

Sleeping
2 HQ Hostel D2
3 Siam Heritage D1

Eating
4 Chennai Kitchen B3
5 Somtam Convent E2

Drinking
6 Balcony E1
7 Telephone E1

Entertainment
8 DJ Station E1
9 G.O.D. E1
10 Tapas Room E1

Information
11 BNH F3

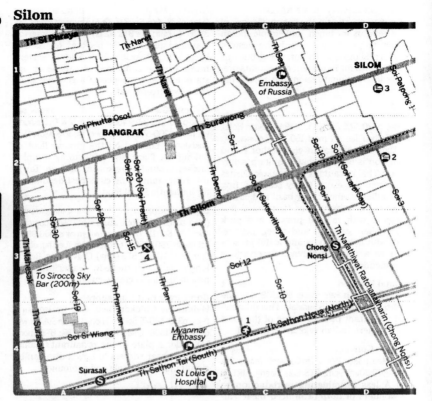

Hippie de Bar BAR
(Map p370; 46 Th Khao San; ⌚6pm-2am; river ferry Tha Phra Athit) Popular with the domestic crowd, Hippie boasts several levels of fun, both indoor and outdoor. There's food, pool tables and a soundtrack you're unlikely to hear elsewhere in town.

Pranakorn Bar BAR
(Map p370; 58/2 Soi Damnoen Klang Tai; ⌚6pm-midnight; klorng taxi Tha Phan Fah) It must have taken a true visionary to transform this characterless multilevel building into a warm, fun destination for a night out.

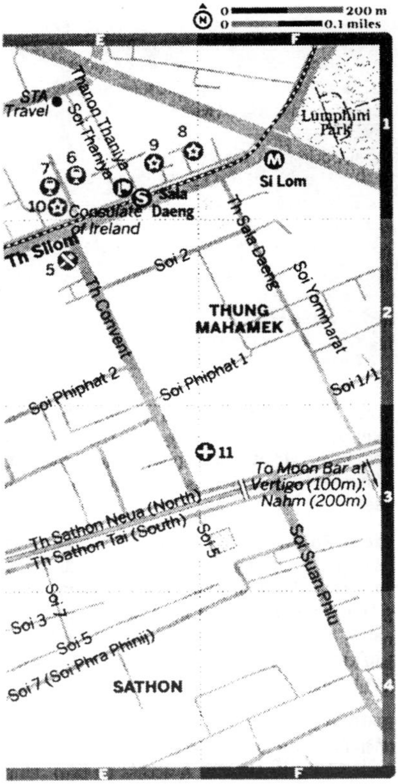

Head for the rooftop for breezy views over Banglamphu.

Rolling Bar BAR
(Map p370; Th Prachathipatai; ⏲6pm-midnight; klorng taxi Tha Phan Fah) An escape from hectic Th Khao San is a good enough excuse to schlep to this quiet canal-side boozer. Live music and capable bar snacks are reasons to stay.

Center Khao San BAR
(Map p370; Th Khao San; ⏲24hr; river ferry Tha Phra Athit) One of many front-row views of the human parade on Th Khao San. The upstairs bar hosts late-night bands.

SILOM, SATHON & RIVERSIDE

Moon Bar at Vertigo BAR
(Off map p380; Banyan Tree Hotel, 21/100 Th Sathon Tai; ⏲5.30pm-1am; MRT Lumphini) Precariously perched on the top of 61 floors of skyscraper, Moon Bar offers a bird's-eye view of Bangkok. Things can get a bit crowded here come sunset, so be sure to show up a bit early to get the best seats.

Sirocco Sky Bar BAR
(Off map p380; The Dome, 1055 Th Silom; ⏲6pm-1am; BTS Saphan Taksin) Descend the sweeping stairs like a Hollywood diva to the precipice bar of this rooftop restaurant that looks over the Mae Nam Chao Phraya.

SIAM SQUARE

Co-Co Walk BAR
(Map p376; 87/70 Th Phayathai; ⏲6pm-1am; BTS Ratchathewi) This covered compound is a lively smorgasbord of pubs, bars and live music popular with Thai university students.

Hyde & Seek BAR
(Map p376; ground fl, Athenee Residence, 65/1 Soi Ruam Rudi; ⏲11am-1am; ❄; BTS Phloen Chit) In addition to Bangkok's most well-stocked bar and some of the city's best cocktails, Hyde & Seek also does tasty and comforting English-inspired bar snacks and meals.

SUKHUMVIT

WTF GALLERY-BAR
(Map p378; www.wtfbangkok.com; 7 Soi 51, Th Sukhumvit; ⏲6pm-1am Tue-Sun; ❄; BTS Thong Lo) No, not that WTF; Wonderful Thai Friendship combines a cozy bar and an art gallery in one attractive package.

Soul Food Mahanakorn BAR-RESTAURANT
(Map p378; ☎0 2714 7708; www.soulfoodmahanakorn.com; 56/10 Soi 55/Thong Lor, Th Sukhumvit; mains 120-250B; ⏲5.30pm-midnight; ❄; BTS Thong Lo) The boozy Thai-inspired cocktails at this popular pub go hand-in-hand with the kitchen's takes on rustic Thai dishes.

Cheap Charlie's BAR
(Map p378; Soi 11, Th Sukhumvit; ⏲Mon-Sat; BTS Nana) There's never enough seating, and the design concept is best classified as 'junkyard', but on most nights this chummy open-air beer corner is a great place to meet everybody, from package tourists to resident English teachers.

Bangkok Bar BAR
(Map p378; Soi Ekamai 2, Soi 63/Ekamai, Th Sukhumvit; ⏲8pm-1am; ❄; BTS Ekkamai) Bounce with Thai indie kids at this fun bar. There's live music, and the eats are strong enough to make Bangkok Bar a dinner destination.

THE PINK MANGO

Bangkok's homosexual community is out and very much open, enjoying lots of local nightspots and even an annual pride parade. **Lesbian Guide to Bangkok** (www.bangkoklesbian.com), **Dreaded Ned** (www.dreadedned.com) and **Fridae** (www.fridae.com) have up-to-date listings and events.

The area around lower Th Silom is Bangkok's gaybourhood. **DJ Station** (Map p380; 8/6-8 Soi 2, Th Silom; ⊙8pm-late; BTS Sala Daeng, MRT Si Lom) and **G.O.D.** (Guys on Display; Map p380; Soi 2/1, Th Silom; cover 280B; ⊙8pm-late; BTS Sala Daeng, MRT Si Lom) get a mixed Thai-*faràng* crowd. For something at conversation level, nearby Soi 4 is home to long-standing **Balcony** (Map p380; www.balconypub.com; 86-88 Soi 4, Th Silom; ⊙5.30pm-1am; BTS Sala Daeng, MRT Si Lom) and **Telephone** (Map p380; 114/11-13 Soi 4, Th Silom; ⊙5pm-1am; BTS Sala Daeng, MRT Si Lom).

Bangkok's lesbian scene is pretty much limited to **Zeta** (29/67 Royal City Ave/RCA, off Phra Ram IX; admission 100B; ⊙8pm-2am; MRT Phra Ram 9 & access by taxi).

Tuba BAR

(Off Map p378; 34 Room 11-12 A, Soi Ekamai 21, Soi Ekamai/63, Th Sukhumvit; ❄; BTS Ekkamai) Part storage room for over-the-top vintage furniture, part friendly local boozer, this bizarre bar certainly doesn't lack in character. Indulge in a whole bottle for once and don't miss the delicious chicken wings.

Bull's Head BAR

(Map p378; ☎0 2259 4444; 595/10-11 Soi 33/1, Th Sukhumvit; ⊙5pm-1am; ❄; BTS Phrom Phong) Bangkok boasts several English-style pubs but the Bull's Head is probably the most authentic of the lot.

☆ Entertainment

Dance Clubs

The trick in Bangkok is to catch the right club on the right night. To find out what is going on, check **Dude Sweet** (www.dudesweet.org), organisers of hugely popular monthly parties, and **Bangkok Recorder** (www.bangkokrecorder.com) for rotating theme nights and visiting celeb DJs. Other sources of info include the listings mag **BK** (http://bk.asia-city.com/nightlife), or if you're partial to the Th Sukhumvit scene, www.thonglor-ekamai.com.

Cover charges for clubs and discos range from 100B to 600B and usually include a drink. Don't even think about showing up before 11pm, and always bring ID. Most clubs close at 2am.

RCA DANCE CLUBS

(Royal City Avenue; off Th Phra Ram IX; MRT Phra Ram 9 & access by taxi) Formerly a bastion of the teen scene, this Vegas-like strip has finally graduated from high school and hosts partiers of every age. Worthwhile destinations include **808 Club** (www.808bangkok.com; admission from 300B), **Flix/Slim** (admission free), **Route 66** (www.route66club.com; admission free) and **Cosmic Café** (admission free).

Tapas Room DANCE CLUB

(Map p380; www.tapasroom.net; 114/17-18 Soi 4, Th Silom; admission 100B; BTS Sala Daeng, MRT Si Lom) You won't find food here, rather the name is an accurate indicator of the Spanish/Moroccan-inspired vibe of this multi-level den.

Ekamai Soi 5 DANCE CLUB

(Map p378; cnr Soi Ekamai 5 & Soi 63/Ekamai, Th Sukhumvit; BTS Ekkamai & access by taxi) This open-air entertainment zone is the destination of choice for Bangkok's young and beautiful – for the moment at least. **Demo** (admission free), with blasting beats and a NYC warehouse vibe, is the epitome of the Alpha Club, while **Funky Villa** (admission free), with its outdoor seating and Top 40 soundtrack, boasts more of a chill-out vibe.

Bed Supperclub DANCE CLUB

(Map p378; www.bedsupperclub.com; 26 Soi 11, Th Sukhumvit; admission from 600B; BTS Nana) This illuminated tube has been a literal highlight of the Bangkok club scene for a good while now. Arrive early to squeeze in **dinner** (mains 450-990B, set meals 790-1850B; ⊙7.30-10pm Tue-Thu, dinner 9pm Fri & Sat), or if you've only got dancing on your mind, come on Tuesday for the popular hip-hop nights.

Club Culture DANCE CLUB

(Map p370 www.club-culture-bkk.com; admission from 200B; Th Ratchadamnoen Klang; klorng taxi Tha Phan Fah) Housed in a seemingly abandoned four-storey building, Club Culture is the quirkiest member of Bangkok's club scene. Opening dates and times can depend on events, so check the website to see what's going on.

Q Bar DANCE CLUB
(Map p378; www.qbarbangkok.com; 34 Soi 11, Th Sukhumvit; admission from 700B; BTS Nana) This darkened industrial space sees a revolving cast of somebodies, nobodies and working girls. Various theme nights fill the weekly calendar.

Café Democ DANCE CLUB
(Map p370; www.cafe-democ.com; 78 Th Ratchadamnoen Klang; admission free; klorng taxi Tha Phan Fah) Up-and-coming DJs present their turntable dexterity at this narrow unpretentious club in Olde Bangkok.

Narz DANCE CLUB
(Map p378; 112 Soi 23, Th Sukhumvit; admission 500B; BTS Asok, MRT Sukhumvit) The former Narcissus has undergone a recent nip and tuck and now consists of three separate zones boasting an equal variety of music.

Live Music

Th Khao San is a hot venue for Thai indie bands. **Brick Bar** (Map p370; basement, Buddy Lodge, 265 Th Khao San; ⊙8pm-1am; ❄; river ferry Tha Phra Athit) hosts live music for an almost exclusively Thai crowd.

Bangkok's jazz scene is strong at **Living Room** (Map p378; ☎0 2649 8888; Level I, Sheraton Grande Sukhumvit, 250 Th Sukhumvit; ⊙6.30pm-midnight; ❄; BTS Asok, MRT Sukhumvit), while rock rules at **Saxophone Pub & Restaurant** (www.saxophonepub.com; 3/8 Th Phayathai; ⊙6pm-2am; ❄; BTS Victory Monument) and tiny **Ad Here the 13th** (Map p370; 13 Th Samsen; ⊙6pm-midnight; ❄; river ferry Tha Phra Athit).

For something more local, check out the stage shows at **Tawandang German Brewery** (cnr Th Phra Ram III & Th Narathiwat Ratchanakharin; ❄; BTS Chong Nonsi & access by taxi) or Thailand's own version of country music at **Raintree** (116/63-64 Soi Th Rang Nam; ⊙6pm-1am; ❄; BTS Victory Monument).

Thai Boxing

Lumphini Stadium (Sanam Muay Lumphini; ☎0 2251 4303; Th Phra Ram IV; MRT Lumphini) and **Ratchadamnoen Stadium** (Sanam Muay Ratchadamnoen; Map p370; ☎0 2281 4205; Th Ratchadamnoen Nok; bus 70, 503, 509, klorng taxi Tha Phan Fah) host Thailand's biggest *muay thai* matches. Ratchadamnoen hosts the matches on Monday, Wednesday, Thursday and Sunday at 6.30pm. Lumphini hosts matches on Tuesday and Friday at 6.30pm and Saturday at 5pm and 8.30pm. Foreigners pay 1000/1500/2000B for 3rd-class/2nd-class/ringside seats (advance reservations needed for ringside). Don't buy tickets from the hawkers hanging round outside the stadium.

Traditional Arts Performances

As Thailand's cultural repository, Bangkok offers visitors an array of dance and theatre performances.

Chalermkrung Royal Theatre THEATRE
(Sala Chalerm Krung; ☎0 2222 0434; www.salachalermkrung.com; cnr Th Charoen Krung & Th Triphet; tickets 800-1200B; ⊙showtime 7.30pm; river ferry Tha Saphan Phut) This art deco theatre provides a striking venue for *kŏhn* (masked dance-drama based on the Ramakian). Don't wear shorts, singlets or sandals when you visit.

Aksra Theatre THEATRE
(☎0 2677 8888, ext 5730; www.aksratheatre.com; 3rd fl, King Power Complex, 8/1 Th Rang Nam; tickets 400-600B; ⊙shows 7.30-8.30pm Mon-Wed, dinner shows 6.30-7pm Thu-Sun; BTS Victory Monument) The ancient art of Thai puppetry was rescued from obscurity by a Thai puppeteer affectionately known as Joe Louis. His children carry on the tradition here.

Shopping

Bangkok is not the place for recovering shopaholics because the temptation to stray from the path is overwhelming. The best of Bangkok's shopping centres line the BTS around Siam Sq. Among your choices are the adjacent **Siam Center & Siam Discovery Center** (Map p376; cnr Th Phra Ram I & Th Phayathai; ⊙10am-10pm; BTS National Stadium or Siam), both good places to pick up local clothing labels, and everyman's **MBK Center** (Mahboonkhrong; Map p376; www.mbk-center.co.th/en; cnr Th Phra Ram I & Th Phayathai; ⊙10am-10pm; BTS National Stadium & Siam), which is just a few air-conditioners and escalators fancier than a street market.

Markets

Don't let the bargaining put you off, it's good fun for seller and buyer.

Chatuchak Weekend Market MARKET
(Talat Nat Jatujak; ⊙9am-6pm Sat & Sun; BTS Mo Chit, MRT Chatuchak Park & Kamphaeng Phet)

DESTINATIONS FROM BANGKOK

DESTINATION	BUS	TRAIN	AIR
Chiang Khong	14 hours/ frequent/493-888B	N/A	N/A
Chiang Mai	9½ hours/ frequent/605-810B	12-15 hours/6 daily/231-581B	70-85 minutes/frequent/from 1490B
Chiang Rai	11-12 hours/ frequent/448-716B	N/A	1¼ hours/frequent/from 1550B
Hanoi (Vietnam)	N/A	N/A	2 hours/4 daily/from 3290B
Ho Chi Minh City (Saigon; Vietnam)	N/A	N/A	1½ hours/5 daily/from 2390B
Lampang	9 hours/ frequent/347-625B	11-12 hours/6 daily/106-1372B	1 hour/1 daily/2405B
Luang Prabang (Laos)	N/A	N/A	1¾ hours/3 daily/from US$173
Mae Sai	13 hours/ frequent/483-966B	N/A	N/A
Mukdahan	10 hours/ frequent/390-502B	N/A	N/A
Nakhon Phanom	11-12 hours/ frequent/450-592B	N/A	40 minutes/1 daily/from 2600B
Nakhon Ratchasima (Khorat)	3 hours/ frequent/154-250B	6 hours/14 daily/100-1010B	N/A
Nan	10-11 hours/ frequent/424-773B	N/A	1¼ hours/1-2 daily/1690B
Nong Khai	10-11 hours/ frequent/350-600B	11-12 hours/3 daily/103-1317B	N/A
Pakse (Laos)	N/A	N/A	2½ hours/1 daily/from US$163
Phnom Penh (Cambodia)	N/A	N/A	1 hour/7 daily/from 2970B
Siem Reap (Cambodia)	N/A	N/A	1 hour/4 daily/from 6635B
Savannakhet (Laos)	see Mukdahan	N/A	1½ hours/1 daily/from US$153
Sukhothai	6-7 hours/ frequent/255-380B	N/A	80 minutes/2 daily/3480B
Surin	7 hours/ frequent/250-372B	7-9 hours/10 daily/73-1146B	N/A
Ubon Ratchathani	8½-10 hours/ frequent/385-473B	8½-12 hours/7 daily/95-1280B	55-65 minutes/2-3 daily/from 1300B
Udon Thani	8-9 hours/ frequent/321-412B	10-11 hours/4 daily/95-1277B	65 minutes/6 daily/from 1386B
Vientiane (Laos)	see Nong Khai	see Nong Khai	1½ hours/4 daily/from US$148

The mother of all markets sprawls over a huge area with 15,000 stalls and an estimated 200,000 visitors a day. Everything is sold here, from snakes to handicrafts to aisles and aisles of clothes.

Pak Khlong Market MARKET

(Flower Market; Th Chakkaphet & Th Atsadang; ⌚24hr; river ferry Tha Saphan Phut) Every night this market near Chao Phraya Mae Nam becomes the city's largest depot for wholesale flowers.

COMMON BANGKOK SCAMS

Commit these classic rip-offs to memory and join us in our ongoing crusade to outsmart Bangkok's crafty scam artists.

» **Gem scam** If anyone offers you unsolicited advice about a gem sale, you can be sure that there is a scam involved.

» **Closed today** Ignore any 'friendly' local who tells you that an attraction is closed for a Buddhist holiday or for cleaning. These are set-ups for trips to a bogus gem sale.

» **Túk-túk rides for 10B** Say goodbye to your day's itinerary if you climb aboard this ubiquitous scam. These alleged 'tours' bypass all the sights and instead cruise to all the fly-by-night gem and tailor shops that pay commissions.

» **Flat-fare taxi ride** Flatly refuse any driver who quotes a flat fare. If the driver has 'forgotten' to put the meter on, just say, 'Meter, kha/khap'.

» **Tourist buses** On long-distance vans originating on Th Khao San, well-organised and connected thieves have hours to comb through your bags. This scam has been running for years but is easy to avoid simply by carrying valuables with you on the bus.

» **Friendly strangers** Be wary of smartly dressed men who approach you asking where you're from and where you're going. As the tourist authorities here pointed out, this sort of behaviour is out of character for Thais and should be treated with suspicion.

Talat Rot Fai MARKET

(Th Kamphaeng Phet; ⏲6pm-midnight Sat & Sun; MRT Kamphaeng Phet) Set in a sprawling abandoned rail yard, this market is all about the retro, from antique enamel platters to second hand Vespas.

Information

ATMs, banks, and currency-exchange kiosks are widespread.

Emergency

Tourist police (☎nationwide call centre 1155; ⏲24hr) English-speaking officers.

Internet Access

Internet cafes charge 20B to 50B per hour. Wi-fi, mostly free of charge, is becoming more and more ubiquitous around Bangkok. For relatively authoritative lists of wi-fi hotspots in Bangkok, go to www.bkkpages.com (under 'Bangkok Directory') or www.stickmanweekly.com/WiFi/BangkokFreeWirelessInternetWiFi.htm.

Media

Bangkok 101 (www.bangkok101.com) A monthly city primer with photo essays and reviews of sights, restaurants and entertainment.

Bangkok Post (www.bangkokpost.net) The leading English-language daily with Friday and weekend supplements covering city events.

BK (http://bk.asia-city.com) Free weekly listings mag for the young and hip.

CNNGo (www.cnngo.com/bangkok) Check the Bangkok pages of this online listings mag for quirky news and reviews.

Medical Services

The following hospitals offer 24-hour emergency service and English-speaking staff. Prices are high, but so is the quality. Use these numbers to call an ambulance.

BNH (Map p380; ☎0 2686 2700; www.bnhhospital.com; 9 Th Convent; BTS Sala Daeng, MRT Si Lom)

Bumrungrad International Hospital (Map p378; ☎0 2667 1000; www.bamrungrad.com; 33 Soi 3/Nana Nua, Th Sukhumvit; BTS Phloen Chit)

Post

Main post office (Th Charoen Krung; ⏲8am-8pm Mon-Fri, 8am-1pm Sat & Sun; river ferry Th Si Phraya)

Tourist Information

Bangkok Information Center (Map p370; ☎0 2225 7612-4; www.bangkoktourist.com; 17/1 Th Phra Athit; ⏲8am-7pm Mon-Fri, 9am-5pm Sat & Sun; bus 32, 33, 64, 82, river ferry Tha Phra Athit) City-specific tourism office provides maps, brochures and directions.

Tourism Authority of Thailand (TAT; ☎1672; www.tourismthailand.org) Head Office (☎0 2250 5500; 1600 Th Petchaburi Tat Mai; ⏲8.30am-4.30pm; MRT Phetchaburi); Banglamphu (Map p370; ☎0 2283 1500; cnr Th Ratchadamnoen Nok & Th Chakrapatdipong; ⏲8.30am-4.30pm; klorng taxi Phan Fah); Suvarnabhumi International Airport (☎0 2134 0040; 2nd fl, btwn Gates 2 & 5; ⏲24hr).

Travel Agencies

Bangkok travel agencies vary greatly in the amount of commission they charge; shop around to compare fares. These are long-running agencies:

Diethelm Travel (☎0 2660 7000; www.diethelmtravel.com; 14th fl, Kian Gwan Bldg II, 140/1 Th Witthayu/Wireless Rd; BTS Phloen Chit)

STA Travel (Map p380; ☎0 2236 0262; www.statravel.co.th; 14th fl, Wall Street Tower, 33/70 Th Surawong; ⊙9am-5pm Mon-Fri, to noon Sat; BTS, MRT Si Lom)

ℹ Getting There & Away

Air

Bangkok has two airports. **Suvarnabhumi International Airport** (☎0 2132 1888; www.bangkokairportonline.com), 30km east of Bangkok, began commercial international and domestic service in September 2006. The airport's name is pronounced *sù·wan·ná·poom*, and it inherited the airport code (BKK) previously used by the old airport at Don Muang. The unofficial airport website has practical information in English, as well as real-time details of arrivals and departures.

Bangkok's former international and domestic **Don Muang Airport** (☎0 2535 1111; www.donmuangairportonline.com), 25km north of central Bangkok, serves a handful of domestic flights.

Bus

Buses using government bus stations are far more reliable and less prone to incidents of theft than those departing from Th Khao San or other tourist centres.

The **Northern & Northeastern bus terminal** (Mo Chit; Map p369; ☎for northern routes 0 2936 2841, ext 311/442, for northeastern routes 0 2936 2852, ext 611/448; Th Kamphaeng Phet; BTS Mo Chit or MRT Kamphaeng Phet & access by taxi), commonly called Mor Chit station *(sà·thaa·nii măw chít)*, serves almost every destination covered in this book, including Aranya Prathet.

Use the **Eastern bus terminal** (Ekamai; Map p378; ☎0 2391 2504; Soi Ekamai/40, Th Sukhumvit; BTS Ekkamai), accessible via BTS to Ekkamai station, if you are headed to Cambodia via Hat Lek or Chanthaburi. Although not covered by this book, southern destinations are handled by the **Southern bus terminal** (Sai Tai Mai; Map p369; ☎0 2435 1199; Th Bromaratchachonanee) in Thonburi. The easiest way to reach the station is by taxi, or you can take bus 79, 159, 201 or 516 from Th Ratchadamnoen or bus 40 from the Victory Monument.

Minivan

Privately run minivans, called *rót đôo*, are a fast and relatively comfortable way to get between Bangkok and its neighbouring provinces. The biggest minivan stop is just north of the Victory Monument (Map p369), with departures for Aranya Prathet (for the Cambodian border; 230B, 3½ hours, from 6am to 6pm) and Muak Lek (for Khao Yai; 120B, 2½ hours, from 8am to 8pm). Directly east of the monument is a minivan to Suvarnabhumi International Airport (40B, one hour, from 5am to 10.30pm).

Train

Bangkok's main train station is **Hualamphong** (Map p369; ☎nationwide call centre 1690, 0 2220 4334; www.railway.co.th; Th Phra Ram IV; MRT Hua Lamphong). It's advisable to ignore all touts here and avoid the travel agencies. To check timetables and prices for other destinations call the **State Railway of Thailand** (☎nationwide call centre 1690; www.railway.co.th) or look at its website.

ℹ Getting Around

Because of parking hassles and traffic jams, hiring a car for getting around Bangkok is not recommended.

Boat

See the boxed text on p373 for the lowdown on water travel in Bangkok.

BTS & MRT

The elevated BTS, also known as the Skytrain *(rót fai fáa)*, whisks you through 'new' Bangkok (Silom, Sukhumvit and Siam Sq). The interchange between the two lines is at Siam station, and trains run frequently from 6am to midnight. Fares vary from 15B to 40B, and most ticket machines only accept coins, but change is available at the information booths.

Bangkok's subway (MRT) is most helpful for people staying in the Sukhumvit or Silom areas to reach the train station at Hualamphong. Otherwise the system is mainly a suburban commuter line. Fares cost 15B to 40B. The trains run frequently from 6am to midnight.

Bus

Bangkok's bus service is frequent and frantic, so a bus map (like *Bangkok Bus Guide* by ThinkNet) is a necessity. Don't expect it to be 100% correct, though; routes change regularly.

Fares for ordinary (non-air-con) buses start at 5B, while air-con buses begin at 11B.

The following bus lines are useful for tourists who are travelling between Banglamphu and Siam Sq:

Bus 15 From Tha Phra, on the Thonburi side of the river, to Sanam Luang (accessible to Wat Phra Kaew) with stops at MBK Center (connect to BTS) and Th Ratchadamnoen Klang (accessible to Th Khao San).

Bus 47 Khlong Toei Port to Department of Lands, along Th Phahonyothin, in northern Bangkok,

GETTING TO CAMBODIA BY LAND

Aranya Prathet to Poipet

This is Thailand's busiest border crossing to Cambodia, as it's the most direct land route to Angkor Wat and a destination for Thais visiting the casino parlours in Poipet.

The Thai border town of Aranya Prathet can be reached by bus, minivan or train from Bangkok. We advise *against* the Th Khao San bus services that go from Bangkok to Siem Reap; we've heard many reports of rip-offs and excessively long trips forcing travellers to overnight at commission-paying guesthouses before crossing the border. If you start out early, the trip through the border can be done in one day, but do note that immigration lines can be long, especially on weekends.

Frequent buses leave from Bangkok's Northern & Northeastern bus terminal (207B, four to five hours), Eastern bus terminal (200B, four hours) and Bangkok's Suvarnabhumi airport (187B, three hours, three times daily). Minivans (230B, 3½ hours, from 6am to 6pm) depart north of the Victory Monument, and there are also two trains (3rd class 48B, six hours, 5.55am and 1.05pm) per day that connect Bangkok's Hualamphong train station with Aranya Prathet. From the train station you'll either need to take a *sŏrngtăaou* (15B), motorcycle taxi (60B) or túk-túk (80B) the final 6km to the border.

After getting stamped out at the **Thai border post** (☎0 3723 0099; ⊙7am-8pm), follow the throng to the Cambodian **border** (⊙7am-8pm); look for the 'Visa on Arrival' sign if you don't have a visa already (see p275 for details on Cambodian visas). On the Cambodian side, there are some touts and scammers who try to 'assist' you, though they are less frequent than in years past. Just continue with border formalities yourself and refer to the Poipet section (p226) for onward travel details.

Pong Nam Ron to Psar Pruhm

It's also possible to cross to Cambodia via the eponymous provincial capital of Chanthaburi Province.

To Chanthaburi, buses leave from Bangkok's Northern & Northeastern bus terminal (187B, 3½ hours, two daily departures) and Eastern bus terminal (187B, 3½ hours, frequent). In Chanthaburi, minivans leave from a stop across the river from River Guesthouse to the border at Pong Nam Ron (150B, 1½ hours, three times daily). From there you can exit the **Thai border** (☎0 3938 7127; ⊙7am-8pm) and cross the **Cambodian border** (⊙7am-8pm) with the usual formalities (for details on Cambodian visas go to p275) to Pailin, which has transport to scenic Battambang for connections to Siem Reap or Phnom Penh. For details on this journey, see p224.

Hat Lek to Cham Yeam

The southernmost border crossing fuses the Thai beach destination of Ko Chang (not covered in this book) with Cambodia's Sihanoukville. The best way to reach this crossing from Bangkok is to travel through the southeastern Thai town of Trat.

To Trat there are buses from Bangkok's Eastern bus terminal (248B, 4½ hours, frequent), Northern & Northeastern bus terminal (248B, 5½ hours, two morning departures) and Suvarnabhumi International Airport (248B, four to 4½ hours, five daily departures). From Trat, take a minivan from the bus station to Hat Lek (120 to 150B) and after crossing the **Thai border** (☎0 3958 8108; ⊙7am-8pm), continue on to Cambodian immigration.

Cambodian tourist visas are available at the **border** (⊙7am-8pm) for US$20, although overcharging in Thai baht is commonplace (for details on Cambodian visas, see p275); payment is usually only accepted in baht at this border. If you try to debate the issue, be prepared for an argument. Be sure to bring a passport photo and try to avoid some of the runner boys who want to issue a health certificate or other 'medical' paperwork.

For details on travelling this route in the opposite direction, see p247.

GETTING INTO TOWN

To/From the Airport

At the time of writing there were still two functioning airports in Bangkok; the vast majority of flights are relegated to shiny new Suvarnabhumi, but some domestic flights still fly in and out of the old Don Muang Airport. If you need to transfer between the two, pencil in *at least* an hour, as the two airports are at opposite ends of town. Minivans run between the two airports from 6am to 5pm (30B to 50B).

SUVARNABHUMI INTERNATIONAL AIRPORT

Local Transport Several air-con local buses serve the airport's public transport centre, a 3km ride on a free shuttle bus from Suvarnabhumi. Bus lines city-bound tourists are likely to use include 551 (Victory Monument), 554 (Don Muang) and 556 (Th Khao San), and minivan line 552 (On Nut BTS station) – fares start at 25B.

From town, you can take the BTS to On Nut, then from near the market entrance opposite Tesco take minivan 522 (25B, about 40 minutes, 6am to 9pm) to the airport. Another alternative is the minivans that park at the east side of the Victory Monument (40B, one hour, from 5am to 10.30pm).

Airport Rail Link In 2010 the much-delayed elevated train service linking central Bangkok and Suvarnabhumi International Airport was finally completed. An express service runs, without stops, between Makkasan and Phaya Thai stations and the airport (15-18 minutes, 150B), from 6am to midnight. Makkasan, also known as Bangkok City Air Terminal (Map p369), is a short walk from MRT Phetchaburi.

The Airport Rail Link is on floor B1 of Suvarnabhumi International Airport.

Taxi As you exit the terminal, ignore the touts and all the signs pointing you to 'official airport taxis' (which cost 700B flat) and descend to the 1st floor to join the generally fast-moving queue for a public taxi. Cabs booked through these desks should always use their meter, but they often try their luck so insist by saying, 'Meter, please'. Toll charges (paid by the passengers) vary between 25B and 45B. Note also that there's an additional 50B surcharge added to all fares departing from the airport, payable directly to the driver.

DON MUANG AIRPORT

There are no longer any express airport buses to/from Don Muang. Slow, crowded public bus 59 stops on the highway in front of the airport and carries on to Banglamphu, passing Th Khao San and the Democracy Monument.

As at Suvarnabhumi, public taxis leave from outside the arrivals hall and there is a 50B airport charge added to the meter fare.

The walkway that crosses from Terminal 1 to the Amari Airport Hotel also provides access to Don Muang train station, which has trains to Hualamphong train station every one to 1½ hours from 4am to 11.30am and then roughly every hour from 2pm to 9.30pm (5B to 10B, one hour).

with stops along Th Phra Ram IV, MBK Center, Th Ratchadamnoen and Sanam Luang.

Taxi

Although many first-time visitors are hesitant to use them, in general, Bangkok's taxis are new and spacious and the drivers are courteous and helpful, making them an excellent way to get around. All taxis are required to use their meters, which start at 35B, and fares to most places within central Bangkok cost 60B to 80B.

It's generally a good idea to get in moving, rather than parked taxis, as the latter often refuse to use their meters. And simply exit any taxi that refuses to use the meter.

Túk-Túk

Some travellers swear by túk-túk, but most have a hard time bargaining a fair price; know how much it should cost to your destination before soliciting a fare. A short trip on a túk-túk should cost at least 50B.

If a túk-túk driver offers to take you on a sightseeing tour, walk away – it's a touting scheme designed to pressure you into purchasing overpriced goods.

NORTHERN THAILAND

With much of today's Thailand resembling relatively flat farmland, it is surprising to encounter the mist-shrouded peaks and valleys that crown the northern reaches of Thailand. Traders and migrants from Asia's mountainous interior trickled through the river valleys bringing with them commerce and cultural attributes now geopolitically partitioned into the Yunan Province of China, Shan state in Myanmar and the various provinces of northern Thailand. These migration routes were a southern spur of the so-called Asian silk route and these mountains are the final southeastern stretch of the great Himalayan range that acted as both a barrier and a conduit. The most enduring symbol of northern Thailand's connection to such seemingly foreign locales as the Tibetan highlands are the minority hill tribes, some of whom claim Tibetan origin but have now dispersed throughout the high-altitude valleys of the region hoping to preserve their traditional way of life.

The history and culture of northern Thailand was shaped by the Lanna kingdom (literally 'Million Rice Fields'), which is believed to have originated near present-day Chiang Saen, a border town on the west bank of the Mekong River. In the 13th century, the kingdom migrated south through Chiang Rai and finally settled in Chiang Mai. It prospered through cooperation with Sukhothai and other city-state neighbours until its defeat in 1556 by the Burmese. The occupation lasted 200 years until the Thai military leader Phaya Taksin began his campaign to push out the Burmese after the fall of Ayuthaya. Once 'liberated', the former Lanna kingdom was beholden to the new Thai kingdom based in Bangkok and never again regained its independence, though its modern descendants continue to speak a unique regional dialect and maintain old food ways and religious traditions.

Chiang Mai

POP 174,000

Chiang Mai is beloved by Thais and tourists for its (relatively) cool climate and its enduring connections to its past as the capital of the northern Thai kingdom of Lanna. It is a city of temples and culture classes and a gateway to the great outdoors of the northern mountains.

Sights

Temples in Town

Chiang Mai's many temples are famous for their distinctive regional architectural styles: intricate woodcarvings, colourful murals and steeply pitched roofs.

A perfect example of Lanna architecture, **Wat Phra Singh** (Th Singarat) owes its fame to the resident Buddha, Phra Singh (Lion Buddha), housed in a small chapel at the back of the compound.

The huge ruined *chedi* at **Wat Chedi Luang** (Th Phra Pokklao) either collapsed during an earthquake in 1545 or from cannon fire in 1775 during the recapture of Chiang Mai from the Burmese. A partial restoration has preserved its 'ruined' look while ensuring it doesn't crumble further.

The large, old teak *wí·hăhn* at **Wat Phan Tao** (Th Phra Pokklao) is one of Chiang Mai's unsung treasures.

Wat Chiang Man (Th Ratchaphakhinai) is believed to be the oldest wat within the city walls and was erected by King Mengrai, Chiang Mai's founder, in 1296. Two famous Buddha images (Phra Sila and the Crystal Buddha) are kept here in a glass cabinet inside the smaller sanctuary to the right of the main chapel.

TEMPLES OUTSIDE OF TOWN

One of Thailand's most famous temples, **Wat Suthep** (Doi Suthep-Pui National Park; admission 30B) overlooks the whole city from its mountainside perch. The temple contains many fine examples of Lanna art and architecture as well as the frequently photographed gold-plated *chedi*, topped by a five-tiered umbrella and enshrining a famous Buddha relic.

The forest temple of **Wat U Mong** (Soi Wat U Mong), dating from Mengrai's rule, has brick-lined tunnels supposedly fashioned around 1380 for a clairvoyant monk; some are still open for exploration.

Built in a forest grove in 1373, **Wat Suan Dok** (Th Suthep) contains a 500-year-old bronze Buddha image and colourful *jataka* murals, but the scenic sunsets over the collection of royal *chedi* are the biggest attraction.

Museums

Lanna history and works of art are documented at the **Chiang Mai National**

Central Chiang Mai

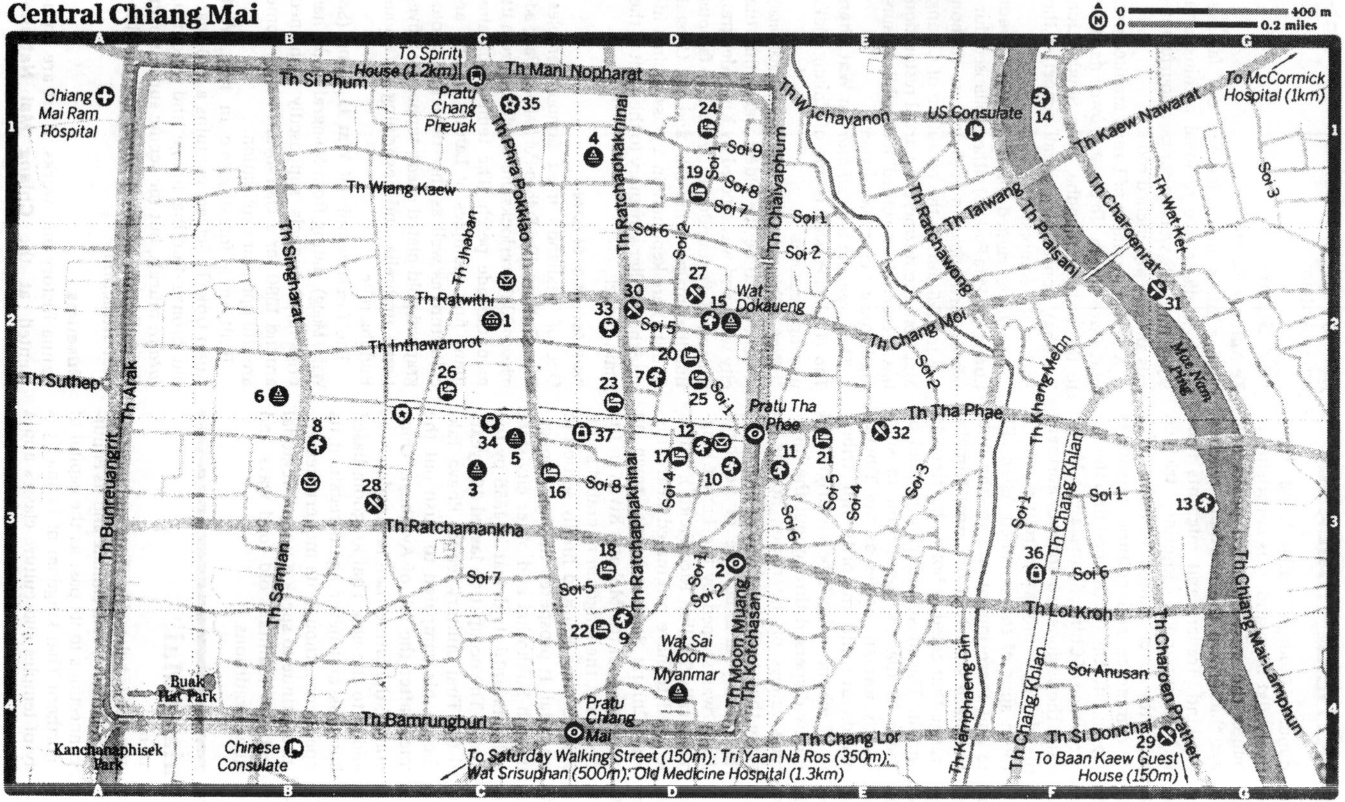

Central Chiang Mai

Sights

1 Chiang Mai City Arts & Cultural Centre ... C2
2 Elephant Nature Park ... D3
3 Wat Chedi Luang ... C3
4 Wat Chiang Man ... D1
5 Wat Phan Tao ... C3
6 Wat Phra Singh ... B2

Activities, Courses & Tours

7 Baan Thai ... D2
8 Chiang Mai Mountain Biking ... B3
9 Chiang Mai Rock Climbing Adventures ... D4
10 Chiang Mai Thai Cookery School ... D3
11 Flight of the Gibbon ... E3
12 Lek Chaiya ... D3
13 Mae Ping River Cruise ... G3
14 Scorpion Tailed River Cruise ... F1
15 Siam River Adventures ... D2

Sleeping

16 3 Sis ... C3
17 Gap's House ... D3
18 Julie Guesthouse ... D3
19 Lamchang House ... D1
20 Mini Cost ... D2
21 Mo Rooms ... E3
22 Sa Thu Boutique House ... D4
23 Tamarind Village ... D2
24 Tri Gong Residence ... D1
25 Vieng Mantra ... D2
26 Villa Duang Champa ... C2

Eating

27 Chiangmai Saloon ... D2
28 Heuan Phen ... B3
29 Just Khao Soi ... G4
30 New Delhi ... D2
31 Riverside Bar & Restaurant ... G2
32 Taste From Heaven ... E3

Drinking

33 Archers ... D2
34 Writer's Club & Wine Bar ... C3

Entertainment

35 North Gate Jazz Co-op ... C1

Shopping

36 Chiang Mai Night Bazaar ... F3
37 Sunday Walking Street ... D3

Museum (☎0 5322 1308; www.thailandmuseum.com; off Th Superhighway; admission 100B; ⏰9am-4pm Wed-Sun) northwest of town.

Chiang Mai's former Provincial Hall has been converted into the **Chiang Mai City Arts & Cultural Centre** (☎0 5321 7793; Th Ratwithi; adult/child 90/40B; ⏰8.30am-5pm Tue-Sun). There are interesting interactive historical displays and glimpses into a building renowned for its architectural restoration.

The **Tribal Museum** (☎0 5321 0872; off Th Chang Pheauk; admission free; ⏰9am-4pm Mon-Fri) at Ratchamangkhla Park is normally worth a visit, although it was being renovated at research time. To get here, head north about 3km from Pratu Chang Pheauk – the museum is on the left-hand side.

Activities

Ping River Trips

Scorpion Tailed River Cruise RIVER CRUISE
(☎08 1960 9398; www.scorpiontailed.com; Th Charoenrat; fare 500B; ⏰5 daily departures) Does history-heavy tours of the river using a traditional-style craft, known as a scorpion-tailed boat.

Mae Ping River Cruises RIVER CRUISE
(☎0 5327 4822; www.maepingrivercruise.com; Th Charoen Prathet; per person 550B; ⏰7-8.30pm) Offers dinner cruises.

Trekking

Chiang Mai is not the only base in northern Thailand for hill-tribe treks but it is the most accessible and thus, most commercial. Most companies offer the same type of tour: a one-hour mini-bus ride to Mae Taeng or Mae Wang (depending on the duration of the trip), a brief hike to an elephant camp, an hour elephant ride to a waterfall, another hour rafting down a river and an overnight in or near a hill-tribe village. One-day treks usually cost around 1000B, while multiday treks (three days and two nights) cost 1500B. Both prices include transport, guide and lunch; in the case of overnight trips, the price also includes lodging (prices will be a bit more in high season). Chiang Mai's Tourism Authority of Thailand office (p395) keeps a list of registered guides.

TREKKING TIPS

Filled with great expectations, many travellers trek through mountainous terrain to hill-tribe villages only to end up disappointed. The hike through the jungle was too short, the hill-tribe villagers were unfriendly and the fellow trekkers were complainers.

Much of this can be avoided if you do your homework. Ask returning trekkers about their experience: did they like the guide, how strenuous was the trip, how rewarding was the village visit etc. Then talk to the agencies that act as brokers: find out how many people will be on the trip (six to 10 is a good range), find out exactly when the tour begins and ends (some three-day treks last less than 48 hours) and be sure you know what the tour does and does not include.

Also, don't overestimate your level of physical fitness: you'll be crossing mountainous terrain in humid weather. The best time to trek is November to February, when the weather is refreshing, there's little or no rain and wildflowers are in bloom.

Trekking can be arranged in numerous towns (but is most popular in Chiang Mai and Chiang Rai) and there are benefits to organising your trek outside popular tourist destinations. Prices tend to be lower and the companies smaller and friendlier, and you usually get into more remote areas. Of course, the downside is that there are fewer companies to choose from and less opportunity to get the lowdown from fellow travellers.

Other Outdoor Activities

See the boxed text on p400 for the award-winning Elephant Nature Park, outside of Chiang Mai.

Flight of the Gibbon ADVENTURE SPORTS
(☎08 9970 5511; www.treetopasia.com; Th Kotchasan; 3hr tours 3000B) This outfit operates a zipline through the forest canopy some 1300m above sea level near Mae Kompong, a high-altitude village, southeast of Chiang Mai. Mountain biking, rock climbing, rafting or hiking can also be tacked on.

Chiang Mai Rock Climbing Adventures ROCK CLIMBING
(☎08 6911 1470; www.thailandclimbing.com; 55/3 Th Ratchaphakhinai; climbing course 2000-6500B) Leads climbing and caving trips to a set of limestone cliffs, known as Crazy Horse Buttress, about 20km east of town.

Siam River Adventures RAFTING
(☎089 515 1917; www.siamrivers.com; 17 Th Ratwithi; tours from 1800B) Runs safety-conscious white-water rafting tours, elephant trekking and village overnight stays.

Chiang Mai Mountain Biking MOUNTAIN BIKING
(☎08 1024 7046; www.mountainbikingchiangmai.com; 1 Th Samlan; tours 1450-2700B) Offers a variety of guided mountain biking (as well as hike-and-bike) tours through Doi Suthep for all levels.

Courses

Buddhist Meditation

Casual introductions to Buddhism are available at 'monk chats' held at Wat Suan Dok, Wat Chedi Luang and Wat Srisuphan. The following have meditation courses and retreats:

Wat Srisuphan MEDITATION
(☎0 5320 0332; 100 Th Wualai; ⏰7-9pm Tue, Thu & Sat) Offers a two-hour introduction to meditation using the four postures: standing, waking, sitting and lying down.

Wat Suan Dok MEDITATION
(☎0 5380 8411, ext 114; www.monkchat.net; Th Suthep; retreats/courses free) Has a two-day meditation retreat every Tuesday and Wednesday; at the end of the month the retreat is extended to four days.

Cooking

Several guesthouses, such as Gap's House, also offer cookery courses. Most courses cost about 1000B per day.

Chiang Mai Thai Cookery School COOKERY COURSE
(☎0 5320 6388; www.thaicookeryschool.com; booking office 47/2 Th Moon Muang) Longest-running school; a portion of profits here funds education of disadvantaged kids.

Baan Thai COOKERY COURSE
(☎0 5335 7339; www.baanthaicookery.com; 11 Soi 5, Th Ratchadamnoen)

Traditional Thai Massage

The following offer in-depth massage courses and shorter foot-reflexology instruction:

Lek Chaiya MASSAGE
(☎0 5327 8325; www.nervetouch.com; 27-29 Th Ratchadamnoen; course from 5000B) Specialises in *jàp sên* (similar to acupressure) and the use of medicinal herbs.

Old Medicine Hospital MASSAGE
(OMH; ☎0 5327 5085; www.thai massageschool.ac.th; 78/1 Soi Siwaka Komarat, Th Wualai; 5-day course 6000B) Very traditional courses with a northern Thai slant.

Festivals & Events

Flower Festival FLOWERS
This is the mother of Chiang Mai festivals held in February and features parades of flower-decorated floats.

Songkran NEW YEAR
The Thai New Year rivals Bangkok with its water pandemonium in mid-April.

Loi Krathong TRADITIONAL
This national festival is celebrated with gusto in Chiang Mai in November.

Sleeping

Most budget guesthouses are clustered on either side of the east moat, and most will arrange free transport from the bus or train station if you call.

IN TOWN

TOP CHOICE **Villa Duang Champa** HOTEL $$
(☎0 5332 7199; www.duangchampa.com; 82 Th Ratchadamnoen; r guesthouse/hotel 700/2500B; ✱@) Duang Champa is an excellent small hotel with simple, beautifully furnished concrete rooms that have tasteful modern fittings. Stick to the hotel as the dark, cramped guesthouse rooms are not a good deal.

Mini Cost HOTEL $$
(☎0 5341 8787; www.minicostcm.com; 19/4 Soi 1, Th Ratchadamnoen; r 750-1050B; ✱@) Apartment-style, contemporary rooms with easy chairs, calming colours and a few touches of Thai-style decor are unusual in Chiang Mai in this price range. It's in a terrific spot too; quiet but accessible to everything around Pratu Tha Phae.

Tamarind Village HOTEL $$$
(☎0 5341 8896-9; www.tamarindvillage.com; 50/1 Th Ratchadamnoen; r 6000-18,000B; ✱@?≋) Tamarind Village has re-created the quiet spaces of a temple with galleried buildings and garden courtyards on the grounds of an old tamarind orchard.

Gap's House GUESTHOUSE $
(☎0 5327 8140; www.gaps-house.com; 3 Soi 4, Th Ratchadamnoen; r 500-750B; ✱@?) Cool, Thai-style wooden rooms planted in a thick jungle garden. Gap's is also famous for its Thai cooking course and nightly vegetarian buffet.

Vieng Mantra HOTEL $$$
(☎0 5332 6640; www.viengmantra.com; 9 Soi 1, Th Ratchadamnoen; r 2000-4500B; ✱@?≋) Smooth, clean lines and a marriage of concrete and wood dominate the Lanna-style building, while rooms are set around an inner courtyard pool and have balconies with sink-in-and-smile cushioned seating.

3 Sis HOTEL $$
(☎0 5327 3243; www.the3sis.com; 1 Soi 8, Th Phra Pokklao; d 1300-1800B; ✱@?) The spacious rooms in the front building are the best deal here, but don't ignore those in the 'vacation lodge', which include lovely wooden floors, clean white walls, fridge and cable TV.

Sa Thu Boutique House HOTEL $$
(☎0 5390 3737; www.sathuboutique.com; 31 Soi Prapokklao, Th Ratchaphakhinai; r 1200-1800B; ≋) Tucked away off busy Ratchaphakhinai Rd, this small boutique gem is freshly opened, beautifully designed and has eager staff.

Julie Guesthouse GUESTHOUSE $
(☎0 5327 4355; www.julieguesthouse.com; 7 Soi 5, Th Phra Pokklao; dm 80B, r 100-350B; ?) Youth central, Julie has a colourful range of rooms and a busy garden cafe.

Lamchang House GUESTHOUSE $
(☎0 5321 0586; 24 Soi 7, Th Moon Muang; r 200B) This old-fashioned Thai house has basic rooms and a small garden restaurant. Bathrooms are shared.

Tri Gong Residence GUESTHOUSE $$
(☎0 5321 4754; www.trigong.com; 8 Soi 1, Th Si Phum; r 700-1000B; ✱@?) Stylish rooms with rattan and teak furniture surrounding a courtyard.

OUTSIDE CENTRE OF TOWN

TOP CHOICE **Mo Rooms** HOTEL $$
(☎0 5328 0789; www.morooms.com; 263/1-2 Th Tha Pae; r 2800-3500B; ✱@≋) The 12 rooms here are all individually designed according

to the animals of the Chinese zodiac – our favourites are the rat, goat and monkey rooms. It's great fun and more like staying at a gallery than a hotel.

Baan Kaew Guest House GUESTHOUSE $$
(✆0 5327 1606; www.baankaew-guesthouse.com; 142 Th Charoen Prathet; r 800B; ❋❧) Set back from the road behind the owner's own residence, this two-storey apartment building is a good, honest deal. Staff are friendly, and the upstairs rooms have small balconies and are light and airy.

Tri Yaan Na Ros BOUTIQUE HOTEL $$$
(✆0 5327 3174; www.triyaannaros.com; 156 Th Wualai; r from 2500B; ❋⊠) This pint-size boutique hotel creates a romantically antique world with its artfully restored house, galleried chambers and narrow walkways – a real honeymoon candidate.

Riverside House GUESTHOUSE $
(✆0 5324 1860; www.riversidehousechiangmai. com; 101 Th Chiang Mai-Lamphun; r 500-800B; ❋❧❧) This friendly and professional set-up has great cheap rooms, the most expensive of which with river views, arranged around a pretty garden.

✕ Eating

You won't lack for dining variety in Chiang Mai, as the city has a down-to-earth assortment for grazing.

[TOP CHOICE] Palaad Tawanron THAI $$
(✆0 5321 6039; Th Suthep; mains 120-320B; ⊙lunch & dinner) Set into a rocky ravine next to a waterfall (in wet season) near Doi Suthep, this spectacularly sited restaurant has a magnificent location, crawling along a rocky ridgeline. Follow the signs at the end of Th Suthep.

Heuan Phen NORTHERN THAI $
(112 Th Ratchamankha; dishes 50-150B; ⊙lunch & dinner) This staple is a tourist's introduction to northern Thai nosh. Daytime meals are served in a large canteen out the front.

New Delhi INDIAN $$
(Th Ratwithi; mains 100-180B; ⊙dinner) Lovingly and expertly prepared, northern Indian food dominates the menu here. Service is patchy, but all will be forgiven when you're tucking into the delectable curries.

Riverside Bar & Restaurant INTERNATIONAL-THAI $$
(Th Charoenrat; mains 100-200B; ⊙10am-1am) This rambling set of wooden buildings has been the most consistently popular riverside place for over 20 years. The food – Thai, Western and vegetarian – is just a minor attraction to the good-times ambience.

Khun Churn VEGETARIAN $
(Soi 17, Th Nimmanhaemin; buffet 100B; ⊙lunch) Set in a minimalist dining space, this expat favourite does a popular daily vegetarian buffet as well as à la carte fruit drinks and Thai vegie mains. It's closed on the 16th of each month.

Hong Tauw Inn THAI $
(95/17-18 Nantawan Arcade, Th Nimmanhaemin; mains 70-130B; ⊙11am-11pm) Decked out in an old-fashioned costume of pendulum clocks and antiques, this intimate restaurant is a starter course on northern Thai cuisine.

Just Khao Soi NORTHERN THAI $
(108/2 Th Charoen Prathet; mains 100-150B; ⊙lunch & dinner) Chiang Mai is famed for its fine *khôw soi*, a Shan-Yunanese concoction of chicken (or, less commonly, beef), spicy curried broth and flat, squiggly wheat noodles. This place offers a gourmet version.

Chiangmai Saloon INTERNATIONAL $$
(30 Th Ratwithi; mains 120-200B; ⊙breakfast, lunch & dinner; ❀) Thais have a deep appreciation of the Wild West, and this cowboy-themed bar delivers with steaks and Tex-Mex.

Spirit House INTERNATIONAL-THAI $$
(Soi Viangbua, Th Chang Pheuak; mains 100-200B; ⊙dinner) An eclectic, antique-decorated place that showcases the freshest ingredients from the market and the owner's quirky personality.

Taste from Heaven VEGETARIAN $
(237-239 Th Tha Phae; dishes 60-110B; ⊙lunch & dinner; ☒) Eat like an elephant at this vegetarian restaurant benefiting the Elephant Nature Park.

☻ Drinking & Entertainment

Most Chiang Mai bars are open from about 5pm to midnight.

Pub BAR
(189 Th Huay Kaew) In an old Tudor-style cottage set well off the road, this venerable Chiang Mai institution semi-successfully calls

up the atmosphere of an English country pub.

Archers BAR
(33/4 Th Ratchaphakhinai;) A chilled-out restaurant-bar, come here for the cold beer and the people-watching – not the food.

Writer's Club & Wine Bar BAR
(141/3 Th Ratchadamnoen) A writers' and expats' hang-out, with English pub grub and big bottles of beer.

At 9 Bar BAR
(Cnr Th Nimmanhaemin & Soi 9) For a bird's-eye view of all the action on Th Nimmanhaemin, pop into this upstairs, open-air bar.

Sudsanan LIVE MUSIC
(Th Huay Kaew) Down a driveway opposite a Shell petrol station, this warmly lit wooden house is one of the best spots in the city to take in some local Thai bands.

North Gate Jazz Co-Op LIVE MUSIC
(Th Si Phum) This tight little jazz club packs in more musicians than patrons, especially for its Tuesday open-mic night.

Warm-Up CLUB
(40 Th Nimmanhaemin) The city's most happening club, with an interior chill-out courtyard surrounded by satellite rooms featuring DJs of every genre.

Shopping

Chiang Mai's leading tourist attraction is the **Night Bazaar** (Th Chang Khlan; 7pm-midnight), which sprawls over several blocks with hundreds of street vendors, several commercial buildings and ordinary shops selling a huge variety of handicrafts, as well as designer goods (both fake and licensed).

A more relaxed and local shopping experience has been cultivated at Chiang Mai's two weekly walking street markets. The **Saturday Walking Street** (Th Wualai; 4pm-midnight Sat), in the historic silversmith district, and the **Sunday Walking Street** (Th Ratchadamnoen; 4pm-midnight Sun), in the heart of the old city, turn the normally busy streets into pedestrian-only bazaars with colourful stalls selling cottage-industry wares, hill-tribe crafts and tasty local food.

Information

You will stumble across banks and ATMs on seemingly every street you visit in Chiang Mai.

Dangers & Annoyances

Years ago some travellers used to report that their belongings (particularly credit cards) stored at Chiang Mai guesthouses had gone walkabout, but we hear fewer of these complaints these days. Beware of bus or minivan services that leave from Bangkok's Th Khao San – some of these services are notoriously unreliable and either under-deliver or, worse, rifle through your bags looking for valuables while you sleep. Also skip the Th Khao San advertisements for a free night's accommodation in Chiang Mai, usually a hook for signing you up for an overpriced trek.

Emergency

Tourist police (nationwide call centre 1155, Chiang Mai 0 5324 7318; Th Faham)

Internet Access

Guesthouses and coffeeshops in Chiang Mai also double as internet cafes, with rates starting at 25B per hour. It is also quite common to have free wi-fi access at most guesthouses and midrange hotels.

Media

1 Stop Chiang Mai (www.1stopchiangmai.com) Website covering city attractions with an emphasis on day trips and outdoor activities.

Chiangmai Mail (www.chiangmai-mail.com) Weekly English-language newspaper.

Chiang Mai Sawadee (chiangmai.sawadee.com) A useful website guide to Chiang Mai, especially when first arriving, with airport information, accommodation and maps.

Citylife (www.chiangmainews.com) Lifestyle magazine profiling restaurants, local culture and people.

Guidelines (www.guidelineschiangmai.com) Monthly advertorial magazine that features respectable historical essays on the north; also a visitors guide.

Where to Eat in Chiang Mai? (http://cm-eat.blogspot.com/) Tips and pics of favourite foodie spots.

Medical Services

Chiang Mai Ram Hospital (0 5322 4880; www.chiangmairam.com; 8 Th Bunreuangrit) The most modern hospital in town, with higher-than-average prices.

McCormick Hospital (0 5392 1777; www.mccormick.in.th; 133 Th Kaew Nawarat) The best-value place for minor treatment.

Post

Main post office (Th Charoen Muang; 8.30am-4.30pm Mon-Fri, 9am-noon Sat & Sun) There's also a branch post office on Th Praisani, near Th Tha Phae.

DESTINATIONS FROM CHIANG MAI

DESTINATION	BUS	TRAIN	AIR
Bangkok	9½ hours/frequent/605-810B/	12-15 hours/6 daily/231-581B	Don Muang: 70 minutes/frequent/from 1490B
			Suvarnabhumi: 1¼ hours/frequent/from 1910B
Chiang Khong	6½ hours/3 daily/215-275B	N/A	N/A
Chiang Rai	3-4 hours/frequent/135-265B	N/A	40 minutes/2 daily/from 1399B
Chiang Saen	3½-4 hours/2 daily/165-220B	N/A	N/A
Nakhon Ratchasima (Khorat)	12 hours/frequent/560-660B	N/A	N/A
Lampang	2 hours/frequent/20-100B	2-3 hours/7 daily/23-102B	N/A
Luang Prabang (Laos)	N/A	N/A	1 hour/1 daily/from 6875B
Mae Sai	5 hours/5 daily/165-320B	N/A	N/A
Nan	6 hours/frequent/150-420B	N/A	45 minutes/2 daily/from 990B
Pai	4 hours/frequent/75-150B	N/A	25 minutes/1 daily/from 1890B
Sukhothai	5-6 hours/frequent/220B	N/A	N/A
Udon Thani	N/A	N/A	80 minutes/1 daily/from 1690B

Tourist Information

Tourism Authority of Thailand office (TAT; ☎nationwide call centre 1672, Chiang Mai 0 5324 8604; Th Chiang Mai-Lamphun; ⊙8.30am-4.30pm) Keeps a list of registered trekking guides, plus maps and brochures.

Getting There & Away

Air

Regularly scheduled flights arrive into and depart from **Chiang Mai International Airport** (☎0 5327 0222; www.chiangmaiairportonline.com), which is 3km south of the centre of the old city. Airport taxis cost a flat 150B. You can charter a túk-túk or red *sŏrngtăaou* from the centre of Chiang Mai to the airport for around 60B to 80B.

In addition to the destinations above, there are also direct flights to Hat Yai, Kuala Lumpur (Malaysia), Phuket, Singapore and Taipei (Taiwan).

Air Asia (☎nationwide call centre 0 2515 9999; www.airasia.com) Flights to Bangkok's Suvarnabhumi International Airport.

Bangkok Airways (☎nationwide call centre 1771, Chiang Mai 0 5328 9338-9; www.bangkokair.com) Flights to Bangkok's Suvarnabhumi International Airport.

Kan Air (☎nationwide call centre 02 551 6111; www.kanairlines.com) Flights to Chiang Rai, Nan and Pai.

Lao Airlines (☎0 5322 3401; www.laoairlines.com) Flights to Luang Prabang (Laos).

Nok Air (☎nationwide call centre 1318; www.nokair.com) Flights to Bangkok's Don Muang Airport, Nan and Udon Thani.

One-Two-Go (☎nationwide call centre 1126; www.flyorientthai.com) Bangkok's Don Muang Airport.

Thai Airways International (THAI; ☎nationwide call centre 02 356 1111, Chiang Mai 0 5321 1044/7; www.thaiair.com) Flights to Bangkok's Suvarnabhumi International Airport.

Bus

There are two bus stations in Chiang Mai. **Chang Pheuak** (☎0 5321 1586) is north of the old city and primarily handles destinations within Chiang Mai province. **Arcade** (☎0 5324 2664), 3km northeast of the old city, handles most long-distance routes. From the town centre, a túk-túk or chartered *sŏrngtăaou* to the Arcade bus terminal should cost about 50B to 60B.

Train

Chiang Mai's **train station** (☎nationwide call centre 1690, Chiang Mai 0 5324 5364; www.

railway.co.th; Th Charoen Muang) is 2.5km east of the old city. Advance booking for overnight sleepers to/from Bangkok is highly advised, especially during peak tourism season and on any Thai holiday.

To check timetables and prices for destinations not indicated opposite, call the **State Railway of Thailand** (nationwide call centre 1690; www.railway.co.th) or look at their website.

Getting Around

Red *sŏrngtăaou* cruise the city and function like shared taxis: flag one down, tell them your destination and they'll nod if they're going that way. They might pick up another fare if the stops are en route. Short trips should cost 20B per person, longer trips 40B.

Túk-túk only do charters and are about 20B more than the *sŏrngtăaou*. Short trips start at 40B; longer trips 60B. At night túk-túk drivers often ask an inflated 100B for return trips from the riverside restaurants to the old city.

Traffic is a bit heavy, but Chiang Mai is small enough that everything is accessible by bike. Rentals cost 30B to 50B a day from guesthouses and various places along the east moat.

Around Chiang Mai

North of Chiang Mai the province becomes mountainous and rugged as it bumps against Myanmar's frontier. Among the highlights are the beautiful Mae Sa Valley and the forested peaks around Chiang Dao. This region is particularly apt for some self-guided exploration.

MAE SA VALLEY & SAMOENG

One of the easiest mountain escapes, the 100km Mae Sa–Samoeng route makes a good day trip with private transport or a country getaway with an overnight in Samoeng.

Head north of Chiang Mai on Rte 107 (Th Chang Pheuak) towards Mae Rim, then left onto Rte 1096. The road becomes more rural but there's a steady supply of tour-bus attractions: orchid farms, butterfly parks, snake farms, you name it.

Only 6km from the Mae Rim turn-off, **Nam Tok Mae Sa** (adult/child 100/50B, car 30B) is a picturesque waterfall that's a favourite weekend getaway for locals.

The road starts to climb and twist after the waterfall entrance. Not far past an elephant camp is the **Queen Sirikit Botanic Gardens** (0 5384 1000; www.qsbg.org; Rte 1096; adult/child 30/10B; 8.30am-5pm), featuring a shorn mountainside displaying 227 hectares of various exotic and local flora for conservation and research purposes. Take the provided bus (30B) or your own car (100B) to get around the whole facility. Motorbikes are not allowed in the gardens.

Opposite the botanic gardens and set high on the hillside, the **Botanic Resort** (0 5381 8628; www.botanicresort.org; Rte 1096; r 1500-4800B;) is all about fresh mountain air, views and relaxation in semiluxurious rooms.

After the botanic gardens the road climbs up into the fertile Mae Sa Valley, once a high-altitude basin for growing opium poppies.

Sitting at the western wedge of the valley, **Proud Phu Fah** (0 5387 9389; www.proudphufah.com; Km17, Rte 1096; r 4500-7000B;) is a small boutique hotel with creature-comfort villas designed to give the illusion of sleeping amid the great outdoors. The open-air restaurant serves healthy Thai food (dishes 100B to 150B) with a panoramic view of the valley.

Eventually the road spirals down into Samoeng, a pretty Thai village. If you want to stay overnight, try the rather rundown **Samoeng Resort** (0 5348 7074; Rte 6033; r 400-500B;). To get here take Rte 1349 from Samoeng (a right-hand turn in the town).

Only part of the route is accessible via public transport. *Sŏrngtăaou* go to Samoeng (70B, 2¾ hours, two morning departures) from the Chang Pheuak bus terminal in Chiang Mai.

CHIANG DAO

In a lush, jungle setting and slammed up against the limestone cliffs of a mighty *doi*, Chiang Dao is a very popular escape from the steaming urban plains of Chiang Mai.

Chiang Dao town isn't much but a dusty crossroads that hosts a colourful **Tuesday morning market** (7am-noon), when hill tribes come to sell their wares. The more charming part of town is 5km west along the road that leads to Tham Chiang Dao (Chiang Dao Cave).

Sights

Some guesthouses rent mountain bikes for 100B a day.

Tham Chiang Dao CAVE

(admission 20B) In the heat of the day, the coolest place in town is the Chiang Dao Cave, a complex said to extend some 10km

EASY RIDER

One of the increasingly popular ways of exploring northern Thailand is from the saddle of a rented motorcycle. Despite the obvious risks of driving in Thailand, motorcycle touring is one of the best ways to explore the countryside at your own pace, and provides the opportunity to leave the beaten track at any moment.

Unless you're specifically intending to go off-road or plan on crossing unpaved roads during the wet season, it's highly unlikely you'll need one of the large dirt bikes you'll see for rent in Chiang Mai. The automatic transmission 110cc to 150cc scooter-like motorcycles found across Thailand are fast and powerful enough for most roads. Rental prices in Chiang Mai start at about 150B per day for a 125cc Honda Wave/Dream, all the way to 1200B per day for a Honda CB1000.

A good introduction to motorcycle touring in northern Thailand is the 100km Samoeng loop, which can be tackled in half a day. The route extends north from Chiang Mai and follows Rtes 107, 1096 and 1269, passing through excellent scenery and ample curves, providing a taste of what a longer ride up north will be like. The 470km Chiang Rai loop, which passes through scenic Fang and Tha Ton along Rtes 107, 1089 and 118, is another popular ride that can be broken up with a stay in Chiang Rai. The classic northern route is the Mae Hong Son loop, a 950km ride that begins in Chiang Mai and takes in Rte 1095's 1864 curves with possible stays in Pai, Mae Hong Son and Mae Sariang, before looping back to Chiang Mai via Rte 108.

The best source of information on motorcycle travelling in the north, not to mention publishers of a series of terrific motorcycle touring-based maps, is **Golden Triangle Rider** (GT Rider; www.gt-rider.com). Their website includes heaps of information on renting bikes (including recommended hire shops in Chiang Mai and Chiang Rai) and bike insurance, plus a variety of suggested tours with maps and an interactive forum.

to 14km into Doi Chiang Dao. There are four interconnected caverns that are open to the public. Tham Phra Non (360m) is the initial segment and is electrically illuminated and can be explored on one's own. To explore the other caves – Tham Mah (735m), Tham Kaew (474m) and Tham Nam (660m) – you can hire a guide with a pressurised gas lantern for 100B for up to five people.

If you just want to wander by yourself, continue to the end of the cave road to **Samnak Song Tham Pha Plong** (Tham Pha Plong Monastic Centre), where Buddhist monks sometimes meditate. A long, steep stairway leads up the mountain to a large *chedi* framed by forest and limestone cliffs.

Doi Chiang Dao MOUNTAIN

Part of the Doi Chiang Dao National Park, Doi Chiang Dao (also called Doi Luang) pokes into the heavens at 2195m above sea level. From the summit, reachable by a two-day hike, the views are spectacular.

Sleeping & Eating

Chiang Dao Nest BUNGALOWS $$

(08 6017 1985; nest.chiangdao.com; r 550-1600B;) Simple, great-value A-frame bungalows get the basics right – comfy beds, privacy and immaculate inside. The restaurant here comes highly recommended.

Malee's Nature Lovers Bungalows BUNGALOWS $$

(08 1961 8387; www.maleenature.com; r 650-1150B;) The cheaper bungalows here are pretty basic but come with high ceilings, fans and decent bathrooms. The more expensive 'honeymoon bungalows' are excellent, with soaring ceilings, fridge and wrap-around porch.

Chiang Dao Rainbow INTERNATIONAL-THAI $$

(set menu 250B) This highly recommended restaurant offers two menus – northern Thai and Greek/Mediterranean.

Getting There & Around

Buses to Chiang Dao (40B, 1½ hours, frequent) leave from Chiang Mai's Chang Pheuak terminal. The buses arrive and depart from Chiang Dao's bus station from where you can catch a *sŏrngtăaou* to your guesthouse. Most drivers charge 150B to deliver passengers to guesthouses on the cave road. Buses also travel to Fang (60B).

DOI ANG KHANG

Welcome to Thailand's 'Little Switzerland', so called for its cool climate and mountain scenery. Doi Ang Khang supports the cultivation of many species of temperate flowers, fruits and vegetables that are considered exotic in Thailand and were introduced as substitutions for opium.

Near the summit of Doi Ang Khang and the Yúnnánese village of Ban Khum is the **Royal Agricultural Station** (www.angkhang. com; admission 50B), showcasing fruit orchards and other flora (such as a Bonsai garden). The restaurant in here serves Thai standards and there are several places to stay.

Close to the station's entry **Angkhang Nature Resort** (☑0 5345 0110; www.oamhotels. com/angkhang; r from 2500B; ❀❁) has accommodation in the way of large bungalows set in a slope behind the main reception building. The on-site restaurant uses locally grown organic produce.

It is possible to get to Doi Ang Khang via public transport, but travelling to points along the mountain will be difficult. You can catch a bus heading to Fang (90B, three hours, every 30 minutes) from Chiang Mai's Chang Pheuak terminal. Tell the driver that you want to get off at the Rte 1249 turn-off. From there you can take a *sŏrngtăaou* to Ban Khum (1500B chartered), which is near the summit.

FANG & THA TON

For most people Fang is just a road marker on the way to Tha Ton, the launching point for river trips to Chiang Rai. If you do hang around this large, bustling town, there are some quiet backstreets lined with little shops in wooden buildings and the Shan/Burmese-style **Wat Jong Paen** (near the New Wiang Kaew Hotel), which has an impressive stacked-roof *wíhăhn*. Along the main street in Fang there are banks offering currency exchange and ATMs.

Tha Ton is a petite settlement plonked on the banks of a pretty bend of the Mae Nam Kok, which is lined by a few riverside restaurants and the boat launch for river trips to Chiang Rai. In Tha Ton, there is a **tourist police office** (☑1155) near the bridge on the boat-dock side.

◎ Sights & Activities

Wat Tha Ton BUDDHIST TEMPLE

In Tha Ton, this temple climbs up the side of a wooded hill. There are nine different levels punctuated by shrines, Buddha statues and a *chedi*. Each level affords stunning views of the mountainous valley towards Myanmar

and the plains of Tha Ton. From the base to the ninth level, it is about 3km or a 30-minute walk.

Local Villages ETHNIC VILLAGES

Within 20km of Fang and Tha Ton you can visit local villages, inhabited by Palaung (a Karen tribe that arrived from Myanmar around 16 years ago), Black Lahu, Akha and Yúnnánese, on foot or by mountain bike or motorcycle. Treks and rafting trips can be arranged through any of Tha Ton's guesthouses or hotels.

🛏 Sleeping & Eating

Most visitors who do stay overnight prefer to stay in Tha Ton.

Apple Resort GUESTHOUSE $

(☑0 5337 3144; garden bungalow incl breakfast with fan/air-con 350/500B, river bungalow incl breakfast 1000/1200B; ❀) Newly opened and right on the river opposite the boat launch (across the other side of the river), Apple Resort is a feel-good place with stylishly decorated bungalows on the riverfront that are light, bright and breezy and come with fantastic front porches right on the waterfront.

Old Tree's House HOTEL $$

(☑08 5722 9002; www.oldtreeshouse.net; bungalow incl breakfast 1200-1400B; ❀❁❃) This is a cleverly designed mini-resort with lots of nooks and crannies and even a platform set in a tree where you can enjoy the views while drying off from the pool. It's 400m past Tha Ton, well signed off the road.

Garden Home HOTEL $$

(☑0 5337 3015; r 600-1800B) A tranquil place along the river, about 150m from the bridge, with thatch-roofed bungalows spaced among lychee trees and bougainvillea. From the bridge, turn left at the Thaton River View Hotel sign.

Chankasen THAI $

(209 Rimnumkok, Tha Ton; mains 60-80B; ☉breakfast, lunch & dinner) The food is fine at this friendly, entrepreneurial Thai spot, but the real puller is the seating right on the river. Conveniently located right alongside the boat dock.

Sunshine Cafe CAFE $

(Tha Ton; breakfast 70B; ☉breakfast & lunch) This is the place to come for freshly brewed coffee (30B) in the morning. Located on the main road, just before the bridge.

PACHYDERM PARTNERS

Thailand's iconic animal has not fared well in the modern age. After the logging ban, these forest fellers faced unemployment, exploitation and the near extinction of the mahout tradition. Recently Thais have begun a homegrown campaign to give the elephants a safe working environment in semi-wild sanctuaries or ecotourism programs. The following are a few of the country's campaigners:

The **Elephant Nature Park** (☎0 5320 8246; www.elephantnaturepark.org; 1 Th Ratchamankha; 1-/2-day tour 2500/5800B) is run by Khun Lek (Sangduan Chailert), who has won numerous awards for her elephant sanctuary in the Mae Taeng valley, 60km from Chiang Mai. The forested area provides a semi-wild environment for elephants rescued from abusive situations or retired from a lifetime of work. Visitors wash the elephants and watch the herd but there is no show or riding.

Thai Elephant Conservation Center (TECC; ☎0 5424 7876; www.thailandelephant.org; child/adult incl shuttle bus 40/80B), 32km from Lampang, covers the usual elephant encounters (shows, bathing, rides and mahout training) but uses the proceeds from the tourist program to underwrite medical treatment for sick elephants. The elephant **show** (⊙10am, 11am & 1.30pm) is less of a circus and more of a historical showing of how elephants were used in the timber industry. Its **mahout training program** (☎0 5424 7875; from 3500B) is one of Thailand's most popular and runs from one to 10 days. Next door, **FAE's Elephant Hospital** (Friends of the Asian Elephant; ☎08 1914 6113; www.elephant-soraida.com; ⊙8am-5pm) is a functioning medical facility for injured elephants. There are no guided tours, but devout fans can stop by to make charitable donations.

Transportation is included in a visit to the Elephant Nature Park. The latter two facilities can be reached by Chiang Mai–bound bus or *sŏrngtăaou* (26B, 40 minutes) from Lampang's bus terminal. Let the driver know where you are headed and get off at the Km 37 marker. Alternatively, you can charter a blue *sŏrngtăaou* for 600B at Lampang's bus terminal.

Getting There & Away

Buses to Fang (90B, three hours, every 30 minutes) leave from the Chang Pheuak bus terminal in Chiang Mai. Air-con minivans make the trip to Fang (150B, three hours, every 30 minutes), leaving from behind the Chang Pheuak bus terminal on the corner of Soi Sanan Kila.

From Fang, yellow *sŏrngtăaou* leave from the market for the 40-minute trip to Tha Ton from 5.30am to 5pm (30B). To Mai Sai (80B to 90B) or Chiang Rai (100B to 110B) directly, take the afternoon bus from the bridge.

From Tha Ton, yellow *sŏrngtăaou* leave from the northern side of the river to Mae Salong (70B, 1½ hours, mornings only).

From Tha Ton you can make a half-day longtail boat trip to Chiang Rai (350B, 12.30pm). The boats are also available for charter hire (2200B, six people).

Lampang

POP 59,000

Constructed as a walled city and boasting magnificent temples and teak mansions, Lampang is a lovely low-key version of Chiang Mai. A vestige of Lampang's connection to the horse-riding tradition that migrated into the kingdom during the Silk Road era are the **horse-drawn carriages** that haul tourists around town. A 15-minute/one-hour ride costs 150/300B.

Sights & Activities

Wat Phra That Lampang Luang BUDDHIST TEMPLE

About 18km to the southwest of Lampang, Wat Phra That Lampang Luang, in the village of Ko Kha, is a beautiful wooden Lanna temple with walls like a medieval castle, and is one of the oldest standing structures in the country. To get here, catch an eastbound *sŏrngtăaou* (20B) on Lampang's Th Rawp Wiang to Ko Kha. From Ko Kha charter a motorcycle taxi (40B) for the remaining 3km to the temple. A *sŏrngtăaou* from Lampang's bus station will make the trip for 350B.

Baan Sao Nak MUSEUM

(85 Th Radwattana; admission 50B; ⊙10am-5pm) Nearby, Baan Sao Nak is a huge teak Lanna-style house supported by 116 teak pillars and furnished with Burmese and Thai antiques.

The house is open to the public as a local museum.

In old-town Lampang, other fine examples of Lanna architecture include **Wat Pongsanuk Tai**, **Wat Si Rong Meuang** and **Wat Si Chum**.

Wat Phra Kaew Don Tao BUDDHIST TEMPLE
(admission 20B; ⏲6am-6pm) Wat Phra Kaew Don Tao is one of the many former homes of the Emerald Buddha, now residing in Bangkok's Wat Phra Kaew.

Th Talat Kao NEIGHBOURHOOD
Th Talat Kao (also known as Kat Korng Ta) is dotted with old atmospheric shophouses and is closed off to vehicular traffic on Saturday and Sunday from 4pm to 10pm for a colourful walking street.

Sleeping & Eating

TOP CHOICE **Riverside Guest House** GUESTHOUSE $$
(☎0 5422 7005; www.theriverside-lampang.com; 286 Th Talad Gao; r 350-900B, ste 1800B; ❄ 📶) Although still within budget range, this leafy compound of refurbished wooden houses is by far the most pleasant place to stay in Lampang. Shaded tables for chatting or eating abound, and motorcycle rental and other tourist amenities are available.

Akhamsiri Home BUDGET HOTEL $
(☎0 5422 8791; www.akhamsirihome.com; 54/1 Th Pahmaikhet; r 450B; ❄ @ 📶) Large cool rooms with TV, fridge and a garden/balcony in a tidy residential compound.

Pin Hotel BUDGET HOTEL $$
(☎0 5422 1509; 8 Th Suandawg; r incl breakfast 600-900B, ste 1300-1800B; ❄ @ 📶) A quiet and clean hotel with all the mod cons.

Aroy One Baht THAI $
(cnr Th Suandawg & Th Talad Gao; mains 15-40B; ⏲4pm-midnight) The local dining table with cheap and delicious Thai food.

Papong NORTHERN THAI $
(125 Th Talad Gao; mains 30-40B; ⏲lunch & dinner) Popular local haunt serving *kà·nŏm jeen*, fresh rice noodles topped with various curries.

Riverside Bar & Restaurant INTERNATIONAL-THAI $$
(328 Th Thipchang; mains 80-210B; ⏲lunch & dinner) Set in a rambling old teak structure on the river with live music, a full bar and an enormous menu.

Information

There are many banks with ATMs along Th Boonyawat.

M@cnet (Th Chatchai; per hr 15B; ⏲9am-10pm) Internet access.

Post office (Th Prisnee; ⏲8.30am-4.30pm Mon-Fri, 9am-noon Sat)

Tourism Authority of Thailand office (TAT; ☎nationwide call centre 1672, Lampang 0 5423 7229; Th Thakhrao Noi; ⏲10am-4pm Mon-Sat) The helpful folks here can provide a decent map of the area and details about local sights and activities.

Getting There & Away

Bangkok Airways (☎nationwide call centre 1771, Lampang 0 5482 1522; www.bangkokair.com) conducts flights between Lampang and Bangkok's Suvarnabhumi Airport (2405B, one hour, once daily), and Lampang and Sukhothai (1915B, 30 minutes, once daily).

Lampang's **bus terminal** is nearly 2km from the centre of town, on the corner of Asia 1 Hwy and Th Chantarasurin – 20B by shared *sŏrngtăaou*. There are frequent daytime departures to Bangkok (347B to 625B, nine hours), Chiang Mai (67B to 134B, two hours), Chiang Rai (143B, 3½ hours) and Sukhothai (162B, 3½ hours).

You can also travel between Lampang and Chiang Mai by train (23B to 50B, three hours). To check timetables and prices for other destinations call the **State Railway of Thailand** (☎nationwide call centre 1690; www.railway.co.th) or look at its website.

Pai

POP 2000

The hippie trail is alive and well in Pai (pronounced more like the English 'bye' not 'pie'), a cool, moist corner of a mountain-fortressed valley. A solid music, art and New Age scene has settled in along with the town's more permanent population of Shan, Thai and Muslim Chinese, though in the high season Pai can feel more like Ko Pha-Ngan without a beach. Diluting the *fa·ràng* factor are visiting Thais from Bangkok and Chiang Mai, who pop in for a long weekend in the country. The town itself can be explored in a matter of minutes, but the real adventure lies along the paths in the hills beyond.

Sights & Activities

Tuckered out on temples? Pai is lean on sights and high on activities, from hikes to

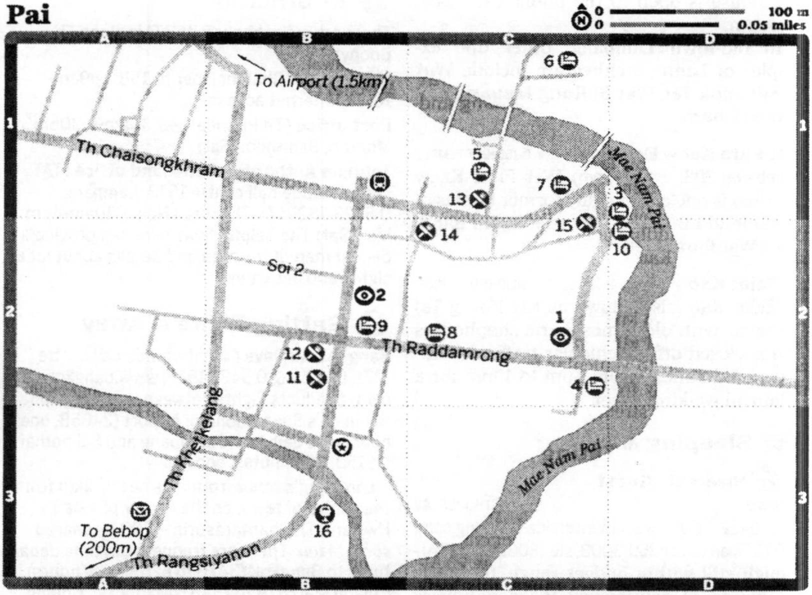

Pai

Sights

1 Pai Traditional Thai Massage....C2
2 Thom's Pai Elephant Camp....B2

Sleeping

3 Baan Pai Village....D1
4 Baan Tawan Guest House....C2
5 Breeze of Pai Guesthouse....C1
6 Pai Country Hut....C1
7 Rim Pai Cottage....C1
8 Tayai's House....C2
9 TTK....B2
10 Villa De Pai....D2

Eating

11 Burger House....B2
12 Je-In Pai....B2
13 Khanom Jeen Nang Yong....C1
14 Mama Falafel....C2
15 Witching Well....C2

Drinking

16 Ting Tong....B3

massages. Guesthouses can organise treks for as little as 700B per day, while rafting excursions start at about 1200B.

Ban Santichon VILLAGE
Approximately 4km outside of Pai, a small market, delicious Yunanese food, tea tasting and pony rides make the village of Ban Santichon not unlike a Chinese-themed amusement park.

Tha Pai Hot Springs HOT SPRINGS
(admission 200/100B; ⌚6am-7pm) A geothermal pool in a local park, 7km southeast of town.

Thai Adventure Rafting RAFTING
(☎0 5369 9111; www.thairafting.com; Th Chaisongkhram) Thai Adventure Rafting has a good safety record and operates two-day whitewater rafting trips from Pai to Mae Hong Son from mid-June to mid-February.

Thom's Pai Elephant Camp ELEPHANT RIDES
(☎0 5369 9286; www.thomelephant.com; Th Rangsiyanon; elephant rides per person 500-1500B) Thom's hauls tourists into the jungle aboard an elephant; more elaborate trips include hot-spring soaks, bamboo rafting and hill-tribe village stays.

Pai Traditional Thai Massage MASSAGE
(PTTM; ☎0 5369 9121; www.pttm1989.com; 68/3 Soi 1, Th Wiang Tai; massage per 1/1½/2hr 180/270/350B, sauna per visit 80B, 3-day massage course 2500B; ⊙9am-9pm) Northern-Thai massage, and during the cool season, herbal sauna, are available here. Three-day massage courses begin every Monday and Friday and last three hours per day.

Sleeping

The most atmospheric accommodation is spread along the banks of Mae Nam Pai. Accommodation can be tight during the Thai tourist season of December to January, and prices drop by as much as 60% during the low season.

IN TOWN

Rim Pai Cottage BOUTIQUE HOTEL $$$
(☎0 5369 9133; www.rimpaicottage.com; Th Chaisongkhram; bungalows incl breakfast 1300-5000B; ✱ ᯤ) The home-like bungalows here are spread out along a secluded and beautifully wooded section of the Nam Pai. The interiors have a romantic feel with their mosquito nets and Thai decorating details, and the open bathrooms are particularly nice.

Baan Pai Village HOTEL $$
(☎0 5369 8152; www.baanpaivillage.com; Th Wiang Tai; bungalows incl breakfast 500-1500B; ✱ @ ᯤ) Comfortable wooden bungalows with stylish interiors sit among winding pathways and soak in the natural landscape. There are also several cheaper riverside bungalows under the name Baan Pai Riverside.

Baan Tawan Guest House BOUTIQUE HOTEL $$
(☎0 5369 8116; www.pai-baantawan.com; 117 Moo 4, Th Wiang Tai; r incl breakfast 1000-3000B, bungalows 1800-3000B; ✱ @ ᯤ) The older, more charming, more expensive, riverside two-storey bungalows made with salvaged teak are the reason to stay here, but there are also spacious rooms in a large two-storey building.

Breeze of Pai Guesthouse BUDGET HOTEL $
(☎08 1998 4597; helendavis2@yahoo.co.uk; Soi Wat Pa Kham; r 400B, bungalows with fan/air-con 500/800B; ✱ ᯤ) This well-groomed complex near the river has attractive rooms and A-frame bungalows that are close to the action but not the noise.

Pai Country Hut BUDGET HOTEL $
(☎08 4046 4458; Ban Mae Hi; bungalows incl breakfast 500B; ᯤ) The bamboo bungalows here are utterly simple, but are tidy and have bathrooms and inviting hammocks. It's the most appealing of several similar places directly across the river.

Villa De Pai HOTEL $$$
(☎0 5369 9109; 87/1 Th Wiang Tai; bungalows incl breakfast 1400-3000B; ᯤ) Slightly aged, but clean and conveniently located riverside bungalows.

TTK GUESTHOUSE $
(☎0 5369 8093; 8/10 Th Ratchadamnoen; r 400-600B; ✱ ᯤ) Set behind the Israeli restaurant of the same name, the rooms here lack any effort at interior design, but are spotless and conveniently located.

Tayai's House GUESTHOUSE $
(☎0 5369 9579; off Th Raddamrong; r 400-600B; ✱) Simple but clean fan and air-con rooms in a leafy compound a short walk from the main drag.

OUTSIDE OF TOWN

Bulunburi BOUTIQUE HOTEL $$$
(☎0 5369 8302; www.bulunburi.com; 28 Moo 5 Ban Pong; bungalows incl breakfast 1350-3300B; ✱ @) Set in a tiny secluded valley of rice fields and streams, the bungalows mostly continue the tasteful design theme established in the attractive lobby, and are large, well equipped and stylish. The hotel is about 2.5km from the centre of town along the road to Mae Hong Song – look for the well-posted turn-off, about 1km from Pai.

Bueng Pai Resort RESORT HOTEL $$$
(☎08 9265 4768; www.paifarm.com; 185 Moo 5 Ban Mae Hi; bungalows 400-1800B; ᯤ ✱) The 12 simple bungalows here are strategically and attractively positioned between a functioning farm and a pond stocked with freshwater fish. Beung Pai is 2.5km from Pai, off the road that leads to Tha Pai Hot Springs – look for the sign.

Pairadise RESORT HOTEL $$
(☎0 5369 8065; www.pairadise.com; 98 Moo 1 Ban Mae Hi; bungalows 800-1500B; ✱ ᯤ) Atop the ridge just east of town, this tidy resort features chic bungalows for the New Age crowd. The spring-fed pond is suitable for swimming.

Sun Hut HOTEL $$
(☎0 5369 9730; www.thesunhut.com; 28/1 Ban Mae Yen; bungalows incl breakfast 900-1900B; ᯤ) In a back-to-nature setting, outside town, this collection of bungalows has a sleepy

hippie ambience. The hotel is 300m east of the Mae Nam Pai along the road that leads to Tha Pai Hot Springs.

Eating

Mama Falafel ISRAELI $
(Soi Wanchaloem; set meals 80-90B; ⏰11am-8pm) This friendly native of Pai has been cooking up tasty falafel, hummus, schnitzel and other Jewish/Israeli faves since 2002.

Witching Well INTERNATIONAL $
(Th Wiang Tai; dishes 40-80B) This foreigner-run place is where to come if you're looking for authentic sandwiches, pasta, cakes and pastries, not to mention the kind of breakfasts you're not going to find elsewhere in Pai.

Khanom Jeen Nang Yong THAI $
(no roman-script sign; Th Chaisongkhram; mains 20B; ⏰lunch & dinner) This place specialises in *kànŏm jeen* – thin rice noodles served with a curry-like broth. It's in the same building as Pai Adventure.

Burger House AMERICAN $
(Th Rangsiyanon; mains 80-210B; ⏰9am-8.30pm) If you are hankering after a big juicy burger this is the place to come.

Je-In Pai VEGETARIAN, THAI $
(Pure Vegetarian Food; Th Raddamrong; mains 40-80B; ⏰10am-8pm) Opposite the District Office, this simple open-air place serves tasty and cheap vegan and vegetarian Thai food.

Drinking & Entertainment

As a general guide to 'downtown' Pai's entertainment scene, most of the open-air and VW van-based cocktail bars are along Th Chaisongkhram; Th Wiang Tai is where you'll find the mostly indoor and chilled reggae-type places; the 'guesthouse' style restaurant-bars with a diverse soundtrack are mostly found on Th Rangsiyanon; and a few live music bars can be found along the eastern end of Th Raddamrong.

Bebop LIVE MUSIC
(Th Rangsiyanon; ⏰6pm-1am) This legendary spot made Pai a musical stage and hosts live bands nightly (from about 9.30pm), playing blues, R&B and rock.

Ting Tong BAR
(Th Rangsiyanon; ⏰7pm-1am) A sprawling compound of bamboo decks, concrete platforms, hidden tables and towering trees, this is one of the larger bars in town.

Getting There & Away

Pai's **airport** is around 1.5km north of town along Rte 1095 and offers a daily connection to Chiang Mai (1890B, 25 minutes) on **Kan Air** (☎nationwide call centre 02 551 6111, Pai 0 5369 9955; www.kanairlines.com).

Buses to Chiang Mai (72B to 150B, four hours, frequent departures from 8am to 4pm) leave from a small **station** on Th Chaisongkhram. Air-con minibuses (150B) also depart hourly from the station and from a travel agency down the street.

Sukhothai

POP 37,000

The Khmer empire extended its influence deep into modern-day Thailand before a formidable rival arose in 1257 to undermine the distant throne's frontier. Naming its capital Sukhothai (Rising Happiness), the ascendant kingdom claimed lands as far north as Vientiane and began to define a cohesive Thai identity by developing a distinctive Thai alphabet as well as architecture and art. All this was accomplished in 150 years, before Sukhothai was superseded by Ayuthaya to the south.

Sights & Activities

Sukhothai Historical Park HISTORICAL PARK
Designated a World Heritage Site, the historical park, also known as *meuang gòw* (old city), contains 21 historic sites that lie within the old walls, with another 70 within a 5km radius. Thailand's Loi Krathong festival is thought to have originated here and is celebrated in November with much historic fanfare.

The park is best reached from town by *sŏrngtăaou* (20B, 30 minutes, frequent departures from 6am to 5.30pm) from the south side of Th Jarot Withithong near Poo Restaurant. Within the old city, bicycles (30B per day) are a great way to explore the grounds and can be rented near the park entrance. **Cycling Sukhothai** (☎0 5561 2519; www.cycling-sukhothai.com; half-/full day 600/750B, sunset tour 300B) offers educational bicycle tours of the area.

Central Zone

This is the historical park's main **zone** (admission 100B, plus per bicycle/motorcycle/car

LOCAL KNOWLEDGE

RONNY HANQUART: MANAGER OF CYCLING SUKHOTHAI

Best temple? Wat Mahathat (p404) and the majestic Buddha statue at Wat Si Chum (p405) are two temples you should not miss.

Best museum? If you are visiting Si Satchanalai-Chaliang Historical Park (p407) then I recommend the excavated kilns along the Yom River (p407).

Best time to visit? Early in the morning is cooler and there are fewer visitors. After a siesta under one of the big trees in the park, you can continue till evening. Sukhothai is green during the monsoon (May to October) and nice and cool during cool season (December to February).

Best place to escape the crowds? The Western Zone (p405) is quite large and has a beautiful natural background. Few tourists go there.

Best sunset? Wat Sa Si (p404) in the Central Zone is a good spot for sunset.

Best non-temple activity? Why not go on a countryside tour by mountain bike? Paddy fields and villages – it's simple and beautiful.

10/30/50B; ⌚6.30am-8pm) and is home to what are arguably some of the park's most well-preserved and impressive ruins. Near the entrance, **Ramkhamhaeng National Museum** (admission 150B; ⌚9am-4pm) provides a modest collection of Sukhothai-era artefacts.

The crown jewel of the old city, **Wat Mahathat**, is one of the best examples of Sukhothai architecture, typified by the classic lotus-bud stupa that features a conical spire topping a square-sided structure on a three-tiered base. Some of the original Buddha images remain, including a 9m standing Buddha among the broken columns.

Wat Si Sawai, just south of Wat Mahathat, has three Khmer-style *prang* and a picturesque moat. **Wat Sa Si** is a classically simple Sukhothai-style temple set on an island. **Wat Trapang Thong**, next to the museum, is reached by the footbridge crossing the large, lotus-filled pond that surrounds it. It remains in use today.

Northern Zone

This **zone** (admission 100B, plus per bicycle/motorcycle/car 10/30/50B; ⌚7.30am-5.30pm), 500m north of the old city walls, is easily reached by bicycle.

In the northwestern corner, **Wat Si Chum** contains a massive seated Buddha tightly squeezed into an open, walled *mondòp*. Somewhat isolated to the north of the city, **Wat Phra Pai Luang** is similar in style to Wat Si Sawai, but the *prang* are larger.

Other Zones

The **western zone** (admission 100B, plus per bicycle/motorcycle/car 10/30/50B; ⌚7.30am-5.30pm) is the most expansive. **Wat Saphaan Hin** is on a hill 3km west of the old city walls, and features a 12.5m-high standing Buddha image looking back towards Sukhothai. Elsewhere, the large, bell-shaped stupa at **Wat Chang Lom**, to the east, is supported by 36 elephants sculpted into its base.

Sleeping

The local taxi mafia is particularly obnoxious here; don't believe anyone who says a guesthouse has closed. Many guesthouses offer free wi-fi, free use of bicycles and free pick-up from the bus terminal.

NEW SUKHOTHAI

Ruean Thai Hotel BOUTIQUE HOTEL **$$$**
(☎0 5561 2444; www.rueanthaihotel.com; 181/20 Soi Pracha Ruammit; r 1200-3600B; ✱@☜✱) At first glance, you may mistake this eye-catching complex for a temple or museum. Rooms have heaps of character and service is both friendly and flawless.

At Home Sukhothai BUDGET HOTEL **$**
(☎0 5561 0172; www.athomesukhothai.com; 184/1 Th Vichien Chamnong; r incl breakfast 400-800B; ✱@☜) The simple but comfortable rooms here really do feel like home. There's a lotus pond out the back, and

virtually every other service, from food to Thai massage, at the front.

Lotus Village BOUTIQUE HOTEL **$$**
(☑0 5562 1484; www.lotus-village.com; 170 Th Ratchathani; r & bungalows incl breakfast 720-2850B; ✻◉🖥️) Village is an apt label for this peaceful compound of elevated wooden bungalows. An on-site spa offers a variety of services.

Ban Thai BUDGET HOTEL **$**
(☑0 5561 0163; banthai_guesthouse@yahoo.com; 38 Th Prawet Nakhon; r without bathroom 200B, bungalows 300-500B; ✻◉🖥️) As friendly as they come, Ban Thai has rooms (the cheapest have shared bathrooms) that sit around a pretty garden.

Sabaidee House BUDGET HOTEL **$**
(☑0 5561 6303; www.sabaideehouse.com; 81/7 Moo 1 Tambol Banklouy; r 200-600B; ✻◉🖥️) Homestay-turned-guesthouse with five attractive bungalows.

Sila Resort BUDGET HOTEL **$**
(✎0 5562 0344; www.sila-resort@hotmail.com; 3/49 Th Kuhasuwan; r 400B, bungalows 500-1000B; ✻◉🖥️) A somewhat Disneyland-like compound a fair hike from the centre of New Sukhothai.

4T Guesthouse BUDGET HOTEL **$$**
(☑0 5561 4679; www.4tguesthouse.ob.tc; 122 Soi Mae Ramphan; r 300-400B, bungalows 600-900B; ✻◉🖥️🏊) Resort-like guesthouse with a variety of budget options.

SUKHOTHAI HISTORICAL PARK
Orchid Hibiscus Guest House BUDGET HOTEL **$$**
(☑0 5563 3284; orchid_hibiscus_guest_house@hotmail.com; 407/2 Rte 1272; r/bungalows 900/1300B; ✻◉🖥️🏊) This collection of rooms and bungalows is set in relaxing, manicured grounds with a swimming pool as a centrepiece and the self-professed 'amazing breakfast' as a highlight. The guesthouse is on Rte 1272 about 500m off Rte 12 – the turn-off is between Km 48 and Km 49 markers.

Vitoon Guesthouse GUESTHOUSE **$**
(☑0 5569 7045; www.vitoonguesthouse.com; 49 Moo 3; r with fan/air-con 300/600B; ✻◉) One of only two budget options within walking distance of the old city, the fan rooms here are showing their age, but the air-con rooms, in a newer building, are spotless and represent a good deal.

 Eating

Sukhothai is known for its *kŭaytĭaw sù-khŏh-thai*, containing a sweet broth, ground peanuts and green beans along with the usual choice of noodles. Try it at **Jayhae** (Th Jarot Withithong; dishes 25-40B; ☺7am-4pm), about 1.3km west of the Mae Nam Yom.

The **night market** (Th Jarot Withithong & Th Rat Uthit) near the bridge has tasty treats and many vendors have bilingual menus.

Dream Café THAI **$$**
(86/1 Th Singhawat; dishes 80-150B; ☺lunch & dinner; ✻) A treasure trove of antiques, this eclectic cafe serves food with character, including a selection of Thai standards and 'stamina drinks'.

Poo Restaurant INTERNATIONAL-THAI **$$**
(24/3 Th Jarot Withithong; dishes 30-150B) This simple restaurant in the heart of town offers breakfasts, hearty sandwiches and tasty Thai dishes, plus traveller information.

ⓘ Information

Post office (Th Nikhon Kasem; ☺8.30am-noon Mon-Fri, 1-4.30pm Sat & Sun)
Sukhothai hospital (☑0 5561 0280; Th Jarot Withithong)
Tourism Authority of Thailand office (TAT; ✎nationwide call centre 1672, Sukhothai 0 5561 6228; Th Jarot Withithong; ☺8.30am-4.30pm) Near the bridge in New Sukhothai, this new office has a decent selection of maps and brochures.
Tourist police (✎nationwide call centre 1155) At Sukhothai Historical Park.

ⓘ Getting There & Away

Sukhothai's airport is 27km from town. There is a minivan service (180B) between the airport and New Sukhothai. **Bangkok Airways** (✎nationwide call centre 1771, Sukhothai 0 5564 7224; www.bangkokair.com; Sukhothai airport) operates flights to Bangkok's Suvarnabhumi Airport (3480B, 80 minutes, twice daily) and Lampang (2115B, 30 minutes, once daily).

The **bus terminal** (✎0 5561 4529; Rte 101) is 1km northwest of New Sukhothai. Options include frequent departures to Bangkok (255B to 380B, six to seven hours), Chiang Mai (218B, six hours), Chiang Rai (249B, nine hours), Lampang (162B, three hours) and Nan (185B, four hours).

ⓘ Getting Around

Transport from the bus terminal into the guesthouse area of New Sukhothai costs 60B in a chartered vehicle or 10B per person in a shared *sŏrngtăaou;* motorbike taxis charge 40B. Poo Restaurant and several guesthouses hire motorcycles.

Around Sukhothai

SI SATCHANALAI-CHALIANG HISTORICAL PARK

Set amid rolling mountains 56km north of Sukhothai, Si Satchanalai and Chaliang were a later extension of the Sukhothai empire. The 13th- to 15th-century ruins in the historical park are in the same basic style as those in Sukhothai Historical Park, but the setting is more rural and covers a 720-hectare area.

The **Si Satchanalai zone** (admission 100B, plus per car 50B; ⏲8am-4.30pm) contains the vast majority of ruins. An **information centre** (⏲8.30am-5pm) distributes free park maps and has a small historical exhibit. Bikes (20B) can be rented near the entrance gate. **Wat Chedi Jet Thaew** has seven rows of stupas in classic Sukhothai style. **Wat Chang Lom** has a *chedi* surrounded by Buddha statues set in niches and guarded by the fine remains of elephant buttresses. Climb to the top of the hill supporting **Wat Khao Phanom Phloeng** for a view over the town and river.

Head east along the riverside for 2km to **Chaliang** (admission free), where you'll find **Wat Phra Si Ratana Mahathat** (admission 20B; ⏲8am-5pm), a very impressive temple with well-preserved *chedi* and a variety of seated and standing Buddhas.

The third zone, which stretches 5km north of Si Satchanalai, is home to more than 200 **kilns** (admission free). Several of the old kilns have been carefully excavated and can be viewed along with original pottery samples at the **Si Satchanalai Centre for Study & Preservation of Sangkhalok Kilns** (admission 100B; ⏲9am-4pm).

The ruins can be visited as a day trip from Sukhothai. If you want to stay, the most convenient accommodation option is at a basic **homestay** (☎08 1935 2835; r & bungalow 500B; ✱📶✈) operation at Chaliang. Other options include **Si Satchanalai Hotel and Resort** (☎0 5567 2666; 247 Moo 2, Rte 101; r 200-500B, bungalows 1200B; ✱), approximately 6km north of the park on the west side of Rte 101, and **Mukda** (no roman-script sign; ☎0 5567 1024; r 200-500B; ✱), at the northern end of Ban Hat Siaw, about 10km from the park.

Si Satchanalai-Chaliang Historical Park is off Rte 101 between Sawankhalok and Ban Hat Siaw. From New Sukhothai, take a Si Satchanalai bus (46B, 1½ hours, 11am) or one of three buses to Chiang Rai (46B) at 6.40am, 9am and 11.30am, and ask to get off at *'meuang gòw'* (old city). The last bus back to New Sukhothai leaves at 4.30pm.

Chiang Rai

POP 62,000

Well-groomed Chiang Rai is more liveable than visitable, as it lacks any major tourist attractions – though the fact that it is much less polluted and more laid-back than Chiang Mai is a good enough reason to visit here.

It's also a good spot for arranging hilltribe treks with companies that try harder than most to help the host tribes.

Sights

Oub Kham Museum MUSEUM
(www.oubkhammuseum.com; 81/1 Military Front Rd; adult/child 300/200B; ⏲8am-6pm) This privately owned museum houses an impressive collection of Lanna paraphernalia, ranging from elaborate to kitschy. The Oub Kham Museum is located 2km outside of the centre town and can be a bit tricky to find; túk-túks will go here for about 50B.

Hilltribe Museum & Education Center MUSEUM
(www.pdacr.org; 3rd fl, 620/25 Th Thanalai; admission 50B; ⏲9am-6pm Mon-Fri, 10am-6pm Sat & Sun) This centre is run by the nonprofit Population & Community Development Association (PDA) but, despite a wealth of information, is underwhelming in its visual presentation.

Wat Phra Kaew BUDDHIST TEMPLE
In the mid-14th century, lightning cracked the *chedi* at this temple, revealing the much-honoured Emerald Buddha (now at Bangkok's Wat Phra Kaew). There is now a near-replica to take its place.

Nearby **Wat Phra Singh** contains a twin of Chiang Mai's revered Phra Singh. About 13km south of town, **Wat Rong Khun** is a unique contemporary take on temple design; hop on a Chiang Mai–bound bus to reach the temple.

Chiang Rai

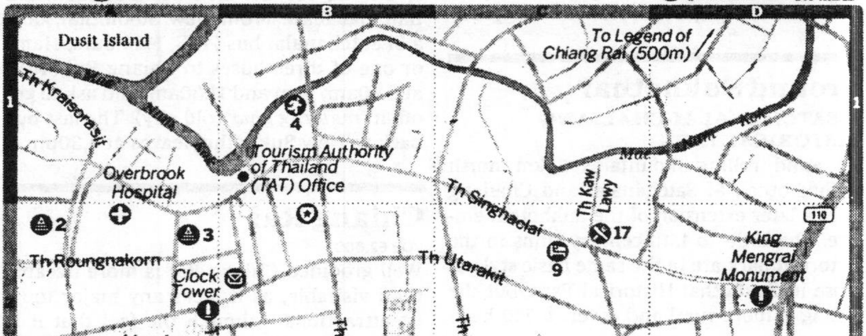

Chiang Rai

Sights

- 1 Hilltribe Museum & Education Center C2
- 2 Wat Phra Kaew A2
- 3 Wat Phra Singh A2

Activities, Courses & Tours

- 4 Akha Hill House B1
- PDA Tours & Travel .... (see 1)

Sleeping

- 5 Baan Bua Guest House B4
- 6 Baan Warabordee C4
- 7 Golden Triangle Inn B3
- 8 Jansom House B4
- 9 Moon & Sun Hotel C2

Eating

- 10 BaanChivitMai Bakery C4
- 11 Doi Chaang B3
- 12 Loong Eed Locol Food D3
- 13 Nam Ngiaw Paa Nuan B4
- 14 Night Market C3
- 15 Old Dutch B3
- 16 Phu-Lae C3
- 17 Somkhuan Khao Soi C2

Activities

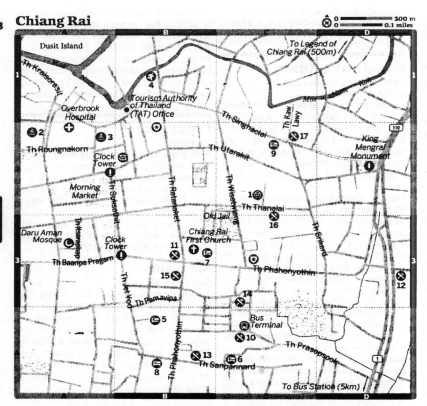

Nearly all travel agencies, guesthouses and hotels offer trekking trips. Rates range from 2500B to 4800B per person for two people for a two-night trek. Generally everything from accommodation to transport and food is included in this price.

The following agencies have a reputation for operating responsible treks and cultural tours, and in some cases profits from the treks go directly to community-development projects.

Mirror Foundation TREKKING
(☏0 5373 7616; www.themirrorfoundation.org; 106 Moo 1, Ban Huay Khom, Tambon Mae Yao) Although its rates are higher than others', trekking with this nonprofit NGO helps support the training of its local guides.

PDA Tours & Travel TREKKING
(☏0 5374 0088; crpdatour@hotmail.com; www.pda.or.th/chiangrai/package_tour.htm; 3rd fl, 620/25 Th Thanalai, Hilltribe Museum & Education Center; ☺9am-6pm Mon-Fri, 10am-6pm Sat & Sun) Offers culturally sensitive tours led by PDA-trained hill-tribe members; profits fund HIV/AIDS education, health clinics and scholarships.

Akha Hill House TREKKING
(☏08 9997 5505; www.akhahill.com; Akha River House) Wholly owned and managed by Akha people.

🛏 Sleeping

Legend of Chiang Rai BOUTIQUE HOTEL $$$
(☏0 5391 0400; www.thelegend-chiangrai.com; 124/15 Moo 21, Th Kohloy; r 3900-5900B, villa 8100B; ✹◉☂🏊) One of the few hotels in town to take advantage of a river location, this upscale resort feels like a traditional Lanna village. The resort is about 500m north of Th Singhaclai.

Ben Guesthouse BUDGET HOTEL $$
(☏0 5371 6775; www.benguesthousechiangrai.com; 351/10 Soi 4, Th Sankhongnoi; r 250-850B, ste 1500-3000B; ✹◉☂🏊) This absolutely spotless compound has a bit of everything, from fan-cooled cheapies to immense suites, not to mention an entire house (12,000B). It's 1.2km from the centre of town, at the end of Soi 4 on Th Sankhongnoi (the street is called Th Sathanpayabarn where it intersects with Th Phahonyothin) – a 60B túk-túk ride.

Baan Warabordee BUDGET HOTEL $$
(☏0 5375 4488; baanwarabordee@hotmail.com; 59/1 Th Sanpannard; r 600-800B; ✹◉☂) This delightful small hotel has rooms decorated in dark woods and light, hand-woven textiles. The owners are friendly and can provide local advice.

Jansom House BUDGET HOTEL $
(☏0 5371 4552; 897/2 Th Jet Yod; r incl breakfast 450-500B; ✹◉☂) This three-storey hotel of-

fers spotless, spacious rooms set around a small courtyard filled with plants.

Moon & Sun Hotel BOUTIQUE HOTEL $$
(☏0 5371 9279; www.moonandsun-hotel.com; 632 Th Singhaclai; r 500-800B, ste 1100B; ✹☂) Bright and sparkling clean, this little hotel offers large modern rooms.

Baan Bua Guest House BUDGET HOTEL $
(☏0 5371 8880; www.baanbuaguesthouse.com; 879/2 Th Jet Yod; r 300-500B; ✹◉☂) This quiet guesthouse consists of a strip of 17 bright green rooms surrounding an inviting garden.

Golden Triangle Inn BUDGET HOTEL $$
(☏0 5371 1339; www.goldentriangleinn.com; 590 Th Phahonyothin; s/d incl breakfast 700/800B; ✹☂) Resembling an expansive Thai home, the 31 simple but attractive rooms here have tile or wood floors and wooden furniture.

🍴 Eating

The **night market** (☺5-10pm) has a decent collection of food stalls.

TOP CHOICE Lung Eed Locol Food NORTHERN THAI $
(Th Watpranorn; mains 30-60B; ☺11.45am-9pm Mon-Sat) To eat like an authentic locol (!), look no further than this rustic but delicious northern-style food shack. The restaurant is on Th Watpranorn near the intersection with the highway.

Nam Ngiaw Paa Nuan VIETNAMESE-NORTHERN THAI $
(Th Sanpannard; mains 10-100B; ☺9am-5pm) This somewhat concealed place serves a unique mix of Vietnamese and northern Thai dishes.

Somkhuan Khao Soi NORTHERN THAI $
(no roman-script sign; Th Singhaclai; mains 25B; ☺8am-3pm Mon-Fri) Friendly Mr Somkhuan sells tasty *kôw soi* from a basic street stall under two giant trees.

Old Dutch DUTCH-INTERNATIONAL $$
(541 Th Phahonyothin; mains 150-300B; ✹) This foreigner-friendly place has a variety of cuisine, not to mention cheap draught beer.

Phu-Lae NORTHERN THAI $$
(673/1 Th Thanalai; mains 80-320B; ☺lunch & dinner; ❄) This air-conditioned restaurant is popular among Thai tourists for its yummy northern Thai dishes.

BaanChivitMai Bakery CAFE $
(www.baanchivitmai.com; Th Prasopsook; 7am-9pm Mon-Sat;) Profits from this Swedish bakery at the bus station support work with orphans.

Doi Chaang CAFE $
(542/2 Th Ratanaket; 7am-11pm;) A smart cafe serving Doi Chaang, the leading Chiang Rai coffee brand.

Information

You'll have no problem finding banks and internet access along Th Phahonyothin.

Overbrook Hospital (0 5371 1366; www.overbrookhospital.com; Th Singhaclai)

Post office (Th Utarakit; 8.30am-4.30pm Mon-Fri, 9am-noon Sat & Sun)

Tourism Authority of Thailand office (TAT; nationwide call centre 1672, Chiang Rai 0 5374 4674; tatchrai@tat.or.th; Th Singhaclai; 8.30am-4.30pm)

Tourist police (nationwide call centre 1155, Chiang Rai 0 5374 0249; Th Phahonyothin; 24hr)

Getting There & Away

Chiang Rai airport (0 5379 8000) is 8km north of town. Taxis run into town from the airport for 200B. Out to the airport you can get a taxi or túk-túk for approximately 250B. **One-Two-Go** (Orient Thai; nationwide call centre 1126; www.flyorientthai.com) flies to Bangkok's Don Muang Airport (1550B, 1¼ hours, twice daily), while **Air Asia** (nationwide call centre 02 515 9999, Chiang Rai 0 5379 3543; www.airasia.com) and **THAI** (nationwide call centre 02 356 1111; www.thaiair.com) fly to Bangkok's Suvarnabhumi International Airport (2164B to 3120B, 1¼ hours, six times daily). **Kan Air** (nationwide call centre 02 551 6111, Chiang Rai 0 5379 3339; www.kanairlines.com) flies to Chiang Mai (from 1399B, 40 minutes, twice daily).

Buses bound for destinations within Chiang Rai Province depart from the **bus station** (Th Prasopsuk) in the centre of town. It's here you'll find buses to Chiang Khong (65B, 2½ hours), Chiang Saen (32B, 1½ hours) and Mae Sai (39B, 1½ hours), both with frequent daytime departures.

If you're heading beyond Chiang Rai, you'll have to go to the **new bus station** (0 5377 3989), 5km south of town on Hwy 1. *Sŏrngtăaou* linking it and the old station run from 5am to 9pm (10B, 20 minutes). There you'll find departures to Bangkok (448B to 716B, 11 to 12 hours), Chiang Mai (142B to 263B, three to seven hours), Lampang (102B to 286B, four to five hours), Nakhon Ratchasima (Khorat; 473B to 710B, 12 to 13 hours) and Sukhothai (223B to 244B, eight hours).

Another way to reach Chiang Rai is by boat on Mae Nam Kok from Tha Ton. For boats heading upriver, go to **CR Pier** (0 5375 0009), 2km northwest of town, via Th Kraisorasit. Passenger boats embark daily at 10.30am, terminating in Tha Ton about four hours later (350B). A charter to Tha Ton costs 3800B at the pier. A túk-túk to CR Pier should cost about 50B.

Golden Triangle

The tri-country border of Thailand, Myanmar and Laos forms the legendary Golden Triangle, a mountainous frontier where the opium poppy was once an easy cash crop for the region's ethnic minorities. As early as the 1600s, opium joined the Asian trade route, along with spices and other natural resources, and enjoyed increased success after the US war in Vietnam when the region became the global heroin (a derivative of opium) supplier. Starting in the 1980s, Thailand began to build infrastructure and introduce crop-substitution programs as well as pursue aggressive law enforcement in order to stamp out opium production. Today Thailand is no longer an opium producer, though its neighbours, especially Myanmar, continue to be players in the drug trade, most recently in the production of methamphetamine, which is shipped across Thailand to feed domestic and international markets. Drug-enforcement officials have renamed the region the Ice Triangle. But for the casual observer, the romanticised past of poppy fields and pack mules is marketed as a tourist attraction.

MAE SALONG (SANTIKHIRI)

POP 20,000

For a taste of China without crossing any international borders, head to this atmospheric village perched on the back hills of Chiang Rai. It's a great place to kick back for a couple of days, and the surrounding area is ripe for exploration.

Sights & Activities

A tiny but interesting **morning market** convenes from 6am to 8am at the T-intersection near Shin Sane Guest House. An **all-day market** forms at the southern end of town, and unites vendors selling hill-tribe handicrafts, shops selling tea and a few basic restaurants.

To soak up the great views from **Wat Santakhiri** go past the market and ascend 718 steps (or drive if you have a car). The

HOME AWAY FROM HOME

Mae Salong was originally settled by the 93rd Regiment of the Kuomintang (KMT), who had fled to Myanmar (Burma) from China after the 1949 Chinese revolution. The renegades were forced to leave Myanmar in 1961 when the Yangon government decided it wouldn't allow the KMT to remain legally in northern Myanmar. Crossing into northern Thailand with their pony caravans, the ex-soldiers and their families settled into mountain villages and re-created a society like the one they'd left behind in Yúnnán.

After the Thai government granted the KMT refugee status in the 1960s, efforts were made to incorporate the Yúnnánese KMT and their families into the Thai nation. Until the late 1980s they didn't have much success. Many ex-KMT persisted in involving themselves in the Golden Triangle opium trade in a three-way partnership with opium warlord Khun Sa and the Shan United Army (SUA). Because of the rough, mountainous terrain and lack of sealed roads, the outside world was rather cut off from the goings-on in Mae Salong, so the Yúnnánese were able to ignore attempts by the Thai authorities to suppress opium activity and tame the region.

Infamous Khun Sa made his home in nearby Ban Hin Taek (now Ban Thoet Thai) until the early 1980s when he was finally routed by the Thai military. Khun Sa's retreat to Myanmar seemed to signal a change in local attitudes and the Thai government finally began making progress in its pacification of Mae Salong and the surrounding area.

In a further effort to separate the area from its old image as an opium fiefdom, the Thai government officially changed the name of the village from Mae Salong to Santikhiri (Hill of Peace). Until the 1980s packhorses were used to move goods up the mountain to Mae Salong, but today the 36km road from Pasang is paved and well travelled. But despite the advances in infrastructure, the town is unlike any other in Thailand. The Yúnnánese dialect of Chinese still remains the lingua franca, residents tend to watch Chinese, rather than Thai, TV, and you'll find more Chinese than Thai food.

In an attempt to quash opium activity, and the more recent threat of *yah bâh* (methamphetamine) trafficking, the Thai government has created crop-substitution programs to encourage hill tribes to cultivate tea, coffee, corn and fruit trees.

wat is of the Mahayana tradition and Chinese in style.

Shin Sane Guest House and Little Home Guesthouse have free maps showing approximate **trekking** routes to Akha, Lisu, Mien, Lahu and Shan villages in the area. Nearby Akha and Lisu villages are less than half a day's walk away.

Shin Sane Guest House arranges four-hour **horseback treks** to four nearby villages for 500B for about three or four hours.

Sleeping & Eating

All accommodation and restaurants are on, or just off, the main road.

Little Home Guesthouse GUESTHOUSE $
(☎0 5376 5389; www.maesalonglittlehome.com; r/bungalows 300/800B; ❄ 🛜) Located near the market intersection, this delightful wooden house holds a few basic but cosy rooms and large and tidy bungalows out the back.

Baan Hom Muen Li BOUTIQUE HOTEL $$
(☎08 4045 8031; osmanhouse@hotmail.com; r incl breakfast 1000-1500B) Located in the middle of town, across from Sweet Maesalong, this new place consists of five rooms artfully decked out in modern and classic Chinese themes.

Saeng Aroon Hotel BUDGET HOTEL $
(☎0 5376 5029; r 300B; ✱ ❄) Next to the teashop of the same name, this new hotel has friendly staff, spacious tiled-floor rooms and great views of the hills. The cheaper rooms share spick-and-span hot-water bathrooms.

Sue Hai CHINESE $
(mains 60-150B; ⏰7am-9pm) This very simple family-run teashop/Yúnnánese restaurant has an English-language menu of local specialities, including local mushrooms fried with soy sauce, or the delicious air-dried pork fried with fresh chili. It also does filling and tasty bowls of home-made noodles. It's roughly in the middle of town.

Sweet Maesalong CAFE $
(mains 45-185B; ⏰8.30am-6pm) If you require a considerably higher degree of caffeine than the local tea leaves can offer, stop by this

cosy modern cafe with an extensive menu of coffee drinks using local beans. Sweet Maesalong is roughly in the middle of town.

Information

There is an ATM at the Thai Military Bank opposite Khumnaiphol Resort, at the southern end of town. An **internet cafe** (per hr 20B; ⏲9am-11pm) can be found next door.

Getting There & Away

To get to Mae Salong by bus, take a Mae Sai–bound bus from Chiang Rai to Ban Pasang (20B, 30 minutes, every 20 minutes from 6am to 4pm). From Ban Pasang, blue *sŏrngtăaou* head up the mountain to Mae Salong (60B, one hour, from 7am to 5pm). To get back to Ban Pasang, *sŏrngtăaou* park near the 7-Eleven. *Sŏrngtăaou* stop running at around 5pm but you can charter one in either direction for about 500B.

You can also reach Mae Salong by road from Tha Ton. Yellow *sŏrngtăaou* bound for Tha Ton stop near Little Home Guesthouse at 8.20am, 10.20am, 12.20pm and 1.50pm (60B, one hour).

MAE SAI

POP 22,000

Thailand's northernmost town peeps over the Mae Nam Sai (Sai River) into Myanmar and is a bustling market crossroads for hill-tribe, Thai and Burmese merchants from the broader Golden Triangle area. The border crossing draws many day trippers heading into Myanmar.

Sights & Activities

Take the steps up the hill near the border to **Wat Phra That Doi Wao**, west of the main street, for views over Mae Sai and Myanmar.

Mae Sai is one of Thailand's primary gem-trading towns, and a walk down Soi 4 will reveal several open-air **gem dealers** diligently counting hundreds of tiny semi-precious stones on the side of the street.

Sleeping & Eating

Khanthongkham Hotel HOTEL $$

(☎0 5373 4222; www.kthotel.com; 7 Th Phahonyothin; r 800-950B, ste 1300-1650B; ❄@📶) Near the border, this hotel features huge rooms that have been tastefully decorated in light woods and brown textiles. Suites are exceptionally vast, and like all rooms, also have flat-screen TVs and user-friendly bathrooms.

Maesai Guest House BUDGET HOTEL $

(☎0 5373 2021; 688 Th Wiengpangkam; bungalows r 200-600B; 📶) A collection of A-frame bungalows that range from simple rooms (shared cold-water showers) to more modern bungalows on the river with terraces and private bathrooms. Located about 300m west of the border near the Mae Nam Sai.

Piyaporn Place Hotel BUSINESS HOTEL $$

(☎0 5373 4511-3; www.piyaporn-place.com; 77/1 Th Phahonyothin; r/ste incl breakfast 800/1800B; ❄@📶) The large, contemporary-styled rooms have wooden floors, a small sofa and the usual four-/five-star amenities like bath, cable TV and minibar. Located about 500m south of the border, near Soi 7.

Bismillah Halal Food MUSLIM-THAI $

(Soi 4, Th Phahonyothin; mains 25-40B; ⏲6am-6pm) Run by Burmese Muslims, this tiny restaurant does an excellent biryani and a dozen other Muslim dishes, from roti to samosa.

Sukhothai Cuisine NOODLES $

(399/9 Th Sailomjoy; mains 30-40B; ⏲7am-4pm) This open-air restaurant in the covered market area near the border serves the namesake noodles from Sukhothai, as well as satay and a few other basic dishes.

An expansive **night market** (⏲5-11pm) unfolds every evening along Th Phahonyothin. During the day, several **snack and drink vendors** (Th Phahonyothin) can be found in front of the police station.

Information

There are several banks with exchange and ATM facilities near the border.

Immigration Main Office (☎0 5373 1008; Rte 110; ⏲8.30am-4.30pm Mon-Fri); Border (⏲7am-6.30pm) There's a main office about 3km from the border near Soi 17 and another at the entrance to the border bridge.

Internet Cafe (per hr 40B) Behind the large Wang Thong Hotel.

Overbrook Clinic (☎0 5373 4422; 20/7 Th Phahonyothin; ⏲8am-5pm) Roughly across from Piyaporn Place Hotel.

Tourist police (☎115) In front of the border crossing before immigration.

Getting There & Away

On the main Th Phahonyothin road, by Soi 8, is a sign saying 'bus stop'. From here *sŏrngtăaou* depart for Sop Ruak (45B, every 40 minutes, 8am to 1pm), terminating in Chiang Saen (50B). Mae Sai's government **bus station** (☎0 5371 1224; Rte 110) is 1.5km from the border; getting there from the border involves a 15B shared *sŏrngtăaou* ride from the corner of Th Phahonyothin and Soi 2 or a 40B motorcycle taxi ride from the stand at the corner of Th Phahonyothin and Soi 4. There are several afternoon departures to Bangkok

GETTING TO MYANMAR (BURMA): MAE SAI TO TACHILEIK

Mae Sai, opposite the Burmese town of Tachileik, is a legal crossing point for foreign tourists. Yet as with all of Myanmar's land crossings, there are several caveats involved and the following information is liable to change, so check the situation locally before you travel.

In general, it's very straightforward to cross to Tachileik for the day and slightly more complicated to get a two-week visa and permission to visit Kengtung, a quiet but interesting outpost of Tai culture 160km north.

The **Thai immigration office** (☎0 5373 1008) is just before the bridge and is officially open from 7am to 6.30pm. After taking care of the usual formalities, cross the bridge and head to the **Myanmar immigration office**. Here you pay 500B and your picture is taken for a temporary ID card that allows you to stay in town for the day; your passport will be kept at the office. On your return to Thailand, the Thai immigration office will give you a new 15-day tourist visa (see p443).

(483B to 966B, 13 hours) from 4pm to 5.45pm, and frequent daytime departures to Chiang Mai (165B to 320B, five hours), Chiang Rai (38B, 1½ hours) and Nakhon Ratchasima (Khorat; 507B to 760B, 15 hours).

Mae Sai is also a legal border crossing into Myanmar.

TACHILEIK & KENGTUNG

There is little to do in **Tachileik** apart from sample Burmese food and shop. There's an interesting morning market and it can be fun to hang about in the teashops.

If you'd like to stay longer or visit Kengtung, proceed directly to the adjacent **tourist information office**. There you'll need three photos, $10 and 50B to process a border pass valid for 14 days; your passport will be kept at the border. It's also obligatory to hire a guide for the duration of your stay. Guides cost 1000B per day (400B of this goes to Myanmar Travels & Tours, a state-run travel agency), and if you haven't already arranged for a Kengtung-based guide to meet you at border, you'll be assigned one by MTT and will also have to pay for your guide's food and accommodation during your stay. Recommended guides include **Sai Leng** (☎95 9490 31470; sairoctor.htunleng@gmail.com), **Freddie** (Sai Yot; ☎95 9490 31934; yotkham@gmail.com) and **Paul** (Sai Lon; ☎95 9490 30464, 95 842 2812).

Kengtung (called Chiang Tung by the Thais and usually spelt Kyaingtong by the Burmese) is a sleepy but historic capital for the Shan State's Khün culture. The Khün speak a northern Thai language related to Shan and Thai Lü, and use a writing script similar to the ancient Lanna script. Built around a small lake and dotted with ageing **Buddhist temples** and crumbling British **colonial architecture**, it's a much more scenic town than Tachileik and one of the most interesting towns in Myanmar's entire Shan State.

Places to stay include the **Princess Hotel** (☎95 842 1319; kengtung@mail4u.com.mm; s/d $30/50; ❄), or the budget-oriented but inconveniently located **Harry's Trekking House** (☎95 842 1418; 132 Mai Yang Rd; r $7-20).

Buses bound for Kengtung (K10,000, five hours) depart from Tachileik's dusty **bus station**, 2km and a 10B *sŏrngtăaou* ride or a 40B motorcycle taxi ride from the border, at about 8am and noon. Alternatively, you can charter a taxi for about 2500B, or if you're willing to wait, get a front/back seat in a share taxi for K15,000/10,000.

For a complete description of Kengtung, see Lonely Planet's *Myanmar (Burma)* guidebook.

CHIANG SAEN

POP 11,000

Despite steady river-barge trade with China, Chiang Saen remains a pretty sleepy town. It is the birthplace of King Mengrai, the acknowledged founder of the Lanna kingdom, which dominated much of northern Thailand in the 14th century. Chiang Saen is only a cross-river ferry ride from Laos, but it is not a legal border crossing for foreigners. It is, however, possible to use the town as a jumping-off point for trips to China.

The small **Chiang Saen National Museum** (702 Th Phahonyothin; admission 100B; ⏰8.30am-4.30pm Wed-Sun) is a nationally run repository of northern Thai artefacts.

Near Pratu Chiang Saen is a **historical park** (admission 50B), preserving the ruins of Chiang Saen's ancient kingdom.

The nearby town of **Sop Ruak**, 9km north, is the official 'centre' of the Golden Triangle and is home to two opium-related

WORTH A TRIP

DAY BOAT TO JINGHONG

Although it was once possible to travel by cargo ship from Chiang Saen to Jinghong in China, now it's only permitted via passenger boat through **Maekhong Delta Travel** (0 5364 2517; www.maekhongtravel.com; 230/5-6 Th Phaholyothin, Mae Sai; one way 820 yuan/3500B; 9am-5pm).

The trip from Chiang Saen to Jinghong takes 15 hours when conditions are good. During drier months (typically March to May) boats don't run, as rocks and shallows can hamper the way. Boats usually depart from Chiang Saen on Monday, Wednesday and Friday at 5am, but this is not set in stone and it's important to call ahead before you make plans.

To do this trip you must already have your visa for China – several guesthouses in town can arrange this for you, but it's quicker to arrange from Chiang Mai or Bangkok. If you already have a visa, tickets can be arranged at most local guesthouses and hotels, or through **Chiang Saen Tour and Travel** (0 5377 7051; chiangsaen2004@yahoo.com; 64 Th Rimkhong; 8am-6pm).

museums. The **House of Opium** (www.houseofopium.com; admission 50B; 7am-7pm) has a small display of poppy cultivation and opium paraphernalia, while 1km north of Sop Ruak is the royally sponsored Mah Fah Luang Foundation's **Hall of Opium** (admission 200B; 8.30am-4pm Tue-Sun), an impressive facility with a multimedia exhibit on the history and effects of opium on individuals and society.

To give bus tourists a taste beyond Thailand's borders, there are several **Mekong River cruises** (400B per boat, 5 people max, 1hr).

There's a handful of places to stay in Chiang Saen. A convenient (though slightly noisy) location opposite the river and night market is the no-frills **Chiang Saen Guest House** (0 5365 0196; 45/2 Th Rimkhong; r 150-650B, bungalows 200B;).

The only reason to stay in or around Sop Ruak is to take advantage of some of northern Thailand's best upscale lodgings. The **Four Seasons Tented Camp** (0 5391 0200; www.fourseasons.com; minimum 3-night stay from 225B;) is among the most truly unique accommodation experiences in Thailand. The 15 tents are luxurious and decked out in colonial-era safari paraphernalia, and guests are encouraged to take in the natural setting (tip: tent 15 looks over an elephant bathing area) and participate in daily activities, which range from mahout training to spa treatments.

Likewise, the **Anantara Golden Triangle Resort & Spa** (0 5378 4084; www.anantara.com; r/ste incl breakfast 16,500/18000B;) takes up a large patch of beautifully landscaped ground directly opposite the Hall of Opium. The rooms combine Thai and international themes, and all have balconies looking over the Mekong.

Kiaw Siang Hai (no roman-script sign; 44 Th Rimkhong; mains 50-200B; 8am-8pm) prepares a huge menu of dishes in addition to the namesake noodle and wonton dishes. The restaurant can be located by the giant ceramic jars out the front. **Evening food vendors** (dishes 30-60B; 4-11pm) set up along the river banks during the dry months.

There's a bus stop near the town's main intersection, with departures to Chiang Mai (165B to 212B, five hours) at 7.15am and 9am, and frequent departures to Chiang Rai (37B, 1½ hours) from 5.30am to 5pm. Blue *sŏrngtăaou* that travel to Sop Ruak (20B) and Mae Sai (50B) wait at a stall at the eastern end of Th Phahonyothin from 7.20am to noon. Parked on Th Rimkhong, green *sŏrngtăaou* go to Chiang Khong (100B, two hours) from 7.30am to noon.

CHIANG KHONG

POP 12,000

A lively border town, Chiang Khong sits at a crucial crossroads in the history of the region. For most of its history, Chiang Khong was a remote but important market town for local hill tribes (including local Mien and White Hmong) and then developed a bustling business as a travellers' gateway to Laos (for details on crossing to Laos, see p415) starting in the 1990s.

The nearby village of **Ban Hat Khrai**, 1.5km south of Chiang Khong, is a riverside fishing village that has long harvested the *plah bèuk* (giant Mekong catfish; *Pangasianodon gigas to ichthyologists*).

This catfish is one of the largest freshwater fish in the world and can measure 2m to 3m in length and weigh up to 300kg. The fish is technically endangered, though fishing is still allowed during the annual migration period between late April and June. Because of limited supply, the meat is a delicacy and can fetch up to 500B or more per kilogram, a price that only high-end Bangkok restaurants can afford.

In Chiang Khong, several banks have branches with ATMs and foreign-exchange services.

There is no shortage of lodging in town, much of it near the river and geared towards the budget market. **Baanrimtaling** (☎0 5379 1613; maleewan_th@yahoo.com; 99/2 Moo 3; dm 100-120B, r 150-450B;) combines a home-like atmosphere and gentle service, although it's outside the centre of town. **Portside Hotel** (☎0 5365 5238; portsidehotel@hotmail.com; 546 Th Sai Klang; r with fan/air-con 300/500B;) is steps from the pier and has good-value rooms. **Khao Soi Pa Orn** (no roman-script sign; Soi 6; mains 15-30B; ⊙8am-4pm) does an excellent local noodle dish; look for the gigantic highway pillar at the eastern end of Soi 6.

Buses depart frequently for Chiang Mai (211B to 272B, 2½ hours) and Chiang Rai (65B, 2½ hours), with a few departures to Bangkok (493B to 888B, 14 hours) between 3.05pm and 4.10pm. Chiang Khong is also a busy crossing point to Laos, with boats going to Luang Prabang and buses to points in Laos and China.

Boats taking up to five passengers can be chartered up the Mekong River to Chiang Saen for 2000B.

Nan

POP 20,000

Due to its remote location, Nan is not the kind of destination most travellers are going to stumble upon. And its largely featureless downtown isn't going to inspire many postcards home. But if you've taken the time to get here, you'll be rewarded by a city rich in both culture and history.

Nan Province is also home to a low-key outdoor adventure scene, and the opening of the international border at Ban Huay Kon (see p418) makes the province a possible gateway to Laos.

Sights

Wat Phumin BUDDHIST TEMPLE

Nan's most famous temple is celebrated for its exquisite murals that were executed during the late 19th century by a Thai Lü artist called Thit Buaphan.

GETTING TO LAOS: CHIANG KHONG TO HUAY XAI

Long-tail boats to Huay Xai, Laos (30B), leave frequently from Tha Reua Bak, a pier at the northern end of Chiang Khong, from 8am to 6pm.

After going through **Thai immigration** (☎0 5379 1332; ⊙8am-6pm) and crossing the river, foreigners can purchase a 30-day visa for Laos upon arrival in Huay Xai for US$30 to US$42, depending on nationality (for more information on Lao visas, see p361). There is an extra US$1 charge after 4pm and on weekends, and if you don't have a passport-style mugshot they'll charge 40B extra.

Once on the Lao side you can continue by road to Luang Nam Tha and Udomxai, or by boat down the Mekong River to Luang Prabang. If you're bound for the capital, **Lao Airlines** (☎8 5621 1026, 8 5621 1494; www.laoairlines.com) has flights from Huay Xai to Vientiane three times a week for US$94.

If time is on your side, the daily **slow boat** (900B, 10am) to Luang Prabang takes two days, including a night in the village of Pak Beng. Avoid the noisy **fast boats** (1450B, 6-7hr) that ply the Huay Xai to Luang Prabang route, as there have been reports of bad accidents. Booking tickets through an agent costs slightly more, but they arrange tickets for you, provide transport from your guesthouse and across the Mekong River, and provide a boxed lunch for the boat ride.

If you already hold a Chinese visa, it's now also possible to go more or less directly to China from Chiang Khong. After obtaining a 30-day Laos visa on arrival in Huay Xai, simply board one of the buses that go directly to the Xishuangbanna town of Mengla (110,000K, eight hours, 8.30am daily) or Jinghong (150,000K, 10 hours, 7.30am Tuesday, Thursday and Saturday) via the Lao border town of Boten.

Details for traversing the border in the opposite direction are on p328.

THE MURALS OF WAT PHUMIN

Wat Phumin is northern Thailand's Sistine Chapel, and the images on its walls are now found on everything from knick-knacks at Chiang Mai's night bazaar to postcards sold in Bangkok. However, despite the happy scenes depicted, the murals were executed during a period that saw the end of Nan as a semi-independent kingdom. This resulted in several examples of political and social commentary manifesting themselves in the murals, a rarity in Thai religious art.

The murals commissioned by Jao Suliyaphong, the last king of Nan, include the *Khaddhana Jataka*, a relatively obscure story of one of the Buddha's lives that, according to Thai historian David K Wyatt in his excellent book, *Reading Thai Murals*, has never been illustrated elsewhere in the Buddhist world. The story, which is on the left side of the temple's northern wall, depicts an orphan in search of his parents. Wyatt argues that this particular tale was chosen as a metaphor for the kingdom of Nan, which also had been abandoned by a succession of 'parents', the Thai kingdoms of Sukhothai, Chiang Mai and Ayuthaya. At roughly the same time as the murals were painted, Nan was fully incorporated into Siam by King Rama V, and much of its territory was allotted to France. Apparent discontent with this decision can be seen in a scene on the west wall that shows two male monkeys attempting to copulate against a background that, not coincidentally according to Wyatt, resembles the French flag.

The murals are also valuable purely for their artistic beauty, something that is even more remarkable if one steps back and considers the limited palette of colours that the artist, Thit Buaphan, had to work with. The paintings are also fascinating for their fly-on-the-wall depictions of local life in Nan during the end of the 19th century. A depiction of three members of a hill tribe on the west wall includes such details as a man's immense goitre and a barking dog, suggesting this group's place as outsiders. Multiple depictions of a man wearing a feminine shawl, often seen performing traditionally female-only duties, are among the earliest depictions of a *gàteui* (transsexual). And in what must be one of the art world's most superfluous cameos, the artist painted himself on the west wall, flirting with a woman. Considering that the murals took Thit Buaphan more than 20 years to complete, we'll allow him this excess.

Nan National Museum MUSEUM
(Th Pha Kong; admission 100B; ⊙9am-4pm) Housed in the 1903-vintage palace of Nan's last two feudal lords, this museum first opened its doors in 1973. In terms of collection and content, it's one of the country's better provincial museums, and has English labels for most items.

🏃 Activities

White-water rafting along Mae Nam Wa, in northern Nan, is popular, but only possible when the water level is high (September to December), and is said to be best during the early part of the wet season.

Nan Adventure Tour RAFTING
(📱08 6701 4777; Th Nokham; 2 days & 1 night per person 3500B, 3 days & 2 nights per person from 4500B) This outfit conducts two- to three-day, all-inclusive, rafting and/or kayaking trips.

Nan Seeing Tour GUIDED TOURS
(📱08 1472 4131; www.nanseeingtour.com; Nan Coffee, Th Sumon Thewarat; 4 person min, 2 days & 1 night per person 1850B, 3 days & 2 nights per person 3850B) This locally run startup conducts two-wheeled expeditions in and around Nan.

🛏 Sleeping & Eating

Pukha Nanfa Hotel BOUTIQUE HOTEL $$$
(📱0 5477 1111; www.pukhananfahotel.com; 369 Th Sumon Thewarat; r 2500-4600B; ❋◉☎) A recent ownership change has transformed the formerly forgettable Nan Fah Hotel into a charming boutique hotel. Old adverts and pictures add to the old world feel, and to top it off, the place is conveniently located and has capable staff.

Fah Place BUDGET HOTEL $
(📱0 5471 0222; 237/8 Th Sumon Thewarat; r 400-500B; ❋☎) The huge rooms here have been decorated with attractive teak furniture, including the kind of puffy inviting beds you'd

normally find at places that charge 10 times this much.

Nan Guest House BUDGET HOTEL $
(☎08 1288 8484; 57/15 Th Mahaphrom; r 250-400B; ❄@☏) Located in a quiet residential area, this longstanding and well-maintained place has spotless spacious rooms, half of which have private hot-water bathrooms. Nan Guest House is at the end of Soi 2, just off Th Mahaphrom.

Pu Som Restaurant NORTHERN THAI $
(no roman-script sign; 203/1 Th Mano; mains 30-70B; ⊙lunch & dinner) The emphasis here is on beef, served in the local style as *lâhp*, or as *néua nêung*, steamed over herbs and served with an incredibly delicious galangal dip.

Yota Vegetarian Restaurant VEGETARIAN THAI $
(Th Mahawong; mains 10-35B; ⊙7am-3pm) Run by the friendliest lady in town who will not let you leave hungry, this is perhaps the best deal in Nan.

Goodview Nan THAI $
(203/1 Th Mano; dishes 35-150B; ⊙11am-midnight) One of the few places in town to take advantage of the views over the Mae Nam Nan, this place works equally well as a dinner date locale or a riverside pub.

Information

You shouldn't have any trouble locating banks and/or internet in Nan, particularly along Th Sumon Thewarat.

Main post office (Th Mahawong; ⊙8.30am-4.30pm Mon-Fri, 9am-noon Sat & Sun) In the centre of town.

Tourist Information Centre (☎0 5475 1169; Th Pha Kong; ⊙8.30am-4.30pm) Opposite Wat Phumin.

Getting There & Away

Destinations from Nan's tiny airport include Bangkok's Don Muang Airport (1690B, 1⅓ hours, one to two times daily) via **Nok Air** (☎nationwide call centre 1318, Nan 0 5477 1308; www.nokair.co.th) and **Solar Air** (☎nationwide call centre 02 535 2455; www.solarair.co.th), and Chiang Mai (990B, 45 minutes, twice daily) via **Kan Air** (☎nationwide call centre 02 551 6111, Nan 0 5477 1308; www.kanairlines.com) and **Nok Mini** (☎nationwide call centre 0 5328 0444; www.nokmini.com). Taxis from the airport to town run from about 100B per person; contact Mr Klay (☎08 6188 0079).

All buses, minivans and *sŏrngtăaou* leave from the bus station at the southwestern edge of town. This includes departures for Bangkok (424B to 773B, 10 to 11 hours) between 8am and 10am, and 6.10pm and 7.45pm; frequent departures to Lampang (120B) and Chiang Mai (223B to 412B, five hours) from 7.30am to 10.30pm; and a single departure to Chiang Rai (176B) at 9am. A motorcycle taxi from the station to the centre of town costs 25B.

Ban Huay Kon, 140km north of Nan, is now a legal border crossing into Laos.

Around Nan

Doi Phu Kha National Park NATIONAL PARK
(☎0 5470 1000; admission 200B) This national park is centred on 2000m-high Doi Phu Kha, the province's highest peak, in Amphoe Pua and Amphoe Bo Kleua in northeastern Nan (about 75km from Nan). There are several Htin, Mien, Hmong and Thai Lü **villages** in the park and vicinity, as well as a couple of **caves** and **waterfalls**, and endless opportunities for forest **walks**. The park headquarters has a basic map and staff can arrange a local guide for walks or more extended excursions around the area, as well as rafting on the Nam Wa. The park is often cold in the cool season and especially wet in the wet season.

The park offers a variety of **bungalows** (☎0 2562 0760; www.dnp.go.th; 2-7 people 300-2500B), and there is a nearby restaurant and basic shop.

To reach the national park by public transport you must first take a bus or *sŏrngtăaou* north of Nan to Pua (50B). Get off at the 7-Eleven then cross the highway to board one of the three daily *sŏrngtăaou* (50B, 30 minutes) that depart at 7.30am, 9.30am and 11.30am.

Ban Bo Luang VILLAGE
Ban Bo Luang (also known as Ban Bo Kleua, or Salt Well Village) is a picturesque Htin village southeast of the Doi Phu Kha National Park where the long-standing occupation has been the extraction of salt from local salt wells.

There is a handful of mostly rustic places to stay in Ban Bo Luang. Rising above the pack is **Boklua View** (☎08 1809 6392; www.bokluaview.com; Ban Bo Luang; r/bungalows incl breakfast 1850B; ❄@☏✖), an attractive and well-run hillside resort overlooking the village and the Nam Mang that runs through it.

There are a few small restaurants serving basic dishes in Ban Bo Luang.

To reach Ban Bo Luang from Nan, take a bus or *sŏrngtăaou* north of Nan to Pua

GETTING TO LAOS: BAN HUAY KON TO MUANG NGEUN

Located 140km north of Nan, Ban Huay Kon is a very quiet village in the mountains near the Lao border. There's a fun **border market** on Saturday mornings, but most will come here because of the town's recent status as an international border crossing to Laos.

After passing the **Thai immigration booth** (☎0 5469 3530; ⊙8am-5pm), foreigners can purchase a 30-day visa for Laos for US$30 to $42, depending on nationality (for more on Lao visas, see p361). There is an extra US$1 or 50B charge after 4pm and on weekends. You can then proceed 2.5km to the Lao village of Muang Ngeun, where you could stay at the **Phouxay Guesthouse** (☎020 214 2826; Nan-Hongsa Rd; r 50,000K), or if your heading onward, to the tiny **'Passenger Car Station'** (☎020 245 0145, 020 244 4130) beside the market, from where *sŏrngtăaou* leave for Hongsa (40,000K, 1½ hours) between 2pm and 4pm, and to Pak Kaen (35,000K, one hour) at around 7.30am and 2pm, arriving in time for the Mekong slowboats to Huay Xai and Pak Beng respectively.

To get to Ban Huay Kon, there are three daily minivans (100B, three hours) that depart Nan at around 5am, 8am and 9am. The only other option is to hop on a bus from Nan to Pon (105B, 2½ hours), which depart every 30 minutes from 6am to 6pm. From Pon you'll need to transfer to one of two daily *sŏrngtăaou* that go the remaining 30km to Ban Huay Kon (100B, one hour) at 9.30am and noon. In the opposite direction, minivans leave Ban Huay Kon at 10am, 1pm and 2.30pm.

There's basic bungalow-style accommodation between Ban Huay Kon and the border. Ask in the village for details.

(50B). Getting off at the 7-Eleven, cross the highway to take the *sŏrngtăaou* that terminate in the village (80B, one hour), departing at 7.30am, 9.30am and 11.30am.

NORTHEAST THAILAND

The personality of the northeast (also known as Isan) is much like the hand-loomed silk that the region is famous for. Its cultural patterns – from language to cuisine – were woven from the ancient kingdoms of neighbouring Cambodia and Laos, long before Bangkok defined the current borders. The resulting textile of people is distinct from and slightly foreign to the rest of Thailand. But nationals from modern-day Laos and Cambodia recognise instant kinship with Thai villagers who grow up speaking either Khmer or Lao (depending on the village) and who have preserved common customs and festivals, some of which have since disappeared outside of Isan's borders.

Isan served as the western frontier of the great Khmer empire, and its plateau (around Nakhon Ratchasima and Surin) was peppered with elaborate temples that formed a trail of religious sentinels facing reverentially towards Angkor Wat. These proud monuments remain today in various states of repair and are still surveying a rural landscape of rice fields ploughed by water buffalo, a view that is surprisingly ancient and incredibly remote from today's population centres.

As Angkor's power waned, the northern provinces of Isan were claimed by the great Lao kingdom of Lan Xang (or Lan Chang, meaning 'Million Elephants'). The greatest amount of Lao influence can be found in Ubon Ratchathani and other riverside towns that have modelled their temple architecture on their northern neighbour's needle-like spires, and some private residences even boast subdued French architecture. In these corners you'll find populations of Thai Catholics and Vietnamese, a result of France's Indochinese adventures.

Not until the rise of the Thai kingdom of Ayuthaya did Nakhon Ratchasima (Khorat) and other city-states in Isan begin to align themselves with the Siamese in central Thailand. The region went largely ignored until the French started to consolidate power in its nearby colonies and again in the 1960s when Isan's proximity to Vietnam and former Indochina was a convenient location for air bases (in Khorat, Khon Kaen, Udon Thani and Ubon Ratchathani) used by US military operations in the region. Today these cities are administrative hubs but their utilitarian facades are sometimes hard to embrace.

Isan is decidedly off the beaten track with the attendant advantages and disadvantages: English is not widely spoken and travel services are at a minimum. But the reward is an insight into a hardworking and welcoming society, defining the identity of the river's social landscape.

Nakhon Ratchasima (Khorat)

POP 215.000

Khorat, the brash gateway to the northeast, is a city you grow to know. This is urban Isan, where the middle class flourishes among sprawling developments and multilane highways. There are some quieter nooks in the old city and a strong regional identity rarely viewed by tourists, most of whom will pass through en route to somewhere else. The collection of craft villages and the Khmer ruins at Phimai, outside town, are reasons to tip your hat to Khorat.

◉ Sights

FREE Thao Suranari Monument MONUMENT
(Th Rajadamnern) In the city centre, a monument honours Thao Suranari, a local heroine who led the inhabitants against Lao invaders during the reign of Rama III (r 1824–51). A holy shrine, the statue receives visitors who offer gifts and prayers or hire singers to perform Khorat folk songs. Behind the memorial is **Chumphon Gate**, the only original city gate still standing.

Maha Viravong National Museum MUSEUM
(Th Rajadamnern; admission 50B; ☉9am-4pm Wed-Sun) For a dose of Khmer and Ayuthaya art, visit this museum, housed in the grounds of Wat Sutchinda.

🛏 Sleeping

Sansabai House BUDGET HOTEL $
(☎0 4425 5144; www.sansabai-korat.com; 335 Th Suranaree; r 270-600B; ✴☎) Surprisingly underpriced, all rooms are bright and spotless with good mattresses, minifridges and little balconies.

Thai Inter Hotel HOTEL $$
(☎0 4424 7700; www.thaiinterhotel.com; 344/2 Th Yommarat; r 650-750B; ✴◉☎) This little hotel tries to be hip by patching together an odd mix of styles, and it pretty much pulls it off. It's got a good (though not so quiet) location near many good restaurants and bars.

V-One HOTEL $$$
(☎0 4434 2444; www.v-onehotelkorat.com; Th Changphurk; r incl breakfast 800-6780B; ✴◉☎▩) The self-proclaimed 'Trendy & Boutique Hotel' is a brash mixture of colours and styles.

✕ Eating

Khorat boasts a local variation on *pàt tai* known as *pàt mèe kohràht*, which is made with a local-style rice noodle. Hunker down to a plate along with Isan's other specialities at **Wat Boon Night Bazaar** (Th Chomphon; ☉5.30-10pm).

Rabiang Pa THAI $$
(284 Th Yommarat; dishes 60-330B; ☉dinner) The leafiest and loveliest restaurant on this stretch of Th Yommarat has a massive picture menu for risk-free ordering.

Cabbages & Condoms THAI $
(Th Seup Siri; dishes 35-200B; ☉lunch & dinner; ✐) Like the original in Bangkok, this is dining for a cause (to help the PDA). It has a leafy terrace on which you can sample a carefully crafted menu of Thai and Western favourites.

ⓘ Information

Emergency
Tourist police (☎0 4434 1777; Hwy 2) Opposite Bus Terminal 2.

Internet Access
Walk two or three blocks and you're bound to pass an internet cafe. Like most, **Plearnta** (Th Rajadamnern; per hr 15B; ☉10am-midnight) stays open late.

Medical Services
Bangkok Hospital (☎0 4442 9999; Th Mittaphap)

Money
Klang Plaza 2 (Th Jomsurangyat) shopping centre has a Bangkok Bank (changes cash only) open daily until 8pm, and an AEON ATM on the 5th floor. There are more extended-hours banks and another AEON ATM at The Mall.

Post
Post office (Th Jomsurangyat; ☉8.30am-10.30pm Mon-Fri, 9am-noon, 4-10.30pm Sat & Sun) Has a stamp museum.

Tourist Information
Tourism Authority of Thailand (TAT; ☎0 4421 3666; tatsima@tat.or.th; Th Mittaphap; ☉8.30am-4.30pm) Next to Sima Thani Hotel.

Nakhon Ratchasima (Khorat)

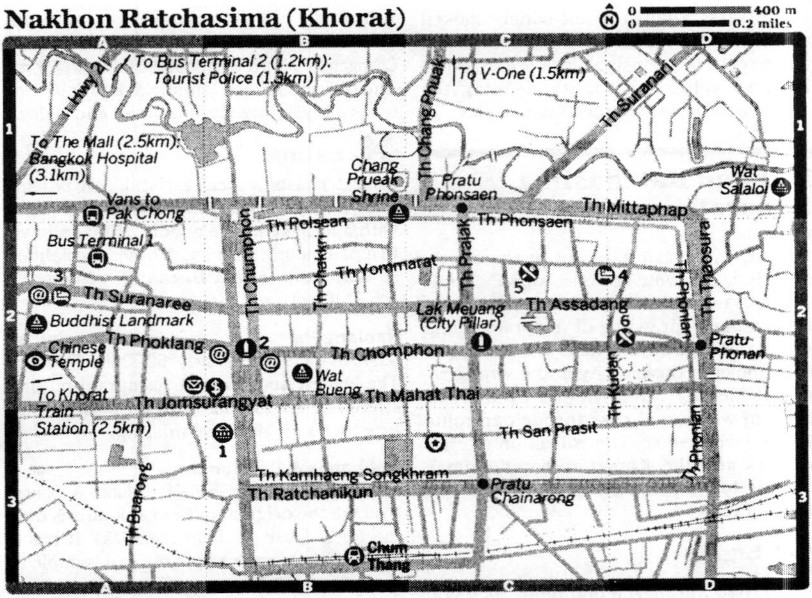

Nakhon Ratchasima (Khorat)

Sights

1 Maha Viravong National Museum B3
2 Thao Suranari Monument B2

Sleeping

3 Sansabai House A2
4 Thai Inter Hotel C2

Eating

5 Rabieng Pa C2
6 Wat Boon Night Bazaar D2

Getting There & Away

There are two bus terminals in Khorat. **Bus Terminal 1** (0 4424 2899; Th Burin) in the city centre serves Bangkok and towns within the province. **Bus Terminal 2** (0 4425 6006) off Hwy 2 has frequent departures to Bangkok (154B to 250B, three hours), Chiang Mai (435B to 653B, 12 to 13 hours), Nong Khai (210B to 420B, six hours), Ubon Ratchathani (203B to 330B, five to six hours) and if you already have a Lao visa, Vientiane (320B, 6½ hours).

Khorat's **train station** (0 4424 2044) has 14 trains daily that connect the city with Bangkok's Hualamphong train station (100B to 1010B, most take six hours), and three to Nong Khai (214B to 368B, 5½ hours). To check timetables and prices for other destinations call the **State Railway of Thailand** (nationwide call centre 1690; www.railway.co.th) or look at its website.

Getting Around

Túk-túk and motorcycle taxis cost between 30B and 70B to most places around town. Several shops on Th Suranari near the intersection with Th Buarong rent motorcycles.

Around Nakhon Ratchasima

PHIMAI

One of Thailand's finest surviving Khmer temples sits at the heart of this innocuous little town, 60km northeast of Khorat. Originally started by Khmer King Jayavarman V in the late 10th century and finished by King Suryavarman I early in the 11th, **Prasat Phimai** (Th Anantajinda; admission 100B; 7.30am-6pm) shares a number of design features with Angkor Wat, including the roof of its 28m-tall main shrine, and may have been its model. Thanks to a superb restoration, Phimai projects a majesty that transcends its modest size.

Phimai National Museum (Th Tha Songkhran; admission 100B; ⊙9am-4pm Wed-Sun), outside the main complex, has a fine collection of Khmer sculpture, including a serene bust of Jayavarman VII, Angkor's most powerful king.

Phimai is usually a day-trip destination, but there are a few places to crash, including **Old Phimai Guesthouse** (☎08 0159 5363; www.phimaigh.com; Th Chomsudasadet; dm 100B, s 170B, d 200-370B; ❄📶).

Buses for Phimai leave from Khorat's Bus Terminal 2 (36B to 50B, 1¼ hours) every half-hour until 10pm.

DAN KWIAN & PAK THONG CHAI

South of Khorat are two of Thailand's most successful craft villages. **Dan Kwian** is known for its rough textured pottery often fired with a rustlike hue. The village was also something of a hideout for protestors who were wanted by the authorities during the tumultuous student-protest era. Buses (14B, 30 minutes) run from near Khorat's south city gate.

Jim Thompson bought much of his silk in **Pak Thong Chai**. Weavers still work hand looms at the **Macchada**, at the southern end of the main road. Buses (30B, one hour) leave Khorat's Bus Terminal 1 every half-hour.

Khao Yai National Park

An easy escape into nature, **Khao Yai** (☎08 6092 6529; admission 400B) incorporates one of the largest intact monsoon forests in mainland Asia and is a Unesco World Heritage Site. Abundant wildlife – including some 200 elephants and one of Thailand's largest hornbill populations – lives among the park's varied terrain. The park has many kilometres of trekking trails and some superb waterfalls (which are at their most majestic after the monsoon rains in October).

Sleeping & Eating

The primary base for foreign tourists visiting the park is the town of Pak Chong, where hotels and guesthouses arrange park tours. You can also visit the park independently without your own transport.

Greenleaf Guest House GUESTHOUSE $
(☎0 4436 5073; www.greenleaftour.com; Th Thanarat, Km 7.5; r 200-300B; 📶) This place has some good-value budget rooms in Pak Chong.

The Jungle House HOTEL $$
(☎0 4429 7183; www.junglehousehotel.com; Th Thanarat, Km19.5; r 800-2200B; ❄📶) The humdrum rooms won't wow you, but this older place has got the jungle vibe down pat. It even has its own elephants (30-minute rides 300B).

Park Accommodation CAMPGROUND $
(☎0 2562 0760; www.dnp.go.th/parkreserve) Offers two campgrounds (30B per person) and bungalows (from 800B) within the park perimeter; the visitor centre rents tents and equipment.

Inside the park there are simple restaurants at the visitor centre, camp sites and some popular waterfalls. In Pak Chong, restaurants can be found along Th Thana.

ℹ Getting There & Away

To reach Khao Yai you need to connect to Pak Chong, which is on the highway between Bangkok (108B to 139B, 2½ hours) and Khorat (60B to 74B, one hour). Pak Chong is also on the train line, but trains are slower than the bus, especially if coming from Bangkok.

Sŏrngtăaou travel the 30km from Pak Chong to the park's northern gate (40B, 45 minutes, frequently 6am to 5pm). It's another 14km to the visitor centre and Thai families piled into pickup trucks often offer a lift. Some shops on Pak Chong's main road hire motorcycles.

Phanom Rung & Around

Crowning the summit of a spent volcano is majestic **Phanom Rung Historical Park** (admission 100B, bike/motorcycle/car 10/20/50B; ⊙6am-6pm), an ancient Angkor-era temple that rises 380m above a far-flung rural landscape. Dating from the 10th to 13th centuries, Phanom Rung faces east towards the sacred capital of Angkor in Cambodia. It was first built as a Hindu monument and features sculpture relating to the worship of Vishnu and Shiva. Later the Thais converted it into a Buddhist temple.

One of the most striking design features is the promenade leading to the main entrance: an avenue sealed with laterite and

> **ℹ COMBO TICKET**
>
> A 150B combo ticket allows entry to both Phanom Rung and Muang Tam at a 50B discount.

sandstone blocks and flanked by sandstone pillars with lotus-bud tops that terminate at a bridge decorated with a *naga* (mythical serpent). The central *prasat* (tower) has a gallery on each of its four sides, and the entrance to each gallery is itself a smaller incarnation of the main tower. The galleries have curvilinear roofs and false-balustrade windows. The craftsmanship at Phanom Rung represents the pinnacle of Khmer artistic achievement, on a par with the bas-reliefs at Angkor Wat.

The rice-growing region around Phanom Rung is peppered with dozens of minor Khmer ruins. Most are little more than jumbled piles of laterite block. Well-maintained **Prasat Meuang Tam** (Lower City; admission 100B; ⊙6am-6pm) gets few visitors, despite sitting only 8km southeast of Phanom Rung.

Sleeping

Phanom Rung can be undertaken as a day trip from Khorat or Surin. But the closest place to lay your head is the town of Nang Rong, which also has vehicle and guide hire. Nang Rong is in Buriram Province and is accessible by bus from Khorat and Surin.

The village of Khok Meuang, nearby Prasat Meuang Tam, runs a **homestay** (☎08 1068 6898; per person incl two meals 300B) program. Another overnight option is slightly pricey **Tanyaporn Homestay** (☎08 7431 3741; dm 150B, r 500B; ❄), southwest of the ruins.

P California Inter Hostel GUESTHOUSE $
(☎08 1808 3347; www.pcalifornianangrong.webs.com; Th Sangkakrit; r 250-700B; ❄@📶) This great place on the east side of town offers bright, nicely decorated rooms with good value in all price ranges. English-speaking Khun Wicha, who's a wealth of knowledge about the area, also provides bikes, rents motorcycles (200B per day) and leads tours.

Honey Inn GUESTHOUSE $
(☎0 4462 2825; www.honeyinn.com; 8/1 Soi Si Kun; r 250-350B; ❄@📶) A long-time travellers' favourite, this welcoming guesthouse is 1km from the bus station and is run by a retired English teacher. Rooms are simple and there's motorcycle hire as well as guided tours.

Cabbages & Condoms HOTEL $$
(☎0 4465 7145; Hwy 24; r 240-1500B; ❄@) This pleasant PDA-run resort (all profits to charity) is ringed by gardens and little lakes west of town, and has a full range of rooms.

Getting There & Away

Phanom Rung is not directly accessible from Isan's major towns. Those coming from or heading to Ubon Ratchathani (125B, five hours, hourly), Surin (60B to 70B, two hours, every half-hour), Khorat (66B to 85B, two hours, hourly), Pak Chong (104B to 140B, 2½ hours, hourly) or Bangkok (275B, five hours, hourly) have the option of getting off at Ban Tako, a well-marked turn-off about 14km east of Nang Rong and waiting for one of the buses or *sŏrngtăaou* from Nang Rong; or just taking a motorcycle taxi (300B return) all the way to Phanom Rung.

To get to the historical park from Nang Rong, hop on a *sŏrngtăaou* (20B, 30 minutes, every half-hour) that leaves from the old market at the east end of town and goes to Ban Ta Pek, where motorcycle taxi drivers charge 200B to Phanom Rung including waiting time.

Motorcycle-taxi drivers will add Meuang Tam onto Phanom Rung for about 150B.

> DON'T MISS
>
> **ELEPHANT ROUNDUP**
>
> Surin's biggest tourist draw is the **Elephant Roundup**, celebrated in November with 10 days of pachyderm pageantry. On the last weekend, there's a buffet spread set out for the creatures and a mock battle involving hundreds of elephants re-enacting their roles as war machines. Tickets for the show start at 40B, but VIP seats (500B) come with shade and English commentary.

Surin & Around

POP 41,000

A distinct Cambodian influence has long infiltrated the border into Surin, which was once the western frontier of the Angkor kingdom and later a safe refuge for Cambodians fleeing conflict in their homeland. Today the province is known for elephants and silk weaving, and the provincial capital of the same name is a good base for visiting nearby craft villages and Khmer ruins.

Sights & Activities

Elephant Study Centre ELEPHANT CENTRE
(☎0 4414 5050; admission 100B; ⊙8.30am-4.30pm) Located in Ban Tha Klang, home to the minority Suai tribe, historically the northeast's elephant herders, the main at-

GETTING TO CAMBODIA: CHONG CHOM TO O SMACH

Because of the casino, there's plenty of minibus (60B, 1½ hours, every 20 minutes) traffic from Surin's bus terminal to the Cambodian **border** (⏲6am-6pm) at Chong Chom, where visas are available on the spot (see p275 for details on getting a Cambodian visa). There's little transport on the Cambodian side. A seat in a 'taxi' will cost 500B for the four-hour drive to Siem Reap, but if you arrive after about 9am you're unlikely to find any Cambodians making the trip and may have to pay 2500B for the whole car. Details for traversing the border in the opposite direction are on p205.

It's also possible to cross from Chong Sa-Ngam, in neighbouring Si Saket Province, to Choam, on the Cambodian side. Visas are available at the border, and the road to Siem Reap is excellent, but the trip can't be done entirely by public transport, making it an expensive option.

traction at this centre is the one-hour **talent show** (⏲10am & 2pm). There's also a little **museum** discussing elephants and elephant training, **elephant rides** (the foreigner price is 200B for 20 minutes) and a **homestay** (per person 200B) program.

If you'd like to spend some quality time with elephants, sign-up for a six-day stay with the Elephant Nature Foundation's **Surin Project** (☎08 4482 1210; www.surinproject.org; 12,000B), which works to improve the elephants' living conditions and provide sustainable income for their owners so they don't need to go begging on city streets.

Sŏrngtăaou run from Surin's bus terminal (50B, two hours, hourly), with the last one returning at 4pm.

Craft Villages VILLAGES

The province's distinct textiles reflect many Khmer influences and use natural dyes and delicate silk fibres. **Ban Tha Sawang** is one of the country's most famous weaving centres, specialising in the intensive hand-woven *pâh yók torng*, which requires four weavers, as well as more mainstream varieties. The village is 8km west of Surin city via Rte 4026, and *sŏrngtăaou* (15B, 20 minutes) run regularly from the market in Surin.

Eighteen kilometres north of Surin via Rtes 214 and 3036 are **Ban Khwao Sinarin** and **Ban Chok**, which are known for silk and silver respectively, though you can buy some of both in each village. Big blue *sŏrngtăaou* to Ban Khwao Sinarin (25B, 1½ hours, hourly) park on an unnamed soi between the fountain and the train station – look for the 'Osram' signs.

Volunteering VOLUNTEERING

Surin is developing something of a voluntourism reputation thanks to **Starfish Ventures** (☎08 1723 1403; www.starfishvolunteers.com), which runs over a dozen projects, ranging from English teaching to home building in surrounding villages. A new Thai-based company, **LemonGrass** (☎08 1977 5300; www.lemongrass-volunteering.com) places volunteer English teachers in classrooms and student camps around the Surin area.

Sleeping

Pirom-Aree's House GUESTHOUSE $

(☎0 4451 5140; Soi Arunee, Th Thungpo; s/d 120/200B) An inconvenient 1km west of the city, the simple wooden rooms (all with shared bathrooms) are surrounded by a shady garden overlooking a former rice paddy. Pirom knows all about the region and can arrange day trips to nearby attractions.

Maneerote Hotel HOTEL $$

(☎0 4453 9477; www.maneerotehotel.com; Soi Poi Tunggor, Th Krungsri Nai; r 400-450B; ❄@📶) This hotel west of the fresh market scores off the charts in the high quality to low prices ratio, though it's a little out of the way.

Surin Majestic Hotel HOTEL $$

(☎0 4471 3980; Th Jitrbumrung; r 900-1200B, ste 1800-4500B; ❄@📶🏊) A shiny top-ender with plenty of extras. Behind the bus terminal.

Eating

Surin has an excellent **night market** (Th Krung Si Nai; ⏲5-10pm) with all the Thai and Isan specialities.

Petmanee 2 NORTHEASTERN THAI $

(no roman-script sign; Th Murasart; dishes 20-80B; ⏲breakfast & lunch) This simple spot between Ruamphet Hospital and Wat Salaloi is Surin's most famous purveyor of *sômđam* (green papaya salad) and *gài yâhng* (grilled chicken).

Larn Chang THAI $
(199 Th Siphathai Saman; dishes 45-220B; ⊙dinner) This old wooden house, with a garden and a rooftop patio, serves tasty Thai and Isan dishes.

Information

Most banks in Surin are on Th Thesaban, south of the train station.

Ruampaet Hospital (☎0 4451 3192; Th Thesaban 1)

Surin Plaza Mall (Th Thesaban 1) Has several banks open evenings and weekends. Located one block west of the fountain.

Tourism Authority of Thailand office (TAT; ☎nationwide call centre 1672, Surin 0 4451 4447; tatsurin@tat.or.th; Th Thesaban 1; ⊙8.30am-4.30pm) Across from Ruampaet Hospital.

Getting There & Away

Surin's **bus terminal** (☎0 4451 1756; Th Jitrbumrung) serves Bangkok (250B to 372B, seven hours), Nakhon Ratchasami (Khorat; 90B to 157B, four hours, every half-hour) and Ubon Ratchathani (105B to 200B, three hours, infrequent during the day).

Surin train station (☎0 4451 1295) is on the line between Bangkok (73B to 1146B, seven to nine hours, 10 daily) and Ubon Ratchathani (81B to 150B, two to five hours, seven daily). To check timetables and prices for other destinations call the **State Railway of Thailand** (☎nationwide call centre 1690; www.railway.co.th) or look at its website.

Nearby Chong Chom is also a legal border crossing into Cambodia.

Ubon Ratchathani

POP 115,000

A veritable metropolis among the rice fields, Ubon Ratchathani (better known as Ubon) claims a deep cultural connection with neighbouring Laos. The city can appear bland but its riverine area along Mae Nam Mun, Thailand's second-longest waterway, is a textbook example of laid-back living. A small trickle of foreigners passes through en route to the Thailand–Laos border crossing at Chong Mek.

Sights & Activities

The main thing Thai visitors want to see is the 7cm-tall Phra Kaew Busarakham (Topaz Buddha) in the *bòht* at **Wat Si Ubon Rattanaram** (Th Uparat). Binoculars are available. Most *faràng* are more fascinated by **Wat Thung Si Meuang** (Th Luang), which has a photogenic *hŏr đrai* (Tripitaka library) on stilts in the middle of a pond and **Wat Jaeng** (Th Nakhon Baan) with its adorable little Lan Xang–style chapel.

Ubon Ratchathani National Museum MUSEUM
(Th Kheuan Thani; admission 100B; ⊙9am-4pm Wed-Sun) Housed in a former palace of the Rama VI era, Ubon National Museum is a good place to delve into Ubon's history and culture.

FREE **Ubon Ratchathani Art & Cultural Centre** MUSEUM
(Rajabhat University, Th Jaeng Sanit; ⊙8.30am-4.30pm Mon-Sat) Ubon is famous for its **Candle Parade** (usually held in July), which evolved out of the tradition of merit-makers donating candles to the temples during the Buddhist Lent retreats. If you're not in town for the parade, check out some of the remarkable specimens at this museum.

Meditation Centres MEDITATION
Ubon Province is equally well known for its forest monastery tradition, founded by meditation master Luang Pu Cha. **Wat Nong Pa Phong** (⊙daylight hr), 9km south of Ubon centre, features the golden *chedi* where Luang Pu Cha's relics are interred and a **museum** (admission free; ⊙8am-4.30pm) displaying his personal possessions. *Sŏrngtăaou* No 3 gets you within 2km; hire a motorcycle taxi (20B) for the remainder of the trip.

English-speaking meditators often retreat to **Wat Pa Nanachat** (www.watpahnanachat.org), a temple opened specifically for foreigners. Any Si Saket–bound bus can drop you on Rte 226, about 500m from the entrance.

Sleeping

Sri Isan Hotel HOTEL $
(☎0 4526 1011; www.sriisanhotel.com; Th Ratchabut; r 380-800B;) Natural light swims through the atrium, brightening the mood of this midranger. The rooms, which come with fridge and TV, are small but standards are high.

Sunee Grand Hotel HOTEL $$$
(☎0 4535 2900; www.suneegrandhotel.com; Th Chayangkun; r incl breakfast 1600-3000B, ste 4250-12,500B;) One of the few hotels in Isan that could hold its own in Bangkok, the Sunee Grand is a stunner and far less expensive than its peers in the capital.

Ubon Ratchathani

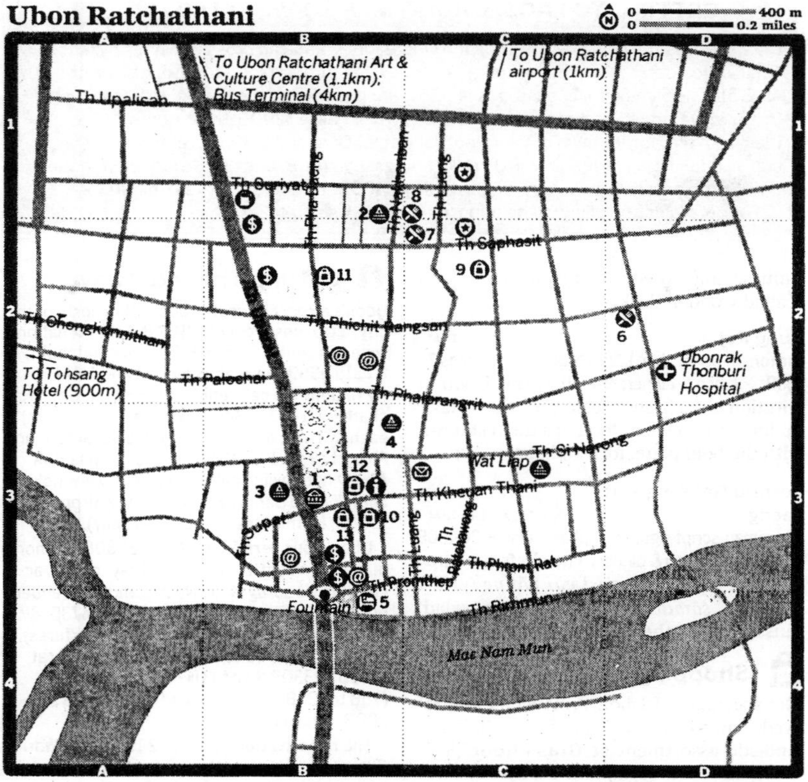

Ubon Ratchathani

Sights

1 Ubon Ratchathani National Museum B3
2 Wat Jaeng B1
3 Wat Si Ubon Rattanaram B3
4 Wat Thung Si Meuang B3

Sleeping

5 Sri Isan Hotel B4

Eating

6 Jumpa-Hom D2
7 Porntip Gai Yang Wat Jaeng C2
8 Rung Roj C1

Shopping

9 Camp Fai Ubon C2
10 Grass-Root B3
11 Punchard B2
12 Punchard 2 .... B3
13 Rawang Thang B3

Tohsang Hotel HOTEL $$
(☎0 4524 5531; www.tohsang.com; Th Palochai; r incl breakfast 1200-1800B, ste 4000B;) The lobby is downright elegant while the rooms are as comfortable as they should be at these prices.

Eating

Jumpa-Hom THAI $$
(Th Phichit Rangsan; dishes 55-1500B; dinner;) One of the classiest places in town, Jumpa-Hom serves pricey but good Thai, Isan,

GETTING TO LAOS: CHONG MEK TO VANG TAO

Chong Mek is the only place in Thailand where foreigners can cross into Laos by land (that is, you don't cross the Mekong). After passing through the **Thai border post** (☎0 4548 5107; ⊙6am-8pm), Lao visas (see p361) are provided at the border with little fuss. Buses leave Ubon Ratchathani for the Lao town of Pakse (200B, three hours), 45 minutes from the border town of Vang Tao, daily at 9.30am and 3.30pm. Alternatively, you can also take a *sŏrngtăaou* from Phibun Mangsahan (40B, one hour, every 20 minutes until 5pm), accessible via minivan from Ubon (100B, 1¼ hours, every 20 minutes).

For details on travelling in the opposite direction, see p342.

Chinese and Western cuisine on a landscaped wooden deck.

Rung Roj THAI $
(no roman-script sign; 122 Th Nakhonban; dishes 30-165B; ⊙lunch & dinner;) What this Ubon institution lacks in service, it more than makes up for with excellent food. It's the restaurant with the bold plate, fork and spoon sign.

Porntip Gai Yang Wat Jaeng NORTHEASTERN THAI $
(no roman-script sign; Th Saphasit; dishes 20-130B; ⊙breakfast, lunch & dinner) The chefs cook up a storm of their renowned *gài yâhng* (grilled chicken), *sômđam* (green papaya salad), sausages and other Isan food.

Shopping

The speciality of Ubon Province is natural-dyed, hand-woven cotton and you'll find a fantastic assortment at **Grass-Root** (87 Th Yutthaphan; ⊙9am-6pm) and **Camp Fai Ubon** (189 Th Thepyoth; ⊙8am-5pm). **Punchard** (158 Th Ratchabut; ⊙9am-8pm) and **Punchard 2** (156 Th Pha Daeng; ⊙9am-8pm) stock a wider array of handicrafts.

Rawang Thang (301 Th Kheuan Thani; ⊙9am-9pm Mon-Sat) sells funky T-shirts and assorted bric-a-brac. The friendly owners are a good source of local information.

Information

29 Internet (Th Nakhonban; per hr 12B)

Post office (Th Luang; ⊙8.30am-4.30pm Mon-Fri, 9am-noon Sat & Sun)

Ubonrak Thonburi Hospital (☎0 4526 0285; Th Phalorangrit) Has a 24-hour casualty department.

Tourism Authority of Thailand office (TAT; ☎nationwide call centre 1672, Ubon Ratchathani 0 4524 3770; 264/1 Th Kheuan Thani; ⊙8.30am-4.30pm)

Tourist police (☎nationwide call centre 1155, Chiang Rai 0 4524 5505; Th Suriyat)

Getting There & Away

Ubon's airport is located about 1km north of the city; a taxi costs only 100B. **Air Asia** (☎nationwide call centre 0 2515 9999, Ubon Ratchathani 0 2515 9999; www.airasia.com) and **THAI** (☎nationwide call centre 0 2356 1111, Ubon Ratchathani 0 4531 3340; www.thaiairways.com) each fly twice a day to Bangkok's Suvarnabhumi Airport (from 1350B, 55 minutes), while **Nok Air** (☎nationwide call centre 1318; www.nokair.com) flies to Bangkok's Don Muang Airport (from 1300B, 65 minutes, three times daily).

Ubon's **bus terminal** (☎0 4531 6085) is north of the town centre, just off Th Chayangkun, accessible via *sŏrngtăaou* No 2, 3 and 10. Frequent buses link Ubon with Bangkok (385B 473B, 8½ to 10 hours, morning and evening departures), Chiang Mai (590B to 893B, 17 hours), Khorat (203B to 330B, five to six hours), Mukdahan (75B to 135B, 3½ hours) and Surin (105B to 200B, three hours).

The **train station** (☎0 4532 1588) is in Warin Chamrap; take *sŏrngtăaou* 2 from Ubon. There's an overnight express train to/from Bangkok (371B to 1280B). All trains also stop in Si Saket, Surin and Khorat. To check timetables and prices for other destinations call the **State Railway of Thailand** (☎nationwide call centre 1690; www.railway.co.th) or look at its website.

Nearby Chong Mek is also a legal border crossing into Laos.

Around Ubon Ratchathani

EMERALD TRIANGLE

A tourism-brochure conceit, the Emerald Triangle refers to the tri-border area of Thailand, Laos and Cambodia. On the Thai side, most of Ubon Ratchathani Province and some of Si Saket Province have been bestowed with this new moniker.

In the northeastern part of Ubon Province, the Mae Nam Mun (Mun River) joins the Mekong River just before it does an oxbow into Laos. The geographic confluence of the two rivers occurs at **Khong Jiam**, where Thais come to see 'Mae Nam Song Si'

(Two-Coloured River). In the wet season the bi-coloured merger is visible from the shore, but the rest of the year boats (200B to 350B) shuttle visitors to the spectacle. Since 2005 the famous and unexplained *naga* fireball phenomenon has appeared here.

Up the Mekong from Khong Jiam is **Pha Taem National Park** (admission 200B), whose centrepiece is a long cliff with views over to Laos and a collection of prehistoric rock paintings that are at least 3000 years old. Mural subjects include fish traps (which look similar to the conical ones still used today), *plah bèuk* (giant Mekong catfish), elephants, human hands and geometric designs.

You can catch a bus from Ubon to Khong Jiam (77B, 2½ hours) at 2.30pm, but there's no public transport to Pha Taem National Park. You can, however, rent a motorcycle (from 200B) from guesthouses in Khong Jiam.

Sitting at the heart of the Emerald Triangle is the little-known **Phu Chong Nayoi National Park** (admission 200B), one of Thailand's wildest and healthiest forests. Most visitors are here to see **Nam Tok Huay Luang**, a waterfall that plunges 40m. There is the usual park accommodation and great stargazing. To get here, catch one of four morning buses from Ubon to Na Chaluai (70B, three hours). From Na Chaluai, túk-túk

can be hired for about 400B for the 20km return journey to Nam Tok Huay Luang.

Mukdahan & Around
POP 34,300

A ho-hum river town, Mukdahan went from forgettable to integral thanks to the 2006 opening of the Thai-Lao Friendship Bridge 2, which links northeastern Thailand to the Lao city of Savannakhet and beyond to Vietnam.

◉ Sights

The city is best known for **Talat Indojin** (Indochina Market), which sets up along the riverfront and sells an unexotic array of cheap food and trinkets.

You have to travel outside of Mukdahan to absorb some of its Indochinese elements. Follow the river-frontage road north of town as it goes under the **Thai-Lao Friendship Bridge 2**, a 1.6km span across the widest reach of the Mekong River within the Thai border. Another 10km north is **Wat Manophirom**, built in 1756 in Lan Xang style.

Another 4.5km north in Ban Wan Yai is **Wat Srimahapo** (Wat Pho Si), a 1916 temple displaying some classical French styles. Continue for 7km to the modern, glass-walled **Our Lady of the Martyrs of Thailand**

NORTHERN THAILAND MUKDAHAN & AROUND

HOMESTAYS AWAY FROM HOME

Isan really reveals its character in the small villages where life and livelihood are tied to the agricultural clock. Homestays are predominantly geared towards domestic tourists, meaning that spoken English is limited and lodging is simpler than the simplest guesthouse (squat toilet, jar basins for bathing and a basic mattress on the floor). But it gives an unparalleled perspective on rural life.

The **Ban Pa-Ao homestay** (☑08 1076 1249; per person incl breakfast 250B) offers the chance to try your hand at silk weaving and brass-smithing, the two village industries. Ban Pa-Ao is northwest of Ubon and is 3.5km off the highway. Buses to/from Yasothon (20B) pass the turn-off, and a motorcycle taxi from the highway should cost 20B.

A village encounter without the self-sufficiency is available at the Australian-owned **Thai House-Isaan** (☑08 7065 4635; www.thaihouse-isaan.com; r incl breakfast 700-1500B; ❀❀❀). Guests visit a family farm, go foraging in the forest and observe other village activities, but sleep in private and modern quarters. Thai House is 60km out of Mukdahan on Hwy 2042. Buses between Mukdahan and Khon Kaen will drop you in Ban Kham Pok (50B, 1½ hours, every half-hour until 4.30pm).

Ban Phu homestay (☑08 5003 7894; per person incl meals 600B) lets you join in daily life – cooking, weaving and farming – and explore nearby mountain caves. English is quite limited in the village, but Khun Puyai Pairit speaks some and will organise *faràng* visits. From Mukdahan's bus terminal catch a *sŏrngtǎaou* to Nong Sung (40B, 1¼ hours, frequently), from where you can take a motorcycle taxi (50B to 60B) or a *sŏrngtǎaou* (about 100B) for the final 6km to Ban Phu.

There are also homestays along the river road between Nakhon Phanom and Nong Khai.

GETTING TO LAOS: MUKDAHAN TO SAVANNAKHET

Since the construction of the Second Thai-Lao Friendship Bridge in 2006, non-Thai and non-Lao citizens are no longer allowed to cross between Mukdahan and Savannakhet by boat.

The Thai-Lao International Bus from Mukdahan's bus terminal (50B, 45 minutes) departs roughly every hour from 7.30am to 7pm, stopping at the **Thai border post** (☎0 4267 4274; ⏰6am-10pm) and the **Lao border post** (⏰6am-10pm), where a 30-day visa on arrival is available for US$20 to US$42, depending on your nationality (for more details on Lao, see p361). If you don't have a photo you'll be charged the equivalent of US$2, and an additional US$1 'overtime fee' is charged from 6am to 8am and 6pm to 10pm on weekdays, as well as on weekends and holidays. The last obstacle is a US$1/40B 'entry fee', and the Thai-Lao International Bus takes you all the way to Savannakhet's bus station.

Details for traversing the border in the opposite direction are on p337.

Shrine (admission free; ⏰8am-5pm, 7am Mass Sun), locally called Wat Song Khan, built to commemorate seven Thai Catholics killed by the police in 1940 for refusing to renounce their faith.

Just beyond the church is **Kaeng Kabao**, a scenic stretch of rocks and rivers enjoyed from bankside restaurants and dry-season beaches. (You will need your own wheels for this trip.)

Sleeping & Eating

Ban Rim Suan HOTEL $
(no roman-script sign; ☎0 4263 2980; Th Samut Sakdarak; r 330B;) This is the best budget deal in the city. Rooms aren't stylish but they aren't depressing either; it's a tad south of the centre and is close to riverside restaurants and bars.

Ploy Palace Hotel HOTEL $$
(☎0 4263 1111; www.ploypalace.com; Soi Ploy 1; r 1050-1800B, ste 5500B;) Rooms at this executive sleep-easy are dated, but are undergoing a slow-motion renovation: be sure to look at several before deciding.

TOP CHOICE **Bao Phradit** NORTHEASTERN THAI $
(no roman-script sign; Th Samran Chaikhongthi; dishes 30-200B; ⏰breakfast, lunch & dinner;) It's a bit of a yomp south of the centre, but this is a real Isan restaurant with dishes like *pàt pèt mu/uu pàh* (spicy stir-fried wild boar) and *gaang wǎi* (rattan curry), all served on a peaceful riverside deck.

Wine Wild Why? THAI $
(Th Samran Chaikhongthi; dishes 40-150B; ⏰lunch & dinner) Housed in an atmospheric wooden building right on the river, this romantic little spot serves delicious Thai food, though the wine list is history.

Night Market THAI-VIETNAMESE $
(Th Song Nang Sathit; ⏰4-9pm) A particularly good spot for eating Isan and Vietnamese dishes.

Getting There & Away

Mukdahan's **bus terminal** (☎0 4263 0486) is on Rte 212, west of town. To get there from the centre catch a yellow *sǒrngtǎaou* (10B, 6am to 5pm) running west along Th Phitak Phanomkhet. There are buses to Bangkok (390B to 502B, 10 hours), with most departing from 5pm to 8pm, Nakhon Phanom (52B to 88B, 2½ hours, every half-hour) via That Phanom (26B to 45B, one hour) and Ubon Ratchathani (75B to 135B, 3½ hours, every half-hour).

Mukdahan is also a legal border crossing into Laos.

That Phanom

A riverside hamlet, That Phanom would be more popular as a sleepy hang-out if it weren't so close to laid-back Laos. What does merit national attention is the looming Lao-style *chedi* at **Wat Phra That Phanom** (⏰5am-8pm), which is something of an icon in the northern parts of Isan. The temple is busiest around full moons because people believe that a visit on these days bestows bountiful happiness.

A lively **riverside market** (⏰7am-2pm Mon & Thu) gathers merchants from both sides of the Mekong.

The **Kritsada Rimkhon Hotel** (☎08 1262 4111; www.ksdrimkhong-resort.com; 90 Th Rimkhong; r 350-500B;) offers a mix of comfy rooms.

When hunger strikes, there is a small **night market** (Th Robbung; ⏰4-10pm) and a clutch of riverside eateries on Th Rimkhong.

Buses depart regularly from the new bus station west of town for Ubon Ratchathani (95B to 167B, 4½ hours), via Mukdahan (26B to 45B, one hour) and Nakhon Phanom (27B to 47B, one hour). Nakhon Phanom also has a *sŏrngtăaou* (35B, 90 minutes, every 15 minutes until 3.30pm) service.

Nakhon Phanom

POP 31,700

In Sanskrit-Khmer, Nakhon Phanom means 'City of Hills', but it refers to the hills across the river in Laos. The fabulous views befit this somnolent town, as does the scattering of graceful French colonial buildings.

◎ Sights

Nakhon Phanom's **temples** have a distinctive style. This was once an important town in the Lan Xang empire and later a vivid Vietnamese and French influence added to the mix. The **Tourism Authority of Thailand** (◻nationwide call centre 1672, Nakhon Phanom 0 4251 3490; Th Sunthon Wijit; ◒8.30am-4.30pm) office has a good city map for a DIY architectural tour.

A Vietnamese community found refuge here after that country's first war for independence against the French. In the nearby village of Ban Na Chok, Ho Chi Minh planned his resistance movement in 1928–29. **Uncle Ho's House** (◻0 4252 2430; admission 50B; ◒daylight hr) and the **community centre** (◻08 0315 4630; admission free; ◒8am-4pm) have displays about his time here.

The new **Former Governor's Residence Museum** (Th Sunthon Wijit; admission free; ◒10am-6pm Wed-Sun) contains photos of Nakhon Phanom past and present.

The city pays respect to the Mekong with the annual **Illuminated Boat Procession** (Lái Reua Fai) in October. The city sets afloat giant bamboo rafts decorated with thousands of handmade lanterns, followed by a week of festivities including boat races and music competitions. Everything in town gets booked up during this period.

⌸ Sleeping & Eating

Windsor Hotel HOTEL $
(◻0 4251 1946; 272 Th Bamrung Meuang; r 250-400B; ✳◉⌨) Despite being housed in a rather intimidating concrete block, this hotel stands out among a lacklustre crowd with decent-value fan rooms.

You're likely to meet the Vietnamese-style baguette sandwiches at some of the river promenade restaurants. Residents flock to the river in the evening to enjoy the cool breezes and sunset views. Mats are laid out for family picnics – an Isan speciality. The city's excellent **night market** (Th Fuang Nakhon; ◒4-9pm) promotes snacking through dinner. The outdoor terrace at the **Indochina Market** (Th Sunthon Wijit; ◒breakfast, lunch & dinner) has choice mountain-view seats.

❶ Getting There & Away

Nok Air (◻nationwide call centre 1318; www. nokair.com) flies daily to/from Bangkok's Don Muang Airport (from 2600B, 40 minutes).

Nakhon Phanom's **bus terminal** (◻0 4251 3444; Th Fuang Nakhon) is west of the town centre. From here buses head to Bangkok (450B to 592B, 11 to 12 hours) between 7am to 8am and 4.30pm to 7pm, Nong Khai (210B, 6½ hours, six daily) and Ubon Ratchathani (116B to 209B, 4½ hours, nine daily) via Mukdahan (52B to 88B, 2½ hours) and That Phanom (27B to 47B, one hour).

Nakhon Phanom is also a legal border crossing into Laos.

River Road: Nakhon Phanom to Nong Khai

From Nakhon Phanom, the river-fronting road loops around the northeastern hump of Thailand to **Beung Kan**, a dusty riverside pit stop, 136km east of Nong Khai, the nearest tourist destination. During the dry season the Mekong recedes here to its

> ### ❶ GETTING TO LAOS: NAKHON PHANOM TO THA KHAEK
>
> At the time of research, work was still being done on a bridge linking Nakhon Phanom in Thailand and Tha Khaek in Laos. Details are unconfirmed, but we were told that buses to Tha Khaek (70B) will run from Nakhon Phanom's bus station between 7am and 6pm and all immigration formalities will be handled at the bridge during the crossing. These developments would make boat crossings, available at the time of research, an option only for locals in the future.
>
> Details for traversing the border in the opposite direction are on p333.

GETTING TO LAOS: BEUNG KAN TO PAKSAN

Although it's rarely done, you can cross the border here to Paksan, but only if you already have your Lao visa (see p361 for details). After leaving the **Thai border post** (☎0 4249 1832; ⊙8am-6pm), a boat (60B, 20 minutes) leaves when eight people show up or you charter it (480B).

Paksan is a busy crossroads and it's generally possible to hop on a bus to points onward, including Vientiane.

For information on crossing in the other direction, see p329.

narrowest point along the Thailand–Laos border. Beyond river trivia, Beung Kan has a few untouristed attractions that might waylay curious visitors.

Buses to Nong Khai (100B, 2½ hours, six daily), Nakhon Phanom (130B, three hours, six daily) and Udon Thani (150B, 4½ hours, 12 daily) park near the old clock tower. Beung Kan is also a legal border crossing into Laos.

Planted on a giant sandstone outcrop, **Wat Phu Tok** (Isolated Mountain Temple; ⊙6am-5pm, closed 10-16 April) is a forest monastery known for its meditative isolation. Seven levels of stairs scramble up the mountain past shrines and monastic residences built in caves and clutching at cliffs. The final flight represents the last ascent to enlightenment and rewards climbers with vistas over the surrounding countryside. If you like what you see, stay awhile at a **homestay** (☎08 0755 0661; per person 200B, meals 100B) in the nearby village of Ban Ahong.

Túk-túk in Beung Kan can be hired for the return journey to/from Wat Phu Tok for about 800B. It's cheaper to take a bus from Bueng Kan to Ban Siwilai (20B, 45 minutes) where túk-túk drivers will do it for 300B to 400B. If you catch an early bus to Bueng Kan, Wat Phu Tok can be visited as a day trip from Nong Khai, although there's no need to backtrack since buses from Siwilai go to Udon Thani (140B, four hours).

Another nearby attraction is the 186-sq-km **Phu Wua Wildlife Reserve,** home to several herds of elephants. The reserve can be easily visited through the well-run **Kham Pia Homestay** (☎0 4241 3578, 08 7861 0601; www.thailandwildelephanttrekking.com; per room 200B, meals 50-90B). Kham Pia is 190km east of Nong Khai and 3km off Rte 212. Buses between Nong Khai (140B, 3½ hours) and Nakhon Phanom (130B, three hours) will drop you off at the Ban Don Chik highway junction, 3km away.

Nong Khai

POP 61,500

A riverside darling, Nong Khai lounges along the leafy banks of the Mekong River, enjoying the river view and its proximity to the Friendship Bridge into Laos, an important border crossing for travellers en route to Vientiane. The town has cultivated one of Isan's few guesthouse scenes and boasts a surreal sculpture park that concretes religious visions into 3-D.

Sights & Activities

Wat Pho Chai BUDDHIST TEMPLE
(Th Phochai; ⊙5am-6pm) Nong Khai's most famous traditional temple is Wat Pho Chai, where a Lan Xang–era Buddha (named Luang Pu Phra Sai) is awash with gold, bronze and precious stones.

Volunteering VOLUNTEERING
Nong Khai has also sprouted grassroots volunteer organisations, like **Open Mind Projects** (☎0 4241 3578; www.openmindprojects.org) and **Travel to Teach** (☎0 8424 60351; www.travel-to-teach.org), which place travellers in teaching and volunteering positions in and around Nong Khai.

Sleeping

Catering to the steady flow of backpackers heading to Laos, Nong Khai's budget offerings are the best in Isan.

Mut Mee Garden Guest House GUESTHOUSE $
(☎0 4246 0717; www.mutmee.com; Soi Mutmee; r 150-1200B; ❄🛜) One of the anchors of Nong Khai as a backpacker paradise, this riverside guesthouse capitalises on its relaxing setting with a friendly thatched-roof restaurant and a small village of simple huts and a few mature residences.

Ruan Thai Guesthouse GUESTHOUSE $
(☎0 4241 2519; 1126/2 Th Rimkhong; r 200-400B, f 1200B; ❄@🛜) This pleasant spot boasts a variety of good-quality rooms from simple

Central Nong Khai

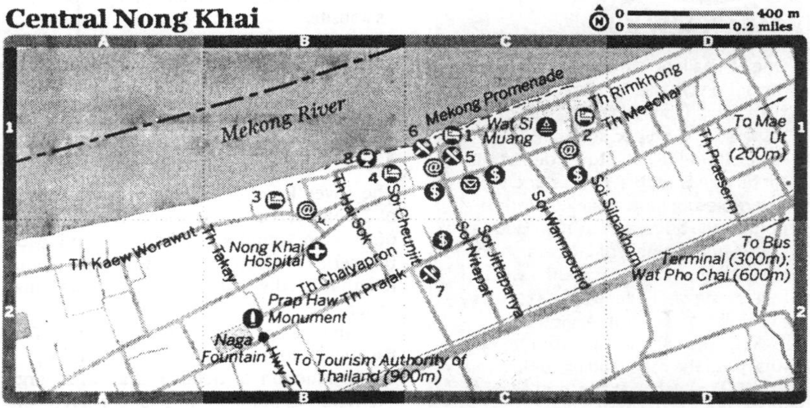

Central Nong Khai

Sleeping

1 Baan Mae Rim Nam ... C1
2 E-San Guesthouse ... C1
3 Mut Mee Garden Guest House ... B1
4 Ruan Thai Guesthouse ... B1

Eating

5 Café Thasadej ... C1
6 Daeng Namnuang ... C1
7 Dee Dee Pohchanah ... C2

Drinking

8 Warm Up ... B1

shared-bathroom basics to a family room in a little wooden cottage.

E-San Guesthouse GUESTHOUSE $
(☎08 6242 1860; 538 Th Khun Muang; r 250-450B; ❄📶) An atmospheric spot just off the river in a restored wooden house. The air-con rooms (with private bathroom) are in a separate modern building.

Baan Mae Rim Nam HOTEL $$
(☎0 4242 0256; www.baanmaerimnam.com; Mekong Promenade; r 500-700B; ❄📶) A new hotel right on the riverfront, this bright yellow building has great rooms with balconies and river views.

Eating & Drinking

Mae Ut VIETNAMESE $
(no roman-script sign; Th Meechai; mains 30-40B; ⊙lunch & dinner) This little place, serving just four items, including fried spring rolls and *khô w gèeab pàhk môr* (fresh noodles with pork), is like your Vietnamese grandma's kitchen. Look for the orange building with tables under a blue awning.

Daeng Namnuang VIETNAMESE $
(Th Rimkhong; dishes 45-180B; ⊙breakfast, lunch & dinner; 📶) This massive river restaurant has grown into an Isan institution and hordes of out-of-towners head home with car boots and carry-on bags stuffed with *nǎam neuang* (pork spring rolls).

Dee Dee Pohchanah THAI $
(no roman-script sign; Th Prajak; dishes 40-230B; ⊙lunch & dinner) Despite having a full house every night, this simple place is a well-oiled machine and you won't be waiting long for its tasty food.

Café Thasadej INTERNATIONAL $$
(387/3 Th Bunterngjit; dishes 60-375B; ⊙breakfast, lunch & dinner) Urban sophistication is rare in Nong Khai, but it is a primary dish at this global kitchen.

Warm Up BAR
(Th Rimkhong; ⊙7pm-2am) This little place rises above, both figuratively and literally, the other bars on this end of Th Rimkhong.

Information

There is no shortage of banks with ATMs and exchange services in town.

Coffee Net (Th Bunterngjit; per hr 30B; ⊙10am-9pm)

Immigration office (☎0 4242 3963; ⊙8.30am-noon & 1-4.30pm Mon-Fri) South of the Friendship Bridge.

DON'T MISS

SALA KAEW KU

One of Thailand's most enigmatic attractions is this fantastical **sculpture park** (admission 20B; ⏰8am-6pm) inspired by a mystic shaman. The larger-than-life sculptures depict the Hindu and Buddhist deities and stories (examples include a pack of anthropomorphic dogs, a 25m-high Buddha statue and a Wheel of Life, which you enter through a giant mouth) and represent one of Thailand's most striking examples of modern religious art.

All buses headed east from Nong Khai pass the road leading to Sala Kaew Ku (10B), which is about 2km east of town, and which is also known as Wat Kaek. It's about a five-minute walk from the highway. Chartered túk-túk should cost 100B to 150B return with a one-hour wait or you can reach it by bike in about 30 minutes.

Nong Khai Hospital (☎0 4241 1504; Th Meechai)

Post office (Th Meechai; ⏰8.30am-4.30pm Mon-Fri, 9am-noon Sat & Sun)

Tourism Authority of Thailand office (TAT; ☎nationwide call centre 1672, Nong Khai 0 4242 1326; Hwy 2; ⏰8.30am-4.30pm Mon-Fri) One kilometre south of town.

Getting There & Away

Nong Khai's **bus terminal** (☎0 4241 1612) is just off Th Prajak, about 1.5km from the main pack of riverside guesthouses. There are departures for Bangkok (350B to 600B, 10 to 11 hours) in the late afternoon and early evening, Nakhon Phanom (210B, 6½ hours, six daily until 12.30pm) and Udon Thani (35B to 47B, one hour, every half-hour), from where you can connect to flights to Bangkok and elsewhere on **Air Asia** (☎nationwide call centre 02 515 9999; www.airasia.com). For those travelling west along the Mekong, the 7.30am bus to Pak Chom continues all the way to Loei (130B, 6½ hours). For Chiang Mai, you have to change at Udon's bus terminal 2 (*bor kŏr sŏr mài*).

Two express trains, one in the morning and the other in the afternoon connect Bangkok (498B to 1317B, 11 to 12 hours) to **Nong Khai train station** (☎0 4241 1592), which is 2km west of downtown. There's also one cheaper rapid train leaving Bangkok in the evening. To check timetables and prices for other destinations call the **State Railway of Thailand** (☎nationwide call centre 1690; www.railway.co.th) or look at its website.

Nong Khai is also a legal border crossing into Laos; see the boxed text opposite for more info.

River Road: Nong Khai to Loei

The River Road (Th Kaew Worawut) west of Nong Khai is lined by flood-plain fields of tobacco, tomatoes and chillies and leads to a series of sleepy market towns and hamlets that hardly make a blip on the national radar.

Mainly a day trip from Nong Khai, **Tha Bo** makes its money by using its noodle – the production of noodles that is. A large Vietnamese population has cornered the rice-noodle industry, a handmade process that occurs on the west side of town near the hospital. From about 5am to 10am you can watch people at the factories making the noodles, and then around 2pm they start the cutting. Afterwards the hairlike strands are set out to dry in the sun.

A yellow bus runs regularly between Nong Khai's bus station and Tha Bo (27B, one hour, every half-hour), taking the scenic riverside route.

At a scenic stretch of the Mekong where giant boulders rise out of the watery depths, **Wat Hin Mak Peng** (⏰6am-7pm) has hidden itself away in a cool bamboo grove. The *tú-dong* monks have taken ascetic vows in addition to the standard 227 precepts, eating only once a day and wearing robes sewn by hand from torn pieces of cloth. Several monuments honour Luang Pu Thet, the wat's revered founding abbot, including a glistening *chedi* housing his few earthly possessions. The current abbot requests that visitors dress politely: no shorts or sleeveless tops.

The temple is midway between Si Chiangmai and Sangkhom. Sangkhom-bound buses from Nong Khai (50B, 2¼ hours) pass the wat, and then it's a longish walk.

Seductively sleepy, the little town of **Sangkhom** is a convenient layover between Nong Khai and Loei. The town looks out at the Lao island of Don Klang Khong (as per border agreements, all river islands belong to Laos) and the river dominates life here. Just after the wet season, the town's main attractions are its waterfalls: the three-tiered **Nam Tok Than Thip** (admission free; ⏰daylight hr), 13km west of Sangkhom (2km off Rte 211), is the most spectacular but **Nam**

Tok Than Thong (admission free; ⏰daylight hr), 11km east of Sangkhom, is easier to get to and has a swimable pool at the bottom. It dries up around April.

Sangkhom's veteran lodge, **Bouy Guesthouse** (☎0 4244 1065; Rte 211; r 200-280B;) has a few simple huts with hammock-strung decks overlooking the river. **Poopae Ruenmaithai** (☎0 4244 1088; Rte 211; r 500-1500B;) is more modern and has better river views.

To Sangkhom, there are usually five buses a day from Nong Khai (55B, three hours) and the earliest of those continues to Loei (70B, 3½ hours).

Loei

The city of Loei is a necessary transport hub but not nearly as endearing as its remote and mountainous countryside, much of which is sparsely inhabited and not easily cultivated. If you need to spend the night, try **Sugar Guest House** (☎08 9711 1975; www.sugarguesthouse.blog.com; 4/1 Th Wisut Titep/Soi 2; r 180-380B;), the cheapest and friendliest place in town.

From Loei's **bus terminal** (☎0 4283 3586) there's usually only one direct bus to Nong Khai (130B, seven hours, 6am), which follows the scenic Mekong River route. Other departures include Bangkok (321B to 640B, 11 hours), Khorat (263B, six hours, hourly) and Udon Thani (66B to 92B, three hours, every half-hour), the latter a major transit hub south of Nong Khai.

Continuing west from Loei into northern Thailand (or vice versa) is a time-consuming but scenic proposition. The closest transit hub is Phitsanulok (139B to 178B, four hours, five daily), from where you can break up your trip with a visit to Sukhothai. There are also six daily departures to Chiang Mai (409B to 526B, 10 hours).

Chiang Khan

Virtually overnight, what was once a sleepy little-known riverside town full of traditional timber houses became a trendy destination for Thais, and now tour buses arrive in Chiang Khan daily. That said, it's far from ruined and we still think it's a good place to visit – it's just no longer great. The photogenic views of the river and the Lao mountains

GETTING TO LAOS: NONG KHAI TO VIENTIANE

The Thai-Lao Friendship Bridge spans the Mekong River between Nong Khai in Thailand and Tha Na Leng in Laos, approximately 20km from the Lao capital, Vientiane. Túk-túks are available from Nong Khai's train station (20B) and bus station (50B) to the Thai border post at the bridge. You can also hop on the Thai-Lao International Bus from Nong Khai bus station (55B, 90 minutes) or Udon Thani bus station (80B, two hours), both of which terminate at Vientiane's Talat Sao bus station. If flying into Udon Thani, a túk-túk from the airport to the city's bus station should cost about 100B.

Regardless of where you're coming from, once in Nong Khai don't be tempted to use a túk-túk driver to get your Lao visa, no matter what they tell you – it will take far longer than doing it yourself and you'll have to pay for the 'service'. Insist they take you straight to the bridge.

After passing the **Thai border post** (☎0 4240 2244; ⏰6.30am-10pm), you'll board a bus (20B, five minutes) that takes you over the bridge to the **Lao border post** (⏰6am-10pm). There, a 30-day visa on arrival is available for US$20 to US$42, depending on your nationality (for more details on Lao visas see p361). If you don't have a photo you'll be charged an extra US$2, and be aware that an additional US$1 'overtime fee' is charged from 6am to 8am and 6pm to 10pm on weekdays, as well as on weekends and holidays. The last obstacle is a US$1/40B 'entry fee', and all that remains is to choose between minivan (100B), túk-túk (250B) or taxi (300B) for the remaining 19km to Vientiane.

It's also possible to cross the bridge by train, as tracks have been extended from Nong Khai's train station 3.5km into Laos, terminating at Dongphasy train station, 23km from central Vientiane. From Nong Khai there are two daily departures (20B to 30B, 15 minutes, 9am and 2.45pm) and border formalities are taken care of at the respective train stations.

For information on crossing in the other direction, see p290.

GREAT BALLS OF FIRE

For a modernised culture, Isan Thais hold fast to their animistic beliefs in guardian spirits. Like many Mekong dwellers, they believe that a mythical serpent-like creature, called *naga*, lives in the river. This creature is the subject of many folk stories and folk festivals. The Mekong communities' long-tail boat races and Nakhon Phanom's illuminated boat procession are intended to honour the Mekong *naga* and are timed to coincide with the end of Buddhist Lent (in October), a holy day celebrated on the 15th waxing moon of the 11th lunar month.

The most spectacular and inexplicable event is the annual occurrence of *bâng fai páyahnâhk* (loosely translated as '*naga* fireballs'), a natural phenomenon along a 300km stretch of the river near Nong Khai. The so-called fireballs are usually small reddish balls of light that appear to shoot or float out of the Mekong River just after dusk before vanishing without a trace. Most claim the *naga* fireballs are soundless, but others say a hissing sound can be heard.

No one can adequately explain the phenomenon: scientists say that methane gas from decomposing plant matter reacts with other chemical compounds and is drawn to the surface by the gravitational pull of the full moon. Others think that some monks have found a way to make a 'miracle'. But residents on both sides of the Mekong are quite content to see the event as a celebratory gesture from the resident *naga*.

Naga fireballs have only recently come to the attention of the rest of Thailand thanks to the 2002 film release of *Mekhong Full Moon Party* (*Sìp Hâh Kâm Deuan Sìpèt*), which fictionalised the event and included dialogue in the Isan dialect (along with subtitles for central Thai speakers). Since then some 40,000 people have invaded little Phon Phisai and dozens of other riverside spots between Sangkhom and Khong Jiam in hopes of sightings. Nong Khai is one of the easiest and most popular places to arrange transport, including Mut Mee Garden Guest House's boat trip (2500B).

The fireball experience is much more than just watching a few small lights rise from the river; it's mostly about watching Thais watching a few small lights rise from the river. And be prepared that the *naga* might not send an annual greeting on the day you come (calculations of the full moon can often vary).

beyond are still there and things remain fairly peaceful in the daytime; before the evening shopping stampede begins.

The Mekong River at this point is reaching its final dramatic stretch of mountainous impediments before it slumps eastward into the flat plateau of greater Isan and beyond. The flood plain of the river is Loei's most fertile area and has the greatest population concentration. You'll find farmers and merchants frolicking at **Kaeng Khut Khu**, a series of rapids about 5km downstream from town. It's a popular recreation spot in the dry season. Most guesthouses arrange boat trips (800B to 1000B for three to four people) to the rapids.

Further east near Na Chan, the Mekong River does a tight turn into Laos heading north to Luang Prabang. The river briefly kisses the Thailand–Laos border along the area once known as the Golden Triangle.

Poonsawasdi Hotel (☎08 0400 8777; www.poonsawasdi.com, in Thai; Soi 9; r 800B; ❄📶) is the town's oldest, and has been creatively jazzed up with coloured wood and antique furnishings. **Chiang Khan Guesthouse** (☎0 4282 1691; www.thailandunplugged.com; 282 Th Chai Khong; s/d/tr 300/450/600B; 📶) is a traditional-style guesthouse, has rooms with shared bathrooms and is all creaking timber and tin roofing. At **Loogmai Guesthouse** (☎08 6234 0011; 112 Th Chai Khong; r 450-550B), oodles of French colonial class converges on the old villa with sparse but atmospheric rooms and an airy river-view terrace.

Sŏrngtăaou to Loei (35B, 1¼ hours) depart about every 15 minutes in the early morning from a stop on Rte 201. From a terminal 300m south, there are also eight buses bound for Khorat (297B, seven hours) that also stop in Loei (34B, 45 minutes) Three companies, departing from offices around town, make the run direct to Bangkok (347B to 479B, 10 hours).

No transport runs direct to Nong Khai. The quickest way there is via Loei and Udon Thani, but for the scenic river route take a

Loei-bound *sŏrngtăaou* south to Ban Tad (20B, 30 minutes), where you can catch the bus to Nong Khai that leaves Loei at 6am. Another option is to hire a car (about 600B) to take you to Pak Chom where there are buses to Nong Khai at 10am, 1pm and 3pm.

GETTING TO LAOS: THA LI TO KAEN THAO

Foreigners can now get Lao visas (see p361 for details), at the seldom-used **Thai-Lao Nam Heuang Friendship Bridge** (⊙8am-6pm) in Amphoe Tha Li, 60km northwest of Loei, but the road to Luang Prabang is rough and public transport is scarce.

From Loei, *sŏrngtăaou* (35B) run to Tha Li, from where infrequent *sŏrngtăaou* (20B) run the remaining 8km between the border.

UNDERSTAND THAILAND

Thailand Today

Political Instability

Following the 2006 coup d'état (the 18th in 70 years), which ousted then Prime Minister, Thaksin Shinawatra, there have been six prime ministers and an increasing sense of social division in Thai society.

Much of this period has been defined by sometimes violent protests by the Yellow Shirts, made up of the educated elite aligned with the monarchy and the military, and the Red Shirts, comprised supporters of the exiled prime minister. In 2008, Yellow Shirt protestors shut down the country's major international airports for two weeks, and in 2010, the opposition Red Shirt protestors staged a two-month siege of Bangkok's central shopping district that ended in violent clashes with the military.

The Red/Yellow conflict came to the forefront in national elections in July 2011. Thanks to Thaksin's populist popularity, the Red Shirt–linked Pheu Thai party dominated, winning 265 of 500 seats. Their candidate for prime minister, Yingluck Shinawatra, Thaksin's younger sister and a political novice, will most likely facilitate the return of her brother to Thailand.

The Ageing King

Thais don't often discuss the topic openly but many are worried about their beloved monarch, Bhumibol Adulyadej. Now 83 years old, he is the world's longest-serving king and is nearly worshipped by his subjects. But as his health has declined, his role in the society at large has diminished. He has been hospitalised since September 2009 and his public appearances are so rare that they make laudatory coverage in Thai national news.

Losing the king will be a national tragedy: he has ruled for more than 60 years and defined through his life what many regarded as the modern Thai man (educated, family-oriented, philanthropic and even stylish). The heir apparent, his son the Crown Prince Vajiralongkorn, has assumed many of the royal duties his father previously performed, but the ongoing political problems complicate a smooth transfer of crown from father to son.

Border Woes

Thailand's border regions have always been hotspots of instability. A violent Muslim insurgency in the country's border region with Malaysia has resulted in nearly 5000 deaths since 2004. In the west, Thailand's border with Myanmar (Burma) is home to an estimated 140,000 refugees. And in 2008, trouble emerged in the country's east, when Prasat Phra Viharn (in Khmer, Prasat Preah Vihear), a Khmer-era temple straddling the border between Thailand and Cambodia, was added to the Unesco Word Heritage List. This sparked a dispute between Thailand and Cambodia over the ownership of the temple and, eventually, several incidents of military conflict, resulting in injuries, deaths and damage to the 11th-century ruins.

History

Rise of Thai Kingdoms

It is believed that the first Thais migrated here from modern-day Yúnnán and Guǎngxī, China, settling into small riverside farming communities.

By the 13th and 14th centuries, what is considered the first Thai kingdom, Sukhothai, began to chip away at the crumbling Angkor empire. The third Sukhothai king, Ramkhamhaeng, developed a Thai writing

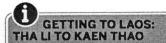

DON'T MISS

PARTYING WITH GHOSTS

The otherwise uninteresting town of Dan Sai has developed a local festival so colourful and outlandish that for three days in June (sometimes July) the town is overrun with something akin to the drunken revelry of Carnival and the ghouls of Halloween.

The raucous **Phi Ta Khon Festival** coincides with the more subdued Buddhist holy day of Bun Phra Wet (Phra Wet Festival, also known as Bun Luang), honouring the penultimate life of the Buddha, Phra Wessandara (often shortened in Thai to Phra Wet). According to the story, when the prince returned to his city the village spirits were so happy that they joined with the human inhabitants in a parade. Most observations of Bun Phra Wet include silk-clad merit-makers intently listening to recitations of the *Mahavessantara Jataka* (past-life stories of the Buddha), which are supposed to enhance the listener's chances of being reborn in the lifetime of the next Buddha.

But Dan Sai's unique twist is the peculiar re-enactment of Phra Wet's return and the participation of the spirits. Villagers don elaborate and wild 'spirit' costumes and masks for a day of *lôw kŏw* (whisky)-fuelled dancing full of sexual innuendo. The revelries culminate with the launching of rockets (a popular fertility ritual in Isan believed to appease the guardian spirits for bountiful rains). The next day, the crowd proceeds to the temple to listen to sermons.

The origins of the festival are not known but some theorise that it is an offshoot of the spirit worship of the ethnic Tai Dam tribe. The dates for the festival are divined by Jao Phaw Kuan, a local spirit medium who invites Phra Upakud (an enlightened monk who transformed himself into a block of white marble to live eternally on the bottom of the Mae Nam Mun) to come to town. Phra Upakud is believed to protect the town from evil spirits.

A couple of villages just outside of Dan Sai run a **homestay** (☎08 9077 2080; dm 150B, tw/tr 400/550B, per meal 70B), organised by some local English teachers. Everything can be arranged at **Kawinthip Hattakham** (75 Th Kaew Asa; ⊙8am-7pm), a craft shop in town that sells authentic Phi Ta Khon masks and other festival-related souvenirs.

Buses between Loei (60B, 1½ hours) and Phitsanulok (94B, three hours) stop in Dan Sai near the junction of Th Kaew Asa and Rte 2013 every couple of hours.

system and built Angkor-inspired temples that defined early Thai art.

Sukhothai was soon eclipsed by another emerging power, Ayuthaya, which was established in present-day Thailand's central plains in 1350. This new centre developed into a cosmopolitan port on the Asian trade route courted by European nations attracted to the region for commodities and potential colonies, though the small nation managed to thwart foreign takeovers. For 400 years Ayuthaya dominated most of present-day Thailand until the Burmese destroyed the capital in 1767.

The Thais eventually rebuilt their capital in present-day Bangkok and established the Chakri dynasty, which continues to occupy the throne today. As Western imperialism marched across the region, King Mongkut (Rama IV, r 1851–68) and his son and successor King Chulalongkorn (Rama V, r 1868–1910) successfully steered Thailand into the modern age without becoming a colonial vassal.

A Struggling Democracy

In 1932 a peaceful coup converted Thailand into a constitutional monarchy loosely based on the British model. Nearly half a century of political chaos followed. During the mid-20th century, a series of anticommunist military dictators wrestled each other for power, successfully suppressing democratic representation and civil rights. Student protests in the 1970s called for a reinstatement of a constitution and the end of military rule. In October 1976, a demonstration on the campus of Thammasat University in Bangkok was quashed by the military, resulting in deaths and injuries. Many activists went underground to join armed communist insurgency groups hiding in the northeast.

In the 1980s and 1990s there were slow steps towards democracy and even a return to a civilian government. During these tumultuous times, King Bhumibol Adulyadej (Rama IX, r 1946–) defined a new political role for the monarchy, as a paternal figure who restrained excesses in the interests of all Thais.

Economic & Political Roller Coaster

During the 1990s, Thailand was one of the so-called tiger economies that imploded in 1997, leading to a recession that lasted nearly three years. Thailand's convalescence progressed remarkably well and it pulled an 'early exit' from the International Monetary Fund's loan package in mid-2003.

The ambitious and charismatic billionaire Thaksin Shinawatra became prime minister in 2001 on a populist platform. He delivered on his promises for affordable health care and village development funds, which won him diehard support among the working class, especially in the impoverished northeast.

He and his party handily swept the 2005 election but his popularity plummeted due to a host of corruption charges. Rumours of his unabated ambitions – to interrupt or even usurp the eventual transfer of the crown from father to son – filtered into the general public, sparking mass protests organised by political rivals and those viewed as loyal to the crown. Behind the scenes Thaksin had earned very powerful enemies as he attempted to eradicate the role that the military continued to play in the government by replacing key appointments with his own loyalists.

On 19 September 2006, army chief Sonthi Boonyaratglin led a bloodless military coup, forcing Thaksin into exile. Political and social instability dominated the next five years, culminating in the 2011 election victory of the Pheu Thai Party, headed by Thaksin's younger sister, Yingluck Shinawatra.

Culture

People

Thais are master chatters and will have a shopping list of questions: where are you from, are you married, do you have children? Occasionally they get more curious and want to know how much you weigh or how much money you make; these questions to a Thai are matters of public record and aren't considered impolite.

Thais are laid-back, good-natured people who live by a philosophy of *sànùk* (fun), and every task is measured on the *sànùk* meter. Thais believe strongly in the concept of 'saving face', that is, avoiding confrontation and endeavouring not to embarrass themselves or other people. All relationships follow simple lines of social rank defined by age, wealth, status, and personal and political power.

About 75% of citizens are ethnic Thais, further divided by geography (north, central, south and northeast). Each group speaks its own Thai dialect and to an extent practises

DOS & DON'TS

- Because Thai money bears a picture of the king, don't step on a dropped bill to prevent it from blowing away.
- Stand respectfully for the national anthem, which is played at 8am and 6pm. (It is not necessary to stand if you're inside a home or building.)
- Rise for the royal anthem, which is played in cinemas before every screening.
- Don't get a tattoo of the Buddha, as the culture ministry is seeking to ban the practice and it is viewed as being sacrilegious.
- Greet people with a smile and a cheery *sàwàtdee kráp* if you're male or *sàwàtdee kâ* if you're female.
- Bring a gift if you're invited to a Thai home and take off your shoes when you enter.
- Lower your head slightly when passing between two people having a conversation or when passing near a monk.
- Dress modestly (cover to the elbows and the ankles) for temple visits and always remove your shoes when you enter any building that contains a Buddha image.
- Never step over someone or their personal belongings.
- Also avoid tying your shoes to the outside of your backpack where they might accidentally brush against someone.

RECOMMENDED READING

» *Being Dharma: The Essence of the Buddha's Teachings* (2001)

» Access to Insight (www.accesstoinsight.org)

» *Thai Folk Wisdom: Contemporary Takes on Traditional Proverbs* (2010), by Tulaya Pornpiriyakulchai and Jane Vejjajiva

» *Sacred Tattoos of Thailand* (2011), by Joe Cummings

regional customs. Politically and economically the central Thais are dominant.

People of Chinese ancestry, many of whom have been in Thailand for generations, make up over 14% of the population. Other large minority groups include Vietnamese in the east, Khmer in parts of the northeast, Lao spread throughout the north and northeast, and Muslim Malays in the far south. Smaller non-Thai-speaking groups include the colourful hill tribes living in the northern mountains.

Religion

Country, family and daily life are all married to Theravada Buddhism (as opposed to the Mahayana schools found in East Asia and the Himalaya). Every Thai male is expected to become a monk for a short period in his life since a family earns great merit when a son 'takes robe and bowl'.

More evident than the philosophical aspects of Buddhism is the everyday fusion with animist rituals. Monks are consulted to determine an auspicious date for a wedding or the likelihood of success for a business. Spirit houses are constructed outside buildings and homes to encourage the guardian spirits to bring good fortune to the site. Food, drink and furniture are all offered to the spirits to smooth daily life.

Roughly 95% of the population practises Buddhism, but there is a significant Muslim community, especially in southern Thailand.

Arts

Classical central Thai music features an incredible array of textures and subtleties, hair-raising tempos and pastoral melodies. Among the more common instruments is the *pèe,* a woodwind instrument with a reed mouthpiece; it is heard prominently at Thai boxing matches. A bowed instrument, similar to examples played in China and Japan, is called the *sor*. The *ránâht èhk* is a bamboo-keyed percussion instrument resembling the Western xylophone, while the *klòoi* is a wooden flute. This traditional orchestra originated as an accompaniment to classical dance-drama and shadow theatre, but these days it can be heard at temple fairs and concerts.

In the north and northeast there are several popular wind instruments with multiple reed pipes, which function basically like a mouth-organ. Chief among these is the *kaan,* which originated in Laos; when played by an adept musician, it sounds like a rhythmic, churning calliope organ.

The best example of modern Thai music is the rock group Carabao, which has been performing for more than 30 years. Another major influence was a 1970s group called Caravan. It created a modern Thai folk style known as *pleng pêua cheewít* (songs for life), which features political and environmental topics. In the 1990s, a respectable alt-rock scene emerged thanks to the likes of Modern Dog and Loso.

On an international scale, Thailand has probably distinguished itself more in traditional religious sculpture than in any other art form. Thailand's most famous sculptural output has been its bronze Buddha images, coveted the world over for their originality and grace.

Temple architecture symbolises elements of the religion. A steeply pitched roof system tiled in green, gold and red represents the Buddha (the Teacher), the Dhamma (Dharma in Sanskrit; the Teaching) and the Sangha (the fellowship of followers of the Teaching).

The traditional Thai theatre consists of dance-dramas using either human dancers or puppets to act out the plot. *Kŏhn*

CLASSIC THAI MOVIES

» *Fun Bar Karaoke* (1997), directed by Pen-Ek Ratanaruang

» *Yam Yasothon* (2005), directed by Petchtai Wongkamlao

» *Fah Talai Jone* (Tears of the Black Tiger; 2000), directed by Wisit Sasanatieng

» *Mekhong Sipha Kham Deuan Sip-et* (Mekong Full Moon Party; 2002), directed by Jira Malikul

is formal masked dance-drama depicting scenes from the *Ramakian* (the Thai version of India's *Ramayana*) and originally performed only for the royal court; *lákon* is a general term covering several types of dance-dramas (usually for nonroyal occasions), as well as Western theatre; *lĭgair* is a partly improvised, often bawdy folk play featuring dancing, comedy, melodrama and music; and *lâkon lék* is puppet theatre.

Environment

Like all countries with high population density, there is enormous pressure on Thailand's ecosystems: 50 years ago about 70% of the countryside was forest, it's now 28%. In response to environmental degradation, the Thai government has created a large number of protected areas since the 1970s. Following devastating floods, exacerbated by soil erosion, logging was banned in 1989.

Though Thailand has a better record than most of its neighbours at protecting endangered species, corruption hinders the efforts and the country is a popular conduit for the illegal wildlife trade.

SURVIVAL GUIDE

Directory A–Z

Accommodation

Thailand offers a wide variety of good-value accommodation. The budget range runs from around 200B for basic rooms (shared bathrooms and fan cooled), while for 400B you'll get air-con and private bathroom. In Bangkok and Chiang Mai, the midrange has become more stylish and interesting these days. In the rest of the country you'll start getting midrange quality at around 600B but the hotels tend to be old and poorly maintained. Top-end in small towns starts above 1500B and in Bangkok above 3000B. Prices in this guide are high-season rates.

The budget breakdown for Bangkok and Chiang Mai is: budget (**$**), under 1000B; midrange (**$$**), 1000B to 3000B; and top end (**$$$**), above 3000B.

For the rest of Thailand: budget (**$**), under 600B; midrange (**$$**), 600B to 1500B; and top end (**$$$**), above 1500B.

Business Hours

The following are standard hours for different types of businesses in Thailand.

Government offices are open from 8.30am to 4.30pm, Monday to Friday. Some close for lunch (noon to 1pm), while others are open Saturday (9am to 3pm).

Bank hours are 9.30am to 3.30pm, Monday to Friday (ATMs are accessible 24 hours a day). All government offices and banks are closed on public holidays (see p442).

Restaurants are generally open from 10am to 10pm. Some specialise in morning meals and close by 3pm.

Local store hours are from 10am to 6pm. Department stores open 10am to 10pm.

Bars open from 6pm to midnight (officially), clubs are open from 8pm to 2am and live-music venue hours are 6pm to 1am. Closing times vary due to local enforcement of curfew laws; bars close during elections and certain religious public holidays.

Customs Regulations

The **customs department** (www.customs.go.th) maintains a helpful website with specific information about customs regulations. Thailand allows the follow items to enter duty free:

» reasonable amount of personal effects (clothing and toiletries)
» professional instruments
» 200 cigarettes
» 1L of wine or spirits

Thailand prohibits the import of the following items:

» firearms and ammunition (unless registered in advance with the police department)
» illegal drugs
» pornographic media

When leaving Thailand, you must obtain an export licence for any antiques reproductions or newly cast Buddha images (except personal amulets). Submitting two front-view photos of the object(s), a photocopy of your passport, along with the purchase receipt and the object(s) in question, to the **Department of Fine Arts** (☎0 2628 5032). Allow four days for the application and inspection process to be completed.

Embassies & Consulates

Foreign embassies are in Bangkok; some nations also have consulates in Chiang Mai.

Australia (Map p369; ☎0 2344 6300; www.thailand.embassy.gov.au; 37 Th Sathon Tai, Bangkok; MRT Lumphini)

Cambodia (Map p369; ☎0 2957 5851-2; 518/4 Pracha Uthit/Soi Ramkamhaeng 39, Bangkok; MRT Phra Ram 9 & access by taxi)

Canada (www.thailand.gc.ca) Bangkok (Map p369; ☎0 2636 0540; 15th fl, Abdulrahim Bldg, 990 Th Phra Ram IV, Bangkok; MRT Si Lom); Consulate Chiang Mai (☎0 5385 0147; 151 Superhighway, Tambon Tahsala)

China (www.chinaembassy.or.th) Bangkok (Map p369; ☎0 2245 7044; www.china embassy.or.th; 57 Th Ratchadaphisek, Bangkok; MRT Phra Ram 9); Consulate Chiang Mai (☎0 5327 6125; 111 Th Chang Lor)

France (www.ambafrance-th.org) Bangkok (Map p369; ☎0 2657 5100; 35 Soi 36, Th Charoen Krung, Bangkok; river ferry Tha Oriental); Consular Section (Map p369; ☎0 2627 2150; 29 Th Sathon Tai, Bangkok; MRT Lumphini); Consulate Chiang Mai (☎0 5328 1466; 138 Th Charoen Prathet).

Germany (Map p369; ☎0 2287 9000; www.bangkok.diplo.de; 9 Th Sathon Tai, Bangkok; MRT Lumphini)

Ireland (Map p380; ☎02 632 6720; www.irelandinthailand.com; Room 407, 4th fl, Thaniya Bldg, 62 Th Silom, Bangkok; BTS Sala Daeng, MRT Si Lom)

Israel (Map p378; ☎0 2204 9200; bangkok.mfa.gov.il; 25th fl, Ocean Tower 2, 25 Soi 19, Th Sukhumvit, Bangkok; BTS Asok, MRT Sukhumvit)

Laos (Map p369; ☎0 2539 6678; www.bkklao embassy.com; 502/1-3 Soi Sahakarnpramoon, Pracha Uthit/Soi 39, Th Ramakamhaeng; MRT Phra Ram 9 & access by taxi)

Myanmar (Burma; Map p380; ☎0 2233 2237; www.mofa.gov.mm; 132 Th Sathon Neua, Bangkok; BTS Surasak)

Netherlands (Map p376; ☎0 2309 5200; www.netherlandsembassy.in.th; 15 Soi Tonson, Th Ploenchit, Bangkok; BTS Phloen Chit)

New Zealand (Map p376; ☎0 2254 2530; www.nzembassy.com; 14th fl, M Thai Tower, All Seasons Place, 87 Th Witthayu, Bangkok; BTS Phloen Chit)

South Africa (Map p376; ☎0 2659 2900; www.saembbangkok.com; 12th fl, M Thai Tower, All Seasons Place, 87 Th Witthayu; BTS Phloen Chit)

UK Bangkok (Map p376; ☎0 2305 8333; ukinthailand.fco.gov.uk; 14 Th Witthayu; BTS Phloen Chit); Consulate Chiang Mai (☎0 5326 3015; British Council, 198 Th Bamrungrat)

USA Bangkok (Map p376; ☎0 2205 4049; http://bangkok.usembassy.gov; 95 Th Witthayu; BTS Phloen Chit); Consulate Chiang Mai (☎0 5310 7777; 387 Th Wichayanon)

Vietnam (Map p376; ☎0 2251 5836-8; www.vietnamembassy-thailand.org; 83/1 Th Witthayu, Bangkok; BTS Phloen Chit)

Food & Drink

Welcome to a country where it is cheaper and tastier to eat out than to cook at home. Markets, pushcart vendors, makeshift stalls, open-air restaurants – prices stay low and cooks become famous in all walks of life for a particular dish.

Take a walk through the day markets to see mounds of clay-coloured pastes moulded into pyramids like art supplies. These are the backbone for Thai *gaang* (curries) and are made of finely ground herbs and seasonings. The paste is taken to home kitchens and thinned with coconut milk and decorated with vegetables and meat to make a meal. Although it is the consistency of soup, *gaang* is ladled onto a plate of rice instead of eaten directly out of the bowl.

For breakfast and for snacks, Thais nosh on *gŏoay đĕeo*, a noodle soup with chicken or pork and vegetables. There are two primary types of noodles to choose from: *sên lék* (thin) and *sên yài* (wide and flat). Before you dig in, add to taste a few teaspoons of the provided spices: dried red chilli, sugar, fish sauce and vinegar. Now you have the true taste of Thailand in front of you.

Not sure what to order at some of the popular dinner restaurants? Reliable favourites are *yam blah mèuk* (spicy squid salad with mint leaves, coriander and Chinese celery), *đôm yam gûng* (coconut soup with prawns, often translated as 'hot and sour soup') or its sister *đôm kàh gài* (coconut soup with chicken and galangal).

Thais are social eaters: meals are rarely taken alone and dishes are meant to be shared. Usually a small army of plates will be placed in the centre of the table, with individual servings of rice in front of each diner. The protocol goes like this: ladle a spoonful of food at a time onto your plate of rice. Using the spoon like a fork and your fork like a knife, steer the food (with the fork) onto your spoon, which enters your mouth.

As an approximate guide, prices for main dishes when eating out are:

» Budget ($): under 150B
» Midrange ($$): 150B to 350B
» Top End ($$$): above 350B

Gay & Lesbian Travellers

Thai culture is relatively tolerant of both male and female homosexuality. However, public displays of affection – whether heterosexual or homosexual – are frowned upon. **Utopia** (www.utopia-asia.com) posts lots of Thailand information for gay and lesbian visitors and publishes a guidebook to the kingdom for homosexuals.

Insurance

A travel-insurance policy to cover theft, loss and medical problems is a good idea. There is a wide variety of policies available, so check the small print. Be sure that the policy covers ambulances or an emergency flight home.

Some policies specifically exclude 'dangerous activities', which can include scuba diving, motorcycling or even trekking. A locally acquired motorcycle licence is not valid under some policies.

Worldwide travel insurance is available at www.lonelyplanet.com/travel_services. You can buy, extend and claim online any time – even if you're already on the road.

Internet Access

You'll find plenty of internet cafes just about everywhere. The going rate is anywhere from 40B to 120B an hour, depending on how much competition there is. Connections tend to be pretty fast and the machines are usually well maintained. Wireless access (wi-fi) is usually available in most hotels and guesthouses.

Legal Matters

In general, Thai police don't hassle tourists, unless you are caught holding drugs. If it's a small amount, you might be able to get away by paying a 'fine', but traffickers are certain to end up in prison.

If you're arrested for any offence, the police will let you make a phone call to your embassy, if you have one, or to a friend or relative if not. Thai law does not presume an indicted detainee to be either 'guilty' or 'innocent' but rather a 'suspect', whose guilt or innocence will be decided in court. Trials are usually speedy.

The **tourist police** (☎1155) usually speak English, often quite well, and offer a range of assistance from providing road conditions during floods to assistance if you've been ripped off or robbed.

Maps

ThinkNet (www.thinknet.co.th) produces high-quality, bilingual city and country maps, including interactive-map CDs. For GPS users in Thailand, most prefer the Garmin units and the associated map products that are accurate and fully routed.

Money

The unit of Thai currency is the bàht, which is divided into 100 satang; coins include 25-satang and 50-satang pieces and baht in 1B, 2B, 5B and 10B coins. Notes are in 20B (green), 50B (blue), 100B (red), 500B (purple) and 1000B (beige). Rarely are other currencies accepted.

Occasionally high-end hotels in Bangkok will quote prices in US dollars; when this is the case we've followed suit. Also note that

TASTY TRAVEL

Thailand's cuisine is intensely regional and virtually every town is associated with a specific dish that's unavailable (or at least not as tasty) outside the city limits. Below are some of the more ubiquitous regional specialities:

» **Chiang Mai** *nâm prík nùm* and *kàab mŏo* (roast chilli 'dip' and deep-fried pork crackling) Available at virtually every market in the city, the two dishes go wonderfully together, ideally accompanied by par-boiled vegies and sticky rice.

» **Lampang** *kôw taan* Deep-fried sticky rice cakes drizzled with palm sugar are a popular treat in this northern town.

» **Nong Khai** *năam neuang* This Vietnamese dish of balls of pork served with rice paper wrappers and a basket of herbs has found a home in northeastern Thailand.

» **Ubon Ratchathani** *gài yâhng* Marinated free-range chicken *(gài bâhn)* grilled over hot coals – a northeastern speciality said to be best in this town.

in certain border sections we've quoted dollars when Thai baht is not accepted.

ATMS & CREDIT CARDS

Debit and ATM cards issued by your home bank can be used at ATMs, which are widespread, to withdraw cash (in Thai baht only). Thai ATMs now charge a 150B foreign-transaction fee on top of whatever currency conversion and out-of-network fees your home bank charges. Cards can also be used for purchases at many shops, hotels and restaurants. The most commonly accepted cards are Visa and MasterCard. Top-end hotels will accept Amex.

MONEYCHANGERS

Banks and private moneychangers (only found in popular tourist destinations) give the best exchange rates and hotels give the worst. Since banks charge commission and duty for each travellers cheque cashed, use large denominations. British pounds and euros are second to the US dollar in general acceptability.

Photography

Memory cards for digital cameras are generally widely available in the more popular formats and available in the electronic sections of most shopping malls. In the tourist areas, many internet shops have CD-burning software if you want to offload your pictures.

Be considerate when taking photographs of the locals. Learn how to ask politely in Thai and wait for an embarrassed nod. In some of the regularly visited hill-tribe areas be prepared for the photographed subject to ask for money in exchange for a picture. Other hill tribes will not allow you to point a camera at them.

Post

The Thai postal system is efficient, inexpensive and reliable, though don't send cash or small valuables, just to be on the safe side. Poste restante can be received in any town that has a post office.

Public Holidays

Government offices and banks close on the following days.

New Year's Day 1 January

Makha Bucha Day Buddhist holy day; February (date varies)

Chakri Day Commemorating the founder of the Chakri dynasty, Rama I; 6 April

Songkran Festival Traditional Thai New Year and water festival; 13–14 April

Coronation Day Commemorating the 1946 coronation of HM the King and HM the Queen; 5 May

Labour Day 1 May

Visaka Bucha Buddhist holy day; May/June (date varies)

Asahna Bucha Buddhist holy day; July (date varies)

Queen's Birthday 12 August

Chulalongkorn Day 23 October

Ork Phansaa The end of Buddhist 'lent'; October/November (date varies)

King's Birthday 5 December

Constitution Day 10 December

New Year's Eve 31 December

Safe Travel

Thailand is not a dangerous country, but there are a few things to watch out for. See p385 for more information on common scams.

Try not to get into an argument with a Thai, especially if alcohol is involved. While foreigners might see a verbal argument as sport, Thais view it as a loss of face and have been known to respond with excessive and unpredictable violence. Especially untrustworthy are the off-duty police officers who are still armed even in civilian settings; there have been several incidents of altercations between foreigners and off-duty police, typically at bars, that have resulted in gun homicides.

Women also need to take care of themselves when travelling or visiting bars alone. Flirtation for the fun of it can often be misunderstood by Thais and can result in unwanted advances or unpredictable retribution if interest isn't mutual.

Telephone

The telephone country code for Thailand is ☎66 and is used when calling the country from abroad. All Thai telephone numbers are preceded by a '0' if you're dialling domestically (the '0' is omitted when calling from overseas). After the initial '0', the next three numbers represent the provincial area code, which is now integral to the telephone number. If the initial '0' is followed by an '8', then you're dialling a mobile phone.

The standard International Direct Dial prefix is ☎001. Economy rates are available with ☎007, ☎008 and ☎009, all of which use Voice over Internet Protocol (VoIP), with varying but adequate sound quality.

Dial ☎100 for operator-assisted international calls or reverse-charges (or collect) call. Alternatively contact your long-distance carrier for their overseas operator number, a toll-free call, or try ☎001 9991 2001 from a CAT phone and ☎1 800 000 120 from a TOT phone.

Payphones and international phone services are being slowly eclipsed by mobile phones. If you have a GSM-enabled handset, you can buy a SIM card (with a Thai telephone number) and prepaid refill cards for 300B to 500B. Rates vary but are typically around 2B per minute domestically and between 5B and 7B for international calls. Roaming charges are quite reasonable in Thailand for those with mobile phones.

Time

Thailand's time zone is seven hours ahead of GMT/UTC (London).

Toilets

Increasingly the Asian-style squat toilet is less of the norm in Thailand. There are still specimens in rural places, but the Western-style toilet is becoming more prevalent and appears wherever foreign tourists can be found.

Even in places where sit-down toilets are installed, the septic system may not be designed to take toilet paper. In such cases there will be a waste basket where you're supposed to place used toilet paper and feminine hygiene products. Some modern toilets also come with a small spray hose – Thailand's version of the bidet.

Tourist Information

The helpful **Tourism Authority of Thailand** (TAT; www.tourismthailand.org) has nearly two-dozen offices throughout the country. Most staff speak English. Check TAT's website for a list of overseas offices, plus plenty of tourism information.

Visas

Thailand's **Ministry of Foreign Affairs** (www.mfa.go.th) oversees immigration and visa issues. In the past five years there have been new rules nearly every year regarding visa extensions; the best online monitor is **Thaivisa** (www.thaivisa.com).

Citizens of 41 countries (including most European countries, Australia, New Zealand and the USA) can enter Thailand at no charge. These citizens are issued a 30-day visa if they arrive by air or 15 days by land.

If you need more time in the country, apply for a 60-day tourist visa prior to arrival at a Thai embassy or consulate abroad. Rules enacted in 2011 state that hotel reservation and documentation of return flight are required for this, but the consensus at writing time is that these rules weren't being enforced across the board.

If you overstay your visa, the penalty is 500B per day, with a 20,000B limit; fines can be paid at any official exit point or at the Bangkok immigration office.

You can extend your stay, for the normal fee of 1900B, at an immigration office. Those issued with a standard stay of 15 or 30 days can extend their stay for seven to 10 days (depending on the immigration office) if the extension is handled before the visa expires. The 60-day tourist visa can be extended by up to 30 days at the discretion of Thai immigration authorities.

Volunteering

There are many wonderful volunteering organisations in Thailand that provide meaningful work and cultural engagement. Volunteer Work Thailand (www.

THAILAND'S IMMIGRATION OFFICES

The following are two common immigration offices where visa extensions and other formalities can be addressed. Remember to dress in your Sunday best when doing official business in Thailand and do all visa business yourself (don't hire a third party). For all types of visa extensions, bring along two passport-sized photos and one copy each of the photo and visa pages of your passport.

» **Bangkok immigration office** (☎0 2141 9889; Bldg B, Government Center, Soi 7, Th Chaeng Watthana; ⏲8.30am-noon & 1-4.30pm Mon-Fri; BTS Mo Chit & access by taxi)

» **Chiang Mai immigration office** (☎0 5320 1755-6; Th Mahidon; ⏲8.30am-4.30pm Mon-Fri)

volunteerworkthailand.org) maintains a database of opportunities.

Women Travellers

Attacks and rapes are not common in Thailand, but incidents do occur. If you return home from a bar alone, be sure to have your wits about you. Avoid accepting rides from strangers late at night or travelling around in isolated areas by yourself - common sense stuff that might escape your notice in a new environment filled with hospitable people.

Getting There & Away

Flights, tours and train tickets can be booked online at www.lonelyplanet.com/bookings.

Entering Thailand

Entry procedures for Thailand, by air or by land, are straightforward: you'll have to show your passport, and you'll need to present completed arrival and departure cards.

Air

Most international flights use Bangkok's Suvarnabhumi Airport (pronounced soo-wanna-poom), though there are a few flights that fly directly to Chiang Mai.

Bangkok is *the* air-travel hub for mainland Southeast Asia and air fares are quite competitive. The major regional carriers include the following:

Air Asia (☎0 2515 9999; www.airasia.com) Bangkok to: Bali (Indonesia), Guangzhou (China), Hanoi (Vietnam), Ho Chi Minh City (Vietnam) Hong Kong (China), Kuala Lumpur (Malaysia), Macau (China), Medan (Indonesia), Penang (Malaysia), Phnom Penh (Cambodia), Shenzen (China), Singapore, Surabaya (Indonesia), Yangon (Myanmar). Chiang Mai to: Kuala Lumpur (Malaysia), Singapore.

Air China (☎0 2634 8991; www.fly-airchina.com) Bangkok to: Běijīng, Chengdu (China).

Bangkok Airways (☎1771; www.bangkokair.com) Bangkok to: Hong Kong (China), Kuala Lumpur (Malaysia), Luang Prabang (Laos), Phnom Penh (Cambodia), Siem Reap (Cambodia), Singapore, Yangon (Myanmar).

China Airlines (☎0 2250 9898; www.china-airlines.com) Bangkok to: Taipei (Taiwan). Chiang Mai to: Taipei.

Garuda Indonesia (☎0 2679 7371; www.garuda-indonesia.com) Bangkok to: Jakarta (Indonesia).

Lao Airlines (☎0 2236 9822; www.laoairlines.com) Bangkok to: Luang Prabang, Pakse, Savannakhet, Vientiane. Chiang Mai to: Luang Prabang (Laos).

Malaysia Airlines (☎0 2263 0565; www.mas.com.my) Bangkok to: Kuala Lumpur (Malaysia).

Myanmar Airways International (☎0 2261 5060; www.maiair.com) Bangkok to: Singapore, Yangon (Myanmar).

Philippine Airlines (☎0 2263 0565; www.philippineairlines.com) Bangkok to: Manila (Philippines).

Royal Brunei Airlines (☎0 2637 5151; www.bruneiair.com) Bangkok to: Brunei.

Singapore Airlines (☎0 2353 6000; www.singaporeair.com) Bangkok to: Singapore.

Thai Airways International (☎0 2288 7000; www.thaiair.com) Bangkok to: Phnom Penh (Cambodia), Denpasar (Indonesia), Hanoi (Vietnam), Ho Chi Minh City (Vietnam), Jakarta (Indonesia), Kuala Lumpur (Malaysia), Manila (Philippines), Penang (Malaysia), Singapore, Vientiane (Laos), Yangon (Myanmar).

Vietnam Airlines (☎0 2655 4137; www.vietnamair.com.vn) Bangkok to: Hanoi (Vietnam), Ho Chi Minh City (Vietnam).

Land

BORDER CROSSINGS

See p35 for the Mekong region's border crossings at a glance.

Cambodia

Cambodian tourist visas are available at most borders for US$20, though some borders charge 1200B. Bring a passport photo and try to avoid some of the runner boys who want to issue a health certificate or other 'medical' paperwork for additional fees.

Laos

It is fairly hassle free to cross into Laos from crossings in northern Thailand and northeastern Thailand. Lao visas (US$30 to US$42) can be obtained on arrival at most borders and applications require a passport photo. You can also pay the visa fee in baht, but the exchange rate is often unfavourable.

Myanmar (Burma)

Most of the land crossings into Myanmar have restrictions that don't allow full access to the country. Border points are also subject to unannounced closures, which can last anywhere from a day to years.

Getting Around

Air

Hopping around the country by air can be quite affordable. Most routes originate in Bangkok at Suvarnabhumi Airport, but a couple of airlines still use the old Don Muang Airport. Airlines for domestic routes include the following:

Air Asia (nationwide call centre 02 515 9999; www.airasia.com)

Bangkok Airways (nationwide call centre 1771; www.bangkokair.com)

Kan Air (nationwide call centre 02 551 6111; www.kanairlines.com)

Nok Air (nationwide call centre 1318; www.nokair.co.th)

Nok Mini (nationwide call centre 0 5328 0444; www.nokmini.com)

One-Two-Go (Orient Thai; nationwide call centre 1126; www.flyorientthai.com)

Solar Air (www.solarair.co.th)

THAI (0 2356 1111; www.thaiair.com)

Bicycle

Single-geared bicycles are available for rent in most tourist towns from around 50B per day. Higher-quality mountain bikes are sometimes available for around 150B per day. Touring the country is also a doable activity as the roads are well sealed and lodging is available along the way.

Boat

The true Thai river transport is the long-tail boat *(reua hăang yao)*, so-called because the propeller is mounted at the end of a long driveshaft extending from the engine. Boats are a common (and highly recommended) means of travel in Bangkok and, to a lesser degree, along the Mekong River in the far north.

Bus

Thai bus service is widespread, convenient and fast, sometimes nail-bitingly so. You're almost always best off travelling with companies operating out of government bus stations (called Baw Khaw Saw) instead of companies contracted out of tourist centres. Tourist-centre bus trips are notoriously corrupt and unreliable, and thefts on the buses are common.

The cheapest buses are the *rót tammádah* that stop in every town and for every waving hand along the way, but this class of bus is a dying breed. Most services are in faster air-con buses, called *rót aa* (air bus). Longer routes offer 2nd-class and 1st-class air-con services; the latter have toilets and better air-con. VIP and Super VIP buses have fewer seats, and hostesses serve snacks.

Car & Motorcycle

Cars, 4WDs or vans can be rented in most large cities. Always verify (ask to see the dated documents) that the vehicle is insured for liability before signing a contract. An International Driving Permit is necessary to drive vehicles in Thailand, but this is rarely enforced for motorcycle hire.

Thais drive on the left-hand side of the road (most of the time!). The main rule to be aware of is that smaller vehicles always yield to bigger ones.

Motorcycle travel is a popular way to get around Thailand. Dozens of places along the guesthouse circuit rent motorbikes for 150B to 300B a day. Motorcycle rental usually requires that you leave your passport, and many provinces require you to wear a helmet.

Recommended car-rental agencies:

Avis (www.avisthailand.com)

North Wheels (www.northwheels.com)

Thai Rent A Car (www.thairentacar.com)

Local Transport

MOTORCYCLE TAXI

Many cities have motorcycle taxis. Rather than cruise the streets they cluster near busy intersections. Fares are from 10B to 30B.

SĂHMLÓR & TÚK-TÚK

Săhmlór, meaning 'three wheels', are pedal rickshaws. The motorised version is called túk-túk because of the throaty cough their two-stroke engines make. In tourist centres, Bangkok especially, many túk-túk drivers are unscrupulously greedy, inflating fares or diverting passengers to places that pay commissions.

You must bargain and agree on a fare before accepting a ride, but in many towns there is a de facto fixed fare anywhere in town.

SŎRNGTĂAOU

Sŏrngtăaou (literally, two rows) are small pick-ups with a row of seats down each side. In most towns *sŏrngtăaou* serve as public buses running fixed routes.

Tours

The better tour companies build their own Thailand itineraries from scratch and choose their local suppliers based on which best serve these itineraries. Many are now offering 'voluntourism' programs, which means that you might buy lunch for an orphanage, visit a hospital or teach an English class in addition to sightseeing. Also see Volunteering (p443) if you're looking for alternative travelling experiences.

Asian Trails (www.asiantrails.info) Tour operator that runs programs for overseas brokers; trips include a mix of on- and off-the-beaten-path destinations.

Hands Up Holidays (www.handsupholidays.com) Voluntourism and village sightseeing programs.

Isan Explorer (www.isanexplorer.com) Custom tours to the northeast.

Mekong Cruises (www.cruisemekong.com) Float down the mighty river aboard an elegant vessel.

Orient Express (www.orient-express.com) High-end luxury tours of common and uncommon places in Thailand.

Tours with Kasma Loha-Unchit (www.thaifoodandtravel.com) Thai cookbook author offers personalised 'cultural immersion' tours of Thailand.

Tiger Trails (www.tigertrailthailand.com) Nature, culture and strenuous trekking tours around Chiang Mai and northern Thailand.

Tour de Thailand (www.tourdethailand.com) Charity bike ride organiser covering touring routes throughout the country.

Train

The **State Railway of Thailand** (☎1690; www.railway.co.th) has four main lines (northern, southern, northeastern and eastern) branching out from Bangkok. Trains are comfortable, but almost always slower and less frequent than buses.

Trains are often heavily booked, so it's wise to reserve well ahead, especially the Bangkok–Chiang Mai overnight trip. You can make bookings at any train station (English is usually spoken) and, for a small fee, through some Bangkok travel agencies.

First-class, 2nd-class and 3rd-class cabins are available on most trains, but each class varies considerably depending on the type of train (rapid, express or ordinary). First class is a private cabin. Second class has individually reclining seats; depending on the train, some cabins have air-con. Non-air-conditioned 3rd class is spartan with bench seating.

Overnight trains have sleeping berths in 1st and 2nd class. Single 1st-class cabins are not available, so if you're travelling alone you may be paired with another passenger.

Understand the Mekong Region

The Mekong Region Today

A Remarkable Turnaround

Rewind just a generation and Cambodia, Laos and Vietnam were pariah states, boycotted by much of the Western world. Scarred by decades of war and instability, the region was considered by many Western experts to be a basket case. How times change. Despite the region's communist history, its leaders proved themselves to be open to Western economic models as they balanced Eastern communism with Western capitalism. Touchdown today and the bad old days seem but a footnote in history. Like the river that runs through it, the Mekong region is well and truly going places.

Economic Highs

Much of the region is closer than it has been for some time thanks to the Association of Southeast Asian Nations (Asean). With the exception of the occasional dispute between Cambodia and Thailand over their shared border (see p231), the countries of the region are at peace and the talk is of cooperation not conflict. All seem to be weathering the global financial crisis better than many of their counterparts in the Western world. Asean is moving towards a free trade area that should liberate commerce between the neighbouring countries of the Mekong region and help keep the economy on track.

Visa-free travel between Asean members and the emergence of budget airlines like Air Asia and Jetstar has kickstarted a regional tourism rush that is redefining travel patterns in the countries of the Mekong region. There are also plans to revolutionise, with China pledging to build a high-speed rail link from Kunming to Bangkok via languid Luang Prabang within the next five years.

Top Travel Reads

A Dragon Apparent (1951) Norman Lewis' classic account of his 1950 foray into Indochine and the last days of French rule.

The River's Tale: A Year on the Mekong (2001) War-protester-turned-foreign-correspondent Edward Gargan sees how this region has come back from the brink.

Phaic Tan: Sunstroke on a Shoestring (2004) This ultimate spoof guidebook is a pastiche of Mekong countries and pokes fun at all of us: locals, travellers and even guidebook authors.

Top Films

Apocalypse Now (1979) Marlon Brando plays Colonel Kurtz, who has gone AWOL, and native, in the wilds of northeast Cambodia. One of the most savage indictments of war ever seen on screen.

The Killing Fields (1984) Iconic film about the Khmer Rouge period.

GDP
(in US$ billions)

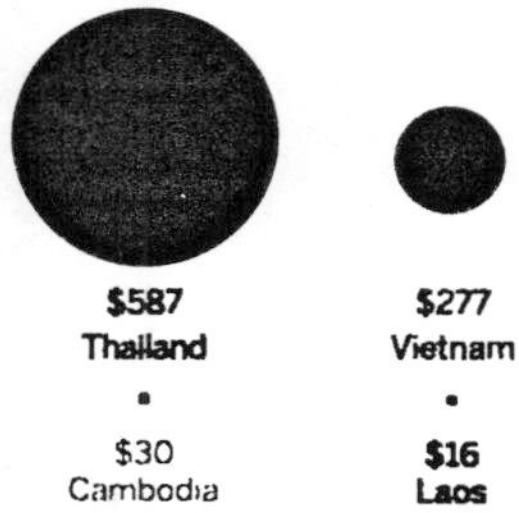

if the Mekong region were 100 people

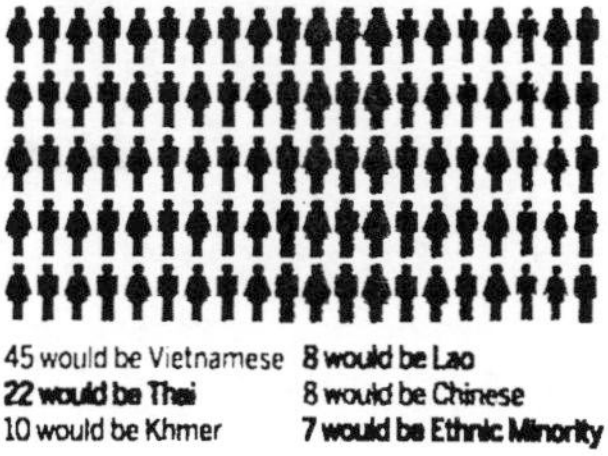

Political Lows

On the flip side of all this development, democracy seems weaker than ever. Laos and Vietnam are old school one-party states with not even the faintest veneer of democracy. Cambodia puts on a good show of traditional ballot box democracy every five years, but the reality is an entrenched political elite that controls every aspect of the state. While the Middle East awakens and revolutions and uprisings spread throughout the Arab world, it seems that Cambodia, Laos and Vietnam have experienced enough turmoil to last a lifetime and the average citizen seems willing to put up with the status quo for now.

Red Shirt, Yellow Shirt

Over in Thailand, politics has been getting very shirty, as governments and hordes of opposition protesters come and go from the capital with alarming regularity. Red Shirts support exiled former Prime Minister Thaksin Shinawatra and are mostly drawn from provincial northern and eastern Thailand. Yellow Shirts support the royal family and the established elite and are generally from Bangkok and central Thailand. For now the Red Shirts are back under the leadership of Thaksin's younger sister Yingluck but it remains to be seen how long the Yellow Shirts, or the army, are willing to stand on the sidelines and watch Shinawatra Plc run the show. A lot also rides on the health of the ageing Thai king, but discuss this in public or over the internet and you might be arrested for *lèse-majesté*. Seriously.

Dam Nations

The Mekong River could be the spark for future conflict. The Mekong is the world's 12th-longest river and 10th largest in terms of volume, and

telling the personal story of photographer Dith Pran's relationship with journalist Sidney Schanberg.

The Quiet American (2002)
Beautiful period film capturing the atmosphere of old Indochine before the advent of war, starring Michael Caine and Brendan Fraser.

Mekong Football

- » Thailand: 119
- » Vietnam: 144
- » Cambodia: 174
- » Laos: 177

Source: World Rankings, www.fifa.com

Best Local Reads

- » *Bangkok Post*, Thailand
- » *Phnom Penh Post*, Cambodia
- » *The Word*, Vietnam

has long been seen as a potentially lucrative source of hydroelectricity. The Chinese have already started damming the river and Laos and Cambodia look set to follow suit. No one really knows what impact this will have downstream, but some environmental experts, such as the WWF, argue convincingly that significant changes to river activity could be disastrous for the Tonlé Sap Lake or the Mekong Delta. The Mekong River Commission is supposed to monitor all developments on the river, but China refuses to join the club. Běijīng is adamant that as long as the river flows through its territory, it has the right to harness its power in any way it sees fit.

The Mekong River is known as Lancang Jiang (Turbulent River) in China; Mae Nam Khong (Mother River of All Things) in Thailand, Myanmar (Burma) and Laos; Tonlé Thom (Great Water) in Cambodia; and Cuu Long (Nine Dragons) in Vietnam.

Big Brother

Relationships with China, Asia's rising superpower, and their membership of Asean are realities that unify all these countries beyond the Mekong River. Běijīng long sought tribute from the Mekong kingdoms in ages past, and still exerts a strong influence on the region through aid and trade. Thus the Mekong countries and China are now on good, if unequal, terms.

Uncharted Waters

Economically, the future is bright. Socially and politically the forecast is cloudy, as the governments of the region struggle to come to grips with expanding populations, urban migration and a widening gap between rich and poor. It will require level heads and good governance to steer these countries to a better future. That said, the remarkable people of the region seem to have a knack for succeeding against the odds, so Asia's century promises much for the Mekong.

Respect Due

» Respect local dress standards, particularly at religious sites. Always remove your shoes before entering a temple, as well as any hat or head covering.

» Nude sunbathing is considered *totally* inappropriate.

» Learn the local greetings in each country – and use them.

» Monks are not supposed to touch or be touched by women.

» No matter how high your blood pressure rises, do not raise your voice or show signs of aggression. This will lead to a loss of face.

» Don't leave a pair of chopsticks sitting vertically in a rice bowl – they can look like the incense sticks that are burned for the dead.

» The people of the Mekong region like to keep a clean house; it's customary to remove shoes when entering a home.

Mekong Region History

This vibrant region has a history as long and dramatic as the Mekong River that cuts through its heart. There have been turbulent moments, there have been calm stretches. Empires have expanded in size only to come crashing down again like the mother river's waters each season. As human habitation has swollen, putting new pressures on this oldest of rivers, so too have the dramas of the region magnified. The Mekong has played host to some of the most brutal wars of the 20th century and the bloodiest revolutions. However, calmer waters lie ahead, as the region is peaceful and relatively stable for the first time in generations.

The history of this great region is also the history of two great civilisations colliding. China and India may be making headlines today as the emerging giants of the 21st century, but it is old news. They have long been great powers and have historically influenced the Mekong region, from art and architecture to language and religion.

Southeast Asian kingdoms were not states in the modern sense, with fixed frontiers, but varied in extent. Outlying *meuang* (principalities or city-states) might transfer their allegiance elsewhere when the centre was weak. That is why scholars prefer the term 'mandala', meaning 'circle of power'.

The Early Years

Modern linguistic theory and archaeological evidence suggest that the first true agriculturalists in the world, perhaps also the first metal workers, spoke an early form of Thai and lived in what we know today as Thailand. The Mekong Valley and Khorat Plateau were inhabited as far back as 10,000 years ago, and rice was grown in northeastern Thailand as early as 4000 BC. China, by contrast, was still growing millet at the time.

According to Lao legend, the mythical figure Khun Borom cut open a gourd in the vicinity of Dien Bien Phu and out came seven sons who spread the Tai family from east to west. Although previous theory had

TIMELINE

4200 BC

Cave dwellers capable of making pots inhabit caves around Laang Spean; archaeological evidence suggests the vessels these people were making are similar to those made in Cambodia today.

c 3000 BC

The region enters the Bronze Age some time before 3000 BC; the Middle East doesn't pass this milestone until 2800 BC and China 1000 years later.

c 2000 BC

The Bronze Age Dong Son culture emerges in the Red River Delta around Hanoi. It's renowned for its rice cultivation and the production of bronzeware, including drums and gongs.

placed the epicentre of Tai culture in southwestern China, recent evidence suggests it may have been in northern Vietnam and part of the Dong Son culture. The Dong Son culture is renowned for its elaborate bronze drums and was a powerful trading kingdom, its merchants penetrating as far south as Alor in Indonesia, where the people still trade in bronze drums.

An Early Empire

Indian culture was disseminated through much of the Mekong region via contact with seafaring Indian merchants calling at trading settlements along the coast of present-day Thailand, Cambodia and Vietnam. Some of these settlements were part of nascent kingdoms, the largest of which was known as Funan to the Chinese, and occupied much of what is southeastern Cambodia today. The Funanese constructed an elaborate system of canals both for transportation and the irrigation of rice. The principal port city of Funan was Oc-Eo in the Mekong Delta and archaeological excavations here tell us of contact between Funan and Indonesia, Persia and even the Mediterranean.

Funan was famous for its refined art and architecture, and its kings embraced the worship of Hindu deities Shiva and Vishnu and, concurrently, Buddhism. The *linga* (phallic totem) was the focus of ritual and an emblem of kingly might, a feature that was to evolve further in the Angkorian cult of the god king.

Vietnam Under Occupation

The Chinese introduced Confucianism, Taoism and Mahayana Buddhism to Vietnam, as well as a written character system, while the Indians brought Theravada Buddhism. Monks carried with them the scientific and medical knowledge of these two great civilisations, and Vietnam was soon producing its own great doctors, botanists and scholars. As the population expanded, the Vietnamese were forced to seek new lands. The ominous Truong Son Mountains prevented westward expansion, so they headed south, bringing them into conflict with first the Chams and later the Khmers.

VIETNAMESE IDENTITY

In AD 679 the Chinese changed the name of Vietnam to Annam, which means the 'Pacified South'. Ever since this era, the collective memory of Chinese domination has played an important role in shaping Vietnamese identity and attitudes towards their northern neighbour.

The Rise of Chenla

From the 6th century the Funan kingdom's importance as a port of call declined, and Cambodia's population gradually settled along the Mekong and Tonlé Sap rivers, where the majority remains today.

Chinese records refer to the rise of the Chenla empire, divided into 'water Chenla' (lower) and 'land Chenla' (upper). Water Chenla was located around Angkor Borei and the temple mount of Phnom Da;

c AD 100
The process of Indianisation begins in the Mekong region, the religions, language, sculpture and culture of India taking root through maritime contact with Cambodia.

245
The Chinese Wei emperor sends a mission to the countries of the Mekong region and is told that a barbarous but rich country called Funan exists in the Delta region.

600
The first inscriptions are committed to stone in Cambodia in ancient Khmer, offering historians the first contemporary accounts of the pre-Angkorian period other than from Chinese sources.

802
Jayavarman II proclaims independence from Java, marking the start of the Khmer empire of Angkor, which controls much of the Mekong region from the 10th to 13th centuries.

and land Chenla in the upper reaches of the Mekong River and east of the Tonlé Sap lake, around Sambor Prei Kuk (p232), one of the first great temple cities of the Mekong region.

What is certain is that the people of the lower Mekong were well known to the Chinese, and gradually the region was becoming more cohesive. Before long the fractured kingdoms of Chenla would merge to become the greatest empire in Southeast Asia.

For a full Cambodian history, from the humble beginnings in the prehistoric period through the glories of Angkor and right up to the present day, seek out a copy of *The History of Cambodia* by David Chandler.

The Khmer Empire

A popular place of pilgrimage for Khmers today, the sacred mountain of Phnom Kulen (p217), to the northeast of Angkor, is home to an inscription that tells us that in 802 Jayavarman II proclaimed himself a 'universal monarch', or a *devaraja* (god king). On his return to Cambodia, he set out to bring the country under his control through alliances and conquests. He was the first monarch to rule all of what we call Cambodia today.

Jayavarman II was the first of a long succession of kings who presided over the rise and fall of the Southeast Asian empire that was to leave the stunning legacy of Angkor. The first records of the massive irrigation works that supported the population of Angkor date to the reign of Indravarman I (877–89). His son Yasovarman I (r 889–910) moved the royal court to Angkor proper, establishing a temple mountain on the summit of Phnom Bakheng (p216).

The Romans of Asia

Like the Romans in Europe, the Khmers built a sophisticated network of highways to connect the outposts of their empire. Roads fanned out from Angkor connecting the capital with satellite cities such as Ayuthaya and Phimai in Thailand and as far away as Wat Phu in southern Laos.

From 1113, King Suryavarman II embarked on another phase of expansion, waging wars against Champa and Vietnam. He is immortalised in

THE LOST KINGDOM OF CHAMPA

The Hindu kingdom of Champa emerged around Vietnam's present-day Danang in the late 2nd century AD. Like Funan, it adopted Sanskrit as a sacred language and borrowed heavily from Indian art and culture. By the 8th century Champa had expanded southward to include what is now Nha Trang and Phan Rang. The Cham were a bellicose bunch who conducted raids along the entire coast of Indochina, and thus found themselves in a perpetual state of war with the Vietnamese to the north and the Khmers to the south. Ultimately this cost them their kingdom, as they found themselves squeezed between two great powers.

938

The Chinese are kicked out of Vietnam after 1000 years of occupation, as Ngo Quyen leads his people to victory in the battle of Bach Dang River, luring the Chinese ships onto sharpened stakes.

1010

Thanh Long, or 'City of the Soaring Dragon', known today as Hanoi or 'bend in the river', becomes Vietnam's capital (and celebrated its 1000th birthday in 2010).

1049

Suryavarman I annexes the Dravati kingdom of Lopburi in Thailand and widens his control of Cambodia, stretching the empire to perhaps its greatest extent.

1113

Suryavarman II commences the construction of Angkor Wat in Cambodia, the mother of all temples and the world's largest religious building; it is dedicated to Vishnu and designed as his funerary temple.

Cambodia as the king who, in his devotion to the Hindu deity Vishnu, bequeathed the world the majestic temple of Angkor Wat (p208).

Suryavarman II had brought Champa to heel and reduced it to vassal status. In 1177, the Chams struck back with a naval expedition up the Mekong and into Tonlé Sap lake. They took the city of Angkor by surprise and put King Dharanindravarman II to death. A year later a cousin of Suryavarman II gathered forces about him and defeated the Chams in another naval battle. The new leader was crowned Jayavarman VII in 1181.

Enter Jayavarman VII

A devout follower of Mahayana Buddhism, Jayavarman VII built the city of Angkor Thom (p209) and many other massive monuments visited by tourists around Angkor today. He is deified by many Cambodians as their greatest leader, a populist who promoted equality, and a socially conscious leader who built schools and hospitals for his people.

Vietnam Kicks Out the Chinese

In the early 10th century, the Tang dynasty in China collapsed. The Vietnamese seized the initiative and launched a long overdue revolt against Chinese rule in Vietnam. In 938, popular patriot Ngo Quyen finally vanquished the Chinese armies at a battle on the Bach Dang River, ending 1000 years of Chinese rule. However, it was not the last time the Vietnamese would tussle with their mighty northern neighbour.

From the 11th to 13th centuries, Vietnamese independence was consolidated under the enlightened emperors of the Ly dynasty. During the Ly dynasty many enemies, including the Chinese, the Khmer and the Cham, launched attacks on Vietnam, but all were repelled.

Sukhothai Stands Up

Several Thai principalities in the Mekong valley united in the 13th and 14th centuries to create Sukhothai (Land of Rising Happiness). Thai princes wrested control of the territory from the Khmers, whose all-powerful empire at Angkor was slowly disintegrating. Sukhothai is considered by the Thais to be the first true Thai kingdom. It was annexed by Ayuthaya in 1376, by which time a national identity of sorts had been forged.

At the same time, an allied kingdom emerged in north-central Thailand known as Lan Na Thai (Million Thai Rice Fields), usually referred to as Lanna, and this included the areas of Luang Prabang and Vientiane in modern-day Laos. Debate rages as to whether Lanna was essentially Lao or Thai and remains an issue of contention between the two peoples today.

AN ANGKOR ACCOUNT

There are very few surviving contemporary accounts of Angkor, but Chinese emissary Chou Ta Kuan lived there in 1296 and his observations have been republished as *The Customs of Cambodia*, a fascinating insight.

1177

The Chams launch a surprise attack on Angkor by sailing up the Tonlé Sap, defeating the powerful Khmers and occupying the capital for four years, before being vanquished by Jayavarman VII.

1238

Sukhothai (Land of Rising Happiness) is born, considered the first Thai kingdom in what is contemporary Thailand. It begins to exert pressure on the ailing Khmer empire.

» Wat Chang Lom (p407), near Sukhothai, Thailand

Lan Xang, the Birth of Laos

As the power of Sukhothai grew, the ascendant Thais began to exert more pressure on the Khmers. The Cambodian court looked around for an ally, and found one in the form of an exiled Lao prince who was being educated at Angkor.

King Jayavarman VIII married Fa Ngum to a Khmer princess and offered him an army of more than 10,000 troops. He pushed north to wrest the middle Mekong from the control of Sukhothai and Lanna. By 1353 he declared himself king of Lan Xang Hom Khao, meaning 'a million elephants and the white parasol'. This was really the last hurrah of the declining Khmer empire and quite probably served only to weaken Angkor and antagonise the Thais.

Within 20 years of its birth, Lan Xang had expanded eastwards to pick off parts of a disintegrating Champa and along the Annamite Mountains in Vietnam. Fa Ngum earned the sobriquet 'The Conqueror' because of his constant preoccupation with warfare. Theravada Buddhism became the state religion in Lan Xang when King Visounarat accepted the Pha Bang, a gold Buddha image from his Khmer sponsors.

By naming his kingdom Lan Xang Hom Khao, Fa Ngum was making a statement. Elephants were the battle tanks of Southeast Asian warfare, so to claim to be the kingdom of a million elephants was to issue a warning to surrounding kingdoms: 'Don't mess with the Lao!'

The Golden Age of Siam

The Thai kings of Ayuthaya grew very powerful in the 14th and 15th centuries, taking over the former Khmer strongholds in present-day central Thailand. Even though the Khmers had been their adversaries in battle, the Thai kings of Ayuthaya adopted many facets of Khmer

THE MONGOLS IN THE MEKONG

The marauding Mongols were to leave an indelible mark on the peoples of the Mekong as they initiated a major shift in the balance of power in the region.

In 1253, Kublai Khan, grandson of Genghis, attacked the Thai state of Nan Chao, which was located in Xīshuāngbǎnnà in the south of Yúnnán. Thais had already been migrating south for several centuries, settling in parts of Laos and northern Thailand. However, the sacking of their capital provoked a mass exodus and brought the Thais into conflict with a waning Khmer empire. The Mongol empire evaporated into the dust of history, but with the sacking of the Thai capital, the die was cast: it was the Thais versus the Khmers, a conflict that has persisted through the centuries to the present day.

In 1288, Kublai Khan planned to attack Champa and demanded the right to cross Vietnamese territory. The Vietnamese refused, but the Mongol hordes – all half a million of them – pushed ahead, seemingly invulnerable. However, they met their match in the legendary general Tran Hung Dao. He defeated them in the battle of Bach Dang River, one of the most celebrated scalps among many the Vietnamese have taken.

1353

Lao prince Chao Fa Ngum is sponsored by his Khmer father-in-law on an expedition to conquer the new Thai kingdoms, declaring himself leader of Lan Xang Hom Khao (Land of a Million Elephants and the White Parasol).

1431

The expansionist Thais sack Angkor definitively, carting off most of the royal court, including nobles, priests, dancers and artisans, to Ayuthaya. It's an irrevocable spiritual and cultural loss to Cambodia.

1516

Portuguese traders land at Danang, sparking the start of European interest in Vietnam. They set up a trading post in Faifo (present-day Hoi An) and introduce Catholicism to the Vietnamese.

1560

King Setthathirat moves the capital of Lan Xang (modern-day Laos) from Luang Prabang to Viang Chan, today known as Vientiane.

culture, including court customs and rituals, language and culture. The cultural haemorrhage that took place with the sacking of Angkor in 1431 continues to strain relations between the two neighbours. Some Thais claim Angkor as their own, while the Khmers bemoan the loss of Khmer kickboxing, classical Khmer dance and Khmer silk to the all-powerful Thai brand.

Angkor's loss was Ayuthaya's gain and it went on to become one of the greatest cities in Asia. It's been said that London, at the time, was a village in comparison. The kingdom sustained an unbroken monarchical succession through 34 reigns from King U Thong (r 1350–69) to King Ekathat (r 1758–67).

SIAM

'Among the Asian nations, the Kingdom of Siam is the greatest. The magnificence of the Ayuthaya court is incomparable.'

Engelbert Campfer, 1690

Vietnamese Expansion

The Chinese seized control of Vietnam once more in the early 15th century, carting off the national archives and some of the country's intellectuals to China – an irreparable loss to Vietnamese civilisation. The poet Nguyen Trai (1380–1442) wrote of this period, 'Were the water of the Eastern Sea to be exhausted, the stain of their ignominy could not be washed away; all the bamboo of the Southern Mountains would not suffice to provide the paper for recording all their crimes.'

In 1418, wealthy philanthropist Le Loi rallied the people against the Chinese. Upon victory in 1428, Le Loi declared himself Emperor Le Thai To, the first in the long line of the Le dynasty. To this day, Le Loi is highly revered as one of the country's all-time national heroes.

THE FALL OF THE KHMER EMPIRE

Some scholars maintain that decline was on the horizon at the time Angkor Wat was built, when the Angkorian empire was at the height of its remarkable productivity. There are indications that the irrigation network was overworked and slowly starting to silt up due to the massive deforestation that had taken place in the heavily populated areas to the north and east of Angkor. Following the reign of Jayavarman VII, temple construction effectively ground to a halt, largely because public works quarried local sandstone into oblivion and the population was left exhausted. The state religion reverted to Hinduism for a century or more and outbreaks of iconoclasm saw Buddhist sculpture vandalised or altered.

The Thais grew in strength and made repeated incursions into Angkor, finally sacking the city in 1431. During this period, perhaps drawn by the opportunities for sea trade with China and fearful of the increasingly bellicose Thais, the Khmer elite began to migrate to the Phnom Penh area. Angkor was abandoned to pilgrims, holy men and the elements.

1707

Lan Xang is divided into three smaller and weaker kingdoms: Viang Chan in central Laos, Luang Prabang in northern Laos and Champasak in southern Laos.

1767

Following several centuries of military rivalry, the Burmese sack the Thai capital of Ayuthaya, forcing its relocation to Thonburi, then to the present-day location of Bangkok.

1772

Cambodia is caught between the powerful Vietnamese and Siamese; the latter burn Phnom Penh to the ground, another chapter in the story of inflamed tensions that persist today.

1802

Emperor Gia Long takes the throne to rule over a united Vietnam for the first time in decades, and the Nguyen dynasty is born, ruling over the country until 1945.

Le Loi and his successors launched a campaign to take over Cham lands to the south, wiping the kingdom of Champa from the map, and parts of eastern Laos were forced to kowtow to the might of the Vietnamese.

The Dark Ages

The glorious years of the Khmer empire and the golden age of Ayuthaya were no guarantee of future success and the 18th century proved a time of turmoil for the region. This was the dark ages when the countries of the Mekong were convulsed by external threats and internal intrigue.

The Continuing Decline of Cambodia

From 1600 until the arrival of the French in 1863, Cambodia was ruled by a series of weak kings who were forced to seek the protection – at a price – of either Thailand or Vietnam. In the 17th century, assistance from the Nguyen lords of southern Vietnam was given on the condition that Vietnamese be allowed to settle in what is now the Mekong Delta region of Vietnam, at that time part of Cambodia and today still referred to by the Khmers as Kampuchea Krom (Lower Cambodia).

In the west, the Thais controlled the provinces of Battambang and Siem Reap from 1794; by the late 18th century they had firm control of the Cambodian royal family.

Saigon began life as humble Prey Nokor in the 17th century, a backwater of a Khmer port in what was then the eastern edge of Cambodia.

The Threat of Burma

Meanwhile, the so-called golden age of Ayuthaya was starting to lose its shine. In 1765, the Burmese laid siege to the city for two years and the capital fell. Everything sacred to the Thais was destroyed, including temples, manuscripts and religious sculpture. The Thais vented their frustrations on their Lao neighbours. If the 17th century had been Lan Xang's very own golden age, the first Lao unified kingdom began to unravel by the end of the century. The country split into the three kingdoms of Luang Prabang, Viang Chan (Vientiane) and Champasak.

Civil War in Vietnam

In a dress rehearsal for the tumultuous events of the 20th century, Vietnam found itself divided in half through much of the 17th and 18th centuries. It wasn't until the dawn of a new century, in 1802, that Nguyen Anh proclaimed himself Emperor Gia Long, thus beginning the Nguyen dynasty. For the first time in two centuries, Vietnam was united, with Hué as its new capital city.

1834

The Vietnamese take control of much of Cambodia during the reign of Emperor Minh Mang and begin a slow revolution to 'teach the barbarians their customs'.

1864

The French force Cambodia into a Treaty of Protectorate, which ironically does prevent the small kingdom being wiped off the map by its more powerful neighbours, Thailand and Vietnam.

1883

The French impose the Treaty of Protectorate on the Vietnamese, bringing together Tonkin in the north, Annam in the centre and Cochinchina in the south, marking the start of 70 years of colonial control.

1893

France gains sovereignty over all Lao territories east of the Mekong, thus consolidating its control over the Mekong region as part of its colony of Indochina.

The French Protectorate

Marco Polo was the first European to cross the Mekong and penetrate the east. In the following centuries many more Europeans followed in his wake, trading in ports as diverse as Ayuthaya and Faifo (Hoi An). However, it was France that was to ultimately claim much of the region as its own.

The concept of 'protectorate' was often employed as a smokescreen by European colonial powers in order to hide their exploitative agenda. However, for the weak and divided kingdoms of Cambodia and Laos, French intervention came not a moment too soon. Both were starting to feel the squeeze as expansionist Thailand and Vietnam carved up their territory. Were it not for the French, it is quite plausible that Cambodia and Laos would have gone the way of Champa, a mere footnote in history, a people without a homeland.

QUOC NGU

One of the most illustrious of the early missionaries was the brilliant French Jesuit Alexandre de Rhodes (1591–1660), widely lauded for his work in devising *quoc ngu*, the Latin-based phonetic alphabet in which Vietnamese is written to this day.

Indochine is Born

France's military activity in Vietnam began in 1847, when the French Navy attacked Danang harbour in response to Emperor Thieu Tri's suppression of Catholic missionaries. Saigon was seized in early 1859 and, in 1862, Emperor Tu Duc signed a treaty that gave the French the three eastern provinces of Cochinchina.

Cambodia succumbed to French military might in 1864, when French gunboats intimidated King Norodom I (r 1860–1904) into signing a Treaty of Protectorate. In Laos, the same technique was employed with much success. In 1893 a French warship forced its way up the Chao Phraya River to Bangkok and trained its guns on the palace. Under duress, the Siamese agreed to transfer all territory east of the Mekong to France and Laos became part of Indochina.

In 1883 the French attacked Hué and imposed the Treaty of Protectorate on the imperial court of Vietnam. The Indochinese Union proclaimed by the French in 1887 may have ended the existence of an independent Vietnamese state, but active resistance continued in various parts of the country for the duration of French rule.

Territorial Losses, Territorial Gains

The French were able to pressure Thailand into returning the northwest provinces of Battambang, Siem Reap and Sisophon to Cambodia in 1907, in return for concessions of Lao territory to the Thais, returning Angkor to Cambodian control for the first time in more than a century.

1907

French authorities negotiate the return of Siem Reap, Battambang and Preah Vihear to Cambodia, under Siamese control since 1794; Laos loses out as territory to the west of the Mekong is conceded in the deal.

1930

Ho Chi Minh establishes the Indochinese Communist Party; it splits into three national communist forces – the Viet Minh in Vietnam, the Khmer Rouge in Cambodia and the Pathet Lao in Laos.

1939

Following a nationalist coup by a pro-fascist military leadership, Siam changes its name to Thailand in an effort to cement control of the Thai peoples in the Mekong region, choosing to side with Japan in WWII.

1941

Japan sweeps through mainland Southeast Asia during WWII, occupying French Indochina in cooperation with pro-Vichy France colonial authorities and winning Thailand's support in return for the promise of territory.

Anglo-French Rivalry

Same old, same old: the English and French have been bickering since the dawn of time. With the British positioned in Burma and the French claiming Indochina, Thailand became a battleground in the struggle for influence.

The Thais are proud of their independent history and the fact they were never colonised. Successive Thai kings courted the Europeans while maintaining their neutrality. It was an ambiguous relationship, best summed up by King Mongkut: 'Whatever they have invented or done, we should know of and do, we can imitate and learn from them, but do not wholeheartedly believe in them.' In the end, it was less a success story for Thai manoeuvring that kept the country independent, but the realisation on the part of the British and the French that a buffer zone prevented open warfare.

One of the first Frenchmen to arrive in Laos was Henri Mouhot, an explorer and naturalist who died of malaria in 1861 near Luang Prabang (where his tomb can still be seen).

Independence Aspirations

Throughout the colonial period, a desire for independence simmered under the surface in Vietnam. Seething nationalist aspirations often erupted into open defiance of the French. Ultimately, the most successful of the anti-colonialists were the communists, who were able to tune into the frustrations and aspirations of the population and effectively channel their demands for fairer land distribution.

The Birth of Communism in Indochina

The story of communism in Indochina is complicated. Keeping it simple, the first Marxist grouping in Indochina was the Vietnam Revolutionary Youth League, founded by Ho Chi Minh in Canton, China, in 1925. This was succeeded in February 1930 by the Vietnamese Communist Party, part of the Indochinese Communist Party (ICP). In 1941, Ho formed the League for the Independence of Vietnam, much better known as the Viet Minh, which resisted the Japanese

FAVOURITES OF THE FRENCH

Vietnam was always the most important element of the colonial equation that was French Indochina. Economically it was the most productive and the French relied on the Vietnamese as administrators in both Cambodia and Laos in much the same way the British relied on the Indians in Burma and beyond. Vietnam developed under the French, while Cambodia and Laos languished. This was to set the pattern for power in Indochina for another century and ensured the Vietnamese were the dominant force in the anti-colonial movement.

1945

Ho Chi Minh proclaims Vietnamese independence on 2 September in Ba Dinh Sq in Hanoi, but the French have other ideas, sparking 30 years of warfare, first against the French, later the Americans.

1953

Cambodia and Laos go it alone with independence from France; almost insignificant sacrifices as the colonial power attempts to cling to control in Vietnam.

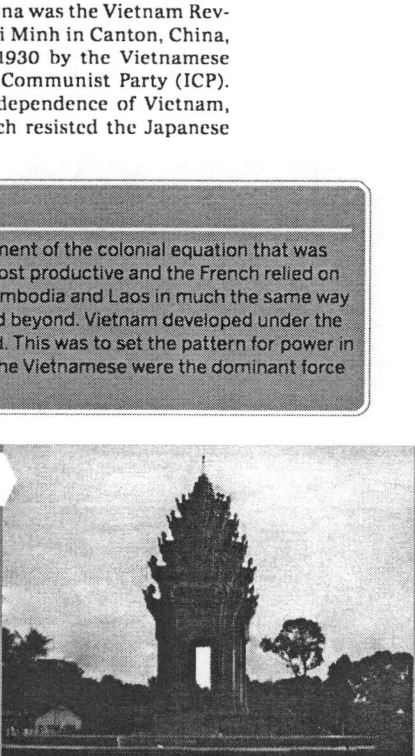

LYNN GAIL / LONELY PLANET IMAGES ©

» Independence Monument, Kompong Chhnang (p218), Cambodia

and carried out extensive political activities during WWII. Ho was pragmatic, patriotic and populist and understood the need for national unity.

WWII

Japanese forces occupied much of Asia, and Indochina was no exception. However, with many in France collaborating with the occupying Germans, the Japanese were happy to let these French allies control affairs.

The main force opposed to both the French and Japanese presence in Indochina was the Viet Minh, which meant Ho Chi Minh received assistance from the US government during this period. As events unfolded in Europe, the French and Japanese fell out and the Viet Minh saw its opportunity to strike.

As WWII drew to a close, the French returned, making the countries 'autonomous states within the French Union', but retaining de facto control. French general Jacques Philippe Leclerc pompously declared: 'We have come to reclaim our inheritance.' The end of the war had brought liberation for France, but not, it seemed, for its colonies.

FAMINE

As WWII drew to a close, Japanese rice requisitions, in combination with floods and breaches in the dikes, caused a horrific famine in which two million of northern Vietnam's 10 million people starved to death.

A False Dawn

By the spring of 1945, the Viet Minh controlled large parts of Vietnam, particularly in the north. On 2 September 1945 Ho Chi Minh declared independence. Throughout this period, Ho wrote no fewer than eight letters to US president Harry Truman and the US State Department asking for US aid, but received no replies.

In the north, Chinese Kuomintang troops were fleeing the Chinese communists and pillaging their way southward towards Hanoi. Ho tried to placate the Chinese, but as the months of Chinese occupation dragged on, he decided 'better the devil you know' and accepted a temporary return of the French.

SIAM REBORN AS THAILAND

Siam transformed itself from an absolute monarchy to a constitutional monarchy in a bloodless coup in 1932. Under nationalist military leader Phibul Songkhram, the country veered off in a fascist direction, changing its name to Thailand in 1939 and siding with the Japanese in WWII in order to seize back Cambodian and Lao territory returned to French Indochina in 1907.

Changing the name of the country from Siam to Thailand was a political masterstroke, as Siamese exclusivity was abolished and everyone was welcome to be a part of the new Thai family, including ethnic minorities and Laotians detached from their homeland by colonial intrigue.

1954

French forces surrender en masse to Viet Minh fighters at Dien Bien Phu on 7 May, marking the end of colonial rule in Indochina.

1955

Cambodia's King Sihanouk abdicates from the throne to enter a career in politics; he founds the Sangkum Reastr Niyum (People's Socialist Community) and wins the election with ease.

1956

Vietnam remains divided at the 17th Parallel into communist North Vietnam, under the leadership of Ho Chi Minh, and 'free' South Vietnam, under the rule of President Ngo Dinh Diem.

1959

The Ho Chi Minh Trail, which had been in existence for several years during the war against the French, reopens for business and becomes the main supply route to the South for the next 16 years.

War with the French

In the face of determined Vietnamese nationalism, the French proved unable to reassert their control. Despite massive US aid and the existence of significant indigenous anticommunist elements, it was an unwinnable war. As Ho said to the French at the time, 'You can kill 10 of my men for every one I kill of yours, but even at those odds you will lose and I will win.'

The whole complexion of the First Indochina War changed with the 1949 victory of communism in China. As Chinese weapons flowed to the Viet Minh, the French were forced onto the defensive. After eight years of fighting, the Viet Minh controlled much of Vietnam and neighbouring Laos. On 7 May 1954, after a 57-day siege, more than 10,000 starving French troops surrendered to the Viet Minh at Dien Bien Phu. This was a catastrophic defeat that brought an end to the French colonial adventure in Indochina. The following day, the Geneva Conference opened to negotiate an end to the conflict, but the French had no cards left to bring to the table.

Independence for Cambodia & Laos

In 1941 Admiral Jean Decoux placed 19-year-old Prince Norodom Sihanouk on the Cambodian throne, assuming he would be naive and pliable. As he grew in stature, this proved to be a major miscalculation. In 1953 King Sihanouk embarked on his 'royal crusade': his travelling campaign to drum up international support for his country's independence.

Independence was proclaimed on 9 November 1953 and recognised by the Geneva Conference of May 1954. In 1955 Sihanouk abdicated, afraid of being marginalised amid the pomp of royal ceremony. The 'royal crusader' became 'citizen Sihanouk' and vowed never again to return to the throne.

Laos was granted independence at the same time. The tragedy for Laos was that when, after two centuries, an independent Lao state was reborn, it was conceived in the nationalism of WWII, nourished during the agony of the First Indochina War, and born into the Cold War. From its inception, the Lao state was torn by ideological division, which the Lao tried mightily to overcome, but which was surreptitiously stoked by outside interference.

Between 1944 and 1945, the Viet Minh received funding and arms from the US Office of Strategic Services (OSS; the CIA today). When Ho Chi Minh declared independence in 1945, he had OSS agents at his side and borrowed liberally from the American Declaration of Independence.

Two Vietnams

After the Geneva Accords were signed and sealed, South Vietnam was ruled by Ngo Dinh Diem, a fiercely anticommunist Catholic. Nationwide elections were never held, as the Americans rightly feared that Ho Chi Minh would win easily. During the first few years of his rule, Diem

1962

The International Court rules in favour of Cambodia in the long-running dispute with Thailand over Preah Vihear, perched on the Dangkrek Mountains; it continues to create friction between the neighbours today.

1963

The assassination of President Diem in Vietnam sees Sihanouk lurch to the left in Cambodia in an attempt to distance himself from the USA; soon after US President Kennedy is assassinated.

1964

The US begins the secret bombing of Laos to try to disrupt North Vietnamese supplies to the guerrilla war in South Vietnam; Air America takes off, the CIA airline allegedly funded by opium and heroin smuggling.

1965

The first US marines wade ashore at Danang as the war in Vietnam hots up, the Americans committing ground troops to avoid the very real possibility of a communist victory.

consolidated power effectively. During Diem's 1957 official visit to the USA, President Eisenhower called him the 'miracle man' of Asia. As time went on Diem became increasingly tyrannical in dealing with dissent.

In the early 1960s, the South was rocked by anti-Diem unrest led by university students and Buddhist clergy. The US decided Diem was a liability and threw its support behind a military coup. A group of young generals led the operation in November 1963. Diem was to go into exile, but the generals got overexcited and both Diem and his brother were killed. He was followed by a succession of military rulers who continued his erratic policies and dragged the country deeper into war.

The War in Vietnam

The campaign to 'liberate' the South began in 1959 with the birth of the National Liberation Front (NLF), nicknamed the Viet Cong (VC) by the Americans. As the communists launched their campaign, the Diem government rapidly lost control of the countryside. In 1964, Hanoi began sending regular North Vietnamese Army (NVA) units down the Ho Chi Minh Trail. By early 1965, the Saigon government was on its last legs. Vietnam was the next domino and could not topple. It was clearly time for the Americans to 'clean up the mess', as one of Lyndon Johnson's leading officials put it.

The Americans Wade Ashore

For the first years of the conflict, the American military was boldly proclaiming victory upon victory, as the communist body count mounted. However, the Tet Offensive of 1968 brought an alternate reality into the homes of the average American. On the evening of 31 January, as Vietnam celebrated the Lunar New Year, the VC launched a series of strikes in more than 100 cities and towns, including Saigon. As the TV cameras rolled, a VC commando team took over the courtyard of the US embassy in central Saigon. The Tet Offensive killed about 1000 US soldiers and 2000 Army of the Republic of Vietnam (ARVN) troops, but VC losses were more than 10 times higher, at around 32,000 deaths. For the VC the Tet Offensive ultimately proved a success: it made the cost of fighting the war unbearable for the Americans.

Simultaneously, stories began leaking out of Vietnam about atrocities and massacres carried out by US forces against unarmed Vietnamese civilians, including the infamous My Lai Massacre. This helped turn the tide and a coalition of the concerned emerged that threatened the establishment. Antiwar demonstrations rocked American university campuses and spilled onto the streets.

THE WAR IN VIETNAM

For a human perspective on the North Vietnamese experience during the war, read *The Sorrow of War* by Bao Ninh, a poignant tale of love and loss that shows the soldiers from the North had the same fears and desires as most American GIs.

1968
The Viet Cong launches the Tet Offensive, a synchronised attack throughout the South that catches the Americans unaware. Iconic images of this are beamed into households all over the USA.

1969
US President Richard Nixon authorises the secret bombing of Cambodia as an extension of the war in Vietnam; the campaign continues until 1973, killing up to 250,000 Cambodians.

1970
Cambodia leader Norodom Sihanouk is overthrown in a coup engineered by his general Lon Nol and cousin Prince Sirik Matak, thus beginning Cambodia's bloody descent into civil war and genocide.

1973
All sides in the Vietnam conflict sign the Paris Peace Accords on 27 January 1973, supposedly bringing an end to the war in Vietnam, but its actually a face-saving deal for the US to 'withdraw with honour'.

Tricky Dicky's Exit Strategy

Richard Nixon was elected president in part because of a promise that he had a 'secret plan' to end the war. Nixon's strategy called for 'Vietnamisation', which meant making the South Vietnamese fight the war without US troops.

The 'Christmas bombing' of Haiphong and Hanoi at the end of 1972 was meant to wrest concessions from North Vietnam at the negotiating table. Eventually, the Paris Peace Accords were signed by the US, North Vietnam, South Vietnam and the VC on 27 January 1973, which provided for a ceasefire, the total withdrawal of US combat forces and the release of 590 US prisoners of war (POWs).

Hitch a ride with Michael Herr and his seminal work *Dispatches*. A correspondent for *Rolling Stone* magazine, Herr tells it how it is, as some of the darkest events of the war in Vietnam unfold around him, including the siege of Khe Sanh.

The End is Nigh

In January 1975 the North Vietnamese launched a massive ground attack across the 17th Parallel using tanks and heavy artillery. Whole brigades of ARVN soldiers disintegrated and fled southward, joining hundreds of thousands of civilians clogging Hwy 1. The North Vietnamese pushed on to Saigon and on the morning of 30 April 1975 their tanks smashed through the gates of Saigon's Independence Palace (now called Reunification Palace). The long war was over, Vietnam was reunited and Saigon was renamed Ho Chi Minh City.

Sideshow: the Civil War in Cambodia

The 1950s were seen as Cambodia's golden years and Sihanouk successfully maintained Cambodia's neutrality into the 1960s. However, the war

A 'SOLUTION' TO THE INDOCHINA PROBLEM

The Geneva Conference of 1954 was designed to end the conflict in Indochina, but the Vietnamese had done a good job of that with their comprehensive defeat of French forces at Dien Bien Phu. Resolutions included: the temporary division of Vietnam into two zones at the Ben Hai River (near the 17th Parallel); the free passage of people across the 17th Parallel for a period of 300 days; and the holding of nationwide elections on 20 July 1956.

Laos and Cambodia were broadly neglected. In Laos two northeastern provinces (Hua Phan and Phongsali) were set aside as regroupment areas for Pathet Lao ('Land of the Lao', or communist) forces. No such territory was set aside in Cambodia, so a group of 1000 Cambodian communists travelled north to Hanoi where they were to remain for the best part of two decades. When they returned to Cambodia to help the revolution in the early 1970s, most were purged under orders from Pol Pot who viewed them as ideologically contaminated by the Vietnamese.

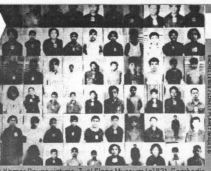

1975

The Khmer Rouge enters Phnom Penh on 17 April, implementing one of the bloodiest revolutions in history; North Vietnamese forces take Saigon on 30 April, renaming it Ho Chi Minh City; Vietnam is reunified.

RACHEL LEWIS / LONELY PLANET IMAGES ©

» Khmer Rouge victims, Tuol Sleng Museum (p182), Cambodia

1978

Vietnam invades Cambodia on Christmas Day in response to border attacks; the Khmer Rouge is overthrown weeks later; a decade-long war between communist 'brothers' begins.

in Vietnam was raging across the border and Cambodia was being slowly sucked into the vortex.

By 1969 the conflict between the Cambodian army and leftist rebels had become more serious, as the Vietnamese sought sanctuary deeper in Cambodia. In March 1970, while Sihanouk was on a trip to France, he was overthrown in a coup by General Lon Nol, his army commander. Sihanouk took up residence in Běijīng and formed an alliance with the Cambodian communists, nicknamed the Khmer Rouge (Red Khmer), who exploited this partnership to gain new recruits.

On 30 April 1970, US and South Vietnamese forces invaded Cambodia in an effort to flush out thousands of Viet Cong and North Vietnamese troops. The Vietnamese communists withdrew deeper into Cambodia.

For the full story on how Cambodia was sucked into hell, read *Sideshow: Kissinger, Nixon and the Destruction of Cambodia* by William Shawcross.

The Secret Bombing

In 1969, the US began a secret program of bombing suspected communist base camps in Cambodia. For the next four years, until bombing was halted by the US Congress in August 1973, huge areas of the eastern half of the country were carpet-bombed by US B-52s, killing thousands of civilians and turning hundreds of thousands more into refugees.

Despite massive US military and economic aid, Lon Nol never succeeded in gaining the initiative against the Khmer Rouge. Large parts of the countryside fell to the rebels and many provincial capitals were cut off from Phnom Penh. On 17 April 1975, Phnom Penh surrendered to the Khmer Rouge.

The Land of a Million Irrelevants

War correspondents covering the conflict in Indochina soon renamed Lan Xang, the land of a million irrelevants. However, the ongoing conflict was very relevant to the Cold War and the great powers were playing out their power struggles on this most obscure of stages. Successive governments came and went so fast they needed a revolving door in the national assembly.

During the US bombing of 1964–73, some 13 million tonnes of bombs – equivalent to 450 times the energy of the atomic bomb used on Hiroshima – were dropped on the Indochina region. This equates to 265kg for every man, woman and child in Vietnam, Cambodia and Laos.

Upcountry, large areas fell under the control of communist forces. The US sent troops to Thailand, in case communist forces attempted to cross the Mekong, and it looked for a time as if the major commitment of US troops in Southeast Asia would be to Laos rather than Vietnam. Both the North Vietnamese and the Americans were jockeying for strategic advantage, and neither was going to let Lao neutrality get in the way.

By mid-1972, when serious peace moves got underway, some four-fifths of the country was under communist control. Unlike Cambodia and Vietnam, the communists were eventually able to take power without a fight. City after city was occupied by the Pathet Lao and in August 1975 they marched into Vientiane unopposed.

1979

China invades northern Vietnam in February to 'punish' the Vietnamese for attacking Cambodia, but observers note that Chinese forces end up humiliated at the hands of the battle-hardened Vietnamese.

1986

Doi moi (economic reform), Vietnam's answer to *perestroika* and the first step towards re-engaging with the West, is launched with a rash of economic reforms.

1989

Vietnamese forces pull out of Cambodia in the face of dwindling support from the Soviet Union under the leadership of a reform-minded President Gorbachev; Vietnam is at peace for the first time in decades.

1991

The Paris Peace Accords are signed in which all Cambodian parties (including, controversially, the Khmer Rouge) agree to participate in free and fair elections supervised by the UN, held in 1993.

The Khmer Rouge & Year Zero

Upon taking Phnom Penh, the Khmer Rouge implemented one of the most radical and brutal restructurings of a society ever attempted; its goal was to transform Cambodia into a Maoist, peasant-dominated agrarian cooperative. Within days of the Khmer Rouge coming to power the entire population of the capital, including the sick, elderly and infirm, was forced to march out to the countryside. Disobedience of any sort often brought immediate execution. The advent of Khmer Rouge rule was proclaimed Year Zero. Currency was abolished and postal services were halted. The country was cut off from the outside world.

Author and documentary film-maker John Pilger was ripping into the establishment long before Michael Moore rode into town. Get to grips with his hard-hitting views on the war in Vietnam at www.johnpilger.com.

Counting the Cost of Genocide

It is still not known exactly how many Cambodians died at the hands of the Khmer Rouge during the three years, eight months and 20 days of its rule. Two million or one-third of the population is a realistic estimate.

Hundreds of thousands of people were executed by the Khmer Rouge leadership, while hundreds of thousands more died of famine and disease. Some zones were better than others, some leaders fairer than others, but life for the majority was one of unending misery and suffering. Cambodia had become a 'prison without walls', as some survivors referred to it at this time.

The Khmer Rouge detached the Cambodian people from all they held dear: their families, their food and their faith. Nobody cared for the Khmer Rouge by 1978, but nobody had an ounce of strength to fight back...except the Vietnamese.

The demise of the Khmer Rouge proved to be a false dawn, as the country was gripped by a disastrous famine that killed hundreds of thousands more who had struggled to survive the Khmer Rouge. Caught in the crossfire of Cold War politics, even the relief effort was about political point scoring and organisations had to choose whether

THE WAR IN VIETNAM IN NUMBERS

In total, 3.14 million Americans served in the US armed forces in Vietnam during the war. Officially, 58,183 Americans were killed or listed as missing in action. The direct cost of the war was officially put at US$165 billion, though its real cost to the economy was double that or more. A total of 223,748 South Vietnamese soldiers had been killed in action; North Vietnamese and VC fatalities have been estimated at one million. Approximately four million civilians (or 10% of the Vietnamese population) were injured or killed during the war.

1997
Southeast Asia experiences an economic crisis similar to the global crisis of 2009; Cambodia is convulsed by a coup and becomes a pariah once more; Laos and Myanmar (Burma) join Asean.

1998
Following a government push on the Khmer Rouge's last stronghold at Anlong Veng, Pol Pot passes away on 15 April 1998; rumours swirl around Phnom Penh about the circumstances of his death.

1999
Cambodia finally joins Asean after a two-year delay, taking its place among the family of Southeast Asian nations welcoming the country back to the world stage.

2000
Millennium fever grips the region as celebrations are held at iconic sites such as the temples of Angkor. Thankfully the millennium bug proves a false alarm.

to work with the UN and the 'free world' on the Thai border or the Vietnamese and their Soviet allies in Phnom Penh.

The Reunification of Vietnam

Vietnam may have been united, but it would take a long time to heal the scars of war. Damage from the fighting extended from unmarked minefields to war-focused, dysfunctional economies; from a chemically poisoned countryside to a population that had been physically or mentally battered. Peace may have arrived, but in many ways the war was far from over.

The party decided on a rapid transition to socialism in the South, but it proved disastrous for the economy. Reunification was accompanied by widespread political repression. Despite repeated promises to the contrary, hundreds of thousands of people who had ties to the previous regime had their property confiscated and were rounded up and imprisoned without trial in forced-labour camps, euphemistically known as re-education camps.

KHMER ROUGE MEMBERS

Several of the current crop of Cambodian leaders were previously members of the Khmer Rouge, including Prime Minister Hun Sen and Head of the Senate Chea Sim, although there is no evidence to implicate them in mass killings.

Brother Enemy

Relations with China to the north and its Khmer Rouge allies to the west were rapidly deteriorating and war-weary Vietnam seemed beset by enemies. An anti-capitalist campaign was launched in March 1978, seizing private property and businesses. Most of the victims were ethnic-Chinese – hundreds of thousands soon became refugees, known to the world as boat people, and relations with China soured further.

Meanwhile, repeated attacks on Vietnamese border villages by the Khmer Rouge forced Vietnam to respond. Vietnamese forces entered Cambodia on Christmas Day 1978. They succeeded in driving the Khmer Rouge from power on 7 January 1979 and set up a pro-Hanoi regime in Phnom Penh. China viewed the attack on the Khmer Rouge as a serious provocation. In February 1979, Chinese forces invaded Vietnam and fought a brief, 17-day war before withdrawing.

Liberation of Cambodia from the Khmer Rouge soon turned to occupation and a long civil war that drained both countries. However, Vietnam had succeeded in stamping its authority on Indochina. Promoted as the masters of the region under the French, the Vietnamese were once more dictating the political destiny of Cambodia and Laos.

Reversal of Fortune

The communist cooperatives in Indochina were a miserable failure and caused almost as much suffering as the wars that had preceded them. Pragmatic Laos was the first to liberalise in response to the economic stagnation, and private farming and enterprise were al-

2001

Thaksin Shinawatra becomes prime minister of Thailand after his party, Thai Rak Thai (Thai Love Thai), sweeps the elections, setting the country on a divisive course.

2004

King Sihanouk abdicates from the throne in Cambodia, closing the chapter on 63 years as monarch, politician and statesman, and is succeeded by his son King Sihamoni.

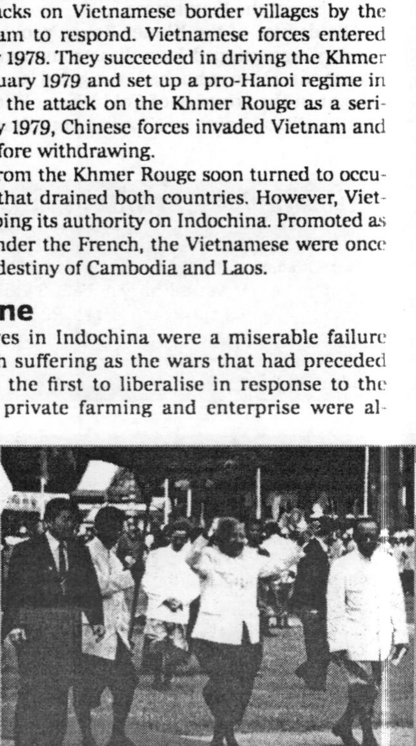

RICHARD I'ANSON / LONELY PLANET IMAGES ©

» King Sihanouk (p265) in Phnom Penh, Cambodia

lowed as early as 1979. However, the changes came too late for the Lao royal family and the last king and queen are believed to have died of malnutrition and disease in a prison camp sometime in the late 1970s. Vietnam was slower to evolve, but the arrival of President Mikhail Gorbachev in the Soviet Union meant *glasnost* (openness) and *perestroika* (restructuring) were in, radical revolution was out. *Doi moi* (economic reforms) were experimented with in Cambodia and introduced to Vietnam. As the USSR scaled back its commitments to the communist world, the far-flung outposts were the first to feel the pinch. The Vietnamese decided to unilaterally withdraw from Cambodia in 1989, as they could no longer afford the occupation. The party in Vietnam was on its own and needed to reform to survive. Cambodia and Laos would follow its lead.

Francois Bizot was kidnapped by the Khmer Rouge, interrogated by Comrade Duch and is believed to be the only foreigner to have been released. Later he was holed up in the French embassy in April 1975. Read his harrowing story in *The Gate*.

A New Beginning

You may be wondering what happened to Thailand in all of this? Well, compared with the earth-shattering events unfolding in Indochina, things were rather dull. Thailand profited as its neighbours suffered, providing air bases and logistical support to the Americans during the war in Vietnam. As the war and revolution consumed a generation in Cambodia, Laos and Vietnam, Thailand's economy prospered and democracy slowly took root, although coups remain common currency right up to the present day. The financial crisis of 1997 shook the country's confidence. More recently, the leadership of billionaire tycoon Thaksin Shinawatra proved very divisive, provoking the military to seize power in 2006. And the south has been gripped by an Islamic insurgency that has claimed hundreds of lives.

Cambodia was welcomed back to the world stage in 1991 with the signing of the Paris Peace Accords, which set out a UN roadmap to free and fair elections. There have been many hiccups along the way, including coups and a culture of impunity, but Cambodia has come a long way

THE SECRET WAR IN LAOS

Before his assassination in 1963, President John F Kennedy gave the order to recruit a force of 11,000 Hmong under the command of Vang Pao. They were trained by several hundred US and Thai Special Forces advisors and supplied by Air America, all under the supervision of the CIA. The secret war had begun.

In 1964 the US began its air war over Laos. According to official figures, the US dropped 2,093,100 tons of bombs in 580,944 sorties. The total cost was US$7.2 billion, or US$2 million a day for nine years. No one knows how many people died, but one-third of the population of 2.1 million became internal refugees.

2006

Vietnam's international rehabilitation is finally complete as it plays host to the glitzy APEC summit, welcoming President George Bush, and formally joins the World Trade Organisation.

2008

Thailand hits the headlines as anti-Thaksin demonstrators occupy the airport, causing mayhem for travellers.

2009

The global economic crisis continues to impact on the region with job losses in the export-dependent countries, shrinking investment, collapsing property prices and uncertain times ahead.

2010

Bangkok is rocked by protests and street violence. Red Shirts occupy the city centre for two months before the army moves in, leading to the deaths or disappearances of 90 people.

from the dark days of the Khmer Rouge. Democracy is hardly flourishing, corruption most certainly is, but life is better for many than it has been for a long time. Attempts to bring the surviving Khmer Rouge leadership to trial continue to stumble along.

Jon Swain's *River of Time* (1995) takes the reader back to an old Indochina, partly lost to the madness of war, and includes first-hand accounts of the French embassy stand-off in the first days of the Khmer Rouge takeover.

Vietnam has followed the Chinese road to riches, taking the brakes off the economy while keeping a firm hand on the political steering wheel. With only two million paid-up members of the Communist Party and around 90 million Vietnamese, it is a road they must follow carefully. However, the economy has been booming and Vietnam's rehabilitation was complete when it joined the World Trade Organisation (WTO) in 2006.

And what of Laos? Still irrelevant to most, but that is wonderful news for visitors who are discovering a slice of older Asia. Hydroelectric power is a big industry and looks set to subsidise the economy in the future. On the flip side, illegal logging remains a major problem, as in Cambodia, with demand for timber in China, Thailand and Vietnam driving the destruction. Tourism has good prospects and Laos is carving a niche for itself as the ecotourism destination of Southeast Asia.

Like the river that binds them, the countries of the Mekong region have a turbulent past and an uncertain future.

2010

The Prime Minister of the Lao PDR, Bouasone Bouphavanh, resigns after more than four years in office, catching political observers off-guard.

2011

Cambodia and Thailand trade blows over the ancient border temple of Prasat Preah Vihear on the Dangkrek Mountains; Asean attempts to broker a lasting settlement.

JOHN ELK III / LONELY PLANET IMAGES ©

» Prasat Preah Vihear (p229)

2011

Protests against China erupt across Vietnam as tensions continue to simmer over the disputed Spratly Islands in the South China Sea.

Ancient Wonders

Historic Cities of Vietnam »
Cambodia, Kingdom of Temples »
Timeless Treasures of Old Laos »
Royal Capitals of Old Siam »

© GLENN BEANLAND / LONELY PLANET IMAGES

Seated Buddha, Ayuthaya (p476), Thailand

Historic Cities of Vietnam

A powerful Cham kingdom once ruled Central Vietnam from My Son. Later Hué became the imperial capital and nearby Hoi An provided a cosmopolitan trade gateway to the wider world.

Hoi An

Discover the historic heart of Hoi An (p107), a centuries-old Vietnamese trading port that has played home to Chinese, Japanese, Dutch, Portuguese and French merchants. The city's beautiful blend of architecture reveals the layers of history here, as successive powers struggled to exert their influence. Spared the ravages of war, Hoi An is now a worthy World Heritage Site and is the most popular stop on the Vietnamese coast.

The Chinese kept their culture alive in the assembly halls and temples that dot the town, reflecting the diverse make-up of the Middle Kingdom. The Japanese bequeathed a classic covered bridge which remains in use today, while the French left their graceful architecture. All of this added up to Hoi An specialising in fusion long before the new generation of gastronomes came to town. Many of the old houses have been preserved to offer a glimpse into the 19th-century life of merchants in old Faifo, as it was once known.

My Son

While the Chams may not have been quite the audacious architects the ancient Khmers were, they certainly knew about beautiful brickwork. Controlling an empire that covered much of south and central Vietnam, the centre of spiritual life was in My Son (p114) when the political capital was in nearby Tra Kieu (Simhapura). Set under the shadow of Cat's Tooth Mountain, the principal temples suffered greatly at the

ANDERS BLOMQVIST / LONELY PLANET IMAGES ©

ANDERS BLOMQVIST / LONELY PLANET IMAGES ©

Clockwise from top left

1. Citadel (p95), Hué 2. Japanese Covered Bridge (p108), Hoi An 3. Cham temple, My Son (p114)

hands of American attacks, but are slowly being restored to their former glory.

The brickwork, later carved and coated in stucco or plaster, is brilliant. Many of the temples would have been finished in gold leaf and must have been an inspiring and imposing sight for pilgrims of old. Modern pilgrims in the shape of tourists travel here today. Arrive early in the morning or late in the afternoon for a more reflective experience.

Hué

Hué (p95) is the intellectual, cultural and spiritual heart of Vietnam. Hué served as the political capital from 1802 to 1945 under the 13 emperors of the Nguyen dynasty. Today Hué's decaying, opulent tombs of the Nguyen emperors and grand, crumbling Citadel comprise a Unesco World Heritage Site.

One of Vietnam's decaying treasures is Hué's Citadel (Kinh Thanh), the erstwhile imperial city on the northern bank of the Song Huong. Construction of the moated Citadel, by Emperor Gia Long, began in 1804. The emperor's official functions were carried out in the Imperial Enclosure, a 'citadel within the Citadel'. Within the Imperial Enclosure is the Forbidden Purple City (Tu Cam Thanh), which was reserved for the private life of the emperor.

Set like royal crowns on the banks of the Song Huong, the tombs of the Nguyen dynasty are an impressive sight. The Tomb of Tu Duc is a majestic site, laced with frangipani and pine trees and set alongside a small lake. The buildings are beautifully designed. The most majestic of the Royal Tombs is the Tomb of Minh Mang, who ruled from 1820 to 1840. This tomb is renowned for its architecture, which blends harmoniously into the natural surroundings.

Cambodia, Kingdom of Temples

While Angkor steals the headlines for obvious reasons (Angkor Wat and Bayon for starters), Cambodia is littered with striking structures from the heyday of the Khmer empire including Koh Ker and Prasat Preah Vihear.

The Temples of Angkor

Heaven on earth, Angkor is the abode of ancient Hindu gods cast in stone. Here you'll find an embarrassment of riches to rival those of the ancient Egyptians of Luxor. The Cambodian god kings of old each strove to better their ancestors in size and scale, culminating in the world's largest religious building, Angkor Wat (p208), and one of the world's weirdest, the Bayon (p209). The hundreds of temples surviving today are but the sacred skeleton of the vast political, religious and social centre of an empire that stretched from Myanmar (Burma) to Vietnam. Here was a city which, at its zenith, boasted a population of one million, a megalopolis of the ancient world.

The temples of Angkor are the heart and soul of the Kingdom of Cambodia, a source of inspiration and national pride to all Khmers as they struggle to rebuild their lives after years of terror and trauma. Today, they are a point of pilgrimage for all Cambodians and no visitor should miss their legendary beauty when passing through the region.

Prasat Preah Vihear

The imposing mountain temple of Prasat Preah Vihear (p229) has the most dramatic location of all of the Angkorian monuments, perched atop the cliff face of Cambodia's Dangkrek Mountains. The views from this most mountainous of temple mountains are breathtaking: lowland Cambodia stretching

KRIS LEBOUTILLIER / GETTY ©

TOM COCKREM / LONELY PLANET IMAGES ©

Clockwise from top left
1. Temple at Koh Ker (p230) 2. Angkor Wat (p208)
3. Prasat Preah Vihear (p229)

as far as the eye can see, and the holy mountain of Phnom Kulen (p217) looming in the distance. The foundation stones of the temple stretch to the edge of the cliff as it falls precipitously away to the plains below.

Known as Prasat Phra Viharn by the Thais, Preah Vihear means 'Sacred Monastery' in Khmer and it was an important place of pilgrimage during the Angkorian period. The 300-year chronology of its construction also offers the visitor an insight into the metamorphosis of carving and sculpture during the Angkor period and there are some impressive touches, including a rendition of the Churning of the Ocean of Milk, later so perfectly mastered at Angkor Wat.

Koh Ker

The history of Cambodia is riven with dynastic spats and political intrigue. One of the most memorable came in the 10th century when Jayavarman IV (r 928–42) threw his toys out of the pram, stormed off to the northeast and established the rival capital of Koh Ker (p230). Koh Ker was the capital for just 15 years, but Jayavarman IV was determined to legitimise his rule through a prolific building program that left a legacy of 30 major temples and some gargantuan sculpture that is on display in the National Museum (p182) in Phnom Penh.

The most striking structure at Koh Ker is Prasat Thom, a seven-storey step pyramid, appearing more Mayan than Khmer, with commanding views over the surrounding forest. Nearby is Prasat Krahom (Red Temple), named after the pinkish Banteay Srei–style stone from which it is built.

2

Timeless Treasures of Old Laos

Laos often feels like a destination lost in time and nowhere is this more palpable than in languid Luang Prabang. Elsewhere lies the enigmatic Plain of Jars and striking Khmer temple of Wat Phu Champasak.

Luang Prabang

Languid and lovely, a visit to lush Luang Prabang (p298) is like travelling back in time to the Asia of old. Dormant for decades, the town survived warfare and communism to emerge as a wonderful living example of a French-colonial town, complete with historic wat and traditional Lao houses. Laos moves at its own pace and seductive Luang Prabang is no exception. Many come for a few days but stay for a few weeks.

The sweeping roof of Wat Xieng Thong (p300) is the most striking of more than 30 ancient temples. Every morning the streets are ablaze with saffron as a stream of monks seeking alms spills out of the wat – an iconic image of Indochina. The Mekong River is a beautiful backdrop for this World Heritage-listed town and it's the perfect way to reach the Pak Ou Caves (p298), a royal repository for thousands of precious Buddha images. Luang Prabang may not be as ancient as some, but this historic town is an absolute wonder.

Wat Phu Champasak

The ancient Khmer religious complex of Wat Phu Champasak (p343) is one of the archaeological highlights of Laos. Stretching 1400m up to the slopes of the Phu Pasak range (also known more colloquially as Phu Khuai or Mt Penis), Wat Phu Champasak is small compared with the monumental Angkor-era sites near Siem Reap in

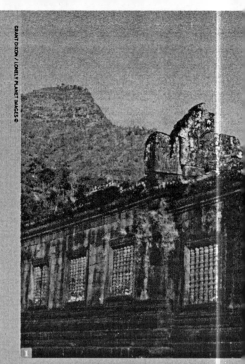

Clockwise from top left
1. Wat Phu Champasak (p343) 2. Wat Xieng Thong (p300), Luang Prabang 3. Plain of Jars (p317), Xieng Khuang Province

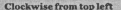

GRANT DIXON / LONELY PLANET IMAGES ©

1

GRANT DIXON / LONELY PLANET IMAGES ©

3

KYLIE MCLAUGHLIN / LONELY PLANET IMAGES ©

2

Cambodia. However, you know the adage about location, location, location – the tumbledown pavilions, ornate Shiva linga sanctuary, enigmatic crocodile stone and tall trees that shroud much of the site in soothing shade add up to give Wat Phu Champasak an almost mystical atmosphere. Unesco declared the complex a World Heritage Site in 2001.

Sanskrit inscriptions and Chinese sources confirm the site has been a place of worship since the 6th century. The temple complex was designed as a worldly imitation of heaven and fitted into a larger plan that evolved to include a network of roads, cities, settlement and other temples. What you see today is the product of centuries of building, rebuilding, alteration and addition, with the most recent structures dating from the late-Angkorian period.

Plain of Jars

Among the most enigmatic sights in Laos, the Plain of Jars (p314) is proof that history remains a mystery in some parts of the Mekong region. Scattered across a plain near Phonsavan (p314) are hundreds of stone jars in many shapes and sizes. Archaeologists continue to debate their function, and theories range from sarcophagi to wine fermenters to rice storage jars.

Nobody really knows how old these curious jars are or where they came from, but they may be linked to the strange stone megaliths in Sam Neua Province. Locals claim they are 2000 years old and have their own explanation for their origin. In the 6th century, the Lao-Thai hero Khun Jeuam travelled to the area to overthrow the cruel despot Chao Angka. To celebrate his victory, locals believe he had hundreds of jars constructed for the fermentation of rice wine. It must have been some party.

Royal Capitals of Old Siam

As Angkor declined, so rose the kingdom of Siam. Its first capital was founded at Sukhothai (Land of Rising Happiness) before moving to a golden age at the court of Ayuthaya.

Sukhothai

Thailand's first capital in the 13th century, Sukhothai (p404) is a World Heritage Site. The site includes the remains of 21 temples within the ancient walls of the *meuang gòw* (old city), and the art and architecture are considered to be the most classic of Thai styles. The city flourished for 200 years and the first Thai script dates from this period.

The graceful architecture of Sukhothai is epitomised by the classic lotus bud stupa, but there are shades of Sri Lanka and Srivijaya in some of the stupas. The largest wat is impressive Wat Mahathat (p405), but Khmer temples such at Wat Si Sawai (p405) suggest this was a spiritual centre long before the Thais established their capital here.

Ayuthaya

The urban setting might be pretty ordinary in comparison with the Angkors and Sukhothais of the region, but Ayuthaya is undoubtedly on the historical A-list of the Mekong region. Eclipsing Sukhothai in the 14th century, this was the glittering capital of the Thai kingdom for more than 400 years, until the Burmese managed to finish what they had started centuries earlier and sacked the capital in 1767.

The historical park includes dozens of temples scattered throughout the town of Ayuthaya. Wat Phra Si Sanphet was once the largest temple here and has an iconic line-up of *chedi*, which draw the crowds. The Burmese left little standing at Wat Phra Mahathat, but this is one of the most photographed places in Thailand thanks to an ancient Buddha head caught in the embrace of a tentacle-like tree root.

Below
Gold Buddha, Ayuthaya

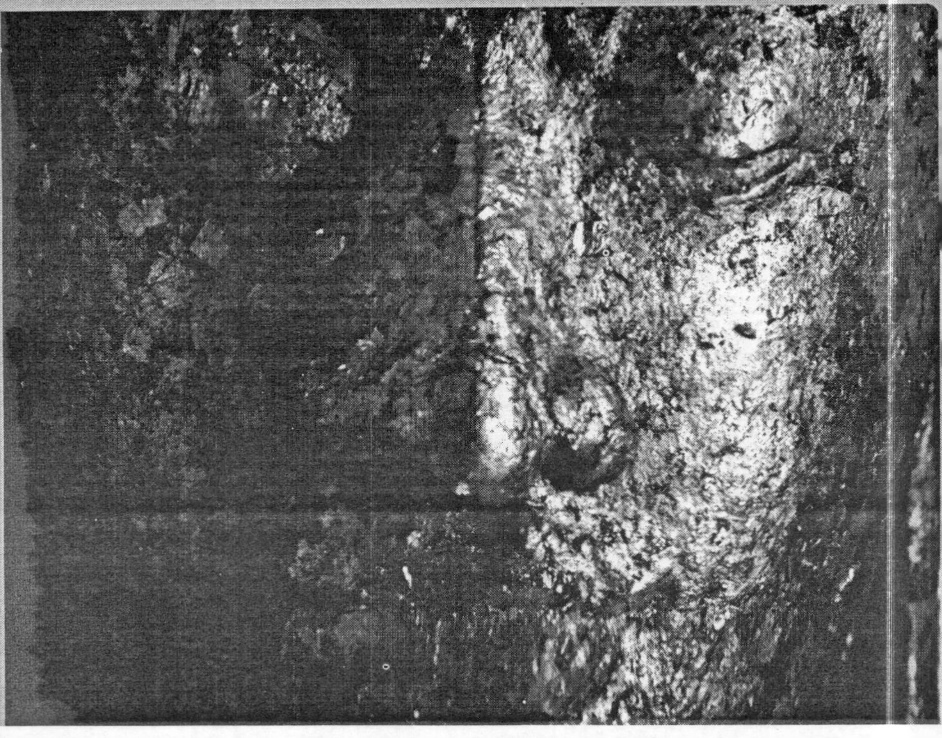

Mekong Region Culture

The Mekong region is not known as Indochina for nothing. Geographically it is the land in between India and China, and culturally it has absorbed influences from both of these mighty civilisations. This is where two of the world's greatest cultures collide. China has shaped the destiny of Vietnam and Yúnnán and continues to cast a shadow over the Mekong region. India exported its great religions, language, culture and sculpture to Cambodia, Laos and Thailand. The border between Vietnam and Cambodia is as significant a sociocultural border as the Himalaya range is a formidable physical barrier between the great rivals of China and India. It is the divide between Sino-Asia to the east and Indo-Asia to the west.

Cambodia was the cultural staging post for the Indianisation of the Mekong region. Indian traders brought Hinduism and Buddhism around the 2nd century and with it came the religious languages of Sanskrit and Pali; Sanskrit forming the root of modern Khmer, Lao

JEAN PIERRE LESCOURRET / LONELY PLANET IMAGES ©

Young novice monks, Chiang Mai (p389), Thailand

and Thai. They also brought their art and architecture, which was redefined so effectively by the ancient Khmers before spreading into Laos and Thailand. Vietnam, meanwhile, was occupied by China for more than a thousand years and, like the Indians, the Chinese brought with them their religion, philosophy and culture. Confucianism and Taoism were introduced and still form the backbone of Vietnamese religion, together with Buddhism.

With a millennium or more of influence from two of the world's most successful civilisations, it is hardly surprising to find such a dynamic variety of culture in the Mekong region today.

KINH

The Mekong region is home to around 85 million Kinh, most living in Vietnam, Cambodia and Laos.

People

As empires came and went, so too did the populations, and many of the countries in the Mekong region are far less ethnically homogenous than their governments would have us believe. It wasn't only local empire building that had an impact, but colonial meddling, which left a number of people stranded beyond their borders. There are Lao and Khmer in Thailand, Khmer in Vietnam, Thai (Dai) in Vietnam and Chinese everywhere. No self-respecting Mekong town would be complete without a Chinatown and in many of the major cities in the region, people of Chinese ancestry may make up as much as half of the population.

The mountains of the Mekong region provide a home for a mosaic of minority groups, often referred to as hill tribes. Many of these groups migrated from China and Tibet and have settled in areas that lowlanders considered too challenging to cultivate. Colourful costumes and unique traditions draw increasing numbers of visitors to their mountain homes. The most popular areas to visit local hill tribes include Mondulkiri (p242) and Ratanakiri (p238) provinces in Cambodia, Luang Nam Tha (p322) and Muang Sing (p325) in northern Laos, Chiang Mai (p389) and Chiang Rai (p407) in northern Thailand, and Sapa (p91) and Bac Ha (p89) in northern Vietnam

Around 18 million Khmers live in Cambodia, Thailand and Vietnam.

Population growth varies throughout the Mekong region. Developed Thailand embraced family planning decades ago and Vietnam has adopted a Chinese model of sorts with a two-child policy in lowland areas. Cambodia and Laos have the highest birth rates and large families remain the rule rather than the exception out in the countryside.

Chinese

Many of the great cities of the Mekong region have significant Chinese communities and in the case of capitals like Bangkok and Phnom Penh, people of at least some Chinese ancestry may make up half the population. The Chinese are much more integrated in the Mekong region than

FACE IT

Face, or more importantly the art of not making the locals lose face, is an important concept to understand in Asia. Face is all in Asia, and in the Mekong region it is above all. Having 'big face' is synonymous with prestige. All families, even poor ones, are expected to have big wedding parties and throw their money around like it is water in order to gain face. This is often ruinously expensive but far less important than 'losing face'. And it is for this reason that foreigners should never lose their tempers with the ...cals; this will bring unacceptable 'loss of face' to the individual involved and end any ...e of a sensible solution to the dispute. Take a deep breath and keep your cool. If ...n't always going according to plan, remember that in countries like Cambo... tourism is a relatively new industry.

in places like Indonesia, and continue to contribute to the economy through investment and initiative. With one eye on history, the Vietnamese are more suspicious of the Chinese than most.

Kinh (Vietnamese)

Despite the Chinese view that the Vietnamese are 'the ones that got away', the Vietnamese existed in the Red River Delta area long before the first waves of Chinese arrived some 2000 years ago. The Kinh make up about 90% of the population of Vietnam. Centuries ago, the Vietnamese began to push southwards in search of cultivable land and swallowed the kingdom of Champa before pushing on into the Mekong Delta and picking off pieces of a decaying Khmer empire. As well as occupying the coastal regions of Vietnam, the lowland Kinh have been moving into the mountains to take advantage of new opportunities in agriculture, industry and tourism.

There are around 12 million Lao people living across the Mekong region, in Laos, Thailand and Cambodia.

Khmer (Cambodian)

The Khmer have inhabited Cambodia since the beginning of recorded history around the 2nd century AD, long before the Thais and Vietnamese arrived in the southern Mekong region. During the subsequent centuries, the culture of Cambodia was influenced by contact with the civilisations of India and Java. During the glory years of Angkor, Hinduism was the predominant religion, but from the 15th century Theravada Buddhism was adopted and most Khmers remain devoutly Buddhist today, their faith an important anchor in the struggle to rebuild their lives. The Cambodian population went to hell and back during the years of Khmer Rouge rule and it is believed that as much as one-third of the population perished as a direct result of their brutal policies.

Lao

Laos is often described as less a nation-state than a conglomeration of tribes and languages. The Lao traditionally divide themselves into four broad families – Lao Loum, Lao Thai, Lao Thoeng and Lao Soung – roughly defined by the altitude at which they live and their cultural proclivities. The Lao government has an alternative three-way split, in which the Lao Thai are condensed into the Lao Loum group. This triumvirate is represented on the back of every 1000 kip bill, in national costume, from left to right: Lao Soung, Lao Loum and Lao Thoeng.

Thai

Thais make up about 75% of the population of Thailand, although this group is commonly broken down into four subgroups: Central Thais or Siamese who inhabit the Chao Praya delta, the Thai Lao of northeastern Thailand, the Pak Thai of southern Thailand, and northern Thais. Each group speaks its own dialect and to a certain extent practises customs unique to its region. Politically and economically, the Central Thais are the dominant group, although they barely outnumber the Thai Lao.

Foreign ethnographers who have carried out field research in Laos have identified anywhere from 49 to 132 different ethnic groups.

Minority Groups

There are many other important minority groups in the region, some rendered stateless by the conflicts of the past, others recent migrants to the region, including the many hill tribes.

CHAM

The Cham people originally occupied the kingdom of Champa in south-central Vietnam and their beautiful brick towers dot the landscape from Danang to Phan Rang. Victims of a historical squeeze between Cambodia and Vietnam, their territory was eventually annexed by the expansionist Vietnamese. Originally Hindu, they converted to Islam in the 16th and 17th centuries and many migrated to Cambodia. Today there are small numbers of Cham in Vietnam and as many as half a million in Cambodia, all of whom continue to practise a flexible form of Islam. The Cham population has intermarried over the centuries with migrating Malay seafarers, introducing an additional ethnic background into the mix.

HMONG

The Mekong region is home to around 45 million Thais, concentrated in Thailand, Laos, Vietnam and Yúnnán.

THAIS

The Hmong are one of the largest hill tribes in the Mekong region, spread through much of northern Laos, northern Vietnam and Thailand. As some of the last to arrive in the region in the 19th century, Darwinian selection ensured that they were left with the highest and harshest lands from which to eke out their existence. They soon made the best of a bad deal and opted for opium cultivation, which brought them into conflict with mainstream governments during the 20th century.

Hmong groups are usually classified by their colourful clothing, including Black Hmong, White Hmong, Red Hmong and so on. The brightest group is the Flower Hmong of northwest Vietnam, living in villages around Bac Ha (p89). There may be as many as one million Hmong in the Mekong region, half of them living in the mountains of Vietnam.

DZAO

The Dzao (also known as Yao or Dao) are one of the largest and most colourful ethnic groups in Vietnam and are also found in Laos, Thailand and Yúnnán. The Dzao practise ancestor worship of spirits, or *ban ho* (no relation to Uncle Ho), and hold elaborate rituals with sacrifices of pigs and chickens. The Dzao are famous for their elaborate dress. Women's clothing typically features intricate weaving and silver-coloured beads and coins – the wealth of a woman is said to be in the weight of the coins she carries. Their long flowing hair, shaved above the forehead, is tied up into a large red or embroidered turban, a sort of skinhead meets Sikh combination.

KAREN

The Karen are the largest hill tribe in Thailand, numbering more than 300,000. There are four distinct groups, the Skaw Karen (White Karen), Pwo Karen, Pa-O Karen (Black Karen) and Kayah Karen (Red Karen). Unmarried women wear white and kinship remains matrilineal. Most Karen live in lowland valleys and practise crop rotation.

Economy

Life for many in the Mekong region has undergone a profound transition in the space of a generation, even if the politics hasn't always come along for the ride. Laos and Vietnam are one-party states which tolerate no opposition. But communism, the mantra for a generation, has taken a back seat to capitalism and the rush to embrace the market. The result is a contradictory blend of ultraliberal economics and ultraconservative politics that has left many inhabitants confused about the country in which they live. They have the freedom to make money but not the basic freedom to voice a political opinion. And the more the average person engages with the outside world – through business, tourism, the internet – the harder this paradox is to swallow.

Corruption remains a cancer throughout the Mekong region. Despite the best intentions of a small minority, the worst intentions of many a politician continues to cost the Mekong countries hundreds of millions of dollars in lost assets. Vietnam has started tackling corruption head on with high-profile executions and prison sentences. Senior party officials have even been put away, but cronyism and nepotism remain alive and well. Laos suffers from corruption, but the small size of the economy has kept enrichment to a minimum for now.

In Cambodia, corruption has been elevated to an art form. When James Wolfensohn, then head of the World Bank, visited Cambodia in 2005 and was asked to sum up the country's problems in three words, his answer was succinct: 'Corruption, corruption, corruption.' Thailand has long suffered from corruption, but Thaksin Shinawatra created a new blend by mixing business and politics to turn the country into 'Shinawatra Plc'. Ultimately it backfired and he was overthrown, but now his younger sister Yingluck Shinawatra has taken the reins of power, it could be business as usual again.

Since shaking off the shadow of Marxist theory, the economies of the Mekong region have been some of the fastest growing in the world. As the global economic crisis continues to unfold, nobody is certain what is in store for the export-oriented region. The Mekong countries were quick to plug themselves into the global economy and now they are likely to share the shock of its continuing collapse. However, the impact may be mild compared to the West, with the economies having to settle for sluggish growth rather than experiencing a full-blown recession. For now their fate is tied to that of the rest of the world, although China may unseat the US as the model of choice for sound economic management in the region.

Thailand is the regional powerhouse with a strong economy underpinned by manufacturing, handicrafts, tourism and agriculture. Vietnam is fast catching up and, like Thailand, is now a major manufacturing centre for automotive assembly and hi-tech gadgetry. Agriculture remains a major industry, with Thailand and Vietnam going head to head for the title of world's largest rice exporter.

The economies of Cambodia and Laos are much smaller by comparison. Cambodia relies heavily on the textile industry and tourism to drive its economy, but agro-industries such as rubber and palm oil

CAO DAISM

A fascinating fusion of East and West, Cao Daism (Dai Dao Tam Ky Pho Do) is a syncretic religion born in 20th-century Vietnam that contains elements of Buddhism, Confucianism, Taoism, native Vietnamese spiritualism, Christianity and Islam – as well as a dash of secular enlightenment thrown in for good measure. The term Cao Dai (meaning high tower or palace) is a euphemism for God. There are an estimated two to three million followers of Cao Daism worldwide.

Cao Daism was founded by the mystic Ngo Minh Chieu (also known as Ngo Van Chieu; born 1878), who began receiving revelations in which the tenets of Cao Dai were set forth.

All Cao Dai temples observe four daily ceremonies: at 6am, noon, 6pm and midnight. If all this sounds like just what you've been waiting for, read more on the official Cao Dai site: www.caodai.org. The most impressive Cao Dai temple is at Tay Ninh (p150), near Ho Chi Minh City.

For a virtual tour of Thai Buddhist architecture around the region, visit www.orientalarchitecture.com/directory.htm.

are growing fast and traditional agriculture and fishing remain very important to the average person. In Laos, the export of hydropower is big business and, if not too contradictory, ecotourism is one of the fastest growing sectors.

Religion

The dominant religions of Southeast Asia have absorbed many traditional animistic beliefs of spirits, ancestor worship and the power of the celestial planets in bringing about good fortune. The Mekong region's spiritual connection to the realm of magic and miracles commands more respect, even among intellectual circles, than the remnants of paganism in Western Christianity. Locals erect spirit houses in front of their homes, while ethnic Chinese set out daily offerings to their ancestors, and almost everyone visits the fortune teller.

Although the majority of the population has only a vague notion of Buddhist doctrines, they invite monks to participate in life-cycle ceremonies, such as funerals and weddings. Buddhist pagodas are seen by many as a physical and spiritual refuge from an uncertain world.

Ancestor Worship

Ancestor worship dates from long before the arrival of Confucianism or Buddhism. Ancestor worship is based on the belief that the soul lives on after death and becomes the protector of its descendants. Because of the influence the spirits of one's ancestors exert on the living, it is considered not only shameful for them to be upset or restless, but downright dangerous.

Animism

Both Hinduism and Buddhism fused with the animist beliefs already present in the Mekong region before Indianisation. Local beliefs didn't

THE LUNAR CALENDAR

Astrology has a long history in China and Vietnam (plus in the Chinese communities of Cambodia, Laos and Thailand), and is intricately linked to religious beliefs. There are 12 zodiacal animals, each of which represents one year in a 12-year cycle. If you want to know your sign, look up your year of birth in the following chart. Don't forget that the Chinese/Vietnamese New Year falls in late January or early February. If your birthday is in the first half of January, it will be included in the zodiac year before the calendar year of your birth. To check the Gregorian (solar) date corresponding to a lunar date, pick up any Vietnamese or Chinese calendar.

Rat (generous, social, insecure, idle) 1924, 1936, 1948, 1960, 1972, 1984, 1996, 2008

Cow (stubborn, conservative, patient) 1925, 1937, 1949, 1961, 1973, 1985, 1997, 2009

Tiger (creative, brave, overbearing) 1926, 1938, 1950, 1962, 1974, 1986, 1998, 2010

Rabbit (timid, affectionate, amicable) 1927, 1939, 1951, 1963, 1975, 1987, 1999, 2011

Dragon (egotistical, strong, intelligent) 1928, 1940, 1952, 1964, 1976, 1988, 2000, 2012

Snake (luxury seeking, secretive, friendly) 1929, 1941, 1953, 1965, 1977, 1989, 2001

Horse (emotional, clever, quick thinker) 1930, 1942, 1954, 1966, 1978, 1990, 2002

Goat (charming, good with money, indecisive) 1931, 1943, 1955, 1967, 1979, 1991, 2003

Monkey (confident, humorous, fickle) 1932, 1944, 1956, 1968, 1980, 1992, 2004

Rooster (diligent, imaginative, needs attention) 1933, 1945, 1957, 1969, 1981, 1993, 2005

Dog (humble, responsible, patient) 1934, 1946, 1958, 1970, 1982, 1994, 2006

Pig (materialistic, loyal, honest) 1935, 1947, 1959, 1971, 1983, 1995, 2007

THE RAMAYANA

The literary epic of the *Ramayana* serves as the cultural fodder for traditional art, dance and shadow puppetry throughout the region. In this epic Hindu legend, Prince Rama (an incarnation of the Hindu god Vishnu) falls in love with beautiful Sita and wins her hand in marriage by successfully stringing a magic bow. Before the couple settle down to marital bliss, Rama is banished from his kingdom and his wife is kidnapped by the demon king, Ravana, and taken to the island of Lanka. With the help of the Monkey King, Hanuman, Sita is rescued, but a great battle ensues. Rama and his allies defeat Ravana and restore peace and goodness to the land. The *Ramayana* is known as the *Reamker* in Cambodia or the *Ramakien* in Laos and Thailand.

simply fade away, but were incorporated into the new religions. The purest form of animism is practised among the ethnic minorities or hill tribes of the region.

Buddhism

The sedate smile of the Buddhist statues decorating the landscapes and temples characterise the nature of the religion in Southeast Asia. Religious devotion within the Buddhist countries is highly individualistic, omnipresent and nonaggressive, with many daily rituals rooted in the indigenous religions of animism and ancestor worship.

Buddhism, like all great religions, has been through a messy divorce, and arrived in the Mekong region in two flavours. Mahayana Buddhism (northern school) proceeded north into Nepal, Tibet, China, Korea, Mongolia, Vietnam and Japan, while Theravada Buddhism (southern school) took the southern route through India, Sri Lanka, Myanmar and Cambodia.

Mahayana Buddhists believe in Bodhisattvas, which are Buddhas that attain nirvana but postpone their enlightenment to stay on earth to save their fellow beings.

Every Buddhist male is expected to become a monk for a short period in his life, optimally between the time he finishes school and starts a career or marries. Men or boys under 20 years of age may enter the Sangha (the monkhood or the monastic community) as novices. Nowadays, men may spend less than one month to accrue merit as monks.

Christianity

Catholicism was introduced to the region in the 16th century by missionaries. Vietnam has the highest percentage of Catholics (8% to 10% of the population) in Southeast Asia outside the Philippines.

For an in-depth look at the beauty of Angkorian-era sculpture and its religious, cultural and social context, seek out a copy of *Sculpture of Angkor and Ancient Cambodia: Millennium of Glory*.

Hinduism

Hinduism ruled the spiritual lives of Mekong dwellers more than 1500 years ago, and the great Hindu empire of Angkor built magnificent monuments to their pantheon of gods. The primary representations of the one omnipresent god include Brahma (the creator), Vishnu (the preserver) and Shiva (the destroyer and reproducer).

The forgotten kingdom of Champa was profoundly influenced by Hinduism and many of the Cham towers, built as Hindu sanctuaries, contain *lingas* (phallic symbols representing Shiva) that are still worshipped by ethnic Vietnamese and ethnic Chinese alike.

Islam

Southeast Asians converted to Islam to join a brotherhood of spice traders and to escape the inflexible caste system of earlier Hindu empires. The Chams may be Muslims, but in practice they follow a localised adaptation of Islamic theology and law. Though Muslims usually pray five times a day, the Chams pray only on Fridays and observe Ramadan (a month of dawn-to-dusk fasting) for only three days.

Taoism

Taoism originated in China and is based on the philosophy of Laotse (The Old One), who lived in the 6th century BC. Little is known about Laotse and there is some debate as to whether or not he actually existed. Taoist philosophy emphasises contemplation and simplicity. The ideal is returning to the Tao (the Way, or the essence of which all things are made), and it emphasises the importance of Yin and Yang.

Tam Giao

Over the centuries, Confucianism, Taoism and Buddhism have fused with popular Chinese beliefs and ancient Vietnamese animism to create Tam Giao (Triple Religion). When discussing religion, most Vietnamese people are likely to say that they are Buddhist, but when it comes to family or civic duties they are likely to follow the moral and social code of Confucianism, and will turn to Taoist concepts to understand the nature of the cosmos.

Living Culture

The Lifestyle»
Trekking in Minority Regions»
Life Among the Minorities»
Food & the Arts»

DAVID GREEDY / LONELY PLANET IMAGES ©

Dzao (p480) and Black Hmong (p480) in Sapa, Vietnam

The Lifestyle

A typical day in the Mekong region starts early. Country folk tend to rise before dawn, woken by the cry of cockerels and keen to get the most out of the day before the sun hots up. This habit has spilled over into the towns and cities and many urban dwellers rise at the crack of dawn for a quick jog, a game of badminton or some tai chi moves. Breakfast comes in many flavours, but Chinese *congee* (rice soup) and noodle soups are universally popular. Food is almost as important as family in this part of the world and that is saying something. Long lunch breaks are common (and common sense, as it avoids the hottest part of the day). The working day winds down for some around 5pm and the family will try to come together for dinner and trade tales about their day.

Traditionally, life in the Mekong region has revolved around family, fields and faith, the rhythm of rural existence continuing for centuries. For the majority of the population still living in the countryside, these constants have remained unchanged, with several generations sharing the same roof, the same rice and the same religion. But in recent decades these rhythms have been jarred by war and ideology, as the peasants were dragged from all they held dear to fight in civil wars, or were herded into cooperatives as communism tried to assert itself as the moral and social beacon in the lives of the people. But Buddhism is back and for many older Mekong residents the temple or pagoda remains an important pillar in their lives.

Traditionally rural agrarian societies, the race is on for the move to the cities. Thailand experienced the growing pains first, and now Cambodia, Laos and Vietnam are witnessing a tremendous shift in the balance of population, as increasing numbers of young people desert the fields in search of those mythical streets paved with gold or, more commonly, jammed with motorbikes.

PETER STUCKINGS / LONELY PLANET IMAGES ©

1

BETHUNE CARMICHAEL / LONELY PLANET IMAGES ©

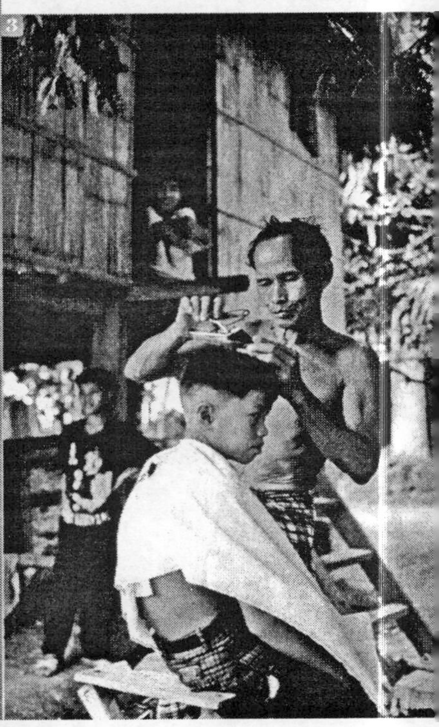

3

Clockwise from top left

1. Con Dao Islands (p127), Vietnam **2.** Aquatic crops, Mekong River, Vientiane (p282), Laos **3.** A haircut in Si Phan Don (p344), Laos

Trekking in Minority Regions

Towering mountains and pancake-flat plains – the contrasting landscapes of the Mekong region have attracted a divergent group of people over the centuries. Discover the diversity of the Mekong with a visit to some of the minority regions.

Mondulkiri Province, Cambodia

1 A world apart from lowland Cambodia, Mondulkiri (p242) offers an enticing blend of forests, dense jungle and hidden waterfalls, and provides a home to the friendly Bunong people, famous for their elephant rearing.

Sapa, Vietnam

2 Sapa (p91) is one of Vietnam's premier trekking centres and a great place to meet minority peoples in this region near the Chinese border. Encounter Hmong and Dzao people and learn about their traditional lifestyles through Hmong-owned trekking agencies.

Luang Nam Tha, Laos

3 Laos is an ethnic melting pot with up to 132 tribal groups, depending on who you believe. Luang Nam Tha (p322) is home to more than 20 of them and homestays are possible during Nam Ha NPA aOKnd Muang Sing treks.

Si Phan Don, Laos

4 Si Phan Don (p344) is the perfect place to experience the languid pace of Lao life. Explore Don Khon (p347) on foot to meet the farmers and fisherfolk who make a living here and experience time that ticks more slowly.

Isan Homestay, Thailand

5 Communication can be tricky and the lodgings basic, but there's no more authentic a window into rural Thai life than a homestay in Isan with a welcoming local family (p427).

NICK RAY / LONELY PLANET IMAGES ©

ANDREW BURKE / LONELY PLANET IMAGES ©

Clockwise from top left

1. Hill-tribe children, Mondulkiri (p242), Cambodia **2.** Dzao women, Sapa (p91), Vietnam **3.** Akha woman, Luang Nam Tha (p322), Laos **4.** Boats at dawn, Si Phan Don (p344), Laos

2

CRAIG LEES / LONELY PLANET IMAGES ©

3

Life Among the Minorities

One of the highlights of a visit to the Mekong region is an encounter with one of the many ethnic minority groups inhabiting the mountains. Many wear incredible costumes, and so elaborate are some of these that it's easy to believe minority girls learn to embroider before they can walk.

While some of these minorities number as many as a million people, it is feared that other groups have dwindled to as few as 100. The areas inhabited by each group are often delineated by altitude, with more recent arrivals settling at a higher altitude. Each hill tribe has its own language, customs, mode of dress and spiritual beliefs. Some groups are caught between medieval and modern worlds, while others have assimilated into modern life.

Most groups share a rural, agricultural lifestyle which revolves around traditional rituals. Most hill-tribe communities are seminomadic, cultivating crops such as rice and using slash-and-burn methods, which have taken a toll on the environment. Hill tribes have among the lowest standards of living in the region and lack access to education, health care and even minimum-wage jobs. While there may be no official discrimination system, cultural prejudice against hill-tribe people ensures they remain at the bottom of the ladder. Put simply, life is a struggle for most minority people.

RESPECT LOCALS

- Always ask permission before taking photos of tribespeople.
- Don't touch totems or sacred items hanging from trees.
- Avoid cultivating a tradition of begging, especially among children.
- Avoid public nudity and don't undress near an open window.
- Don't flirt with members of the opposite sex. Don't drink or do drugs with villagers.

DAN GAIR / LONELY PLANET IMAGES ©

1

DAN GAIR / LONELY PLANET IMAGES ©

3

Clockwise from top left

1. Hill-tribe women, Sapa (p91), Vietnam **2.** Villagers in Mondulkiri (p242), Cambodia **3.** Women at market, Sapa (p91), Vietnam

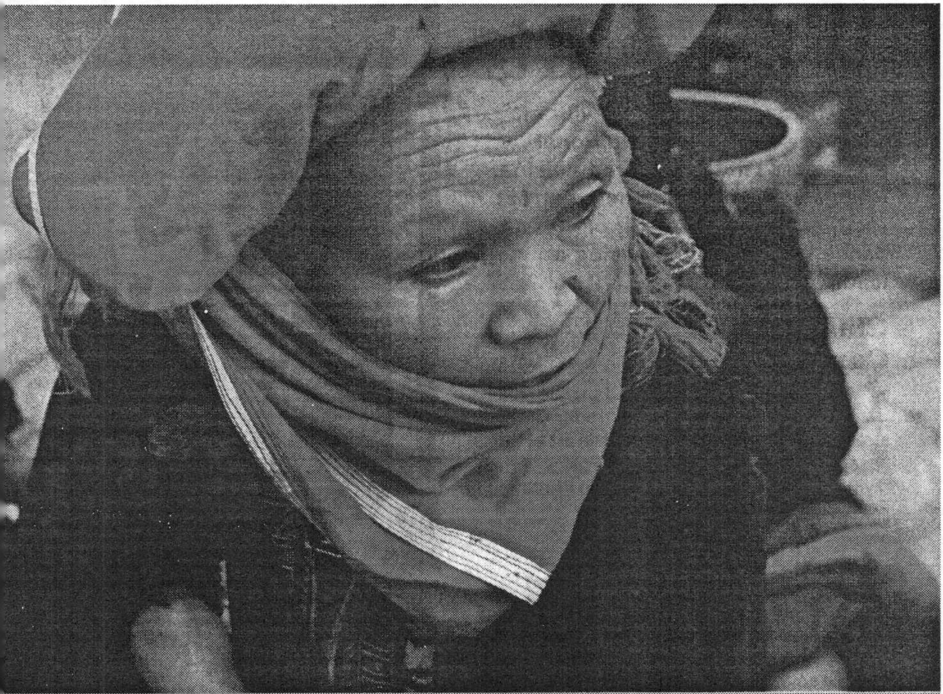

2

Food & the Arts

The Mekong is home to a vibrant cultural scene, from traditional arts to artistically inspired cuisine. Plunge in by sampling some street food, catching a live gig or classical dance show, or by browsing a leading museum.

Classical Dance, Cambodia

1 Cambodia's royal ballet is a tangible link with the glory of Angkor. Its traditions stretch long into the past, when the art of the *apsara* (nymph) resounded to the glory of the divine king. Catch a performance in Phnom Penh (p193) or Siem Reap (p204).

Hanoi Street Food, Vietnam

2 Dive into Hanoi's wonderful street food scene (p67), famous for *bun cha* (barbecued pork), sticky rice, fried eels and *pho* (noodle soup). Vendors crowd pavements with smoking charcoal burners, plastic stools and expectant queues of canny locals.

Live Music, Thailand

3 The Thais love to rock. The live music scene in cities like Bangkok (p382) and Chiang Mai (p394) is something to savour. Bars host live jams and blues sessions and cover bands belt out pop anthems.

Chiang Mai, Thailand

4 Undisputed capital of northern Thailand, Chiang Mai (p389) is also culinary heaven. The fastest way to a Thai is through the stomach and a cooking course is a rewarding insight into Thai culture.

Traditional Arts & Ethnology Centre, Laos

5 Have you ever wondered 'who's who' in the kaleidoscope of groups that make up Laos' rich tribal tapestry? A visit to Luang Prabang's excellent cultural centre (TAEC; p300) will help you distinguish between Hmong, Akha and Khamu tribes.

FELIX HUG / LONELY PLANET IMAGES ©

1

SALLY DILLON / LONELY PLANET IMAGES ©

2

Right

1. *Apsara* dancer, Angkor Wat (p208), Cambodia
2. Street food, Hanoi (p69), Vietnam

Survival Guide

Directory A–Z

This chapter includes general information about the Mekong region. For specific information for each country, check out the Directory section at the end of each country chapter.

Accommodation

The Mekong region has something for everyone – from dives to the divine – and we cover them all. Prices are quoted in the local currency or US dollars throughout this book based on the preferred currency of the particular property. Accommodation prices listed are high-season prices for rooms with attached bathroom, unless stated otherwise. An icon is included if air-con is available; otherwise, assume that a fan will be provided.

Accommodation costs vary slightly across the region, but prices are consistently affordable compared with those found in the West. Check the Directory section in individual country chapters for the budget breakdown used within that chapter.

Across the region, when it comes to budget we are generally talking about family-run guesthouses or minihotels where the majority of rooms cost less than US$25. Budget rooms generally come well equipped for the money, so don't be surprised to find air-con, hot water and a TV for US$15 or less.

For midrange, we are referring to rooms ranging from US$25 to around US$75, a range which secures some pretty tasty extras in this region. At the lower end of this bracket, many of the hotels are similar to budget hotels but with bigger rooms or balconies. Splash a bit more cash and three-star touches are available, such as access to a swimming pool and a hairdryer hidden away somewhere.

At the upper end are a host of international-standard hotels and resorts that charge from US$100 a room to US$750 a suite. These are mostly restricted to big cities and major tourist centres. Some of these are fairly faceless business hotels, while others ooze opulence or history. There are some real bargains when compared with the Hong Kongs and Singapores of this world, so if you fancy indulging yourself, the Mekong region is a good place to do so. Most top-end hotels levy a tax of 10% and a service charge of 5%, displayed as ++ ('plus plus') on the bill.

Peak tourist demand for hotel rooms in the region comes at Christmas and New Year, when prices may rise by as much as 25%. There is also a surge in many cities during Chinese New Year (Tet in Vietnam), when half the population is on the move. Try to make a reservation in advance at these times so as not to get caught out without a bed.

> **BOOK YOUR STAY ONLINE**
>
> For more accommodation reviews by Lonely Planet authors, check out hotels.lonelyplanet.com. You'll find independent reviews, as well as recommendations on the best places to stay. Best of all, you can book online.

Camping

With the exception of the national parks in Thailand and some high-end experiences in Cambodia, Laos and Vietnam, the opportunities for general camping are pretty limited.

Guesthouses & Hotels

There is an excellent range of guesthouses and hotels in the Mekong region, no matter what your budget. As tourism is a relatively recent phenomenon in Cambodia, Laos and Vietnam, there are lots of newly built places that are excellent value for money.

There is some confusion over the terms 'single', 'double', 'double occupancy' and 'twin', so let's set the record straight here. A single contains one bed, even if two people sleep in it. If there are two beds in the room, that is a twin, even if only one person occupies it. If two people stay in the same room, that is double occupancy. In some hotels 'double' means twin beds, while in others it means double occupancy.

While many of the newer hotels have lifts (elevators), older hotels often don't and the cheapest rooms are at the end of several flights of stairs. It's a win-win-win situation: cheaper rooms, a bit of exercise and better views. Bear in mind that power outages are possible in some towns and this can mean 10 flights of stairs just to get to your room.

Many hotels post a small sign warning guests not to leave cameras, passports and other valuables in the room. Most places have a safety deposit system of some kind, but if you're leaving cash (not recommended) or travellers cheques, be sure to seal the loot in an envelope and have it countersigned by staff.

Homestays

Homestays are a popular option in parts of the Mekong region, but some countries are more flexible than others about the concept. Homestays are well established in parts of Thailand and Vietnam, and many treks through minority areas in the far north include a night with a local family to learn about their lifestyle. Homestays are just starting up in Cambodia and Laos, but many visitors end up staying with local families when motorbiking in remote areas.

For more on homestays in Laos see p357; in Thailand, see p427; and in Vietnam, see p165.

Activities

There are plenty of activities to keep visitors busy in the Mekong region. Go on the water, go under the water, crank up the revs on a motorbike or cruise down a slope on a mountain bike, the possibilities abound. Thailand is the adventure capital of the region, with Vietnam fast catching up, but every country has something to offer. For more on outdoor activities and adventures in the region, see p40.

> **THE NATIONAL DISH**
>
> If there's just one dish you try, make it one of these. These are the dishes that capture the cuisine of the country in a single serving. Enjoy.
>
> **Cambodia** *Amok* (baked fish in coconut leaves)
> **Laos** *Làap* (spicy salad with meat or fish)
> **Thailand** *Đôm yam gûng* (hot and sour soup with shrimp)
> **Vietnam** *Pho bo* (rice noodle soup with beef)

Business Hours

Business hours are reasonably standard across the region. Most government offices, embassies and businesses open between 8am and 9am and close around 4pm to 5pm. Government offices and some businesses break for lunch, usually just one hour in Thailand, often two hours in Cambodia, Laos and Vietnam. Banks often keep shorter hours (until about 3.30pm) but don't close for lunch. Banks are also open on Saturday morning.

Small businesses such as shops may keep much longer hours – from 7am to 7pm or later – and don't close at weekends. Markets are usually open from dawn until dusk, although most cities have at least one night market that rumbles on after dark.

Local restaurants open and close early, serving breakfast from 6am and winding down dinner before 9pm. Fancy restaurants usually stay open until about 11pm. Opening hours for bars vary dramatically depending on the country in question and the mood of the government that month. It is usually possible to drink or dance into the wee hours, although places in Laos tend to close before midnight, while places in Cambodia stagger on all night.

Customs Regulations

Customs regulations vary little around the region. Drugs and firearms are strictly prohibited – a lengthy stay in prison is a common sentence. Check the Customs Regulations sections in the Directories of the country chapters for specific details.

Discount Cards

The International Student Identity Card (ISIC) is the official student card, but is

> **INSURANCE ALERT!**
>
> Do not visit the Mekong region without medical insurance. Hospitals are often basic, particularly in remote areas. Anyone with a serious injury or illness may require emergency evacuation to Bangkok or Hong Kong. With an insurance policy costing no more than the equivalent of a bottle of beer a day, this evacuation is free. Without an insurance policy, it will cost US$10,000 or more.

of limited use in the Mekong region. Some domestic and international airlines provide discounts to ISIC cardholders, but because knock-offs are so readily available, the cards carry little power.

Electricity

Most countries work on a voltage of 220V to 240V at 50Hz (cycles); note that 240V appliances will happily run on 220V. You should be able to pick up adaptors in electrical shops in most of the main towns and cities.

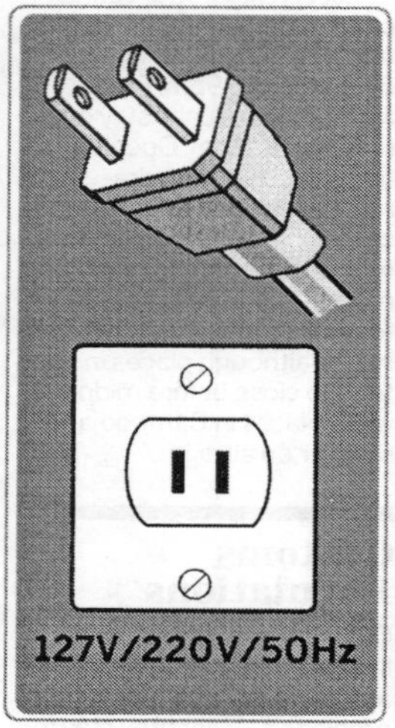

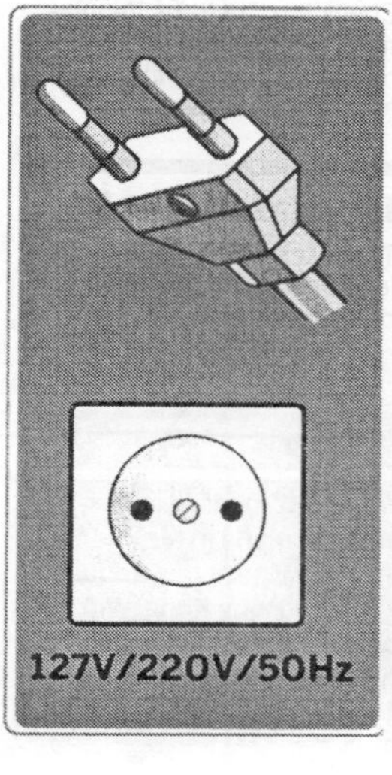

Embassies & Consulates

It's important to realise what your own embassy – the embassy of the country of which you are a citizen – can and can't do to help if you get into trouble.

Generally speaking, it won't be much help in emergencies if the trouble you're in is remotely your own fault. Remember that you are bound by the laws of the country you are in. Your embassy will not be sympathetic if you end up in jail after committing a crime locally, even if such actions are legal in your own country.

In genuine emergencies you might get some assistance, but only if other channels have been exhausted. For example, if you need to get home urgently, a free ticket home is exceedingly unlikely – the embassy would expect you to have insurance. If you have all your money and documents stolen, it might assist with getting a new passport, but a loan for onward travel is out of the question.

Most travellers should have no need to contact their embassy while in the Mekong region, although if you're really going off the trail it may be worth letting your embassy know. However, be sure to let them know when you return. In this way valuable time, effort and money won't be wasted looking for you while you're relaxing on the beach somewhere in a different country.

For details of embassies and consulates in the Mekong region see the Directory sections in the individual country chapters.

Food

This is arguably the best region in the world when it comes to sampling the local cuisine. The food of China, Thailand and Vietnam needs no introduction, but Laotian and Khmer cuisine is also a rewarding experience. See the Food & Drink sections of each country chapter for the full story. For drinkers, there is plenty to get excited about, from divine fruit shakes and coffee with a kick to micro-brewed beers and home-made hooch.

Food is fantastic value throughout the region. Street snacks start from as little as US$0.50, meals in local restaurants start at US$1.50 and even a serious spread at a decent restaurant will only be in the US$10 to US$20 range.

Gay & Lesbian Travellers

Thailand, Cambodia and Laos have the most progressive attitudes towards homosexuality. While same-sex displays of affection are part of most Asian cultures, be discreet and respectful of the local culture. Extra vigilance should be practised in Vietnam, where authorities have arrested people on charges of suspected homosexual activities. There is not usually a problem with same-sex couples checking into rooms throughout the region, as it is so common among travellers.

Check out **Utopia Asian Gay & Lesbian Resources** (www.utopia-asia.com) for more information on gay and lesbian travel in Asia. Other links with useful pointers for gay travellers include www.gayguide.net and www.outandabout.com.

Insurance

A travel insurance policy to cover theft, loss and medical

problems is essential. There's a wide variety of policies available, so check the small print. For more information about the ins and outs of travel insurance, contact a travel agent or travel insurer.

Some policies specifically exclude 'dangerous activities', which can include scuba diving, motorcycling and even trekking. A locally acquired motorcycle licence is not valid under some policies. Check that the policy covers ambulance rides and emergency flights home.

Also see p511 for further information on health insurance and p508 for more information on car and motorcycle insurance.

Worldwide travel insurance is available at www.lonelyplanet.com/travel_services. You can buy, extend and claim online anytime – even if you're already on the road.

Internet Access

Email and internet services are available throughout the region. Access points in the Mekong region vary from internet cafes to post offices and hotels. The cost is generally low and the connection speeds pretty reasonable. Wi-fi access is increasingly common in major cities and is often free in cafes and bars. See the country chapters for further details.

Legal Matters

Be sure to know the national laws before unwittingly committing a crime. In all of the Mekong region countries, using or trafficking drugs carries stiff punishments that are enforced, even if you're a foreigner. See p499 for more on the risks associated with drugs in the region.

If you are the victim of a crime, contact the tourist police, if available; they are usually better trained to deal with foreigners and foreign languages than the regular police force.

TRAVEL ADVISORY WEBSITES

Travel advisories are government-run websites that update nationals on the latest security situation in any given country, including the countries of the Mekong region. They are useful for checking out dangerous countries or during dangerous events, but these official sites tend to be pretty conservative to cover themselves, stressing dangers where many would feel they don't always exist.

» **Australia** (www.dfat.gov.au/travel)

» **Canada** (www.voyage.gc.ca)

» **New Zealand** (www.mft.govt.nz/travel)

» **UK** (www.fco.gov.uk/travel)

» **USA** (www.travel.state.gov)

Maps

Country-specific maps are usually sold in English bookstores in capital cities. Local tourist offices and guesthouses can also provide maps of smaller cities and towns. There aren't many maps that cover the Mekong region as a whole. There are some good maps of Indochina that include Bangkok and Northeast Thailand: check out Nelles *Vietnam, Laos & Cambodia* map at a scale of 1:1,500,000.

Money

Most experienced travellers will carry their money in a combination of travellers cheques, credit/bank cards and cash. You'll always find situations in which one of these cannot be used, so it pays to carry all three.

ATMs

In most large cities ATMs are widespread, but before relying on this option review the individual country's Money section for specifics.

Some banks back home charge for withdrawals overseas. Shop around for an account that offers free withdrawals. Similarly, some local banks in the region charge for withdrawals, particularly in Cambodia and Vietnam, although the sums are small.

Black Market

There is still something of a black market in moneychanging in Laos and Vietnam. However, given the

HAPPINESS IS A STATE OF MIND

'Don't worry, be happy' could be the motto for the Mekong region, but in some backpacker centres the term 'happy' has taken on a completely different connotation. Seeing the word 'happy' in front of 'shake', 'pizza' or anything else does not, as one traveller was told, mean it comes with extra pineapple. The extra is usually marijuana, added in whatever quantity the shake-maker deems fit. For many travellers 'happy' is a well-understood alias, but there are others who innocently down their shake or pizza only to spend the next 24 hours floating in a world of their own.

MAKING YOUR MONEY GO FURTHER

Many parts of the region remain mired in poverty. Support local businesses by buying locally made products. Eat in local restaurants where possible and dine in villages rather than taking picnics from town. Use local guides for remote regions, including indigenous minority peoples. Consider the option of homestays where they are available and support national park programs by visiting one of the many protected areas in the region.

When bargaining for goods or transport, remember the aim is not to get the lowest possible price, but one that's acceptable to both you and the seller. Coming on too strong or arguing over a few cents does nothing to foster positive feelings towards foreign visitors. Don't ask the price unless you're interested in actually buying it. If you become angry or visibly frustrated then you've lost the bargaining game.

Begging is common in many countries of the region and the tug on the shirtsleeve can become tiresome for visitors after a time. However, try to remember that many of these countries have little in the way of a social-security net to catch the fallen. It is best to keep denominations small to avoid foreigners becoming even more of a target than they already are. Avoid giving money to children, as it is likely going straight to a 'begging pimp' or family member. Food is an option, but better still is to make a donation to one of the many local organisations trying to assist in the battle against poverty.

tiny differences in rates and the huge chance that you'll be ripped off, it is not really worth pursuing this path.

Credit Cards

Credit cards are widely accepted in the region. Thailand leads the way, where almost anything can be paid for with plastic. However, things dry up beyond major tourist centres or bigger towns, so don't rely exclusively on credit cards. It is quite common for the business to pass on the credit-card commission (usually 3%) to the customer in Cambodia, Laos and Vietnam, so check if there is an additional charge before putting it on the plastic. Also check your monthly bills carefully in case some scamster clones your card while you are paying for something on your travels.

Exchanging Money

The US dollar is the currency of choice in the Mekong region. It is widely accepted as cash in Cambodia, Laos and Vietnam, and can be easily exchanged in Thailand. Other major currencies are also widely accepted by banks and exchange bureaus, but the rates get worse the further you get from a major city. The Thai baht is also accepted throughout Laos and in parts of western Cambodia.

Tipping

Tipping is not a traditional practice but is greatly appreciated, particularly in the poorer countries of the region where salaries remain low. Locals sometimes don't tip, but tourism has introduced the concept to hotels and restaurants, as well as to tour guides and drivers.

Travellers Cheques

Travelling with a stash of travellers cheques can help if you hit an ATM-free zone. Get your cheques in US dollars and in large denominations, say US$100 or US$50, to avoid heavy per-cheque commission fees. Keep careful records of which cheques you've cashed and keep this information separate from your money, so you can file a claim if any cheques are lost or stolen.

Photography

For those travelling with a digital camera, most internet cafes in well-developed areas let customers transfer images from the camera to an online email account or storage site. Flash memory is also widely available and most internet cafes can burn shots onto a DVD. Before leaving home, find out if your battery charger will require a power adaptor by visiting the website of the **World Electric Guide** (www.kropla.com/electric.htm).

Print film is readily available in cities and larger towns throughout the region. The best places to buy camera equipment or have repairs done are Bangkok, Ho Chi Minh City and Phnom Penh.

If you're after some tips, check out Lonely Planet's *Travel Photography: A Guide to Taking Better Pictures*, written by travel photographer Richard I'Anson.

Photographing People

You should always ask permission before taking a person's photograph. Many hill-tribe villagers seriously object to being photographed, or they may ask for money in exchange; if you want the photo, you should honour the price.

Post

Postal services are generally reliable across the region. Of course, it's always better to leave important mail and parcels for the big centres such as Bangkok and Hanoi.

There's always an element of risk in sending parcels home by sea, though as a rule they eventually reach their destination. If it's something of value, it's worth considering air freight – better still, register the parcel or send it by courier. Don't send cash or valuables through government-run postal systems.

Poste restante is widely available throughout the region and is the best way of receiving mail. When getting people to write to you, ask them to leave plenty of time for mail to arrive and to print your name very clearly.

Public Holidays

For full details on public holidays in each of the Mekong region countries, see the individual country Directory sections. Allegedly, Cambodia has the most public holidays in the world. Chinese New Year (or Tet in Vietnam) is the one holiday common to all countries and can have a big impact on travel plans, as businesses close and all forms of transport are booked out. Cambodia, Laos and Thailand also celebrate their own new year at the same time in the middle of April and mass water fights are common.

Safe Travel

Commissions

It could be the taxi driver, it might be the bus driver or even the friendly tout who latches on to you at the train station. Commissions are part and parcel of life in Asia, and the Mekong region is no exception. Thailand is getting better, while Cambodia and Vietnam are arguably getting worse. Laos doesn't have much of a problem just yet. Many places in the region refuse to pay commissions to touts, and hence you might be told a certain hotel or guesthouse is closed. Don't believe it unless you have seen it with your own eyes.

Drugs

The risks associated with recreational drug use and distribution have grown to the point where all visitors should exercise extreme caution even in places with illicit reputations. A spell in a local prison can be truly torturous. With heightened airline security worldwide, customs officials are zealous in their screening of both luggage and passengers.

Pollution & Noise

Pollution is a growing problem in the major cities of the region. Bangkok has long been famous as a place to chew the air rather than inhale. However, Ho Chi Minh City and Phnom Penh also have problems of their own. Laos remains blissfully pollution-free for the most part.

Remember the movie *Spinal Tap*? The soundtrack of the cities in this region is permanently cranked up to 11. Not just any noise, but a whole lot of noises that

SHOP 'TIL YOU DROP

Recovering shopaholics beware...the Mekong region offers some incredible opportunities to shop 'til you drop. Bangkok is the gateway to the region and also one of the world's best-known shopping destinations. Everything that is produced in the Mekong region, from textiles to handicrafts, state-of-the-art electronics to suspect antiques, ends up in Bangkok's malls and markets. Browse Chatuchak Weekend Market (p383) for the best range in the region.

Cambodia is famous for its superb silk, as are Laos and Thailand. There is good-quality silver throughout the region, but purity can be questionable. There are fine handicrafts, including excellent woodcarving, intricate lacquerware and striking stone carving, in all the countries of the region. The ethnic minorities of the region are also in on the act and produce a range of handicrafts and colourful clothing that make popular keepsakes. Art is increasingly popular, with Thailand, Vietnam and Yúnnán leading the way. Antiques are a popular purchase, but be aware that there are a lot of fakes about. If the price seems too good to be true, it probably is. Precious stones is another area where it's almost always too good to be true. Bangkok is the gem scam capital of Asia, but buying precious stones anywhere in the region is a risk unless you really know what you are doing.

There are some great clothing and electronic stores in the region. Bangkok is the fashion capital of the Mekong region, offering everything from Prada to Kevin Clein (yes, there are lots of fakes). Cambodia and Vietnam both produce a lot of textiles for export, so it's easy to pick up high-street names for a fraction of the price back home. When it comes to electronics, Bangkok is the most reliable place, but Cambodia is sometimes a cheaper option thanks to a lack of tax and duty.

just never seem to stop. At night there is most often a competing cacophony from motorbikes, discos, cafes, video arcades, karaoke lounges and restaurants. If your hotel is near any or all of these, it may be difficult to sleep. Fortunately most noise subsides around 10pm or 11pm, as few places stay open much later than that. Unfortunately, however, locals are up and about from around 5am onwards.

One last thing...don't forget the earplugs.

Queues

What queues? Most locals in the Mekong region don't queue, they mass in a rugby scrum, pushing towards the counter. When in Rome... This is first-seen, first-served, so take a deep breath, muscle your way to the front and wave your passport or papers as close to the counter as you can.

Scams

Every year Lonely Planet gets hundreds of letters and emails from hapless travellers reporting that they've been scammed in this region. In almost all cases there are two culprits involved: a shrewd scam artist and the traveller's own greed.

Two perennial scams involve card games and gemstones. If someone asks you to join a card game be extremely wary. If the game involves money, walk away – it's almost certainly rigged. As for gemstones, if there really were vast amounts of money to be made by selling gems back home, savvy businesspeople would have a monopoly on the market already. Don't believe the people who say that they support their global wanderings by re-selling gemstones; in reality they support themselves by tricking unsuspecting foreigners.

Other common scams include losing money on black-market exchange deals; having your rented bicycle or motorbike 'stolen' by someone with a duplicate key; and dodgy drug deals that involve police extortion. There are many more so it pays to keep your antennae up during a trip through the Mekong region.

See the Safe Travel sections in the individual country chapters for local scams.

Theft

Theft in this part of the world is usually by stealth rather than by force. Keep your money and valuables in a money belt worn underneath your clothes. Be alert to the possible presence of snatch thieves, who will whisk a camera or a bag off your shoulder. Don't store valuables in easily accessible places such as packs that are stored in the luggage compartment of buses, or the front pocket of daypacks.

Violent theft is very rare but occurs from time to time – usually late at night and after the victim has been drinking. Be careful when walking alone late at night and don't fall asleep in taxis.

Always be diplomatically suspicious of overfriendly locals. Don't accept gifts of food or drinks from someone you don't know. In Thailand, thieves have been known to drug travellers for easier pickings.

Finally, don't let paranoia ruin your trip. With just a few sensible precautions most travellers make their way across the region without incident.

Unexploded Ordnance (UXO) & Landmines

The legacy of war lingers on in Cambodia, Laos and Vietnam. Laos suffers the fate of being the most heavily bombed country per capita in the world, while all three countries were on the receiving end of more bombs than were dropped by all sides during WWII. There are still many undetonated bombs and explosives out there, so be careful walking off the trail in areas near the Laos–Vietnam border or around the Demilitarised Zone (DMZ). Cambodia suffers the additional affliction of landmines, some 4 to 6 million of them according to surveys. Many of these are located in border areas with Thailand in the north and west of the country, but it pays to stick to marked paths anywhere in Cambodia.

Violence

Violence against foreigners is pretty rare and is not something you should waste much time worrying about, but if you do get into a flare-up with some locals, swallow your pride and back down.

YABA DABA DO? YABA DABA DON'T!

Watch out for *yaba*, the 'crazy' drug from Thailand, known as *yama* in Cambodia, and also, rather ominously, as the Hindu god of death. Known as ice or crystal meth back home, it's not just any old diet pill from the pharmacist, but homemade meta-amphetamines produced in labs in Myanmar (Burma), Cambodia, Laos, Thailand and elsewhere. The pills are often laced with toxic substances, such as mercury, lithium or whatever else the maker can find. *Yaba* is a dirty drug and more addictive than users would like to admit, provoking powerful hallucinations, sleep deprivation and psychosis. Steer clear of the stuff unless you plan on an indefinite extension to your trip to the Mekong region.

You are the outsider. You don't know how many friends they have nearby, how many weapons they are carrying or how many years they have studied kickboxing.

Telephone

Telephone systems vary widely across the Mekong region. For international calls, most countries have calling centres (usually in post offices) or public phone booths that accept international phonecards. Each country's system is different, so check the Telephone section in each country's Directory before making a call.

These days, the cheapest and most popular option is to use an internet-based phone system to make calls. Anyone with a Skype or Yahoo Messenger account can simply sign in and start talking to friends if there's a headset available. Many of the internet cafes in the region have headsets and webcams. Otherwise you can pay a small charge to make a call, often as little as US$0.10 a minute to countries in the West. Some budget and midrange hotels in the region have switched over to internet-based telephone systems for their guests.

You can take your mobile (cell) phone on the road with you and get respectable coverage in major population centres. Not all mobile phones, especially those from the USA, are outfitted for international use. Check with your service provider for global-roaming fees and other particulars. Double-check the rates before you start calling, or even texting away, as prices can be prohibitively high. Consider buying a local SIM card for a local network if you plan to make a lot of local telephone calls. Some phones are 'locked' by the issuing company back home, but most telephone shops in the Mekong region can 'unlock' them in seconds for a small charge. Many of the local mobile operators offer cheap international calls via the internet, making a local SIM a good option.

Fax services are available in most countries across the region. Try to avoid the business centres in upmarket hotels – tariffs of 30% and upwards are often levied on faxes and international calls.

YOU WANT MASSAGE?

Karaoke clubs and massage parlours are ubiquitous throughout the region. Sometimes this may mean an 'orchestra without instruments', or a healthy massage to ease a stiff body. However, more often than not, both these terms are euphemisms for some sort of prostitution. There may be some singing or a bit of shoulder tweaking going on, but ultimately it is just a polite introduction to something naughtier. Legitimate karaoke and legitimate massage do exist in the bigger cities, but as a general rule of thumb, if the place looks sleazy, it probably is.

Time

Cambodia, Laos, Thailand and Vietnam are seven hours ahead of Greenwich Mean Time or Universal Time Coordinated (GMT/UTC). When it is midday in Bangkok or Hanoi, it is 10pm the previous evening in San Francisco, 1am in New York, 5am in London, 6am in Paris and 3pm in Sydney.

Toilets

As tourism continues to grow in the region, sit-down toilets are increasingly common. Apart from the very cheapest guesthouses, most rooms include a sit-down toilet, as do restaurants and other businesses catering to foreigners. However, in rural areas it is another story and squat toilets are common.

Even in places where sit-down toilets are installed, the plumbing may not be designed to take toilet paper. In such cases, the usual washing bucket will be standing nearby or there will be a waste basket in which you place used toilet paper.

Public toilets are common in department stores, bus and train stations and large hotels. Elsewhere you'll have to make do; while on the road between towns and villages it's acceptable to go discreetly behind a tree or bush. In landmine- and UXO-affected countries such as Cambodia and Laos, stay on the roadside and do the deed, or grin and bear it until the next town.

Tourist Information

All the countries in the Mekong region have government-funded tourist offices with varying degrees of usefulness. Thailand offers by far the most efficient tourism information service. When it comes to the rest, better information is often available from dedicated internet sites, guesthouses and travellers' cafes, or your fellow travellers, rather than through the state-run tourist offices. See each country's Directory for more on tourist information.

Travellers with Disabilities

Travellers with serious disabilities will likely find the Mekong region a challenging

THE ABUSE OF INNOCENCE

The sexual abuse of children by foreign paedophiles is a serious problem in some parts of the Mekong region, particularly Cambodia and Vietnam. Many child prostitutes are sold into the business by relatives. These sex slaves are either trafficked overseas or forced to cater to domestic demand and local sex-tourism operators.

Fear of contracting HIV/AIDS from mature sex workers has led to increasing exploitation of (supposedly as-yet uninfected) children. Unicef estimates that there is close to one million child prostitutes in Asia – one of the highest figures in the world.

Paedophiles are treated as criminals in the region and several have served or are serving jail sentences as a result. Many Western countries have introduced much-needed legislation that sees nationals prosecuted in their home country for having underage sex abroad. Visitors can do their bit to fight this menace by keeping an eye out for suspicious behaviour on the part of foreigners. Don't ignore it. Try to pass on any relevant information such as the name and nationality of the individual to the embassy concerned.

End Child Prostitution & Trafficking (Ecpat; www.ecpat.org) is a global network aimed at stopping child prostitution, child pornography and the trafficking of children for sexual purposes, and has affiliates in most Western countries. **Childsafe International** (www.childsafe-international.org), operating out of Cambodia, , now covers Laos and Thailand as well, and aims to educate businesses and individuals to be on the lookout for children in vulnerable situations.

place to travel. Even the more modern cities are very difficult to navigate for the mobility- or vision-impaired. Tactical problems include the chaotic traffic, a lack of lifts in smaller hotels, high kerbs and uneven pavements (sidewalks) that are routinely blocked by parked motorbikes and footstalls. In general, care of a person with a disability is left to close family members throughout the region and it's unrealistic to expect much in the way of public amenities. Bus and train travel is tough, but rent a private vehicle with a driver and almost anywhere can become accessible.

The Travellers With Disabilities forum on Lonely Planet's **Thorn Tree** (www.lonelyplanet.com) is a good place to seek the advice of other disabled travellers.

International organisations that can provide information on mobility-impaired travel include:

Accessible Journeys (☎610-521 0339; www.disabilitytravel.com)

Mobility International USA (☎541-343-1284; www.miusa.org; PO Box 10767, Eugene, OR 97440, USA)

Royal Association for Disability & Rehabilitation (Radar; ☎020-7250 3222; www.radar.org.uk; 12 City Forum, 250 City Rd, London EC1V 8AF, UK)

Society for Accessible Travel & Hospitality (SATH; ☎212-447-7284; www.sath.org; 347 Fifth Ave, Ste 610, New York, NY 10016, USA)

Visas

Visa rules vary depending on the point of entry. Many nationalities do not require a visa for Thailand and are given 30 days on arrival. For Cambodia and Laos, a visa is required, but is issued on arrival at airports and most land borders. For Vietnam, it is necessary to arrange a visa in advance. For more details, see the Visas section in each country's Directory.

Get your visas as you go rather than all at once before you leave home; they are often easier and cheaper to get in neighbouring countries and visas are only valid within a certain time period, which could interfere with an extended trip.

Procedures for extending a visa vary from country to country. In some cases, extensions are quite complicated, in others they're a mere formality. Remember the most important rule: treat visits to embassies, consulates and borders as formal occasions and look smart for them.

In some countries in the Mekong region, you are required to have an onward ticket out of the country before you can obtain a visa to enter. In practice, however, as long as you look fairly respectable, it's unlikely that your tickets will be checked.

Volunteering

There are fewer opportunities for volunteering than one might imagine there would be in a region that remains predominantly poor. This is partly due to the sheer number of professional development-workers based here, and development is a pretty lucrative industry these days. For details on local volunteer projects in the region see individual country chapters.

The other avenue is professional volunteering

through an organisation back home that offers one- or two-year placements in the region. One of the largest is **Voluntary Service Overseas** (VSO; www.vso.org.uk) in the UK, but other countries have their own organisations, including the **US Peace Corps** (www.peacecorps.gov), **VSO Canada** (www.vsocan.org), **Australian Volunteers International** (AVI; www.australianvolunteers.com) and **Volunteer Service Abroad** (VSA; www.vsa.org.nz). The UN also operates its own volunteer program; details are available at www.unv.org. Other general volunteer sites with links all over the place include www.worldvolunteerweb.org and www.volunteerabroad.com.

Women Travellers

While travel in the Mekong region for women is generally safe, there are several things visitors can do to make it hassle-free.

Keep in mind that modesty in dress is culturally important across all Southeast Asia. Causes for commotion include wearing the ever-popular midriff T-shirt that inadvertently sends the message that you're a prostitute. At the beach, save the topless sunbathing for home rather than this conservative region of the world. This is particularly important when travelling from Thailand to Cambodia or Laos. Thailand may be very Westernised with an 'anything goes' atmosphere, but Cambodia and Laos are much more traditional. Walking around Angkor or Luang Prabang dressed like you are going to a full-moon party won't impress the locals.

Solo women should be on guard especially when returning home late at night or arriving in a new town at night. While physical assault is rare, local men often consider foreign women as being exempt from their own society's rules of conduct regarding members of the opposite sex.

Use common sense about venturing into dangerous-looking areas, particularly alone or at night. If you do find yourself in a tricky situation, try to extricate yourself as quickly as possible – hopping into a taxi or entering a business establishment and asking them to call a cab is often the best solution.

Treat overly friendly strangers, both male and female, with a good deal of caution.

Many travellers have reported small peepholes in the walls and doors of cheap hotels, some of which operate as boarding houses or brothels (often identified by their advertising 'day use' rates). If you can, move to another hotel or guesthouse.

Work

The range of jobs available in the region is quite staggering, but many of the better jobs such as working with the UN or for international corporations are appointments from overseas or from a pool of well-qualified locals. The main opportunities for people passing through the region are teaching English (or another European language), landing a job in tourism or starting a small business such as a bar or restaurant.

Teaching English is the easiest way to support yourself in the Mekong region. For short-term gigs, the large cities such as Bangkok, Ho Chi Minh City and Phnom Penh have a lot of language schools and a high turnover. **Payaway** (www.payaway.co.uk) provides a handy online list of language schools and volunteer groups looking for recruits for its regional programs.

Tourism has brought plenty of job opportunities to the region. Most of these deservedly go to locals, but there are opportunities for wannabe guesthouse or hotel managers, bartenders, chefs and so on. This can be a pretty memorable way to pass a few months in a different culture.

Starting up a business is a possibility, but tread with caution. Many a foreigner has been burned in the region. Sometimes it's an unscrupulous partner, other times it's the local girlfriend, or boyfriend, who changes their mind and goes it alone. Sometimes the owners burn out themselves, drinking the profits of the bar or dabbling in drugs. Do your homework regarding ownership laws and legal recourse in the event of a dispute. That said, there are many success stories in the region, where people came for a holiday and built an empire.

Transitions Abroad (www.transitionsabroad.com) and its namesake magazine cover all aspects of overseas life, including landing a job in a variety of fields. The website also provides links to other useful sites and publications for those living abroad.

Transport

This chapter gives an overview of the transport options for getting to the Mekong region, and getting around once there. For more specific information about getting to (and around) each country, see the relevant sections in each chapter. For general details of the region's border crossings, see p33.

GETTING THERE & AWAY

Entering the Region

All the countries in the region have international airports, but Bangkok is far and away the most important hub. There are long-haul flights linking Hanoi and Ho Chi Minh City (Saigon) to Europe and North America, but Phnom Penh and Vientiane are only accessible via a regional gateway such as Bangkok, Hong Kong or Singapore.

When it comes to land borders, Thailand is linked to Malaysia for those visiting more of Southeast Asia. Myanmar (Burma) looks like a tantalising option for overland travel to India, but this is not currently permitted. Both Laos and Vietnam share borders with China for those heading deeper into Asia or planning an epic overland trip to or from Europe.

Flights, tours and rail tickets can be booked online at www.lonelyplanet.com/bookings.

Passport

To enter the Mekong region countries, your passport must be valid for at least six months from your date of entry, even if you're only staying for a few days. You may be refused entry if your passport doesn't have enough blank pages available for a visa. When checking into hotels in Vietnam, staff will request a copy of your passport.

Air

For specific information on airports and airlines operating to (and around) each country in the Mekong region, see the Air sections of the relevant chapter.

Tickets

The major Asian gateways for cheap flights are Bangkok, Hong Kong and Singapore. Bangkok is the best place to shop for onward tickets and tickets around the region.

To research and buy a ticket on the internet, try these services:

Cheapflights (www.cheapflights.com) No-frills website with a number of destinations.

Kayak (www.kayak.com) Reliable fare comparison website.

Lonely Planet (www.lonelyplanet.com) Use the Trip Planner service to book multistop trips.

Lowest Fare (www.lowestfare.com) They promise... 'the lowest fares'.

CLIMATE CHANGE & TRAVEL

Every form of transport that relies on carbon-based fuel generates CO_2, the main cause of human-induced climate change. Modern travel is dependent on aeroplanes, which might use less fuel per kilometre per person than most cars but travel much greater distances. The altitude at which aircraft emit gases (including CO_2) and particles also contributes to their climate change impact. Many websites offer 'carbon calculators' that allow people to estimate the carbon emissions generated by their journey and, for those who wish to do so, to offset the impact of the greenhouse gases emitted with contributions to portfolios of climate-friendly initiatives throughout the world. Lonely Planet offsets the carbon footprint of all staff and author travel.

STA Travel (www.statravel.com) Leading student travel agency with cheap fares, plus separate websites for the UK, Australia and New Zealand.

Trailfinders (www.trailfinders.co.uk) Popular UK flight specialist.

Travel.com (www.travel.com) This website also has numerous destinations.

Travelocity (www.travelocity.com) Popular US website for flights.

Round-The-World & Circle Asia Tickets

Bucket shops, consolidators and online search engines offer cheap tickets to the region. If Asia is one of many stops on a global tour, consider a round-the-world (RTW) ticket, which allows a certain number of stops within a set time period as long as you don't backtrack; for more information, talk to a travel agent.

Circle Asia fares are offered by various airline alliances for a circular route originating in the USA, Europe or Australia and travelling to two destinations in Asia, including Southeast and East Asia. Contact individual airlines or a travel agent for more info.

Bangkok is easily the best-connected city in the region, with flights to the Indian subcontinent, the Far East, Central Asia and the Middle East. Japan is well connected to the region, with flights to many of the larger cities, as is South Korea.

Land

The land borders between the Mekong region and the rest of Asia include the Lao and Vietnamese northern borders with China and the frontier that Thailand shares with Malaysia and Myanmar.

See p33 for general details of the region's border crossings.

Sea

Apart from a few cruises that call at ports in Thailand, Vietnam and, occasionally, Cambodia, there are no real options for travelling to the Mekong region by sea.

Tours

Tours through the Mekong region are offered by travel agencies worldwide. Tours come in every shape and size from budget trips to ultimate indulgences. Tours are not bad value when you tally everything up (flights, hotels, transport), but then again it's a cheap region in which to travel.

It's easy enough to fly into Bangkok or another major city in the region and make travel arrangements from there. See individual country chapters for recommended local travel agents. The main saving through booking before arrival is time, and if time is more precious than money, a prebooked tour is probably right for you.

For a rewarding trip through the Mekong region, consider contacting the following.

Australia

Adventure World (☎02-8913 0755; www.adventureworld.com.au) Adventure tours throughout the region.

Intrepid Travel (☎1300 360 667; www.intrepidtravel.com.au) Small-group tours for all budgets with an environmental, social and cultural edge.

Peregrine (☎02-9290 2770; www.peregrineadventures.com) Small-group and tailor-made tours supporting responsible tourism.

New Zealand

Adventure World (☎09-524 5118; www.adventureworld.co.nz) A wide range of adventure tours covering the region.

Pacific Cycle Tours (☎03-972 9913; www.bike-nz.com) Mountain-bike tours through Indochina, plus hiking trips.

UK

Audley Travel (☎01604-234855; www.audleytravel.com) Popular tailor-made specialist covering all of Vietnam.

Cox & Kings (☎020-7873 5000; www.coxandkings.co.uk) Well-established high-end company, strong on cultural tours.

Explore (☎0870-333 4001; www.explore.co.uk) Long-running company with affordable adventure trips.

Hands Up Holidays (☎0776-501 3631; www.handsupholidays.com) This company brings guests closer to the people of the Mekong through its responsible holidays with a spot of volunteering.

Wild Frontiers (☎020-7376 3968; www.wildfrontiers.co.uk) Adventure specialist with themed tours and innovative adventures.

USA

Asia Transpacific Journeys (☎800-642 2742; www.asiatranspacific.com) Group tours and tailor-made trips across the Asia-Pacific region.

Distant Horizons (☎800-333 1240; www.distanthorizons.com) Educational tours for discerning travellers.

Myths & Mountains (☎775-832 5454; www.mythsandmountains.com) Well-respected high-end adventure-travel company.

GETTING AROUND

See p33 for general details of the region's border crossings.

Air

Air travel is a mixed bag in the Mekong region. Some routes are now a real bargain, as no-frills regional carriers such as **Air Asia** (www.airasia.com) offer heavily discounted fares. However, on many other routes, there may only be one carrier and prices are high.

One of the best airlines in the region is **Bangkok Airways** (www.bangkokairways.com), billing itself as Asia's boutique airline. It links some of the most popular places in the Mekong region and offers a high level of service. Among the national carriers, **Thai Airways** (www.thaiair.com) has the best reputation, but **Vietnam Airlines** (www.vietnamairlines.com) has upped the level of its game in recent years.

For a quick look at the most popular routes in the region, see the air routes map.

A little caution is necessary when buying tickets from travel agents. Carefully check the tickets to make sure that the dates meet your specifications and confirm with the airline as soon as possible.

Most airports in Southeast Asia charge a departure tax, so make sure you keep some local currency in reserve if it is not included in the ticket price.

Air Passes

The national airlines of Southeast Asian countries frequently run promotional deals from select Western cities or for regional travel. **Airtimetable.com** (www.airtimetable.com) posts seasonal passes and promotions.

Bangkok Airways offers a Discovery Pass (in conjunction with Lao Airlines), which includes domestic coupons for US$88 in Thailand and US$70 in Laos, plus international coupons from US$120 per sector (US$200 for longer distances).

Bicycle

Touring Southeast Asia on a bicycle has been steadily growing in popularity. Many long-distance cyclists start in Thailand and head into Indochina for some challenging adventures.

Mekong Region Air Routes

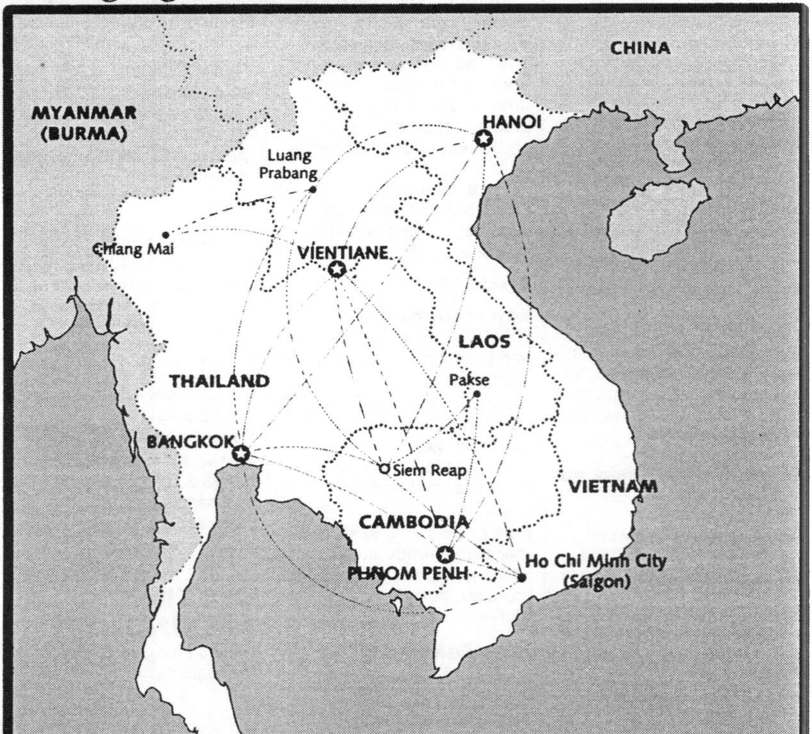

ROAD DISTANCES (KM)

	Bangkok	Battambang	Chiang Mai	Dalat	Halong City	Hanoi	Ho Chi Minh City (Saigon)	Hoi An	Hué	Luang Prabang	Kratie	Pha Taem National Park	Phnom Penh	Sapa	Si Phan Don	Siem Reap	Sihanoukville	Sukhothai Historical Park	Lampang
Battambang	335																		
Chiang Mai	589	797																	
Dalat	977	759	1458																
Halong City	1361	1090	1018	1184															
Hanoi	1238	1041	896	1133	127														
Ho Chi Minh City (Saigon)	761	452	1197	226	1264	1206													
Hoi An	1101	863	1237	509	703	644	706												
Hué	1090	904	1141	593	601	542	797	100											
Luang Prabang	879	818	480	1458	675	616	1258	803	642										
Kratie	738	467	1195	410	1215	1156	201	596	696	1138									
Pha Taem National Park	533	427	1010	658	949	891	687	566	466	976	233								
Phnom Penh	564	245	1050	430	673	615	196	677	577	1151	278	546							
Sapa	1090	1164	767	1365	397	339	1528	826	726	326	1395	1142	1437						
Si Phan Don	567	410	1009	634	949	891	427	477	377	990	240	323	350	1292					
Siem Reap	355	139	841	627	1243	1184	378	719	819	892	391	330	263	1235	334				
Sihanoukville	549	404	1077	634	1446	1387	412	975	1075	1142	481	550	198	1438	533	447			
Sukhothai Historical Park	420	749	246	1387	805	746	1029	914	814	326	1023	878	832	736	925	653	907		
Lampang	510	912	76	1464	1034	975	1130	1060	960	373	1142	988	972	733	1017	757	973	164	
Vientiane	530	644	704	1059	665	665	968	758	658	257	811	740	859	578	714	656	859	228	390

Vietnam is a great place to take a bicycle. Traffic is relatively light away from National Hwy 1A, buses take bicycles and the entire coastal route is feasible, give or take a few hills. In Cambodia and Laos, road conditions can make two-wheeling more challenging, but light traffic, especially in Laos, makes pedalling more pleasant than elsewhere.

International standard bicycles and components can be bought in Bangkok and Phnom Penh, but most cyclists bring their own. Bikes can travel by air; ask about extra charges and shipment specifications.

Boat

Boats are a major feature of the Mekong region, both on the mother river itself and up and down the smaller rivers of the region. River cruising is becoming increasingly popular and there are several options to idle away some time on the Mekong. In the far north, there are boat connections between Jǐnghóng in Yúnnán and Chiang Saen in Thailand (see the boxed text, p414). The leisurely *Luang Say* cruise is a fine way to link Huay Xai and Luang Prabang with a night in Pak Beng. See p329 for details. For those on a budget, there are plenty of public boats running this way.

There are several companies that offer luxury boat cruises between Ho Chi Minh City and Siem Reap via Phnom Penh:

Indochina Sails (www.indochina-sails.com)

Jayavarman VII (www.heritage-line.com)

Pandaw Cruises (www.pandaw.com)

Toum Teav Cruises (www.cfmekong.com)

There are also fast boats plying the Mekong between Chau Doc and Phnom Penh for those who want to explore the Mekong Delta without backtracking to Ho Chi Minh City. For more details see the border crossing boxed text, p154.

SURVIVING THE STREETS

Wherever you roam in the region, you'll have to cross some busy streets eventually, so if you don't want to wind up like a bug on a windscreen, pay close attention to a few pedestrian survival rules. Foreigners frequently make the mistake of thinking that the best way to cross a busy street in the Mekong region is to run quickly across, but this could get you creamed. Most locals cross the street slowly – very slowly – giving the motorbike drivers sufficient time to judge their position so they can pass on either side. They won't stop or even slow down, but they will try to avoid hitting you. Just don't make any sudden moves.

Bus

Bus travel has become a great way to get around with improved roads throughout the region. Thailand offers by far the most comfortable buses. Cambodia and Vietnam have a pretty impressive network of buses connecting major cities, although these dry up in remote areas. Buses in Laos are reasonable on the busiest routes, but pretty poor elsewhere.

In most cases, land borders are crossed via bus; these either travel straight through the two countries with a stop for border formalities, or require a change of buses at the appropriate border towns.

Be aware that theft does occur on some long-distance buses; keep all valuables on your person, not in a stowed bag.

Car & Motorcycle

Motorcycles are a great way to get up close and personal with the region, although drive carefully to ensure you don't get too up close and personal. Motorcycles are available for hire or purchase, but require more safety precautions (such as a helmet, wet-weather gear and a quick brake test) than many visitors realise.

It is advisable to hire a car or motorcycle in a certain locality rather than depend upon it for regional travel. You could cover Thailand by car pretty easily and enjoy well-signposted, well-paved roads. Vietnam has decent roads these days, but self-drive is not possible. Road conditions in Laos and Cambodia vary, although sealed roads are now the norm; both countries offer brilliant motorbiking for experienced riders, not forgetting the incredible mountain roads of northern Vietnam.

Driving Licence

Self-drive car hire is only really possible in Thailand. If you are planning to do any driving, get an International Driving Permit (IDP) from your local automobile association before you leave your home country; IDPs are inexpensive and valid for one year.

There are some fantastic motorbiking opportunities in the region, but it is usually a case of no licence required.

Hire

Thailand is the only place with Western self-drive car-hire chains, although Laos also has a self-drive option now. However, vehicles with driver are available at very reasonable rates in all countries of the region. For rural areas of Cambodia, Laos and Vietnam, 4WDs are necessary. Guesthouses and families rent motorcycles cheaply throughout the region, usually for around US$5 to US$10 a day. In Cambodia and Laos, 250cc dirt bikes are available and are a lot of fun if you know how to handle them. In Thailand, motorbikes of every shape and size are available, but to rent a bigger bike you will need to show a licence.

Insurance

Get insurance with a motorcycle if at all possible. The more-reputable motorcycle-hire places insure all their motorcycles; some will do it for an extra charge. Without insurance you're responsible for anything that happens to the bike. To be absolutely clear about your liability, ask for a written estimate of the

MOTORCYCLE TIPS

Most Asians are so adept at driving and riding on motorcycles that they can balance the whole family on the front bumper, or even take a quick nap as a passenger. Foreigners unaccustomed to motorcycles are not as graceful. If you're riding on the back of a motorcycle remember to relax. For balance hold on to the back bar, not the driver's waist. Tall people should keep their long legs tucked in as most drivers are used to shorter passengers. Women (or men) wearing skirts should always ride side-saddle and collect longer skirts so that they don't catch in the wheel or drive chain. Enjoy the ride.

replacement cost for a similar bike.

Insurance for a hired car is also necessary. Be sure to ask the car-hire agent about liability and damage coverage.

Motorcycle Tours

Specialised motorbike tours through Indochina are growing in popularity. It is a great way to get off the trail and explore remote regions. Two wheels can reach the parts that four wheels sometimes can't, traversing small trails and traffic-free back roads.

For specialised companies in each country, see the individual country chapters. One company that runs adventurous trips covering Laos and Vietnam, and sometimes Cambodia, is Hanoi-based **Explore Indochina** (☎091-309 3159; www.exploreindochina.com).

Road Rules

Basically, there aren't many, arguably any. Drive cautiously. An incredible number of lives are lost on roads in this region every year, particularly around major holidays. Size matters and the biggest vehicle wins by default, regardless of circumstances – might makes right on the road. The middle of the road is typically used as an invisible third lane, even if there is oncoming traffic. And the horn is used to notify other vehicles that you intend to pass them. Be particularly careful about children on the road; it's common to find kids playing hopscotch in the middle of a major highway. Livestock on the road is also a menace; hit a cow on a motorbike and you'll both be hamburger.

Safety

Always check a vehicle thoroughly before you take it out. Look at the tyres for treads, check for oil leaks, test the brakes. You may be held liable for any problems that weren't duly noted before your departure. When driving a motorcycle, wear protective clothing and a helmet. Long trousers, long-sleeved shirts and shoes are highly recommended as protection against sunburn and as a second skin if you fall. If your helmet doesn't have a visor, then wear goggles, glasses or sunglasses to keep bugs, dust and other debris out of your eyes.

FARE'S FAIR?

This is the million-dong question: 'Am I being quoted the right fare or are they completely ripping me off?' Well, there's no easy answer, but here are some guidelines to help you navigate the maze.

Airfares are usually fixed, although web fares differ depending on when you book and what dates you want to travel. Rail fares are also fixed, although naturally there are different prices for different classes. Bus fares are a bit more complicated. If you buy the ticket from the point of departure (ie the bus station), then the price is usually fixed and very reasonable. However, should you board the bus along the way, then there is a chance the driver or conductor will overcharge. This is more prevalent in more remote areas, where prices may be four or five times what the locals pay. Most boat fares for ferries or hydrofoils are fixed, but not for small local boats or some tourist boats.

When it comes to local transport, local bus prices are usually fixed and displayed by the door. Taxis are mostly metered and very cheap, but some taxis have dodgy meters that run fast. Cyclo (pedicab), motorbike taxi and túk-túk fares are most definitely not fixed and you need to bargain. Local transport prices throughout this book are indicative; the actual price of a ride depends on the wiliness of the driver and your negotiating skills.

Hitching

Hitching is never entirely safe in any country in the world and is not recommended. Travellers who decide to hitch should understand that they are taking a small but potentially serious risk. People who do choose to hitch will be safer if they travel in pairs and let someone know where they are planning to go.

Locals do flag down private and public vehicles for a lift, but some sort of payment is usually expected.

Local Transport

Beyond urban centres, personal ownership of cars in the region is not that common, so local transport in towns and cities is a roaring trade. Anything motorised is often modified to carry passengers – from Thailand's high-octane three-wheeled chariots, known as túk-túk, to the Cambodian motorbike and trailer (remorks). Metered taxis are now common in Thailand and Vietnam, and have finally made an appearance in Cambodia, but are still a rarity in Laos. Motorcycle taxis are another popular way to get around, but watch out for the hot exhaust – many a visitor has returned from the region with a souvenir burn on their leg.

In large cities, extensive public bus systems either travel fixed routes or do informal loops around the city picking up passengers along the way. Bangkok, Hanoi and Ho Chi Minh City have efficient bus networks, but there is no such thing in Phnom Penh or Vientiane.

Bangkok boasts a state-of-the-art light-rail and underground system that make zipping around town feel like time travel. At the other end of the scale, the bicycle rickshaw still survives in the region, assuming such aliases as *săhmlór* in Laos and Thailand and cyclo in Cambodia and Vietnam.

Animals still make up a percentage of the local transport in very remote areas, and it is possible to ride an ox cart through remote parts of Cambodia and Laos in the wet season, or trek on an elephant through the wilds of Thailand, Laos or Cambodia.

Train

Thailand and Vietnam have efficient railway networks, including the option of comfortable air-con sleeper berths. Cambodia's railways are in a severely dilapidated state and passenger services are currently not offered, while poor old Laos has no railways at all, save a short link to Thailand via the Friendship Bridge to Nong Khai. Partly due to these missing links, there aren't many international trains in the region. Thai trains serve the Thai border towns of Nong Khai (for crossing into Laos) and Aranya Prathet (for crossing into Cambodia). In Vietnam, there are local trains to the Chinese border towns of Lang Son and Lao Cai. There is also a twice-weekly international service between Hanoi and Beijing.

Plans are afoot for the construction of a high-speed rail link between Kūnmíng- and Bangkok, passing via Luang Prabang and Vientiane. Touted for 2015, it seems a little ambitious given the terrain that will need to be navigated through Laos.

Health

Travellers tend to worry about contracting infectious diseases when in the tropics, but infections are a rare cause of serious illness or death in travellers. Pre-existing medical conditions such as heart disease, and accidental injury (especially traffic accidents), account for most life-threatening problems. Becoming ill in some way, however, is relatively common. Fortunately, most common illnesses can either be prevented with some sensible behaviour or be treated easily with a well-stocked traveller's medical kit.

The following advice is a general guide and does not replace the advice of a doctor trained in travel medicine.

BEFORE YOU GO

Pack medications in their original, clearly labelled, containers. A signed, dated letter from your physician describing medical conditions and medications, including generic names, is a good idea. If carrying syringes or needles, be sure to have a physician's letter stating their medical necessity.

If taking any regular medication, bring a double supply in case of loss or theft. In most Mekong region countries, you can buy many medications over the counter without a doctor's prescription, but it can be difficult to find some of the newer drugs.

Insurance

Even if you're fit and healthy, don't travel without health insurance. Declare any existing medical conditions, as the insurance company *will* check if the problem is pre-existing and will not pay up if undeclared. Adventure activities such as rock climbing sometimes require extra cover. If your health insurance doesn't cover you for medical expenses abroad, consider getting extra insurance. If you're uninsured, emergency evacuation is expensive. Bills of more than US$100,000 are not uncommon.

Find out in advance if the insurance plan will make payments directly to providers or reimburse later for overseas health expenditures. In many countries doctors expect payment in cash. Some prefer a policy that pays doctors or hospitals directly rather than having to pay on the spot and claim later. If claiming later, keep all documentation.

Vaccinations

Specialised travel-medicine clinics are the best source of information, as they stock all available vaccines and can give specific recommendations for each region. The doctors will take into account factors such as past vaccination history, length of trip, activities and existing medical conditions.

Most vaccines don't produce immunity until at least two weeks after they're given, so visit a doctor four to eight weeks before departure. Ask for an International Certificate of Vaccination (otherwise known as the yellow booklet), which will list all the vaccinations given.

Recommended Vaccinations

The World Health Organization (WHO) recommends the following vaccinations for travellers to the Mekong region:

Adult diphtheria and tetanus Single booster recommended if you haven't had one in the previous 10 years.

Hepatitis A Provides almost 100% protection for up to a year; a booster after 12 months provides at least another 20 years' protection.

Hepatitis B Now considered routine for most travellers. Given as three shots over six months. A rapid schedule is also available, as is a combined vaccination with hepatitis A. Lifetime protection occurs in 95% of people.

Measles, mumps and rubella (MMR) Two doses of MMR are required unless you have had the diseases. Many young adults require a booster.

Polio Only one booster is required as an adult for lifetime protection.

Typhoid Recommended unless your trip is less than a week long and only to developed cities. The vaccine offers around 70% protection, lasts for two to three years and comes as a single shot.

Required Vaccinations

The only vaccine required by international regulations is for yellow fever. Proof of vaccination is only required if you have visited a country in the yellow-fever zone within the six days before entering the Mekong region. If travelling to the Mekong region from Africa or South America, check to see if proof of vaccination is required. It is only likely to be an issue if flying directly from an affected country to a major gateway such as Bangkok.

Medical Checklist

Recommended items for a personal medical kit:

- antibacterial cream, eg Muciprocin
- antibiotics for diarrhoea, such as Norfloxacin or Ciprofloxacin; for bacterial diarrhoea Azithromycin; for giardiasis or amoebic dysentery Tinidazole
- antifungal cream, eg Clotrimazole
- antihistamine – there are many options, eg Cetrizine for daytime and Promethazine for night
- anti-inflammatory such as Ibuprofen
- antiseptic, eg Betadine
- antispasmodic for stomach cramps, eg Buscopan
- contraceptives
- decongestant, eg Pseudoephedrine
- DEET-based insect repellent
- diarrhoea treatment – consider an oral rehydration solution (eg Gastrolyte), diarrhoea 'stopper' (eg Loperamide) and antinausea medication (eg Prochlorperazine)
- first-aid items such as scissors, plasters, bandages, gauze, thermometer (but not one with mercury), sterile needles and syringes, safety pins and tweezers
- indigestion medication, eg Quickeze or Mylanta
- paracetamol
- Permethrin to impregnate clothing and mosquito nets
- steroid cream for allergic or itchy rashes, eg 1% to 2% hydrocortisone
- sunscreen and hat
- throat lozenges
- thrush (vaginal yeast infection) treatment, eg Clotrimazole pessaries or Diflucan tablet
- Ural or equivalent if you're prone to urine infections

Websites

There is a wealth of travel health advice on the internet. For further information, **Lonely Planet** (www.lonelyplanet.com) is a good place to start. The **World Health Organization** (www.who.int/ith) publishes a superb book called *International Travel & Health,* which is revised annually and is available online at no cost.

Another website of general interest is **MD Travel Health** (www.mdtravelhealth.com), which provides complete travel health recommendations for every country and is updated daily. The **Centers for Disease Control & Prevention** (CDC; www.cdc.gov) website also has good general information.

Further Reading

Lonely Planet's *Healthy Travel – Asia & India* is a handy pocket-sized book that is packed with useful information, including pretrip planning, emergency first aid, immunisation and disease information, and what to do if you get sick on the road. Other recommended references include *Traveller's Health* by Dr Richard Dawood and *Travelling Well* by Dr Deborah Mills – check out www.travellingwell.com.au.

IN THE MEKONG REGION

Availability & Cost of Health Care

Most capital cities in the Mekong region now have clinics that cater specifically to travellers and expats. These clinics are usually more expensive than local medical facilities, but are worth utilising, as they usually offer a superior standard of care. Additionally, they understand the local system and are aware of the safest local hospitals and best specialists. They can also liaise with insurance companies should you require evacuation. Recommended clinics are listed under Information in the capital-city sections of country chapters in this book. It is difficult to find reliable medical care in rural areas.

Self-treatment may be appropriate if your problem is minor (eg traveller's diarrhoea), you are carrying the appropriate medication and you cannot attend a recommended clinic. If you think you may have a serious disease, especially malaria, do not waste time – travel to the nearest quality facility to receive attention. It is always better to be assessed by a doctor than to rely on self-treatment.

Buying medication over the counter is not recommended, as fake medications and poorly stored or out-of-date drugs are common.

The standard of care in the Mekong region varies from country to country:

Cambodia There are some international clinics in Phnom Penh, and one in Siem Reap, that provide primary care and emergency stabilisation.

Laos There are few reliable facilities in Laos; the nearest good facilities are in northern Thailand.

Thailand There are some very good facilities in Thailand, particularly in Bangkok. This is the city of choice for expats living in the Mekong region who require specialised care.

Vietnam Government hospitals are overcrowded and basic. In order to treat foreigners, a facility needs to obtain a special licence. The private clinics in Hanoi and Ho Chi Minh City are very good.

Infectious Diseases

Cutaneous Larva Migrans

Risk All countries.

This disease, caused by dog hookworm, is common on the beaches of Thailand. The rash starts as a small lump, then slowly spreads in a linear fashion. It is intensely itchy, especially at night. It is easily treated with medications and should not be cut out or frozen.

Dengue

Risk All countries.

This mosquito-borne disease is becoming increasingly problematic throughout the Mekong region, especially in the cities. As there is no vaccine available it can only be prevented by avoiding mosquito bites. The mosquito that carries dengue bites day and night, so use insect-avoidance measures at all times. Symptoms include high fever, severe headache and body ache (dengue used to be known as breakbone fever). Some people develop a rash and experience diarrhoea. There is no specific treatment, just rest and paracetamol – do not take aspirin as it increases the likelihood of haemorrhaging. See a doctor to be diagnosed and monitored.

Filariasis

Risk All countries.

This mosquito-borne disease is very common in the local population, yet very rare in travellers. Mosquito-avoidance measures are the best way to prevent this disease.

Hepatitis A

Risk All countries.

A problem throughout the region, this food- and water-borne virus infects the liver, causing jaundice (yellow skin and eyes), nausea and lethargy. There is no specific treatment for hepatitis A; you just need to allow time for the liver to heal. All travellers to the Mekong region should be vaccinated against hepatitis A.

Hepatitis B

Risk All countries.

The only sexually transmitted disease that can be prevented by vaccination, hepatitis B is spread by body fluids, including sexual contact. In some parts of the Mekong region, up to 20% of the population carry hepatitis B, and usually are unaware of this. The long-term consequences can include liver cancer and cirrhosis.

Hepatitis E

Risk All countries.

Hepatitis E is transmitted through contaminated food and water and has similar symptoms to hepatitis A, but is far less common. It is a severe problem in pregnant women and can result in the death of both mother and baby. There is currently no vaccine, and prevention is by following safe eating and drinking guidelines.

HIV

Risk All countries.

HIV is now one of the most common causes of death in people under the age of 50 in Thailand. The country in the region with the worst and most rapidly increasing HIV problem is Vietnam. Heterosexual sex is now the main method of transmission in these countries.

Influenza

Risk All countries.

Present year-round in the tropics, influenza (flu) symptoms include high fever, muscle aches, runny nose, cough and sore throat. It can be very severe in people over the age of 65 or in those with underlying medical conditions such as heart disease or diabetes; vaccination is recommended for these individuals. There is no specific treatment, just rest and paracetamol.

Japanese B Encephalitis

Risk All countries.

While rare in travellers, this viral disease, transmitted by mosquitoes, infects at least 50,000 locals each year. Most cases occur in rural areas and vaccination is recommended for travellers spending more than one month outside of cities. There is no treatment, and a third of infected people will die while another third will suffer permanent brain damage. Highest-risk areas include Thailand and Vietnam.

Malaria

Risk All countries.

For such a serious and potentially deadly disease, there is an enormous amount of misinformation concerning malaria. You must get expert advice about whether your trip will actually put you at risk. Many parts of the Mekong region, particularly city and resort areas, have minimal to no risk of malaria, and the risk of side effects from the prevention tablets may outweigh the risk of actually getting the disease. For most rural areas in the region, however, the risk of contracting the disease far outweighs the risk of any tablet side effects. Remember that malaria can be fatal. Before you travel, seek medical advice on the right medication and dosage for you.

Malaria is caused by a parasite transmitted by the bite of an infected mosquito. The most important symptom of malaria is fever, but general symptoms such as headache, diarrhoea, cough or chills may also occur. Diagnosis can only be made by taking a blood sample.

Two strategies should be combined to prevent malaria – mosquito avoidance and antimalarial medications. Most people who catch malaria are taking inadequate or no antimalarial medication.

Travellers are advised to prevent mosquito bites by taking the following steps:

» Use a DEET-based insect repellent on exposed skin. Wash off at night, as long as you are sleeping under a mosquito net. Natural repellents such as citronella can be effective, but must be applied more frequently than products containing DEET.

» Sleep under a mosquito net that is impregnated with Permethrin.

» Choose accommodation with screens and fans (if not air-conditioned).

» Impregnate clothing with Permethrin in high-risk areas.

» Wear long sleeves and trousers in light colours.

» Use mosquito coils.

» Spray your room with insect repellent before going out for your evening meal.

There is a variety of medications available. Derivatives of Artesunate are not suitable as a preventive medication. They are useful treatments under medical supervision.

The effectiveness of the Chloroquine and Paludrine combination is now limited in most of the Mekong region. Common side effects include nausea (40% of people) and mouth ulcers. Generally not recommended.

The daily Doxycycline tablet is a broad-spectrum antibiotic that has the added benefit of helping to prevent a variety of tropical diseases, including leptospirosis, tick-borne disease, typhus and meliodosis. The potential side effects include photosensitivity (a tendency to sunburn), thrush in women, indigestion, heartburn, nausea and interference with the contraceptive pill. More serious side effects include ulceration of the oesophagus. You can help prevent this by taking your tablet with a meal and a large glass of water, and never lying down within half an hour of taking it. It must be taken for four weeks after leaving the risk area.

Lariam (Mefloquine) has received much bad press, some of it justified, some not. This weekly tablet suits many people. Serious side effects are rare but include depression, anxiety, psychosis and seizures. Anyone with a history of depression, anxiety, other psychological disorders, or epilepsy should not take Lariam. It is considered safe in the second and third trimesters of pregnancy. Tablets must be taken for four weeks after leaving the risk area.

Malarone is a combination of Atovaquone and Proguanil. Side effects are uncommon and mild, usually nausea and headache. It is the best tablet for scuba divers and for those on short trips to high-risk areas. It must be taken for one week after leaving the risk area.

A final option is to take no preventive tablets but to have a supply of emergency medication should you develop the symptoms of malaria. This is less than ideal, and you'll need to get to a good medical facility within 24 hours of developing a fever. If you choose this option the most effective and safest treatment is Malarone (four tablets once daily for three days).

Measles

Risk All countries.

Measles remains a problem in some parts of the Mekong region. This highly contagious bacterial infection is spread via coughing and sneezing. Most people born before 1966 are immune as they had the disease in childhood. Measles starts with a high fever and rash and can be complicated by pneumonia and brain disease. There is no specific treatment.

Meliodosis

Risk Cambodia, Laos and Thailand.

This infection is contracted by skin contact with soil. It is rare in travellers, but in some parts of northeast Thailand up to 30% of the local population is infected. The symptoms are very similar to those experienced by tuberculosis sufferers. There is no vaccine but it can be treated with medications.

Rabies

Risk All countries.

Still a common problem in most parts of the Mekong region, this uniformly fatal disease is spread by the bite or lick of an infected animal – most commonly a dog or monkey. You should seek medical advice immediately after any animal bite and commence post-exposure treatment. Having pre-travel vaccination means the post-bite treatment is greatly simplified. If an animal bites you, gently wash the wound with soap and water, and apply iodine-based antiseptic. If you are not pre-vaccinated you will need to receive rabies immunoglobulin as soon as possible.

Schistosomiasis

Risk All countries.
Schistosomiasis is a tiny parasite that enters your skin after you've been swimming in contaminated water – travellers usually only get a light infection and hence have no symptoms. If you are concerned, you can be tested three months after exposure. On rare occasions, travellers may develop 'Katayama fever'. This occurs some weeks after exposure, as the parasite passes through the lungs and causes an allergic reaction – symptoms are coughing and fever. Schistosomiasis is easily treated with medications.

Sexually Transmitted Diseases (STDS)

Risk All countries.
Sexually transmitted diseases (STDs) most common in the Mekong region include herpes, warts, syphilis, gonorrhoea and chlamydia. People carrying these diseases often have no signs of infection. Condoms will prevent gonorrhoea and chlamydia but not warts or herpes. If after a sexual encounter you develop any rash, lumps, discharge, or pain when passing urine, seek immediate medical attention. If you have been sexually active during your travels, have an STD check on your return home.

Strongyloides

Risk Cambodia, Laos and Thailand.
This parasite, transmitted by skin contact with soil, is common in travellers but rarely affects them. It is characterised by an unusual skin rash called *larva currens* – a linear rash on the trunk that comes and goes. Most people don't have other symptoms until their immune system becomes severely suppressed, when the parasite can cause an overwhelming infection. It can be treated with medications.

Tuberculosis

Risk All countries.
While tuberculosis is rare in travellers, medical and aid workers and long-term travellers who have significant contact with the local population should take precautions. Vaccination is usually only given to children under the age of five, but adults at risk are recommended to have pre- and post-travel TB testing. The main symptoms are fever, cough, weight loss, night sweats and tiredness.

Typhoid

Risk All countries.
This serious bacterial infection is spread via food and water. It gives a high and slowly progressive fever, headache, and may be accompanied by a dry cough and stomach pain. Typhoid is diagnosed by blood tests and treated with antibiotics. Vaccination is recommended for all travellers spending more than one week in the Mekong region, or travelling outside of the major cities. Be aware that vaccination is not 100% effective so you must still be careful with what you eat and drink.

Typhus

Risk All countries.
Murine typhus is spread by the bite of a flea, whereas scrub typhus is spread via a mite. These diseases are rare in travellers. Symptoms include fever, muscle pains and a rash. You can avoid these diseases by following general insect-avoidance measures. Doxycycline will also prevent them.

Traveller's Diarrhoea

Traveller's diarrhoea is by far the most common problem that affects travellers – between 30% and 50% of people will suffer from it within two weeks of starting their trip. In more than 80% of cases, traveller's diarrhoea is caused by bacteria (there are numerous potential culprits), and therefore responds promptly to treatment with antibiotics. Treatment will depend on your situation – how sick you are, how quickly you need to get better, where you are and so on.

Traveller's diarrhoea is defined as the passage of more than three watery bowel-actions within 24 hours, plus at least one other symptom such as fever, cramps, nausea, vomiting or feeling generally unwell.

Treatment consists of staying well hydrated; rehydration solutions such as Gastrolyte are the best for this. Antibiotics such as Norfloxacin, Ciprofloxacin or Azithromycin will kill the bacteria quickly.

Loperamide is just a 'stopper' and doesn't get to the cause of the problem. It can be helpful, for example, if you have to go on a long bus ride. Don't take Loperamide if you have a fever, or blood in your stools. Seek medical attention quickly if you do not respond to an appropriate antibiotic.

Amoebic Dysentery

Amoebic dysentery is very rare in travellers but is often misdiagnosed by poor-quality labs in the Mekong region. Symptoms are similar to bacterial diarrhoea, ie fever, bloody diarrhoea and generally feeling unwell. You should always seek reliable medical care if you have blood in your diarrhoea. Treatment involves two drugs: Tinidazole or Metronidazole to kill the parasite in your gut and then a second drug to kill the cysts. If left untreated, complications such as liver or gut abscesses can occur.

Giardiasis

Giardia lamblia is a relatively common parasite in travellers. Symptoms include nausea, bloating, excess gas, fatigue and intermittent diarrhoea. The parasite will eventually go away if left untreated but this can take months. The treatment of choice is Tinidazole, with Metronidazole being a second option.

Environmental Hazards

Air Pollution

Air pollution, particularly vehicle pollution, is an increasing problem in most of the Mekong region's major cities. If you have severe respiratory problems speak with your doctor before travelling to any heavily polluted urban centres. This pollution also causes minor respiratory problems such as sinusitis, dry throat and irritated eyes. If troubled by the pollution, leave the city for a few days and get some fresh air.

Diving

Divers and surfers should seek specialised advice before they travel, to ensure their medical kit contains treatment for coral cuts and tropical ear infections, as well as the standard problems. Divers should ensure their insurance covers them for decompression illness – get specialised dive insurance through an organisation such as **Divers Alert Network** (DAN; www.danseap.org).

Food

Eating in restaurants is the biggest risk factor for contracting traveller's diarrhoea. Ways to avoid diarrhoea include eating only freshly cooked food, and avoiding shellfish and food that has been sitting around in buffets. Peel all fruit, cook vegetables and soak salads in iodine water for at least 20 minutes. Eat in busy restaurants where there is a high turnover of customers.

Heat

Many parts of the Mekong region are hot and humid throughout the year. For most people it takes at least two weeks to adapt to the hot climate. Swelling of the feet and ankles is common, as are muscle cramps caused by excessive sweating. Prevent these by avoiding dehydration and excessive activity in the heat. Take it easy when you first arrive. Don't eat salt tablets (they only aggravate the gut), but drink rehydration solution or eat salty food. Treat cramps by stopping activity, resting, rehydrating with double-strength rehydration solution, and gently stretching.

Dehydration is the main contributor to heat exhaustion. Symptoms include weakness, headache, irritability, nausea or vomiting, sweaty skin, a fast, weak pulse, and a normal or slightly elevated body temperature. Treatment involves getting out of the heat and/or sun, fanning the person and applying cool wet cloths to the skin, laying the person flat with their legs raised and rehydrating them with water containing a quarter of a teaspoon of salt per litre. Recovery is usually rapid, but it is common to feel weak for some days afterwards.

Heatstroke is a serious medical emergency. Symptoms come on suddenly and include weakness, nausea, a hot, dry body with a body temperature of more than 41°C, dizziness, confusion, loss of coordination, seizures, and eventually collapse and loss of consciousness. Seek medical help and commence cooling by getting the person out of the heat, removing their clothes, fanning them and applying cool, wet cloths or ice to their body, especially to the groin and armpits.

Prickly heat is a common skin rash in the tropics, caused by sweat being trapped under the skin. The result is an itchy rash of tiny lumps. Treat by moving out of the heat and into an air-conditioned area for a few hours and by having cool showers. Creams and ointments clog the skin so they should be avoided. Locally bought prickly heat powder can be helpful.

Insect Bites & Stings

Bedbugs don't carry disease but their bites are very itchy. They live in the cracks of furniture and walls and then migrate to the bed at night to feed on you. You can treat the itch with an antihistamine.

DRINKING WATER

» Never drink tap water.

» Bottled water is generally safe – check the seal is intact at purchase.

» Boiling water is the most efficient method of purifying it.

» The best chemical purifier is iodine. It should not be used by pregnant women or those people who suffer with thyroid problems.

» Water filters should filter out viruses. Ensure your filter has a chemical barrier such as iodine and a small pore size, ie less than four microns.

Lice inhabit various parts of your body but most commonly your head and pubic area. Transmission is via close contact with an infected person. Lice can be difficult to treat and you may need numerous applications of an antilice shampoo such as Permethrin. Pubic lice are usually contracted from sexual contact.

Ticks are contracted after walking in rural areas. They are commonly found behind the ears, on the belly and in armpits. If you have had a tick bite and experience symptoms such as a rash at the site of the bite or elsewhere, or fever or muscle aches, you should see a doctor. Doxycycline prevents tick-borne diseases.

Leeches are found in humid rainforest areas. They do not transmit any disease but their bites are often intensely itchy for weeks afterwards and can easily become infected. Apply an iodine-based antiseptic to any leech bite to help prevent infection.

Bee and wasp stings mainly cause problems for people who are allergic to them. Anyone with a serious bee or wasp allergy should carry an injection of adrenaline (eg an Epipen) for emergency treatment. For others, pain is the main problem – apply ice to the sting and take painkillers.

Most jellyfish in the waters of Cambodia and Vietnam are not dangerous, just irritating. First aid for jellyfish stings involves pouring vinegar onto the affected area to neutralise the poison. Do not rub sand or water onto the stings. Take painkillers, and if you feel ill in any way after being stung seek medical advice. Take local advice if there are dangerous jellyfish around and keep out of the water.

Parasites

Numerous parasites are common in local populations in the Mekong region; however, most of these are rare in travellers. The two rules for avoiding parasitic infections are to wear shoes and to avoid eating raw food, especially fish, pork and vegetables. A number of parasites are transmitted via the skin by walking barefoot, including strongyloides, hookworm and cutaneous *larva migrans*.

Skin Problems

Fungal rashes are common in humid climates. There are two that commonly affect travellers. The first occurs in moist areas that get less air, such as the groin, armpits and between the toes. It starts as a red patch that slowly spreads and is usually itchy. Treatment involves keeping the skin dry, avoiding chafing and using an antifungal cream such as Clotrimazole or Lamisil.

Cuts and scratches become easily infected in humid climates. Take meticulous care of any cuts and scratches to prevent complications such as abscesses. Immediately wash all wounds in clean water and apply antiseptic. If you develop signs of infection, such as increasing pain and redness, see a doctor. Divers and snorkellers should be particularly careful with coral cuts as they can be easily infected.

Snakes

The Mekong region is home to many species of both poisonous and harmless snakes. Assume that all snakes are poisonous and never try to catch one. Always wear boots and long pants if walking in an area that may have snakes. First aid in the event of a snakebite involves pressure immobilisation via an elastic bandage firmly wrapped around the affected limb, starting at the bite site and working up towards the chest. The bandage should not be so tight that the circulation is cut off, and the fingers or toes should be kept free so the circulation can be checked. Immobilise the limb with a splint and carry the victim to medical attention. Do not use tourniquets or try to suck the venom out.

Antivenin is available for most species in the urban centres of Thailand or Vietnam, but not readily available in Cambodia and Laos.

Sunburn

Even on a cloudy day sunburn can occur rapidly. Always use a strong sunscreen (at least factor 30), making sure to reapply after a swim, and always wear a wide-brimmed hat and sunglasses outdoors. Avoid lying in the sun during the hottest part of the day (10am to 2pm). If you become sunburnt, stay out of the sun until you have recovered, apply cool compresses and take painkillers for the discomfort. One percent hydrocortisone cream applied twice daily is also helpful.

Language

WANT MORE?

For in-depth language information and handy phrases, check out Lonely Planet's *Southeast Asia Phrasebook*. You'll find it at shop.lonelyplanet.com, or you can buy Lonely Planet's iPhone phrasebooks at the Apple App Store.

This chapter offers basic vocabulary to help you get around the countries covered in this book. Read our coloured pronunciation guides as if they were English, and you'll be understood. Some of the phrases have both polite and informal forms – these are indicated by the abbreviations 'pol' and 'inf'. The abbreviations 'm' and 'f' indicate masculine and feminine gender respectively.

KHMER

In our pronunciation guides, vowels and vowel combinations with an h at the end are pronounced hard and aspirated (with a puff of air).

The symbols are read as follows: aa as the 'a' in 'father'; a and ah shorter and harder than aa; i as in 'kit'; uh as the 'u' in 'but'; ii as the 'ee' in 'feet'; eu like 'oo' (with the lips spread flat); euh as eu (short and hard); oh as the 'o' in 'hose' (short and hard); ow as in 'glow'; u as the 'u' in 'flute' (short and hard); uu as the 'oo' in 'zoo'; ua as the 'ou' in 'tour'; uah as ua (short and hard); œ as 'er' in 'her' (more open); ia as the 'ee' in 'beer' (without the 'r'); e as in 'they'; ai as in 'aisle'; ae as the 'a' in 'cat'; ay as ai (slightly more nasal); ey as in 'prey'; o as the 'ow' in 'cow'; av like a nasal ao (without the 'v'); euv like a nasal eu (without the 'v'); ohm as the 'ome' in 'home'; am as the 'um' in 'glum'; ih as the 'ee' in 'teeth' (short and hard); eh as the 'a' in 'date' (short and hard); awh as the 'aw' in 'jaw' (short and hard); and aw as the 'aw' in 'jaw'.

Some consonant combinations in our pronunciation guides are separated with an apostrophe for ease of pronunciation, eg 'j-r' in j'rook and 'ch-ng' in ch'ngain. Also note that k is pronounced as the 'g' in 'go'; kh as the 'k' in 'kind'; p as the final 'p' in 'puppy'; ph as the 'p' in 'pond'; r as in 'rum' but hard and rolling; t as the 't' in 'stand'; and th as the 't' in 'two'.

Basics

Hello.	ជំរាបសួរ	johm riab sua
Goodbye.	លាសិនហើយ	lia suhn hao-y
Excuse me./ Sorry.	សុំទោស	sohm toh
Please.	សូម	sohm
Thank you.	អរគុណ	aw kohn
Yes.	បាទ/ចាស	baat/jaa **(m/f)**
No.	ទេ	te

Numbers – Khmer

1	មួយ	muy
2	ពីរ	pii
3	បី	bei
4	បួន	buan
5	ប្រាំ	bram
6	ប្រាំមួយ	bram muy
7	ប្រាំពីរ	bram pii
8	ប្រាំបី	bram bei
9	ប្រាំបួន	bram buan
10	ដប់	dawp

What's your name?

អ្នកឈ្មោះអី? — niak ch'muah ei

My name is ...

ខ្ញុំឈ្មោះ ... — kh'nyohm ch'muah ...

Accommodation

I'd like a room ...	ខ្ញុំសុំបន្ទប់ ...	kh'nyohm sohm bantohp ...
for one person	សំរាប់ មួយនាក់	samruhp muy niak
for two people	សំរាប់ ពីរនាក់	samruhp pii niak

How much is it per day?

តំលៃមួយថ្ងៃ ប៉ុន្មាន? — damlay muy th'ngay pohnmaan

Eating & Drinking

Do you have a menu in English?

មានមីនុយជាភាសា អង់គ្លេសទេ? — mien menui jea piasaa awnglay te

I'm vegetarian.

ខ្ញុំតមសាច — kh'nyohm tawm sait

The bill, please.

សូមគិតលុយ — sohm kuht lui

beer	ប៊ៀរ	bii-yœ
coffee	កាហ្វេ	kaa fey
tea	តែ	tai
water	ទឹក	teuk

Emergencies

Help!

ជួយខ្ញុំផង! — juay kh'nyohm phawng

Call the police!

ជួយហៅប៉ូលិសមក! — juay hav polih mao

Call a doctor!

ជួយហៅគ្រូពេទ្យមក! — juay hav kruu paet mao

Where are the toilets?

បង្គន់នៅឯណា? — bawngkohn neuv ai naa

Shopping & Services

How much is it?

នេះថ្លៃប៉ុន្មាន? — nih th'lay pohnmaan

That's too much.

ថ្លៃពេក — th'lay pek

I'm looking for the ...	ខ្ញុំរក ...	kh'nyohm rohk ...
bank	ធនាគារ	th'niakia
market	ផ្សារ	p'saa
post office	ប្រៃសណីយ	praisuhnii
public telephone	ទូរស័ព្ទ សាធារណៈ	turasahp saathiaranah

Transport & Directions

Where is a/the ...?

... នៅឯណា? — ... neuv ai naa

bus stop

ចំណតឡានឈ្នួល — jamnawt laan ch'nual

train station

ស្ថានីយរថភ្លើង — s'thaanii roht plœng

What time does the ... leave?	... ចេញម៉ោង ប៉ុន្មាន?	... jein maong pohnmaan
boat	ទូក	duk
bus	ឡានឈ្នួល	laan ch'nual
train	រថភ្លើង	roht plœng
plane	យន្តហោះ	yohn hawh

LAO

Lao is a tonal language, meaning that many identical sounds are differentiated only by changes in the pitch of a speaker's voice. Pitch variations are relative to the speaker's natural vocal range, so that one person's low tone isn't necessarily the same pitch as another person's. There are six tones in Lao, indicated in our pronunciation guides by accent marks on letters: low tone (eg di̖i), high (eg heúa), rising (eg sǎam), high falling (eg sâo) and low falling (eg khào). Note that no accent mark is used for the mid tone (eg het).

The pronunciation of vowels goes like this: i as in 'it'; ii as in 'feet'; ai as in 'aisle'; aa as the 'a' in 'father'; a as a short aa; ae as the 'a' in 'bad'; eh as the 'a' in 'hate'; oe as the 'u' in 'fur'; eu as the 'i' in 'sir'; u as in 'flute'; uu as in 'food'; ao as in 'now'; aw as in 'jaw'; o as in 'phone'; oh as in 'toe'; ia as in 'Ian'; ua as in 'tour'; iu as in 'yew'; and awy as the 'oy' in 'boy'.

Also keep in mind the distinction between the following consonant sounds: k is pronounced as a hard 'k' (a bit like 'g'); kh as the 'k' in 'kite'; p as a hard 'p' (a bit like 'b'); ph as the 'p' in 'put'; t as a hard 't' (a bit like 'd'); and th as the 't' in 'tip'.

Basics

Hello.	ສະບາຍດີ	sábąai-dìi
Goodbye.	ສະບາຍດີ	sábąai-dìi
Excuse me./Sorry.	ຂໍໂທດ	khǎw thòht
Please.	ກະລຸນາ	ga-lú-náa
Thank you.	ຂອບໃຈ	khàwp jại
Yes./No.	ແມ່ນ/ບໍ່	maan/baw

What's your name?
ເຈົ້າຊື່ຫຍັງ jâo seu nyǎng

My name is ...
ຂ້ອຍຊື່ ... kháwy seu ...

Accommodation

Where's a ...?	... ຢູ່ໃສ?	... yùu sǎi
campsite	ບ່ອນຕັ້ງເຄັ້ມ	born dâng kêm
guesthouse	ເຮືອນພັກ	héu-an pak
hotel	ໂຮງແຮມ	hóhng háem

Do you have a ...?	ເຈົ້າມີ ... ຫວ່າງບໍ່?	jôw mii ... wâhng baw
double room	ຫ້ອງນອນ ຕຽງຄູ່	hàwng náwn tìang khuu
single room	ຫ້ອງນອນ ຕຽງດ່ຽວ	hàwng náwn tìang diaw

Numbers – Lao

1	ນຶ່ງ	neung
2	ສອງ	sǎwng
3	ສາມ	sǎam
4	ສີ່	sii
5	ຫ້າ	hàa
6	ຫົກ	hók
7	ເຈັດ	jét
8	ແປດ	pàet
9	ເກົ້າ	kâo
10	ສິບ	síp

How much is it per ...?	... ເທົ່າໃດ?	... thao dại
night	ຄືນລະ	khéun-la
person	ຄົນລະ	khón-la

Eating & Drinking

Please bring the ...	ຂໍ ... ແດ່	khǎw ... dae
bill	ແຊັກ	saek
menu	ລາຍການອາຫານ	láai-kąan ąa-hǎan

What do you have that's special?
ມີຫຍັງພິເສດບໍ່ míi nyǎng phi-sèt baw

I'm a vegetarian.
ຂ້ອຍກິນແຕ່ຜັກ khàwy kịn tae phák

beer	ເບຍ	bịa
coffee	ກາເຟ	kąa-féh
tea	ຊາ	sáa
water	ນ້ຳ	nâm

Emergencies

Help!	ຊ່ວຍແດ່!	suay dae
Go away!	ໄປເດີ້!	pại dôe

Call the police!
ຊ່ວຍເອີ້ນຕຳຫລວດແດ່! suay ôen tam-lùat dae

Call a doctor!
ຊ່ວຍຕາມຫາໝໍໃຫ້ແດ່! suay tąam hǎa mǎw hài dae

I'm lost.
ຂ້ອຍຫລົງທາງ khàwy lǒng tháang

Where are the toilets?
ຫ້ອງສ້ວມຢູ່ໃສ? hàwng sùam yuu sǎi

Shopping & Services

I'm looking for the ...	ຂ້ອຍຊອກຫາ ...	khàwy sâwk hǎa ...
bank	ທະນາຄານ	thanáakháan
post office	ໄປສະນີ (ໂຮງສາຍ)	pại-sá-nii (hóhng sǎai)
telephone	ໂທລະສັບ	thóhlasáp

How much (for) ...?
... ເທົ່າໃດ? ... thao dại

The price is very high.
ລາຄາແພງຫລາຍ láakháa pháeng lǎai

Transport & Directions

Where is the ...?	... ຢູ່ໃສ?	... yùu sǎi
bus station	ສະຖານີລົດ ປະຈຳທາງ	sathǎanii lot pájạm tháang
bus stop	ບ່ອນຈອດລົດ ປະຈຳທາງ	bawn jàwt lot pájạm tháang

When will the ... leave?	... ຈະອອກ ຈັກໂມງ	... já àwk ják móhng
boat	ເຮືອ	héua
bus	ລົດ	lot
minivan	ລົດຕູ້	lot tûu
plane	ເຮືອບິນ	héua bǐn

THAI

In Thai the meaning of a syllable may be altered by means of tones. In standard Thai there are five tones: low (eg bàht), mid (eg dee), falling (eg mâi), high (eg máh) and rising (eg sǎhm). The range of all tones is relative to each speaker's vocal range, so there is no fixed 'pitch' intrinsic to the language.

In our pronunciation guides, the hyphens indicate syllable breaks within words, and for ease of pronunciation some compound vowels are further divided with a dot, eg mêu·a-rai (when).

The vowel a is pronounced as in 'about', aa as the 'a' in 'bad', ah as the 'a' in 'father', ai as in 'aisle', air as in 'flair' (without the 'r'), eu as the 'er' in 'her' (without the 'r'), ew as in 'new' (with rounded lips), oh as the 'o' in 'toe', or as in 'torn' (without the 'r') and ow as in 'now'.

Note also the pronunciation of the following consonants: b (a hard 'p' sound, almost like a 'b', eg in 'hip-bag'); đ (a hard 't' sound, like a sharp 'd', eg in 'mid-tone'); and r (as in 'run' but flapped; often pronounced like 'l').

Basics

Hello.	สวัสดี	sà-wàt-dee
Goodbye.	ลาก่อน	lah gòrn
Excuse me.	ขออภัย	kŏr à-pai
Sorry.	ขอโทษ	kŏr tôht
Please.	ขอ	kŏr
Thank you.	ขอบคุณ	kòrp kun
Yes.	ใช่	châi
No.	ไม่	mâi

What's your name?
คุณชื่ออะไร kun chêu à-rai
My name is ...
ผม/ดิฉัน pŏm/dì-chăn
ชื่อ... chêu ... (m/f)

Accommodation

Where's a ...?	... อยู่ที่ไหน	... yòo têe năi
campsite	ค่ายพักแรม	kâi pák raam
guesthouse	บ้านพัก	bâhn pák
hotel	โรงแรม	rohng raam
youth hostel	บ้าน เยาวชน	bâhn yow-wá-chon

Do you have a ... room?	มีห้อง ... ไหม	mee hôrng ... măi
single	เดี่ยว	dèe·o
double	เตียงคู่	đee·ang kôo

Eating & Drinking

What would you recommend?
คุณแนะนำอะไรบ้าง kun náa-nam à-rai bâhng
I'd like (the menu), please.
ขอ (รายการ อาหาร) หน่อย kŏr (rai gahn ah-hăhn) nòy
I don't eat (red meat).
ผม/ดิฉันไม่กิน (เนื้อแดง) pŏm/dì-chăn mâi gin (néu·a daang) (m/f)
Cheers!
ไชโย chai-yoh
Please bring the bill.
ขอบิลหน่อย kŏr bin nòy

beer	เบียร์	bee·a
coffee	กาแฟ	gah-faa
tea	ชา	chah
water	น้ำดื่ม	nám dèum

Numbers – Thai

1	หนึ่ง	nèung
2	สอง	sŏrng
3	สาม	săhm
4	สี่	sèe
5	ห้า	hâh
6	หก	hòk
7	เจ็ด	jèt
8	แปด	ɓàat
9	เก้า	gôw
10	สิบ	sìp

Emergencies

Help!	ช่วยด้วย	chôo·ay dôo·ay
Go away!	ไปให้พ้น	ɓai hâi pón

I'm lost.
ผม/ดิฉัน หลงทาง — pŏm/dì-chăn lŏng tahng (m/f)

Call the police!
เรียกตำรวจหน่อย — rêe·ak đam·ròo·at nòy

Call a doctor!
เรียกหมอหน่อย — rêe·ak mŏr nòy

I'm ill.
ผม/ดิฉันป่วย — pŏm/dì-chăn ɓòo·ay (m/f)

Where are the toilets?
ห้องน้ำอยู่ที่ไหน — hôrng nám yòo têe năi

Shopping & Services

I'd like to buy ...
อยากจะซื้อ ... — yàhk jà séu ...

How much is it?
เท่าไร — tôw-rai

That's too expensive.
แพงไป — paang ɓai

Transport & Directions

Where's ...?
... อยู่ที่ไหน — ... yòo têe năi

What's the address?
ที่อยู่คืออะไร — têe yòo keu à-rai

Can you show me (on the map)?
ให้ดู (ในแผนที่) ได้ไหม — hâi doo (nai păan têe) dâi măi

A ... ticket, please.	ขอตั๋ว ...	kŏr đŏo·a ...
one-way	เที่ยวเดียว	têe·o dee·o
return	ไปกลับ	ɓai glàp

boat	เรือ	reu·a
bus	รถเมล์	rót mair
plane	เครื่องบิน	krêu·ang bin
train	รถไฟ	rót fai

VIETNAMESE

Vietnamese is written in a Latin-based phonetic alphabet, which was declared the official written form in 1910.

In our pronunciation guides, a is pronounced as in 'at', aa as in 'father', aw as in 'law', er as in 'her', oh as in 'doh!', ow as in 'cow', u as in 'book', uh as in 'but' and uhr as in 'fur' (without the 'r'). We've used dots (eg dee·úhng) to separate the combined vowel sounds. Note also that d is pronounced as in 'stop', đ as in 'dog', and ğ as in 'skill'.

Vietnamese uses a system of tones to make distinctions between words – so some vowels are pronounced with a high or low pitch. There are six tones in Vietnamese, indicated in the written language (and in our pronunciation guides) by accent marks on the vowel: mid (ma), low falling (mà), low rising (má), high broken (mã), high rising (má) and low broken (mạ). The mid tone is flat.

The variation in vocabulary between the Vietnamese of the north and the south is indicated by (N) and (S) respectively.

Basics

Hello.	*Xin chào.*	sin jòw
Goodbye.	*Tạm biệt.*	daạm bee·ụht
Excuse me./Sorry.	*Xin lỗi.*	sin lõy
Please.	*Làm ơn.*	laàm ern
Thank you.	*Cảm ơn.*	ğaảm ern
Yes.	*Vâng./Dạ.* (N/S)	vuhng/ yạ
No.	*Không.*	kawm

What's your name?
Tên là gì? — den laà zeè

My name is ...
Tên tôi là ... — den doy laà ...

Accommodation

Where's a ...?	*Đâu có ... ?*	đoh ğó ...
campsite	*nơi cắm trại*	ner·ee ğúhm chại
hotel	*khách sạn*	kaák saạn
guesthouse	*nhà khách*	nyaà kaák

I'd like a ...	*Tôi muốn ...*	doy moo·úhn ...
single room	*phòng đơn*	fòm dern
double room	*phòng giường đôi*	fòm zuhr·èrng đoy

How much is it per ...?	*Giá bao nhiêu một ...?*	zaá bow nyee·oo mạwt ...
night	*đêm*	đem
person	*người*	nguhr·eè

Eating & Drinking

I'd like the menu.
Tôi muốn thực đơn. doy moo·úhn tụhrk đern

What's the speciality here?
Ở đây có món gì đặc biệt? ér đay kó món zeè dụhk bee·ụht

I'm a vegetarian.
Tôi ăn chay. doy uhn jay

I'd like ...
Xin cho tôi ... sin jo doy ...

Cheers!
Chúc sức khoẻ! júp súhrk kwả

The bill, please.
Xin tính tiền. sin díng dee·ùhn

beer	*bia*	bi·a
coffee	*cà phê*	ğaà fe
tea	*chè/trà* (N/S)	jà/chaà
water	*nước*	nuhr·érk
wine	*rượu nho*	zee·oọ nyo

Emergencies

Help!
Cứu tôi! ğuhr·oó doy

Leave me alone!
Thôi! toy

I'm lost.
Tôi bị lạc đường. doi beẹ laạk đuhr·èrng

Please call the police.
Làm ơn gọi công an. laàm ern gọy ğawm aan

Please call a doctor.
Làm ơn gọi bác sĩ. laàm ern gọy baák seẽ

I'm ill.
Tôi bị đau. doy beẹ đoh

Where is the toilet?
Nhà vệ sinh ở đâu? nyaà vẹ sing ér đoh

Shopping & Services

I'd like to buy ...
Tôi muốn mua ... doy moo·úhn moo·uh ...

How much is this?
Cái này giá bao nhiêu? ğaí này zaá bow nyee·oo

It's too expensive.
Cái này quá mắc. ğaí này gwaá múhk

bank	*ngân hàng*	nguhn haàng
market	*chợ*	jẹr
post office	*bưu điện*	buhr·oo đee·ụhn
tourist office	*văn phòng hướng dẫn du lịch*	vuhn fòm huhr·érng zũhn zoo lịk

Transport & Directions

Where is ...?
... ở đâu? ... ér đọh

What is the address?
Địa chỉ là gì? đee·ụh cheẻ laà zeè

Can you show me (on the map)?
Xin chỉ giùm (trên bản đồ này). sin jeẻ zùm (chen baản dàw này)

I'd like a ... ticket.	*Tôi muốn vé ...*	doy moo·úhn vá ...
one way	*đi một chiều*	đee mạt jee·oò
return	*khứ hồi*	kúhr haw·eè

boat	*thuyền*	twee·ùhn
bus	*xe buýt*	sa beét
plane	*máy bay*	máy bay
train	*xe lửa*	sa lủhr·uh

Numbers – Vietnamese

1	*một*	mạwt
2	*hai*	hai
3	*ba*	baa
4	*bốn*	báwn
5	*năm*	nuhm
6	*sáu*	sóh
7	*bảy*	bảy
8	*tám*	dúhm
9	*chín*	jín
10	*mười*	muhr·eè

This glossary is a list of Cambodian (C), Lao (L), Thai (T) and Vietnamese (V) terms you may come across in the Mekong region.

ao dai (V) – traditional Vietnamese tunic and trousers
APEC – Asia-Pacific Economic Cooperation
apsara (C) – heavenly nymphs or angelic dancers
Asean – Association of Southeast Asian Nations

bąasĭi (L) – sometimes written as 'basi' or 'baci'; a ceremony in which the 32 *khwăn* are symbolically bound to the participant for health and safety
baht (T) – the Thai unit of currency
baray (C) – ancient reservoir
BE (L, T) – Buddhist Era
boeng (C) – lake
BTS (T) – Bangkok Transit System (Skytrain)
bun (L) – festival
buu dien (V) – post office

Cao Daism (V) – Vietnamese religious sect
Cham (C, V) – ethnic minority descended from the people of Champa; a Hindu kingdom dating from the 2nd century BC
chedi (T) – see *stupa*
Chenla (C, L, V) – Pre-Angkorian *Khmer* kingdom covering parts of Cambodia, Laos and Vietnam
Chunchiet (C) – ethnolinguistic minority
CPP (C) – Cambodian People's Party
cyclo (C, V) – bicycle rickshaw

devaraja (C) – god king
DMZ (V) – the misnamed Demilitarised Zone, a strip of land that once separated North and South Vietnam
dong (V) – the Vietnamese unit of currency
duong (V) – road, street; abbreviated as 'Đ'

Ecpat – End Child Prostitution & Trafficking

faràng (T) – Western, Westerner; foreigner
Funan (C, V) – first *Khmer* kingdom, located in Mekong Delta area

HCMC (V) – Ho Chi Minh City (Saigon)
Hoa (V) – ethnic Chinese, the largest single minority group in Vietnam

Indochina – Vietnam, Cambodia and Laos, the French colony of Indochine; the name derives from Indian and Chinese influences
Isan (T) – general term used for northeastern Thailand

jataka (C, L, T) – stories of the Buddha's past lives, often enacted in dance-drama
jumbo (L) – a motorised three-wheeled taxi, sometimes called a *túk-túk*

karst – limestone peaks with caves, underground streams and potholes
khao (T) – hill, mountain
khlong (T) – canal
Khmer (C) – ethnic Cambodians; Cambodian language
Khmer Rouge (C) – literally Red *Khmers*, the commonly used name for the Cambodian communist movement responsible for the genocide in the 1970s
khwăn (L) – guardian spirits of the body
Kinh (V) – the Vietnamese language
kip (L) – the Lao unit of currency
ko (T) – island
koh (C) – island
krama (C) – chequered scarf

lákhon (C, T) – classical dance-drama
linga (C, L, T, V) – phallic symbol

mae nam (L, T) – river
Mahayana – literally, 'Great Vehicle'; a school of Buddhism that extended the early Buddhist teachings; see also *Theravada*
meuang (L, T) – city
MIA (C, L, V) – missing in action, usually referring to US personnel
Montagnards (V) – highlanders, mountain people; specifically the ethnic minorities inhabiting remote areas of Vietnam
moto (C) – motorcycle taxi
Mt Meru – the mythical dwelling place of the Hindu gods, symbolised by the Himalayas
múan (L) – fun, which the Lao believe should be present in all activities
muay thai (T) – Thai boxing

nâam (L, T) – water, river
naga (C, L, T) – mythical serpent-being
NTAL (L) – National Tourism Administration of Lao
NVA (V) – North Vietnamese Army

Pali – ancient Indian language that, along with *Sanskrit*, is the root of Khmer, Lao and Thai
Pathet Lao (L) – literally, 'Country of Laos'; both a general term for the country and the common name for the Lao communist military during the civil war
phansăa (T) – Buddhist lent
phnom (C) – mountain
phu (L) – hill or mountain
POW – prisoner of war
prasat (C, T) – tower, temple
psar (C) – market

quan (V) – urban district

quoc ngu (V) – Vietnamese alphabet

Ramakian (T) – Thai version of the *Ramayana*

Ramayana – Indian epic story of Rama's battle with demons

Reamker (C) – *Khmer* version of the *Ramayana*

remork (C) – (or *remorque-moto*) a motorised three-wheeled pedicab

riel (C) – the Cambodian unit of currency

roi nuoc (V) – water puppetry

rót fai fáa (T) – Skytrain; *BTS*

săhmlór (T) – three-wheeled pedicab

Sanskrit – ancient Hindu language that, along with *Pali*, is the root of *Khmer*, Lao and Thai

sànùk (T) – fun

soi (L, T) – lane, small street

song (L, V) – river

Songkran (T) – Thai New Year, held in mid-April

sŏrngtăaou (L, T) – small pick-up truck with two benches in the back

SRV (V) – Socialist Republic of Vietnam (Vietnam's official name)

stung (C) – small river

stupa – religious monument, often containing Buddha relics

talat (L) – market

Tam Giao (V) – literally, 'triple religion'; Confucianism, Taoism and Buddhism fused over time with popular Chinese beliefs and ancient Vietnamese animism

Tao (V) – the Way; the essence of which all things are made

TAT (T) – Tourism Authority of Thailand

tat (L) – waterfall

Tet (V) – Lunar New Year

thâat (L) – Buddhist *stupa*, reliquary; also written as 'that'

thànŏn (L, T) – road, street, avenue; abbreviated as *'Th'*

Theravada – a school of Buddhism found in Cambodia, Laos and Thailand; this school confined itself to the early Buddhist teachings unlike *Mahayana*

tonlé (C) – major river

tripitaka (T) – Buddhist scriptures

túk-túk (L, T) – motorised *săhmlór*

UNDP – United Nations Development Programme

UXO (C, L, V) – unexploded ordnance

VC (V) – Viet Cong or Vietnamese Communists

vihara (C) – temple sanctuary

wâi (L, T) – palms-together greeting

wat (C, L, T) – Buddhist temple-monastery

wihăhn (T) – sanctuary, hall, dwelling

xe om (V) – motorbike taxi (also *Honda om*)

xich lo (V) – see *cyclo*

behind the scenes

SEND US YOUR FEEDBACK

We love to hear from travellers – your comments keep us on our toes and help make our books better. Our well-travelled team reads every word on what you loved or loathed about this book. Although we cannot reply individually to postal submissions, we always guarantee that your feedback goes straight to the appropriate authors, in time for the next edition. Each person who sends us information is thanked in the next edition – and the most useful submissions are rewarded with a free book.

Visit **lonelyplanet.com/contact** to submit your updates and suggestions or to ask for help. Our award-winning website also features inspirational travel stories, news and discussions.

Note: We may edit, reproduce and incorporate your comments in Lonely Planet products such as guidebooks, websites and digital products, so let us know if you don't want your comments reproduced or your name acknowledged. For a copy of our privacy policy visit lonelyplanet.com/privacy.

OUR READERS

Many thanks to the travellers who used the last edition and wrote to us with helpful hints, useful advice and interesting anecdotes:

Mark Allen, Michel Alov, Sebastian Arabito, Kate Atkinson, Reinier Bakels, Stephanie Barnard, Sara Bengtsson, Patricio Berumen, Anjali Bhasin, Angelique Bryce, Henrik Dam, Kathrin Damm, Frederik De Bleser, Leticia Duboc, Becca Ebels, Allie Edwards Williams, Emma, Carla Figueiredo, Alexandra Finch, Karyne Framand, David Glover, Charlie Gower-Smith, Kylie Greenshields, Paruth Hann, Christopher Hoare, Carl Hollis, Ariel Jacob, Gillian Jeens, Johno, Jon, Denis Kearney, Sebastian Koch, Michael Leboldus, Lia, Markus Lindner, Johanna Meier, Michelle, Judith & Bill Page, Leo Paton, Mathieu Pelletier, Paul Phillips, Paulina Pirart, Harel R, Anthony Ranville, Claire Roberts, Julia Sahin, Morgan Schofield, Steffen Schulze-Ketelhut, Sofia, Anne Sommer, Jean Stewart, Stacey Sudlow, Brenda Sutherland, Yaiza Taihuttu, Caroline Theyse, Ben Thompson, Stijn Timmer, Denise Turcinov, Alex Twose, Marieke Van Bovene, Tim Van Der Velden, Kelly Walsh, Konstantin Willmann

AUTHOR THANKS

Nick Ray

As always a huge and heartfelt thanks to the people of the Mekong region, whose warmth and humour, stoicism and spirit make it a happy yet humbling place to be. Biggest thanks are reserved for my lovely wife Kulikar Sotho, as without her support and encouragement the adventures would not be possible. And to our young children Julian and Belle for enlivening our lives immeasurably.

Many thanks to my Mum and Dad for their many visits to this part of the world. And thank you to my Cambodian family for welcoming me warmly and understanding my not so traditional lifestyle. Thanks to fellow travellers, residents, friends and contacts in the Mekong region who have helped shaped my knowledge and experience here. There is no room to thank everyone, but you all know who you are, as we meet for beers regularly enough.

Thanks also to my co-authors Iain Stewart, Austin Bush, Rich Waters and Greg Bloom, all seasoned authors and good friends, for going the extra mile to ensure this is a worthy new edition.

Finally, thanks to the Lonely Planet team who have worked on this title. The author may be the public face, but a huge amount of work goes into making this a better book behind the scenes and I thank you all for your hard work.

Greg Bloom

The cumulative knowledge of 'the gang' in Phnom Penh was elemental in writing this book – you know who you are. Special thanks to Stephen & Rachel for snouting around Snooky with me, and to Lina, Steve G and colleague-slash-cagey-Phnom-Penh-vet Nick. A nod to daughter Anna for her Phnom Tamao insight, and for enduring climbs up Phnom Chisor and Udong, and to her mama for holding down the fort.

Austin Bush

Thanks to talented Lonely Planeters Ilaria Walker, David Connolly and Bruce Evans; fellow writers Tim Bewer, Alan Murphy and China Williams; and the kind folks on the ground in Thailand including Joe Cummings, Greg Glachant, Craig Harrington, Richard Hermes, Natchaphat Itthi-chaiwarakom, Maher Satter, David Thompson, Pailin Wedel and Patrick Winn.

Iain Stewart

Many thanks to Ilaria and the Melbourne team for inviting me aboard another Southeast Asia title and to my co-pilots in Vietnam: Nick, Peter and Brett. I was greatly aided by kings of the highway Vinh Vu and Mark Wyndham, Ben and Bich in Phong Nha, Tam in Dong Ha, and a great crew in Hoi An including the Dive Bar boys, Neil and Caroline and Dzung the tennis ace.

Richard Waters

Thanks first of all to my fiance, Ali and my kids Finn and Aggie who watch me disappear with a pack on my back at regular intervals. Thanks, too, to my commissioning editor, Ilaria Walker, who continues to send me to enchanting jungles. In Laos my gratitude to Michel Marcel Saada, COPE, MAG, Matt Verborg, WWF, Green Discovery, Adri Berger, Zuela Guesthouse, Les 3 Nagas, Derek Beattie, Sousath Travel and Mr Somkiad. And finally Mark at Apple, Regent St who fixed my Mac.

ACKNOWLEDGMENTS

Climate map data adapted from Peel MC, Finlayson BL & McMahon TA (2007) 'Updated World Map of the Köppen-Geiger Climate Classification', *Hydrology and Earth System Sciences*, 11, 163344.

Cover photograph: Shadow Puppets. Siem Reap, Cambodia, Antony Giblin/Lonely Planet Images

Many of the images in this guide are available for licensing from Lonely Planet Images: www.lonelyplanetimages.com.

THIS BOOK

This third edition of *Vietnam, Cambodia, Laos & Northern Thailand* was coordinated by Nick Ray, Lonely Planet veteran and aficionado of all things Indochina. Nick wrote the Plan Your Trip, Understand and Survival Guide chapters and worked with fellow Phnom Penh local Greg Bloom to write the Cambodia chapter. Nick and Greg were assisted by three of Lonely Planet's most charming, handsome and talented writers: Austin Bush wrote the Northern Thailand chapter, Iain Stewart wrote the Vietnam chapter and Richard Waters wrote the Laos chapter. Research for the previous edition was done by the following: Brett Atkinson, Mark Beales, Tim Bewer, Greg Bloom, Austin Bush, Robert Carmack, Peter Dragicevich, David Lukas, Morrison Polkinghorne, Nick Ray, Iain Stewart, Richard Waters and China Williams. The Health chapter is based on content supplied by Dr Trish Batchelor. This guideBook was commissioned in Lonely Planet's Melbourne office, and produced by the following:

Commissioning Editor Ilaria Walker
Coordinating Editor Nigel Chin
Coordinating Cartographer Xavier Di Toro
Coordinating Layout Designer Mazzy Prinsep
Managing Editors Bruce Evans, Kirsten Rawlings
Managing Cartographers Shahara Ahmed, David Connolly
Managing Layout Designers Chris Girdler, Jane Hart
Assisting Editors Carolyn Bain, Paul Harding, Kim Hutchins, Kristin Odijk, Helen Yeates
Assisting Cartographer James Leversha
Cover Research Sabrina Dalbesio
Internal Image Research Rebecca Skinner
Illustrator Javier Zarracina
Language Content Annelies Mertens, Branislava Vladisavljevic
Thanks to Elin Berglund, Barbara Delissen, Ryan Evans, Chris Girdler, Briohny Hooper, Corey Hutchison, Alex Leung, Catherine Naghten, Trent Paton, Angela Tinson, Gerard Walker, Jeanette Wall

index

ABBREVIATIONS

C	Cambodia
L	Laos
NPA	National Protected Area
T	Thailand
V	Vietnam

000 Map pages
000 Photo pages

I

J

K

000 Map pages
000 Photo pages

L

M

000 Map pages
000 Photo pages

Q

R

S

X

Y

Z

000 Map pages
000 Photo pages

how to use this book

These symbols will help you find the listings you want:

- Sights
- Beaches
- Activities
- Courses
- Tours
- Festivals & Events
- Sleeping
- Eating
- Drinking
- Entertainment
- Shopping
- Information/ Transport

These symbols give you the vital information for each listing:

- Telephone Numbers
- Opening Hours
- Parking
- Nonsmoking
- Air-Conditioning
- Internet Access
- Wi-Fi Access
- Swimming Pool
- Vegetarian Selection
- English-Language Menu
- Family-Friendly
- Pet-Friendly
- Bus
- Ferry
- Metro
- Subway
- Tram
- Train

Reviews are organised by author preference.

Look out for these icons:

TOP CHOICE	Our author's recommendation
FREE	No payment required
	A green or sustainable option

Our authors have nominated these places as demonstrating a strong commitment to sustainability – for example by supporting local communities and producers, operating in an environmentally friendly way, or supporting conservation projects.

Map Legend

Sights
- Beach
- Buddhist
- Castle
- Christian
- Hindu
- Islamic
- Jewish
- Monument
- Museum/Gallery
- Ruin
- Winery/Vineyard
- Zoo
- Other Sight

Activities, Courses & Tours
- Diving/Snorkelling
- Canoeing/Kayaking
- Skiing
- Surfing
- Swimming/Pool
- Walking
- Windsurfing
- Other Activity/ Course/Tour

Sleeping
- Sleeping
- Camping

Eating
- Eating

Drinking
- Drinking
- Cafe

Entertainment
- Entertainment

Shopping
- Shopping

Information
- Post Office
- Tourist Information

Transport
- Airport
- Border Crossing
- Bus
- Cable Car/ Funicular
- Cycling
- Ferry
- Metro
- Monorail
- Parking
- S-Bahn
- Taxi
- Train/Railway
- Tram
- Tube Station
- U-Bahn
- Other Transport

Routes
- Tollway
- Freeway
- Primary
- Secondary
- Tertiary
- Lane
- Unsealed Road
- Plaza/Mall
- Steps
- Tunnel
- Pedestrian Overpass
- Walking Tour
- Walking Tour Detour
- Path

Boundaries
- International
- State/Province
- Disputed
- Regional/Suburb
- Marine Park
- Cliff
- Wall

Population
- Capital (National)
- Capital (State/Province)
- City/Large Town
- Town/Village

Geographic
- Hut/Shelter
- Lighthouse
- Lookout
- Mountain/Volcano
- Oasis
- Park
- Pass
- Picnic Area
- Waterfall

Hydrography
- River/Creek
- Intermittent River
- Swamp/Mangrove
- Reef
- Canal
- Water
- Dry/Salt/ Intermittent Lake
- Glacier

Areas
- Beach/Desert
- Cemetery (Christian)
- Cemetery (Other)
- Park/Forest
- Sportsground
- Sight (Building)
- Top Sight (Building)

OUR STORY

A beat-up old car, a few dollars in the pocket and a sense of adventure. In 1972 that's all Tony and Maureen Wheeler needed for the trip of a lifetime – across Europe and Asia overland to Australia. It took several months, and at the end – broke but inspired – they sat at their kitchen table writing and stapling together their first travel guide, *Across Asia on the Cheap*. Within a week they'd sold 1500 copies. Lonely Planet was born.

Today, Lonely Planet has offices in Melbourne, London and Oakland, with more than 600 staff and writers. We share Tony's belief that 'a great guidebook should do three things: inform, educate and amuse'.

OUR WRITERS

Nick Ray

Coordinating author, Cambodia A Londoner of sorts, Nick comes from Watford, the sort of town that makes you want to travel. He lives in Phnom Penh with his wife Kulikar and his young children Julian and Belle. He has written for countless guidebooks on the Mekong region, including Lonely Planet's *Cambodia*, *Vietnam* and *Laos* books, as well as *Southeast Asia on a Shoestring*. When not writing, he is often out exploring the remote parts of Cambodia as a location scout and manager for TV and film, including for the movies *Tomb Raider* and *Two Brothers*. Motorbikes are a passion and he has travelled through most of Indochina on two wheels.

Read more about Nick at: lonelyplanet.com/members/nickray

Greg Bloom

Phnom Penh & South Coast Cambodia After five years in Manila, Greg crossed the pond to 'small town' Phnom Penh in 2008 and immediately took a liking to the city and its residents. He's spent ample time researching its restaurants and bars ever since. When not writing about Southeast Asia, Greg can be found snouting around the former Soviet Union (he was editor of the *Kyiv Post* in another life) or running around on Asia's ultimate frisbee fields. Read about his trips at www.mytripjournal.com/bloomblogs.

Read more about Greg at: lonelyplanet.com/members/gbloom4

Austin Bush

Northern Thailand Austin came to Thailand in 1998 on a language scholarship to Chiang Mai University. The lure of city life and a need for employment and spicy food led Austin to Bangkok. City life, employment and spicy food have kept him there since. But escaping Bangkok, particularly for northern Thailand's mountains, is one of his favourite things about writing for this guide. Austin is a freelance writer and photographer who often focuses on food. Samples of his work can be seen at www.austinbushphotography.com.

Read more about Austin at: lonelyplanet.com/members/osten_th

Iain Stewart

Vietnam Iain Stewart first visited, and was captivated by, all the countries in this guidebook as a traveller in 1991 armed with a trusty Lonely Planet or two. He's now a Brighton-based writer, specialising in hot countries a long way from his English seaside abode. Iain has written over 30 guidebooks for six publishers on destinations as diverse as Ibiza and Indonesia.

Read more about Iain at: lonelyplanet.com/members/stewpot

Richard Waters

Laos Richard lives with his family in the Cotswolds, and, since his early years driving a battered motor-home around Central America, has had invisible wings on his heels that insist on seeing what's over the next hill. It's usually a jungle. He's worked and travelled in Laos for the last 10 years and it's still his favourite country. When he's not working for Lonely Planet he writes and photographs for British national newspapers and magazines. To read some of his blurb visit: www.richardwaters.co.uk.

Published by Lonely Planet Publications Pty Ltd
ABN 36 005 607 983
3rd edition – Feb 2012
ISBN 978 1 74179 823 4
© Lonely Planet 2012 Photographs © as indicated 2012
10 9 8 7 6 5 4 3 2 1
Printed in Singapore

Although the authors and Lonely Planet have taken all reasonable care in preparing this book, we make no warranty about the accuracy or completeness of its content and, to the maximum extent permitted, disclaim all liability arising from its use.

All rights reserved. No part of this publication may be copied, stored in a retrieval system, or transmitted in any form by any means, electronic, mechanical, recording or otherwise, except brief extracts for the purpose of review, and no part of this publication may be sold or hired, without the written permission of the publisher. Lonely Planet and the Lonely Planet logo are trademarks of Lonely Planet and are registered in the US Patent and Trademark Office and in other countries. Lonely Planet does not allow its name or logo to be appropriated by commercial establishments, such as retailers, restaurants or hotels. Please let us know of any misuses: lonelyplanet.com/ip.